Communications
in Computer and Information Science   324

Tianyuan Xiao   Lin Zhang
Minrui Fei (Eds.)

AsiaSim 2012

Asia Simulation Conference 2012
Shanghai, China, October 27-30, 2012
Proceedings, Part II

 Springer

Volume Editors

Tianyuan Xiao
Tsinghua University
Department of Automation
National CIMS Engineering Research Center
Beijing 100084, China
E-mail: xty-dau@tsinghua.edu.cn

Lin Zhang
Beihang University
School of Automation Science and Electrical Engineering
Beijing 100191, China
E-mail: johnlin9999@163.com

Minrui Fei
Shanghai University
School of Mechatronics Engineering and Automation
Shanghai 200072, China
E-mail: mrfei@staff.shu.edu.cn

ISSN 1865-0929   e-ISSN 1865-0937
ISBN 978-3-642-34389-6   e-ISBN 978-3-642-34390-2
DOI 10.1007/978-3-642-34390-2
Springer Heidelberg Dordrecht London New York

Library of Congress Control Number: 2012949581

CR Subject Classification (1998): I.6, I.2, H.4, H.3, C.2, D.2, I.4

Typesetting: Camera-ready by author, data conversion by Scientific Publishing Services, Chennai, India

Printed on acid-free paper

Springer is part of Springer Science+Business Media (www.springer.com)

Preface

The Asia Simulation Conference and the International Conference on System Simulation and Scientific Computing 2012 (AsiaSim & ICSC 2012) was formed to bring together outstanding researchers and practitioners in the field of modeling and simulation and scientific computing areas from all over the world to share their expertise and experience.

AsiaSim & ICSC 2012 was held in Shanghai, China, during October 27–30, 2012. It was constituted by AsiaSim and ICSC. AsiaSim is an annual international conference organized by three Asia Simulation Societies: CASS, JSST, and KSS since 1999. It has now become a conference series of the Federation of Asia Simulation Societies (ASIASIM) that was established in 2011. ICSC is a prolongation of the Beijing International Conference on System Simulation and Scientific Computing (BICSC) sponsored by CASS since 1989. AsiaSim & ICSC 2012 was organized by the Chinese Association for System Simulation (CASS) and Shanghai University. In the AsiaSim & ICSC 2012 conference, technical exchanges between the research community were carried out in the forms of keynote speeches, panel discussions, as well as special sessions. In addition, participants were also treated to a series of social functions, receptions, and networking sessions, which served as a vital channel to establish new connections, foster everlasting friendships, and forge collaborations among fellow researchers.

AsiaSim & ICSC 2012 received 906 paper submissions from eight countries. All papers went through a rigorous peer-review procedure including pre-review and formal review. Based on the review reports, the Program Committee finally selected 298 good-quality papers for presentation at AsiaSim & ICSC 2012, from which 267 high-quality papers were then sub-selected for inclusion in five volumes published in the Springer *Communications in Computer and Information Science* (CCIS) series.

This proceedings volume includes 63 papers covering five relevant topics including modeling theory and technology, M&S technology on synthesized environments and virtual reality environments, pervasive computing and simulation technology, embedded computing and simulation technology, and verification/validation/accreditation technology. All of these offer us plenty of valuable information and would be of great benefit to the technical exchange among scientists and engineers in modeling and simulation fields.

The organizers of AsiaSim & ICSC 2012, including the Chinese Association for System Simulation and Shanghai University, made enormous efforts to ensure the success of AsiaSim & ICSC 2012. We hereby would like to thank all the members of the AsiaSim & ICSC 2012 Advisory Committee for their guidance and advice, the members of the Program Committee and Technical Committee and the referees for their effort in reviewing and soliciting the papers, and the members of the Publication Committee for their significant editorial work. In particular, we would like to thank all the authors for preparing, contributing, and presenting their excellent research works. Without the high-quality submissions and presentations from the authors, the success of the conference would not have been possible.

Finally, we would like to express our gratitude to the National Natural Science Foundation of China, the Japanese Society for Simulation Technology, Korea Society for Simulation, the Society for Modeling and Simulation International, International Association for Mathematics and Computer in Simulation, Federation of European Simulation Societies, Science and Technology on Space System Simulation Laboratory, Beijing Electro-Mechanical Engineering Institute, Shanghai Electro-mechanical Engineering Institute, and Shanghai Dianji University for their support in making this conference a success.

July 2012   Bo Hu Li
                                                                Qinping Zhao

AisaSim & ICSC 2012 Organization

Honorary Chairs

Chuanyuan Wen, China   Robert M. Howe, USA   Osamu Ono, Japan
Sung-Joo Park, Korea   Myoung-Hee Kim, Korea   Mahammad Obaidat, USA

Sadao Takaba, Japan   Xingren Wang, China   Zongji Chen, China

General Chairs

Bo Hu Li, China
Qinping Zhao, China

General Co-chairs

Koyamada Koji, Japan   Jonghyun Kim, Korea   Axel Lehmann, Germany
Qidi Wu, China   Song Wu, China   Zicai Wang, China
Xianxiang Huang, China   Khalid Al-Begain, UK

International Program Committee

Chairs

Tianyuan Xiao, China
Lin Zhang, China

Co-chairs

Bernard Zeigler, USA   Tuncer Ören, Canada   Ralph C. Huntsinger, USA

Xiaofeng Hu, China   Fengju Kang, China   Soo-Hyun Park, Korea
Satoshi Tanaka, Japan   Zaozhen Liu, China   H.J. Halin, Switzerland
Xudong Pan, China   Kaj Juslin, Finland   Roy E. Crosbie, USA
Ming Yang, China   Xiaogang Qiu, China   Satoshi Tanaka, Japan
Jin Liu, China   Min Zhao, China   Shiwei Ma, China

Technical Committee

Agostino Bruzzone, Italy   Anxiang Huang, China   Yoonbae Kim, Korea
Yu Yao, China   Fei Xie, USA   Toshiharu Kagawa, Japan

Giuseppe Iazeolla, Italy   Mhamed Itmi, France   Haixiang Lin,
                                                     The Netherlands

Henri Pierreval, France   Hugh HT Liu, Canada   Shengen Zhou, China

Wolfgang Borutzky,   Jong Sik Lee,Korea   Xiaolin Hu, USA
  Germany

Yifa Tang, China   Wenhui Fan, China   Mingduan Tang, China

Long Wang, China   Doo-Kwon Baik, Korea   Shinsuke Tamura, Japan

Pierre Borne, France   Ratan Guha, USA   Reinhold Meisinger,
                                                     Germany

Richard Fujimoto, USA   Ge Li, China   Jinhai Sun, China

Xinping Xiong, China   Gary S.H. Tan,   Francesco Longo, Italy
                             Singapore

Hong Zhou, China   Shin'ichi Oishi, Japan Zhenhao Zhou, China

Beike Zhang, China   Alain Cardon, France   Xukun Shen, China

Yangsheng Wang, China   Marzuki Khalid,   Sergio Junco, Argentina
                             Malaysia

Tieqiao Wen, China   Xingsheng Gu, China   Zhijian Song, China

Yue Yang, China   Yongsheng Ding, China Huimin Fan, China

Ming Chen, China

Secretaries

Ping Zhang, China
Li Jia, China

Publication Chairs

Huosheng Hu, UK
Fei Tao, China

Special Session Chair

Shiwei Ma, China

Organizing Committee

Chairs

Minrui Fei, China
Yunjie Wu, China

Co-chairs

Ping Zhang, China
Linxuan Zhang, China
Noriyuki Komine, Japan
Kang Sun Lee, Korea

Members

Shixuan Liu, China
Baiwei Guo, China
Yulin Xu, China
Xin Li, China
Qun Niu, China
Shouwei Gao, China

Xiao Song, China
Gang Zhao, China
Tingzhang Liu, China
Li Jia, China
Min Zheng, China

Ni Li, China
Yanxia Gao, China
Shaohua Zhang, China
Xin Sun, China
Ling Wang, China

Awards Committee

Chair

Zongji Chen (China)

Co-chairs

Axel Lehmann (Germany)
Soo-Hyun Park (Korea)
Wakae Kozukue (Japan)

Members

Satoshi Tanaka (Japan)
Sung-Yong Jang (Korea)
Wenhui Fan (China)
Yifa Yang (China)
Xiao Song (China)

Table of Contents – Part II

The First Section: Networked Modeling and Simulation Technology

The Second Section: Modeling and Simulation Technology of Continuous System, Discrete System, Hybrid System, and Intelligent System

The Third Section: High Performance Computing and Simulation Technology

The Fourth Section: Cloud Simulation Technology

Network Synchronization Mechanism Design Based on MMORPG

Jianwei Li[1], Hualei Wu[2], Xiaowen Li[3], and Shixi Chen[1]

[1] College of Physics and Information Engineering,
Fuzhou University, Fuzhou 350002, China
[2] Xiamen City University, Xiamen 361000, China
[3] Longyan University, Longyan 364000, China

Abstract. Based on the reason of network synchronization and the existing synchronization mechanisms, this article adopts the idea of message partition, IOCP and the thread pool technology, improves Time Warp algorithm and Dead Reckoning Algorithm, designs a integrated solution of synchronization between server and client to mitigate the synchronization problems in MMORPG. In the experiment, we compare and analysis the effect of traditional synchronous solutions and the effect of our solution, it is shown that this system can better solve the synchronization problem in MMORPG.

Keywords: MMORPG, Network Synchronization, Concurrent Access.

1 Introduction

In massively multiplayer online role-playing game(MMORPG), real-time interaction and collaboration between multi-players are particularly important, that ensures the consistency of each player's screen display in case of natural network latency, avolidless packet loss and limited bandwidth. Some inherent limitations of network environment cause the network latency, such as time for basic electron migration and time for routers routing. The synchronization algorithms used by the server and the client and the server's strategy for concurrent access can reduce the network latency to varying degrees. Exploring each component in network transmission, we can achieve a better solution of synchronization in MMORPG through a comprehensive comparison and improvement.

Synchronization mechanism can be broadly classified into two categories: one is conservative synchronization algorithm [1], and the other is synchronization algorithm based on optimistic forecast [2]. Conservative synchronization algorithm is the strategies that process after ensuring safety and accuracy of the data, includes Lock_step [3] algorithm, Synchronization Authentication algorithm [1] and Fixed-time Bucket [4] algorithm. Conservative synchronization algorithms ensure the consistency of each player, but there are a lot of shortages in concurrency processing such as slow response and the extra waiting time. Synchronization algorithm based on optimistic forecast is the strategies that forecast before execution, then test and correct after detect errors. Synchronization algorithms based on optimistic forecast include

T. Xiao, L. Zhang, and M. Fei (Eds.): AsiaSim 2012, Part II, CCIS 324, pp. 1–8, 2012.

Time Warp [5] algorithm, Active/Passive Detection algorithm [6], Multi-table algorithm [7] and Dead Reckoning algorithm [8] and so on.

Because conservative synchronization algorithm is not suitable for the demanding and fast-paced online game, MMORPG generally use synchronization algorithm based on optimistic forecast in order to let the players not feel the latency. This article compares the synchronization algorithms for clients and servers, then chooses strategies which fit for MMORPG to research and implement.

2   Synchronization Mechanism Analysis

According to the reason of synchronization problem, this article divides synchronization mechanism into three sections: client to server synchronization, server broadcasting, client to client synchronization.

2.1   Client to Server Synchronization

(1) Synchronization Validity. Most of the existing MMORPG use synchronization validity strategy [1]. When player delivers a moving request, client-side does not act first, but execute after the server's logic validity.

This Two-way relay [9] conservative synchronization strategy causes long time-delay and frequently packets sending on client computer. So it is not fit for MMORPG.

(2) Time Warp. In Time Warp, the server will record the game state before the task's execution. When sever receives events sequence error, it will rollback and undo the events which occur between recording game state and executing this event [9]. There are two methods to record the state: mass state storage and incremental state storage.

This method ensures synchronization by detection and correction, is more suitable for interactive online games. However the cycle length of the state recording and the excessive contents may cause excessive CPU usage.

2.2   Server Broadcasting

(1) Active Detection Algorithm. Active Detection algorithm used the observer mode, which means each observed object maintains a list of observer [6]. When an object enters the scene, it needs to traverse all objects within the visible range and build relations with the appropriate objects. When the observed object leaves the scene, the server needs to notify all its observers. Then the observers will judge whether to dissolve the observation relationship.

This algorithm enables the server to avoid seeking other broadcasting objects every time when broadcasting. Sever only need to send it to the observers on the list. However, each object maintains a list of observers will lead to a large storage spending.

(2) Passive Detection Algorithm. Relative to Active Detection algorithm, Passive Detection algorithm [6] is based on the observers in observer mode. Passivity is reflected in logging out of the observation relationship. On the observation list, whether to dissolve the observation relationship in real time does not directly affect the client's display, Passive Detection is used only when observed object acts.

Passive Detection algorithm has a disadvantage that when an object leaves the scene all the objects in the scene must be traversed to determine whether it's that object's observed object, then dissolve the observation relationship. However, Passive Detection avoids traversing objects when any object moves. It reduces the spending of synchronizing the observation list. This system will use Passive Detection algorithm to process server broadcasting [6].

2.3   Client-to-Client Synchronization

While syncing, server only play the role of forwarding.

(1) Multi-table. Multi-table is also known as semi-server synchronization [7]. According to the message type of broadcasting, it needs to build some list on the client-side, then let the clients make decision by themselves according to the state of native clients. When the clients decide to create or destroy an individual object, the ultimate decision will be sent directly to each client on the list, then ensure synchronization between the clients by checking the time difference.

The prototype of this program is Mutual synchronization [7], which is based on optimistic estimates of future network. Currently this solution is only on thought, not been completely achieved. Most of the decision-making authority is on the client-side. It effectively saves the server's resources and reduces the error caused by network latency, but it cannot effectively prevent the plug-in. This system will use this idea for reference.

(2) Dead Reckoning Algorithm. Dead Reckoning is from the distributed motion simulation system of the United States Department of Defense, is a predicted project based on position/orientation. For a client, when message arrives, active objects on the display are updated. At the same time, the client can make conjectures by the history and the present state of active objects and let active objects keep on moving.

When the difference between forecast and reality reach the predicted level, the client which sent out motion will send the package to correct. Furthermore, in Dead Reckoning, there are about nine algorithms to move the local entity to the updated location. "Point-to-Point", "Liner", "Quadratic" algorithms [10] are often be used.

"Point-to-Point" and "Liner" algorithm will cause the speed and the direction changes rapidly. It will cause less real sense. Based on the former, "Quadratic" algorithm adds the acceleration to the path equation, so that entity moves more realistically. But as time change, the acceleration won't change, so the effect is not ideal.

The path expression [11] is as follow:

$$NewPos = OldPos + Velocity * Time + 1/2 * Acceleration * (Time)^2 \qquad (1)$$

This article will improve this equation so that the path will be more reality.

3   Synchronization Mechanism Design

This system designs a synchronization strategy of MMORPG in two ways: reduce network natural delay and reduce network traffic.

3.1   Message Processing Strategy

This system builds message administration and message buffer between the server and the client, and then logically divides messages into important and non-critical messages according to the ratio of 1:3. For important messages, client does not act first, but send the message to the server. After verification, server broadcasts to the relevant objects, then the client acts. For non-critical information, the client makes decision directly and sends the verification message to the server for authentication at the same time. If they are not consistent, repair it.

3.2   Server IOCP and Thread Pool Technique

This system uses IOCP (I/O completion ports) and thread pool technique to process the concurrent access of multiple threads on the server [12,13].

IOCP is actually FIFO queue that the system maintains. Because pushing into the queue is an overlapping event notification, so it's called completion port. System creates a completion port object to manage the overlapped I/O, and open up thread pool, create a certain amount of threads to make the non-I/O processing and I/O processing can be overlapping operated in parallel.

When initializing the server, threat pool technique will open a group of threats previously. Based on the experiment, the number of this system's work threads is two times of the number of the processing units. While the work thread is processing assignment, it will be removed from the thread pool and will be back after the assignment.

The combination of IOCP and thread pool technology not only reduces the time-consuming and system resources expending of creating and destroying a large number of the thread, but also reduces the expending of the thread scheduling and context switching.

3.3   Comprehensive Improvement on the Client-Side

On the server side, according to the experiment's situation and the optimistic speculation, this system chooses the client which is sending acting message to predict and calculate, then appends the predicted information to the package. So the server and the client receiving the information do not need to predict and calculate again, it is easy for timely correct the error of the predicted information.

When the client receives the message, Time Warp algorithm can be used [14].

Time Warp records the game state and the interval is instructions time (one or a small amount of instructions); and the interval to record state in this article is some kind of delay (this article we use 100ms). When there is a conflict with the fact, the system will search the farthest state record that need to be computed and re-execute the instructions from that record.

At the same time, how the game entity moves more realistically in the client's screen is one of the synchronization problems. This system will improve "quadratic" algorithm in Dead Reckoning to get a cubic equation formula.

Define four position parameters [14]: The first parameter P1 is the position where the entity starts to act, the second parameter P2 is the position of the entity after one second running, the third parameter P3 is the position one second before the predicted final position End, the fourth parameter P4 is End:

$$P_1 = Start \tag{2}$$

$$P_2 = P_1 + V \tag{3}$$

$$P_3 = P_4 - V \tag{4}$$

$$P_4 = End \tag{5}$$

Each parameter has x, y, z coordinates, the equations are as follows:

$$x = At^3 + Bt^2 + Ct + D \tag{6}$$

$$y = Et^3 + Ft^2 + Gt + H \tag{7}$$

$$z = It^3 + Jt^2 + Kt + L \tag{8}$$

Variable t represents time, set the value between 0 and 1, and then we can work out each coefficient to determine the track.

This cubic equation not only makes the motion path smoother, but also avoids blunt bending of entities by taking the description of the entities' motion direction in updated message package into account. When the updated packet arrives, simply calculate P4. It makes players feel more real and smooth.

4   Experimental Results

Based on the designed synchronization mechanism, this system experiments the system in campus network. The server's configuration is: software platform: Windows2008 systems; hardware configuration: CPU INTEL E5620 2400MHz, RAM 4G. Figure 1 shows the screenshot on the game client-side.

Fig. 1. Screenshot on the game client-side

Experiments show that IOCP can improve the limiting number of the clients that server can accept. Select model and event selection model can only reach about 60 concurrent connections. The number of connections in IOCP model can reach about 5000, shown as Table 1.

Table 1. Maximum connection comparison with I/O model

I/O Model	Select model	Event selection model	Asynchronous selection model	IOCP model
maximum connection	60	62	4023	5014

Excellent performance of IOCP also reflects in time and space consumption. The tests can be concluded that time and space consumption of the server-side based on IOCP model is significantly less than the sever based on asynchronous choice and the time for accepting connections goes linearly with the number of connections, shown as Table 2 and Table 3.

Table 2. Connection time consumption comparison with I/O model (s)

Number of connections	Asynchronous selection model	Completion port model
2000	5.3240s	2.0634s
3000	10.5621s	3.1345s
4000	18.2560s	4.6723s

Table 3. Connection space consumption comparison with I/O model (Byte)

Number of connections	Asynchronous selection model	Completion port model
2000	19493672B	4982345B
3000	34102356B	5623142B
4000	48012742B	17312568B

Table 4. Data after the improvement of Time Warp algorithm

Experiment NO.	Synchronous delay (ms)	Execution time(s)	The number of instructions	Time-consuming (s)	Roll-back time (s)	Number of Roll-back	Time-consuming of Roll-back (s)
1	50	6.16	40,640	0.14	1.16	816	1.41
2	100	6.45	46,124	0.14	1.24	873	1.40
3	50,100	9.14	59,865	0.15	1.31	924	1.42
4	50,100,110	14.35	78,924	0.14	1.54	1,089	1.41
5	50,100,450	13.87	99,429	0.13	3.35	2,369	1.42

This system improves Time Warp algorithm and uses random number to experiment. It can be conclude that because of cancelling to recover the outdated memory scene, the number of re-execution instructions and the rollbacks obviously reduces and the overall performance is improved, shown as Table 4.

5   Conclusions

Based on the reason of network synchronization and the existing synchronization mechanisms, this article adopts the idea of message partition, IOCP and the thread pool technology, improves Time Warp algorithm and Dead Reckoning Algorithm, designs a integrated solution of synchronization between server and client to mitigate the synchronization problems in MMORPG. In the experiment, we compare and analysis the effect of traditional synchronous solutions and the effect of our solution.

Experiments show that this solution can better solve the synchronization problem in online games. But there still exists shortness in this article, the synchronization problem of online games is unavoidable, future work will focus on reducing the amount of information between client and server and improving the smooth motion display on the client-side.

Acknowledgments. This project is sponsored by the National Science Foundation of China (Grant No. 31100415), the Science Foundation of the Fujian Province, China (Grant No. 2010J01255), and Education Department of Fujian Province (No.JA09005; No.JA10038).

References

1. He, G.Q., Pan, Z.G., Li, Y.Q.: Virtual fitness integrated synchronous technology of online games. Computer Aided Design and Computer Graphics 20(2), 103–114 (2008)
2. Su, N.Y., Wu, X.Y., Lie: Multi-core platforms based on optimistic parallel discrete event simulation. Journal of System Simulation 22(4), 858–863 (2010)
3. Shunsuke, M., Masaru, K., Tatsuhiro, Y.: Minimization of latency in Cheat-Proof Real-Time gaming by trusting Time-Stamp servers. In: 2007 International Conference on Cyberworlds, pp. 202–206 (October 2007)
4. Anurag, A.: Fine Tuning of Fuzzy Token Bucket Scheme for Congestion Control in High Speed Networks. In: Proceedings of the 2010 Second International Conference on Computer Engineering and Applications of the IEEE ICCEA, vol. 1, pp. 170–174 (March 2010)
5. Zhang, W., Sina, M., Jun, W.: A simulated annealing technique for optimizing Time Warp Simulation. In: Proceedings of the 2010 Second International Conference on Computer Modeling and Simulation of the IEEE ICCMS, vol. 2, pp. 197–201 (January 2010)
6. Qian, X., Shen, X.F., Dai, G.J.: Clapping and Broadcasting Synchronization in Wireless Sensor Network. In: Proceedings of the 2010 Sixth International Conference on Mobile Ad-hoc and Sensor Networks, pp. 140–145 (December 2010)
7. Chen, Q.X., Wang, C.S.: The synchronization technology in on-line game engine. Journal of Software 8(3), 100–102 (2009)
8. Cameron, R., Ahmed, H., Cong, L.: Energy-Efficient gaming on mobile devices using Dead Reckoning-based power management. In: Proceedings of the 2010 Sixth International Conference on Mobile Ad-hoc and Sensor Networks (November 2010)
9. Zhang, J., Zhang, H., Chen, C.: A MMORPG synchronization mechanism for wireless networks. Journal of Jiangnan University (Natural Science Edition) 6(5), 565–569 (2007)
10. Yeung, S.F., Lui John, C.S.: Hack-proof synchronization protocol for multi-player online games. Multimedia Tools and Applications, 305–331 (2009)
11. Liang, B., Chen, L.T., Cai, H.B.: Dead Reckoning technology in on-line game application. Application Research of Computers 24(9), 231–314 (2007)
12. Wang, R.B., Li, F.Q., Shi, Y.X.: Implementation of on-line game server communication layer based on IOCP mechanism. Computer Engineering and Applications 45(7), 75–81 (2009)
13. Wang, W.W., Zhao, W.D., Wang, Z.C.: Network communication module design on high performance server. Computer Engineering 35(3), 103–114 (2009)
14. Chen, M.R.: MMOG network engine synchronization technology research and design. University of Electronic Science and Technology, Sichuan (2006)

Research of Networked Control System Based on Predictive Functional Control

Daogang Peng[1,2], Jiajun Lin[2], Yue Wu[1], and Hao Zhang[1]

[1] School of Electric Power and Automation Engineering,
Shanghai University of Electric Power, Shanghai 200090, China
[2] School of Information Science and Engineering,
East China University of Science and Technology, Shanghai 200237, China
jypdg@163.com, jjlin_ecust@126.com

Abstract. As a hotspot in the field of the control theory research and control engineering application, networked control system (NCS) has drawn the domestic and foreign researchers' attention. The essence of NCS is that all kinds of information such as reference input, control input, object output etc can exchange data by the different components of networked control system, such as sensors, controllers and actuators and so on. As a model based advanced control technology, predictive functional control has the same advantages as model predictive control, its algorithm and principle are simple and can be easily realized. Takes the first-order plus time-delay system in typical industry process control system for example, the networked control system based on predictive functional control is designed in this paper, and the simulation platform by using TrueTime toolbox based on Matlab platform is constructed. The simulation result has shown that the control scheme is effective and feasible, and it can be used in engineering application.

Keywords: Networked control system, Predictive functional control, Predictive control, Advanced control technology.

1   Introduction

Predictive control, also known as model predictive control (MPC) is an advanced control technology based on model. Its main features are briefed as follows: the diversity of predictive models, temporality of rolling optimization, adaptability of online correction and industrial applicability and son on. Model predictive control consist of model algorithmic control(MAC), dynamic matrix control(DMC), generalized predictive control(GPC), predictive functional control(PFC), etc. Among them, the PFC views the structure of control input as critical issue, it can overcome the control input problems that other predictive control strategy usually have when the control law is uncertain. At the same time, it has strong tracking ability and robustness also.

Networked control system(NCS) developed to be a hotspot in field of the control theory research and control engineering application during 1990s. Its main advantages are fewer cables, easier expansion, simple diagnosis and maintenance, high flexibility,

T. Xiao, L. Zhang, and M. Fei (Eds.): AsiaSim 2012, Part II, CCIS 324, pp. 9–17, 2012.

resource sharing and remote control etc. The essence of NCS is that all kinds of information such as reference input, control input, object output etc can exchange data by the different components of networked control system, such as sensors, controllers and actuators and so on.

Takes the first-order plus time-delay system in typical industry process control system for example, the networked control system based on predictive functional control is designed in this paper. The simulation research has shown that the control scheme is effective and feasible, and it can be used in engineering application.

2   Principles of Predictive Functional Control

Predictive function control belongs to the category of model predictive control which keeps all the advantages MPC has and, at the same time, makes the control input it produced more regularity. Besides, PFC also reduces the amount of calculation effectively to meet the fast requirements of control algorithm asked by controlled object. Moreover, PFC still has some basic features which MPC has, such as prediction model, reference trajectory, rolling optimization and feedback correction.

2.1   Predictive Model

PFC uses the state variable model to predict the next output of controlled object. Generally speaking, the inner model is usually used as prediction model to predict controlled object's next output. For the system of single input and single output(SISO), the prediction model output $y_m(k)$ consists two parts: free output and functional output of model.

(1) Free output of model $y_1(k)$: The output at k moment is the output without considering the new control action at this moment, free output can be formulated as follow:

$$y_1(k) = F(X(k)) \tag{1}$$

Where $X(k)$ is the data known at k moment, it consists two parts: the value of output and controlled quantity and the set value of input at next moment. F is the mathematical expression of predictive model of controlled objects, it can be expressed by linear difference equation and convolution formula.

(2) Functional output of model $y_f(k)$: It is the new model respond after control action is added. Unlike other predictive control, PFC regard the structure of input is the key to ensure the control performance. In PFC, the new control action will be expressed as the linear combination of some known functions of $f_n(n=1,\cdots,N)$.

$$u(k+i) = \sum_{n=1}^{N} \mu_n f_n(i), i = 0, \cdots, P-1 \tag{2}$$

Where $f_n (n = 1, \cdots, N)$ is called base function, $f_n(i)$ is the value of base function at $t = iT_s$ moment. T_s is the sampling period, P is the length of predictive optimization time, μ_n is the coefficient linear combination.

Instead of independent value in time domain, the new system input in PFC is the combination of base functions. So, the change of system output it caused is not the simple plus of the control effect, it is the linear superposition responses of various base functions. The choice of base functions will depends on features of controlled object and its set value. For example, the step function, slope function and index function can be used.

The output of model function can be formulated as:

$$y_f(k+i) = \sum_{n=1}^{N} \mu_n g_n(i), i = 1, \cdots, P \tag{3}$$

Where $g_n(i)$ is the model output under the influence of $f_n(i)$. It can calculated offline. Therefore, the model output can be formulated as:

$$y_m(k) = y_1(k) + y_f(k) \tag{4}$$

2.2   Reference Trajectory

Reference trajectory is a trajectory which requires that the final output must track the set value. It is fully determined by the designer's request to closed-loop response of system who designs predictive controller. As for asymptotically stable system, it usually chooses the first order index function.

The reference trajectory can be described as follows:

$$y_r(k+i) = \alpha_r y(k) + (1 - \alpha_r) r(k) \tag{5}$$

Where $\alpha_r = e^{(-T_s/T_r)}$ is the attenuation coefficient, T_s is the sampling period, T_r is the transit time when the output get 95% of the expect reference trajectory. $r(k)$ is the set value and $y(k)$ is the process output.

It can avoid over control and makes the output reach the set value smoothly by using this reference trajectory. It also can be seen that if α_r is bigger the stability of system is better while speed of responds is getting worse. Therefore, in the design of predictive control, α_r is a critical parameter to the robust and dynamic characteristics of closed-loop system.

2.3   Receding Optimization

In PFC, the future control variables are calculated by iteration and optimization. The optimization in PFC is time limited, the performance index is time varying. Similarly, future control is realized by iteration and optimization and other steps in PFC. Optimization goal is to find a group of weighted coefficient $\mu_n (n = 1, \cdots, N)$ and makes the prediction output approach expectation of reference trajectory in time domain. The most common method is to minimize the sum of square error of optimization point between reference trajectory and process predictive output. The formulation of the minimization is:

$$J_P = \min(\sum_{i=P_1}^{P_2} (y_r (k + i) - y_P (k + i))^2) \tag{6}$$

$$y_P (k + i) = y_m (k + i) + e(k + i) \tag{7}$$

Where P_1 and P_2 are the upper and lower limit in optimization time domain. $y_P (k + i)$ is the expect output of process and $y_m (k + i)$ is the output of the model at $k + i$ moment. $e(k + i)$ is the future error.

2.4   Feedback Correction

PFC use calculation method which is out of time or frequency domain to correct the error of model. In practical system, the influences such as model mismatch, parameter time-variance, secondary input and noise will cause error between the output of predictive model and the practical system. So, it is necessary to predict the error of future optimization domain and there are many predict methods. Among them, it can use the future error and it is formulated as follows:

$$e(k + i) = y(k) - y_m (k) \tag{8}$$

Where, $y(k)$ is the output of controlled object and $y_m (k)$ is the output of predictive model at k moment.

3   Networked Control System Based on Predictive Functional Control

3.1   Structure of Control System

The directly relative field devices between networked control system and control loops involve sensors, controllers and actuators and so on, and these types of devices belong to the network nodes in the networked control system. Every node can execute several different tasks according to its own hardware configuration. The essence of NCS is that all kinds of information such as reference input, control input, object output etc can exchange data by the different components of networked control system, such as sensors, controllers and actuators and so on. Each node in the NCS is connected by control network, which has many advantages such as resource sharing, fewer wires, easy to expand and maintenance and so on. While the information transmission of uncertainties is found because of the introduction of network which has transmission time delay, network package lost, package wrong sequence and some other errors.

Figure 1 shows the structure of predictive function control based on networked control system, in which sensors are used to collect signal and transmit it to predictive functional controller though the network path periodically. The controller calculates the signal by predictive functional control algorithm and sends it to actuator, which can control the object by the signal.

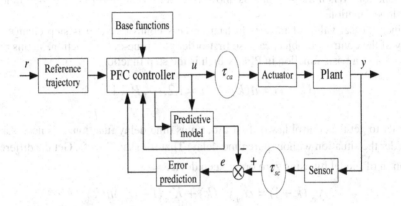

Fig. 1. Structure of NCS based on PFC

In NCS, the detection signals and control signals are sent by different kinds of information in the form of data packet in networked control system. Therefore, the sensor send detection signals to the controller periodically by time-driven mode while the controller uses either time-driven mode or event-driven mode. The controller and actuator calculate and execute the latest date packet information in a steady time interval when they are both time-driven mode. On the other side, when they both use event-driven mode, the controller calculates the new control variable when the controller received a date packet and the actuator doesn't work until it receives the date packet of control variable.

3.2 Algorithms of Predictive Functional Control

In the process of industrial production, many controlled objects can be described by first-order plus time-delay function. Those high order asymptotic stability objects can be simplified in the form of first-order plus time-delay plant. Even some cascade control system can use PID to build a control loop in vice loop link, and view vice loop and primary loop as controlled object, and then makes the system a first-order plus time-delay plant by adjusting parameters of PID. So it has great practical value to study the predictive function control based on networked control system for first-order plus time-delay system.

The predictive model of PFC is as follow:

$$G_m(s) = \frac{K_m}{T_m s + 1} e^{-T_d s} \tag{9}$$

In the algorithms of PFC, control precision is determined by basis function. Generally, step function and slope function can satisfy this request. When the first order object and its set value change with stepping, only one function is needed and it is step function. While when set value includes slope signal, the step function and slope function are both needed. When the set value is below or equal to the threshold θ, control input is step function. When the set value is above threshold θ, control input is step function and slope function.

Since the set value of most industrial process control system is step change, and many of the controlled object can use first-order plus time-delay function, so this paper only choose a basis function in PFC, which is the step function.

$$u(k+i) = u(k) \qquad i = 1, 2, \cdots, P-1 \tag{10}$$

In order to get the control law of first-order plus time-delay function, it is necessary to consider the situation without pure time-delay, That is to say $T_d = 0$. Get the difference equation of model by using zero order keep device.

$$y_m(k+1) = \alpha_m y_m(k) + K_m(1 - \alpha_m)u(k) \tag{11}$$

Where $\alpha_m = e^{-T_s/T_d}$.

According to formulas of (10) and (11), using mathematical induction can get:

$$y_m(k+P) = \alpha_m^P y_m(k) + K_m(1 - \alpha_m^P)u(k) \tag{12}$$

For the optimization target of formula (6), get $P_1 = P_2 = P$, and assume:

$$\frac{\partial J_P}{\partial u(k)} = 0 \tag{13}$$

According to formulas of (6), (7), (8), (10), (12) and (13), the control value at k moment is as follow:

$$u(k) = \frac{r(k+P) - a_r^P r(k) - y(k)(1 - a_r^P)}{K_m(1 - a_m^P)} + \frac{y_m(k)}{K_m} \tag{14}$$

When pure time-delay link is added in the system, that is to say $T_d \neq 0$, and according to Smith predictive control theory, PFC will use the model when $T_d = 0$ and it need correction after plant output.

Suppose $D = T_d/T_s$, then the correction method of plant output is as follow:

$$y_v(k) = y(k) + y_m(k) - y_m(k-D) \tag{15}$$

Where $y_v(k)$ is the modified process output value. Then formula (8) can be described as:

$$e(k+i) = y_v(k) - y_m(k) \tag{16}$$

Replace $y(k)$ with $y_v(k)$ in formula (14) , then the PFC control output when controlled object is first-order plus pure time-delay plant can be described as:

$$u(k) = \frac{r(k+P) - a_r^P r(k) - y_v(k)(1-a_r^P)}{K_m(1-a_m^P)} + \frac{y_m(k)}{K_m} \tag{17}$$

4   Simulation Studies

In order to indentify the validity of networked control system of PFC, simulation platform is built by TrueTime under Matlab environmental. Take typical first-order plus time-delay system in practical industrial production process for example, the model is:

$$G_m(s) = \frac{K}{Ts+1} e^{-\tau s}$$

In this paper, the parameters of the controlled object are $K = 1.5$, $T = 20s$, $\tau = 10s$. It is the predictive model of PFC also which has the form of formula (9). In the process of simulation, the simulation model will not change whether controlled object matches it or not. PFC takes the step function as its basis function, where $P = 45, T_r = 0.95s$ and sampling time $T_s = 1$.

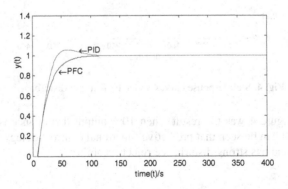

Fig. 2. Step response curves of the two control strategies

In order to prove the predictive functional control strategy has more advantages than normal PID control strategy, both of the simulation researches were built. Figure 2 was the step response results of the two control strategies.

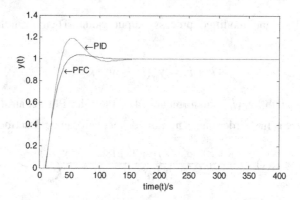

Fig. 3. Step response curves of parameters increased model

Figure 3 was the step response results when all parameters of the controlled object include proportional coefficient, time constant and time delay increased 20%. It can be seen from the simulation results that the system dynamic quality of predictive functional control strategy is better than traditional PID control.

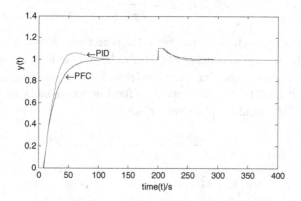

Fig. 4. Step response curves under 10% output disturbance

In addition, figure 4 was the result when 10% output disturbance is added in the control system. It can be seen that predictive functional control strategy can overcome the disturbance and has strong disturbance rejection ability.

5   Conclusions

As a hotspot in the field of the control theory research and control engineering application, networked control system has advantages of fewer cables, easier expansion, simple diagnosis and maintenance, high flexibility, resource sharing and remote control, etc. As a model based advanced technology, the predictive functional control can overcome the control input problems that other MPC usually have when the control law is uncertain. At the same time, its tracking ability and robustness is also pretty well. This paper takes the first-order plus time-delay system in typical industry process control system for example, designed the networked control system based on predictive functional control strategy and the simulation results has shown that the control scheme is effective and feasible and has good robustness and stability.

Acknowledgments. This work was supported by the State Key Program of National Natural Science Foundation of China under Grant No. 61034004.

References

1. Wang, G., Han, P., Wang, D.: Predictive Functional Control and Its Application Study. Journal of System Simulation 14(8), 1087–1091 (2002)
2. Zhang, Q., Zhang, W.: Time-stamped predictive functional control in networked control systems. Control Theory & Applications 23(1), 126–130 (2006)
3. Wang, T., Xu, D., Han, P., et al.: Application of PFC algorithm in networked control system with long time delay. In: Pro. of the 27th Chinese Control Conference, Kunming, Yunnan, China, July 16-18, pp. 185–189 (2008)
4. Zhou, L., Wang, T., Han, P., et al.: Study and application of predictive functional control in networked control system. In: Pro. of the 7th World Congress on Intelligent Control and Automation, Chongqing, China, June 25-27, pp. 6236–6240 (2008)
5. Wu, J., Fei, R.: Application of Predictive Functional Control in Deterministic Networked Control Systems. Journal of East China University of Science and Technology 32(7), 876–879 (2006)
6. Wang, Z., Jiang, J., Li, L.: Research on predictive functional control of long delay networked control systems. Chinese Journal of Scientific Instrument 29(5), 1006–1010 (2008)
7. Liu, C., Chen, Z., Dong, E.: Predictive functional control application in networked control system. Journal of Tianjin University of Technology 25(1), 29–32 (2009)

A Wireless Sensor Network Location Algorithm Based on Firefly Algorithm[*]

Song Cao[1], Jianhua Wang[2], and Xingsheng Gu[1]

[1] Key Laboratory of Advanced Control and Optimization for Chemical Process,
Ministry of Education, East China University of Science and Technology,
Rd. Meilong 130, 200237 Shanghai, China
[2] School of Electrical and Electronic Engineering, Shanghai Institute of Technology,
Rd. Haiquan 100, 201418 Shanghai, China
wjh@sit.edu.cn

Abstract. Wireless sensor network(WSN) is getting more attention from the society for its underlying application value. The position of the nodes is very important in some pictures. This paper proposes a new method of localization of target nodes based on the Firefly Algorithm(FA).We introduce the Firefly Algorithm and improve it . We discuss performance of our method based on the numerical simulations compared with other localization algorithm.

Keywords: wireless sensor works, localization, firefly algorithm.

1   Introduction

With the development of radio frequency(RF) integrated circuit and network technology, the application of WSN in the field of healthcare, natural habitat monitoring, home automation, traffic management, and military has got more attention, and the search in WSN has become a hot spot recently [1,2]. Usually, WSN is consist of thousands of sensor nodes which are spatially distributed across an area of interest to cooperatively monitor environmental condition. Each sensor node is equipped with a radio transceiver, a microcontroller, and a battery, so that they can communicate with each other wirelessly.

Location awareness is required for many wireless sensor network application, so it is necessary to locate the senor nodes. Equipping every sensor nodes with GPS or locating them manually is costly and unpractically. Hence, various localization schemes for assigning geographical coordinates to each node in a sensor network system are proposed [3].

Localization algorithms can be divided into range-based and range-free algorithms.

The basic principle of range-based algorithms is that firstly we get the distance—through the ways like TOA [4]、TDOA [5]、AOA[6]、RSSI [7]—between one

---

[*] This work is supported by:1.Key Program of Shanghai Committee of Science and Technology(No.11510502700);2.Shanghai Municipal Natural Science Foundation(No.11Z R1409800).

T. Xiao, L. Zhang, and M. Fei (Eds.): AsiaSim 2012, Part II, CCIS 324, pp. 18–26, 2012.

unlocalized node and the anchor nodes ($M \geq 3$)which are equipped with GPS and located around the unlocalized one within communication range, then trilateration, triangulate-on, Maximum likelihood Estimation or some heuristic methods are applied to locate the sensor nodes. The typical heuristic methods which are used in location include particles swarm optimization(PSO), simulated annealing(SA) [8], Genetic algorithm (GA) [9] and so on, The range-free algorithms are based on the network connectivity ,and the typical range-free algorithms are MAP[10], W-Centroid [11], DV-Hop [12], APIT [13].

In the paper, we talk about the range-based algorithms and propose a new heuristic method based on FA. The remained parts of the paper are organized as follows.Section2 provides a description of the FA and a improved FA is shown. The proposed WSN localization based on improved FA is explained in Section 3.The simulation are give in Section 4.Section 5 concludes.

2   Firefly Algorithm

2.1   The Standard Firefly Algorithm

Firefly Algorithm is proposed by scholar Yang in literature [14].FA models the phenomenon that the fireflies flash and attract each others in nature. It is one kind of colony searching technology.

For a maximization problem, the brightness can simply be proportional to the value of the objective function. Based on these three rules, three definitions are given as following in the Firefly algorithm.

1. The light intensity $I(r)$ can be expressed as

$$I(r) = I_0 e^{-\gamma r^2} .$$ (1)

Where I_0 is the original light intensity, γ is the fixed light absorption coefficient, r is the distance.

2. As the attractiveness is proportional to the light intensity, so we can get the attractiveness β

$$\beta(r) = \beta_0 e^{-\gamma r^2} .$$ (2)

Where β_0 is the attractiveness at $r = 0$.

3. When a firefly i is attracted by a firefly j ,the firefly i moves to the firefly j and the state of firefly i can be defined as

$$x_i = x_i + \beta_0 e^{-\gamma r_{ij}^2} (x_j - x_i) + \alpha \varepsilon_i .$$ (3)

Where x_i, x_j is the state of firefly i and firefly j respectively, the third term is randomization with α being the randomization parameter, and ε_i is a vector of random numbers drawn from a Gaussian distribution or uniform distribution.

2.2   The Improved Firefly Algorithm

In the paper, we proposed an improved FA, called FA1.We make change in two points as following.

2.2.1   Change β_0

In the basic FA, β_0 is a constant. In our FA1, we define

$$\beta_0 = a - \frac{a - 0.01}{MaxGeneration} k \qquad (4)$$

Where a is a constant, MaxGeneration is the max iteration , k is a variable representing the k th iteration.

Introduce it into function(2),we can get

$$\beta = (a - \frac{a - 0.01}{MaxGeneration} k) e^{-\gamma r^2} \qquad (5)$$

The main reason to do this lies in that we hope to explore the search space globally in the beginning of iterations ,while ,with the iteration goes, searching locally and more intensively is needed. Hence, that β_0 decrease gradually can make it.

2.3   Move the Bad-State Fireflies to the Better Place

We find a ubiquitous picture in our simulation that there are some fireflies cannot converge to extremum mostly, therefore these fireflies make no sense but increase complexity of algorithm in the later stage of iteration. We decide to move these bad-state fireflies(N_bad) to the adjacent area of the current best firefly at some moment in the later stage. The area is the circle taken current best as the center with radius R

$$R = 0.05 * L * \sqrt{DM} \qquad (6)$$

Where L is the length of the side of search area, DM is dimension.

$$N\_bad = 0.2 * n \qquad (7)$$

Where n is the number of fireflies.

So the pseudo code of the FA can be changed   as following[14]

```
FA1
Objective function f(x) , x=(x_1,...,x_i)^T
Generate initial polulation of fireflies x_i(i=1,...,n) ;
Light intensity I_i at x_i is determined by f(x_i) ;
```

```
Define light absorption coefficient γ ,the parameter a ;
While (t<MaxGeneration)
For i=1:n all n fireflies
  For j=1:n all n fireflies(inner loop)
  If( I_i < I_j )

    Move firefly i towards j;
  End If
  If k reach a setted value k=| η *MaxGeneration|
    move the badfireflies to the better place;
  End If
  vary attractiveness with distance r via exp[-rγ];

  evaluate new solutions and update light intensity;
  end for j
End for i
Postprocess results and visualization;
```

The simulation through stand test function on part 4 shows that our proposed algorithm FA1 is better than standard one.

3   FA-Based Localization Algorithm

3.1   Problem Definition

Range-based one-hop localization in a network of a total of n+m sensor nodes estimates the coordinates of n target nodes using a priory information about the location of m anchor nodes and the pair-wise distance information d_{ij} between the ith anchor and the jth target node.Thus, for a 2D localization problem,a total of 2n unknown coordinates, $\theta = [\theta_x , \theta_y]$,where $\theta_x = [x_1, x_2, \cdots, x_n], \theta_y = [y_1, y_2, \cdots, y_n]$ are to be estimated using the anchor node coordinates $[x_{n+1}, x_{n+2}, \cdots, x_{n+m}]$ $[y_{n+1}, y_{n+2}, \ldots, y_{n+m}]$ [15].

The position estimation of coordinate of target nodes can be formulated as an optimization problem in which the mean squared range errors between the target node and neighboring anchor nodes can be considered as the objective function for this problem. The underlying range measurement techniques result in the ranging errors, especially for RSSI which can suffer from large errors(±50%) [16] .In this paper, we assume that the distance measurement errors are independent Gaussian random variables with zero mean and known variance σ_d^2, even though the assumption of the uncorrelated Gaussian range measurement errors will not represent all practical scenarios, this assumption is a good starting point for exposing error trends in a multi-hop sensor network environment according to other studies [17]. Thus we have

$$d_i = \sqrt{(x-x_i)^2 + (y-y_i)^2} \qquad (8)$$

$$\hat{d}_i = d_i * (1.0 + Gaussian\ Noise() * Noise\ Factor) \tag{9}$$

where (x, y), (x_i, y_i) is the coordinate of the target node and anchor node respectively. d_i, $\hat{d}_i$ is the real and measurement distance between (x, y) and (x_i, y_i) respectively.

Then the objective function can be got

$$f(x, y) = \sum_{i=1}^{M} (\sqrt{(x-x_i)^2 + (y-y_i)^2} - \hat{d}_i)^2$$

$$\tag{10}$$

3.2   The FA1-Based WSN Localization

For the existence and instability of measure errors, the estimated positions of target nodes are corresponding to the fluctuation of measure errors, sometimes estimated position is very close to the real one, while sometimes errors are relative great. To solve the problem, average of multi-estimated position ---the typical technology of reducing error---is introduced. Coupled with FA1, each target node performs the following steps:

```
Step1 Get the distance between target nodes and the
      neighborhood anchor nodes;
Step2 Generate new fireflies,calculate the values of
      the objective function f(x₀);
Step3 if k≠0 compare the light intensity of firefl-
      is,and move the fireflies to the brighter ones
      according to the light intensity of firefli-
      es,and move the fireflies to the brighter ones
      according to function(3).After the movement,the
      new state x'ₖ produce.If k=|η*MaxGeneration|,then move
      the n' bad-state fireflies to the adjacent area of
      the current best firefly. If k=MaxGeneration
      then end the iteration and skip to Step5,else
      k=k+1,xₖ=x'ₖ;
Step4 calculate the values of the objective function
      f(xₖ),skip to Step3;
Step5 if the times of estimation are equal to N, then
      average the total estimation results, else skip
      to Step1;
```

The FA1-based localization can make a good performance, but sometimes the gross error confuses us because of the convergence of FA1 to the local optimum. To solve the problem, we propose a solution , called FA2 for simplicity:

Step1 get the averaged estimated location through FA1 - Based localization;

Step2 calculate the distances between the N estimated locations and the averaged one,called D_i ($1 \leq i \leq N$).

Step3 if D_i is greater than a threshold value φ ,get rid of the corresponding estimated location.

Step4 if the number of discarded estimated location is greater than ζ,just discard the worst estimated locations,for that the number of estimated location affect the localization.

Step5 re-average the rest estimated location,and take the result as the location of target node.

4   Simulation Results and Discussion

In this section firstly the comparison between FA1 and standard FA are given, then we talk about the performance between FA1-based,FA2-based and Malguki[18] localization methods. Both target and anchor nodes deploy statically in a square area. For simplisity,there are only three anchors and one target node. Irrespective of the underlying ranging method, the measured distances between a target node and the anchor nodes in its transmission range are assumed to be blurred by additive white Gaussian(AWG) noise only.

4.1   The Comparison between FA1 and Standard FA

The proposed algorithm was tested on five standard functions, which are Sphere, Rosenbrock, Rastrigin, Ackely and Schewefel.The parameters(MG mean the Maxgeneration, PS means the population size) of FA1 and standard FA are shown in table1,and the results(in 10 ,20 and 30 dimensions) are the mean fitness of the value founded in 30 times separated run with independent seeds. As shown in table2 FA1 has better performance than standard Firefly algorithm.

Table 1. The parameters of Stand-FA and FA1

	γ	α	MG	PZ	Beta0	η	a
FA	0.01	0.7	5000	30	1	-	-
FA1	0.01	0.7	5000	30	-	0.6	1

Table 2. Comparison between standard firefly algorithm and FA1 throught test functions

Fun	Dim	FA-Average and Std	FA-Best	FA1-Averag and Std	FA1-Best
Sphere	10	0.0618 ± 0.0122	0.0254	0.0488 ± 0.0131	0.0211
	20	0.3268 ± 0.0418	0.1975	0.3085 ± 0.0376	0.2182
	30	0.8790 ± 0.1337	0.6407	0.7411 ± 0.1196	0.5900
Rosenb-rok	10	13.6374 ± 1.4664	10.7820	11.9939 ± 1.2186	9.2268
	20	1.7950 ± 7.3867	37.7546	46.3651 ± 3.9442	36.2564
	30	120.8810 ± 21.7240	98.5459	99.0491 ± 8.0865	78.3138
Rastrig-in	10	16.5409 ± 3.0757	10.0972	16.3561 ± 4.059	9.5459
	20	75.1082 ± 7.1237	60.0441	66.3648 ± 7.2644	52.4111
	30	143.3815 ± 12.2115	113.7362	136.5052 ± 11.1509	103.3671
Ackley	10	2.6262 ± 4.8415	0.5252	1.0725 ± 0.6272	0.6478
	20	19.3094 ± 0.1895	18.8281	18.2710 ± 1.4690	11.7658
	30	19.8430 ± 0.1288	19.5877	19.6932 ± 0.1637	19.3376
Schwef-el	10	0.6492 ± 0.0803	0.4474	0.5589 ± 0.0646	0.3850
	20	2.1964 ± 0.2010	1.8465	1.9201 ± 0.1990	1.3177
	30	922.5036 ± 2774	4.5465	7.0935 ± 71.9515	3.5058

4.2   Comparison among FA1,FA2 and Malguki

We make comparisons among FA1-based algorithm, FA2-based algorithm and Malguki. The Noise Factor ranges from 0 to 1.And the results are average of 100 times simulation. In the FA2-based algorithm, φ and ζ are very important. We chose $\zeta = 7$ for simplicity. When Noise Factor range from 0 to 1,the constant φ is not advisable. So φ should change corresponding to Noise Factor. To get φ,we make simulation based on FA1, Noise Factor ranging from 0 to 1.We repeat the simulation for 100 times for different Noise Factor, recording the biggest D every time, then average the total biggest D which is the right φ after appropriate adjustment.Table3 shows the results.

Table 3. The threshold value of φ

NR	0	0.1	0.2	0.3	0.4	0.5	0.6	0.7	0.8	0.9	1.0
φ	0	9.5	13.4	18.0	20.7	22.9	25.6	35.2	45.3	50.0	55.9

Fig.1-3 show the effection of Noise Factor on the average error ,best error and stand deviation separately. It is obvious that the FA1-based algorithm and FA2-based algorithm are both better than Malguki in the three aspects(average error, best error, standard deviation). At the same time, the FA2-based algorithm are better then FA1-based algorithm slightly.

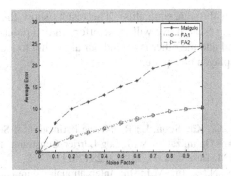

Fig. 1. The effection of nosie factor on average error

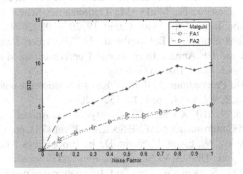

Fig. 2. The effection of noise factor on STD

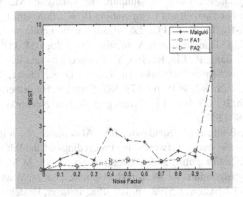

Fig. 3. The effection of noise factor on best error

5   Conclusions

In this paper, the localization algorithm based on firefly algorithm have been proposed. We give the detailed analysis of the improvement of standard firefly algorithm and the effection of some parameters on the average error. In addition, we compare our algorithm with Malguki algorithm through simulation. The results show that our algorithms are better than it. For further research, we will make effort on two points, one is the effection on energy of our method and the other is extend our algorithm to more complex situation that more nodes are displayed on square.

References

1. Hong Anh, N., Hao, G., Kay-Soon, L.: Real-Time Estimation of Sensor Node's Position Using Particle Swarm Optimization With Log-Barrier Constraint. IEEE Transactions on Instrumentation and Measurement 60, 3619–3628 (2011)
2. Low, K.S., Win, W.N.N., Er, M.J.: In: International Conference on Computational Intelligence for Modelling, Control and Automation, 2005 and International Conference on Intelligent Agents, Web Technologies and Internet Commerce, vol. 2, pp. 271–276 (2005)
3. Niewiadomska-Szynkiewicz, E., Marks, M.: Optimization Schemes Forwireless Sensor Network Localization. Int. J. Appl. Math. Comp. 19, 291–302 (2009)
4. Priyantha, N.B., Chakraborty, A., Balakrishnan, H.: The Cricket location-support system. In: Proceedings of the 6th Annual International Conference on Mobile Computing and Networking, pp. 32–43. ACM, Boston (2000)
5. Girod, L., Estrin, D.: Proceedings 2001 IEEE/RSJ International Conference on Intelligent Robots and Systems, 3, vol. 1313, pp. 1312–1320 (2001)
6. Niculescu, D., Badri, N.: INFOCOM 2003. Twenty-Second Annual Joint Conference of the IEEE Computer and Communications. IEEE Societies, 3, vol.1733, pp. 1734–1743 (2003)
7. Girod, L., Bychkovskiy, V., Elson, J., Estrin, D.: In: Proceedings 2002 IEEE International Conference on Computer Design: VLSI in Computers and Processors, pp. 214–219 (2002)
8. Zhongcheng, S., Fei, S., Rui, W.: In: 2nd International Conference on Biomedical Engineering and Informatics, BMEI 2009, pp. 1–5 (2009)
9. Qingguo, Z., Jinghua, W., Cong, J., Junmin, Y., Changlin, M., Wei, Z.: In: Fourth International Conference on Natural Computation, ICNC 2008, vol. 1, pp. 608–613 (2008)
10. Kuo-Feng, S., Chia-Ho, O., Jiau, H.C.: Localization with mobile anchor points in wireless sensor networks. IEEE Transactions on Vehicular Technology 54, 1187–1197 (2005)
11. Shen, X., Wang, Z., Jiang, P., Lin, R., Sun, Y.: Connectivity and RSSI Based Localization Scheme for Wireless Sensor Networks. In: Huang, D.-S., Zhang, X.-P., Huang, G.-B. (eds.) ICIC 2005. LNCS, vol. 3645, pp. 578–587. Springer, Heidelberg (2005)
12. Niculescu, D., Nath, B.: DV Based Positioning in Ad Hoc Networks. Telecommunication Systems 22, 267–280 (2003)
13. He, T., Huang, C., Blum, B.M., Stankovic, J.A., Abdelzaher, T.: Range-free localization schemes for large scale sensor networks. In: Proceedings of the 9th Annual International Conference on Mobile Computing and Networking, pp. 81–95. ACM, San Diego
14. Yang, X.-S.: Firefly Algorithms for Multimodal Optimization. In: Watanabe, O., Zeugmann, T. (eds.) SAGA 2009. LNCS, vol. 5792, pp. 169–178. Springer, Heidelberg (2009)
15. Gopakumar, A., Jacob, L.: Performance of some metaheuristic algorithms for localization in wireless sensor networks. International Journal of Network Management 19, 355–373 (2009)
16. Fubao, W., Long, S., Fengyuan, R.: Self-localization systems and algorithms for wireless sensor networks. Journal of Software16, 857–868 (2005)
17. Savvides, A., Garber, W.L., Moses, R.L., Srivastava, M.B.: An analysis of error inducing parameters in multihop sensor node localization. IEEE Transactions on Mobile Computing 4, 567–577 (2005)
18. Arias, J., Zuloaga, A., Lázaro, J., Andreu, J., Astarloa, A.: Malguki: an RSSI based ad hoc location algorithm. Microprocessors and Microsystems 28, 403–409 (2004)

Simulation Research on DSDV and AODV Protocol in Tactical Unit Network

Houmin Li, Lijun Pan, and Rui Fan

Department of Equipment Command and Administration, AAFE,
100072 Beijing, China
lihmzzu@163.com

Abstract. Ad Hoc Network and its potential application were introduced, typical proactive routing protocol DSDV and typical on-demand routing protocol AODV were analyzed and compared. Modeling and simulation for DSDV protocol and AODV protocol in tactical unit network were projected under VRNET Developer platform. Results show that DSDV protocol has pretty performance in network environment with fewer nodes, low mobility and high real-time requirements, and AODV protocol is more fit for network environment with many nodes and high mobility.

Keywords: ad hoc network, routing protocols, DSDV, AODV.

1   Introduction

Military communications in modern warfare often has no fixed communication infrastructures, and Precision-guided Weapons have a serious threat to communication network relied on fixed facilities. To solve these problems, such network is needed, the network does not require fixed base stations, distributed without a central management, with high mobility, has the ability of survivability, deployment rapidly, and self-organized, it meets tactical communications [1]. Ad Hoc Networks arise under this background, and it has been widely applied in military, rescue, explore and wireless personal communications.

Ad Hoc Network is a no-center, self-organized and multi-hop wireless network. Each node in the network is a host and has routing function, all nodes can move randomly, the network will not be paralyzed as failure of some nodes, and it has a strong survivability. Compared with the traditional wireless network, it can realize point to point communication without depending on the base station or other fixed facilities.

In Ad Hoc Networks, topology changes frequently caused by node mobility and wireless channel fading and interference, so traditional internet routing protocols can not be used directly. Distributed operating routing protocols should be used, and routing loops must be avoided. Because of limited resource-poor nodes, routing protocol should be able to support the operation of sleep. Taking into account of Ad Hoc application environment, routing protocol must provide security protection [2].

T. Xiao, L. Zhang, and M. Fei (Eds.): AsiaSim 2012, Part II, CCIS 324, pp. 27–36, 2012.

Many routing protocols have been proposed for Ad Hoc Networks, in accordance with the different route discovery strategies, routing protocols can be divided into proactive routing protocols, on-demand routing protocols and hybrid networking protocols [3].

1) Proactive routing protocols are also named table-drive routing protocols, The primary characteristic of proactive approaches is that each node in the network broadcasts routing packet, and maintains a route to other nodes in the network at all times. Typical routing protocols include DSDV, OLSR and FSR.

2) On-demand routing protocols are also known as reactive routing protocols, routes are only discovered when they are actually needed. When a source node needs to send data packets to destination, it checks its routing table to determine whether it has a route. If no routes exist, it performs a route discovery procedure to find a path to the destination. Typical routing protocols include AODV, DSR and FSR.

3) The characteristics of proactive and reactive routing protocols can be integrated in various ways to form hybrid networking protocols. Hybrid networking protocols may exhibit proactive behavior given a certain set of circumstances, while exhibiting reactive behavior given a different set of circumstances. The typical routing protocols include ZRP and SRL.

Typical proactive routing protocol DSDV and Typical on-demand routing protocol AODV will be analyzed and compared. Modeling and simulation for DSDV protocol and AODV protocol in tactical unit network will be projected under VRNET Developer platform. According to the analysis of simulation results, some suggestion will be given in selecting routing protocol for building tactical unit networks.

2   DSDV and AODV Work Process Analysis

2.1   DSDV Routing Protocol

The Destination-Sequenced Distance Vector (DSDV) routing protocol is a distance vector protocol. DSDV utilizes per-node sequence numbers to avoid the counting to infinity problem common in many distance vector protocols. A node increases its sequence number whenever there is a change in its local neighborhood. When given a choice between two routes to a destination, a node always selects the route with the greatest destination sequence number. Because DSDV is a proactive protocol, each node maintains a route to every other node in the network. The routing table contains the following information for each entry, such as destination IP address, destination sequence number, next-hop IP address, hop count, and install time. Every time interval, each node broadcasts its current sequence number to its neighbors, along with any routing table updates. The routing table updates as the form:

< destination IP address, destination sequence number, hop count>

DSDV defines two types of updates: full and incremental. Full updates are transmissions of a node's entire routing table; these updates are performed relatively infrequently. Incremental updates only include those routing table entries that have changed size since the last full update.

DSDV protocol is fit for small network, and the network topology changes slowly. The main advantage of DSDV is to eliminate routing loops, fast convergence speed, and with small end-to-end delay. The primary disadvantage is it still consumes energy and network bandwidth when the network is idle, it is difficult to adapt to network with rapidly moving nodes. DSDV does not support one-way channel.

2.2   AODV Routing Protocol

AODV is a reactive protocol that discovers and maintains routes on demand, and AODV protocol standardization was completed in July 2003 by Inter Engineering Task Force (IETF) Mobile Ad Hoc Network (MANET) [4].

When a route to a target station is needed, the AODV protocol broadcasts a route-request packet that is then disseminated throughout the network. It places the destination node's IP address, the last known sequence number for that destination, and the source's IP address and current sequence number in this packet. The RREQ also contains a hop count and a RREQ ID, to gather with the RREQ ID, uniquely identifies a RREQ and can be used to detect duplicates. When the target station or a valid route to the target station is found, a route-reply message is sent back to the requesting station by means of a unicast message. While this message travels towards the requesting station, routes are set up inside routing tables of the traversed stations.

Two types of Route maintenance was applied with AODV. One optimization is the source repair. When a link break along an active path occurs, the node upstream of the break then creates a route error (RERR) message and sends this message to its upstream neighbors that were also utilizing the link. Once the source node receives the RERR, it can repair the route if the route is still needed. Another optimization is the local repair. When a link break occurs, instead of sending a RERR to the source, the node upstream of the break can try to repair the link locally itself.

The AODV routing protocol was designed for Mobil Ad Hoc Networks with dozens to thousands of mobile nodes, it is able to handle low, medium and relatively high rate of movement, and it also be able to handle various level of data communication.

The advantages of AODV routing protocol include distance vector mechanism, support for intermediate nodes reply, the node stores only needed rout, and the use of destination sequence number to avoid routing loops. The disadvantage of AODV is that it does not support one-way channel.

2.3   Qualitative Comparison between DSDV and AODV

It can be seen that they both make use of the distance vector algorithm. The difference is that DSDV protocol broadcasts periodically to maintain routing information, as long as routes are available, delay is very small. The primary disadvantage of DSDV is that the control overhead will be very large in large networks or in networks with rapidly moving nodes. AODV protocol just requires maintaining the needed routing, thus reducing the burden on the network, and making it has advantages in terms of routing overhead, bandwidth and power consumption. However, AODV needs to route discovery, then increases route discovery delay.

Table 1. Qualitative Comparison between DSDV and AODV

Comparison	DSDV	AODV
Routing Protocol Type	Proactive	On-demand
Algorithm Type	Distance Vector	Distance Vector
Packet Forwarding	By-hop	By-hop
Periodic Broadcast	Yes	No
Route Discovery Delay	Low	High
Routing Overhead	High	Low
Energy Consumption	High	Low
Bandwidth Consumption	High	Low

3   Measures of Routing Protocols

Based on the characteristics of the battlefield environment, measures of routing protocols include:

1) Packet Delivery Rate: the number of packets correctly received by destination nodes divided by the number of packets sent by source nodes. The higher the value, the more data packets sent to destination nodes successfully, and vice versa.

2) Average End-to-End Delay: time used by sending packet from source nodes to destination nodes. The smaller the delay, the stronger the network transmission capacity is.

3) Routing Overhead: the number of routing control packets sent by all network nodes within simulation time. Routing overhead is an important indicator to measure protocol performance, and it can be used to compare the scalability, ability of adapting to network congestion and efficiency of routing protocol.

4   Measures of Routing Protocols

4.1   Simulation Tools

Simulation is performed under VRNET Develop platform. VRNET Developer is an object-oriented discrete event network emulator, and it makes use of C++ object-oriented method for modeling and simulation. It has the development of whole Chinese interface, completely open to simulation kernel code and protocols, many communication protocol libraries, with these characteristics, VRNET Developer is fit for military communications simulation system which has relatively high demand of customized.

4.2   Routing Protocol Performance Simulation

In battlefield environment, the speed of the node affects the change of network topology, node density has a direct impact on the complexity of the network topology, and network load directly affects its performance. Therefore the main factors affecting the performance of Ad Hoc tactical unit network include node moving speed, node density and network load. Different simulation scenarios are designed to study the impact of these factors on the performance of DSDV routing protocol and AODV routing protocol.

The Impact of Node Speed on Routing Protocols. Take tank company tactical unit network as background to study the impact of node speed on the performance of routing protocols. Tank company tactical network has 10 nodes, node speed is about 36-72Km/h, node communication distance is generally 20-30Km, the source node packet size is generally about 1KB, and the time interval is about 1s [5].

Simulation nodes at the MAC layer use 802.11 CSMA/CA mechanism, wireless communication distance of node is 300m generally, but communication distance of radio in military communications is much longer, so when use node to simulate radio, the actual battlefield network's coverage area should be narrow accordingly. According to it, simulation model of tank company tactical network is build. The specific configuration is shown in Table 2.

Table 2. Tank company network services configuration

Services	Configuration
Node Number	10
Simulation Scene Area	2000m×2000m
Mobility Model	Group Mobility Model
Node Moving Speed(mps)	1、10、20、30
Packet Size(byte)	1024
Transmission Frequency	1s
Destination Node	Random
Simulation Time	600s

Square area simulates such a situation: nodes move freely around each other, there is a reasonable path and spatial diversity to use routing protocols [6].

In simulation, The rate and direction of node movement change over time, therefore the concept of mobility model is proposed, the substance of the mobile model is through a statistical point of view to represent the node movement model[7]. In Group mobility model, each group has a center, the center called the cluster head, which is the leader of the group nodes. Movement of the cluster head represents the movement trend of the entire group. The group nodes movement is in accord with the cluster head, but allows a certain degree of deviation. Because the group mobility characteristic is obvious in the battlefield environment, so the model is fit to simulate the node movement in the battlefield.

Packet size is 1024B, and the packet sending rate is 1s, which is close to the VHF Radio transfer rate of the new generation.

To ensure the accuracy of simulation results, five different seeds are used in each scene, finally we get the average simulation results.

The following is a tank company tactical Network simulation scenario.

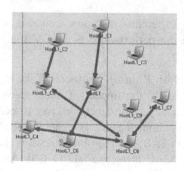

Fig. 1. Tank company tactical network

In Figure 1, there are 10 nodes, the middle one HostL1 is company commander vehicle, it is also the cluster head node of the group, and the rest nodes are ordinary members. The distance between the cluster head node and the ordinary node is approximately 200m, the transmission rate of all nodes is 8kbps, and the service is Continuous Bit Rate (CBR).

In the case of the parameters configuration as described above, simulation results are as follows:

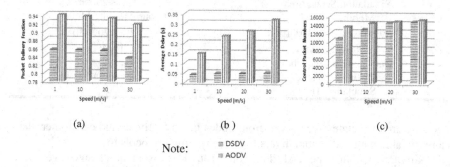

(a)   (b)   (c)

Note: ≡ DSDV
            ‖‖ AODV

Fig. 2. (a) Packet Delivery Rate. (b) Average Delay. (c) Routing Overhead.

It can be seen from Figure 2: with the increase of nodes speed, the performance of DSDV and AODV become bad.

In terms of average end-to-end delay, the faster the nodes move, the more rapidly the network topology changes, then AODV convergence slower, resulting in the delay rise. Because DSDV is a proactive protocol, so each node maintains a route to every other node in the network, the benefit is that when a route is needed, the route is immediately available.

In terms of packet arrival rate and routing overhead, the performance of AODV remains good, while DSDV perform worse when nodes move rapidly. Rapidly moving nodes lead to DSDV routing table often fail, then packet loss, but AODV has avoided this phenomenon successfully. With the accelerated speed of node, the DSDV routing incremental update message and the AODV routing request packet are increased, but the impact of speed changing on DSDV is greater than on AODV.

The Impact of Network Size on Routing Protocols. Take tank company tactical network and tank battalion tactical network as background respectively, to research the impact of network size on routing protocol performance. The tank battalion tactical network scenarios shown in Figure 3.

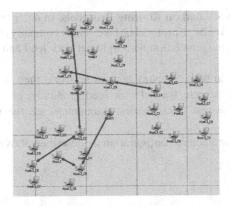

Fig. 3. Tank battalion tactical network

In Figure 3, there are 31 nodes, the middle one HostY1 is battalion commander vehicle, it is also the cluster head of the entire battalion, and HostL1, HostL2, HostL3 is the cluster head of its company respectively. The distance between the battalion cluster head and the company cluster head is 300m, and the distance between the company cluster head and the ordinary company nodes is 200m. The rest configuration parameters are the same as Table 2.

Simulation results are as follows:

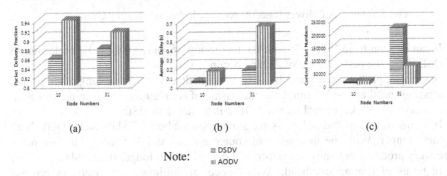

(a)   (b)   (c)

Note: ≡ DSDV
     ⦀ AODV

Fig. 4. (a) Packet Delivery Rate. (b) Average Delay. (c) Routing Overhead.

It can be seen from Figure 4:

Packet delivery rate of AODV is above 0.92, while Packet delivery of DSDV is about 0.88, AODV performs better.

The average end-to-end delay of each routing protocol becomes longer. Because of the increasing nodes, leading to some routing hops increase, therefore the average end-to-end delay becomes longer. As an active routing protocol, DSDV has a shorter delay.

With the increasing of nodes, routing control packets become more. DSDV broadcasts routing control packets periodically, while AODV sends routing control packets only when needed, so routing control packets of DSDV are much more than AODV.

The Impact of Network Load on Routing Protocols. In order to research the impact of network load on routing protocols, take tank company tactical network as background, and carry out simulation with light network load and heavy network load respectively.

There are 10 nodes in tank company tactical network, then set 2, 5 and 10 source nodes respectively to increase the network load gradually, and destination node is selected randomly. The rest configuration parameters are the same as previously described.

In the case of the parameters configuration as described above. Simulation results are as follows:

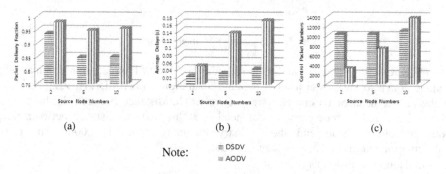

(a)   (b)   (c)

Note: ≡ DSDV
         ‖‖ AODV

Fig. 5. (a) Packet Delivery Rate. (b) Average Delay. (c) Routing Overhead.

It can be seen from Figure 5: with the increasing of source nodes, the performance of DSDV and the performance of AODV become worse.

In terms of packet arrival rate, because of the node storage queue length and packet processing speed are both limited, the increasing of source node result in packets loss. In this case, the packet arrival rate of AODV is higher than DSDV.

In terms of end-to-end delay, as the same reason above, DSDV and AODV both become longer. With the increasing of source nodes, AODV needs to initiate route discovery process frequently, its end-to-end delay is much longer than DSDV.

In terms of routing overhead, AODV needs to initiate route discovery process frequently, so the number of routing control packets increase dramatically. As an active routing protocol, routing control packets of DSDV changes little.

4.3   Conclusions of Simulation Results

Take tank company tactical network and tank battalion tactical network as background respectively, a series of simulation experiments are performed and simulation results are analyzed, conclusions are summarized as follows:

1) When nodes move slowly, DSDV and AODV both perform good. When nodes move rapidly, AODV performance remains good, but DSDV performance is badly. This shows that DSDV is fit for networks changing relatively slow.

2) When nodes in the network are fewer, the performance of DSDV and AODV are more or less. With the increasing of nodes, the packet arrival rate of DSDV rise a little, the end-to-end delay become much shorter, and the routing overhead become more less. The performance of AODV changes little. This shows that DSDV is more suitable for smaller networks.

3) With the increasing of source nodes, the packet arrival rate of DSDV declines sharply, but its end-to-end delay and routing overhead change very little. The packet arrival rate of AODV changes not much, but its end-to-end delay and routing overhead both increase much. This shows that network size have an important impact on both DSDV and AODV.

5   Summarize

In every simulation scene, the average end-to-end delay of DSDV is shorter than AODV, while the packet arrival rate of AODV has advantage. When network nodes are less and the nodes movement is slow, DSDV and AODV both have good performance. With the increasing of node and high mobility, the routing overhead of AODV performs better than DSDV. With the increasing of source nodes, the performance of DSDV and AODV both become worse.

Simulation results show that DSDV is fit for tactic unit network with fewer nodes, low mobility and light load, and the real-time performance of DSDV is good. While AODV performs well in tactic network with more nodes and rapid nodes movement, and the packet arrival rate performance of AODV is good. With heavy load, DSDV has advantage.

In a word, AODV is much fit for tactic network, but it also has some disadvantages, such as it does not support one-way channel, its end-to-end delay is long and its poor security. In the future, Effort should be made to decline routing overhead and the end-to-end delay of AODV, and enhance its security to fit tactic unit network well.

References

1. Yu, Q.: Tactical Communications Theory and Technology. Electronic Industry Press, Beijing (2009)
2. Liu, P., Zhou, X., Yang, H.: Wireless Ad Hoc Networks DSR Routing Protocol Simulation and Performance Analysis. Micro-Computer Information(Monitoring and Control Automation) (2009)
3. Zhang, H.: Wireless Ad Hoc Networks Routing Protocol Study and Implementation. Journal of Xi'an Electronic Science and Technology University (2009)

4. IETF RFC 3561. Ad hoc On-demand Distance Vector(AODV) Routing. The Internet Society, USA (2003)
5. Lin, H.: Ad Hoc Tactical Network Simulation Study. Journal of Chongqing University (2005)
6. Chen, L., Zeng, X., Cao, Y.: Mobile Ad Hoc Networks——Self-organizing Packet Radion Networks. Electronic Industry Press, Beijing (2006)
7. Wang, D.: Ad Hoc Network Mobility Model. Journal of Xi'an Electronic Science and Technology University (2009)

The Transmission Power Control Method for Wireless Sensor Networks Based on LQI and RSSI[*]

Shang Jin, Jingqi Fu, and Liming Xu

School of Mechatronic Engineering and Automation,
Shanghai University, Shanghai, China
{jinshang521,xuliming826}@163.com,
jqfu@staff.shu.edu.cn

Abstract. Improving energy efficiency to prolong the lifetime is a key research issue of the wireless sensor networks. Appropriately adjusting the nodes transmission power is very important to reduce the network energy consumption. This paper proposes a transmission power control method based on LQI and RSSI which can dynamically adjust the network energy consumption and improve the energy efficiency of the wireless sensor nodes. The test conducted on a wireless network established in the lab shows that the transmission power control method can save the nodes energy effectively as well as significantly prolong the lifetime of the network.

Keywords: WSN, LQI, RSSI, energy consumption, transmission power control.

1 Introduction

Wireless sensor network (WSN) consists of a large number of low-power sensor nodes. The main function of the WSN is to collect the information from the surrounding environment and send them to the sink.

Usually the sensor node carries limited resources and cannot be recharged. Therefore, it becomes a key research issue on improving the energy efficiency and prolonging the network lifetime.

2 Energy Consumption Model and Distribution

2.1 Energy Consumption Model

Consider the energy consumption model in [5]. The energy consumption of the nodes consists of circuit propagation loss and power amplification loss. Node sends l bits

---
[*] This work is supported by Key Project of Science and Technology Commission of Shanghai Municipality under Grant 11DZ1121602. Shanghai Key Laboratory of Power Station Automation Technology.

T. Xiao, L. Zhang, and M. Fei (Eds.): AsiaSim 2012, Part II, CCIS 324, pp. 37–44, 2012.

data to a sink. The distance between the node and the sink position is d. Equation (1) is the energy consumption of sending data, (2) is the energy consumption of receiving data.

$$
\begin{cases}
E_{member} = lE_{elec} + l\varepsilon_{fs}d^2 & if \quad d < d_0 \\
E_{member} = lE_{elec} + l\varepsilon_{amp}d^4 & if \quad d > d_0
\end{cases}
\tag{1}
$$

$$
E_{RX}(l) = lE_{elec}
\tag{2}
$$

E_{elec} is the circuit propagation loss. If the propagation distance is smaller than the threshold value d_0, then the power amplification loss should be considered in the free space model. Otherwise, the power amplification loss should be considered in the multiple-routine attenuation model. $\varepsilon_{fs}, \varepsilon_{amp}$ are the energy needed to amplify the power in the two models respectively.

2.2   Energy Consumption Distribution

Using the above mentioned energy consumption model, [6-7] have presented the distribution of the WSN energy consumption. The energy consumption is affected by the transmitted data amount, transmitting speed and the emission radius. Specific relationships are shown in the Fig. 1 to Fig. 3 as is shown below.

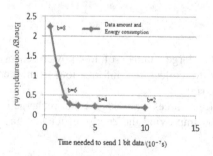
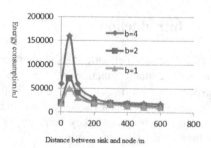

Fig. 1. Relation of energy and time needed to transmit 1 bit data

Fig. 2. Energy consumption under different transmitting speed

For the same size of data, when the code rate is settled, the higher the transmitting speed, the larger bit number of one code is. However, the energy consumption increases as well. When the transmitting speed is settled, the energy consumption increases by the increasing number of data transmitted. If the transmitting speed and the data amount are stable, in a short reach transmission, the smaller emission radius, the lower energy consumption is while the nodes transmission power directly determines the emission radius.

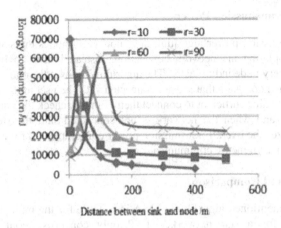

Fig. 3. Energy consumption under different emission radius

If screenshots are necessary, please make sure that you are happy with the print quality before you send the files.

3   Typical Methods of Transmission Power Control

It is difficult to effectively adjust the data amount and transmitting speed because of the restriction of the application or the limitation of the hardware. However, it is much easier to adjust the transmission power for there are many transmission power adjustable RF chips which can be used to control the energy consumption precisely.

The transmission power control method can be used in different aspects of local and global. Common algorithms are: Local Mean Algorithm (LMA), Fixed Transmission Power, (FTP) and Diverse Transmission Power (DTP) [8].

3.1   Local Mean Algorithm

Local mean algorithm is a typical method of controlling the number of neighbors by adjusting the transmission power. The algorithm defines upper and lower limits. If the neighbor number is bigger than the upper limit, then decrease the transmission power by a proportional amount. If the neighbor number is smaller than the lower limit, then increase the transmission power by a proportional amount. The adjustment is done when the number of neighbors is among the limit.

3.2   Fixed Transmission Power

The fixed transmission power algorithm sets an arbitrary transmission power for all nodes in the same network. Assume that the network characteristics are already known. Thus, the minimum transmission power needed for global communication can be calculated. This minimum transmission power is set as the global transmission power.

3.3   Diverse Transmission Power

The diverse transmission power algorithm does not set all nodes the same transmission power when completing the network connection. Instead it tries to find a minimum power level for every node individually. The algorithm chooses the one with the smallest distance among the node pairs that are not connected yet. Then set transmission power of these two nodes to value sufficient to connect them. Finally, check the connectivity of the resulting network and when the network is not connected start the steps again. This algorithm minimizes the overall transmission power consumption for the entire network, but it may result in asymmetric communication.

3.4   Analysis and Comparison

Of all the above mentioned algorithms, LMA is suitable for the multi-hop network. It is too complex for a star network.   FTP only concerns about the minimum transmission power and neglects the date transmission QoS. DTP combines the advantages of the LAM and FTP. It provides transmission power control method in the global area, but the local area transmission power control method is not included.

In this paper, we propose a transmission power control method which is more efficient in power control.

4   The Transmission Power Control Method Base on LQI and RSSI

4.1   LQI and RSSI

LQI (Link Quality Indicator) indicates the energy and quality of the data received. Its value is based on the signal strength and the signal-to-noise ratio (SNR). It is calculated by the MAC layer and transmitted to the upper layer. Generally it is related to the probability of receiving the correct data. RSSI (Receive Signal Strength Indicator) is the value of difference between the optimal received signal strength and the actual receive signal strength. The dynamic range of LQI is larger than RSSI, and LQI has a higher resolution. Nevertheless RSSI has a faster response speed than LQI, so that RSSI can reflect the network status more rapidly. Combining LQI and RSSI to evaluate the network status can have more accuracy and fast response, thus helps to adjust the transmission power more effectively and precisely.

4.2   Transmission Power Control Method Based on LQI and RSSI

The transmission power control method is an algorithm proposed by this paper intending to dynamically adjust the transmission power in wireless sensor networks. Assume that the network is a single-hop network. The working principles are as follows:

All the nodes are set to an initial transmission power when the nodes are started. There is a vector table of transmission power stored in the node. The vector table contains all the transmission power levels for example the RF chip CC2530 from Texas Instrument has 16 levels of transmission power. The sink stores a threshold table of LQI and RSSI which defines the upper and lower limit of LQI and RSSI values. Refer to [9] to define the thresholds or consider the actual applicative requirements to set the value.

After the network is established, nodes start to send data to the sink. The sink calculates the LQI and RSSI value when the date is received. It compares the LQI and RSSI value with the threshold value stored in the sink. The sink judges the RSSI value each time it receives the data. If the RSSI is lower than the threshold value, the sink will tell the node to increase the transmission power. If the RSSI value is appropriate, then the node transmission power will stay the same. The sink judges the LQI every 100 pieces of data. The value judged by the sink is the mean value of last 100 LQI values. If both the mean LQI value and the RSSI value are larger than the threshold value, then the sink tells the node to decrease two levels of transmission power. If the mean LQI value is higher than the threshold value and the RSSI is not, then the sink tells the node to suspend the transmission power. If the mean LQI value is lower than the threshold value, then increase the transmission power. Otherwise, keep the nodes transmission power the same as last time. The node adjusts the transmission power based on the command sent by the sink. The strategy of increasing the transmission power is to choose a middle level between the current power level and the maximum power level. If there are two middle levels, then choose the bigger one. If the node does not receive the acknowledgement from the sink in a certain time of waiting, then the node will increase the transmission power by itself, and send the data again. The retransmission mechanism should be considered under the actual application circumstances.

4.3   Algorithm Flow Chart

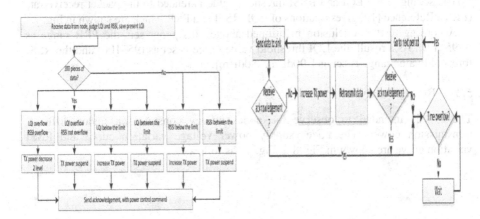

•   **Fig. 4.** The flow chart of sink   **Fig. 5.** The flow chart of node

5   The Test on an Single-Hop Network

5.1   Environment Settings

The test is conducted on a single-hop star network. In order to verify the algorithm only in the aspect of whether it can control the energy consumption or not, the network will be established on one sink and three nodes. Each test consists of one sink and one node. The three nodes transmission power are set respectively as follows: maximum transmission power (4.5dBm), initial transmission power (-10dBm), adjustable transmission power. Each node carries the same power resource (2×1.5V dry batteries). The test is conducted under the same environmental conditions. The node sends data every 2 seconds and works for 96 hours if possible. The test platform is as shown in Fig. 6.

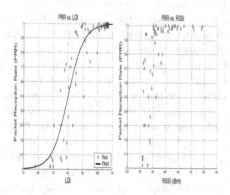

Fig. 6. Factual picture of the test platform   **Fig. 7.** PRR vs. LQI and PRR vs. RSSI

The setting of the LQI and RSSI threshold value is related to the packet receive rate (PRR). Reference [10] gives relations of LQI, RSSI and PRR which are shown in Fig. 7.

According to the conclusion mentioned above, this paper sets the PRR range as [0.95, 1.0]. As a result, the LQI threshold value range is set as [95, 100] and the RSSI threshold value range is set as [-90dBm, -80dBm].

5.2   Results Analysis

The test is intended to observe the nodes energy consumption under different transmission power. The nodes supply power voltage variation curve and RSSI variation curve are shown in Fig. 8 to Fig. 10 as follows.

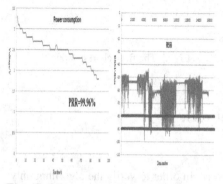

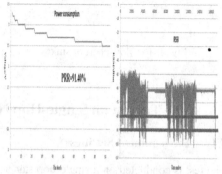

Fig. 8. Max transmission power node voltage and RSSI

Fig. 9. Initial transmission power node voltage and RSSI

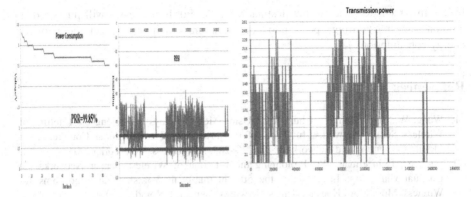

Fig. 10. Adjustable transmission power node voltage and RSSI

Fig. 11. Adjustable transmission power variation curve

In the figures above, the thick lines represent the upper and lower limits of RSSI value.

The Fig. 8 shows that the node using the maximum transmission power maintains a pretty high PRR (99.96%) and RSSI while the supply power voltage drops quickly. The Fig. 9 shows that the node using the initial power has lower energy consumption but the time that the RSSI is below the lower limit is longer and the PRR (91.40%) is not acceptable. The Fig.10 shows that the node using adjustable transmission power makes a balance between energy consumption and PRR (99.85%) while the RSSI stays between the limits mostly of the running time.

Fig. 11 is the variation curve of the adjustable transmission power node. The transmission power levels are represented by numbers from 5 to 249 which mean - 22dBm to 4.5dBm. From the curve we can see that most of the testing time the nodes transmission power stays at a low level which helps the node to save energy.

The result accords with the expected goal which means that the algorithm of dynamically controlling the transmission power can improve the energy efficiency and prolong the network life time as well as ensure that the network communication is unimpeded.

6   Summarization and Prospect

The transmission power control method based on LQI and RSSI proposed in this paper make an balance between transmission power and packet receive rate. Through the test, it shows that the algorithm can improve the network energy efficiency and prolong the network lifetime.

If the network topology is more complex than the single-hop network, for instance a multi-hop network, the algorithm proposed by this paper does not have a control strategy for adjusting global energy distribution which may lead to energy hole.

In the further research, we will try to add a power control command forwarding strategy. Thus, the algorithm proposed in this paper can be used in a multi-hop network. When the power control command is sent from the sink, it will be forwarded by the intermediate nodes to the destination node. Furthermore we will put the data amount and transmitting speed into consideration which also affect the network energy consumption.

References

1. Wang, W., Srinivasan, V., Chua, K.C.: Using Mobile Relays to Prolong the Lifetime of Wireless Sensor Networks. In: Proc. of the 11th Annual International Conference on Mobile Computing and Networking, pp. 270–283. ACM Press, New York (2005)
2. Soro, S., Heinzelman, W.: Prolonging the Lifetime of Wireless Sensor Networks via Unequal Clustering. In: Proc. of the 5th International Workshop on Algorithms for Wireless, Mobile, Ad Hoc and Sensor Networks. Denver, Colorado (2005)
3. Shi, G.-T., Liao, M.-H.: Movement-Assisted Data Gathering Scheme with Load-Balancing for Sensor Networks. Movement-Assisted Data Gathering Scheme with Load-Balancing for Sensor Networks. Journal of Software 18(9), 2235–2244 (2007)
4. Monks, J.P., Ebert, J.P., Wolisz, A., Mei, W., Hwu, W.: A study of the Energy Saving and Capacity Improvement Potential of Power Control in Multi-Hop Wireless Networks. In: Workshop on Wireless Local Networks, also Conf of Local Computer Networks(LCN), Tampa, Florida, USA (November 2001)
5. Nhatre, V., Rosenberg, C.: Design Guidelines for Wireless Sensor Networks: Communication, Clustering and Aggregation. Ad Hoc Networks 2(1), 45–63 (2004)
6. Raghunathan, V., Schurgers, C., Park, S., Srivastava, M.B.: Energy aware wireless microsensor networks. IEEE Signal Processing Magazine 19(2), 40–50 (2002)
7. Zeng, Z.-W., Chen, Z.-G., Liu, A.-F.: Energy-Hole Avoidance for WSN Based on Adjust Transmission Power. Chinese Journal of Computers 33(1), 12–22 (2010)
8. Kubisch, M., Karl, H., Wolisz, A., Zhong, L.C., Rabaey, J.: Distributed Algorithms for Transmission Power Control in Wireless Sensor Networks. In: 2003 IEEE Wireless Communications and Networking, WCNC 2003, March 16-20, vol. 1 (2003)
9. Xu, H., Tu, Y.-Q., Xiao, W., Guo, B., Xu, G.-B.: The Power Control Method in Sensor Networks of LQI-based Mean Value. Journal of Logistical Engineering University 25(2), 56–59 (2009)
10. Gungor, V.C., Sastry, C., Song, Z., Integlia, R.: Resource-Aware and Link Quality Based Routing Metric for Wireless Sensor and Actor Networks. In: Proceeding of IEEE ICC, Glasgow, UK, pp. 3364–3369 (2007)

Research on ZigBee Wireless Meter Reading System in Opnet Simulator

Yinfang Wang and Shiwei Ma

School of Mechatronics Engineering & Automation,
Shanghai Key Laboratory of Power Station Automation Technology,
Shanghai University, NO.149, Yanchang Rd.
200072 Shanghai, China
masw@shu.edu.cn

Abstract. The paper aims to evaluate the performance of a ZigBee wireless meter reading system using Opnet. At first, a scheme of distributed meter reading system is proposed. In order to simulate the real system, an energy module special for CC2530 is added in Opnet. Then the necessary parameter configurations for it are considered. At last, the simulation environment of the proposed system is set up. According to the monitored global and local statistics, it comes to the conclusion that the scheme has the distinguishing characteristics of the smaller end-to-end delay, the few packet loss as well as lower energy consumption and can be well applied in the factual meter reading system.

Keywords: Wireless meter reading system, ZigBee, Opnet.

1   Introduction

Wireless sensor network (WSN) is a distributed network of nodes with limited energy. And it can collect the physical or environmental conditions, such as pressure, motion, temperature, etc. The standards like IEEE 802.15.4 and ZigBee have provided in this field, which have an effect on the commercial applications like health, home control, wireless meter reading, etc. ZigBee is a set of communication protocols for small coverage, low rate wireless network [1]. It can operate at the 868MHz frequency band at a data rate of 20 kbps in Europe, 916 MHz band at 40 kbps in the USA and 2.4 GHz at 250kbps worldwide. ZigBee architecture is accordance with the international ISO, which is comprised of the physical layer, IEEE 802.15.4 MAC, network layer and application layer. It supports multiple topologies like star, tree and mesh network. Two kinds of nodes are used: full function devices (FFD) and reduced function devices (RFD). The former can be configured as coordinator and communicate with any other devices. The latter can access to the network and only communicate with FFDs or coordinator, not with another RFD.

The current dominating network tools are NS2 and Opnet. Opnet can simulate heterogeneous network that uses multiple communication protocols. Besides, it encompasses libraries including the models for the equipments and protocols for many of the best known communication technologies [2]. Opnet encompasses several

T. Xiao, L. Zhang, and M. Fei (Eds.): AsiaSim 2012, Part II, CCIS 324, pp. 45–53, 2012.

fixed or mobile components of a ZigBee network – ZigBee coordinator, ZigBee router, ZigBee end device. Besides, the ZigBee model is newly added in Opnet 14.5 and above. The most noticeable limitation of the ZigBee model is the incomplete implementation of the beaconing capability [3]. So the nodes can't enter into the sleeping mode periodically to save energy in the simulation. But these limitations can't hinder the convenience and accuracy to simulate the network.

This paper is organized as follows. In Section 2, a distributed ZigBee meter reading system is proposed. In Section 3, we describe the node modeling and energy module for the system. In Section 4, we build the simulation system and analyze the simulation results. In Section 5, the conclusive remark is come up.

2   ZigBee Wireless Meter Reading System

In general, wireless meter reading system is a multi-layer and distributed structure [4], and consists of meter management center, smart meter, wireless sensor network, public network, etc. In this paper, the schematic diagram of the overall ZigBee meter reading system is shown in Figure 1. Obviously the wireless sensor network includes concentrator, router and collector. Each wireless meter-reading area, such as District 1#, establishes a mesh network in the circle of the specific coordinator. Collector achieves the meter data by RS485 bus, and then sends the nearest router or coordinator. Besides, a router extends the scope of network. In addition, the wireless communication chips for three kinds of nodes are CC2530 in the wireless network.

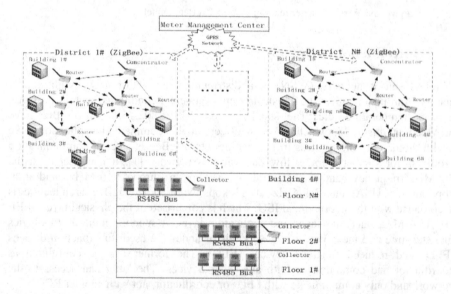

Fig. 1. The schematic diagram of ZigBee wireless meter reading system

3   Node Modeling and Energy Module for ZigBee

3.1   Network Nodes Modeling

Before the simulation, network node modeling is necessary. The modeling mainly involves the radio channel modeling, concentrator and router modeling as well as collector modeling.

In Opnet, the establishment of radio channel can be realized by the wireless transceiver. In the physical layer of ZigBee, there are 27 physical radio channels: one in the 868MHz, ten in the 915MHz and sixteen in the 2.4GHz [5]. The attributes of transceiver can be set in the node model of ZigBee. The main attribute configurations are as follows: 2.4GHz frequency band, 5MHz in the bandwidth, the modulation for O-QPSK (MSK), the data transmission speed of 250kbps and the technology of Direct Sequence Spread Spectrum (DSSS), the spreading code of 8.

The functions of concentrator are same as ones of ZigBee coordinator. And the main attribute configurations of it are as follows: application traffic (no traffic), frequency band (2450MHz), transmit power (0.005), channel sensing duration (0.1s), PANID (0x0001), ACK Mechanism (enabled), reception power threshold (-85dBm), etc. Besides, the configurations of router are the same as ones of concentrator above, except for the item of ACK Mechanism. The functions of collector are same as mobile ZigBee end device. The configurations of collector are the same as router above, except for the item of application traffic (parent) and altitude. And the altitude value of collector is increasing with the step of layer.

Considering that Opnet ZigBee model is capable of handling range about 1200 meters at the default settings for transmission power and reception power (0.05) [3]. However, the power of transceiver is set as 0.005 in this paper. And the communication range is about 100 meters which is similar to one of CC2530.

3.2   Energy Process Module

There is incomplete implementation for the beacon enable mode. So it is difficult to simulate periodical wake-up and sleeping in Opnet. Energy consumption of CC2530 mainly comes from the periods of receiving and transmitting [6]. Regardless of the sleeping mode, a energy module is built in the node model of ZigBee (Figure 2).

The current for CC2530 is 24mA in the receiving mode and 29mA when in the transmitting mode by 1 dBm [7]. According to the 3dB principle, the current is 58mA when it is in 3 dBm for transmitting. The current is 14.5 mA and 7.25mA separately when in -3dBm and -6dBm. So the corresponding configuration is shown on the left side of Figure 3. The initial energy is configured as 2AA batteries of 34560 Joule.

The statistics for the energy module containing the global statistic and local statistics is shown on the right side of Figure 3. Consumed Energy (Joule) belongs to the global statistic. Remaining Energy (Joule) and Consumed Energy (Joule) belong to the local statistics.

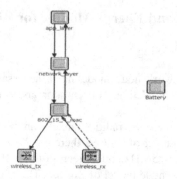

Fig. 2. Node model of ZigBee network

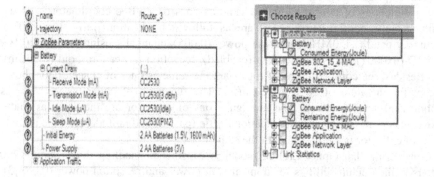

Fig. 3. Energy configuration and statistics of node

4   Simulation Design and Results

The simulation tool used in this article is Opnet 14.5. The simulation scenario is 360000 square meters (600 meters multiply by 600 meters). The interferences for adjacent networks can be reduced into the minimum by means of mutiple channels technology in ZigBee. The simulation may simplify into ZigBee network of a single coordinator in sub-district, such as District 1#.

At present, the buildings between six and eighteen layers are the majority in metropolis. However, the others are in the minority. Besides, building with eighteen layers is the trend in the future. So it is assumed that each building has the same floor of eighteen layers in the paper. The height of each floor is 3 meters for the building. The simulation that we developed is aimed to evaluate the performance of real wireless meter reading system based on ZigBee. These projects are introduced next.

Project 1 contains several comparative scenarios including the network topology scenarios, node placement scenarios, acknowledgement mechanism scenarios. In order to simulate the larger mesh network, we must modify the network parameters, such as the maximum children, maximum router, maximum depth, etc. And it has been proved that the network with the modified parameters works well. A case in point is that the maximum of children, router and depth are set as 35, 15 and 5 separately for these simulations. Afterward, the placement scenarios are in the implement. After running the simulation for this project, there is a coupled statistic concerning the limitation of the node identification, where the nodes with the same x position and y position as well as the different altitudes are treated as a node. So the collectors of a building are placed in the slightly different x and y position in the following projects.

From the comparative acknowledgment mechanism scenarios, the end-to-end delay makes few differences among the networks with and without the acknowledgement mechanism. Despite of the acknowledgments will increase slightly the overhead as well as the throughput and delay of the MAC (Figure 4). The acknowledgement mechanism will improve the performance of wireless meter reading system. So the acknowledgment enables in the following project.

In the conclusion, these basic experiments and established parameters are beneficial to the next project.

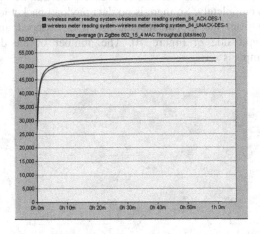

Fig. 4. Throughput of MAC for established mesh network

Project 2 encompasses one scenario (Figure 5). It is a distributed network with 14 supervised areas, where a building stands. There is a router and six collectors in every area. The network adopts the mesh topology. So there are one concentrator, fourteen routers and eighty-four (fourteen multiply by six) collectors in the network. The configurations for a variety of nodes are shown in the previous section.

The global statistics monitored are: end-to-end delay, load, traffic sent (packets and bps), traffic received (packets and bps), consumed energy (Joule), throughout, data dropped and retransmission attempts. The local statistics collected are traffic sent (packets and bps) in the ZigBee application, load and data traffic sent (packets and bps) in the MAC.

From the statistics concerning the data traffic for a collector (Figure 6), obviously the traffic header including the network and MAC layer is up to about 262 bps. It is possible to remark that the overhead traffic can be up to about 50% of total traffic which is generated by each collector with 208 bits per second. Hence, collector can store the multiple meter values at first and package the values together to send the network for the purpose of the efficiency in the real meter reading system.

End-to-end delay is shown in Figure 7. The delay fluctuates with 0.0081s during an hour. But the delay also decreases when some nodes consume their energy and fail. So the delay can meet the request for the wireless meter reading system.

The local statistic of remaining energy and consumed energy of a collector is shown in Figure 8. Each collector is powered by 2AA batteries. The initial energy is 34560 Joule. The consumed energy of collector grows linearly at the proportion of 0.02 on the right side of Figure 8. And the total consumed energy for each collector is 1.1 Joule during an hour. The global statistic of the remaining energy is shown in Figure 9. And the remaining energy curve of the network reduces slightly on the stable phase during an hour. Hence, the design of meter reading system can maintain about one year for the consideration of the consumption for the peripheral interface such as RS485, RS232.

The synthetic curve for the global statistics of send traffic and traffic receive at the application level is shown on the left side of Figure 10. It can be figured out that the two curves overlap completely. So there is no data payload packet loss. In addition, it is better to prove from the global statistic for data dropped and retransmission attempts on the right side of Figure 10. The number of the data dropped and retransmission attempts is zero.

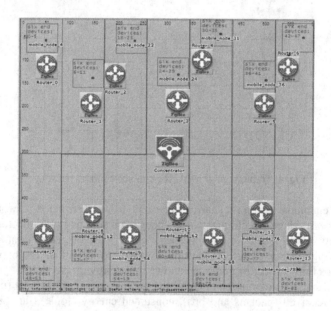

Fig. 5. Scenarios used to simulate the actual meter reading system

Throughput is shown in Figure 11. It can be demonstrated that the throughput is still below 28 kbps, which is much lower than the highest throughput of 250 kbps in ZigBee.

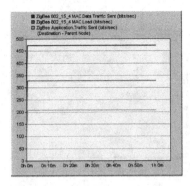

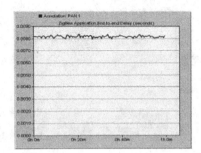

Fig. 6. Data traffic for one collector

Fig. 7. The global statistic of end-to-end delay (second)

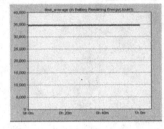

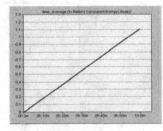

Fig. 8. The local statistic of the remaining energy and the consumed energy (Joule) for an collector

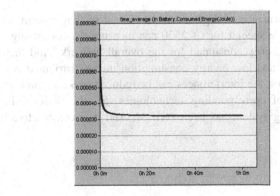

Fig. 9. The global statistic of the remaining energy (Joule)

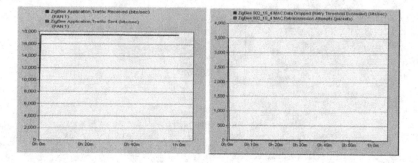

Fig. 10. The global statistic of send traffic and traffic receive at the application level on the left side. The global statistic for data dropped and retransmission attempts on the right side.

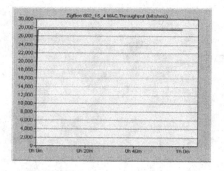

Fig. 11. The global statistic of throughout in MAC

5   Conclusions

In this paper, the performance of ZigBee wireless meter reading system is evaluated. Firstly, a energy module special for CC2530 can measure the consuming energy for every node and total energy consumed for the overall network. And there is small delay, few packet loss and low energy consumption in the distributed network with one coordinator. Besides, the interferences can be reduced into minimum for adjacent networks by means of corresponding technologies. So the reasonability for the proposed meter reading system has been verified. And it is constructive to the real meter reading system.

References

1. Baronti, P., Pillai, P., Chook, V.W.C., Chess, S., Gotta, A., Fun Hu, Y.: Wireless sensor networks: A survey on the state of the art and the 802.15.4 and ZigBee standards. Computer Communications 30, 1655–1695 (2007)
2. Marghescu, C., Pantazica, M., Brodeala, A., Svasta, P.: Simulation of a wireless sensor network using OPNET. In: 2011 IEEE 17th International Symposium for Design and Technology in Electronic Packaging(SIITME), Timisoara, Romania, pp. 249–252 (2011)
3. Opnet. Opnet Help
4. Cao, S.: Wireless Automatic Meter Reading System for Resident Power User Based on Smart Electricity Meter. J. Electrical Technology 8, 112–116 (2010)
5. ZigBee Alliance: ZigBee Wireless Networking (2002)
6. Farahani, S.: ZigBee Wireless Networks and Transceivers. USA (2008)
7. Texas Instruments Inc. CC2530Fx Datasheeet,
   http://www.ti.com/lit/ds/symlink/cc2530.pdf

Network-in-the-Loop Simulation Platform
for Control System

Xiaowei Chen, Yang Song, and Jia Yu

Shanghai Key Laboratory of Power Station Automation Technology,
Department of Automation,
School of Mechatronical Engineering & Automation, Shanghai University,
Shanghai 200072, China
y_song@shu.edu.cn

Abstract. In order to research how the real network influences the control system, a Network-in-the-loop simulation platform is established in this paper. The platform consists of two simulation modules and two communication interfaces. Plant modeling and controller design is based on Matlab whereas communication interfaces programming is complemented in Visual C++. In this scheme, data is exchanged between Matlab and VC++ by Dynamic Data Exchange (DDE) technology, while Windows Socket is used for networked transmission design. On the platform, users can design and imitate the real networked control online. Besides, the real-time delay data is obtained in Simulink environment. Finally, according to the simulation experiment of DC motor servo system, the validity of the simulation platform is demonstrated.

Keywords: Network-in-the-loop, Synchronization, NCS simulation.

1   Introduction

In recent years, embedded, distributed and pervasive systems have gained a significant importance in a number of applications, including exploration, industrial automation, and remotely operated vehicles. These applications go under the general name of Networked Control Systems (NCSs). The NCS is a kind of closed-loop feedback systems. The sensor, controller and actuator of NCS communicate through network. Comparing with the traditional control system, NCS has an advantage of low cost, convenient diagnosis and maintenance.

While NCS brings a broad vision to the control system, it also has some restraints. The communication delay and package loss caused by network, make the control system more complex to analyze and design. A considerable number of studies on the relationship between network and control system are reported. The simulation of NCS plays an important role in the validation of these works. In the simulation of NCS, both the control and communication aspects have to be taken into account. While simulation methods of traditional control systems only imitate the control principle, they are not suitable for NCS. To address this problem, many NCS simulation platforms are proposed.

T. Xiao, L. Zhang, and M. Fei (Eds.): AsiaSim 2012, Part II, CCIS 324, pp. 54–62, 2012.

The general method of NCS simulation is utilizing a toolbox, Truetime [1-3]. The network block of Truetime can imitate network such as Ethernet, CAN, TDMA, FDMA, and so on. But Truetime is lack of the simulation of high-level network protocols, like TCP and UDP. For this reason, several authors choose network simulator such as NS2 to imitate the communication module of NCS [4]. But it is quite difficult for new users, because there are few user-friendly manuals. And above simulation approaches are based on virtual network which is not exactly the same as real network. Thus, several simulation frameworks based on real industrial control network such as CAN and ProfiBus have been proposed [5], [6]. In these networks, time delay is less than the sampling period, and there is almost no package lost. But in NCS, delay and package dropout both exist, and delay may be more than sampling period. So these frameworks just reflect the relationship between control and a special network. With the rapid development of Internet, Internet-based NCS has been widely applied in many fields, and the realization of Internet-based simulation and control is significant.

In this paper, the Network-in-the-loop Simulation Platform is established based on Internet. The concept of network-in-the-loop means that real network is inserted into the closed control loop, and both control data and sensor data is transmitted through real network, instead of virtual network. And the influence of real network can be reflected completely, especially when the NCS contains time-depended parameters. On the platform, users can design plant and controller models in Matlab according to their different needs, and they can also collect the delay data of NCS online.

2 Relevant Background and Technology

Based on Matlab and Internet, a few distanced laboratories are built to share resources and information [7-11]. Users can create Matlab applications that use the capabilities of the World Wide Web to send data to Matlab for computation and to display the results in a Web browser. But these laboratories have some restraints: (1) users can only choose plant from existing devices of laboratory, or select a control algorithm from those provided by laboratory; (2) the code of distant controller/plant is downloaded to a local computer to operate together with local plant/controller, so that the control systems is still a local-control system.

In order to solve the above two problems, the Network-in-the-loop Simulation Platform is designed based on Visual C++ and Matlab. The implementation of remote real-time simulation can be divided into two steps: (1) establish simulation model of controller on client and model of plant on server; (2) communicate through Internet between simulation models. Step (1) can be finished by users according to their special needs. Step (2) is achieved by Socket technology and Dynamic Data Exchange (DDE) technology.

Windows Socket is the open, widely used programming interface under Windows Operating System, and supported by multiple protocols. It is also the most common application programming interface on TCP/IP network and Internet. So Socket is used for networked communication between is based applications of Visual C++. While DDE technique is utilized code for data interaction between Visual C++ and MATLAB. The primary function of DDE is to allow Windows applications to share data.

3   Network-in-the-Loop Simulation Platform

3.1   The Structure and Realization of the Platform

The framework of network-in-the-loop simulation platform is Client/Server structure. On both client and server side, there is a MFC communication interface and a Simulink model. Each side can be divided into three parts: simulation model, the date exchange interface between VC++ and Matlab, VC++ networked communication module. Fig.1 shows the structure of network-in-the-loop simulation platform.

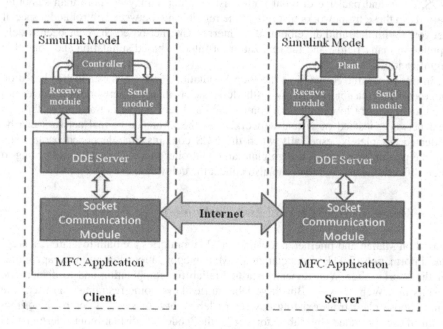

Fig. 1. Structure of Network-in-the-loop Simulation Platform

The controller and plant model is set up by Simulink. The VC++ networked communication module is MFC applications. Data interaction between VC++ and Matlab relies on DDE conversation. The DDE server of the conversation is registered in MFC application whereas the DDE client is realized by S-function in Simulink.

Fig.2 shows the simulation flow of the platform. The MFC application on the server of this platform should be run first to start the service; then run the client MFC application and connect to the server; open the controller model on the client and begin to simulate; open the server plant simulation model to start simulation and data transmission. The default case is that the controller model is the initiator of data transmission. The data exchange is launched after the server responses.

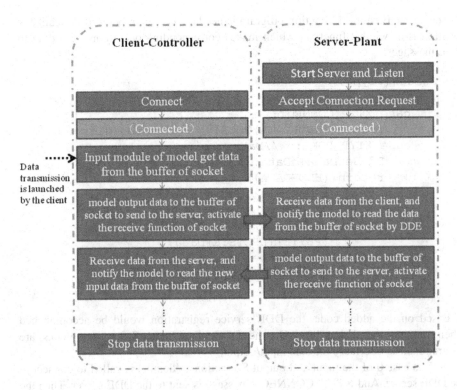

Fig. 2. The flow of Network-in-the-loop Simulation Platform

Data Interface Module. DDE conversation is conduct between DDE client program--Matlab simulation model, and DDE server program--MFC application. What should be done first is to add code into MFC dialog initialization module for the DDE server initialization and registration:

```
if(DdeInitialize(&idInst,
                (PFNCALLBACK)DdeCallback,
                APPCMD_FILTERINITS|
                CBF_FAIL_EXECUTES|
                CBF_SKIP_CONNECT_CONFIRMS|
                CBF_SKIP_CONNECT_CONFIRMS,
                0))
{
    MessageBox("DDE initialization failed•");
    return(FALSE);
}
DdeNameService(idInst,hszApp,0,DNS_REGISTER);
```

Then a DDE callback function program is needed. The main body of the callback function is a switch() function, which makes corresponding operations according to DDE messages:

```
switch(wType)
{
    case XTYP_CONNECT:
        return((HDDEDATA)TRUE);   //Connect allowed
    case XTYP_POKE:   //Data coming
        DdeGetData(hData,(PBYTE)stmp,255,0);
        return((HDDEDATA)DDE_FACK);
    case XTYP_ADVREQ:    //Data update
    case XTYP_REQUEST:    //Data request
        return(DdeCreateDataHandle(idInst,
                (PBYTE)(LPCTSTR)Data,
                Data.GetLength()+1,
                0,Item,wFmt,0));  //Return data
}
```

Based on the added code, the DDE service registration would be accomplished when running the dialog box. On the DDE client side, S-function blocks are programmed as interfaces for data input/output.

Both in case 0 of the input and output S-functions, ddeinit() is called to connect to the DDE server. And XTYP_CONNECT message is sent to the DDE server. Then the callback function allows the connection by returning TRUE. After conversation is established, ddepoke() function is called in case 3 of the output S-function when the Simulink model has data to export. Computer system sends XTYP_POKE message to the callback function, and then the DdeGetData() function receives data. While in the input S-function, ddereq() function would send out a data request to the DDE server when the model wants input data. Then the callback function will respond to XTYP_REQUEST message and transfer the data to simulation model.

Networked Communication Module. VC++ network communication module realizes data transmission between the client and the server of the simulation platform. The communication process is that: (1) the server creates a listening socket which is a blocking socket, and listens to the connection request from the client; (2) the client establishes a socket and requests for connection; (3) the server creates a new socket for communication after accepting the connection request, and begins to exchange data.

In the server program of Network-in-the-loop Simulation Platform, the network communication socket is a custom socket class which derived from the non-blocking socket class. The custom class can capture activation events of Socket to call corresponding response functions. Once receiving the output data of the plant model the server would inspire FD_WRITE event immediately. Then the OnSend () function of the communication socket will send the output data to the client. After that, the server immediately activates FD_READ to accept the data from the controller, and gives the returned data to the simulation model.

In the client program of Network-in-the-loop Simulation Platform, the data flow is similar with the server program. The main difference is that the socket used by the client program is blocking, for realizing the synchronization of models.

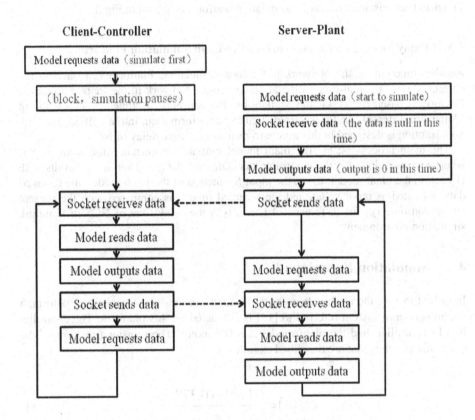

Fig. 3. Data Sending and Receiving Process

3.2   Synchronization of the Network-in-the-Loop Simulation Platform

As we all know, Simulink is a pseudo-real-time simulation environment. Its simulation time is a different concept from the actual time. And it corresponds with the model complexity and execution speed of computer. Because the simulation speed of controller and plant may be inconsistencies even if they have the same simulation time step, the synchronization between the client and the server of Network-in-the-loop Simulation Platform should be taken into account.

For simulation tools and models which are connected by Socket interface, the synchronization can be solved by blocking the read/write operations of socket [12]. Choose blocking socket class to transfer data in the client program. If the plant model has not yet simulated while the controller model has began to run, the client program would block on OnReceive() function, and simulation of controller would also pause at time zero. Until the plant model begins to simulate, the server sends data and the client receives data successfully, and then the controller model continues to simulate. The data transmission process on simulation platform is shown in Fig.3.

3.3   Delay Testing on the Network-in-the-Loop Simulation Platform

Another function of the Network-in-the-loop Simulation Platform is to access the current delay in real-time simulation process. Network-in-the-loop Simulation Platform is based on VC++ and Matlab, but the concepts of "time" in VC++ and in Matlab are different. And it is very difficult to transform them into a unified standard. So a solution is designed in this article to measure the time delay of NCS.

The main process is: (1) the plant model outputs the current simulation time t_1 when it exports data; (2) the controller calculates the data, and sends the results with t1 back to the plant model; (3) in the input S-function of the plant model, the received data is treated as input value, and the received time t_1 is compared with the present simulation time t_2. The difference of t_1 and t_2 is the delay time of NCS in Simulink simulation environment.

4   Simulation Experiment

In order to verify the effectiveness of the Network-in-the-loop Simulation Platform, a DC motor servo system referred to [13] is simulated on this platform. The controller is a PI controller, and the plant model is a DC motor. The transfer functions of the controller and the plant are described as follows:

$$G_C(s) = \frac{0.1701s + 0.378}{s}, \tag{1}$$

$$G_P(s) = \frac{2029.826}{(s+26.29)(s+2.296)}. \tag{2}$$

Divide the DC motor servo system into two models, controller and plant. The controller run on the server of Network-in-the-loop Simulation Platform whereas the plant on the client. And they constitute a feedback control system through network. Run the server on a computer in Shanghai whereas the client on another computer in Hefei. Simulation results are shown as Fig.4.

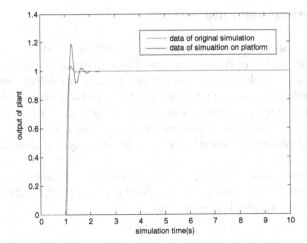

Fig. 4. The comparison of data between original simulation which is without network and simulation on Network-in-the-loop Simulation Platform

It can be seen from Fig.4, due to the network, control system on the Network-in-the-loop Simulation Platform has larger overshoot and longer oscillation time. Fig.5 shows the delay of the feedback control system on Network-in-the-loop Simulation Platform.

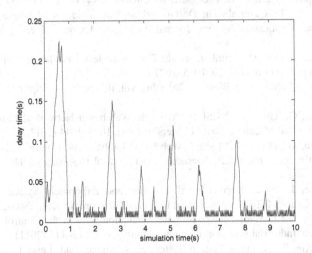

Fig. 5. The delay of DC motor system on Network-in-the-loop Simulation Platform

5   Conclusions and Future Work

This paper established a Network-in-the-loop Simulation Platform to realize the networked communication of data between two Simulink models by Socket technology. And real network is introduced into the simulation process of feedback control system. Instead of the method of modeling for network and off-line simulation which are used by other simulation platforms, the Network-in-the-loop Simulation Platform connects with an actual network for real-time simulation, and gathers the current delay time online which reflects the influence of network factors on the control system accurately.

Acknowledgments. This work is partially supported by National Nature Science Fund of China (60904016), Shanghai Rising-Star Program (11QA1402500), Excellent Youth Instructor of Shanghai University (2011).

References

1. Peng, D., Zhang, H., Lin, J., et al.: Simulation Research for Networked Cascade Control System Based on Truetime. In: Proceeding of the 8th World Congress on Intelligent Control and Automation, Taipei, Taiwan, pp. 486–488 (2011)
2. Sun, J., Deng, W., Li, L., et al.: Matlab-based Simulation Platform for Networked Control System. Process Automation Instrumentation 31(3), 19–22 (2010)
3. Qian, M., Shan, Y., Xie, G.: The Application of OPC Toolbox on the Simulation of Network Control Systems. Microcomputer Information 23(4-3), 117–119 (2007)
4. Shan, S., Du, Y., Li, Q., et al.: The Design and Implementation of NS2-based Simulation Semi-physical Verification System. Journal of Beijing Union University 24(4), 17–19 (2010)
5. Scarpella, E., Marcos, D., Friml, J., et al.: Control of leaf vascular patterning by polar auxin transport. Genes & Dev. 20, 1015–1027 (2006)
6. Murray, J.D.: Mathematical Biology, 3rd edn., vol. II, pp. 71–81. Springer, New York (2005)
7. Pang, Z., Liu, G., Qiao, Y.: NCSLab: A Whole Web-based Networked Control System Laboratory. Journal of Central South University 42(4), 1005–1014 (2011)
8. Qiao, Y., Liu, G., et al.: NCSLab: A Web-based Global-scale Control Laboratory with Rich Interactive Features. IEEE Transaction on Industrial Electronics 57(10), 3253–3265 (2010)
9. Wu, M., She, J., et al.: Internet-based Teaching and Experiment System for Control Engineering Course. IEEE Transaction on Industrial Electronics 55(6), 2386–2396 (2008)
10. Zhou, Y., Hu, N.: Development of Remote Simulation System for Control Technology Based on Web. Industrial Instrumentation & Automation 3, 112–115 (2011)
11. Huang, Q., Xie, S.: Adaptive Control System of Nonlinear Tank Level Based on RTW. Automation & Instrumentation 10, 19–30 (2011)
12. Quanglia, D., Muradore, R., Bragantini, R., et al.: A SystemC / Matlab Co-simulation Tool for Networked Control Systems. Simulation Modeling Practice and Theory 23, 71–86 (2012)
13. Yodyium, T., Chow, M.Y.: Control methodologies in networked control systems. Control Engineering Practice 11(10), 1099–1111 (2003)

Command and Control Evolutive Network Models for Command Substitution

Lidong Qian and Xiao Song

Science and Technology on Aircraft Control Laboratory,
School of Automation Science and Electrical Engineering, Beihang University,
100191 Beijing, China

Abstract. Due to the damage of commander or command post in battlefield, it often appears the substitution of command right of C2 (Command and Control) nodes. Firstly, this paper analyzes information exchanging in C2 network and builds a classic army C2 network. Secondly, three kinds of command substitution such as backup-command, junior-command and bypass-command are concluded according to the actual combat, which also means that three evolutive networks are built based on the three evolutive rules. It shows that the original network and its evolutions all present different degree of complex network characteristics. Finally, based on communication decision-making model, it shows the diversity of synchronization in different networks with Netlogo simulation software and draws the conclusion that the synchronization of network by using backup-command is better than other two evolutive networks.

Keywords: command substitution, backup-command, junior-command, bypass-command, synchronization.

1 Introduction

Affected by the rapid development of technology and the substantial jump of automated management, it demands C2 relationship with a high degree of flexibility in informational battlefield. In some certain situations, the adaptive adjustment in the relationship of partial C2 and collaboration will make a great influence on the warring quality as well as the operational network topology.

In this paper, a model of C2 system composed of different organizational structures and armed forces is established on the basis of learning the activity characters of network centric C2. Besides, the changes of network characters under different evolutive rules are quantitatively and qualitatively analyzed, which provides the theoretical foundation for the study and test of the C2 system.

2 Description of C2 Organizational Structure

The general relationships of C2 include not only the relationship of commanding between the upper and the lower levels, but also the collaborative relationship between the posts at the same level. Throughout this, the information flow is also true. Besides

T. Xiao, L. Zhang, and M. Fei (Eds.): AsiaSim 2012, Part II, CCIS 324, pp. 63–70, 2012.

the information flow for the vertical command and control, there are a large number of intelligent information flows for horizontal collaboration, which makes up a complex structure of the network information system.

Organizational structure determines the collaboration within the organization. At the same time, the collaboration within the organization largely determines whether the process execution is good. According to this above, the whole C2 structure can be seen as a coupled network of command information and intelligence information. The relationships of information exchange between C2 nodes are shown in Figure 1 as well as the process of their behavior.

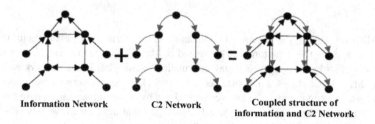

Information Network   C2 Network   Coupled structure of
                                          information and C2 Network

Fig. 1. Description of the coupled structure of information and C2 network in C2 organization

3   Construction of C2 Network Topology Model

This paper takes a classic army as an example and it builds basic C2 agencies according to the need of actual battle. We use "S-level C2 member – T-level C2 member – Y-level C2 member – L-level C2 member" corresponding to the actual top-down hierarchical command relationships, which is shown in Figure 2.

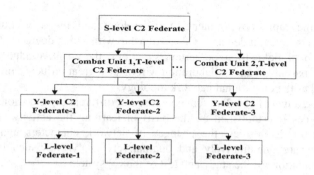

Fig. 2. Hiberarchy structure of C2 federate

According to corresponding theories about complex network, it defines nodes set as $V = \{v_1, v_2, \cdots, v_n\}$ and edges set as $E = \{e_1, e_2, \cdots, e_m\}$, which makes up the diagram $G = (V, E)$. As for C2 nodes in the same C2 hiberachy, two nodes have edge linked when there are information and intelligence flows between them. Otherwise, there is no edge between them. And as for C2 nodes in different C2 hiberachy, if there are direct channels to command the information flow between two C2 nodes which means there are direct affiliation relations between two C2 nodes, it can be considered that there is edge linked between the two nodes.

The L-level units are classified as three categories in corresponding to the three kinds of nodes in the network in order to reflect some actions in modern combat process, such as detecting, decision-making and so on.

Sensor S: It is on behalf of the system of reconnaissance and surveillance. It includes the units that can provide perception of combat space. Besides, sensors can receive the observed phenomenon from other nodes and send them to decision points.

Decision point D: It is on behalf of the C2 center. It can receive the information from sensors or influencers.

Influencer I: It is on behalf of the units that can cause soft or hard damage. It receives the instructions from decision points and attacks enemy units.

In modern combat circulation theory, it can be seen that the combat process is a circulation that sensors find targets and send the information to decision points, and then after analyzing the situation, the decision points command influencers to take some combat actions. On the basis of theory above, the C2 network based on JBS C2 structure can be established by using social network analysis software Ucinet and the network topology is shown in Figure 3.

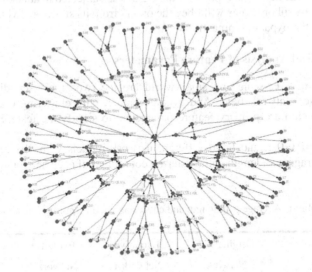

Fig. 3. C2 Network topology structure

4   Evolution of C2 Network Topology Structure

The execution of combat mission requires C2 relationship with a high degree of flexibility. And the fixed C2 relationship can't satisfy the need of actual combat.

It should make some adaptive adjustment in the relationship of partial C2 and collaboration timely according to the requirements of actual battlefield. And then, it will convert information advantages into decision-making advantage from the entire battlefield.

4.1   Construction of Evolutive Rules

On the basis of describing the activity characters of network centric C2, it simulates the evolution of C2 system by defining different evolutive rules, measures network characteristic parameters in different stages and analyzes characters of evolutive networks. The main evolutive rules discussed in this paper are as follows.

Evolutive rule 1: Selecting some nodes randomly with the probability P1 in C2 network. When the node that represents the C2 unit is subjected to attack from enemies and damaged, its subordinates will obey the orders from some corresponding units that are at the same level with their original superiors, which means that it implements the backup-command.

Evolutive rule 2: Selecting some nodes randomly with the probability P2 in the C2 network. When the node that represents the C2 unit is subjected to attack from enemies and damaged, the command of one of its subordinates will be elevated and it will command other subordinates to take some military actions in the combat environment, which means that it implements junior-command.

Evolutive rule 3: Selecting some nodes randomly with the probability P3 in the C2 network. When the node that represents the C2 unit is subjected to attack from enemies and damaged, its subordinates will obey the orders from its superiors, which mean that it implements the bypass-command.

4.2   Statistical Analysis of Feature Parameters

The Features of Free-scale and small-world are the two significant discoveries in current complex network field. And average path length, clustering coefficient and degree distribution are primary feature parameters to signify the feature of complex network.

Set P1=P2=P3=0.2, and build different network models with different evolutive rules. The average path length and clustering coefficient of each network are shown in table 1.

Table 1. Average path length and clustering coefficient of C2 network

	Original C2 Network	Evolutive Network 1	Evolutive Network 2	Evolutive Network 3
Average path length	6.796	6.727	6.614	5.350
Clustering coefficient	0.235	0.330	0.295	0.216

It can be seen from the table above the average path length of Evolutive Network 3 is shorter than other networks as the result of Evolutive Network 3 implements bypass-command, which will shorten the time and procedure during information processing.

At the same time, from the clustering coefficient of the networks above, we can conclude that the C2 network and its evolutive networks established in this paper have their high aggregation. The high aggregation is the trend of the war in future and it is also an essential feature of C2 network. Specially, the clustering coefficient of Evolutive Network 1 is larger than other networks, which indicates that the subordinates of some C2 units are on the increase in the C2 network.

The dynamic changes of C2 network will implement the effective links between C2 units, which will make C2 units and the entire combat system integrated together. And the C2 network will improve its stability significantly. When some nodes in the network are destroyed, the holistic stability of C2 network will not be affected as all C2 units compose a network structure. What's more, the substitution between C2 nodes under certain conditions makes the regenerative capacity of overall command structure more stronger, which will improve the freedom of C2 units and the ability to command the combat.

5   Synchronization Analysis of C2 Network

Research on synchronization in informational combat will help us understand how some special C2 network converts information advantage, collaboration advantage and structure advantage into combat advantage. Synchronization of C2 network means that through communication, C2 units have consensus about battlefield as well as possible and take coordinate actions on the basis of perception, transmission and sharing of battlefield situations.

5.1   Communication Decision-Making Model

In C2 network, the inceptive opinions of C2 units to some combat plan or the threat of an enemy may be different from each other. This paper takes a value from 0 to 1 to describe the degree of perception of combat situation. In addition, it analyzes the synchronization by building communication decision-making model. Communication decision-making model is the process that different opinions influence each other and come to the final opinions. In the same complexity of inceptive opinions, the more concentrated of final opinions and the time that they spend on forming the final opinions is shorter, the synchronization of entities communication network will be better.

We suppose that at time t, the value of agent i to some situation is $z_i(t) \in [0,1]$.

When agent i is communicates with other agents, it will keep its original value if the difference of their values is larger than some limited value like $d_{ij}(0 < d_{ij} < 1), |z_i(t) - z_j(t)| > d_{ij}$. Otherwise, agent i will adjust its value according to values of other agents:

$$z_i(t+1) = z_i(t) - u \bullet [z_i(t) - \frac{(z_j(t) + z_k(t) + z_z(t) + \cdots)}{n}] \qquad (1)$$

Among them, u_i is the accepted degree and d_{ij} is the contained degree.

There are three steps to build communication decision-making model:

Firstly, initialize the communication condition: (1) Determine the category and scale of generated network. (2) Initialize values of agents, and the value will be a stochastic value from 0 to 1 generated by computer to show the original opinion of each agent. (3) Determine the feature of communication, which means determining the accepted degree d and the contained degree u.

Secondly, Simulation: (1) Determine communication strategy. (2) Agent i communicates with other corresponding agents according to communication strategies and rules, and then makes some adjustment with its value, which is called a communication round. (3) Back to the second step until it has conducted scheduled rounds

Thirdly, expression of communication opinion mode: record the value of each agent after a communication round.

5.2   Simulation Analysis

In order to reflect the communication of units based on the classic army structure veritably, it adopts local communication between nodes in closed system. Local communication means that each node only communicates with other nodes within the scope in certain group. In other words, each C2 unit only communicates with its superior, subordinates and the units at the same level.

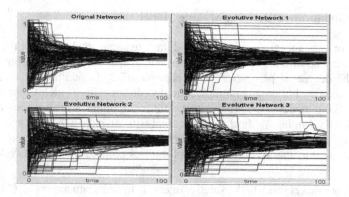

Fig. 4. Communication state of each node

It conducts experiments with Netlogo simulation tool. Set P1=P2=P3=0.2 and build the original network and three evolutive networks. Initialize values of each node in the network and determine features of communication. In this experiment, the accepted degree d is set to 0.3 and the contained degree u is set to 0.4. When communication round gets to 100, record values of each nodes and analyze synchronization of the network.

From the diagram above, we can see that there are few nodes that form the consistent opinion at the beginning of communication. With the increase of communication round, each node adjusts its opinion according to the opinions of its neighbouring nodes and finally they come to the final opinions.

Specially, the opinions of the original network and Evolutive Network 1 are more concentrated than Evolutive Network 2 and Evolutive Network 3. Besides, the time that they spend on forming the final opinions are shorter than Evolutive Network 2 and Evolutive Network 3. That is to say, through communication, synchronization of the original network and Evolutive Network 1 are better than Evolutive Network 2 and Evolutive Network 3. When some nodes in C2 network are subjected to attack and damaged, the method of backup-command will contribute to having consensus about battlefield and taking coordinate actions.

6   Conclusions

From the perspective of improving the stability of C2 network, a model of C2 system based on a classic army structure was established on the basis of analyzing information exchanging in C2 network. Besides, it constructed different evolutive rules to make some adjustment to C2 network, which improved the capability for C2 units to control the battlefield. In addition, the feature of small-world and scale-free were discovered in the C2 network and its evolutive networks according to the theory of complex networks. At the end of this paper, it conducted some experiments with Netlogo simulation tool and found that with the method of backup-command, it contributed to taking coordinate actions and improving operational efficiency when some C2 units were subjected to attack and damaged. Characteristic analysis of C2 relationship network and its evolutions will enhance the stability of the whole C2 network, which will provide theory bases for analyzing and optimizing C2 networks.

Acknowledgements. This research was supported by grant 61104057 and 61074144 from the Natural Science Foundation of China and National key lab of Virtual Reality Technology and System. The authors thank the reviewers for their comments.

References

1. Zhu, T., Chang, G., Zhang, S., Guo, R.: Research on Model of Command and Control Information Cooperation Based on Complex Networks. Journal of System Simulation 20(22), 6058–6060 (2008)
2. Ma, X., Sun, K., Wang, H.: Research on Network Topology of Command and Control Organization based on Theory of Complex Networks. Fire Control & Command Control 35(2), 69–71 (2010)
3. Wang, X., Li, X., Chen, G.: Complex Network Theory and Its Application. Tsinghua University Press, Beijing (2009)

4. Alberts, D.S., Hayes, R.E.: Power to the Edge: Command, Control in the Information Age, pp. 213–222. CCRP Publications Series, Washington, DC (2003)
5. Liu, H., Zhang, L.: Analysis on Opinion Emergence of Group Communication. Complex Systems and Complexity Science 1(4), 45–52 (2004)
6. Bao, X.: Modeling and Analysis of Combat Synchronization Based on Complex Networks. National Univ. of Defense Technology, Changsha (2009)
7. Chen, L., Huang, J., Zhang, W.: Research on Complex Network Topology Model of Network Warfare. Electronics Optics & Control 15(6), 4–7 (2008)
8. Wang, H., Guo, J., Li, X., Chang, G.: Research of C2 System Modeling and Simulation in NCO. Journal of System Simulation 19(9), 1897–1901 (2007)

Stochastic Stability Analysis of MIMO Networked Control Systems with Multi-quantizers

Haoliang Bai, Dajun Du[*], Minrui Fei, and Zhihua Song

Shanghai Key Laboratory of Power Station Automation Technology,
School of Mechanical Engineering & Automation, Shanghai University,
Shanghai 200072
ddj@shu.edu.cn

Abstract. This paper is concerned with stochastic stability analysis of MIMO NCSs with multi-channel communication constrain and multi-quantizers. With communication constrains treated as packet disordering and quantization error treated as sector-bounded uncertainty, the closed-loop system is firstly modeled as a Markov jump linear system (MJLS). A stochastically stable condition has then been derived, and the main results are further extended to MIMO NCSs with parameter uncertainty. Finally, simulation results confirm the effectiveness of the proposed method.

Keywords: Networked control systems, packet disordering, quantization, stochastic stability, Markov jump linear system.

1   Introduction

Networked control systems (NCSs), with many advantages such as low cost, less wiring, simple installation and maintenance, have been employed in many industrial fields [1-2]. However, the network is not always a reliable communication medium, network nondeterministic issues, such as packet dropout, network-induced delay and packet disordering (out-of-order), will appear when they share a common network with the limited network bandwidth. This may lower even deteriorate the stability and control performance of the systems [3-4]. Moreover, to reduce the network load, signals are usually quantized before being transmitted, which will inevitably produce quantization errors that further deteriorate the NCSs performance.

Communication constrain problems have been studied in the past decades. Different models and control strategies have been developed to solve these problems. Network nondeterministic issues in feedback channel are treated as time-varying delay in [5]. Using a discard-packet strategy, network nondeterministic issues are treated as data packet dropout in the MIMO NCSs, and a sufficient condition of asymptotical stability is then given in [6]. By treating network nondeterministic issues as packet out of order with a supposed disorder upper bound, a Markov jumping model is proposed in [7].

---

[*] Corresponding author.

T. Xiao, L. Zhang, and M. Fei (Eds.): AsiaSim 2012, Part II, CCIS 324, pp. 71–81, 2012.
© Springer-Verlag Berlin Heidelberg 2012

Most researches have been done on the quantized control of NCSs with single quantizer [8-10], including linear/nonlinear systems with the quantized state/control input. However, single packet can carry only limited information. In practical application, sensors and actuators may be placed at different positions, a large number of data packets need be transmitted by multi-channels. Therefore, the research on MIMO quantized control systems is an important issue [11-12]. Network induced-delay and packet loses are modeled as Markov chain in [11], where multi-quantizers are adopted. The quantized state feedback stabilization problem was developed for MIMO systems by using a sector bound method and the LMI technology in [12].

However, the above existed works do not consider both network communication constrains and quantization for MIMO NCSs. This paper mainly investigates stochastic stability analysis for MIMO NCSs with multi-channel communication constrain and multi-quantizers. The paper is organized as follows. Section 2 gives problem formulation and modeling. Section 3 presents Stochastic Stability Analysis of MIMO Networked Control Systems. The main results are further extended to MIMO NCSs with parameter uncertainty in Section 4. Section 5 describes the simulation results, followed by a conclusion in Section 6.

2   Problem Formulation and Modeling

Consider a MIMO discrete-time linear time-invariant (LTI) system as:

$$x_{k+1} = Ax_k + Bu_k, \tag{1}$$

where $x_k = [x_1(k), x_2(k), ..., x_n(k)] \in R^n$ and $u_k = [u_1(k), u_2(k), ..., u_m(k)] \in R^m$ are the state and control input, A and B are known constant matrices.

In the paper, each plant state is quantized before entering the network channel. Therefore n quantizers are set and denoted as $q[\cdot] = [q_1[\cdot], ..., q_n[\cdot]]^T$. Furthermore, every quantizer is assumed to be symmetric. To the benefit of owning a wide range of the signal level, the logarithmic quantizer is chosen. For each quantizer (e.g. $q_p[\cdot]$, $p = 0, 1, ..., n$), the quantization levels are expressed by $v_p = \{\pm \rho_p^d \mu_0^{(p)}$, $d = 0, \pm 1, \pm 2, ...\} \bigcup \{0\}$, where $0 < \rho_p < 1, \mu_0^p > 0$.

As the density of logarithmic quantizer is proportional to ρ, we take ρ as the density of logarithmic quantizer. Thus, the associated quantizer is described as follow

$$q_p[\varepsilon] = \begin{cases} \rho_p^d \mu_0^{(p)} & if\ \dfrac{1}{1+\delta_p} \rho_p^d \mu_0^{(p)} < \varepsilon \leq \dfrac{1}{1-\delta_p} \rho_p^d \mu_0^{(p)}, \varepsilon > 0 \\ 0 & if\ \varepsilon = 0 \\ -q[-\varepsilon] & if\ \varepsilon < 0 \end{cases} \tag{2}$$

where $\delta_p = (1 - \rho_p)/(1 + \rho_p)$.

Using the sector bound method [12], the quantization error for given quantization density can be defined as

$$e_p(k) = q_p(x_p(k)) - x_p(k) = \Delta_p(k)x_p(k), \tag{3}$$

where $\Delta_p(k) \in [-\alpha_p, \alpha_p], p \in [1,...n]$, $\alpha_p = (1 - \rho_p)/(1 + \rho_p)$, ρ_p is the quantization destiny of the pth channel.

Remark 1. From the quantization error, it can be seen that quantization error $\Delta_p(k) \in (-\alpha_p, \alpha_p)$ has nothing to do with the time for any channel, i.e., $\Delta_p(k) = \Delta_p(k-1) = ... = \Delta_p(k-h) \, (p = 1,...,n)$.

Suppose that the network only exists between the sensor nodes and the control node. The data packet out-of-order, packet dropout and network-induced delay are inevitably introduced in each channel. These issues are taken into account within one framework, i.e., which are considered as data packet out-of-order using a concept of maximum disorder upper bound [7]. The maximum time delay and successive package losses numbers for each channel are remarked as $\tau_p(k)$ and η, where $0 \le \tau_p(k) \le \tau T \, (p = 1,...,n)$, and let $h = \tau + \eta$. Then, we set $q_p(k) = q_p(x_p(k))$ $(p = 1,...,n)$ denoting the state signal being quantized in the pth channel at sampling instant k. Consider a sequence of packets being quantized, $q_p(k-h), q_p(k-(h-1)),$ $\cdots, q_p(k-i),..., q_p(k)$, the corresponding expected arrival sequence numbers are $1, 2,$ ..., $h+1$ (i.e., $h+1-i$; $i=0,1,...,h$) and the sequence number of packet actually be received can be marked as $R_p^k(i)$. Therefore, the displacement value of the packet can be describe as: $d_p^k(h+1-i) = R_p^k(i) - (h+1-i)$. Furthermore, whether the packets arrive early or late than their expected value can be formulized as

$$\delta_p(d_p^k(h+1-i)) = \begin{cases} 1 & d_p^k(h+1-i) \le 0 & early\ or\ normal \\ 0 & d_p^k(h+1-i) > 0 & late \end{cases} \tag{4}$$

For the pth channel, $\chi_p^k(i) = \Pi_{j=0}^{i-1}\left(1 - \delta_p(d_p^k(h+1-j))\right)\delta_p(d_p^k(h+1-i))$ and $\Pi_{j=0}^{-1}\left(1 - \delta_p(d_p^k(h+1-j))\right) = 1$ are defined. It guarantees that the newest signal in the pth channel is executed. So the states of the $h+1$ packets become $\chi_p^k(0)q_p(k)$, $\chi_p^k(1)q_p(k-1)$, ..., $\chi_p^k(h)q_p(k-h)$. Moreover, define $w_p(k)$ to represent which packet is eventually adopted as

$$w_p(k) = \sum_{i=0}^{h} \chi_p^k(i)(1 + \Delta_p(k-i))x_p(k-i). \tag{5}$$

Remark 2. It can be found that $\chi_p^k(i)=1$ or 0 and $\sum_{i=0}^h \chi_p^k(i)=1$, which is determined by the displacement value of the packets. This provides a path to describe the state signal through the network.

After the state signals are quantized and transmitted to the controller node via all n channels, they can be expressed as

$$w_k = (I+\Delta)M_k\xi_k, \tag{6}$$

where $w_k = [w_1(k)^T, w_2(k)^T, ..., w_n(k)^T]$, $M_k = [\chi^k(0)\ \chi^k(1)...\ \chi^k(h)]$, $\Delta = diag$ $\{\Delta_1\ \Delta_2\ ...\ \Delta_n\}$, $\chi^k(i) = diag(\chi_1^k(i)\ \chi_2^k(i)...\ \chi_n^k(i))$, $\xi_k = [x_k^T\ x_{k-1}^T\ ...\ x_{k-h}^T]^T$.

Consider the following state feedback law

$$v_k = K_s w_k, \tag{7}$$

where K_s is the feedback gain.

Combine (7) into (6), we have

$$u_k = v_k = K_s w_k = K_s(I+\Delta x)M_k\xi_k. \tag{8}$$

Substitute (8) into (1), yeilding

$$x_{k+1} = Ax_k + BK_s(I+\Delta)M_k\xi_k = \tilde{A}\xi_k, \tag{9}$$

where $\bar{\bar{A}} = [A, \underbrace{0, ..., 0}_h]$, $\tilde{A} = \bar{\bar{A}} + BK_s(I+\Delta)M_k$.

Remark 3. For all n channels with the maximum disorder upper bound $h>0$, we can get $s \in \Re = [1, r], r = (h+1)^n$, i.e. there exist r packet disordering situations/modes. At the kth sampling instant, one kind of arriving sequence of the sampled multi-channel packets to the controller node corresponds to a different controller parameter K, so the controller parameter K_s in (7) indicates that the controller is dynamic. In fact, the closed-loop system (9) is a Markov jump linear system, in which $\{r_k\}$ is a discrete-time homogeneous Markov chain that take values in $\Re = \{1, ..., r\}$ and r_k denotes the different jump mode. The transition probability matrix of r_k is $TP = [\pi_{sj}]$. That means r_k jump from mode s to mode j with the probability π_{sj} : $\pi_{sj} = \Pr\{r_{i+1}=j|$ $r_k = s\}$, where $\pi_{sj} > 0$ and $\sum_{j=1}^r \pi_{sj} = 1$.

3 Stochastic Stability Analysis of MIMO Networked Control Systems

Definition 1: The discrete-time Markov jump linear system (9) is stochastically stable, if for any initial condition (φ_0, s_0), there exist $\lim\limits_{h\to\infty} \sum\limits_{k=0}^{h} E(x_k^T x_k) < \infty$.

Lemma1 [13]: Given matrices W, D and E of compatible dimensions with W symmetric, then $W + DFE + E^T F^T D^T < 0$ hold for all $F^T F \leq I$ if and only if there exists a constant $\varepsilon > 0$ such that $W + \varepsilon DD^T + \varepsilon^{-1} E^T E < 0$.

Theorem 1: For the given quantization error of the form in (6), a scalar h and real matrices K_s, if there exist symmetric positive-definite matrices $P_s(s=1,...,r)$, $R_l(l=1,..,h)$, such that (10) hold, then the closed system (9) is stochastic stable.

$$\Phi_s = \theta_s + \sum_{j\in\Im} \pi_{sj} \tilde{A}^T P_j \tilde{A} < 0, \tag{10}$$

where $\theta_s = diag(-P_s + \sum\limits_{l=1}^{h_1} R_l, -R_1,...,-R_h)$, $\tilde{A} = \bar{\bar{A}} + BK_s(I+\Delta)M_k$, $\bar{\bar{A}} = [A, \underbrace{0,...,0}_{h}]$.

Proof: Choosing a Lyapunov-Krasovskii functional as follow

$$V_k = \underbrace{x_k^T P_s x_k}_{V_{1,k}} + \underbrace{x_{k-1}^T R_1 x_{k-1}}_{V_{2,k}} + \underbrace{\sum_{l=k-2}^{k-1} x_l^T R_2 x_l}_{V_{3,k}} + ... + \underbrace{\sum_{l=k-h}^{k-1} x_l^T R_h x_l}_{V_{h+1,k}},$$

where $P_s(s=1,...,r)$ and $R_l(l=1,...,h)$ are symmetric positive-definite matrices. Considering (9), $EV_{1,k+1} = E(x_{k+1}^T P_s x_{k+1}) = \sum\limits_{j\in\Im} \pi_{sj}\{(\tilde{A}\xi_k)^T P_j \tilde{A}\xi_k\} = \sum\limits_{j\in\Im} \pi_{sj}\xi_k^T \tilde{A}^T P_j \tilde{A}\xi_k$.

Finally, $\Delta V(k) = EV(k+1) - V(k) = \xi_k^T \theta_s \xi_k + \sum\limits_{j\in\Im} \pi_{sj}\xi_k^T \tilde{A}^T P_j \tilde{A}\xi_k$. If (10) holds, $\Delta V(k)$

$\leq \xi_k^T \theta_s \xi_k \leq -\beta \xi_k^T \xi_k \leq -\beta x_k^T x_k$, where $\beta = \min\{\lambda_{\min}(-\Theta_s), s\in\Im\}$, $\Im \in [1,(h+1)^n]$.

Summing up both sides of the above equality from $k=0$ to $k=l$ and let $\ell=\infty$, we got $\lim\limits_{h\to\infty} EV(h+1) - V(\varphi_0, s_0) \leq -\beta\lim\limits_{h\to\infty} \sum\limits_{k=0}^{h} E(x_k^T x_k)$. Considering $\lim\limits_{h\to\infty} EV(h+1) = 0$,

then we have $\lim\limits_{h\to\infty} \sum\limits_{k=0}^{h} E(x_k^T x_k) \leq (1/\beta)V(\varphi_0, s_0) < \infty$, where φ_0 and s_0 are the condition of the system. Thus the stochastic stability is proved.

Noted that parameter uncertainty Δ is contained in (10), and theorem 1 can not directly get the controller gain K_s in (7). Thus, the following theorem is given to easily get the controller K_s for the closed-control system (9).

Theorem 2: For the given quantization error upper bound matrix G and a scalar h, if there exist symmetric positive-definite matrices $P_s(s=1,...,r)$, $R_l(l=1,..,h)$, real matrices K_s, and a scalar $\varepsilon > 0$, such that (11) hold, then the closed system (9) is stochastic stable.

$$
\begin{bmatrix}
\theta_s \\
F_{1s} & -P_1 \\
F_{2s} & 0 & -P_2 \\
\cdots & \cdots & & \cdots \\
F_{rs} & 0 & & \cdots & -P_r \\
0 & J_{1s} & J_{2s} & \cdots & J_{rs} & -\varepsilon I \\
\varepsilon\sqrt{G}M_k & 0 & & \cdots & & & -\varepsilon I
\end{bmatrix} < 0, \qquad (11)
$$

where $F_{qs} = \sqrt{\pi_{sq}}(P_q\bar{\bar{A}} + P_q BK_s M_k)$ $(q=1,...r)$, $J_{qs} = \sqrt{\pi_{sq}}K_s^T B^T P_q$ $(q=1,...r)$, $G = diag\{\rho_1^2, \rho_2^2, ..., \rho_n^2\}$.

Proof: By Schur complement and Lemma 1, substituting $\tilde{A} = \bar{\bar{A}} + BK_s(I+\Delta)M_k$ and split the inequality according to uncertain item Δ, we can obtain

$$
\begin{bmatrix}
\theta_s + \varepsilon M_k^T \Delta^T \Delta M_k \\
\sqrt{\pi_{s1}}(\bar{\bar{A}} + BK_s M_k) & -P_1^{-1} \\
\sqrt{\pi_{s2}}(\bar{\bar{A}} + BK_s M_k) & 0 & -P_2^{-1} \\
\cdots & \cdots & & \cdots \\
\sqrt{\pi_{sr}}(\bar{\bar{A}} + BK_s M_k) & 0 & & \cdots & -P_r^{-1} \\
0 & \sqrt{\pi_{s1}}K_s^T B^T & \sqrt{\pi_{s2}}K_s^T B^T & \cdots & \sqrt{\pi_{sr}}K_s^T B^T & -\varepsilon I
\end{bmatrix} < 0.
$$

It is easy proved that $\Delta\Delta^T = \Delta^T\Delta < G$ (supposed known constant diagonal matrix containing quantization information in all communication channels), therefore, establish of the above inequality is guaranteed by the following inequality.

$$\begin{bmatrix} \theta_s + \varepsilon M_k^T G M_k & & & & \\ \sqrt{\pi_{s1}}(\overline{\overline{A}} + BK_s M_k) & -P_1^{-1} & & & \\ \sqrt{\pi_{s2}}(\overline{\overline{A}} + BK_s M_k) & 0 & -P_2^{-1} & & \\ ... & ... & & ... & \\ \sqrt{\pi_{sr}}(\overline{\overline{A}} + BK_s M_k) & 0 & & ... & -P_r^{-1} \\ 0 & \sqrt{\pi_{s1}}K_s^T B^T & \sqrt{\pi_{s2}}K_s^T B^T & ... & \sqrt{\pi_{sr}}K_s^T B^T & -\varepsilon I \end{bmatrix} < 0.$$

Using Schur complement again and pre- and post-multiplying both sides of above inequality by $diag(\underbrace{I,...,I}_{r+2},\varepsilon)$, we can obtain

$$\begin{bmatrix} \theta_s & & & & & * \\ \sqrt{\pi_{s1}}(\overline{\overline{A}} + BK_s M_k) & -P_1^{-1} & & & \\ \sqrt{\pi_{s2}}(\overline{\overline{A}} + BK_s M_k) & 0 & -P_2^{-1} & & \\ ... & ... & & ... & \\ \sqrt{\pi_{sr}}(\overline{\overline{A}} + BK_s M_k) & 0 & & ... & -P_r^{-1} \\ 0 & \sqrt{\pi_{s1}}K_s^T B^T & \sqrt{\pi_{s2}}K_s^T B^T & ... & \sqrt{\pi_{sr}}K_s^T B^T & -\varepsilon I \\ \varepsilon\sqrt{G}M_k & & & & & -\varepsilon I \end{bmatrix} < 0.$$

It is obvious that both P_s and P_s^{-1} exists in above inequality, multiply both sides of above inequality with $diag(I, P_1,..., P_r, I, I)$. Therefore, (11) is obtained and this complete the proof.

Remark 4. It is clear that inequality (11) is a set of BMIs because it contains P_s, $K_s(s=1,...,r)$ and $P_s(s=1,...,r)$ coupled together with K_s in some items. However, for fixed K_s and ε, (11) is LMIs for $P_s(s=1,...,r)$ and $R_l(l=1,...,h)$. Furthermore, (11) is LMIs for K_s and ε if $P_s(s=1,...,r)$ and $R_l(l=1,...,h)$ are fixed. Therefore, the BMIs in (11) can be solved by the 'alternate' algorithm [14].

4   Stochastic Stability Analysis of Parameter-Uncertain MIMO Networked Control Systems

The above results can be extend to parameter uncertainties of the plant as

$$x_{k+1} = (A + \Delta A)x_k + (B + \Delta B)u_k, \tag{12}$$

where the parameter uncertainties are norm-bounded with the following form $[\Delta A \ \Delta B] = HF(k)[E_1 \ E_2]$, $F(k)$ is an unknown matrix reflecting the uncertainty of model parameters and satisfies $F(k)^T F(k) \leq I$, H, E_1, E_2 are known constant matrices with appropriate dimensions.

Using (8) and (1), it follows that

$$x_{k+1} = (A + \Delta A)x_k + (B + \Delta B)u_k = \tilde{A}\tilde{\xi}_k , \tag{13}$$

where $\tilde{A} = \bar{\bar{A}} + HF(k)\bar{E}_1 + BK_s(I + \Delta x)M_k + HF(k)E_2 K_s(I + \Delta x)M_k$, $\bar{\bar{A}} = [A, 0, ..., 0]$,

$\bar{E}_1 = [E_1, 0, ..., 0]$. Similar as the previous case, we obtain theorem 3 to guarantee the closed-loop system (13) of stochastic stable and obtain the related controller.

Theorem 3: For the given quantization error upper bound matrix G, constant matrices H, $E1$, $E2$ and a scalar h, if there exist symmetric positive-definite matrices $N_s(s = 1, ..., r)$, $\bar{R}_l(l = 1, .., h)$, real matrices K_s, and scalars $\varepsilon_1 > 0, \varepsilon_2 > 0$, such that (15) hold, then the closed system (13) is stochastic stable.

$$\begin{bmatrix} \theta_s & & & & & * \\ \sqrt{\pi_{s1}}F_s & -N_1 + \varepsilon_1 \pi_{s1}HH^T & & & & \\ \cdots & \cdots & \cdots & & & \\ \sqrt{\pi_{sr}}F_s & \varepsilon_1 \sqrt{\pi_{sr}\pi_{s1}}HH^T & \cdots & -N_r + \varepsilon_1 \pi_{sr}HH^T & & \\ \bar{E}_1 J_s & 0 & \cdots & & -\varepsilon_1 I & \\ 0 & \sqrt{\pi_{s1}}K_s^T B^T & \cdots & \sqrt{\pi_{sr}}K_s^T B^T & K_s^T E_2^T & -\varepsilon_2 I \\ \varepsilon_2 \sqrt{G}M_k M_s & 0 & \cdots & & & -\varepsilon_2 I \end{bmatrix} < 0 \tag{14}$$

where $F_s = \bar{\bar{A}}M_s + BK_s M_k M_s$, $J_s = \bar{E}_1 M_s + E_2 K_s M_k M_s$, $M_s = diag(\underbrace{P_s^{-1}, ..., P_s^{-1}}_{h+1})$,

$N_s = P_s^{-1}(s = 1, ..., r)$, $\theta_s = diag(N_s + \sum_{l=1}^{h} \bar{R}_l, -\bar{R}_1, ..., -\bar{R}_h)$, $\bar{R}_l = P_s^{-1}R_l P_s^{-1}(l = 1, ..., h)$.

Proof: The proof is similar to that in theorem 2, and thus is omitted.

5   Simulation Example

Consider the following two-input and two output unstable discrete system $x_{k+1} = \begin{bmatrix} -0.3 & -0.6 \\ -1.2 & 0.5 \end{bmatrix} x_k + \begin{bmatrix} -0.5 & 0.8 \\ 0.5 & -0.5 \end{bmatrix} u_k$ .The newest packets executed by controller subject to Markov process, with the assumption of $h=2$ as the maximum disorder upper bound for each channel. For the 1st channel, there are three packet (i.e., $q_{1(k-2)}, q_{1(k-1)}, q_{1(k)}$) that can be chosen at sampling instant k. It is similar to 2nd channel, thus there are 9 cases for the newest packets that will be used in two input channels.

A Markov chain, taking values from a finite set $\Re = \{1, 2, ..., 9\}$, is used to describe the disordering.

Different channels need different quantization destinies in practical application. In the first experiment, the quantization destinies are set $\rho_1 = 0.8$, $\rho_2 = 0.9$ for channel 1 and channel 2, respectively, and the quantization error upper bound matrix $G = diag(0.0123, 0.0028)$ is got. By setting the initial values $x_0 = (2, -3)$, $P_s = diag(0.1, -0.2)$ $(s = 1, ..., 9)$ and $R_l = diag(0.1, 0.3)(l = 1, ..., 4)$, the controller gains are obtained according to Theorem 2 and the 'alternate' algorithm as follows

$$K_1 = \begin{bmatrix} 7.2693 & -0.6789 \\ 4.9098 & 0.3178 \end{bmatrix}, K_2 = \begin{bmatrix} 7.1875 & 0 \\ 4.8736 & 0 \end{bmatrix}, K_3 = \begin{bmatrix} 7.3859 & 0 \\ 4.8521 & 0 \end{bmatrix}, K_4 = \begin{bmatrix} 0 & -1.6444 \\ 0 & -0.3331 \end{bmatrix}$$

$$K_5 = \begin{bmatrix} 0 & 0 \\ 0 & 0 \end{bmatrix}, K_6 = \begin{bmatrix} 0 & 0 \\ 0 & 0 \end{bmatrix}, K_7 = \begin{bmatrix} 0 & -2.2290 \\ 0 & -0.5713 \end{bmatrix}, K_8 = \begin{bmatrix} 0 & 0 \\ 0 & 0 \end{bmatrix}, K_9 = \begin{bmatrix} 0 & 0 \\ 0 & 0 \end{bmatrix}.$$

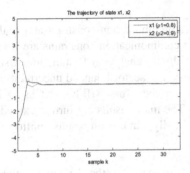

Fig. 1. Trajectory of state of x1 and x2

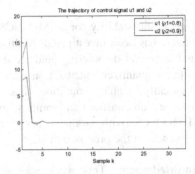

Fig. 2. Trajectory of control signal u1 and u2

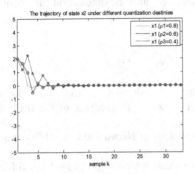

Fig. 3. Trajectory of state of x1 under different quantization destinies

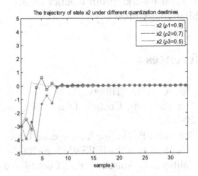

Fig. 4. Trajectory of state of x2 under different quantization destinies

Simulation results including state trajectory and control signal are demonstrated as Figs. 1 and 2. It is seen that the system is stochastically stable under the proposed control strategy.

In the second experiment, to observe the influence of different quantization error on system performance, we set three groups of different quantization destinies for each channel and the other initial values are same as the 1st experiment. Figs. 3 and 4 show the results for the two channels under different quantization destinies. It is found that the coarser the quantization destiny, the slower for the states to converge, and the coarser quantization destinies produce the larger quantization error. However, it is well known that the higher quantization destiny will consume the more bandwidth. For limited bandwidth, coarser quantization destinies help in reducing the network congestion because less information is transmitted. Therefore, it is necessary that there is a trade-off between quantization destinies and the network congestion or dynamic response of the system.

6   Conclusions

The stochastic stability for MIMO NCSs with communication constrain and multi-quantizers has been investigated. Multi-channel communication constrains are firstly treated as packet disordering, and are described by an analytical formulation. Using logarithmic quantizer, quantization error is regarded as sector-bounded uncertainty. A stochastically stable condition has been derived for MIMO NCSs with communication constrain and multi-quantizers. The main results are further extended to MIMO NCSs with parameter uncertainties. Finally, simulation results confirm the effectiveness of the proposed method.

Acknowledgment. This work was supported in part by the National Science Foundation of China (61074032, 60834002, 51007052, 61104089), Science and Technology Commission of Shanghai Municipality (11ZR1413100), the cultivating foundation for the youth teacher of Shanghai colleges and the innovation fund project for Shanghai University.

References

1. Moyne, J.R., Tilbury, D.M.: The Emergence of Industrial Control Networks for Manufacturing Control, Diagnostics, and Safety Data. J. Proceedings of the IEEE. 95, 29–47 (2007)
2. Antsaklis, P., Baillieul, J.: Special Issue on Technology of Networked Control Systems. J. Proceedings of the IEEE 95, 5–8 (2007)
3. Baillieul, J., Antsaklis, P.J.: Control and Communication Challenges in Networked Real-time Systems. J. Proceedings of the IEEE 95(1), 9–28 (2007)
4. Yang, R.N., Shi, P., Liu, G.P., Gao, H.J.: Network-based Feedback Control for System with Mixed Delays Based on Quantization and Dropout Compensation. J. Automatica 47, 2805–2809 (2011)

5. Wang, S.B., Meng, X.Y., Chen, T.W.: Wide-area Control of Power Systems Through Delayed Network Communication. J. IEEE Transactions on Control Systems Technology 20(2), 495–503 (2012)
6. Du, D.J., Fei, M.R., Jia, T.G.: Modelling and Stability Analysis of MIMO Networked Control systems with multi-channel random packet losses. J. Transactions of the Institute of Measurement and Control, doi:10.1177/0142331211406605
7. Li, J.N., Zhang, Q.L., Yu, H.B., Cai, M.: Real-time Guaranteed Cost Control of MIMO Networked Control Systems with Packet Disordering. J. Journal of Process Control 21(6), 967–975 (2011)
8. Coutinho, D.F., Fu, M.Y., De Souza, C.E.: Input and Output Quantized Feedback Linear Systems. J. IEEE Trans. on Automatic Control 55(3), 761–766 (2010)
9. Zhang, J., Lam, J., Xia, Y.: Observer-based Output Feedback Control for Discrete Systems with Quantised Inputs. J. IET Control Theory and Applications 3(5), 478–485 (2010)
10. Liberzon, D.: Hybrid Feedback Stabilization of Systems with Quantized Signals. J. Automatica 39(9), 1543–1554 (2003)
11. Rasool, F., Nguang, S.K., Krug, M.: Robust H∞ Output Feedback Control of Networked Control Systems With Multiple Quantizers. In: 6th IEEE Conference on Industrial Electronics and Applications, pp. 1541–1546 (2011)
12. Fu, M.Y., Xie, L.: The Sector Bound Approach to Quantized Feedback Control. J. IEEE Transactions on Automatic Control 50, 1698–1711 (2005)
13. Wang, Y., Xie, L., de Souza, C.E.: Robust Control of a class of uncertain non-linear systems. J. System Control Letters 19, 139–149 (2002)
14. Goh, K.C., Turan, L., Safonov, M.G., Papavassilopoulos, G.P., Ly, J.H.: Baffine Matrix Inequality Properties and Computational Methods. In: Proceedings of the American Conference, Maryland, pp. 850–855 (1994)

Remote Iterative Learning Control System with Duplex Kalman Filtering

Wenju Zhou[1,2], Minrui Fei[1,*], Haikuan Wang[1], Xiaobing Zhou[1], and Lisheng Wei[3]

[1] Shanghai Key Laboratory of Power Station Automation Technology,
School of Mechatronics Engineering and Automation,
Shanghai University, Shanghai 200072, China
[2] School of Information and Electronic Engineering, Ludong University,
Yantai 2640025, China
[3] School of Information and Electronic Engineering, Anhui Polytechnic University,
Wuhu 201002, China
mrfei@staff.shu.edu.cn

Abstract. This article investigates the iterative learning control (ILC) problem for a remote network control systems under wireless network condition. To reduce wireless channel noise, a novel method of duplex Kalman filtering is firstly presented and combined into the remote ILC system. The convergence of system is analyzed and the convergence condition is given. The merit of the propose method is also verified by comparing the fluctuations boundaries of the two cases with Kalman filtering and without Kalman filtering. Finally, simulation results confirm that the tracking accuracy is greatly improved in comparison with other approaches under different cases of ILC and Kalman filtering.

Keywords: Wireless network control systems, Remote iterative learning control (RILC), Kalman filtering.

1 Introduction

In a wireless network control systems, the control signals are all exchanged by the wireless channel which makes the analysis and control design more complicated than classical transmission medium cable. As a result, the signals transmitted by the wireless channel will be distorted badly and the performance of remote network control systems will be degraded and even failed [3],[4]. In wireless network control systems research there have been numerous efforts to attenuate channel noise and compensate for data dropouts [5],[6],[7]. Specifically, if the plant is to be operated repetitively, there is a surprising advantage to using the iterative learning control (ILC) [3]. However the non-repeatable stochastic channel disturbance cannot be cut down only depend on ILC method. Since the influence of stochastic noise to histories is not repeatable on the control action, the influence of noise will be amplified on the output [8]. Therefore, we have to find other way to solve this problem. A Kalman filtering is

---

* Corresponding author.

T. Xiao, L. Zhang, and M. Fei (Eds.): AsiaSim 2012, Part II, CCIS 324, pp. 82–91, 2012.
© Springer-Verlag Berlin Heidelberg 2012

an optimal method for minimizing the influence of process and measurement noise when estimating error [9]. In fact, however, Kalman filtering used in ILC design methods have been suggested in the literature [10]. But only single Kalman filtering at controller side have been considered. In this paper, we propose an approach which duplex Kalman filtering adopts on the remote iteration learning control systom, and the convergence of this novel approach has been analyzed. We use the Kalman filter along the time axis toestimate the real measurement error $e_k(t)$ and the input $u_k(t)$.

The Kalman filter is of iteration nature, which prouduces two dimensions iterations along orthogonal directions, i.e., the iteration axis and the time axis. Finally, theoretical proofs and simulation results show that the incorporation of duplex Kalman filtering into RILC system will significantly reduce the fluctuation boundary of output error and improve RNCS performance.

This paper is organized as follows. In section 2 we formalize the problem of RILC system with a method of duplex Kalman filtering. In section 3, we analyze the convergence of the system and investigate the fluctuation boundary of the output. In section 4 we simulate an example to prove the correctness of the theorems and lemmas proposed in section 3. Finally, in section 5, we state our conclusions and give directions for future work.

2   Formulations RILC System with Duplex Kalman Filtering

The structure of developed remote iterative learning control system with duplex Kalman filtering is shown in Fig.1, where the input $u_k(t)$ will be transmitted from the controller node to actuator nodes by wireless channels [10]. The wireless channel noise $v_k(t)$ between the controller and to the actuator will disturb the input $u_k(t)$. $y_d(t)$ denotes the reference signal, which is stored in memory, and the output $y_k(t)$ to track $y_d(t)$ as closely as possible by manipulating the input variable $u_k(t)$. The output error $e_k(t)$ denotes the difference between a reference signal $y_d(t)$ and the output variable $y_k(t)$. The discrete-time-varying dynamical systems represented by Fig.1 can be described by the following difference equations:

$$x_k(t+1) = A(t)x_k(t) + B(t)\hat{u}_k(t) , \tag{1.a}$$

$$y_k(t) = C(t)x_k(t), \tag{1.b}$$

$$e_k(t) = y_d(t) - y_k(t) , \tag{1.c}$$

$$e'_k(t) = e_k(t) + w_k(t) , \tag{1.d}$$

$$u_{k+1}(t) = u_k(t) + L(t)\hat{e}_k(t+1) , \tag{1.e}$$

$$u'_k(t) = u_k(t) + v_k(t) , \tag{1.f}$$

with $x_k(0) = 0$ for all $k \in [1, 2, \cdots, \infty)$. Here t indicate time index, and k denotes the number of operation cycle, and system state vector $x_k(t) \in \mathbb{R}^p$, system control input vector $u_k(t) \in \mathbb{R}^r$, system output vector $y_k(t) \in \mathbb{R}^q$, $\forall t \in [0, \cdots, T]$ for some positive integer. $L(t)$ is the appropriate gain matrix.

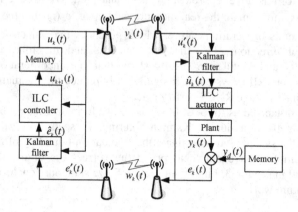

Fig. 1. Structure of RILC system with duplex Kalman filtering

The key point in (1) is how to get $\hat{e}(t)$ and $\hat{u}(t)$. We use two Kalman filters which are added in the closed loop for obtaining $\hat{e}(t)$ and $\hat{u}(t)$ from $e'(t)$ and $u'(t)$ respectively.

The Kalman filtering state equation and the filtering process for $e'(t)$ can be described by following recursive equations:

State equation:

$$x_{ek}(t+1) = A_e(t)x_{ek}(t) + B_e(t)\hat{u}_k(t),\tag{2.a}$$

$$e'_k(t) = C_e(t)x_{ek}(t) + y_d(t) + w_k(t),\tag{2.b}$$

State Propagation and Estimate:

$$\bar{x}_{ek}(t) = A_e(t-1)\hat{x}_{ek}(t-1) + B_e(t-1)\hat{u}_k(t-1),\tag{2.c}$$

$$\hat{x}_{ek}(t) = \bar{x}_{ek}(t) + K_k(t)(e'_k(t) - y_d(t) + C_e(t)\bar{x}_{ek}(t)),\tag{2.d}$$

Covariance and Gain Propagation:

$$\bar{P}_k(t) = A_e(t-1)\hat{P}_k(t-1)A_e(t-1)^T + B_e(t-1)QB_e(t-1)^T,\tag{2.e}$$

$$K_k(t) = -\bar{P}_k(t)C_e(t)^T(C_e(t)\bar{P}_k(t)C_e(t)^T + R)^{-1},\tag{2.f}$$

$$\hat{P}_k(t) = \bar{P}_k(t) - K_k(t)C_e(t)\bar{P}_k(t)\tag{2.g}$$

Where $K(t)$ is the Kalman gain matrix, $P(t)$ is the covariance of the estimated state error, Q and R denote the covariance of wireless channel noise $v_k(t)$ and $w_k(t)$, respectively. ⁻ stands for the propagated state, ˆ stands for the corrected state error using the Kalman gain matrix, The relation expression between adjacent trails can be written as following:

$$\hat{P}_k(0) = \hat{P}_{k-1}(T) .$$
(3)

This equation can also be written as $\hat{P}_k(t) = \hat{P}(kn+t)$. Thus, the time axis become infinite, i.e. time parameter $kT + t \to \infty$ when $k \to \infty, t \in [1,T]$. Our target is to find $\hat{e}(t)$, estimate of measurement error $e'(t)$.

According to (2c)~(2g), $\hat{x}_{ek}(t)$ can be obtained.

Using $\hat{e}_k(t) = y_d(t) - \hat{y}_k(t)$ and (1b), we get

$$\hat{e}_k(t) = y_d(t) - C_e(t)\hat{x}_{ek}(t) .$$
(4)

Similarly, for $u'(t)$, the Kalman filtering state equation and the filtering process can be also shown as:

State equation:

$$x_{uk}(t+1) = A_u(t)x_{uk}(t) + B_u(t)\hat{e}_k(t)$$
(5.a)

$$u'_k(t) = C_u(t)x_{uk}(t) + v_k(t)$$
(5.b)

State Propagation and Estimate:

$$\overline{x}_k(t) = A_u(t-1)\hat{x}_k(t-1) + B_u(t-1)\hat{e}_k(t-1) ,$$
(5.c)

$$\hat{x}_k(t) = \overline{x}_k(t) + K_k(t)(u'_k(t) - C_u(t)\overline{x}_k(t)),$$
(5.d)

Covariance and Gain Propagation:

$$\overline{P}_k(t) = A_u(t-1)\hat{P}_k(t-1)A_u(t-1)^T + B_u(t-1)QB_u(t-1)^T ,$$
(5.e)

$$K_k(t) = -\overline{P}_k(t)C_u(t)^T (C_u(t)\overline{P}_k(t)C_u(t)^T + R)^{-1} ,$$
(5.f)

$$\hat{P}_k(t) = \overline{P}_k(t) - K_k(t)C_u(t)\overline{P}_k(t) .$$
(5.g)

Estimate value $\hat{u}_k(t)$ is obtained,

$$\hat{u}_k(t) = C_u(t)\hat{x}_{uk}(t) .$$
(6)

Using the Kalman filtering and selecting the appropriate gain matrix $L(t)$ can guarantee following relationship hold:

$$\lim_{k \to \infty} \|e_k(t)\| \to 0, \forall t \in [0,\cdots,T] ,$$
(7.a)

$$\lim_{k \to \infty} u_k(t) \to u_d(t), \forall t \in [0, \cdots, T],$$
(7.b)

$$\lim_{k \to \infty} y_k(t) \to y_d(t), \forall t \in [0, \cdots, T].$$
(7.c)

That is, the following difference equation is satisfy

$$x_d(t+1) = A(t)x_d(t) + B(t)u_d(t),$$
(8.a)

$$y_d(t) = C(t)x_d(t).$$
(8.b)

3   Convergence and Fluctuation Boundary Analysis

In this section, we compare the method using duplex Kalman filtering that proposed in this paper with that of using single side Kalman filtering [11]. We will derive the fluctuation boundary of the measurement error in the norm sense.

Consider the discrete-time-varying dynamical system described by (1) ~ (8), it includes the channel noise $v_k(t)$ and $w_k(t)$. For the convenience of investigation, we assume that all the parameters mentioned in (1) ~ (8) satisfy the properties and bounds stated as follows.

1) System (8) is stable for $t \in [0, T]$, with $T < \infty$.

2) Let $v_k(t)$ and $w_k(t)$ be sequences of zero-mean white Gaussian noise with covariance Q and R, respectively. They are bounded in the sense of $\|v_k(t)\| \le b_v$ and $\|w_k(t)\| \le b_w$ for $\forall k, k \in [0, \infty), t \in [0, T]$. b_v and b_w are positive constants.

3) System returns to the same initial conditions at the star of each trial, i.e. $x_k(0) = \hat{x}_k(0) = x_d(0) = 0$, and each iteration has the same finite length, i.e. $t \in [0, T]$, with $T < \infty$.

4) The matrices $A(t)$, $B(t)$, $C(t)$ and $L(t)$ are defined in $\mathbb{R}^{p \times p}$, $\mathbb{R}^{p \times r}$, $\mathbb{R}^{q \times p}$ and $\mathbb{R}^{r \times q}$, respectively. Their bounds can be stated as $\|A(t)\| \le b_a$, $\|B(t)\| \le b_b$, $\|C(t)\| \le b_c$ and $\|L(t)\| \le b_l$.

Remark

The symbol $\|\cdot\|$ represents vector or matrix norm which can be described as

$\|x\| = (x^T x)^{\frac{1}{2}}$, where $x \in \mathbb{R}^p$ is the vector,

$\|C\| = [\lambda_{\max}(C^T C)]^{\frac{1}{2}}$, where $C \in \mathbb{R}^{p \times n}$ is the matrix, and $\lambda_{\max}$ represents the max eigenvalue of matrix $C^T C$.

$\|f(\cdot)\| = \sup_{t \in [0, T]} \|f(t)\|$.

$\|f(\cdot)\|_\lambda = \sup_{t \in [0, T]} \|f(t)\| \lambda^t, \quad 0 < \lambda < 1.$

Theorem 1. Suppose that iterative learning control system (1) ~ (8) satisfies assumptions 1) ~ 4), and the following inequality:

$$\|I - L(t)C(t+1)B(t)\| \le \rho < 1 \tag{9}$$

holds for all $t \in [0,T]$, then the control input $u_k(t)$ converges to a neighborhood of the desired control input $u_d(t)$ for $t \in [0,T]$ as $k \to \infty$. Furthermore, the radius of the neighborhood is zero, if the bound b_v and b_w are zero.

Proof: From (1) and (2), we get

$$\begin{aligned}
\Delta \hat{x}_k(t+1) = {} & (A(t) + K_k(t+1)C(t+1)A(t))\Delta \hat{x}_k(t) \\
& - K_k(t+1)C(t+1)A(t)\Delta x_k(t) + B(t)\Delta \hat{u}_k(t) \\
& - K_k(t+1)w_k(t+1)
\end{aligned} \tag{10}$$

$$\begin{aligned}
\Delta u_{k+1}(t) = {} & \Delta u_k(t) - L(t)C(t+1)B(t)\Delta \hat{u}_k(t) \\
& - L(t)C(t+1)\Phi_k(t)\Delta \hat{x}_k(t) + L(t)C(t+1)\Psi_k(t)\Delta x_k(t) \\
& + L(t)C(t+1)K_k(t+1)w_k(t+1)
\end{aligned} \tag{11}$$

where $\Delta u_k(t) \triangleq u_d(t) - u_k(t)$; $\Delta \hat{x}_k(t) \triangleq x_d(t) - \hat{x}_k(t)$; $\Delta x_k(t) \triangleq x_d(t) - x_k(t)$; $\Phi_k(t) \triangleq A(t) + K_k(t+1)C(t+1)A(t)$; $\Psi_k(t) \triangleq K_k(t+1)C(t+1)A(t)$. In order to facilitate the writing, we omit some subscript.

Due to Kalman filtering is convergence. We can suppose $\Delta \hat{u}_k(t) = \Delta u_k(t) + r(t)$, where $r(t)$ is a any tiny amount and bounded, i.e. $\|r(t)\| = \varepsilon_0 < \infty$.

Consequently, taking the norm $\|\cdot\|$ both sides of the equation (11), we have

$$\begin{aligned}
\|\Delta u_{k+1}(t)\| \le {} & \rho \|\Delta u_k(t)\| + b_l b_c b_\varphi \|\Delta \hat{x}_k(t)\| + b_l b_c b_\psi \|\Delta x_k(t)\| \\
& + b_l b_c b_\theta b_v + b_l b_{ck} b_w + b_\theta \varepsilon_0
\end{aligned} \tag{12}$$

Where $\forall t, t \in [0,T]$, $b_\varphi = \|\Phi_k(t)\|$, $b_\psi = \|\Psi_k(t)\|$, $b_\theta = \|K_k(t+1)C(t+1)B(t)\|$, $b_{ck} = \|C(t+1)K_k(t+1)\|$.

Take norms on both sides of equation (10) and using the discrete Bellman-Gronwall lemma, we get

$$\begin{aligned}
\|\Delta \hat{x}_k(t)\| \le {} & b_\varphi^t \|\Delta \hat{x}_k(0)\| + \sum_{j=1}^{t-1} b_\varphi^{t-j-1}(b_\psi \|\Delta x_k(j)\| \\
& + b_b \|\Delta u_k(j)\| + b_\theta b_v + b_k b_w + b_b \varepsilon_0)
\end{aligned} \tag{13}$$

Substitute (13) in (12), and multiply both sides by λ^t, with $0 < \lambda < 1$, finally, we have

$$\|\Delta x_k\|_\lambda \le b_b \lambda \frac{1 - b_a^T \lambda^T}{1 - b_a \lambda} \|\Delta u_k\|_\lambda + \varepsilon_2 \ , \tag{14}$$

$$\|\Delta u_{k+1}\|_\lambda \le \tilde{\rho} \|\Delta u_k\|_\lambda + \tilde{\varepsilon} \ , \tag{15}$$

where
$$\varepsilon_1 \triangleq b_l b_c (b_\theta b_v + b_k \varepsilon_0 + b_k b_w) \frac{b_\varphi \lambda (1 - b_\varphi^T \lambda^T)}{1 - b_\varphi \lambda} + b_l b_c b_\theta b_v + b_l b_{ck} b_w + b_\theta \varepsilon_0 \quad,$$

$$\varepsilon_2 = b_b b_v \lambda \frac{1 - b_a^T \lambda^T}{1 - b_a \lambda},$$

$$\tilde{\rho} \triangleq \rho + b_l b_c b_b b_\varphi \lambda \frac{1 - b_\varphi^T \lambda^T}{1 - b_\varphi \lambda} + b_l b_c b_b b_a \lambda \frac{1 - b_a^T \lambda^T}{1 - b_a \lambda} + b_l b_c b_b b_\varphi b_a \lambda^2 \frac{(1 - b_\varphi^T \lambda^T)(1 - b_a^T \lambda^T)}{(1 - b_\varphi \lambda)(1 - b_a \lambda)},$$

$$\tilde{\varepsilon} \triangleq (b_l b_c b_\psi + b_l b_c b_\psi b_\varphi \lambda \frac{1 - b_\varphi^T \lambda^T}{1 - b_\varphi \lambda}) \varepsilon_2 + \varepsilon_1.$$

Apparently, choose λ small enough so that $\tilde{\rho} < 1$.

Thus, inequation (15) is a contraction in $\|\Delta u\|_\lambda$. When the operations increase, i.e. $k \to \infty$, we get

$$\limsup_{k \to \infty} \|\Delta u_k\|_\lambda \leq \frac{\tilde{\varepsilon}}{1 - \tilde{\rho}}. \tag{16}$$

Inserting (16) in (14), we get

$$\limsup_{k \to \infty} \|\Delta x_k\|_\lambda \leq b_b \lambda \tilde{\varepsilon} \frac{1 - b_a^T \lambda^T}{(1 - \tilde{\rho})(1 - b_a \lambda)} + b_b b_v \lambda \frac{1 - b_a^T \lambda^T}{1 - b_a \lambda}. \tag{17}$$

Finally, we have

$$\|e_k(t)\|_\lambda \leq b_c \|\Delta x(t)\|_\lambda. \qquad \bullet \tag{18}$$

And this implies

$$\limsup_{k \to \infty} \|e_k(t)\|_\lambda \leq b_c b_b \lambda \tilde{\varepsilon} \frac{1 - b_a^T \lambda^T}{(1 - \tilde{\rho})(1 - b_a \lambda)} + b_c \varepsilon_2. \tag{19}$$

Clearly, we have the result that if the condition (9) holds for all $t \in [0, T]$, then the control input $u_k(t)$ converges to a neighborhood of the desired control input $u_d(t)$ and measurement error $e_k(t)$ converges to a fixed puniness bound for $t \in [0, T]$ as $k \to \infty$. Especially, if the noise bound b_v and b_w are zero, i.e. $b_v = b_w = 0$, we get $\varepsilon_1 = (b_l b_c b_b \frac{b_\varphi \lambda (1 - b_\varphi^T \lambda^T)}{1 - b_\varphi \lambda} + b_\theta) \varepsilon_0$, $\varepsilon_2 = 0$, and $\tilde{\varepsilon} = \varepsilon_1$. For Kalman filtering,

$\lim_{k \to \infty} \Delta \hat{u}_k(t) = \Delta u_k(t)$. Hence, $\lim_{k \to \infty} \varepsilon_0 = 0$. we have $\limsup_{k \to \infty} \|e_k(t)\|_\lambda = 0$ as result.

More detailed proof process, please refer to the literature [11]. This proof is similar to the convergance proof of one side Kalman filtering.

4   Experimental Result

A model of a unicycle-type mobile robot, which has two independent driving wheels on the same axis, is given in literature [12]. We control the mobile robot through the wireless signal. The motion of the mobile robot can be described in a discrete-time domain as

$$\begin{bmatrix} x_k(t+1) \\ y_k(t+1) \\ \theta_k(t+1) \end{bmatrix} = \begin{bmatrix} x_k(t) \\ y_k(t) \\ \theta_k(t) \end{bmatrix} + \Delta T \begin{bmatrix} \cos\theta_k(t) & 0 \\ \sin\theta_k(t) & 0 \\ 0 & 1 \end{bmatrix} (\begin{bmatrix} u_{1k}(t) \\ u_{2k}(t) \end{bmatrix} + \begin{bmatrix} v_{1k}(t) \\ v_{2k}(t) \end{bmatrix}), \tag{20}$$

where $x(t)$ and $y(t)$ are the Cartesian coordinates of the mobile robot in the world frame. $\theta_k(t)$ denotes the orientation angle of the robot. ΔT denotes the sampling time, which is $0.001s$. $u_{1k}(t)$ and $u_{2k}(t)$ are the linear and angular velocity respectively. $v_{1k}(t)$ and $v_{2k}(t)$ are zero-mean Gaussian white noises with variance $Q_1 = 0.2$ and $Q_2 = 0.2$ respectively.

The learning law formulizes to be

$$\begin{bmatrix} u_{1k}(t+1) \\ u_{2k}(t+1) \end{bmatrix} = \begin{bmatrix} u_{1k}(t) \\ u_{2k}(t) \end{bmatrix} + L \begin{bmatrix} \cos\theta_k(t) & \sin\theta_k(t) & 0 \\ 0 & 0 & 1 \end{bmatrix} (\begin{bmatrix} e_{xk}(t+1) \\ e_{yk}(t+1) \\ e_{\theta k}(t+1) \end{bmatrix} + \begin{bmatrix} w_{1k}(t+1) \\ w_{2k}(t+1) \\ w_{3k}(t+1) \end{bmatrix}), \tag{21}$$

where $L = 0.5$. $e_{xk}(t)$, $e_{yk}(t)$ and $e_{\theta k}(t)$ denote the error of measurement. They can be got by following expressions:

$$e_{xk}(t) = x_d(t) - x_k(t) \quad , \quad e_{yk}(t) = y_d(t) - y_k(t) \quad ,$$

$e_{\theta k}(t) = \theta_d(t) - \theta_k(t)$.

$w_{1k}(t)$, $w_{2k}(t)$ and $w_{3k}(t)$ are zero-mean Gaussian white noises with variance $R_1 = R_2 = R_3 = 0.2$.

The desired output trajectory is circle-shape, which can be described as $x_d^2(t) + y_d^2(t) = r^2 \quad t \in [0,400]$. Where $r=1m$, which denotes radius.

We simulated the mobile robot with three conditions. First, we performed simulation tests for 100 iterations without channel noise. Second, we add perturbation to both the input $[u_{1k}(t) \quad u_{2k}(t)]^T$ of wireless channels and the measure error $[e_{xk}(t) \quad e_{yk}(t) \quad e_{\theta k}(t)]$ of wireless channels in remote ILC mobile robot system without Kalman filtering. Last, we use Kalman filtering in last simulation. The Fig.2 shows the mobile robot path-tracking of the simulations above. As shown in this figure, the full line represents the desire path. The dotted line represents the 100th iteration path-trajectory of the mobile robot without channel noise. The star line represents the 100th iteration path-trajectory of the mobile robot with stochastic channel noise. The solid line show the trajectory of the mobile robot at 100th iteration, which controlled by wireless channel signal with stochastic noise and estimated by the Kalman filtering. Obviously, the proposed in the paper is closer to desire trajectory than these of the case without the Kalman filtering, while the wireless channel signal have been disturbed by stochastic noise. As shown in this figure, the top right shows the maximum absolute value of measure error $e_{xk}(t)$, the bottom-left figure shows the maximum absolute value of measure error $e_{yk}(t)$, and the bottom-left figure presents the maximum absolute value of measure error $e_{\theta k}(t)$ in the iteration process. The circle lines and dotted line represent the cases these RILC robot system with channel noise have not smoothed by Kalman filtering. The triangle lines and full line indicate the cases of this paper present method. The star lines show the cases that these RILC robot system without channel noise. Obviously, the maximum absolute value of measure error of the RILC mobile robot system with the Kalman filter on time axis as show in the figure with up triangle line and full line become smaller than these of the cases without the Kalman filter be shown in figure with circle lines and dotted line. These imply that the trajectory of mobile robot with Kalman filtering is closer to desire trajectory than these of the case without the Kalman filtering, this case is also presented in Fig. 2. This example means that the theorem.1 presented in this paper above are also very accurate.

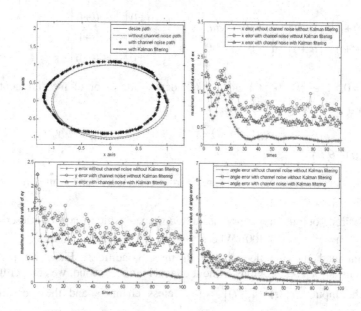

Fig. 2. Simulation results of mobile robot path-trajectory

5   Conclusions

In this paper, a new Kaman filtering scheme to attenuate wireless channel noise for the RILC network system was developed. The key idea of the suggested method is that the time index of trails is connected as a whole time axis, and the measurement error is estimated online with Kalman filtering on this time axis, which is infinite when the number of iterations is infinite. As the main contribution of this paper, it was analyzed and proved that the base-line error of the uncertain RILC system caused by the channel noise can be significantly reduced by the suggested Kalman filtering and ILC scheme. Simulations results indicate that the Kalman filtering along time axis and RILC along iteration axis can be considerably reduced wireless channel noise as compared to the case of RILC without Kalman filtering.

Acknowledgments. This work was supported in part by the National Natural Science Foundation of China under Grant No.61074032 and No.61104089, Science and Technology Commission of Shanghai Municipality under Grant No.10JC1405000, Natural Science Foundation of Anhui Province of China under grant 1208085QF124, Foundation of Anhui Educational Committee under grant KJ2011B010.

References

1. Du, D., Fei, M., Song, Y., Li, X.: Brief survey and prospect of networked control systems. Chinese Journal of Scientific Instrument 32(3), 713–720 (2011)
2. Yang, T.C.: Networked control system: a brief survey. IEE Proceedings-Control Theory and Applications 153(4), 403–412 (2006)
3. Fang, Y., Yan, H.-C.: Error analysis for remote nonlinear iterative learning control system with wireless channel noise. Journal of Shanghai University (English Edition) 15(1), 7–11 (2011)
4. Ahn, H.-S., Moore, K.L., Chen, Y.Q.: Iterative Learning Control: Robustness and Monotonic Convergence for Interval Systems. Springer, London (2007)
5. Fei, M., Yi, J., Hu, H.: Robust Stability Analysis of an Uncertain Nonlinear Networked Control System Category. International Journal of Control, Automation, and Systems 4(2), 172–177 (2006)
6. Hespanha, J.P., Naghshtabrizi, P., Xu, Y.: A survey of recent results in networked control systems. Proceedings of the IEEE 95(1), 138–162 (2007)
7. Li, T.J., Fujimoto, Y.: Control system with high-speed and real-time communication links. IEEE Transactions on Industrial Electronics 55(4), 1548–1557 (2008)
8. Elia, N.: Remote stabilization over fading channels. Systems & Control Letters 54, 237–249 (2005)
9. Pana, Y.-J., Marquez, H.J., Chen, T.: Stabilization of remote control systems with unknown time varying delays by LMI techniques. International Journal of Control 79(7), 752–763 (2006)
10. Zhou, W.J., Fei, M.R., et al.: A method of Kalman filtering for remote iterative learning control system with wireless channel noise. In: Fourth International Workshop on Advanced Computational Intelligence, Wuhan, Hubei, China, October 19-21, pp. 365–369 (2011)
11. Zhou, W.J., Fei, M.R., Du, D.D., et al.: Convergence of Remote Iterative Learning Control System With Kalman Filtering. In: International Conference on System Simulation, Shanghai, China, April 6-9, pp. 445–450 (2012)
12. Kang, M.K., Lee, J.S., Han, K.L.: Kinematic Path-Tracking of Mobile Robot Using Iterative Learning Control. Journal of Robotic Systems 22(2), 111–121 (2005)

Prognostics for Aircraft Control Surface Damage Based on Fuzzy Least Squares Support Vector Regression (FLS-SVR)

Lei Dong, Zhang Ren, and Qingdong Li

Science and Technology on Aircraft Control Laboratory
Beihang University, Beijing 100191, China
jack19830108@sina.com

Abstract. The trends of flight control system state parameters which can be measured are indirect manifestations of surface damage. In order to predict the changes of states trend more accurately, an algorithm based on fuzzy least squares support vector regression (FLS-SVR) was presented. This approach reconstructed the phase space of multivariate time series using K-L transformation method. A FLS-SVR model was built with the new information priority theory according to apply a fuzzy membership to each input point. The SVR parameters were optimized by genetic algorithm (GA) to improve the accuracy of the model. In order to verify the validity of FLS-SVR algorithm, the prognostics and analysis of surface damage trend were performed. The simulation result demonstrates the prognostics model has good predictive ability.

Keywords: Prognostic, support vector regression, fuzzy membership, least squares, genetic algorithm.

1 Introduction

In recent years, with the development of equipment maintenance theory and related technologies, the prognostics technology is rapidly developed. In the structural analysis of complex systems, prognostics technique is a very complex issue. Especially for the flight control system, it is an important part which affects the safety of aircraft. Predict important parameters reflecting the performance of system status to achieve monitoring the flight control system can enhance the ability of early fault detection [1], [2], [3].

When the aircraft surface failure, the flight status will have a huge non-linear change, and the fault degree will be developed soon. The traditional linear prognostics model is no longer applicable. Therefore, the neural network technology has been used to predict the failure of such a complex nonlinear system such as study [4]. However, it was not considered the learning algorithm of neural network based on empirical risk minimization exist the problems of "owe learning" and "over learning". In comparison, support vector regression (SVR) extended by the support vector machines (SVM) can take into account the experience risk and generalization ability

T. Xiao, L. Zhang, and M. Fei (Eds.): AsiaSim 2012, Part II, CCIS 324, pp. 92–101, 2012.

of the learning algorithm. It not only do not exist the problems of "owe learning" and "over learning" but also avoid the problems of high dimension sample and local minimum. In these years, a growing number of scholars have used it for prognostics of nonlinear systems.

Least squares support vector regression (LS-SVR) adheres to the advantages of structural risk minimization principle and modeling capabilities using small samples. It changes the constraints of SVR into equality from inequality so as to make a quadratic programming convert to solve linear equations. This approach simplifies the computational complexity and improves the learning efficiency.

In this paper, we reconstructed the phase space of multivariate time series using K-L transformation method and applied a fuzzy membership to each input point of SVR so as to build a FLS-SVR model with the new information priority theory. The SVR parameters were optimized by genetic algorithm (GA) to improve the accuracy of the model. The prognostics and analysis of surface damage trend was performed and the simulation result demonstrates the prognostics model has good predictive ability.

The rest of this paper is organized as follows. The K-L transformation method will be described in Section 2. The FLS-SVR model will be derived in Section 3. Section 4 will present the genetic algorithm for parameter optimization. In Section 5, the experiment of the improved algorithm on aircraft surface fault prognosis has been discussed. Some concluding remarks are given in Section 6.

2 Phase-Space Reconstruction

The method converts the scalar time series to vectors in an m-dimensional Euclidean space. In multivariate time series $X(t) = [x_1(t),...,x_n(t)]^T$ $(t=1,2,...,N)$, $x_1(t),...,x_n(t)$ are the value of n parameters at time t. The reconstruction method of multivariate time series is the same as single variable time series to select the appropriate embedding dimension and delay time. Then, the embedding delay vector of multivariate time series is,

$$X_n = \begin{bmatrix} x_1(t) & x_1(t-\tau_{d1}) & \cdots & x_1(t-(m_1-1)\tau_{d1}) \\ \vdots & \vdots & \vdots & \vdots \\ x_i(t) & x_i(t-\tau_{di}) & \cdots & x_i(t-(m_i-1)\tau_{di}) \\ \vdots & \vdots & \vdots & \vdots \\ x_n(t) & x_n(t-\tau_{dn}) & \cdots & x_n(t-(m_n-1)\tau_{dn}) \end{bmatrix}^T \tag{1}$$

Where m_i is embedding dimension and τ_{di} is delay time.

Recent studies show that the quality of the phase-space is determined jointly by m_i and τ_{di}. Therefore, study [5] proposed to get m_i and τ_{di} by using the embedding delay window τ_{wi}.

$$\tau_{wi} = (m_i - 1)\tau_{di} \tag{2}$$

For each time series, τ_{wi} can be determined according to the correlation between elements of the observation points. In order to contain enough predictive information,

τ_{wi} usually take a larger value in an optional range. For τ_{di}, if its value is too large, it will increase the difficulty of calculation and loss the nature connection between data. If its value is too small, the information is not exposed easily. Takens theorem considers that τ_{di} which is not the best will only affect the Euclidean geometry of attractor and the calculation of correlation dimension. Therefore, τ_{di} is generally selected smaller value.

Karhunen-Loeve (K-L) transformation is a special kind of orthogonal linear transformation which is similar to Fourier transformation and Walsh transformation. Select a single variable time series from equation (1) and its complete expression after phase-space reconstruction is,

$$X_i = \begin{bmatrix} x_i(t) & x_i(t-1) & \cdots & x_i(t-M+1) \\ x_i(t-\tau_{di}) & x_i(t-1-\tau_{di}) & \cdots & x_i(t-M+1-\tau_{di}) \\ \cdots & \cdots & & \cdots \\ x_i(t-(m_i-1)\tau_{di}) & x_i(t-1-(m_i-1)\tau_{di}) & \cdots & x_i(1) \end{bmatrix} \quad (3)$$

Where $M = t - (m_i - 1)\tau_{di}$.

And the covariance matrix of X_i is,

$$\bar{Z}_x = E\left\{ \left(X_i - \bar{X}_i \right) \left(X_i - \bar{X}_i \right)^T \right\} \quad (4)$$

Then, the m-dimensional real symmetric matrix of $\bar{Z}_x$ is,

$$\bar{Z}_x = \begin{bmatrix} c_{11} & c_{12} & \cdots & c_{1m} \\ c_{21} & c_{22} & \cdots & c_{2m} \\ \cdots & \cdots & & \cdots \\ c_{m1} & c_{m2} & \cdots & c_{mm} \end{bmatrix} \quad (5)$$

From equation (5), m eigenvalues λ_i and their eigenvectors V_{1i} ($i=1,2,\ldots,m$) can be obtained by the covariance matrix. Then, the orthogonal transformation of V_1 is presented as

$$V_2 = V_{1i} V_{1j}^T = \begin{cases} 1 & i = j \\ 0 & i \neq j \end{cases} \quad (i, j = 1, 2, \cdots, m) \quad (6)$$

We complete the K-L transformation with $Y = V_2^T X$. Y is a combination of the re-distribution of a variety of information in X and each vector contains all the information of X. So we can give up the vectors whose eigenvalues are smaller than others in covariance matrix and the vectors of the remaining eigenvalues retain most information of the original signal [6].

3   FLS-SVR Model

For a given training data set $(x_i, y_i) \in R^d \times R^h$, $(i = 1, 2, \cdots l)$, l is the number of samples. In the situation of samples are nonlinear, we can map the samples to a high dimensional feature space from their original feature space through a nonlinear mapping function $\Phi(\bullet)$. Then, a nonlinear fitting problem in the original feature space is changed into a linear fitting problem in high dimensional feature space. Therefore, we can use linear function of high dimensional feature space to fit the sample sets.

$$f(x) = w^T \cdot \Phi(x) + b \tag{7}$$

Where x is input sample, w is vector of weight and b is threshold.

Considered the function complexity and the fitting error, regression prognostics problem can be expressed as a constrained optimization problem according to structural risk minimization principle.

$$\min_{w,b,\xi} J(w,\xi) = \frac{1}{2} \sum_{j=1}^{h} w_j^T w_j + \frac{1}{2} \gamma \sum_{i=1}^{l} \sum_{j=1}^{h} \xi_{ij}^2 \tag{8}$$

$$s.t. \quad y_{ij} = w_j^T \cdot \Phi(x_i) + b_j + \xi_{ij} \quad i = 1, 2, \cdots l \ \ j = 1, 2, \cdots, h$$

Where γ is a constant and it can be regarded as a regularization parameter, ξ is a measure of error in the SVR and we usually call it slack variable.

For regression prognostics problem, it is often that the training points are more important if the distance is larger between the training points and the measured point. So a fuzzy membership associated with each training point is used. For multivariate time series after phase space reconstruction, we make the vector of fuzzy membership is,

$$S_i = \left[s_{11}^i, s_{21}^i, \cdots, s_{m_1 1}^i, s_{12}^i, s_{22}^i, \cdots, s_{m_2 2}^i, \cdots, s_{uv}^i, \cdots, s_{m_n n}^i \right]^T \tag{9}$$

$$u = 1, 2, \cdots, m_v \quad v = 1, 2, \cdots, n$$

Where m is the embedding dimension and n is the number of parameters. We make the fuzzy membership s_{uv}^i be a function of (p, η, m, u, v).

$$s_{uv}^i = f(p, \eta, m, u, v) \tag{10}$$

Where p is the position of the point in the multivariate input samples and η is lower bound of fuzzy memberships. For one of n parameters, we make the last point be the most important and choose its fuzzy membership is 1, and make the first point of m_i input points be the least important and its fuzzy membership is η. By applying the boundary conditions, we can get the multivariate fuzzy membership function is,

$$s_{uv}^i = \eta_i + (1 - \eta_i) \left(\frac{p_{uv} - p_{1v}}{m_v} \right)^2 \tag{11}$$

Then, we can reconstruct function (8) as

$$\min_{w,b,\xi} J(w,\xi) = \frac{1}{2}\sum_{j=1}^{h} w_j^T w_j + \frac{1}{2}\gamma\sum_{i=1}^{l}\sum_{j=1}^{h} S_i \xi_{ij}^2 \tag{12}$$

In order to solve the optimization problem, it needs to establish Lagrange equation and converts the constrained optimization problem into an unconstrained optimization problem.

$$L(w,b,\alpha,\xi) = \frac{1}{2}\sum_{j=1}^{h} w_j^T w_j + \frac{1}{2}\gamma\sum_{i=1}^{l}\sum_{j=1}^{h} S_i \xi_{ij}^2$$
$$- \sum_{i=1}^{l}\sum_{j=1}^{h} \alpha_{ij}\left[w_j^T \Phi(x_i) + b_j + \xi_{ij} - y_{ij}\right] \tag{13}$$

Where α_{ij} is Lagrange multiplier. According to the Karush-Kuhn-Tucker (KKT) condition, we can get

$$\begin{cases} \dfrac{\partial L}{\partial w_j} = w_j - \sum_{i=1}^{l} \alpha_{ij} \cdot \Phi(x_i) = 0 \\[2mm] \dfrac{\partial L}{\partial b_j} = \sum_{i=1}^{l} \alpha_{ij} = 0 \\[2mm] \dfrac{\partial L}{\partial \xi_{ij}} = \alpha_{ij} - \gamma \cdot S_i \cdot \xi_{ij} = 0 \\[2mm] \dfrac{\partial L}{\partial \alpha_{ij}} = w_j^T \cdot \Phi(x_i) + b_j + \xi_{ij} - y = 0 \end{cases} \tag{14}$$

Elimination of w and ξ, we can get the linear equations as

$$\begin{bmatrix} 0 & e \\ e & \Omega + \dfrac{I}{\gamma S_i} \end{bmatrix} \begin{bmatrix} b \\ \alpha \end{bmatrix} = \begin{bmatrix} 0 \\ Y \end{bmatrix} \tag{15}$$

Where

$$Y = \begin{bmatrix} y_{11} & y_{12} & \cdots & y_{1h} \\ y_{21} & y_{22} & \cdots & y_{2h} \\ \cdots & \cdots & & \cdots \\ y_{l1} & y_{l2} & \cdots & y_{lh} \end{bmatrix} \qquad \alpha = \begin{bmatrix} \alpha_{11} & \alpha_{12} & \cdots & \alpha_{1h} \\ \alpha_{21} & \alpha_{22} & \cdots & \alpha_{2h} \\ \cdots & \cdots & & \cdots \\ \alpha_{l1} & \alpha_{l2} & \cdots & \alpha_{lh} \end{bmatrix} \tag{16}$$

And I is a identity matrix, $e = [1,1,\cdots,1]^T$, $\Omega_{ij} = \Phi(x_i) \cdot \Phi(x_j) = K(x_i, x_j)$, $K(x_i, x_j)$ is kernel function. Then, the prognostics model of FLS-SVR is,

$$y_j(x) = \sum_{i=1}^{l} \alpha_{ij} K(x, x_i) + b_j \tag{17}$$

We choose $K(x_i, x_j) = \exp\left(-\|x_i - x_j\|^2 / 2\sigma^2\right).$

4   Parameter Optimization

The parameters γ and σ greatly affect the performance of the FLS-SVR model. Therefore, GA which is a biologically motivated adaptive system based on natural selection and genetic recombination is used to search for better combination of the parameters. We can obtain the optimal solution after a series of iterative computations using GA. The process of optimizing γ and σ with GA is described as below.

1) Encoding parameters and Population initialization: The parameters γ and σ of FLS-SVR model are represented by a chromosome composed of float number code which can avoid decoding and coding repeatedly. As the parameters have their range respectively, binary encoding is adopted. Then, randomly generate an initial population of chromosomes to present the values of two parameters.

2) The construction of fitness function: The fitness function is the unique information and plays a critical role to measure GA's performance. In this study, root mean square relative error (RMSRE) is used as the fitness function.

$$Fitness = \sqrt{\frac{1}{l} \sum_{i=1}^{l} \left(\frac{y_i - \hat{y}_i}{y_i}\right)^2} \tag{18}$$

Where y_i is actual value and $\hat{y}_i$ is predictive value.

3) Selection operation: Based on the fitness function, compare the best chromosome A_{best} of the old generation and the best chromosome B_{best} of the new generation, the worst chromosome of the new generation is replaced by A_{best} if B_{best} is better than A_{best}, and B_{best} is replaced by A_{best} if A_{best} is better than B_{best}. The selection method can avoid the drawback of high fitness chromosome occupies population quickly in early stage.

4) Crossover and mutation operation: It is the main method to produce new individuals by simulating the process of biological evolution. Define the crossover probability P_c and P_m, we can get the function of crossover and mutation is,

$$P_{c,m} = \begin{cases} P_{c_1,m_1} - \dfrac{\left(P_{c_1,m_1} - P_{c_2,m_2}\right)\left(fit_{max} - fit_i'\right)}{fit_{max} - fit_{avg}} & fit_i' \geq fit_{avg} \\ P_{c_1,m_1} & fit_i' < fit_{avg} \end{cases} \tag{19}$$

Where fit_{max} is the maximum fitness, fit_{avg} is the average fitness and fit_i' is the larger fitness of two crossover individuals [7].

5) Offspring forms a new population in the next generation and replaces the old population. The evolutionary process proceeds until stop conditions are satisfied and then the best chromosomes are presented as a solution.

5　Experimental Analysis

5.1　Prognostic Strategy for Aircraft Control Surface Damage

In practice, the parameters can be detected on the aircraft is limited and the collected data is often affected by noise so that the prediction accuracy reduces. Thus, the samples pretreatment is needed and then choose the cofactors which have a strong correlation with the parameter to be predicted. The prognostics framework for aircraft control surface damage based on FLS-SVR is shown in Fig.1.

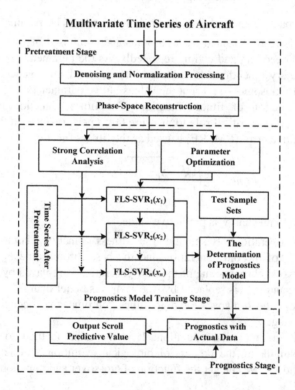

Fig. 1. This shows the prognostics framework for aircraft control surface damage based on FLS-SVR. The prognostic strategy for aircraft control surface damage is divided into three stages. There are pretreatment stage, prognostics model training stage and prognostics stage.

The prognostics steps are as follows:

Step 1: The multidimensional parameter time series sample data are obtained from six-degree-of-freedom closed-loop flight control system model. Deal the sample data for denoising and normalization processing and reconstruct the phase space of the sample data using K-L transformation method.

Step 2: Do Strong correlation analysis for the sample data and find the optimal parameters of FLS-SVR by GA.

Step 3: We can get one-step prognostic value using the trained FLS-SVR model and add the value to the original sample data while removing the oldest data. Repeat the step 2 and 3 to achieve rolling prognostics.

5.2   Simulation and Analysis

There are many types of aircraft surface damage fault. In this paper, we mainly discuss the failure of aircraft rudder damage. When the rudder has some damages, the change of yaw rate r is the most obvious. So this paper only discusses the parameter r. Fig.2 shows the signal of parameter r with noise and the sampling period is 0.05s. The rudder damages at 22s and the degree of damage increases with time.

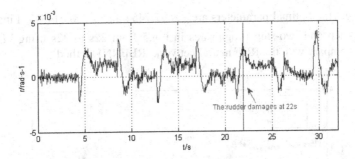

Fig. 2. This shows the signal of parameter r with noise. The rudder damages at 22s and the degree of damage increases with time. It can be seen from the figure, the signal is cyclical changes before 22s and non-cyclical changes after 22s.

Denoising by wavelet transform method and the result is shown in Fig.3.

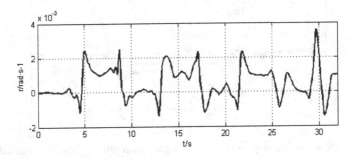

Fig. 3. This shows the signal of parameter r after denoising by wavelet transform method

Assuming the initial altitude of aircraft is 5000m, the initial speed is 0.69Ma and the initial trim conditions are zero. In this paper, we use the roll angle ϕ as a cofactor to predict r. After reconstruct the phase space of the sample data using K-L transformation method, we can get $m_\phi = 7$, $m_r = 5$ and $\tau_{d\phi} = \tau_{dr} = 1$. Then, use the method of GA to optimize the parameters γ and σ. The fitness curve is shown in Fig.4.

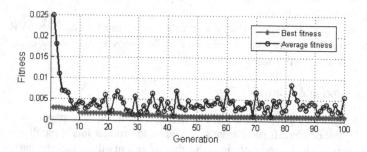

Fig. 4. This shows the fitness curve. The blue and circle curve is average fitness curve while the red and asterisk one is the best fitness curve.

We can get the optimal parameters are γ is 97.7454 and σ is 0.014877. Finally, we do the one-step and two-step prognostics in Fig.5 from 22s to 32s using FLS-SVR model and compare with the RBF neural network (RBFNN) method.

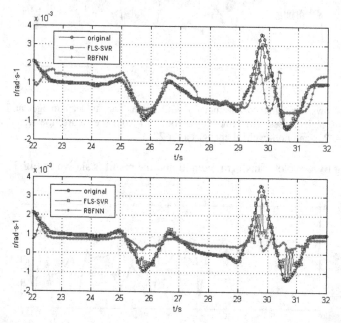

Fig. 5. This shows the one-step and two-step prognostics results of FLS-SVR and RBFNN

It can be seen that both the FLS-SVR method and the RBF neural network method can predict the trend of parameter r well when the rudder damages. However, Table 1 indicates whatever one-step prognostic or two-step prognostic, the FLS-SVR method is better than the RBFNN method.

Table 1. This shows the performance comparison of the FLS-SVR and RBFNN

Performance indicators	One-step prognostic (RBFNN)	One-step prognostic (FLS-SVR)	Two-step prognostic (RBFNN)	Two-step prognostic (FLS-SVR)
MAPE	0.6775	0.6020	1.6683	0.9056
MSE	0.0007	0.0006	0.0074	0.0012

6   Conclusions

The simulation results show that the FLS-SVR method can predict the trend of parameter r well when the rudder damages and compare with the RBF neural network method to prove that the prognostic accuracy of proposed method is better. However, this method also has some shortcomings. After multi-step rolling prognostics, the accuracy decreases gradually. Therefore, how to interacts the prognostic data and training data together and create a dynamic prognostics model to increase accuracy is the direction for further research.

Acknowledgements. This work was supported under National Natural Science Foundation of China, under grant (60874117, 61101004), and the Programe of Introducing Talents of Discipline to Universities, under grant B07009.

References

1. Belkharraz, A.I., Sobel, K.: Direct adaptive control for aircraft control surface failures. In: Proceedings of the American Control Conference, pp. 3905–3910. IEEE, Piscataway (2003)
2. Weiss, J.L., Willsky, A.S., Looze, D.P., et al.: Detection and isolation of control surface effectiveness failures in high performance aircraft. In: IEEE NAECON, pp. 552–559 (1985)
3. Zhang, Y.Z., Deng, J.H.: On-Line fault mode prediction and fault detection for control surface damage. Journal of Northwestern Polytechnical University 21, 298–301 (2003)
4. Li, B., Zhang, W.G., Ning, D.F., Yin, W.: Fault prediction system of airplane steer surface based on neural network model. Journal of System Simulation 20, 5840–5842 (2008)
5. Rosenstein, M.T., Collins, J.J., De Luca, C.J.: Reconstruction expansion as a geometry based framework for choosing proper delay yime. Physica D: Nonlinear Phenomena 73, 82–98 (1994)
6. Schouten, J.C., Coppens, M.-O., Takens, F., van den Bleek, C.M.: Chaotic attractor learning and how to deal with nonlinear singularities. In: The IEEE 2000 Adaptive Systems for Signal Processing, Communications, and Control Symposium, AS-SPCC 2000, October 1-4, pp. 466–470 (2000)
7. Srinivas, J., Catnaik, L.M.: Adaptive probabilities of crossover and mutation in genetic algorithm. IEEE Transactions on SMC 24, 656–667 (1994)

The SOS Simulation of Network-Centric Information System Based on Agent

Fang Zhou and Shaojie Mao

The Information System Important Laboratory of the 28th Research Institute of China
Electronics Technology Group Corporation, Nanjing, 21007
326zhoufang@163.com

Abstract. In this paper, the concept, composition and architecture of network-centric information system are firstly introduced. Secondly, the methodology of Agent-based modeling (ABM) is used to establish the simulation model of command and control (C2) node of network-centric information system. At last, a method based on the information associated network is proposed to solving the problem of the System of System (SOS) simulation on network-centric information system. Through analyzing the information interactive relationship between information system nodes, the interactive contents are real-time computed and stored in a two-dimension table. So according to the information interactive relationship and interactive contents, the SOS running effect of network-centric information system can be high fidelity simulated.

Keywords: Network-Centric, System of System Simulation, Agent Simulation, Information Associated Network.

1   Introduction

With the development of information technology and network technology, the mode of military information system should be transited from the hierachical mode based on platform-centric to the flat mode based on network-centric [1-2].

At present, many scholars at home and abroad are developing the research about the large system of system simulation. Some of them utilize the complex ecosystem theory, multi-agent modeling and simulation method, complex networks theory to do some system simulation researches. In paper [3], the author designed an agent-based simulation framework, including simulation entity type, the relationships and interfaces, the interior architecture and behavior rules. The SOS combat simulation modeling under the information war is established with the complex network and multi-agent theory in paper [4]. And some other relative simulation researches can be referenced by papers [5-7].

But the problem of the inter-relationship between entities is not perfectly resolved under the above papers. In this paper, the problem on SOS simulation of network-centric information system is studied. The C^2 model of node is established based on the multi-agent. And a dynamic information inter-relationship table between nodes of application system is built based on the information associated network.

T. Xiao, L. Zhang, and M. Fei (Eds.): AsiaSim 2012, Part II, CCIS 324, pp. 102–109, 2012.

2   Network-Centric Information System

The network-centric military information system is designed based on the grid network structure and web service technology. It is composed by the distributed sensors, the C^2 system, the weapon control system backed up the military information infrastructure. The military information infrastructure is constituted by communication networks, computing infrastructure and common support services [8-9]. The structure and the layered structure are described as fig 1:

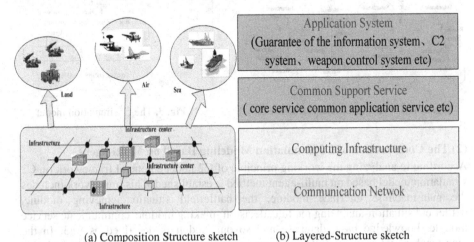

(a) Composition Structure sketch   (b) Layered-Structure sketch

Fig. 1. Network-centric information system

3   The SOS Simulation of Network-Centric Information System

3.1   The Entity Simulation of Application System

The constituent entities of application system can be abstracted to detection node, intelligence processing node, C^2 node, fighting node. Considering that there are many results about modeling problem of the detection node, intelligence processing node and fighting node [10], so this problem is not discussed in this paper. And the multi-agent method is used to establish the simulation model of different level C^2 node in this paper, the detail step is described as follows:

(1) Establishing the Composition Structure of Different Level C^2 Node
Each C^2 node of application system will be abstracted to a C^2 agent, the inter-relationship between different C^2 nodes can be reflected by the interaction behavior between C^2 agents. Those agents within the same level can corporative make decision scheme, and the superior C^2 agent can directive distribute operation mission or send operation plan to those subordinate C^2 agent or weapon system. The detail structure is described as fig2:

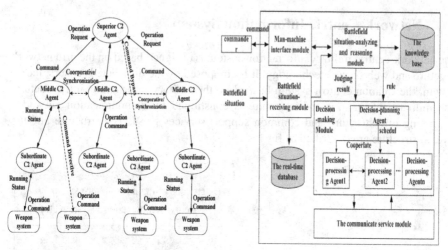

Fig. 2. The sketch of C² agent structure of   **Fig. 3.** The C² simulation model

(2) The Construction of C2 Simulation Modeling Based on Multi-agent

According to analyzing the working principle of C2 node, a general framework on C2 simulation model based on multi-agent method is established. This framework includes the man-machine interface module, the battlefield situation-achieving module, battlefield situation-analyzing module, decision -making module, communicate service module, knowledge base, database and so on. And it is described as fig3. In the man-machine interface module, commander can send intervention order through this module. And the visualization of real-time situation and the running process can be displayed on this module. The battlefield situation- receiving module receives the battlefield situation/intelligence information in order to accomplish the decision-making. The decision-making module is the core processing part of C2 agent. It includes multi agents that accomplish the decision-planning and scheme-making mission. Among them, the decision-planning agent will receive result from the battlefield situation-analyzing module and utilize operation rule from knowledge base in order to develop operation decision. The decision-processing agent will receive the result from the decision-planning agent in order to form the operation Scheme, and it is scheduled and controlled by the decision-planning agent. Each agent has its own decision-making rule (storing in the knowledge base), so it can automatic command and decision-making according to the operation rule and battlefield environment. The knowledge base stores the operational rules, target base, environment information base and so on. And it is used to support the battlefield situation-analyzing module dealing with situation and offer the rule reasoning toward the decision-making module.

3.2   The SOS Simulation of Network-Centric Information System

The information associated network is defined as a logistic network that is composed by system inner entity and information associated relationship between those entities. And the inner entity is defined as a network node; the information associated relationship is defined as a network edge. There are some complex relationships between application system entity and resource service node. In order to clearly reflect the information interactive mechanism, the SOS simulation method based on information associated network is presented in this paper. The detail is described as fig4:

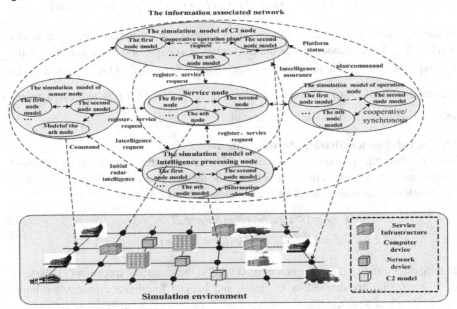

Fig. 4. The sketch of SOS simulation based on information associated network

Considering the topology structure of above information associated network, a dynamic two-dimension table is established to store the relationship between different entities. The content of this table will be real-time updated during the simulation process. So it is very important to analyze the information relationship between the application system entity and services node.

Firstly, the application system node and service node are expressed as follows: $D=\{D1,D2,D3,...Dm\}$ is defined as the detection node set. $I=\{I1,I2, I3,...In\}$ is defined as the intelligence processing node set. $C=\{C1,C2,C3,...Cr\}$ is defined as the all kinds of C2 node set. $F=\{F1,F2,...Fs\}$ is defined as the operation unit node set. $S=\{S1,S2,...St\}$ is defined as the service node set.

Secondly, we should establish the dynamic information interactive relationship between different node according to the running process and mode of application system.

(1) The Intelligence Detecting-Processing Relationship: D-I

This relationship is used to describe the information interaction between detecting node and intelligence-processing node. The detecting node sends the original intelligence information to intelligence-processing node. The intelligence -processing node receives and fuses that information, then sends the management and control command to detecting node in order to control the working status.

$$S-I = \{< sender, receiver, inf, T >$$
$$inf = \{< f_{DI}(D_i, I_j, t), f_{ID}(I_j, D_i, t) >, i = 1...m, j = 1...n\} \quad (1)$$

In the expression (1), the inf is defined as the interactive information between sender and receiver, T is expressed as transmitting delay, D_i is expressed as the detecting node, I_j is expressed as the intelligence-processing node, $f_{DI}(D_i, I_j, t)$ is expressed as the information from D_i to I_j node at the time of t, $f_{ID}(I_j, D_i, t)$ is expressed as the information from I_j to D_i node at the time of t.

(2) The Intelligence-Sharing Relationship: I-I
This relationship is used to describe information interactive between different intelligence- processing nodes; it will reflect the intelligence-sharing degree. Generally this relationship is bidirectional and can be described as follows:

$$I-I = \{< sender, receiver, inf, T >$$
$$inf = \{< f_I(I_i, I_j, t) >, i, j = 1, 2...n\} \quad (2)$$

In the expression (2), the definition of term "inf" is the same as expression (1), the term of "Ii" and "Ij" are defined as the main and backup intelligence processing node, $f_I(I_i, I_j, t)$ is expressed as the fusion information and synchronization information from Ii to Ij node at the time of t, and the replaced information under the condition of the main node (Ii) broken-down.

(3) The C2- Intelligence Relationship: C-I
This relationship is used to describe information interactive between C2 and intelligence processing node. Generally this relationship is bidirectional and can be described as follows:

$$C-I = \{< sender, receiver, inf, T >$$
$$inf = \{< f_{CI}(C_i, I_j, t), f_{IC}(I_j, C_i, t) >, i = 1...r, j = 1...n\} \quad (3)$$

In the expression(3), the definition of term "inf" is the same as expression (1), $f_{CI}(C_i, I_j, t)$ is expressed as the intelligence-subscribed request information from C^2 node (Ci) to intelligence node (Ij), and $f_{CI}(C_i, I_j, t)$ is expressed as the subscribed intelligence information from Ij to Ci.

(4) The C2 Relationship: C-C
This relationship is used to describe information interactive about all kinds of C^2 nodes, and will reflect the control and cooperative decision process between different C^2 nodes. It is defined as follows:

$$C-C = \{< sender, receiver, inf, T >$$
$$inf = \{< f_C(C_i, C_j, t) >, i, j = 1, 2...r\} \tag{4}$$

In the expression(4), $f_C(C_i, C_j, t)$ is expressed as the operational plan、command and planning request、operational result information etc when C_i and C_j are lied in the different level. Also $f_C(C_i, C_j, t)$ will be expressed as the cooperative operation plan and command when C_i and C_j are lied in the same level.

(5) The C2-Operation Relationship: F-C
This relationship is used to describe information interactive about C^2 node and operational unit node. It is defined as follows:

$$F-C-I = \{< sender, receiver, inf, T >$$
$$inf = \{< f_{FC}(F_i, C_j, t), f_{CF}(C_j, F_i, t) >, i = 1...t, j = 1...r\} \tag{5}$$

In the expression(5), $f_{CF}(C_j, F_i, t)$ is expressed as the control command、target indication information at the time of t from C^2 node(C_j) to operation unit node(F_i), and $f_{FC}(F_i, C_j, t)$ is expressed as the militancy and platform status information from F_i to C_j.

(6) The Operation Unit Cooperate Relationship: F-F
This relationship is used to describe information interactive during the process of cooperate fighting between the operational unit node. It is defined as follows:

$$F-F = \{< sender, receiver, inf, T >$$
$$inf = \{< f_F(F_i, F_j, t) >, i, j = 1, 2...s\} \tag{6}$$

In the expression (6), $f_F(F_i, F_j, t)$ is expressed as the synchronization information on running status and operation cooperative information from the operational unit node F_i to F_j node.

(7) Source Serves Relationship: S-S
This relationship is used to describe information interactive between the application system entity and service node, and it will efficient describe the process of service-requesting and service- responding. It is defined as follows:

$$S - S = \{< sender, receiver, inf, T >$$
$$inf = \{< f_{SN}(N_i, S_j, t), f_{NS}(S_j, N_i, t) >, \qquad (7)$$
$$N_i \in \{D, C, F\}, j = 1, 2...t\}$$

In the expression(7), the term "S_j" is denoted as the service node that owning different function, such as the enrolling service、 distributing serves、 dynamic connecting service and so on, The term "N_i"is denoted as the application system entity. $f_{SN}(N_i, S_j, t)$ is expressed as all kinds of service -requesting from N_i to S_j, including the user-enrolled information, intelligence-requesting information and so on. $f_{NS}(S_j, N_i, t)$ is expressed as the request-processed information from S_j to N_i。

On the basis of above analyzing, we can establish the two-dimension information interactive table as described table1:

Table 1. The information interactive table

	Detection node		Intelligence processing node		C2 node		Operation unit node		Service node	
	D_1 $\cdots$ D_m		I_1 $\cdots$ I_n		C_1 $\cdots$ C_r		F_1 $\cdots$ F_s		S_1 $\cdots$ S_t	
Detection node $D_1 \cdots D_m$	$0 \cdots \cdots$; $\cdots 0 \cdots$; $0 \cdots 0$		$f_{DI}(D_1 I_1 t) \cdots f_{DI}(D_1 I_n t)$; $\cdots \cdots \cdots$; $f_{DI}(D_m I_1 t) \cdots f_{DI}(D_m I_n t)$		$f_{SC}(S_1 C_1 t) \cdots f_{SC}(S_1 C_r t)$; $\cdots \cdots \cdots$; $f_{SC}(S_m C_1 t) \cdots f_{SC}(S_m C_r t)$		$f_{DF}(D_1 F_1 t) \cdots f_{DF}(D_1 F_s t)$; $\cdots \cdots \cdots$; $f_{DF}(D_m F_1 t) \cdots f_{DF}(D_m F_s t)$		$f_{NS}(D_1 S_1 t) \cdots f_{NS}(D_1 S_t t)$; $\cdots \cdots \cdots$; $f_{NS}(D_m S_1 t) \cdots f_{NS}(D_m S_t t)$	
Intelligence processing node $I_1 \cdots I_n$	$f_{ID}(I_1 D_1 t) \cdots f_{ID}(I_1 D_m t)$; $\cdots \cdots \cdots$; $f_{ID}(I_n D_1 t) \cdots f_{ID}(I_n D_m t)$		$0 \cdots f_{II}(I_1 I_n t)$; $\cdots 0 \cdots$; $f_{II}(I_n I_1 t) \cdots 0$		$f_{IC}(I_1 C_1 t) \cdots f_{IC}(I_1 C_r t)$; $\cdots \cdots \cdots$; $f_{IC}(I_n S_1 t) \cdots f_{IC}(I_n C_r t)$		$0 \cdots 0$; $\cdots \cdots \cdots$; $0 \cdots 0$		$f_{NS}(I_1 S_1 t) \cdots f_{NS}(I_1 S_t t)$; $\cdots \cdots \cdots$; $f_{NS}(I_n S_1 t) \cdots f_{NS}(I_n S_t t)$	
C2 node $C_1 \cdots C_r$	$f_{CD}(C_1 D_1 t) \cdots f_{CS}(C_1 D_m t)$; $\cdots \cdots \cdots$; $f_{CD}(C_r D_1 t) \cdots f_{CD}(C_r D_m t)$		$f_{CI}(C_1 I_1 t) \cdots f_{CI}(C_1 I_n t)$; $\cdots \cdots \cdots$; $f_{CI}(C_r I_1 t) \cdots f_{CI}(C_r I_n t)$		$0 \cdots f_{CI}(C_1 C_r t)$; $\cdots 0 \cdots$; $f_{C}(C_1 C_1 t) \cdots 0$		$f_{CF}(C_1 F_1 t) \cdots f_{CF}(C_1 F_s t)$; $\cdots \cdots \cdots$; $f_{CF}(C_r F_1 t) \cdots f_{CF}(C_r F_s t)$		$f_{NS}(C_1 S_1 t) \cdots f_{NS}(C_1 S_t t)$; $\cdots \cdots \cdots$; $f_{NS}(C_r S_1 t) \cdots f_{NS}(C_r S_t t)$	
Operation unit node $F_1 \cdots F_s$	$f_{FD}(F_1 D_1 t) \cdots f_{FD}(F_1 D_m t)$; $\cdots \cdots \cdots$; $f_{FD}(F_s D_1 t) \cdots f_{FD}(F_s D_m t)$		$0 \cdots 0$; $\cdots \cdots \cdots$; $0 \cdots 0$		$f_{FC}(F_1 C_1 t) \cdots f_{FC}(F_1 C_r t)$; $\cdots \cdots \cdots$; $f_{FC}(F_s C_1 t) \cdots f_{FC}(F_s C_r t)$		$0 \cdots 0$; $\cdots \cdots \cdots$; $0 \cdots 0$		$f_{NS}(F_1 S_1 t) \cdots f_{NS}(F_1 S_t t)$; $\cdots \cdots \cdots$; $f_{NS}(F_s S_1 t) \cdots f_{NS}(F_s S_t t)$	
Service node $S_1 \cdots S_t$	$f_{SN}(S_1 D_1 t) \cdots f_{SN}(S_1 D_m t)$; $\cdots \cdots \cdots$; $f_{SN}(S_t D_1 t) \cdots f_{SN}(S_t D_m t)$		$f_{SN}(S_1 I_1 t) \cdots f_{SN}(S_1 I_n t)$; $\cdots \cdots \cdots$; $f_{SN}(S_t I_1 t) \cdots f_{SN}(S_t I_n t)$		$f_{SN}(S_1 C_1 t) \cdots f_{SN}(S_1 C_r t)$; $\cdots \cdots \cdots$; $f_{SN}(S_t C_1 t) \cdots f_{SN}(S_t C_r t)$		$f_{SN}(S_1 F_1 t) \cdots f_{SN}(S_1 F_s t)$; $\cdots \cdots \cdots$; $f_{SN}(S_t F_1 t) \cdots f_{SN}(S_t F_s t)$		$0 \cdots f_{S}(N_1 N_s t)$; $\cdots 0 \cdots$; $f_{S}(S_t S_1 t) \cdots 0$	

The SOS simulation method based on information associate network can efficiently solve the problem of one to one mutual function during the operation simulation of traditional information system, it can reflect the SOS character, complicacy during the process of system running under the condition of network-centric battlefield environment.

4   Conclusions

The SOS simulation of network-centric system is an effective approach that can reflect the stability of system running. And the simulation on information interactive relationship is a difficult and important problem. Considering this demand, the simulation method based on agent is used to build the C^2 system simulation model in this paper. The interactive modeling method based on information associate network is presented to establish the information interactive relationship between the nodes of system, and it will be an effective method that simulating the effect of system SOS running.

Acknowledgements. This paper is supported by the Key Program of GAD Science Foundation of China [Grant No. 9140A06010611DZ3802].

References

1. David, S.A.: The agility advantage: a survival guide for complex enterprise and endeavors. CCRP Publication Series, Washington, DC (2011)
2. Huo, X.-H., Han, X.-Y., Gu, Y.-G.: A Way to build the networked command and control Systems based component technology. Fire Control & Command Control 10, 45–49 (2011)
3. Tang, S., Yu, W., Zhu, Y., et al.: Agent-based simulation and analysis of networking air defense missile systems. Systems Engineering and Electronics 32(12), 2632–2637 (2012)
4. Jin, W.-X., Xiao, T.-Y.: Simulation on Evolutive Behavior of System-of-Systems (SoS) Created for Net-Centric Operations (NCO) Based on Complex System Theory. Journal of System Simulation 22(10), 2435–2445 (2010)
5. Cheng, Y., Jiang, J.: The simulation research of integrated combined operation command system based on multi-agent. Military Operations Research and Systems Engineering 20(3), 3–7 (2006)
6. Zhao, Y., Zhang, M., et al.: Research on the C2 Modeling in Weapon and Equipment System of System Warfare Simulation. The Computer Simulation 26(2), 18–22 (2009)
7. Huang, J., Li, Q., et al.: The framework research of SOS simulation model based on agent-combining. Systems Engineering and Electronics 7, 1553–1557 (2011)
8. Jiang, W., Cui, Z.: Net-Centric environment of information service and the development of military field. Command Information System and Technology 2(4), 10–16 (2011)
9. Zhou, X., Zhang, Y., et al.: Information Sharing Scheme for Network Centric Command Information System. Command Information System and Technology 2(3), 14–18 (2011)
10. Mao, S., Ju, Z., Li, Y., et al.: The technology of C4ISR simulation test, Bijing (2011)

Modeling on 3D Atmospheric Transmission
of Infrared Radiation

Zhifeng Li, Xu Geng, Fan Li, and Li Zhang

Shanghai Institute of Mechanics and Electricity Engineering, Shanghai, 200233

Abstract. On the basis of analysis atmosphere, a new method of calculating the atmosphere transmissibility is introduced. The 3D model of atmospheric transmission of infrared radiation is established for calculating atmospheric transmittance, thermal emission, and single scatter solar radiance along sensor-to-target lines-of-sight (LOS) within a three-dimensionally varying atmosphere. This model analysis the various factors which affect the infrared radiation of atmospheric transmission. The calculation results of atmosphere transmissibility not only consider the atmosphere layering situation along the vertical direction but also atmosphere molecules distribution variable along the horizontal direction. Finally, the simulation images show in this paper.

Keywords: 3D model of atmospheric, Single scatter solar radiation, Path radiation.

1 Introduction

Atmospheric transmittance is one of the most important influent factors in infrared radiation. In the process of infrared imaging, especially in remote imaging, scattering and absorption in the atmosphere have a very important impact on imaging. Also, the atmospheric transmittance and the radiation effects should be calculated quantificationally in infrared imaging simulation system. Therefore, the atmospheric radiation transmission model has been concerned by designers and researchers and paid much more attention on it. The 2D atmospheric radiation transmission model is commonly used, such as LOWTRAN, MODTRAN, which only considered the calculation of atmospheric radiation transmission effect, extinction and the background radiation along vertical direction. This paper established a 3D atmosphere radiation transmission models. This model is a MODTRAN4-based module for calculating atmospheric transmittance, thermal emission, and single scatter solar radiance within a three-dimensional varying atmosphere.

2 The Atmosphere on the Influence of the Infrared Radiation Transmission

Attenuation [1] is the weaken processes of infrared radiation through atmospheric, which can be express with atmospheric transmittance τ as:

T. Xiao, L. Zhang, and M. Fei (Eds.): AsiaSim 2012, Part II, CCIS 324, pp. 110–118, 2012.
© Springer-Verlag Berlin Heidelberg 2012

$$\tau = \exp(-\sigma \times x) \tag{1}$$

Where σ is the attenuation coefficient, x is the length of infrared transmission paths.

The atmosphere radiation transmission is mainly affected by absorption of atmospheric molecules and the scattering effect of suspended particles in the atmosphere (the aerosol that often says namely). Therefore,

$$\sigma = \alpha + \gamma \tag{2}$$

Here α is the absorption coefficient, mainly from molecules absorption in the atmosphere, γ is the scattering coefficient, mainly from the gas and the aerosol scattering. α and γ are related to the wavelength.

Atmosphere radiation transmission is attenuated by the absorption of atmospheric molecules. The composition of atmosphere which produced the selective absorption effect mainly contained water vapor, carbon dioxide and ozone. Water vapor is a variable composition in atmosphere, which changing with the temperature, pressure, height and position, especially pressure. According to the Beer-Lambert law [4], the infrared radiation power will be attenuated by atmospheric absorption. The monochromatic radiation fluxes $p(\lambda, x)$ transmitted with a distance x can be expressed as:

$$p(\lambda, x) = p(\lambda, 0) \times \exp[-\alpha(\lambda)] \tag{3}$$

Where $p(\lambda, 0)$ is the incident monochromatic radiation flux, $\alpha(\lambda)$ is the absorption coefficient in the equation.

Scattering is produced by non-uniformity of the medium. The density fluctuation of gas molecular in atmospheric and various kinds of suspended particles are scattering element. Scatting does not change the spectral distribution of radiation, but change the spatial distribution. It is the reason that the radiation will be attenuated after scatted in their original path. The attenuation of infrared radiation along the x direction with wavelength λ can be expressed as [5]:

$$p(\lambda, 0) = p(\lambda, x) \exp[-\gamma(\lambda)x] \tag{4}$$

Here, $\gamma(\lambda)$ is the scattering coefficient, $p(\lambda, 0)$ is the monochromatic radiation fluxes before the scattering with distance x while $p(\lambda, x)$ is after.

Atmospheric scattering will be composed of molecular scattering and aerosols scattering. The scattering coefficient $\gamma(\lambda)$ is

$$\gamma(\lambda) = \gamma_{mol}(\lambda) + \gamma_{aer}(\lambda) \tag{5}$$

Here $\gamma_{mol}(\lambda)$ and $\gamma_{aer}(\lambda)$ represent the molecular scattering and the aerosol scattering coefficient, respectively.

The scattering can be divided into two categrides-Raley scattering and Mie scattering. We define the angular distribution of the sky radiation caused by diffuse scattering to be phase function. The molecular scattering phase function is given by the classic formula of isotropic scattering

$$P_M(\psi) = 0.06050402 + 0.0572197\cos^2\psi \tag{6}$$

Here ψ is the scattering angle between the observer direction and the sun direction.

The aerosol phase function $P_A(\psi, g)$ can be approximate given by double Henyey Greenstein function:

$$P_A(\psi, g) = \frac{1}{2}\frac{1-g^2}{(1-2g\cos\psi+g^2)^{3/2}} \tag{7}$$

Where ψ is scattering angle of the sky radiation, g is the asymmetry factor.

Besides the atmospheric absorption and the scattering, the atmospheric turbulence also has an impact on the radiation signal through the atmosphere transmission of infrared radiation. Since many factors can influence infrared radiation, it is difficult to realize during the simulation. Therefore, the atmospheric turbulence factor can be ignored.

3   Modeling and Analysis

Atmosphere can be divided into n levels along vertical direction because the atmospheric pressure, temperature, gas density and humidity usually changing with attitudes. Considering the variable factors of carbon dioxide, vapor and ozone in the horizontal direction [3], atmosphere is divided into M molecular extinction interval again. We can set the baseline characteristics and spectral properties of the atmosphere at first. Once the atmospheric properties are defined, the propagation and emission of radiation along a given line-of-sight (LOS) can be calculated. As shown in the Fig.1, a LOS is divided into sub-paths and segment, propagation proceeds by calculating the local contribution of the each segment to the total emission and scattered solar radiation beginning with the end segment and proceeding to the segment ending at the observer location. An approximate solution is obtained by using a correlated-k band model. The band model accumulates spectral values for the transmission, emission, and solar scattering at sub-band resolution and then computes the final in-band LOS values as weighted averages. Atmospheric boundary must be higher than the cloud top height, but less than the top layer height in the atmosphere. Default value is 20km.

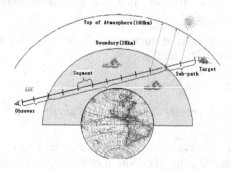

Fig. 1. MOD 3D++ Line-Of-Sight Concepts

3.1   Setting the Properties and Spectral Characteristics of Baseline Atmosphere

MODTRAN4 has been modified to output a set of files which can be used to set the spectral characteristics of a baseline atmosphere. These files contain key atmospheric profile information, including

- Spectral resolution and band pass,
- K-distribution weighting factors,
- Baseline pressure dependent profiles for H_2O, CO_2 and O_3 g/m^3,
- Profile scale factors used in each MODTRAN calculation,
- Scattering cross-sections, extinction cross-sections, and scattering asymmetry factors for aerosols, clouds and rain,
- Molecular scattering cross-sections,
- Molecular extinction cross-section data.

In addition, the three-dimensional atmospheric properties for the current local environment are required and include the local pressure, temperature and density. The local properties are

- Pressure in atmospheres $[ATM]_o$.
- Temperature in Kelvin $[K]_o$.
- Aerosol extinction $[KM^{-1}]$
- Cloud particle density in grams per meter cubed $[gm/m^3]_o$.
- Rain Rate in millimeter per hour raised to the 0.63 power $[(mm/hr)^{0.63}]_o$.
- Gaseous H_2O density in grams per meter cubed $[gm/m^3]_o$.
- Gaseous CO_2 density in grams per meter cubed $[gm/m^3]_o$.
- Gaseous O_3 density in grams per meter cubed $[gm/m^3]_o$.

The rain rate in millimeter per hour is raised to the 0.63 power because the rain extinction in MODTRAN4 is modeled as varying linear with this term, and the calculation will execute more rapidly if the data is stored this way.

3.2   Calculation of the Atmospheric Properties and Optical Properties on Sub-path

Each section is divided into front-end (sensor port), endpoint in the segment and end point (remote sensor port). The atmospheric characteristics of the three endpoints mentioned above can be obtained respectively through the interpolation. Since clouds and rain in each segment has a certain structure of distribution, the density of cloud particles and rainfall must be modified according to formula (8) and (9)

$$Avg_{cloud} = (Beg_{cloud} + 2 \times Cen_{could} + End_{cloud})/4 \tag{8}$$

Here Avg_{cloud}、Beg_{cloud}、Cen_{cloud}、End_{cloud} represent the density of cloud particles within the interval、the front point of interval, middle of the interval and the end point of interval, respectively.

$$Avg_{rain} = (Beg_{rain} + 2 \times Cen_{rain} + End_{rain})/4 \tag{9}$$

Here Avg_{rain}、 Beg_{rain}、 Cen_{rain}、 End_{rain} represent the precipitation within the interval、 middle of the interval at the front point of interval, end point of interval, respectively.

3.3   Calculation of the Optical Properties on Sun Path

For each sub-path, there are two endpoints. A line from the endpoint of sub-path to the solar position must have an intersection with top of Atmosphere. The path from the intersection to the endpoint of sub-path is called solar path. First of all, determine whether the minimum distance that the sub-path to geocentric is smaller than the radius of the earth or not, if so, which indicates the interval endpoint is located below the horizon. Then the optical depth data of the sun path can be set as the maximum value. Otherwise, we must calculate the average atmospheric properties which contain the weighted pressure and the average atmospheric pressure of aerosol, clouds and rain, the average density of water vapor, carbon dioxide and ozone. The average density of water vapor, carbon dioxide and ozone needs to be corrected, and the empirical formula follows as

Define wat firstly:

$$wat = \frac{Avg_{h_2o}}{(Nprof_{h_2o} - 1) \times Avg_{press}} \tag{10}$$

Where Avg_{h_2o} and Avg_{press} are the average density of water vapor and the average density of atmospheric, respectively. $Nprof_{h_2o}$ is the number of water vapor contours ($Nprof_{h_2o} > 1$ and take the integer value).

If both satisfy the conditions (a) $Avg_{h_2o}(i) > wat \times Avg_{press}(i)$ and conditions (b) $Avg_{press}(i) > Avg_{press}$, the following formula would be established:

$$\begin{cases} Ratio & = Avg_{press}(i) / Avg_{press} \\ Avg_{h_2o}' = Avg_{h_2o} \times Ratio \\ Avg_{co_2}' = Avg_{co_2} \times Ratio \\ Avg_{o_3}' = Avg_{o_3} \times Ratio \\ Avg_{press}' = Avg_{press} \times Ratio \end{cases} \tag{11}$$

Where i is an integer value, it means the number of layers in atmosphere along vertical direction. Avg_{h_2o}、 Avg_{co_2}、 Avg_{o_3}、 Avg_{press} represent the average density water vapor, carbon dioxide, ozone and average atmospheric pressure before corrected on the solar path, respectively. Avg_{h_2o}'、 Avg_{co_2}'、 Avg_{o_3}'、 Avg_{press}' are the average density water vapor, carbon dioxide, ozone and average atmospheric pressure after corrected on the solar path, respectively. $Avg_{h_2o}(i)$、 $Avg_{press}(i)$ are the average water vapor density and average pressure in the atmosphere layer i, respectively.

3.4 Calculation of the Molecular Extinction Coefficient

According to the interpolation of molecular extinction properties table, the pressure interpolation factor, the location of water vapor profile, interpolation factor of water vapor, carbon dioxide and ozone, respectively represent the water vapor, carbon dioxide, and ozone distribution in the horizontal direction. For any optical extinction segment in the horizontal direction, the molecular extinction coefficient is available through the multi-dimensional linear interpolation, Method is as follows:

Molecular extinction coefficients in the baseline spectral databases is represented as $xmol(i,j,m)$, where i is an integer value represented the number of molecular extinction segment in the horizontal direction, j is the molecular atmospheric pressure, m is the number of the atmosphere in the vertical direction.

$$xmf[n] = xmol(i, P_{h_2o} + n - 4, m) + F_{press} \times [xmol(i, P_{h_2o} + n - 4, m - 1) \qquad (12)$$
$$- xmol(i, P_{h_2o} + n - 4, m)]$$

Where n take the integer value, traverse calculation through section [0,7], we could get $xmf[0] \cdots xmf[7]$ 8 results, then interpolation with ozone interpolation factor F_{o_3}.

$$xmo[n] = xmf[n] + F_{o_3} \times (xmf[n+1] - xmf[n]) \qquad (13)$$

Here, n take 0,2,4,6 and we could get $xmo[0]$, $xmo[2]$, $xmo[4]$, $xmo[6]$ four values, interpolated with carbon dioxide interpolation factor F_{co_2}:

$$xmco[n] = xmo[n] + F_{co_2} \times (xmo[n+2] - xmo[n]) \qquad (14)$$

Where n were taken 0,4 can be calculated in $xmco[0]$ and $xmco[4]$. Finally, interpolate this two values with the water vapor interpolation factor F_{h_2o}.

$$ME = xmco[4] + F_{h_2o} \times (xmco[4] - xmco[0]) \qquad (15)$$

ME represents molecular extinction coefficient of each sub-segment.

3.5 Calculation of the Atmospheric Transmission and Path Radiance of Monochromatic Radiation

The optical depth in each sub-path caused by continuous attenuation medium (aerosol, clouds and rain) basic remained unchanged, where i is the number of molecular extinction segment, j is the number of the sub-path. Then the optical thickness of sub-path number j is:

$$dep_{cn}(j) = x_{aer} \times \rho_{aer} + x_{cld} \times \rho_{cld} + x_{rain} \times \rho_{rain} \qquad (16)$$

Here x_{aer}、x_{cld}、x_{rain} represent spectra extinction coefficients of aerosol, cloud and rain in sub-segment, respectively. ρ_{aer}、ρ_{cld}、ρ_{rain} respectively indicated the aerosol optical depth, average density of cloud particle and precipitation in sub-segment.

For the molecular extinction sub-path number i, segment j, the $dep_{cn}(j)$ is:

$$dep_{seg}(i, j) = L_{seg}(j) \times [dep_{cn}(j) + ME(i, j) \times D_{avg}(j)] \qquad (17)$$

Where $L_{seg}(j)$、$D_{avg}(j)$ represent the length of the sub-path and the average density of molecules within the segment, respectively.

Atmospheric transmission $T_{sf}(i,j)$ function is calculated by substituting function $deps_{seg}(i,j)$ into the formula (1). Absorption rate of each molecule $A_{seg}(i,j)$ in extinction interval also can be obtained:

$$A_{seg}(i,j) = 1 - T_{seg}(i,j) \tag{18}$$

According to Max Planck's law and Kirchhoff's law, the molecular extinction interval segment number i, the path radiation in the sub-path number j can be obtained

$$Ems_{seg}(i,j) = A_{seg}(i,j) \times Plank(T_f) + 2 \times [Plank(T_f) - Plank(T_c)] \times A_{seg}(i,j) \tag{19}$$

Here, $Plank(T)$ is the Planck formula, T_f represents absolute temperature of the front-end point of the segment, T_c represents the absolute temperature at the midpoint.

According to Bayes' law, using the following formula:

$$T_{seg}(i) = \prod_{j=0}^{N-1} T_{seg}(i,j) \tag{20}$$

Atmospheric transmittance of the molecular extinction sub-path $T_{seg}(i)$ can be get. And the path radiance of molecular extinction interval number i can be calculated by using the following formula:

$$Ems_{seg}(i) = \sum_{j=0}^{N-1} [Ems_{seg}(i,j) \times \prod_{k=0}^{j-1} T_{seg}(i,k)] \tag{21}$$

Finally the atmospheric transmittance of monochromatic radiation T_{spec} can be get by the following formula:

$$T_{spec} = \sum_{i=0}^{M-1} [T_{seg}(i) \times W(i)] \tag{22}$$

And the path radiation of monochromatic radiation E_{spec} can also be obtained:

$$E_{spec} = \sum_{i=0}^{M-1} [Ems_{seg}(i) \times W(i)] \tag{23}$$

Here, M is the total number of section of the molecular extinction, $W(i)$ represents the width molecular extinction segment number i.

3.6   Calculation of Single Scatter Solar Radiation of Monochromatic Radiation

The optical depth which generated by attenuation medium with the initial segment on the solar path remained largely unchanged on the whole molecular extinction interval. $deps_{cn}(j)$ is the optical depth function from the end-point of the jth path on the solar path. The optical depth function is given by

$$deps_{cn}(j) = x_{xaer} \times \rho_{saer} + x_{scld} \times \rho_{scld} + x_{srain} \times \rho_{srain} \qquad (24)$$

Here i is the number of molecular extinction interval, j is the number of sub-band, x_{saer} 、 x_{scld} 、 x_{srain} represent aerosol extinction coefficients of spectra, cloud and rain , respectively. ρ_{saer} 、 ρ_{scld} 、 ρ_{srain} respectively indicated the aerosol optical depth, average density of cloud particle and precipitation.

The scattering coefficient $S_{seg}(j)$ of path j can be obtained by following formula

$$S_{seg}(j) = (S_{aer} \times \rho_{aer} + S_{cld} \times \rho_{cld} + S_{rain} \times \rho_{rain}) \times P_A(\psi, g) + S_{mol} \times D_{avg}(j) \times P_M(\psi) \,(25)$$

Where S_{aer} is the aerosol spectra scatter coefficients of layer j, S_{cld} is cloud scatter coefficients of layer j, S_{rain} is rain scatter coefficients of layer j, S_{mol} is molecular scatter coefficients of layer j, $P_M(\psi)$ is molecular scatter phase function, the function $P_A(\psi, g)$ can be written by formula (7).

The molecular extinction $SME(i, j)$ on sun's path can be calculated by molecular extinction interpolation table with the whole optical depth $deps_{seg}(i, j)$ is given by

$$deps_{seg}(i, j) = deps_{cn}(j) + SME(i, j) \times D_{savg}(j) \qquad (26)$$

Here $D_{savg}(j)$ is the average molecular density of path j.

Atmospheric transmission $T_{sf}(i, j)$ function was calculated by substituting function $deps_{seg}(i, j)$ into the formula (1).

Similarly, the atmospheric transmission $T_{sb}(i, j)$ with the end segment of each sub-path can be obtained by radiation characteristic on solar path of next segment, and the average transmission $T_{sol}(i, j)$ [2] terms:

$$T_{sol}(i, j) = T_{sf}(i, j) \times \int_0^1 (\frac{T_{seg}(i, j) \times T_{sb}(i, j)}{T_{sf}(i, j)})^x d_x \qquad (27)$$

The single scatter solar radiation coefficients $SE_{ssct}(i)$ with the visual range given is given by

$$SE_{ssct}(i) = \sum_{j=0}^{N-1} [T_{sol}(i, j) \times S_{seg}(j) \times \prod_{i=0}^{j-1} T_{seg}(i)] \qquad (28)$$

Here N is the total band layer of visual range. The single scatter solar radiation S_{spec} can be written

$$S_{spec} = I_0 \sum_{i=0}^{M-1} [SE_{ssct}(i) \times W(i)] \qquad (29)$$

Where M is the total number of molecular extinction, $W(i)$ is the width interval of molecular extinction, I_0 is the solar radiation on the top of the atmosphere.

4   Simulation Example

To observe the image of the atmospheric effects, the 3D model of atmospheric transmission is used in infrared imaging simulation system. The simulation image received form sensors model is composed by a target and the background which add the atmospheric transmission effects. In this example, we simulate the infrared image with a aircraft and a terrain clutter models. The simulation time is 10 seconds, and the image frame rate is 2Hz. The aircraft is behind the background in the simulation initial moment, as the time past, it is move from the back of terrain clutter to the up. The simulation result show in Fig,2.

Fig. 2. Simulation result

5   Conclusions

This paper has developed the 3D model of atmospheric transmission for calculating the ratio of atmospheric transmission, path radiation and single scatter solar radiation. The modeling considered the attenuation of infrared radiation which affected by $H2O$, $CO2$ and $O3$ uneven distribution of the horizontal direction. This method generate spectral data by MODTRAN4 which using a simplified way for processing. Because of lacking measured data, only the operating performance of the modeling can be tested. The next step is concentrated in improving the accuracy and realism of the model.

References

1. Accetta, J.S., et al.: The Infrared and Electro-Optical Handbook. SPIE Optical Engineer Press, USA (1993)
2. Acharya, P.K.: Multiple Scattering and Bi-Directional Reflectance Distribution Function Upgrades to MODTRAN. In: Optical Spectroscopic Techniques and Instrumentation for Atmospheric and Space Research III, vol. 3756. SPIE Proceeding, USA (1999)
3. Dobbs, B.M.: The Incorporation of Atmospheric Variability Into DIRSIG. Center for Imaging Science Rochester Institute of Technology, USA (January 16, 2005)
4. Zhong, R.-H., et al.: Infrared Seeker of Aerodynamic missile. Astronautic Publishing House, Beijing (1994)
5. Zhang, J.-Q., Fang, X.-P.: Infrared Physics. Xidian University Publishing House, Xi'an (2004)

Link Prediction Based on Weighted Networks

Zeyao Yang, Damou Fu, Yutian Tang, Yongbo Zhang,
Yunsheng Hao, Chen Gui, Xu Ji, and Xin Yue

College of Computer Science and Technology, Jilin University, China
{yangzeyao,yutiantang1990,zhangyongbo0523,haoyunsheng1201,
guiallanchen,yxleonardo}@gmail.com, fudamou@gmail.com.cn,
sov_matrix@126.com

Abstract. Link Prediction can make networks more complete. However, because of restraint of algorithm, traditional link-prediction measures cannot make full use of weight information to analyze the network. To solve this problem, this paper proposes a new method based on weighted networks, and the new method synthesizes and improves existent methods so that the predictor could make use of weight information in the network. We apply the new method to three real networks (astro-ph, cond-mat and hep-th). The result of experiment demonstrates that new method is more precise, and this method provides people with a new idea about how to better analyze weighted networks.

Keywords: complex network, link prediction, weighted network.

1 Introduction

With the development of research on complex networks, more and more people pay attention to analyzing social network. Social network is abstracted as graph structure. In this structure, nodes represent people or agents, and links between nodes represent relation or interactions [1].

At the same time, with the development of Internet and wide application of Web 2.0 technology, the online social networks have made an enormous progress [2]. The online social networks are usually the replicas of real social circle of the people. For example, Facebook and Renren both encourage users to provide real information. However, it is impossible that users add all of their friends by searching their friends' names, so the system has to recommend potential friends for users. Link prediction is a method that predicts the state of networks at next moment based on the information at current state, which could be used to infer un-link friends in the social networks. If the inference is accurate enough, it would obviously help website improve user experience, and attract more customers.

Based on link prediction in weighted networks, this paper proposes a new link-prediction method to help website recommend miss friends for users.

T. Xiao, L. Zhang, and M. Fei (Eds.): AsiaSim 2012, Part II, CCIS 324, pp. 119–126, 2012.

2   Related Works

Link prediction in network not only includes prediction for miss link, but also includes prediction for future link. As a part of data mining field, link prediction has been under research. Paper [3] applies Markov chain to analyze and predict path; Paper [5] uses property of nodes to predict networks; Paper [6] uses structure information and nodes' property to predict networks [6]; Paper [7] defines similarity between nodes based on property of nodes, and then uses similarity to predict.

Though applying external information such as node property could succeed in predicting some links, it is sometimes impossible to acquire external information (e.g. users' information is secret in many online social networks). Moreover, even though property information is available, the reliability of information cannot be guaranteed, because some users' information is not true in online social networks.

In recent years, link-prediction methods based on network structure have received more attention. Paper [1] defines similarity based on topological structure, and analyzes link-prediction effect of different measures in collaboration networks. Paper [8] demonstrates existence of hierarchical structure in social networks, and then proposes a link-prediction method based on hierarchical structure. Compared with property information, network structure is accessible and reliable. Furthermore, methods based on topological structure are universal, so these methods could avoid instituting different measures for different networks.

Existent link-prediction methods define predictor and quantify information in networks according to link-prediction algorithm, then calculate proximity that two nodes that do not currently link with each other link at next moment. If a couple of nodes that do not connect with each other have higher proximity, and they are more possibly to link at next moment. These are some representative measures of link prediction: Common Neighbors measure, *Jaccard* measure, *Adamic / Adar* measure, and $Katz^{\beta}$ measure [1]. Through the experiment, all of these measures are useful for predicting future network state [1].

However, now most of measures are based on unweight graph, because it is difficult to quantify relationship among nodes in traditional social networks (e.g. it is difficult to quantify personal relationship). As a result, most of existent measures are implemented based on unweight network.

In the online social networks, though users' personal information and communication contents are secret, frequency of communication and exchange visit could be obtained easily. System could make use of these information to quantify the relationship among users and obtain weight. Because existent methods cannot make full use of weight information, they are deficient in weighted network.

Moreover, another significant difference between traditional networks and online networks is that online networks usually have larger scale, so link-prediction method for online social networks needs to adapt large data. Most of existent methods, however, are aiming at traditional and relatively small networks, so they could not adapt to online social network.

Due to above deficiencies of existent methods, this paper proposes a method to link prediction based on weighted network.

3   Method

3.1   Build Weight Graph

Since new method is bases on graph theory, so it is necessary to firstly: construct weigh network:

1) Because new method recommends possible link for all nodes, weigh graph selects random node S become center. Put S into network
2) Put s' neighbors into network
3) Put neighbors of s' neighbors into network
4) Put links who connect two nodes in the network into sub-network

Considering weighted undirected network G (V, E), where V is the set of nodes and E is the set of links. For each pair of non-connection nodes $s, t \in V$, t is called possible node, we assign a score for the possibility that s connect with t at next moment. All are sorted in decreasing order, and the t which is at the top are most likely to link with s.

Under normal conditions, s is more likely to link with node which has common neighbors with s, so this paper only considers two layer nodes.

3.2   Reduced Graph

In the network, there are possibly some wrong links, called spurious links [9]. For example, users could add some unfamiliar or unknown 'friends'. The interference of these links is greater than contribution of them [9], so this paper proposes a simple method to reduce the number of spurious links in network.

We define a sieve C, and delete links that are edge of s and weight is smaller than C, as well as links that are not edge of s and weight is smaller than $aC(a > 1)$. If a path from a node to another has longer lengthen, and the path is less meaningful (Katz measure [1]). As a result, we adopt sieve C for links that are edges of s and sieve $aC(a > 1)$ for links that are not edges of s.

Reduced graph decreases the impact from unnecessary links and improves link-prediction effect.

3.3   Link-Prediction Measures

We improve existent measures so that they could make use of the weight to predict network, which is the core of the new method. Prediction measures are divided into three kinds---neighbor measure, path measure and stochastic measure.

1) Neighbour Measure

Two nodes possess more common neighbors, they are more likely to link. As we know, if two people have many common friends, they are possibly at same circle of friends. Assume s and t as center node and possible node, and then proximity can be defined:

$$neighbor(s,t)_1 = \Gamma(s) \cap \Gamma(t)$$

Where $\Gamma(s), \Gamma(t)$ is set of neighbours of s and t.

Links between a neighbour and s and between this neighbor and t possess higher weight, and then this neighbour devotes more contributions for *proximity* of s and t. As in common sense, a person that is the best friend with other two people which are usually friends.

$$neighbor(s,t)_2 = \sum_{m \in \Gamma(s) \cap \Gamma(t)} \frac{(Weight(s,m)-C)+(Weight(t,m)-C)}{4}$$

Where $Weight(s,m)$ means weight of link between s and m, and C is sieve.

A common neighbour of s and t possesses less degrees, it devotes more contribution for *proximity* (*Adamic / Adar* [1]).

$$neighbor(s,t)_3 = \sum_{z \in \Gamma(s) \cap \Gamma(t)} \frac{1}{\log(\Gamma(z))}$$

Neighbor measure is sum of above three aspects:

$$neighbor(x, y) = neighbor(s,t)_1 + neighbor(s,t)_2 + neighbor(s,t)_3$$

2) Path Measure

There are more paths from s to t, *proximity* of t is higher. For example, two users in online social network have many paths, and then the two users could exchange more information.

$$path(s,t)_1 = pathNum(s,t)$$

Where $pathNum(s,t)$ is the number of paths from s to t.

Weight on the path from s to t is higher, *proximity* of t is higher.

$$path(s,t)_2 = \sum_l \frac{SumWeight(l)-PaceNum(l)*C}{PaceNum(l)}$$

Where l are all paths from s to t, and $SumWeight(l)$ is sum of weight in the path, and $PaceNum(l)$ is length of path.

3) Stochastic Measure

Because stochastic measure is random and is not influenced by human factor, this measure is possible effectual and precise than neighbor measure and path measure. As a result, stochastic measure cannot be ignored.

This paper defines a simple stochastic measure: some pets are emitted from s, and they prefer to choice the path whose weight is higher. According to the number of pets who arrives a node, *proximity* is endowed different value.

$$random(s,t) = destination(s,t)$$

Where *destination*(s,t) is the number of pets that arrive t.

3.4   Recommend

We integrate above measures:

$$proximity(s,t) = neighbor(s,t) + paht(s,t) + random(s,t)$$

The node whose *proximity* is at the top is recommended to link with s.

4   Experiment and Discussion

This paper applies new method to three different data sets (http://www-personal.umich.edu/~mejn/netdata/), and discusses the prediction result.

Because new method is bases on graph theory, we assume that network is $G = \langle V, E \rangle$, and edge $e = \langle u, v \rangle \in E$ represents relationship between u and v

This paper is aiming at restoring miss links in the social network, so we randomly delete 1000 links in the network and then recommend link for node that is a vertex of deleted link. If the result of recommendation is deleted link, the method returns success, otherwise failure. We define the accuracy of prediction as the number of success divide the number of prediction.

We choose several representative measures from the data sets, and get following table 1.

Table 1. Different measures' accuracies in astro-ph, cond-mat and hep-th

Measure	astro-ph	cond-mat	hep-th
Common-neighbor	48.7%	47.3%	36.5%
Path	45.6%	46.2%	34.2%
Jaccard	14.3%	16.1%	11.8%
Adamic/Adar	49.9%	49.6%	34.7%
Preferential Attach	10.1%	16.9%	19.1%
Katz ($\beta = 0.25$)	49.4%	48.9%	36.4%

Firstly, we define C is equal with 0.1, and apply new method on three data sets. The result is showed by table 2.

Table 2. When C is equal with 0.1, the accuracies of new method

Method	astro-ph	cond-mat	hep-th
New Method	73.5%	70.2%	57.8%

Comparing new method with existent methods, we get figure 1.

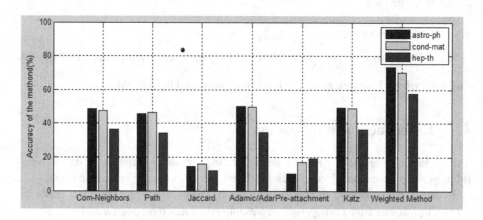

Fig. 1. The accuracies of new method with existent methods

The result demonstrates that new method has higher accuracy.

Discussion of Parameter: Because new method in this paper uses parameter, so the value of the parameter is very important. As the sieve value, *C* not only influences the second step, but also influences neighbor measure and path measure. As a result, this paper discusses parameter *C* specially.

We endow *C* different value and get table 3.

Table 3. Accuracies of applying different C in three data sets

C	astro-ph	cond-mat	hep-th
0.0	70.2	68.4	50.2
0.1	73.5	70.2	57.8
0.2	50.4	55.6	52.4
0.3	35.9	37.4	40.5
0.4	29.7	22.2	26.6

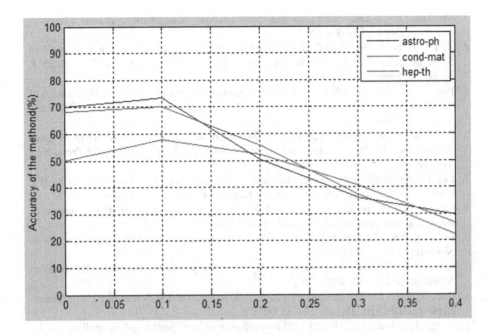

Fig. 2. Accuracies of applying different C in new method

The result demonstrates that when *C* is equal with 0.1 new method is the most efficient. Different networks have their own characteristics, so the users are able to adjust the *C* to make the method adapt different situation.

5   Conclusion and Future Work

This paper proposes a new link-prediction method based on weighted network. One main contribution of the model is that it provides a direct and efficient way to predict miss links. Another contribution of this model is that it integrates and improves existent method and makes them more suitable for weighted network and scaled data. By experiments, we demonstrate that the new method can performance as well as we expected.

With the great development of online social network, link prediction is becoming more important. This paper proposes a model that emphasizes weight information, and provides a new idea for link prediction in online social network.

References

1. Liben-Nowell, D., Kleinberg, J.: The link-prediction problem for social networks. J Am. Soc. Inform. Sci. Technol. 58(7), 1019–1031 (2007)
2. Kumar, R., Novak, J., Tomkins, A.: Structure and evolution of online social networks. In: Proceedings of the ACM SIGKDD 2006, pp. 611–617. ACM Press, New York (2006)

3. Sarukkai, R.R.: Link prediction and path analysis using markov chains. Computer Networks 33(1-6), 377–386 (2000)
4. Zhu, J., Hong, J., Hughes, J.G.: Using Markov Chains for Link Prediction in Adaptive Web Sites. In: Bustard, D.W., Liu, W., Sterritt, R. (eds.) Soft-Ware 2002. LNCS, vol. 2311, pp. 60–73. Springer, Heidelberg (2002)
5. Popescul, A., Ungar, L.: Statistical relational learning for link prediction. In: Proceedings of the Workshop on Learning Statistical Models from Relational Data, pp. 81–87. ACM Press, New York (2003)
6. O'Madadhain, J., Hutchins, J., Smyth, P.: Prediction and ranking algorithms for event-based network data. In: Proceedings of the ACM SIGKDD 2005, pp. 23–30. ACM Press, New York (2005)
7. Lin, D.: An information-theoretic definition of similarity. In: Proceedings of the 15th Intl. Conf. Mach. Learn., pp. 296–304. Morgan Kaufman Publishers, San Francisco (1998)
8. Clauset, A., Moore, C., Newman, M.E.J.: Hierarchical structure and the prediction of missing links in networks. Nature 453, 98–101 (2008)
9. Holland, P.W., Laskey, K.B., Leinhard, S.: Stochastic blockmodels: First steps. Social Networks 5, 109–137 (1983)
10. Getoor, L., Diehl, C.P.: Link mining: a survey. ACM SIGKDD Explorations Newsletter 7(2), 3–12 (2005)
11. Brin, S., Page, L.: The anatomy of a large-scale hypertextual Web search engine. Comput. Netw. & ISDN Syst. 30(1-7), 107–117 (1998)
12. Tong, H., Faloutsos, C., Pan, J.Y.: Fast random walk with restart and its applications. In: Proceedings of the 6th Intl. Conf. Data Min., pp. 613–622. IEEE Press, Washington, DC (2006)
13. Shang, M.S., Lü, L., Zeng, W., et al.: Relevance is more significant than correlation: Information filtering on sparse data. Europhys. Lett. 88(6), 68008 (2009)

Research on Product Comprehensive Information Modeling

Xinghui Dong, Yuwei Zhao, Ying Liu, and Yuanyuan Li

School of Energy, Power and Mechanical Engineering,
North China Electric Power University,
Beijing, China
dongxh2007@gmail.com, {zyw163happy,zgjsyclyy}@126.com,
913618466@qq.com

Abstract. To meet the demand of information model ,this article analyzed the evolution for information model, presented and clarified the concept, ideas and content derived from product comprehensive information model; through the detailed and concise classification to the information of lifecycle, drew the composition structure of product comprehensive information model, and built product comprehensive information model from both overall and local aspects; at the same time, provided the expression form for product comprehensive information model and the document type to access its information as well.

Keywords: information model, lifecycle, diversity, comprehensive information theory.

1   Introduction

The information model is the basis of the information expression, and its method is no other than to meet its requirements to the development of information technology. However, recently researchers have mainly focused on a partial information modeling for full life cycle and the information expression has still been a coverage area; even for the classification and expression to full life cycle, their talking has mostly been ambiguous, not clearly; in addition, the information graphical representation, especially for the relationship information, has rarely been reflected in the information model too.

In short, in the researches to information modeling, information expression has been in an average level on completeness, accuracy, legibility, diversity and so on, except that research on consistency and sharing, while their points are geometry/ topology information and semantic information, obtained some achievements. However, no double completeness, accuracy, legibility and diversity are very important to express information well. Therefore, while meeting consistency and sharing requirements, product information model should also appeal to the four requirements.

1) Completeness [1,2,3]. Besides the geometry/topology information and non-geometric information including engineering semantic information, that is

T. Xiao, L. Zhang, and M. Fei (Eds.): AsiaSim 2012, Part II, CCIS 324, pp. 127–134, 2012.

semantic information, product information model should contain value information, that is utility information in management, evaluation and process serving the whole product life cycle.

2) Accuracy [3]. For information, as an important aspect of achieving the effective storage, precise and detailed classification preferably facilitates the efficient management to information and other follow-up processing.

3) Legibility. Making people preferably obtaining information is the purpose to build product information model. Legibility is just about an approach to improve the efficiency to read information, make it easier and faster for people to access effective information data.

4) Diversity [1]. To meet the information requirements from all stages in the product life cycle need to build product information model with covering both overall and local aspects on information expression.

Thus,based on the STEP product data exchange standards and the building information model (BIM), this article studied on the modeling method of product information model for the purpose to meet requirements, including completeness, accuracy, accessibility and diversity, to information.

2   Product Comprehensive Information Model

For catering to requests to product information model in completeness, accuracy, accessibility and diversity, this paper proposes an idea called product comprehensive information model. Product comprehensive information model is an life-cycle-oriented information integration model based on comprehensive information theory [4] and BIM (Building Bnformation Modeling) basic connotation.

By the above definition, it is clear that product comprehensive information model embodies the following: four information integration ideas and their content:

1) Comprehensive Information Theory [4]. Comprehensive information theory, based on epistemology, is the formulation by the subject about the "the motion status and its change way", and the trinity on certainty information, logical information and utilitied information, including the form, content and value in the "status-way". Graphic representation is as follows:

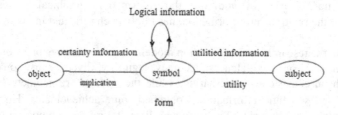

Fig. 1. Comprehensive information theory [4]

Compared to the ontology, only focusing on the thing itself and describing the information unconditionally, epistemology expression to information is conditional, also containing subject-related information (content and value) in addition to the information from the thing itself (form). In conclusion, epistemology possesses two advantages: containing more information; adding the subject in epistemology makes the information expression closer to natural language, more easily acceptable. That is the difference between product comprehensive information model and the related researches on information model based on ontology.

2) BIM Basic Connotation [5,6]. BIM is the project process to design, construction and operation by using digital model. It integrates various construction organizations, throughout the building life-cycle process, have characteristics about completeness, relevance and consistency in the model information.

3) Life-cycle Oriented. Refering to comprehensive information theory and BIM theory, entire information model should contain information in the life cycle and all associated information, focusing on the lifecycle.

4) Information Integration. That, integrating full information in life-cycle model and applying to establishment to models in different stages, different process, is the unified model.

The Division to information based on epistemology, in comprehensive information theory, makes classification clear, straightforward and yet not lacking any information, and can be used to satisfy the completeness and legibility to information model, from the perspective that subject acts on object; Completeness, relevance and consistency reflected in BIM basic connotation, together with the object-oriented lifecycle concepts, make the completeness to information greater; The concept about object in object-oriented life cycle presents that product information model has a very strong pertinence, plus information theory, apply to promoting information precision; Information integration unifies information and models in different stages, different process, integrated and diverse.

2.1   Information Classification

As is widely known, STEP standards summarises the information to three layers: physical layer, logical layer and application layer. Taking this standard and comprehensive information theory, product comprehensive information model divides information throughout the life cycle into three classes: entity information, technology information and utility information.

1) Entity Information [7,8]
Entity information in product comprehensive information model, that is the form(logical information) expressed in comprehensive information theory, reflecting some original information the product itself owned, mainly contains geometry/topology information, material property, volume/quality information, product entire composition layout information, basic status information(in process) and so on. It is the basic to others, and is basic information carrier, with all information throughout, must possess.

2) Technology Information [7]
Content (logical information) in the formulation by the subject about the "the motion status and its change way", is just about the expression form to process information in comprehensive information theory. Technology information is the core, the relevancy and the joint in the whole information system. It controls entity information, utility

information and their relationship, sustains the frame throughout the whole model and is the director to carry out the work-flow process in the lifecycle. Assembly technology information, process and manufacture technology information, management regulations, maintenance rules and so on, belong to technology information.

Assembly technology information comprises assembly plan, assembly accuracy, assembly relationship, assembly sequence, assembly path, assembly regulations (technology requirements), assembly tools and their relevant information, and so on, in the product assembly course, and is basic information in assembly information model. Process and manufacture technology information covers process technology regulations(technology requirements), process accuracy, process methods, process surface quality, process and manufacture equipments and their relevant information, and so on, in the course to process and manufacture, and directs accomplishment to every part in process and manufacture. Management regulations mainly set the general principle must followed in the management course to product information, and rule the whole management course. Maintenance rules are the basic technology requirements and operational regulation/details.

3) Utility Information [7]

Utility information, that is value(utilitied information) in comprehensive information theory, serving the whole life cycle and managing information from every application, contains mainly management information, evaluation information, technology sustaining information (service/maintenance/recycle), the work-flow in the whole life cycle and so on. For utility information, the best point lies in that it reflects the subject's role on the expression to information model.

Management information, used to expressing organization and management to product data, includes component information (quantity, stock and so on) , management messages in various BOMs, version information, component characteristics information and process characteristics information, organization information to staff and so on. Evaluation information reflects work-flow operational status and product quality status. Technology sustaining information expresses cost and quality in service, maintenance and recycle.

All in all, These three categories include various information in the product life cyclestatic/dynamic, course, functions and so on, reflecting physical, logical, and application in the STEP standards. This information classification, concise and strong generality, plays a key role on the establishment to information model and effectively accessing to information and management will, and also satisfies the accuracy requirement to information.

2.2   Structure and Expression

(1) Structure

According to information classification to product comprehensive information model, this paper expresses separately entity information, utility information and technology information from three forms: tree structure, this life-cycle course and elements described, and draws a sketch of overall structure to product information model as fig.2:

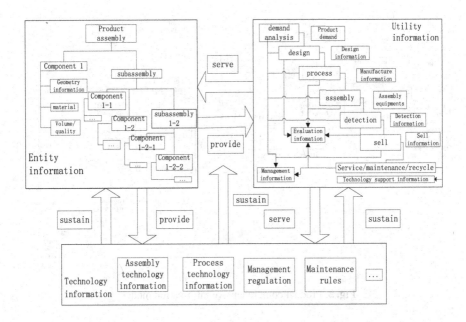

Fig. 2. Product comprehensive information structure

In fig.2, product assembly sequence can be expressed in two forms: serial number, such as $z_1 - z_2 - z_i - ... - l_i$, and ladder graphics. In serial number expression, z represents subassembly, and its subscript represents the product assembly sequence place where this subassembly is; l represents component, and its subscript represents the product assembly sequence place where this component in. Entire information model, as a whole, comprises interrelated entity information, technology information and utility information, and can be subdivided into manufacture information model, assembly information, management information model and other sub-models. Different sub-model contains different information, but all its information can be divided into entity information, technology information and utility information.

(2) Expression

Expression to product information model tends to reflect the subject role and to facilitate computer management to product data. This article, from global and local product information model, shows product comprehensive information in the form of product structure tree and table.

a) Global Product Comprehensive Information Model

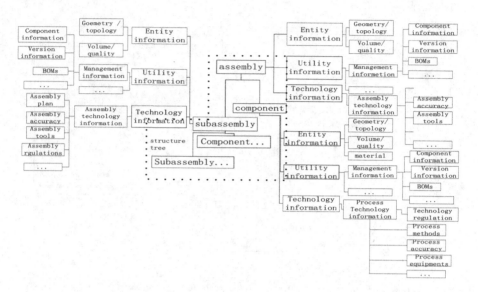

Fig. 3. Product comprehensive information model

Fig.3 is the integration expression to product comprehensive information model. This figure shows almost information in product life cycle, and meanwhile, together with fig.2, reflects the form to express assembly sequence information lying on ladder graphics.

b) Local Comprehensive Information Model

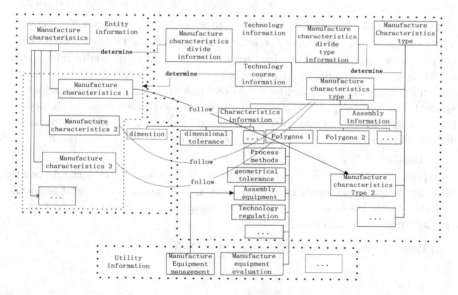

Fig. 4. Component manufacture comprehensive information model [8,9]

Fig.4 reflects the product comprehensive information modeling in the local parts manufacture. In the figure, entity information mainly includes the size and basic characteristics to the manufactured parts, in which characteristics dividing and ladder characteristic manufacture procedure are determined separately by manufacture characteristics dividing and process in technology information, and every manufacture feature must comply with the provisions of the technical requirements, operating procedures, processing methods in each manufacturing feature type; technology information mainly consists of two parts in regulatory information for restricting and supporting the entity and the utility; utility information is used for the organization and management to the product manufacture course and manufacture equipments, as well as evaluating quality to manufacture, in which the assessment to manufacture quality can be used in the process parts for adjusting or amending the process course, and as a reference to technicists, it indirectly reflects the process situation of manufacture features in entity parts as well.

In conclusion, product comprehensive information model is applicable for the global and local processes. Thus, it can solve the unification and diversity to information.

(3) Document Type

In a model, information may be expressed directly or attached to the models, existing in model property. However, directly reflecting the information in models need various documents: BOM table, technical documentation, drawings, data sheets and process card and so on. Fig.5 shows the basic document type to the information in product comprehensive information model.

document class / information class		BOM	technical document	engineering drawing	data sheet	process chart
entity information	geometry/topology information			yes		
	material property	yes				
	volume/quality				yes	
	structural allocation information	yes		yes		yes
	course information		yes			
technology information	assembly technology information — assembly plan		yes			
	assembly accuracy	yes		yes	yes	yes
	assembly relationship	yes	yes			yes
	assembly sequence	yes				yes
	assembly path			yes		yes
	assembly tools	yes			yes	yes
	assembly regulation		yes			
	process technology information — process methods		yes			yes
	process accuracy	yes		yes	yes	yes
	process surface quality		yes		yes	yes
	process equipments	yes				
	process technology regulations		yes			yes
	management regulations		yes			yes
	maintenance rules		yes			yes
Utility information	management information	yes	yes			
	evaluation information	yes	yes		yes	
	technology sustaining information		yes			
	flow information	yes	yes			

Fig. 5. Basic document type

The description to the file type is used to express product information, also facilitate the establishment to product information.

3   Conclusions

This paper puts foreword product comprehensive information model theory by analyzing the demand to entire information model and introducing comprehensive information theory and the idea of building information modeling. In this case, the lifecycle graphical description has become a trend for the development to information technology. Therefore, the study on product comprehensive information model will provide a theoretical model reference for the current development of information visualization techniques in face of lifecycle and play a role on guiding the implementation to data management.

References

1. Liu, X.-M., He, Y.-L.: Product Lifecycle Information Mode. Journal of Chongqing University (Natural Science Edition) 25(1), 138–140 (2002)
2. Liu, Z., Wang, P., Ai, Y.: Research on process-oriented virtual assembly modeling technology for product information. China Mechanical Engineering 22(1) (January 2011)
3. Hu, J.-X., Zhou, L.-S., Wei, W., Jia, Z.-N.: Research on information model of tooling rapid design for aircraft engines. Manufacturing Automation 32(12) (December 2010)
4. Zhong, Y.-X.: Comprehensive Information Based Methodology for Natural Language Understanding. Journal of Beijing University of Posts and Telecommunications 27(4) (August 2004)
5. He, G., Huang, M.: Explanation on Ten Most Popular BIM Terms. Journal of Information Technology in Civil Engineering and Architecture 2(2) (2010)
6. Zhang, J.: Research and application on BIM technology. Construction Technology (January 2011)
7. Li, Y., Wan, L., Xiong, T.: Product Lifecycle Data Modeling Based on Domain. Journal of Computer-Aided Design &Computer Graphics 22(2) (February 2010)
8. Jiang, Y., Qiao, L.: Research and Application of 3D Feature Part Information Mode. New Technology & New Process (5) (2008)
9. Ge, C., Qiao, L.H.: Manufacturing feature information modeling and instantiation. Computer Integrated Manufacturing Systems 16(12) (December 2010)

Research on Structure of Communication Network in Smart Grid

Feng Ran[1], Hailang Huang[2], Tao Wang[2], and Meihua Xu[2]

[1] Research and Development Center of Microelectronics, Shanghai University,
Shanghai 200072, China
[2] School of Mechatronics Engineering and Automation, Shanghai University,
Shanghai 200072, China

Abstract. As the next generation of power systems, smart grid is a high degree integration of electric power, communication and automatic control. A safe, effective and intelligence communication platform is the precondition of building Smart grid. This paper introduces an overview of power communication in nowadays, analyzes and probes the structure and safe strategy of communication network in Smart grid. Several key technologies of communication safety in Smart grid are summarized and generalized. This paper has important reference value to the research area of the communication safety of Smart grid.

Keywords: Power Communication, SDH, PTN, ASON.

1   Introduction

Because of its unique economic and social benefits, Smart grid has become one of the hottest researches for the next generation of grid. Europe and other developed countries have studied smart grid technology for 30 years and have borne fruit. In China, the research was started very later, but developing rapidly and China has already mastered part of the core technology. Whether domestic or foreign, there are many technical problems which have to be solved before building the intelligent grid. In fact, most smart grid technologies have been used in communications and other industries [1]. It's important for researchers and academics to integrate and apply these technologies into power system. Today, not only SDH which is used in electric power communication network in nowadays, but also PIN and ASON technology are gradually improved. They are playing an important role in smart grid in the near future In China.

2   Synchronous Digital Hierarchy

SDH(Synchronous Digital Hierarchy) network is a kind of comprehensive information transport network which has the functions of multiple connection, transmission line and information interchange. Comparing to other network equipments, SDH optical

T. Xiao, L. Zhang, and M. Fei (Eds.): AsiaSim 2012, Part II, CCIS 324, pp. 135–142, 2012.

transmission equipment has a lot of advantages [2]. SDH has become one of the most important transmittal forms in the modern high-capacity fiber optic network.

SDH network topology is formed by the arrangement of network nodes (network elements) and the transmission line. Chain, star, tree, ring and mesh-shaped are the basic structures of SDH. In order to increase self-healing function, SDH usually adopts circular way. When the SDH network fails, it only takes about 50ms to recovery. It shows great superiority in SDH network. Self-healing ring structure can be divided into two categories: channel protection ring and multiplex section protection ring [2].

2.1   SDH Channel Protection Ring

Channel protection ring is usually achieved by two optical fibers, one fiber optic used for transmission signal service, called S fiber, the other is used for protection, called P fiber. Under normal circumstances, protection segment is used to send business signals under abnormal circumstances. It is used to protect the entire ring. The maximum operational capacity in the channel ring is STM-N. If the capacity meets the requirements, we can use networking channel protection ring fashion through fair and foul. Two-fiber unidirectional path protection ring structure is shown in Fig 1.

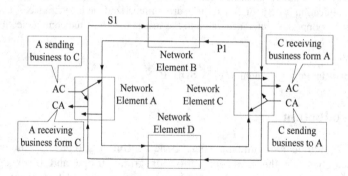

Fig. 1. Two-fiber unidirectional path protection ring structure

For SDH protection ring, one failure point doesn't affect the normal operation of the business. This characteristic gives SDH a lot of advantages such as high reliability, protection action of the small part and short time of protection switching, which make SDH can be widely used in many occasions.

2.2   SDH Multiplex Section Protection Ring

The most common networking mode in SDH multiplex section protection ring is Two-fiber bidirectional multiplex section protection ring, which is known as multiplex section shared protection ring. It is mainly composed by the main optical fiber and standby. Under normal circumstances, the main ring is used to transmit primary business, and the standby ring is used to send additional business. A typical Two-fiber bidirectional multiplex section protection ring is shown in Fig 2.

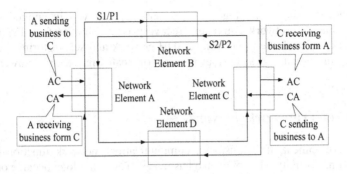

Fig. 2. Two-fiber bidirectional multiplex section protection ring

When multiplex section protection ring appeared abnormal in operation, especially the two fibers were cut off or forming isolated nodes [3], the AIS signals would be inserted to not affect the communication and avoid appearing misuse. For example, if the two fibers between node B and node C were cut off, AIS signals would be inserted in node B and C. When A sent business to node C, the data-signal would transmit along the direction of S1/P1 form node A to B. Then with the help of inserted AIS, the data-signal would transmit along the direction of S2/P2 form node B to A, and finally arrived at node C. At this time, the AIS signals which were inserted in node C would be in action. At last, the data-signal would be transmitted from S2/P2 to S1/P1, which made C receive business form A. Similarly, when C sent business to A, the data-signal would be transmitted along the direction noted in diagram. The network elements have recovered before misuses get the fault message. The process is shown in Fig 3.

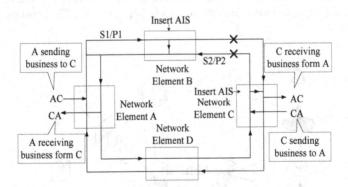

Fig. 3. SDH multiplex section protection ring protecting communications

SDH transmission technology plays more and more important role in Telecommunications for Electric Power System field today. Using Self-healing ring network to provide reliable and stable information Transport Channel become one of the key technology in SDH networking communication. As its business demanding increasing constantly, the coverage of SDH transit network in modern electric power system becomes larger, and the number of related node raises constantly. Although

SDH Self-healing ring technology is very maturely and widely applied to power communication, the network equipment recovery is still not perfect. Especially in large network, to break the protection of SDH network and self-restoring technology will be an important work in the process of realizing electric power system intelligence.

3 Packet Transport Network

With the development of IP business, communications network function becomes more and more diversity. Grouping also has made PTN technology became one of the most important characteristics of network. Packet Transport Network not only inherited the SDH-based MSTP (Multi-Service Transport Platform) core ideology, but also has very lower total cost of ownership (TCO) and statistical multiplexing features [4]. It makes the PTN network have high availability and reliability, efficient bandwidth management and traffic engineering, convenient OAM and network management, scalability, high security advantages. PTN is one of essential parts in the next-generation communications networks.

3.1 PTN Network Mode

The core of Packet Transport Network is package switching. At present, the packet transport network technology primarily has several different systems, mainly can be divided into two broad categories. They are the Ethernet transmission technology with enhanced technology and multi-protocol label switching (MPLS). Multi-protocol label switching (MPLS-TP, also known as T-MPLS) is representative of MPLS and the Ethernet Provider Backbone Bridging - Traffic Engineering (PBB-TE, also known as PBT) is the representative of Enhancements [4]. One of PTN network model is shown in Fig 4.

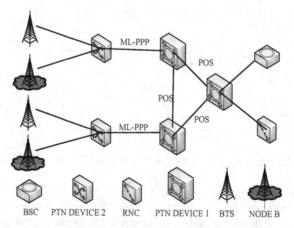

Fig. 4. PTN communication networking model

PTN has different networking patterns, including three typical structures. They are PTN+OTN networking, PTN independent networking and PTN+MSTP hybrid networking [5]. They have different characteristics and advantages, and their network structure will be the focus of the next generation PTN.

(1) PTN+MSTP Hybrid Networking

It's inevitable for transport network evolution from circuit to packet transporting, which adapts to the development of business. But the evolution can't happen very soon. Now the network must be in accordance with the actual situation of the MSTP deployed step by step construction of PTN. PTN equipment should be fully considered the network level with the MSTP network interconnection. It is important that the PTN equipment can be flexibility inserted into the existing MSTP network level without affect its expanding way.

(2) PTN + OTN Network Mode

The most important characteristic of PTN+OTN network mode is that it uses the OTN devices as its core layer and PTN devices as its convergence layer and the access layer. OTN devices of the core layer, providing the Ethernet physical line interface, bearing PTN packet service, mapping to ODUK and crossing based on ODUK, are primarily applied in backbone layer in which cross-scheduling of large particles of OTN system are needed. According to by-packet scheduling of the small particles, the access layer and the convergence layer maintain users and service one by one, and then takes end-to-end control and transmission in packet network.

Some issues can't be solved by traditional WDM devices such as large particles for wavelength-level cross, low bandwidth utilization and poor overall crossing capacity owing to small crossing particles of SDH devices reasons. Integrated with the features of PTN and OTN, the schedule of large-capacity and the adjustments of fine particle can be well solved for different business models to achieve a better transmission. According to the flow of business, the flow characteristics and the characteristics of transmission technology, Mesh network which is used in the core layer and ring or chain network mode is adopted in the convergence layer and the access layer for abundant connection of light direction, high utilization of fiber resource and flexible business scheduling.

As emerging technologies, PTN and OTN will play a critical role in the next generation of optical transmission network. Theoretically speaking, PTN+OTN network model has been entirely feasible. It is believed that broader development space of the application of PTN and OTN will come with the development of technology.

(3) PTN Independent Network Model

PTN independent network model is that all devices use PTN equipment from access layer to core layer. Due to the independent network model, the network structure is clear, and the network becomes available for management and maintenance and suitable for the emergence of a large number IP service access.

3.2   PTN Network Protection

The protection method supported by PTN network mainly contains protection within network and other protection of dual homing network. It is listed as follows:

(1) Protection within Network

In the PTN network, the protection can be divided into chain network protection and ring network protection. The ring network protection contains two kinds of protection mechanisms, they are and Steering wrapping which is mainly applied.

(2) Other Protection of Dual Homing Network

3.3   Time Synchronization

In PTN network, we currently achieve time synchronization with IEEE 1588v2. IEEE 1588v2 has been defined 3 clock modes. They are ordinary clock OC, the boundary clock BC and transparent clock TC. Network start-side and terminal devices are usually OC. The device has only one port, this port is used as a SLAVE (slave port) or MASTER (master port). BC is a network intermediate node clock device, the device has more ports. One port can be used as SLAVE. Other ports are used as the MASTER. The transferring time can be achieved step by step. TC is a network intermediate node device clock. It can be divided into E2E TC (End to End TC) and the P2P TC (Peer to Peer TC) models.

In the PTN network, IEEE 1588v2 time synchronization has two models, namely, BC mode and TC models. BC (Boundary Clock) mode is more widely used.

4   Automatically Switched Optical Network

The traditional Optical Transport Network is an optoelectronic hybrid network combined with SDH/SONET and WDM equipment. Because of using fixed link connection mode in network, the assignment of bandwidth is basically static, which leads it lack real time service provision power in network, and also constrain its flexibility, reliability and extensibility [6]. ASON(Automatically Switched Optical Network) can make up he deficiency of SDH network well because it is dynamics, flexibility, high efficiency and intelligence in setting up network. ASON firstly introduced signal and routing to transport network. Then through intelligent control level to construct call and connection, a new intersection in switching, transmission, data three field was added again realizing truly Routing settings, End-to-End business schedule and automatic network recovery. It is a great breakthrough for Optical Transport Network, which is considered widely as the mainstream technology for next generation optical network.

4.1   Characteristics of ASON Network

The traditional transmission network is composed of network level and transport level. However, ASON network has three levels, and import new control level. Intelligent control layer is introduced to establish a connection which is realized by means of distributed signaling contributes [7]. Compared to traditional synchronous digital hierarchy SDH network, we can find that ASON network has distinct characteristics and advantages.

(1) Intelligent Switching Network

ASON has independent and intelligent control level to complete the function of call and connection control. Its characteristic such as becoming flexible, reliable, scalable intelligent switching optical network can makes it insurance for network smooth upgrade.

(2) Effective Network of Protection and Good Self-healing

When the network failure, the management plane and control plane of ASON cooperate to ensure that the error information can be disseminated accurate and timely, backup and restored route can be started quickly, and then increase the system robustness and self-healing of network.

(3) Dynamic Network Resource Allocation and Scheduling

Under the control of ASON control plane, it automatically complete the discovery of network adjacent and topology structure, distributed route computing, and establish, remove and revise the end-to-end optical channel.

(4) Good Equipment Interoperability and Powerful Extensions

Because of the modular of ASON network, different network operators can be well interconnected by defining unified, standard network interfaces.

4.2   ASON Network Architecture

ASON network architecture includes three levels: transport plane, control plane and management plane. In the traditional SDH network, a control plane is added between transmission equipment and network management plant. Various planes (CCI) are connected through the relevant interfaces. ASON architecture is shown in Fig 5.

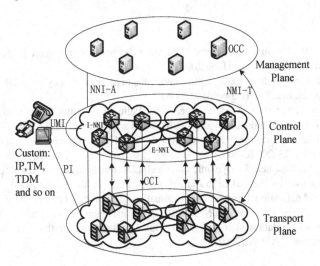

Fig. 5. ASON network architecture

ASON has several interfaces. They are user network interface (UNI), internal network node interface (I-NNI), external network node interface (E-NNI), connection control interface (CCI), the interface between management plane and control plane and the interface between management plane and Transport plane. UNI is business interface, I-NNI is a network interface, and E-NNI has business and network interface features.

5   Conclusions

Benefited from the development of information technology, the safety and reliability of Power Communication Systems have greatly increased. Especially after the MSTP network structure based on SDH used in special Power Communication network, more advanced network equipment and perfect Communication Systems are springing up constantly. As the improving of PTN and ASON technology, the idea and operation Method of traditional transmission network were changed greatly, and have been profoundly influenced in its development. Intellectualization will be an inexorable trend of Optical Transport Network for electric power. Its advanced technology ascendancy must push the revolution and development of communication optical fiber transmission network for electric power and communication system for electric power greatly.

Acknowledgements. The authors would like to acknowledge the financial support by Shanghai-AM Fund under Grant No. 09700714000, Grant No.09530708600, and also to acknowledge the financial support by National Science and Technology Ministry under Grant No. 2009GJC00031.

References

1. Belhomme, R., Deasuarcr, Valtorta, G.: Active demand for the smart grids of the future. Smart Grids for Distribution (June 2008)
2. Gao, F.: The research of multiplexing and transmission efficiency of SDH. Submitted to Optical Communication Technology (2008)
3. Cárdenas, J.P., Santiago, A., Mouronte, M.L., Feliú, V., Benito, R.M.: Complexity in the SDH network. International Journal of Bifurcation and Chaos (2009)
4. Li, Z.: The development and application of PTN. Telecommunications Network Technology 10, 25–29 (2008)
5. Huang, H., Li, X., Chen, J.: Dynamic branch elimination algorithm for topological design of PTN mesh networks. Submitted to Journal of Computer Applications (2010)
6. Zhang, Y.: Application Research of Automatically Switched Optical Network ASON in Metropolitan Area Transmission Networks. Southwest Jiaotong University (2007)
7. ITU-T Recommendation G.8080/Y.1304-2001, Architecture for the Automatic Switched Optical Networks, ASON (2003)

Analysis of Information Encryption
on Electric Communication Network

Feng Ran[1], Hailang Huang[2], Junwei Ma[2], and Meihua Xu[2]

[1] Research and Development Center of Microelectronics, Shanghai University,
Shanghai 200072, China
[2] School of Mechatronics Engineering and Automation, Shanghai University,
Shanghai 200072, China

Abstract. The greatly improvement of electric power automation is making electric power system increasingly depend on the information networks to ensure its safety, reliable and efficient operation. This paper introduces the general situation of electric power system and power information network system in nowadays. Finally, two typical encryption algorithms DES and RSA are analyzed and compared, and software program based on QT is used to prove the principle of the encryption algorithms. This paper also has some reference value for the research on security of electric power telecommunication.

Keywords: Power Communication, Information Security, DES, RSA.

1   Introduction

Electric power network security means that the hardware, software and data in this system are protected, and not damaged, changed, and leaked because of the accidental or malicious reasons, ensuring the electric power system in normal operation [1-3]. Network security is information security in essence. In order to ensure the security of information, one can introduce many technologies, such as encryption technology, access control technology, the authentication technology and security auditing technology and so on. But so far, the most important security tool for network and communication automation is encryption [4-5]. This paper analyzed and compared two kinds of encryption methods, and realized the encryption principle by software programming.   At last, the paper put forward a point of view that choosing different encryption methods according to different information security classification.

The foundation of modern power grids system is to build a high-speed, two-way, real-time, and integrated communication system, which will enter millions of households just like power grids. This creates two closely-knit networks: power grid and communication network, given the name of electric power communication network [6-9]. It is playing a pivotal role in the security and economic operation of power grid, and improving the information systems automation in domestic grid enterprises. Moreover, because of the particularity of electricity power system, any slight network security problem may lead to disastrous consequences, and then bring

T. Xiao, L. Zhang, and M. Fei (Eds.): AsiaSim 2012, Part II, CCIS 324, pp. 143–150, 2012.

to the enterprise immeasurable economic loss. Obviously, establishing the protection system of electric power network relates to the national economic development.

At present, most of the electric power information systems use plaintext transmission in China, which leads to electric power data more easily to be modified, monitored, forged, and deleted, and so on. Even if power information system adopts efficient protection software against hackers and all system vulnerabilities are repaired, plaintext transmission also can bring great security risk without any encryption measure [10].

2   Information Encryption Technology

2.1   Overview of Information Encryption Technology

Encryption is a process that plaintext can be converted into ciphertext, and the transform of data encryption and decryption is controlled by key. Encryption and decryption using the same key or not, base on which modem password technology can be classified into symmetrical encryption algorithm and asymmetric encryption algorithm. Symmetrical encryption algorithm is characterized by fast, simple and efficient. However, it has low security because both sides use the same key. In addition, each time a couple of users use symmetrical encryption algorithm, it needs one key that others do not know, which leads to geometrical progression of the number of keys with the users increase. As a result, key management becomes the burden of the users.

In asymmetric encryption algorithm, encryption and decryption use different keys. It is almost impossible to deduce another key from one key, and key management is simple. However, the algorithm is complex and low efficiency. Usually, it applies to a distributed system.

Presently the commonly used symmetrical encryption technology has Data Encryption Standard (DES), Triple Data Encryption Standard (3DES)[11], and Advanced Encryption Standard (AES)[12-13]. The key length for DES is 56 bits. 3DES is the improvement of DES, and with triple DES, each 64 bit block is encrypted under three different DES keys, which can increase encryption strength. AES, a new encryption standard, the key length of which has 128, 192 and 256 bits, is the replacement of DES. So far, it has never been broken. Currently, asymmetric encryption technology used mainly has RSA and ECC, and 1024 bits RSA is the most widely used asymmetric encryption technology [14].

2.2   Flow of Data Encryption in Power Information System

Electric Power Information System Transmission Model is shown in figure 1. Signal Source M sends out data signals m, which then can be converted into Ciphertext C through encryption devices (realized by hardware such as DES or by software such as RSA). When the Ciphertext is transmitted to the receiver, it can be decrypted with the key received. However, illegal invaders may crack or tamper the ciphertext in a transmission link. So the most ideal Encryption Technology for Electric Power Information System is to ensure that the encrypting files shall not be illegal broken and the integrity of the information.

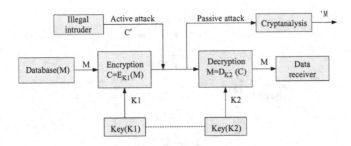

Fig. 1. Electric power communication system data transmission mode

3   DES and RSA Algorithms

There are two kinds of typical data encryption algorithms: data encryption standard and public-key encryption algorithm RSA (which stands for Rivest, Shamir and Adleman who first publicly described it), from which most of the encryption algorithms nowadays are developed. Although they have been used for a long time, they still have very strong practicability. The following article provides a detailed explanation of the two algorithms.

3.1   Data Encryption Algorithm

Data Encryption Algorithm, a symmetrical encryption algorithm, is widely used in POS, ATM cards, Intelligent Cards (IC) for gas stations and highway toll, etc. In addition, in order to keep the key data safe, the DES Algorithm is also used in credit card holder's PIN Encryption transmission, two-way authentication between IC card and POS, and MAC calibration for data packets of financial transaction. To believe that with the electric power communication network gradually formed, the classic DES algorithm will radiate its vigour of youth.

DES is the archetypal block cipher-an algorithm that takes a fixed-length string of plaintext bits and transforms it through a series of complicated operations into another ciphertext bitstring of the same length. In the case of DES, the block size is 64 bits. DES also uses a key to customize the transformation, so that decryption can supposedly only be performed by those who know the particular key used to encrypt. The key ostensibly consists of 64 bits; however, only 56 of these are actually used by the algorithm. Eight bits are used solely for checking parity, and are thereafter discarded. Hence the effective key length is 56 bits, and it is never quoted as such. Every 8th bit of the selected key is discarded, that is, positions 8, 16, 24, 32, 40, 48, 56, 64 are removed from the 64 bit key leaving behind only the 56 bit key.

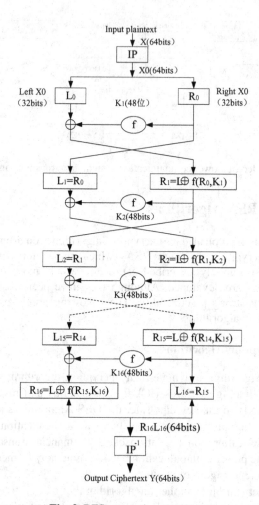

Fig. 2. DES encryption algorithm

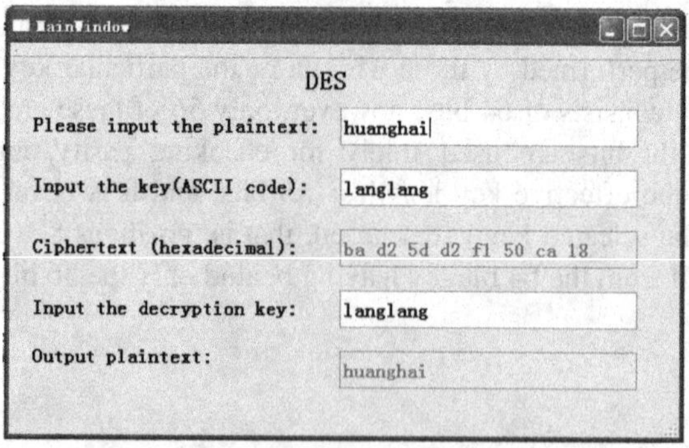

Fig. 3. DES algorithm test

Software programming was used to realize the principle of DES algorithms. First, C++ language programs based on QT were used to descript the mechanism, and then debugging and running the programs. After the plaintext was input, the programs could remind you of inputting the key. Next, the programs converted the plaintext into ciphertext. Finally, when the ciphertext was transmitted to receiver, it would be decrypted by the same key. The DES test programs are shown in fig.3.

DES algorithm has very high security. So far, there are no efficient methods to attack DES except for exhaustive searches method. According to the theoretical calculation, the exhaustion space is 256 for a 56 bits key, which means that if a computer checks one million keys per second, it will need nearly 2285 years to test all the keys. So it is difficult for illegal users to break encrypted data information. DES algorithm is can be used to both encryption and decryption because of its symmetric properties. By regularly updating the keys of source and destination end in communication network, it can further improve the privacy of data.

3.2   RSA Algorithm

RSA is one of the most influential public key encryption algorithm, and it can resist all password attack known now, and has been recommended by ISO for public key data encryption standard. RSA algorithms based on a very simple arithmetical facts: two large prime numbers is easy to be multiplied by, but then the product of theirs is extremely difficult to be facorized. Therefore the product may be used as public key encryption. Furthermore, the RSA algorithm does not need Online Key Server, and has simple Key Distribution Protocol, both of which greatly simplify the key management. In addition to encryption function, the RSA system can provide digital signature.

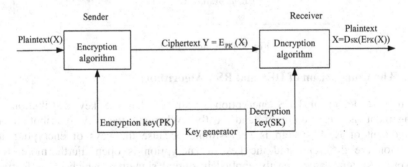

Fig. 4. Public key cryptosystem

The keys for the RSA algorithm are generated by the following ways:

(1) Compute n = p*q. For security purposes, the prime integers p and q should be chosen at random, and should be of similar bit-length. Prime integers can be efficiently found using a primality test. n is used as the modulus for both the public and private keys.

(2) Compute $\varphi(n) = (p-1)(q-1)$, where φ is Euler's totient function. The number of $\varphi(n)$ is less than n, and is prime to n.

(3) Choose an integer e such that $1 < e < \varphi(n)$, e and $\varphi(n)$ are coprime. e is released as the public key exponent.

(4) Determine $d = e^{-1} \bmod \varphi(n)$, d is kept as the private key exponent.

(5) Obtain the public key and private key: public key(encryption key) PK = {e, n}; private key(decryption key) SK = {d, n}.

Software programming was used to realize the principle of RSA algorithms. First, C++ language programs were used to descript the mechanism, and then debugging and running the programs. After the prime integers p and q were chosen at random, the programs can remind you of inputting the public key exponent e (e equal to79). Next, The programs computed the private key, and then converted the plaintext into ciphertext. When the ciphertext was transmitted to receiver, it would be decrypted by the private key. The RSA testing is shown in fig.5.

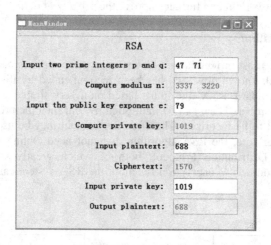

Fig. 5. RSA algorithm test

3.3   The Comparison of DES and RSA Algorithms

The biggest defect of DES encryption system is that the key distribution and management is very complex and costly. Whereas, the key distribution and management of RSA system is very simple because the keys of encryption and decryption are different, and the key of encryption is open. Furthermore, RSA encryption system can be easily applied in digital signature, which can effectively protect the integrity of the data.

The main shortcoming of RSA is that the generation of keys is quite complicated because of the technical limitations of the prime producing. Therefore, it is difficult for RSA encryption system to realize once a secret key. What's more, the packet length is too big, which leads to high cost and slow speed of the operation. Along with the development of decomposition technique, the length is still increasing, which goes against the standardization of data format.

4   Encryption Scheme of Electric Power Communication System

In view of the trends of the development of electric power networks in the future, the electric power information encryption is special important. According to the different features of the encryption methods, they can be classified into software-based encryption and hardware-based encryption and so on. Symmetrical encryption system such as DES has fast speed of encryption and decryption, and the algorithms do not need to be kept confidential, so manufacturers can develop low-cost chips to realize data encryption in mass production. So, if one adopts DES encryption methods, he can choose hardware encryption devices, while for the Advanced Encryption Standard (AES) algorithm, software-based encryption is more reasonable.

At the same time, with the amount of information of electric power communication increasing, a technical scheme that different security levels for electric power data adopt different encryption methods is put forward. So, for the power data of lower level, such as daily power datas, one may choose DES algorithms as economic and feasible encryption scheme. On the contrary, the key data of electric power have higher security levels, and one may choose more complicated and stronger RSA encryption algorithm, and even 3DES. Of course, specific encryption algorithms also depends on the conditions that the electric power communication system is vulnerable to attack.

5   Conclusions

With the rapid development of the electric power communication technology, the requirements for network information security are also further enhanced, and more advanced encryption methods will be applied in the electric power communication special network. According to the characteristics of communication technology and taking the corresponding encryption methods, which not only ensures the special channel bandwidth of the electric power communication network, effectively improves the security of the whole electric power system.

References

1. Chen, Y.-J., Zhang, H.-F., Dang, Q.: Design and Application of Electronic Official Document Security Transmission Platform for Power Grid. Electric Power Information Technology (11), 75–79 (2011)
2. Hu, Y., Dong, M., Han, Y.: Consideration of Information Security for Electric Power Industry. Automation of Electric Power Systems 7, 1–4 (2002)
3. Xin, Y.: Development Trend of Power System Dispatching Automation Technology in 21st Century. Power System Technology 25(12), 1–10 (2001)
4. Yang, L.-L.: Technique of Mixed Cryptography and its Application in Network and Communication Security. Computer Knowledge and Technology (5), 1077–1078 (2009)
5. Rabah, K.: Data Security and Cryptographic Techniques-A Review. Information Technology Journal 3(1), 106–132 (2004)

6. Lei, S.: Security Communication of Real-Time Data in Power Information System. Electronic Design Engineering. Huazhong University of Science and Technology, 10–30 (2005)
7. You, C.: The Research of Information Security in Power Communication. Computer & Telecommunication (9), 55–57 (2009)
8. Wang, Y., Xin, Y., Xiang, L., et al.: Security and Protection of Dispatching Automation Systems and Digital Networks. Automation of Electric Power Systems 25(21), 5–8 (2001)
9. Baumeister, T.: Literature Review on Smart Grid Cyber Security. University of Hawaii, America (2010)
10. Feng, D.-G., Wang, X.-Y.: Progress and prospect of some fundamental research on information security in china. J. Comput. Sci. & Technol 21(5), 740–755 (2006)
11. Xia, Y.-B., Zhang, L.-L.: Research on One-Time Pad Cryptographic Scheme Based on DES and RSA. Jiangxi Electric Power (06), 38–40 (2011)
12. Xiao, G., Bai, E., Liu, X.: Some New Developments on the Cryptanalysis of AES. Acta Electronica Sinica 31(10), 1549–1553
13. Akkar, M.-L., Giraud, C.: An Implementation of DES and AES, Secure against Some Attacks. In: Koç, Ç.K., Naccache, D., Paar, C. (eds.) CHES 2001. LNCS, vol. 2162, pp. 309–318. Springer, Heidelberg (2001)
14. Feng, H.-J., Ma, H., Yang, B.: New Traitor Tracing Scheme Based on RSA. Application Research of Computers 24(5), 135–136 (2007)

Using Distance-Based Outlier Detection Method to Handle the Abnormal Gateway in WSN

Wei Su, Jingqi Fu, and Haikuan Wang

Shanghai Key Laboratory of Power Station Automation Technology,
School of Mechanical Engineering and Automation,
Shanghai University, Shanghai, 200072, China
suwei_100@shu.edu.cn

Abstract. The gateway of wireless sensor network (WSN) plays a key role in the network system. Its stability and reliability is very important to the WSN. The abnormal of gateway will make the network sequence disorder. The node can't report its data to the gateway, and it will need much more power consumption. In this paper, we propose a star topology network and the redundant node can monitor the node data and realize the gateway working status detection. We establish the relevant mathematical model based on the distance-based outlier detection method (DBODM) to analysis the gateway. When the deviation value is more than a certain threshold, the redundant node changes the nodes' working patterns through sending the intelligent decision message, to realize the node working in low power consumption.

Keywords: Gateway Abnormal, Redundant Node, Distance-based Outlier Detection, Outliers Factor.

1 Introduction

WSN has been widely used in area of environmental monitoring [1], habitat monitoring [2], health monitoring [3], industrial monitoring [4], etc. In all the application, the gateway plays an important role in the network system. Usually it does not allow an error. But the wireless sensor network often deployed in the bad environment, it may face a variety of network attacks that can lead to the failure of the gateway. And sometimes the gateway may power down or the software update. Due to its sudden happening of the anomalies, the gateway does not send message to the sensor node. As a result, the sensor nodes will wait for the network command for a long time, and the data collected by the sensor nodes can't be sent out successfully. The energy consumption of the energy constraint nodes increase sharply. As a result, the network must have good fault tolerance with the gateway failure.

Regarding to the variety of threats to the failure of the gateway, Jing Deng [5] propones an idea that relocation the gateway in the network topology can enhance resiliency and mitigating the scope of damage. It can reduce the network attack to the gateway in the particular area, but it can't deal with a wide range network attack. Most of the time, the gateway must be deployed in the specific area. Delphine

T. Xiao, L. Zhang, and M. Fei (Eds.): AsiaSim 2012, Part II, CCIS 324, pp. 151–159, 2012.
© Springer-Verlag Berlin Heidelberg 2012

Christin [6] puts forward a multiple routing to multiple gateways as a strategy to provide tolerance against individual gateway base station attacks or compromise. An adaptive and fault tolerant protocol for multiple gateways is presented in the article [7]. It is highly scalable, because uses clustering and allows network to recover from gateway failure using neighbor gateways as backup. Similar multi-gateway architecture is discussed in the article [8] and results are rather optimistic. It would be beneficial to increase the number of deployed gateways in order to extend the lifetime of sensors and provide a more predictable sensor-to-gateway transmission times [9]. Of course, the more deployment of the gateways, the more cost is needed.

Although the architecture of multi-gateways can increase the network fault tolerance, it still has problems. How can the nodes operate if all the gateways power down. In order to keep low power consumption, the nodes must know the gateway real-time state whether the gateway is well or not. In this way, the nodes can operate in the different sequences according to the gateway state. As a result, the gateway failure events must be accurately detected.

The gateway failure can be viewed as an outlier in all the gateway state. The measurements that are significantly deviated from the normal pattern of sensed data can be defined as outliers [10]. The potential sources of outliers include noise and errors, events, and malicious attacks on the network. Outliers caused by other sources need to be identified as they contain important information about events that are of great interest to the researchers [11].

In our research, we mine all the gateway state datasets on the time dimension to find the gateway abnormal status. We construct a star topology WSN, and based on this network using the function of redundant node to analysis the gateway status through the distance-based outlier detection to get the gateway real-time statue. The node can enter into the low consumption mode, when receiving the gateway abnormal message from the redundant node.

This paper is organized as follows. In section 2, a star topology WSN system is constructed and energy reduction model is put forward. In section 3, the distance-based outlier detection method (DBODM) is proposed to detect the gateway statue. In section 4, the gateway abnormal network sequence is put forward, and with this time sequence the node power consumption is compared with the gateway normal time sequence. The result shows the node energy consumption can reduce greatly in the gateway failure circumstances. Finally, our work is summarized in the last section.

2   System Construction and Energy Reduction

This paper constructs a WSN of multiple clusters. As illustrated in Figure 1, each star cluster is constituted of nodes, redundant node and gateway.

Gateway is the cluster head node in each cluster, and mainly achieves the function of management the operation of each node and redundant node. Including sending the time synchronization frame, command frame, receiving the data frame, and extracting the relevant features of attribute parameters from the data frame, then retransmit the these parameters to the redundant node. The gateway is the key component of the entire network, it needs high reliability requirements, usually are not allowed to failure, once the error appears, the node will fail to send the data and the energy consumption will increase greatly.

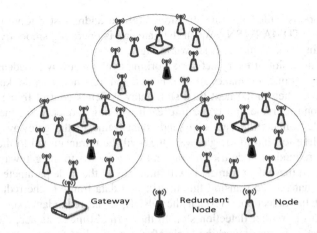

Fig. 1. The Network System Structure

Redundant node on one hand works as a routing node transmitting the data that cannot be directly transmitted to the gateway successfully. On the other hand, redundant node operated as a network data warehouse receiving the gateway's character value which shows the gateway's own state to do gateway status outlier detecting in the outlier time slot of each network cycle. When the analysis result shows that the gateway is error, it works as a temporary coordinator to make the node working in the mode of low power consumption.

The node works as a network terminal to collect the different data in the different physical position, and sends data to the gateway. The energy-constrain nodes do not change the battery and need to work for a long time. So that, when the gateway device is normal, the network working time sequence needs well designed to make the node decrease the energy consumption. Otherwise, when the gateway is abnormal, the nodes can get the gateway abnormal information, decreasing the date change with the gateway, and increasing the sleeping time slot.

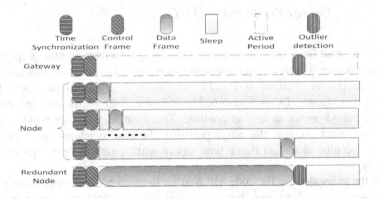

Fig. 2. Network Working Time Sequence

This network is called as time division multiple address star topology wireless sensor network (TDMASWSN). When the gateway is operating smoothly, the whole network working time sequence is shown in Fig.2.

In the first time slot of every network working cycle, gateway broadcasts the time synchronization frame to make all the nodes and redundant node keeping time synchronization. Then in the next time slot, gateway sends control frame, each node received its control frame and come into each working sequence. In the third time slot, each node collects the data and sends data frame to the gateway. If the data frames are failure to send to the gateway, they will be retransmitted to the redundant node, then the redundant node tries to transmit these frames to the gateway. When the gateway received these data frames, it will integrate all the node parameters to form a gateway state matrix, and transmit this matrix as a data frame to the redundant node used for its status detection. Through the DBODM, the redundant node knows the gateway's status in outlier detection slot. In the normal time sequence, the node will sleep in the rest of network working cycle after sending data frames successfully and the redundant node will sleep after the outlier detection time slot until the end of the network cycle.

In WSN, the resource-constrain sensor node usually uses the battery power, and battery replacement is difficult. Therefore, reducing the energy consumption of the sensor nodes to extend its lifetime is one of the major goals of network designing. The lifetime of the sensor node is also an important indicator to evaluate the network performance.

In duty-cycled operation, every node follows a sleep-wakeup-communicate cycle, where the majority of the cycle is spent in the low-power sleep state [12].This process, which relies on hardware support for implementing sleep states, permits the average power consumption of a node to be reduced by many orders of magnitude. An expression for the energy reduction obtainable through duty-cycling can be derived (1), where DC is the duty cycle (defined as the fraction of the cycle that the node is active for the artical[12]), and P_{sleep}[W] and P_{active}[W] are the power consumptions of the node in sleep mode and active mode respectively.

$$Energy\ Reduction = (1 - DC)(1 - \frac{P_{sleep}}{P_{active}}) \tag{1}$$

It can be observed from (1) that decreasing the DC (thus increasing the proportion of time spent sleeping) increases the reduction in energy. Similarly, an increase in the energy reduction is obtained as P_{sleep}[W] decreases or P_{active}[W] increases. In the network time sequence, DC is determined by software, if the DC is well designed, and the active period works as less as possible. The node lifetime can prolong. In the figure 2, we must decrease the active period of the time synchronization time slot, control frame time slot, data frame time slot to make much more energy reduction effectively.

When the gateway fails, the node will wait for the network time synchronous frame and command frame for a long time, after collecting the data, the sensor node will also transmit the data frame for time and time again. The network DC increases sharply, as a result, the node lifetime decreases rapidly. In order to working for a long time, the sensor node must take actions, such as reducing the nodes waiting time, do not collect and send the data frame to decrease the DC period. All the taking measures have the premise that the sensor node can obtain the message of gateway fault. In order to get the gateway state, we use the distance-based outlier detection method (DBODM). The redundant node realizes the gateway state monitoring.

3   Distance-Based Outlier Detection Method

We set up a time division multiple address star topology wireless sensor network (TDMASWSN), the nodes in this network are distributed deployed in the isomorphism network measurement environment.

Suppose X(t) is the gateway state value in the t period, D(t) is the gateway dataset in the t period, and $D(t)=X(1)\cap...\cap X(t)$, it can be included that $D(t-1)\subset D(t)$, $X(t)\subset D(t)$. If the gateway state value X(t) of the dataset D(t) is bigger than distance feature threshold, X(t) can be considered as deviating from the general data features of the gateway datasets. It is an outlier.

The distance-based outlier detection deviation calculation formula can be expressed as follows,

$$X(t)\_dev = \frac{1}{2}\left(\min_{i=1}^{t-1} |X(t)-X(i)| + |X(t)-X(t)\_avg| \right) \quad (2)$$

X(t)_dev is the deviation value in the t period.
X(i) is the outlier coefficient of the i network cycle.
X(t)_avg is the average historical outlier coefficient.

X(t), X(i) and X(t)_avg update with the increasing of network monitoring time. The formula (2) described the gateway outlier factor based on the distance outlier detection method in the t network cycle. The first half of formula (2) shows the minimum distance of present moment outlier coefficient to the historical outlier coefficient. And the second half of the formula (2) means the distance between the outlier coefficients of present moment to the historical average outlier coefficient. If there are some outliers in the historical dataset, these data need to be removed, when doing the outlier detection of present moment.

The result of outlier detection X(t)_dev needs to be compared with the minimum distance of outlier threshold dmin. The threshold is a very reliable value that can determine whether the gateway is normal through the many experiments results in different circumstance.

If the result of deviation value shows X(t)_dev≥dmin, it means the gateway is abnormal, the nodes need to run in the low power consumption mode.

If the result of deviation value shows X(t)_dev<dmin, it means the gateway is operating well, all the devices in the network can operate in normal working sequence smoothly.

4   Gateway Abnormal Networking Time Sequence

The redundant node analyses the gateway state through the DBODM in Outlier detection slot. When the gateway is abnormal, the redundant node sends gateway abnormal message frame to all the nodes which belong to this gateway. And the nodes come into the low power time sequence. In the low power mode, the nodes do not collect data and send the data frames. The specific network time sequence is shown in Figure 3.

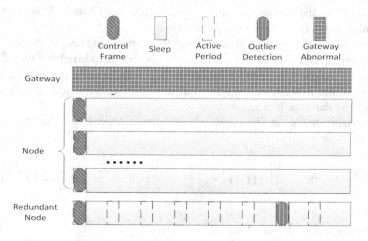

Fig. 3. Gateway abnormal network time sequence

When the network is abnormal, the redundant node has judged the gateway's state in the previous cycle. At the beginning of current network cycle, the redundant node sends the gateway abnormal message frame to the nodes. When the nodes received this message, they will immediately enter into the sleep mode until the end of the current cycle. The redundant node also enters into sleep after sending the gateway abnormal message. And it will wake-up regularly in the rest of the cycle to listen the gateway recovery message. If the redundant node does not receive the gateway recovery message, it means the gateway is still in the abnormal state. The nodes still need to work in the lower power mode in the next network cycle.

In this network time sequence, the sensor node can reduce the power consumption greatly. Because the node does not need to sample and transmit the date and it also does not need to waiting for the gateway commands.

Lots of the factors can affect the node's life. Such as the design of the node software and hardware, the node's network time sequence, the node's network cycle, the node's data load, noise interference in the network channel.

In this paper, we mainly aim at solving the problems of the node's waiting time in the time synchronization and control frame slot; resend the data in the data frame slot. Make the node working in the low power condition. When the gateway is abnormal, effectively improving the node working schedule, reducing the node's power consumption to increase its working life.

Through the distances-based detection method (DBODM), the nodes' working sequence is shown in fig6. In this application, the node life is directly influenced by the network cycle, the length of the data frame and the times to resend the data. We compared the node life when the gateway is in good condition, when the gateway is abnormal, and using the distance-based method when the gateway is abnormal. And the result is shown below.

In fig 4, the relation between network cycle and node life, we can find that the node life is increasing with the increasing of the network cycle, because according to formula 1, the longer the network cycle is, the smaller DC is. And the node life through the DBODM is the longest. If the node sends longer data frame, it need more time to transmit the data at one time. It will cost much more power consumption. Fig 5 and fig 6 show that the node life time is decreasing with increasing of the data frame length. But fig 7 shows that data frame length has no impact on the node life, because using the DBODM the nodes know the gateway state, they do not sample and transmit the data during the gateway abnormal sequence.

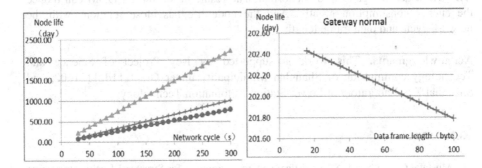

Fig. 4. Network cycle and node life relation   **Fig. 5.** Data frame length and node life relation in normal sequence

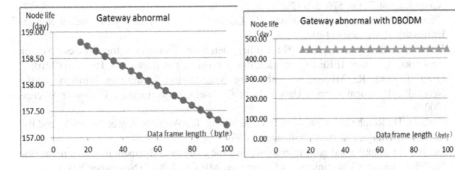

Fig. 6. Data frame length and node life relation in gateway abnormal sequence

Fig. 7. Data frame length and node life relation with distance-based outlier detection method

5   Conclusions

In this paper we construct a typical star topology WSN. According to this feature, the corresponding mathematical model is established to detect the outlier of the gateway datasets. In the experiment, we power down the gateway artificially for some times to generate the abnormal state. Examining whether the redundant node can intelligently judging the gateway state. The experiment result shows that through distance-based outlier detection method the redundant node can get the gateway state. When the gateway is abnormal, the redundant node makes an intelligence decision to inform the node going to the low power consumption time sequence. In this way, the node life time can be extended. In addition, when the gateway back to normal operation, the network also has the ability to recover from the former sequence. The experimental results show that the node can get the gateway abnormal information effectively and access into sleep when the gateway is abnormal. We analysis and compare the node life when the gateway is in good condition, the gateway is abnormal, and using the DBODM when the gateway is abnormal. The result shows the DBODM can reduce the energy consumption greatly. And the node life has close relations with the network cycle and data frame length.

Acknowledgments. This work is supported by Key Project of Science and Technology commission of Shanghai Municipality under Grant 11dz1121602, and Shanghai Key Laboratory of Power Station Automation Technology

References

1. Mustafa, G., Catbas, F.N.: Statistical pattern recognition for Structural Health Monitoring using time series modeling: Theory and experimental verifications. Mechanical Systems and Signal Processing 23(7), 2192–2204 (2009)
2. Vihonen, J., Ala-Kleemola, T., Kerminen, R., Jylhä, J., Visa, A.: On sequential on-line outlier detection and a linescan application. In: IEEE International Conference on Acoustics, vol. 3, pp. 576–579 (2006)
3. Chandola, V., Banerjee, A., Kumar, V.: Outlier detection: a survey. Technical Report, University of Minnesota (2007)
4. Yang, Z., Nirvana, M., Paul, H.: Outlier Detection Techniques for Wireless Sensor Networks: A Survey. IEEE Communications Surveys & Tutorlals 12(2), 159–170 (2010)
5. Deng, J., Han, R., Mishra, S.: Enhancing Base Station Security in Wireless Sensor Networks. Technical Report, University of Colorado, Department of Computer Science (2003)
6. Christin, D., Reinhardt, A., Mogre, P.S., Steinmetz, R.: Wireless Sensor Networks and the Internet of Things: Selected Challenges (2009)
7. Su, W.: An adaptive and fault-tolerant scheme for gateway assignment in sensor networks. In: IEEE Military Communications Conference, MILCOM 2004 (November 2004)
8. Dutta, P., Hui, J., Jeong, J., Kim, S., Sharp, C., Taneja, J., Tolle, G., Whitehouse, K., Culler, D.: Trio: Enabling Sustainable and Scalable Outdoor Wireless Sensor Network Deployments. In: Proceedings of the Fifth International Conference on Information Processing in Sensor Networks Special Track on Platform Tools and Design Methods for Network Embedded Sensors, IPSN/SPOTS 2006 (April 2006)

9. Younis, M., Munshi, P., Gupta, G., Elsharkawy, S.M.: On Efficient Clustering of Wireless Sensor Networks. In: Second IEEE Workshop on Dependability and Security in Sensor Networks and Systems (DSSNS 2006), Columbia, MD (April 2006)
10. Garces, H., Sbarbaro, D.: Outliers detection in environmental monitoring databases. Engineering Applications of Artificial Intelligence 24, 341–349 (2011)
11. McKenna, S.A., Hart, D., Katherine, K., Victoria, C., Wilson, M.: Event detection from water quality time series. In: Proceedings of the World Environmental and Water Resources Congress (2007)
12. Dutta, P.K., Culler, D.E.: System software techniques for low-power operation in wireless sensor networks. In: Proc. Int'l Conf. Computer Aided Design (ICCAD 2005), San Jose, CA, USA, pp. 925–932 (November 2005)

Security in Underwater Acoustic Sensor Network: Focus on Suitable Encryption Mechanisms[*]

Ji Eon Kim[1], Nam Yeol Yun[1], Sardorbek Muminov[1],
Soo Hyun Park[1, **], and Ok Yeon Yi [2]

[1] Ubiquitous System Lab., Graduate School of BIT, Kookmin University, Korea
[2] Dept. of Mathematics, Kookmin University, Korea
{un1730,anuice,smuminov,shpark21,oyyi}@kookmin.ac.kr

Abstract. Underwater acoustic sensor network (UWASN) technology is advancing recently, and research is increasing rapidly. UWASN can be applicable to many fields such as underwater monitoring, underwater resource exploration, ocean data collection, and military purposes. Existing terrestrial wireless sensor network security mechanisms have not been applied to UWASNs due to interference such as multipath propagation, signal fading, limited bandwidth, slow data rates, and long transmission delays. UWASNs also require security mechanisms and algorithms to maintain data confidentiality and integrity. Security-related research is being actively conducted, but it is still in its nascent stages. Therefore, when considering a UWASN protocol stack, the application layer, when sending data to its sub-layer, needs to encrypt the payload for information security. In this paper, we consider the requirements and security issues of UWASNs. We also discuss applicable security algorithms that are suitable for UWASN.

Keywords: Security, Underwater Acoustic Sensor Network, Encryption.

1 Introduction

Recently, UWASNs have been applied to many fields such as underwater environmental monitoring, underwater resource exploration, oceanic data collection, disaster prevention, and tactical surveillance. However, there are many sources of underwater interference in communication between nodes such as bandwidth limitation, multi-path propagation, padding, long end-to-end propagation delays, high data error rates, temporary losses of connectivity, and limited battery power. Acoustic communication has limited bandwidth due to long propagation delay and low data transfer rates. An underwater channel can be broken easily during transmission due to amplitude modulation and multipath occurrence. For this reason, it is difficult to apply the security mechanism used in terrestrial wireless network to UWASNs [1], [2].

---

[*] This work was supported by the IT R&D program of MKE/KEIT. [10041841, Development of Core Technologies for Growth Management of Migratory Fishes in Littoral Sea Agriculture].
[**] Corresponding author.

T. Xiao, L. Zhang, and M. Fei (Eds.): AsiaSim 2012, Part II, CCIS 324, pp. 160–168, 2012.

In UWASNs, sensed information must be processed and managed safely. Furthermore, secure transmission among nodes should be guaranteed. Therefore, security in UWASNs should be sufficiently strong to provide secure services and protect against attacks. The actual data transmitted from the upper layer is the payload. When considering the UWASN protocol stack, before the application layer sends data from the sub-layer, it needs to encrypt the payload. In this paper, we discuss UWASN security issues and analyze strengths and weaknesses of existing concepts by applying this mechanism.

The remainder of this paper is organized as follows. In Section 2, we consider underwater security field-related works. In Section 3, we examine the characteristics and structure of UWASNs. Section 4 analyzes UWASN security issues, and we find the most appropriate basic encryption algorithms for UWASN. In the last section, we conclude our paper and outline future works.

2   Related Works

Research on UWASN security continues to be in its nascent stages owing to various restrictions. However, the necessity of security technology for UWASN is growing rapidly. In this section, we describe ongoing research on UWASNs and security-related technologies.

In [3], the authors focused on UWASN security issues. They analyzed UWASN and its characteristics. The application environments of UWASN were studied, and the goals and challenges of UWASN security were investigated. The performance of wireless sensor networks (WSNs) and adhoc sensor networks (ASNs) was compared by the contributors. If nodes are damaged, or damage occurs in the network, nodes can be destroyed. Therefore, the node's security is remains essential. WSN and ASN cannot apply the security protocols developed for UWASN. Therefore, a security protocol for UWASN needs to be suitable for underwater environment. Based on the above studies, security threats are classified according to their potential harm to a UWASN. Corresponding countermeasures against those threats are taken into consideration.

In [4], the authors analyzed threats and attacks on UWASN security. Owing to the characteristics of UWASNs and underwater channels, UWASNs are vulnerable to malicious attacks. A layered security system has limits against a blended attack, and in order to overcome these limitations in a UWASN, the proposed security mechanism is necessary. Sensor nodes can be easily intercepted by an enemy and are at risk of information packet tampering. If the network applies traditional techniques such as cipher, message digest, or digital certificates, the message size is increased. To solve these problems of a cryptographic suite for UWASNs, [5] proposed an encryption method that avoids expansion of the message size and provides confidentiality, authentication, and key management. To avoid ciphertext size expansion, in the present study, a cipher text stealing (CTS) mode was used. A CTS mode is used in a block cipher, and the encryption mode is one-of-a-kind. The mode handles plaintext without limiting its length and generates cipher text with the same length as the plaintext. In addition, there is no padding, and message expansion does not occur. A CTS mode is the same size because it uses plaintext and ciphertext. In the present study, we selected a hash algorithm that operates regardless of the input message size and produces an encrypted message of the same size in addition to message authentication. Conversely, a hash algorithm with a long fixed length data is used to abbreviate the data. For example, the SHA-256 hash algorithm can convert 1500 bytes of input data to a 160-bit abbreviation.

In [2] and [3], the authors stated security issues and basic requirements, but encryption is not considered the foundation of security. However, a recently published paper [4] considers the encryption scheme as a proposed concept, and the UWASN project has proposed an encryption method that can be applied. In this paper, we determine appropriate cryptographic algorithms for basic UWASNs.

3   Overview of UWASN

UWASNs have many more restrictions than terrestrial sensor networks. Owing to these limitations, many problems occur when we apply terrestrial security mechanisms. Therefore, we must consider the characteristics of UWASNs in order to ensure security. The characteristics of sonar sensor networks are as follows.

3.1   Characteristics

1. Acoustic communication: The most important feature of UWASN is its use of acoustic signals instead of RF signals. Owing to the special underwater environment, RF signals are subject to severe attenuation and limited bandwidth. For this reason, an RF signal at a node's maximum transmission power is not able to spread more than 1 m.
2. Long propagation delay: Synchronization between nodes is difficult to establish, and the time taken for transmission between packets increases the probability of impulse owing to which underwater communication system will have reduced efficiency. Battery life is also an often-encountered problem.
3. Multi-pass, fading phenomenon: The effects of water make this problem worse.
4. Lower baud rate: While RF communication propagates at 3×10^8 m/s, sound propagates underwater at 1500 m/s, which is remarkably slow by comparison.

3.2   Cluster-Based Architecture

Figure 1 shows an underwater communication system (UCS). It consists of underwatersensor nodes, underwater syncnodes, underwater relay node, and a configured surface gateway. Underwatersensor nodescollect data in the underwater environmentandtransfer it tothe sync node. Then, the sync node merges received data from the cluster and transmits it to the surface gateway through the relay nodes. The collected data can then be transmitted to the base station by the surface gateway.

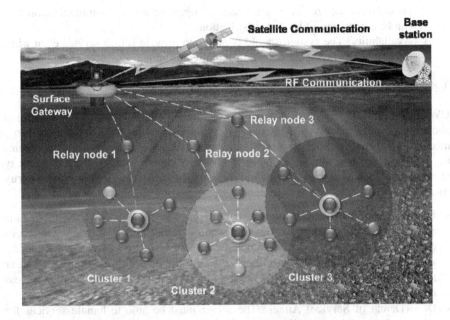

Fig. 1. Underwater Communication System

4   Security in UWASN

UWASNs have been used in various fields of interest in the marine environment with increasing need for security. Compared to the research in security for wireless sensor networks, UWASN security research is in its nascent stage. UWASNsare very vulnerable owing to restrictions and special circumstances compared to terrestrial sensor networks, because the system operates in a limited environment and data are stored in place for an extended time,creating a high risk of attack. Security mechanisms for an underwater environment are difficult to apply owing to the limited bandwidth. Therefore, for underwater security, appropriate security mechanisms and security requirements must be defined simultaneously [6].

In the Section 4, the basic security requirements and security issues of the security scheme for UWASNs are discussed.

4.1   Basic Requirements

The following are the three requirements to be fulfilled for basic UWASN security.

1) Confidentiality: Underwater sensor nodes communicate acoustically. If another entity collects the transmitted data, it can be easy to retrieve the original data. Therefore, the system must be protected from eavesdropping.

2) Authentication and Integrity: If an underwater sensor node does not require identification or message authentication, an attacker node can easily participate in communication inside the network. If an attack node collects

packet information and ID information from wiretapping, communication data can be compromised by data falsification.

3) Availability: The system should continue to provide robust service even when the network is being threatened by a malicious node.

4.2   Security Issues

UWASN security is weak due to network limitations such as acoustic communication and long propagation times. Moreover, it is impossible to adopt existing security mechanisms meant for wireless sensor networks. UWASN requires new technologies to build secure networks. However, UWASNscannot fulfill typical security requirements such as confidentiality and integrity. Next, we discuss UWASN security issues [7], [8].

- Data Encryption: After sensing data is collected through the UWASN, the data is encrypted using the next key. When the data is retransmitted, this key guarantees confidentiality and integrity. To implement security in underwater sensor nodes, they require basic security algorithms. Because the environment limits the sensor node's memory, power, etc., the encryption algorithm must be small, use less memory, and have a low processor load.

- DoS (Denial of Service) Attack: The server must be able to handle services for other nodes and prevent the system from being suspended or shut down when sensor nodes are lost in normal operations or by depletion of energy resources.

- Eavesdropping: Listening to information intercepted by a third person is called "tapping," and this type of attack is likely to occur by falsifying information. If authentication features are not in place for underwater nodes, the attacking node can easily participate in the network. In this case, the attacker sends packets containing node information, and data can be easily exposed. Utilizing this data, they can attack by falsifying the node's information. To prevent this, an authentication procedure and integrity verification capability iscritical.

- Message Authentication: In the case of encrypted data, third parties or by an attacker, the node cannot know the content of the data to be retransmitted over the network. We can authenticate the signature of the information source to verify the source of the information in the message.

4.3   Encryption Algorithm

The protocol stack of a UWASN is composed of an application layer, transport layer, network layer, MAC layer, and physical layer. If data is sent from an upper layer to a lower layer, the data needs a header added to the payload in each layer. Figure 2 shows the process of data encryption. The lowerlayer adds its header, in front of which another new security header may be added. The new security header contains several security parameters for the receiver that needs to retrieve data securely. After adding the headers, the entire message,New_Security_Header–Header–Data, is entered into a message-authenticated code algorithm such as AES-CBC-MAC with a shared secret key, and the output value message integrity code (MIC) is added at the end of the entire message. The value of the MIC ensures that the every single bit in the entire message including the shared key involved in this calculation is authentic.

Then, the receiver having the same shared key recalculates its own MIC value and compares it with that received. If the two MIC values are different, the receiver can discard the entire received message. After adding the MIC value (8-bit, 16-bit, 32-bit, 64-bit, etc.) at the end of the entire message, the encryption algorithm encrypts the data and the MIC.

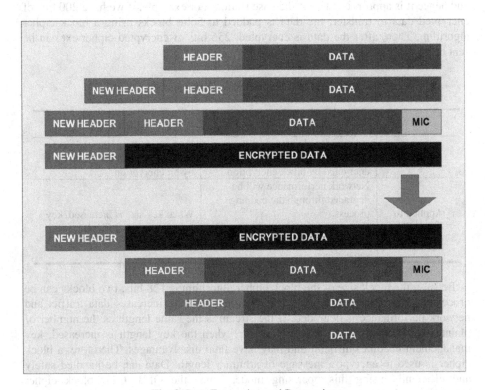

Fig. 2. Data Encryption and Decryption

Obviously, the encryption uses both the security header and the new header, but the new header is not encrypted. The receiver follows the process inversely to ensure that all the data is authentic and the entire message is originated from a known device.

The data could arrive as a justifiable object that the receiver cannot identify. In this case, the data can be guaranteed safely through the MIC. Additional MIC data can be generated and added to the message. However, in order to ensure stability, it is essential that at least the length of the MIC is used.

The next most important issue is applying an encryption algorithm. In this paper, we suggest that a transmitter and receiver use the same key for data encryption and decryption. Symmetric keys are divided into stream and block ciphers. However, for device or user authentication, control data authentication, sensing data authentication, confidentiality, and data availability for UWASNs, a symmetric key encryption algorithm is the only possible solution. Because the key size of a symmetric key algorithm is relatively smaller than an asymmetric key, a symmetric key-based encryption algorithm such as AES or ARIA is suitable for a lower-powered UWASN.

However, a symmetric key encryption algorithm used for encrypting plaintext from a cipher key that is also used for decryption has the advantage of speed and is suitable for an underwater communication environment.

In other words, when considering the structure shown in Figure 1, a UWASN can be managed through the base station rather than using a symmetric and public key, and hence it is appropriate to use the base station. For example, if we have 200 bits of encrypted data to transfer, the data is padded to 56bit blocks using a block cipher algorithm. Then, after the data is encrypted, 256 bits of encrypted ciphertext can be sent back.

Table 1. Symmetric cryptographic

	Block Cipher	Stream Cipher
Process	An array of plaintext is divided into blocks that are sequentially encrypted by block encryption	Each character in the plaintext stream is immediately encrypted by bit encryption.
Applied to UWASN	Network performance will be degraded through the padding process. Depending on the operating mode, stream ciphers could have the same effect.	When key size is increased, key management is difficult.

Because the block size of the block cipher algorithm is 128 bits, two blocks can be processed. When we perform block encryption, padding increases data traffic, and network performance is degraded. If the stream is the same length as the number of plaintext bits, it will be efficient. However, when the key length is increased, key management becomes difficult and may have fatal disadvantages. Therefore, a block cipher is used to encrypt a message of arbitrary length. Data can be handled safely and efficiently using this operating mode. Thus, the OFB, CTR block cipher algorithm in the form of a stream cipher is considered for data encryption because stream ciphers can give the same effect through those operating modes.

Table 2. Comparison of security requirements

	Stream Cipher	Block Cipher
Confidentiality	Y	Y
Integrity	N	Y
User/Device Authentication	N	Y
Message Authentication	N	Y

Table 2 compares the security requirements. All cryptographic algorithms guarantee confidentiality. A block cipher uses the proper operation mode, and MIC provides confidentiality and integrity of data. Stream cipher keys are used for processing because without a key, the entire system is vulnerable. In fact, it becomes vulnerable and can be cracked. However, if a block cipher with fixed input and fixed-length repetitive rounds is used, the system can perform safely and efficiently through the configured encryption.

A UWASN that uses a hash algorithm regardless of the size of the input produces a result of the same size. A hash algorithm is used to encrypt input message of arbitrary length, and other compression functions use a fixed length. However, a cryptographic hash function algorithm features existing one-way functions. This algorithm should not be used when the data size is reduced because it does not have the capability of decoding the data and is difficult to use while sending and receiving.

5   Conclusion

Interest in UWASNs is increasing, and related research studies are also in progress. However, as mentioned before, underwater environment is a special environment that has many restrictions. Considering this restriction, UWASN security research is still incomplete. If a UWASN doesn't not consider security requirements, data can be exposed or a malicious node can attack the system. A UWASN requires basic security mechanisms such as confidentiality, integrity, and authentication.

In this paper, we explored security study trends and the security issues of UWASNs. A suitable encryption algorithm for an aquatic environment was investigated. Considering an underwater protocol stack, when the application layer sends data from a sub-layer, sending an encrypted payload is simple and safe. However, when we apply security mechanisms to UWASNs, the amount of data increases. Therefore, we added a minimum amount of data and considered the mechanisms for underwater operation. UWASNs are typically used to monitor marine traffic and for military purposes. Therefore, the Cryptographic Module Validation Program (CMVP) algorithm with guaranteed stability should be used. A block cipher algorithm such as SEED or ARIR two might have advantages, and should be considered in future studies.

Acknowledgment. This work was supported by the IT R&D program of MKE/KEIT. [10041841, Development of Core Technologies for Growth Management of Migratory Fishes in Littoral Sea Agriculture].

References

1. Shin, S.Y., Namgung, J.I., Park, S.H.: SBMAC: Smart Blocking MAC mechanism forVariable UW-ASN (Underwater Acoustic Sensor Network) Environment. Sensors 10(1) (January 2010)
2. Yun, N.-Y., Kim, Y.-P., Muminov, S., Lee, J.-Y., Shin, S.-Y., Park, S.-H.: Sync MAC Protocol to control Underwater Vehicle basedon Underwater Acoustic Communication. In: Proc. of IEEE/IFIPInternational Conference on Embedded and Ubiquitous Computing, Melbourne, pp. 452–456 (2011)

3. Dong, Y., Liu, P.: Security consideration of Underwater Acoustic Networks. In: International Congress on Acoustics, ICA 2010 (2010)
4. Cong, Y., Yang, G., Wei, Z., Zhou, W.: Security in underwater Sensor network. In: International Conference on Communication and Mobile Computing (2010)
5. Dini, G., Lo Duca, A.: A Cryptographic Suite for Underwater Cooperative Applications. In: Computers and Communications (ISCC), pp. 870–875 (2011)
6. Perrig, A., Stankovic, J., Wagner, D.: Security in Wireless Sensor Networks. Communications of the ACM 47(6), 53–57 (2004)
7. Hu, F.: Security considerations in ad hoc sensor networks. Ad Hoc Networks 3(5), 69–89 (2005)
8. Domingo, M.C.: Securing underwater wireless communication networks. IEEE Wireless Communications (February 2011)

Towards a Biological More Plausible Artificial Neural Networks

Junaidi Bidin and Muhamad Kamal M. Amin

Graduate School of Electronic System Engineering,
Malaysia-Japan International Institute of Technology (MJIIT),
University Technology Malaysia Kuala Lumpur Campus, Kuala Lumpur, Malaysia
junaidi.bidin@gmail.com, m_kamal@ic.utm.my

Abstract. This paper presents a simulation of a biological more plausible neural network system. The system modeled a Spiking Neural Network for self-organized architecture. Recently, Spiking Neural Networks have been much considered in an attempt to achieve a more biologically realistic neural network which was coined as the third generation Artificial Neural Networks. Spiking neurons with delays to encode the information is suggested. Thus, each output node will produce a different timing which enables competitive learning. The suggested mechanism is designed and analyzed to perform self-organizing learning and preserve the inputs topology. The simulation results show that the model is feasible to perform a self-organized unsupervised learning. The mechanism is further assessed in real-world dataset for data clustering problem.

Keywords: Spiking Neural Network(SNN), Self-organized.

1 Introduction

Neural network is a key concept in the creation of machine learning. A neural network is a network of interconnecting elements called neurons which were first inspired by studies of the human brain. The advantages of neural networks over other possible solution are their ability to learn or trained. Many applications such as pattern recognition, classification and many more have used neural networks method. Despite this success, biological more inspired neural networks should be studied to realize the true potential of neural networks.

Recently, Spiking Neural Networks (SNN) has been much considered in attempt to achieve a more biologically inspired artificial neural network. The objective of the Spiking Neural Networks (SNN) as the name implies, tries to overcome this over simplification of the ANN system and emulate the pulse system to come out with a more biologically realistic neural system.

The motivation of implementing Spiking Neural Networks (SNN) is mainly because a single pulse or spike emitted by a neuron is able and sufficient to carry information [1], [3]. This has been clearly understood from the real biological neuron's point of view where our nervous system communicates through pulses. The pulse is also known as a "spike" to indicate its short and transient nature. Neurons are

T. Xiao, L. Zhang, and M. Fei (Eds.): AsiaSim 2012, Part II, CCIS 324, pp. 169–176, 2012.
© Springer-Verlag Berlin Heidelberg 2012

affected by incoming spikes and generate a spike when the membrane potential becomes larger than a threshold.

Conventional ANNs, both digital and analog networks, however, ignore this pulsing system and simply assume a set of real or binary numbers to represent its network communication and computation. Although the pulse system is a very simple mathematical model, it is very difficult to apply into practical computing and signal processing applications, since the system requires to be encoded temporally. Despite this, the pulse dynamics of the neurons has been studied extensively in recent years. These studies have led to many theoretical analyses and model development as well as exploring its computational capability to the common ANN application and hardware implementation.

This basic computation yet very important feature of the real neurons may guide direction to investigate a more biological plausible neural network. For this reason, we extend the basic SNN to a more advanced learning in neural networks i.e. unsupervised learning which is more appropriate model for some aspects of biological learning (e.g. somatotopic map [2]).

The organization of the paper is as follows. Section 2 describes the self-organized network architecture. Section 3 and 4 provide the experimental results and discussion.

2   Self-Organized SNN Architecture

There exist various kinds of spiking neuron models. The neuron model presented here is based on the Spike Response Model introduced by Gerstner [1]. This model is further structured to form a self-organized SNN architecture. The network architecture is illustrated in Fig. 1. The diagram illustrates the basic architecture of self-organized SNN. The presynaptic neurons are each of them connected to all the postsynaptic neurons (the output layer). In this diagram the inputs are n dimensional elements and the output has 5x5 layer structure. Every time a set of n dimensional element input is presented to the network, a spike potential with different delays travel across each connection. The Self-Organized SNN architecture can be categorized into three main processes i.e. initialization, delay adjustment and self-organization.

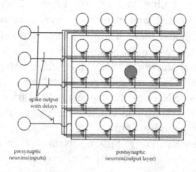

Fig. 1. A basic architecture of 5x5 self-organized SNN

2.1   Initialization

In this stage, the presynaptic neurons (as illustrated in Fig.1) are preprocessed before the learning phase. Initial random values of inputs(x) are set and transform into temporal inputs(S). The pre-processing of any information, before going into the network is encoded by the time difference between the inputs (x) and some reference point (t_r) .Assumption is made that each neuron is firing only once i.e. one spike per neuron, each neuron of the input layers hold the value of each inputs; dependent on the dimension of the inputs.

$$(S) = (t_r) - (x) \tag{1}$$

Having temporally transformed the inputs, a random set of delay values are set to each input-output connection which results in each connection now has a different value of delay.

Another important point in the initialization process of the SNN is the response function (ε). There exist various response functions in the past literature [7].This response function which represent the postsynaptic potentials (PSP) are described in different ways but regardless of the model used, the response function is meant to represent the a spike form. In this model we used the following equation.

$$\varepsilon = \frac{t}{t_{peak}} \exp\left(1 - \left(\frac{t}{t_{peak}}\right)\right) \tag{2}$$

2.2   Delay Adjustment

The connection strength of the input-output strength can be determined by delays instead of weights. The delay is given by the difference between the presynaptic neuron firing time and the time the postsynaptic potential starts rising. In this manner, each input neuron that produced temporal input values will have delays value added. Thus an equation can be written as follows:

$$\varepsilon(t - t_i^f - delay) \tag{3}$$

and since in Self Organized SNN architecture, a single network connect between the input neuron and output neuron layer, the postsynaptic potential (PSP) sum at the output layer can be written in the following form.

$$PSP = \sum_{n=1} \varepsilon(S_n - delay_n) \tag{4}$$

Note that the time interval $(t - t_i^f)$ in (eq. (3)) is replaced with *temporal input* (S) since the data input that is coded temporally is now the presynaptic firing spike that travels to its postsynaptic output.

The delays play very important roles in the computation of the network, because the entire memory of the proposed unsupervised SNN is stored inside the delayed connections between the input and output layer. These delays are adjusted in each step or epoch. An epoch occurs when training data is presented to the network and the delays are adjusted based on the results of this item of training data. The adjustments to the delays should produce a network that will yield more favorable results the next time the same training data is presented. Epochs continue as more and more data is presented to the network and the delays are adjusted.

Eventually, the return on these delay adjustments will decrease to the point that it is no longer valuable to continue with this particular set of delays. When this happens the entire delay matrix is reset to new random values. This forms a new cycle. The final delay matrix to be used will be the best delay matrix determined from each of the cycles.

2.3   Self-Organization

The Self-Organized SNN organizes its neurons into an input network layer and an output network layer. Each neuron in the input layer is connected to each neuron in the output layer. The two-dimensional output layers act as a map where each neuron is positioned. For this winning measurement we use the shortest Euclidean distance $\|temporal\ inputs - delays\|$ between the input and the competing neurons.

The winning neuron is the one whose delay vector is closer to the input vector. This winning node in the winner take all contest then has its delays modified to make them more like the actual values input. At time t+1, another pattern is presented. It is either similar to the previous inputs, in which case the delays of the winning node are adjusted still more, or it is a new pattern, which activates different neurons and results in a different set of delays being modified.

At the same time, the neurons close to the winner get their delays modified greatly in the direction of the input neurons' values. Neurons far from the winner get their delays modified very little. This computation can be done by updating the delays of the winning neurons and its neighborhood. The equation can be written as follows:

$$\Delta delay = \alpha h(i,i^*)((S) - delay) \tag{5}$$

$$h(i,i^*) = \exp\left(-\frac{|r_i - r_{i^*}|^2}{2\sigma^2}\right) \tag{6}$$

In this work, the common Gaussian neighborhood kernel $h(i,i^*)$ is used. This function is basically a bell curve centered at the winning neuron i^*. The r_i and r_{i^*} are the positions of neuron i and i^* which measure the topographic distance between node i and i^*. As the training progresses, the σ which is the width of the neighborhood kernel should gradually decrease to zero or approaching zero.

During learning, the nodes that are topographically close together up to a certain distance will activate each other to learn from the same input. Hence, the topology of the output map preserves the information gathered from all the input patterns. The topological ordering property is a direct consequence of the delay update equation that forces the delay vector of the winning neuron to move toward the input vector. The delay updates also move the delay vectors of the closest neurons along with the winning neuron. Together these caused the whole output space to become appropriately ordered.

As a conclusion, the Self Organized SNN process can be briefly described as a process where for each sample input vector, the winner neuron and its neighbors are changed closer to the sample in the input space. In other words the network is trained through number of iteration and various processes to learn the input samples.

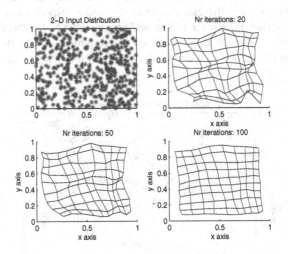

Fig. 2. The top left diagram shows a two-dimensional input vectors distributed randomly. Rest of the diagrams show the output of self-organized spiking neurons after 20, 50 and 100 iterations.

Fig. 2 displays a simulation result of the above mentioned algorithm. In this case the inputs are two-dimensional which is sequentially feed and applied to the network. Each input is assigned with an arbitrarily small value of delay. The output activation is calculated at each run by measuring the difference of the inputs and the delays value. Through this process, the node that fired the quickest spike is chosen as the winner. These processes continue to iterate which in this case 100 iterations were chosen. As we can see from the diagram, at various iteration the network gradually learn to map the inputs.

3 Experimental Results

The proposed Self-Organized SNN was further assessed with real-world dataset for data clustering. The objective was to analyze the effectiveness of the architecture on data analysis exploration. The Glass Identification dataset from UCI Repository [7] was used for the experiment.

This data is the study of classification of types of glass which was motivated by criminological investigation. The objective of the investigation is to use the glass left at the scene of the crime as evidence, therefore the type of glass has to be correctly identified. The Glass Identification datasets class distribution has 214 instances. This dataset is classified into two main classes: window glass and non-window glass, with 7 types of glasses collected.

The experiment is carried out using the MATLAB technical computing language and its built-in Neural Network Toolbox for Self Organizing Maps. However, certain parameters of the original Toolbox have to be modified in order to accommodate the Spiking Neural Networks parameters. Some of the parameters that need to be included in the toolbox are the calculation of the spike response function (eq. (**2**)). Another main important parameter in the Self Organized SNN is the delay function. Some modification was made in the distance programming file so that the distance computation is based on the spike delay. The value for the delay is setup between the range of [0, 1].

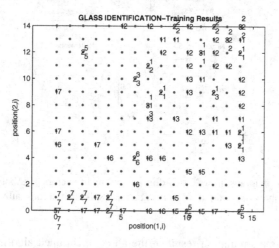

(a) Training results

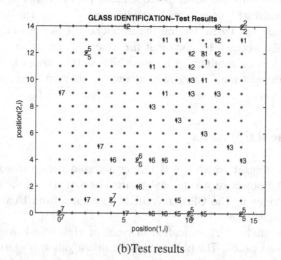

(b)Test results

Fig. 3. Training and Test results with 1000 epochs

Fig.3 shows the training and testing result of this data. The simulation was run for 1000 epochs. The figure shows the clusters results of the Glass dataset. It clearly classified the windows (legend no. 1, 2, 3) cluster and non-windows (legend no. 5, 6, 7) cluster classes. It also shows the sub- clusters of the 7 types of glasses. The sub-clusters of the 7 type's glasses, however, did not cluster to each of its class attribute.

Fig. 4 shows an increased training and testing result of this data. The training cycle was increased to 10000 epochs. The objective was to see if the sub-cluster of the 7 type's glasses can produce better results. Unfortunately, the sub- clusters did not produce better results, although the non-windows and windows classification clustered almost perfectly.

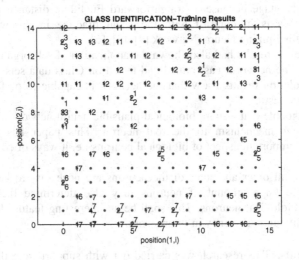

(a) Training results

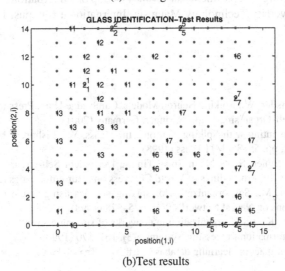

(b)Test results

Fig. 4. Training and Test results with 10000 epochs

4   Discussion and Conclusions

The experimental results showed that Spiking Neural Networks is able to be implemented in self-organized learning. Few publications have been reported relating to the implementation of Spiking Neural Network in self-organization networks [4], [5], [6]. However, the research on Self-Organizing Spiking Neural Network is still an open discussion. Researchers reported different models with different approaches.

The Self-Organized SNN which was presented in this paper, contribute another perspective of the Spiking Neural Networks unsupervised learning. The learning computes the delay of the input-output neurons for its competitive process. This method is an advantage because a straightforward Euclidian distance measurement can be used. This is in contrast with the usual practice in the weighted sum computation of the Spiking Neural Network [4], [5], [6].

The experimental results had also shown the application of self-organized SNN on data clustering. The network was trained and tested on Glass data sets. The training and testing simulation results show that the network is capable to perform to some extend the desired results.

It is understandable that a more biological plausible neural network should ideally produce a similar mechanism to the real neuron. This paper has analyze and investigated one important aspect of biological neurons i.e. it ways of communication through pulses.

However, several other attributes of the neurons are necessary to be considered. For example, the huge amount of neurons may also determine the intelligence computation of biological neurons. This shall be an interesting feature for extending the SNN capability and efficiency in future work.

Acknowledgments. This research was carried out with support from the Electronic System Engineering Department at Malaysia-Japan International Institute of Technology, University Technology Malaysia, International Campus, Kuala Lumpur, Malaysia.

References

1. Gerstner, W., Kistler, W.: Spiking Neuron Models. Cambridge Univ. Press (2002)
2. Kohonen, T.: Self-Organising Maps. Springer, Germany (2001)
3. Maass, W.: Computing with Spiking Neurons. In: Maass, W., Bishop, C.M. (eds.) Pulsed Neural Network, pp. 55–85. MIT Press (1998)
4. Panchev, C., Wermter, S.: Hebbian Spike-Timing Dependent Self-Organization in Pulsed Neural Networks. In: Proceedings of World Congress on Neuroinformatics (2001)
5. Ruf, B., Schmitt, M.: Self-organization of spiking neurons using action potential timing. IEEE Transactions on Neural Networks 9(3), 575–578 (1998)
6. Sala, D.M., Cios, K.J.: Self-organization in networks of spiking neurons. Australian Journal of Intelligent Information Processing Systems 5(3), 161–170 (1998)
7. UCI repository of machine learning databases, http://archive.ics.uci.edu/ml

Modeling and Simulation Methodology
of Multifield Coupling for Hypersonic Vehicle

Ping Ma, Tao Chao, and Ming Yang[*]

Control and Simulation Center, Harbin Institute of Technology
150080 Harbin, China
{pingma,chaotao,myang}@hit.edu.cn

Abstract. Multifield coupling among gas flow, heat transfer, structure deformation and flight control is an important phenomenon for hypersonic vehicle. The coupling mechanism can be simplified according to simulation purpose. Typical simulation tests for different phases of hypersonic vehicle guidance, navigation and control (GNC) system design process are presented and the coupling boundaries are also given. Multifield coupling simulation time advancement scheme is proposed and calculation method for each field is presented. Multifield coupling simulation platform design method methodology is presented and an integrated numerical simulation platform prototype, consisting of geometry configuration design, mesh grid generation, trajectory optimization, GNC, aero-thermo-elastic coupling calculation, simulation results visualization and analysis software is designed. The functions of CSC-MPCSim are demonstrated through modeling and simulation of a flight vehicle with a configuration similar to X-43 hypersonic flight vehicle designed by NASA of the USA.

Keywords: Modeling, Simulation, Hypersonic Vehicle, Multifield coupling.

1   Introduction

It is realized that during the high speed flight in the atmosphere, flight vehicle suffers tight coupling among multiple physics field, such as gas flow, heat transfer, structure deformation and flight control [1]. Numerical simulation is a useful way to explore the multifield coupling mechanism of hypersonic vehicles.

Previous researches about multifield coupling for hypersonic vehicle focus on three aspects. The first aspect focuses on numerical analyses of the coupling mechanism among gas flow, heat transfer and structure deformation. McNamara [2] studied the aeroelastic behavior of a low aspect ratio three-dimensional wing using third order piston theory. The second aspect focus on the analyses of the effects to flight control of hypersonic aerothermoelasticity and control oriented aerothermoelastic modeling. Falkiewicz [3] modeled the aerothermoelastic characteristics of aerodynamic fins of hypersonic vehicle in order to evaluate the effect of structure deformation to flight

---

[*] Corresponding author.

T. Xiao, L. Zhang, and M. Fei (Eds.): AsiaSim 2012, Part II, CCIS 324, pp. 177–184, 2012.
© Springer-Verlag Berlin Heidelberg 2012

control system. The third aspect is generic multifield or multiphysics simulation software development. M4 Engineering Corporation developed ASTEP, which consists of geometry module used to modeling structure and generate mesh grid, trajectory module to simulate trajectory motion, trim module used to guide flight vehicle following the reference vehicle, aero-propulsion module used to simulate aerodynamic force and prolusion force, heat module used to simulate temperature field and structure module used to simulate structure characteristics [4]. Advanced Dynamics is also developing an Integrated Variable-Fidelity Tool Set for Modeling and Simulation of multifield coupling [5]. University of Colorado, Zona Technology Inc. and University of Maryland are doing some studies using an integrated Aero-Servo-Thermo-Propulsion-Elasticity method [6].

This paper focuses on modeling and simulation method of hypersonic vehicle multifield coupling among aerodynamics, heat, structure and GNC system (called control for short), especially control oriented aerothermoelastic modeling, aerothermoelastic effects on control modeling and integrated modeling and simulation platform design. The rest of the paper is organized as follows. Section 2 introduces multifield coupling of hypersonic vehicles briefly, including classification of the coupling, two different ways to simulate the coupling and presents three typical coupling simulation tests for GNC system design process. Section 3 describes multifield coupling model, and the coupling boundaries among these physics field. Section 4 presents time advancement scheme in multifield coupling simulation and model solving method for each physics field. Section 5 provides a simulation platform design example and conclusions are given in section 6.

2   Overview of Multifield Coupling

Hypersonic flight vehicle multifield coupling is distinguished by the interaction of multiple physics field, especially the followings: interaction between gas flow and heat transfer (aero-thermo coupling), interaction between gas flow and structure deformation (aero-elastic coupling), interaction between heat transfer and structure deformation (thermo-elastic coupling), interaction between gas flow and flight control (aero-control coupling) and interaction between structure deformation and flight control (structure-control coupling). Temperature field, structure field and flow field can be described as an integrated field (called aero-thermo-elastic field), which leads us to fig. 2. From fig. 2, it can be concluded that aero-thermo-elastic field computation does not evolve control field, and the coupling between aero-thermo-elastic field and control field can be achieved through information exchanges after the computation of each field, so when we develop a multifield coupling simulation platform these two fields can be developed separately.

3   Coupling Multifield Simulation Model

This section describes the coupling boundaries of multifield coupling which provides enough information for coupling simulation method research, while detail descriptions of the model of each field are omitted, which interested readers are referred to reference [7~9].

Aero-elastic coupling is boundary coupling, and its coupling boundary is computation mesh grid interfaces of these two fields overlap, and stress of fluid and solid substances on coupling interface satisfies

$$\vec{r}_s(\tau) = \vec{r}_f(\tau) \tag{1}$$

$$N(r_s, \tau) = -N(r_f, \tau) \tag{2}$$

where, $\vec{r}_s$ is solid substance position vector on coupling interface, $\vec{r}_f$ is fluid substance position vector on coupling interface and N is the stress.

Thermo-elastic coupling is domain coupling, and the solving domain of temperature field and structure field overlap. So the equations of structure fields consists of temperature, and the equations of temperature fields consists of deformation work, as described in the following

$$\rho c \frac{\partial T}{\partial t} = \nabla \cdot (\nabla k T) - T_0 \beta \frac{\partial e}{\partial t} - \nabla \cdot q + \varphi \tag{3}$$

$$(\lambda + G)\nabla\theta + G\nabla^2 u_n + F_n - \frac{\alpha_0 E}{1 - 2\nu}\frac{\partial T}{\partial y^n} = \rho \frac{\partial^2 u_n}{\partial t^2} \tag{4}$$

$$\theta = \frac{\partial u}{\partial x} + \frac{\partial v}{\partial y} + \frac{\partial w}{\partial z} \tag{5}$$

$$e = \frac{1}{3\lambda + 2G}\Theta + 3\alpha_0 \Delta T \tag{6}$$

$$\beta = (3\lambda_0 + 2G)\alpha_0 \tag{7}$$

$$T(x, y, z)|\Gamma_1 = T(x, y, z) \tag{8}$$

$$-\lambda \left(\frac{\partial T}{\partial n}\right)_w |\Gamma_2 = q \tag{9}$$

$$-\lambda \left(\frac{\partial T}{\partial n}\right)_w |\Gamma_3 = h(T - T_f) \tag{10}$$

where, ρ is density, c is specific heat capacity, k is thermal-conductivity coefficient, q is heat flux density, F is volume force, u is displacement, α_0 linear expansion coefficient of the material, ν is Poisson ratio, T_0 is thermo deformation reference temperature, λ_0 and G are lame constant, $\Theta = \sigma_x + \sigma_y + \sigma_z$, $\sigma_x, \sigma_y, \sigma_z$ is positive strain in x , y, z direction, φ is heat source in unit volume, k, c, ρ, λ, G is the function of temperature, h is heat convection coefficient, T_f is the flow temperature, $\Gamma_1, \Gamma_2, \Gamma_3$ is the boundary of temperature field computation domains.

Aero-thermo coupling is boundary coupling. When radiation is omitted, the coupling boundary is

$$T_f = T_s, \quad q_f = q_s \tag{11}$$

where, q_s is the heat flux density of heat transfer on the coupling boundary; q_f is the heat flux density of heat convection on the coupling boundary.

When radiation is not omitted and the surface of the flight vehicle is an opaque interface, the coupling boundary is

$$T_f = T_s, \quad q_f + q_r = q_s \tag{12}$$

where, q_s is the heat flux density of heat convection and radiation on the coupling boundary.

Aero-control coupling is boundary coupling, for aerodynamic deflections cause the changing of the aerodynamic forces and moments acting on the vehicle, i.e.

$$F = F(\delta_\varphi, \delta_\psi, \delta_\gamma, x) \tag{13}$$

$$x = [h, V, \varphi, \psi, \gamma]^T \tag{14}$$

where, x is flight states, F is aerodynamic forces and moments, h is height, V is the velocity, $\delta_\varphi, \delta_\psi, \delta_\gamma$ is elevator, rudder and aileron deflection respectively, φ is pitching angle, ψ is yawing angle and γ is rolling angle.

From structure mechanics, flexible vibrating can be described as

$$y(x,t) = \sum_1^n q_{x1yi}(t) W_{x1yi}(x) \qquad i = 1, 2, \cdots, n \tag{15}$$

Where, $W_{x1yi}(x)$ is the i order vibrating shape function of position x and $q_{x1yi}(t)$ is the general coordinates of i order vibrating shape function.

Assume that attitudes and rates of angle measuring devices are located at the center of mass of the flight vehicle. Due to flexible vibrating, the measured values of attitudes are the sum of the attitudes of equivalent rigid body and increments caused by vibrating, i.e.

$$\varphi_s = \varphi + \sum_1^n q_{x1yi}(t) W'_{x1yi}(X_{\varphi s}) \tag{16}$$

Where, $X_{\varphi s}$ is the location of attitude sensor along axis $o_1 x_1$; φ_s is the measured value of attitude; φ is the attitude of equivalent rigid body; $W'_{x1yi}(X_{\varphi s})$ is the derivative of ith order vibrating shape function with respect to $X_{\varphi s}$.

Similarly, the measured value of rate of angle is the sum of equivalent rigid body rate of angle and increment cause by vibrating, i.e.

$$\dot{\varphi}_{gs} = \dot{\varphi} + \sum_{1}^{n} q'_{x1yi}(t) W'_{x1yi}(X_{\varphi gs}) \tag{17}$$

Where, $X_{\varphi gs}$ is the location of rate of angle sensor along axis $o_1 x_1$; $\dot{\varphi}_{gs}$ is the measured value of rate of angle; $\dot{\varphi}$ is the rate of angle of equivalent rigid body; $q'_{x1yi}(t)$ is the derivative of general coordinates of ith order vibrating shape function with respect to time; $W'_{x1yi}(X_{\varphi gs})$ is the derivative of ith order vibrating shape function with respect to $X_{\varphi gs}$.

4   Multifield Simulation Method

Multifield simulation time advancement scheme is as the following.

STEP 1: Initialize flight height, Mach, fin deflections, velocity, mass, simulation step etc. and set simulation time t=0;

STEP 2: Read aerodynamic forces and moments and structure deformation information provided by aero-thermo-elastic field, the location of sensor;

STEP 3: Calculate position, velocity, attitudes, and rates of angle measure by sensor according to sensor model;

STEP 4: Calculate guidance law commands according to sensor measured values and reference trajectory values and transit them to control law module;

STEP 5: Calculate control law commands according to sensor measured values and guidance law commands, and transit them to actuators;

STEP 6: Calculate aerodynamic fins deflection angles according to control law commands and actuator model;

STEP 7: Integrate flight motion equations using numerical integration method, such as Runge-Kutta method;

STEP 8: Output flight position, velocity, attitudes, rates of angle, and fin deflections for the next time period.

5   Multifield Coupling Simulation Platform Design Example

We developed a multifield coupling simulation platform prototype using the presented design method described previously. It consists of data saving and human-machine interactive interface functions in addition to those functions discussed previously. Data saving and human-machine interactive interface software are developed in C++ language, and all the other software are integrated with the human-machine interactive interface, as shown in fig. 1.

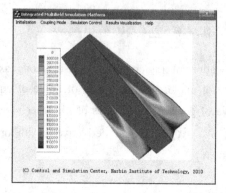

Fig. 1. Human-machine interactive interface of multifield simulation platform prototype

A typical flight vehicle with a configuration like the X-43 of NASA of the USA is used to give an example of multifield coupling simulation. Two types of tests with aero-control coupling and aero-elastic-control coupling are performed. The reference trajectories for these two tests are the same, which are generated by trajectory optimization software, CSC-TO, based on CFD computation.

The flight control laws for the two tests are the same, which are designed using classical Proportional-Integrative-Derivative (PID) control method. The flow field, temperature field and structure field of the flight vehicle with Mach 10 as the entrance condition is shown in fig.2. The aerodynamic pressure on the surface of the flight vehicle is 37.9Pa~1.95e6Pa, and the pressure on the back is much lower than that of the belly. The temperature distribution is shown in fig.3, it is obvious that the nose of the flight vehicle has the highest temperature, and because there is a large temperature gradient, the deformation caused by heat transfer is also large, which in the nose region can be as large as 4mm.

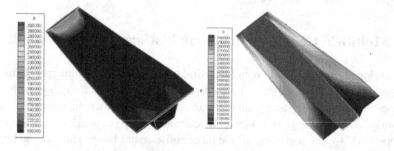

Fig. 2. Surface pressure of the flight vehicle at Mach=10

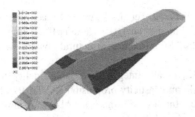

Fig. 3. Temperature distribution of flight vehicle at Mach=10

6   Conclusions

The way to simulate multifield coupling in this paper is to analyze coupling boundaries of the fields, build simulation model using existing sophisticated modeling tool in each physics field and use integrated platform to integrate these simulation model. Trajectory optimization, control field computation, aero-thermo-elastic field, simulation results visualization software are integrated into a single multifield coupling simulation platform, in which, optimization trajectory is used to get optimal reference trajectory, control field computation software is used to calculate aerodynamic fin deflections and other flight parameters, aero-thermo-elastic coupling software is used to simulate the coupling among flow field, temperature field and structure field, and the simulation results are visualized through figures of temperature distribution, stress distribution, flight trajectory etc.. The example of a flight vehicle with a configuration like that of X-43 shows that the platform is capable of multifield coupling simulation, and the proposed modeling and simulation method for multifield coupling is an effective way to explore the coupling mechanism of flow field, temperature field, structure field and control field.

It is worth noting that the reliability of the simulation results needs to be checked through wind tunnel test or other physics tests and the verification, validation and accreditation of the simulation platform prototype is a further research direction.

Acknowledgments. This work is supported by the Innovative Team Program of the National Natural Science Foundation of China under Grant No. 61021002.

References

1. Bertin, J.J., Russell, M., Cummings, M.: Fifty years of hypersonics: where we've been, where we're going. Progress in Aerospace Sciences 39, 511–536 (2003)
2. McNamara, J.J., Friedmann, P.P., Powell, K.G.: Aeroelastic and aerothermoelastic vehicle behavior in hypersonic flow. In: Proceedings of AIAA 13th International Space Planes and Hypersonic Systems and Technologies
3. Falkiewicz, N.J., Cesnik, C.E.: Thermoelastic formulation of a hypersonic vehicle control surface for control-oriented simulation. In: Proceedings of the 2009 AIAA Guidance, Navigation and Control Conference, Chicago, Illinois, USA (2009)

4. Roughen, K., Baker, M., Seber, G., et al.: A system for aerothermodynamic, servo, thermal, elastic, propulsive coupled analysis (ASTEP). In: Proceedings of 47th AIAA/ASME/ASCE/AHS/ASC Structure, Structural Dynamics, and Materials Conference, Rhode Island, USA

5. Hu, R., Xue, L., Qu, K., et al.: Integrated variable-fidelity tool set for modeling and simulation of aeroservothermoelasticity-propulsion (ASTE-P) of aerospace vehicles from subsonic to hypersonic. In: Proceedings of AIAA Atmospheric Flight Mechanics Conference, Chicago, Illinois, USA

6. Starkey, R.P., Liu, D.D., Chen, P.C., et al.: Integrated aero-servo-thermo-propulsion-elasticity (ASTPE) method for hypersonic scramjet vehicle design/analysis. In: Proceedings of 48th AIAA Aerospace Sciences Meeting including the New Horizons Forum and Aerospace Exposition, Orlando, Florida, USA (2010)

7. Anderson, J.: Fundamentals of Aerodynamics, 3rd edn. McGraw-Hill, Inc. (2001)

8. Chandrupatla, T., Belegundu, A.: Introduction to Finite Elements in Engineering, 3rd edn. Prentice-Hall, Inc. (2002)

9. Siegel, R., Howell, J.: Thermal Radiation Heat Transfer. Taylor and Francis, New York (2002)

Research on Target Electro-optical Tracking Based Fuzzy Disturbance Observer Controller

Ying Liu[1], Zhenghua Liu[2], and Le Chang[2]

[1] Beijing Changan Auto Engineering Research Co. Ltd., Beijing, China
[2] School of Automation Science & Electrical Engineering, Beihang University, Beijing, China

Abstract. The compound axis control technique is a quick and effective approach to improve the accuracy of high precision target tracking systems. However, traditional disturbance observer controller can not inhibit all-domain noises and can not achieve ideal performance. The robust control method based on fuzzy disturbance observer(FDO) is introduced in this paper, and the method is applied to the electro-optical tracking system together with the Kalman Filter. Compared to the traditional method, the method based on FDOB can inhibit high-frequency noise and compensate low-frequency interference better finally.

Keywords: compound-axis system, servo system, fuzzy disturbance observer, Kalman filter.

1   Introduction

The compound axis control technique is an effective means to improve the accuracy and bandwidth of high precision electro-optical tracking systems, so that it is broadly used in the field of aerospace, aeronautics, astronomy and military engineering. A compound axis system consists of two subsystems, so-called main system and subsystem separately. The subsystems can be controlled separately. The main system works in a large scope with narrow bandwidth and low accuracy. On the other hand, the subsystem works in a small scope, with a broad bandwidth, fast response, and high precision. The superposition of two subsystems can achieve high precision tracking within a wide range [1].

The idea of robust DOB approach proposed by Japanese scholar K. Ohnishi in 1987, appears in the paper [2-3], which have been applied into many angular tracking systems before. However, this traditional DOB controller has some shortcomings such as lacking in restrictions of high-domain frequency noise. In 2002, a paper of "A Fuzzy Disturbance Observer and Its Application", written by Euntai Kim, describes this FDO method in detail [4]. The novel FDO algorithm, not only restricts the low-domain frequency noise, for instance, system frictions, but also well fits the high-domain frequency noise and solves the high frequency disturbances [5]. Lately, FDO is studied and applied into some industrial servo system step by step by some scholars.

The traditional DOB controller is difficult to further improve the dynamic performance of low frequencies and suppress the interference, because of the limitation of this method itself. Therefore, the combination of the FDO robust controller and

T. Xiao, L. Zhang, and M. Fei (Eds.): AsiaSim 2012, Part II, CCIS 324, pp. 185–193, 2012.
© Springer-Verlag Berlin Heidelberg 2012

Kalman filter technique is applied in the compound-axis optical tracking platform valuably.This paper is organized as follows. The theory and models of compound axis systems are introduced in Section 2, the robust control method based on fuzzy disturbance observer is described in Section 3, and Section 4 demonstrates the effectiveness of the method finally.

2   Compound Axis Control Systems

A typical compound axis control system with two detectors is shown in Figure 1, where $A_1(s)$ and $A_2(s)$ represent the transfer functions of the two subsystems separately, $G_1(s)$ and $G_2(s)$ describe the controlled object of two subsystems, and R and Y stand for the reference input and output.

The basic principal of the compound axis control is to divide the system into two parts, the main system and the subsystem. The main system undertakes the task of coarse regulation, and the subsystem compensates the error of main system at the basis of main system. The final result of output is the superposition of the main and subsystem. This method compensates the precision requirement which cannot achieved by single axis control, relatively easy to be applied in the electro-optical tracking systems [5].

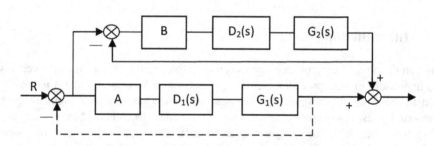

Fig. 1. Theoretical diagram of Compound-axis system

A typical high-precision servo motion control system usually includes feed-forward section, closed-loop control section, and friction compensation section. The advantage of the method based on the combination of feed-forward and feedback is that, tracking performance of the system can be considered separately with the stability. The feed-forward control is used to realize the tracking performance without affecting the stability, while the closed-loop control ensures the system stability and robustness against external interferences and parameter vibrations. For a mechanic servo system directly driven by motors, friction is the most important part of torque disturbance sources. The design of friction compensator is essential to improve the system's tracking ability. Generally, the model based feed-forward method is used to compensate frictions, because friction disturbances is similar to step disturbances, which can be inhibited by introducing equivalent compensation before the friction torque affects the system adversely [3-5].

3   Structure and Theory of Improved FDO

3.1   Fuzzy System Description

Basic fuzzy logic system consists of four parts: fuzzy rule, fuzzy Inference machine, fuzzification and defuzzification. By using the rule of IF-THEN, Fuzzy Inference machine can acquire that the input variables $x = (x_1, x_2, ..., x_n)^T \in R^n$ can map the output variables $y \in R$, where, the Number I fuzzy rule is described as:

R^i : If x_1 is A_1^i and ... and x_n is A_n^i, then y is y^i.

Where, A_1^i, ..., A_n^i and y^i are defined as fuzzy set of the domain of R. By using weighted average method, thereby the output of fuzzy system can be described as

$$y(x) = \frac{\sum_{i=1}^{r} y^i \left(\prod_{j=1}^{n} \mu_{A_j^i}(x_j) \right)}{\sum_{i=1}^{r} \left(\prod_{j=1}^{n} \mu_{A_j^i}(x_j) \right)} = \hat{\theta}^T \xi(x) \tag{1}$$

Where, let r be numbers of fuzzy rules, $\hat{\theta}^T = (y^1, y^2, ..., y^r)$ is the adjusted

parameter variables, $\xi(x) = \frac{\prod_{j=1}^{n} \mu_{A_j^i}(x_j)}{\sum_{i=1}^{r} (\prod_{j=1}^{n} \mu_{A_j^i}(x_j))}$ is defined as fuzzy basis function.

Given by the following n-phase nonlinear control system

$$\dot{x}_1 = x_2$$
$$\vdots \tag{2}$$
$$\dot{x}_{n-1} = x_n$$

$$\dot{x}_n = [\alpha(x) + \Delta\alpha(x)] + [\beta(x) + \Delta\beta(x)]u + d$$

Where u is the system input, $x = (x_1, x_2, \cdots, x_n)^T$ is the observable state of the control system, $\alpha(\bullet)$ and $\beta(\bullet)$ can be described as defined nominal functions. $\Delta\alpha(\bullet)$ and $\Delta\beta(\bullet)$ are described as accordingly uncertainties, d is symbol for exterior disturbance.

Let equation(2) redefine as follows

$$\dot{x}_n = \alpha(x) + \beta(x)u + \Delta\alpha(x) + \Delta\beta(x)u + d$$
$$= \alpha(x) + \beta(x)u + \Omega_x(x, u) \tag{3}$$

Where $\Omega_x(x, u)$ contains self-errors of system model and exterior disturbances, we need solve the following problem: how to design a fuzzy control system $\hat{\Omega}_x(x, u)$, which can be approached the actual disturbances and realize the aims to observe, finally can be used for compensating for overall disturbances.

3.2   Design of FDO Controller

Assumptions 1: Suppose x belongs to the compact set M_x, the ideal parameter vector θ^* is defined as

$$\theta^* = \arg \min_{\theta \in M_\theta} \left[\sup_{x \in M_X} | \Omega_x(x) - \hat{\Omega}_x(x | \hat{\theta}) | \right] \tag{4}$$

Still more, suppose parameter vector θ^* lies in the convex space,

$$M_\theta = \{ \theta \mid \|\theta\| \le m_\theta \} \tag{5}$$

Where m_θ is the design parameter.

Considering the equation(3) including the nonlinear system, if we need design the FDO controller $\hat{\Omega}_x(x, u | \hat{\theta})$ to observe the uncertain disturbance, a suitable adjusting method can be supplied for adjusting the parameter $\hat{\theta}$.

Theorem 1: considering the following dynamic system

$$\dot{\mu} = -\sigma \mu + p(x, u, \hat{\theta}) \tag{6}$$

where,

$$p(x, u, \hat{\theta}) = \sigma x_n + \alpha(x) + \beta(x) u + \hat{\Omega}_x(x, u | \hat{\theta}), \tag{7}$$

Define a new variable "the error of disturbance observation"

$$\zeta \equiv x_n - \mu \tag{8}$$

If the adjusted parameter of the FDO controller can be regulated online by equation(8), the result is bounded, thereby the error of DOB "ζ" will convergence into a wantonly little neighborhood.

$$\dot{\hat{\theta}} = \gamma \zeta \xi(x, u) \tag{9}$$

Prove: let equation(7) rewrite in the following style

$$\dot{\mu} = \alpha(x) + \beta(x) u + \hat{\Omega}_x(x, u | \hat{\theta}) + \sigma(x_n - \mu) \tag{10}$$

By using equation (9) and equation(10), we can get that

$$\dot{\zeta} = -\sigma \zeta + \Omega_x(x, u) - \hat{\Omega}_x(x, u | \hat{\theta}) \tag{11}$$

From the supposition(1) and omnipotent approaching function of fuzzy system, the actual disturbance of the control system can be acquired by adding a reconfigured error $\varepsilon(x,u)$ into FDO controller,   thereby

$$\Omega_x(x,u) = \hat{\Omega}_x(x,u\,|\,\theta^*) + \varepsilon(x,u) \tag{12}$$

$$|\varepsilon(x,u)| \leq \bar{\varepsilon} \tag{13}$$

Where, upper bound $\bar{\varepsilon}$ can be monished by adding fuzzy rules. Let equation (13) subsist into equation (11), the error dynamic equation of disturbance observance will be

$$\dot{\zeta} = -\sigma\zeta + \hat{\Omega}_x(x,u\,|\,\theta^*) - \hat{\Omega}_x(x,u\,|\,\hat{\theta}) + \varepsilon(x,u) \tag{14}$$

Define parameter error $\tilde{\theta} = \theta^* - \hat{\theta}$,   by using fuzzy basis functions we get

$$\dot{\zeta} = -\sigma\zeta + \tilde{\theta}^T\xi(x,u) + \varepsilon(x,u) \tag{15}$$

Define quasi-lyapunov function

$$V = \frac{1}{2}\zeta^2 + \frac{1}{2\gamma}\tilde{\theta}^T\tilde{\theta} \tag{16}$$

Differentiate equation(16),   let equation(15) subsist into equation(16), we can get

$$\dot{V} = \zeta\dot{\zeta} + \frac{1}{\gamma}\tilde{\theta}^T\dot{\tilde{\theta}}$$

$$= -\sigma\zeta^2 + \zeta\tilde{\theta}^T\xi(x,u) + \zeta\varepsilon(x,u) + \frac{1}{\gamma}\tilde{\theta}^T\dot{\tilde{\theta}} \tag{17}$$

$$= -\sigma\zeta^2 + \tilde{\theta}^T\{\zeta\xi(x,u) + \frac{1}{\gamma}\dot{\tilde{\theta}}\} + \zeta\varepsilon(x,u)$$

Choose a adjustable method of fuzzy rule

$$\dot{\hat{\theta}} = -\gamma\zeta\xi(x,u), \tag{18}$$

Thereby,

$$\dot{V} = -\sigma\zeta^2 + \zeta\varepsilon(x,u)$$

$$= -\sigma\zeta^2 + \zeta\varepsilon(x,u) + \left\{\frac{\sigma}{2}\zeta^2 + \frac{1}{2\sigma}\varepsilon^2(x,u)\right\} - \left\{\frac{\sigma}{2}\zeta^2 + \frac{1}{2\sigma}\varepsilon^2(x,u)\right\} \tag{19}$$

$$= -\frac{\sigma}{2}\zeta^2 + \frac{1}{2\sigma}\varepsilon^2(x,u) - \left(\sqrt{\frac{\sigma}{2}}\zeta - \sqrt{\frac{1}{2\sigma}}\varepsilon(x,u)\right)^2$$

$$\leq -\frac{\sigma}{2}\zeta^2 + \frac{1}{2\sigma}\varepsilon^2(x,u)$$

When $|\zeta| > \dfrac{\bar{\varepsilon}}{\sigma}$, $\dot{V} < 0$. Under the condition of the bounded $\hat{\theta}$, the error of DOB will also be consistently bounded, the designed FDO controller can track the undefined disturbance of Ω_d effectively.

4   Simulation Results

This paper takes an electro-optical tracking system for example, and simulate with the compound axis control method based on fuzzy disturbance observers. The equivalent control block diagrams of main and subsystems are shown as Figure 2 and Figure 3. A delay part is added to the main system to approximate the actual system. Considering the time delay of feedback signal, a Kalman filter is added between the delay part and the control block to compensate the time delay of television sampling. The design of control block takes the method of ZPETC(Zero Phase Error Tracking Control) and PID, which ensures good performance of both   stable-state characteristic and dynamic characteristic.

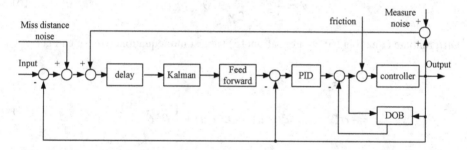

Fig. 2. The control loop structure diagram of the main system

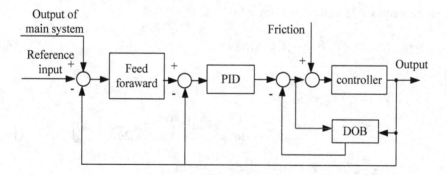

Fig. 3. The control loop structure diagram of the sub system

In the control system, FDO control parameters are: $\gamma = 1500$, $\sigma = 95$, fuzzy rule is defined as seven and used by Gaussian style. In the main system, the plant is a DC motor, whose math model can be described as

$$G_1(s) = \frac{1}{0.00752s^2 + 0.1879s} \tag{8}$$

And in the subsystem, the plant is a voice coil motor, whose math model is

$$G(s) = \frac{1}{0.06875s^2 + 0.625s} \tag{9}$$

Construct the system in the Simulink platform. The system has three inputs, the original input signal, the encoder noise and the miss distance noise separately. The current position gets from the superposition result of encoder output and the miss distance. Considering the delay of television sampling, the Kalman Filter is used to estimate the current actual position and inhibit the noise. The encoder output is mixed with 1.6''-mean-square white noise, and the miss distance noise is added with 4''-mean-square white noise.

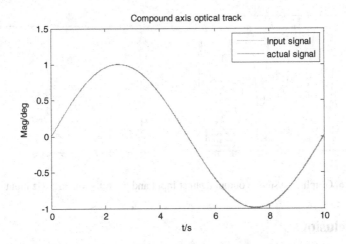

Fig. 4. Graph of system's output against input and the error with 0.1 Hz input

Input with sinusoidal signal with amplitude of 1 and angular frequency of 0.1 Hz, the system's output graphs against input and the error are showed as Figure 4.

Input with sinusoidal signal with amplitude of 0.5 and angular frequency of 1 Hz, the system's output graphs against input and the error are showed as Figure 5.

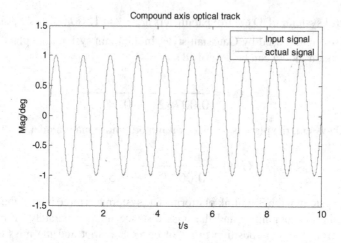

Fig. 5. Graph of system's output against input and the error with 1 Hz input

Input with sinusoidal signal with amplitude of 0.5 and angular frequency of 1.5 Hz, the system's output graphs against input and the error are showed as Figure 6.

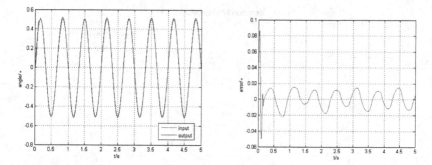

Fig. 6. Graph of system's output against input and the error with 1.5 Hz input

5   Conclusions

Compared with the traditional method, the control method based on fuzzy disturbance observers evidently improves the tracking precision of the system. With this method, the tracking error is reduced to arc sec level from arc min level, and the ability to suppress low-frequency interference and high-frequency noise is enhanced. This method is demonstrated to be effective to improve the control accuracy of compound axis tracking systems.

Of course, considering the fact that noise in the television sampling progress, waveform is distorted after the Kalman filter, and the control input may vibrate. While used in real application, mechanic parts wear may occur because of the vibration, which also reduces the life of the machine. As a result, the prediction filtering of original signal with noise is worth to be explored further.

Acknowledgments. The paper is supported by Aeronautics Fund of China (2009ZA02001).

References

1. Li, W.: Research on the Control Strategy of Compound-axis Electro-optical tracking systems. Graduate School of Chinese Academy of Sciences (Changchun Institute of Optics, Fine Mechanics and Physics) (2005) (in Chinese)
2. Wu, Y.: Summary of flight motion simulator. Chinese Science Information 8, 100–104 (2005) (in Chinese)
3. Liu, Q.: Current motion theory and application research for high accuracy servo-systems. Beihang University (2002) (in Chinese)
4. Shim, H., Jo, N.H., Son, Y.: A new disturbance observer for non-minimum phase linear systems. In: Proceedings of the American Control Conference, pp. 3385–3389. IEEE, Washington (2008)
5. Kim, E.: A fuzzy disturbance observer and its application to control. IEEE Trans. on Fuzzy Systems 10(1), 77–84 (2002)
6. Liu, T.: The Research of Compound-axis Servo Control Technique of O-E Tracking System. Graduate School of Chinese Academy of Sciences (Changchun Institute of Optics, Fine Mechanics and Physics) (2005) (in Chinese)
7. Liu, Z., Wang, J.: Robust Backstepping Control for Flight Motion Simulator Based on Nonlinear Disturbance Observer. Journal of System Simulation 20(19), 5354–5357 (2008)
8. Liu, Q., Er, L.: Disturbance Observer Based Robust Tracking Control of High Precision Flight Simulator. Journal of Beijing University of Aeronautics and Astronautics 29(2), 181–184 (2003) (in Chinese)

Comparison on H∞ Filter and Kalman Filter for Initial Alignment of SINS on Static Base

Bo Yang and Xiuyun Meng

Beijing Institute of Technology, Beijing, 100081

Abstract. This paper discusses two kinds of initial alignment for Strap-down Inertial Navigation System(SINS), one is based on Kalman filter, and the other is based on H∞ filter. Through modeling, simulating and comparing, it can be concluded that using the former, with given system model and the noise characteristics, the leveling misalignment angles converge relatively rapid, but the azimuth misalignment angle converges relatively slow. If there is too large disturbance on system model, Kalman filter would be prolonged, even be emanated. However, the standard Kalman filter performances can be improved by using H∞ filter. The latter performs better than the former in azimuth alignment and equivalent to the former in level alignment. And H∞ filter can also greatly enhances the robustness of the system. So H∞ filter is an available method for the initial alignment.

Keywords: SINS, initial alignment, the H∞ filter, Kalman filter.

1   Introduction

The main task of initial alignment for Strap-down Inertial Navigation System(SINS) is to determine the attitude matrix and calibrate sensors error. Domestic and foreign scholars have made a lot of research using Kalman filter technology [1~3]. Based on the equations of system state and measurement variables, It is good to use Kalman filter estimating the system state from the measured data. Compared with conventional filtering methods, the advantage of Kalman filter is that it is not only it include not only .the constant error of inertial sensitive components, but also the random error of them. The selection of Kalman filter parameters P0, Q and R also have great impact on its performance, including the accuracy and convergence speed of the state. If there is too large noise with uncertain characteristics, The filter would be prolonged, even be emanated.

In recent years, some scholars [4~7] proposed taking H∞ filter instead of Kalman filter on initial alignment for SINS, and have made a lot of research and simulations. Studies show that H∞ filter can effectively suppress the impact of uncertainty in system model and noise, thereby improving the performance of Kalman filter. The performance of these two methods is discussed by lots of simulations.

T. Xiao, L. Zhang, and M. Fei (Eds.): AsiaSim 2012, Part II, CCIS 324, pp. 194–201, 2012.
© Springer-Verlag Berlin Heidelberg 2012

2   Kalman Filter for Initial Alignment on Static Base

2.1   Design of Kalman Filter for Initial Alignment

For initial alignment on static base, Kalman filter is usually after the analytic coarse alignment, also known as "fine alignment". Assume the analytic coarse alignment for SINS has be finished, then the error-angles of "math platform" are small angles. After the geographical location of carriers has been accurately measured, it can be used a 10-order Kalman filter to calculate the attitude angle and speed of carriers, as well as the error of inertial instruments.

Suppose the state equation of SINS is:

$$\dot{X} = AX + BW, Z = CX + V . \tag{1}$$

After discretized, the system model become:

$$X_k = \Phi_{k,k-1} X_{k-1} + \Gamma_{k,k-1} W_{k-1}, Z_k = H_k X_k + V_k . \tag{2}$$

Where,

$$\Phi_{k,k-1} \approx e^{A(t_{k-1})T} = \sum_{n=0}^{\infty} \frac{[A(t_{k-1}) \cdot T]^n}{n!}, \Gamma_{k,k-1} = \sum_{n=0}^{\infty} \frac{[A(t_{k-1}) \cdot T]^n \cdot T}{(n+1)!} . \tag{3}$$

T is sampling period of Kalman filter. $X_{k,k-1}$ represents one step prediction of X_k. $\Phi_{k,k-1}$ represents one step state transition moment of the discrete system. $Z_k \in R^m$、 $W_k \in R^r$ are separately observation vector and the system noise vector. $\Gamma_{k,k-1} \in R^{n \times r}$ is system noise-driven matrix. $H_k \in R^{m \times n}$、 $V_k \in R^m$ are separately measurement matrix and measurement noise vector. For a standard Kalman filter, it is known that $\{W_k\},\{V_k\}$ are unrelated white noise sequence with zero mean. Covariance matrix of measurement noise R and system noise Q are also unrelated with X0.

State vector X is:

$$X = [X_1 X_2]^T = [\delta v_x \quad \delta v_y \quad \psi_x \quad \psi_y \quad \psi_z |\nabla_x \quad \nabla_y \quad \varepsilon_x \quad \varepsilon_y \quad \varepsilon_z]^T . \tag{4}$$

The error model equations of SINS on static base is equation (5).

$$
\begin{bmatrix} \dot{\delta v}_x \\ \dot{\delta v}_y \\ \dot{\psi}_x \\ \dot{\psi}_y \\ \dot{\psi}_z \\ \dot{\nabla}_x \\ \dot{\nabla}_y \\ \dot{\varepsilon}_x \\ \dot{\varepsilon}_y \\ \dot{\varepsilon}_z \end{bmatrix}
=
\begin{bmatrix}
0 & 2\omega_{ie}\sin L & 0 & -g & 0 & c_{11} & c_{12} & 0 & 0 & 0 \\
-2\omega_{ie}\sin L & 0 & g & 0 & 0 & c_{21} & c_{22} & 0 & 0 & 0 \\
0 & 0 & 0 & \omega_{ie}\sin L & -\omega_{ie}\cos L & 0 & 0 & c_{11} & c_{12} & c_{13} \\
0 & 0 & -\omega_{ie}\sin L & 0 & 0 & 0 & 0 & c_{21} & c_{22} & c_{23} \\
0 & 0 & \omega_{ie}\cos L & 0 & 0 & 0 & 0 & c_{31} & c_{32} & c_{33} \\
0 & 0 & 0 & 0 & 0 & 0 & 0 & 0 & 0 & 0 \\
0 & 0 & 0 & 0 & 0 & 0 & 0 & 0 & 0 & 0 \\
0 & 0 & 0 & 0 & 0 & 0 & 0 & 0 & 0 & 0 \\
0 & 0 & 0 & 0 & 0 & 0 & 0 & 0 & 0 & 0 \\
0 & 0 & 0 & 0 & 0 & 0 & 0 & 0 & 0 & 0
\end{bmatrix}
\begin{bmatrix} \delta v_x \\ \delta v_y \\ \psi_x \\ \psi_y \\ \psi_z \\ \nabla_x \\ \nabla_y \\ \varepsilon_x \\ \varepsilon_y \\ \varepsilon_z \end{bmatrix} . \tag{5}
$$

Where, ∇_i, $\varepsilon_i (i = x, y, z)$ are measured values accelerometers and gyros. As alignment time is very short, the attitude matrix can be seen as a unit matrix.

The random noise vector is:

$$W(t) = \begin{bmatrix} w_{v_E} & w_{v_N} & w_{\psi_E} & w_{\psi_N} & w_{\psi_U} & 0 & 0 & 0 & 0 & 0 \end{bmatrix}^T. \tag{6}$$

Where, $W(t) \sim N(0, Q)$. B is the unit matrix of the same dimensions with matrix A_i .Speed vector is usually selected as observables in the measurement equation(the second equation of (1)).

Where,

$$V_k = \begin{bmatrix} V_x(t) \\ V_y(t) \end{bmatrix}, H_k = \begin{bmatrix} 1 & 0 & 0 & 0 & 0 & 0 & 0 & 0 & 0 & 0 \\ 0 & 1 & 0 & 0 & 0 & 0 & 0 & 0 & 0 & 0 \end{bmatrix}. \tag{7}$$

For standard Kalman filter, the filtering algorithm are as follows:

1) State prediction equation:

$$\hat{X}_{k,k-1} = \Phi_{k,k-1} \hat{X}_{k-1}. \tag{8a}$$

2) Filtering equation:

$$\hat{X}_k = \Phi_{k,k-1} \hat{X}_{k-1} + K_k [Z_k - H_k \Phi_{k,k-1} \hat{X}_{k-1}]. \tag{8b}$$

3) Prediction of error variance matrix:

$$P_{k,k-1} = \Phi_{k,k-1} P_{k-1} \Phi_{k,k-1}^T + \Gamma_{k,k-1} Q_{k-1} \Gamma_{k,k-1}^T. \tag{8c}$$

4) Filter gain equation:

$$K_k = P_{k,k-1} H_k^T [H_k P_{k,k-1} H_k^T + R_k]^{-1}. \tag{8d}$$

5) Filtering estimate of error variance matrix:

$$P_k = [I - K_k H_k] P_{k,k-1}. \tag{8e}$$

From equation (8c)~(8e), it can be concluded that when P_0, Q_k, R_k change in the same multiples, the gain matrix K_k remains the same. when R_k becomes large, the gain K_k smaller. If either P_0 or Q_k becomes small, the $P_{k,k-1}$ smaller, so smaller is K_k . Conversely, vice versa. From the formulas above, it can be roughly deduced that the gain matrix K_k is proportional to Q_k and inversely proportional to R_k . So it's important to select these parameters to optimize the performance of the filter.

2.2   Results and Analysis of Kalman Filter

Different initial value makes a big difference to the performance of filter. Specific methods are as follows.

Selection of Initial Value. The initial value of vector $X(0)$ is zero, Kalman filter $P(0)$、Q、R all take the corresponding values of moderate precision gyroscope. Initial misalignment angle of three axis takes 1 degree, The constant drift of gyroscope takes 0.5 (°)/h, random drift 0.1 (°)/h. The initial deviation of accelerometer takes $0.3 \times 10^{-3}g$, random deviations $0.05 \times 10^{-3}g$. Precision of speed takes 0.1 m/s, The latitude of SINS is 45°. Kalman filter period T takes 0.05s. Therefore the initial value of the Kalman filter are as follows:

$$X0 = [0,0,0,0,0,0,0,0,0,0]^T.$$

$$Q = \text{diag}\{(0.05 \times 10^{-3}g)^2, (0.05 \times 10^{-3}g)^2, (0.1 \ (°)/h)^2, (0.1 \ (°)/h)^2, (0.1 \ (°)/h)^2, 0, 0,$$
$$0, 0, 0\}.$$

$$P = \text{diag}\{(0.1 \ \text{m/s})^2, (0.1 \ \text{m/s})^2, (1°)^2, (1°)^2, (1°)^2, (0.3 \times 10^{-3}g)^2, (0.3 \times 10^{-3}g)^2, (0.5$$
$$(°)/h)^2, (0.5 \ (°)/h)^2, (0.5 \ (°)/h)^2\}.$$

$$R = \text{diag}\{(0.1 \ \text{m/s})^2, (0.1 \ \text{m/s})$$

Simulation Results and Analysis. Figure 1 shows the simulation results of leveling misalignment angles and azimuth misalignment angle curve.

It can be seen from the figure, the estimate error in horizontal directions converge very fast, but much slower in azimuth angle error. When $R = \text{diag}\{(0.1 \ \text{m/s})^2, (0.1 \ \text{m/s})^2\}$, according to figure 1(a), convergence time of level misalignment angle is within 10s, precision for 63", while azimuth angle convergence time is 100s, precision about 56'. However, if the measurement noise R increases 10 times, that is $R = \text{diag}\{(1 \ \text{m/s})^2, (1 \ \text{m/s})^2\}$, according to figure 1(b), convergence time of level misalignment angle is 30", and convergence time of azimuth angle is about 260s.

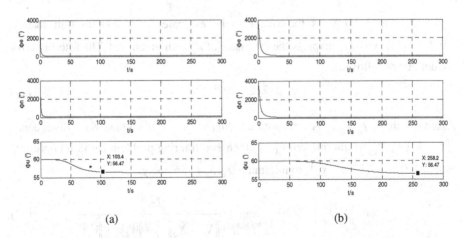

(a)   (b)

Fig. 1. Simulation results of Kalman filter on static base. Fig (a) is the result according to the selected initial values, and fig (b) is the result when R increase 10 times. ϕ_e and ϕ_n represent east misalignment angle and north misalignment, ϕ_u represents azimuth misalignment angle.

This example shows that R is important to the performance of filter. If R is selected too large, observation noise will also increase, thus delaying the time of the filter to stabilize, increasing the error of the filter and even leading to the divergence of the filter. On the contrary, if R is a very small, our observation technology must be improved, which is very difficult to achieve in practical applications. Moreover, the calculated statistics will not be fully used, thereby reducing the accuracy of the filter or change the filter results.

3   Initial Alignment of H∞ Filter on Static Base

At first, the problem of H∞ filtering is described, and then a H∞ filter is designed for initial alignment of SINS on static base.

3.1   Description of H∞ Filtering Problem

For the discrete-time systems described as equation (2), initial state of system is X_0, $\hat{X}_0$ represent a estimate value of X_0, and the initial estimate error is defined as follow:

$$P_0 = E\left\{ [X_0 - \hat{X}_0][X_0 - \hat{X}_0]^T \right\} .$$
(9)

Here, system noise and observation noise is arbitrary, namely, system initial state X_0, system noise W_k, and observation noise V_k are some unknown disturbances input.

Usually, it's hoped to take advantage of observations y_k to estimate arbitrary linear combination of state X_k:

$$Z_k = L_k X_k .$$
(10)

Where, $L_k \in R^{q \times n}$, if X_k is the vector to be estimated, L_k take as unit matrix. Let $\hat{Z} = F_f(y_0, y_1, \cdots y_k)$ express the estimates of Z_k with given $\{y_k\}$. The filtering error are defined as follows:

$$e_k = \hat{Z}_k - L_k X_k$$
(11)

Assume that $T_k(F_f)$ is transition function from unknown disturbance $\{(x_0 - \hat{x}_0), W_k, V_k\}$ to filtering error $\{e_k\}$, then H∞ filtering problem is to find optimum estimate $\hat{Z}_k = F_f(y_0, y_1 \cdots y_k)$, to minimum $\|T_k(F_f)\|_\infty$, namely:

$$\gamma^2 = \inf_{F_f} \|T_k(F_f)\|_\infty^2 = \inf_{F_f} \sup_{X_0, W \in h_2, V \in h_2} \frac{\|e_k\|_2^2}{\|X_0 - \hat{X}_0\|_{P_0^{-1}}^2 + \|W_k\|_2^2 + \|V_k\|_2^2}$$
(12)

Where P_0 is a positive definite matrix.

The optimal solution is too conservative in practice, it is usually need to seek a suboptimal solution of the H∞ filtering problem. For given $\gamma > 0$, that is to seek a suboptimal estimate $\hat{Z}_k = F_f(y_0, y_1 \ldots y_k)$, which makes $\left\| T_k\left(F_f(t)\right) \right\|_\infty \leq \gamma$.

For the given $\gamma > 0$, if $\left[\Phi_k, \Gamma_k\right]$ is full rank, then the filter meeting the conditions of $\left\| T_k\left(F_f(t)\right) \right\|_\infty \leq \gamma$ exists if and only if for all k:

$$P_k^{-1} + H_k^T H_k - \gamma^2 L_k^T L_k > 0 \tag{13}$$

Where P_k satisfy the Riccati equation:

$$P_{k+1} = \Phi_k P_k \Phi_k^T + \Gamma_k \Gamma_k^T - \Phi_k P_k \begin{bmatrix} H_k^T & L_k^T \end{bmatrix} R_{e,k}^{-1} \begin{bmatrix} H_k \\ L_k \end{bmatrix} P_k \Phi_k^T \tag{14}$$

Where,

$$R_{e,k} = \begin{bmatrix} I & 0 \\ 0 & -\gamma^2 I \end{bmatrix} + \begin{bmatrix} H_k \\ L_k \end{bmatrix} P_k \begin{bmatrix} H_k^T & L_k^T \end{bmatrix} \tag{15}$$

If the above formula is established, an available H∞ filter is given as follows:

$$\hat{Z}_k = L_k \hat{X}_k. \tag{16}$$

Here $\hat{X}_k$ can be calculated according to the following recursive formula:

$$\hat{X}_{k+1} = \Phi_k \hat{X}_k + K_{k+1}\left(y_{k+1} - H_{k+1}\Phi_k \hat{X}_k\right). \tag{17}$$

$$K_{k+1} = P_{k+1}H_{k+1}^T\left[I + H_{k+1}P_{k+1}H_k^T\right]^{-1} \tag{18}$$

By comparing, it can be seen that the structure of Kalman filter and H∞ filter has a lot in common. In fact, when $\gamma \to \infty$, H∞ filter will degenerate into Kalman filter. That is to say, if the norm index is removed, H∞ filter is equivalent to Kalman filter. Therefore in the design of H∞ filter, γ is set as small as possible, under the condition that the Riccati equation solution P is definite positive.

3.2   H∞ Filter Design for Initial Alignment on Static Base

For the SINS error equation described as (3), the interference of acceleration a_d and angular velocity w_d are introduced, the dynamic equation of system is as follow:

$$\begin{bmatrix} \delta \dot{V}_E \\ \delta \dot{V}_E \\ \dot{\psi}_E \\ \dot{\psi}_N \\ \dot{\psi}_U \end{bmatrix} = \begin{bmatrix} 0 & 2\omega_{ie}\sin L & 0 & -g & 0 \\ -2\omega_{ie}\sin L & 0 & g & 0 & 0 \\ 0 & 0 & \omega_{ie}\sin L & -\omega_{ie}\cos L & 0 \\ 0 & -\omega_{ie}\sin L & 0 & 0 & 0 \\ 0 & \omega_{ie}\cos L & 0 & 0 & 0 \end{bmatrix} \begin{bmatrix} \delta V_E \\ \delta V_E \\ \psi_E \\ \psi_N \\ \psi_U \end{bmatrix} + \begin{bmatrix} \nabla_E + a_{dE} \\ \nabla_N + a_{dN} \\ \varepsilon_E + w_{dE} \\ \varepsilon_N + w_{dN} \\ \varepsilon_U + w_{dU} \end{bmatrix}. \quad (19)$$

Now using the state feedback H∞ control for initial alignment, the generalized state space realization is designed as:

$$\dot{x}(t) = Ax(t) + B\omega(t), \quad y(t) = Cx(t) + D\omega(t), \quad Z(t) = Lx(t). \quad (20)$$

Where,

$$\omega(t) = \begin{bmatrix} \nabla_E + a_{dE} & \nabla_N + a_{dN} & \varepsilon_E + w_{dE} & \varepsilon_N + w_{dN} & \varepsilon_U + w_{dU} \end{bmatrix}^T. \quad (21)$$

represents the interference vector, $x = \begin{bmatrix} \delta V_E & \delta V_N & \psi_E & \psi_N & \psi_U \end{bmatrix}^T$ is the state vector, $Z(t) = Lx(t)$ is the observation vector, and $y(t) = Cx(t) + D\omega(t)$ is the output vector. Under these assumptions (random drift of gyro and random deviations of accelerometer are bounded, in this case, can be set to less than 0.01), the H∞ filter for SINS initial alignment is simulated.

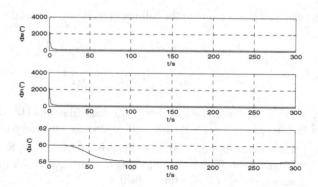

Fig. 2. Simulation of H∞ filter for SINS initial alignment on static base. ϕ_e and ϕ_n represent east misalignment angle and north misalignment, ϕ_u represents azimuth misalignment angle

3.3   Results Analysis of H∞ Filtering

Figure 2 shows the simulation results of H∞ filter with parameter γ =0.3. It can be seen that the convergence time of level misalignment angles are 10s, and the azimuth angle is 70s. Change of system noise and measurement noise R make little difference to the performance, but if γ is too large, there is also divergence problems for H∞ filter like Kalman filter. A good selection can both enhance the robustness of system and filtering precision. In fact, Kalman filter is a special case of H∞ filter, when γ tends to infinitely great, H∞ filter is equivalent to Kalman filter.

4   Conclusions

With the deduced SINS model on static base, the relevant H∞ filter and Kalman filter are designed, and the performance of the two filters is compared. The simulation result shows that Kalman filter is good in static base condition and H∞ filter method performs better than standard Kalman filer when there is large disturbance on system model. Kalman filter is good in dealing system with white noise like static base. Azimuth misalignment angle divergent much slower than horizon misalignment angle. Using H∞ filter can improve system sensitivity to noise and the divergence speed of azimuth. As long as parameter γ is suitable and noise variance bounded, H∞ filter can effectively suppress the uncertainty of interference from modeling and noise. This paper focus on the static base model, other base model is also to be simulated. Filtering algorithms also need to be optimized. In a word, compared with Kalman filter, H∞ filter performs better in robustness and convergence, proved to an available method for initial alignment.

References

1. Wan, D., Fang, J.: Initial Alignment of Inertial Navigation. M. Southeast University Press, Nanjing (1998)
2. Bar-Itzhack, I.Y., Berman, N.: Control Theoretic Approach to Intertial Navigation System. Journal of Guidance and Control 11(3), 237–245 (1988)
3. Sun, B., Du, X.: The Research of Initial Alignment Technology in SINS. Beijing Institute of Technology Master's Degree Thesis (2006)
4. Feng, S., Yuan, X.: H∞ Filtering and Its Application in INS Ground Alignment. Journal of Nanjing University of Aeronautics and Astronautics 30(4), 383－387 (1998)
5. Nie, L., Wu, J., Tian, W.: H∞ Filtering and Its Application in INS Alignment. Journal of China Inertial Technology, 11(6), 39－43 (2003)
6. Lv, S., Xie, L., Chen, J., Yao, X.: Parameter Optimization of H∞ Filter in Initial Alignment of SINS Alignment. Fire Control & Command Control 35(6), 67－69 (2010)
7. Zhu, L., Bao, Q., Zhang, Y.: Comparison on Kalman Filter and H∞ Filter for Initial Alignment of SINS. Journal of China Inertial Technology 13(3), 4－9 (2005)

Self-generating Interpretable Fuzzy Rules Model from Examples

Meng Li[1], Zhiwei Hu[1], Jiahong Liang [1], and Shilei Li[2]

[1] College of Mechanical Engineering and Automation,
National University of Defence Technology, 410073 Changsha, P.R. China
[2] Department of Information Security, College of Electronic Engineering,
Naval University of Engineering, 430000, Wuhan, P.R. China
{mengshuqin1984,huzhiwei_nudt,lingjiahong_nudt,
stoneli}@163.com

Abstract. In this paper, we propose a powerful method for automatically generating interpretable fuzzy rules model from a set of given training examples (i.e. numerical data) which are sampled from an unknown function. Self-generating fuzzy rules from examples can be used as a common method for simulation such as behavior simulation for virtual humans and CGF. Our method consists of two steps: Step 1 automatically extracts a fuzzy rule base which can approximate the unknown function with an approving accuracy by introducing a homologous Gaussian-shaped membership function. Step 2 improves its interpretability by deriving linguistic rules from fuzzy if-then rules with consequent real numbers. In this way, we achieve the balance between the accuracy and interpretability of the generated rules. Finally, we show the availability of our method by applying it to the problem of function approximation.

Keywords: Fuzzy modeling, fuzzy rule, rule extraction, fuzzy system design, orthogonal transformation.

1 Introduction

Fuzzy rule based modeling has become an active research field in recent years because of its unique merits in solving complex nonlinear system identification and control problems. Primary advantages of this approach include the facility for the explicit knowledge representation in the form of If–Then rules, the mechanism of reasoning in human understandable terms, the capacity of taking linguistic information from human experts and combining it with numerical information, and the ability of approximating complicated nonlinear functions with simpler models [1]. This paper is concerned with considering regression or function approximation problems. Our principal goal is to learn an unknown functional mapping between input and output vectors, using a set of known training samples. Once this mapping is generated, it can be used for predicting the output values given new input vectors. So our method can be used to construct models for simulation systems.

T. Xiao, L. Zhang, and M. Fei (Eds.): AsiaSim 2012, Part II, CCIS 324, pp. 202–209, 2012.

Historically, fuzzy rule bases have been constructed by knowledge acquisition from experts while the weights within neural nets have been learned from data [2], [3]. The most straightforward approach is to define rules and membership functions subjectively by studying a human operator. However, consulting an expert may be difficult and/or expensive; furthermore, translating the human operator's experience directly into the fuzzy linguistic values can be influenced by the intuition of the operators and designers, so that the fuzzy control rules may be incomplete or even contradict each other [4]. So, the goal of this paper is establishing a rule base which provides an effective way to capture the approximate and inexact nature of complex nonlinear systems from samples.

Recently, various methods were proposed for automatically generating fuzzy if-then rules from examples. Some methods involved iterative learning procedures or complicated rule generation mechanisms such as genetic-algorithm-based methods, least-squares methods, a fuzzy c-means method and a fuzzy-neuro method [5]. But most of these approaches predefined the membership functions in the antecedent part of the fuzzy rules or fixed the membership functions in the antecedents and even in the consequence of the rules. This fixed structure helps the application of the symbolic minimization step proposed in previous works. However, the distribution of the membership functions (shape and location) has a strong influence on the performance of the systems. Our method is elicited from Hector's work which presented a systematic approach to a self-generating fuzzy rule-table for function approximation [4]. But, he focused much on the accuracy of the rules, ignored the interpretability of the extracted rules.

The organization of the rest of this paper is as follows. At first, we make some changes on Hector's systematic approach to a self-generating a precise fuzzy rule base. Then we analyze mechanisms to improve the interpretability in precise fuzzy rule base: translating the rules with consequent real numbers into linguistic rules. In this way, we acquire a balance between accuracy and interpretability of the rules. Numerical experiments and conclusions are presented at the end of this paper.

2   Self-generating Fuzzy Rules from Examples

2.1   Formulation of the Problem

We consider the problem of approximating a continuous multi-input single-output function to clarify the basic ideas of our approach. The examples are represented by a set D, derived from an unknown function or system F. Each vector datum $(\vec{x}^k; z^k)$ of the examples can be expressed as $(x_1^k, x_2^k, \cdots, x_N^k; z^k)$, with $\vec{x}^k \in R^N$, $z^k \in R$ and $k = 1, 2, \cdots, K$, where N is the number of input variables and K is the number of examples. A fuzzy system comprises a set of IF-THEN fuzzy rules $R_{i_1 i_2 \cdots i_N}^*$. In this paper, we have adopted the fuzzy model with constant consequent constituents to illustrate the proposed methods. This type of fuzzy model has the following form [5]:

IF x_1 is $X_1^{i_1}$ AND x_2 is $X_1^{i_2}$ AND$\cdots$AND x_N is $X_N^{i_N}$ THEN $z = R_{i_1 i_2 \cdots i_N}$　　　(1)

where $X_m^{i_m} \in X_m^1, X_m^2, \cdots, X_m^{n_m}$ with n_m being the number of membership functions of the m-th input variable and $R_{i_1 i_2 \cdots i_N}$ is the numeric consequence of the rule. We use $\mu_{X_m^{i_m}}(x_m^k)$ to represent the membership degree of the m-th input of the k-th vector datum. The fuzzy function can be expressed as:

$$\tilde{F}(\vec{x}^k; R, C) = \frac{\sum_{i_1=1}^{n_1}\sum_{i_2=1}^{n_2}\cdots\sum_{i_N=1}^{n_N}\left(R_{i_1 i_2 \cdots i_N} \cdot \prod_{m=1}^{N} \mu_{X_m^{i_m}}(x_m^k)\right)}{\sum_{i_1=1}^{n_1}\sum_{i_2=1}^{n_2}\cdots\sum_{i_N=1}^{n_N}\left(\prod_{m=1}^{N} \mu_{X_m^{i_m}}(x_m^k)\right)}$$　　　(2)

We can see that the fuzzy output not only depend on the input vector, but also on the consequent of the rules and on all the parameters that describe the membership functions C. the soul of this section can be depicted as that of finding a configuration C and generating a set of fuzzy rules $R_{i_1 i_2 \cdots i_N}^*$ from a data set D of K input-output pairs $(x_1^k, x_2^k, \cdots, x_N^k; z^k)$, such that the fuzzy system $\tilde{F}(\vec{x}^k; R, C)$ correctly approximates the unknown function or system F considering the trade-off between complexity and accuracy. The goal function to be minimized is the sum of squared errors:

$$J(R, C) = \sum_{k \in D}\left(e^2(\vec{x}^k)\right)^2$$　　　(3)

where $e^2(\vec{x}^k) = F(\vec{x}^k) - \tilde{F}(\vec{x}^k; R, C)$.

Use 10-point type for the name(s) of the author(s) and 9-point type for the address(es) and the abstract. For the main text, please use 10-point type and single-line spacing. We recommend the use of Computer Modern Roman or Times. Italic type may be used to emphasize words in running text. Bold type and underlining should be avoided.

2.2　Finding the Optimum Rules for a Fixed Membership Function Configuration

The first step of our algorithm is to acquire the optimum rule conclusion under the condition that the distribution and number of membership functions are fixed. Observing (2), $\tilde{F}$ is not only a continuous and differentiable expression as a linear function of the consequent of the rules $R_{i_1 i_2 \cdots i_N}$. When the membership function configuration is fixed, we have the following equation:

$$\frac{\partial J(R, C)}{\partial R_{j_1 j_2 \cdots j_N}} = -2 \cdot \sum_{k \in D}\left[\left(F(\vec{x}^k) - \tilde{F}(\vec{x}^k; R, C)\right) \cdot \left(\frac{\partial \tilde{F}(\vec{x}^k; R, C)}{\partial R_{j_1 j_2 \cdots j_N}}\right)\right] = 0$$　　　(4)

Substituting (2) in (4) and introducing the following notation:

$$S_{i_1 i_2 \cdots i_N, j_1 j_2 \cdots j_N} \equiv \sum_{k \in D} \left(\frac{\prod_{m=1}^{N} \mu_{X_m^{i_m}}(x_m^k)}{\sum_{i_1=1}^{n_1} \sum_{i_2=1}^{n_2} \cdots \sum_{i_N=1}^{n_N} \left(\prod_{m=1}^{N} \mu_{X_m^{i_m}}(x_m^k) \right)} \bullet \frac{\prod_{m=1}^{N} \mu_{X_m^{j_m}}(x_m^k)}{\sum_{i_1=1}^{n_1} \sum_{i_2=1}^{n_2} \cdots \sum_{i_N=1}^{n_N} \left(\prod_{m=1}^{N} \mu_{X_m^{i_m}}(x_m^k) \right)} \right) \qquad (5)$$

$$S_{F, j_1 j_2 \cdots j_N} \equiv \sum_{k \in D} \left(F(\vec{x}^k) \bullet \frac{\prod_{m=1}^{N} \mu_{X_m^{j_m}}(x_m^k)}{\sum_{i_1=1}^{n_1} \sum_{i_2=1}^{n_2} \cdots \sum_{i_N=1}^{n_N} \left(\prod_{m=1}^{N} \mu_{X_m^{i_m}}(x_m^k) \right)} \right) \qquad (6)$$

We obtain a set of linear equations:

$$\sum_{i_1=1}^{n_1} \sum_{i_2=1}^{n_2} \cdots \sum_{i_N=1}^{n_N} \left(R_{i_1 i_2 \cdots i_N} \bullet S_{i_1 i_2 \cdots i_N, j_1 j_2 \cdots j_N} \right) = S_{F, j_1 j_2 \cdots j_N} \qquad (7)$$

where j_m ranges from 1 to n_m. This expression represents $n_1 * n_2 * \cdots * n_N$ linear equations. Depending on (7), we can obtain the consequents of the rules for a predefined membership function distribution. In this paper, the configuration of membership function of input variables is assumed to be a homologous Gaussian form:

$$\mu_{X_m^{i_m}}(x_m^k) = \begin{cases} \exp\left(\dfrac{\left(x_m^k - c_m^{i_m}\right)^2}{2\left(\sigma_{R,m}^{i_m}\right)^2} \right) R\left(x_m; c_m^{i_m}, c_m^{i_m+1}\right) & \text{if } i_m = 1 \\[2ex] \exp\left(\dfrac{\left(x_m^k - c_m^{i_m}\right)^2}{2\left(\sigma_{L,m}^{i_m}\right)^2} \right) L\left(x_m; c_m^{i_m-1}, c_m^{i_m}\right) + \exp\left(\dfrac{\left(x_m^k - c_m^{i_m}\right)^2}{2\left(\sigma_{R,m}^{i_m}\right)^2} \right) R\left(x_m; c_m^{i_m}, c_m^{i_m+1}\right) & \text{if } i_m \neq 1 \text{ and } i_m \neq n_m \\[2ex] \exp\left(\dfrac{\left(x_m^k - c_m^{i_m}\right)^2}{2\left(\sigma_{L,m}^{i_m}\right)^2} \right) L\left(x_m; c_m^{i_m-1}, c_m^{i_m}\right) & \text{if } i_m = n_m \end{cases}$$

$$(8)$$

where $R\left(x_m; c_m^{i_m}, c_m^{i_m+1}\right) = \begin{cases} 1 & \text{if } x_m \geq c_m^{i_m} \\ 0 & \text{otherwise} \end{cases}$ $L\left(x_m; c_m^{i_m-1}, c_m^{i_m}\right) = \begin{cases} 1 & \text{if } x_m \leq c_m^{i_m} \\ 0 & \text{otherwise} \end{cases}$. $\sigma_{R,m}^{i_m}$ is

the real number which makes $c_m^{i_m+1}$ be the upper alpha quantile $z_{R,\alpha}$, if $R\left(x_m; c_m^{i_m}, c_m^{i_m+1}\right) = 1$. Accordingly, $\sigma_{L,m}^{i_m}$ is the real number which makes $c_m^{i_m-1}$ be the lower alpha quantile $z_{L,\alpha}$, if $L\left(x_m; c_m^{i_m-1}, c_m^{i_m}\right)=1$. Obviously, the location of the membership function is controlled by $c_m^{i_m}$, of which the shape is controlled by $z_{R,\alpha}$ and $z_{L,\alpha}$. In this paper, we make $\alpha \le 0.005$ which ensure that each input variable will have a nonzero membership value in at most two fuzzy sets (i.e. the values less than α are ignored).

2.3   Tuning the Parameters of Membership Function to Find the Global Optimum Solution

In order to find the global optimum rules, we firstly achieve a near-optimum solution by seeking the distribution of centers that produces equally distributed errors throughout all the areas defined [4]. That is, we use Hector's method to tune the centers of the membership function based on (9).

$$\Delta c_m^{i_m} = \begin{cases} -bp_m^{i_m} & \text{if } p_m^{i_m} \ge 0 \\ bp_m^{i_m} & \text{if } p_m^{i_m} < 0 \end{cases} \tag{9}$$

where $p_m^{i_m}$ is the slope of $e^2\left(\vec{x}^k\right)$ in the scope of $\left[c_m^{i_m-1}, c_m^{i_{m+1}}\right]$. But Hector's method is based on the triangular membership function. If we fix α to one value, then our method is the same to Hector's, except that they have different membership functions. In our method, α is tuned based on (10).

$$\Delta \alpha : \begin{cases} \Delta \alpha_L = -Tp_m^{i_m} & \text{if } p_m^{i_m} \ge 0 \\ \Delta \alpha_R = Tp_m^{i_m} & \text{if } p_m^{i_m} < 0 \end{cases} \tag{10}$$

b and T are the user defined parameters. They are tuned interactively to guarantee that the centers of the membership functions remain their order unchanged and the errors distribute equally throughout all the areas. Once we have a configuration assumed to be a near optimum one, then a method to find a local minimum is employed, thus reaching the desired minimum [4]. We use gradient descent method to find the desired minimum of error distribution. In this process, $c_m^{i_m}$ and α are the independent variables and according to our method, α provides us a useful way to give the membership function enormous freedom to ensure $min\left(\sum_{x_m^k \in \left[c_m^{i_m-1}, c_m^{i_{m+1}}\right]} e^2\left(\vec{x}^k\right)\right)$. The process of our method is illustrated in Fig. 1.

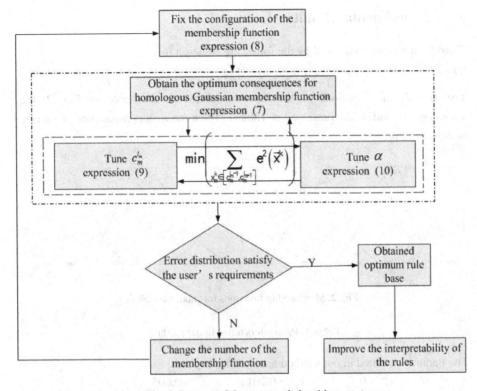

Fig. 1. Process of the proposed algorithm

2.4   Improving the Interpretability in Precise Fuzzy Rule Base

So far, we have obtained the optimum rule base in the previous section. However, we must translate consequent real numbers into linguistic labels in the consequent part to improve the rules' interpretability.   Suppose that the output $R_{i_1 i_2 \cdots i_N}$ of the obtained rules is divided into N fuzzy sets $B_1, B_2, \ldots, B_N$ which are defined by triangle-shaped function and associated with the membership functions $\mu_{B_1}, \mu_{B_2}, \ldots, \mu_{B_N}$. In this method, the obtained fuzzy if-then rules in (1) are represented by two linguistic rule tables: a main rule table and a secondary rule table [5]. The main rule table consists of the following fuzzy if-then rules, which are best fitting to the consequent real number.

IF x_1 is $X_1^{i_1}$ AND x_2 is $X_1^{i_2}$ AND$\cdots$AND x_N is $X_N^{i_N}$ THEN $z = B_{i_1 i_2 \cdots i_N}^*$ with $\varpi_{i_1 i_2 \cdots i_N}^*$ (11)

where $B_{i_1 i_2 \cdots i_N}^*$ is the consequent fuzzy set characterized $\varpi_{i_1 i_2 \cdots i_N}^*$ which is the degree of certainty defined as $\varpi_{i_1 i_2 \cdots i_N}^* = \mu_{B_{i_1 i_2 \cdots i_N}^*}\left(R_{i_1 i_2 \cdots i_N}\right) = max\left\{\mu_{B_i}\left(R_{i_1 i_2 \cdots i_N}\right) \mid i = 1, 2, \ldots, N\right\}$.

Analogously, the formations of the secondary rule table are the same as (11), except that $B_{i_1 i_2 \cdots i_N}^*$ is substituted by the consequent fuzzy set with the second best fitting to $R_{i_1 i_2 \cdots i_N}$ and $\varpi_{i_1 i_2 \cdots i_N}^*$ is substituted accordingly.

3   Experimental Results

Consider the function defined by the following equation [6]:

$$F(x_1, x_2) = 1.5(1 - x_1) + e^{(2x_1 - 1)} \sin\left(3\pi(x_1 - 0.6)^2\right) + e^{3(x_2 - 0.5)} \sin\left(4\pi(x_2 - 0.9)^2\right) \quad x_1, x_2 \in [0,1] \quad (12)$$

The membership functions of the input variables are illustrated in Fig. 2, the associated $c_m^{i_m}$ and α are presented in Table 1. The numerical consequence of the rule is shown in Fig. 3.

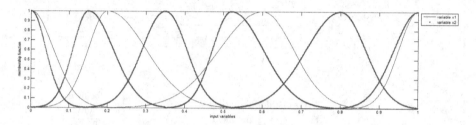

Fig. 2. Membership functions for input variables

Table 1. Parameters tuned in our method

The Parameters tuned in our method are as follows:

$$x_1 : \frac{c_m^{i_m}}{(\alpha_L, \alpha_R)} : \begin{array}{llll} c_1^{1_1} = 0 & c_1^{2_1} = 0.201 & c_1^{3_1} = 0.605 & c_1^{4_1} = 1 \\ \alpha_R = 3.86 \times 10^{-3} & (0.51, 0.34) \times 10^{-3} & (4.13, 0.52) \times 10^{-3} & \alpha_L = 0.24 \times 10^{-3} \end{array}$$

$$x_2 : \frac{c_m^{i_m}}{(\alpha_L, \alpha_R)} : \begin{array}{llll} c_2^{1_2} = 0 & c_2^{2_2} = 0.153 & c_2^{3_2} = 0.347 & c_2^{4_2} = 0.519 \\ \alpha_R = 0.62 \times 10^{-3} & (0.31, 2.2) \times 10^{-3} & (4.56, 3.71) \times 10^{-3} & (0.83, 0.54) \times 10^{-3} \end{array}$$

$$\begin{array}{ll} c_2^{5_2} = 0.805 & c_2^{6_2} = 1 \\ (4.07, 4.33) \times 10^{-3} & \alpha_L = 3.86 \times 10^{-3} \end{array}$$

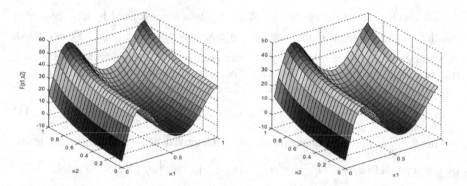

Fig. 3. Original output surface (Left) and output surface obtained by our method

4   Summary

The rules extracted by our method will approximate the unknown system with higher accuracy as α is introduced. From the experiment results, it can be seen that the proposed self-generating fuzzy rule algorithm can assign appropriate membership function configuration to the input variable and achieve an approving approximating accuracy. In the end we derive linguistic rules from rules with consequent real numbers, which improve the interpretability of the extracted rule base.

Acknowledgments. This paper was supported by national natural science foundation (61170160).

References

1. Yen, J., Wang, L.: Simplifying Fuzzy Rule-Based Models Using Orthogonal Transformation Methods. IEEE Transactions on Systems, Man, and Cybernetics—Part B: Cybernetics 29(1) (1999)
2. Driankov, D., Hellendoorn, H., Reinfrank, M.: An Introduction to Fuzzy Control. Springer, Berlin (1993)
3. Sudkamp, T., Hammell, R.J.: Interpolation, completion and learning fuzzy rules. IEEE Trans. Syst., Man, Cybern. 24, 332–342 (1994)
4. Pomares, H., Rojas, I., Ortega, J., Gonzalez, J., Prieto, A.: A Systematic Approach to a Self-Generating Fuzzy Rule-Table for Function Approximation. IEEE Transactions on Systems, Man, and Cybernetics—Part B: Cybernetics 30(3) (2000)
5. Nozaki, K., Ishibuchi, H., Tanaka, H.: A simple but powerful heuristic method for generating fuzzy rules from numerical data. Fuzzy Sets and Systems 86, 251–270 (1997)
6. Cherkassky, V., Gehring, D., Mulier, F.: Comparison of adaptive methods for function estimation from samples. IEEE Trans. Neural Networks 7, 969–984 (1996)

Modeling and Simulation on Pulse Compression of Hybrid-Modulation Signal Based on Simulink

Biao Wu, Kaining Xiao, Guoqin Shen, Ning Zhou, and Zhaohui Han

Electronic System Engineering Company of China, Beijing, China, 100079
kingwb9190@yahoo.com.cn

Abstract. The principle of the hybrid-modulation signal and the method of its pulse compression are introduced, and then the simulation model of pulse compression is established by Simulink. Some difficult problems and their solutions in the process of simulation are analyzed here, and the results of simulation are given. According to the analysis, it is known that the simulation realizes the pulse compression of the hybrid-modulation signal, and it can offer reference not only for the modeling and simulation of radar system, but also for the research of the radar signal digital processing technology.

Keywords: hybrid-modulation, pulse compression, linear frequency modulation, phase encoding.

1   Introduction

Recently, with the rapid development of the radar ECM, the requirement of the radar signal is higher and higher. The counter-reconnaissance capability of the traditional linear frequency modulation (LFM) signal is so poor that the radar signal is easily intercepted and captured by the enemy. However, the phase-encoded signal is so sensitive to Doppler frequency that it only adapt to the condition that Doppler frequency is low. The hybrid-modulation signal combines the LFM signal with the phase-encoded signal. It overcomes some shortcomings of the two signals which are the LFM signal and the phase-encoded signal, has the characteristics of low probability intercept (LPI) which can make the signal difficult to be found, and can improve the gain in the process of the radar signal. So it could be used in all kinds of low intercept radar systems in general.

Simulink is a kind of fashionable simulation platform of object-oriented dynamic system under the circumstance of the MATLAB language in recent international. In the process of establishing the simulation model, it achieves graphic designing of human-machine interface, and combines the process of the simulation tests with the analysis of simulation results. Simultaneously, the function of the Simulink integration circumstance is sustained by MATLAB, so it can directly use the very scientific calculation function of MATLAB. Simulink makes use of the method of module-combination to make the user set up the computer model of dynamic system rapidly and correctly.

T. Xiao, L. Zhang, and M. Fei (Eds.): AsiaSim 2012, Part II, CCIS 324, pp. 210–216, 2012.

2   Principal and Pulse Compression Method of the Hybrid-Modulation Signal

2.1   Principal of the Hybrid-Modulation Signal

The Hybrid-modulation Signal is a new kind of signal which adapts to apply in the pulse compression radar. It combines advantages of the LFM with that of the phase-encoded signals. Then the LFM signal is modulated in every code of the phase-encoded signal.

Suppose the mathematic expression of the LFM signal is

$$u_L(t) = \frac{1}{\sqrt{T}} \exp(j\pi k t^2)[\varepsilon(t) - \varepsilon(t-T)]$$

Phase code use the BC signal and its pulse function is

$$u_B(t) = \frac{1}{\sqrt{P}} \sum_{m=0}^{P-1} c_m \delta(t - mT)$$

Here, $\varepsilon(t)$ is step function; $\delta(t)$ is impulse function; T is the width of subpulse; P is the length of code; k is chirp slope of the LFM; c_m is a random sequence, take $\{c_m = \pm 1\}$; The hybrid-modulation Signal is the convolution form of the LFM and the BC pulse function:

$$u(t) = u_L(t) \otimes u_B(t) = \frac{1}{\sqrt{PT}} \sum_{m=0}^{P-1} c_m [\exp(j\pi k t^2)(\varepsilon(t) - \varepsilon(t-T))] \otimes \delta(t - mT)$$

$$= \frac{1}{\sqrt{PT}} \sum_{m=0}^{P-1} \exp[j\pi k (t - mT)^2] \cdot c_m \cdot [\varepsilon(t - mT) - \varepsilon(t - (m+1)T)]$$

Seen from the above formula, LFM-BC radar signal is a kind of hybrid-modulation signal formed through dividing the wide pulse into several subpulses, carrying out phase encoding and linear frequency modulation between the subpulses. This kind of hybrid-modulation signal isn't sensitive to the Doppler basically and doesn't produce obvious peak value excursion phenomenon though the gain declines slightly. So it has the advantages of the two signals, which are the LFM signal and phase-encoded signal, and can make up the disadvantages of the two signals at the same time. LFM-BC signal is an important kind of hybrid-modulation signal.

2.2   The Pulse Compression Method of the Hybrid-Modulation Signal

Before the pulse compression, firstly the matched filter of relevant radar transmitting signal must be achieved. In the practical engineering, the process of the pulse compression is realized in the frequency domain, thus the fast Fourier transform

(FFT) algorithm can be used to improve the calculating speed. And then the result of the processing of the pulse compression could be achieved through multiplying the frequency response of the radar echo and that of the matched filter and the inverse fast Fourier transform (IFFT). Because the convolution processing is not used, the computational complexity is greatly reduced. Therefore, during the simulation of pulse compression processing, the first thing is to acquire the matched filter or compression coefficient of pulse compression radar

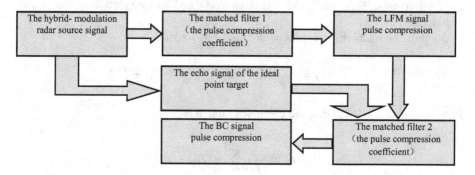

Fig. 1. The Pulse Compression Procession of the Hybrid-modulation Signal

It needs two steps to dispose pulse compression of the LFM-BC hybrid-modulation signal that firstly to deal with the LFM signal and secondly to process the BC signal. There are also two steps to generate the pulse compression coefficient during the pulse compression processing. Firstly, the needed LFM pulse compression coefficient is generated by making use of a code. Secondly, the LFM pulse compression is processed using the theoretical hybrid-modulation signal. Then the needed BC pulse compression coefficient is produced by using the result of the theoretical LFM pulse compression processing. Finally, the BC pulse compression coefficient and the ideal object echo signal are used to finish the second pulse compression. So the final pulse compression result of the hybrid-modulation signal is achieved. The pulse compression process of the hybrid-modulation signal is as the figure 1 shown.

After two pulse compression disposal finished, the extent of output signal becomes $P \times \sqrt{D}$ times of the input signal (P is the length of the BC, D is the compression ratio of LFM signal), so the ratio of signal to chirp is effectively improved. Of course, two matching filter function can be combined into one filter function, so the pulse press of the hybrid-modulation signal can be finished by one pulse compression.

3   Simulink Simulation Model of the Hybrid-Modulation Signal Pulse Compression

The model uses the algorithm of frequency domain to match filtrate wave, viz. using FFT and IFFT to achieve FIR, which algorithm is as the figure 2 shown. In the figure 2, u(n) is the disperse expression of the hybrid signal, and L is the wide sampling point number of the hybrid-modulation signal. According to the relationship of the cyclic convolution and the linear convolution, N which is the point number of FFT must meet the condition of N>=L+M-1. In the practical treatment, N usually adopts the power hypo-square of two.

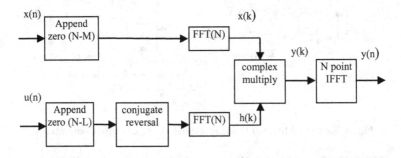

Fig. 2. Frequency-Domain Pulse Compression Block Diagram

According to the pulse compression algorithm analysis of the hybrid-modulation signal, the matched filter of the LFM pulse compression in code is set up firstly, as the figure 3 is shown.

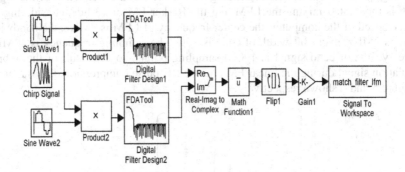

Fig. 3. Simulink Model of LFM Pulse Compression

Here, match_filter_lfm is the matching coefficient of the LFM pulse compression in code of the first pulse compression. In the processing, it is outputted to the workspace in order to achieve the LFM pulse compression of the hybrid signal.

The model in the next step is LFM pulse compression of the hybrid-modulation signal, and then the BC pulse compression matching-coefficient is achieved across conjugation and reversal. In addition, the BC pulse compression is treated with the echo signal of the ideal object, finally the pulse compression signal of the hybrid-modulation signal is achieved. The model is as the figure 4 shown.

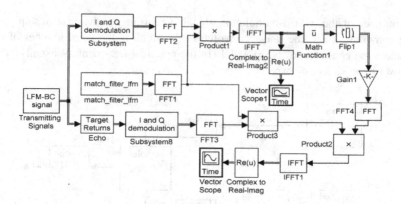

Fig. 4. Simulink Model of Hybrid-modulation signal Pulse Compression

Here, the difficult problem of filling zero in FFT mainly is settled by the way of the frame treatment of DSP module in Simulink.

4   The Result and Analysis of the Simulation

If the signal of the radar system sending out in the middle frequency is the signal which is modulated mixing the LFM and the Barker FM of 13 bits, considering the manage speed of the computer, the center frequency of LFM is 2MHz, the bandwidth of FM is 2MHz, every bit width of code is 10μs, the sampling frequency is 40MHz, the delay time of echo signal is 10000 sampling points, so the result of the hybrid-modulation signal during the linear FM and the BC pulse compression disposal are as the figure 5 and 6 shown respectively.

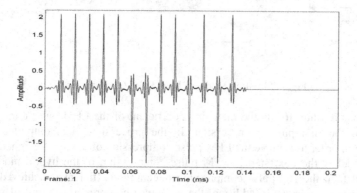

Fig. 5. The Simulation Result of LFM Pulse Compression

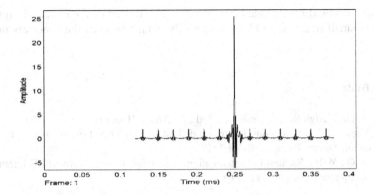

Fig. 6. The Simulation Result of hybrid-modulation signal Pulse Compression

In figure 5, after the hybrid-modulation signal across the matched filter of the LFM pulse compression, every envelope of outputting pulse in code is approximately sin c(x). Under the circumstances of multi-objective, the side-lamella of big objective can flood the nearby main signal of fewer objectives causing the objective loss. In order to improve the distinguishing ability of multi-objective, the side-lamella can be restrained by the technology of adding right. If an ideal point object in 37.5km via the delay time of echo signal is 0.25ms(10000 sampling points), when the hybrid-modulation signals are disposed by 13 barker pulse compression, the main lamella appears in 0.25ms, as the figure 6 is shown. During the second pulse compression, the outputting width is P times of the first pulse compression and the width of the whole pulse compression is $P \times \sqrt{D}$ times. The pulse compression result of the hybrid-signal equal the BC compression result which width is 1/B and code length is $P \times \sqrt{D}$. Therefore, the Doppler influence of the hybrid-signal is smaller than the pure position code.

Seen from the simulation results, during the twice pulse compression disposal, the pulse width is greatly decreased. And the whole pulse compression ratio is approximately equal the multiply the two pulse compression. On the premises of the radar influence distance, the better capacity to discriminate distances and the measure precision are obtained.

5   Conclusions

The paper begins from the principle of the hybrid-modulation signal, and sets up the simulating model of the hybrid-modulation signal pulse compression using Simulink. According to the analysis of the results, the model realizes the simulation of pulse compression on the hybrid-modulation signal preferably and provides support for development of radar system simulation on Simulink and the research on the technology of radar digital signal processing. In course of setting up the simulation model, the powerful simulation capability of Simulink has been realized. Its modeling time is short comparatively, the model is simple and clear and the calculating precision is high. At the same time the model, evaluating result and the validating system action could be amended conveniently in any step of the system design. And the fund is small so that it will be spread easily. So it can be used extensively in every field.

References

1. Wehner, D.R.: High Resolution Radar, 2nd edn. Artech House (1995)
2. Bell Mark, R.: Information Theory and Radar Wavform Design. IEEE Trans. on Information Theory 79(5), 1578–1597 (1993)
3. Schrich, G., Wiley Richard G.: Interception of LPI Radar Signals. In: IEEE International Radar Conference, pp. 108–111 (1990)

The Reentry Trajectory Optimization for Lifting Vehicle by Using Gauss Pseudospectral Method

Yuxing Yang and Xiuyun Meng

School of Aerospace Engineering, Beijing Institute of Technology,
Beijing, China
yangyx_bit@sina.com

Abstract. To obtain the flight trajectory for lifting vehicle after reentry atmosphere, the Gauss pseudospectral method is used to convert the reentry trajectory optimization problem of three-dimension for the vehicle into a nonlinear programming problem. The path constraints include the heat flux peak on stagnation point and maximum dynamic pressure and the terminal constraints include the vehicle's height and position, and the optimal performance index is the minimum total heat absorption. The angle of attack and bank angle are chosen as control variables. The result of simulation indicates that the GPM is effective to solve trajectory optimization problem, and can satisfy the above optimization index and constraint condition.

Keywords: lifting vehicle, gauss pseudospectral method, reentry trajectory, nonlinear programming.

1 Introduction

Compared with traditional ballistic and ballistic-lifting vehicle, the lifting vehicle can provide a relatively higher lift so that the reentry trajectory is suitable for soft landing, which can reduce the impact load of payload and improve the landing accuracy. This kind of vehicle usually changes the trajectory by aerodynamic force to make sure that the reentry trajectory will meet the requirements. However, it is so complex and difficult, because the vehicle need not only to satisfy the path constraints include the strong heat flux and dynamic pressure but also to fall into the specified area for attack or recycle, which makes the reentry trajectory to be limited into a narrow range [1]. So we must choose an optimization method to find a trajectory that can fit the path contraints and terminal contraints.

The optimization of reentry trajectory is generally nonlinear optimal control problems with state constraints and control constraints. At present, most numerical methods for solving optimal control problems fall into two general categories: indirect methods and direct methods. In an indirect method, the optimal control problems are converted to the Two-point boundary value problem based on minimum principle. The primary advantages of indirect methods are a high accuracy in the solution and the assurance that the solution satisfies the first-order optimality conditions. However, for a nonlinear system, it's very hard to solve the Two-point boundary value problems

T. Xiao, L. Zhang, and M. Fei (Eds.): AsiaSim 2012, Part II, CCIS 324, pp. 217–227, 2012.

by using numerical methods, because it is so difficult to get the transversality condition and an accurate initial guess of the state, which is usually required. In a direct method, the continuous-time optimal control problem is transcribed directly to a nonlinear programming problem (NLP) instead of solve the necessary optimality conditions. The resulting NLP can be solved numerically by well developed algorithms which attempt to satisfy a set of conditions associated with the NLP.The direct method is more effective in solving complex practical problem, so it is widely used in the reentry trajectory optimization. The Gauss pseudospectral method(GPM) is proposed by Benson in 2005, it is one kind of direct method. The critical contribution by Benson is that he proved GPM is exactly equivalent to the first order necessary conditions in optimal control theory. Huntington has solved the problem of optimal spacecraft formation configuration by using GPM [2].

2   The Gauss Pseudospectral Method

The main idea of GPM: the unknown state and control variables are discretized in a series of Gauss points, then the Lagrange interpolating polynomials are used to approximate the true status and control. The dynamic equation is approximated by differentiating the state approximation. So the continuous-time optimal control problem is converted into a parameter optimization problem with some algebraic constraints.

The trajectory optimization problems are generally nonlinear optimal control problems with state constraints and control constraints. Mathematical description: determine the control $u(t) \in R^m$, that minimizes the Bolza cost functional [3]:

$$J = \phi(X(t_f), t_f) + \int_0^{t_f} g(X(t), U(t), t)dt \qquad (1)$$

involving the state $x(t) \in R^n$, initial time t_0 and final time t_f, subject to the dynamic constraint

$$\dot{x} = f(x(t), u(t), t), \quad t \in [t_0, t_f] \qquad (2)$$

the boundary condition

$$\varphi(x(t_0), t_0, x(t_f), t_f) = 0 \qquad (3)$$

and inequality path constraint

$$c[X(t), U(t), t] \le 0 \qquad (4)$$

First the Gauss quadrature formula is given by:

$$\int_{-1}^{1} f(\tau)d\tau = \sum_{i=1}^{N} \omega_i f(\tau_i) + E \qquad (5)$$

where, τ_i is the independent variable on the i th Gaussian point, E is the error remainder term, N gauss points are null points of the n order Legendre polynomials. ω_i is the gauss weight, shown as:

$$\omega_i = \int_{-1}^{1} \prod_{k=1, k \neq i}^{N} \frac{t - t_k}{t_i - t_k} dt \qquad (6)$$

Note that the time interval in the optimal control problem spans $t \in [t_0, t_f]$, yet spans $\tau \in [-1,1]$ in GPM, we should do the follow transformation:

$$t = \frac{(t_f - t_0)\tau + (t_f + t_0)}{2} \qquad (7)$$

Let $\eta = \{\tau_1, \cdots, \tau_N\}$ be the set of N Legendre-Gauss(LG) points, they lie on the interior of the interval $(-1,1)$ are strictly increasing, then appends the point $\tau_0 = -1$ to the set η for a total of N+1 points on the interval $[-1,1)$. An approximation to the state with a basis of N+1 Lagrange interpolating polynomials $L_i(\tau)(i = 0, \cdots, N)$ is formed as follows:

$$x(\tau) \approx X(\tau) = \sum_{i=0}^{N} L_i(\tau)x(\tau_i) \qquad (8)$$

where

$$L_i(\tau) = \prod_{j=0, j \neq i}^{N} \frac{\tau - \tau_j}{\tau_i - \tau_j} \qquad (9)$$

Similarly, the control variables can be approximated as:

$$u(\tau) \approx U(\tau) = \sum_{i=0}^{N} L_i^*(\tau)u(\tau_i) \qquad (10)$$

where

$$L_i^*(\tau) = \prod_{j=1, j \neq i}^{N} \frac{\tau - \tau_j}{\tau_i - \tau_j} \qquad (11)$$

It is noteworthy that, N+1 points include N Gauss Points and a initial point are used to approximate state, while only N Gauss points are used to the control.

The dynamic equations is approximated by differentiating the state approximation of Eq.(8) as follows:

$$\dot{x}(\tau_k) \approx \dot{X}(\tau_k) = \sum_{i=0}^{N} \dot{L}_i(\tau_k)X(\tau_i) = \sum_{i=0}^{N} D_{ki}(\tau_k)X(\tau_i) \qquad (12)$$

the differentiation matrix $D \in R^{N(N+1)}$, is determined as:

$$D_{ki} = \dot{L}_i(\tau_k) = \sum_{l=0}^{N} \frac{\prod\limits_{j=0, j\neq i, j}^{N} (\tau_k - \tau_j)}{\prod\limits_{j=0, j\neq i}^{N} (\tau_i - \tau_j)} \tag{13}$$

where $k = 1, 2, \cdots, N \; ; i = 0, 1, \cdots, N$

By Eq.(6), the differential equations are converted into a series of algebraic constraints:

$$\sum_{i=0}^{N} D_{ki} X(\tau_i) - \frac{t_f - t_0}{2} f(X(\tau_k), U(\tau_k), \tau_k; t_0, t_f) = 0, (k = 1, \cdots, N) \tag{14}$$

Since X_f is absent in the state approximation of Eq.(8), it must be constrained in other ways to ensure that it satisfies the state dynamic equations. According to the state dynamics:

$$X(\tau_f) = X(\tau_0) + \frac{t_f - t_0}{2} \sum w_k f(X(\tau_k), U(\tau_k), \tau, t_0, t_f) \tag{15}$$

Lastly, the integral term in the cost functional of Eq. (1) can be approximated with a Gauss quadrature, resulting in

$$J = \phi(X_0, t_0, X_f, t_f) + \frac{t_f - t_0}{2} \sum_{k=1}^{N} \omega_k g(X_k, U_k, \tau_k; t_0, t_f) \tag{16}$$

boundary constraint

$$\varphi(X_0, t_0, X_f, t_f) = 0 \tag{17}$$

and path constraint

$$C(X_k, U_k, \tau_k; t_0, t_f) \leq 0 \tag{18}$$

Eq.(14)-(18) define a NLP whose solution is an approximate solution to the continuous Bolza problem. X_k, U_k, τ_k are the parameters to be optimized. Performance index is Eq.(16), constraints consist of Eq.(14), (15), (17)and(18). In this way, the continuous-time optimal control problem is transformed to nonlinear programming problems.

The Sequential Quadratic Programming(SQP), also known as the constrained variable metric method, is used to solve the NPL in this paper. In the algorithm, a inital value of parameters shuold be given, which has a direct impact on the performance of the algorithm[4].

3   The Problem of Reentry Trajectory Optimization

This paper selects the Common Aero Vehicle(CAV) designed by the U.S.A to be the object of study. CAV is a maneuvering reentry vehicle capable of carrying a payload down from a suborbital or orbital atmospheric reentry and either impacting a target directly or dispensing in less than one hour. In order to hold a good cross-range, CAV has relatively high hypersonic lift to drag(L/D). The hypersonic L/D associated with CAVs are nearly in the 2.0-3.0 range. The fight control for the reentry is essential, we have to make sure not only that the stagnation point heat flux and dynamic pressure are within allowed limits, but also the CAV reaches in range of the carried weapons. Therefore, it is very important to get a reentry trajectory meet the above requirements [5].

3.1   The Dynamic Model for Reentry

Assuming the Earth is a uniform sphere rotating around its own axis, and ignoring the influence of the Earth's rotation, we get the simplified three DOF nonlinear equations of motion:

$$\frac{dr}{dt} = v \sin \vartheta \tag{19}$$

$$\frac{d\lambda}{dt} = \frac{v \cos \vartheta \cos \zeta}{r \cos \phi} \tag{20}$$

$$\frac{d\phi}{dt} = \frac{v \cos \vartheta \sin \zeta}{r} \tag{21}$$

$$\frac{dv}{dt} = -\frac{D}{m} - g \sin \vartheta \tag{22}$$

$$v \frac{d\vartheta}{dt} = \frac{L}{m} \cos \sigma - g \cos \vartheta \tag{23}$$

$$v \frac{d\zeta}{dt} = \frac{L \cos \sigma}{m \cos \vartheta} - \frac{v^2}{r} \cos \vartheta \cos \zeta \tan \phi \tag{24}$$

where, r is the geocentric distance from vehicle, λ, ϕ for the latitude and longitude, ϑ for the flight path angle, ζ for the heading angle, m for the mass;g is the acceleration of gravity as a function of the height: $g = \frac{\mu}{r^2}$, μ for the Earth's gravitational constant; D and L for the drag and lift, are given respectively by:

$$D = 0.5 \rho V^2 C_D S_{ref} \tag{25}$$

$$L = 0.5\rho V^2 C_L S_{ref} \tag{26}$$

C_D and C_L are the drag coefficient and lift coefficient, S_{ref} is the reference area, ρ is the atmospheric density, the approximation here is

$$\rho = \rho_0 e^{-\beta(r-r_e)} \tag{27}$$

Where, ρ_0 for atmospheric density on sea-level, r_e for the radius of the Earth, $\beta = 1/7200$.

The relevant data of the reentry vehicle studied in this paper are from CAV-L, its mass is 816.48kg, and the effective reference area is 0.32258 m², detailed aerodynamic parameters as shown in Table 1 and Table 2[4].

Table 1. The lift coefficient of CAV(C_L)

AOA	Mach 3.5	Mach 5	Mach 8	Mach 15	Mach 20	Mach 23
10°	0.3401	0.3264	0.3108	0.2856	0.2760	0.2739
15°	0.5786	0.5358	0.4883	0.4491	0.4349	0.4319
20°	0.7975	0.7291	0.6731	0.6137	0.5975	0.5966

Table 2. The drag coefficient of CAV(C_D)

AOA	Mach 3.5	Mach 5	Mach 8	Mach 15	Mach 20	Mach 23
10°	0.1838	0.1483	0.1295	0.1226	0.1210	0.1217
15°	0.2691	0.2505	0.2308	0.2187	0.2150	0.2159
20°	0.4197	0.3861	0.3599	0.3388	0.3379	0.3409

In hypersonic flight conditions, the aerodynamic coefficients can be simplified as the function of the angle of attack, generally

$$C_L = a_0 + a_1\alpha + a_2\alpha^2 \tag{8}$$

$$C_D = b_0 + b_1\alpha + b_2\alpha^2 \tag{29}$$

We otain the vaule by fitting the the aerodynamic with Mach 8:

$a_0 = -0.0223$, $a_1 = 0.0319$, $a_2 = 0.0001$; $b_0 = 0.0103$, $b_1 = 0.0064$, $b_2 = 0.0006$

3.2   Performance Index and Constraints

Boundary Conditions. For the CAV, the initial state should be determined according to the reentry conditions, the initial height is set as 120km here; the terminal state should be determined according to Terminal Area Energy Management(TAEM), the height is set as 18km. Considering the general condition about the reentry of lifting vehicle, the initial and terminal value of the state are chosen as follows[6]

$$r_0 = 6498 \text{ km} , V_0 = 7.315km / h , \lambda_0 = \phi_0 = 0° , \vartheta_0 = -1.5° , r_f = 6396 \text{ km}$$

Path Constraints. Except for the boundary conditions, the reentry should satisfies the constraints of the heat flux peak on the stagnation poin, dynamic pressure and overload.

Constraint of the heat flux peak on the stagnation poin[7]:

$$\frac{C}{\sqrt{R}} \sqrt{\rho} V^{3.08} \leq \dot{Q}_{max} \tag{30}$$

where C is a constant, the value is 30.5; R for the curvature radius of the vehicle, here R=0.15m; $\dot{Q}_{max}$ for the allowed heat flux peak, which is set to$1200W / cm^2$.

Constraint of dynamic pressure:

$$0.5\rho V^2 \leq q_{max} \tag{31}$$

q_{max} is the allowed maximum dynamic pressure and is set to$1.5 \times 10^5 N / m^2$.

Constraint of overload

$$\frac{\sqrt{(L^2 + D^2)}}{G} \leq n_{max} \tag{32}$$

G for gravity, n_{max} is the allowed maximum overload and is set to 4.

Constraints of Control. For the control of lifting vehicle, the attack angle and bank angle should be within the allowed range. That is:

$$10° \leq \alpha \leq 40° \tag{33}$$

$$-90° \leq \sigma \leq 90° \tag{34}$$

Performance Index. The trajectory of lifting vehicle is relatively flat, but the voyage and total time are longer. This leads to smaller heat flux peak but longer heating time and higher heat absorption. So the total heat absorption minimum is one of the most important performance index. The expression is:

$$J = \int_{t_0}^{t_f} \frac{C}{\sqrt{R}} \sqrt{\rho} V^{3.08} dt \tag{35}$$

4   Mathematical Simulation

The CAV for the model, with the full consideration of the path constraints and terminal constraints, the Matlab code was developed based on GPM. The number of Gauss nodes is 40, the configurations are accordance with the contents in section 2. In addition, there is an estimate of the given state and control on the starting point and end point, accurate estimates is conducive to the faster convergence of the algorithm. The time course of height and position are shown in Fig.1 and 2.

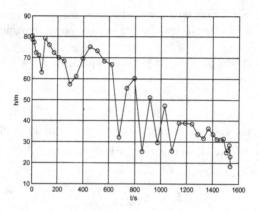

Fig. 1. The relationship between heght and time

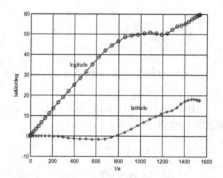

Fig. 2. The relationship between position and time

Fig.1 shows the curve of altitude in the reentry, we can learn from the figure that the CAV declines in oscillation form, and achieves 18km at the end of trajectory. In Fig.2, the changes of latitude and longitude reflect the CAV is closing to the target gradually.

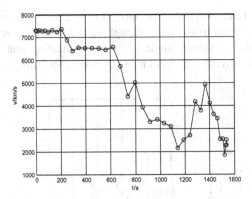

Fig. 3. The relationship between speed and time

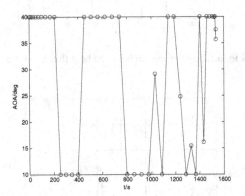

Fig. 4. The relationship between the AOA and time

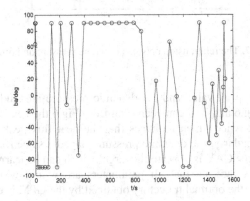

Fig. 5. The relationship between bank angle and time

Fig.3 shows the trend of speed. The optimal time course of control are shown in Fig.4 and 5. It can be seen from Fig.4, throughout the process of reentry the flight of CAV is almost at the maximum angle of attack, indicating that the high angle of attack is very helpful to reduce the total heat absorption for lifting vehicle.

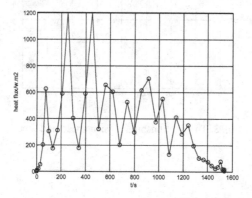

Fig. 6. The relationship between heat flux and time

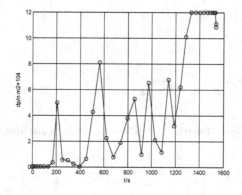

Fig. 7. The relationship between dynamic pressure and time

Also the heat flux peak value and the dynamic pressure are studied in this paper, they are shown in Fig.6 and 7. It can been seen from Fig.6 the heat flux on stagnation point reach the peak twice,which indictaes that the heat flux peak played a limited role in the flight. Simularly, the dynamic pressure played a same role by maintaining the maximum when the CAV is close to the target,which can be learned in Fig.7.

The above figures indicate that all parameters are within within the scope of constraints. Therefor, the optimal trajectory obtained by the GPM is entirely feasible.

5   Conclusions

The reentry trajectory optimization for lifting vehicle by using Gauss Pseudospectral Method is studied in this paper. The optimal performance index is the minimum total heat absorption taking into accounts the path constraints and terminal constraints. The simulation results indicate that the designed trajectory can satisfy the performance index and constraints well. This study also shows that GPM is a very effective method to the trajectory optimization problem.

References

1. Zhao, H.: Reentry dynamics and guidance. National Defense University Press, M. Changsha (1997)
2. Huntington, G.T., Rao, A.V.: Optimal spacecraft formation con-figuration using a Gauss pseudospectral method. In: Proc. of the AAS/AISS Space Flight Mechanics Meeting (2005)
3. Todd, H.G.: Advancement and Analysis of a Gauss Pseudospectral Transcription for Optimal Control Problems. Massachusetts Institute of Technology, Cambridge (2007)
4. Shi, G.: Using the Sequential Quadratic Programming algorithm to solve nonlinear programming problems. Lanzhou University (2009)
5. George, R.: The common aero vehicle: Space delivery system of the future. In: AIAA Space Technology Conference and Exposition, Albuquerque (1999)
6. Yong, E.: Study on Trajectory Optimization and Guidance Approach for Hypersonic Glidereentry Vehicle. National Defense University (2008)
7. Phillips, T.H.: A common aero vehiclemode:l Description and employment guide. Report of Schafer Corporation for AFRL and AFSPC (2003)

Intelligent Remote Wireless Streetlight Monitoring System Based on GPRS

Meihua Xu[1], Mengwei Sun[2], Guoqin Wang[1], and Shuping Huang[2]

[1] School of Mechatronical Engineering and Automation, Shanghai University
[2] Microelectronic R&D Center, Shanghai University, Shanghai, China
smw@shu.edu.cn

Abstract. According to the development trend of the streetlight, this paper presents a remote and wireless streetlight monitoring system based on GPRS. GPRS stands for General Packet Radio Service, it has a lot of advantages like widely used, high transmission speed, low power consumption and so on. The system uses microcontroller chip MSP430F2274 and wireless transceiver chip CC2500. The whole network consists of the control center and up to 100 groups of control network, and each control network has up to 100 terminal nodes, terminal nodes measure humidity, current, voltage and other information, and send these information to the transition points by the RF wireless transceiver module, then the transition points transmit information to the control center through GSM/GPRS networks. The control center will deal with the data so that it can know the situation of each streetlight. According to the result the control center gives orders to each streetlight to control the switch state and illumination of them.

Keywords: GPRS, remote monitoring, wireless transceiver, streetlight.

1 Introduction

With global increasing pressure on resources and environment, the request that the society has on environment protection, energy saving and emission reduction, sustainable development is increasing day by day. The government of China is trying hard to find a new way which can has a good return, low emission, sustainable and the price is low. Today more than half of people on the world live in the city, we must implement the low carbon production mode and life-style, reduce the abuse of natural resources. Then we can have the sustainable development. As the indispensable equipment, streetlights are everywhere whether in the city or in the town. How to enhance the management, monitoring and intelligent control of the illumination of the streetlights is important to reduce energy consumption and emission, and achieve low carbon development.

This paper aims at the need for remote and wireless streetlight monitoring system, relies on the GPRS network of China Mobile to build a remote and wireless monitoring

T. Xiao, L. Zhang, and M. Fei (Eds.): AsiaSim 2012, Part II, CCIS 324, pp. 228–237, 2012.

system platform based on GPRS which can cover all streetlight networks in the urban area. This system incorporates advanced GPRS wireless communication technology, the computer control technology, data acquisition technology, database technology, with huge streetlight network which needed to be monitored as its object [1]. This system will collect and process the data and send them to remote control center through GPRS to provide reference for the manager so that it can know the real time working situation of the equipment, and then to realize fault diagnosis, timely alarm, data analysis, meanwhile the system can intelligently regulate and control the illumination of streetlights from far away according to the real time environmental condition.

We can reduce the labor intensity of the technician and improve work efficiency by using this remote and wireless streetlight monitoring system. This system becomes very important especially in some high risk environment where engineer cannot easily reach, because it can monitor the equipment from far away, and avoid the risk of working in the dangerous situation. The control of the switch and the illumination of the streetlights can sharply reduce the power consumption and prolong their service life. At the same time, this method can make contribution to the realization of green, low carbon, sustainable economic development.

2   The Hardware Design of Remote and Wireless Streetlight Monitoring System

2.1   Overall Design of System

Fig.1 shows the overall frame diagram of the remote and wireless streetlight monitoring system. The sink node is installed in the control center, the control center detect all kinds of working situation of every streetlight through GSM/GPRS network, including voltage, current, temperature, humidity, illumination. The control center automatically controls the switch state and illumination of the streetlights to save energy and protect the whole streetlight system. The system contains up to 100 groups of control networks, and each group of control network has 100 terminal nodes at most, in the end of each group of control network, there is a special node calls transition node, it is installed on the streetlight and contains a GSM/GPRS module so that it can communicate with the terminal node and the sink node. The terminal node is also installed on the streetlight.

In each group of control network, every terminal node connects to each other in a daisy-chained way, and sends the data packet to the previous node in turn, when the data packet arrives in the transition node, the data packet will be sent to the sink node in the control center through GPRS. By using GPRS, each group of control network builds a communication bridge with the sink node, and it can obviously increase the communication distance because GPRS do not have the distance limitation.

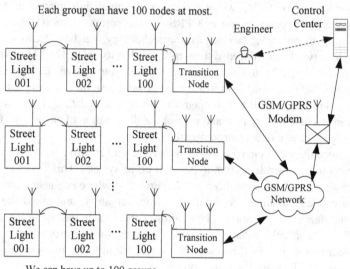

Fig. 1. System Frame Diagram

The remote and wireless streetlight monitoring system can provide a real-time picture of the whole streetlight network for the workers in the control center in order to manager the system easily. Once some measured data of any nodes becomes anomaly, such as high humidity, high temperature and short circuit, the system will alarm automatically and inform the engineer, or cut down the power to protect itself. The control center can control the streetlights on the basis of the measured data, for example, when morning turn off the lights automatically; when dark or rainy the lights will be turn on; when traffic is not heavy, the control center will turn on every other streetlight or turn on one side streetlights. Meanwhile all the data is saved in the database in the control center to be read anytime and be researched to establish the scheme of the streetlight control.

The whole system contains 3 kinds of nodes. They are terminal node, the transition node and the sink node. The structure of them will be present in the next section.

2.2 Hardware Structure of the Terminal Node

Fig2 shows the hardware structure of the terminal node. The terminal node is mainly made up of micro-controller module, RF wireless transceiver, MCU power management module, memory, current and voltage detection module, humidity measuring module, relay control module, JTAG debug interface and LED display module.

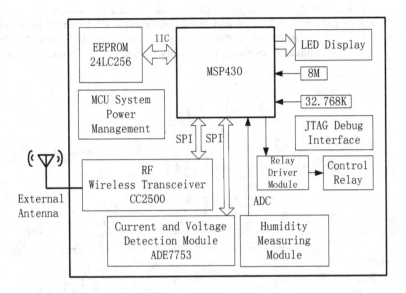

Fig. 2. Hardware Structure of the Terminal Node

2.2.1 Micro-controller Module

This paper uses MSP430F2274 from TI in the micro-controller module. MSP430 is the center of the whole terminal node, it receives the data from the current and voltage detection module, RF wireless transceiver module and humidity measuring module [2]. At the same time, MSP430 will detect the temperature itself, and then MSP430 will process and analysis these data, at last give orders to the relay control module to switch on or off the streetlights and send the data to the RF wireless transceiver to communicate with other terminal nodes or the transition node.

MSP430F2274 is an ultralow-power mixed signal microcontroller with two built-in 16-bit timers, a universal serial communication interface, 10–bit A/D converter with integrated reference and data transfer controller (DTC), two general purpose operational amplifiers and thirty two I/O pins. MSP430F2274 needs very low voltage range from 1.8V to 3.6V, so it can be powered by the battery [3]. MSP430 has five low power modes such as active mode, standby mode, off mode, etc. When works at active mode, the current is 250µA; when works at standby mode, the current is 0.7µA; when works at off mode, the current is only 0.1µA. So it is optimized to achieve extended battery life in the remote and wireless streetlight monitoring system. Even though powered by the battery the terminal node can work for an enough long time.

MSP430 is integrated with A/D converter, multiplier, timer, comparator and some other modules. Additionally the micro-controller has rich peripherals, so MSP430F2274 is the best choice in this paper.

2.2.2 RF Wireless Transceiver Module

In this paper, we use CC2500 RF wireless transceiver from TI, the CC2500 is a low-cost 2.4 GHz transceiver designed for very low-power wireless applications. The circuit is intended for the 2400-2483.5MHz ISM and SRD frequency band. The RF transceiver is integrated with a highly configurable baseband modem. The modem supports various modulation formats and has a configurable data rate up to 500kbps. CC2500 provides extensive hardware support for packet handling, data buffering, burst transmissions, clear channel assessment, link quality indication, and wake-on-radio [4].

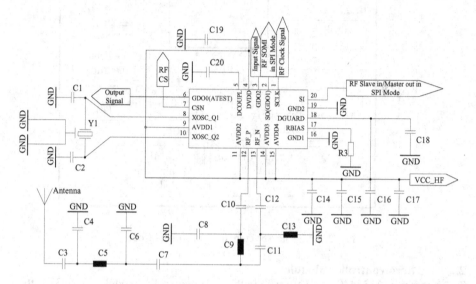

Fig. 3. Principle Scheme of RF Wireless Transceiver Module

Fig.3 shows the principle scheme of RF wireless transceiver module. The function of RF wireless transceiver module is transmitting data to and receiving data from the other terminal nodes and the transition node in the group of the control network. The pin CSN is the RF chip selected signal, it decides when the chip is on, when it is off; the pin SCLK is the RF clock signal, it decides the working clock of the CC2500 chip; the pin SO is the RF slave out/master in in the SPI mode, and SI is the RF slave in/master out in the SPI mode, they decide the working way in the SPI mode; the pin GDO2 is the input signal and the pin GDO0 is the output signal, they receive and transmit signals to the micro-controller module; pin RF_P and PF_N link to the antenna circuit, they control the working status of the antenna.

The terminal node is installed on the streetlight, so it requires that all the members of the node do not occupy too much space. At the same time, the terminal node is powered by the battery, it is important to save energy. The CC2500 chip can meet the two requirements, and it has a very small volume and has low power consumption, it is suitable for the terminal node. Meanwhile, the CC2500 has the very high sensitivity and an efficient SPI interface. So it can transmit and receive data in a really high speed and can detect the feeble signal to get the necessary information. At last, we install an external antenna in the terminal node. Using this antenna, the signal is enhanced and transceiver distance is increased so that the other nodes can easily receive the data packet even though they are in distant places.

2.2.3 Current and Voltage Detecting Module

The function of the current and voltage detecting module includes: detecting the current and the voltage of the streetlight; calculating the power of each streetlight and send the data to the micro-controller module through SPI interface. MSP430 will deal with the data received from the detecting module, to decide what to do next. When the current, the voltage or the power exceeds the limit, the MSP430 chip can give orders to CC2500 to send information to the control center through other nodes. The control center can alarm or cut off the power automatically.

This paper uses the ADE7753 chip from ADI [5]. It is a chip with an advanced, high accuracy measuring circuit. ADE7753 can adjust to large variations in environmental conditions and time. This chip incorporates two second-order 16-bit $\sum$-Δ ADCs, a digital integrator, reference circuitry, temperature sensor, energy measurements, line-voltage period measurement, and rms calculation on the voltage and current. These blocks can fit the meets in the detecting module. The on-chip digital integrator can enable direct interfaced to current sensors with di/dt output. The chip can measure active, reactive and apparent energy. And in active energy measurement it has less than 0.1% error over a dynamic range of 1000 to 1 at 25°C. ADE7753 is powered by 5V, so we can also use battery to supply the energy. Another advantage of this chip is that when it works, it does not cost a lot of power.

2.2.4 Other Modules

The function of the humidity measuring module includes: measuring the humidity of the environment; turning the humidity signal into the voltage signal; sending the data to the micro-controller module. The function of the relay control module includes: receiving the commands from the micro-controller module, and controlling the switch state and the illumination of the streetlight. The function of the LED display module is to display the real-time state of the streetlight and the terminal node. The function of the memory is saving important data. It will not lose the information when power off. It ensures the security of the data.

2.3 Hardware Structure of the Transition Node

Fig.4 shows the hardware structure of the transition node. It is made up of micro-controller module, RF wireless transceiver module, MCU system power management, memory, GSM/GPRS module, GSM power management module, reset management module, SIM, JTAG debug interface, LED display module.

The modules in the transition node are similar to the modules in the terminal node. The difference between them is that the terminal node has the current and voltage measuring module while the transition node has the GSM/GPRS module and some other related modules. The micro-controller module mainly control the RF wireless transceiver module, LED display module and the GSM/GPRS module. The function of the RF wireless transceiver module is sending data to and receiving data from the terminal node with the external antenna. CC2500 receives orders from MSP430 in SPI

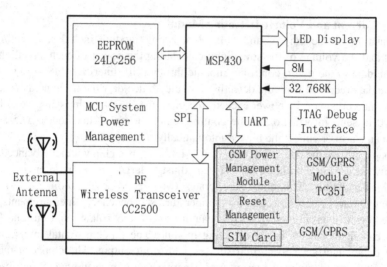

Fig. 4. Hardware Structure of the Transition Node

interface. The GSM power management module supply necessary energy to the GSM/GPRS module and the reset management module; GSM/GPRS module is the bridge of the sink node and the transition nodes. The GSM/GPRS module also has an external antenna. The antenna increase the communication distance of the transition node. The sink node in the control center gives orders to the transition nodes through GPRS, and then the transition nodes send the data to the terminal nodes in their group. When the terminal nodes want to upload data, they will first send data to the transition node in turn. The transition nodes then transmit the data to the sink node to finish a communication.

2.4   Hardware Structure of the Sink Node

Fig.5 shows the hardware structure of the sink node. It contains GSM power management module, GSM/GPRS module, reset management module, SIM, USB controller module and USB interface.

The GSM power management module, the reset management module, SIM work together to ensure the GSM/GPRS module can work steadily. Their functions are similar to the modules in the transition node. GSM/GPRS module communicates with the transition nodes by the external antenna through GPRS. This paper uses CY7C68013 from Cypress as the USB controller. It has an internal embedded 51 MCU. With the USB controller, the control center can exchange information with the GSM/GPRS module, and then send the data to other nodes. It has a really high transmit speed, low power consumption, and small volume, so it can meet the need of the design.

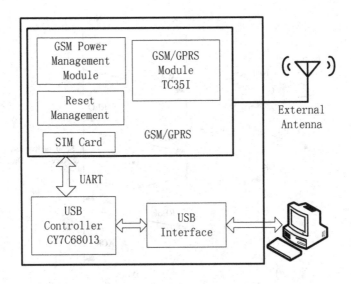

Fig. 5. Hardware Structure of the Sink node

3   Software Design of the Monitoring System

The transmission protocol used in this paper is based on the SimpliciTI transmission protocol. The SimpliciTI protocol has two major advantages: low power consumption and occupying small memory. This ensures the transmission protocol in this paper takes little resource and keeps low power consumption while working efficiently. The monitoring system adopts the thought of three-time-handshaking from TCP protocol to accomplish the establishment and acknowledgement of the link. TCP protocol has a lot of advantages like reliable, high stability, easy to connect and so on [6]. By combining the two different protocols together, the new protocol can have many advanced characteristics and functions. It can detect the situation like data losing; data corruption. When not receiving data, it can automatically send data again. When finding mistakes, it can deal with the emergency and alarm promptly.

Fig.6 shows the working timing diagram of the nodes. It has 5 kinds of data packets, INIT, REQ, RESP, WAIT, and ACK. By using these packets, the system can control all the nodes, and know any information that it needs.

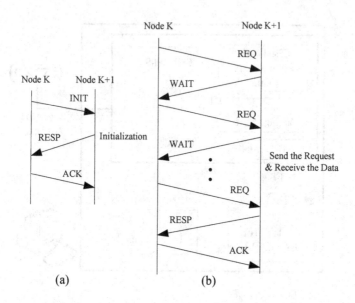

Fig. 6. Working Timing Diagram: (a) this is initialization; (b) this is a process of sending the request and receiving the data

When working, the sink node in the control center transmits an INIT data packet to the transition nodes through GPRS, and then the transition node will send the INIT data packet to the terminal node in the group of the control network. Taking node K and node K+1 as an example, the node K sends an INIT packet to the next node K+1; when the node K+1 receives the INIT packet, it will return a RESP packet to node K; node K sends an ACK packet to acknowledge that it has received the RESP packet. There are numbers in the INIT packet. When the initialization finished, every node has a sole number so that we can distinguish the different nodes. When a node breaks, it will cost a lot of time if we send the engineer to check every node. Having these numbers, in the control center, we can get the number of the broken node, and then we can locate the node. It can save time and reduce labor intensity.

When the control center wants to know the data information of the nodes, it will send a REQ packet. Taking node K and node K+1 as an example, node K sends a REQ packet to the node K+1; when node K+1 has the data that node K needs, it will return RESP packet; when node K+1 does not have the data, it will return a WAIT packet to node K; node K will continue to transmit REQ packet until it receives RESP packet; when node K receives the RESP packet, it will send an ACK packet to finish this communication. This kind of transmission protocol makes the whole process safe and efficient.

4   Conclusions

This paper accomplished the remote and wireless monitoring system. The whole system can monitor the statement of every streetlight. When finding anomalous situations, the control center can make countermeasures immediately, like cutting off the power, alarming, informing the engineers, etc. The nodes in the monitoring system are powered by the batteries and have not too much room. In consideration of this, the chips in the nodes do not take too much space and have the advantage of low power consumption. If the monitoring system can take the place of the traditional streetlight control system, it will be good to the green, low carbon and sustainable economic development of our country.

Acknowledgment. The authors would like to acknowledge the financial support by Shanghai Annual Plan for Absorption and Innovation of Technology Imported under Grant No. 11XI-15.

References

1. Jing, C., Shu, D., Gu, D., Liu, B.: Streetlight Power Cable Monitoring System Based on Wireless Sensor Networks. In: Proc. IEEE Symp. Information Acquisition, pp. 1284–1288. IEEE Press (August 2006), doi:10.1109/ICIA.2006.305936
2. Zhang, Y.: Wireless Temperature Control System Based on MSP430. Friend of Science Amateurs 1, 137–138 (2009), doi:CNKI:SUN:KXZB.0.2009-01-074
3. Texas Instruments Company. MSP430x22x2, MSP430x22x4 Family User's Guide
4. Zhang, P., He, N.: USB interfaces wireless data acquisition system based on MSP430 and CC2500. Electronic Design Engineering 18(2), 12–14 (2010), doi:CNKI:SUN: GWDZ.0.2010-02-008
5. Kong, J., Zhong, R., Cai, J.: High precision and multi-function energy metering system with IC ADE7753. Application of Electronic Technique 1, 78–79 (2009), doi:CNKI:SUN: DZJY.0.2009-01-030
6. Meyer, M.: TCP performance over GPRS. In: Proc. IEEE Symp. WCNC 1999, pp. 1248–1252. IEEE Press (September 1999), doi:10.1109/WCNC.1999.79693

Research of Time-Delay Chaotic Systems via Linear Feedback*

Hua Wang**, Xin Wang, Xianhai Shen, and Xuliang Zhang

School of Mechatronics Engineering and Automation,
Shanghai Key Laboratory of Power Station Automation Technology,
Shanghai University, Shanghai, 200072, China
wanghua609@yahoo.com.cn

Abstract. Based on the Razumikhin theorem of time-delay systems, this paper discusses chaos control and synchronization of chaotic systems with time-varying lags. A novel method for time-delay chaotic systems is derived. Linear and feasible controller is designed to control and synchronize Lorenz system with time-varying lags. The proposed controller can realize chaos control even though there exist unknown time-varying lags. This method can be applied to a class of systems with different time-varying delays too. Numerical simulation results are given to show the effectiveness of the proposed method.

Keywords: Lorenz system, Chaos Synchronization, Lyapunov-Razumikhin function, Time-delay, Linear controller.

1 Introduction

As a very interesting phenomenon, chaos has been intensively investigated in many fields. Especially, chaos synchronization has attracted strong attention due to its powerful potential application in laser physics, secure communication, biomedical and many other fields [1-5].

Many methods have been presented to achieve chaos control and synchronization, such as the passive control method[6], backstepping design method [7], adaptive control method[8,9], sliding mode control[10,11] and control Lyapunov function (CLF) method [12,13], etc. However, most the controllers designed with these above methods are nonlinear, which are more difficult to be implemented in application than linear controllers. Consequently, the design of novel linear controllers is a very meaningful and valuable work [14,15].

Recently, there has been a substantial increase of activities on chaotic systems with time-varying lags [16-20]. Time-delay chaotic phenomenon is frequently encountered

---

* Supported by Natural Science Foundation of Shanghai(11ZR1412400), Innovation Fund of Shanghai University, the Scientific Special Research Fund for Training Excellent Young Teachers in Higher Education Institutions of Shanghai (No. shu10044) and the "11th Five-Year Plan" 211 Construction Project of Shanghai University.
** Corresponding author.

T. Xiao, L. Zhang, and M. Fei (Eds.): AsiaSim 2012, Part II, CCIS 324, pp. 238–247, 2012.
© Springer-Verlag Berlin Heidelberg 2012

in engineering, biology and other fields [16]. Based on the Lyapunov-Krasovskii stability theory, Zhang etc. [17] proposed a new method to realize chaos synchronization for a chaotic system with time-varying lags. In Ref.[18], two different chaotic time-delay systems are presented. Based on the analysis of error dynamical systems, time-delay correlative controller is applied to achieve synchronization [18]. As a hotspot in chaos study, chaotic Lur'e systems are paid more attention [19,20]. In Ref. [19], an adaptive scheme for the stabilization and synchronization of chaotic Lur'e systems is proposed. A feedback controller is designed using the invariant principle of functional differential equations. In Ref. [20], based on an extended Lyapunov-Krasovskii function, the authors presented a delay dependent criterion for the error system. The proposed controllers are nonlinear.

Because linear controller is simple and easy to be implemented in application, we will propose a linear controller to realize chaos control and synchronization for delay chaotic systems. Based on the Razumikhin theorem of time-delay systems, this paper is focused on Lorenz system with time-varying lags.

2   Main Results

2.1   Preliminaries

Consider the following Lorenz chaotic system [18]:

$$\begin{cases} \dot{x}_1 = mx_2(t-\tau) - mx_1 \\ \dot{x}_2 = rx_1 - x_2 - x_1x_3 \\ \dot{x}_3 = x_1x_2 - bx_3(t-\tau) \end{cases} \tag{1}$$

Where m, r, b are the system parameters, $\tau = \tau(t)(0 \le \tau \le \tau_m)$ is the time-varying lag. This advanced Lorenz system may be in the chaotic state through the suitable selection of time delay τ and the system parameters.

Lemma 1 [21]. Razumikhin showed that for a time-delay system to be asymptotically stable, it is sufficient to require

$$\dot{V}(x(t)) < -w(\|x(t)\|) \quad \text{whenever}$$
$$V(t+\theta, x(t+\theta)) \le p(V(t,x(t))) \quad \text{for all } \theta \in [-\tau, 0].$$

where $p(\bullet)$ is a continuous nondecreasing function satisfying $p(s) < s$ for all $s > 0$.

Inspired by this lemma, we can discuss the stability of time-delay systems using the Lyapunov function $V(x(t)) = x^T(t)Px(t)$, setting $w(s) = \varepsilon s^2$ and $p(s) = (1+\varepsilon)s$ with $\varepsilon > 0$. This means that the system is stable if

$$\dot{V}(x(t)) + \alpha[(1+\varepsilon)V(x(t)) - V(x(t)-\tau)] < -\varepsilon\|x(t)\|^2 \tag{2}$$

for some $\alpha \ge 0$.

2.2   Chaos Control

Consider the following controlled time-delay Lorenz system:

$$\begin{cases} \dot{x}_1 = mx_2(t-\tau) - mx_1 + u_1 \\ \dot{x}_2 = rx_1 - x_2 - x_1x_3 + u_2 \\ \dot{x}_3 = x_1x_2 - bx_3(t-\tau) + u_3 \end{cases} \tag{3}$$

Where m, r, b are the system parameters. τ is the system delay. u_1, u_2 and u_3 are the control inputs. We will design a linear controller as

$$u_1 = -l_1x_1, u_2 == l_2x_2, u_3 = --l_3x_3$$

where l_1, l_2 and l_3 are the controller gains to be determined later.

To carry out the stability analysis, consider the following candidate Lyapunov function $V(x)$ for the time-delay system (3)

$$V(x_1, x_2, x_3) = \frac{1}{2}x_1^2 + \frac{1}{2}x_2^2 + \frac{1}{2}x_3^2 \tag{4}$$

Calculate its derivation along the solutions of system (3) and we can get

$$\dot{V}(x(t)) + \alpha[(1+\varepsilon)V(x(t)) - V(x(t-\tau))]$$

$$= x_1\dot{x}_1 + x_2\dot{x}_2 + x_3\dot{x}_3$$

$$+ \frac{\alpha}{2}[(1+\varepsilon)(x_1^2 + x_2^2 + x_3^2) - (x_1^2(t-\tau) + x_2^2(t-\tau)) + x_3^2(t-\tau))]$$

$$= mx_1x_2(t-\tau) - mx_1^2 + x_1u_1 + rx_1x_2 - x_2^2 - x_1x_2x_3 + x_2u_2 + x_1x_2x_3 - bx_3x_3(t-\tau) + x_3u_3$$

$$+ \frac{\alpha}{2}[(1+\varepsilon)(x_1^2 + x_2^2 + x_3^2) - (x_1^2(t-\tau) + x_2^2(t-\tau)) + x_3^2(t-\tau))]$$

$$\leq \frac{m^2}{2\alpha}x_1^2 + \frac{\alpha}{2}x_2^2(t-\tau) - mx_1^2 + x_1u_1 + rx_1x_2 - x_2^2 + x_2u_2 + \frac{b^2}{2\alpha}x_3^2 + \frac{\alpha}{2}x_3^2(t-\tau)$$

$$+ x_3u_3 + \frac{\alpha}{2}[(1+\varepsilon)(x_1^2 + x_2^2 + x_3^2) - (x_1^2(t-\tau) + x_2^2(t-\tau)) + x_3^2(t-\tau))]$$

$$= \frac{m^2}{2\alpha}x_1^2 - mx_1^2 + x_1u_1 + rx_1x_2 - x_2^2 + x_2u_2 + \frac{b^2}{2\alpha}x_3^2 + x_3u_3$$

$$+ \frac{\alpha}{2}(1+\varepsilon)(x_1^2 + x_2^2 + x_3^2) - x_2^2(t-\tau)$$

$$\leq -(m - \frac{m^2}{2\alpha} - \frac{\alpha(1+\varepsilon)}{2} - \frac{r}{2} + l_1)x_1^2 - (1 - \frac{\alpha(1+\varepsilon)}{2} - \frac{r}{2} + l_2)x_2^2 - (-\frac{b^2}{2\alpha} - \frac{\alpha(1+\varepsilon)}{2} + l_3)x_3^2$$

Let controller gains l_1, l_2 and l_3 satisfy the following inequalities:

$$\begin{cases} m - \dfrac{m^2}{2\alpha} - \dfrac{\alpha(1+\varepsilon)}{2} - \dfrac{r}{2} + l_1 > \varepsilon \\ 1 - \dfrac{\alpha(1+\varepsilon)}{2} - \dfrac{r}{2} + l_2 > \varepsilon \\ -\dfrac{b^2}{2\alpha} - \dfrac{\alpha(1+\varepsilon)}{2} + l_3 > \varepsilon \end{cases} \tag{6}$$

where $\alpha \geq 0, \varepsilon \geq 0$ and ε can be selected arbitrarily small. Some literature chooses α as some fixed value such as 1. Then, we have

$$\dot{V}(x(t)) + \alpha[(1+\varepsilon)V(x(t)) - V(x(t)-\tau)] < -\varepsilon(x_1^2 + x_2^2 + x_3^2)$$

according to Razumikhin sufficient condition, the controlled Lorenz time-delay system(3) is asymptotically stable. This means that when the control parameters are selected as

$$\begin{cases} l_1 > \dfrac{m^2}{2\alpha} - m + \dfrac{r}{2} + \dfrac{\alpha(1+\varepsilon)}{2} + \varepsilon \\[2mm] l_2 > -1 + \dfrac{r}{2} + \dfrac{\alpha(1+\varepsilon)}{2} + \varepsilon \\[2mm] l_3 > \dfrac{b^2}{2\alpha} + \dfrac{\alpha(1+\varepsilon)}{2} + \varepsilon \end{cases}$$

the linear controller $u_1 = -l_1 x_1, u_2 = -l_2 x_2, u_3 = -l_3 x_3$ can suppress the chaotic phenomenon in the delay chaotic system (3) .

Remark 1. when the system parameters are selected as $m = 10, r = 28, b = \dfrac{8}{3}$, we can let $\alpha = 10$ and $\varepsilon = 0.1$. Then, we can further conclude the control parameters $l_1 > 14 + 6\varepsilon, l_2 > 18 + 6\varepsilon, l_3 > 5.36 + 6\varepsilon$. Therefore, the controller can be designed as $u_1 = -15x_1, u_2 = -19x_2, u_3 = -6x_3$.

Remark 2. It can bee seen that the proposed linear controller is independent of the time-varying lags. This means that the proposed controller can realize chaos control even though there exist unknown time-varying lags.

2.3   Chaos Synchronization

In this section, we study chaos synchronization of the time-delay Lorenz chaotic system. The master chaotic system is

$$\begin{cases} \dot{x}_1 = mx_2(t-\tau) - mx_1 \\[2mm] \dot{x}_2 = rx_1 - x_2 - x_1 x_3 \\[2mm] \dot{x}_3 = x_1 x_2 - bx_3(t-\tau) \end{cases} \tag{7}$$

where m, r, b are the system parameters, τ is the time delay.

The slave system is

$$\begin{cases} \dot{y}_1 = my_2(t-\tau) - my_1 + u_1 \\[2mm] \dot{y}_2 = ry_1 - y_2 - y_1 y_3 + u_2 \\[2mm] \dot{y}_3 = y_1 y_2 - by_3(t-\tau) + u_3 \end{cases} \tag{8}$$

Our aim is to design a controller to make the slave system (8) asymptotically synchronize the master system (7).

Denote the error state as $e_1 = y_1 - x_1, e_2 = y_2 - x_2, e_3 = y_3 - x_3$. Subtracting Eq.(7) from Eq.(8), we can get the following error dynamic system:

$$\begin{cases} \dot{e}_1 = me_2(t-\tau) - me_1 + u_1 \\ \dot{e}_2 = re_1 - e_2 - y_1 y_3 + x_1 x_3 + u_2 \\ \dot{e}_3 = y_1 y_2 - x_1 x_2 - be_3(t-\tau) + u_3 \end{cases} \tag{9}$$

From the fact that

$$\begin{cases} x_1 x_3 - y_1 y_3 = -e_1 e_3 - e_1 x_3 - e_3 x_1 \\ y_1 y_2 - x_1 x_2 = e_1 e_2 + e_1 x_2 + e_2 x_1 \end{cases} \tag{10}$$

Consequently, the error system(9) can be rewritten in the following form:

$$\begin{cases} \dot{e}_1 = me_2(t-\tau) - me_1 + u_1 \\ \dot{e}_2 = re_1 - e_2 - e_1 e_3 - e_1 x_3 - e_3 x_1 + u_2 \\ \dot{e}_3 = e_1 e_2 + e_1 x_2 + e_2 x_1 - be_3(t-\tau) + u_3 \end{cases} \tag{11}$$

In the following, based on the Razumikhin theorem of time-delay systems, we will design a linear controller to globally stabilize the error system (11).

For system (11), consider the following positive function:

$$V(e_1, e_2, e_3) = \frac{1}{2}e_1^2 + \frac{1}{2}e_2^2 + \frac{1}{2}e_3^2 \tag{12}$$

Because the states of chaotic systems are bounded, we can assume that there exist two positive constants M, N, such that $|x_2| \le M, |x_3| \le N$. Therefore

$$\dot{V}(e(t)) + \alpha[(1+\varepsilon)V(e(t)) - V(e(t-\tau))]$$

$$= e_1 \dot{e}_1 + e_2 \dot{e}_2 + e_3 \dot{e}_3 + \frac{\alpha}{2}[(1+\varepsilon)(e_1^2 + e_2^2 + e_3^2) - (e_1^2(t-\tau) + e_2^2(t-\tau)) + e_3^2(t-\tau))]$$

$$= me_1 e_2(t-\tau) - me_1^2 + e_1 u_1 + re_1 e_2 - e_2^1 - e_1 e_2 e_3 - e_1 e_2 x_3 - e_2 e_3 x_1 + e_2 u_2$$

$$+ e_1 e_2 e_3 + e_1 e_3 x_2 + e_2 e_3 x_1 - be_3 e_3(t-\tau) + e_3 u_3$$

$$+ \frac{\alpha}{2}[(1+\varepsilon)(e_1^2 + e_2^2 + e_3^2) - (e_1^2(t-\tau) + e_2^2(t-\tau)) + e_3^2(t-\tau))]$$

$$\le \frac{m^2}{2\alpha}e_1^2 + \frac{\alpha}{2}e_1^2(t-\tau) - me_1^2 + e_1 u_1 + re_1 e_2 - e_2^2 - Ne_1 e_2 + e_2 u_2 + Me_1 e_3 + \frac{b^2}{2\alpha}e_3^2 + \frac{\alpha}{2}e_3^2(t-\tau) + e_3 u_3$$

$$+ \frac{\alpha}{2}[(1+\varepsilon)(e_1^2 + e_2^2 + e_3^2) - (e_1^2(t-\tau) + e_2^2(t-\tau)) + e_3^2(t-\tau))]$$

$$= -(m - \frac{m^2}{2\alpha} - \frac{\alpha(1+\varepsilon)}{2} + l_1)e_1^2 - (1 - \frac{\alpha(1+\varepsilon)}{2} + l_2)e_2^2$$

$$-(-\frac{b^2}{2\alpha} - \frac{\alpha(1+\varepsilon)}{2} + l_3)e_3^2) + (r - N)e_1 e_2 + Me_1 e_3 - \frac{\alpha}{2}e_1^2(t-\tau)$$

$$\le -(m - \frac{m^2}{2\alpha} - \frac{\alpha(1+\varepsilon)}{2} + l_1)e_1^2 - (1 - \frac{\alpha(1+\varepsilon)}{2} + l_2)e_2^2$$

$$-(-\frac{b^2}{2\alpha} - \frac{\alpha(1+\varepsilon)}{2} + l_3)e_3^2 + (r - N)e_1 e_2 + Me_1 e_3$$

$$\le -(m - \frac{m^2}{2\alpha} - \frac{\alpha(1+\varepsilon)}{2} - \frac{r-N}{2} - \frac{M}{2} + l_1)e_1^2$$

$$-(1 - \frac{\alpha(1+\varepsilon)}{2} - \frac{r-N}{2} + l_2)e_2^2 - (-\frac{b^2}{2\alpha} - \frac{\alpha(1+\varepsilon)}{2} - \frac{M}{2} + l_3)e_3^2 \tag{13}$$

Design the controller gains satisfying the following inequality

$$
\begin{cases}
m-\dfrac{m^2}{2\alpha}-\dfrac{\alpha(1+\varepsilon)}{2}-\dfrac{r-N}{2}-\dfrac{M}{2}+l_1>\varepsilon \\[2mm]
1-\dfrac{\alpha(1+\varepsilon)}{2}-\dfrac{r-N}{2}+l_2>\varepsilon \\[2mm]
-\dfrac{b^2}{2\alpha}-\dfrac{\alpha(1+\varepsilon)}{2}-\dfrac{M}{2}+l_3>\varepsilon
\end{cases}
\tag{14}
$$

where $\alpha, M, N \geq 0, \varepsilon > 0$. ε is a small constant and it can be selected arbitrarily small. Then,

$$
\dot{V}(e(t))+\alpha[(1+\varepsilon)V(e(t))-V(e(t)-\tau)]<-\varepsilon(e_1^2+e_2^2+e_3^2)
\tag{15}
$$

From Razumikhin theorem we know that if the control parameter satisfies the following conditions

$$
\begin{cases}
l_1>\dfrac{m^2}{2\alpha}-m+\dfrac{r-N}{2}+\dfrac{M}{2}+\dfrac{\alpha(1+\varepsilon)}{2}+\varepsilon \\[2mm]
l_2>-1+\dfrac{r-N}{2}+\dfrac{\alpha(1+\varepsilon)}{2}+\varepsilon \\[2mm]
l_3>\dfrac{b^2}{2\alpha}+\dfrac{M}{2}+\dfrac{\alpha(1+\varepsilon)}{2}+\varepsilon
\end{cases}
\tag{16}
$$

the error system(11) is asymptotically stable.

Remark 3. Similarly, if the parameters are selected as $m=10$, $r=28$, $b=\dfrac{8}{3}$, $\alpha=10$, we can conclude $l_1>2+6\varepsilon, l_2>-12+6\varepsilon, l_3>23.5+6\varepsilon$. When the controller is designed as $u_1=-3x_1, u_2=0, u_3=-24x_3$, the slave system(8) can asymptotically synchronize the master system(1). Figs3-5 are provided to illustrate the effectiveness of the developed controller.

Remark 4. From the design process of the controller we can see that two control inputs μ_1 and μ_3 are enough to stabilize the error system(11). The controller is simpler than that designed in the chaos control problem.

Remark 5. Compared with the controller designed in Refs.[17-20], the linear controller presented in the study of synchronization is more feasible and easy to be implemented.

3   Numerical Simulation

In this section, we give the numerical simulation results of the delay Lorenz system. The chaotic attractors of system(1) are presented in Figs.1-2 with $\tau=0.2$. From these Figs, we can see that the time-delay Lorenz system exhibits many interesting dynamical behaviors.

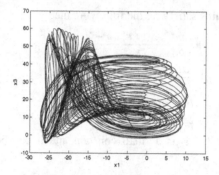

Fig. 1. Phase of two states in system(1), i.e., x_1 versus x_3 when $\tau = 0.2$

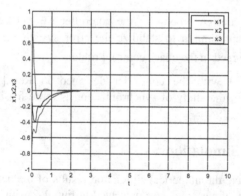

Fig. 2. Phase of two states in system(1), i.e., x_2 versus x_3 when $\tau = 0.2$

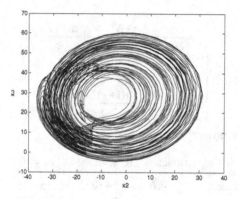

Fig. 3. Time responses of the system(3) with the proposed controller

The numerical results of chaos control and synchronization are given respectively. With the linear control law designed in section2.2, simulation result is shown as Fig.3 with the initial value $(x_1, x_2, x_3)^T = (0, -1, 1)^T$. Fig.3 shows that the time-delay Lorenz system can be stabilized to the origin (0,0,0).

In the simulation of chaos synchronization, the initial states of the drive and response system are $(x_1, x_2, x_3)^T = (-3, 5, 6)^T$, $(y_1, y_2, y_3)^T = (3, 1, 2)^T$ respectively. The initial condition of the error system is $(e_1, e_2, e_3)^T = (6, -4, -4)^T$. From the simulation results we can get $M \approx 36, N \approx 60$. Figs.4-5 show the synchronization of the chaotic time-delay system with the proposed linear controller. As illustrated in Fig.5, we can observe that the trajectories of the slave system can asymptotically approach those of the master system.

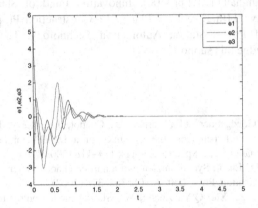

Fig. 4. The error dynamics of synchronization with the proposed controller

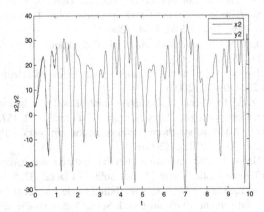

Fig. 5. The time response of x_1 and y_1

4   Conclusions

Based on Razumikhin theorem, a novel method is developed to realize chaos control and synchronization of the time-delay Lorenz system. Even if there exist unknown time-varying lags, the presented linear can still realize chaos control of the time-delay Lorenz system. Also, we have designed a linear controller independent of time-delay to realize chaos synchronization. It can be seen that the presented method can be applied in other time-delay chaotic systems with disturbance and linear controller can be derived too. Numerical simulation results are provided to illustrate the effectiveness of the proposed controller.

Acknowledgements. The author would thank the support from the Natural Science Foundation of Shanghai(11ZR1412400), Innovation Fund of Shanghai University, Shanghai University "11th Five-Year Plan" 211 Construction Project and Shanghai Key Laboratory of Power Station Automation Technology. The authors, hereby, gratefully acknowledge this support.

References

1. Udaltsov, V.S., Goedgebuer, J.P., Larger, L., Cuenot, J.B., Levy, P., Rhodes, W.T.: Communicating with hyperchaos: the dynamics of a DNLF emitter and recovery of transmitted information. Opt. Spectrosc. 95(1), 114–118 (2003)
2. Lu, J.A., Wu, X.Q., Lu, J.: Synchronization of a unified chaotic system and the application in secure communication. Phys. Lett. A 305, 365–370 (2002)
3. Wang, H., Han, Z.Z., Xie, Q.Y., Zhang, W.: Sliding mode control for chaotic systems based on LMI. Commun. Nonlinear Sci. Numer. Simul. 14(4), 1410–1417 (2009)
4. Wang, H., Han, Z.Z., Zhang, W., Xie, Q.Y.: Chaotic synchronization and secure communication based on descriptor observer. Nonlinear Dyn. 57, 69–73 (2009)
5. Yassen, M.T.: Adaptive chaos control and synchronization for uncertain new chaotic dynamical system. Phys. Lett. A 350, 36–43 (2006)
6. Wang, F.Q., Liu, C.X.: Synchronization of unified chaotic system based on passive control. Physica D 225, 55–60 (2007)
7. Li, G.H.: Projective synchronization of chaotic system using backstepping control. Chaos Solitons Fractals 29, 490–494 (2006)
8. Tao, C.H., Liu, X.F.: Feedback and adaptive control and synchronization of a set of chaotic and hyperchaotic systems. Chaos, Solutions and Fractals 32, 1572–1581 (2007)
9. Cao, J.D., Lu, J.Q.: Adaptive synchronization of neural networks with or without time-varying delay. Chaos 16(1), 013133 (2006)
10. Tavazoei, M.S., Haeri, M.: Determination of active sliding mode controller parameters in synchronizing different chaotic systems. Chaos Solitons Fractals 32, 583–591 (2007)
11. Yan, J.J., Hung, M.L., Liao, T.L.: Adaptive sliding mode control for synchronization of chaotic gyros with fully unknown parameters. J. Sound Vibration 298, 298–306 (2006)
12. Wang, H., Han, Z.Z., Zhang, W., Xie, Q.Y.: Synchronization of unified chaotic systems with uncertain parameters based on the CLF. Nonlinear Anal: Real World Appl. 10(5), 715–722 (2009)

13. Wang, H., Han, Z.Z., Xie, Q.Y., Zhang, W.: Finite-time synchronization of uncertain unified chaotic systems based on CLF. Nonlinear Anal: Real World Appl. 10(5), 2842–2849 (2009)
14. Wang, H., Han, Z.Z., Zhang, W., Xie, Q.Y.: Chaos control and synchronization of unified chaotic systems via linear control. Journal of Sound and Vibration 320, 365–372 (2009)
15. Wang, H., Han, Z.Z., Zhen, M.: Synchronization of hyperchaotic systems via linear control. Commun. Nonlinear Sci. Numer. Simulat. 15, 1910–1920 (2010)
16. Sun, J.: Global synchronization criteria with channel time-delay for chaotic time-delay systems. Chaos, Solitons & Fractals 21, 967–975 (2004)
17. Zhang, X.H., Cui, Z.Y., Zhu, Y.Y.: Synchronization and circuit experiment simulation of chaotic time-delay systems. In: IEEE 2009 Pacific-Asia Conference on Circuits, Communications and System (2009)
18. Li, L.X., Peng, H.P., Yang, Y.X., Wang, X.D.: On the chaotic synchronization of Lorenz systems with time-varying lags. Chaos, Solitons and Fractals 41, 783–794 (2009)
19. Lu, J.Q., Cao, J.D.: Adaptive Stabilization and Synchronization for Chaotic Lur'e Systems With Time-Varying Delay. IEEE Transactions on Circuits and Systems-I:Regular Paper 5(35), 1347–1357 (2008)
20. Yalcin, M.E., Suykens, J.A.K., Vandewalle, J.: Master-slave synchronization of Lure systems with time-delay. Int. J. Bifurcat Chaos 11(6), 1707–1722 (2001)
21. Razumikhin, B.S.: On the stability of systems with a delay. Prikl. Mat. Mekh 20, 500–512 (1956) (Russian)

Research on Matching Pattern
of Land Used Transfer Alignment

Yajing Yu, Qing Li, and Zhong Su

Institute of Intelligence Control, Beijing Information Science and Technology University,
Beijing 100101, China

Abstract. Aiming at the problem of initial alignment of land used strap-down inertial navigation system (SINS), pointed out the advantages and particularity of the moving base transfer alignment. Make the system error as the state variables of transfer alignment model, and the relationship between matching pattern of transfer alignment and system state observer was studied, if matching patterns are different, the form of measurement equation will be different. So matching pattern is the key factor to affecting transfer alignment performance. Simulate and analysis different matching patterns to get alignment results respectively, and summarizes the principle of choosing combination matching patterns according to different terrain conditions.

Keywords: land used, transfer alignment, matching pattern, terrain condition, SINS.

1 Introduction

The primary factor to ensure the inertial navigation system working properly is initial alignment, the accuracy and time of initial alignment impact on system performance directly. According to the reference information used in alignment process are different, initial alignment is mainly divided into static base self-aligned and moving base transfer alignment. Compared with the traditional self-aligned, transfer alignment needs less time and requirements of inertial sensors are lower [1][2]. Therefore, the transfer alignment technology becomes a focus of research.

In the transfer alignment algorithm design, the algorithm structure depends on the choice of measure matching parameters. It's a key factor to affect the transfer alignment algorithm performance. So the research of matching pattern is particularly important. Transfer alignment matching method can be divided into two categories, calculation parameters match (speed matching, position matching, etc.) and measurement parameters match (angular rate matching, attitude matching, acceleration matching, etc.) [7].

At present, the research of ship-borne and airborne transfer alignment is more at home and abroad, and this technology has a wide range of applications in sea and air filed[3]. But, for the research of land used transfer alignment characteristics and matching patterns are not specific enough.

T. Xiao, L. Zhang, and M. Fei (Eds.): AsiaSim 2012, Part II, CCIS 324, pp. 248–257, 2012.

This paper is organized as follows. In section 2, the characteristics and principle based on the land used SINS are analyzed. In section 3, several kinds of matching patterns are given. In section 4, different matching patterns in two motor solutions are presented and simulated separately, the simulation results are compared and selection principle of land used matching pattern is presented. Finally, our work of this paper is summarized in the last section.

2   Particularity of Land Used Transfer Alignment

In practical application, lever-arm effect error, data measurement delay error, vector flexible deformation and vibration error are the main factors of influence land used transfer alignment. Most of the factors are closely related to terrain condition. In the process of alignment, motor solutions and strength are limited by terrain condition. Several typical terrain and its characteristics as follow.

Table 1. Typical Terrain and Characteristics

terrain	Temperature differential	relief	motor way
plain	small	gentle	more, accelerate quickly
gobi	big	rugged	more, accelerate quickly
desert	big	rugged	more, accelerate slowly
hill	small	gentle	less, accelerate quickly
marsh/wet land	small	gentle	more, accelerate slowly

Land used SINS transfer alignment belong to moving base transfer alignment. The diversity and complexity of terrestrial environment lead to the diversity and complexity of error factors. Compared with airborne and ship-borne transfer alignment, land used transfer alignment has its own characteristics.

1)   Great differences lie between maneuver manner and maneuver strength of the land-used carrier.

2)   The structural displacement of the land-used carrier consists of long-term deformation and dynamical deformation. The long-term deformation is comprised of mechanical installation errors, the structural ageing of the carrier and the structural displacement caused by operation temperature change. The dynamical deformation is related to topographic situations. Different topographic situations cause different types of dynamical deformations.

3)   The reference of the land-used INS is close to the equipment system (within 10m generally). The lever arm effects of the master INS and the slave INS is low, as well as their time-delay problem.

4)   The land-used carrier speed up or down quite often. So the acceleration alignment needs to be quick. Every topographic situation lead a vibration for the moving carrier. So the error caused by vehicle body vibration cannot be neglected.

The preconditions for building a error model are:

1) MINS has high accuracy, whose navigation error is negligible.
2) SINS has low accuracy.

DEFINITION for several coordination systems

1) Geocentric inertial coordination system (Sys. I) -- $X_i Y_i Z_i$;
2) Earth coordination system (Sys. E) -- $X_e Y_e Z_e$;
3) Geographic coordination system (Sys. G) -- NED ;
4) Carrier coordination system (Sys. B) -- $OX_b Y_b Z_b$.

This paper uses the geographic coordination system as its navigation coordination system.

INS's attitude misalignment angle is:

$$\dot{\phi} = -\omega_{in}^n \times \phi - C_b^n \varepsilon_g^b + \eta_\phi .$$

Velocity error is:

$$\delta \dot{V}_e^n = f^n \times f + C_b^n \varepsilon_a^b - (2\omega_{ie}^n + \omega_{en}^n) \times \delta V_e^n + \eta_v ,$$

where η_ϕ and η_V are noise vectors.

We need to consider the inertial devices error and the vector $\tilde{r}^a$ standed for the lever arm between MINS and SINS while we are doing transfer alignment. The model considered is:

$$\dot{\varepsilon}_a^b = 0 \quad \dot{\varepsilon}_g^b = 0 \quad \dot{\tilde{r}}^a = 0 .$$

Other systems could be used if the specific transfer alignment matching algorithms need them.

3   Transfer Alignment Matching Pattern

Generally speaking, the estimation precision of calculation parameters match method is higher than measurement parameters match method in the same conditions, but the speed of alignment is lower than measurement parameters match method [5].

3.1   Velocity Matching

Velocity matching transfer alignment is a initial alignment method using filtering algorithm to estimate the error of slave INS by comparing the velocity output between the master and slave INS. The velocity marching transfer alignment algorithm is shown in Figure 1.

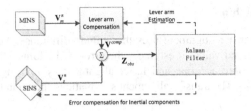

Fig. 1. Block diagram for the velocity marching transfer alignment

The velocity of the MINS can be compensated by lever arm effects.

$$V_m^{comp} = V_m^n + C_a^n \left[\left(\omega_{ia}^a - \omega_{ie}^a \right) \times r^a \right]$$

The velocity observed value of SINS is:

$$\tilde{V}_s^n = V_s^n + \delta V_s^n = V_m^n + C_a^n \left[\left(\omega_{ia}^a - \omega_{ie}^a \right) \times \tilde{r}^a \right] + C_a^n \dot{\tilde{r}}^a + \delta V_s^n$$

Then

$$Z_{V_{obs}} = \tilde{V}_s^n - V_m^{comp} .$$

Considering

$$\tilde{r}^a = r^a + \delta r^a$$

where δr^a is the vector error of lever arm.

Because of the carrier flexure, we have

$$\delta r^a = \delta r_{Stat}^a + \delta r_{Dyn}^a ,$$

whose dynamic component can be processed as noise, namely, $\delta \dot{r}_{Stat}^a = 0$.

To sum up, we concluded the measurement equation is:

$$Z_{V_{meas}} = \delta V_s^n + C_a^n \left(\omega_{ea}^a \times \right) \delta r_{Stat}^a + v_v$$

3.2   Location Matching

Location matching is a technologic maturely alignment method uses the location differences between the master INS and slave INS as the observed value of Kalman filter.

Observe based on location is better than that based on velocity under the circumstances of strong vibrations, for the reason that location matching requires less while dealing with flexural vibration. Velocity matching have a strict requirement on accuracy while computing the compensation of lever arm effects. In contrast, location matching has a relatively less requirements on computations and difficulty.

3.3   Attitude Matching

Attitude matching transfer alignment uses the attitude differences between master and slave INS as its observed value. It estimates the error by building a Kalman filter. This matching realizes a more accurate and faster alignment by revising the misalignment angles of the slave INS. The transfer alignment schematic is shown in Figure 2.

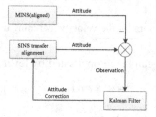

Fig. 2. The transfer alignment schematic

The attitude observed value can be obtained by multiplying the direction cosine matrix of MINS by that of SINS:

$$Z_{obs}^{att} = \tilde{C}_b^n \tilde{C}_a^b C_n^a$$

where

$$\tilde{C}_b^n = [I - \Phi] C_b^n = C_b^n - \varphi \times C_b^n \quad ,$$

$$\Phi = \varphi \times = \begin{bmatrix} 0 & -\delta\gamma & \delta\beta \\ \delta\gamma & 0 & -\delta\alpha \\ -\delta\beta & \delta\alpha & 0 \end{bmatrix} .$$

Suppose the attitude error angle(ζ) from the MINS coordination to the SINS coordination is small.
Then

$$\tilde{C}_a^b = [I - \zeta \times] C_a^b \quad .$$

In summary, the attitude measurement equation is

$$Z_{meas}^{att} = \begin{bmatrix} Z_{obs}^{att}(2,3) \\ Z_{obs}^{att}(3,1) \\ Z_{obs}^{att}(1,2) \end{bmatrix} = \varphi + C_b^n \zeta + v_\varphi$$

where v_φ is the attitude measurement noise.

3.4   Angular Velocity Matching

Angular velocity transfer alignment uses the angular velocity differences between MINS and SINS as the observed value of Kalman filter. It observes the misalignment angle between MINS and SINS, so that it can revise the attitude matrix for SINS to achieve the alignment purpose. The schematic for this alignment is in Figure 3.

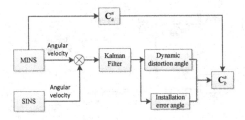

Fig. 3. The schematic for angular velocity transfer alignment

The angular velocity observation equation is:

$$Z_{obs}^{\omega} = \tilde{\omega}_{ib}^{n} - \omega_{ia}^{n} .$$

The measurement equation is:

$$Z_{meas}^{\omega} = \left[\omega_{ia}^{n} \times \right] \varphi + \tilde{C}_{b}^{n} \delta \omega_{ib}^{b} + v_{\omega} ,$$

where $v_{\omega} = \tilde{C}_{b}^{n} C_{a}^{b} \omega_{ab}^{a} .$

3.5   Velocity-Attitude Matching

Generally speaking, attitude measurement cannot efficiently estimate the accelerometer constant bias. However, attitude matching is still doing better in estimated accuracy and convergence rate then velocity matching. Consequently, this paper introduced velocity-attitude matching transfer alignment algorithm combines the advantages of attitude matching and velocity matching. Velocity-attitude matching transfer alignment algorithm has made a great progress in estimating accuracy and alignment time, especially for the gyro bias drift.

Considering the viberation for the carrier, the complexity of accurately modeling the flexure and the calculation and robustness of the Kalman filter, we suppose the misalignment angle ζ is walking randomly. Then we have

$$\dot{\zeta} = \eta_{flex} .$$

We can properly adjust the variance of the process noise (η_{flex}) to compensate the error caused by modeling.

3.6   Velocity-Angular Velocity Matching

Compared with the acceleration matching, velocity matching is more suitable for the transfer alignment in carrier vibration and flexure effect. And the lever arm compensation can be realized more easily in that matching. But meanwhile, compared with the attitude matching, velocity angle matching is more sensitive for the angular motion of the carrier. Therefore, we combined velocity matching with angular velocity matching into a hybrid matching, whose block diagram is in Figure 4.

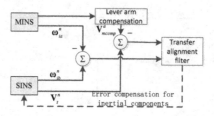

Fig. 4. The block diagram for the velocity-angular velocity matching transfer alignment

The alignment algorithm of the velocity-angular velocity matching can be got by the mentioned measurement equations of the velocity matching and angular velocity matching.

4   Experimental Result

4.1   Parameter Design

The experiment uses the gyroscope data and accelerometer data generated by the SINS emulator. The device installation error is ignored. The performance parameters of the inertial devices are:

MINS gyroscope random drift: $0.01^\circ / h$;
MINS gyroscope scale factor error: 10^{-4} ;
MINS accelerometer's random constant bias: $\nabla_x = \nabla_y = 5 \times 10^{-5} g$;
MINS accelerometer random drift: $10^{-5} g$;
MINS accelerometer scale factor error: 10^{-4} ;
SINS gyroscope random drift: 10^{-4} ;
SINS gyroscope scale factor error: 10^{-4} ;
SINS accelerometer's random constant bias: $\nabla_x = \nabla_y = 5 \times 10^{-3} g$;
SINS accelerometer random drift: $10^{-3} g$;
SINS accelerometer scale factor error: 10^{-4} ;
Initial misalignment angle: $\phi = [1^\circ \quad 1^\circ \quad 1^\circ]$

4.2   Maneuver Scheme

Scheme One: Uniform Motion in a Straight Line
In this scheme, the rate of attitude angle change and course angle change are both zero, as well as the acceleration in track coordinate systems.

While the carrier is doing uniform motion in a straight line, its north-oriented velocity is 12m/s, and its east-oriented velocity is 12m/s, too.

Scheme Two: Sigmoid Maneuver

When carriers are doing sigmoid maneuvering, the angular velocity is only happened in the course. Because of the sigmoid trace, the acceleration needs to be separated into two directions.

$$V_N = V \cos \omega t$$
$$\dot{V}_N = -V \omega \sin \omega t$$
$$V_E = V \sin \omega t \cdot sign[\sin \omega t]$$
$$\dot{V}_E = V \omega \cos \omega t \cdot sign[\sin \omega t]$$

where v_N, v_E represent the north-oriented and east-oriented velocity separately.

The maneuver acceleration is:

$$\left| \dot{V}_N \right| = \left| \dot{V}_E \right| = V \omega = \varsigma \cdot \frac{2\pi}{T}$$

where $T = \frac{2\pi}{\omega}$ is the maneuver cycle, usually, $T = \frac{2}{3} T_0$.

The mathematical model of the sigmoid maneuver can be described as followed:

$$\omega(t) = \begin{bmatrix} 0 & 0 & \omega \end{bmatrix}^T$$
$$\alpha(t) = \begin{bmatrix} \dot{V}_E & \dot{V}_N & 0 \end{bmatrix}^T$$

where ω is the course angular velocity.

While the carrier is sigmoid maneuvering, the north-oriented velocity is 10m/s, the course swing range is 15°, and the swing frequency is 0.5Hz.

4.3   The Result

The simulation figures for all transfer alignment matching modes in two maneuver ways are shown as followed.

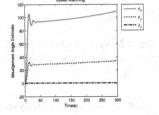 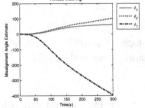

Fig. 5. Velocity matching misalignment angles' estimation in uniform motion in a straight line   **Fig. 6.** Attitude matching misalignment angles' estimation in uniform motion in a straight line

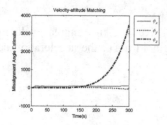

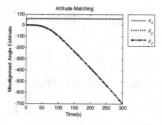

Fig. 7. Velocity-attitude matching misalignment angles' estimation in uniform motion in a straight line

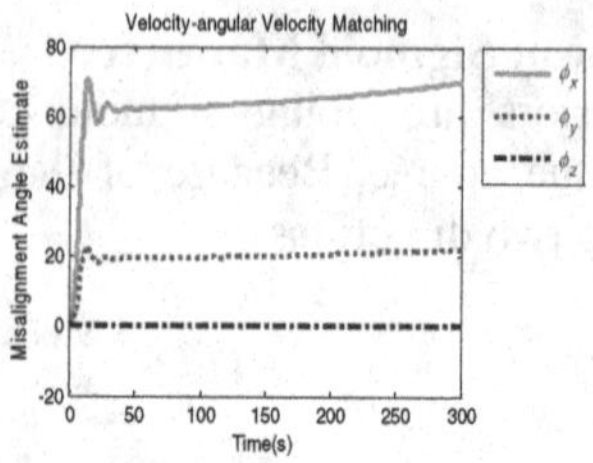

Fig. 8. Velocity-angular velocity matching misalignment angles' estimation in uniform motion in a straight line

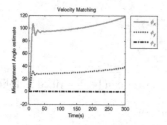

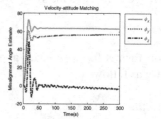

Fig. 9. Velocity matching misalignment angles' estimation in sigmoid maneuver

Fig. 10. Attitude matching misalignment angles' estimation in sigmoid maneuver

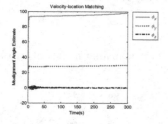

Fig. 11. Velocity-location matching misalignment angles' estimation in sigmoid maneuver

Fig. 12. Velocity-attitude matching misalignment angles' estimation in sigmoid maneuver

From the above figures, we find that velocity matching and velocity-angular velocity matching can estimate the misalignment angle effectively in the uniform motion in a straight line. Nevertheless, velocity-attitude matching and velocity-location matching can do that in a sigmoid maneuver.

According to the above experimental results, we can obtain the selection principles of these matching modes.

1) According to the present matching mode studies, as far as the observation is concerned, the linear movement mixed angular movement matching algorithm is the best constitution. Generally speaking, the alignment performance of the combined matching modes is better than the singular ones.
2) The matching mode we select needs to be capable of reducing the impact of vibration and the flexure of the carriers. When a matching mode is sensitive to some error, we should avoid using this matching mode, or at least avoid using it individually.
3) The topographic condition restricts the way and the strength of the maneuver. We hope matching mode can realize transfer alignment under low-dynamic condition in actual applications. That is to say, matching mode can use any carrier's low amplitude movement to speed up the alignment progress and improve the alignment accuracy.

Therefore, according to the character of the land INS, we propose the requirements for alignment performance. Then we can get suitable matching mode in light of the above selection principles.

5   Conclusions

Aiming at the characters of the land used carrier, this paper studied the principle and the specificity of the land used SINS transfer alignment. Then it analyzed different matching modes and did relevant emulations. At last, we got the matching modes selection principles by analyzing the experimental results.

Acknowledgments. The authors would like to thank the Institute of Intelligence Control, University of Beijing Information Science & Technology, China, for qruipment access and technical support. This work was supported by National Natural Science Foundation of China (Grant No. 61031001, 60972118).

References

1. Su, Z. (ed.): Inertial Technology. National Defence Industry Press, Beijing (2010)
2. Spalding, K.: An Efficient Rapid Transfer Alignment Filter. In: Guidance and Control Conference, Hilton Head Island, USA, pp. 1276–1286 (1992)
3. Wang, S., Deng, Z.L.: Technique Review of Transfer Alignment for Inertial Navigation Systems on Moving Base. Nanotechnol. 11, 2 (2003)
4. Li, Q.S., Dong, J.X.: The Application of Angular Rate Matching to Transfer Alignment for Airborne Weapons 29, 3 (2009)
5. Gao, X.W.: Study of Transfer Alignment Techniques in Strap-down Navigation System (2007)
6. Luan, H.Z., Mao, Y.L.: Study on a Method of Rapid Transfer Alignment. In: International Conference on Mechatronic Science. Electric Engineering and Computer (2011)
7. Ding, G.Q.: To Research on the Transfer Alignment Problems of Inertial Navigation Systems (2010)

The Design of Simulation System of GPS/INS Ultra-tight Integration under High Dynamic Environment

Zhen Ji, Chuanjun Li, and Xingcheng Li

School of Aerospace Engineering, Beijing Institute of Technology
Beijing, China
2120100058@bit.edu.cn

Abstract. When the carrier to do a high dynamic motion, it will lead the tracking error to increase, then the degree of nonlinearity of the detector will become large and the equivalent gain response will reduce, so it may lead the satellite signal to loss lock. This paper studies the simulation system of GPS/INS ultra-tight integration under high dynamic environment, it simulates two kinds of dynamic models and the results show the superiority of ultra-tight integration. When the GPS single interrupted, it can continue tracking by INS and it's able to quickly restore the tracking when signal recovery. Ultra-tight integration also provides a possible for GPS anti-jamming technology.

Keywords: high dynamic, GPS+INS, ultra-tight integration, simulation.

1   Introduction

With the development of modern warfare, traditional GPS receiver can't afford to the requirement of tracking and positioning under harsh environment, so GPS + INS technology comes into being. It combines GPS's(Global Positioning System) characteristics: all-weather, all-round, continuous, real-time and the INS's(Inertial Navigation System) characteristics: it's not affected by external interference. Not only satisfy the prolonged work requirements while maintaining a certain degree of accuracy, it also can select three operating modes: pure INS, pure GPS and GPS+INS mode of operation. GPS + INS simulation system provides experimental platform to study high dynamic GPS + INS integrated navigation system's dynamic performance and anti-jamming performance.

2   System Architecture

The system includes: the host computer, trajectory generator, the INS emulator, the GPS emulator, and the Integrated Kalman Filter. The INS emulator includes IMU simulation and INS mechanical arrange; The GPS emulator includes a GPS simulator and a GPS receiver. The system block diagram is shown in Figure 1.

T. Xiao, L. Zhang, and M. Fei (Eds.): AsiaSim 2012, Part II, CCIS 324, pp. 258–264, 2012.

Firstly, the host computer generates trajectory file by MATLAB, then send the trajectory instruction to the trajectory generator through a serial port, the trajectory generator is to ensure the update of trajectory is real-time. The trajectory generator sends the real-time trajectory data to the IMU simulation and GPS simulator. The IMU simulation simulates three-axis attitude angles (or angular rate) and acceleration of the object by the trajectory data, then send them to INS mechanical arrange to calculate the object's PVA(Position, Velocity, Attitude). GPS simulator simulates object's flying scene real-time by the receiving trajectory data then generates the GPS single and sends the single to the GPS receiver by RF. The GPS receiver calculates the object's PVT(Position, Velocity, Time). The Integrated Kalman Filter sets the differences between PVA and PVT as measured values, and the filtering results correct the INS for keeping the INS errors in the small range and it can select the system mode according to the needing. Finally, the filter results are sent to the host computer to analysis. In addition, the system time is synchronized by the GPS receiver.

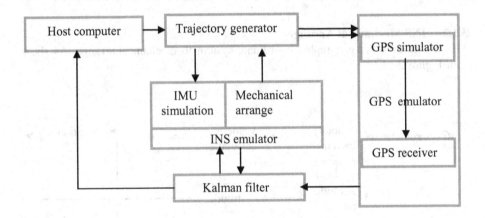

Fig. 1. The system block diagram

Ultra-tight integration mainly uses the I and Q-channel data of the receiver tracking loop with the position, velocity, attitude of INS output. Receiver tracking loop is controlled by the navigation filter which is different from the ordinary receiver tracking loop. Ultra-tight integration structure can take advantage of speed information that the INS provide to assist the receiver tracking loop, so it can eliminate the vector of the dynamic and the receiver has good performance in high dynamic environment.

3   System Implementation

3.1   INS Emulator

3.1.1   IMU Simulation

IMU simulation combines the output data of the trajectory generator and the model of noise to simulate the information about acceleration and angular rate. Error model is as follows:

$$f^b = (I + Ka)[I + (\Delta C_a^b)^T] \cdot f_{in}^b + \nabla^b + w_a^m + w_a \tag{1}$$

$$w^b = (I + Kg)[I + (\Delta C_g^b)^T] \cdot w_{in}^b + \varepsilon^b + w_g^m + w_g \tag{2}$$

Ka, Kg for scale factor error; ΔC_a^b, ΔC_g^b for installation error; ∇^b, ε^b for zero error; w_a^m, w_g^m for markov process; w_a, w_g for normal distribution white noise.

3.1.2   INS Mechanical Arrange

This article uses the geographic coordinate system to mechanical arrange. As show n in Figure 2.

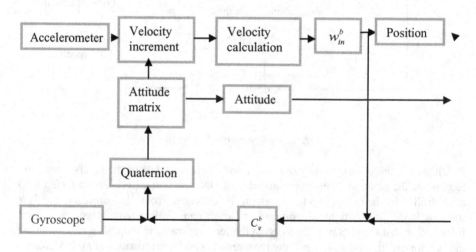

Fig. 2. INS mechanical arrange

Using the Quadruple Order Runge Kutta to update quaternion and using first order Euler to correct the velocity.

3.2   GPS Emulator

3.2.1   GPS Simulator

We use the GNSS7700 of SPIRENT as the GPS simulator. Trajectory generator send the dates of the simulator trajectory to simulator at the speed of 100Hz through RS232 serial port .Then the simulator generates the current aircraft flying scene and simulates the GPS signal that the aircraft receiving. Finally, the GPS signal is send to the GPS receiver through RF.

3.2.2   GPS Receiver

The elevation of satellite decides which satellite can be used by receiver. The formula for elevation as follows:

$$E = \arctan \frac{\cos(\varphi_p - \varphi_s)\cos L_p - \dfrac{R}{R+H}}{\sqrt{1 - [\cos(\varphi_p - \varphi_s)\cos L_p]^2}} \tag{3}$$

R is the radius of the earth; H is the distance between the ground and the satellite; φ_p and L_p are the longitude and latitude of the receiver; φ_s is the longitude of the satellite. If the elevation below 10^0, we consider the satellite is invisible.

Satellite positioning takes at least four satellites. Positioning accuracy and GDOP is inversely proportional. Firstly, we choose the largest elevation of the satellite, then calculate the volume to choose the other three satellites.

After determining the Galaxy, we can calculate the pseudorange between the receiver and the four satellites. Pseudorange formula is:

$$\rho_k^j = [(X^j - X_K)^2 + (Y^j - Y_K)^2 + (Z^j - Z_K)^2]^{\frac{1}{2}} + b_k - c\delta t^j + \delta\rho_{K_n}^j + \delta\rho_{K_p}^j + v_k^j \tag{4}$$

ρ_k^j is the pseudorange between the receiver k and the satellites j; (X^j, Y^j, Z^j) represents satellite j's position; (X_K, Y_K, Z_K) represents coordinates of the receiver; c is for the speed of light; δt^j is clock offset of the satellite; $b_k = c\delta t_k$ (δt^k is clock offset of receiver); $\delta\rho_{K_n}^j$ is the delay of ionospheric; $\delta\rho_{K_p}^j$ is the delay of the troposphere; v_k^j is the random error of the receiver. We can obtain the X_K, Y_K, Z_K, b_k from the formula. Figure 3 is flow charts of the GPS receiver.

3.3   Trajectory Generator Simulates Two Kinds of Models of High Dynamic

Two kinds of models of high dynamic: one is linear acceleration which has phase step with 50g, the acceleration is a constant; the other is circular motion or turn which has radial acceleration with 50g.All the velocity and derivative are the sinusoidal waveform.

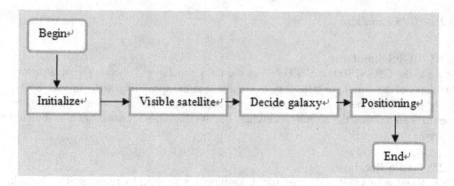

Fig. 3. Flow charts of the GPS receiver

3.4   Mathematical Model of Ultra-tight Integration System

Mathematical model of ultra-tight integration system has two sectors: the first sector is INS, a total of 18 state quantities are INS error; the second is GPS, state quantities are the GPS clock offset and frequency error.

Mathematical model of ultra-tight integration system as follows:

$$\dot{X}(t) = F(t)X(t) + G(t)W(t) \tag{5}$$

$$Z(t) = H(t)X(t) + V(t) \tag{6}$$

4   Simulation Results

Users' initial position : N34.00000, W118.00000, height is 0m, Initial Heading angle is 90^0, pitch angle and roll angle are all 0^0. INS system error: horizontal posture errors is 300'', azimuth angle error is 600''; the velocity error of each direction is 2 m/s; the errors of longitude and latitude are 20m, the error of height is 50m. Due to space constraints only introduce the simulate results under the linear acceleration with the acceleration about 50g. Figure 4 to Figure 9 are the error of the position and velocity that output by INS, GPS and GPS+INS Ultra-tight integration. Da sh-dot-line shows INS, dotted line shows GPS, solid line shows GPS+INS.

As can be seen from the graph, GPS+INS Ultra-tight integration has higher precision.

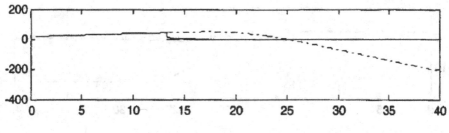

Fig. 4. The error of latitude

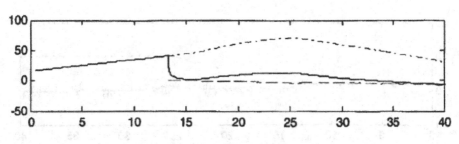

Fig. 5. The error of longitude

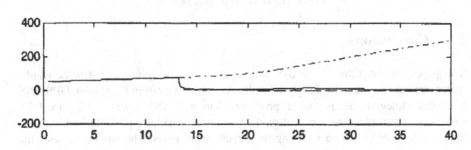

Fig. 6. The error of elevation

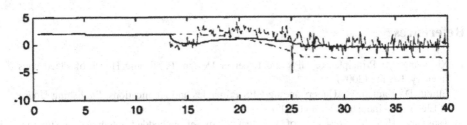

Fig. 7. The error of speed of east

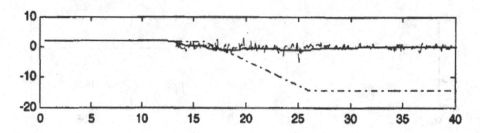

Fig. 8. The error of speed of north

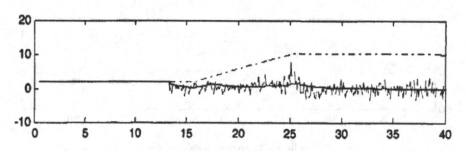

Fig. 9. The error of speed of heaven

5   Conclusions

This paper simulates the GPS + INS ultra-tight integration system and gets the results under two kinds of models of high dynamic. As can be seen from the results, GPS+INS Ultra-tight integration has higher precision than pure INS system and pure GPS system, so it can meet the needs of modern war and provides a possible for GPS anti-jamming technology while reducing the development costs. The simulation uses the idealized processing in some way, so we must do some algorithm optimization in the future.

References

1. Xie Gang, C.: Principles of GPS and Receiver Design. Publishing House of Electronics Industry, Beijing (2009)
2. Elliott, D., Kaplan, C.: Understanding GPS Principles and Applications. Publishing House of Electronics Industry, Beiing (2005)
3. Tangkang Hua, T.: Research of key technology of embedded integrated navigation. National University of Defense Technology (2008)
4. Jennifer Denise Gautier, S.: GPS/INS Generalized Evaluation tool (GIGET) for The Design and Testing of Integrated Navigation Systems (2003)

Location Based on Passive RFID
by Using Least Squares SVM

Panfeng Niu[1], Zengqiang Chen[1], Yibo Li[2], and Qinglin Sun[1]

[1] Department of Automation,
Nankai University, Tianjin, 300071, China
[2] Department of Communication Engineering,
Beijing Institute of Technology, Beijing, 100081, China
npfeng900@163.com, {chenzq,sunql}@nankai.edu.cn,
191981249@qq.com

Abstract. In this paper, two location algorithms are mentioned. One is LANDMARC, which has a good performance of anti-interference, but it is an approximate estimate and cannot get an accurate result. It heavily depends on the empirical formula and the layout of reference tags. The other algorithm proposed in this paper is the location algorithm based on least squares SVM. It uses the least squares SVM to get the mapping of RSSI to distance, and then gets the position results by using least-squares method. According to the simulation, it has a better performance comparing to LANDMRC.

Keywords: Passive tag, Location algorithm, Received Signal Strength Indicator, Least Squares Support Vector Machine.

1   Introduction

Radio Frequency Identification (RFID) is an automatic identification technology, which can automatically identify targets and collect certain digital information via using radio waves [1]. In recent years, with the booming of entire RFID industry, the research on RFID location system gradually becomes a public concern. RFID location system aims at getting the position of RFID reader or tag. It is very suitable for small area positioning because of its non-contact, non-line of sight, high sensitivity and low cost [2]. Most RFID location systems are on a basis of principles of Angle of Arrival (AOA), Time of Arrival (TOA) and Received Signal Strength Indicator (RSSI). However, the majority of RFID location system is still placed in the experimental and theoretical research stage. At present, the most famous RFID location systems are LANDMARC system [3], RADAR system [4], SpotOn system [5] and so forth.

The object of this research in terms of RFID location system based on passive RFID is to get the position of passive tags. Like most location system, the location algorithm discussed in this paper is based on the principle of RSSI.

T. Xiao, L. Zhang, and M. Fei (Eds.): AsiaSim 2012, Part II, CCIS 324, pp. 265–274, 2012.

2   Related Work

The tag in the passive RFID does not have any power. Its operating power is obtained from ratio frequency waves emitted from reader antenna. Then, it responds its modulated backscatter signal (MBS) to the reader antenna.

In the location algorithm, the RFID signal propagation model is assumed to be unknown, whereas the RFID signal propagation model is indispensable in the simulation. Here the RFID signal is represented as Log-distance Path Loss Model [6]:

$$PL(d) = PL(d_0) + 10n\log_{10}(\frac{d}{d_0}) + X_\sigma(dB) \tag{1}$$

where $PL(d)$ is the free space path loss for distance d , d_0 is an arbitrary reference distance (usually 1m), n is the path loss exponent and X_σ is zero mean Gaussian random variable with variance $\sigma^2(dB)$.

Define $P_r(d)$ as the RSSI received by reader antenna for distance d . P_t is antenna's transmission power, then

$$P_r(d) = P_t - PL(d_0) - 10n\log_{10}(\frac{d}{d_0}) + X_\sigma(dB). \tag{2}$$

The parameters of equation (2) in this paper's simulation are: $d_0 = 1$m, $n = 2.4$, $P_t = 30$dBm, $X_\sigma \sim N(0, 0.25)$.

3   LANDMARC

The core theory of LANDMARC proposed by Lionel M. Li and Yunhao Liu is to use reference tags to estimate the position of target tag. Initially, LANDMARC is used in the system based on active RFID; but it also satisfies passive RFID. This algorithm cannot get very accurate results. These reference tags serve as the reference point for the system.

3.1   Principle

Suppose there are M readers and N reference tags in the system. The positions of reference tags are (x_i, y_i) $(i = 1, 2, 3...N)$. And define each reference tag's RSSI vector as $P_i = (P_{i,1}, P_{i,2}, P_{i,3}, ..., P_{i,M})$, where $P_{i,j}(i = 1, 2...N; j = 1, 2...M)$ is the RSSI of reference tag i received by reader j. For target tag, its RSSI vector is $S = (S_1, S_2, S_3, ..., S_M)$, where $S_j(j = 1, 2...M)$ is the RSSI of target tag received by reader j.

Define the distance degree of target tag and reference tag i as E_i:

$$E_i = |S - P_i| = \sqrt{(S_1 - P_{i,1})^2 + (S_2 - P_{i,2})^2 + \cdots + (S_M - P_{i,M})^2} \, . \tag{3}$$

The smaller E_i is, the closer target tag to reference tag i is. Then, we choose k reference tags of minimum values of E_i, recording their distance degrees as $\tilde{E}_i (i = 1, 2 \ldots k)$ and their positions as $(\tilde{x}_i, \tilde{y}_i)(i = 1, 2 \ldots k)$. Define relevant weight w_i as

$$W_i = \left(\tilde{E}_i^2 \right)^{-1} \bigg/ \sum_{i=1}^{k} \left(\tilde{E}_i^2 \right)^{-1} . \tag{4}$$

Ultimately, the estimated position $(\bar{x}_0, \bar{y}_0)$ of target tag is computed as follows:

$$\begin{cases} \bar{x}_0 = \sum_{i=1}^{k} \left(W_i \cdot \tilde{x}_i \right) \\ \bar{y}_0 = \sum_{i=1}^{k} \left(W_i \cdot \tilde{y}_i \right) \end{cases} . \tag{5}$$

At last, define the location error as $e = \sqrt{(\bar{x}_0 - x_0)^2 + (\bar{y}_0 - y_0)^2}$, where (x_0, y_0) is the real position of target tag.

3.2 Stimulation of LADMARC

There is a square area of 6×6m (Fig 1), 4 reader antennas, 25 reference tags are placed in this area. The height of antennas is 1m, and the height of all tags (reference tags and target tags) is 0m.

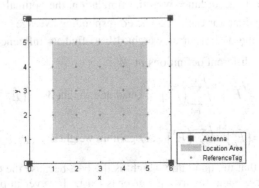

Fig. 1. Layout of simulation environment

The effective location area is the gray area of Fig 1. Suppose each antenna's transmission power is 40dBm, then the signal strength of position (x, y) is:

$$P_r(x, y) = \sum_{i=1}^{4} \{40 - 30 - 24 \log_{10} d_i + N(0, 0.25)\} \tag{6}$$

where $d_i (i = 1, 2, 3, 4)$ is the distance between antenna i and position (x, y). Thus we can easily get the distribution field of signal strength in the environment.

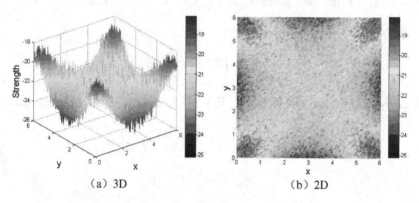

(a) 3D   (b) 2D

Fig. 2. The distribution field of RF-signal strength

Suppose tags can obtain all the power from the ratio frequency waves in their position showing in the Fig 2, and can translate it into its backscatter signal without any loss. According to the principle of LANDMARC, the position of target tag then can be readily calculated. At first, define $k=4$, which means the target tag's position is estimated through 4 nearer reference tags. The location error is inevitable. Even the noise is declined to zero ($X_\sigma \sim N(0,0)$), there is an average error of around 0.1m.

The location error is not constant for different k. The value of k ought not to be too big or too small. In accordance with the simulation, the optimal k is 4 after five thousand tests being done for each k. The corresponding average error is 0.1750m.

We also change the definition of weight W_i to find its influence to the location error. There are four different definitions of W_i:

Linear weight $W_i = \left(\tilde{E}_i\right)^{-1} \Big/ \sum_{i=1}^{k} \left(\tilde{E}_i\right)^{-1}$; Quadratic weight $W_i = \left(\tilde{E}_i^2\right)^{-1} \Big/ \sum_{i=1}^{k} \left(\tilde{E}_i^2\right)^{-1}$;

Cubic weight $W_i = \left(\tilde{E}_i^3\right)^{-1} \Big/ \sum_{i=1}^{k} \left(\tilde{E}_i^3\right)^{-1}$; Logarithm weight $W_i = \left(\log \tilde{E}_i\right)^{-1} \Big/ \sum_{i=1}^{k} \left(\log \tilde{E}_i\right)^{-1}$.

Fig 3: (a) shows that the quadratic weight is the best because the error distribution is relatively centralized, and the average error is least. However in practice, different environment means different definition of W_i. If we want to improve the accuracy of LANDMRC, the definition of W_i will be a researching direction.

The layout of reference tags is another factor taking into account. According to the simulation, the triangle layout is better than the square layout. However, the superiority of triangle layout is not quite obvious (Fig 3: (b)). Besides, the density of reference tags significantly affects the location accuracy. The denser layout is, the higher accuracy will be. Nevertheless, it is infeasible to use too many reference tags since it is inconvenient and wasteful. Thus it is necessary to figure out the balance level.

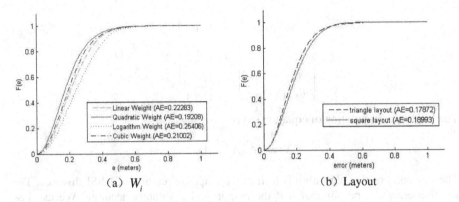

(a) W_i (b) Layout

Fig. 3. Cumulative percentile of error for W_i and layout

(AE means Average Error of experiment)

4   Location Based on LS-SVM

Unlike LANDMARC, target tag's position is not estimated via reference tags. It is directly computed by means of the target tag's RSSI. An important work of this approach is to find the mapping of RSSI to distance by using least squares support machine (LS-SVM).

4.1   Principle

Suppose there are M readers, and their positions are (x_i, y_i) $(i = 1, 2...M)$. As for target tag, we can get its RSSI on every reader and then map the RSSI vector to the distance vector as $(d_1, d_2, ..., d_M)$. According to the geometrical knowledge, we get the simultaneous equations:

$$
\begin{cases}
(\overline{x}_0 - x_1)^2 + (\overline{y}_0 - y_1)^2 = d_1^2 \\
(\overline{x}_0 - x_2)^2 + (\overline{y}_0 - y_2)^2 = d_2^2 \\
\quad \cdots \\
(\overline{x}_0 - x_M)^2 + (\overline{y}_0 - y_M)^2 = d_M^2
\end{cases}
\Rightarrow
\begin{cases}
\overline{x}_0 m_1 + \overline{y}_0 n_1 = l_1 \\
\overline{x}_0 m_2 + \overline{y}_0 n_2 = l_2 \\
\quad \cdots \\
\overline{x}_0 m_{M-1} + \overline{y}_0 n_{M-1} = l_{M-1}
\end{cases}
\tag{7}
$$

where $(\overline{x}_0, \overline{y}_0)$ is the position of target tag and $m_i = x_{i+1} - x_i$, $n_i = y_{i+1} - y_i$,

$$l_i = \frac{1}{2}\Big[\big(d_i^2 - d_{i+1}^2\big) - \big(x_i^2 - x_{i+1}^2\big) - \big(y_i^2 - y_{i+1}^2\big)\Big], \ i = 1, 2, ..., M - 1.$$

Equations (7) can be represented as

$$AX = b \tag{8}$$

where

$$A = \begin{bmatrix} m_1 & n_1 \\ m_2 & n_2 \\ \vdots \\ m_{M-1} & n_{M-1} \end{bmatrix}, b = \begin{bmatrix} l_1 \\ l_2 \\ \vdots \\ l_{M-1} \end{bmatrix}, X = \begin{bmatrix} \overline{x}_0 \\ \overline{y}_0 \end{bmatrix}.$$

The least-squares solution of equation (8) is

$$\hat{X} = \big(A^T A\big)^{-1} Ab. \tag{9}$$

The key point of this algorithm is to find the mapping relation of RSSI-distance. The location error can be eliminated if the mapping is absolutely accurate. We use LS-SVM to get the mapping. LS-SVM is a powerful methodology for solving problems in nonlinear function estimation [7]. It's a reformulation to standard SVM, which is proposed by J.A.K Suykens and J.Vandewalle.

Given a training data set of n points $\{(x_1, y_1), \cdots, (x_n, y_n)\}$ with input data as $x_i = (x_i^1, x_i^2, \cdots, x_i^m)^T \in X = R^m, i = 1, 2, ..., n$ and corresponding target output data as $y_i \in Y = R, i = 1, 2, ..., n$. The nonlinear function estimation modeling takes the form as

$$f(x) = w^T \varphi(x) + b \tag{10}$$

where $\varphi(x)$ denotes the high dimensional feature space which is nonlinearly mapped from the input space. The unknown variables w and b are estimated by regularization and structural risk principle. Based on the structural risk minimization principle, we can get:

$$\begin{cases} \min\limits_{w,e} \ J(w, e) = \dfrac{1}{2} w^T w + \dfrac{C}{2} \sum\limits_{i=1}^{n} e_i^2 \\ s.t. \qquad y_i = w^T \varphi(x_i) + b + e_i \quad i = 1, 2, ..., n \end{cases} \tag{11}$$

where $e = (e_1, e_2, \cdots, e_n)^T$ is the random errors and $C \geq 0$ is a regularization parameter in determining the trade-off between minimizing the training errors and minimizing the model complexity. To solve the optimization problem above, the corresponding Lagrange function is given by

$$L(w,b,e,\alpha) = \frac{1}{2}w^T w + \frac{C}{2}\sum_{i=1}^{n} e_i^2 - \sum_{i=1}^{n} \alpha_i(w^T \varphi(x_i) + b + e_i - y_i) \qquad (12)$$

where $\alpha_i (i = 1, 2, \ldots, n)$ is the Lagrange multiplier. According to the Karush-Kuhn-Tunker conditions, the bellowing formula can be got:

$$\begin{cases} \dfrac{\partial L}{\partial w} = 0 \Rightarrow w - \sum_{i=1}^{n} \alpha_i \varphi(x_i) = 0 \\[2mm] \dfrac{\partial L}{\partial b} = 0 \Rightarrow \sum_{i=1}^{n} \alpha_i = 0 \\[2mm] \dfrac{\partial L}{\partial e} = 0 \Rightarrow Ce_i - \alpha_i = 0 \\[2mm] \dfrac{\partial L}{\partial \alpha} = 0 \Rightarrow w^T \varphi(x_i) + b + e_i - y_i = 0 \end{cases} \qquad (13)$$

Eliminating e_i and w, equation (13) can be changed into:

$$\begin{pmatrix} K(x_1,x_1)+\dfrac{1}{C} & K(x_1,x_2) & \cdots & K(x_1,x_n) & 1 \\ K(x_2,x_1) & K(x_2,x_2)+\dfrac{1}{C} & \cdots & K(x_2,x_n) & 1 \\ \vdots & \vdots & \ddots & \vdots & \vdots \\ K(x_n,x_1) & K(x_n,x_2) & \cdots & K(x_n,x_n)+\dfrac{1}{C} & 1 \\ 1 & 1 & \cdots & 1 & 0 \end{pmatrix} \begin{pmatrix} \alpha_1 \\ \alpha_2 \\ \vdots \\ \alpha_n \\ b \end{pmatrix} = \begin{pmatrix} y_1 \\ y_2 \\ \vdots \\ y_n \\ 0 \end{pmatrix} \qquad (14)$$

where $K(x_i,x_j) = \varphi(x_i)^T \bullet \varphi(x_j)$ is defined as kernel function. Any function that satisfies Mercer's condition [8] can be used as the kernel function.

Finally, the parameters $(\alpha_1, \alpha_2, \cdots, \alpha_n)^T$ and b can be worked out from equation (14) and then LS-SVM model for function estimation can be expressed as:

$$f(x) = w^T \varphi(x) + b = \sum_{i=1}^{n} \alpha_i K(x_i, x) + b \cdot \qquad (15)$$

In the whole process, regularization parameter C and kernel function $\varphi(x)$ needs to be chosen artificially.

4.2   Simulation

The environment of simulation is similar to LANDMARC. First, the mapping relation of RSSI-distance needs to be acquired. In the simulation, Back Propagation (BP) neural network is compared with LS-SVM. They all need some sample data for training. Here we use the layout of Fig 1 to get the sample data. Each reader antenna collects 25 RSSI values, in total of 100 samples. After training, the input is RSSI and the output is distance no matter the model is BP or LS-SVM.

Following are the parameters of BP: one-size input layer for the value of RSSI; one-size output layer for the value of distance; one hidden layer of size 10; the transfer function of hidden layer $\sigma(x) = 1/(1+e^{-x})$; and the transfer function of output layer $\sigma(x) = x$.

What we use in our simulation is a matlab toolbox called LS-SVMLab [9], which is developed by a project group of K.U. Leuven University. Radial Basis Function (RBF) is chosen as the kernel function of LS-SVM model:

$$K(x_i, x_j) = \exp\left(-\frac{|x_i - x_j|^2}{\sigma^2}\right). \tag{16}$$

The kernel function parameter σ^2 and regularization parameter C are gained through matlab function "tunelssvm": $\sigma^2 = 13.4227, C = 29.5465$.

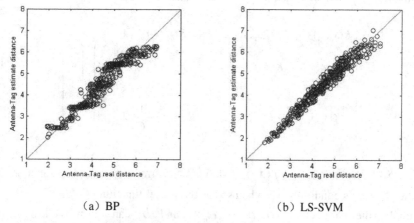

(a) BP   (b) LS-SVM

Fig. 4. Comparison of BP and LS-SVM

100 target tags are randomly placed in the location area to test the performance of BP and LS-SVM. Fig 4 reveals that the performance of LS-SVM is better. Compared with BP, LS-SVM has better convergence, faster calculating speed and less occupation of computation resources. In consequence, LS-SVM is more suitable for the problems of small sample and nonlinear. Additionally, it is our optimal choice to map RSSI to distance. Then according to the location algorithm based on LS-SVM, we can eventually get the position of target tag. From the Fig 5: (b), the location average error is only 0.12547m, which is much less than that of LANDMAC.

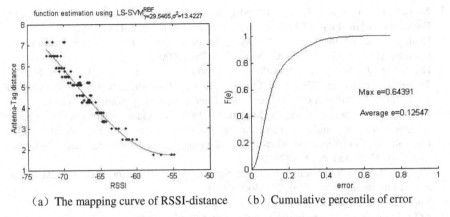

(a) The mapping curve of RSSI-distance   (b) Cumulative percentile of error

Fig. 5. The simulation results of LS-SVM

5   Conclusions

In conclusion, while the location algorithm based on LS-SVM is proposed, the location algorithm of LANDMARC is mentioned in great detail. The LANDMARC has an advantage of strong anti-interference even though its accuracy primarily depends on practical experience and empirical formula. In order to increase the location accuracy, it is necessary to place more readers and reference tags. Nevertheless, this approach would bring about inconvenience to practice. By contrast, the location algorithm based on LS-SVM has more accurate results, but the difficulty is to find the precise mapping relation of RSSI-distance. LS-SVM, therefore at this point, is introduced to get the mapping relation by our research. According to the simulation, the location performance is better than LANDMARC and it does not need so many reference tags. In future work, this algorithm will be tested in practice and then be improved.

Acknowledgement. This work was supported in part by the Natural Science Foundation of China Under Grants of 61174094 and 60904064, the Specialized Research Fund for the Doctoral Program of Higher Education of China Under Grant 20090031110029, the Tianjin Nature Science Foundation under Grant 10JCZDJC15900.

References

1. Liu, Y., Du, H., Xu, Y.: The Research and Design of the Indoor Location System Based on RFID. In: 2011 Fourth International Symposium on Computational Intelligence and Design (ISCID), vol. 2, pp. 87–90 (2011)
2. Liu, Y., Yang, G.: Indoor Location Algorithm on RFID and Its Improvement. In: 2011 3rd International Conference on Computer Research and Development (ICCRD), vol. 2, pp. 56–59 (2011)

3. Ni, L.N., Liu, Y., Lau, Y.C.: LANDMARC: indoor location sensing using active RFID. In: Proceedings of the First IEEE International Conference, pp. 407–415 (2003)
4. Bahl, P., Padmanabhan, V.N.: RADAR: An in-building RF-based user location and tracking system. In: IEEE INFOCOM, pp. 775–784 (2000)
5. Hightower, J., Want, R., Borriello, G.: SpotON: An Indoor 3D Location Sensing Technology Based on RF Signal Strength. Technical Report UW CSE, University of Washington, Department of Computer Science and Engineering, Seattle WA (2000)
6. Klozar, L., Prokopec, J., Hanus, S., Slanina, M., Fedra, Z.: Indoor channel modeling based on experience with outdoor urban measurement – Multislope modeling. In: 2011 IEEE International Conference on Microwaves, Communications, Antennas and Electronics Systems (COMCAS), pp. 1–4 (2011)
7. Suykens, J.A.K., Vandewalle, J.: Least Squares Support Vector Machine Classifiers. Neural Processing Letters 9(3), 293–300 (1999)
8. Vapnik, V.N.: Statistical Learning theory. John Wiley&Sons, New York (1988)
9. http://www.esat.kuleuven.be/sista/lssvmlab
10. Choi, J.S., Lee, H., Engels, D.W.: Passive UHF RFID-Based Localization Using Detection of Tag Interference on Smart Shelf. IEEE Transactions on Systems Man and Cybernetics, Part C: Application and Reviews 42, 268–275 (2012)
11. Zhang, W., Li, C., Zhong, B.: LSSVM Parameters Optimizing and Non-Linear System Prediction Based on Cross Validation. In: Fifth International Conference on Natural Computation, ICNC 2009, vol. 1, pp. 531–535 (2009)

Performance Robustness Comparison
of Active Disturbance Rejection Control
and Adaptive Backstepping Sliding Mode Control[*]

Ying Kang[1], Donghai Li[2], and Dazhong Lao[1]

[1] School of Aerospace Engineering, Beijing Institute of Technology, Beijing 100081, China
[2] State Key Lab. of Power Systems, Dept. of Thermal Engineering,
Tsinghua University, Beijing 100084, China
monica1987mail@163.com,
lidongh@mail.tsinghua.edu.cn

Abstract. Active disturbance rejection control and sliding mode control are two control approaches which are claimed to have good ability and strong robustness in the control of the systems with internal uncertainties and external disturbances. But the systematic comparisons of these two control schemes are lacking in the extant literatures. In this study, Monte-Carlo experiment is adopted to test the performance robustness of these two control schemes based on the same nominal disturbance rejection ability. Simulation results show that the second-order linear active disturbance rejection control has very good performance robustness, especially for the plants with integrating element, the high order plants and the nonlinear plants.

Keywords: Second-order linear active disturbance rejection control, Adaptive backstepping sliding mode control, Performance robustness, Monte-Carlo experiment.

1 Introduction

With the development of modern industry, more and more large-scale and complicated industrial systems gradually appear. In practice, however, accurate mathematical models of most systems are difficult to obtain, internal uncertainties and external disturbances always exist. Good performance robustness is hoped to achieve which means that a controller is not only able to ensure the stability but also can achieve good dynamic performance of the system with internal uncertainties and external disturbances [1].

Both the second-order active disturbance rejection control (ADRC) and the sliding mode control (SMC) are claimed to be excellent control approaches in the control of the systems with internal uncertainties and external disturbances [1,2]. But the systematic comparison of this two control schemes are lacking in the extant literatures. On the other hand, most studies of active disturbance rejection control (ADRC) were based on

---

[*] This work is supported by the National Natural Science Foundation of China (Grant No.51176086 and Grant No.51076071).

T. Xiao, L. Zhang, and M. Fei (Eds.): AsiaSim 2012, Part II, CCIS 324, pp. 275–285, 2012.

the comparison with proportional-integral-derivative (PID) controllers, lacking of comparison with other more advanced control approaches which have relatively mature theories and application technologies. This will restrict the development and application of ADRC in some extent. Therefore, this paper will make a comparative study of the second-order linear ADRC (LADRC) and the adaptive backstepping SMC. On the condition of the same disturbance rejection ability we compare the performance robustness of the two control schemes based on second-order LADRC and adaptive backstepping SMC.

In the 1990s, Han proposed ADRC based on the advantages of PID control and the modern control theory [3]. The PID eliminates the error based on the error, while the modern control theory is based on internal mechanism description [4]. By introducing the tracking differentiator (TD) and nonlinear feedback control law ADRC overcomes two disadvantages of PID, which are unreasonable obtaining method of control error and the form of error feedback law restricted to weighted sum. Moreover, extended state observer (ESO) is innovatively designed which regards the lumped disturbance (internal uncertainties and external disturbances) of system as an augmented state and estimates it using the state observer. Thus, the system can be transformed into a unit gain double integrator. However, the tuning procedure of nonlinear ADRC is very complicated due to its large number of parameters. The tuning is usually relied on the experiences of the engineers. Gao [5] used linear gains in place of the original nonlinear gain in ADRC. Thus, the number of parameters was reduced obviously. The linear ADRC not only keeps the good control capacity of nonlinear ADRC, but also make the tuning more realistic and efficient.

Since the 1950s, the theories and application technologies of sliding mode control has become more and more mature [6]. SMC achieved very good results in mechanical and electrical control system, servo control system, space and vehicle control system, robotics control system and inverted pendulum control system and so on [1]. Adaptive backstepping SMC is proposed according to the traditional sliding mode control, backstepping method and adaptive control [7]. Therefore, it inherits the advantages of the traditional SMC which are good disturbance rejection ability and strong robustness. By using the backstepping method, it decomposes a complex system into several low order subsystems and designs a Lyapunov function and stabilising function for each subsystem, until finishes the whole design of the control law. Furthermore, adaptive control method is adopted to overcome the disadvantage of the traditional SMC which is the demand to know the upper bound of the lumped uncertainty. Thus, adaptive backstepping SMC is able to make the system meet the Lyapunov stability condition and enhance the robustness and adaptability of the system. It is a rather representative control method of the sliding mode variable structure control.

In this study, Monte-Carlo experimental method is adopted to analyze and compare the time-domain performance robustness of second-order LADRC and adaptive backstepping SMC. The organization of this paper is as follows: In Section 2, system description and problem formulation are presented. Moreover the principles and design methods of second-order LADRC and adaptive backstepping SMC are briefly described. In section 3, the numerical simulations of performance robustness aiming at six typical plants including four linear plants and two nonlinear ones are performed. Besides, the results of the simulation are analyzed. Finally, Section 4 ends this paper with some concluding remarks.

2   Problem Formulation and Algorithm Theory

2.1   Problem Formulation

Consider the following n-order system:

$$
\begin{cases}
\dot{x}_1 = x_2 \\
\quad \vdots \\
\dot{x}_i = x_{i+1} \\
\dot{x}_n = F(x_1,\cdots,x_n,a_i)+bu+d \\
y = x_1
\end{cases}
\tag{1}
$$

where $(x_1,\cdots,x_n)\in R^n$, $a_i(i=1,\cdots,n)\in R$, $y\in R$ and $u\in R$ are the state vector, the constant parameters, the output and the control input of system, respectively, $F(x_1,\cdots,x_n)$ can be a linear or nonlinear function of $(x_1,\cdots,x_n)$, d is the load disturbance. Here suppose that the parameters a_i perturb in the $\pm10\%$ range of their nominal value which represents that there are some of the internal uncertainties in the model of the system.

The purpose of controller design is to make the system meet the following requirements [8] that the system asymptotically tracks stepwise reference input changes, and the settling time and overshoot $\sigma\%$ are smaller than desired value. Secondly, the process output y comes back to reference input r quickly and the impact of disturbance is low. Thirdly, for a 10% change in parameters a_i, the system is stable with good control performance.

2.2   Second-Order LADRC

The structure of second-order LADRC system [1] is illustrated in Fig.1. It mainly includes the linear extended state observer (*LESO*), the error feedback control law u_0 and the control input u.

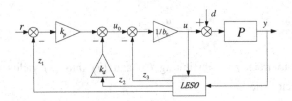

Fig. 1. Structure of second-order LADRC

where P is the plant. Two external signals act on the control loop, namely the system reference input r and the load disturbance d, respectively. k_p, k_d and b_0 are the control parameters.

To illustrate the algorithm theory of second-order LADRC, we rewrite system (1) as:

$$y^{(n)} = F(x_1, \cdots, x_n, a_i) + bu + d .$$

(2)

Since the models of most industrial systems can be transformed into second-order ones, the system (2) can be rewritten as:

$$\ddot{y} = F(x_1, \cdots, x_n, a_i) + \ddot{y} - y^{(n)} + bu + d = f + b_0 u ,$$

(3)

where $f = F(x_1, \cdots, x_n, a_i) + \ddot{y} - y^{(n)} + d + (b - b_0)u$ is the lumped disturbance of the control system.

Regard f as the augmented state variable, namely x_3, then the system can be rewritten as:

$$\begin{cases} \dot{x}_1 = x_2 \\ \dot{x}_2 = x_3 + b_0 u \\ x_3 = f \\ y = x_1 \end{cases}$$

(4)

Set the state observer for the system, namely the linear extended state observer ($LESO$):

$$\begin{cases} e = y - z_1 \\ \dot{z}_1 = z_2 + \beta_1 e \\ \dot{z}_2 = z_3 + \beta_2 e + b_0 u \\ \dot{z}_3 = \beta_3 e \end{cases}$$

(5)

Therefore, z_1, z_2, z_3 will track the state variables x_1, x_2, x_3 of system (3), respectively when the parameters $\beta_1, \beta_2, \beta_3$ of $LESO$ are set reasonably.

From Fig 1, it can be known that error feedback control is

$$u_0 = k_p e - k_d z_2 ,$$

(6)

and the control input is

$$u = \frac{u_0 - z_3}{b_0} .$$

(7)

If z_3 is able to track f , substituting (6) and (7) into (3) yields the closed-loop dynamic characteristic

$$\ddot{y} + k_d \dot{y} + k_p y = k_p r .$$

(8)

Taking the Laplace transform yields the close-loop transfer function

$$G_d(s) = \frac{y(s)}{r(s)} = \frac{k_p}{s^2 + k_d s + k_p} .$$

(9)

As proposed in [5], we simplify the problem by making $\beta_1, \beta_2, \beta_3$ a function of ω_o (observer bandwidth) and k_p, k_d a function of ω_c (control bandwidth):

$$s^3 + \beta_1 s^2 + \beta_2 s + \beta_3 = (s + \omega_o)^3; s^2 + k_d s + k_p = (s + \omega_c)^2. \tag{10}$$

Thus

$$k_p = \omega_c^2, k_d = 2\omega_c \; ; \; \beta_1 = 3\omega_0, \beta_2 = 3\omega_0^2, \beta_3 = \omega_0^3. \tag{11}$$

Such that there are only three parameters need to be tuned, that is b_0, ω_c, ω_0.

2.3   Adaptive Backstepping SMC

To describe the algorithm theory of adaptive backstepping SMC, the system (2) can be rewritten as

$$y^{(n)} = f(x_1, \cdots, x_n, a_{nom}) + bu + \theta \;, \tag{12}$$

where a_{nom} denote the nominal value of a_i, $\theta = f(x_1, \cdots, x_n, \Delta a_i) + d$ is the lumped uncertainty including the load disturbances d and internal uncertain $f(x_1, \cdots, x_n, \Delta a_i)$ results from parameters perturbation .

Define the tracking error and its n-order derivatives as follows [9]:

$$\begin{cases} z_1 = y - r \\ z_2 = x_2 - \alpha_1(x_1) \\ \cdots \\ z_n = x_n - \alpha_{n-1}(x_1, \cdots, x_{n-1}) \end{cases}, \tag{13}$$

where $\alpha_i (i = 1, \cdots, n-1)$ is the stabilising function to be determined.

To design the backstepping controller, we assume that not only r but also its derivatives $\dot{r}, \cdots, r^{(n)}$ are all bounded functions of time. The lumped uncertainty θ is assumed to be bounded and changes slowly, i, e.

$$|\theta| \leq \bar{\theta}, \dot{\theta} = 0. \tag{14}$$

The design method of adaptive backstepping SMC is described step-by-step as follows:

Step 1: take derivative of the tracking error z_1

$$\dot{z}_1 = \dot{x}_1 - \dot{r} = x_2 - \dot{r} = z_2 + \alpha_1(x_1) - \dot{r}. \tag{15}$$

Then the first Lyapunov function is chosen as:

$$V_1 = \frac{1}{2} z_1^2, \tag{16}$$

and its derivative is

$$\dot{V}_1 = z_1 \dot{z}_1 = z_1 (z_2 + \alpha_1 (x_1) - \dot{r}).$$

(17)

Define the stabilizing function:

$$\alpha_1 = -c_1 x_1 + \dot{r},$$

(18)

then the derivative of V_1 is

$$\dot{V}_1 = z_1 \dot{z}_1 = -c_1 z_1^2 + z_1 z_2.$$

(19)

It is easily to know that if $z_2 = 0, \dot{V}_1 \le 0$, z_1 is asymptotically stable. But in general, $z_2 \ne 0$. Thus there is necessary to define the second stabilising function α_2 to make z_2 has the desired stability.

Step k $(k = 2,3,\cdots n-1)$: the $k-th$ Lyapunov function is chosen as:

$$V_k = V_{k-1} + \frac{1}{2} z_k^2 = \frac{1}{2}(z_1^2 + \cdots + z_k^2).$$

(20)

Define the $i-th$ stabilizing function:

$$\alpha_k = -c_k z_k + \dot{\alpha}_{k-1},$$

(21)

where $\alpha_k = \alpha(x_1, x_2, \cdots, x_k), \dot{\alpha}_{k-1} = \sum_{i=1}^{k-1} \frac{\partial \alpha_{k-1}}{x_i} \cdot \dot{x}_i = \sum_{i=1}^{k-1} \frac{\partial \alpha_{k-1}}{x_i} \cdot x_{i+1}$.

Then we can get the derivative of V_i :

$$\dot{V}_k = -(c_1 z_1^2 + \cdots + c_k z_k^2) + z_k z_{k+1}.$$

(22)

Step n : since θ is unknown in practical application [10], the upper bound $\bar{\theta}$ is difficult to determine. Therefore, an adaptive law is proposed to adapt the value of the lumped uncertainty $\hat{\theta}$. Then a Lyapunov candidate is chosen as:

$$V_n = V_{n-1} + \frac{1}{2}\sigma^2 + \frac{1}{r}(\theta - \hat{\theta})^2$$

(23)

with the sliding surface

$$\sigma = k_1 z_1 + \cdots + k_{n-1} z_{n-1} + z_n$$

(24)

where $r(>0)$ is the adaptive gain coefficient, $k_i > 0$. If we take the derivative of the Lyapunov function, and according to (14), then

$$\dot{V}_n = \dot{V}_{n-1} + \sigma \dot{\sigma} - \frac{2}{r}(\theta - \hat{\theta})\dot{\hat{\theta}} = \dot{V}_{n-1} + \sigma(k_1 \dot{z}_1 + \cdots + k_{n-1}\dot{z}_{n-1} + \dot{z}_n) - \frac{2}{r}(\theta - \hat{\theta})\dot{\hat{\theta}}$$

$$= \dot{V}_{n-1} + \sigma(\sum_{i=1}^{n-1} k_1 (z_{i+1} - c_i z_i - z_{i-1}) + \sum_{i=1}^{n-1} \frac{\partial \alpha_{n-1}}{\partial x_i} + f + bu + \varphi(x)\hat{\theta}) - \frac{2}{r}(\theta - \hat{\theta})\dot{\hat{\theta}}.$$

(25)

Use the exponential reaching law:

$$\dot{\sigma} = -h[\sigma + \beta \operatorname{sgn}(\sigma)] \tag{26}$$

where $h > 0, \beta > 0$. The structure of exponential reaching law is simple and can achieve good process quality by choosing the value of h and β [11].

According to (25) and (26), an adaptive backstepping sliding mode control law u is proposed as:

$$u = -\frac{1}{b} \{ \sum_{i=1}^{n-1} k_i (z_{i+1} - c_i z_i - z_{i-1}) + \sum_{i=1}^{n-1} \frac{\partial \alpha_{n-1}}{\partial x_i} x_{i+1} + f(x) + \varphi(x)\hat{\theta} + h[\sigma + \beta \operatorname{sgn}(\sigma)] \}. \tag{27}$$

The adaptation laws for $\dot{\hat{\theta}}$ is designed as:

$$\dot{\hat{\theta}} = r\sigma\varphi(x). \tag{28}$$

It is used to estimate the parameter θ in real time. Then, substituting (27) and (28) into (25), the following equation can be obtained:

$$\dot{V}_n = -\sum_{i=1}^{n-1} c_i z_i^2 + z_{n-1} z_n - h\sigma^2 - h\beta|\sigma|. \tag{29}$$

Thus (29) can be rewritten as

$$\dot{V}_n = -z^T Q z - h\beta|\sigma| \le 0, \tag{30}$$

where $z^T = [z_1 \quad z_2 \quad \cdots \quad z_n]$, Q is a symmetric matrix with the following form:

$$Q = \begin{bmatrix} c_1 + hk_1^2 & hk_1 k_2 & \cdots & hk_1 k_{n-1} & hk_1 \\ hk_1 k_2 & c_2 + hk_2^2 & \cdots & hk_2 k_{n-1} & hk_2 \\ \vdots & \vdots & \cdots & \vdots & \vdots \\ hk_1 k_{n-1} & hk_2 k_{n-1} & \cdots & c_{n-1} + hk_{n-1}^2 & -\frac{1}{2} + hk_{n-1} \\ hk_1 & hk_2 & \cdots & -\frac{1}{2} + hk_{n-1} & h \end{bmatrix}. \tag{31}$$

Q can be guaranteed a positive definite by choosing the value of parameters $c_i, k_i (i = 1, 2, \cdots n - 1), h$.

As a result, the stability of the proposed adaptive backstepping SMC system can be guaranteed. The detailed proof of stability can be found in [9]. Therefore the backstepping sliding mode control system is asymptotically stable even if parametric uncertainty, external disturbance exist. All the parameters of adaptive backstepping SMC need to be tuned are $c_i, h, \beta, k_i, \gamma, (i = 1, 2, \cdots, n)$, n is the order number of each plant.

3   Numerical Simulations of Performance Robustness Comparison

3.1   Simulation Examples

To investigate the time-domain performance robustness of the proposed second-order LADRC and adaptive backstepping SMC, the following four typical linear simulation examples and two nonlinear ones are considered.

$$P_1: \frac{1}{(s+1)(2s+1)} \qquad P_2: \frac{1}{(5s-1)(2s+1)} \qquad P_3: \frac{2}{s(s+1)^2} \qquad P_4: \frac{3}{(20s+1)(s+1)(0.1s+1)^2}$$

$$P_5: \begin{cases} \dot{x}_1 = x_2 \\ \dot{x}_2 = \sin(0.25\pi t)x_1 + x_2^2 + 0.2\cos(0.2\pi t) - u \\ y = x_1 \\ x_1(0) = 0, x_2(0) = 0 \end{cases} \qquad P_6: \begin{cases} \dot{x}_1 = x_2 \\ \dot{x}_2 = sign(\sin(0.05t)) + 1.5u \\ y = x_1 \\ x_1(0) = 0, x_2(0) = 0 \end{cases}$$

where P_1 is a common second-order plant, P_2 is an second-order plant including a unstable pole , P_3 is an third-order plant with integrating element, P_4 is a high-order plant which order is fourth, P_5 and P_6 are two second-order nonlinear plants.

3.2   Dynamic Response Based on the Same Nominal Disturbance Rejection Ability

Design second-order LADRC and adaptive backstepping SMC for the abovementioned six plants. Under the condition that the parameters of the plants are nominal, add a step load disturbance d to the control input at half of the simulation time. The value of d is 100% of the reference input.

For the fairness of performance robustness comparison, the same disturbance re-jection ability are achieved by ensuring the similar dynamic process (Overshoot as low as possible, settling time as short as possible) and the same absolute error integral IAE of the two control systems. This target will be reached by tuning the parameters of the two control schemes. Controller parameters tuning results are in Table 1, the dynamic response processes and control inputs are in Table 2.

Table 1. Parameters of two controllers

Plant	LADRC				SMC			
	b_0	ω_0	ω_c	(c_i)	h	β	(k_i)	γ
P_1	0.5	37	6	(1)	10	0.08	(2,1)	100
P_2	0.1	18.5	16.5	(1,2)	62	0.1	(10)	116
P_3	1.8	57.5	0.7	(0.5,0.5)	0.5	0.3	(0.1,0.1)	25
P_4	0.49	59.5	1.44	(0.9,3,4)	19	0.8	(3.9,5.8,6)	32
P_5	-1	52.5	12.5	(1,2)	79	0.04	(6,1)	80.5
P_6	1.5	30.5	9.1	(1)	72	0.08	(4,5)	92.7

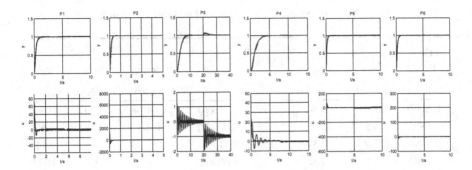

Fig. 2. The dynamic response and control inputs of LADRC (*solid line*) and SMC (*dash dotted line*)

3.3   Comparison of Time-Domain Performance Robustness

Monte-Carlo experimental method is adopted to compare the time-domain perfor-mance robustness of the two controllers, which is described as follows:

Let the parameters of the plants perturb 500 times within ±10% of their nominal values and perform 500 times of step response experiment. Meanwhile, plot the time-domain performance indices settling time and overshoot on the plane of $t_s - \sigma\%$. The more closer the performance index points are to the bottom left corner of the plane, the better dynamic property the control system has. And the more inten-sive the points are distributed, the better performance robustness the control system has. Furthermore, the distribution range, mean and variance of each performance index are given for a better comparison. Results of Monte-Carlo experiment are in Fig.3, performance indices are in Table 2.

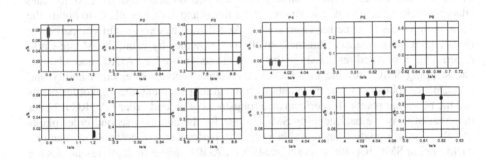

Fig. 3. Monte-Carlo experiment results of LADRC (*above*) and SMC (*bottom*)

Table 2. The range, mean and variance of performance indices

P	Con-troller	IAE	Settling time (s)			Overshoot (%)		
			Range	Mean	Var	Range	Mean	Var
		$(\times 10^{-4})$				$(\times 10^{-4})$	$(\times 10^{-4})$	$(\times 10^{-10})$
P_1	LADRC	15	0.90	0.90	5.71×10^{-29}	6.648-8.5	7.591	9.39
	SMC	15	1.21	1.21	4.00×10^{-30}	0.4-1.5	0.872	2.68
P_2	LADRC	1.8	0.34	0.34	7.41×10^{-30}	31-33	32	7.11
	SMC	1.8	0.32	0.32	1.60×10^{-29}	67	67	0.073
P_3	LADRC	2200	8.71-8.73	8.72	2.73×10^{-5}	24-27	26	24.0
	SMC	2200	6.90-6.92	6.90	6.22×10^{-6}	39-45	41	68.5
P_4	LADRC	130	4.00-4.01	4.01	2.25×10^{-5}	3.3-5.2	4.085	9.38
	SMC	130	4.03-4.05	4.04	3.12×10^{-5}	15-17	16	5.26
P_5	LADRC	20	0.52	0.52	1.69×10^{-29}	4.9-5.1	5.0	0.078
	SMC	20	0.51-0.52	0.51	7.37×10^{-6}	23-25	24	18.9
P_6	LADRC	29	0.63	0.63	1.11×10^{-29}	0.94-2.3	1.51	6.34
	SMC	29	0.71	0.71	1.43×10^{-29}	50-56	54	77.9

It can be seen from the simulated results, for P_1 and P_2 the performance robustness of SMC is better than that of LADRC. While for P_3, P_4, P_5, P_6, LADRC is better than SMC. Moreover the conclusion is supported by lots of numerical experiments.

4   Conclusions

This study has designed two control schemes based on second-order LADRC and adaptive backstepping SMC for the six typical linear and nonlinear plants to obtain the same nominal disturbance rejection ability. And then it has successful compared the time-domain performance robustness of the two schemes by using the Monte-Carlo experiment. Simulated results show that both the second-order LADRC and adaptive backstepping SMC are able to achieve very good disturbance rejection ability and performance robustness. For the plants with integrating element, the high order plants and the nonlinear plants, the performance robustness of second-order LADRC is better than that of adaptive backstepping SMC. While for the common second-order plants and the plants including an unstable pole, the performance robustness of adaptive backstepping SMC is better than second-order LADRC. More in-depth researches are expected in the future.

References

1. Xing, C., Donghai, L., Zhiqiang, G., Chuanfeng, W.: Tuning Method for Second-order Active Disturbance Rejection Control. In: Proceedings of the 30th Chinese Control Conference, CCC, pp. 6322–6327 (2011)

2. Dewen, Z.: Research on Sliding-Mode Control of Discrete Uncertain Systems with Time-delays. Ocean University of China (2009) (in Chinese)
3. Jingqing, H.: Auto disturbance rejection control and its applications. Control and Decision 13(1), 19–23 (1998) (in Chinese)
4. Jingqing, H.: Active disturbance rejection control. National Defense Industry Press, Beijing (2008) (in Chinese)
5. Zhiqiang, G.: Scaling and Bandwidth-Parameterization based Controller Tuning. In: Proceedings of the American Control Conference, vol. 6, pp. 4989–4996 (2003)
6. Weibing, G.: Theoretical basis of Variable structure control. Science and Technology of China Publishing House, Beijing (1990) (in Chinese)
7. Pourmahmood, M., Khanmohammadi, S.: Synchronization of two different uncertain chaotic systems with unknown parameters using a robust adaptive sliding mode controller. Communications in Nonlinear Science and Numerical Simulation 16(7), 2853–2868 (2001)
8. Xing, C.: Active disturbance rejection controller tuning and its applications to thermal processes. Tsinghua University (2009) (in Chinese)
9. Xiangzhe, W.: Study on the backstepping adaptive variable structure control for the nonlinear power system. Nanjing University of Science and Technology (2010) (in Chinese)
10. Lin, F.J., Shen, P.H., Hsu, S.P.: Adaptive backstepping sliding mode control for linear induction motor drive. IEEE Proceedings Electric Power Applications, 184–194 (2002)
11. Jinkun, L.: MATLAB Simulation for Sliding Mode Control. Tsinghua University Press, Beijing (2006) (in Chinese)

Research and Simulation of Surface Fitting Algorithm Based on Surface Patches Splicing[*]

Xiaoping Qiao[1], Hesheng Zhang[1,2], Jinxing Xu[1], and Xiaojin Zhu[1,**]

[1] School of Mechatronics Engineering and Automation, Shanghai University,
Shanghai, 200072, P.R. China
[2] Shanghai Institute of Aerospace Electronic Technology,
China Aerospace Science and Technology Corporation, Shanghai, 201109, P.R. China
mgzhuxj@shu.edu.cn

Abstract. According to differential geometry of surface theories, this paper researches on a surface fitting algorithm based on surface patches splicing. Space curved surface is decomposed into several surface patches, and then, surface model is established based on the quadratic equation. During the establishment of multiple nonlinear equations, the equal mean curvature and continuous surface works as boundary constraint conditions. For each patch, the nonlinear equations are solved by using single rank inverse Broyden quasi Newton method to obtain the parametric equation of the surface patch. Through the recursion, the patches can be spliced and it can realize the surface reconstruction. Finally, simulations are carried out in the Matlab environment and the experimental results show that the surface fitting algorithm can effectively reconstruct the large deformation surface, so it is feasible for space surfaces reconstruction.

Keywords: Surface patches, Surface reconstruction, Single rank inverse Broyden quasi Newton method.

1 Introduction

With the development of the aerospace industry and technological progress, the structure of the spacecraft is increasingly complex and huge. And without damping outer space, it is prone to nonlinear low frequency vibration which results in the structure of the spacecraft, especially space solar panel substrate deformation. In addition, it often needs to complete a variety of difficult missions for high performance aircraft, such as substantial flip, quick movements, high-altitude flight in adverse weather conditions, which easily cause the deformation of the wing. Although the above two kinds of structure of deformation have different reasons, the lack of active monitoring of the above key structural deformation is what they have in

---

[*] This research is supported by program of National Nature Science Foundation of China (No.51175319), and key program of Shanghai Municipal Education Commission.
[**] Corresponding author.

T. Xiao, L. Zhang, and M. Fei (Eds.): AsiaSim 2012, Part II, CCIS 324, pp. 286–295, 2012.
© Springer-Verlag Berlin Heidelberg 2012

common. And the solar panels and wings are a plate-type structure, so research on a new real-time monitoring technology for the plate-type structure has far-reaching significance to the aerospace industry [1,2].

Before realizing the deformation detection of the plate-type structure, it is necessary to obtain the physical information from the structure, and then the surface can be fitted and reconstructed with the corresponding space surface fitting algorithm. The traditional surface fitting algorithms [3,4] are mostly based on the coordinate values of the fixed space point, but for the aerospace structure the traditional algorithms are not suitable because of its movement causing not getting definite position information and limit of the data transmission bandwidth. For the research thinking, the fiber Bragg grating sensing network is implanted into the structure based on non-visual sensing method; it realizes the fitting and reconstruction of structure through obtaining discrete sensing information from the structure. Among them, the related fitting and reconstruction algorithm and experiment validation is one of the key problems in this field. Scholars from all over the world actively study on it from different ideas and angles [5,6], for example, Rapp put forward using pair wise orthogonal FBG sensors and modal displacement matrix method to estimate the displacement field of two-dimensional board; Xiaojin Zhu realized the shape reconstruction of the flexible solar panel structure's low-frequency vibration and visualization based on curvature information and three-dimensional surface fitting algorithm. The above-mentioned study and research results has played a positive role in the development of structure strain detection and morphology real-time reconstruction based on FBG sensor network, but due to the difference in research background, application occasion, sensors arrangement, the above methods all have their application limitation. For example, current surface fitting algorithms based on curvature information rarely reflect the structural bending and torsion deformation. So the related theory method and technology need further study in depth.

With the background of plate-type structure deformation monitoring and morphological reconstruction, this paper researches on a surface fitting algorithm based on orthogonal curvature information according to differential geometry of surface theories. Space curved surface is decomposed into several surface patches, and then, the surface patch model is established based on the quadratic equation. For each patch, the nonlinear equations which are established through analysis of the boundary constraint conditions are solved by using single rank inverse Broyden quasi Newton method to obtain the parametric equation of the surface patch. Through the recursion and splicing, it can realize the surface reconstruction. In the simulation, the template surface is a quadric surface and it gets the solution of nonlinear equations with the numerical method. The results show that the algorithm can effectively achieve the reconstruction of the complex space surface.

2   Space Curved Surface Fitting Based on Surface Patch Splicing

The input conditions of the algorithm are the normal curvature of two orthogonal directions detected by the sensors and the related arc length information; the output result is the entire shape of the space curved surface.

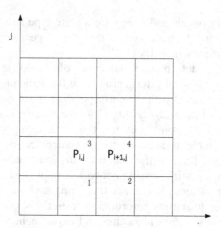

Fig. 1. FBG sensors distribution

As shown in Fig.1, it takes one of the surface patches as the object of study. Through the detection of the FBG sensors, the mutually perpendicular normal curvature information of the four corners of the surface patches is available, which are $K_{i,j}^{n1}$, $K_{i,j}^{n2}$ $(i, j = 1,2,3,4)$. The principal curvatures of the monitoring points on the surface are indicated by $K_{1(i,j)}$, $K_{2(i,j)}$. The angle between the normal curvature of the any direction and principal curvature is $\varphi_{i,j}$, according to the theory of surface Euler formula, the relationship between the normal curvatures of a point on the surface along a direction and the two principal curvatures is:

$$\begin{cases} K_{i,j}^{n1} = K_{1(i,j)} \cos^2 \varphi_{i,j} + K_{2(i,j)} \sin^2 \varphi_{i,j} \\ K_{i,j}^{n2} = K_{1(i,j)} \sin^2 \varphi_{i,j} + K_{2(i,j)} \cos^2 \varphi_{i,j} \end{cases}. \tag{1}$$

The sum of the above two formulas is Eq.2.

$$K_{i,j}^{n1} + K_{i,j}^{n2} = K_{1(i,j)} + K_{2(i,j)}. \tag{2}$$

The mean curvature of a point on the surface is defined as Eq.3.

$$K_{1(i,j)} + K_{2(i,j)} = 2H_{i,j}. \tag{3}$$

Where $H_{i,j}$ can be determined by the first and second fundamental quantity of the surface and shown as Eq.4.

$$H_{i,j} = \frac{EN - 2FM + GL}{2(FG - F^2)}. \tag{4}$$

Where the E, F, G in Eq.4 are called the first fundamental quantity and the L, M, N are called the second fundamental quantity, which can be calculated according to the parametric equation of the surface .

Where n is the unit normal vector. Then Eq.5 is calculated according to Eq.2, Eq.3, and Eq.4.

$$(K_{i,j}^{n1} + K_{i,j}^{n2}) = \frac{EN - 2FM + GL}{FG - F^2}. \tag{5}$$

Then Eq.6 can be deduced from Eq.5.

$$g_{xy} = \frac{EN - 2FM + GL}{FG - F^2} - (K_{i,j}^{n1} + K_{i,j}^{n2}). \tag{6}$$

Assuming the surface as a general quadratic surface equation:

$$f_{xy}(x, y) = a_1 + a_2 x + a_3 y + a_4 xy + a_5 x^2 + a_6 y^2. \tag{7}$$

Where $a_1, a_2, a_3, a_4, a_5, a_6$ are undetermined coefficients

Then the first and second fundamental quantity can be determined from Eq.8.

$$\begin{cases} E = 1 + (a_2 + a_4 y + 2a_5 x)^2 \\ F = (a_2 + a_4 y + 2a_5 x)(a_3 + a_4 x + 2a_6 y) \\ G = 1 + (a_3 + a_4 x + 2a_6 y)^2 \\ L = 2a_5 / \sqrt{(a_2 + a_4 y + 2a_5 x)^2 + (a_3 + a_4 x + 2a_6 y)^2 + 1} \\ M = a_4 / \sqrt{(a_2 + a_4 y + 2a_5 x)^2 + (a_3 + a_4 x + 2a_6 y)^2 + 1} \\ N = 2a_6 / \sqrt{(a_2 + a_4 y + 2a_5 x)^2 + (a_3 + a_4 x + 2a_6 y)^2 + 1} \end{cases} \tag{8}$$

The normal curvature of the four control points on the surface patch meet Eq.6, which can get four constraint equations. In the boundary conditions, the left of the surface is fixed which means the point 1 and point 3 of the surface is known, and then two boundary constraint equations are achieved. From above, it can get six equations.

This paper uses the single rank inverse Broyden quasi Newton method[7,8] to solve the nonlinear equations. Assuming the nonlinear equations $F(a) = 0$, where $a = (a_1, a_2, a_3, a_4, a_5, a_6)^T, F(a) = (g_1(a), g_2(a), g_3(a), g_4(a), f_1(a), f_2(a))^T$ the iterative formula is Eq.9.

$$a^{(k+1)} = a^{(k)} - [A_k]^{-1} F(a^{(k)}), k = 0, 1, 2... \tag{9}$$

Which $a^{(0)}$ is the initial approximation, $a^{(k)}$ is the k-th iteration approximation, matrix A_k is the approximation of $F'(a^{(k)})$, and the initial value is the unit matrix.

The Taylor expansion of $F(a)$ in $a^{(k+1)}$ is Eq.10.

$$F(a^{(k)}) \approx F(a^{(k+1)}) + A_{(k+1)}(a^{(k)} - a^{(k+1)}) . \tag{10}$$

When $(a^{(k)} - a^{(k+1)}) \neq 0$, then

$$\begin{cases} p^{(k)} = (a^{(k+1)} - a^{(k)}) \\ q^{(k)} = F(a^{(k+1)}) - F(a^{(k)}) \end{cases} . \tag{11}$$

From Eq.10 and Eq.11, Eq.12 can be deduced.

$$A_{(k+1)} p^{(k)} = q^{(k)} . \tag{12}$$

The above equation can not determine $A_{(k+1)}$. It is supported to be Eq.13.

$$A_{(k+1)} = A_{(k)} + \Delta A_{(k)} . \tag{13}$$

Which $\Delta A_{(k)}$ is incremental matrix and $rank(\Delta A_{(k)}) = 1$. It is expressed as:

$$\Delta A_{(k)} = u^{(k)} (v^{(k)})^T , (u^{(k)}, v^{(k)} \in R^n) . \tag{14}$$

Then Eq.15 can be deduced from Eq.12, Eq.13 and Eq.14.

$$[A_{(k)} + u^{(k)} (v^{(k)})^T] p^{(k)} = q^{(k)} . \tag{15}$$

When $(v^{(k)})^T p^{(k)} \neq 0$,

$$u^{(k)} = \frac{q^{(k)} - A_{(k)} p^{(k)}}{(v^{(k)})^T p^{(k)}} . \tag{16}$$

For reducing the computational complexity, $A_{(k)}^{-1}$ can be used $B_{(k)}$ instead, according to Sherman-Morrison[9],

$$(A + uv^T)^{-1} = A^{-1} - \frac{A^{-1} uv^T A^{-1}}{1 + v^T A^{-1} u} . \tag{17}$$

Which $A \in R^{n \times n}, v^T A^{-1} u \neq -1, u, v \in R^{n \times n}$

$$[A_{(k)} + u^{(k)}(v^{(k)})^T]^{-1} = (A_{(k)} + \Delta A_{(k)})^{-1} = A_{(k+1)}^{-1} = B_{(k+1)}. \tag{18}$$

Usually $v^{(k)} = p^{(k)}$, when $(p^{(k)})^T B_{(k)} q^{(k)} \neq 0$, then Eq.19 can be deduced from Eq.17 and Eq.18.

$$B_{(k+1)} = B_{(k)} - \frac{[B_{(k)} q^{(k)} - p^{(k)}](p^{(k)})^T B_{(k)}}{(p^{(k)})^T B_{(k)} q^{(k)}}. \tag{19}$$

So the iterative formula of single rank inverse Broyden quasi Newton method is Eq.20.

$$\begin{cases} a^{(k+1)} = a^{(k)} - B_{(k)} F(a^{(k)}) \\ p^{(k)} = (a^{(k+1)} - a^{(k)}) \\ q^{(k)} = F(a^{(k+1)}) - F(a^{(k)}) \qquad k = 0,1,2... \\ B_{(k+1)} = B_{(k)} - \dfrac{[B_{(k)} q^{(k)} - p^{(k)}](p^{(k)})^T B_{(k)}}{(p^{(k)})^T B_{(k)} q^{(k)}} \end{cases} \tag{20}$$

Which $a^{(0)}$ need input and $B_{(0)}$ is unit matrix

According to Eq.20, it can obtain the equation of the patch. Then the coordinate of point 1, 3 can be calculated from the equation. Through recursive method and splicing of the surface, the whole space surface can be achieved. Single rank inverse Broyden quasi Newton method which used in this paper is an effective for solving nonlinear equations, which avoid calculating the inverse matrix and reduce the amount of computation. To some extent, cumulative error is reduced. At the same time compared to the fixed point, single rank inverse Broyden quasi Newton method has a faster convergence rate.

3   Simulation and Experimental Analysis

The template surface in the simulation is a quadric surface whose size is 300mm * 400mm, and the parametric equation of the surface is given as the following:

$$f_{xy}(x, y) = 1 + x + y + x * y + x^2 + y^2. \tag{21}$$

Before the simulation, it is certain to obtain the curvature information of the template surfaces. The relationship between the orthogonal normal curvature and the first and second fundamental quantities of the surface is shown as Eq.5. From which, the curvature information is got and it can be regard as input information to verification of the algorithm. In the simulation, the most important part is the implementation of single rank inverse Broyden quasi Newton method in Matlab. The following are the main steps of the algorithm coding:

1) Give the initial $a^{(0)}$ and the precision ε;

2) Calculate $F(a^{(0)})$ and $B_{(0)}$; (Generally $B_{(0)}$ is an identity matrix, F is a nonlinear equations)

3) When k=0, 1, 2......To calculate $a^{(k+1)}$, $F(a^{(k+1)})$ and $p^{(k)}$ respectively, which can be got from Eq.22;

$$\begin{cases} a^{(k+1)} = p^{(k)} + a^{(k)} \\ p^{(k)} = -B_{(k)} * F(a^{(k)}) \end{cases}$$ (22)

If $\left\| p^{(k)} \right\| < \varepsilon$, go to step (4); Else, to calculate Eq.23

$$\begin{cases} q^{(k)} = F(a^{(k+1)}) - F(a^{(k)}) \\ B_{(k+1)} = \dfrac{B_{(k)} + (p^{(k)} - B_{(k)} * q^{(k)}) * (p^{(k)})^T * B_{(k)}}{(p^{(k)})^T * B_{(k)} * q^{(k)}} \end{cases}$$ (23)

4) Output $a^{(k+1)}$;

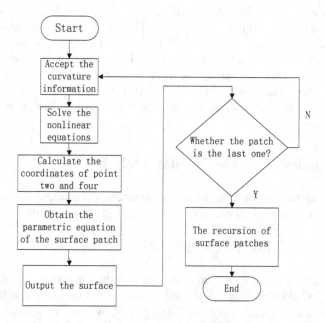

Fig. 2. The flow chart of surface fitting algorithm

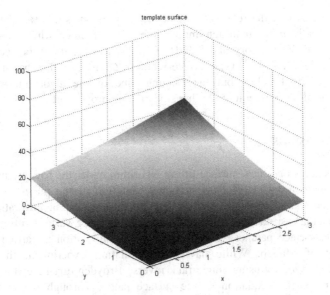

Fig. 3. The image of quadric surface

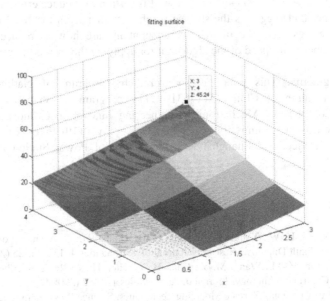

Fig. 4. Simulation result with the surface patches splicing algorithm

The flow chart of space surface fitting algorithm based on surface patch stitching is shown in Fig.2. In the Matlab environment, the above algorithm is encoded to test whether it is effective or not. The template surface of the algorithm is a quadric surface which is shown in Fig.3. Through the simulation, the result is got, which can be seen in Fig.4. According to the simulation, it can be calculated that the maximum fitting error is 24mm; the relative error of the same point is 0.53%. The simulation experiment needs more than ten minutes in the computer which has a system configuration of 2G memory and 2.3GHz CPU frequency. It can be seen from the simulation results that the space surface reconstruction algorithm based on surface patch stitching is feasible, but the running time of the algorithm is too long. Therefore, the algorithm requires further study and improvement.

4   Conclusions

This paper studies on a new surface fitting algorithm under the background of active monitoring technology oriented to structural vibration of the plate-type structures such as spacecraft's solar panel substrate and airplane's wing. The quadratic surface is used as a template surface, and then, it studies on a space surface fitting algorithm based on the surface patches splicing. Finally, the simulation is carried out in the environment of Matlab. While having a simulation experiment, the nonlinear equations are solved by using single rank inverse Broyden quasi Newton method to obtain the parametric equation of the surface patch. Through the recursion, the template surface can be reconstructed effectively. Because the algorithm uses the method of numerical analysis and recursion, it is certain to produce error and the error is being bigger and bigger as the surface patch is farther from the fixed end. In the related further research, the main research contents are how to reduce error and improve the operation speed of the algorithm for applying the method to practice.

Acknowledgments. This paper is sponsored by program of National Nature Science Foundation of China (51175319), key program of Shanghai Municipal Education Commission, Mechatronics Engineering Innovation Group project from Shanghai Education Commission, Shanghai University "11th Five-Year Plan" 211 Construction Project and Shanghai Key Laboratory of Power Station Automation Technology.

References

1. Jiang, L.-X., Li, H.-W., Yang, G.-Q., Yang, Q.-R., Huang, H.-Y.: A Survey of Spacecraft Autonomous Fault Diagnosis Research. Journal of Astronautics 4, 1320–1326 (2009)
2. Liu, T.-X., Lin, Y.-M., Wang, M.-Y., Chai, H.-Y., Hua, H.-X.: Review of the Spacecraft Vibration Control Technology. Journal of Astronautics 1, 1–12 (2008)
3. Zhu, X.: Free Curve and Surface Modeling Techniques. Science Press, Beijing (2000)
4. Lin, Z.: Research and Implement of Surface Reconstruction Technology in Reverse Engineering. Suzhou University (2006)
5. Fan, H.: Key Technique of Dynamic Surface Measurement and Visualization Based on FBG Sensing. Shanghai University (2007)

6. Rapp, S., Kang, L., Han, J., Mueller, U., Baier, H.: Displacement Field Estimation for a Two-Dimensional Structure Using Fiber Bragg Grating Sensors. Smart Materials and Structures 18, 025006, 12 (2009)
7. Wang, B.: Single rank inverse Broyden quasi Newton method and its realization in MATLAB for nonlinear equations. Journal of Yunnan University 30, 144–148 (2008)
8. An, H., Bai, Z.: Broyden Method for Nonlinear Equation in Several Variables. Mathematica Numerica Sinica 26(4), 385–400 (2004)
9. Du, T., Shen, Y., Jia, T.: Numerical Analysis and Experiments. Science Press, Beijing (2006)

Convergence Analysis of Variational Iteration Method for Caputo Fractional Differential Equations*

Zhiwu Wen**, Jie Yi, and Hongliang Liu

School of Mathematics and Computational Science,
Xiangtan University, Hunan 411105, China
wenzhiwu@xtu.edu.cn

Abstract. In this paper, the variational iteration method is applied to solve initial value problems of Caputo fractional differential equations. The convergence of the variational iteration method for solving the initial value problems of the kind of equation has been proved. The numerical examples show the efficiency of the variational iteration method for solving the initial value problems of the kind of equation.

Keywords: Fractional differential equation, Variational iteration method, Caputo derivatives, Convergence.

1 Introduction

Consider the initial value problem of the fractional differential equations

$$\begin{cases} {}_a^C D_t^\alpha y(t) = f(t,\ y(t)), & n-1 < \alpha \le n, \\ y^{(k)}(0) = y_0^k, & k = 0, \ldots, n-1, \end{cases} \tag{1}$$

where $t \in [0,T]$, $y^{(k)}(t)$ is the kth derivative of y, $f : [0,T] \times C \longrightarrow C$, and fulfill a Lipschitz condition

$$|f(t,u_1) - f(t,u_2)| \le L|u_1 - u_2|, \quad t \ge 0, \quad u_1, u_2 \in C,$$

where L is Lipschitz constant, we define norm $\| y \|_\infty = \max\limits_{0 \le t \le T} |y(t)|$. ${}_a^C D_t^\alpha y(t)$ is Caputo fractional derivative, for positive real number α, $0 \le n-1 < \alpha \le n$, we define α order Caputo derivatives of the function $f(t)$ in inter of $[a,b]$ as

$$
{}_a^C D_t^\alpha f(t) = \begin{cases} \dfrac{1}{\Gamma(n-\alpha)} \displaystyle\int_a^t \dfrac{f^{(n)}(\tau)d\tau}{(t-\tau)^{\alpha-n+1}}, if\ \alpha \in [n-1, n), \\ \dfrac{d^n}{dt^n} f(t), & if\quad \alpha = n \in N. \end{cases} \tag{2}
$$

---

* This work is supported by projects NSF of China (10971175), Specialized Research Fund for the Doctoral Program of Higher Education of China (No. 20094301110001), Program for for Changjiang Scholars and Innovative Research Team in University of China (IRT1179), the Aid Program for Science and Technology, Innovative Research Team in Higher Educational Institutions of Hunan Province of China.
** Corresponding author.

T. Xiao, L. Zhang, and M. Fei (Eds.): AsiaSim 2012, Part II, CCIS 324, pp. 296–307, 2012.
© Springer-Verlag Berlin Heidelberg 2012

Diethelm et.al. in [1] proved that Eq.(1) can be equivalent to the following Volterra integral equation

$$y(t) = \sum_{j=0}^{\lceil \alpha \rceil - 1} y_0^{(j)} \frac{t^j}{j!} + \frac{1}{\Gamma(\alpha)} \int_0^t (t - \tau)^{\alpha - 1} f(\tau, \ y(\tau)) d\tau. \qquad (3)$$

let

$$g(t) = \sum_{j=0}^{\lceil \alpha \rceil - 1} y_0^{(j)} \frac{t^j}{j!},$$

and the equation(3) can be transformed into the form

$$y(t) = g(t) + \frac{1}{\Gamma(\alpha)} \int_0^t (t - \tau)^{\alpha - 1} f(\tau, \ y(\tau)) d\tau. \qquad (4)$$

Basis of idea of Xu[2] and Ghorbani [3] et.al., variational iteration methods(also VIM) for the integral equation (4) read the following iteration form,

$$y_{n+1}(t) = g(t) + \frac{1}{\Gamma(\alpha)} \int_0^t (t - \tau)^{\alpha - 1} f(\tau, \ y_n(\tau)) d\tau, \quad n = 1, 2, \cdots. \qquad (5)$$

We use initial value $y_0(t) = y_0^{(0)} + y_0^{(1)} t + \cdots + y_0^{(n-1)} t^{n-1}$ and start to iterate, using the N-th iterative value $y_N(t)$ to approximate exact solution of Eq.(1)

$$y(t) = \lim_{n \to \infty} y_n(t).$$

Because of it's describing matter memory function and inherited domino offect, the problem (1) can be more accurately simulated realism problem (see [4-6]). Many authors have presented many numerical methods for adomian decomposition method, linear multistep method, collocation method, predictor-corrector method, etc. applied to fractional differential equations (see [7-12]).

Variational iteration method(VIM) is a method about analytical solution and appoxima analytical solution, and it has less computation amount than adomian decomposition method and new iterative methods. These cause pepole's wide interest in the (VIM)(such as [11,13-15]). Especially, the paper [16] obtains general convergence results of fractional-oder and integer orders with no delays for the initial value problem of the differential equations, respectively. In this paper, we discuss variational iteration method of solving Caputo fractional-oder differential equations,and prove the convergence of the method. Moreover, simulation experiments were competed to show the effective aspects of the algorithm.

2   Convergence Analysis

Theorem 2.1. Assume that $y(t), y_i(t) \in C[0, T], i = 1, 2, \cdots$, Then from (5), we get the true solution $y(t)$ of solution sequences convenge at the problem (1).

Proof. First of all,from the paper [6], we know that $y(t)$ is unique, let $E_i(t) = y_i(t) - y(t), i = 1, 2, \cdots$, apparently

$$y(t) = g(t) + \frac{1}{\Gamma(\alpha)} \int_0^t (t - \tau)^{\alpha-1} f(\tau,\ y(\tau)) d\tau. \tag{6}$$

From (5) and (6), we have

$$E_{n+1}(t) = \frac{1}{\Gamma(\alpha)} \int_0^t (t - \tau)^{\alpha-1} [f(\tau,\ y_n(\tau)) - f(\tau,\ y(\tau))] d\tau. \tag{7}$$

Hereinafter, we discuss two things of $0 < \alpha < 1$ and $\alpha \geq 1$. If $\alpha \geq 1$, for $\forall t \in [0, T]$, and $\tau \in [0, t]$, then $(t - \tau)^{\alpha-1}$ is bounded, if let

$$M = \max_{0 \leq \tau \leq t, 0 \leq t \leq T} |(t - \tau)^{\alpha-1}|,$$

then make use of Lipschitz condition, we have $|E_{n+1}(t)|$

$$\leq \frac{1}{\Gamma(\alpha)} \int_0^t |(t - \tau)^{\alpha-1}| \cdot |f(\tau,\ y_n(\tau)) - f(\tau,\ y(\tau))| d\tau$$

$$\leq \frac{M \cdot L}{\Gamma(\alpha)} \int_0^t |y_n(\tau) - y(\tau)| d\tau$$

$$= \frac{M \cdot L}{\Gamma(\alpha)} \int_0^t |E_n(\tau)| d\tau,$$

Making use of the recurrence relational expression, we have $|E_{n+1}(t)|$

$$\leq \frac{M^2 \cdot L^2}{[\Gamma(\alpha)]^2} \int_0^t \int_0^{\tau_1} |E_{n-1}(\tau_2)|\ d\tau_2\ d\tau_1$$

$$\vdots$$

$$\leq \frac{M^{n+1} \cdot L^{n+1}}{[\Gamma(\alpha)]^{n+1}} \int_0^t \int_0^{\tau_1} \int_0^{\tau_2} \cdots \int_0^{\tau_n} |E_0(\tau_{n+1})|\ d\tau_{n+1} \cdots d\tau_3\ d\tau_2\ d\tau_1,$$

From this, we have $\|E_{n+1}(t)\|_\infty$

$$\leq \left[\frac{M \cdot L}{\Gamma(\alpha)}\right]^{n+1} \max_{0 \leq t \leq T} \int_0^t \int_0^{\tau_1} \int_0^{\tau_2} \cdots \int_0^{\tau_n} |E_0(\tau_{n+1})|\ d\tau_{n+1} \cdots d\tau_3\ d\tau_2\ d\tau_1$$

$$\leq \left[\frac{M \cdot L}{\Gamma(\alpha)}\right]^{n+1} \cdot \frac{T^{n+1}}{(n+1)!} \|E_0(t)\|_\infty.$$

Because M, L, T, $\Gamma(\alpha)$,$\|E_0(t)\|_\infty$ are constant, then we have

$$\lim_{n \to \infty} \|E_{n+1}(t)\|_\infty \leq \lim_{n \to \infty} \left[\frac{M \cdot L \cdot T}{\Gamma(\alpha)}\right]^{n+1} \cdot \frac{\|E_0(t)\|_\infty}{(n+1)!}$$

$$= 0.$$

When $0 < \alpha < 1$

$$|E_{n+1}(t)| \leq \frac{L}{\Gamma(\alpha)} \int_0^t (t - \tau)^{\alpha-1} |y_n(\tau) - y(\tau)| \, d\tau$$

$$= \frac{L}{\Gamma(\alpha)} \int_0^t (t - \tau)^{\alpha-1} |E_n(\tau)| \, d\tau,$$

Let

$$J^\alpha f(t) = \frac{1}{\Gamma(\alpha)} \int_0^t (t - \tau)^{\alpha-1} f(\tau) \, d\tau,$$

we have

$$|E_{n+1}(t)| \leq L \cdot J^\alpha |E_n(t)|,$$

According [6], the operator J^α meet the following complex relation

$$J^\alpha \cdot J^\alpha f(t) = J^{\alpha+\alpha} f(t) = J^{2\alpha} f(t),$$

therefore, we have

$$|E_{n+1}(t)| \leq L^2 \cdot J^{2\alpha} |E_{n-1}(t)|$$

$$\vdots$$

$$\leq L^{n+1} \cdot J^{(n+1)\alpha} |E_0(t)|$$

$$= L^{n+1} \cdot \frac{1}{\Gamma(n\alpha + \alpha)} \int_0^t (t - \tau)^{n\alpha+\alpha-1} |E_0(\tau)| \, d\tau$$

$$\leq \frac{L^{n+1} \cdot \|E_0(t)\|_\infty}{\Gamma(n\alpha + \alpha)} \int_0^t (t - \tau)^{n\alpha+\alpha-1} \, d\tau$$

$$= \frac{L^{n+1} \cdot \|E_0(t)\|_\infty}{\Gamma(n\alpha + \alpha)} \cdot \frac{t^{n\alpha+\alpha}}{(n\alpha + \alpha)}.$$

Based on [17], we have

$$\Gamma(n\alpha + \alpha) \sim \sqrt{2\pi} \, e^{-n\alpha} (n\alpha)^{n\alpha+\alpha-\frac{1}{2}},$$

then

$$\frac{L^{n+1} \cdot t^{n\alpha+\alpha}}{\Gamma(n\alpha + \alpha)(n\alpha + \alpha)} \sim \frac{L^{n+1} \cdot t^{n\alpha+\alpha}}{\sqrt{2\pi} \, e^{-n\alpha} (n\alpha)^{n\alpha+\alpha-\frac{1}{2}}} \cdot \frac{1}{(n\alpha + \alpha)},$$

For L of Lipschitz constant, we can find the bounded real number L_1, and make

$$L_1^\alpha = L,$$

then

$$\frac{L^{n+1} \cdot t^{n\alpha+\alpha}}{\sqrt{2\pi} \, e^{-n\alpha} (n\alpha)^{n\alpha+\alpha-\frac{1}{2}}} \cdot \frac{1}{(n\alpha + \alpha)}$$

$$= \frac{1}{\sqrt{2\pi} \cdot e^\alpha} \cdot \left(\frac{L_1 t e}{n\alpha} \right)^{n\alpha+\alpha} \cdot \frac{(n\alpha)^{\frac{1}{2}}}{(n\alpha + \alpha)}.$$

When $0 \leq t \leq T$, we have

$$\|E_{n+1}(t)\|_\infty \leq \frac{\|E_0(t)\|_\infty}{\sqrt{2\pi} \cdot e^\alpha} \cdot \frac{(L_1 T e)^{n\alpha+\alpha}}{(n\alpha)^{n\alpha+\alpha}} \cdot \frac{(n\alpha)^{\frac{1}{2}}}{(n\alpha+\alpha)},$$

Because $\|E_0(t)\|_\infty$, L_1, T are constants, the convergence rate of the method is $\|E_{n+1}(t)\|_\infty \leq \frac{\|E_0(t)\|_\infty}{\sqrt{2\pi} \cdot e^\alpha \alpha^{\frac{1}{2}}} \cdot \frac{1}{(1+\frac{1}{n})^{\frac{1}{2}}}$, then we get

$$\lim_{n\to\infty} \|E_{n+1}(t)\|_\infty$$

$$\leq \lim_{n\to\infty} \left(\frac{\|E_0(t)\|_\infty}{\sqrt{2\pi} \cdot e^\alpha} \cdot \frac{(L_1 T e)^{n\alpha+\alpha}}{(n\alpha)^{n\alpha+\alpha}} \cdot \frac{(n\alpha)^{\frac{1}{2}}}{(n\alpha+\alpha)} \right)$$

$$\leq \frac{\|E_0(t)\|_\infty}{\sqrt{2\pi} \cdot e^\alpha} \cdot \lim_{n\to\infty} \left(\frac{(L_1 T e)^{n\alpha+\alpha}}{(n\alpha)^{n\alpha+\alpha}} \right)$$

$$= 0.$$

3   Numerical Example

In this section, some illustrative examples are given to show the efficiency of the VIM for solving the problem(1). All of the computations have been done by using the MAPLE software.

Example 1. Consider the following fractional-order homogeneous linear equation

$$_a^C D_t^\alpha f(t) = -y(t), \quad 0 < \alpha < 2, \tag{8}$$

Initial conditions are

$$y(0) = 1, \quad y'(0) = 0, \tag{9}$$

The exact solution is

$$y(t) = E_\alpha(-t)^\alpha,$$

where $E_\alpha(z)$ is simple coefficiential Mittag-Leffler function

$$E_\alpha(z) = \sum_{j=0}^\infty \frac{z^j}{\Gamma(\alpha j + 1)}, \quad \alpha > 0.$$

Here the variable z can be a complex number.

First of all, from (4), we can make the problems (8)–(9) for the following Volterra integral equation

$$y(t) = 1 - \frac{1}{\Gamma(\alpha)} \int_0^t (t-\tau)^{\alpha-1} y(\tau) d\tau,$$

secondly from iteration form (5), we get the following variational iteration form

$$y_{n+1}(t) = 1 - \frac{1}{\Gamma(\alpha)} \int_0^t (t-\tau)^{\alpha-1} y_n(\tau) d\tau, \quad n = 1, 2, 3, \cdots.$$

We use the initial value $y_0(t) = 1$ and begin to iterate, then get the following iterative value

$$y_1(t) = 1 - \frac{1}{\Gamma(1+\alpha)}t^{\alpha},$$

$$y_2(t) = 1 - \frac{1}{\Gamma(1+\alpha)}t^{\alpha} + \frac{1}{\Gamma(1+2\alpha)}t^{2\alpha},$$

$$y_3(t) = 1 - \frac{1}{\Gamma(1+\alpha)}t^{\alpha} + \frac{1}{\Gamma(1+2\alpha)}t^{2\alpha} - \frac{1}{\Gamma(1+3\alpha)}t^{3\alpha},$$

$$\vdots$$

When $\alpha = 0.25$, $\alpha = 1.25$ and $t = 0.1$,the immediate errors of analytical solution and numbercial solution are shown in Table 1 and Table 2 separately, The n in Tables delegate iterative times. From the Tables, we can find that numerical solutions converge extra solutions, and these test the conclusion of Theorem 2.1. When $\alpha = 0.25$, $\alpha = 1.25$, analytical solutionnumbercial solution and their errors are shown in Table 3 and Table 4 separately, from these tables, we can make out that numerical results are exactness comparatively.

Table 1. $\alpha = 0.25$

n	exact solution	VIM	error
3	0.6094871084	0.5429262386	-6.656E-02
6	0.6094871084	0.6170817456	7.595E-03
9	0.6094871084	0.6088193625	-6.677E-04
12	0.6094871084	0.6095355083	4.840E-05
15	0.6094871084	0.6094840997	-3.009E-06
18	0.6094871084	0.6094872735	1.651E-07
21	0.6094871084	0.6094871007	-7.700E-09
24	0.6094871084	0.6094871088	-4.000E-10

Table 2. $\alpha = 1.25$

n	exact solution	VIM	error
1	0.9513080798	0.9503671855	-9.409E-04
2	0.9513080798	0.9513187184	1.064E-05
3	0.9513080798	0.9513079970	-8.280E-08
4	0.9513080798	0.9513080803	5.000E-10
5	0.9513080798	0.9513080798	0
6	0.9513080798	0.9513080798	0

Table 3. $\alpha = 0.25$

t	exact solution	VIM	error
0.1	0.6094871084	0.6094871088	-4.000E-10
0.2	0.5665511819	0.5665511824	-4.000E-10
0.3	0.5408913015	0.5408913044	-2.900E-09
0.4	0.5225338734	0.5225338973	-2.380E-08
0.5	0.5082446751	0.5082448063	-1.312E-07
0.6	0.4965553359	0.4965558667	-5.307E-07
0.7	0.4866725890	0.4866743184	-1.729E-06
0.8	0.4781185882	0.4781233943	-4.806E-06
0.9	0.4705829898	0.4705948377	-1.185E-05
1.0	0.4638527608	0.4638793120	-2.655E-05

Table 4. $\alpha = 1.25$

t	exact solution	VIM	error
0.1	0.9513080798	0.9513080798	0
0.2	0.8871936706	0.8871936703	3.000E-10
0.3	0.8182314798	0.8182314731	6.700E-09
0.4	0.7478252531	0.7478251968	5.630E-08
0.5	0.6778687280	0.6778684398	2.882E-07
0.6	0.6095662530	0.6095651647	1.088E-06
0.7	0.5437236057	0.5437202754	3.330E-06
0.8	0.4808857365	0.4808769974	8.739E-06
0.9	0.4214139751	0.4213935827	2.039E-05
1.0	0.3655344400	0.3654910643	4.338E-05

Example 2. Consider the following fractional-order relaxation-oscillation equation

$$\begin{cases} {}_a^C D_t^\alpha y(t) + Ay(t) = f(t), & 0 < \alpha \leq 2, \\ y^{(k)}(0) = 0, & (k = 0, 1), \end{cases} \tag{10}$$

where $A = 1$, $f(t) = 1$, the extra solution of the equation is

$$y(t) = \int_0^t G(t-\tau)d\tau, \quad G(t) = t^{\alpha-1}E_{\alpha,\alpha}(-t^\alpha),$$

$E_{\alpha,\beta}(z)$ is Mittag-Leffler function,

$$E_{\alpha,\beta}(z) = \sum_{j=0}^{\infty} \frac{z^j}{\Gamma(\alpha j + \beta)}, \quad \alpha > 0, \ \beta > 0.$$

where the variable z can be a complex number. First of all, from (4), we can make the problem (10) for the following Volterra integral equation

$$y(t) = \frac{1}{\Gamma(\alpha)} \int_0^t (t-\tau)^{\alpha-1}(1-y(\tau))d\tau,$$

secondly from iteration form (5), we get the following variational iteration form

$$y_{n+1}(t) = \frac{1}{\Gamma(\alpha)} \int_0^t (t-\tau)^{\alpha-1}(1-y_n(\tau))d\tau,$$

We use the initial value $y_0(t) = 0$ and begin to iterate.

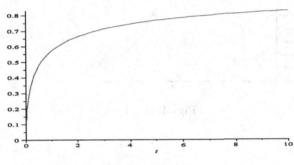

Fig. 1. $\alpha = 0.5$

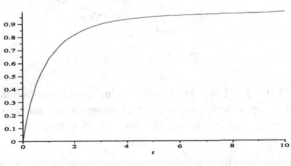

Fig. 2. $\alpha = 0.9$

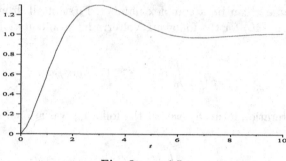

Fig. 3. $\alpha = 1.5$

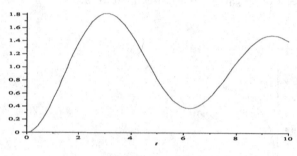

Fig. 4. $\alpha = 1.9$

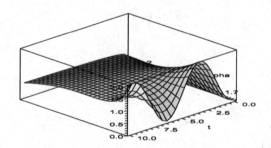

Fig. 5. $0 < \alpha < 2$

When $\alpha = 0.5, 0.9, 1.5, 1.9$ in equation, the images of numbercial solution are shown in Figs. 1–4 separately. The image was shown on α from 0 to $2(0 < \alpha < 2)$ in Figs. 5, this image was shown on the process of solution from relaxation to oscillation .

Example 3. Consider the following nonlinear fractional-order predator-prey system

$$\begin{cases} {}_a^C D_t^{\alpha_1} x(t) = x(t) - x(t)y(t), \\ {}_a^C D_t^{\alpha_2} y(t) = -y(t) + x(t)y(t), \end{cases} \tag{11}$$

Initial conditions are

$$x(0) = 1, \quad y(0) = 0.5. \tag{12}$$

First of all, from (4), we can make the problems (11)–(12) for the following Volterra integral equations

$$
\begin{cases}
x(t) = 1 + \dfrac{1}{\Gamma(\alpha_1)} \displaystyle\int_0^t (t-\tau)^{\alpha_1-1} x(\tau)\, d\tau \\
\qquad - \dfrac{1}{\Gamma(\alpha_1)} \displaystyle\int_0^t (t-\tau)^{\alpha_1-1} x(\tau) y(\tau)\, d\tau, \\
y(t) = 0.5 - \dfrac{1}{\Gamma(\alpha_2)} \displaystyle\int_0^t (t-\tau)^{\alpha_2-1} y(\tau)\, d\tau \\
\qquad + \dfrac{1}{\Gamma(\alpha_2)} \displaystyle\int_0^t (t-\tau)^{\alpha_1-1} x(\tau) y(\tau)\, d\tau.
\end{cases}
$$

secondly from iteration form (5), we get the following variational iteration form

$$
\begin{cases}
x_{n+1}(t) = 1 + \dfrac{1}{\Gamma(\alpha_1)} \displaystyle\int_0^t (t-\tau)^{\alpha_1-1} x_n(\tau)\, d\tau \\
\qquad - \dfrac{1}{\Gamma(\alpha_1)} \displaystyle\int_0^t (t-\tau)^{\alpha_1-1} x_n(\tau) y_n(\tau)\, d\tau, \\
y_{n+1}(t) = 0.5 - \dfrac{1}{\Gamma(\alpha_2)} \displaystyle\int_0^t (t-\tau)^{\alpha_2-1} y_n(\tau)\, d\tau \\
\qquad + \dfrac{1}{\Gamma(\alpha_2)} \displaystyle\int_0^t (t-\tau)^{\alpha_1-1} x_n(\tau) y_n(\tau)\, d\tau.
\end{cases}
$$

We use the initial value $x_0(t) = 1, y_0(t) = 0.5$ and begin to iterate, then get the following iterative value

$$x_1(t) = 1 + \frac{0.5}{\Gamma(1+\alpha_1)} t^{\alpha_1},$$

$$y_1(t) = 0.5,$$

$$x_2(t) = 1 + \frac{0.5}{\Gamma(1+\alpha_1)} t^{\alpha_1} + \frac{0.25}{\Gamma(1+2\alpha_1)} t^{2\alpha_1},$$

$$y_2(t) = 0.5 + \frac{0.5}{\Gamma(1+\alpha_1+\alpha_2)} t^{\alpha_1+\alpha_2},$$

$$\vdots$$

When $\alpha_1 = 0.5, \alpha_2 = 0.6$ and $\alpha_1 = 1, \alpha_2 = 1$, the images of numbercial solution are shown in Fig.6–Fig.7 separately. From these images, we can make out that results are coincident with result in [12].

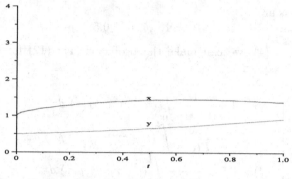

Fig. 6. $\alpha_1 = 0.5, \alpha_2 = 0.6$

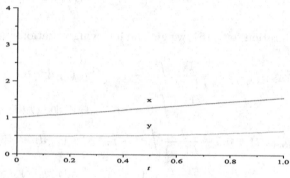

Fig. 7. $\alpha_1 = 1.0, \alpha_2 = 1.0$

4   Conclusions

From these above example, we can make out variational iteration method applies to fractional-order differential equation of linear and nonlinear. Because of memorability of fractional operator, this cause that the time of many computation methods is long, and make terribly heavy weather etc. In this article, we use the MAPLE software to compute these problems, computational process is succinct, computational time is short, computational result is high precision, and convergent speed in some problems is very quick to extra solution, these advantage is compelling for other methods. From this section, we can make out high efficiency of variational iteration method.

References

1. Diethelm, K., Ford, N.J.: Analysis of fractional differential equations. Journal of Mathematical Analysis and Applications 265, 229–248 (2002)
2. Xu, L.: Variational iteration method for solving integral equations. Computers and Mathematics with Applications 54, 1071–1078 (2007)
3. Ghorbani, A., Nadjufi, J.S.: An effective modification of He's variational iteration method. Nonlinear Analysis: Real World Applications 10, 2828–2833 (2009)

4. Bagley, R.L., Calico, R.A.: Fractional order state equations for the control of viscoelastically damped strucures. Journal of Guidance, Control and Dynamics 14, 304–311 (1991)
5. Koeller, R.C.: Application of fractional calculus to the theory of viscoelasticity. Journal of Applied Mechanics 51, 299–307 (1984)
6. Pudlubny, I.: Fractional Differential Equations. Academic Press, San Diego (1999)
7. Saha Ray, S., Bera, R.K.: An approximate solution of a nonlinear fractional differential equation by Adomian decomposition method. Applied Mathematics and Computation 167, 561–571 (2005)
8. Momani, S., Al-Khaled, K.: Numerical solutions for systems of fractional differential equations by the decomposition method. Applied Mathematics and Computation 162, 1351–1365 (2005)
9. Yu, Q.: Numerical Approximation of the Fractional Reaction-diffusion Equation. Master Paper, Xiamen University (2007)
10. Momani, S., Odibat, Z.: Numerical comparison of methods for solving linear differential equations of fractional order. Chaos, Solitons and Fractals 31(5), 1248–1255 (2007)
11. Momani, S., Odibat, Z.: Numerical approach to differential equations of fractional order. Journal of Computational and Applied Mathematics 207, 96–110 (2007)
12. Diethelm, K., Ford, N.J., Freed, A.D.: A predictor-corrector approach for the numerical solution of fractional differential equation. Nonlinear Dynamics 29(14), 3–22 (2002)
13. Yu, Z.H.: Variational iteration method for solving the multi-pantograph delay equation. Physics Letters A 372, 6475–6479 (2008)
14. Zhang, Y.: Application for some Fractional Ordinary Differential Equation sbout new iteration method. Master Paper, Xiangtan University (2009)
15. Salkuyeh, D.K.: Convergence of the variational iteration method for solving linear systems of ODEs with constant coefficients. Computers Math. Applic. 56, 2027–2033 (2008)
16. Odibat, Z.: A study on the convergence of variational iteration method. Mathematics and Computer Modelling 51, 1181–1192 (2010)
17. Abramowitz, M., Stegun, I.A.: Handbook of Mathematical Functions. Nauka, Moscow (1979)

Fluid Motion Estimation Based on Energy Constraint

Han Zhuang and Hongyan Quan

East China Normal University Science Building B219
No. 3663 Zhongshan North Road, Shanghai
hyquan@sei.ecnu.edu.cn

Abstract. This paper presents a method for motion estimation of fluid flow in natural scene. Due to drastic brightness changes in images sequence, previous methods based on continuity equation or brightness consistency constraint cannot be applied in this context well. We define Brightness Distribution Matrix (BDM) to present regional brightness. In the initialization of motion field, the BDM consistency between original point and corresponding point is used as a constraint. Towards the incorrect motion vector caused by drastic brightness change, we denoise to the initial motion field by statistical method, and then a novel smoothness constraint is applied to optimization for denoised motion field. The results of natural fluid flow in images show the validity of our method and the obtained motion field can be used to process 3D recovery for fluid flow.

Keywords: Motion field, energy function, fluid.

1   Introduction

Motion estimation of liquid has great importance in a number of scientific areas and our daily life. In the area of pattern recognition, motion field allows the facial expression recognition [1, 2]. In the environmental science, motion field also used to tracing the ice floes [3]. Moreover, motion field provide valuable information to the numerical models of weather prediction or ocean circulation analysis [4, 5]. In the field of fluid mechanic, displacement field can be used to calculate div and curl fields of liquid [6]. In the area of medical supplementary, motion field is applied to the matching of the medical images [7]. Motion field also play an important role in image recovery [8].

In all these domains, motion field has to be obtained from cameras. However, images only provide brightness information of fluid flow. Moreover brightness changes irregularly in images series, one must face the complex task of utilizing the patterns recorded in the images to obtain motion field. Since then, motion estimation of liquid flow is under widely researching. One or more new method would be proposed almost every year.

Due to slight and drastic brightness changes, we propose 3 step estimation method. Firstly, focusing in region of slight brightness changes, we defined the BDM to present regional brightness. In the initialization of motion field, BDM consistency between original point and corresponding is used as a constraint. Towards stable

T. Xiao, L. Zhang, and M. Fei (Eds.): AsiaSim 2012, Part II, CCIS 324, pp. 308–318, 2012.

liquid flow in images sequence, our initial motion field has high accuracy. However in the region with drastic brightness change, our initial motion vector may be incorrect. We thus denoise to initial motion field to wipe out incorrect motion vectors by statistical method. In motion field of fluid flow, one motion vector should be similar to its neighboring motion vectors. We thus assume: if informed motion of neighboring motion vectors, the incorrect motion vector in the region can be obtained by optimization. In next step, blank position in the denoised motion field, are estimated by optimization method. In optimization, a novel energy function is defined, which is composed of two terms: one is the data term of BDM consistency constraint and the other one is of promoted smoothness constraint. By minimizing the energy function, we obtain new motion vectors to replace incorrect motion vectors.

This method has three characteristic:

1. It has high accuracy property in the estimation of steady fluid flow and slight motion can be detected in our method.
2. It can be used to estimate the region with abrupt brightness changes.
3. It can be implemented quickly and be widely used in numbers of science area.

In next section, we will introduce related work. The initialization procedure will be described in section 3. Denoising method will be given in section 4. We will introduce optimization method using the energy constraint in section 5. Results of experiments will be discussed in section 6 and followed by summary in section 7.

2   Related Work

In recent years, a lot of methods of motion estimation had been proposed. B.Horn and B.Schunck [9] proposed the brightness consistency constraint and brought us the first method for estimate motion of objects in images. Lucas and Kanade [10] applied the pyramid model which reduces the limitation of location window and promoted the accuracy of estimation. But slight brightness change would decrease the accuracy of method based on brightness consistency. M.Tiastare [11], S.Uras and F.Girosi [12] used gradient consistency constraint as a new constraint in optical flow model, which improve its robustness facing little brightness variation. Due to the great displacement in images, Thomas Corpetti *et al.* [13] applied continuity equation into optical flow model. To improve the accuracy when estimating satellite images of cloud, Zhou *et al.* [14] the Affine motion model to estimate the velocity of cloud motion. Nakajima *et al.* [15] applied the Navier-Stikes equation and a continuity equation as velocity constraint. Elise [16] modified traditional smoothness constraint for Schlieren Image. To estimate the motion field with abrupt changes, H.Sakain [17] proposed a method based on wave generation. However methods above contain brightness consistency constraint or continuity equation constraints. And continuity equation and brightness consistency constraint cannot be applied to region of drastic or slight brightness changes well.

3   Initialization for Motion Field Based on BDM Constraint

The motion of point in image is determined by the motions of corresponding points. In fluid flow, the regional brightness of one point is similar to its corresponding point's. In the paper, we derive a formula that demonstrates the change of brightness of local region of one point to the corresponding point:

$$R(x, y, t) = R(x + u, y + v, t + 1) .$$
(1)

Where $R(x, y, t)$ denotes the brightness of local region of point (x, y) .

Regional brightness consistency is not a novel theory in PIV. And in the field of PIV, regional brightness consistency derives the methods of estimating motion by image matching. The brightness of local region used to be described as:

$$R(x, y, t) = \begin{pmatrix} I(x - w, y - w, t) & \cdots & I(x + w, y - w, t) \\ \vdots & \ddots & \vdots \\ I(x - w, y + w, t) & \cdots & I(x + w, y + w, t) \end{pmatrix}.$$
(2)

Where w denotes the size of sampling window, $I(x, y, t)$ is the brightness at point (x, y) at time t .

Although regional brightness is constant approximately, in images sequence, slight brightness changes are frequent. If we use formula 2 to present regional brightness, the slight brightness changes will be reflected obviously. Consequently, the results of formula 1 may be decrease by these slight changes, and we may obtain incorrect motion vectors. With this fact, we must design a new data structure to presents the brightness of local region of one point. Towards stable fluid flow, shape changes are slight. A new constraint based on shape and brightness is demanded. Shape description matrix describes shape of images and Wang Y et al. [19] had applied it to the retrieval of images. We add the brightness dimension into the shape description matrix and define the brightness distribution matrix.

We define BGM to present the brightness in sampling window size of $w \times w$, and we obtain:

$$BDM(x, y, t) = \begin{pmatrix} S^0(x,y,t) & \cdots & S^4(x,y,t) \\ \vdots & \ddots & \vdots \\ S^{20}(x,y,t) & \cdots & S^5(x,y,t) \end{pmatrix}.$$
(3)

Where $S^L(x, y, t) = \begin{pmatrix} D_{r_0} & \cdots & D_{r_3} \\ \vdots & \ddots & \vdots \\ D_{r_{12}} & \cdots & D_{r_{15}} \end{pmatrix}$, L is the brightness level, r_i $(i = 0...15)$ is

one of sub block in GDM, D_{r_i} is the value that sum up the coordinate of all pixels which brightness owning to level L.

The BDM has 25 brightness levels, w is 16 and sub block size is 4×4. Every point obtains its corresponding BDM with Formula 3. The BDM can describe shape and brightness set around one point.

As we mentioned above, the motion of point in image is determined by the motions of corresponding points. We assume BDM of one point and its corresponding point are equal approximately. Then we get a novel constraint based on BDM:

$$BDM(x, y, t) = BDM(x + u, y + v, t + 1). \tag{4}$$

Where $BDM(x, y, t)$ is the BDM at point (x, y) at time t.

Since the image is discrete, every point can be regarded as a particle and image matching method is used to obtain motion vectors. We define the motion vector as $d = (u, v)$ and the objective function defined as:

$$D(d) = D(u, v) = \sum_{L=0}^{24} \sum_{r=0}^{15} S^L(x, y, t) - S^L(x + u, y + v, t + 1) . \tag{5}$$

Where r is the index of each sub block in BDM.

In the process of image matching, we design a searching window size of 8×8 at the same position of the original point, in next image of images sequence. Objective value is defined as the value of formula 5. We calculate objective value for every point in the searching window, using formula 5 and the displacement between original point and current point of searching window. In this paper, the point with minimal objective value is the corresponding point. Thus motion vector can be obtained with the original point and corresponding point.

4   Denoising to Motion Field

B.Horn and B.Schunck [9] proposed the smoothness consistency constraint:

$$\nabla^2 u = \frac{\partial^2 u}{\partial x^2} + \frac{\partial^2 u}{\partial y^2}, \nabla^2 v = \frac{\partial^2 v}{\partial x^2} + \frac{\partial^2 v}{\partial y^2} . \tag{6}$$

In several optical flow methods [9, 17, 20], a regularization term of energy function had been derived from Formula 6. Because of drastic brightness changes, the initial motion field of method, based on brightness consistency constraint or continuity equation, may contain some incorrect motion vectors. And if we input incorrect motion vectors into energy function and process iteration calculation, the accuracy of motion field would be decreased.

In fluid flow, points have similar motion direction in small region. We thus assume: one motion vector is incorrect, if its direction is different from most motion vectors in this region. This kind of motion vectors would be wiped out from our motion field. However these motion vectors may be correct, if it exist in the boundary of the region. This case will be discussed in section 5.

In our denoising method, we separate the image into several sub blocks $r_i(i = 0,1...15)$ and process statistic in each sub block size of 60×60. Dir_i $(i = 0...3)$ is defined as the number of motion vectors in each quadrant, in each sub blocks. We obtain Dir_i by adding up the number of each motion vector in each direction. We assume the direction presented by Dir_{max} is the main motion direction of this sub block and motion vectors have different direction from this are incorrect vectors. Then we wipe out the incorrect motion vectors from our motion field. Denoised motion field is obtained, and the motion vectors of these points can be used to optimization for blank position in the denoised motion field. In the next section we will discuss our optimization method.

5   Optimization Based on Energy Constraint

Kass et al. [21] proposed the snake model which developed interactive techniques for guiding minimizing of energy:

$$E_{snake}^* = \int_0^1 E_{int}(v(s)) + E_{image}(v(s)) + E_{con}(v(s))ds$$

(7)

Where $v(s) = (s(x), s(y))$ and E_{int} denotes the energy from spline itself and E_{image} presents the force from image, E_{con} is the external constraint force.

With the energy force, the function can be minimized and spline appears automatically. The theory of active contour model has been widely studied and extended. Energy function is widely used in optical flow [13], [16], [17], [20]. A number of methods [16], [20] defined data term about continuity equation and regularization:

$$E(u,v) = E_{data}(u,v) + \alpha E_{regularization}(u,v) .$$

(8)

Where $E_{data}(u,v)$ derives from continuity equation and $E_{regularization}(u,v)$ derives formula 6. The parameter α balances the influence of two force term in the function. Each term has different drawbacks towards light changes of situation in image sequence, so this kind of energy functions cannot estimate region with abrupt brightness change well. As we mentioned, in motion field of fluid, the motion vector should be similar to neighboring motion vectors. And we assume: if informed motion of neighboring motion vectors, the points can be optimization calculation. Since denoised motion field has been obtained in section 3, we can define a term of novel smoothness constraint:

$$E_{image}(u,v) = \sum_{i=x-n}^{x+n} \sum_{j=y-n}^{y+n} (u - u_{ij})^2 + (v - v_{ij})^2 . \qquad (9)$$

Where u_{ij} and v_{ij} are components of motion vector of point (x, y) in denoised motion field, along x and y direction respectively, and n is the size of the searching window.

On the other hand, the corresponding point has similar brightness set with original point. We thus define a constraint term base on equation (4):

$$E_{Data}(u,v) = \sum_{i=x-n}^{x+n} \sum_{j=y-n}^{y+n} D(s(x, y), s(x + u_{ij}, y + v_{ij})) . \qquad (10)$$

Where u_{ij} and v_{ij} are components of motion vector of point (x, y) along x direction and y direction respectively, in denoised motion field.

Finally, we get our energy function:

$$E(u,v) = E_{image}(u,v) + \alpha E_{con}(u,v) . \qquad (11)$$

As we mentioned above, motion vectors in the boundary of one sub block, may has different direction with other motion vectors. Since then, due to points at the boundary of the sub block, α can be set as relatively small value.

Each point can be regarded as a particle, and a searching window size of 8×8 is defined. In optimization, motion vector of each point can be obtained by retrieving the searching window. We obtain motion vector by finding out corresponding point which has minimal energy among the searching window.

The complete algorithm is summarized as:

1. Initialization for motion field.
    1.1 Obtain BGM for each point by formula 3.
    1.2 For every point in original image:
        a. Choose the first point in searching window: if the displacement between the original point and current point in searching window minimize the formula 5, then go to Step a, else go to Step c.
        b. Choose the next point in searching window: if the displacement between the original point and current point in searching window minimize the formula 5, then go to Step c, else go to Step b.
        c. Choose current point in searching window as corresponding point and the displacement between original point and current point record as motion vector of original point.

2. Denoising for initial motion field.
    2.1 Separate initial motion field to 16 sub blocks.
    2.2 The direction of the most motion vectors defined as regional direction of each sub block
    2.3 For every point in motion field:
        a.   If the direction of current motion vector has the same direction with regional direction of local sub block, then go to Step b.
        b.   Wipe out current point from motion field.
3. Optimization calculation for blank position in denoised motion field:
    3.1 For every point in original image:
        a.   Choose the first point in searching window: if the displacement between the original point and current point in searching window minimize the formula 11, then go to Step c, else go to Step b.
        b.   Choose the next point in searching window: if the displacement between the original point and current point in searching window minimize the formula 11, then go to Step c, else go to Step b.
        c.   Choose current point in searching window as corresponding point and the displacement between original point and current point record as motion vector of original point.

6   Experiment

We implement our algorithm under windows XP, using VC6.0 and OpenCV. To show the validity of our method, we process experiment in 3 sections. In section 6.1, real images are used to test our method. In section 6.2, the comparison with existing methods is introduced. We will discuss the error in experiment on synthetic images Yosemite in section 6.3.

6.1   Experiment on Real Images

We test our method with several series of images in DynTex dynamic texture library [22].

The images on the left column are the original images in the images sequence, and the images on the right column are our experiment results. In experiment results, red arrows demonstrate the motion vectors obtained from initialization and green arrows demonstrate the motion vectors obtained by optimization.

Experiment results show the validity of our method. For instance, result of "6489b10", demonstrates that this method estimate motion for region with drastic brightness change well. Result of "6483710" shows that, motion vectors are longer and have correct direction, in the region with larger displacement. Moreover, in such a large region having similar regional brightness, motion is difficult to be detected, but our method estimation in this kind of region is correct. I can be seen that this method has high accuracy and robustness in most case of real images with drastic brightness changes, slight and large displacement.

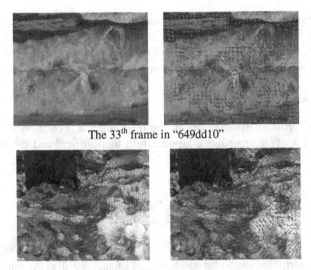

The 33th frame in "649dd10"

The frame 0th in "6483710"

Fig. 1. Our experiment results using real images

6.2   Comparison with Existing Method

To demonstrate the advantage of our method, we process our comparison experiment with other methods [23, 24], using Yosemite and images sequences [22]. In each following groups of images, the image on the top left is the original image, and the image on the top right is the results using method in [23], the image on bottom left is the method using [24], the image on the bottom right is the result using our method.

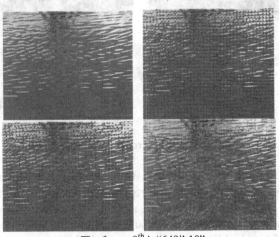

The frame 0th in "649ib10"

Fig. 2. Comparison of experiment results from real images and synthetic images

From this part of experiment, it can be seen that the advantage of our method over other existing methods. For instance, the result from"649ib10" shows, our method have robustness in the region with slight displacement or drastic brightness changes, while existing method cannot apply to this context well.

6.3   Error Analyze

To analyze the error in the experiment, the 0th frames in Yosemite are used in this paper. We will analyze error using ground truth motion field and the error function defined as:

$$Error = \frac{\sum_{i=0}^{n_x}\sum_{j=0}^{n_y}|u_{ij} - u_{ij}'| + |v_{ij} - v_{ij}'|}{\|P\|} . \tag{12}$$

Where n_x and n_y are the width and height of image, $\|P\|$ is the number of pixels of the image, u_{ij} and v_{ij} denote components of motion vector in our motion field at point (i, j) respectively, u_{ij}' and v_{ij}' are components of motion vector in ground truth motion field at point (i, j) .

In this series of experiment, the size of searching window is 7×7 .The experiment results are shown in Fig. 3.The images on the left column are our experiment results and the right column is the original images. We calculate error for each group of experiment using formula 12. The error of results from 0th is 1.40.

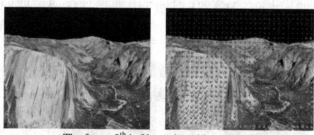

The frame 0th in Yosemite without cloud

Fig. 3. Experiment results of Yosemite

It can be seen from the results of frame 0th that, in region with large displacement, the motion vectors are larger than that in region with small displacement. Moreover, in region with small displacement, the motion vectors also have be estimated correctly. And the error obtained with formula 12, shows the motion field we obtained is reliable. Experiment in this section demonstrates the high accuracy of this method.

7   Summary

Motion estimation for fluid flow is hot topic in computer vision, and a number of new methods are reported in recent years. However, frequent and irregular brightness change makes this problem complex.

Due to drastic brightness changes, we define the BDM at first, which is used as a constraint in initialization and optimization. To improve the accuracy of estimation, we denoise to initial motion field by statistical method. At last, in optimization, it use a novel energy function based on BDM consistency constraint and promoted smoothness constraint.

This paper presents a new method for estimate motion field for fluid flow. It can be used as initialization in other scientific areas such as 3D recovery and pattern recognition. It can estimate motion field for region with drastic or slight brightness well. With this fact, it can be used to estimate for complex environment.

The experiment on real images shows that this method can adapt to images of natural scenes well. Its validity and robustness can be seen from the experiment about comparison and error analyze.

In future work, we will do researches about 3D recovery and 3D motion estimation for fluid flow.

Acknowledgements. We wish to thank Mao-Mao Wu and Ming-Qi Yu for their comments and suggestions. We would also like to thank the Natural Science Foundation of Shanghai Science and Technology Commission in China (grant 11ZR1411100) and the Undergraduate Innovation Foundation of Shanghai Undergraduate Science and Innovation Commission in China (grant KY2011-51S) for funding this project.

References

1. Yu, M.-S., Li, S.-F.: Dynamic Facial Expression Recognition Based on Optical Flow. Journal of Microelectronics and Computer 22, 113–119 (2005)
2. Yang, G.-L., Wang, Z.-L., Wang, G.-J., Chen, F.-J.: Facial Expression Recognition Based on Optical Flow for Non-rigid Motion Analysis. Journal of Computer Science 34, 213–229 (2007)
3. Das Peddada, S., McDevitt, R.: Least Average Residual Algorithm(LARA) for Tracking the Motion of Arctic Sea Ice. IEEE Trans. Geoscience and Remote Sensing 34(4), 915–926 (1996)
4. Ottenbacher, A., Tomasini, M., Holmund, K., Schmetz, J.: Low-Level Cloud Motion Winds from Metrosat High-Resolution Visible Imagery. Weather and Forecasting 12(1), 175–184 (1997)
5. Cohen, I., Herlin, I.: Non Uniform Multiresolution Method for Optical Flow and Phase Portrait Models: Environmental Applications. International Journal of Computer Vision 33(1), 29–49 (1999)
6. Lu, Z., Liao, Q., Pei, J.: A PIV Approach Based on Nonlinear Filter. Journal of Electronics & Information Technology 32(2) (2010)

7. Shu, X., Kang, S., Long, Y.: Method of medical image registration based on optical flow field. Computer Engineering and Applications 44, 191–198 (2008)
8. Nogawa, H., Nakajima, Y., Sato, Y.: Acquisition of Symbolic Description from Flow Fields: A New Approach Based on a Fluid Model. IEEE Trans. Pattern Analysis Machine Intelligence 19, 58–63 (1997)
9. Horn, B., Schunck, B.: Determining optical flow. Artificial Intelligence 17, 185–203 (1981)
10. Lucas, B.D., Kanade, T.: An Iterative Image Registration Technique with an Application to Stereo Vision. In: Proceedings of Imaging Understanding Workshop, pp. 121–130 (1981)
11. Tistarelli, M.: Multiple Constraints for Optical Flow. In: Eklundh, J.-O. (ed.) ECCV 1994. LNCS, vol. 800, pp. 61–70. Springer, Heidelberg (1994)
12. Uras, S., Girosi, F., Verri, A., Torre, V.: A computational approach to motion perception. Biological Cybernetics 60, 79–87 (1988)
13. Corpetti, T., Memin, E., Perez, P.: Dense Estimation of fluid flows. IEEE Transactions on Pattern Analysis and Machine Intelligence 24(3) (2002)
14. Zhou, L., Kambhamettu, C., Goldof, D.B.: Fluid structure and motion analysis from multi-spectrum 2D cloud image sequence. In: IEEE Conference on Computer Vision and Pattern Recognition, pp. 744–751 (2000)
15. Nakajima, Y., Inomata, H., Nogawa, H., Sato, Y., Tamura, S., Okazaki, K., Torii, S.: Physics-based flow estimation of fluids. Pattern Recognition 36, 1203–1212 (2003)
16. Arnaud, E., Mémin, É., Sosa, R., Artana, G.: A fluid motion estimator for schlieren image velocimetry. In: Leonardis, A., Bischof, H., Pinz, A. (eds.) ECCV 2006. LNCS, vol. 3951, pp. 198–210. Springer, Heidelberg (2006)
17. Sakaino, H.: Fluid Motion Estimation Method based on Physical Properties of Waves. In: IEEE Conference on Computer Vision and Pattern Recognition (2008)
18. Fitzpatrick, J.M., Pederson, C.A.: A Method for Calculating Fluid Flow in Time Dependent Density Images. Electronic Imaging 1, 347–352 (1988)
19. Wang, Y., Zhai, H., Mu, G.: Shape description matrix and its application to color-image retrieval and recognition. Science in China E 47, 159–165 (2004)
20. Brox, T., Bruhn, A., Papenberg, N., Weickert, J.: High Accuracy Optical Flow Estimation Based on a Theory for Warping. In: Pajdla, T., Matas, J(G.) (eds.) ECCV 2004. LNCS, vol. 3024, pp. 25–36. Springer, Heidelberg (2004)
21. Kass, M., Witkin, A., Terzopoulos, D.: Snakes: Active contour models. International Journal of Computer Vision, 321–331 (1987)
22. DynTex dynamic texture library,
    http://projects.cwi.nl/dyntex/index.html
23. Deqing Sun, S., Stefan, R., Michael, J.B.: Secrets of optical flow estimation and their principles. In: Proceedings of the IEEE Conference on Computer Vision and Pattern Recognition, San Francisco, California (2010)
24. Nilanjan, R.: Computation of fluid and particle motion from a time-sequenced image pair: A Global Outlier Identification Approach. IEEE Transactions on Image Processing 10(20), 2925–2936 (2011)

Numerical Simulation of Discrete Gust Response for a Free Flexible Aircraft

Dong Guo[*], Min Xu, and Shilu Chen

College of Astronautics, Northwestern Polytechnical University, Xi'an, P.R. China
guodong@mail.nwpu.edu.cn

Abstract. Gust response analysis plays a very important role in large aircraft design. This paper presents a methodology for calculating the flight dynamic characteristics and gust response of free flexible aircraft. A multidisciplinary coupled numerical tool is developed to simulate detailed aircraft models undergoing arbitrary free flight motion in the time domain, by Computational Fluid Dynamics (CFD), Computational Structure Dynamics (CSD) and Computational Flight Mechanics (CFM) coupling. To achieve this objective, a structured, time-accurate flow-solver is coupled with a computational module solving the flight mechanics equations of motion and a structural mechanics code determining the structural deformations. A novel method to determine the trim state of flexible aircraft is also stated. First, the field velocity approach is validated, after the trim state is attained, gust responses for the one-minus-cosine gust profile are analyzed for the longitudinal motion of a slender-wing aircraft configuration with and without the consideration of structural deformation.

Keywords: Numerical Simulation, Computational Flight Mechanics (CFM), Multi-disciplinary Coupled, Gust Response.

1 Introduction

Modern aircraft design requires the evaluation of dynamic loads in response to discrete and random gust excitations. Gust response affects many aspects of aircraft characteristics, including stability and control, dynamic structural loads, flight safety and easement. The Federal Aviation Regulations require that the aircraft structure can withstand discrete gusts of certain profile, intensity and gradient [1].

Flight mechanics and aeroelasticity can be often treated as separate discipline, namely, flight mechanics and aeroelasticity. The first one concerned principally with rigid aircraft experiencing large motions (commonly known as Rigid Body Approximation-RBA), while the second aims mainly to the analysis of elastic aircraft experiencing relatively small deformations. The idea to not consider cross-coupling effects between these two disciplines has been commonly justified by the large frequency separation of the characteristic motion which is typical of conventional structures. Nowadays, the focus on weight minimization for aircraft, leads toward more

---

[*] Corresponding author.

T. Xiao, L. Zhang, and M. Fei (Eds.): AsiaSim 2012, Part II, CCIS 324, pp. 319–327, 2012.

and more flexible vehicles. The resulting underlying structures may not exhibit the usual wide frequency separation among the rigid body degrees of freedom and the remaining elastic modes. So that the approach mentioned above can lead to mistakes/errors in analyses of flight performance, flying qualities, and control systems design. In these cases, an integrated analysis of flight mechanics and aeroelasticity is necessary from the very early stages of preliminary design [2].

Another reason which substantiates the development of an integrated approach is high-altitude; long-endurance (HALE) unmanned aerial vehicles (UAVs) are recently receiving considerable attention from the technical community. Cesnik[3-6] showed that when the nonlinear flexibility effects are taken into account in the calculation of trim and flight dynamics characteristics, the predicted aeroelasitc behavior of the complete aircraft turns out to be very different from what it would be without such effects. The Helios accident also highlighted our limited understanding and limited analytical tools necessary for designing very flexible aircraft and to potentially exploit aircraft flexibility. The number one root cause/recommendation from NASA was "more advanced, multidisciplinary (structures, aeroelastic, aerodynamics, atmospheric, materials, propulsion, controls, etc.) time-domain analysis methods appropriate to highly flexible, morphing vehicles [be developed]." [7]

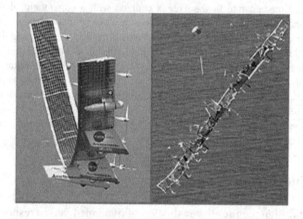

Fig. 1. HP03-2 Mishap

For all of the reasons stated, a better understanding of the flight dynamics/aeroelasticity of these vehicles is required. Although there are commercial software tools capable of dealing with pieces of the problem, there is no commercially available software that integrates all of the disciplines needed for such investigation as discussed here.

The intention here is not to investigate complex flight mechanics behavior, but to describe the development of a tool which can be used for this purpose. This paper illustrates a multidisciplinary coupled numerical tool to simulate detailed aircraft models undergoing arbitrary free flight motion in the time domain, by Computational Fluid Dynamics (CFD), Computational Structure Dynamics (CSD) and Computational Flight Mechanics (CFM) coupling. A substantial part of this work is devoted to the development of an integrated aircraft flight mechanics model as generic as possible, which comprises the structure vibration influence, without loss of : the simplicity of the equations; the similarity to the classical RBA; and perhaps the most important, the physical understanding of the interactions. As in Ref.8 the modal decomposition technique is used to represent the structural dynamic. The CFD solver developed by MFDCL (Multidisciplinary Flight Dynamic and Control Laboratory, College of Astronautics, Northwestern Polytechnical University), will be used to compute the unsteady aerodynamics loads in this work.

2   Numerical Approach

2.1   Flight Model—A Review

The dynamic equations of motion for the elastic aircraft are then derived from first principles using Lagrange's equation [9]:

$$\frac{d}{dt}\left(\frac{\partial T}{\partial \dot{q}_i}\right) - \frac{\partial T}{\partial q_i} + \frac{\partial U}{\partial q_i} = Q_i \tag{1}$$

The resulting equations from the application of Eq. (1) may be expressed as follows. Equations for rigid-body translational accelerations:

$$M(\dot{u} + qw - rv + g\sin\theta) = X$$
$$M(\dot{v} + ru - pw - g\cos\theta\sin\phi) = Y \tag{2}$$
$$M(\dot{w} + pv - qu - g\cos\theta\cos\phi) = Z$$

Equations for rigid-body rotational accelerations:

$$I_x\dot{p} - (I_{xy}\dot{q} + I_{xz}\dot{r}) + (I_z - I_y)qr + (I_{xy}r - I_{xz}q)p + (r^2 - q^2)I_{yz} = L$$
$$I_y\dot{q} - (I_{xy}\dot{p} + I_{yz}\dot{r}) + (I_x - I_z)pr + (I_{yz}p - I_{xy}r)q + (p^2 - r^2)I_{xz} = M \tag{3}$$
$$I_z\dot{r} - (I_{xz}\dot{p} + I_{yz}\dot{q}) + (I_y - I_x)pq + (I_{xz}q - I_{yz}p)r + (q^2 - p^2)I_{xy} = N$$

Equations for elastic degrees of freedom:

$$\ddot{\eta}_i + 2\varsigma_i\omega_i\dot{\eta}_i + \omega_i^2\eta_i = Q_{\eta_i}/m_i \tag{4}$$

The means of the symbols are followed by reference [9].

2.2   CFD Solver

The behavior of the fluid flow affecting the object of interest is simulated with the EU3D-Code, a CFD tool developed by the Multidisciplinary Flight Dynamics and Control Laboratory. A full discussion of the code and turbulence models implemented is given in reference [10]. The EU3D-Code solves the compressible, three-dimensional, time-accurate Euler and RANS equations using a finite volume formulation. The Code is based on a structured-grid approach. The grids used for simulations in this paper were created with the grid generator Gridgen. The Code contains several upwind schemes, FDS-Roe, FVS-Vanleer, AUSM+ and AUSMpw+. LUSGS and dual time step marching scheme LUSGS- τ TS is also available.

2.3   Coupled Solution Procedure

The coupling flow chat is showed in Fig.2:

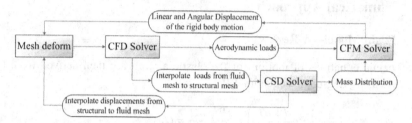

Fig. 2. CFD-based multidisciplinary coupled numerical simulation flow chart

The Infinite Plate Spline (IPS) method by Harder and Desmarais is applied to exchange the boundary information between the fluid mesh and the structure mesh [11]. A modified TFI method is employed here to account for the control surface deflections and the rigid motion of the aircraft [10]. Fig.3 illustrates the flow girds updated by TFI.

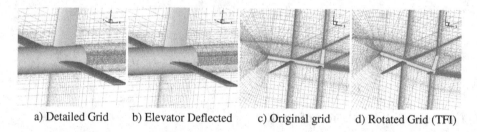

a) Detailed Grid   b) Elevator Deflected   c) Original grid   d) Rotated Grid (TFI)

Fig. 3. Deformation of the grid

2.4   Trim Process

So far we have obtained a multidisciplinary coupled numerical tool to simulate the flexible aircraft in time-domain. The next step is generally necessary to first solve the so-called trim problem. The solution of the trim problem is iteratively sought in a manner as outlined in Fig.4; it consists of three different nested iteration-levers [8, 12]:

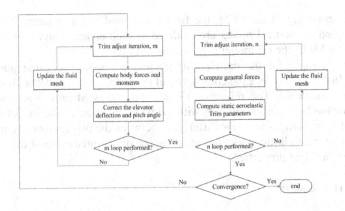

Fig. 4. Flow chart for the deformable trim process

3   Numerical Model and Results

Because it is hard to find the structural data of a flexible vehicle, a wing-body-tail aircraft configuration with slender wings (aspect ratio 33.33) designed by the author, as shown in fig.5(a), which may not be reasonable, is selected as a test case for the numerical simulation. The total length of the fuselage is 30m. The detail geometric properties and mass properties are included in Table 1.

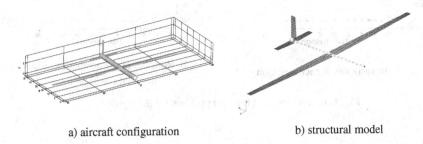

a) aircraft configuration   b) structural model

Fig. 5. Slender-wing HALE aircraft configuration and structural model

Table 1. Geometry of the Slender-wing model

	Wing	HTP	VTP
Span	75m	16m	8m
Root Chord	3.0m	2.0m	2.0m
Tip Chord	1.5m	1.2m	1.2m
Airfoil	NACA 4415	NACA 0012	NACA 0012
Incidence Angle	2.0°	2.0°	0°
Wing Area: 168.75m²	Wing-to-HTTP: 15m		Wing-to-Nose: 12m

In the modeling of the FEM, the fuselage is modeled as a beam. The wing, the elevators and the vertical rudder are modeled as shell element, and contacted with the fuselage by MPC, the FE model is presented in Fig.5 (b).

As an example for the coupled simulation, a one-minus-cosine gust has been defined. In detail, to reduce the complexity of the problem, a symmetric flight condition has been considered. The reference flight condition is Mach 0.5 at sea level. The simulation has been performed both with a rigid and with an elastic model. One goal of the simulations is to assess of the differences between the two approaches, most notably to see whether an elastic model has an influence on the prediction of the aerodynamic loads and the flight properties.

3.1   Trim Results

In case of a stationary, straight symmetrical flight, all asymmetric equations of motion reduce to zero. Two cases were considered, the rigid-run and elastic-run. In this work, the iteration number $m = n = 5$, the ending conditions is $\left| x^{(n+1)} - x^{(n)} \right| \le 1.0e-6$. For the rigid-run, Fig.6 shows the convergence history of the trim problem for the rigid run. Fig.7 presents the convergence of the trim problem for the elastic-run.

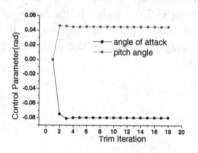

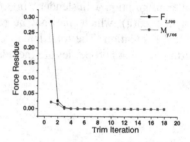

a. Trim variables at each iteration

b. Residual of the normal force and moment coefficient

Fig. 6. Convergence of the trim problem for the rigid-run

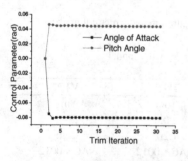

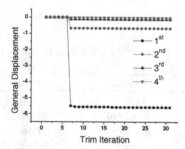

a. Trim variables at each iteration

b. Values at each trim step iteration

Fig. 7. Convergence of the trim problem for the elastic-run

The final deformed shape is depicted in Fig.8 (a). Fig.8 (b) shows the difference in chord-wise Mach distribution for the rigid and deformable trim configurations.

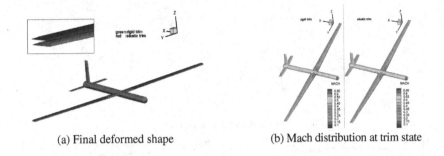

(a) Final deformed shape   (b) Mach distribution at trim state

Fig. 8. Comparison of trimmed state between the rigid-run and elastic-run

3.2   Free-Flying of the Longitudinal Flight

In general, gust disturbance is stochastic. In this paper, the gust model is simplified as a discrete gust having one-minus-cosine velocity profile. The velocity profile is shown in Fig.9.

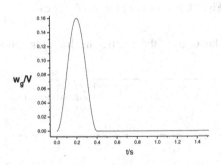

Fig. 9. Time variation of gust speed

The so-called field velocity approach, developed by Baeder [13], is used to calculate the gust response. With this gust velocity profile, the displacement in translations, plunging and the angular displacement in pitch are shown in Fig.10. As illustrated by these figures, the free model ends up in an almost steady ascent. The motion of the aircraft should evolve into a 'phugoid' transient (altitude/horizontal speed oscillation). However, the duration of the period is much longer than what one would expect to capture with this type of analysis.

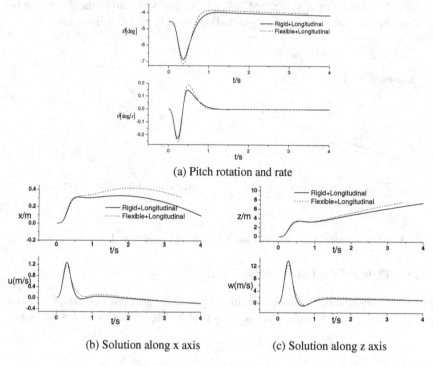

(a) Pitch rotation and rate

(b) Solution along x axis   (c) Solution along z axis

Fig. 10. Response for the free flying case

Fig.11 shows the time histories of the coefficients lift, drag and pitching moment.

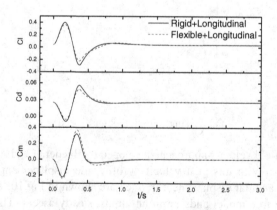

Fig. 11. Time histories of the coefficients of lift, drag and pitching moment

4   Conclusions

In the present paper, a multidisciplinary coupled numerical tool to simulate detailed aircraft models undergoing arbitrary free flight motion in the time domain was illustrated. The simulation tool combines time-accurate aerodynamic, aeroelastic and flight-mechanic calculations to achieve this objective. This type of problems requires the use of sophisticate fluid-dynamics models, in order to capture the relevant dynamic effects of unsteady transonic flow, including aerodynamic loads that depend on unsteady compressibility effects.

A novel method for CFD-based maneuver trim analysis was presented. The method belongs to the category of closed coupled aeroelastic analyses, in which the flow analysis, elastic deformations, and trim computations are performed within the CFD code, within a single run. The results of trim and transient analysis applied to a slender wing HALE aircraft show the soundness of the proposed procedure.

References

1. Anon, Gust and Turbulence Loads. Code of Federal Regulations, Aeronautics and Space, Part 25.341, National Archives and Records Administration, Office of the Federal Register (January 2003)
2. Silvestre, F.J., Paglione, P.: Dynamics and Control of a Flexible Aircraft. AIAA 2008-6876
3. Patil, M.J., Hodges, D.H., Cesnik, E.S.: Nonlinear Aeroelasticity and Flight Dynamics of High-Altitude Long Endurance Aircraft. Journal of Aircraft 38(1), 88–94 (2001)
4. Su, W., Cesnik, C.E.S.: Nonlinear Aeroelasticity of a Very Flexible Blended-Wing-Body Aircraft. AIAA 2009-2402
5. Shear, C.M., Cesnik, C.E.S.: Nonlinear Flight Dynamics of Very Flexible Aircraft. In: AIAA Atmospheric Flight Mechanics Conference and Exhibit, San Francisco, CA, August 15-18 (2005)
6. Su, W., Cesnik, C.E.S.: Dynamic Response of Highly Flexible Flying Wings. AIAA 2006-1636
7. Noll, T.E., Brown, J.M., Perez-Davis, M.E.: Investigation of the Helios Prototype Aircraft Mishap, http://www.nasa.gov/pdf/64317main_helios.pdf
8. Cavagna, L., Masarati, P., Quaranta, G.: Simulation of Maneuvering Flexible Aircraft by Coupled Multibody/CFD. In: Multibody Dynamic 2009, ECCOMAS Thematic Conference (2009)
9. Waszak, M.R., Schmidt, D.K.: Flight Dynamics of Aeroelastic Vehicles. AIAA Journal of Aircraft 25(6), 563–571 (1988)
10. Yao, W.: Nonlinear Aeroelastic System Simulation in Time Domain [Ph.D]. Northwestern Polytechnical University, Xi'an, China (2009)
11. Harder, R.L., Desmarais, R.N.: Interpolation Using Surface Splines. Journal of Aircraft 9(2), 189–191 (1972)
12. Raveh, D.E.: Maneuver Load Analysis of Overdetermined Trim Systems. Journal of Aircraft 45(1), 119–129 (2008)
13. Parameswaran, V., Baeder, J.D.: Indicial Aerodynamic in Compressible Flow-Direct Computational Fluid Dynamic Calculations. Journal of Aircraft 34(1), 131–133 (1997)

A Study of Wireless Mobile Node Localization Algorithm Based on MCL and HS

Yan Chen and Jingqi Fu

School of Mechatronic Engineering and Automation, Shanghai University
Shanghai, China
chenysh903@163.com,
jqfu@staff.shu.edu.cn

Abstract. This paper proposes the methods to improve the Monte Carlo (MCL) algorithm for the wireless mobile node localization. It combines the anchor boxes constructed by different power signals with the node location information in the previous time to reduce the sampling region. Through sampling and filtering in this region, we adopt the Harmony Search (HS) algorithm to optimize the obtained samples and then calculate the estimated value of the node location. Moreover, the RSSI ranging is used to assist localization. And it takes full advantage of the nodes information with high availabilities. The simulation results show that the improved algorithm reduces the requirements of anchors density and improves the sampling filter efficiencies and the localization accuracy.

Keywords: node localization, MCL algorithm, HS algorithm, RSSI.

1   Introduction

Wireless sensor network (WSN) is a new network with combination of sensor technology, communication technology, distributed information processing technology, and software programming technology and others [1].

With the developments of WSN technologies and practical applications, mobile localization for WSNs is getting more and more attention. In 2004, Lingxuan Hu proposed a mobile WSN localization algorithm based on MCL [2]. Some improvement algorithms appeared one after another on this basis, such as MCB [3], MSL [4] and so on. With the developing of technologies of low-power, microprocessor and FPGA etc., intelligent algorithms are used in WSN node localization to be a new research direction. It is worthy of further research on how to improve MCL algorithm, combine with the advantages of other algorithms.

2   Monte Carlo(MCL) Algorithm

The Monte Carlo method [2] is an analysis method for random probabilities. By filtering to obtain coincident particles and with cycle iteration, the best position of the

T. Xiao, L. Zhang, and M. Fei (Eds.): AsiaSim 2012, Part II, CCIS 324, pp. 328–337, 2012.

unknown node is achieved. Fig. 1 shows the schematic diagram of MCL sampling region and filtering conditions.

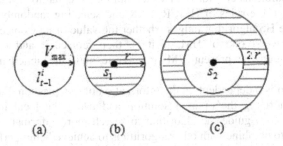

(a)   (b)   (c)

Fig. 1. Schematic diagram of sampling region and filtering condition

In the forecast period, it is supposed that we only know the moving speed of the node to be located is no more than V_{max}. The possible location of the node l_t^i in current moment is in the circle whose circle center is some possible location l_{t-1}^i in the previous moment and radius is V_{max}, as Fig. 1(a). In Fig. 1(b), s_1 is the single-hop anchor, and r is the communication radius. In Fig. 1(c), s_2 is the two-hop anchor. The shadow in Fig. 1 shows the positions according the filtering conditions (1).

$$filter(l)=\{\forall s\in S_1, d(l,s_1)\leq r\}\wedge\{\forall s\in S_2, r<d(l,s_2)\leq 2r\}.\tag{1}$$

Where, l is the sampling point, $d(l,s_1)$ is the distance from l to s_1. $d(l,s_2)$ is the distance from l to s_2.

After filtering, because some samples are been filtered, it should repeat forecast and filtration until the samples' number is enough. Finally the mean of samples is as the node location.

3   Harmony Search(HS) Algorithm

Harmony Search (HS) algorithm [5-6] is a new intelligent optimization algorithm proposed by Geem which is presented by comparing music with optimal issue. Table1 briefly describes the analogy of the optimal issue and music performance.

Table 1. Analogy of Optimal Issue and Music Performance

Analogy Element	Optimization Process	Implementation Process
Optimum state	Global optimization	Excellent harmony
Evaluated by...	Objective function	Esthetics evaluation
Evaluate with...	Designed variable value	Pitch of musical instrument
Process unit	Each iteration	Each practice

The HS algorithm initializes the Harmony memory size (HMS), Harmony memory considering rate (HMCR) and Pitch adjusting rate (PAR) at first. Then, it will generate initial solutions arbitrarily of which number is equal to HMS to be stored in HM. According to the rules of HMCR, PAR and selecting randomly generating the new solution, the HS algorithm judges whether the value of new objective function is better than the worst one of HM. If it is, then replace it and update the HM. Otherwise, maintain the present HM and iterate until the anticipated iteration is achieved.

This algorithm is independent on the information of the question. Furthermore, it is capable of memorizing the optimal solution and using the local information and global information to guide the algorithm to search more information. At the same time, it is easier to combine with other algorithms to achieve better performance.

4   The Improved Algorithm Based on MCL and HS

This paper improves the main disadvantages of MCL algorithm. The algorithm makes the anchors transmit beacon signals of different powers to intercommunicate information with the unknown nodes, gets all of the single-hop and two-hop anchor boxes of the nodes, and construct the square with the node position in previous time as its center and $2V_{max}$ as its side length. Then we use the intersection of the anchor boxes and square as the sampling area to reduce sampling range. We strengthen the filtering conditions, adopt HS algorithm to optimize the filtered samples, and then calculate the estimated location of the node. This paper also uses the RSSI ranging and information of the positioned nodes to assist localization, thus improving the localization accuracy.

4.1   Initialization Stage

Anchors Information Transmission
Firstly anchors transmits two beacon signals with different powers, corresponding to the communication radius of $0.5r$ and r, where r is achieved by maximal power. And the unknown nodes transmit the signals with the maximal power. The anchors flood broadcast their own information. Then unknown nodes receive and forward the anchors information within the single-hop to neighbor nodes, and get the information of the two-hop neighbor anchors from the neighbor nodes, and then store the anchors' energies in series. Thus the possible existing areas of unknown nodes are been reduced by two-hop communication range.

Error Compensation of RSSI Ranging
This paper uses Received Signal Strength Indication (RSSI) as the auxiliary information for localization. Because RSSI values will be affected by various factors outside, such as a variety of reflection, humidity, etc. to cause the errors and influences localization accuracies [7]. In this paper we firstly compensate the errors of RSSI ranging and generate errors fitting curve. The specific steps are as follows.

(a).Anchors i, j calculate the distance d_{ij} between each other within the communication range and get the measurement distance d_{ij}' by the RSSI value. Via the routing nodes these values are transmitted to sink nodes in network and stored as an array in series.

Here, RSSI value between anchors is calculated by the logarithmic theoretical model [8], and then the distance d_{ij}' is calculated as is showing in (2).

$$d_{ij}' = d_0 * 10^{\frac{p_r(d_0) - p_r(d)}{10 n}}.$$ (2)

Where, $p_r(d_0)$ is the received signal strength at the reference distance d_0 which is gotten by measurement. Its unit is dBm. $p_r(d)$ is the received signal strength of the node. d is the measurement distance. n is the pass loss exponent, as a constant. Here $n = 2$.

(b).Define $E_{ij} = d_{ij} - d_{ij}'$ as the propagation error. Build the fitting curve by least square method with RSSI value as abscissa and E_{ij} as ordinate, generating the fitting equation.

(c).Transmit the fitting curve information to unknown nodes in network. Then with the information the checked distance d_{check} between the anchor and node is calculated.

4.2 Sampling and Filtering Stage

Determination of Sampling Region

Fig. 2 shows the localization constraint schematic. In Fig. 2, s_1, s_2 and s_3 are anchors, and p_1, p_2 are unknown nodes. p_2' is the location of p_2 in the previous time.

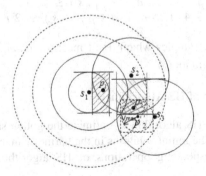

Fig. 2. The localization constraint schematic

We calculate the upper, lower, left and right tangent of the communication radius with the anchor as the center, and take the minimum rectangle surrounded by tangents which includes the unknown nodes as the sampling region. This region is named the anchor box. In Fig. 2, the solid line circles represent the communication radiuses in single-hop. The large dotted line circles are communication radiuses in two-hop. The red shadow of the rectangle in the left is the anchor box obtained by s_1 and s_2 including p_1 location. Fig. 2 also shows that p_1 is the neighbor of p_2 and p_2 is in the two-hop range of s_1. The blue shadow where p_2 is in is the anchor box built by s_1, s_2 and s_3. We use the previous time location p_2' and the maximal speed V_{max} to construct a small square, and then overlap with the anchor box to be as the sampling region of p_2, as the smaller red shadow where p_2 is in shows in Fig. 2.In this area, we select N samples randomly as predictive values. Here the number of N is 50. Then we filter these values and get the samples who meet the conditions.

Determination of Filtering Conditions

During the time from t to $t+1$, the node P receives the information including the anchors' information transmitting with two powers in the communication radius and the anchors' information forwarding by the neighbor nodes.

We assume some conditions as follows. $S1$ is the set of anchors communicating with the node P by $0.5r$, and $S2$ is the set of anchors communicating with P by r in single-hop. $S3$ is the set of anchors communicating by $0.5r$ in two-hop, and $S4$ is the set of anchors communicating by r in two-hop. $p_{t+1}^i(x_{t+1}^i, y_{t+1}^i)$ is anyone of N samples of the node P. i is from 1 to N. s stands for the anchor. $d(p_{t+1}^i, s)$ is the distance between the sample and the anchor. The filtering condition is as (3).

$$\begin{aligned}
&\{\forall s \in S1, d(p_{t+1}^i, s) \le 0.5r\} \\
&\wedge \{\forall s \in S2, 0.5r \le d(p_{t+1}^i, s) \le r\} \\
&\wedge \{\forall s \in S3, r \le d(p_{t+1}^i, s) \le 1.5r\} \\
&\wedge \{\forall s \in S4, 1.5r \le d(p_{t+1}^i, s) \le 2r\}
\end{aligned} \qquad (3)$$

We use (3) to filter the samples which don't meet the requirements, retain the rest, and then get N samples in loops.

4.3   The Application of HS Algorithm

In this paper, we adopt HS algorithm to optimize the gotten samples. By calculating the objective function, the initial solutions in the harmony memory are obtained. And then we run the corresponding operations of HS algorithm to produce the new harmony memory.

Definition of the Objective Function

The objective function is used to judge the virtues or defect degree of the solution. The objective function value $obj(p_i)$ is calculated as (4).

$$obj(p_i) = 1 / \sum_{m=1}^{3} \alpha_m^2 (d_{mcheck} - d_{m,i})^2 . \tag{4}$$

Where, i is sample point from 1 to N. p_i is the i th sample value of the node p. m from 1 to 3 is the number of the nearest anchor away from p. d_{mcheck} is the checked distance between p and m. $d_{m,i}$ is the distance between i and m. α_m is inversely proportional to d_{mcheck}, reflecting the measurement accuracy of distance between p and m.

Generation of the New Harmony

The algorithm selects HMS initial solutions (harmonies) with the best objective function values into the harmony memory (HM). Here, HMS is 40. The methods of generating the new harmony p_i are as (5) and (6).

Firstly, we select the value from the harmony memory.

$$p_i = \begin{cases} p_i \in HM & ,if \quad r1 < HMCR \\ p_{obj_{min}} + r1(p_{obj_{max}} - p_{obj_{min}}) & ,otherwise \end{cases} \tag{5}$$

Where, $HMCR$ is the harmony memory considering rate. Here it is 0.9. $p_{obj_{min}}$ is the solution with the minimal objective function value, and $p_{obj_{max}}$ is the maximal one. $r1$ is a random number uniformly distributing on 0 to 1.

Secondly, if the new harmony is from the harmony memory, we will do the fine adjustment for it. The operation is as (6).

$$p_i = \begin{cases} p_i + r2 * bw & ,if \ r2 < PAR \\ p_i & ,otherwise \end{cases} \tag{6}$$

Where, PAR stands for Pitch adjusting rate. Here, it is 0.3. bw is fine adjustment bandwidth. Here, it is 0.01. $r2$ is a random number uniformly distributing on 0 to 1.

Finally, the algorithm compares the objective function value of the new harmony with the minimal one, and then leave the best solution to update the harmony memory.

4.4   Termination Condition of the Algorithm

This paper makes the maximal iteration number of the HS algorithm as the termination criteria. That is to say, while the algorithm runs to the maximal iteration number $N1$, it terminates. Here, $N1$ is 10.

Now we calculate the weight w_t^i of the solution p_t^i in the harmony memory as is showing in (7).

$$w_t^i = 1 / \sum_{m=1}^{3} (d_{mcheck} - d_{m,i}) . \tag{7}$$

Where, p_t^i stands for the i th solution in the memory at moment t , and w_t^i is its weight. i from 1 to HMS is the number of the solution in the harmony memory. m , d_{mcheck} and $d_{m,i}$ are as in (4).

Then, we use (8) to normalize the weight w_i of the node p .

$$w_i = w_t^i / \sum_{i=1}^{HMS} w_t^i . \tag{8}$$

Lastly, the estimated location of the unknown node (x_p, y_p) is calculated in (9).

$$(x_p, y_p) = (\sum_{i=1}^{HMS} w_i x_i , \sum_{i=1}^{HMS} w_i y_i) . \tag{9}$$

Where, x_i and y_i stand for the abscissa and ordinate of the solution i separately.

In addition, for the located node p , we define its availability η_p in (10).

$$\eta_p = 1 - \sum_{m=1}^{3} \left| \sqrt{(x_p - x_m)^2 + (y_p - y_m)^2} - d_{mcheck} \right| / \sum_{m=1}^{3} d_{mcheck} . \tag{10}$$

Where, m and d_{mcheck} are as in (4). x_m and y_m represent the abscissa and ordinate of these anchors. If η_p is larger than or equal to λ which depends on the actual situation, we will take this node p as an available node and use its location information for assisting the neighbor node localization.

5   Simulation Analysis

In this paper, the simulation software is MATLAB 7.0. We set the size of simulation region is 300 by 300 square meters and the maximal communication radius r of the node is 30 meter. The anchors are motionless and uniformly distributed. The speed of unknown node is randomly selected from 0 to $V_{\max}$. Here, the initial $V_{\max}$ is $0.2r$. The nodes move as the Random Waypoint model. We simulate and analysis MCL, MCB and the improved algorithm which is named MCHS. Here, we take the localization error as the performance index of the algorithm, which is the ratio of the Euclidean distance from the estimated location to the actual location and communication radius.

Fig. 3 shows node localization errors are reduced as the algorithm execution time goes on. Our algorithm, which has built the RSSI error fitting curve, taking full use of the located node information and optimizing the sample values with HS algorithm, shows higher accuracy than the traditional MCL algorithm and MCB algorithm. Throughout the all execution time, the error of the algorithm in this paper is decreased gradually and the localization accuracy is better than the other two algorithms.

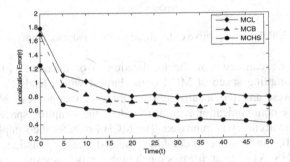

Fig. 3. Relationship curve of localization error and time

Fig. 4 is the curve of MCL, MCB and MCHS algorithms' localization errors changing with anchors density, which is the average number of anchors in single-hop. At the beginning, the three algorithms' errors are large while the anchors density is low. But the MCHS's error is smaller than the others because of using the located nodes information to assist localization. Comparing with MCL and MCB, MCHS algorithm uses the anchors information to optimize the sample space and decreases the error by adopting the intelligent algorithm which improves the localization accuracy. With the increasing number of anchors, the errors all get smaller and smaller, and the curves variation tends to be stable.

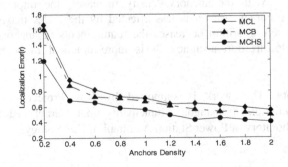

Fig. 4. Relationship curve of localization error and anchors density

Fig. 5 shows the affection of nodes movement on localization accuracy. The nodes maximal moving speed has direct effect on the range of sampling space.

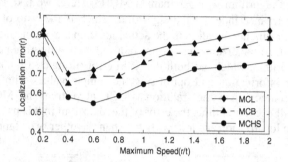

Fig. 5. Relationship curve of localization error and maximum speed

From Fig. 5 we can see that the localization error decreases firstly and then increases. The sampling space of MCL is the largest which leads to that sampling efficiency is lowest and the localization accuracy is the poorest. MCB uses the overlapping of the communication regions to reduce the sampling space as a result of which the location accuracy is improved. The MCHS reduces the sampling region on the basis of MCB. Furthermore, it combines the distance information and optimizes the sample with HS. As a result, it gains much higher efficiency samples and then it is less affected by the nodes maximum moving speed.

6   Conclusions

In this paper, on the premise that the anchors are static and the common nodes move randomly in the network, we improve the MCL algorithm, reduce the sampling region and enhance the filtering conditions. Besides, we build the RSSI error fitting curve and adopt the HS algorithm to optimize the samples, getting an effective localization algorithm for mobile sensor networks. The simulation results show that the algorithm proposed in this paper has the higher accuracy than MCL and MCB. The performances on the time, anchors density and node maximum speed are all improved, as well. With the anchors density increases, the improved algorithm reaches a higher accuracy. And it is less affected by the nodes maximum moving speed. The improved algorithm decreases the requirements of anchors density and gets the higher localization accuracy. It is more practical in some application scenarios.

Acknowledgments. This work is supported by Key Project of Science and Technology commission of Shanghai Municipality under Grant 11dz1121602, and Shanghai Key Laboratory of Power Station Automation Technology.

References

1. Li, X.W., Xu, Y.J., Ren, F.Y.: Techniques for Wireless Sensor Networks, pp. 1–11. Beijing Institute of Technology Press, Beijing (2007)
2. Hu, L., Evans, D.: Localization for mobile sensor networks. In: Proceedings of Mobile Computing and Networking, pp. 45–47 (2004)
3. Baggio, A., Langendoen, K.G.: Monte-Carlo Localization for Mobile Wireless Sensor Networks. In: Cao, J., Stojmenovic, I., Jia, X., Das, S.K. (eds.) MSN 2006. LNCS, vol. 4325, pp. 317–328. Springer, Heidelberg (2006)
4. Rudafshani, M., Datta, S.: Localization in wireless sensor networks. In: Proc. of the 6th International Symposium on Information Processing in Sensor Networks, pp. 51–60 (2007)
5. Geem, Z.W., Kim, J.H., Loganathan, G.: A new heuristic optimization algorithm: harmony search. Simulation 76(2), 60–68 (2001)
6. Yong, L.-Q.: Advances in Harmony Search Algorithm. Computer System Application 20(7), 244–248 (2011)
7. Peng, B.: Research Localization Algorithm in Wireless Sensor Network Based on RSSI Ranging-Error Compensation. Dalian University of Technology, 29–33 (2008)
8. Fang, Z., Zhao, Z., Guo, P.: Analysis of Distance Measurement Based on RSS. Journal of Sensor Technology 20(11), 2526–2530 (2007)

The Research on Association Rules Mining with Co-evolution Algorithm in High Dimensional Data

Wei Lou, Lei Zhu[*], and Limin Yan

School of Mechatronics Engineering and Automation, Shanghai University,
NO.149, Yanchang Rd. 200072 Shanghai, China
zl8650@163.com

Abstract. This paper adopts a co-evolution algorithm, which utilizes improved genetic algorithm and particle swarm optimization algorithm to iterate two populations simultaneously. Meanwhile, the mechanism of information interaction between these two populations is introduced. Finally, experiments and application have been made to prove that on the premise of acceptable time complexity, not only does the co-evolution algorithm inherit the superiority of traditional genetic algorithm such as reducing the number of scanning the database effectively and generating small-scale candidate item sets, but also avoid the phenomenon of premature through comparing the properties of co-evolution algorithm, traditional genetic algorithm and particle swarm optimization algorithm when used in association rules mining. High quality association rules can be found when adopted the co-evolution algorithm, especially in high-dimension database.

Keywords: Association rules mining, Co-evolution, Genetic algorithm (GA), Particle swarm optimization (PSO) algorithm.

1 Introduction

The association rules mining is an important branch of data mining research, which can help decision-makers in different areas to identify a potential relationship among the data items in a large database, so many scholars are eager to study this knowledge discovery problem [1]. As a classic frequent item set generation algorithm, Apriori algorithm is a milestone in association rules mining. However, as the study goes further contiguously, the two major defects of the Apriori algorithm are gradually revealed [2]:

① The algorithm must spend a lot of time dealing with large-scale candidate item sets.
② The algorithm needs to repeatedly scan the database for pattern matching to the candidate item sets.

Theoretically speaking, the Apriori algorithm can ensure the high precision of the results. However, when used to deal with massive, high dimensional data, the runtime

---

[*] Corresponding author.

T. Xiao, L. Zhang, and M. Fei (Eds.): AsiaSim 2012, Part II, CCIS 324, pp. 338–346, 2012.

is considerable, or even impossible to finish in limited years. For the defects of the Apriori algorithm researchers have proposed many improved algorithm to compensate for its shortcomings, such as FP-growth algorithm proposed by J.Han et.al [3], Partition algorithm proposed by A.Savasere [4]. Compared to the Apriori algorithm, the performance of these algorithms have been significantly improved, but when used in massive high-dimensional data, the use of these algorithms to mining rules is still unrealistic on some occasion [1].

In this paper we use a co-evolution algorithm, which is on the basis of the standard GA and imports optimized PSO algorithm. The algorithm is able to share historical information and current status to search out high-quality association rules in high-dimensional data set.

2   Co-evolution Concepts

Co-evolution concept is first proposed by Ehrlich and Raven who discuss the evolution between plants and herbivorous insects. Its core idea is: the interaction of populations is indispensable conditions for survival of each other. In long-term evolutionary process, they are interdependent and coordinate. They improve the individual and whole performance [5]. By introducing this concept, the evolution is not only related with its own population, but also affected by the population having contact with it. Co-evolution concept has a very wide range, including the proposed multi PSO of co-evolution algorithm, co-evolutionary genetic algorithm and so on. In this paper we use co-evolution of "GA-PSO", taking GA and PSO to iterate each other. Combined with co-evolution concept, the two populations can co-evolve, in order to search out high quality of association rules in the high-dimensional data set. In order to achieve this idea, we design an information exchange mechanism, named interoperability. Let information pass between the two populations to achieve the purpose of co-evolution.

3   Search Strategies of Co-evolution Algorithms

3.1   Improvement of GA Search Strategy

The GA makes the following improvements to ensure that the information can be passed between the two populations.

① Encoding Rules
Solution space of association rule mining corresponds to the entire transaction database, so this method takes a real number array to encode [6].The number of elements in an array of real numbers corresponds to transaction database field. The number of element values represents the attribute values of the field.

② Fitness Function
In this paper, the fitness function is design by the support and confidence of association rules, in Eq. (1)

$$F\left(R_{j}\right)=\omega_{s}\frac{Support\left(R_{j}\right)}{minsupp}+\omega_{c}\frac{Confidence\left(R_{j}\right)}{minconf} \tag{1}$$

Where *Support* (R_j), *Confidence* (R_j) are a new rule support and confidence formed through genetic manipulation.

minsupp is a minimum support threshold and *minconf* is minimum confidence threshold, which is given by user. When $\dfrac{Support\left(R_{j}\right)}{minsupp}\geq 1, \dfrac{Confidence\left(R_{j}\right)}{minconf}\geq 1$,

$\omega_{s}+\omega_{c}=1$, $\omega_{c}\geq 0, \omega_{s}\geq 0$.

R_j meets the requirements of the rules; otherwise, this rule will be eliminated in the next generation.

③ **The Determination of the Genetic Operators**
In this paper we use single-point crossover method to determine the crossover operator. The crossover probability is another important element to design the crossover operator. We adjust the crossover probability dynamically according to the fitness value of different stages. The adjustment strategies of crossover probability are shown in Eq. (2): crossover probability of the high fitness individual should be small, and crossover probability of the low fitness individual should be larger.

$$P_{c}=\begin{cases}\dfrac{P_{cmax}-P_{cmin}}{1+\exp\left[\dfrac{2\left(f'-\overline{f}\right)}{f_{max}-\overline{f}}\right]}+P_{cmin} & , \quad f'\geq\overline{f}\\[4mm] P_{cmax} & , \quad f'<\overline{f}\end{cases} \tag{2}$$

Where P_{cmax} and P_{cmin} respectively denote the upper and lower limits of the crossover probability P_c. The values are 0.9 and 0.3 in this paper.

f_{max} is the maximum fitness value of individuals in the current population.
$\overline{f}$ is the average fitness value of the current population.
f' is the larger fitness value of two cross-individual.

④ **Mutation Operator Design**
We select the variant individuals in mutation probability P_m based on the improved method of uniform variation [7]. Then each individual variety in turn to ensure each

mutated values in the allowed range. In this paper, the mutation probability is related to iterations number. The Eq. (3) is as follows:

$$
P_m = \begin{cases} P_{mmin} + \dfrac{t}{T_{max}} & , \quad 0 \le \dfrac{t}{T_{max}} \le \left(P_{mmax} - P_{mmin} \right) \\[4mm] \dfrac{P_{mmax}}{P_{mmax} - P_{mmin} - 1} \times \dfrac{t}{T_{max}} + \dfrac{P_{mmax}}{P_{mmin} + 1 - P_{mmax}} & , \quad \left(P_{mmax} - P_{mmin} \right) \le \dfrac{t}{T_{max}} \le 1 \end{cases} \tag{3}
$$

Where P_{mmax} and P_{mmin} are the upper and lower limits of P_m, our values are 0.1 and 0.001.

T_{max} is the maximum number of iterations.

t is the current number of iterations.

3.2   Improvement of PSO Search Strategy

Since the genetic algorithm individual has not a memory function, each individual can only reflect the current state but cannot reflect historical status. The magnitude and direction of the evolution do not get rid of the randomness and blindness, so GA is slow in late convergence period and get premature convergence easily. Therefore we introduce a PSO with individual memory function. GA and PSO are equally applicable in encoding rules and designing fitness function. In this section, we focus on improvement of particles update formula and control parameter selection.

① **Particles Update Formula**

Standard PSO algorithm aims at continuous function to search operations, while PSO algorithm will be applied to the field of association rule mining in this paper. The solution space is the entire database, belonging to discrete domain, so discrete improvements of the original particle must be made. We put forward *sigmoid* function: $S\left(v_{id}^t \right) = 1 / \left(1 + \exp\left(-v_{id}^t \right) \right)$, which will be updated as the particle position probability. Specific location updates formula, such as Eq. (4) and Eq. (5) shows.

$$
v_{id}^{t+1} = \omega \times v_{id}^t + c_1 \times r_1 \times \left(p_{id}^t - x_{id}^t \right) + c_2 \times r_2 \times \left(p_{gd}^t - x_{id}^t \right) \tag{4}
$$

$$
\begin{cases} x_{id}^{t+1} = x_{id}^t + fix\left(v_{id}^{t+1} \right) & , \quad rand(\ ) < S_{id}^{t+1} \\[2mm] x_{id}^{t+1} = x_{id}^t & , \quad rand(\ ) \ge S_{id}^{t+1} \end{cases} \tag{5}
$$

Where $fix()$ round up v_{id}^{t+1}, $rand(\ )$ generates a random number between [0, 1].

② **Control Parameter Selection**

The value of w should be decreasing. Therefore, we use nonlinear regulation strategies of w, such as Eq. (6).

$$w(t) = w_{min} + (w_{max} - w_{min}) \exp\left(-3 \times (t / T_{max})^2\right) \tag{6}$$

Where w_{max} and w_{min} are upper and lower of inertia weight w, we use 0.9 and 0.4.

t is the number of current iteration.
T_{max} is maximum number of iterations.

4   Co-evolution Algorithms

Co-evolution algorithm flow chart is shown in Fig. 1, which Step3 uses the idea of co-evolution, defining the collaborative operation method. It helps to avoid premature convergence when the traditional GA is used in association rule mining. The specific steps are described as follows:

Step1: Two initial populations are randomly generated according to the target database. POP_1 and POP_2 use respectively the search strategy of PSO and GA to search for association rules. Two populations use the same coding rules, the fitness function, population size and the maximum evolution generation.

Step2: We initialize the two populations with various parameters: weight, determine the minimum support threshold for association rules *minsupp*, the minimum confidence threshold *minconf* and constraints of previous item sets and later item sets.

Step3: We scan the database to calculate the two populations in the individual's fitness value. Then we retain eligible individuals' access to their respective next-generations and eliminate non-compliant individual. We compare fitness value of the global best individual G^{pso} in POP_1 and best individual G^{ga} in POP_2. Individuals with larger fitness values will replace the best individual of other populations, as a basis for the next generation of evolution.

Step4: We judge condition whether or not to meet the termination condition. If the number of iterations has reached the maximum number of iterations then the algorithm ends, switch to Step 6; or continue to the next step.

Step5: The speed and location of POP_1 are updated in accordance with the Eq.(4) and Eq.(5) then produce next generation. POP_2 are operated in genetic manipulation to get the next generation. Then we go to Step3 to evaluate fitness value.

Step6: Output association rules.

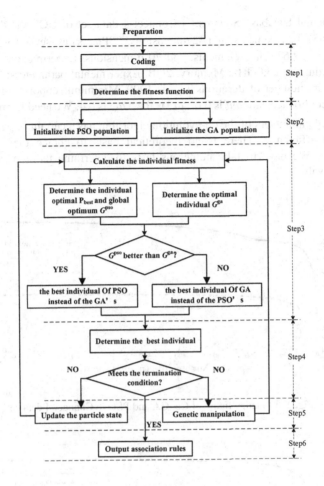

Fig. 1. Co-evolution algorithm process

When the individuals in POP_1 fall into local minima, the individuals no longer determine the next location just based on the experience of their own groups, and will draw on the best individual of POP_2. Using excellent individual in POP_2, we can guide individual which has been plunged into the local optimum value to deviate from the original local minima. So we get the global optimum with greater probability.

5   Experiments Analysis and Application

The co-evolution algorithm is programmed with MATLAB7.6 (R2008a) under Windows XP. We compare GA, PSO, as well as co-evolution algorithm by tracking runtime and the average fitness value of population.

Experimental Database Sources: ①Connect-4 data set of UCI, the data set has a total of 67,557 data elements, and 42 dimensions. ②Plants data set of UCI, the data set has a total of 22,632 data elements, and 70 dimensions. Experimental environment: CPU: Intel dual-core3.0GHz; Memory: 2GB. Experimental parameters: Population is 30, Maximum number of iterations T_{max} is 1000, Minimum support *minsupp* is 0.45, Minimum confidence *minconf* is 0.6, ω_s is 0.6, ω_c is 0.4. We need to emphasize that experimental parameters of the co-evolution algorithm has a certain impact on solving results and efficiency. There is no theoretical basis to choice them in practical applications. We have to take numerous tests to determine these parameters as a reasonable value.

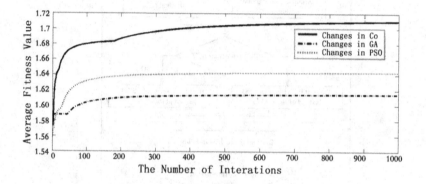

Fig. 2. Tendency figure of Co, GA and PSO in Connect-4 data set

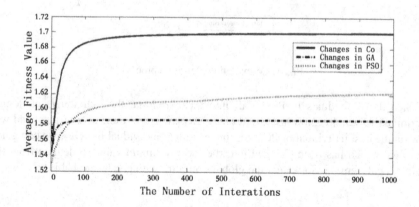

Fig. 3. Tendency figure of Co, GA and PSO in Plants data set

The evolutionary process of the three algorithms on the Connect-4 data set and Plants data set are shown in Fig. 2 and Fig. 3. The dimensions of two data sets are 42 and 70, belonging to high-dimensional data sets. As Fig. 2, Fig. 3 reflects similar information, so we take example of Fig. 2 to analyze the characteristics of the three algorithms. It can be seen from Fig. 2, the individual quality of co-evolution algorithm was significantly better than the GA and PSO in the early evolution. With the increasing number of iterations, the GA has been caught the premature convergence and could not get out after 40 iterations. Compared with the GA, the individual quality of PSO has been improved, but also faces the dilemma that cannot jump out of local optimal solution. In the iterative process, co-evolution algorithm also has the phenomenon of premature convergence. There is a clear inflection point at 180 iterations, showing that the algorithm guide individual deviation from the original local minima.

Table 1. The Runtime of Co, GA and PSO

Runtime(s)	Connect-4	Plants
Co	4946.13s	3765.79s
GA	3601.43s	2658.95s
PSO	2153.56s	1769,68s

It can be seen from Table 1, co-evolution algorithm has no advantage in runtime relative to the other two algorithms, but entirely within an acceptable range.

6   Conclusions

This paper presents a co-evolution algorithm using GA and PSO to iterate the two populations. We introduce a mechanism for information exchange between populations, so that the two populations can co-evolve. Proved by experiments, runtime of co-evolution algorithm is slightly longer compared to the other two global optimization algorithms. But the runtime is acceptable. Compared to the other two algorithms, co-evolution algorithm not only is superior in the mining quality, but also has a significant advantage in the ability to jump out of local optimal solution.

References

1. Han, J., Kamber, M.: Data Mining: Concepts and Techniques, 2nd edn., pp. 146–155. China Machine Press (2011)
2. Agrawal, R., Imielinski, T., Swami, A.: Mining Association Rules between Sets of Items in Large Databases. In: Proc. 1993 ACM-SIGMOD Int. Conf. Management of Databases, pp. 20–72. ACM Press, Washington, DC (1993)
3. Han, J., Pei, J., Yin, Y.: Mining frequent patterns without candidate generation. In: Proceedings of the 2000 ACM-SIGMOD International Conference on Management of Data, Dallas, Texas, pp. 1–12. ACM Press (2000)

4. Savasere, A., Omiecinski, E., Navathe, S.: An efficient algorithm for mining association rules in large databases. In: Dayal, U., Gray, P.M.D., Nishio, S. (eds.) Proceedings of the 21th International Conference on Very Large Databases(VLDB 1995), Zurich, pp. 432–443. Morgan Kaufmann Publisher (1995)
5. Wiegand, R.P.: An analysis of cooperative co-evolutionary algorithms. George Mason University, Fairfax (2003)
6. Sharma, S.K., Irwin, G.W.: Fuzzy coding of genetic algorithms. IEEE Trans. Evolutionary Computation, 344–355 (2003)
7. Thierens, D.: Adaptive mutation rate control schemes in genetic algorithms. In: Proceedings of the 2002 Congress on Evolutionary Computation, CEC 2002, vol. 1, pp. 980–985 (2002)
8. Shi, Y., Eberhart, R.C.: Parameter Selection in Particle Swarm Adaptation. In: Porto, V.W., Waagen, D. (eds.) EP 1998. LNCS, vol. 1447, pp. 591–600. Springer, Heidelberg (1998)

Simulated Annealing Algorithm
in the Application of Thermal Reliability

Shaoxin Tian, Zhong Su, Xiaofei Ma, and Xu Zhao

Institute of Intelligence Control, Beijing Information Science & Technology University,
Beijing, 100101, China

Abstract. According to the influence of temperature on the lifespan of electronic devices, this paper uses the simulated annealing algorithm to optimize the layout of array distributed electronic components, and the finite element method to verify the result. The results show that it can effectively lower the high temperature of the electronic components through the layout optimization. The highest temperature and the average temperature are decreased by 10.49% and 10.41% respectively in this simulation, which indicates the simulated annealing algorithm can effectively solve the problem of layout optimization of components on the printed circuit board and avoid large-scale computing in the traditional algorithm. This algorithm is of practical value in the field of engineering.

Keywords: simulated annealing algorithm, array distribution, finite element, high temperature, thermal layout optimization.

1   Introduction

With the rapid development of microelectronic technique, the integrated level of electronic components in the electronic equipment is getting higher and higher. Because of the special requirements of the continuing miniaturization, high performance and space adaptability development of the electronic components, which lead to the increasing in the number of components, the size decreasing of the equipment, the layout of the components on the PCB will be more compact, and this may ultimately leads to unreasonable layout which will cause too high local temperature to make the reliability of the system reduced [1~2]. According to a report, about 55% of the reasons that caused the electronic equipment out of work are caused by higher temperature comparing to a specified one, so it is quite important to reduce the local temperature of electronic equipment through reasonable layouts.

As is shown in Figure 1, high temperature has great effect on electronic elements, the relationship between the component failure rate and junction temperature is exponential. According to some statistical data, once the temperature of electronic equipment in civil aviation is lowered by 1℃, its failure rate will fall 4% [3]. Therefore, it is very important to control the temperature. In the case of natural convection, the layout design of electronic components is one of the most effective ways in thermal design to control the temperature. From the present research home

T. Xiao, L. Zhang, and M. Fei (Eds.): AsiaSim 2012, Part II, CCIS 324, pp. 347–354, 2012.

and abroad, we can see that most of the thermal designs are proposed through experience and tests. In general, they have to wait for the completion of the design to change the layout through test measuring, but this will increase the design cost greatly, and it cannot ensure a best layout. The simulated annealing algorithm is a global optimization algorithm, and it can be particularly applied in combinatorial optimization problems which contain a large-scale array distributed electronic components. This algorithm is of high operation rate and flexible application. In this paper, the simulated annealing algorithm is used to reduce the local temperature of the array distributed electronic components to improve the whole equipment adaptability to high temperature, and we put forward an available solution for the optimization design of the electronic equipment.

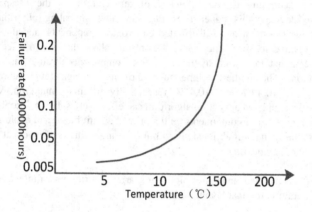

Fig. 1. The relation diagram between component failure rate and junction temperature

2   The Model of Simulated Annealing Algorithm

The simulated annealing algorithm is derived from the principle of solid annealing. In the solid annealing progress, the solid is heated to a high enough temperature, then we let it slowly cooled. When the solid is heated, its internal particles become disordered as the temperature rises, and their internal energy will increase accordingly. When the solid is cooled slowly, its particles become more and more orderly, and this process can reach an equilibrium state at each temperature, finally it reaches the ground state at room temperature, and under this condition the energy of the particles will reduce to the minimum. When we use solid annealing principle to simulate combinatorial optimization problems, we set the internal energy value to be the objective function value, and transform the temperature T to the control parameter s, now we get the simulated annealing algorithm which can be used to solve the combinatorial optimization problems [4~6]. When dealing with this kind of problems, we firstly get the initial values and the control parameter s, and then we continually do an iterative process in the following steps: generating new solutions, calculating objective function values, calculating the differences of objective function values, accepting or discarding. In the iteration process, the value of s is decaying gradually, and when the algorithm terminates under a given condition, the final value of s is the approximate optimal one. This is a heuristic random search process which is based on the Monte Carlo Iteration Method.

In this paper, the maximum temperature value of the components is defined as the energy of the system, and all possible electronic components layouts constitute the solution space. It's determined by the control parameter s whether or not to receive the transfer from current solutions to new solutions. According to the Metropolis rule, the probability of accepting a new solution is given by the following expression:

$$P(i \rightarrow j) = \begin{cases} 1, t_j \leq t_i \\ \exp\left(\dfrac{t_i - t_j}{s}\right), t_j \geq t_i \end{cases} \tag{1}$$

Where s is the control parameter, t_i is the maximum temperature of current solution, t_j is the maximum temperature of new solution. Here $0 \leq P \leq 1$. When the new

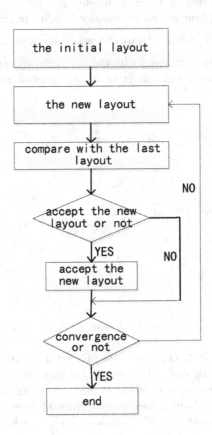

Fig. 2. The flow chart of the layout optimization algorithm program

solution t_j is smaller than the current solution t_i or when the two are equal, the new layout will be accepted completely; when the new solution t_j is larger than the current solution t_i, we will not deny this new solution directly as the normal layout optimization does, instead we adopt the poor new solution at a certain rate according to Metropolis rule. In addition to fully adopt the optimal solution, we also adopt the other poor solutions as a reference within the limits of a certain probability, and this is the essential difference between the simulated annealing algorithm and local search algorithm. The initial value of S is a large one, so we may get some poor solutions. But with its value decreasing, we can avoid the defect of local search algorithm and ensure to obtain the global optimal solution of combinatorial optimization problems. The flow chart of this layout optimization algorithm program is shown in Figure 2.

3   The Calculation Process and Results

According to the energy balance principle, the differential equation of heat conduction is deduced from the energy balance of some micro unit inside the object. Take the node (i, j) for an example, we can get the temperature relationships between the node and its surrounding nodes with the use of the energy balance [7]. Figure 3 shows the thermal equilibrium diagram of the internal nodes of the electronic components.

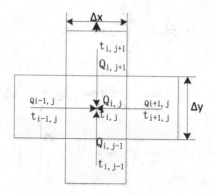

Fig. 3. Thermal equilibrium diagram of the nodes

Considering that a PCB contains a lot of related electronic components, if we assume that the shape, the size and the material of these electronic components are all the same, but the current(or the power of each electronic component is different) flowing through the electronic components is different, then we get the layout of the electronic components on the PCB shown in Fig.4, where the great rectangle represents the PCB, the small ones represent electronic components on the PCB.

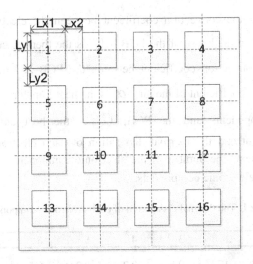

Fig. 4. The layout diagram of the electronic components on the PCB

According to the energy balance principle, we can also get that the sum of the total heat flowing into the control volume and the heat generating inside the control volume is equal to the sum of the total heat flowing out of the control volume and the internal energy increment of the control volume. And we can get the energy balance equation through the research[8~9]. The description of the equation is as follows: the sum of the heat that flowed into the node (i, j) from the $(i+1, j), (i-1, j), (i, j-1), (i, j+1)$, that generated inside the components, and that absorbed in the components' self-cooling progress and that transferred from the PCB is zero.

We can assume that there are five channels between the air and the electronic components on each plane, including four heat flux channels between the component and its surrounding ones and one heat convection channel between the air and the component. There is a thermal equilibrium among the effects of heat generation, heat conduction and convection cooling which is shown in the following equation.

$$\frac{t_{i+1,j}-t_{i,j}}{\dfrac{1}{l_{y1}\bullet l_c}(\dfrac{l_{x1}}{\lambda_c}+\dfrac{l_{x2}}{\lambda_g})}+\frac{t_{i-1,j}-t_{i,j}}{\dfrac{1}{l_{y1}\bullet l_c}(\dfrac{l_{x1}}{\lambda_c}+\dfrac{l_{x2}}{\lambda_g})}+\frac{t_{i,j-1}-t_{i,j}}{\dfrac{1}{l_{x1}\bullet l_c}(\dfrac{l_{y1}}{\lambda_c}+\dfrac{l_{y2}}{\lambda_g})}+\frac{t_{i,j+1}-t_{i,j}}{\dfrac{1}{l_{x1}\bullet l_c}(\dfrac{l_{y1}}{\lambda_c}+\dfrac{l_{y2}}{\lambda_g})}$$

$$+l_{x1}l_{y1}\alpha_c(T_\infty-T_{i,j})+\frac{T_\infty-T_{i,j}}{\dfrac{1}{l_{x1}l_{y1}}(\dfrac{1}{\alpha_h}+\dfrac{1}{\alpha_p}+\dfrac{l_p}{\lambda_p})}+Q^n=0 \qquad (2)$$

where l_c is the thickness of all electronic components, l_{x1} and l_{y1} is the length and width of the electronic components, l_{x2} and l_{y2} is the gaps between each two electronic components, λ_c is the thermal conductivity coefficient of the electronic components, α_c is the convection coefficient between the electronic components and the air; l_p is the thickness of the PCB, λ_p is the thermal conductivity of the PCB, α_p is the convection coefficient between the PCB and the air; λ_g is the thermal conductivity coefficient of the air; α_h is the heat transfer coefficient between the electronic components and the PCB, $Q_{i,j}^n$ is the heat emitting from each electronic component and the thermal dissipation of each electronic component is different, n represents the number of the electronic components, (i, j) represents the locations of the electronic components.

Table 1. The thermal dissipation of each electronic component

number	1	2	3	4	5	6	7	8
power (w/cm²)	0.231	0.231	0.562	0.231	0.231	0.5	0.5	0.231
number	9	10	11	12	13	14	15	16
power (w/cm²)	0.751	0.831	0.562	0.562	0.214	0.214	0.751	0.5

There is a total of 4 × 4 array of electronic components distributing on the PCB, and these sixteen chips are evenly distributed. The size of the PCB is 65mm × 65mm × 1.5mm, and the size of each chip is 10mm × 10mm × 5mm with a 15mm center distance between each two chips. The thermal dissipation of each electronic component is shown in Table1.

The layout of the electronic component before the optimization is as follows:

arry_best =
    1   2   3   4;   5   6   7   8;
    9   10   11   12;   13   14   15   16.

The simulation result is shown in Figure 5.

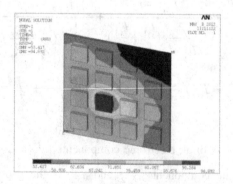

Fig. 5. The temperature distribution before optimization

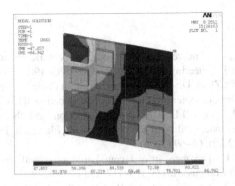

Fig. 6. The temperature distribution after optimization

According to the iteration flow chart shown in Figure 2, if the new maximum temperature is lower than the one last time, the new layout will be adopted; otherwise we have to devise the distribution again and then calculate again. The layout of the electronic component after the optimization is shown as follows:

arry_best1 =
| 10 | 7 | 11 | 13; | 12 | 1 | 6 | 8; |
| 15 | 4 | 2 | 3; | 16 | 9 | 5 | 14. |

The simulation results by using the ANSYS is shown in Figure 6. Comparing Figure 5 with Figure 6, we can see that the temperature range before optimization is from 53.417°C to 94.892°C, the temperature range after optimization is from 47.857°C to 84.942°C. The maximum temperature after optimization is about 10.49% lower than the maximum temperature before optimization, and the maximum temperature of most of the electronic components is significantly reduced compared with that before the optimization. The results show that the re-layout of components using the simulated annealing algorithm can greatly reduce the temperature of the electronic components, and therefore it can greatly improve the thermal reliability of electronic equipment.

4 Conclusions

This paper applies the simulated annealing algorithm to the thermal layout optimization design of electronic components, then use the ANSYS to get the simulation results verified. The results show that the simulated annealing algorithm can solve the optimization problem of the layout of the electronic components on the PCB, and this algorithm has some certain versatility, so it can greatly improve the adaptability of electronic components to high temperature.

Acknowledgments. This work is supported by the National Natural Science Foundation of China (GrantNo.61031001,60972118); 71F120907, 502812300; 40405100304, 9071223301;PHR201106226,PHR201006115.

References

1. Zhang, H.J., Zhang, Y.: The research of layout problem Based on simulated annealing algorithm. Computer Engineering and Design 27(11), 1985–1988 (2006)
2. Zhou, X.G., Liu, G.X., Zhao, D.: The layout optimization of electronic components based on genetic algorithm. The Computer Engineering and Application 4(17), 100–103 (2007)
3. Qiu, L.F., Fang, B.Z., Lu, J.L.: The present situation and the demand of electronic information products' adaptability to the environment. Electronic Product Reliability and Environmental Test 24(2), 66–69 (2006)
4. Yang, Y.Z., Xie, G.J.: The gate array layout based on simulated annealing algorithm. Microelectronics and Computer 27(4), 115–117, 121 (2010)
5. Sun, C.C., Lin, D.: The research of layout Based on sequence and the simulated annealing algorithm. Microelectronics and Computer 26(1), 210–213, 67 (2010)
6. Zhang, Y.P., Feng, Q.K., Yu, X.L.: The thermal analysis and design of multi-chip module (MCM). Power Electronics 43(2), 67–69 (2009)
7. Ankur, J., Robert, E.J., Huang, Z.H., et al.: Thermal Modeling and Design of 3D of Integrated Circuits. In: IEEE. Int. 2008: Thermal and Thermo-mechanical Phenomena in Electronic Systems, pp. 1139–1145. IEEE, USA (2008)
8. Huang, Y.F., Zhang, R.B., Ling, W.S.: The analysis of heat reliability of the key component on PCB board. Micro Computer Information 21(2), 164–166 (2005)
9. Qi, J.-Y.: Application of Improved Simulated Annealing Algorithm in the Facility Layout Design. In: Proceedings of the 29th of Chinese Control Conference, Beijing, China, July 29-31, pp. 5224–5227 (2010)

Parallel Simulation Based on GPU-Acceleration

Jun Du, Qiang Liang, and Yongchun Xia

NO.21, Dujiakan, Fengtai District, Academy of Armored Force Engineering,
Beijing, China

Abstract. GPU has much intensive computation capacity and wide bandwidth, and with the advantage of high performance and low power cost, the heterogeneous architecture of CPU and GPU make good effect in many fields. With the appearance of CUDA that carried out by Nvidia, the GPU is used for general-purpose computation is easier and cheaper, there are many high performance computation questions in simulation field, such as the simulation of the electromagnetic environment, the solution of higher order differential equations, the simulation data processing, large-scale combat simulation and so on, among these, some of the questions that are involved data-intensive computation, are suitable for acceleration by GPU. With the development and maturity of GPGPU, the heterogeneous parallel computation will play an important role in parallel simulation.

Keywords: paralle simulation, GPU acceleration, general-purpose computation, heterogeneous paralleling.

1   Introduction

Recently, In order to meet need of 3D game and visual simulation, Graphic Process Unit(GPU) is being upgraded quickly, its FPS has been much higher than the synchronous CPU's, and its woke mode has become from fixed pipelining to programmable pipelining. As the same time, limited by the technology and power wastage, the frequency of processors could not been improved much more in a short time, accordingly, the Moore's law about computer development has changed as that future computer's will not more quickly but more widely. So, the latest CPU adopts multi-cores architecture to improve parallel process capacity, while the GPU is multi-cores architecture essentially and has much more cores than CPU. It is assured that GPU will play an important role in the parallel simulation computation field.

2   General-Purpose Computation on GPU

2.1   Background of GPGPU

GPU is a high level parallel data stream processor which makes optimization to vector computation, and it has two types of streaming Processor, which are vertex shader and pixel shader. Vertex shader is multiple instructions multiple data (MIMD), while pixel

T. Xiao, L. Zhang, and M. Fei (Eds.): AsiaSim 2012, Part II, CCIS 324, pp. 355–362, 2012.

shader is single instruction multiple data (SIMD), taking data stream as process unite, they are good at dealing with date stream.[1] In view of this, a new research field is initiated, which is defined as general-purpose computation on graphics process (GPGPU) and focus on how to use GPU solving more extensive computation question besides computer graphics.

GPGPU take heterogeneous mode as its compute policy, which take CPU to execute the complex logical operation and transaction management that is not suitable for data parallel computation, when take GPU to execute compute-intensive data parallel computation. Making use of powerful computation and high-bandwidth of GPU to make up the inadequate performance of CPU, GPGPU has prominent advantage in cost and cost-effective.

2.2   Characteristic of GPGPU

There are some common characteristic in algorithm that is used in graphics applications, algorithm-intensive, highly parallel, simple control, multi-step execution and feed forward pipelining, the applications which have or could been convert to have these characteristic can have good performance on GPU, while the following restrictions need to be considered.

(1) Precision
The data precision is important of large-scale scientific computation, Currently, the accuracy of floating-point operation has improve to 32 bit from 24 bit, some graphics have support 64 bit double floating-point operation, but the speed is much slower than floating-point operation, about from 8 to 12 times.

(2) Data Types
As far as now, only the float-point can be read and operated by GPU, and other data type such as string, date need to special treatment.

(3) Additional Spending in Communication
GPU only can operate the data that in graphic memory, so additional time need to be spent on copying data from memory to graphic memory.

(4) Integer Arithmetic Instruction
GPU doesn't have integer arithmetic units, so it can't execute integer arithmetic instruction which is usually used in database operation.

(5) No Random Access
GPU reads and writes date in a sequential way and can't read or write value randomly, which limit the algorithm development and application.

(6) Branching Structure
SIMD mode in which GPU works, affect the efficiency of pipelining greatly and sometimes even lead to interruption.

2.3   Platform of GPGPU

As a processor that specially executes the graphic operation, GPU has its own storage unit with a special way accessing data, and it's main user, game makers usually use non-standard programming mode to develop application, which lead to is expensive and difficult for developing General-Purpose computation. In order to break this status and make much easier to use General-Purpose computation capacity of GPU for common developer, some famous software and hardware manufacturers release some platforms and tools, which promote the development and progress of the GPGPU. The most popular product is CUDA from NVIDIA, because following two reasons.

(1) Hardware

The architecture of GPU that supports CUDA has been significantly improved, one aspect is application of unified device architecture, which could make more effective use of computing resource that distribute in vertex shader and pixel shader. The other aspect is the introduction of on-chip shared memory, which support random write and thread communication. These two aspects of improvement make CUDA more suitable for GPGPU.

(2) Software

CUDA uses C language as its development language, and don't need the help of graphic API to develop general-purpose application, so developers can easily migrate from CPU programming mode with C language to GPU programming mode with CUDA, and don't need to study specific instruction and structure of the graphics chip. The most advantage of CUDA is greatly reducing the threshold of GPU programming, and if grasping C language, the developers could program using programming environment and SDK provided by CUDA.

3   GPGPU and Parallel Simulation

3.1   Comparison of CPU and GPU Hardware Architecture

In the view of architecture, the CPU and GPU designed according to different design ideas, as shown by Fig1.

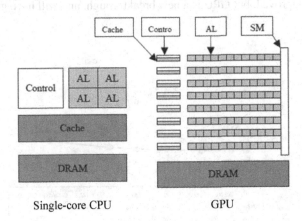

Fig. 1. Hardware Architecture of CPU and GPU

The architecture of the CPU is designed following the principle that executing instructions in parallel and computing data in parallel, which takes into account the parallelism, versatility, their balance of program execution and data operations, so CPU is the most complex chip in computer. Compare to GPU, there are not much repeat designed parts, but the complexity comes from the realization, such as program branch prediction, speculative execution, the implementation of multiple nested branch, relativity of instruction and data when execute instruction and operate data, consistency of multi-core co-processing, and some other complex logic.

GPU is actually a collection of hardware that realizes a set of graphics functions, which are mainly used in the computation for graphic render, including Pixels drawing, light and shadow processing and 3D coordinate transformation. Graphics computation is characterized by the data-intensive computation, and architecture of GPU is designed to fit numerical operation of the matrix data, a large number of re-designed computing units, such operation can be divided into many independent numerical computing threads without logical relativity like the program execution.

3.2   Comparison of CPU and GPU Computation Capacity

GPU has separate memory system, which has much higher bandwidth than the system memory. When GPU works, the work load transferred from the CPU into GPU memory thought the PCI-E bus, according to the level of the architecture in top-down distribution. In PCI-E 2.0 specification, the data transmission speed of each channel has reached 5.0Gbit / s, and 16 slots can provide 5.0×16Gbit /s=10GB/s, while effective bandwidth can reach 8GB / s, because of effect of PCI-E data packet, the actual bandwidth available is about 5-6GB / s.

The GPU's performance of floating-point operations and parallel computation is far better than CPU's, as described by graph 2. So Making the GPU as a CPU's coprocessor that executes floating-point operation can improve the computation capacity of PC very much. If you consider a deeper level, the CPU has encountered a bottleneck, whether the efficiency or the number of cores is difficult to obtain significantly improved, but GPU is a new breakthrough, and will have great potential.

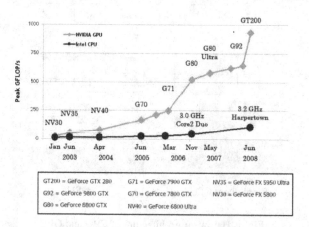

Fig. 2. Comparison of CPU and GPU Computation Capacity

3.3   Application of GPGPU in Parallel Simulation

The rapid development of GPGPU especially the appearance of "CPU+GPU"mode, making GPGPU gradually applied in all areas of scientific computation, such as FFT (Fast Fourier Transform)[2], string matching algorithms[3], scientific visualization[4], real-time infrared image generation[5], genetic algorithm acceleration[6], database operations[7]. The simulation field involves a large number of high-performance parallel computations, such as, the simulation of the electromagnetic environment, the solution of higher order differential equations, the simulation data processing, large-scale combat simulation and so on, they can all involve the GPGPU to solve specific questions.

4   Design of Parallel Simulation Algorithm with GPGPU

The essence of acceleration based on GPU is CPU and GPU heterogeneous parallel computation, and the design of algorithm divided into following three steps: pre-assessment, design and optimization.

4.1   Pre-assessment

Not all parallel simulation algorithms are suitable to be complied and run on the GPU, so before designing the algorithm, some evaluation should be done.

(1) Does the Data Accuracy Meet the Need of Simulation?

At present, the floating-point operation of GPU uses the IEEE 754-1985 standard, when executing MAD instructions, GPU will cut out the very small mantissa in multiply operation and make rounding operation in the subsequent add computation. Compared to CPU, the error of MAD single-precision floating operation of GPU, and the double-precision arithmetic unit which is far less than single-precision arithmetic unit, can only provide one tenth or one eighth double-precision operations capacity relative to single-precision floating operation. In summary, the current GPU cannot be achieved the simulation algorithm with high accuracy.

(2) Can the Expected Performance Increase Be Acquired?

First, computational performance of transplanted algorithm should be considered, if it has a good performance when running on CPU in serial mode, it is difficult to improve performance in parallel mode on GPU. The heterogeneous computation of CPU and GPU is actually a process that CPU products data while GPU consumes data, who result in performance decreased brought by communication between each other, and the shorter time spent on by arithmetic execution, the effect is more serious, the extreme situation is the cost of communication exceed to the performance improvements of GPU computation, leading to performance decreased not increased. Second, the proportion of parallel part of transplanted algorithm should be observed, however the parallel part of the algorithm speed up, the speedup will not exceed the constant value that parallel part divide serial. Therefore, if the limit can't meet the requirements of the algorithm, it is not suitable for direct parallelization, acquiring other solution.

4.2   Algorithm Design

(1) Task Division

The serial simulation algorithm should be divided into two parts, parallel part executed by GPU and serial part executed by CPU, then the parallel part need to more division that using data partitioning for data-intensive algorithms while computation partitioning for the numerical algorithm. In addition, it is common that serial processing algorithm running on CPU may not be suitable for GPU and data structure on CPU may not fit GPU and its parallel processing, the results of task division is the distinguish between a number of CPU processing steps and several GPU core procedures.

(2)Thread Mapping

The thread function should be designed according to thread blocks structure, when simulation algorithm is transferred to the GPU, and distribute the computation task to thread in blocks, differing from coarse MIMD of CPU, GPU thread execution model is SIMD, that same instructions operate the different data. Using Warp or Half-Warp which is the width of the instruction stream multiprocessor to do thread-task mapping, can obtain high efficiency in most cases.

4.3   Performance Optimization

(1) Memory Access Optimization

Memory bandwidth is the most important performance bottleneck in GPGPU, whose goal is to handle large-scale problem, so accessing to the global memory frequently is not avoid, as a result, the condition that aligning first address and accessing to address continuous is first thing t to consider, when assessing global memory, whether to meet the merge assess will lead to large affects to algorithm efficiency. In addition, in order to tilt to the general purpose computing, the GPU provides a multi-level memory, which accelerated obviously general purpose computing is shared memory, texture memory and constant memory. There are no uniform optimized rules, and different algorithms need designed different data reuse strategy according to the characteristics of the problem characteristics and storage characteristics data reuse strategy. Memory access optimization is the key and difficult points of the GPU performance optimization.

(2) Communication Optimization

Most of GPU is connected to CPU by PCI-E bus, which is far less than the GPU chip memory and the GPU chip memory bandwidth, thus, GPU is more suitable for dealing with iterative computation, that once the data upload, it can by use repeated by GPU, so as to fully reduce the communication overhead between CPU and GPU.

(3) Instruction Stream Optimization

Streaming Multiprocessors of GPU read instruction for each thread in the warp, then execute them, and finally write calculated results to memory in the warp. Therefore, the effective instruction throughput depends not only on theoretical instruction throughput but also the memory latency and bandwidth. Following means could be taken to increase instruction throughput.

- Avoid the use of low throughput instructions;
- Optimizing each type of memory to use bandwidth effectively;
- Trying to use more mathematical calculation to cover the access latency, while ensuring each stream processor to have enough active threads.

The algorithm design and performance optimization of GPGPU are not isolated, for example, the merger of the global memory access restricts the way of data storage and the division of tasks, task partitioning also affect thread instruction stream. Thus, in practice, the CPU and GPU heterogeneous parallel simulation algorithm can first design a usable version, based on which, don't make iterative improvement untie achieve the desired results.

5   Trajectory Simulation with GPGPU

Trajectory simulation is ubiquitous in the combat simulation, and it is a typical question of solution of higher order differential equations, because of its strong representation, it is chosen to validate the acceleration of GPGPU, using Runge-Kutta algorithm to solve two order differential equations of Trajectory as follow.

$$\frac{dv_x}{dt} = -CH(y)F(v)\cos\theta = -C\prod(y)F(v)\cos\theta\,\tau_{0N}/\tau \tag{1}$$

$$\frac{dv_y}{dt} = -CH(y)F(v)\sin\theta - g = -C\prod(y)F(v)\sin\theta\,\tau_{0N}/\tau - g \tag{2}$$

$$\frac{dx}{dt} = v_x \tag{3}$$

$$\frac{dy}{dt} = v_y \tag{4}$$

$$v = \sqrt{v_x^2 + v_y^2} \tag{5}$$

$$\theta = tg^{-1}\frac{v_y}{v_x} \tag{6}$$

The experiments run on a GeForce G210m graphics adapter and Intel Core2Duo clocked at 2.2G Hz with CUDA SDK and C compiler environment, and the execution time of GPU include data operation and the data exchange between dedicated graphics memory and main memory. In experiment, the execution time of CPU and GPU are compared through changing the number of Trajectory.

When the number of trajectory is less than 1024, GPU execution speed is not fast than CPU, and the data-intensive computation advantage of GPU didn't taken out.

When the trajectory number is greater than 1024, the GPU acceleration benefits begin to appear, GPU acceleration benefits more and more obviously with the increase of trajectory number, mainly due to large-scale and high-throughput data operations can hide the delay caused by accessing memory and transferring data.

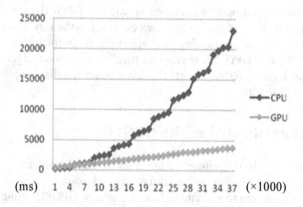

Fig. 3. Execution time of experiment

6   Conclusions

With the rapid increase of computation capacity of GPU with relative software platform support, high performance computation has gradually entered the desktop platform, for the common scientific and technical personnel, HPC is no longer beyond the reach. With the help of this cost-effective computation resource, many simulation computation questions seems unable to solve can be solved in another way.

References

1. Nvidia. NVIDIA CUDA Compute Unified Device Architechture Programming Guide [OL] (2008)
2. Wu, E.-H.: The Technology Status and Challenge of GPGPU. Software Paper 15(10), 1493–1504 (2004)
3. Xiao, J.: Ability Test for Matrix-Multiplication and FFT Based on CUDA. Computer Engineering 35(10) (2009)
4. Zhang, Q.-D.: Research on String Matching Algorithms Based on GPU. Computer Application 26(7), 7 (2006)
5. Mao, H.-Q.: The Research on the 3D Real-time Rendering Optimized Base on GPU, p. 3. Wuhan University (2010)
6. Li, Y.: The Research of Real-time Infrared Image Generation Based on GPU. Xi'An University of Electronic Science & Technology (2007)
7. Yang, Z.-L.: Acceleration Algorithm of Electromagnetic calculation Based on GPU. Electronic Paper 35(6), 6 (2007)
8. Tan, C.-F.: Research on the Parallel Implementation of Genetic Algorithm on CUDA Platform. Computer Engineering & Science (2009)

Quantization Based Real-Time Simulation
of Continuous System in Distributed Environment

Wei Zhang and Jiangyun Wang

School of Automation Science and Electrical Engineering, Beihang University,
100191Beijing, China

Abstract. Continuous system must be discretized for computer simulation.
There is a kind of methods such as QSS method that discretizes the continuous
system based on the discretization of the state space except the classical methods
such as Euler, Runge-Kutta, etc. It is proved that the quantization based method
would reduce the redundant caculation while guarantee the accuracy. It has
always been proved that QSS method would guarantee the stability and
convergence under some conditions. QSS method discretizes the continuous
system to discrete-event model and each model could be treated as a federate in
HLA. The real-time simulation in HLA is supported by a special federate called
RTFederate. At last, an example would be introduced to prove the method.

Keywords: QSS method, distributed simulation, continuous system, real-time
simulation.

1 Introduction

This paper mainly researches on a method for the real-time simulation of continuous
system in HLA distributed environment. Continuous system must be discretized for
computer simulation. Classical methods such as Euler, Runge-Kutta are based on the
discretization of time and this would cause redundant caculation when the system state
variables change slowly.

Another way to do the discretization is based on the discretization of state space such
as QSS method. QSS method is a variable step method without iterated caculation. It
would reduce the redundant caculation while guarantee the accuracy and when used in
distributed simulation the community would be simple.

The paper uses QSS method for continuous system discretization and mainly
researches on a way to keep the real-time synchronization in HLA distributed
simulation environment.

2 QSS Method

Consider a continuous system model

$$\begin{cases} \dot{x}(t) = f\big(x(t), u(t)\big) \\ y(t) = g\big(x(t), u(t)\big) \end{cases} \tag{1}$$

T. Xiao, L. Zhang, and M. Fei (Eds.): AsiaSim 2012, Part II, CCIS 324, pp. 363–369, 2012.

$x(t)$ represents a set of state variables, $u(t)$ represents a set of input variables, $\dot{x}(t)$ represents a set of state derivate variables, $y(t)$ represents a set of output variables, $f(\bullet)$ represents the state transform function, $g(\bullet)$ represents the output function.

$$q(t) = \begin{cases} d_{i+1} & if \quad x(t^-) = d_{i+1} \wedge i < r \\ d_{i-1} & if \quad x(t^-) = d_i - \varepsilon \wedge i > 0 \\ d_i & otherwise \end{cases} \tag{2}$$

Define a set of quantizated state variables $q(t)$ fits (2).

Let $D = \{d_0, d_1, ..., d_r\}$ be a set of real number where $d_i < d_{i+1}$ with i be a nonnegative integer and if the quantum Δq be a constant number then $d_i - d_{i-1} = \Delta q$ would also be a constant number. ε represents a small hysteresis, article [2] proves the necessity to use it.

Substitute $x(t)$ on the right side of the equal mark in (1) with $q(t)$. The approximated model is as (3) shows.

$$\begin{cases} \dot{x}(t) = f(q(t), u(t)) \\ y(t) = g(q(t), u(t)) \end{cases} \tag{3}$$

It has been proved in article [1] that if $u(t)$ have piecewise constant and bounded trajectories and $f(\bullet)$ is continuous and bounded in any bounded domain, then $q(t)$ have piecewise constant trajectories, $\dot{x}(t)$ also have piecewise constant trajectories, $x(t)$ have continuous piecewise linear trajectories and $y(t)$ have piecewise constant trajectories.

3   Real-Time Simulation of Continuous System in HLA

3.1   RTFederate Module

This special module is created to support real-time simulation. It would be an independent federate in HLA. The time management mode would be set on Constrained and Regulation.

RTFederate mainly has three parts: Time Memory, Real Timer and RTI Interface. Time Memory need to set a least time step defined as T_{min}, it would be a positive integer.

RTFederate module would get the allowed advance time from RTI through RTI Interface and then add it to the Time Memory. If the value T in Time Memory is smaller than T_{min}, Time Memory would request time advance with T_{min} through RTI

Interface. Otherwise, Time Memory would transfer the value T to Real Timer and then reset the value T to zero. Real Timer would count $\lfloor T \rfloor$ of unit time. $\lfloor T \rfloor$ means the largest integer which is smaller than T. At the end of the count, Real Timer would request time advance with T_{min} through RTI Interface.

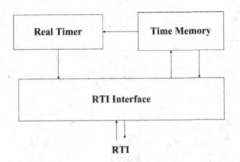

Fig. 1. The structure of RTFederate module

3.2   Real-Time Simulation

Each of the subsystems would be discretized with QSS method and be treated as a federate in HLA. The time management mode of all of the federates would be set on Constrained and Regulation as RTFederate module does. In HLA RTI would allow time advance only if all of the federates under that mode request and the least requested time step would be allowed. Figure 2 shows the procedure of time advance.

Especially, only if RTFederate request, RTI would allow time advance. So the simulation speed would be controlled by RTFederate module and then it would support real-time simulation.

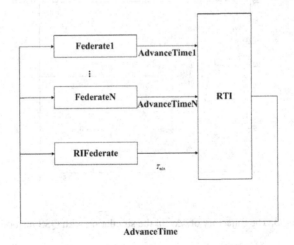

Fig. 2. The procedure of time advance

4   Example

Consider a plane vertical control system as (6) shows

$$
\begin{bmatrix} \dfrac{d\Delta\bar{v}}{dt} \\ \dfrac{d\Delta\alpha}{dt} \\ \dfrac{d\Delta\theta}{dt} \\ \dfrac{d\Delta q}{dt} \end{bmatrix} = \begin{bmatrix} -X_v & -X_\alpha & -X_\theta & 0 \\ -Z_v & -Z_\alpha & 0 & 1 \\ 0 & 0 & 0 & 1 \\ -M_v + M_\alpha Z_v & -M_\alpha + M_\alpha Z_\alpha & 0 & -M_q - M_\alpha \end{bmatrix} \begin{bmatrix} \Delta\bar{v} \\ \Delta\alpha \\ \Delta\theta \\ \Delta q \end{bmatrix} \tag{6}
$$
$$
+ \begin{bmatrix} -X_{\delta_T} & 0 \\ 0 & -Z_{\delta_e} \\ 0 & 0 \\ -M_{\delta_T} & -M_{\delta_e} + M_\alpha Z_{\delta_e} \end{bmatrix} \begin{bmatrix} \Delta\delta_T \\ \Delta\delta_e \end{bmatrix}
$$

The input variables are the angle of the elevator $\Delta\delta_e$ and the thrust control $\Delta\delta_T$. The output variables are the changed speed of the plane $\Delta\bar{v}$, the angle of attack $\Delta\alpha$ and the pitch angle $\Delta\theta$.

The system is discretized with QSS method, the quantum is 0.001 and so as the hysteresis, initial conditions are $\Delta\bar{v} = \Delta\alpha = \Delta\theta = \Delta q = 0$, $\Delta\delta_e = 2°$, $\Delta\delta_T = 0°$. Figure 3 showes the trajectory of $\Delta\bar{v}$, x axes represents the caculation times, y axes represents the value of $\Delta\bar{v}$.

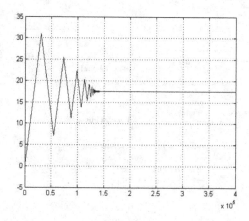

Fig. 3. The trajectory of $\Delta\bar{v}$ in the simulation with QSS method

Table 1 showes the step time around the first peak value and table 2 showes the step time in relative stable value. As the value of $\Delta\bar{v}$ getting closed with the peak value, the step grew bigger. Compare table 1 and table 2, it is apparently that when the trajectory went into a relative state the step got bigger. The result proves that the QSS method reduces the redundant caculation and improves the simulation efficiency.

Table 1. The step time around the first peak value

StepTime(s)	0.001475	0.001476	0.001477	...	0.010535	0.010806
$\Delta\bar{v}$	30.0008	30.0018	30.0028	...	31	31.001

Table 2. The step time in relative stable value

StepTime(s)	0.247985	0.482912	0.147666	0.180637	0.3733	0.252046
$\Delta\bar{v}$	17.51415	17.51515	17.51517	17.51496	17.51419	17.51373

For comparison, the paper also simulated the system with classical method as four order Runge-Kutta method and the step was fixed at 0.001.

Figure 4 showes the result. x axes represents the simulation time and y axes represents the value of $\Delta\bar{v}$.

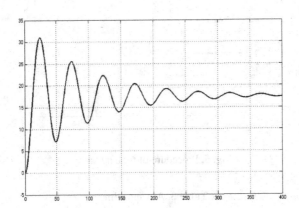

Fig. 4. The trajectory of $\Delta\bar{v}$ in the simulation with Runge-Kutta

In Figure 4 one unit time means 1000 caculation times as the step be set at 0.001. Afterabout 300 of unit time the trajectory reached the relative stable value, it needed $300\times1000 = 300000$ times of caculation and to reach the same value, simulation with QSS method just needed about 140000 times of caculation. The comparision also proves that QSS method could reduce the redundant caculation and improve the simulation efficiency.

To be simulated in distributed environment each of the state variables would be treated as a federate and in addition with RTFederate module it has five federates in total.

Federate1: $\dfrac{d\Delta\bar{v}}{dt} = -X_v \cdot \Delta\bar{v} - X_\alpha \cdot \Delta\alpha - X_\theta \cdot \Delta\theta - X_{\delta_T} \cdot \Delta\delta_T$

Federate2: $\dfrac{d\Delta\alpha}{dt} = -Z_v \cdot \Delta\bar{v} - Z_\alpha \cdot \Delta\alpha + \Delta q - Z_{\delta_e} \cdot \Delta\delta_e$

Federate3: $\dfrac{d\Delta\theta}{dt} = \Delta q$

Federate4: $\dfrac{d\Delta q}{dt} = (-M_v + M_{\dot{\alpha}}Z_v) \cdot \Delta\bar{v} + (-M_\alpha + M_{\dot{\alpha}}Z_\alpha) \cdot \Delta\alpha$
$\qquad\qquad - (M_q + M_{\dot{\alpha}}) \cdot \Delta q - M_{\delta_T} \cdot \Delta\delta_T + (M_{\dot{\alpha}}Z_{\delta_e} - M_{\delta_e}) \cdot \Delta\delta_e$

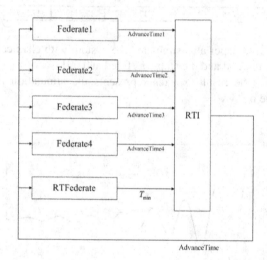

Fig. 5. Procedure of time advance

Table 3. Advance time

AdvanceTime1	∞	21.4062	13.1519	...	0.0085	0.0082
AdvanceTime2	0.3846	0.2787	0.2188	...	0.0085	0.0082
AdvanceTime3	0.3846	0.2787	0.2188	...	0.0085	0.0082
AdvanceTime4	0.0036	0.0036	0.0037	...	0.0085	0.0082
T_{min}	0.01	0.01	0.01	...	0.01	0.01
AdvanceTime	0.0036	0.0036	0.0037	...	0.0085	0.0082

Table 4. Allowed advance time

caculation point	0	1	2	3	4
StepTime(s)	0.003605	0.003633	0.003662	0.003691	0.003722

Figure 5 showes the procedure of time advance and table 3 shows the advance time list. In first step Federate 1 request time advance with ∞, Federate 2 request time advance with 0.3846 and so as Federate 3, Federate 4 request time advance with 0.0036, T_{min} is set at 0.01, so least of them, 0.0036, would be the allowed advance time.

Table 4 showes the allowed advance time in first five steps. As $T_{min} = 0.01$, the initial allowed advance time is 0.003605 which is smaller than T_{min}, so that value would be added into the Time Memory in RTFederate module and the time advance procedure goes on. The third allowed advance time is 0.003662, the value would be added to the Time Memory and then $T = T + 0.003662$, as $T = 0.01087 > T_{min}$ Time Memory would transfer T to Real Timer to do the time count and reset T to zero. The unit real time step in Real Timer is $0.001s$,so T would be modified as $T = T \times 1000$, the Real Timer would count $\lfloor T \rfloor = 10ms$ and then the time advance procedure goes on.

5   Conclusions

The paper discretizes the continuous system using QSS method which is based on the quantization of the state space to improve the simulation efficiency. QSS method transforms the continuous system to the discrete-event model. The paper introduces a method to support the real-time simulation in HLA distributed environment. QSS method guarantees the stability and convergence under some conditions and so it is not adapted to all the continuous system simulation. It is needed to extend the application range in the future.

References

1. Kofman, E., Junco, S.: Quantized StateSystems. A DEVS approach for continuoussystem simulation. Technical ReportLSD0004, LSD, FCEIA, UNR (2000); To appear in Transactions of SCS
2. Kofman, E.: A Third Order Discrete Event SimulationMethod for Continuous System Simulation. Latin American Applied Research 36(2), 101–108 (2006)
3. Zeigler, B., Kim, T.G., Praehofer, H.: Theory ofModeling and Simulation, 2nd edn. Academic Press, New York (2000)
4. Zeigler, B., Lee, J.S.: Theory ofquantized systems: formal basis for DEVS/HLAdistributed simulation environment. In: SPIE Proceedings, vol. 3369, pp. 49–58 (1998)
5. Kofman, E.: Discrete Event Simulation of Hybrid Systems. Technical Report LSD0205, LSD, UNR (2002); SIAM Journal on Scientific Computing 25, 1771–1797 (2004)

Modified Self-adaptive Strategy
for Controlling Parameters in Differential Evolution

Tam Bui[1], Hieu Pham[1], and Hiroshi Hasegawa[2]

[1] Graduate School of Engineering and Science,
Shibaura Institute of Technology, Japan
tambn-sme@mail.hut.edu.vn, pnh112@gmail.com
[2] College of Systems Engineering and Science,
Shibaura Institute of Technology, Japan
h-hase@shibaura-it.ac.jp

Abstract. In this paper, we propose a new technical to modify the self-adaptive Strategy for Controlling Parameters in Differential Evolution algorithm (MSADE). The DE algorithm has been used in many practical cases and has demonstrated good convergence properties. It has only a few control parameters as NP (Number of Particles), F (scaling factor) and CR (crossover), which are kept fixed throughout the entire evolutionary process. However, these control parameters are very sensitive to the setting of the control parameters based on their experiments. The value of control parameters depend on the characteristics of each objective function, so we have to tune their value in each problem that mean it will take too long time to perform. We present a new version of the DE algorithm for obtaining self-adaptive control parameter settings that show good performance on numerical benchmark problems.

Keywords: Differential Evolution (DE), Global search, Multi-peak problems, Local search.

1   Introduction

Deferential evolution DE is an optimization technique originally proposed by Storn and Price [1]. In DE, new individuals are generated by mutation and crossover, which uses the variance within the population to guide the choice of new search points. Although DE is very powerful, DE sometime falls into local optimum and has a slow convergence speed in the last period of iterations. The aim of this work is to modify self-adaptive the scaling factor F by ranking the population and applying formula of sigmoid function depend on the rank number of population size to estimate the F value. The results show that our algorithm with modified self-adaptive control parameter settings is better than or at least comparable to the standard DE algorithm and evolutionary algorithms from literature when considering the quality of the solutions obtained. All the algorithms are applied to the some benchmark functions and compared based on some different metrics.

T. Xiao, L. Zhang, and M. Fei (Eds.): AsiaSim 2012, Part II, CCIS 324, pp. 370–378, 2012.

The section 2 gives a briefly introduce to the DE and related work of DE. Section 3 describes MSADE. Section 4 evaluates the Performance of MSADE on the six benchmark test functions and experiment results. A few conclusions are given in Section 5.

2   Review of DE and Related Work

2.1   Differential Evolution (DE)

Differential evolution (DE), proposed by Storn and Price [1], is a very popular evolutionary algorithm (EA). Like other EAs, DE is a population-based stochastic search technique. It uses mutation, crossover, and selection operators at each generation to move its population toward the global optimum minimum. At each generation G, DE creates a mutant vector $v_i^G = \left(v_{i,1}^G, v_{i,2}^G \dots v_{i,D}^G \right)$ for each individual x_i^G (called a target vector) in the current population.

In this paper, we will use DE/target-to-best/1 mutation scheme as follow.

$$v_{i,j}^{G+1} = x_{i,j}^G + F*(x_{best}^G - x_{i,j}^G) + F*(x_{r_1,j}^G - x_{r_2,j}^G) \tag{1}$$

where r_1 and r_2 are distinct integers randomly selected from the range [1, NP] and are also different from i. The parameter F is called the scaling factor, which amplifies the difference vectors. x_{best} is the best individual in the current population.

After mutating, DE performs a binomial crossover operator on x_i^G and v_i^G to generate a trial vector $u_i^G = \left(u_{i,1}^G, u_{i,2}^G \dots u_{i,D}^G \right)$.

$$u_{i,j}^{G+1} = \begin{cases} v_{i,j}^{G+1} & if \ rand_{i,j} \le CR \ or \ j == j_{rand} \\ x_{i,j}^G & otherwise \end{cases} \tag{2}$$

where i = 1, ..., NP, j = 1, ..., D , j_{rand} is a randomly chosen integer in [1, D], $rand_j$ (0, 1) is a uniformly distributed random number between 0 and 1 which is
Generated for each j, and CR $\in$ [0, 1] is called the crossover control parameter. Due to the use of j_{rand}, the trial vector u_i^G differs from target vector x_i^G.

The selection operator is performed to select the better one between the target vector x_i^G and the trial vector u_i^G to enter the next generation.

$$x_i^{G+1} = \begin{cases} u_i^{G+1} & if \ f(u_i^{G+1}) \le f(x_i^G) \\ x_i^G & otherwise \end{cases} \tag{3}$$

DE Algorithm: Require: Max_iter, Number of particles
NP, Crossover constant CR, and Scaling factor F.
Begin
1: Initialize the population.

$$x_i^G = lb_j + rand_j*(ub_j - lb_j)$$

(4)

$rand_j$ a random number in [0,1].
2: Evaluate the population.

3: For each individual x_i^G do.

4: Mutation: DE creates a mutation vector v_i^G in (1).

5: Crossover: DE creates a trial vector u_i^G in (2).

6: Apply Greedy Selection: To decide whether or not it
should become a member of next generation, the trial
u_i^G is compared to target vector x_i^G in (3).

7: Memorize the best solution found so far.
8: Repeat 2 to 7 until terminal condition.
9: return best solution.
End.

2.2   Related Work of DE

This section reviews some papers that compare a different extension of DE with the
original DE. After that, we concentrate on papers that deal with parameter control in
DE.

There have been many research works on controlling search parameters of DE. DE
Control parameters include the population size NP, the scaling factor F, and the
crossover control parameter CR.

Storn and Price [1] argued that these three control parameters are not difficult to set
for obtaining good performance. They suggested that NP should be between 5D and
10D, F should be 0.5 as a good initial choice and the value of F smaller than 0.4 or
larger than 1.0 will lead to performance degradation, and CR can be set to 0.1 or 0.9.

J.Teo [9] proposed an attempt to dynamic self-adaptive populations in differential
evolution, in addition to self-adapting crossover and mutation rates; they showed that
DE with self-adaptive populations produced highly competitive results compared to a
conventional DE algorithm with static populations.

J.Brest [2] presented another variant of DE algorithms SaDE, which uses different
self-adaptive mechanisms applied on the control parameters: The step length F and
crossover rate CR are produce factors F and CR in a new parent vector.

$$F_i^{G+1} = \begin{cases} F_l + rand_1 * F_u & if \ rand_2 \leq \tau_1 \\ F_i^G & otherwise \end{cases}$$

(5)

$$CR_i^{G+1} = \begin{cases} rand_3 * & if \ rand_4 \leq \tau_2 \\ CR_i^G & otherwise \end{cases}$$

(6)

where $rand_1$, $rand_2$, $rand_3$ and $rand_4$ are uniform random values $\in [0, 1]$. τ_1 and τ_2 represent probabilities to adjust factors F and CR, respectively. Author set $\tau_1=\tau_2=0.1$. Because $F_l = 0.1$ and $F_u = 0.9$, the new takes a value from $[0.1, 0.9]$ in a random manner. The new CR takes a value from $[0, 1]$. F_i^{G+1} and CR_i^{G+1} are obtained before the mutation process.

In the Brest [2], the F and CR value are achieved by (5) and (6), the main point of this problem is using the randomly principle to produce F and CR value for each individual in each iteration. Because Brest [3] used the randomly principle in (5) and (6), it does not know how that method is reliable and do not have any theory to explain why that approach can get good convergence? Overcome this problem, we should develop a new method to adaptive control parameter and this method is more stable, next section will introduce MSADE.

3   Modified Self-adapting Parameters – New Version of DE Algorithm

In the multi-point search of the DE, individuals move from their current points to new search points in the design space of design variables. For example, as shown in Fig.1, the individual A requires a slight change to the values of the design variables to obtain the global optimum solution. On the other hand, individual B cannot reach a global optimum solution without a significant change, and in addition, individual C has landed in a local optimum solution. Such a situation, in which the good individual and the low individual are intermingled, can generally occur at any time in this search process. Therefore, we have to recognize each individual's situation and propose a suitable design variables generation process for each individual's situation in the design space.

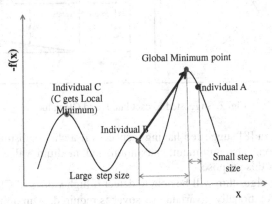

Fig. 1. Example of individual situations

In The MSADE method, the distance for a search point can be changed by controlling the F factor for determining the neighborhood range. To do this, H.Hasegawa and S.Tooyama [10] proposed APGA/VNC approach in which author used sigmoid function to control neighborhood parameter. In this paper, we will sort all the individuals by estimating their fitness and then rank them by these sorting results show in Figure 2. A ranked individual is labeled with this rank number and assigned F that corresponds with this number. The formula for the F (Scalar factor) by sigmoid function as follows.

$$F_i^G = \frac{1}{1+\exp(\alpha * \dfrac{i-\dfrac{NP}{2}}{NP})} \quad with \ F^{LB} \le F_i^G \le F^{UB} \tag{7}$$

$$\begin{cases} F_i^G = F^{UB} & if \ F_i^G \ge F^{UB} \\ F_i^G = F^{LB} & if \ F_i^G \le F^{LB} \end{cases} \tag{8}$$

where α, i, NP, F^{LB}, and F^{UB} denote the gain of the sigmoid function, particle of ith in NP, Number of Particles, the lower boundary condition of the F, and the upper boundary condition of the F, respectively. From our experiment we assign F^{LB}=0.15, and F^{UB} =0.95.

The gait of F chart depends on the sign and gain of α Fig.2. When individual at good fitness same as individual A in Fig.1 will have small step size of F factor and otherwise with individual B. From this view, the MSADE method automatically adapts F factor to obtain design variable generation accuracy for each individual's situation and individual's fitness. As a result, we believe that it will steadily provide a global optimum solution and reduce the calculation cost.

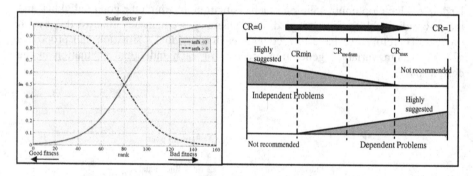

Fig. 2. Suggested to caculate F and CR values

G.Reynoso-Meza [8] suggested having a success if a child substitutes its parent in the next generation. The minimum, maximum and medium value on such set of success is used for this purpose.

In this way, the algorithm will be able to detect if high values of CR are useful, and furthermore, if a rotationally invariant crossover is required. A minimum base for CR around its median value is incorporated to avoid stagnation around a single value, Fig.2 shows this principle, and so we propose the ideas behind this adaptive mechanism for the crossover:

The control parameter CR is adapted as follows:

$$CR_i^{G+1} = \begin{cases} rand_2 * & if \quad rand_1 \leq \tau \\ CR_i^{G} & otherwise \end{cases} \tag{9}$$

where: $rand_1$ and $rand_2$ are uniform random values $\in [0, 1]$, τ represents probabilities to adjust CR, same as [2] we assign $\tau = 0.10$.

After that we adjust CR as follows:

$$\begin{cases} CR_i^{G+1} = CR_{min} & if \quad CR_{min} \leq CR_i^{G+1} \leq CR_{medium} \\ CR_i^{G+1} = CR_{max} & if \quad CR_{medium} \leq CR_i^{G+1} \leq CR_{max} \end{cases} \tag{10}$$

where: CR_{min}, CR_{medium} and CR_{max} denote the low value, median value and high value of crossover parameter respectively. From our experiment in many trials, we assign $CR_{min}=0.10$, $CR_{medium}=0.50$ and $CR_{max}=0.95$.

The purpose of our approach is that user does not need to tune the good values for F and CR, which are problem dependent. The rules for Modified self-adapting control parameters are quite simple; therefore, the new version of the DE algorithm does not increase the time complexity, in comparison to the original DE algorithm.

4   Experiments

In this section, the first experiment is to be test for turning the α parameter MSADE, after that test in comparing the robustness of the MSADE method with some reference methods as: SaDE Brest [2], PSO J.Kenedy and ABC D.Karaboga. These experiments are performed 30 trials for every function.

4.1   Benchmark Functions

To estimate the stability and convergence to the optimal solution of MSADE, We will use 6 benchmark functions with 20 dimensions.

4.2   Test to Get Good Value of α in MSADE

As mention above we know that the gait of sigmoid function is depend on the sign and value of α, Fig.2 shows the relationship of F and Rank depend on the α. In this section, we test to get best value of α. Number of Population $NP = 160$, Maximum iteration Max_Iter = 3000, accurate $\alpha = 10^{-6}$, $\tau = 0.1$ and alpha value $\alpha = -20 \div 20$.

As in Fig. 3, the solutions of all the benchmark functions with 20 dimensions reach their global optimum solutions with accurate $\varepsilon = 10^{-6}$. However, the result of $\alpha < 0$ is better than that of $\alpha > 0$. The SP, AC, and GR function are good with α from -10 to 10 but with RO, RI and RA function is not good at that value, from -10 to 20 maybe they are not change when we change α value, for best value of all function we will choose $\alpha = -10$ for next test.

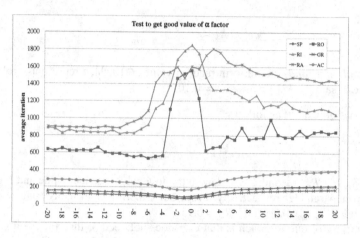

Fig. 3. Result of test to get good value of α

4.3   MSADE and Some Approaches Are Compared in This Test with Same Accurate

Population size was NP=160, and accurate ε=10^{-6} compare the iteration, τ = 0.1, max_iter = 5000, at which the optimum is satisfy. If the success rate of the optimal solution was not 100% - is shown in Table 1.

Table 1. Average of iterations requred by MSADE and some approaches

Function	PSO	ABC	SaDE	MSADE
SP	1029.03	288.00	150.13	**139.67**
RO	-	-	1281.80	**596.20**
RI	-	-	2264.00	**841.33**
GR	932.07	247.37	118.27	**106.67**
RA	-	565.83	2825.50	1537.27
SP	1290.90	524.53	278.13	**256.17**

As in Table.1, the MSADE gets global optimum at less iteration than that of SaDE in all functions.The MSADE is also better than PSO and ABC in converange speed and stability.

4.4   Test with Maximum Iteration Compares the Mean of Global Minimum and Std (Standard Deviation)

In this experiment we will test with NP= 160, D = 20 dimensions, τ = 0.1 and max_iter=1500 for each function as in table 2.

As in table 2, the result test shows that the average of fitness value and std of MSADE is better than SaDE. In comparison with other approaches PSO and ABC, MSADE is good result for three functions SP, RI and RO, ABC is good at two functions GR and RA, SaDE good at AC function from this view we can conclude that MSADE is outstanding in all approaches.

Table 2. Average of global minimum and the standard deviation

Function	PSO		ABC		SaDE		MSADE	
	mean	std	mean	std	mean	std	mean	std
SP	5.92E-56	2.40E-55	1.75E-37	1.73E-37	6.80E-71	8.52E-71	**2.25E-77**	0.1
RO	14.70	24.80	0.68	1.00	2.07E-08	9.40E-08	**0**	0
RI	6.49E+03	5.03E+03	2680.0	648.0	0.00181	0.00226	**1.04E-10**	2.90E-10
GR	3.33E-17	5.09E-17	**0**	0	1.11E-16	2.47E-32	1.37E-16	4.70E-17
RA	11.90	4.85	**0**	0	7.61	1.59	0.03	0.09
SP	7.43E-15	1.94E-15	7.67E-15	6.38E-16	**7.31E-15**	8.86E-16	1.35E-14	3.70E-15

Fig.4 and Fig.5 shows the convergence graph of some benchmark functions, the convergence Rosenbrock, Ridge and Ratrigin function the convergence of MSADE method is better than that of SaDE method.

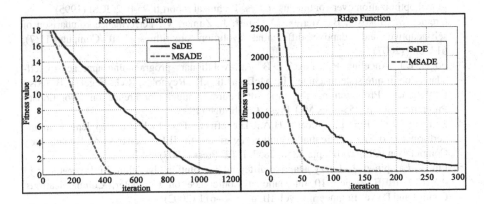

Fig. 4. Convergence graph of Rosenbrock and Ridge functions

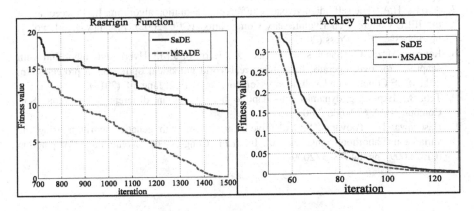

Fig. 5. Convergence graph of Rastrigin and Ackley functions

5 Conclusions

In this paper, a new modified of self-adaptive differential evolution is proposed for solving global optimization problems. The main idea is to change the scalar factor F by sigmoid function after ranking population in their fitness value and adjust the control parameter CR to balance the abilities of DE in exploitation and exploration. Six benchmark functions are used to validate the performance of the MSADE compared to SaDE. The results show that MSADE outperforms both in most function minimization. The results are also proved that the convergence speed of MSADE is faster that SaDE.

References

1. Storn, R., Price, K.: Differential evolution - a simple and efficient adaptive scheme for global optimization over continuous spaces. Technical report tr-95-012, ICSI (1995)
2. Greiner, S., Bokovic, B., Mernik, M., Brest, J., Zumer, V.: Performance comparison of self-adaptive and adaptive differential evolution algorithms. Soft Computer 11(7), 617–629 (2007)
3. Fogel, L.J., Angeline, P.J., Fogel, D.B.: An evolutionary programming approach to self-adaptation in nite state machines. In: McDonnell, J.R., Reynolds, R.G., Fogel, D.B. (eds.) Evolutionary Programming IV: Proc. of Fourth Annual Conference on Evolutionary Programming, pp. 355–365. MIT Press, Cambridge (1995)
4. Soliman, O.S., Bui, L., Abbass, H.A.: The effect of a stochastic step length on the performance of the differential evolution algorithm. In: IEEE Congress on Evolutionary Computation (CEC 2007), pp. 2850–2857. IEEE Press (2007)
5. Liu, J., Lampinen, J.: Fuzzy adaptive differential evolution algorithm. In: Proceedings of the 17th IEEE Region 10 International Conference on Computer, Communications, Control and Power Engineering, vol. III, pp. 606–611 (2002)
6. Price, K.V.: An introduction to differential evolution. In: New Ideas in Optimization, pp. 79–108. McGraw-Hill Ltd., London (1999)
7. Abbass, H.A.: The self-adaptive pareto differential evolution algorithm. In: Proceedings of the IEEE Congress on Evolutionary Computation (CEC 2002), Piscataway, NJ, vol. 1, pp. 831–836. IEEE Press (2002)
8. Reynoso-Meza, G., Sanchis, J., Blasco, X., Herrero, J.M.: Hybrid DE algorithm with adaptive crossover operator for solving real-world numerical optimization problems. In: 2011 IEEE Congress on Evolutionary Computation (CEC), June 5-8 (2011)
9. Teo, J.: Exploring dynamic self-adaptive populations in differential evolution. Soft Comput. 10(8), 673–686 (2006)
10. Hasegawa, H., Tooyama, S.: Adaptive plan system with genetic algorithm using the variable neighborhood range control. In: IEEE Congress on Evolutionary Computation (CEC 2009), pp. 846–853 (2009)

Research on a Integrated Real-Time Simulation Platform for Aircraft Control System

Chao Shen, Xiaohang Chang, Jinxia Liu, and Jingyan Han

Beijing Electromechanical Engineering Institute, Beijing 100074, China

Abstract. In order to meet the requirements of hardware-in-the-loop simulation for aircraft control system, an integrated real-time simulation platform is presented, then its functions, working principal, and architecture are introduced in detail. Analyzed several key technologies such as memory database, real-time simulation and general simulation modeling; with the advantages of high universality, integration and flexibility, this platform can effectively support the development and execution of real-time and hardware-in-the-loop simulation.

Keywords: flight control, hardware-in-the-loop simulation(HIL), real-time simulation platform, integration.

1   Introduction

The applications of flight control and management system in aircraft control have greatly improved complex control ability for aircraft, but at the same time it brings more technical challenges in flight control system development. The main part of the flight control and management system is a set of integrative control software running over the control computer. Along with its performance greatly improved taking the advantage of the cooperative work mode and enhanced interface support of modern CPU, more critical requirements was brought forward such as computing performance, interface diversity and simulation scheduling ability of the simulation platform.

In order to meet the requirements to support the whole development cycle simulation for flight control and management system, an integrated real-time simulation platform is presented. It has the capabilities of real-time model calculating, various types of interface communication implementing HIL simulation by fulfilling the data exchanging between simulated equipment and physical equipment. In addition, the platform also offers overall testing procedure management to keep the simulation testing procedure safe and efficient.

The platform provides common-purpose simulation developing environments and a set of simulation toolkits to facilitate the development, debugging, calculating, transportation of simulation model and the simulation process run-time control, the design and development periods of simulation systems, to standardize the criterion of simulation equipment development, also improving the simulation accuracy and credibility.

T. Xiao, L. Zhang, and M. Fei (Eds.): AsiaSim 2012, Part II, CCIS 324, pp. 379–385, 2012.

2   Capabilities of the Simulation Platform

The main functions of the integrated real-time simulation platform include: simulation tasks scheduling and management, simulation model developing and debugging, real-time simulation operating, interface data processing and human-computer interaction. Specific functions are as follows:

2.1   Simulation Tasks Scheduling and Management

The platform provides simulation tasks scheduling and management function to implement simulation initial state configuration, functional units scheduling and the simulation procedure management, including setting simulation working mode, scheduling software module, initializing simulation parameters, starting, stopping, and quitting system, etc.

2.2   Simulation Model Developing and Debugging

By constructing a simulation development environment which provides visual modeling toolkit based on general-purpose algorithms and model libraries, users can easily accomplish adding, deleting and updating simulation model, defining input and output parameters, calculating and debugging simulation model.

2.3   Simulation Process Real-Time Control

Based on the capabilities of accurate and stable frame periodicity control, the platform can offer real-time simulation model calculating control and real-time interface communication with external equipment.

2.4   Interface Data Processing

With MMDB and shared memory, the platform help users to manage the relations between model I/O variables and its mapped interface memory, the definition of model I/O variables and the storage of simulation files.

2.5   Human-Computer Interaction

Human-Computer interaction module of the platform provides various types of controls such as text display control, indicator light control and graphic display control to show user important information, warning and error messages. On the other hand, with the assistance of this function module; user can perform initial parameter configuration, simulation task work mode setting and simulation process control.

3   Working Principle

Based on MMDB and shared memory techniques, real-time simulation model calculating control and real-time interface communication solutions, the platform offers a universal software framework to integrate different types of software module and I/O communication configuration module to meet the requests of various simulation applications, offering a quick solution for real-time simulation system construction. The system working principle is showed in figure 1.

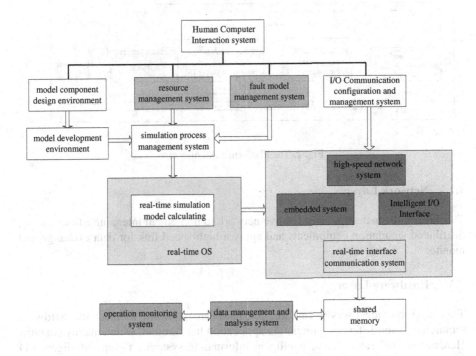

Fig. 1. Working principle of the platform

4   Architecture

The architecture in figure 2 has five layers, includes: network layer、hardware layer 、service layer、function layer the application layer .This architecture is expedient to make a real-time simulation system using different hardware platform and software modules to fulfill the different demands. The hardware platform is distributed in the network, and the software is divided in modules according to their specific function and the layer where they lie.

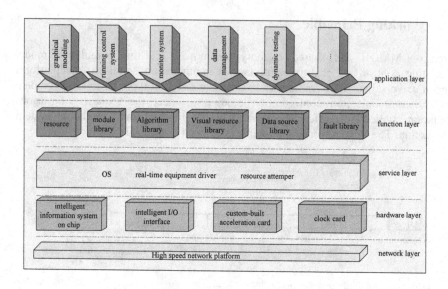

Fig. 2. The Platform's Architecture

4.1   Network Layer

This layer utilizes the optical reflective network to implement interconnections among distributed simulation equipments and apply a high-speed link for data exchange and monitor.

4.2   Hardware Layer

This layer provide users a configurable hardware platform to meet the hardware requirements for different   simulation application background, which mainly contains Hardware Accelerator Cards, intelligent information system on chip, intelligent I/O interface cards, ect.

4.3   Service Layer

Service layer realizes real-time device driving and hardware resources scheduling based on real-time operation system, making support for users to assemble specific functions such as graphic modeling and simulation procedure monitoring.

4.4   Function Layer

As the core of the platform architecture, function layer contains general-purpose knowledge repository, model repository, data resource repository, algorithms library, visualization Resource library, real-time scheduling API library, display control library and so on.

During simulation execution these software modules exchange the runtime data through the shared memory and the MMDB.

4.5   Application Layer

Application layer provides application-specific software modules including environment of graphical modeling, environment of real-time execution, real-time simulation monitoring module and data management module.

With the assistant of the software module mentioned above, users can integrate specific simulation applications, for example, with the environment of the graphical modeling, user could develop and debug the simulation models, define the input/output parameters and configure the corresponding relationships between these parameters and physical I/O Card, with the clock control and frame time control functions supplied by the environment of real-time execution could help user to ensure real-time model calculating and data communication, with the real-time monitoring module users could construct the application of real-time data display and communication state monitor, with the data management module users could implement centralized data acquisition, control and storage.

5   Key Technique

5.1   Universal Simulation and Modeling

According to the characteristic and requirement of simulation of the aircraft control system, the platform integrates all resources now we have to buildup different document libraries, which locate in different layers, such as file repository, algorithms library、 module repository、 model library, file repository is mainly used to store original data, including aerodynamic data files, booster files, engine files, algorithm library mainly includes integral algorithms, interpolation algorithms, coordinate conversion algorithms, filtering algorithms, matrix algorithms and other numerical algorithms we used continually; model library can be built up by associating module library with algorithms library ,which can be set with different parameters. According to these ways, we can realize the standardization and general purpose of simulation model.

5.2   Real-Time Running of Simulation

Real-time is the kernel capability which supports the real-time running of simulation. The platform takes many techniques to satisfy the real-time requirement of aircraft simulation, such as custom-tailor operating system, time synchronization, real time algorithm, real time communication etc.

5.3   The Technology of Real-Time Data Exchange

To ensure the performance of integrated real-time simulation platform, the data exchange management module should not only manage the data but also satisfy the real time requirement.

To accommodate the different data type which produced during the simulation process, the platform uses database and file system to build up disk-based database and uses DLL to build up main-memory database. The data exchange strategy based on disk-based and main-memory database is showed in figure 3:

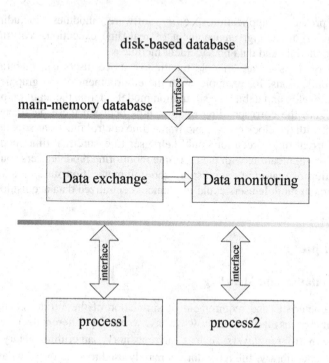

Fig. 3. Sketch map of the data exchange strategy

6   Summary

To cope with the long-standing problems lying on the flight control HIL simulation system such as lacking of high-level layout, weak reusability of simulation resources, long design and integrating period, a real-time integrated simulation platform is presented.

Firstly, an efficient and unified measure to manage various types of simulation resources is realized grounded on constructing a simulation resource repository. Secondly, with the flexibility of the multi-layer architecture, the platform allows users to set up simulation applications quickly using configuration tools to integrate corresponding software modules and hardware devices. As a highly opening simulation platform, it provides a convenient graphic modeling environment for users to implement simulation model development and debugging as well. In conclusion, this platform could offer users effective solutions for assuring real-time execution performance and reliability of complex interface communication could be accommodate to the typical types of practical simulation background.

References

1. Cheng, F., Gao, Q., Lu, C., Jiang, Z.: Research on Simulation Support System Based on Windows. Journal of System Simulation 12(2), 193–198 (2001)
2. Wang, C., Lu, C.-D., Sui, Z.: Research on Simulation Integration Support Platform. Journal of System Simulation 15(7), 956–961 (2003)
3. Cui, H., Xiao, H., Yang, Y., Li, Z., Xie, Z.: The Research on the Development of an Integrative Process Simulation and Control Support Platform. Computer Engineering and Applications 14, 111–114 (2004)
4. Luo, B., Chen, H., Shang, Q.-M., Shi, D.-Y.: Research and Implementation of Simulation Integration Support Platfrom. Journal of Wuhan University of Technology 28(2), 94–96 (2006)
5. Lin, X.-Y., Song, Z.-G.: Design Plan for Missile-borne Software System Testing. Science Technology and Engineering 9(4), 911–918 (2009)
6. Cao, J.-G., Li, Y.-L., He, L.-S.: Application of Memory Ring in Real-time Simulation & Testing Computer Simulation 5, 85–122 (2006)

The Application of Dynamical Management Based on Ontology-Based Simulation Case-Based Description and Reasoning

Xiayi Gong[1], Bohu Li[1], Xudong Chai[2], Yabin Zhang[1], and Mu Gu[2]

[1] Beijing University of Aeronautics and Astronautics,
Beijing, 100191, China
[2] Beijing Simulation Centre, Beijing, 100039, China
gongwhite56167@sohu.com

Abstract. To meet the requirement of simulation resource description dynamical management by the technology of simulation system environment dynamically building in Cloud Simulation Platform(CSP), the application of dynamical management based on ontology-based simulation case-based description and reasoning has been presented. This method could generate description intelligently, when simulation users cannot give the exact one, so as to provide the basis for dynamical building in CSP. With the CBR, the paper mainly discussed the ontology-based expression and reasoning. Finally, the description of simulation case and the ontology-based reasoning rule are present to show the feasibility and effectiveness.

Keywords: cloud simulation, simulation case-based description, ontology, reasoning.

1   Introduction

In recent years, as an effective tool for understanding and reconstruction of the objective world, modeling and simulation technology has been a tremendous development, forms the integrated technology system, and goes forward the "digitalization, virtualization, networking, intelligentialization, integration, collaboration "as the characteristics of modernization in this area [1]. Based on the simulation grid, based on the concept of "cloud computing", it integrates the virtualized, pervasive computing and high performance computing technology further, builds new network modeling and simulation platform - cloud simulation platform [2] which provides a new modeling and simulation usage pattern. Simulation users meet their individual needs simulation platform based on cloud fast, efficient and flexible access to simulation services without concern of simulation resources required where and how to use, cloud simulation platform constructs the simulation system operating environment intelligently, based on the description of the simulation task,   the whole process will be without human intervention.

Automated, intelligent building simulation runtime environment must be based on the accurate description of the simulation resources and the environment needs. Environmental needs of the simulation resource description contain the information of

T. Xiao, L. Zhang, and M. Fei (Eds.): AsiaSim 2012, Part II, CCIS 324, pp. 386–394, 2012.

the operating environment and performance of two types of demand, the operating environment determines the cloud simulation platform how to organize the simulation resources to build the operating environment, performance requirements determines the cloud simulation platform to what parameters to configure the operating environment. However, in practice, the simulation user can not accurately describe environmental performance requirements of the simulation resources, this is because: (1) Simulation users are often difficult to grasp the exact value of the environmental performance requirements of the simulation model; (2) The same simulation model has different requirements in different simulation applications. Therefore, the cloud simulation platform must be able to provide a dynamic simulation resources to describe the management methods, when the simulation user is difficult to give an accurate description of the operating performance of the simulation model needs to intelligently generate descriptions for simulation users automatically , it can give accurate description, automated, intelligent organization of simulation resources on-demand services.

Currently, there is little research on description of the dynamic simulation resources management, mainly because of the computer or network simulation platform based on the center in the past, simulation resources have been deployed in advance in accordance with the design of simulation applications, there is no need for simulation description dynamic management of resources. User-centered Cloud simulation platform is concerned about the simulation needs of the users how to meet the simulation tasks required for simulation resources and operating environment, this paper combines the characteristics of simulation resources described in the simulation platform with dynamic management, the application of dynamical management based on ontology-based simulation case-based description and reasoning has been presented., which gives an accurate description of the simulation model performance requirements for simulation users automatically, and effectively supports the autonomy and dynamically building of the simulation system operating environment.

2   The Idea of Simulation Resources to Describe the Dynamic Management

The dynamic management goal of Simulation resources description is to provide a more accurate basis for cloud simulation run dynamic environment. Figure 1 shows the cloud simulation runtime environment dynamically building process is based on virtualization technology, and simulation knowledge base is the key to make the simulation resources describe the dynamic management. When description of every simulation task is finished, the simulation knowledge base will save simulation tasks and simulation resources as knowledge preservation, and when the new simulation task is submitted, cloud simulation platform forms the current simulation tasks based on existing knowledge and reasoning in the simulation knowledge base, the performance requirements of the simulation resources, and demand information will be updated to the description of the simulation resources, in the end of the simulation tasks, description of the can be corrected simulation resources according to the operating status of the simulation resources, together with the simulation tasks as the new knowledge to be saved. Cloud simulation platform simulation will achieve self-learning process by knowledge base, with the increase of simulation applications, knowledge capacity and credibility of simulation knowledge base have been improving.

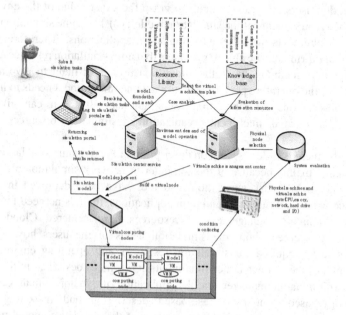

Fig. 1. The cloud simulation runtime environment dynamically building process is based on virtualization technology

Description of the simulation tasks and simulation resources are considered as a simulation case, then the above process is actually a CBR, (Case-Based Reasoning) [4], the CBR is a new kind of machine learning and reasoning method, its core idea is to reuse past problem-solving experience to solve new problems. A description of the cloud simulation resources is using ontology technology [5], with a strong knowledge of skills and characteristics to support a strong reasoning ability, making ontology-based case-based reasoning process take full advantage of domain knowledge to obtain more accurate results [6]. Case-based reasoning based on ontology is becoming a hotspot. Reasoning cycle consists of four basic process 4R cycle (Retrieve, Reuse, Revise, Retain) [7-8], corresponding to the description of the simulation cases, adaptation and reasoning, revised and expanded, which is shown in Figure 2.

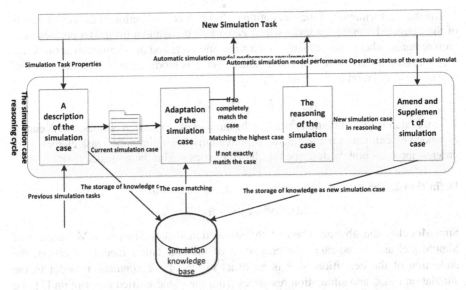

Fig. 2. Describe the dynamic management simulation CBR cycle-based simulation resources of the body of case-based reasoning

On case-based reasoning, this paper focuses on the description of the ontology-based simulation case and the reasoning, explaining how to automatically give the performance requirements of the simulation resources in the current simulation tasks based on the existing simulation case description, in order to achieve the dynamic management of the simulation of resource description.

3   Ontology-Based Simulation Case Description

The case description needs to extract to establish the elements information of the case object, and information is stored as formatted form.Ontology-based simulation case description is based on the ontology language to describe such information, as the form of formatted storage in the Knowledge Base. Simulation resources to describe the dynamic management involves the simulation of the application of the simulation model needs, the needs of the simulation model for the simulation environment, simulation applications, simulation models and simulation environment as a case study describing the elements of information.

Description 1. The definition of a simulation case is defined as:

$$\text{Simu App} = <\text{Id}, \text{A}, \{\text{Mi}\}> \ (\text{i} \in \text{N})$$

Among them, the Id stands for the simulation case number, A represents the set of attribute information of the simulation task, {Mi}stands for a collection of instances of the simulation model of the simulation tasks required.

Attribute information of the simulation tasks set A is a collection of the key elements of the extracted simulation tasks which can affect the simulation model performance requirements, where two elements of the simulation rate and the simulation entities size are most directly affected. For convenience, Set A is modified by simulation rate and size of the simulation entities, namely:

$$A = \{K, S\}$$

Where K stands for simulation rate, S is the number of simulation entities. Set A can be expanded by extraction in the practical application of new simulation task elements , in order to more accurately describe the characteristics of simulation tasks.

Definition 2. The case of the simulation model is defined as:

$$SimuModel = <P, T, E>$$

SimuModel is the abstract class of the simulation model M,namely M instance of SimuModel and P indicates the properties of the simulation model collection, the collection of the definition of P is an exact match of the simulation model in the simulation tasks, and simulation resources from the cloud unified description [7], the basic properties, functional properties and use the property to extract feature information and to expand set P, will not repeat the definition; T said that within the simulation model solving step; E simulation model run depends instance of the simulation environment.

Definition 3. Simulation environment case is defined as:

$$SimuEnv = <O, \{Si\}, C, M, N, D> (i \bullet N)$$

SimuEnv dependent simulation model running in the definition simulation environment E is an abstract class, namely E for SimuEnv instance. SimuEnv is defined by extracting the attributes of information elements in cloud simulation unified resources.O is the operating system, {Si} represents the collection of software, C stands for the CPU, M said that memory, N denotes the network and D network latency.

OWL DL is one of the three languages of OWL, which provides a powerful logical reasoning ability, based on OWL DL reasoning with the completeness and credibility of [9-10]. Ontology-based case expression abstract syntax of OWL DL. Describe the rules of OWL DL-based simulation case is defined as follows: userdef that custom namespace prefix, $i \in [1, n]$, n is the dimension of feature vector:

Definition 4. Simulation case class is defined as:
```
Case: Class (userdef: Case partial owl: Thing);
```

Definition 5. Objects corresponding to the concept of class Oi is defined as:
```
for i = 1 to m {
Class (userdef: Oi partial owl: Thing);
 }
```

m is the number corresponding to the concept of class.

Definition 6. Attribute definitions of the six simulation cases. The properties of the simulation cases are divided into two categories Dpi and OPi, where DPi represents a value type, and the OPi represents object type, domain of DPi and OPi is the Case, range of OPi is Oi,:

```
for i = 1 to, k1 {
        DatatypeProperty (userdef: DP i domain (userdef:
Case));
    }
    for i = 1 to k2, {
        ObjectProperty (userdef: OPi domain (ex: Case) range
userdef: (Oi));
    }
    k1 is the number of properties of the value type, and k2
is the number of attributes of the object type.
```

So, describing structure of the rules of simulation cases is shown in Figure 3 based on Definition 1, the definition 2 and definition 3.

Class(userdef:SimuApp partial owl:Thing);

Class(userdef:SimuModel partial owl:Thing);

Class(userdef:SimuEnv partial owl:Thing);

Class(userdef:Soft partial owl:Thing);

DatatypeProperty(userdef:Id domain(userdef: SimuApp));

DatatypeProperty(userdef:K domain(userdef: SimuApp));

DatatypeProperty(userdef:S domain(userdef: SimuApp));

ObjectProperty(userdef:hasModel   domain(userdef: SimuApp)   range(userdef:
SimuModel));

DatatypeProperty(userdef:N domain(userdef: SimuModel));

DatatypeProperty(userdef:F domain(userdef: SimuModel));

DatatypeProperty(userdef:T domain(userdef: SimuModel));

ObjectProperty(userdef:hasEnv domain(userdef: SimuModel) range(userdef: SimuEnv));

DatatypeProperty(userdef:O domain(userdef: SimuEnv));

DatatypeProperty(userdef:C domain(userdef: SimuEnv));

DatatypeProperty(userdef:M domain(userdef: SimuEnv));

DatatypeProperty(userdef:N domain(userdef: SimuEnv));

DatatypeProperty(userdef:D domain(userdef: SimuEnv));

Fig. 3. The description rules structure based on the simulation case of OWL DL

Current simulation tasks can also be defined in this method, but Id in the definition of 1 and E values in the definition 2 are null, in which E is given by the simulation case-based reasoning, Id is given as new knowledge stored in the simulation of knowledge in the simulation case amended.

4   Simulation Case-Based Reasoning Based on Ontology

Simulation case of ontology-based adaptation is needed before carrying out the simulation case-based reasoning, it is the case for the current query matched with each case in the case of space, selecting one of the most similar cases, not introduced in detail.However, due to the cloud simulation platform for a wide range of simulation applications and various types of simulation applications, due to limited simulation cases in knowledge base, there may be not satisfied with the degree of similarity of the adaptation of the final simulation case as a result of the simulation case adapter failure. In this case, the corresponding simulation model description requirements must be obtained through simulation CBR performance.

Simulation CBR problem can be described as the current simulation case s and the simulation case space Q for each simulation case q fit, when the simulation case does not fit, the highest simulation case q on the basis of similarity, based on Q in all simulation cases and cases described in the domain ontology knowledge T, modify the formation of a new simulation case p, with the s adaptation. Of the current simulation case s of all the characteristics of $s = \{e1, e2, ..., en\}$ ($n \in N$), and used to match the characteristics is $s' = \{e1, e2, ... em\}$ ($m < n$), all the features of the highest similarity simulation case of q for $q = \{f1, f2, ... fn\}$ ($n \in N$), and s match the characteristics of $q' = \{f1, f2, ... fk\}$ ($k < m$), it certainly has $q' \subseteq s'$. Other characteristics of key value corresponds to how to modify the case to fix the problem is when you change the characteristics of the s'-q 'in q value of s' and q' adaptation.

Ontology-based description logic, a simulation case with the current simulation tasks describe features associated with relationships can be created, matching based on ontology inference rules to determine the need to modify the characteristics, resulting in the adaptation failure simulation case, the simulation model performance requirements description can be calculated based on existing simulation case knowledge.Simulation knowledge base of the cloud simulation platform supports the custom ontology reasoning rules, the simulation user can fix custom ontology reasoning rules by actual simulation application needs.

After Ontology-based inference rules determining the modified characteristics, modifying the corresponding changes is necessary based on the contents of matching features. We can consider knowledge base already in the simulation case as simulation knowledge base, such as from the case

$$q1=\{f1,f2,...,fn\}, q2=\{f'1,f'2,...,f'n\}, q3=\{f''1,f''2,...,f''n\},...$$

The relationship between the first m features $R = \{(f1, f'1, f'' 1), (f2, f'2, f'' 2), ..., (fm, f'm, f'' m)\}$ can be summarized, the same as the role of other characteristics. The matching features to modify the contents of a given target case, other characteristics of the modified value will be obtained. Modifying the value of the specific calculation algorithm does not belong to the research focus of this paper, will not be discussed here.

The computational been solution to a multivariate solving problems may produce multiple solutions, randomly selecting any of them a solution as recommended values in the simulation model performance requirements description.

Through case-based reasoning performance requirements of the simulation model description has been obtained, but new simulation case obtained by the case of reasoning is not the actual simulation runtime and, therefore, cannot serve as a new simulation case knowledge which is necessary to carry out a simulation case amendment of the next section.

5   Conclusions

To meet the requirement of simulation resource description dynamical management by the technology of simulation system environment dynamically building in Cloud Simulation Platform(CSP), the application of dynamical management based on ontology-based simulation case-based description and reasoning has been presented. With the CBR, the paper mainly discussed the ontology-based expression and reasoning. Finally, the description of simulation case and the ontology-based reasoning rule are present to show the feasibility and effectiveness. Cloud simulation platform simulation knowledge base through this method can achieve the described automation of simulation resources and the environment needs to provide an accurate basis for intelligent dynamic management, laying the foundation for dynamically building of cloud simulation platform. In order to achieve the accuracy of the simulation case study description and adaptation, the expansion of the simulation cases are described in the practical application features. Cloud simulation platform based on simulation knowledge base has a self-learning mechanism, capacity, credibility and intelligence in the simulation knowledge base will increase, and cloud simulation platform will be more and more intelligent.

References

1. Li, B., Chai, X., Zhu, W.: Some Focusing Points in Development of Modern Modeling and Simulation Technology. Journal of System Simulation 16(9), 1871–1877 (2004)
2. Li, B., Chai, X.: Networked Modeling & Simulation Platform Based on Concept of Cloud Computing—Cloud Simulation Platform. Journal of System Simulation 21(17), 5292–5299 (2009)
3. Zhang, Y., Li, B., Chai, X., Hou, B., Ren, L.: Research on Virtualization-based Simulation Environment Dynamically Building Technology for Cloud Simulation. In: 2010 International Conference on Information Security and Artificial Intelligence, vol. 3, pp. 582–586 (2010)
4. Schank, R.C.: Dynamic Memory: A Theory of Reminding and Learning in Computers and People. Cambridge University Press (January 28, 1983)
5. Zhang, Y., Chai, X., Hou, B., Ren, L.: Research on Virtual Simulation Resource Modeling in Cloud Simulation. In: 2010 International Conference on Information Security and Artificial Intelligence, vol. 3, pp. 394–398 (2010)
6. Xie, H., Li, J.: Research of case-based reasoning model based on ontology. Application Reasearch of Computers 26(4) (2009)

7. Yang, J., Zhao, Q.: Research and application of CBR's progression. Computer Engineering and Design 29(3) (2008)
8. Yang, T.: Research on Framework of Ontology Based Case-based Reasoning System. Nanjing University of Aeronautics and Astronautics, Nanjing
9. McGuinness, D.L., van Harmelen F.: 2003 OWL web ontology language overview. Technical report, World Wide Web Consortium (W3C) (2003) Internet, http://www.w3.org/TR/owl-features
10. Patel-Schneider, P.F., Hayer, P., Horrocks, I. (eds): OWL Web ontology language semantics and abstract syntax [EB/OL] (2004), http://www.w3.org/TR/owl-semantics/
11. Salton, G., Buckley, C.: Term-weighting approaches in automatic text retrieval. Information Processing & Management 24(5), 513–523 (1988)
12. Bergmann, R., Stahl, A.: Similarity Measures for Object-Oriented Case Representations. In: Smyth, B., Cunningham, P. (eds.) EWCBR 1998. LNCS (LNAI), vol. 1488, pp. 25–36. Springer, Heidelberg (1998)

Virtual Machine Task Allocation for HLA Simulation System on Cloud Simulation Platform

Shaoyun Zhang[1], Zhengfu Tang[2], Xiao Song[1], Zhiyun Ren[1], and Huijing Meng[1]

[1] Science and Technology on Aircraft Control Laboratory, School of Automation Science, Beihang University, Beijing 100191, China
[2] Key Lab. of Complex Aviation System Simulation, Beijing 100076, China
sy.zhang2000@gmail.com

Abstract. A new yet promising technology, Cloud computing, can benefit large-scale simulations by providing on-demand, everywhere simulation services to users. In order to enable multi-task and multi-user simulation tasks with Cloud computing, Cloud Simulation Platform (CSP) is proposed and developed. To promote the running efficiency of HLA systems on CSP, this paper proposes an approach addressing the Virtual Machine task allocation problem, which is divided into two levels of task allocation steps. The first-level uses a heuristic algorithm to optimize the mapping from federates (of HLA system) to virtual machines (of CSP) and aims to achieve load balance on virtual machines in CSP. The second-level dispatches the subtasks of federate to the cores of virtual machines to minimize the makespan (schedule length) of the federate which uses a DAG based list scheduling algorithm: the EST (Earliest-Start-Time) algorithm. Experiments show that the two-level task allocation strategy effectively improves the running efficiency of HLA system on CSP.

Keywords: task allocation, Cloud Simulation Platform, HLA, DAG, heuristic algorithm.

1 Introduction

In order to provide users with the ability to acquire modeling and simulation resources on demand through the network, Cloud Simulation Platform (CSP) [1] is proposed which integrates Cloud computing technology with network modeling and simulation technology, virtualization technology, pervasive computing and high-performance computing technology. Virtualization technology is a key technology of CSP. It can provide unified encapsulation form for varieties of heterogeneous simulation resources, thus shielding the heterogeneity of the hardware architecture and software environment, and achieving high quality of sharing and transparent use of simulation resources.

The High Level Architecture (HLA) has been a milestone in distributed simulation, so it is also an important kind of application in CSP. But the HLA systems running on CSP have different features. First, the system scale is larger and it consists of more entities (federates). Second, the HLA system in CSP is running on *virtual machines*

T. Xiao, L. Zhang, and M. Fei (Eds.): AsiaSim 2012, Part II, CCIS 324, pp. 395–403, 2012.

(VMs) which shields the heterogeneity of environment and is easier to be migrated. Third, the CSP supports multi-user, it means that the resources are not dedicated in CSP. All these differences call for new techniques to ensure the high efficiency and result correctness of HLA system running in CSP. In this paper, we focus on the task allocation for HLA simulation systems in Cloud Simulation Platform and propose a two-level allocation strategy to improve the efficiency of the HLA system running on Cloud Simulation Platform.

Efficient task allocation is critical for achieving high performance in simulation systems [2]. And because of its key importance, it has been extensively studied and various strategies have been proposed in the literature. These strategies can be classified into two main categories: one for load balancing ([5], [8]) and another for minimizing the makespan ([4], [6], [7], [9]). Most of the strategies for load balancing use heuristic algorithms such as clustering algorithms and guided random search algorithms et al, to seek for the approximation optimal mappings from jobs to limited number of resources. And the strategies for minimizing the makespan mainly focus on the job that can be decomposed to numbers of tasks with precedence constrains. These jobs can be represented by directed acyclic graphs (DAG), and these strategies usually base on the DAGs and use the algorithms such as list scheduling algorithms and duplication-based algorithms et al.

However, these strategies do not work well with HLA system. In HLA system there are a number of federates that need to be allocated to limited number of resources and federates can be decomposed to subtasks (logic process) in the meanwhile. Therefore, the HLA system needs task allocation strategies that have the both functionalities mentioned above, i.e. the functionality of achieving load balance in the mappings from federates to resources and the functionality of minimizing the makespan of federates. Moreover, the Cloud Simulation Platform has many different features from traditional simulation platforms. The virtualization technology in CSP shields the heterogeneity of resources and the dynamic building technique of virtual machine makes it easier for task migration. Therefore, the task allocation problem of HLA system on CSP is different from other ones, thus is necessary to be researched.

2   The Two-Level Task Allocation Strategy

The allocation strategy takes account of the features of both HLA system and the CSP. The HLA system consists of a lot of federates, and a federate usually produces small resource overhead, so it causes resource waste if allocating only one federate to one VM. Therefore, a federate clustering strategy is needed to be researched to allocate several federates to one VM, taking into account of the computation and communication demands of federates and aiming at load balance of VMs.

Then federates can be decomposed to a set of subtasks with precedence constrains, so they can be represented by directed acyclic graphs (DAGs), of which the nodes represent the subtasks and the edges represent the communication relationship between subtasks. By allocating the nodes of DAGs on the same VM to the cores of the VM, the second level allocation strategy aims to minimize the makespan of federates on the VM. Fig. 1 shows a straightforward illustration of the Two-level Task Allocation Strategy.

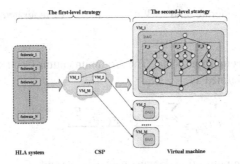

Fig. 1. The Two-level Task Allocation Strategy

2.1 The First-Level Allocation Strategy

In CSP, there generally has a limiting range for the performance configuration of VMs. If the VM's configuration is out of the range, the CSP will not be able to support it. This algorithm uses the ideal performance configuration which is defined as the intermediate value of the limiting range. The executing rate of the ideal performance configuration is R_I, and the communication speed is C_I.

For a HLA system with N federates, the total computing demand, T_s, is defined as

$$T_s = \sum_{i=1}^{N} T_i, \tag{1}$$

where T_i is the computing demand of *federate$_i$* (i=1,2,...N). Under ideal performance configuration (virtual machine is configured with ideal performance configuration), the number of virtual machines that are required is M, which is defined by

$$M = T_s / R_I. \tag{2}$$

Therefore, the allocation problem that the first-level strategy deals with can be formulated as the problem of searching for the optimal mapping from N federates to M virtual machines. This problem has been proved to be NP-Complete [3], so it is very difficult to find the optimal mapping.

Before introducing the details of the strategy, we define some indices that are used in our strategy.

2.1.1 Some Indices Used by the Strategy

Computing Occupation Rate. The Computing Occupation Rate of VM_k (the k_{th} virtual machine) is defined as

$$OR_k = \frac{\sum_{F_i \in S(VM_k)} T_i}{R_I}, \tag{3}$$

where F_i is the i_{th} federate, and $S(VM_k)$ is the set of federates that are allocated to VM_k.

Communication Occupation Rate. The Communication Occupation Rate between VM_p and VM_q is defined as

$$OC_{pq} = \frac{\sum_{F_i \in S(VM_p), F_j \in S(VM_q)} E_{ij}}{C_I}, \qquad (4)$$

where E_{ij} is the communication demand between F_i and F_j.

Performance Index. The Performance Index of a mapping m is defined as

$$\delta(m) = \max(OR_k, OC_{pq}), \ k, p, q = 1, 2, \cdots, M, \qquad (5)$$

i.e. the Performance Index of a mapping m is the maximum value of the Computing Occupation Rate and the Communication Occupation Rate of the mapping.

According to the Indices defined above, the object of first-level allocation is to find a mapping m^* so that

$$\delta(m^*) = \min(\delta(m)), \qquad (6)$$

2.1.2   Description of the Strategy

The first-level allocation strategy uses a heuristic searching algorithm, so first we build the searching-tree of the problem.

Searching-Tree of the Problem. In the allocation problem, the root node of the searching tree represents an empty mapping, the leaf nodes represent complete mappings and the nodes between them represent partial mappings. The parent node can generate several child nodes by adding a new Federate to the mapping which will produce several new mappings. In the searching tree, each child node can be a parent node and generates its child nodes until all federates are allocated. Then the optimal mapping m^* can be found by searching in the whole complete mappings.

In order to use the heuristic algorithm, the heuristic function needs to be defined.

Heuristic Function. The heuristic function $f(n)$ of node n is defined as the performance index of the mapping m_n that is represented by node n.

$$f(n) = \delta(m_n), \qquad (7)$$

When a new generation of child nodes is generated, the child node with the minimum value of heuristic function is selected as the parent node of next generation. This method can significantly reduce the searching space, and get the approximate optimal mapping with fewer overheads.

The algorithm is described in Fig. 2. First, sort federates in descending order of computing demands and allocate them in turn. Allocate one federate in each step and this operation generates M child nodes (M is the number of VMs) which represent M new mappings. For each child node, calculate the Computing Occupation Rate and Communication Occupation Rate of the mapping it represents, and get the heuristic value of it. Then select the node with minimum heuristic value as the parent node of next generation. When all federates are scheduled, the selected mapping with the minimum heuristic value is the approximation optimal mapping of allocation problem.

1	Sort federates in a list in descending order of computing demands;
2	while there are allocated federates in the list
3	Select the first federate from the list;
4	Generate M child nodes;
5	Compute the heuristic value, $f(n)$, for each node;
6	Allocate the federate according to the mapping that is represented by the node with the minimum $f(n)$ value, n_k ;
7	Select the node n_k as the parent node of next step;
8	end while

Fig. 2. The heuristic algorithm used in the First-level Task Allocation Strategy

2.2   The Second-Level Task Allocation Strategy

In HLA system, the simulation step size can be reduced by reducing the execution time of federates in each step, and this is conducive to meeting the demand of real-time or super real-time simulation. Exploiting the parallelism of the subtasks of federates and using the multi-cores virtual machine can effectively reduce the execution time of federates. Therefore, the second level allocation strategy uses a DAG based scheduling algorithm to dispatch the subtasks of federates to the cores of VMs to reduce their execution time.

As mentioned above, a federate can be represented by a DAG. The weight of the node represents the computing demand of the subtask and the weight of edge represents the communication volume between two subtasks. For several federates on a VM, their DAGs can be integrated as one larger DAG for scheduling, as shown in Fig. 3.

The DAG1, DAG2 and DAG3 in Fig. 3 represent three federates on the VM. The pseudo entry node and pseudo exit node are used to integrate the three DAGs to one DAG. And their computing demand and communication volume are zero, so they have no effects on task allocation.

The second-level task allocation strategy (Fig. 4) uses a list scheduling algorithm, EST (Earliest-Start-Time) algorithm, to schedule the nodes of DAG. The EST algorithm has two major phases: the task prioritizing phase and the processor selection phase.

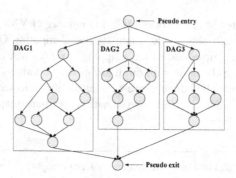

Fig. 3. The DAGs of federates on a VM

First, we introduce a graph attribute of the DAG that is used by the algorithm.

The Height of the Node. The *height* of the node n_i in a DAG is the maximum path length from n_i to the exit node. The path length is the sum of the weights of the nodes and edges on the path. Therefore, the *height* of node n_i is defined as

$$height(n_i) = T_i + \max_{n_i \in succ(n_i)} \{E_{ii} + height(n_i)\}, \tag{8}$$

where $succ(n_i)$ is the set of n_i's immediate successors. The *height* is computed recursively by traversing the DAG upward, starting from the exit task. For the exit task, n_{exit}, the height is

$$height(n_{exit}) = T_{exit}. \tag{9}$$

Task Prioritizing Phase. In this phase, the height of each node is computed and the priority of each node is set to be the *height* of it. A task list is generated by sorting the nodes in descending order of their *height*.

1	Recursively compute the *height* of each task, starting from the exit task;
2	Sort the tasks in a task list in descending order of *height* value;
3	While there are unscheduled tasks in the list
4	Select the first task, n_i, from the list for allocating;
5	for each processor p_k
6	Compute $EST(n_i, p_k)$ value;
7	Allocate task n_i to the processor p_k with the minimum value $EST(n_i, p_k)$;
8	end while

Fig. 4. The Second-level Task Allocation Strategy

Processor Selection Phase. In this phase, each task from the task list is allocated to the processor with the Earliest Start Time for it. The Earliest Start Time for task n_i on processor p_k is defined as

$$EST(n_i, p_k) = \max\{EFT(n_j, p_k), Data_{ik}\}, \tag{10}$$

where n_j is the previous task on processor p_k before n_i, and $Data_{ik}$ is the complete time of required data of n_i transmitted to p_k. $EFT(n_j, p_k)$ is the Earliest Finish Time of n_j on p_k which is defined as

$$EFT(n_j, p_k) = EST(n_j, p_k) + T_j, \tag{11}$$

As an illustration, Fig. 6 shows the allocation result obtained by the second-level allocation strategy for the sample DAG of Fig. 5. Table 1 gives the computing demand and *height* of each node. And the schedule order is { n_1, n_6, n_4, n_5, n_2, n_3, n_8, n_9, n_7, n_{10} }. The schedule length is 103.

Table 1. The computing demand and *height* of each node

Node	n_1	n_2	n_3	n_4	n_5	n_6	n_7	n_8	n_9	n_{10}
Computing Demand	10	13	12	8	15	20	5	18	21	12
height	108	73	59	78	77	79	32	53	53	12

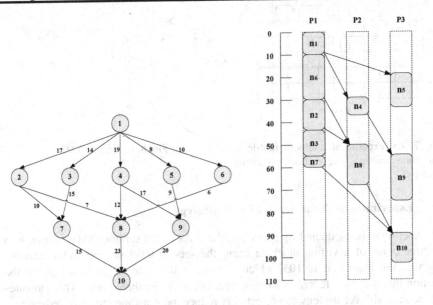

Fig. 5. A Sample DAG

Fig. 6. Allocation result of DAG in Fig. 5 by using the Second-level Allocation Strategy

3   Experiment Results and Analysis

3.1   Experiment with the First-Level Allocation Strategy

The experiment uses a HLA system with one hundred federates. The computing demand of each federate is random value from 1 to 100, and the communication demand between two federates is random value from 0 to 3. The unit of computing demand and communication demand are MIPS (Million Instructions per Second) and Mbps (Million bits per second). The ideal performance configuration of virtual machines are set as R_l =400MIPS, C_l =100Mbps.

The performance of the first-level allocation strategy is compared with the random allocation strategy which randomly allocates federates to virtual machines. Fifty experiments have been conducted and the results are shown in Fig. 7. The vertical coordinate is the performance index value of mapping generated by the strategy. The results show that the performance index value of the mapping generated by the random allocation strategy is high (whose average value is 2.27 in the experiments) and it changes in a large range, while the performance index value of the mapping generated by the first-level allocation strategy slightly oscillates around the value 1, which ensures the VMs' performance configuration is within the limiting range of CSP and thus the HLA system can acquire high running efficiency.

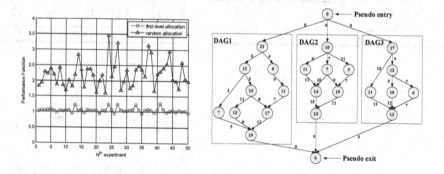

Fig. 7. The experiment results of first-level allocation strategy and random allocation strategy

Fig. 8. A Sample DAG

3.2   Experiment with the Second-Level Strategy

The experiment is conducted by allocating the tasks of the sample DAGs in Fig. 8 to the three cores of a virtual machine using the second-level strategy. The schedule length of the algorithm is 105, which is smaller than the schedule length in the situation that the three federates running separately on the three cores. This indicates that the second-level strategy can effectively reduce the schedule length of federates.

4   Conclusions

This paper proposes a two-level task allocation strategy for HLA system on Cloud Simulation Platform. The first-level allocation strategy dispatches federates to virtual machines using a heuristic searching algorithm and gets an approximation optimal mapping which ensures the load balance of the system. The second-level strategy uses a DAG based list scheduling algorithm to schedule the subtasks of federates on virtual machines and effectively reduces the makespan of federates. The experiment results show that the two-level task allocation strategy has good performance in balancing the load of the system and reducing the makespan of federates, thus effectively improving the efficiency of the HLA system running on Cloud Simulation Platform.

Acknowledgements. This research was supported by grant 61104057 and 61074144 from the Natural Science Foundation of China, National key Lab of Virtual Reality Technology and System and the Graduate Student Innovation Practice Foundation of Beihang University in China. The authors thank the reviewers for their comments.

References

1. Li, B.H., Chai, X.D., Hou, B.C., et al.: Networked Modeling & Simulation Platform Based on Concept of Cloud Computing-Cloud Simulation Platform. Journal of System Simulation 21(17), 5292–5299 (2009)
2. Topcuoglu, H., Hariri, S., Wu, M.Y.: Performance-Effectvie and Low-Complexity Task Scheduling for Herogeneous Computing. In: IEEE Transachtions on Parallel and Distributed Systems, pp. 260–274. IEEE Press, New York (2002)
3. Gary, M.R., Johnson, D.S.: Computers and Intractability: A Guide to the Theory of NP-Completeness. W.H. Freeman and Company (1979)
4. Kwok, Y., Ahmad, I.: Dynamic Critical-Path Scheduling: An Effective Technique for Allocating Task Graphs to Multi-processors. IEEE Transaction on Parallel and Distributed System, 506–521 (1996)
5. Boukerche, A., De Grande, R.E.: Dynamic Load Balancing Using Grid Services for HLA-Based Simulations on Large-Scale Distributed Systems. In: Proceedings of 13th IEEE/ACM International Symposium on Distributed Simulation and Real Time Applications (DS-RT 2009), pp. 175–183 (2009)
6. Audsley, N., Burns, A., Richardson, M., et al.: Applying new scheduling theory to static priority pre-emptive scheduling. Software Engineering Journal, 284–292 (1993)
7. Stavrinides, G.L., Karatza, H.D.: Scheduling multiple task graphs in heterogeneous distributed real-time systems by exploiting schedule holes with bin packing techniques. Simulation Modelling Practice and Theory, 540–552 (2011)
8. Du, Z.H., Wang, M., Chen, Y.N.: The Triangular Pyramid Scheduling Model and algorithm for PDES in Grid. Simulation Modelling Practice and Theory, 1678–1689 (2009)
9. Sih, G.C., Lee, E.A.: A Compile-Time Scheduling Heuristic for Interconnection-Constrained Heterogeneous Processor Architectures. IEEE Transaction on Parallel and Distributed Systems, 175–187 (1993)

HLA Collaborative Simulation Oriented Virtual Machine Task Scheduling Strategy

Zhiyun Ren[1,2], Xiao Song[1,2], Lin Zhang[2], and Shaoyun Zhang[1,2]

[1] Science and Technology on Aircraft Control Laboratory,
Beihang University, Beijing 100191, China
[2] School of Automation Science and Electrical Engineering,
Beihang University, Beijing 100191, China
rzy0801@163.com

Abstract. Aim at the lack of embedded load balancing mechanism in HLA simulation system and the heterogeneity of resources in the network modeling and simulation platform, the study of the initial deployment of HLA simulation task is performed. At first, a unified description model of the federation is established based upon the repulsion and pull relationship between federates; And then, using the analysis of the unified description model, a first detect first combine based coarse combination algorithm is proposed; Taking full consideration of load balance and the late migration efficiency, a Huffman coding tree based fine-grained combination algorithm is put forwarded. Finally, cloud computing simulation platform---CloudSim is utilized to perform the simulation experiment, the result demonstrates that the algorithm improves the management efficiency, fault tolerance and QoS of the resource.

Keywords: HLA simulation, initial deployment, load balance, Huffman coding, CloudSim.

1   Introduction

With the development of simulation technology, the slow-running characteristic of the HLA [1] system in distributed environment is gradually known. The reason is that the load imbalance of simulation resource may emerge inevitably in the running process. Therefore, keeping the load balance of simulation resource through task scheduling becomes one of the most important ways to improve the resource utilization and speed up the simulation process [2] [3] [4]. However, the HLA standard concerns only with the simulation coordination, without consideration of the performance issues of distributed resources which process the simulation task, lacking embedded load balancing mechanism [5] [6]. Hence study one task scheduling mechanism which fits the HLA standard, can effectively improve the utilization and the throughput of the heterogeneous distributed simulation resources, which is also an important strategy to promote the further development of HLA standard.

Network modeling and simulation platform provides personalized simulation environment for simulation users anytime, anywhere, effectively and transparently,

T. Xiao, L. Zhang, and M. Fei (Eds.): AsiaSim 2012, Part II, CCIS 324, pp. 404–412, 2012.
© Springer-Verlag Berlin Heidelberg 2012

without any concern of the specific details of the simulation environment organizations and even the background management of the simulation resource, hence the simulation stuff can focus on the work related to the emulation services itself. The network modeling and simulation platform not only meets the user's mobile office needs, but also solve the deficiencies of the HLA standard in resource management. Therefore, it has become an important direction in the further development of today's simulation technology.

However, the distribution and heterogeneity of the hardware resources in large-scale distributed simulation platform, the diversification of the software environment, the complexity of the multi-disciplinary simulation models have greatly increased the difficulty of resource management in the simulation platform. Virtualization technology (VT) encapsulates the simulation application models and software packages to a relatively independent execution environment, and deploys it to the underlying physical machine (PM) simulation platform in the form of virtual machine (VM), achieving the exclusive distribution of the virtual machines and improving the resource utilization on the basis of ensuring the normal operation of the simulation tasks. Hence, VT is gradually penetrated into the simulation of large-scale distributed resource management platform.

Therefore, with the usage of virtualization technology, this paper performs the deployment research of HLA simulation task for large-scale distributed resource management platform. An HLA simulation task can be described as a simulation federation composed by a number of federates, the federate is executed with a certain mutual relationship in parallel. Therefore, the HLA simulation task scheduling problem is concentrated on how to deploy federates to the physical servers.

Task scheduling in non-virtualized environment and task scheduling in a virtualized environment is essentially different. The former is to deploy the simulation task in a physical machine which is running; while task-oriented virtual environment deployment process is to deploy the simulation task in a virtual machine, and the virtual machine is created according to the simulation task granularity.

The remainder of this paper is structured as follows. Recent study about virtual machine allocation is presented in Section II. In Section III, a unified description model of the federation is established based upon the repulsion and pull relationship between federates; Based upon the analysis of the unified description model, a first detect first combine based coarse combination algorithm and a Huffman coding tree based fine-grained combination algorithm are put forwarded in Section IV. In Section V, cloud computing simulation platform-- CloudSim is utilized to perform the simulation experiment and the result is analyzed. Finally, the conclusion and future work is conducted in Section 6.

2   Related Research

An algorithm with good performance is always for the specific research questions. The allocation problem of simulation tasks is no exception. To study an effective allocation algorithm of simulation tasks, the first is to establish a unified description of the simulation system which is conducive to the allocation of resources.

However, the majority of recent research did not establish a unified description of simulation system [7], and makes it be solved urgently. The resource requirements of a single simulation task is simple integrated as computing and communication costs [8] [9] in some research, ignoring the coupling between subtasks. There are also some research abstracts the subtasks as DAG diagram according to the timing, logic and communication relationship between subtasks, and then a variety of static scheduling algorithm are used for the deployment of the tasks in DAG diagram. GL Park [10], who proposed a low complexity scheduling algorithm, improved the priority node selection criteria in list scheduling algorithm. Using this algorithm, the worst performance case under common input in DAG is analyzed, getting the worst and best performance case under the DAG tree structure. M. Houshmand [11] combined the list scheduling method with the simulated annealing algorithm, that is to use the list scheduling algorithm firstly to seek the initial solution of simulated annealing algorithm, and then use the simulated annealing algorithm iteratively to seek the approximate optimal solution. However, the HLA simulation systems are usually composed by a number of federates, assuming that conservative time advance mechanism is adopted in the system, then the federates are parallel tasks and interact with each other in each simulation step, therefore the federates can't be expressed as a DAG, this kind of algorithms are not useful for HLA simulation task.

The target system is pretreated to achieve a reasonable division of the network of the processing unit by fuzzy clustering method, making the processing unit with better performance can be clustered with preference in the task scheduling process, thus, thus narrowing the search space, reducing the time consumed in the task scheduling process. In order to shorten the time consumed in task scheduling and improve the performance of task scheduling, paper[12] proposed a task scheduling algorithm based on multidimensional performance clustering of grid resource MPCGSR (multidimensional performance clustering of the grid service resources). Based on the large number, heterogeneous and diverse characteristics of service resource in grid environment, this algorithm build a hyper-graph model, combine the small-world theory, and converge with the service resource in multi-dimension, at last, match the task and the clustered resource and realize the scheduling. However, in such algorithms, the unified description focuses on the resource, the purpose of this study is mapping the simulation tasks to virtual machines, the virtual machine is dynamically configured based on the granularity of combined task, thus virtual machine clustering problem does not exist. Therefore, it is not suitable for the problems proposed in this paper.

This paper proposed a task combination and load balance based deployment strategy for federates and virtual machine, on the basis of the establishment of unified description specification for HLA simulation tasks which is qualitatively and quantitatively combined, the resource requirement of each federate and the repulsion and interaction relationship between different federates.

3   The Unified Description Model for HLA Simulation Task

The unified description of HLA simulation task is the key point of choosing simulation resource from the virtualization resource pool and the basis of various resources interaction. To facilitate the interoperability of simulation system and the reuse of simulation components, the HLA object model is described from two aspects, one is used to describe each federate in the federation. The other is used to describe the mutual relationship between federates, namely the HLA federation object model.

3.1   The Unified Description Model of One Single Federate

Federate is the basis unit of a federation, therefore the description of a HLA simulation task is based on the description of a single federate.

Definition 3.1. The description model of federate:
VSA= <UUID, Name, Description, Function, Resource, Environment, OtherInfo>
Where, *UUID*(Universally Unique Identifier) denotes the dynamic instance flag of the federate. *Name* means the name of the federate, it is to facilitate the memory and search for users. *Description* means the description of federate, for the usage of the federate; *Function* means the specific functional requirements of the simulation application, including the input and output and others. *Resource* means the computational overhead of the application, it is a comprehensive assessment of the resource usage (including CPU, memory and network bandwidth); *Environment*= {OS, Swlist} means the environment information required in the running process of the federate, including the operation system and simulation software list and so on; *OtherInfo* means the other description information, which is generally reserved as information space.

3.2   The Unified Description Model of Federation

As said above, federate is a basic unit of federation, federation in this paper is viewed as a set of federates and there is some kind of interactive relationship between federates.

Definition 3.2. The description model of virtual simulation system:
VSS= <UUID, Name, Description, Function, {VSA}, Communication, OtherInfo>
    It is similar with the definition of federate, but still exist some difference.
    {VSA} denotes the composition of the federation, is a description set of federates; *Relation* denotes the interaction frequency between federates, it implicit the communication tightness between federates. Virtual machine is the carrier of federate, so deploy closely related federates can effectively reduce the communication overhead and improve the simulation efficiency. Therefore, viewing *Relation* as an element of the federation description model provides enough information for multi-layer federate composition algorithm.

4   Multi-layer Composition Algorithm for Simulation Federate

It is not advisable to map one single federate to a virtual machine, since the granularity of a single federate may be relatively small. Assign a separate virtual machine for it may cause that the system overhead could be greater than the simulation overhead, resulting in serious waste of resource. Therefore, an initial composition algorithm is established with a goal of balance the granularity in the virtual machine.

4.1   Repulsion and Pull Analysis of Federates

Assume that there are n federates in a federation, then there are two aspects that needs to be considered in federate composition process.

- **Repulsion Relationship:** Two federates can't be deployed in the same virtual machine. Considering the fact that different federates need different running environment, and different running environment may exist some kind of repulsion, operation system repulsion, software incompatible and so on.

- **Pull Relationship:** Two federates should be deployed in the same virtual machine as far as possible. Due to the modeling characteristics, the communication conditions may vary with each other, resulting in the pull relationships between federates. Therefore, in order, deploy federates with close communication into the same virtual machine is advisable.

Therefore, the analysis of federates is based on the repulsion and pull relationship.

4.2   The Coarse-Grained Combination Algorithm of Federates

Because the combined federates will be deployed in the same virtual machine, it should be avoided the federate is conflict combine with each other. As the repulsion relationship is priority to the pull relationship. Through this mechanism, a pre-optimization is made before running to reduce the communication overhead and improve the simulation efficiency. Therefore, a crude combination algorithm based on the first detected the first combined notion is presented.

4.3   The Fine-Grained Combination Algorithm of Federates

As described in the previous section, a crude combination strategy is achieved according to the communication relationship and environment requirement. However, while federates are too many, this combination result can't be used as the ultimate strategy, because the crude combination is only considered from the perspective of simulation stability and ignore the balance management of simulation resource. While in the combination process, on one hand, the granularity should not be two large to facilitate the virtual machine migration; on the other hand, it should not be too small to ensure the resource utilization.

In this paper, an effective combination approach is proposed as shown in Figure 2.

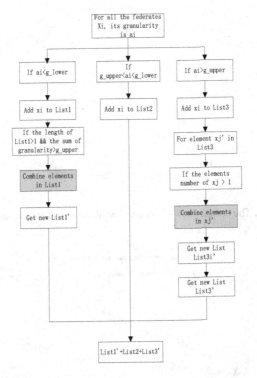

Fig. 1. The flow chart of fine-grained combination algorithm

In the process, some combination strategies are got, the balance and the minimum granularity could be achieved, and then use the objection of the problem, the ultimate optimal strategy is obtained.

5   Simulation Experiment

The open source cloud computing simulation platform "CloudSim" is extended in this paper, the idea of the proposed algorithm is tested based on the source code. Each data entity is analyzed firstly, including: Federation, Federate, Cloudlet, Vm, Host, DataCenter. To facilitate the elaboration, social network diagram is used to describe their relationship, which is shown below:

The federate combination algorithm is compared with the deployment strategy which doesn't adopt the combination algorithm. In the simulation process, 10 groups of simulations are performed, the federate number of them are 100, 200, 300, 400, 500, 600, 700, 800, 900 and 1000. To facilitate the whole running of the simulation, the deployment process of federates to virtual machine adopts the crude-grained and fine-grained combination algorithm, the deployment process of virtual machine to physical machine adopts iqr-mc algorithm. The purpose of federate combination is to reduce the number of virtual machines in running process and improve the resource utilization on the assurance of QoS.

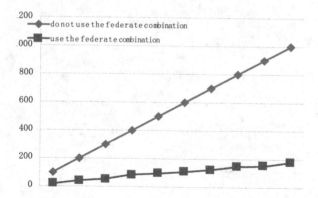

Fig. 2. The comparison of vm number along with federate number

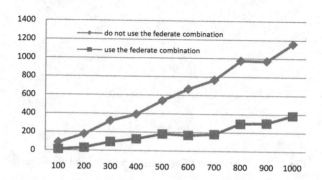

Fig. 3. The comparison of vm migration number along with federate number

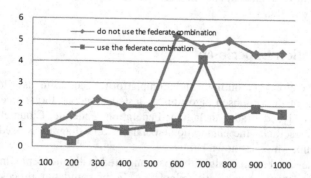

Fig. 4. The comparison of SLA violation percentage along with federate number

According to the above simulation results, the number of virtual machine and the migration number of virtual machine are greatly reduced when adopt the federate combination algorithm, hence the manage efficiency and fault tolerance are greatly improved when the simulation is in progress. On the other hand, the combination algorithm decreases the SLA violation greatly from the perspective of platform users and ensures the quality of service.

6   The Conclusion and Future Work

The initial deployment problem of HLA simulation task caused by the lack of embedded load balancing mechanism in HLA simulation system and the heterogeneity of resources in the network modeling and simulation platform are closely around and deeply researched, what's more a creative simulation task combination strategy based on Huffman coding tree is proposed in this paper, hence improve the utilization and fault tolerance and the QoS of the simulation resource. However, the improvement is on the cost of simulation time, there are still some issues that need further study.

(1) **Design a Dynamic Migration of Virtual Machine Based Scheduling Policy.** The background environment of Network modeling and simulation platform is datacenter in cloud, where virtualization technology is extensively used to form a shared virtual resource pool to use the resource more flexible and cost effective. However the dynamic migration of virtual machine is the most widely used technology and design an effective task scheduling strategy is the further work.

(2) **Solve the More Complex Task Scheduling Problem That Can Be Further Decomposed.** The deployment problem researched in this article focuses on federate which can't be decomposed, without further consideration of complex task which can be decomposed. This schedule of this kind of task should think over the sequence of constraints, the network communication overhead and so on, which is more complex. Therefore, further research should be done to solve this kind of task.

Acknowledgements. This research was supported by grant 61104057, 61074144 from the Natural Science Foundation of China, the 863 project 2011AA040501 and the Graduate Student Innovation Practice Foundation of Beihang University in China. The authors thank the reviewers for their comment.

References

1. S.I.S.C. (SISC). IEEE Standard for Modeling and Simulation (M&S) High Level Architecture (HLA) Framework and Rules. IEEE Computer Society (September 2000)
2. Yang, J., Tan, G., Wang, R.: A survey of dynamic load balancing strategies for parallel and distributed computing. Acta Electronica Sinica 38(5), 1122–1130 (2011) (in Chinese)
3. Jiang, J., Zhang, M.X., et al.: Study on load balancing algorithms based on multiple resources. Acta Electronica Sinica 30(8), 1148–1152 (2002) (in Chinese)
4. Zheng, B.G.: Achieving High Performance on Extremely Large Parallel Machines: Performance Prediction and Load Balancing. UIUC, Urbana (2005)
5. EI Ajaltouni, E., Boukerche, A., Zhang, M.: An Efficient Dynamic Load Balancing Scheme for Distributed Simulations on a Grid Infrastructure. In: Proceedings of the 12th 2008 IEEE/ACM International Symposium on Distributed Simulation and Real-Time Applications, pp. 61–68. IEEE Computer Society (2008)

6. Boukerche, A., De Grande, R.E.: Dynamic Load Balancing Using Grid Services for HLA-Based Simulations on Large-Scale Distributed Systems. In: Proceedings of the 13th 2009 IEEE/ACM International Symposium on Distributed Simulation and Real-Time Applications, pp. 175–183. IEEE Computer Society (2009)

7. Zhang, Y., Li, B., et al.: Research on Virtualization-based Simulation Environment Dynamically Building Technology for Cloud Simulation. In: Proceedings of ISAI, pp. 1754–1769 (2010)

8. De Grande, R.E., Boukerche, A.: Self-Adaptive Dynamic Load Balancing for Large-Scale HLA-based Simulation. In: Proceedings of the 2010 IEEE/ACM International Symposium on Distributed Simulation and Real-Time Applications, pp. 14–21. IEEE Computer Society (2010)

9. De Grande, R.E., Boukerche, A.: Distributed Dynamic Balancing of Communication Load for Large-Scale HLA-based Simulations. In: Proceeding of the 14th 2010 IEEE/ISCC International Symposium on Computers and Communications, pp. 1109–1114. IEEE Computer Society (2010)

10. Park, G.L., Shirazi, B., Marquis, J., et al.: Decisive path scheduling: a new list scheduling method. In: Proceedings of the International Conference on Parallel Processing, Bloomington, pp. 472–480. IEEE (1997)

11. Houshmand, M., Soleymanpour, E., Salami, H., et al.: Efficient scheduling of task graphs to multiprocessors using a combination of modified simulated annealing and list based scheduling. In: Proceedings of the 3rd International Symposium on IITSI, Jinggangshan, pp. 350–354. IEEE (2010)

12. Chen, Z., Yang, B.: Task Scheduling Based on Multidimensional Performance Clustering of Grid Service Resource. Journal of Software 20(10), 2766–2775 (2009)

Scenario Driven Lifecycle Automation
of Net-Centric Simulation

Ying Cai, Rusheng Ju, Xu Xie, Mei Yang, and Kedi Huang

College of Mechatronics Engineering and Automation,
National University of Defense Technology, 410073, Changsha, Hunan, P.R. China
Caiying_cn@126.com,
jrscy@hotmail.com,
{xiexu,meiyang,Kedihuang}@nudt.edu.cn

Abstract. Interoperability and process automation are two major problems in realizing collaborated simulation in a net-centric environment. In this paper, we propose a scenario driven architecture to solve these problems. By retrieving 5"W" element from simulation scenario, a data exchange model is generated for promoting interoperability between federations. Meanwhile, the COA (Course of Action) element of the scenario is used to generate the simulation instance lifecycle model which can be used for automating simulation lifecycle. Applications show that formalized simulation scenario enables interoperability between different federations and lifecycle automation of net-centric simulation.

Keywords: net-centric simulation, simulation scenario, COA, interoperability, simulation lifecycle automation, data exchange model, resource discovery.

1   Introduction

The recent development of Cloud Computing provides a compelling value proposition for organizations to outsource and obtain resources on demand over the Internet [1]. Cloud computing is supposed to fulfill the requests submitted by clients transparently; therefore customers like M&S (modeling and simulation) engineers can focus on the solving the problem itself instead of wasting time preparing its execution environment [2]. Due to the fact that current Cloud Computing does not well solve the problem of sharing resources among different vendors, we have presented a hybrid sharing architecture in our previous research [3]. However, before it is applied to simulation in a net-centric environment, following problems should be settled:

First, to realize collaboration among different organizations, interoperability should be guaranteed. DIS (Distributed Interactive Simulation) and HLA (High Level Architecture) treated this problem by defining PDU (Protocol Data Unit) and FOM (Federate Object Model) respectively, assuming that all models can be expressed by some kind of common Übermodel representing the truth completely and free of contradictions [4]. This assumption isn't always achievable in net-centric environment. Web service provides a promising approach to promote interoperability;

T. Xiao, L. Zhang, and M. Fei (Eds.): AsiaSim 2012, Part II, CCIS 324, pp. 413–420, 2012.

however, how to promote interoperability in an appropriate level [5] for net-centric simulation is still a problem;

Second, lifecycle automation is needed for net-centric simulation. There are two reasons. 1) How to choose the right resources? It is unrealistic for the customers to choose the resources manually from the numerous options in the cloud, especially considering the huge numbers of resources needed for one military operation simulation; 2) How to schedule the services in the lifecycle of a simulation? The lifecycle of simulation involves many steps; each deals with complex operations and collaborations. Net-centric simulation environment should provide for automating the whole process.

As an important element in M&S, simulation scenario serves as a bridge between concept model and simulation execution. It is an embodiment of concept model as well as an abstract for the simulation execution. Scenario includes the models, services, tasks, COA (Course of Action) and the context for running a simulation, which can be of great help for the interoperability and automation design of net-centric simulation.

The remainder of this paper is organized as follows: section 2 introduces scenario related concepts and formalizes the simulation scenario. Section 3 proposes the scenario driven architecture and presents the designs. Section 4 applies the method to a military simulation case and finally section 5 concludes the paper.

2   Simulation Scenario Formalization

At first, we review some scenario related concepts before extracting information from simulation scenario.

In Wikipedia, a scenario is defined as a synthetic description of an event or series of actions and events. A scenario is also an account or synopsis of a projected course of action, events or situations. However, we can hardly find consensus on definition for simulation scenario because simulation is always project specific and the definitions are related to the domain of project, such as[6],[7]. However, consensus exists over the following opinions: first, simulation scenario is different from scenario. Second, it embodies scenario control measures during simulation. Third, simulation scenario is different from simulation script which is an instance depending on platforms and applications.

The descriptions above demonstrate that simulation scenario contains the context of events and COA information, which can be used to promote interoperability and automation respectively. In the following part, we will present how to use this information in detail. And for convenience, scenario is also used as simulation scenario in this paper.

2.1   How to Promote Interoperability?

Although simulation scenario contains the situation and course of action element for semantic understanding, interoperability cannot be automatically achieved because of the heterogeneity of interface between different organizations. A common data exchange model should be built and complied with.

In order to achieve interoperability at pragmatic level, interactions should contain at least 5"W" element of the activity, namely: who, when, where, what and why. Thus we construct our data exchange model named DataExModel as below:

DataExModel={ who when where what why}

Since COA also contains 5"W" elements, it is easy to construct DataExModel by retrieving the counterparts in COA. Interactions are described in the self-describing language of XML according to the data exchange model. And a corresponding XML schema is also defined for explanation and verification. Therefore, by parsing the message though the data exchange model, pragmatic interoperability between different services can be achieved.

2.2   How to Promote Automation

In general, simulation in the net-centric environment contains three steps like other simulations: the preparation phase, the execution phase and the results treatment phase. Automation of the lifecycle means the control model should obtain enough information for the whole of process in a sequential way. For different phases of simulation, different needs should be satisfied. Firstly, the resources should be prepared before and during the simulation process, which means resources discovery should be carried out automatically. Secondly, the process of simulation execution should be presented in a manner which the simulation engine is capable to recognize. Thirdly, the results can be displayed and assessed automatically.

The COA element in the standard of C-BML (Coalition Battle Management Language) is a well defined schema for the structure of the course of action in military domain. In order to achieve more generality, the military domain elements are pruned away and the COA is formalized as below:

COA $= \{ObjectHandle, Name, EntityOwnerHandle, COAPurpose, Rules,$
        $COAStatus, COAPhases\}$

$COAPhases = \{ObjectHandle, PhaseSequence, Name, Rules, PhaseEvents\}$

$PhaseEvents = \{ObjectHandle, EventSequence, Name, EventStatus, EventEffect,$
        $Triggers, Activity\}$

$Triggers = \{ObjectHandle, Name, TriggerType, TriggeringEvent, RelativeTime,$
        $RelativeTime, EntityOwnerHandle\}$

$Activity = \{ObjectHandle, Name, TriggerHandle, ActivityData, EntityOwnerHandle\}$

$ActivityData = \{COAHandle, Task\};$

$Entity = \{ObjectHandle, Name, Property, Relation\};$

where ObjectHandle is a Universal Unique IDentifier (UUID) of the object; Name is an unabbreviated designation; EntityOwnerHandle stands for the UUID reference to the Entity that owns a particular item of data as part of that Entity's plan. COA is composed of a series of COAPhases sequenced by PhaseSequence; while COAPhases is composed of a series of PhaseEvents sequenced by EventSequence; PhaseEvents is composed of a series of Activities triggered by Triggers. For each Activity, the Entity (through EntityOwnerHandle element to find) presents the "Who". The Task element provides the "What" and "Why". The Trigger data (through TriggerHandle element to find) tells the "When" and "Where" the task will be triggered.

Once the COA element of a simulation is formalized as above, it is easy to achieve lifecycle automation of net-centric simulation. There is no need to rewrite the request for resources. Each entity stands for a resource needed for simulation so that information extracted from Entity element can be used for automatic resource discovery. It is feasible to convert the COA into an event list which can be recognized by simulation engine and executed automatically. Besides, since results are generated with 5"W" information, it is helpful for display and estimation.

3   Designs

3.1   Simulation Scenario Driven Architecture

Since the 5"W" data exchange model and description of COA have been formalized, we embed them into the design of simulation system. Fig.1 shows the simulation scenario driven architecture for net-centric simulation. It is similar to grid protocol architecture1 in the bottom layers and Cloud Architecture in the upper layers, which enables it to promote resource sharing in a Grid Computing way and transparent control in a Cloud Computing way. The shadow block is where federations join. Communication module and Supervisory Control module over the federations provide interoperability and automation of the simulation.

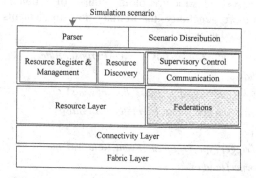
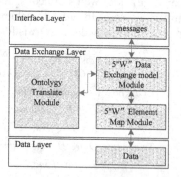

Fig. 1. Simulation scenario driven architecture   **Fig. 2.** Three-layer communication architecture

Imported simulation scenario is parsed by the Parser module and distributed by Scenario distribution module to the resource discovery module and federations of the simulation. Resource discovery module leverages this information for preparing all the resources which is then distributed to federations. Federations communicate with each other by the Communication module and process under the control of Supervisory control module according to the COA of scenario. Since all the information is contained in the simulation scenario which has been formalized in section 2, interoperability and automation lifecycle of the simulation can be realized.

3.2   Three-Layer Communication Module

We adopt the three-layer architecture for the design of Communication Module. The three-layer architecture is a classic design pattern in a client-server architecture, which contains the user interface layer as the top layer; the business logic layer as the second layer; and data layer as the bottom layer. This architecture benefits in that it separates the concern of each layer and any of the three layers can be modified independently.

We replace the middle layer with the data exchange layer as shown in Fig.2. Three sub-modules are designed for this layer, including the 5"W" Data Exchange Model module, the 5"W" Element Mapper module and an Ontology Translate module which is used for semantic analysis and translation in case the ontology is different between the federations.

When communications between different federations begins, the sender firstly maps the data into the 5"W" element and then wraps the data by data exchange module into a message with context. On the other hand, the receiver decomposes the message by exchange module with the help of ontology module and then distributed the data to the counterpart of the COA elements.

Since the 5"W" data model can be extracted from the simulation scenario, pragmatic interoperability can be achieved.

3.3   Simulation Scenario Based Automation

According to the phases of simulation defined in section 2, two things are compulsory: resource discovery and control of simulation.

(1) Resource Discovery

In a net-centric environment, a common resource discovery process is: the customer requests for resources; then the discovery agent receives the request and returns the service that matches the most. The representation of request is important because combining sufficient and understandable information in the request is the basis for the whole discovering process. However, to represent the information is very hard work considering the numbers of models needed in one simulation.

Since resource information is included in simulation scenario, there's no need to rewrite the request and it is easy to retrieve the information from a formalized simulation scenario as defined in section 2 for resource discovery. Thus for every matching process:

Firstly the scenario is parsed by discovery agent and the request for the simulation is divided to single requests for each model;

Secondly, the match engine compares the requests with the registered resources, makes reasoning based on domain knowledge base, calculates the similarity and returns the top scored result;

At last, the result is mapped to the UUID of Entity.

(2) COA Based Lifecycle Automation

Collaborated simulation can be difficult because the time advance relationships between federates often are complex. Traditionally the engineer should manually turn the scenario into a running script for the computer to follow. It wastes a lot of time and the scenario script is hard for reuse due to heterogeneity. The COA element of a scenario can reflect this information.

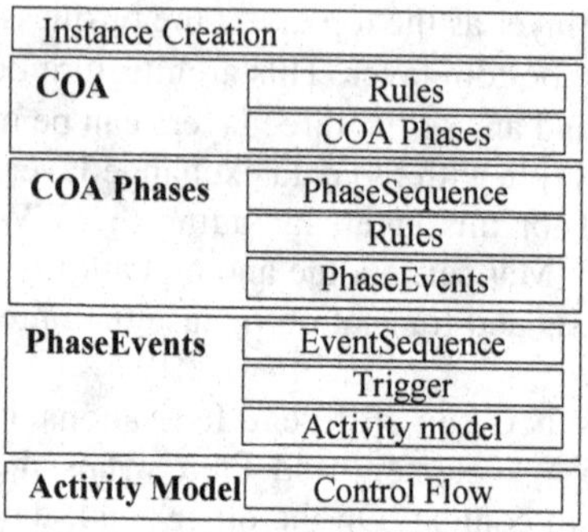

Instance Creation		
COA	Rules	
	COA Phases	
COA Phases	PhaseSequence	
	Rules	
	PhaseEvents	
PhaseEvents	EventSequence	
	Trigger	
	Activity model	
Activity Model	Control Flow	

Fig. 3. Simulation Instance Lifecycle Model

Based on the COA description in section 2, a Simulation instance lifecycle model is built, as is shown in Fig. 3. Though this model, it is simple to control the process according to the COA and control system can easily parse this information and execute simulation automatically.

This model can be easily embedded into other platform as well, such as a Grid Computing system; it will be described in the next section.

4   Applications

In this section, we present an application of our method to a military simulation case.

Since MSDL (Military Simulation Description Language) [6] has been approved as a standard by SISO (Simulation Interoperability Standards Organization) and widely accepted by organization in military simulation domain, we employ a MSDL based sample scenario from [8] as a draft simulation scenario. Because the current version of the MSDL standard in balloting under SISO does not contain a specification of the COA structure [9] we adopt the COA model defined in its draft version [10] for supplement.

4.1   Step 1: Simulation Scenario Formalization

The draft scenario is converted to a standardized one as introduced in section 2. In MSDL, model resource requirements are defined in Unit element and Equipment element in Organizations component, thus they are mapped to the Entity element for resource discovery.

The activity model of COA in C-BML is then mapped to 5"W" data model for data exchange according to Fig. 4.

Once simulation scenario is formalized, interoperability can be achieved.

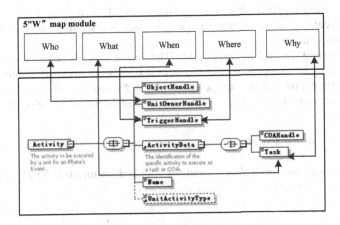

Fig. 4. Activity element mapping to "5W" data model

4.2 Step 2: Process Automation

4.2.1 Simulation Scenario Based Resource Discovery

In this sample, there are 212 Units and 576 EquipmentItems, 760 Entities in total. It takes a lot of work to write request for each of them were it not carried out by simulation scenario driven method. The UnitSymbolModifiers element in Unit element specifies the modifiers of unit symbol. It is an xs:all compositor comprised of the elements, including almost all the information needed for discovering the model.

Descriptions of model in UnitSymbolModifiers Element Structure are converted to relation diagram which makes the querying process more efficient. And since the models can be searched separately, it can be automatically conducted in parallel.

4.2.2 Simulation Instance Lifecycle Model Based Control

Simulation instance lifecycle model can be converted to workflow to assist the control of simulation. For those who want to use web computing resources such as Grid Computing, it is easy to embed the model into the legacy architecture. Taking Grid Workflow Execution Language [11] for example, by replacing the instance lifecycle model with simulation instance lifecycle model defined in Fig. 3, simulation can be deployed on the Open Grid Services Architecture.

5 Conclusions

In this paper, we propose a scenario driven architecture to support interoperability and automation for net-centric simulations. Information in a simulation scenario is retrieved to build the data exchange model, which enables interoperability at pragmatic level. Simulation instance lifecycle model generated from the COA element of scenario can be used to control the process of the simulation, which benefits in the following ways:

1) Automated resource discovery is supported. By using the Entity element in simulation scenario as the resource request, resources discovery can be conducted in parallel automatically;

2) Automated control is supported. The simulation instance lifecycle model generated from the COA element of formalized simulation scenario enables automatic control of simulation in a net-centric environment. Moreover, this model can be easily embedded into other mature platforms, which can be of great help for preserving legacy system.

Furthermore, formalized simulation scenario can also promote the reuse of the scenarios.

In conclusion, our simulation scenario driven architecture will be of great value to the net-centric simulations.

References

1. Foster, I., Zhao, Y., Raicu, L., et al.: Cloud Computing and Grid Computing 360-Degree Compared. In: GCE 2008, pp. 1–10 (2008)
2. Li, B.H., Cai, X.D., et al.: Networked Modeling and Simulation Platform based on the Concept of Cloud Computing-Cloud Simulation. Journal of System Simulation 21(7), 5292–5299 (2009)
3. Cai, Y., Yang, M., Huang, K.D.: Resource Sharing Architecture for Simulation Based on Hybrid Pattern. Journal of System Simulation 7(23), 89–93 (2011)
4. Tolk, A., Diallo, S.Y.: Using a Formal Approach to Simulation Interoperability Specify Languages for Ambassador Agents. In: Proceedings of the 2010 WSC, pp. 359–370. IEEE CS Press (2010)
5. Tolk, A., Muguira, J.A.: The Levels of Conceptual Interoperability Model. In: 2003 Fall Simulation Interoperability Workshop, paper 03F-SIW-007 (2003)
6. Scenario Definition Language Study Group. S.: Standard for: Military Scenario Definition Language (MSDL) SISO-STD-007-2008,
   http://www.sisostds.org/digitalLibrary.aspx?command=core_Dow nload&EntryId-29782 (last access June 10, 2011)
7. Lima, G., Nascimento, F.M.: Simulation Scenarios: a Means of Deriving Fault Resilience for Real-Time Systems. In: 11th Brazilian Workshop on Real-Time and Embedded Systems, pp. 1–12 (2007)
8. Scenario Definition Language Study Group, SampleMSDL,
   http://www.sisostds.org/digitalLibrary.aspx?command=core_Dow nload&EntryId-31559 (last access June 10, 2011)
9. Blais, C.: Military Scenario Definition Language (MSDL): How Broadly Can It Be Applied. In: 2008 Spring SIW, paper 08S-SIW-002 (2008)
10. Scenario Definition Language Study Group, S.: Specifications for: Military Scenario Definition Language (MSDL), Initial Draft (April 2005)
11. Cybok, D.: A Grid workflow infrastructure. Concurrency and Computation: Practice and Experience 18, 1243–1254 (2006)
12. Tolk, A., Diallo, S., Dupigny, K., et al.: A Layered Web Services Architecture to Adapt Legacy Systems to the Command & Control Information Exchange Data Model (C2IEDM). In: 2005 Euro Simulation Interoperability Workshop, Toulouse, France, paper 05E-SIW-034. ACM Press (2005)

Research on Co-simulation Task Scheduling
Based on Virtualization Technology
under Cloud Simulation

Chen Yang[1], Xudong Chai[2], and Faguang Zhang[1]

[1] School of Automation Science and Electrical Engineering,
Beihang University, 100191 Beijing, China
[2] Beijing Simulation Center, 100854, Beijing, China
wzhyoung@163.com, xdchai@263.net, davidfaguang@gmail.com

Abstract. By introducing virtualization technology, cloud simulation platform can break tight coupling between soft simulation resources (OS, software, model, etc) and computing resources, shield the heterogeneity of underlying computing hardware, and flexibly divide computing resources, which makes the simulation task scheduling agile, transparent and efficient. Due to the characteristics of co-simulation: consistency and close coupling of time and space, one abstract description model of both co-simulation task and computing resources in cloud simulation is proposed, and then two task scheduling models based on different objectives and constraints are put forward, including models for green energy-saving and minimal time span respectively. Finally, the aforementioned scheduling models applied in one aircraft virtual prototype co-simulation are discussed in detail which proves their advantages, and also future work is presented.

Keywords: cloud simulation, co-simulation task scheduling, virtualization technology.

1 Introduction

At present, the widely used High-level architecture [1] provides one general development framework and methodology of large scale distributed simulation systems, which promotes reuse and interoperability of simulation model [2], however it does not inherently support resource management and task scheduling for co-simulation, especially in most applications simulation resources and federates are statically bound together [3], which makes co-simulation scheduling difficult to achieve.

[4], [5] presented their detailed research on collaborative task scheduling and distributing under grid environment, but they mainly focus on computing task which differs greatly from co-simulation task-requires intensive interaction and time synchronization. Researchers have combined M&S and grid computing technologies together to form the simulation grid which can achieve dynamic share and reuse, collaborative interoperability, optimally scheduling and execution of various

T. Xiao, L. Zhang, and M. Fei (Eds.): AsiaSim 2012, Part II, CCIS 324, pp. 421–430, 2012.

simulation resources in the grid or federation [6]. The simulation grid primarily enables the necessary conditions for co-simulation scheduling. [7] put forwards one simulation grid scheduling framework based on monitored node state information (including static and dynamic scheduling but no corresponding algorithms). [8] did solid works on optimal static allocation and dynamic load division of optimistic discrete event simulation, but this method can only be applied to simulations with few nodes, because it contains the ratio of the task load to the total capacity of all nodes, which can be very close to zero if there exist a great many nodes under grid or cloud computing environment. [9] proposed a dynamic and adaptive load balancing method of the HLA-based large scale simulation in simulation grid, but the author does not consider difficulties for scheduling the task among heterogeneous grid nodes, resource contentions and runtime conflicts between multiple tasks in one grid node. [10] took into account both computation and communication factors in establishing an node selection model and one corresponding genetic-based solving algorithm is presented, but the selection model assumes that all users need the optimal nodes, which is not always suitable.

Additionally, the strong heterogeneity and uneven performance of nodes, and the instability of communication performance in simulation grid both lead to restrictions on task scheduling, and even more simulation grid lacks fully support for fine-grained resource share, multi-user online use, high efficient fault-tolerance, etc [11].

In order to address the aforementioned problems in distributed simulation, the concept, connotation and patterns of cloud simulation were presented in [11], [12]. In cloud computing field, there exists much research literature on task allocation based on Map-Reduce programming model and hardware resource scheduling in VMM (virtual machine monitor) and SLA-based individual application scheduling using VM [13], however research on co-simulation oriented scheduling with considerations for time and space consistency and synchronization is lacked. Combining the co-simulation requirement with the characteristics of virtualized simulation resource in cloud simulation, the author first proposed an abstract description model of co-simulation task and simulation resource, and then two task scheduling models based on different objectives and constraints are put forward, including models for green energy-saving and minimal time span respectively. Finally, the elementary analysis of one aircraft virtual prototype co-simulation and future work are presented.

Unless special instructions, the co-simulation task scheduling in this paper is based on HLA and refers to the static scheduling in the initial stage of simulation.

2   Co-simulation Task Scheduling in Cloud Simulation

2.1   Requirements and Problems in Co-simulation Scheduling

All federates constituting the simulation system run collaboratively to accomplish the co-simulation task. During the process of simulation, each federate need to 1) choose and execute the simulation models according to the application logic, 2) interact with other federates. As a result, the main factors affecting the efficiency of co-simulation lie in the computing capacity of host node and the communication capacity between the nodes.

In fact, the execution of each federate relies on the operating system (OS) and software environment. For example, the computation of Adams model in federates needs the Adams software, and federates also have the portability problem between different OSs. In the traditional network modeling and simulation environment, the running environment heterogeneity limits the available physical machines (PMs) for federates and also the scheduling algorithm of co-simulation task will be badly affected.

2.2   The Virtualization-Based Co-simulation Scheduling Approach

Virtualization technology is introduced into cloud simulation, which offers a new and more effective way to address the problems above. Virtualization technology can be used to provide one unified standard encapsulating form for various heterogeneous simulation resources, which can shield the heterogeneity of hardware architectures, system environments and simulation resources, so as to make the scheduling of the simulation task more flexible, as shown in the figure 1. More specifically, they are 1) static scheduling: via quick deployment and start of virtual instruments to create the simulation running environment, 2) dynamic scheduling: via dynamic configuration or live migration of virtual machines (VMs) to enable runtime adjustment of simulation environment. Especially, multiple virtual running environments can run in one PM, thus making scheduling of federates more flexible and efficient.

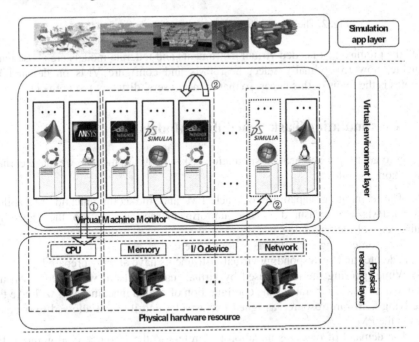

Fig. 1. Collaborative scheduling enabling technology in cloud simulation

The whole scheduling routine is to decompose simulation task to federate models, then map federate models to VMs, and map VMs with proper configuration to executing PMs, as shown in figure 2. Moreover federates under different OSs can execute in one PM with the help of system virtualization technology.

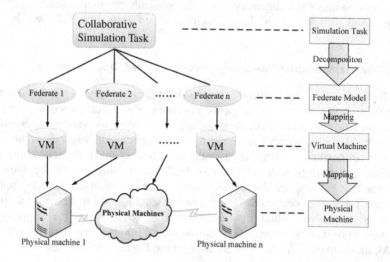

Fig. 2. The whole scheduling routine of co-simulation task

On the premise that needed virtual instruments and federate models are chosen and available, how to optimally select host PMs and configure VMs on demand by federates is the focus of this paper, so that to meet users' different requirement.

3   Co-simulation Task Scheduling Models

In order to get proper and neat co-simulation task scheduling models, we make certain assumptions as follows:

1) The computing capability of each PM and the communication capability between PMs are measured in one uniform metric, and so do the capability requirements of the federation.

2) Every processing core of PMs is homogeneous.

3) Federates and corresponding virtual instruments have already prepared.

4) While ignoring the loss caused by virtual machine itself, we directly map the requirement of each federate to the configuration of virtual machine. VM will take the underlying hardware resource assigned exclusively, and it is not allowed to oversell cores in the PM.

5) The demand of one co-simulation task refers to the resource configuration for simulation models, which can meet users' basic quality requirement of simulation.

6) The computation requirement of one single federate cannot exceed the most powerful PM. This is reasonable, because it is common that there exist ten more cores in one physical node with the booming multi-core technology.

In the course of operation, the undirected weighted graph which is composed of the computing and communication capability needed by co-simulation task can be obtained by 3 means: 1) using the test set and test bed [14]; 2) via the history running records of co-simulation system in the case library; 3) evaluating the complexity of the algorithm and programming language.

The requirement of federate models can be described as five element set:

$$Co-SimTask =< Fed, Env, Comp, CompC, Comm > \tag{1}$$

Where, $Fed = \{FM_1, FM_2, \ldots, FM_{Num}\}$ denotes the federate model set,

$|Fed| = Num$ refers to number of federates,

$Env = \{< OS, SoftSet > (FM_i) | FM_i \in Fed\}$, $< OS, SoftSet >$ denotes the OS and software requirement of federate,

$Comp = \{N_{compute}(FM_i) | FM_i \in Fed\}$, $N_{compute}$ is defined as the performance demand of federates,

$CompC = \{N_{core}(FM_i) | FM_i \in Fed\}$, N_{core} refers to the needed number of physical cores allocated for virtual machine that is host to federate, and if the computation demand is mapped as non-integer, N_{core} is assigned as the closest upward integer,

$Comm = \{N_{net}(FM_i, FM_j) | FM_i, FM_j \in Fed\}$, N_{net} denotes the demanded communication capability.

Similarly, the physical computation resource can be described as:

$$Resource =< ND, CP, CPR, CM > \tag{2}$$

Where, $ND = \{Node_1, Node_2, \ldots, Node_k\}$ denotes k physical nodes,

$CP = \{NR_{compute}(i) | i \in ND\}$, $NR_{compute}$ refers to computation performance of the physical node,

$CPC = \{NR_{core}(i) | i \in ND\}$, NR_{core} denotes the number of cores in one physical node,

$CM = \{NR_{net}(i, j) | i, j \in ND\}$, NR_{net} is defined as the communication performance between physical nodes.

We assumes scheduling map as:

$$Fed \rightarrow ND$$

$$FM_i \rightarrow Node_j$$

We use the number of physical nodes: $p = N_{node}$, which can be denoted as $\{Node_1, Node_2, \cdots, Node_p\}$.

(1) The Scheduling Model for Green Power

Under the constraint that simulation system performance meets the minimal demand, based on virtualization technology, this model aims at finding the scheduling solution for co-simulation task with least physical nodes in order to reducing the operating nodes, improve the efficiency of computation resource, and save energy.

Messages exchanged between federates in one physical node are not through networks, but through the underlying virtual machine monitor directly. Thus the delay can be negligible comparing to the common network delay. So the communication constraint imposed on federates in one physical node can be removed.

$$\min p = N_{node}$$

$$s.t. N_{node} \leq k$$

$$\sum_{SM(FM_i)=Node_m} N_{core}(FM_i) \leq NR_{core}(Node_m), \forall 0 < m \leq N_{node}$$

$$\sum_{SM(FM_i)=Node_m, SM(FM_j)=Node_n} N_{net}(FM_i, FM_j) \leq NR_{net}(Node_m, Node_n),$$

$$\forall 0 < m \leq N_{node}, Node_m \neq Node_n$$

(3)

The three constraints denote respectively that the number of nodes allocated should less than that of available nodes; the cores for all federates scheduled to one node should be limited by cores in that node; the aggregate communication between federates in one node and federates in another node should be restricted by the communication capability of these two nodes.

(2) The Scheduling Model for Minimal Time Span

The main idea of this model is using enough physical nodes to reduce the time span during the execution of co-simulation and to reduce the cost of time. In ideal case, the computation task of simulation model can be mapped to physical node according to the proportion of total simulation task and the total computing capacity. It needs to be guaranteed that the communication capacity between physical nodes is greater than the communication command between simulation models.

At present, multi-machine virtualization technology waits for further research. The existing technology cannot seamlessly integrate the resource on several physical nodes as one logical virtual computing resource very well. Thus, simulation federate model cannot be scheduled to cross-node VM and the computing capacity distributed to federate model shouldn't be stronger than the maximum computing capacity of a single physical node. $NRA_{core}(FM_i)$ refers to the number of cores allocated to federate model FM_i in order to gain best performance of whole system.

$$Min\left\{ \left| r - \frac{\sum_{SM(FM_i)=Node_m} NRA_{core}(FM_i)}{\sum_{SM(FM_i)=Node_m} N_{core}(FM_i)} \right|, \forall 0 < m \leq N_{node} \right\}$$

$$s.t. \ r = \frac{Max\{NR_{core}(Node_j)\}}{Max\{N_{core}(FM_i)\}}, FM_i \in Fed, 0 < j \leq N_{node}$$

$$NRA_{core}(FM_i) = N_{core}(FM_i) \times r, FM_i \in Fed$$

$$\sum_{SM(FM_i)=Node_m, SM(FM_j)=Node_n} N_{net}(FM_i, FM_j) \leq NR_{net}(Node_m, Node_n),$$

$$\forall 0 < m \leq N_{node}, Node_m \neq Node_n$$

(4)

The objective is that most federates get maximal proportional cores for computation, where r is the ratio of most powerful computing resource to maximal require of computing power among all federates. The other equation constrain refers to that the ratio of cores allocated for each federates to their demands should be according with r. The last inequality constraint denotes federates in another node should be restricted by the communication capability of these two nodes.

As presented above, we can see that two scheduling models have distinct purpose, one for basic performance with more interest on energy saving or fundamentally money saving, the other for best performance considering less on resource consuming but more on less time. This is evident when there exist 32 more cores in one PM which can provide powerful computing capability, some multi-disciplinary virtual prototypes care more on verifying the design of real physical system, and some simulation applications are collaboratively executing with real system needing badly for quick simulation result to guide operation of real system. This is also an extremely important issue when users access the simulation service on public simulation cloud with billing metrics for resource allocation.

4   Application Example

Currently, based on the research fruits of cloud simulation, the author team has developed one cloud simulation platform prototype "COSIM-CSP", which has been applied in areas of multidisciplinary collaborative simulation of virtual prototyping and large-scale system-level co-simulation [11], [12].

The collaborative simulation design system of an aircraft virtual prototype is mainly made up of five federate models (shown in table 1), five domain modeling and simulation tools (Fluent for fluid federate, MATLAB for control federate, ADAMS for multi-body dynamics federate, EASY5 for hydraulics federate, CATIA for three dimensional visualization), HLA-RTI and computer system. Table 1 shows the running environment and performance requirement of simulation models.

Table 1. The requirement of federate models

No.	Simulation Model	Software List	OS	Performance Demand
1	Fluid Simulation Model	Fluent, RTI	Redhat Linux	8core, memory 4GB
2	Undercarriage Control Model	Matlab, RTI	Windows	1core, memory 1GB
3	Undercarriage Hydraulic Model	Easy5, RTI	Windows	1core, memory 1GB
4	Landing Gear Multi-body Dynamics Model	Adams, RTI	Windows	1core, memory 1GB
5	3D Model	CATIA, RTI	Windows	2core, memory 2GB

The typical physical node connected together by Gigabit Switch is 2 CPU (each 4 core inside), memory 8G. In our test case, the communication delay and bandwidth are not the bottleneck, due to the large time spent on solving of federate models. Because according to statistics, under the above ideal environment simulation time advances 35 seconds (16 steps) in one minute of wall clock-one step needs 3.75

seconds, but in LAN the network delay is at the level of millisecond. In the traditional way, distributed domain participants need 5 physical machines with different OS and software to launch M&S activities in parallel.

(1) The scheduling model for green power

Using brute search method, one possible solution for green energy-saving model can be:

Table 2. One solution for the green energy-saving scheduling model

Solutions	PM No.	Co-simulation task scheduling
scheduling plan 1	1# 4GB memory left	VM(1, 8 core, Memory 4GB)
	2# 3 core, 3GB memory left	VM(2, 1 core, Memory 1GB), VM(3, 1 core, Memory 1GB), VM(4, 1 core, Memory 1GB), VM(5, 2 core, Memory 2GB)

Comparing to traditional methods, 3 physical machines are saved. Even though the co-simulation task can be scheduled to 2 physical machines under grid simulation environment in theory, however there exist severe security and resource contention problems.

(2) The Scheduling Model for Minimal Time Span

Fluid Simulation Model needs 8 cores, which are the maximum cores that one node can provide. Moreover, the performance of co-simulation system largely depends on the slowest federate, so just upgrading other federates resource configuration except Fluid federate can exert limited effect on performance enhancement. So we assume that basic demand of Fluid Simulation Model is 4 cores, 4GB Memory, and give the solutions. Here

$$r = \frac{Max\{NR_{core}\left(Node_j\right)\}}{Max\{N_{core}\left(FM_i\right)\}} = 8/4 = 2,$$

and the configuration of the whole system is doubled. So, according to formula (3), using brute search method, two typical scheduling plans can be:

Table 3. Solutions for the minimal time span scheduling model

Solutions	PM No.	Font size and style
scheduling plan 1	1# resource exhausted	VM(1, 8 core, Memory 8GB)
	2# resource exhausted	VM(3, 2 core, Memory 2GB), VM(4, 2 core, Memory 2GB), VM(5, 4 core, Memory 4GB)
	3# 6 core, 6GB memory left	VM(2, 2 core, Memory 2GB)
scheduling plan 2	1# resource exhausted	VM(1, 8 core, Memory 8GB)
	2# 2 core, 2GB memory left	VM(3, 2 core, Memory 2GB), VM(4, 2 core, Memory 2GB), VM(2, 2 core, Memory 2GB)
	3# 4 core, 4GB memory left	VM(5, 4 core, Memory 4GB)

Using the minimal time span model, the performance can be possibly enhanced doubly, while the computation resources are efficiently utilized (less than traditional 5 physical nodes), so that avoiding the case that limited performance enhancement is gained with more computation resources.

So we can see that using two scheduling models, different performance and result are gained which are both better than traditional methods-1 model needs minimal physical machines giving out basic performance and 2 model needs 3 physical machines giving out double performance reducing the time consumption of simulation.

5   Conclusions and Future Work

The author primarily proposed two static scheduling models for co-simulation task, and then based on the two models elementary discussion and analysis are put forward which shows the advantage of co-simulation scheduling in cloud simulation.

Form the discussion above, we can see that co-simulation in Cloud Simulation has some new characteristics as follows by introducing virtualization technology:

(1) Multiple heterogeneous tasks can execute in one node;
(2) Each application has one isolated running environment, avoiding interference and conflicts;
(3) In case that static scheduling of task leads to poor performance in some simulation time, dynamic reconfiguration or live migration of running environment can be implemented for better simulation system performance.

So future work includes:

(1) The scheduling method across the whole simulation process including runtime dynamic adjustment, and the complete supporting framework;
(2) Some intelligent optimization algorithm to solve the two scheduling models;
(3) Multiple co-simulation task scheduling methods, which enables multi-user online mode.

References

1. IEEE Standard 1516 Standard for M&S HLA-Framework and Rules. The Institute of Electrical and Electronics Engineers, New York (2010)
2. Li, Z., Cai, W., Tuner, S.J., Pan, K.: Federate migration in a service oriented HLA RTI. In: Procs of international Symposium on Distributed Simulation and Real-Time Applications, pp. 113–121. IEEE Press, New York (2007)
3. Wu, L., Du, Z.H.: A dynamic knowledge-based task scheduling algorithm in simulation grid environment. Journal of Computer Research and Development 45(2), 261–268 (2008)
4. Zhang, W.Z., Tian, Z.H.: Multi-Cluster Co-Allocation Scheduling Algorithms in Virtual Computing Environment. Journal of Software 18(8), 2027–2037 (2007) (in Chinese)
5. Banino, C., Beaumont, O.: Scheduling Strategies for Master-Slave Tasking on Heterogeneous Processor Platforms. IEEE Trans. Parall. Distr. Syst. 15(4), 1–12 (2004)

6. Li, B.H., Chai, X.D., Hou, B.C.: Research and Application on CoSim (Collaborative Simulation) Grid. In: The Proceeding of MS-MTSA 2006 (2006)
7. Fu, Y.F., Bai, X.J.: Scheduling Method of Resource for Simulation System based on Grid. In: The International Conference on Computational Intelligence and Software Engineering (2009)
8. Zhang, Y.X., Yao, Y.P.: A dynamic partitioning algorithm based on approximate local search for optimistic parallel discrete event simulation. Chinese Journal of Computers 33(5), 813–821 (2010)
9. Grande, R.E.D., Boukerche, A.: Self-Adaptive Dynamic Load Balancing for Large-Scale HLA-based Simulations. In: 14th IEEE/ACM Symposium on Distributed Simulation and Real-Time Applications (2010)
10. Song, C.F., Li, B.H., Chai, X.D.: Node selection in simulation grid. Journal of Beijing Univ. Aero. Astro. 35(1), 56–60 (2009)
11. Li, B.H., Chai, X.D., Hou, B.C.: A networked modeling & simulation platform based on the concept of cloud computing-"cloud simulation platform". J. Sys. Sim. 21(17), 5292–5299 (2009) (in Chinese)
12. Li, B.H., Chai, X.D., Hou, B.C.: New advances of the research on cloud simulation. In: Proceedings of Asia Simulation Conference. Springer, Japan (2011)
13. Wang, Q.B., Jin, X.: Virtualization and cloud computing. Publishing House of Electronics Industry, Beijing (2010) (in Chinese)
14. Wang, Q.J., Gui, X.L.: Multi-start most steep hill-climbing algorithm for grid node selection based on execution cost model. J. Xi'an JiaoTong Univ. 37(8) (2003) (in Chinese)

A Service Encapsulation Method
in Cloud Simulation Platform

Wensheng Xu[1], Lingjun Kong[1], Nan Li[2], and Jianzhong Cha[1]

[1] School of Mechanical, Electronic and Control Engineering,
Beijing Jiaotong University, Beijing 100044, China
[2] School of Material and Mechanical Engineering,
Beijing Technology and Business University, Beijing 100037, China
{wshxu,08116294,jzcha}@bjtu.edu.cn,
linan@th.btbu.edu.cn

Abstract. In a cloud simulation platform, there exist a large number of simulation software tools that need to be encapsulated as services that can be invoked conveniently when required in the product development process. An appropriate architecture for encapsulating and managing these software tools are needed to facilitate the management of these simulation resources. In this paper, the service object-oriented architecture (SOOA) is adopted to construct the service sharing environment for engineering software on the dynamic network, and the SOOA-based two-stage service encapsulation method for engineering software is proposed. With this method, simulation software tools can be encapsulated and deployed as services conveniently without the need of programming, and the encapsulated services can be invoked and accessed conveniently through a standard Web browser via the cloud simulation platform portal.

Keywords: service encapsulation, cloud simulation, simulation software tools, service object-oriented architecture.

1   Introduction

In a cloud simulation platform there exist a large number of engineering software tools such as CAD, CAE, CAM, CAPP, etc. that can facilitate the design and analysis activities in a product development process. Since these software tools are normally expensive and they should be utilized conveniently by as most developers as possible, and they should be integrated dynamically and flexibly for specific product development processes, an appropriate architecture for managing these engineering software tools needs to be adopted to encapsulate these software tools as services and then manage these services. These simulation resources should be conveniently invoked or launched dynamically by product developers. Encapsulating engineering software tools as services is a very useful approach to realize the sharing and management of the distributed simulation resources in a cloud simulation platform.

T. Xiao, L. Zhang, and M. Fei (Eds.): AsiaSim 2012, Part II, CCIS 324, pp. 431–439, 2012.

In recent years, Service Object-Oriented Architecture (SOOA) has evolved rapidly from traditional Service Oriented Architecture (SOA) which is basically Service Protocol-Oriented Architecture (SPOA) [1]. The comparison of SPOA and SOOA is shown in Fig.1. In SPOA, the service protocol between service providers and service requestors is fixed beforehand, the network environment is assumed constant, reliable, and no latency exists, so it cannot adapt to the dynamic network environment very well. In contrast, SOOA is protocol neutral, execution neutral and co-location neutral [2], and the service requestor does not need know the location of the service provider and the communication protocol beforehand. The service proxy is the key in SOOA: the service proxy is generated, configured and published by the service provider, so it knows the location and the communication protocol of service provider. After the service requestor gets the service proxy, it can access the service without knowledge of the specific communication protocol and the location of the service provider. In the locating process of the service registry, multicast is used as the discover protocol for service providers and service requestors, so the location of the service registry does not need to be known beforehand either. Because of the features of SOOA, it can provide a fundamental sharing environment for engineering software tools even when these tools and the network environment are dynamic and less reliably available.

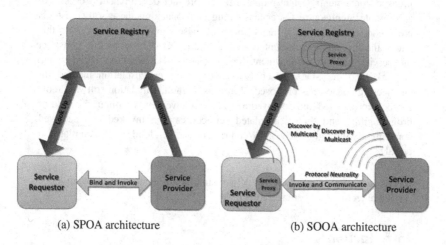

(a) SPOA architecture   (b) SOOA architecture

Fig. 1. Comparison between SPOA and SOOA

In this paper, a service encapsulation method based on SOOA for engineering software tools is proposed to achieve the efficient sharing of engineering software resources in the cloud simulation platform, and the Jini middleware [3] is used as the implementation of SOOA. The framework of a cloud simulation platform is first analyzed (Section 2), then the SOOA-based service encapsulation process for engineering software is proposed (Section 3), and an application case for encapsulating an engineering software tool is presented (Section 4), and finally the conclusions are given (Section 5).

2   Service Encapsulation in the Cloud Simulation Platform

2.1   Framework of Cloud Simulation Platform

The layered framework of a cloud simulation platform is shown in Fig. 2. The framework can be divided basically into five layers: resource layer, encapsulation layer, service layer, task management layer and platform portal layer.

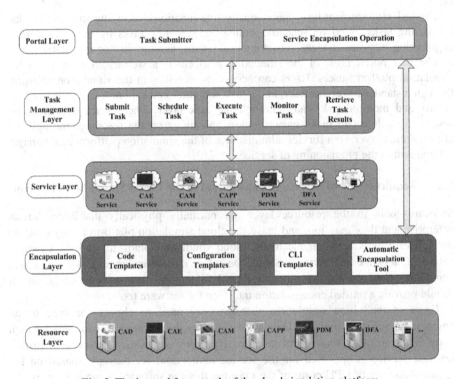

Fig. 2. The layered framework of the cloud simulation platform

In the resource layer, there are different kinds of engineering software tools, such as Computer Aided Design (CAD), Computer Aided Engineering (CAE), Computer Aided Manufacturing (CAM), Computer Aided Process Planning (CAPP), Product Data Management (PDM), Design for Assembly(DFA), and other engineering software tools. For each type of software, there are normally a number of copies that are running on different physical or virtual machines that provide the same functions.

The service encapsulation layer is responsible for encapsulating engineering software tools as services, so users of the cloud simulation platform can easily invoke various services. Service encapsulation is a key issue in the cloud simulation platform as it affects the efficiency and effectiveness of the cloud simulation platform and the management approach of the platform. The automatic encapsulation tool can take advantage of code templates, configuration templates and Command-Line Interface (CLI) templates to construct services, as explained in Section 3.

After encapsulation, the engineering software resources are presented as services in the service layer. The service layer contains various engineering software services, such as CAD service, CAE service, CAM service, CAPP service, DFA service, and other services, which are corresponding to the physical resources in the resource layer.

The task management layer has basically five functions: receiving submitted tasks, scheduling tasks based on schedule strategies, executing tasks by invoking remote engineering software services, retrieving task results, and monitoring task states.

The user portal layer of the simulation platform is a web-based entry point for simulation platform users. Users can access the services in the simulation platform through a standard Web browser, and a task submitter can submit a task, retrieve task results and monitor task states through the task layer. The service encapsulation operation module can make encapsulation operations on the resources through the encapsulation layer, so a service administrator of the simulation platform can manage, list and search the provisioning of services.

2.2   Requirements of Service Encapsulation in the Cloud Simulation Platform

Software tools in the resource layer are normally physically distributed in an enterprise and they may join and leave the cloud simulation platform at any time, so the software tools are dynamic to the cloud simulation platform, and the dynamic nature of network and services should be taken into consideration [4]. The cloud simulation platform acts as a resource pool for engineering software tools, and it should provide a unified encapsulation interface for software tools.

Users of the cloud simulation platform only need to choose the type of an engineering software tool and then invoke it, they do not need to care about which copy of the software tool of the specified type they are using. Of course, if further level of service is specified for the service invocation, for example, based on the required number of CPU cores of the machine that the software is running on, or the memory size the machine has or the required speed of the CPU of the machine, then some qualified service may be selected by the cloud simulation platform for the service request.

The service encapsulation process should be easy to follow, and it should be system administrator-oriented, not programmer-oriented, and the administrator of the platform should encapsulate the software tools as services conveniently by a simple procedure through a standard Web browser without secondary development of the software.

The encapsulated services can be used by any users in the distributed departments of an organization, but only the individual or the department who owns the software has the highest priority of usage. So the service should be manageable according to the owner's privileges and requirements.

3   SOOA-Based Service Encapsulation Process

3.1   Encapsulation Interface of Engineering Software

In order to meet the encapsulation requirements in the cloud simulation platform discussed above, Jini [3] as an implementation of SOOA is used as the fundamental architecture for encapsulating engineering software on the dynamic network.

In order to encapsulate the engineering software as services, the invocation interface of engineering software is needed as the encapsulation interface. There are normally two kinds of invocation interface for engineering software: API (Application Programming Interface) and CLI (Command-Line Interface) [5]. The encapsulation of engineering software based on API is focused on how to encapsulate some features of the software into a general service or how to encapsulate engineering software for a specific engineering application[6,7], and it usually needs secondary development of the software because of the APIs of different engineering software are normally different. So the API is not suitable for the uniform encapsulation interface of service for different engineering software. On the contrary, the CLIs of different software are only different in CLI executor, CLI parameters and parameter order, but the invoking method is the same that the software can be invoked by command-line. So the CLI can be used as the uniform encapsulation interface for different engineering software tools to realize the service encapsulation without secondary development.

3.2   Two-Stage Service Encapsulation

The two-stage service encapsulation process of engineering software is shown in Fig. 3. It is actually the process of filling the encapsulation templates with the relevant information for the engineering software. The basic service template includes the code template and the configuration template. In the first stage encapsulation, the relevant engineering software information is incorporated into the basic service template, such as interface name, method name, command-line template, service template description, operator name and etc., and it can then generate the type service template, i.e. the interface template for a specific type of engineering software with standard service interface.

In the second stage encapsulation, the relevant service information including service name, service instance number, service description, software name, software path, software description and etc. is incorporated into the interface template to generate the engineering software service. The generated service is the encapsulated Jini-based service which can be invoked through the Jini interface [3], and it mainly has three components: provider jars, requestor jars and the configuration file. The provider jars and the configuration file are used by the service provider to register service in the Jini Lookup Service and encapsulate the CLI of the engineering software. The requestor jars are used by service requestors to invoke the engineering software service.

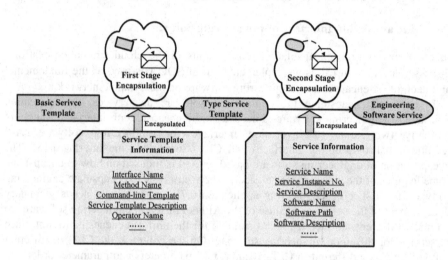

Fig. 3. The two-stage service encapsulation process

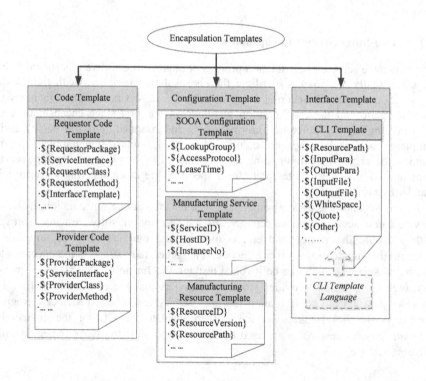

Fig. 4. Structure of the encapsulation templates

3.3   Encapsulation Templates

Encapsulation templates include code templates, configuration templates and interface templates which are key to the encapsulation process, whose structure is shown in Fig.4. The templates are all constructed in VTL (Velocity Template Language) which can facilitate string substitution operations [8]. The code templates are used to generate program code of the simulation service, including requestor code templates and provider code templates. The service management function of engineering software is implemented with the code template with four management operations: start service, pause service, resume service and stop service. The configuration templates are implemented by the mechanism of Jini configuration [9] and it can be dynamically loaded by SOOA-based service programs with necessary service information and software resource information. The interface templates are the CLI templates for various software tools. Template instantiation of the interface template into the Java interface class for service providers of HyperMesh software is shown in Fig. 5.

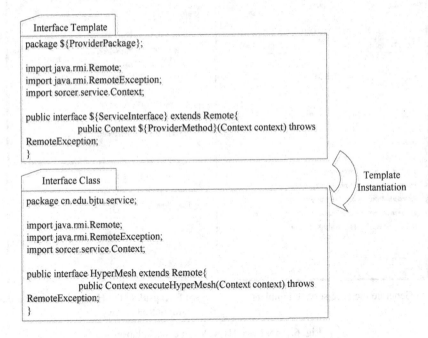

Fig. 5. Template instantiation of the interface template for HyperMesh software

4   Implementation of the Encapsulation Process

The service encapsulation process is implemented in the automatic encapsulation tool and the service encapsulation operation module in the cloud simulation platform. For example, for encapsulating HyperMesh software in the first stage encapsulation, the platform administrator can choose the CLI template and fill in the relevant service information such as service interface, service method, interface template, etc., as shown in Fig. 6(a), and then generate the HyperMesh interface template.

In the second stage encapsulation, the platform administrator can instantiate the HyperMesh interface by filling in the relevant information of specific resource information, such as the service name, instance number, resource path, etc., as shown in Fig. 6(b), and then encapsulate a HyperMesh software as a simulation Jini service through the HyperMesh interface template, and then deploy the encapsulated service in a selected remote host computer. Then platform users can access and utilize the service through a standard Web browser. Service requestors can also request this HyperMesh service along with other services through the Jini interface, therefore various services can be integrated through the Jini interfaces and form a composite service for users to invoke.

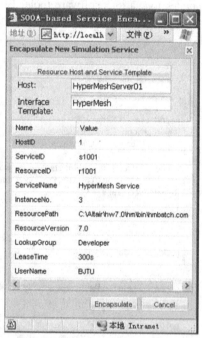

(a) Generate the type service template   (b) Encapsulate the HyperMesh software as a simulation service

Fig. 6. Two-stage HyperMesh encapsulation

5   Conclusions

The SOOA-based service encapsulation process for engineering software tools is proposed to realize the efficient sharing of engineering software resources in the cloud simulation platform. Software engineering tools can be encapsulated and deployed as Jini services by the platform administrator without programming skills through a web browser, and the encapsulated services can be accessed and utilized through a standard Web browser or by Jini interfaces. With this service encapsulation method, an engineering software tool in a cloud simulation platform can be easily encapsulated and deployed as a service once the service templates are ready for the specified software, and service management and service invocations in the cloud simulation platform can then be conveniently implemented.

Acknowledgments. This research is supported by the National Natural Science Foundation of China (No. 51175033) and the General Program of Science and Technology Development Project of Beijing Municipal Education Commission (KM201210011007).

References

1. Sobolewski, M.: SORCER: Computing and Metacomputing Intergrid. In: 10th International Conference on Enterprise Information Systems, pp. 74–85. Springer, Berlin (2008)
2. Yu, J.Q., Cha, J.Z., Lu, Y.P., Xu, W.S., Sobolewski, M.: A CAE-integrated Distributed Collaborative Design System for Finite Element Analysis of Complex Product Based on SOOA. Advances in Engineering Software 41, 590–603 (2010)
3. The Apache River Project, http://river.apache.org
4. Deutsch, P.: https://blogs.oracle.com/jag/resource/Fallacies.html
5. The Wikipedia Project,
   http://en.wikipedia.org/wiki/Command-line_interface
6. Fan, L.Y., Wang, Y.L., Chen, G., Han, Y.B., Xiao, T.Y.: CAD Software Encapsulation System Based on CORBA. Computer Engineering and Applications 39, 61–62 (2003) (in Chinese)
7. Zhang, G.H., Jiang, P.Y., Zhou, G.H.: Portalet-based Encapsulation for CAx Software. Computer Integrated Manufacturing Systems 12, 1134–1140 (2006) (in Chinese)
8. The Apache Velocity Project, http://velocity.apache.org
9. Newmarch, J.: Foundations of Jini 2 Programming. Apress, New York (2006)

CAE Services on Cloud Computing Platform in South Korea

Sang-Hyun Cho

KITECH, 7-47, Songdo-Dong, Yeonsu-Ku,
Incheon, 406-840, South Korea
chosh@kitech.re.kr

Abstract. We, KITECH, had developed CAE software for casting industries(foundries) over last 10 years, and distributed the developed CAE package for foundries in south korea. But the gorwth rate of market for CAE technologies becomes slower because of expensive prices of CAE tools and lacks of trials for introducton of new technologies into their manufacturing workplaces. So that we have been developing new concept market for CAE tehcnologies for last 5 years, and built cloud platform services for CAE in south korea, and it is ISC(Internet Simulation Center). We setup cluster computing systems, datacenter for infrastructure, and developed various services and relational interfaces to serve cloud computing services. So that we have loaded 4 CAE contents into our cloud computing platform, and are providing CAE services to domestic users.

Keywords: ISC, cloud computing, CAE, foundry.

1 Introduction

We had developed and propagated CAE software package to foundries over last 10 years, and it has many functions based on CFD, and heat transfer analysis to predict and analyze physical phenomena of casting processes. But up to date, the CAE market of foundry does not recognize necessities of CAE technologies, moreover price of software packages does not drop down. These situations make CAE market smaller than ever. In South Korea, we have more than 600 foundries, and average sale of them is less than 1 million US dollars per year. These environmental elements delay the introduction of scientific tools to workplaces, and concerns about industry weakening are on increasing.

From the viewpoint of CAE developer, development of new CAE technology is marking time, so that investments for CAE are being focused mainly not on solvers, but on user interfaces including pre and post processors.

To resolve situational difficulties, we have constructed cloud computing platforms for CAE, and started to provide services to SMEs (Small and Medium sized Enterprises).

T. Xiao, L. Zhang, and M. Fei (Eds.): AsiaSim 2012, Part II, CCIS 324, pp. 440–446, 2012.

2   Development of Cloud Computing Platform for CAE

Cloud computing services are already active markets for various fields such as desktop virtualization, database, web services, development environments, and also data-center. Especially, the commercial services for mobile offices [1] and web-based data storages [2] are already are fully activated in South Korea, and Amazon web service [3] and Google Apps [4] had been providing computing resources over the internet.

Microsoft has incorporated their cloud platform, Windows Azure [5], into Visual Studio 2010 package to provide not only development tools but also computing resources, and Apple introduces iCloud services [6] to synchronize personal data between multi-platform devices such as iPhone, iPod, iPad and Macintoshes. All these services are hidden over the clouds, so that users do not need to know where their data or servers exist. These cloud computing services are made up of three major services such as PaaS(Platform as a Service), SaaS(Software as a Service), and IaaS(Infrastructure as a Service). In CAE area, cloud-based services have been developed in South Korea, and it was focused mainly on casting simulation field [7], [8].

2.1   Concept of Cloud-Based CAE Services

ISC is the name of cloud computing platform developed for CAE services and its concept is shown in Fig. 1.

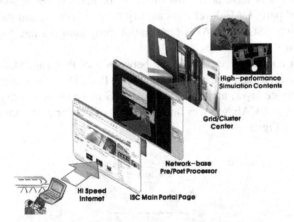

Fig. 1. Concepts of CAE services based on cloud computing

Normally, CAE software is made up of two parts, and they are solver for massive calculation and UI(User Interface) for input/output manipulations. So that UI gathers user's input and save them into local storages, and then solver starts to calculate according to input data. In ISC environment, solvers exist at cluster system side, and UI is distributed through internet, and installed at personal computers. After UI is installed, and the network connection is established, users can use CAE contents just as locally installed full CAE packages. This model differs exactly from simple client-server model or desktop virtualization technologies.

2.2   Development of Cloud-Based CAE Services

To develop and provide ISC services, the system structure shown in Fig. 2 can be introduced.

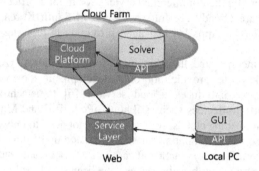

Fig. 2. Schematics of CAE services based on cloud computing

As is, solver and UI should exist independently, and both of them should be installed on cluster system and local PCs. Methods of distribution for UI packages can be .asp or activeX technologies. The distributed UI packages differ from normal CAE packages because they have additional function for network-based job management. To promote third party CAE developers modify their own codes and then upload their own packaged into ISC farm, APIs (application programming interfaces) should be provided to them.

After internet connection establishment between user PCs and ISC, UI manipulate users' input and send data and request signals to ISC. The sent requests from users arrive at ISC service layer, and cloud platform OS or services identify user requests and data to carry out CAE services and functions of platform OS are divided into 4 sections shown in Fig. 3

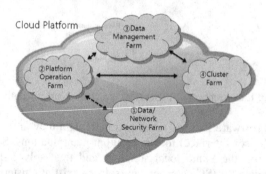

Fig. 3. ISC platform functions for cloud computing services

2.3   IaaS

To provide CAE software and computing resources as IaaS, we built up cluster platforms made up of over 100 servers for calculation and all them are interconnect through ethernet and infiniband switches. In addition to calculation servers, many servers for service monitoring and controls, big storages and security-relation systems were introduced. To ensure safety of users' data, specialized backup and encryption solutions were also applied to ISC system.

2.4   API for 3rd Party Developers

Aims of ISC services are to setup cloud computing platform and to propagate CAE technologies to SMEs. It is different with desktop virtualization which runs under server-client concept, so that all CAE contents of ISC should have uniform structures to be loaded into ISC and to be distributed through internet. Namely, solvers and UI including user interface should be separated completely, run independently.

The solvers at cloud platform and GUI at client side should introduce some specific APIs (Application Programming Interfaces) into their own source codes when off-line to on-line migration work is carried out. In this time, the necessities for simplicity of ISC API are important point not for ISC operator but for third party developer. Because, to expand this kind of services, cloud platform should provide the fastest migration methods to third party developers. In consideration with this point, ISC API was designed and developed.

Fig. 4. Components of ISC API

2.5   Test Beds

In developing CAE software for ISC, test beds are necessary to test or debug the developed codes, but ISC is not stand-alone packages but network-based complex services, so that it is not easy to make test environment for third party developers. To make a solution for this problem, we are providing test environment through internet. If the developer is registered at ISC as certificated developer, we provided virtualized test zone through internet, and then the developer can upload their own codes to virtual environment and test them under fully similar environment with ISC.

3   ISC Services

We, ISC, are planning to provide at least one CAE contents for six manufacturing fields, and six manufacturing fields are casting, forging, heat treatment, welding, surface treatment and plastic injection moldings shown in Fig. 5.

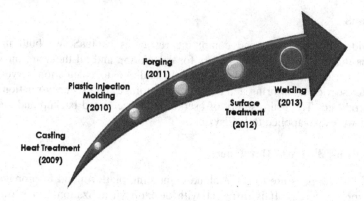

Fig. 5. CAE content roadmap for ISC services

To use ISC services, user can access to ISC web site, and then register the login account through registration pages. After the authentication operations by ISC operator, new password will be sent to user according to user's email address which is registered already by user. Then user can open ISC service page shown in Fig. 6.

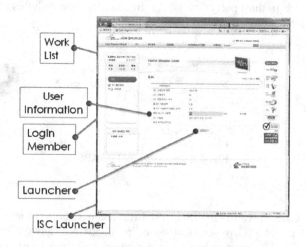

Fig. 6. ISC service page for authenticated users

User can select the services at ISC user's page, and then the UI will be installed to user's local PC through internet. UI have two running modes and they are on/off-line modes. If the internet connection between ISC and user's PC has been established without problem, UI will launch as on-line mode with job managing window, otherwise, UI will launch as off-line mode for only post-processing operations.

In Fig. 7, the CAE services on ISC are shown.

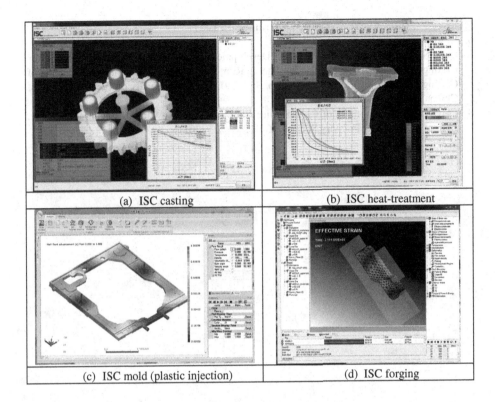

| (a) ISC casting | (b) ISC heat-treatment |
| (c) ISC mold (plastic injection) | (d) ISC forging |

Fig. 7. CAE contents of ISC

4   Conclusions

Manufacturing industries are encountering with hard situations, and they want to increase benefits and decrease defects and errors. To achieve high efficiencies, new manufacturing technologies should be applied to working places with scientific tools, but investments for CAE tools do not grow considerably because of prices of CAE tools and risk of investment. So that we developed cloud-base CAE services, which includes SaaS, IaaS and PaaS, and started to provided services to domestic users by free. We have over 600 uses in South Korea, and user number increases gradually. We wish to expand CAE service concept based on cloud computing to various industries with more varieties, so that new coming market can be born.

References

1. http://office.microsoft.com/ko-kr/web-apps/
2. http://home.ucloud.olleh.com
3. http://aws.amazon.com
4. http://www.google.com/apps/

5. http://www.microsoft.com/windowsazure/
6. http://www.apple.com/icloud/
7. Cho, S.-H., Kim, J.-T., Choi, J.-K.: Development of Integrated Simulation Portal for Casting Processes on the Net. In: 7th Pacific Rim International Conference on Modeling of Casting and Solidification Processes, pp. 353–360. Dalian University of Technology Press, China (2007)
8. Cho, S.-H.: Development of CAE Service Platform Based on Cloud Computing Concept. Journal of the Korea Foundry Society 31(4), 218–223 (2011)

Author Index

book similar to the research addressed in the conference. Most of the accepted full papers competed for the best paper and best student paper awards, which finally were attributed to Jesús Gimeno, Pedro Morillo, Juan Manuel Orduña, and Marcos Fernández for "An Occlusion-Aware AR Autoring Tool for Assembly and Repair Task" and Tomokazu Ishikawa, Yonghao Yue, Kei Iwasaki, Yoshinori Dobashi, and Tomoyuki Nishita for "Visual Simulation of Magnetic Fluid."

The paper by Gimeno et al. proposes an easy-to-use Kinect-based authoring tool oriented to the development of augmented reality applications for the execution of industrial sequential procedures. Ishikawa et al. focus on the simulation of magnetic fluids and propose an efficient method by combining a procedural and the smoothed particle hydrodynamics approach. The proposed method simulates overall behaviors of the magnetic fluids method and generates visually plausible results within a reasonable computational cost.

Concerning the other papers, we would like to mention: "Muscle Fibers Modeling" by J. Kohout et al., which describes a method for representing muscles by a realistic chaff of fibers that are automatically generated in the volume defined by the surface mesh of the muscle which itself automatically wraps around bones as they move; "Patchworks Terrains" by L. Rocca et al. presents a new method for the management, multi-resolution representation, and rendering of large-terrain databases. This method provides a Ck representation of terrain, with k depending on the type of base patches and supports efficient updates of the database as new data come in; "Visualization of Long Scenes from Dense Image Sequences Using Perspective Composition" by S. Fang and N. Campbell presents a system for generating multi-perspective panoramas for long scenes from dense image sequences by combining different perspectives, including both original and novel perspectives; "Distance-Adapted 2D Manipulation Techniques for Large High-Resolution Display Environments" by A. Lehmann and O. Staadt presents an intuitive overview+detail technique in large high-resolution display environments where users may interact bimanually at different distances to manipulate high-resolution content with the appropriate accuracy; "Sketching Fluid Flow — Combining Sketch-Based Techniques and Gradient Vector Flow for Lattice-Boltzmann Initialization" by S. Ferreira Judice and G.A. Giraldi proposes an intuitive fluid flow initialization for computer graphics applications. They use a combination of sketching techniques and gradient vector flow to obtain a smooth initialization for the simulation using a lattice Boltzmann method (LBM).

The four selected IVAPP papers are not only excellent representatives of the field of information visualization but also form quite a balanced representation of the field itself. In particular, they cover both, application and theory; they use a wide and diverse range of data types (flow fields, geospatial data, trees, and high-dimensional point sets); they use visualization for various tasks (search for individual data points, exploration of data sets, visualization of structures in the data, etc.); and they employ many of the tools and methods that are crucial in information visualization (data analysis, computer graphics, information design, interaction design, etc.). Above all, they are almost as diverse and exciting as the field of information visualization itself.

Specifically, flow visualization is represented by the paper "Space–Time Visualization of Dynamics in Lagrangian Coherent Structures of Time-Dependent 2D Vector Fields" by Sven Bachthaler, Filip Sadlo, Carsten Dachsbacher, and Daniel Weiskopf, who discuss space–time visualizations of time-dependent vector fields and finite-time Lyapunov exponent fields. A Web-based system for geovisualization is presented in the paper "Comparative Visualization of Geospatial-Temporal Data" by Stefan Jänicke, Christian Heine, Ralf Stockmann, and Gerik Scheuermann. This system provides interactive visualizations for the comparison of multiple geospatial and temporal data sets. Tree visualization is employed in the paper "Scaffold Hunter" by Karsten Klein, Nils Kriege, and Petra Mutzel, who present an interactive tool for the exploration and analysis of chemical databases. The fourth paper, "Interpretation, Interaction, and Scalability for Structural Decomposition Trees" by René Rosenbaum, Daniel Engel, James Mouradian, Hans Hagen, and Bernd Hamann, investigates visualizations of high-dimensional, scattered point sets using structural decomposition trees. Among the four selected papers, it therefore represents visualization of the most abstract data.

It is not to be expected that any single reader is equally interested in all four of the selected IVAPP papers; however, the diversity of these papers makes it very likely that all readers can find something of interest in this selection.

VISIGRAPP 2012 included four invited keynote lectures, presented by internationally renowned researchers, whom we would like to thank for their contribution to reinforce the overall quality of the conference, namely, in alphabetical order: Sabine Coquillart (INRIA, France), Zoltan Kato (University of Szeged, Hungary), Sabine Süsstrunk (Ecole Polytechnique Fédérale de Lausanne (EPFL, Switzerland) and Colin Ware (University of New Hampshire, USA). Professor Zoltan Kato kindly accepted to write a brief resume of his intervention published herein.

We wish to thank all those who supported VISIGRAPP and helped to organize the conference. On behalf of the Organizing Committee, we would like to especially thank the authors, whose work was the essential part of the conference and contributed to a very successful event. We would also like to thank the members of the Program Committee, whose expertise and diligence were instrumental ensuring the quality of the final contributions. We also wish to thank all the members of the Organizing Committee, whose work and commitment was invaluable. Last but not least, we would like to thank Springer for their collaboration in getting this book to print.

December 2012

Gabriela Csurka
Martin Kraus
Robert S. Laramee
Paul Richard
José Braz

Organization

Conference Chair

José Braz — Polytechnic Institute of Setúbal, Portugal

Program Co-chairs

GRAPP

Paul Richard — University of Angers, France

IVAPP

Martin Kraus — Aalborg University, Denmark
Robert S. Laramee — Swansea University, UK

VISAPP

Gabriela Csurka — Xerox Research Centre Europe, France

Organizing Committee

Sérgio Brissos	INSTICC, Portugal
Marina Carvalho	INSTICC, Portugal
Helder Coelhas	INSTICC, Portugal
Patrícia Duarte	INSTICC, Portugal
Bruno Encarnação	INSTICC, Portugal
Liliana Medina	INSTICC, Portugal
Carla Mota	INSTICC, Portugal
Raquel Pedrosa	INSTICC, Portugal
Vitor Pedrosa	INSTICC, Portugal
Daniel Pereira	INSTICC, Portugal
Cláudia Pinto	INSTICC, Portugal
José Varela	INSTICC, Portugal
Pedro Varela	INSTICC, Portugal

GRAPP Program Committee

Francisco Abad, Spain
Marco Agus, Italy
Tremeau Alain, France
Marco Attene, Italy
Dolors Ayala, Spain
Jacob Barhak, USA
Rafael Bidarra, The Netherlands
Jiri Bittner, Czech Republic
Manfred Bogen, Germany
Willem F. Bronsvoort,
    The Netherlands
Stephen Brooks, Canada
Stefan Bruckner, Austria
Emilio Camahort, Spain
Maria Beatriz Carmo, Portugal
L.G. Casado, Spain
Teresa Chambel, Portugal
Hwan-gue Cho, Republic of Korea
Miguel Chover, Spain
Ana Paula Cláudio, Portugal
Sabine Coquillart, France
António Cardoso Costa, Portugal
Victor Debelov, Russian Federation
John Dingliana, Ireland
Arjan Egges, The Netherlands
Francisco R. Feito, Spain
Petr Felkel, Czech Republic
Jie-Qing Feng, China
Fernando Nunes Ferreira, Portugal
Luiz Henrique de Figueiredo, Brazil
Ioannis Fudos, Greece
Alejandro García-Alonso, Spain
Miguel Gea, Spain
Mashhuda Glencross, UK
Enrico Gobbetti, Italy
Stephane Gobron, Switzerland
Peter Hall, UK
Anders Hast, Italy
Vlastimil Havran, Czech Republic
Nancy Hitschfeld, Chile
Toby Howard, UK
Andres Iglesias, Spain
Insung Ihm, Republic of Korea

Jiri Janacek, Czech Republic
Frederik Jansen, The Netherlands
Juan J. Jimenez, Spain
Andrew Johnson, USA
Pieter Jorissen, Belgium
Chris Joslin, Canada
Josef Kohout, Czech Republic
Marc Erich Latoschik, Germany
Miguel Leitão, Portugal
Heinz U. Lemke, Germany
Suresh Lodha, USA
Adriano Lopes, Portugal
Steve Maddock, UK
Joaquim Madeira, Portugal
Claus B. Madsen, Denmark
Nadia Magnenat-Thalmann,
    Switzerland
Stephen Mann, Canada
Michael Manzke, Ireland
Adérito Fernandes Marcos, Portugal
Ramon Molla, Spain
Guillaume Moreau, France
David Mould, Canada
Gennadiy Nikishkov, Japan
Marc Olano, USA
Samir Otmane, France
Georgios Papaioannou, Greece
Alexander Pasko, UK
Giuseppe Patané, Italy
Daniel Patel, Norway
João Pereira, Portugal
Steve Pettifer, UK
Ruggero Pintus, Italy
Denis Pitzalis, Cyprus
Dimitri Plemenos, France
Anna Puig, Spain
Enrico Puppo, Italy
Paul Richard, France
Inmaculada Rodríguez, Spain
Przemyslaw Rokita, Poland
Manuel Próspero dos Santos, Portugal
Rafael J. Segura, Spain
Roberto Seixas, Brazil

Alexei Sourin, Singapore
A. Augusto Sousa, Portugal
Milos Sramek, Austria
Frank Steinicke, Germany
Ching-Liang Su, India
Veronica Sundstedt, Sweden
Jie Tang, China
Matthias Teschner, Germany
Daniel Thalmann, Singapore
Juan Carlos Torres, Spain
Anna Ursyn, USA

Pere-Pau Vázquez, Spain
Luiz Velho, Brazil
Andreas Weber, Germany
Daniel Weiskopf, Germany
Alexander Wilkie, Czech Republic
Michael Wimmer, Austria
Burkhard Wuensche, New Zealand
Lihua You, UK
Jian J. Zhang, UK
Jianmin Zheng, Singapore

GRAPP Auxiliary Reviewers

Hugo Álvarez, Spain
Carlos Ogayar Anguita, Spain
Jan Baumann, Germany
António Coelho, Portugal
Vitor Cunha, Portugal
Alexandra Diehl, Argentina
Ángel Luis García Fernández, Spain
Martin Fischbach, Germany
Anton Gerdelan, Sweden
Joel Glanfield, Canada
Saskia Groenewegen, The Netherlands
Ralf Habel, Austria
Feifei Huo, The Netherlands
Björn Krüger, Germany

Francisco Lopez Luro, Sweden
Peter Mindek, Slovak Republic
Przemyslaw Musialski, Austria
Harold Nefs, The Netherlands
Luís Oliveira, Portugal
Andreas Pusch, Germany
Luigi Rocca, Italy
Rui Rodrigues, Portugal
Vasiliki Stamati, Greece
Andrej Varchola, Austria
Andreas Vasilakis, Greece
Yu Wang, USA
Dennis Wiebusch, Germany

IVAPP Program Committee

Lisa Sobierajski Avila, USA
Maria Beatriz Carmo, Portugal
Carlos Correa, USA
Chi-Wing Fu, Singapore
David Gotz, USA
Charles Hansen, USA
Pheng-Ann Heng, Hong Kong
Seokhee Hong, Australia
Ingrid Hotz, Germany
Tony Huang, Australia
Andreas Kerren, Sweden

Martin Kraus, Denmark
Denis Lalanne, Switzerland
Robert S. Laramee, UK
Chun-Cheng Lin, Taiwan
Peter Lindstrom, USA
Lars Linsen, Germany
Giuseppe Liotta, Italy
Kwan-Liu Ma, USA
Krešimir Matkovic, Austria
Silvia Miksch, Austria
Klaus Mueller, USA

Luis Gustavo Nonato, Brazil
Steffen Oeltze, Germany
Benoît Otjacques, Luxembourg
Alex Pang, USA
Margit Pohl, Austria
Christof Rezk-Salama, Germany
Paul Richard, France
Adrian Rusu, USA
Heidrun Schumann, Germany
Han-Wei Shen, USA
Aidan Slingsby, UK

Shigeo Takahashi, Japan
Melanie Tory, Canada
Chaoli Wang, USA
Matt Ward, USA
Tino Weinkauf, Germany
Huub van de Wetering,
   The Netherlands
Jarke van Wijk, The Netherlands
Hsu-Chun Yen, Taiwan
Ji Soo Yi, USA
Xiaoru Yuan, China

IVAPP Auxiliary Reviewers

Bilal Alsallakh, Austria
Ilya Boyandin, Switzerland
Wallace Casaca, Brazil
Nathaniel Cesario, USA
Andrew Crowell, USA
Danilo Eler, Brazil
Florian Evequoz, Switzerland
Paolo Federico, Austria
Theresia Gschwandtner, Austria
Yi Gu, USA
Yifan Hu, USA

Paulo Joia, Brazil
Tim Lammarsch, Austria
Jun Ma, USA
Philipp Muigg, Austria
Jose Gustavo Paiva, Brazil
Adam Perer, USA
Paulo Pombinho, Portugal
Huamin Qu, Hong Kong
Confesor Santiago, USA
Jun Tao, USA
Björn Zimmer, Sweden

VISAPP Program Committee

Henrik Aanæs, Denmark
Luis Alexandre, Portugal
Emmanuel Audenaert, Belgium
Sileye Ba, France
Reneta Barneva, USA
Arrate Muñoz Barrutia, Spain
Olga Bellon, Brazil
Hugues Benoit-Cattin, France
Diego Borro, Spain
Adrian Bors, UK
Alain Boucher, Vietnam
Valentin Brimkov, USA
Alfred Bruckstein, Israel
Xianbin Cao, China

Barbara Caputo, Switzerland
Pedro Latorre Carmona, Spain
Gustavo Carneiro, Portugal
Vicent Caselles, Spain
M. Emre Celebi, USA
Vinod Chandran, Australia
Chin-Chen Chang, Taiwan
Jocelyn Chanussot, France
Samuel Cheng, USA
Hocine Cherifi, France
Albert C.S. Chung, Hong Kong
Laurent Cohen, France
David Connah, UK
Carlos Correa, USA

Charalambos Poullis, Cyprus
Bogdan Raducanu, Spain
Ana Reis, Portugal
Paolo Remagnino, UK
Alfredo Restrepo, Colombia
Eraldo Ribeiro, USA
Elisa Ricci, Italy
Alessandro Rizzi, Italy
Marcos Rodrigues, UK
Jarek Rossignac, USA
Adrian Rusu, USA
Joaquin Salas, Mexico
Ovidio Salvetti, Italy
Jagath Samarabandu, Canada
Mário Forjaz Secca, Portugal
Fiorella Sgallari, Italy
Lik-Kwan Shark, UK
Gaurav Sharma, USA
Li Shen, USA
Maryam Shokri, Canada
Chang Shu, Canada
Luciano Silva, Brazil
Bogdan Smolka, Poland
Ferdous Ahmed Sohel, Australia
Mingli Song, China
Lauge Sørensen, Denmark
José Martínez Sotoca, Spain
Ömer Muhammet Soysal, USA
Jon Sporring, Denmark
Joachim Stahl, USA
Filippo Stanco, Italy
Liana Stanescu, Romania
Changming Sun, Australia

Yajie Sun, USA
Shamik Sural, India
David Svoboda, Czech Republic
Tamás Szirányi, Hungary
Ryszard Tadeusiewicz, Poland
Johji Tajima, Japan
Tolga Tasdizen, USA
João Manuel R.S. Tavares, Portugal
YingLi Tian, USA
Hamid Tizhoosh, Canada
Shoji Tominaga, Japan
Georgios Triantafyllidis, Greece
Yulia Trusova, Russian Federation
Muriel Visani, France
Frank Wallhoff, Germany
Tiangong Wei, New Zealand
Joost van de Weijer, Spain
Christian Wöhler, Germany
Stefan Wörz, Germany
Qingxiang Wu, UK
Pingkun Yan, USA
Vera Yashina, Russian Federation
Yizhou Yu, USA
Jun Zhang, Japan
Yonghui (Iris) Zhao, USA
Jianmin Zheng, Singapore
Huiyu Zhou, UK
Yun Zhu, USA
Zhigang Zhu, USA
Li Zhuo, China
Peter Zolliker, Switzerland
Ju Jia (Jeffrey) Zou, Australia

VISAPP Auxiliary Reviewers

Hadi Aliakbarpour, Portugal
Luis Almeida, Portugal
Hugo Álvarez, Spain
Beatriz Andrade, Brazil
Aasa Feragen, Denmark
Shibo Gao, China
Xiaoyin Guan, UK
Gabriel Hartmann, New Zealand

Søren Hauberg, Denmark
Jurandir Santos Junior, Brazil
Denis Khromov, Russian Federation
Alexey Kurakin, Russian Federation
Yugang Liu, Singapore
Sebastià Massanet, Spain
Arnau Mir, Spain
Sandino Morales, New Zealand

Gabriele Pieri, Italy
Stefan Posch, Germany
José Prado, Portugal
Mahdi Rezaei, New Zealand
Jan Richarz, Germany
Stefan Robila, USA
Luis Santos, Portugal
Maurício Pamplona Segundo, Brazil
Pierluigi Taddei, Italy

JunLi Tao, New Zealand
Archil Tsiskaridze, Russian Federation
Szilard Vajda, Germany
Shuang Wang, USA
Qing Wu, USA
Qijun Zhao, USA
Yingxuan Zhu, USA

Invited Speakers

Sabine Süsstrunk

Ecole Polytechnique Fédérale de Lausanne
(EPFL) Switzerland

Colin Ware
Sabine Coquillart
Zoltan Kato

University of New Hampshire, USA
INRIA, France
University of Szeged, Hungary

Table of Contents

Part II: Information Visualization Theory and Applications

Part III: Computer Vision Theory and Applications

Invited Paper

Linear and Nonlinear Shape Alignment
without Correspondences

Zoltan Kato

Department of Image Processing and Computer Graphics,
University of Szeged, P.O. Box 652., 6701 Szeged, Hungary
kato@inf.u-szeged.hu

Abstract. We consider the estimation of diffeomorphic deformations aligning a known binary shape and its distorted observation. The classical solution consists in extracting landmarks, establishing correspondences and then the aligning transformation is obtained via a complex optimization procedure. Herein we present an alternative solution which works without landmark correspondences, is independent of the magnitude of transformation, easy to implement, and has a linear time complexity. The proposed universal framework is capable of recovering linear as well as nonlinear deformations.

Keywords: Registration, Shape, Matching, Affine transformation, Planar homography, Thin plate splines.

1   Introduction

Registration is a crucial step when images of different views or sensors of an object need to be compared or combined. Application areas include visual inspection, target tracking in video sequences, super resolution, or medical image analysis. In a general setting, one is looking for a transformation which aligns two images such that one image (called the *observation*, or moving image) becomes similar to the second one (called the *template*, or model image). Due to the large number of possible transformations, there is a huge variability of the object signature. In fact, each *observation* is an element of the orbit of the transformations applied to the *template*. Hence the problem is inherently *ill-defined* unless this variability is taken into account.

When registering an image pair, first we have to characterize the possible deformations. From this point of view, registration techniques can be classified into two main categories: physical model-based and parametric or functional representation [1]. Herein, we deal with the latter representation, which typically originate from interpolation and approximation theory.

From a methodological point of view, we can differentiate *feature-based* and *area-based* methods. *Feature-based* methods [2] aim at establishing point correspondences between two images. For that purpose, they extract some easily detectable features (*e.g.* intersection of lines, corners, etc.) from the images and then use these points to compute the closest transformation based on a similarity metric. Searching for the best transformation usually requires an iterative algorithm like the iterative closest point (ICP) algorithm, which requires that the deformation be close enough to identity. The main

G. Csurka et al. (Eds.): VISIGRAPP 2012, CCIS 359, pp. 3–14, 2013.

drawback of these methods is thus the assumption of a limited deformation and high computational cost. Their main advantage is that as long as a sufficient number of point matches are available, one can usually find an optimal aligning transformation implying that these algorithms are less sensitive to occlusions. *Area-based* methods [3,4] treat the problem without attempting to detect salient objects. These methods are sometimes called correlation-like methods because they use a rectangular window to gain some preliminary information about the distortion. They search the position in the observation where the matching of the two windows is the best and then look for sufficient alignment between the windows in the template and in the observation. The drawback of this family of methods is also the high computational cost and the restricted range of distortions.

In many situations, the variability of image features is so complex that the only feasible way to register such images is to reduce them to a binary representation and solve the registration problem in that context. Therefore binary registration (*i.e.* shape alignment) is an important problem for many complex image analysis tasks. Herein, we will present a generic framework for recovering linear [5,6,7,8] and nonlinear [9,10] deformations of binary objects without correspondences.

2   Registration Framework

Let us denote the point coordinates of the *template* and *observation* by $\mathbf{x} \in \mathbb{R}^n$ and $\mathbf{y} \in \mathbb{R}^n$ respectively. Corresponding point pairs $(\mathbf{x}, \mathbf{y})$ are related by an unknown diffeomorphism $\phi : \mathbb{R}^n \to \mathbb{R}^n$ such that

$$\mathbf{y} = \phi(\mathbf{x}) \quad \Leftrightarrow \quad \mathbf{x} = \phi^{-1}(\mathbf{y}), \tag{1}$$

where $\phi^{-1} : \mathbb{R}^n \to \mathbb{R}^n$ is the corresponding inverse transformation. Note that ϕ^{-1} always exists since a diffeomorphism is a bijective function such that both the function and its inverse have continuous mixed partial derivatives. The goal of registration is to recover the aligning transformation ϕ.

Classical approaches would establish a set of point correspondences $\{(\mathbf{x}_i, \mathbf{y}_i)\}_{i=1}^{N}$ and, making use of Eq. (1), define a *similarity metric* $S(\{(\mathbf{x}_i, \mathbf{y}_i)\}, \hat{\phi})$ which characterizes the geometric alignment of the point pairs $\{(\mathbf{x}_i, \hat{\phi}(\mathbf{y}_i))\}$ achieved by a particular transformation $\hat{\phi}$. The solution is usually obtained via an iterative optimization procedure, where S is maximized (or equivalently, the *dissimilarity* is minimized). Such procedures require a good initialization (*i.e.* the transformation must be close to identity) and are computationally expensive as the evaluation of S requires the actual execution of each intermediate transformation. Furthermore, landmark extraction and correspondence implicitly assumes, that one can observe some image features (*e.g.* gray-level of pixels [11]) f and g that are *covariant* under the transformation

$$f(\mathbf{x}) = g(\phi(\mathbf{x})) = g(\mathbf{y}). \tag{2}$$

However, lack of characteristic features (*e.g.* binary images, printed art) or changes in features (*e.g.* illumination changes, mulimodality) make landmark extraction and matching unreliable in many cases. Segmentation of such images is often straightforward and

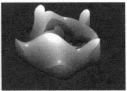

Fig. 1. The effect of applying a polynomial (left) and a trigonometric (right) ω function can be interpreted as a consistent colorization or as a volume

is available as an intermediate step of a complex image analysis task. Herein, we will discuss a generic correspondence-less framework which works well in such situations.

Since correspondences are not available, Eq. (1) cannot be used directly. However, individual point matches can be integrated out yielding the following integral equation:

$$\int_{\mathcal{D}} \mathbf{y} d\mathbf{y} = \int_{\phi(\mathcal{F})} \mathbf{z} d\mathbf{z}, \tag{3}$$

where $\mathcal{D}$ corresponds to the *observation* shape's domain and $\phi(\mathcal{F})$ is the transformed *template* shape's domain. Note that computing the latter integral involves the actual execution of the transformation ϕ on $\mathcal{F}$, which might be computationally unfavorable. Therefore, let us rewrite the above integrals over the *template*'s domain $\mathcal{F}$ and *observation*'s domain $\mathcal{D}$ by making use of the integral transformation $\mathbf{z} \mapsto \phi(\mathbf{x})$ and $d\mathbf{z} \mapsto |J_\phi(\mathbf{x})| d\mathbf{x}$:

$$\int_{\mathcal{D}} \mathbf{y} d\mathbf{y} = \int_{\mathcal{F}} \phi(\mathbf{x}) |J_\phi(\mathbf{x})| d\mathbf{x}, \tag{4}$$

where $|J_\phi(\mathbf{x})|$ is the Jacobian determinant of the transformation ϕ. Note that the above equation corresponds to a system of n equations, where n is the dimension of the shapes. Although the space of allowed deformations is low dimensional, determined by the number of free parameters k of the deformation ϕ, n is typically 2 (planar shapes) or 3 (3D objects), which is not sufficient to solve for all parameters of a real deformation. Therefore we need a general mechanism to construct new equations. Indeed, Eq. (1) remains valid when a function $\omega : \mathbb{R}^n \to \mathbb{R}$ is acting on both sides of the equation

$$\omega(\mathbf{y}) = \omega(\phi(\mathbf{x})), \tag{5}$$

and the integral equation of Eq. (4) becomes

$$\int_{\mathcal{D}} \omega(\mathbf{y}) d\mathbf{y} = \int_{\mathcal{F}} \omega(\phi(\mathbf{x})) |J_\phi(\mathbf{x})| d\mathbf{x}. \tag{6}$$

Adopting a set of nonlinear functions $\{\omega_i\}_{i=1}^{\ell}$, each ω_i generates a new equation yielding a system of ℓ independent equations. Hence we are able to generate sufficient number of equations by choosing $\ell \geq k$. Intuitively, each ω_i generates a consistent coloring of the shapes and the equations in Eq. (6) match the volume of the applied ω_i function over the shapes (see Fig. 1). The parameters of the aligning transformation ϕ are then simply obtained as the solution of the nonlinear system of equations Eq. (6). In practice,

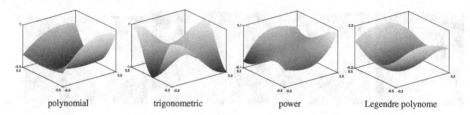

Fig. 2. Various ω functions

usually an overdetermined system is constructed (*i.e.* $\ell > k$), which is then solved in the *least squares sense* by minimizing the algebraic error. Hereafter, we will omit the integration domains from the equations.

What kind of ω functions can be used to generate these independent equations? From a theoretical point of view, only trivial restrictions apply: the functions must be integrable and rich enough (*i.e.* generate a non-constant colorization). Furthermore, they have to be unbiased: each equation should have an equally balanced contribution to the algebraic error, which can be achieved by normalizing the images into the unit square (or cube in 3D) around the origin and the range of the ω functions should also be normalized [10]. Some examples can be seen in Fig. 2. From a practical point of view, we have to solve a system of integral equations meaning that intermediate deformations need to be evaluated hence complexity is highly dependent on image size. If we could get rid of the integration in the equations, then considerable speed-up could be achieved. Fortunately, the equation of Eq. (6) can be reduced to a plain polynomial system under the following conditions [5,10]:

1. The deformation ϕ is given as a linear combination of basis functions. Note that the most common transformation groups, such as linear, polynomial and thin plate spline deformations are of such form, while other diffeomorphisms can be approximated by their Taylor expansion.
2. The adopted set of nonlinear functions $\{\omega_i\}_{i=1}^{\ell}$ are polynomial.

Let us now briefly overview how to use our framework for some typical deformation classes.

3   Linear Deformations

In the case of linear deformations, the diffeomorphism ϕ becomes a non-singular linear transformation matrix $\mathbf{A}$ and the identity relation takes the following simple form:

$$\mathbf{A}\mathbf{x} = \mathbf{y} \quad \Leftrightarrow \quad \mathbf{x} = \mathbf{A}^{-1}\mathbf{y}. \tag{7}$$

Since the Jacobian is simply the determinant of $\mathbf{A}$, which can be computed as the ratio of the areas of the two planar shapes to be aligned, we can easily construct a system of polynomial equations [5,6]:

$$\int \omega(\mathbf{x})d\mathbf{x} = \frac{1}{|\mathbf{A}|} \int \omega(\mathbf{A}^{-1}\mathbf{y})d\mathbf{y}. \tag{8}$$

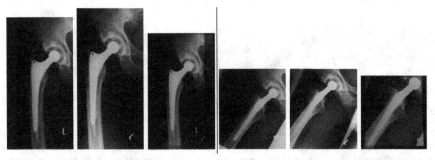

Fig. 3. Fusion of hip prosthesis X-ray image pairs by registering follow up images using a 2D affine transformation (typical CPU time is around 1 sec. in Matlab)

Obviously, the choice of ωs is crucial as our goal is to construct a system which can be solved. It is easy to see that a polynomial system, which is certainly straightforward to solve, is obtained when $\omega(x) = x^i$ (see [5]). From a geometric point of view, for $\omega(x) \equiv x$ Eq. (8) simply matches the center of mass of the *template* and *observation* while for $\omega(\mathbf{x}) = [x_1^i, x_2^i, 1]^T$, Eq. (8) matches the center of mass of the shapes obtained by the nonlinear transformations ω. In the 2D affine case, we have to solve a system of polynomial equations of the following form, where q_{ki} denotes the unknown elements of the inverse transformation $\mathbf{A}^{-1}$

$$|\mathbf{A}| \int x_k = q_{k1} \int y_1 + q_{k2} \int y_2 + q_{k3} \int 1, \tag{9}$$

$$|\mathbf{A}| \int x_k^2 = q_{k1}^2 \int y_1^2 + q_{k2}^2 \int y_2^2 + q_{k3}^2 \int 1 + 2q_{k1}q_{k2} \int y_1 y_2$$
$$+ 2q_{k1}q_{k3} \int y_1 + 2q_{k2}q_{k3} \int y_2, \tag{10}$$

$$|\mathbf{A}| \int x_k^3 = q_{k1}^3 \int y_1^3 + q_{k2}^3 \int y_2^3 + q_{k3}^3 \int 1 + 3q_{k1}^2 q_{k2} \int y_1^2 y_2$$
$$+ 3q_{k1}^2 q_{k3} \int y_1^2 + 3q_{k2}^2 q_{k3} \int y_2^2 + 3q_{k1}q_{k2}^2 \int y_1 y_2^2$$
$$+ 3q_{k2}q_{k3}^2 \int y_2 + 3q_{k1}q_{k3}^2 \int y_1 + 6q_{k1}q_{k2}q_{k3} \int y_1 y_2. \tag{11}$$

The above system of equations can be readily solved either by a direct solver found *e.g.* in Matlab [5] or by a classical LSE solver like the *Levenberg-Marquardt* algorithm [7]. Some registration examples can be seen in Fig. 3, where hip prosthesis X-ray image pairs are aligned using a 2D affine transformation. The goal is to fuse post operative follow-up scans of the hip prosthesis to check loosening of the implant. Note that correspondence-based methods are challenged by lack of corner-like landmarks and the nonlinear radiometric distortion between follow-ups. However, segmentation of the implant is straightforward, hence binary registration is a viable option here. In spite of the inherent modeling error (the physical transformation of the implant is a 3D rigid motion followed by a projection), our method was able to find a precise alignment. This is

Fig. 4. Registration of pelvic CT data: superimposed registered 3D bone models (typical CPU time is around 0.25 sec for 1 megavoxel objects using our Java demo program). The first two cases show good alignment. Even the third one provides a good approximation of the true alignment.

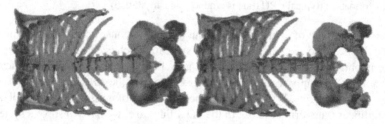

Fig. 5. Registration of thoracic CT data: superimposed registered 3D bone models. Perfect alignment is not possible due to the relative movements of the bone structure. Affine alignment results are used as a good starting point for *e.g.* lymph node detection.

mainly due to the fact, that images are taken in a standard position of the patient, hence affine transformation is a good approximation.

3.1 Registration of 3D Objects

The extension of the polynomial equations to 3D objects [6,7,8] is relatively straightforward. However, numerical implementation has to be carefully designed. Therefore, both in 2D and 3D we examined two different types of solution methods: iterative least-squares solutions and direct analytical solutions.

- In case of a direct method, limited number of equations can be used (according to the degree of freedom of the n-dimensional affine transformation), while an iterative approach allows for an overdetermined system, which may give more stability.
- Direct methods may provide many hundreds or even thousands of possible solutions, many (or even all) of them may be complex thus a solution selection scheme has to be used to produce only one real solution from these. Iterative methods provide a single real solution, but the search may fall into local minima. To avoid such local minima, usually a sophisticated search strategy is necessary.
- Direct methods can provide full affine solutions only, but in case of iterative methods restrictions to lower degree of freedom transformations are easy to impose.

We found that the direct approach gives more stable results, but the iterative one is more precise. It is also possible to combine the two approaches: The direct approach provides the initialization of the iterative one.

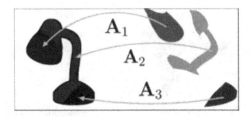

Fig. 6. Affine puzzle: reconstructing the complete template object from its deformed parts

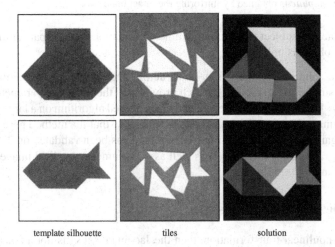

template silhouette   tiles   solution

Fig. 7. Two solutions of the Tangram puzzle. The average alignment runtime was about 50 sec. in Matlab.

Another issue is discretization error, which might be particularly problematic in 3D. For that purpose, we extended our method by investigating the case when the segmentation method is capable of producing *fuzzy object*s instead of a binary result in both 2D and 3D. It has been shown that the information preserved by using fuzzy representation based on area coverage may be successfully utilized to improve precision and accuracy of our equations [6,7]. The result of a series of synthetic tests showed that fuzzy representation yields lower registration errors in average. In Fig. 4 and Fig. 5, some registration results on 3D medical images are shown.

3.2   Affine Puzzle

The affine puzzle problem can be formulated as follows: Given a binary image of an object (the *template*) and another binary image (the *observation*) containing the fragments of the *template*, we want to establish the geometric correspondence between these images which reconstructs the complete *template* object from its parts. distortion is a global nonlinear transformation with the following constraint (see Fig. 6):

– the object parts are distinct (*i.e.* either disconnected or separated by segmentation),
– all fragments of the *template* are available, but

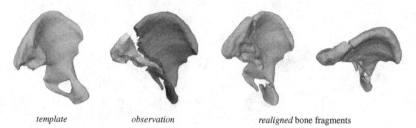

template   observation   *realigned* bone fragments

Fig. 8. Bone fracture reduction (CPU time in Matlab was 15 sec. for these 1 megavoxel CT volumes). The *template* is obtained by mirroring the intact bone.

- each of them is subject to a different affine deformation, and the partitioning of the *template* object is unknown.

The proposed solution [9] consists in constructing and solving a polynomial system of equations similar to Eq. (9)–(11), which provides all the unknown parameters of the alignment. We have quantitatively evaluated the proposed algorithm on a large synthetic dataset containing 2D and 3D images. The results show that the method performs well and robust against segmentation errors. The method has been validated on 2D real images of a tangram puzzle (see Fig. 7) as well as on volumetric medical images applied to surgical planning (see Fig. 8).

4   Nonlinear Deformations

When ϕ is a nonlinear transformation, then the Jacobian $J_\phi(\mathbf{x})$ is not a constant anymore and thus Eq. (6) has to be used directly:

$$\int \omega_i(\mathbf{y})d\mathbf{y} = \int \omega_i(\phi(\mathbf{x}))|J_\phi(\mathbf{x})|d\mathbf{x}, \quad i = 1, \dots, \ell \tag{12}$$

From a practical point of view, this means that our method can be applied to any diffeomorphism ϕ for which one can compute its Jacobian $J_\phi(\mathbf{x})$. Of course, in order to obtain an overdetermined system, ℓ has to be larger than the number of free parameters of ϕ.

4.1   Planar Homography

The simplest such deformation is a plane projective transformation (or planar homography), which is a linear transformation in the projective plane $\mathbb{P}^2$ [12,10]:

$$\mathbf{y}' = \mathbf{H}\mathbf{x}' \tag{13}$$

where $\mathbf{y}', \mathbf{x}' \in \mathbb{P}^2$ are the homogeneous coordinate representations of $\mathbf{y}, \mathbf{x} \in \mathbb{R}^2$. In the Euclidean plane $\mathbb{R}^2$, however, planar homography is a nonlinear transformation due to projective division by the third (homogeneous) coordinates, and the Jacobian is of the following form:

$$|J_\phi(\mathbf{x})| = \begin{vmatrix} \frac{\partial \phi_1}{\partial x_1} & \frac{\partial \phi_1}{\partial x_2} \\ \frac{\partial \phi_2}{\partial x_1} & \frac{\partial \phi_2}{\partial x_2} \end{vmatrix} = \frac{|\mathbf{H}|}{(H_{31}x_1 + H_{32}x_2 + 1)^3} . \tag{14}$$

Fig. 9. Registration of traffic sign images using a plane projective deformation model. The first column shows the *template*s, while the second, third, and fourth columns show the registration result as an overlayed yellow contour for SIFT, Shape Context, and our method, respectively.

Substituting back ϕ and J_ϕ into Eq. (12), we obtain a system of equations for the unknown transformation parameters which can be solved in the least-squares sense via the *Levenberg-Marquardt* algorithm.

Since the system is solved by minimizing the algebraic error, proper normalization is critical for numerical stability. For that purpose, the *template* and *observation* coordinates are normalized into $[-0.5, 0.5]$ by applying appropriate scaling and translation. Moreover the range of the ω functions should also be normalized into $[-1, 1]$ in order to ensure a balanced contribution of the equations to the algebraic error. This can be achieved by dividing the integrals with the maximal magnitude of the integral over the unit circle containing the objects [10]:

$$N_i = \int_{\|\mathbf{x}\| \leq \frac{\sqrt{2}}{2}} |\omega_i(\mathbf{x})| d\mathbf{x} \tag{15}$$

Some registration results on traffic sign images can be seen in Fig. 9.

4.2 Thin Plate Splines

A broadly used class of parametric deformation models are splines, in particular thin plate splines (TPS) [13,14]. TPS models are quite useful whenever a parametric free-form registration is required but the underlying physical model of the object deformation is unknown or too complex. Given a set of control points $\mathbf{c}_k \in \mathbb{R}^2$ and associated mapping coefficients $a_{ij}, w_{ki} \in \mathbb{R}$ with $i = 1, 2, j = 1, 2, 3$ and $k = 1, \ldots, K$, the TPS interpolating points $\mathbf{c}_k$ is given by [14]

$$\varphi_i(\mathbf{x}) = a_{i1}x_1 + a_{i2}x_2 + a_{i3} + \sum_{k=1}^{K} w_{ki}Q(\|\mathbf{c}_k - \mathbf{x}\|), \qquad (16)$$

where $Q : \mathbb{R} \to \mathbb{R}$ is the *radial basis function*

$$Q(r) = r^2 \log r^2 .$$

The local parameters are also required to satisfy the following additional constraints [14], meaning basically that the TPS at infinity behaves according to its affine term:

$$\sum_{k=1}^{K} w_{ki} = 0 \quad \text{and} \quad \sum_{k=1}^{K} c_{kj}w_{ki} = 0, \quad i, j = 1, 2 . \qquad (17)$$

Note that parameters include 6 global affine parameters a_{ij} and $2K$ local coefficients w_{ki} for the control points. In classical correspondence based approaches, control points are placed at extracted point matches, and the deformation at other positions is interpolated by the TPS. When correspondences are available, the exact mapping of the control points are also known which, using Eq. (16), provides constraints on the unknown parameters. Therefore in such cases, a TPS can be regarded as an optimal *interpolating* function whose parameters are usually recovered via a complex optimization procedure [13,14].

However, we are interested in solving the TPS registration problem without correspondences. Therefore in our approach, a TPS can be considered as a parametric model to *approximate* the underlying deformation field [10]. Control points (*i.e.* radial basis functions) can be placed *e.g.* on a uniform grid in order to capture local deformations everywhere. Obviously, a finer grid would allow a more refined approximation of the deformation field at the price of an increased number of free parameters.

To construct our system of equations Eq. (12), we need the Jacobian $|J_\varphi(\mathbf{x})|$ of the transformation φ, which is composed of the following partial derivatives ($i, j = 1, 2$) [10]

$$\frac{\partial \varphi_i}{\partial x_j} = a_{ij} - \sum_{k=1}^{K} 2w_{ki}(c_{kj} - x_j)\big(1 + \log(\|\mathbf{c}_k - \mathbf{x}\|^2)\big) . \qquad (18)$$

The system is then solved as in the previous section [10]. Fig. 10 shows some registration results on multimodal medical images using a TPS deformation model.

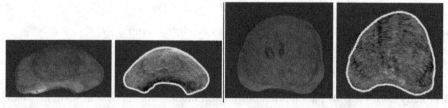

Fig. 10. Alignment of MRI (left) and US (right) prostate images using a TPS deformation model with 25 control point placed on a 5×5 uniform grid. The contours of the registered MRI images are overlaid on the US images.

5 Conclusions

A unified framework for correspondence-less registration of binary shapes has been presented. The method is applicable both for linear and non-linear deformations. In this paper, some of the most important transformation models have been considered (affine, projective and this plate splines) and the efficiency of the method has been demonstrated on medical images as well as on traffic sign matching. Furthermore, the method is not only usable for classical transformations, but it can also solve special problems like the affine puzzle. Demo implementations of our method are also available from http://www.inf.u-szeged.hu/~kato/software/ as follows:

- *Affine Registration of Planar Shapes*: JAVA code with a direct solver (only runs under Windows).
- *Affine Registration of 3D Objects*: JAVA code with multi-threading (≈ 0.2sec. CPU time for megavoxel volumes).
- *Nonlinear Shape Registration without Correspondences*: Implements planar homography, extension to other nonlinear deformations is relatively easy.

Acknowledgements. This research was partially supported by the grant K75637 of the Hungarian Scientific Research Fund; the grant CNK80370 of the National Innovation Office (NIH) & the Hungarian Scientific Research Fund (OTKA); the European Union and co-financed by the European Regional Development Fund within the projects TÁMOP-4.2.2/08/1/2008-0008 and TÁMOP-4.2.1/B-09/1/KONV-2010-0005.

The author gratefully acknowledges the contributions of Csaba Domokos, Jozsef Nemeth, and Attila Tanács from University of Szeged, Hungary.

The fractured bone CT images were obtained from the University of Szeged, Department of Trauma Surgery and were used with permission of Prof. Endre Varga, MD.

Pelvic CT studies and hip prosthesis Xray images were provided by Endre Szabó, Ádám Perényi, Ágnes Séllei and András Palkó from the Radiology Department of the University of Szeged.

Thoracic CT studies were provided by László Papp from Mediso Ltd., Hungary.

References

1. Holden, M.: A review of geometric transformations for nonrigid body registration. IEEE Trans. Med. Imaging 27, 111–128 (2008)
2. Belongie, S., Malik, J., Puzicha, J.: Shape matching and object recognition using shape context. IEEE Transactions on Pattern Analysis and Machine Intelligence 24, 509–522 (2002)
3. Heikkilä, J.: Pattern matching with affine moment descriptors. Pattern Recognition 37, 1825–1834 (2004)
4. Hagege, R., Francos, J.M.: Parametric estimation of multi-dimensional affine transformations:an exact linear solution. In: Proceedings of International Conference on Acoustics, Speech, and Signal Processing, vol. 2, Philadelphia, USA, pp. 861–864. IEEE (2005)
5. Domokos, C., Kato, Z.: Parametric estimation of affine deformations of planar shapes. Pattern Recognition 43, 569–578 (2010)

6. Tanács, A., Domokos, C., Sladoje, N., Lindblad, J., Kato, Z.: Recovering Affine Deformations of Fuzzy Shapes. In: Salberg, A.-B., Hardeberg, J.Y., Jenssen, R. (eds.) SCIA 2009. LNCS, vol. 5575, pp. 735–744. Springer, Heidelberg (2009)
7. Tanács, A., Sladoje, N., Lindblad, J., Kato, Z.: Estimation of linear deformations of 3D objects. In: Proceedings of International Conference on Image Processing, Hong Kong, China, pp. 153–156. IEEE (2010)
8. Tanacs, A., Kato, Z.: Fast linear registration of 3D objects segmented from medical images. In: Proceedings of International Conference on BioMedical Engineering and Informatics, Shanghai, China, pp. 299–303. IEEE (2011)
9. Domokos, C., Kato, Z.: Affine Puzzle: Realigning Deformed Object Fragments without Correspondences. In: Daniilidis, K., Maragos, P., Paragios, N. (eds.) ECCV 2010, Part II. LNCS, vol. 6312, pp. 777–790. Springer, Heidelberg (2010)
10. Domokos, C., Nemeth, J., Kato, Z.: Nonlinear shape registration without correspondences. IEEE Transactions on Pattern Analysis and Machine Intelligence 34, 943–958 (2012)
11. Hagege, R., Francos, J.M.: Parametric estimation of affine transformations: An exact linear solution. Journal of Mathematical Imaging and Vision 37, 1–16 (2010)
12. Nemeth, J., Domokos, C., Kato, Z.: Recovering planar homographies between 2D shapes. In: Proceedings of International Conference on Computer Vision, Kyoto, Japan, pp. 2170–2176. IEEE (2009)
13. Bookstein, F.L.: Principal warps: Thin-Plate Splines and the Decomposition of deformations. IEEE Trans. Pattern Anal. Mach. Intell. 11, 567–585 (1989)
14. Zagorchev, L., Goshtasby, A.: A comparative study of transformation functions for nonrigid image registration. IEEE Transactions on Image Processing 15, 529–538 (2006)

Part I
Computer Graphics Theory
and Applications

An Easy-to-Use AR Authoring Tool
for Industrial Applications

Jesús Gimeno[1], Pedro Morillo[1], Juan Manuel Orduña[2], and Marcos Fernández[1]

[1] Instituto de Robótica, Universidad de Valencia, Paterna (Valencia), Spain
{Jesus.Gimeno,Pedro.Morillo,Marcos.Fernandez}@uv.es
[2] Departamento de Informática, ETSE, Universidad de Valencia, Spain
Juan.Orduna@uv.es

Abstract. Augmented Reality (AR) applications have been emerged last years as a valuable tool for saving significant costs in maintenance and process control tasks in industry. This trend has been stimulated by the appearance of authoring tools that allow the fast and easy development of AR applications. However, most of current AR authoring tools are actually programming interfaces that are exclusively suitable for programmers, and they do not provide advanced visual effects such as occlusion or object collision detection.

This paper proposes an easy-to-use AR authoring tool oriented to the development of AR applications for the execution of industrial sequential procedures. Unlike other recent easy-to-use AR authoring tools, this software framework allows non-programming users to develop both marker-based and markerless AR solutions for different mobile hardware platforms, including occlusion capabilities. In order to validate the proposed AR authoring tool, we have developed four AR applications belonging to different industrial areas. The evaluation results show that overlaying 3D instructions on the actual work pieces reduces the error rate for an assembly task by more than a 75% particularly diminishing cumulative errors common in sequential procedures. Also, the results show that the time required by non-programming users to develop the AR prototypes using our tool was more than 90% lower than the time required for developing the same prototypes with computer graphics programmers. These results validate the tool as a general-purpose AR authoring tool for industrial AR applications.

Keywords: Augmented Reality, Authoring Tools, Non-immersive Desktop.

1   Introduction

Augmented Reality (AR) applications have been emerged last years as a valuable tool for saving significant costs in maintenance and process control tasks in industry. The term Augmented Reality (AR) defines computer graphic procedures or applications where the real-world view is superimposed by computer-generated objects in real-time [1]. Augmented Reality (AR) systems have been widely used in numerous applications such as medical procedures, scientific visualization, manufacturing automation, cultural heritage and military applications [2].

G. Csurka et al. (Eds.): VISIGRAPP 2012, CCIS 359, pp. 17–32, 2013.

Assembly, maintenance and even repair tasks in industry environments are some of the direct application fields of AR tools, and a lot of proposals have been made in these industrial areas [3, 4]. However, most of the proposed AR systems have been specifically developed for enhancing certain procedures in the domain of the problem.

One of the main problems that prevents AR applications to become popular is the lack of AR authoring platforms that allow unqualified users in computer graphics to easily generate AR applications. There are popular software libraries like ARToolKit and ARToolKitPlus [5] that use OpenGL, VRML or OpenScene-Graph [6] to represent the 3D models on the real images in real time. However, the use of these and others computer graphics libraries requires programming skills to generate AR applications, and every AR development should be constructed from the scratch.

In order to avoid these problems, AR authoring tools were proposed a decade ago [7]. The main advantage of AR authoring tools is that they do not rely on time and cost consuming recompilation steps, and therefore the changes and enhancements in the development of AR systems are fast and efficiently completed. In this sense, numerous platforms have been developed for the prototyping of AR applications last years [8–11]. Moreover, a recent work even classifies the existing AR tools depending on the use of external libraries, and the programming knowledge required for using them [12]. This later work also classifies AR development tools into two categories: AR-related software framework and GUI-based AR authoring tools.

Industrial environments shows specific characteristics different from other application context. For example, once a mechanic begins to physically manipulating objects in a task, he does not always need the visual information provided by the display [13] to complete certain steps of a given industrial procedure. On the other hand, solving the occlusion problem is crucial in these environments. This problem arises in AR systems when a computer-generated object closer to the viewer obscures the view of real elements farther away along the line-of-sight [14]. If the occlusion problem is not properly solved, then the developed tool does not significantly facilitate workers their actual on-the-job tasks. This fact is especially evident in AR systems for assembly or repair/maintenance purposes, because of the cluttered backgrounds and the frequent occlusions in these types of industrial environments [15].

Figure 1 shows an example of the occlusion problem when a custom AR system has been used in the on-site repair process of an engine. The left picture of this figure shows how a non-ocludded 3D computer-generated plastic coolant hose is visualized over the engine indicating the mechanic a misleading final location of the oil cooler. In this sense, the AR tool seems to indicate that the current hose should be located into one of the coolant pipes located in the front side of the engine as observed from the user's point of view. On the contrary, the right picture of the same figure shows how this augmented plastic coolant hose has been correctly occluded by the foreground real objects in the scene, indicating the proper location of the coolant pipe within the back side of the engine.

Fig. 1. An example of the occlusion problem in an AR system for industrial purposes

In this paper, we propose an easy-to-use AR authoring tool oriented to the development of AR applications for the execution of industrial sequential procedures. Unlike other recent easy-to-use AR authoring tools, this software framework, called SUGAR, allows non-programming users to quickly developing both marker-based and markerless ARsolutions for different mobile hardware platforms, including occlusion capabilities.

In order to validate the proposed AR authoring tool, we have developed four AR applications belonging to different industrial areas. The evaluation results show that overlaying 3D instructions on the actual work pieces reduces the error rate for an assembly task by more than a 75% particularly diminishing cumulative errors common in sequential procedures. Also, the results show that the time required by non-programming users to develop the AR prototypes using our tool was more than 90% lower than the time required for developing the same prototypes with computer graphics programmers. These results validate the tool as a general-purpose AR authoring tool for industrial AR applications. SUGAR allows describing industrial task, such as assembly, repairing and maintenance procedures as a set of sequential steps including different digital contents: video, images, text, manufacture's manuals, and Augmented Reality information. Since our AR authoring tool does not use a proprietary format, any kind of device (PDA/smartphones, TabletPC, See-Through goggles, etc.) could be used for the AR applications generated by the proposed tool. Moreover, the iterative development process of an AR application and the corresponding maintenance phase can be completed with our tool by developers with non-programming skills. Our approach uses Kinect [16] for computing a depth map of the scene to produce occlusion effects, greatly reducing the cost for solving the occlusion problem. The application examples show that, unlike other recent easy-to-use AR authoring tools [12], the proposed tool can be used as a general-purpose and low-cost framework for generating different maintenance and repair AR applications.

Also, this paper describes some experiments that test the relative effectiveness of AR instructions in assembly, maintenance and repair tasks. In this sense, three instructional media were compared to evaluate the performance of the developed AR applications: a printed manual, computer assisted instruction (CAI) using a TabletPC display, and CAI utilizing a head-mounted display. The evaluation results show that overlaying 3D instructions on the actual work pieces reduced the error rate for an assembly task by 79%, particularly diminishing cumulative errors (errors due to previous assembly mistakes). Moreover, the time required by non-programming users using SUGAR to develop the AR prototypes was much lower (approximately a 95%) than the time required for developing the same prototypes with expert programmers. These results validates the proposed tool as a general-purpose AR authoring tool for industrial AR applications.

The rest of the paper is organized as follows: Section 2 shows some related work about AR authoring tools for maintenance and repair tasks. Section 3 describes in detail the proposed AR authoring tool. Next, Section 4 shows different application examples of the proposed tool, and Section 5 shows the performance evaluation of AR instructions in an assembly task using the proposed tool. Finally, section 6 shows some concluding remarks and the future work to be done.

2   Related Work

Augmented Reality has been tested in manufacturing environments since more than one decade ago [3]. The potential of AR systems led to national research projects like ARVIKA [4]. Although ARVIKA included mature concepts for integrating physical and digital workspaces in a common scenario, the final AR procedures resulted very poor in terms of intuitive interaction mechanisms, functionality and usability. At the same time, another work proposed a prototype hardware and a software framework for supporting a wide range of maintenance categories with AR [17].

More recently, the most remarkable developments in the field of AR technologies for manufacturing purposes were collected in a survey [18]. Also, another work proved that an AR application was more efficient than an enhanced baseline system in reducing time and head movement during the localization portion of maintenance tasks [13]. The authors were especially encouraged to achieve these results with a population of professionally-trained mechanics working in a field setting, who expressed support for this approach.

Finally, another recent work includes a question examination mechanism in the AR authoring tool [12]. From a pedagogical point of view, examination is an important method in understanding the efficacy of a system of learning, and this feature can be a valuable tool also in manufacturing environments. However, the target users of the proposed authoring tool are high school students, and the examination mechanism is limited in that study to this population.

3   An Overview of SUGAR

SUGAR (which stands for System for the development of Unexpensive and Graphical Augmented Reality application) is an open-source software platform designed to enable a rapid prototyping of low-cost AR systems. Our framework is oriented to develop complex AR software applications based on procedural simulations, which are modeled following an easy-to-use AR authoring editor.

This AR editor generates an exchange file, describing the AR procedure, which can be loaded into different AR devices not requiring high computational power.

Figure 2 shows the workflow for the development of AR applications using SUGAR. The SUGAR editor allows users with non-programming skills the creation of Augmented Reality procedures based on steps. The main challenge when creating an Augmented Reality application is to achieve a correct overlap (registration) between the real world and the virtual information that is added on the real world. SUGAR allows the creation of virtual contents through an easy edition mechanism based on real world photos. The user takes photos of the real scenarios to be augmented, and is on these photos where the virtual content is edited. The ARToolKitPlus-based markers are automatically generated with a simple calibration step, in such a way that the user should only paste the AR markers on the real object in order to visualize the augmented scene. Therefore, SUGAR bridges the gap between virtual information and the real world, offering the user an easy way of creating virtual contents according to reality.

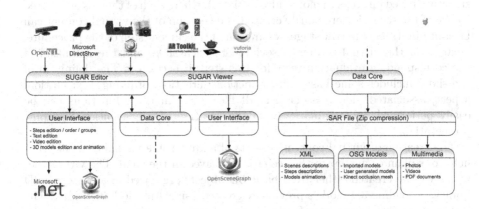

Fig. 2. Proposed workflow for the development of AR applications using SUGAR

The SUGAR modules can be classified in two groups: description of the real world, and virtual content edition. The first group includes those modules necessary for creating the scenarios where the virtual contents will be displayed. Each scenario is composed of an image of the real environment, some AR markers that are generated automatically, and a depth map (the latter one only is presented if a Kinect is available when the photo is taken). In order to create this scenario, two wizards guide the user through some easy stages. The first stage, called the *PhotoKinect Wizard module*, displays the real-time image of the markers camera and allows taking photos storing at the same time the depth image. This depth information will be used later in order to produce correct occlusions. The other wizard, called *Locations wizard*, allows the user the creation of a scenario from either a conventional photo or a photo captured with AR markers. This wizard is also split into four easy substages: first, the desired images are loaded. Then, the wizard allows to draw a rectangle indicating a flat area where the markers can be located. The two final substages consists of the introduction of the flat area defined within the real image and the number of AR markers to be used. After these steps, the scenario is ready for editing the virtual contents. The virtual models will be adjusted to the size of the real object to be augmented by using the size information introduced by the user. At any moment, the user can select a scenario and print the associated markers in order to paste these markers on a real object. This simple wizard allows a user with neither programming, nor ARToolKit/ARToolKitPlus knowledge, the creation of an AR marker with the proper size and the corresponding associated configuration file. The absence to this editor would require that the user selects the images of the markers to be used (he also locates the markers in the correct position) and he finally creates a configuration file with the description of the size, location and rotation matrix of each of the markers within the image.

After the creation of the scenarios, the other group of modules includes the procedures for defining the virtual information. The editor of SUGAR uses a structure based on steps (denoted also as slides), where each of them is associated to one of the scenarios previously created. The edition of the virtual content can be split into three different stages: definition of the current step of the procedure, creation of the virtual content associated to each slide, and the definition of the corresponding evaluation tests for this step, if necessary. The definition of the slides includes some basic office functions: creation, ordering, text edition, aspect, associated video, associated pdf files, etc. All these functions can be easily performed, in a similar way to the creation of a conventional graphic presentation.

The creation of virtual content consists of adding some virtual elements that help to explain each step to the scenario displayed in the slide. The virtual elements can be created either from basic 3D objects organized in an internal 3D library, or loading 3D models previously created using Autodesk 3DS Max. The included 3D library consists of cubes, spheres, planes, cones, etc., which can be grouped to generate more complex models, and allows changing their textures, colors, or other properties. Also, we have developed an animation module based on keyframes that allows to animate the virtual objects. In order to allow the creation of 3D models that are appropriate for the scenario to be augmented, the 3D scene includes a template with the photo that is used as the model, and even (depending on the type of scenery) a mesh created from the picture taken with Kinect. Using this reference, the user only has to locate the virtual models on the template. This way of creating a scene, starting from a reference image, allows the location of the virtual elements and their size adjustment. The absence of this template would force the user not only to accurately measure the location of each virtual element and its orientation on the real object according to the ARToolKitPlus marker, but also requiring from the user a certain level of knowledge in 3D design, computational trigonometry and the use of the ARToolKitPlus library.

Figure 2 also shows how we have created a *Test Wizard* for the test edition process. This module can easily generate three kinds of questions: true/false questions, multiple answer questions, and selection on the image. The latter one consists of asking the user to mark a concrete area on the image (for example, a car battery). When creating the test, the user enters the photo and he marks each vertex of the correct area with the mouse.

The software architecture of SUGAR is based on a modular approach oriented to develop procedural AR systems. Basically, the SUGAR framework consists of two applications: an easy-to-use editor for AR procedures and an AR light viewer. Both applications share some software modules permitting them to reuse 3D-tracking data structure models, and visualization code.

Although the AR editor and AR viewer share the same software module, each application includes a different user's interface. Thus, the graphical user interface of the AR editor has been developed on Windows Forms and includes some components, developed on OpenSceneGraph, in order to offer high-performance 3D graphical capabilities when users create and edit the AR procedures. In this sense, the OpenNI software library allows accessing the depth map of the real scene using the Kinect device. Moreover, the Microsoft DirectShow API enables high-quality playback of streaming video and audio to be attached to the steps of the industrial (maintenance, repair or even assembly) procedures. In contraposition to this multiview 3D application, the AR viewer corresponds to a light Windows application, developed on Qt/C++ [19], embedding a reduced version of the OpenSceneGraph framework and including a reduced set of primitives for this 3D high-level library tool. Since Qt/C++ is a cross-platform development framework, the same source code for a Qt application can be compiled on different operating systems without changes. In this sense, the "SUGAR Viewer" has been ported to Symbian and Android operative systems with minimum changes within the initial source code. The reduced computation workload of this multiplatform application allows the viewer to be executed on low-power general purpose processors to execute the AR procedures in on-site industrial environments.

The "Data Core" module also includes the definition and the basic properties of the exchange file format for the SUGAR framework, denoted as SAR files. These files are generated by the AR editor to be imported by the SUGAR multiplatform viewers. Basically, the SAR files are zip-compressed archives containing a structured representation of AR applications, and the corresponding multimedia content, that can be attached to the steps of the modeled AR procedures for industrial task. The organization of the digital content, including the depth maps obtained from the Kinect device, has been defined using XML files, providing a flexible configuration mechanism.

Additionally, SUGAR provides not only marker-based, but also markerless ARsolutions for different mobile hardware platforms. Unlike in the marker-based AR systems, inmarkerless AR some actual objects of the environment are used as a target to be tracked in order to place 3D virtual objects. This approach improves the most common disadvantages of the marker-based AR systems since it is not necessary that artificial intrusive markers which are included as a part of the real environment. In order to estimate the position, orientation and the three-dimensional movement of the camera from the captured images, the markerless AR systems includes tracking algorithms based on natural features where elements, such as corners of edges, are recognized in the scene in real-time [20]. Although these algorithms are computationally expensive, they have been ported to mobile platforms [21, 22]. In order to port SUGAR to these platforms, we have selected Vuforia [23], released by the ARM-processor company Qualcomm at the end of the 2011, as the markerless-based tool for computer vision and Augmented Reality to be integrated in SUGAR. Unlike another approaches such as NyARToolkit NFT or AndAR, VuforiaSDK supports for more than 400 different smartphones and tablet models, and it tracks real objects on the current frame with a impressive fluidityand reliability. This high-level, out-of-the-box AR SDK acts as a mobile middleware and mobile data processing component, and it is interfaced to the kernel module of SUGAR. As an example, figure 3 shows a snapshot of SUGAR for a markerless system. The left side of the figure shows the interface of the proposed editor, while the right side show how the Augmented Reality image is displayed by a Samsung Galaxy Note terminal.

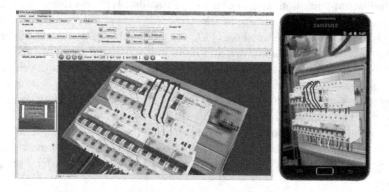

Fig. 3. Snapshot of SUGAR (left image: editor, right image: AR viewer running on a Samsung Galaxy Note) for a markerless application

4   Application Examples

In order to validate our AR editor as an efficient tool for the rapid prototyping of AR applications for assembly, maintenance and repair purposes, we have tested our tool in four different application examples belonging to various industrial areas. Concretely, these application examples are the following procedures: the replacement of the cut heading within a lathe machine (metal machining area), the assembly of a computer starting from its basic components (computer and electronics manufacturing area), the repair of the admission system in a mobile lighting tower (maintenance of heavy machinery area), and the review of the

Table 1. Decomposition of the procedures in steps

Procedure Groups	Steps	AR Steps
PROC 1	6	51	26
PROC 2	5	25	20
PROC 3	7	58	32
PROC 4	4	15	10

spark plugs and the ignition coils on a BMW M3 E92 (420CV) engine (automobile maintenance area). We have denoted these procedures as *PROC 1* to *PROC 4*, respectively. Table 1 shows the amount of steps, gathered into groups, needed to complete each one of the tasks. Since not all the steps recommended by the manufacturer need visual indications to be completed, this table also shows, for each procedure, the number of steps that actually include AR contents.

In order to help in the completion of these tasks, SUGAR authoring tool was used to prototype two different AR systems (for each of the four procedures considered): a computer assisted instruction system using a TabletPC system (we will denote this AR system as S2) and a computer assisted instruction system using a head-mounted display (we will denote this AR system as S3). Concretely, the S2 system was developed on a Dell Latitude XT1 TabletPc (Intel Core 2 Duo at 1.2GHz, 2GB RAM, ATI Radeon Xpress 1250, Windows 7 Professional) including a LCD-CCFL 12.1-inch screen for outdoor environments, reaching up to 400cd/m2 of brightness. The S3 system consists of the same Dell Latitude XT1 but connected to an "AR Vision 3D HMD", which is a full stereoscopic video see-through AR device including a binocular SVGA (1024x768) displays and two separate 752x480 (60 FPS) color cameras. In order to illustrate the considered application examples, Figure 4 shows a snapshot of the proposed AR editor (SUGAR Editor) when implementing Procedure 1, while Figure 5 shows a snapshot of the SUGAR tool when used for Procedure 3.

Figure 4 and Figure 5 show the interface of the proposed AR editor for sequential procedures included in SUGAR. The easy-to-use interface of the editor is very similar to the most common graphic presentation programs (such as Microsoft PowerPoint, Apple KeyNote, Open Office Impress, etc.), and it consists of a large view of the current step of the modeled procedure along with a view of the rest of steps (as a slide sorter) on the left side of the screen. The editor allows non-programming users to create AR applications consisting of a set of sequential steps handled by AR markers. In this sense, the toolbars on the top of the window allow to include multimedia contents such as video, images, text, manuals and AR information into the steps of the AR procedure.

Figure 5 shows the "Affine Transformation Toolbar" that appears when 3D models (modeled using Autodesk 3DS Max or selected from a library included within the applications) are included into the current step of the procedure. This toolbar allows rotating, scaling, translating and defining animation for the 3D models that will be visualized by the user when the system recognize the AR markers located as a part of the environment. Also, the button located at the right upper corner of the screen allows to load a depth map of the real scene using

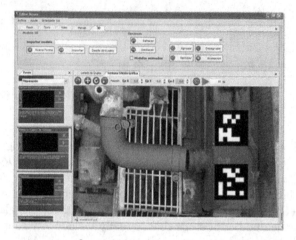

Fig. 4. Snapshot of SUGAR editor for Procedure 1

Fig. 5. Snapshots of the SUGAR editor and light AR viewer (Android and Symbian versions) for Procedure 3

Fig. 6. Real use of the S2 system in Procedure 1

the Kinect device. This feature is needed when the 3D model for the current step of the AR procedure needs occlusion capabilities. Finally, this figure shows on the right side the Augmented Reality images that two different client terminals (with different operating systems) display. Figure 6 illustrates the use of the S2 system when Procedure 1 was tested in a real industrial environment.

5   Performance Evaluation

The performance evaluation of Augmented Reality authoring tools results in a complex task, since it is very difficult to quantitatively show the utility or effectiveness of the proposed methodology and tools. The measurement of costs reduction in software development and maintenance neither results an easy task. The main reasons are the lack of objective metrics in not only Augmented Reality, but also Virtual Reality, and the qualitative and even fuzzy nature of most software engineering studies [24].

A possible way of evaluating the performance of Augmented Reality tools is a qualitative, user-centered approach [25]. According to recent studies [26], the observations and questionnaire are the basis for a qualitative analysis. The questionnaire consists of several questions where the participants in the evaluation of the AR tool can freely answer on their experience of the AR system. The questions are usually related to overall impression of the AR system, experienced difficulties, experienced positive aspects, what they would change in the system and whether it is possible to compare receiving AR instructions to receiving instructions from an instructor. However, a qualitative approach does not allow neither to compare different AR tools on a fair basis, nor to evaluate their performance in comparison with traditional training or guidance tools. On the contrary, a quantitative analysis can allow a fair comparison of different tools. Some metrics like cost efficiency, development time and maintainability have been proposed for a quantitative analysis [27]. However, that work does not define concrete criteria for assigning values to the three metrics, and only the development time is accurately measured.

We propose a quantitative approach for the performance evaluation of the AR tool in some industrial environments. In order to measure the complexity of the assembly, repair and maintenance tasks, we have followed the criteria proposed in [28]. Therefore, we have classified the complexity of the Procedure1 (application examples described in Section 4) as Very High, the complexity of Procedure 2 as Normal, and the complexity of Procedures 3 and 4 as High.

In order to measure the performance provided by the AR systems prototyped with SUGAR, we have first measured the average completion time required by fifteen different users in order to completely execute each of the considered procedures. All the users were experts technicians in their area, but a training session was performed prior to the performance evaluation in order to allow the users to get in contact with the AR technology. The same users were used for performing the four procedures, in order to avoid any skew in the results due to the different skill of different populations. However, the fifteen users were divided into four groups, and the sequence of procedures executed by each group was different, in order to avoid skews in the experimental results due to the potential training with the technology. Moreover, not only it was the first time that the users executed the considered procedures, but also any of the groups repeated the same procedure using different systems, in order to avoid the benefit with the knowledge and experience that they acquire before.

For comparison purposes, the users also performed the considered procedures exclusively using a printed manual provided by the manufacturer. We have denoted this "system" as S1. Table 2 shows, in its three mostlef columns, the average completion times required when using each system for all the procedures considered. As it could be expected, the average completion times for systems S2 and S3 are much lower than the ones achieved with S1 system. Also, this table shows that the times achieved with S3 (computer assisted instructions (CAI) using a head-mounted display) are lower than the ones achieved with S2 (CAI using a TabletPC display), reaching even less than half the time required for the same procedure with system S1 (in Procedures 1, 3 and 4). These results show the significant benefits that AR systems can provide to assembly, repair and maintenance tasks.

Table 2. Completion times and average number of repeated stages with different systems

Procedure	Complet. Time			Repeated (times)		
	S1	S2	S3	S1	S2	S3
PROC 1	4h 30min	2h 30min	1h 45min	12.25	2.65	3.30
PROC 2	50min	35min	30min	7.51	1.26	4.65
PROC 3	6 h	3h 30min	2h 45 min	14.13	2.40	3.60
PROC 4	2h	1h 15min	50min	4.33	1.23	1.57

In order to get a more in-depth analysis of the results shown in the most left half of Table 2 shows the mistakes made when executing the AR procedures for all the considered experiments. Concretely, this half of Table 2 shows the average number of steps in the experiments that were repeated by the qualified participants because of human errors. As it could be expected, the direct visual guidance provided by the Augmented Reality devices in systems S2 and S3 resulted in a significant decrease in the number of repeated stages, compared to the use of manufacture's manuals in S1. The system S2 provides the lowest number of repeated stages. Since the execution of assembly and maintenance/repair tasks are often incremental processes, where the results of previous steps are the input of next steps, undetected mistakes in preceding stages (denoted as cumulative errors) result in repeating all the previous affected tasks, starting where the mistake was committed. For this reason, the number of the repeated tasks grows exponentially as the errors made by the participants increase. Nevertheless, the differences between S2 and S3 systems become significant even if taking into account this fact, showing that immersive Augmented Reality does not provide the best performance in industrial environments.

Nevertheless, Table 2 does not actually measure the performance of SUGAR, but the prototypes developed with this AR authoring tool. In order to measure the performance achieved with SUGAR, we have asked two different teams to develop the prototypes whose results are shown in Table 2. One of the teams (we will denote this one as Team 1) was composed of AR programmers, and the other one (we will denote this one as Team 2) was exclusively composed of expert technicians. As a reference, we asked Team 1 to develop the prototype following the classic AR development approach, by writing, compiling and debugging source code. In this sense, Team 1 developed the AR prototypes using Microsoft Visual Studio 2010 as C++ development framework, OpenSceneGraph 2.9.7 as 3D graphics visualization toolkit and ARToolKitPlus 2.2 as software library for AR purposes. In order to measure the performance of SUGAR, we asked Team 2 to develop the same prototypes with SUGAR.

Table 3 shows the development times (in working days) required by each team. The column labeled as "Team" shows the team, the column labeled as "Param." shows the specific parameter of the development time measured by each row, and the other four columns shows the results for each procedure. The parameters measured are the following ones: SLOC measures the final number of source lines of code included within the final AR prototype, while FPS indicates the framerate (in frames per second) achieved using the test hardware. The parameter CT measures the number of working days required by the team for completing the coding stage of the prototype. The parameter DT measures the number of working days required by the team for completing the debugging/adjusting stage, and the parameter TT measures the total time required for the development of the prototype (the sum of CT and DT parameters).

Table 3. Source-code sizes and development times

Team	Param.	PROC 1	PROC 2	PROC 3	PROC 4
1	SLOC	71853	64710	76254	53695
	FPS	28	44	32	50
	CT	95	76	108	59
	DT	15	10	17	6
	TT	110	86	125	65
2	SLOC	79215	71523	37749	60101
	FPS	31	40	35	50
	CT	3	3	2	2
	DT	1	1	2	1
	TT	4	4	4	3

Table 3 shows that the size of the source code generated by SUGAR is roughly a 10% higher than the source code created by traditional AR programming. However, this slight increase of the source code does not have an effect on the graphic performance of the AR application. Moreover, Table 3 also shows that the time required by non-programming users with SUGAR to develop the AR prototypes are less than 5% of the ones required for developing the same prototypes with programmers. These differences of orders of magnitude show the potential that an intuitive AR authoring tool like SUGAR can provide to industrial environments. Moreover, the ease of use of SUGAR allows to avoid the need for programming skills, exclusively requiring the expertise of technicians in that field for developing AR prototypes. Also, any potential change required by the prototype can also be made by technicians, without the need of programming skills.

6   Conclusions and Future Work

In this paper, we have proposed an easy-to-use AR authoring tool, which allows the easy creation of interactive Augmented Reality applications without any programming knowledge. This authoring tool includes an easy-to-use editor for AR procedures and an AR light viewer, which share non-proprietary exchange files describing the AR procedures. The proposed tool allows the development of AR applications with occlusion capabilities to be used in on-site industrial procedures, where a certain level of depth-perception is necessary. Unlike other recent proposals, our tool does not rely on expensive or unavailable 3D models, and it uses Kinect for computing a depth map of the scene.

The performance evaluation of the proposed AR authoring tool includes both a qualitative and a quantitative assessment. Concretely, we have tested four AR applications, belonging to different industrial areas, using different instructional media. The performance evaluation results show that the registration of geometric models to the real-world counterparts in industrial procedures significantly facilitate workers their actual on-the-job tasks. The direct visual guidance provided by the AR devices significantly decrease the number of repeated stages when compared to commonly used manufacture's manuals.

Also, the time required by users with non-programming skills to develop the AR prototypes using our tool was much lower than the time required for developing the same prototypes with expert programmers when following a classical development of AR systems. These results shows the potential of our approach and validates it as a general-purpose AR authoring tool for industrial AR applications.

As a future work to be done, we are working on new versions of the light viewer for iOs and Windows Phone devices. Moreover, SUGAR pretends to integrate a new tracking module, based on natural features, to improve the current Augmented Reality experience provided by the tool when executing on-site industrial tasks.

Acknowledgements. This work has been jointly supported by the Spanish MICINN and the European Commission FEDER funds under grants Consolider-Ingenio CSD2006-00046 and TIN2009-14475-C04-04.

References

1. Azuma, R.: A survey of augmented reality. Presence: Teleoperators and Virtual Environments 6(4), 355–385 (1997)
2. Cawood, S., Fiala, M.: Augmented Reality: A Practical Guide. Pragmatic Bookshelf (2008)
3. Baird, K., Barfield, W.: Evaluating the effectiveness of augmented reality displays for a manual assembly task. Virtual Reality 4, 250–259 (1999)
4. Friedrich, W.: Arvika-augmented reality for development, production and service. In: Proceedings of the IEEE/ACM International Symposium on Mixed and Augmented Reality, ISMAR 2002, pp. 3–4 (2002)

5. Wagner, D., Schmalstieg, D.: Artoolkitplus for pose tracking on mobile devices. In: Proceedings of 12th Computer Vision Winter Workshop, CVWW 2007, pp. 139–146 (2007)
6. Burns, D., Osfield, R.: Open scene graph a: Introduction, b: Examples and applications. In: Proceedings of the IEEE Virtual Reality Conference, VR 2004, p. 265 (2004)
7. Haringer, M., Regenbrecht, H.T.: A pragmatic approach to augmented reality authoring. In: Proceedings of the 1st International Symposium on Mixed and Augmented Reality, ISMAR 2002, p. 237. IEEE Computer Society, Washington, DC (2002)
8. Ledermann, F., Schmalstieg, D.: April: A high-level framework for creating augmented reality presentations. In: Proceedings of the IEEE Virtual Reality Conference, VR 2005, pp. 187–194 (2005)
9. Schmalstieg, D.: Rapid prototyping of augmented reality applications with the studierstube framework. In: Proceedings of the Workshop of Industrial Augmented Reality, IAR, IEEE/ACM International Symposium on Mixed and Augmented Reality, ISMAR 2005 (2005)
10. Hampshire, A., Seichter, H., Grasset, R., Billinghurst, M.: Augmented reality authoring: generic context from programmer to designer. In: Proceedings of the Australasian Computer-Human Interaction Conference, OZCHI 2006, pp. 409–412 (2006)
11. Seichter, H., Looser, J., Billinghurst, M.: Composar: An intuitive tool for authoring ar applications. In: Proceedings of the IEEE/ACM International Symposium on Mixed and Augmented Reality, ISMAR 2008, pp. 177–178 (2008)
12. Wang, M., Tseng, C., Shen, C.: An easy to use augmented reality authoring tool for use in examination purpose. Human-Computer Interaction 332, 285–288 (2010)
13. Henderson, S.J., Feiner, S.: Evaluating the benefits of augmented reality for task localization in maintenance of an armored personnel carrier turret. In: Proceedings of the 2009 8th IEEE International Symposium on Mixed and Augmented Reality, pp. 135–144. IEEE Computer Society (2009)
14. Breen, D.E., Whitaker, R.T., Rose, E., Tuceryan, M.: Interactive occlusion and automatic object placement for augmented reality. Computer Graphics Forum 15(3), 11–22 (1996)
15. Sang-Cheol, P., Sung-Hoon, L., Bong-Kee Sinb, S., Seong-Whan, L.: Tracking nonrigid objects using probabilistic hausdorff distance matching. Pattern Recognition 38(12), 2373–2384 (2005)
16. Santos, E.S., Lamounier, E.A., Cardoso, A.: Interaction in augmented reality environments using kinect. In: Proceedings of the 2011 XIII Symposium on Virtual Reality, SVR 2011, pp. 112–121. IEEE Computer Society, Washington, DC (2011)
17. Schwald, B., Laval, B.D., Sa, T.O., Guynemer, R.: An augmented reality system for training and assistance to maintenance in the industrial context. In: Proceedings of 11th International Conference in Central Europe on Computer Graphics, Visualization and Computer Vision, pp. 425–432 (2003)
18. Ong, S.K., Yuan, M.L., Nee, A.Y.C.: Augmented reality applications in manufacturing: a survey. International Journal of Production Research 46(10), 2707–2742 (2008)
19. Blanchette, J., Summerfield, M.: C++ GUI Programming with Qt 4. Open Source Software Development Series. Prentice-Hall (2008)
20. Simon, G., Berger, M.O.: Reconstructing while registering: A novel approach for markerless augmented reality. In: ISMAR, pp. 285–294. IEEE Computer Society (2002)

21. Wagner, D., Reitmayr, G., Mulloni, A., Drummond, T., Schmalstieg, D.: Pose tracking from natural features on mobile phones. In: Proceedings of the 7th IEEE/ACM International Symposium on Mixed and Augmented Reality, ISMAR 2008, pp. 125–134. IEEE Computer Society, Washington, DC (2008)

22. Klein, G., Murray, D.: Parallel tracking and mapping on a camera phone. In: Proceedings of the 2009 8th IEEE International Symposium on Mixed and Augmented Reality, ISMAR 2009, pp. 83–86. IEEE Computer Society, Washington, DC (2009)

23. Qualcomm incorporated: Vuforia sdk 1.5 (2012),
    http://www.qualcomm.com/solutions/augmented-reality

24. Seo, J., OhM, S.: Pvot: An interactive authoring tool for virtual reality. International Journal of Computer Science and Network Security (IJCSNS) 7(4), 17–26 (2007)

25. Traskback, M., Koskinen, T., Nieminenl, M.: User-centred evaluation criteria for a mixed reality authoring application. In: Proc. of Tenth International Conference on Human-Computer Interaction, HCI, pp. 1263–1267 (2003)

26. Nilsson, S., Johansson, B., Jönsson, A.: A Holistic Approach to Design and Evaluation of Mixed Reality Systems. Human-Computer Interaction Series. In: The Engineering of Mixed Reality Systems, pp. 33–55. Springer (2010)

27. Abawi, D.F., Luis, J., Arcos, L., Haller, M., Hartmann, W., Huhtala, K., Träskbäck, M.: A mixed reality museum guide: The challenges and its realization. In: Proceedings of the 10th International Conference on Virtual Systems and Multimedia, VSMM 2004 (2004)

28. Campbell, D.J.: Task complexity: A review and analysis. Academy of Management Review 13(1), 40 (1988)

Fast Realistic Modelling of Muscle Fibres

Josef Kohout[1], Gordon J. Clapworthy[2], Saulo Martelli[3], and Marco Viceconti[3]

[1] University of West Bohemia, Plzeň, Czech Republic
besoft@kiv.zcu.cz
[2] University of Bedfordshire, Luton, U.K.
[3] Istituto Ortopedico Rizzoli, Bologna, Italy
http://graphics.zcu.cz/Projects/Muskuloskeletal-Modeling

Abstract. In this paper, we describe a method for automatic construction of arbitrary number of muscle fibres in the volume of a muscle represented by its surface mesh. The method is based on an iterative, slice-by-slice, morphing of predefined fibres template into the muscle volume. Our experiments with muscles of thighs and pelvis show that in most cases, the method produces realistic fibres. For some muscles, especially, those with large attachment areas, some imperfections are observable; however, results are acceptable anyway. As our sequential VTK-based C++ implementation is capable of producing 128 fine fibres within a muscle of 10K triangles in 380 ms on commodity hardware (Intel i7), the method is suitable for interactive educational medical software. We believe that it could also be used in clinical biomechanical applications to extract information on the current muscle lever arm and fibre path.

Keywords: Muscle modelling, Muscle fibres, VTK.

1 Introduction

Knowledge of muscle fibres is essential for physiotherapists, surgeons and orthopedists, especially for effective rehabilitation programs that aim at improving the quality of life of patients suffering from neuromuscular disorders (more than 0.1% of general population in UK [7]), for planning optimal muscle surgery (e.g., muscle auto-transplantation), and prediction of forces having impact on joints.

Studying traditional anatomical atlases (e.g., Gray's atlas [2]) is a common option to gain this knowledge. However, the full understanding requires an excellent imagination skill of the student since they need to reconstruct 3D models in their minds. Digital 3D anatomical atlases seem to be a better alternative. However, as far as we know, most of them display muscle fibres on the muscle surface only, thus not providing information about muscle interior, or do not display them at all, and, therefore, they provide a limited insight.

Ng Thow Hing [6] represents a muscle with a B-spline solid fitted to raw muscle surface data extracted from a set of parallel images and to internal fibre points obtained from an autopsy. Muscle fibres can be then generated simply by constructing iso-curves within the solid. Although accurate, this technique is rather impractical because of its the complexity of B-spline fitting procedure.

G. Csurka et al. (Eds.): VISIGRAPP 2012, CCIS 359, pp. 33–47, 2013.

A different approach is described by Blemker & Delp in [1]. In their model, a muscle is represented by 3D finite-element hexahedral mesh whose cells contain information about the direction of the muscle fibres present in its volume. This mesh is constructed as follows. A surface model of the muscle to be represented is obtained from the input medical images. The user then has to create, manually, a hexahedral cubical template mesh that contains the whole muscle in its interior. Unlike the approach by Ng Thow Hing, muscle fibres arrangement is not derived from a real muscle but it is given in a predefined cubical template that consists of a set of interpolated rational Bézier spline curves connecting two muscle attachment areas highlighted on this template. This template of the fibre geometry is mapped into this template hexahedral mesh. Finally, the template mesh is projected into the volume of muscle by a proprietary mapping method available in the commercial TrueGRID (XYZ Scientific Applications) software. Although much easier definition of muscle fibres is presented, the dependence on an expensive commercial tool together with the large memory consumption (because of 3D mesh) renders this approach also quite impractical.

Representing a muscle with a triangular surface mesh is very popular, especially, due to its simplicity and low memory requirements. As far as we know, however, no method is currently available for an automatic construction of muscle fibres in the muscle volume defined by its mesh surface. Hence, in this paper, we describe a simple iterative technique based on a slice-by-slice morphing of predefined fibres template (defined by Blemker & Delp) into the interior of the muscle, employing mapping technique described in [3].

The remainder of this paper is structured as follows. In the next section, we give a brief brings an overview of our method; details are described in sections 3. Section 4 presents the experiments that were performed. Section 5 concludes the paper and provides an overview of possible future work.

2   Method Overview

Our method is designed to process any muscle represented by its surface mesh for which information about its attachment areas, i.e., about sites at which the muscle is attached to the bone is available. This information is typically provided as two sets of landmarks, one for the origin and the other for the insertion area, specified by an expert. Every landmark is fixed to an underlying bone, so that when bones move (during the simulation of various activities), so do landmarks. The number of landmarks in the set define the accuracy of the fibres generated. We note that for many muscles, it is sufficient to specify just one landmark. Fig. 1 shows an example of muscles and their landmarks.

For each muscle, it is also necessary to specify what type of muscle fibres it contains, if parallel, fanned, curved or pennate, and to define the requested number of fibres to be constructed and their resolution, i.e., the number of segments along its length. It is important to point out that all these settings can be specified by an expert and then stored in the atlas data, so that no input is required from an ordinary user (e.g., a student of medicine).

According to the specified type of muscle, our method selects the appropriate predefined template with fibres geometry (defined by Blemker & Delp [1]). This is a unit cube

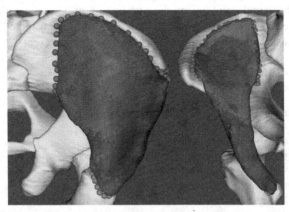

Fig. 1. Gluteus Medius (left) and Iliacus (right) with their attachment areas. The origin area is blue, the insertion area is red.

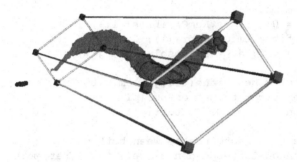

Fig. 2. The best fitting of the parallel fibres template for the sartorius muscle. The origin area defined in the template (a rectangle with four points) and specified by the user (a cloud of points) on the bone is blue, while the insertion area is red.

describing the space of an arbitrary number of muscle fibres (analytically expressed by rational Bézier spline curves) and containing also information about attachment area. The method picks the requested number of fibres, exploiting Sobol points sampling[4], and then samples the picked fibres to get poly-lines of the requested resolution. In the next step, we find an affine transformation of the template such that the attachment areas of the transformed template best correspond to those of the muscle – see Fig. 2. Naturally, the fibres generated in the previous step undergo the same transformation.

The transformed template fibres are then morphed successively into the interior of the muscle. The morphing is done successively by slicing both the oriented bounding box (OBB) of the transformed cube with its fibres and the muscle surface and mapping the contour of the OBB onto the contour of the muscle using generic barycentric coordinates [3].

For muscles with wide attachment areas, the paths of muscle fibres generated by the process described so far are unrealistic in a proximity of such an area since the fibres tend to meet in a common point instead of spreading over the whole area. To correct this, we cut out the part of the fibre that is close to the attachment area and replace it by a line segment whose end-point lies on the surface of muscle in the region defined by the attachment area and that has the direction derived from the trimmed fibre. Finally, the muscle fibre is smoothed to eliminate noise that might be present.

Pseudo-Code of the Method

```
void Decomposition([in] Surface ms, [in] AttachmentAreas oi,
   [in] MuscleSettings ss, [out] Polylines fibres)
{
   //select the appropriate template
   FibreTemplate tm = GetTemplate(ss.MuscleType);

   //generate template fibres
   tm.GenerateFibres(ss.NumOfFibres, ss.Resolution);

   //transform the template with its fibres so that
   //attachment areas are aligned
   tm.Transform(ms, oi);
   for (int i = 0; i < ss.NumOfFibres; i++) {
      Polyline fib = tm.GetFibre(i);
      for (int j = 0; j <= ss.Resolution; j++)
      {
         Plane pl = new Plane(fib[j], tm.GetMainAxis());
         Polygon tmc = tm.GetContour(pl);
         Polygon mc = ms.GetContour(pl);

         //make correspondence between both contours
         MakeContourCorrespondence([ref] tmc, [ref] mc);

         //calculate barycentric coordinates for point fib[j]
         //in template contour and reconstruct the point
         //in the target contour (muscle contour)
         Double[] bc = tmc.GetBarycentricCoords(fib[j]);
         mc.ReconstructCoords(bc, [out] fib[j]);
      }

      //Filter the fibre and smooth it
      FilterFibre(ms, oi, [ref] fib);
      SmoothFibre([ref] fib, ss.SmoothSettings);
      fibres.Add(fib);
   }
}
```

3   Details

In this section, we describe all steps of the method, we have just outlined, in detail.

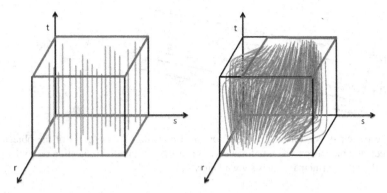

Fig. 3. The template of parallel (left) and pennate (right) fibres. The origin area is blue, the insertion area is red.

3.1 Template Construction

Following the ideas presented by Blemker & Delp [1], the template is a unit cube with defined the origin and insertion areas on its bottom and top faces, respectively. The areas are connected by Bézier curves (of degree varying from 2 to 4 depending on the muscle type) which will represent the muscle fibres – see Figure 3. Generally, the cube can contain an infinite number of curves, so there is no limit on the number of fibres that can be represented; each fibre is a Bézier curve $C(t)$ of real parameter t whose control polygon can be identified by a pair of real parameters r, s.

To create the requested number of fibres, the parametric space r, s must be sampled. Ng-Thow-Hing [6] suggests the use of Sobol sampling [4] which produces a better distribution of fibres within the muscle volume than random or uniform sampling, especially when the number of fibres is relatively low (up to hundreds), which is typical in this context. The fibre curves retrieved are sampled in the parameter space, t, to produce poly-lines of as many segments as the value of the required resolution.

3.2 Template Fitting

We assume that the principal axis of the muscle coincides with one of the axes of the cube. The origin of the principal axis is calculated as the centroid of the muscle, i.e., the mean of coordinates of surface vertices. The direction of the principal axis can be determined easily as the difference between the centroid of the insertion area and the centroid of the origin area. In a case that the attachment area is so complex that its centroid does not fit the data well, the direction is determined differently as the eigenvector with the largest eigenvalue obtained for the first-order covariance matrix:

$$\frac{1}{N-1} \cdot \begin{pmatrix} C_{0,0} & C_{0,1} & C_{0,2} \\ C_{0,0} & C_{1,1} & C_{1,2} \\ C_{,0} & C_{2,1} & C_{2,2} \end{pmatrix} \tag{1}$$

$$C_{i,j} = \sum_{k=0}^{N-1} (V_{k,i} - O_i) \cdot (V_{k,j} - O_j) \tag{2}$$

Fig. 4. The principal axis (dashed red line) oriented bounding boxes (grey) of the object. Red axis + green and blue arrows denote local coordinate frames. Parallel projection on to the plane perpendicular to the principal axis is shown below.

where $O = (O_0, O_1, O_2)$ is the origin of the principal axis and $V_{i,0}, V_{i,1}, V_{i,2}$ are the Euclidean coordinates of the surface vertex V_i ($i = 0 \dots N - 1$; N is the number of surface vertices).

Having aligned u_0 with the principal axis, we choose any two vectors v_0 and w_0 so that (u_0, v_0, w_0) forms an orthogonal set. These vectors are successively rotated around the principal axis by a small angle (we use $5°$), which results in a set of frames (u_0, v_i, w_i), as depicted in Fig. 4. For each frame, the minimal oriented bounding box of the muscle surface is constructed based on vectors u_0, v_i, w_i.

From these bounding boxes, we must choose the one whose origin and insertion areas (see Figure 3) best match the muscle origin and insertion areas that are specified either by the action lines of the muscle or manually by an expert. To do so, for each point of the template origin area (defined as a rectangle for most templates) we find the closest point on the muscle origin area and, likewise, for each point of the template insertion area, the closest point on the muscle insertion area. The Euclidean distances between the pairs of points found are summed – the best configuration is the one with the minimal sum. The result of fitting sartorius muscle is shown in Fig. 2.

3.3 Template Morphing

After the template has been transformed to fit the muscle, the template is morphed into the muscle so that its boundary becomes the surface of the muscle and its internal fibres (represented by poly-lines) are mapped into the muscle interior.

The morphing uses a sweeping paradigm: a plane perpendicular to the principal axis of the muscle moves from one face of the template to the opposite face, stopping at each point F_j of fibre poly-lines that has not yet been processed. This plane cuts both the template box and the surface of the muscle producing a rectangle from the template and a polygon contour from the surface.

Let us assume that vertices of both polygons are oriented clockwise and that the contour polygon is formed of m segments, where $m \geq 1$. Our task is to subdivide the sides of the template rectangle in such a manner that the resulting polygon is also formed of m segments, and to establish a correspondence between the vertices of both polygons (rectangle template and contour polygon).

The algorithm starts with the detection of the vertex of the muscle contour that is closest to the first vertex P_0 of the muscle contour from previous slice or, if there is

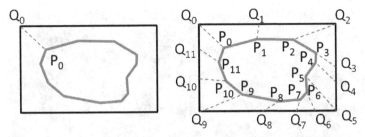

Fig. 5. Establishing correspondence between the rectangle and muscle contour

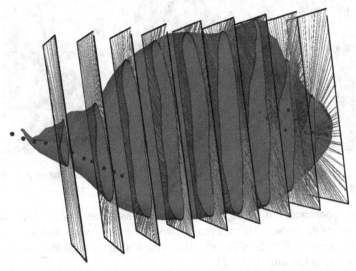

Fig. 6. Correspondence between contours of Gluteus Medius and its template polygons

no previous slice, to the first vertex Q_0 of the template rectangle. The vertices of the muscle contour are relabelled so that the detected vertex is the first one. This vertex denoted as P_0 is set to correspond to vertex Q_0. We note that such strategy was adopted to diminish unnatural twisting of fibres within the volume of muscle.

Now, the chain of vertices $P_0...P_m$ must be split into four parts, where each part corresponds to one side of the input rectangle. The split must be such that the overall error, given as the sum of errors for every part, is minimal. Let k be the ratio of the rectangle perimeter to the contour perimeter. The error for a given part of the chain is computed as the square of the difference between the size of the rectangle side associated with the part and the sum of the lengths of the segments formed by the vertices in the part, scaled by the constant k. After that, a side of the rectangle can be easily subdivided into as many segments as there are segments in the corresponding part of the chain. The ratios between the segment lengths are, of course, preserved. Establishing the correspondence between the polygons is straightforward: the vertex P_i corresponds to the vertex Q_i – see Fig. 5 and Fig. 6.

Hormann & Floater [3] proposed an approach that allows to express the coordinates of the fibre poly-line point F_j (where the cutting plane has currently stopped) with

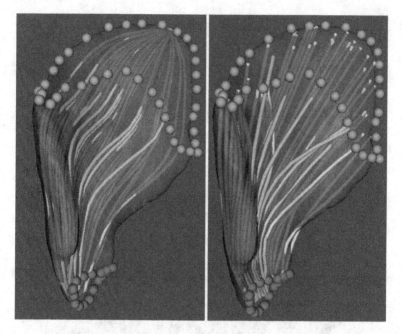

Fig. 7. Muscle fibres of Gluteus Medius before (left) and after (right) filtering of parts too close to attachment areas

respect to the coordinates of the segmented rectangle as the sum of $\lambda_i \cdot Q_i$, where the λ_i are real non-negative weights such that their sum equals 1. Once the weights λ_i are computed, the new coordinates of the poly-line point within the muscle contour $P_0 \ldots P_m$ are simply given as the sum of $\lambda_i \cdot P_i$.

As the cutting of the muscle surface is clearly the bottleneck of the decomposition, we process not only all fibre poly-line points lying on the cutting plane but also those in its close proximity. Hence, the minimal number of slices used is equal to the specified resolution of fibres. Naturally, the worst-case number of slices used is given as the requested number of fibres times their resolution.

3.4 Fibres Filtering

For muscles with large attachment areas, particularly, the process described so far may produce fibres with unacceptable unrealistic paths in the proximity of their attachment areas, as it is illustrated in Fig. 7 left. Hence, we need to change the path in the proximity of the attachment area to provide users with a better correspondence with the reality – see Fig. 7 right.

To do so, we construct two cutting planes perpendicular to the principal axis passing through the extremal (in the direction of the principal axis) landmarks of attachment areas. These planes are used to cut out the unwanted parts of fibres. In the next step, it is necessary to reconstruct the cut parts of fibres. Having a fibre $P_0 \ldots P_m$ whose part in proximity of the insertion area must be reconstructed, we add a new segment (P_m, P_{m+1}), where P_{m+1} is a new point such that it lies on the surface of muscle, in

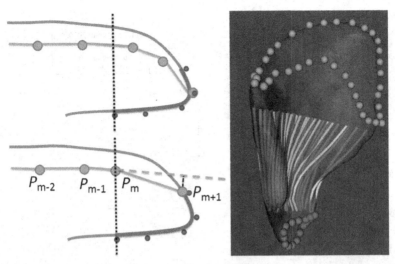

Fig. 8. Illustration of the trimming and reconstruction of a fibre – fibres are yellow, the attachment area red, the cutting plane is dotted black. Right: fibres of Gluteus Medius after trimming.

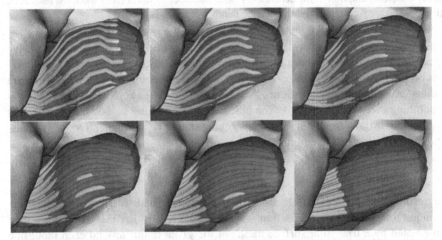

Fig. 9. Fibres of Quadratus Femoris without smoothing (top left) and with smoothing using 1, 5 (top right), 10 (bottom left), 20 and 100 (bottom right) smoothing steps

the insertion area, and is closest the ray defined by the segment (P_{m-1}, P_m). We note that the extraction of triangles belonging to the insertion area can be done by cutting out the larger part of the surface at the place of surface contour defined by the points obtained from projecting the landmarks onto the surface of muscle. The reconstruction of the part in the proximity of the origin area is similar. Fig. 8 demonstrates the process.

3.5   Fibres Smoothing

Clearly, the smoothness of the produced fibres depends upon both the resolution and the shape of the muscle. If the muscle bend or abruptly changes its dimensions, the

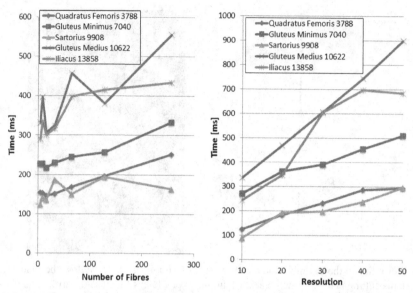

Fig. 10. Time consumption in the dependency on the number of fibres (left) when the resolution is fixed and on the resolution (right) when the number of fibres is fixed

fibres may be too noisy, in which case the poly-lines may have to be smoothed. We use an iterative process – the more smoothing steps it takes, the smoother the poly-lines become. At each step, the coordinates of the inner points P_i of the poly-line are modified according to the equation: $P_i' = (P_{i-1} + k \cdot P_i + P_{i+1})/(k + 2)$, where k is a smoothing constant – we use 4. The influence of smoothing is shown in Fig. 9. It is apparent that using a small number of smoothing steps (we recommend 5 steps) results in quite smooth but realistic fibres.

3.6 Application

The resulting smoothed muscle fibres can be then visualise using any rendering technique for poly-lines visualisation – we use a VTK [9] filter that generates a tube (represented by a triangular surface mesh) of the given radius around each input line segment. We also believe that these fibres can be passed to any solver predicting lever arms characteristics from the paths of the action lines, which, in most cases, should bring an increased accuracy to these predictions because the accuracy generally increases with the number of input poly-lines passed to the solver and whilst a muscle is typically represented by a couple of action lines only (it is because action lines cannot be constructed automatically), one could easily generate an arbitrary number of fibres using the proposed technique.

4   Experiments and Results

Our approach was implemented in C++ (MS Visual Studio 2010) under the Multimod Application Framework – MAF [10], which is a visualisation system based mainly on

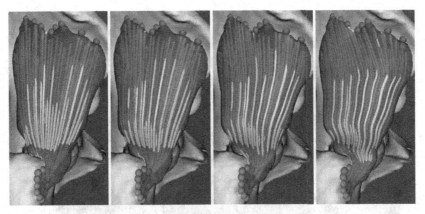

Fig. 11. Fibres of Iliacus with the specified resolution of 10, 20, 30 and 50 segments

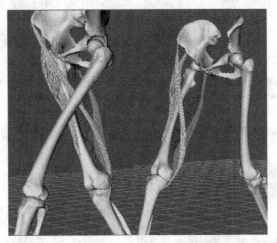

Fig. 12. Fibres of four selected muscles (sartorius – green, rectus femoris – yellow, biceps femoris – red and semimembranosus – fuchsia) during the movement at two different frames

VTK [9]. This framework is designed to support the rapid development of biomedical software. It is particularly useful in multimodal visualisation applications, which support the fusion of data from multiple sources and in which different views of the same data are synchronised, so that when the position of an object changes in one view, it is updated in all the other views. Our implementation was integrated into the Muscle-Wrapping software[1], which is a part of the larger LHPBuilder software being developed within the VPHOP project [11]. We tested our implementation on various real data sets of muscles of thighs and pelvis with typical sizes about 15K vertices on Intel Core i7 2.67 GHz, 12 GB DDR3 1.3GHz RAM with Windows 7 Pro x64.

Fig. 10 show that the time required for the overall process grows proportionally with the number of triangles in the surface mesh of the muscle, the requested number of

---

[1] http://graphics.zcu.cz/Projects/Muskuloskeletal-Modeling

Fig. 13. Our visualisation of gluteus minimus muscle in comparison with the visualisation obtained from http://www.biodigitalhuman.com/ online anatomical atlas (bottom right corner)

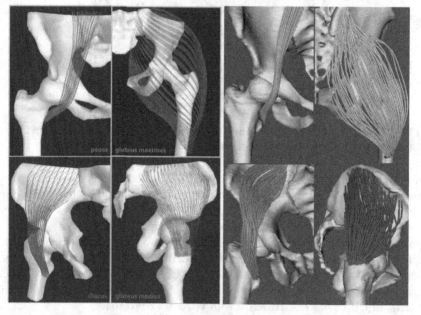

Fig. 14. Muscle fibres of psoas, gluteus maximus, illiacus and glutes medius produced by the method by Blemker et al. (left) and by our method (right). Left picture was taken from [1].

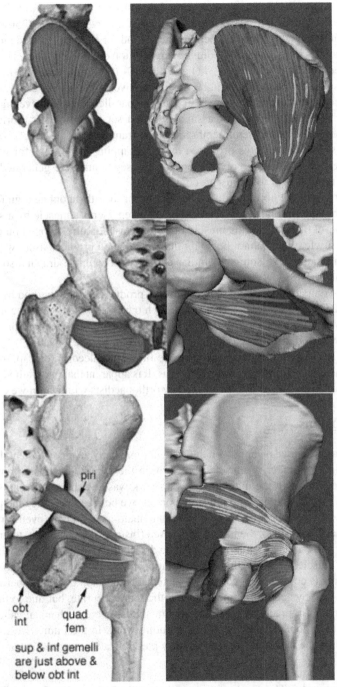

Fig. 15. Comparison of produced fibres of Gluteus Medius (top), Obturator Ext. (middle), and Piriformis, Quadratus Femoris and Obturator Int. (bottom) with those in Richardson's anatomical atlas [8]

fibres to be produced and their resolution, and that this growth has almost linear trend. It is important to point out that even for very large number of fibres (256) and large resolution (50 segments), times are bellow one second for a typical muscle model of 10 thousand triangles (e.g., Gluteus Medius). As resolution of 20–30 segments is sufficient for any tested muscle (see also Fig. 11) and also 50–100 fibres usually bring visually plausible results, the method is suitable for interactive visualisation; especially, if we take into account that our implementation could be parallelized to run even faster.

Fig. 12 shows the wrapping of a small selected set of muscles (sartorius, rectus femoris, biceps femoris and semimembranosus) at frames t = 0.00, 0.25, 0.50 and 0.75 of the walk sequence of 1.56 s produced by our wrapping method [5] for which fifty parallel fibres represented by poly-lines of 14 line segments were generated in about 300 ms per frame (for all four muscles considered).

A comparison of the fibres produced by our approach with an online digital anatomical atlas is brought in Fig. 13. As this online atlas represents a muscle by a surface of a quite low level of detail and its muscle fibres only as a texture mapped onto the surface of the muscle, there cannot be doubt that our method provides users with a more realistic visualisation. We note that similar conclusions could be drawn also for other anatomical atlases.

When we compare our results with the results produced by the method by Blemker et al. [1] – see Figure 14, it is clear that although our method may produce unrealistic path for a couple of fibres, the majority of produced fibres resemble those produced by its much slower, and, therefore, impractical, counterpart.

Finally, Fig. 15 brings a comparison of the fibres produced by our approach with those illustrated in a traditional anatomical atlas. It is apparent that our method produces quite realistic fibres. This is also confirmed by orthopaedists with whom we cooperate.

5   Conclusions

This paper has presented an approach that can automatically, in a convenient time, generate an arbitrary number of muscle fibres within the volume of muscle represented by its surface. Although the main goal of our work was to enhance educational tools used by both medical experts and physiotherapists, we believe that, since the produced fibres quite well correlate with those depicted in anatomical atlases (even for muscles with large attachment sites), the fibres can be used (instead of action lines) to predict the muscle lever arm on the articular joints and the distribution of fibre length (which is an input for the muscle force-length-velocity relationship to define the boundaries within which the force is constrained) with an expected accuracy somewhere in between predictions provided by action-line methods and the more accurate, but due to their large time-consumption impractical, finite-element methods. A biomechanical validation is, however, still required. This is a part of our future work. In the future, we would like also to speed up the decomposition process by parallelization to make it run in almost real time.

Acknowledgements. This work was supported by the Information Society Technologies Programme of the European Commission under the project VPHOP (FP7-ICT-223865). The authors would like to thank the various people who contributed to the realisation of the MAF and LHPBuilder software and to various people who provided condition under which the work could be done.

References

1. Blemker, S.S., Delp, S.L.: Three-dimensional representation of complex muscle architectures and geometries. Annals of Biomedical Engineering 33(5), 661–673 (2005),
   http://www.springerlink.com/index/10.1007/s10439-005-1433-7
2. Gray, H.: Anatomy of the Human Body. Lea & Febiger (1918),
   http://www.bartleby.com/107/
3. Hormann, K., Floater, M.S.: Mean value coordinates for arbitrary planar polygons. ACM Transactions on Graphics 25(4), 1424–1441 (2006),
   http://portal.acm.org/citation.cfm?doid=1183287.1183295
4. Joe, S., Kuo, F.Y.: Constructing sobol sequences with better two-dimensional projections. Society 30(5), 2635–2654 (2008),
   http://link.aip.org/link/doi/10.1137/070709359/html
5. Kohout, J., Clapworthy, G.J., Martelli, S., Wei, H., Viceconti, M., Agrawal, A.: Fast muscle wrapping. Computers & Graphics (2011) (submitted for publication)
6. Ng-Thow-Hing, V.: Anatomically-based models for physical and geometric reconstruction of humans and other animals. Ph.D. thesis, University of Toronto, Canada (2001)
7. Pohlschmidt, M., Meadowcroft, R.: Muscle disease: the impact, Muscular Dystrophy Campaign (January 2010), http://www.muscular-dystrophy.org
8. Richardson, M.: Muscle Atlas of the Extremities. Amazon Whispernet (2011)
9. Schroeder, W., Martin, K., Lorensen, B.: The Visualization Toolkit, 3rd edn. Kitware Inc. (2004), http://www.worldcat.org/isbn/1930934122
10. Viceconti, M., Astolfi, L., Leardini, A., Imboden, S., Petrone, M., Quadrani, P., Taddei, F., Testi, D., Zannoni, C.: The multimod application framework. In: International Conference on Information Visualisation, pp. 15–20 (2004),
    http://doi.ieeecomputersociety.org/10.1109/IV.2004.1320119
11. VPHOP: The osteoporotic virtual physiological human (2010), http://vphop.eu

Patchwork Terrains: Multi-resolution Representation from Arbitrary Overlapping Grids with Dynamic Update

Luigi Rocca[1], Daniele Panozzo[2], and Enrico Puppo[1]

[1] DIBRIS, University of Genoa, Genoa 16146, Italy
[2] IGL, ETH Zurich, Zurich, Switzerland
{rocca,puppo}@disi.unige.it, panozzo@inf.ethz.ch

Abstract. We present a radically new method for the multi-resolution representation of large terrain databases. Terrain data come as a collection of regularly sampled, freely overlapping grids, with arbitrary spacing and orientation. A multi-resolution model is built and updated dynamically off-line from such grids, which can be queried on-line to obtain a suitable collection of patches to cover a given domain with a given, possibly view-dependent, level of detail. Patches are combined to obtain a C^k surface, with k depending on the type of base patches. The whole framework is designed to take advantage of the parallel computing power of modern GPUs.

1 Introduction

Management of huge terrain datasets is a challenging task, especially for virtual globes, like Google Earth and Microsoft Virtual Earth, and GIS modules performing analyses in hydrography, land use, road planning, etc. In fact, such applications may need to cope with terabytes of data.

Digital Elevation Maps (DEMs) consist of collections of grids, which may have different resolutions and different orientations. In order to support interactive data manipulation, it is necessary to rapidly fetch a suitable and properly organized subset of data, which is relevant for the problem at hand. Continuous Level Of Detail (CLOD) models support dynamic extraction of representations for a given domain at a given accuracy. However, to the best of our knowledge, all CLOD models in the literature are based on static data structures that cannot be updated dynamically [12].

In this paper, we present an approach to CLOD terrain modeling that is radically different from previous literature. Its salient features can be summarized as follows (see Figure 1):

1. Our method provides on-line a compact C^k representation of terrain at the desired accuracy over a given domain, with a degree of smoothness k selected depending on application requirements. This representation is obtained by blending a collection of freely overlapping rectangular patches, of different sizes and orientations, which locally approximate different zones of terrain at different detail.

G. Csurka et al. (Eds.): VISIGRAPP 2012, CCIS 359, pp. 48–66, 2013.

Fig. 1. A view-dependent query executed on the Puget Sound Dataset with an on-screen error of one pixel. The wedge is the portion of domain intersected by the view frustum for an observer placed above its apex. The different colors represent patches of different sizes.

2. Starting from the input DEMs, we produce a large collection of small patches of different sizes and accuracies, and we store them in a spatial data structure indexing a three-dimensional space. Such embedding space has two dimensions for the spatial domain, and a third dimension for the approximation error. Every patch is represented as an upright box: its basis corresponds to the domain covered by the patch; its height corresponds to the range of accuracies for which the patch is relevant. We optimize the range of accuracies spanned by each patch, so that the number of patches used to represent a given LOD is minimized. Independent insertion of patches in the spatial index can be performed easily and efficiently, and the result is order independent, thus dynamic maintenance of the database is supported.
3. CLOD spatial queries are defined by specifying a surface in the embedding space, which encodes space culling and detail requirements altogether. Such queries are executed on-line by finding the set of boxes that intersect this user-defined surface.
4. The extracted representation can be resampled on-the-fly to produce an adaptive (possibly view-dependent) tessellation with arbitrary connectivity.

This paper describes the general framework, alongside with two proof-of-concept implementations. The first implementation provides a C^0 representation that can be efficiently sampled in real-time in the GPU. The second implementation provides a smooth C^2 representation which and can be used for computationally intensive GIS tasks. We present results obtained on a moderately large dataset containing about 256M points.

2   Related Work

Overall, known approaches to terrain modeling and rendering can be subdivided into three categories, reviewed in the following. The first category is better suited for modeling purposes, while the other two categories are specifically designed for rendering. Our proposal belongs to none of them, and it can be tailored to both rendering, and other GIS tasks.

CLOD Refinement. These methods produce triangle meshes, which approximate terrain according to LOD parameters that can vary over the domain. They are mostly used for modeling and processing purposes, since they provide an explicit representation, with the desired trade-off between accuracy and complexity. Specific CLOD methods, tailored for rendering, build clusters of triangles in a preprocessing steps, possibly at different resolutions [2,4,6]. Clusters are selected on-the-fly at rendering time and passed to the GPU in batches: the rendering primitive is not anymore a single triangle, but rather a triangle strip encoding a large zone of terrain. Recent surveys on CLOD refinement methods can be found in [12,20].

Geometry Clipmaps. In the approach presented in [9], a set of nested regular grids centered about the viewer are stored in the GPU memory, and used for rendering. As the viewpoint moves, the Geometry Clipmaps are updated in video memory. Tessellation is performed directly in the GPU. This method requires that input comes as a single uniform grid at high resolution, and it takes advantage of the intrinsic coherence of height maps to compress the input, thus reducing the amount of data that are passed to the GPU. Very high frame rates can be obtained, even for huge datasets.

GPU Ray-Casting. The use of ray-casting for rendering height maps is well studied in the literature, and different GPU techniques that achieve real-time frame rates have been developed in recent years. Methods for real-time rendering of meshes and height maps represented as Geometry Images have been proposed in [3,11,15]. However, all these methods were not designed to work with large terrain datasets. In [5], a tiling mechanism is used to support real-time rendering on arbitrarily large terrains. Ray-casting methods can be used only for the purpose of rendering, since they do not produce an explicit multi-resolution representation. In [16] a method is proposed, which exploits fast GPU wavelet mechanisms to support both ray-casting rendering and interactive editing of huge terrain datasets. Also this method requires input data to come as a single regular grid at high resolution. In [1], a hybrid approach that combines ray casting and mesh-based rendering has been proposed.

3   Patchwork Terrains

In this Section, we describe our technique: in Subsection 3.1, we define the type of patches we use; then, in Subsection 3.2, we describe how patches are blended to form a C^k representation of terrain; finally, in Subsection 3.3, we describe the multi-resolution model, the order-independent algorithm for the dynamic insertion of patches and the spatial queries.

3.1   From Grids to Patches

We assume a two-dimensional global reference system Π on which we define the domain D of the terrain, where all input grids are placed. A grid is a collection of regularly sampled height values of terrain. In addition to the matrix of samples, every grid is defined by an anchor point, an angle that defines its orientation, and grid steps in both directions (see Figure 2). In the following, we will use the term *vertex* to denote a sample point on the grid, and the term *cell* to denote a rectangle in D spanned by a 2×2

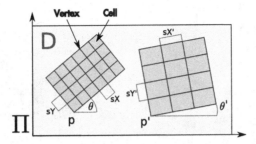

Fig. 2. The terrain is covered by a set of regularly sampled grids. Every grid has its own anchor point p, orientation angle θ and different sample steps for the two axes sX and sY.

grid of adjacent vertices. The *accuracy* of a grid also comes as a datum, and it is the maximum error made by using the grid to evaluate the height of any arbitrary point on terrain.

We aim at defining parametric functions that represent small subsets of vertices of the grid, called *patches*. A single patch is defined by an anchor point, its height, its width, and the coefficients that describe the parametric function. For the sake of simplicity, we will consider the height and width of every patch to be equal, hence the domain of every patch will be a square. Extension to rectangular patches is trivial.

We consider two types of patches: *perfect* patches interpolate the samples of the original terrain; while *approximating* patches represent the terrain ad a lower level of detail and accuracy. We assign an error to each patch, namely the accuracy ε of the input grid for a perfect patch; and $\varepsilon + \delta$ for an approximating patch, where δ denotes the maximum vertical distance between the input grid and the approximating patch. We will denote as *kernel* a rectangular region inside every patch, while the rest of the patch will be denoted as its *extension zone*. The extension zone will be used for the purpose of merging different patches, and the ratio between the sizes of the kernel and of the extension zone provides a trade-off between efficiency and smoothness of transition between different patches, which will be clarified later on.

The type of function defining a patch will vary depending on the application. In Section 4.1 we provide specific examples. Our technique, however, can be used with any kind of parametric function: depending on the application, it may be convenient to use either a larger collection of simpler patches, or a smaller collection of more complex patches. The rest of this section is generic in this respect.

Note that, unlike splines, our patches may freely overlap, without any fixed regular structure.

3.2 Merging Patches

Given a collection of freely overlapping patches, we blend them to produce a smooth function that represents the whole terrain spanned by this collection. In order to obtain a C^k surface that is efficient to evaluate, we use a tensor product construction, starting from the one dimensional, compactly supported radial basis function defined in [21]. Our weight function is defined as:

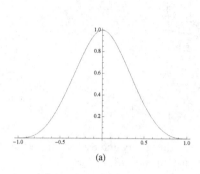
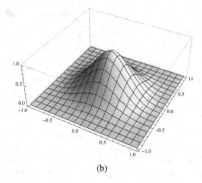

(a)   (b)

Fig. 3. C^2 weight functions: (a) 1D function w, plotted between -1 and 1. (b) 2D function W, plotted with x,y between -1 and 1, with the parameter d set to 1.

$$W(x,y,d) = \frac{w(x/d)w(y/d))}{\int_{-1}^{1}\int_{-1}^{1} w(x/d)w(y/d)\, dxdy}$$

for $x, y \in [-d, d]$ and 0 elsewhere. The 1-dimensional weight $w(t)$ is a C^k function with compact support, as defined in [21]: see Figure 3 for the C^2 case and Section 4.1 for further details. It is easy to see that the weight function W has the following properties:

1. It has compact support in $[-1, 1] \times [-1, 1]$;
2. Its derivatives up to order k vanish on the boundary of its support;
3. It is C^k in $[-1, 1] \times [-1, 1]$;
4. It has unit volume.

The first three conditions guarantee that the weight function has limited support, while being C^k everywhere. This is extremely important for efficiency reasons, as we will see in the following. Property 4 is useful, since it naturally allows smaller (and more accurate) patches to give a stronger contribution to the blended surface.

For every patch P, we define its weight function $W^P(x, y)$ as a translated and scaled version of W, such that its support corresponds with the domain of P:

$$W^P(x, y) = W(|x - P_x|, |y - P_y|, P_s)$$

with P_x and P_y the coordinates of the center of P and P_s the size of P.

A collection of C^k patches $P^1, P^2, ..., P^n$ placed on a domain D, such that every point of D is contained in the kernel of at least one patch, defines a C^k surface that can be computed using the following formula:

$$f(x, y) = \frac{\sum_{i=0}^{n} P_f^i(x, y)W^{P^i}(x, y)}{\sum_{i=0}^{n} W^{P^i}(x, y)} \tag{1}$$

with P_f^i the function associated with patch P^i.

Note that the surface is C^k inside D since it is defined at every point as the product of C^k functions and the denominator can never vanish since every point in D belongs to the interior of the domain of at least one patch. The summation actually runs only over patches whose support contains point (x, y), since the weight function will be zero for all other patches.

At this point, terrain can be described with an unstructured collection of patches. To use this method on large datasets, we still miss a technique to efficiently compute this representation at a user-defined LOD.

3.3 The Multi-resolution Model

We build a multi-resolution model containing many patches at different LODs, each patch being defined by a small number of parameters, and we provide a simple and efficient algorithm to extract a minimal set of patches covering a given region of interest at a given LOD, possibly variable over the domain.

We define a 3D embedding space, called the *LOD space*, in which two axes coincide with those ones of the global reference system Π, while the third axis is related to approximation error. For simplicity, we will set a maximum allowed error, so that LOD space is bounded in the error dimension. In this space, every patch will be represented as an upright box (i.e., a parallelepiped), having its basis corresponding to the spatial domain of the patch, and its height corresponding to the range of approximation errors, for which the patch is relevant. The bottom of the box will be placed at the approximation error of the patch, while its top will be set to a larger error, depending on its interaction with overlapping boxes, as explained in the following.

In this section, patches will be always treated as boxes, disregarding their associated functions. We will consider open boxes, so that two boxes sharing a face are not intersecting. For a box B, we will denote as $B.min$ and $B.max$ its corners with minimal and maximal coordinates, respectively. Furthermore for a point p in LOD space, we will denote its three coordinates as $p.x$, $p.y$ and $p.z$.

Given a collection of patches embedded in LOD space, a view of terrain at a constant error e can be extracted by gathering all boxes that intersect the horizontal plane $z = e$. More complex queries, which may concern a region of interest as well as variable LOD, can be obtained by cutting the LOD space with trimmed surfaces instead of planes.

To informally describe our approach, let us consider the examples depicted in Figure 4. Figure 4(a) shows two non-overlapping patches embedded in LOD space: P_1 is a perfect patch with zero error, and its box extends from zero to maximum error in the LOD space. This means that P_1 will be used to approximate its corresponding part of terrain at all LODs. On the contrary, patch P_2 is an approximating patch: it has its bottom set at its approximation error, while its top is again set at maximum error. Patch P_2 will be used to represent its part of terrain at any error larger or equal than its bottom, while it will not be used at finer LODs.

In Figure 4(b), a larger patch P_3 is added to our collection, which has a larger error than P_1 and P_2 and also it completely covers P_1. A cut at an error larger than the error of P_3 would extract all three patches, but P_1 is in fact redundant, since its portion of terrain is already represented with sufficient accuracy from P_3, which also covers a larger domain. In order to obtain a minimal set of patches, in Figure 4(c) patch P_1 is shortened in LOD space, so that its top touches the bottom of P_3. Note that we cannot

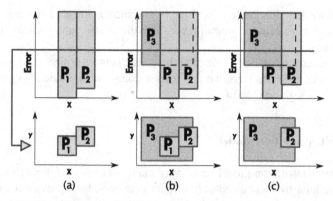

Fig. 4. Boxes of patches in LOD space, with a cut shown by the blue line: (a) Two independent patches P_1 and P_2; (b) A third patch P_3 is added: patch P_1 becomes redundant for the given cut; (c) P_1 is shortened to obtain a minimal set of patches for every cut of the spatial index

shorten P_2 in a similar way, because a portion of its spatial domain is not covered by any other patch.

This simple example leads to a more complete invariant that patches in LOD space must satisfy to guarantee that minimal sets are extracted by cuts. We first formally describe this invariant, then we provide an algorithm that allows us to fill the LOD space incrementally, while satisfying it. This algorithm builds the multi-resolution model and the result is independent of the order of insertion of patches. Implementation will be described later in Section 4.2.

We define a global order $<$ on patches as follows: $P < P'$ if the area of P is smaller than the area of P'; if the two areas are equal, then $P < P'$ if $P.min.z > P'.min.z$, i.e., P is less accurate than P'.

Since both the spatial extension and the approximation error of a patch P are fixed, the spatial invariant is only concerned with the top of P, i.e., with its maximal extension in the error dimension.

Patch Invariant. A patch P must not intersect any set of patches, such that the union of their kernels completely covers the kernel of P, and each patch is greater than P in the global order $<$. Also, the patch P cannot be extended further from above without violating the previous condition.

In other words, this invariant states that a patch is always necessary to represent terrain at any LOD, in its whole extension in the error domain, because that portion of terrain cannot be covered by larger patches. If all the patches in the model satisfy this property, we are sure that we will obtain a minimal set of patches whenever we cut the model with horizontal planes of the form $z = c$. The second part of the invariant enforces patches to span all levels of error where their contribution is useful for terrain representation, thus maximizing the expressive power of the model. More general cuts will also extract correct representations in terms of LOD, but minimality is not guaranteed.

Let us consider inserting a new patch P into a collection of patches that satisfy the invariant. If the new patch does not satisfy the invariant, we shorten it at its top. This is done through Algorithm 1 described below. Note that a patch may be completely wiped out by the shortening process: this just means that it was redundant. After the insertion of P, only patches that intersect P may have their invariance property invalidated, so we fetch each of them and we either shorten or remove it, again by Algorithm 1. All this process is done through Algorithm 2. Shortening patches that were already in the model does not invalidate invariance of other patches, so no recursion is necessary.

Algorithm 1. cutter(Patch P, SetOfPatches ps)

 1: sort *ps* in ascending order wrt min.z
 2: current = {}
 3: last = {}
 4: **for** $P' \in ps$ **do**
 5:     **if** P ¡ P' **then**
 6:         current = current $\cup \{P'\}$
 7:         **if** the patches in current cover P **then**
 8:             last = P'
 9:             **break**
10:         **end if**
11:     **end if**
12: **end for**
13: **if** not (last == {}) **then**
14:     **if** last.min.z ¡ P.min.z **then**
15:         Remove P
16:     **else**
17:         P.max.z = P'.min.z
18:     **end if**
19: **end if**

Algorithm 2. add-patch(Patch P).

 1: ps = patches that intersect P
 2: cutter(P, ps)
 3: **for** $P' \in ps$ **do**
 4:     **if** P' still intersects P **then**
 5:         ps' = patches that intersect P'
 6:         cutter(P', ps')
 7:     **end if**
 8: **end for**

It is easy to see that all patches in a model built by inserting one patch at a time through Algorithm 2 satisfy the invariant. We also show that the result is independent on the order patches were added.

Order Independence. The structure of a model built by repeated application of Algorithm 2 is independent of the insertion order of patches.

Proof. The height of the box associated to a patch depends only on the spatial position and minimal error of the other patches inserted in the spatial index. The invariant guarantees that all boxes have their maximum allowed size in the error dimension, with respect to all other patches in the model. Therefore, the final result only depends on what patches belong to the model. □

To summarize, the algorithm shown allows us to dynamically build and update a spatial data structure that automatically detects and discards redundant data. Queries are executed on-line by cutting such structure with planes or surfaces. Extracted patches are merged, as explained in Section 3.2, to produce the final terrain representation.

This completes the theoretical foundations of our technique. We discuss the implementation details in Sections 4 and 5, while we provide benchmarks and results in Section 6.

4   Implementation of the Spatial Index

This section describes a possible implementation of the general framework presented in Section 3, which has been kept as simple as possible for the sake of presentation. In Section 4.1 we describe the construction of patches, while in Section 4.2 we describe the implementation of the spatial index.

4.1   Generation of Patches

We describe two types of patches: bilinear patches provides a C^0 representation of the terrain that can be used for rendering purposes; while bicubic patches provide a C^2 representation, trading speed for increased terrain quality.

We use patches at different scales, which are generated from sub-grids of the various levels of a mipmap of terrain data. Each patch is a rectangle that covers a set of samples of the terrains. The patch must represent the terrain it covers, and its size depends on the density of grid samples. Patches may also cover mipmaps, thus allowing to represent larger zones of the terrain with less samples.

For every level of the mipmap, we build a grid of patches such that the union of their kernels form a grid on the domain, and the intersections of their kernels are empty. The size of the kernel with respect to the size of the patch is a parameter controlled by the user, that we denote σ. Any value $0 < \sigma < 1$ produces a C^k terrain representation; different values can be used to trade-off between quality and performance: small values of σ improve the quality of blending between patches; conversely, large values reduce the overlapping between different patches, thus improving efficiency, but transition between different patches may become more abrupt, thus producing artifacts. In our experiments, we obtained satisfactory results by using $\sigma = 0.9$.

Bilinear Patches are formed by a grid of samples and they are simply produced by bilinear interpolation of values inside every 2x2 sub-grid of samples. These patches are C^0 in their domain, and the blending function we use is $w(t) = (1 - |t|)$.

Bicubic Patches are formed by a grid of samples, as in the case of bilinear patches. To define a piecewise bicubic interpolating function we compute an interpolant bicubic spline with the algorithm described in [13]. These patches are C^2 in their domain, and the blending function we use is $w(t) = (1 - |t|)^3(3|t| + 1)$.

4.2   Spatial Index

The spatial index must support the efficient insertion and deletion of boxes, as well as spatial queries, as explained in Section 4.3. An octree would be an obvious choice, but it turns out to be inefficient, because large patches are duplicated in many leaves. We propose here a different data structure that is more efficient for our particular application.

Given a patch P, we define its *z-span* to be the interval $[P.min.z, P.max.z]$ of errors for which P is relevant, and the *z-ceiling* of P to be the highest value of its z-span. We build a quadtree over the first two dimensions. For the sake of brevity, we will refer with the same symbol q to a node in the quadtree and to its related quadrant in the spatial domain. We store at every node q (either internal or leaf) a set of patches that intersect the domain of q. Not all intersecting patches are stored, but just the first t patches that have the highest z-ceilings, and that are not stored in any ancestor node of q. We use a threshold t of 64 in our experiments. There is no guarantee that a patch is stored in exactly one node, but in our experiments a patch is always stored in less than two nodes on average. We define the *z-span* of node q to be the smallest interval that contains th union of all patches stored at q.

The quadtree fulfills the following invariant: *for a quadrant q of the quadtree, let $[z_q, Z_q]$ be its span, then: all patches intersecting q and having a z-ceiling larger than Z_q are stored in the ancestors of q; all patches intersecting q and having a z-ceiling between z_q and Z_q are stored in q; and all patches intersecting q and having a z-ceiling smaller than z_q are stored in the children of q.* This kind of structure is similar to Multiple Storage Quadtrees [14] and it can be exploited to support spatial queries, as explained in the following subsection.

Inserting a new box in the tree is simple. Starting at the root, a box B is inserted in the node(s) that intersects its spatial domain, if and only if either the number of patches in such node does not exceed its capacity, or the z-ceiling of the new box is larger than the z-ceiling of the last box in the list at that node; in the latter case, the last box of the list (which has the minimum z-ceiling in the list) is moved downwards in the tree. Otherwise, the new patch is moved downwards in the tree.

4.3   Spatial Queries

As explained in Section 3.3, queries are specified by a surface in LOD space. The projection of such a surface in the spatial domain is the region of interest (ROI) of the query, which will drive traversal of the quadtree. The z-values of the surface define the error tolerance at each point in the ROI, and will provide thresholds to prune the search.

At query time, the quadtree is traversed top-down, and quadrants that intersect the ROI are visited. For each such quadrant q, its z-span $[z_q, Z_q]$, is compared with the z-interval $[z_t, Z_t]$ spanned by the portion of query surface intersecting q. If $Z_q < z_t$, then the search is pruned at q; if $z_q > Z_t$ then the patches stored at q are discarded and the search is propagated to the children of q; otherwise the list of patches is scanned and a patch P is selected if and only if its z-span intersects the z-interval spanned by the query surface on the domain of P. Traversal of the list can be interrupted as soon as a patch having a span that does not intersect interval $[z_t, Z_t]$ is found (as that patch, and all subsequent patches, are more accurate than needed).

View-Dependent Queries. For applications such as view-dependent rendering, the accuracy of the extracted representation should smoothly decrease with distance from the viewpoint, so that larger patches can be used on far portions of terrain, thus reducing the computational load, without introducing visual artifacts. We perform a view-dependent query by cutting the LOD space with a skewed plane, which aims at extracting a model with a constant screen error, for a given viewpoint.

In [7] a method was proposed that computes the maximum error in world coordinates that we can tolerate, in order to obtain an error in screen coordinates smaller than one pixel. Such a method defines a surface in LOD space that we could use to make view-dependent queries in our spatial index. However, the resulting surface is complex and the related intersection tests would be expensive. We use an approximation of such a method that allows us to cut the spatial index with a plane, which provides a conservative estimate of the correct cutting surface: we obtain a surface that is correct in terms of screen error, while it could be sub-optimal in terms of conciseness. To compute the cutting plane, we ignore the elevation of the viewer with respect to the position of the point, obtaining the following formula:

$$\delta_{screen} = \frac{d\lambda\delta}{\sqrt{(e_x - v_x)^2 + (e_y - v_y)^2}},$$

with e being the viewpoint, v the point of the terrain where we want to compute the error, d the distance from e to the projection plane, λ the number of pixels per world coordinate units in the screen xy coordinate system, δ the error on world coordinate and δ_{screen} the error in pixels.

This plane is reduced to a triangle by clipping the zones outside the view frustum. The spatial index is then cut with this triangle, and the intersection between boxes in the index and the triangle are efficiently computed with the algorithm of [19], after an appropriate change of reference system has been performed on the box.

5   Terrain Tessellation

In this section, we discuss in detail how a terrain represented as a collection of patches, as extracted from the spatial index, can be resampled to obtain a tessellated model. We describe general principles concerning the resampling operation, and we provide a CPU and a GPU implementation.

So far, we have shown how to extract a parametric C^k representation of terrain at the desired LOD from the spatial index. Let G be a grid on the domain of terrain and let S be the set of extracted patches. To render the terrain, we rasterize it by imposing G on the domain and by evaluating the parametric surface only at its vertices, using equation (1). The computation can be performed efficiently by observing that the weight function associated with a patch P is zero for all the vertices of G that lies outside the domain of P. Thus, for every patch P^i in S, we need to evaluate P_f^i and W^{P^i} just for the vertices of G that lie in the domain of P^i.

Note that sampling the terrain at a certain coordinate is an indipendent operation. We use grids only for convenience - irregular triangulations could be used just as easily. In the following paragraphs, we suggest two simple but effective ways to support uniform as well as view-dependent resampling.

Uniform Resampling. A uniform rendering is easily obtained by imposing a regular grid on the terrain domain. Note that this resampling operation is decoupled from the desired LOD, already obtained by querying the spatial index, and can be tailored to application needs.

View-Dependent Resampling. A view-dependent rendering is obtained by imposing a position-dependent grid on the terrain domain. We produce a grid in screen space that has approximately the same number of samples as the number of pixels on the screen. By projecting this grid on the terrain domain we obtain a trapezoidal grid with a high density of vertices in the neighborhood of the viewer, and progressively lower densities as we move farther. This technique is similar to the Persistent Grid Mapping proposed in [8].

5.1 CPU Resampling

To efficiently perform the resampling operation in CPU, we have built a two-dimensional spatial index on the domain on the terrain. This spatial index contains the position of all vertices of G and allows us to rapidly fetch all vertices contained in the domain of a patch, exploiting the fact that only a small subset of patches in S has a non-zero contribution to a particular vertex. Note that this spatial index has to be built just once, since the grid is uniform or depends only on the position of the viewer. If a viewer moves in subsequent frames, we do not move the grid, but we rather translate and rotate the patches returned by the query to place the grid in the desired position. By using this spatial index, we can efficiently extract the vertices that lie in every patch and incrementally compute Equation (1). Note that the implementation can be easily parallelized on multi-core CPUs with a multi-thread implementation, since every vertex can be sampled independently.

5.2 GPU Resampling

We have developed an experimental GPU implementation using the nVidia CUDA language. It works using vertices as parallelization points. Every GPU thread resamples a vertex and runs through all extracted patches, searching for the relevant ones. Despite still being a basic prototype, results are promising (as shown in section 6). Ideas for a complex GPU data structure specifically tailored to the patchwork model are discussed in section 7.

6 Results

In this Section we present the results obtained with our prototype implementation on a dataset over the Puget Sound area in Washington. Experiments were run on a PC with a 2.67Ghz Core i5 processor equipped with 8Gb of memory and a nVidia GTX275 graphic card. The dataset is made up of 16,385 × 16,385 vertices at 10 meter horizontal and 0.1 meter vertical resolution [17]. Our framework produces a single frame to be rendered in two main phases: a query to the spaial index, in order to obtain a set of patches representing the terrain at the desired LOD; and a tessellation phase, where points on a grid covering the desired domain on the terrain are sampled from the set of patches. If this second task is performed on the GPU or on another computer, patches need to be transferred on the system bus or on a network. As we will show, queries are extremely efficient even using a single core, easily scaling up to hundreds of queries per second. The critical phases become transmission and tessellation. Our current GPU prototype yields interactive frame rates and we expect that an optimized GPU implementation, which will be the focus of our future work, will be able to obtain interactive frame rates on larger terrains with HD quality.

We present results produced using bilinear patches unless otherwise stated. Section 6.6 discusses performance when bicubic patches are used.

6.1 Pre-processing

The pre-processing computations executed by our system can be divided in three phases: mipmap generation, error evaluation and construction of the spatial index. Table 1 reports our preprocessing times for the full dataset, and for two scaled versions. Note that pre-processing is performed online, i.e. it is possible to add new data to a precomputed dataset without the need to rebuild it from scratch. This feature is unique of our method since, at the best of our knowledge, it is not available in any other work in the literature [12].

In our experiments, each patch covers a grid of 32x32 samples, while its kernel is made of the central 28x28 pixels.

Table 1. Time and space required to preprocess and store the multi-resolution model. From left to right: the time required to compute the mipmap, to evaluate the error associated with each patch and to build the spatial index; the space required to store the mipmaps, the patches and the spatial index.

Dataset		Preprocessing Time				Space overhead			
samples	size	Mipmap	Error	Index	Total	Mipmaps	Patches	Index	Total
1k × 1k	2M	0.1s	0.6s	0.05s	0.75s	702k	18k	12k	732k
4k × 4k	32M	0.9s	10s	0.83s	11.73s	11.2M	301k	202k	11.7M
16k × 16k	512M	12.6s	169s	14.6s	196.2s	179M	4.8M	3.2M	187M

The majority of time is spent on the first two phases, which would be simple to execute in parallel on multiple cores, unlike the last phase, which involves complex data structures.

6.2 Space Overhead

On average, our multi-resolution model requires approximately 35% space more than the original dataset. A breakdown of the space occupied by the various components of our model is shown in Table 1. The majority of space is taken by the mipmap.

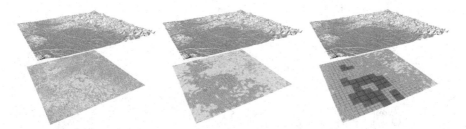

Fig. 5. Puget Sound Dataset (16k x 16k samples) rendered with error thresholds of 5, 20 and 50 meters. The colors on the bottom represent the size of the patch used to approximate the terrain. Blue and cyan corresponds to large patches, used to approximate flat zones, while red and orange indicates small patches required to represent fine details.

There is a trade-off between the space occupied by the multi-resolution model and the size of patches. Smaller patches increase adaptivity but take more space since they must be inserted and stored in the spatial index.

6.3   Spatial Index Queries

Uniform queries. Our system is able to execute 800 uniform queries per second with a 50m error. Queries with no error slow down the system to 55 queries per second. Note that the latter queries return the maximum number of patches at the highest level of detail possible.

Figure 5 shows the results of three different queries performed with an error threshold of 5, 20 and 50 meters. Smaller patches are used to correctly represent fine details, while large patches are used in flat zones, even with a very low error threshold. High frequency detail is obviously lost as error increases.

View-dependent Queries. A single view-dependent query representing a portion of terrain 15km long with an on-screen error of one pixel extracts approximately 250 patches and requires only 2.5ms. Thus, our system is able to query the spatial index at very high frame rates, meaning that the CPU time required by queries for every frame is negligible.

Figure 6 shows the number of view-dependent queries per second executed by our prototype and the number of extracted patches at different screen error thresholds. The use of progressive spatial queries could further increase performance.

6.4   Transmission of Patches

To the GPU. As shown in Figure 7, sending all the extracted patches to the GPU takes a neglibile amount of time. Transmission of hundreds of patches (more than enough for high quality rendering) to the GPU requires less than a millisecond.

On a Network. We have simulated the minimal traffic required to send patches on a network during a fly over the Puget Sound dataset at different speeds: only a few kb per frame are required to send the difference between two queries to the GPU (see

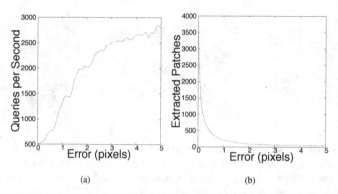

(a) (b)

Fig. 6. Number of queries per second (a) and number of extracted patches (b) while performing view-dependent queries at different screen error thresholds

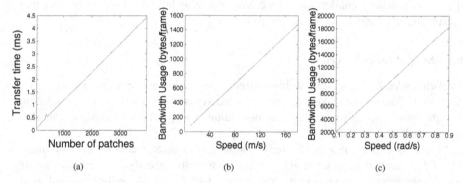

(a) (b) (c)

Fig. 7. (a) Time required to send a certain number of patches to the GPU on the system bus. (b) During a straight fly over terrain at different speeds, only a few bytes per frame must be sent through the network to update the set of patches to the viewpoint. (c) A rotation of the viewpoint requires slightly more bandwidth. Both (b) and (c) were performed with an allowed screen error of three pixels and every query extracted 70 patches on average, representing a portion of terrain 15km long.

(b) and (c) in Figure 7). Every patch that has to be sent to the GPU uses 4106 bytes, while the removal of a patch requires only to transfer its unique identifier (4 bytes). This makes our framework suitable for a client/server architecture since a reasonably low bandwidth is required to achieve high quility interactive rendering. Development of incremental queries would make it even more suitable.

6.5　GPU Tessellation

Our GPU prototype already obtains interactive frame rates with a laptop-screen sized resampling grid (see Fig. 8). As expected, its performances scale linearly with the number of sampling points. We expect a future optimized implementation, as sketched in section 7, to easily reach interactive frame rates for HD resolutions.

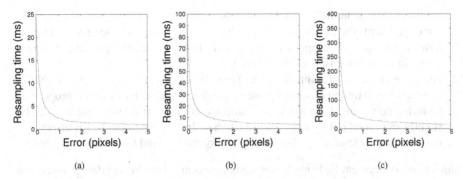

Fig. 8. Time required to resample the terrain on the GPU using a 256×256 grid (a), a 512×512 grid (b) and a 1024×1024 grid (c) while performing view-dependent queries at different screen error thresholds

6.6 Differences with Bicubic Patches

Changing type of patches influences differently the various steps of our framework. The preprocessing step is slowed down thirty times: this is due to the huge increase of the computational cost required for the evaluation of the bicubic patches. The construction of the spatial index is almost unaffected by the modification, since the only information that it needs is the maximal error associated with every patch. The space used is similar. The evaluation of the terrain is greatly slowed down. Currently, only a CPU implementation exists. While our current implementation can be used just for modeling purposes, a highly optimized GPU implementation would be required to reach interactive frame rates.

7 Concluding Remarks

7.1 Benefits

The main advantage of our method is the possibility to efficiently update the system with new heterogeneous grids, by automatically detecting and removing redundant data. Furthermore, our technique produces a multi-resolution C^k surface instead of a discrete model. The actual evaluation of the surface, which is the only computationally intensive task, can be demanded to the GPU, while keeping the communication between CPU and GPU limited. Texture and normal map can be easily integrated, since they can be associated to every patch and interpolated, with the same method used for the height values.

The space overhead is moderate, being approximately the same as the space used for a mipmap pyramid. The spatial index involves a negligible overhead, and it can be maintained in main memory even for huge terrain databases.

7.2 Limitations

Some limitations of our current approach come from the lack of certain theoretical bounds:

1. On the maximum number of patches that may overlap at a single point of terrain. In our experiments the number of overlapping patches never exceeded six, and it was four on average, but computation of Formula 1 at each sampling point may result computationally intensive even in this case.
2. On the accuracy of a sampled point. When evaluating the point, a patch that is as precise as required is surely present, given the spatial index query properties. Unfortunately, using Formula 1 the contribute of the most accurate patch could be slightly smoothed out by neighboring patches. In our experiments this effect was undetectable by human eye, but having a theoretical bound would be preferable.

Futhermore, our current GPU implementation is optimized neither for data transfer, nor for computational balance, as all data are transferred to the GPU at each frame, and all threads process all patches. We believe that a speedup of orders of magnitude could be gained with an optimized implementation, as outlined in the following.

7.3   Future Work

Our current work is proceeding in several directions to extend our current model and implementation. Our aim is to overcome the limitations outlined in the previous section.

New blending Function. We are exploring a blending function that will allow us to use only the most accurate patch for any point that falls within its kernel, while blending only at transitions between the extension zone of a more accurate patch and the kernel of a less accurate patch. This new method will allow us to improve accuracy and greatly speedup computation altogether, providing us with a theoretical bound on the error and performing blending only on very small (usually just two) and limited number of patches.

Optimized GPU Tessellation. Computational load of GPU processors can be greatly improved by a proper distribution of patches to multiprocessors. In the CUDA architecture, a fixed number (usually 16 or 32) of threads belong to the same "warp". A block of threads, formed by multiple warps, is executed cuncurrently and shares a fast memory between its threads that can be used as an explicit cache called "shared memory" (see [10]). We are exploring a novel GPU parallel data structure that could exploit the fact that both sample points and patches share the same 2D geometrical domain. We may allocate sample points to threads in such a way that threads within a given warp map to neighboring samples. Then, we assign to the shared memory in the block just the patches that contain such samples. This can be done in a pre-computation phase on the GPU, where each thread works on a patch; followed by an evaluation phase, where each thread evaluates a sample point. With this strategy, every thread works just on a subset of all patches, already cached inside the shared memory, thus greatly speeding up the tessellation phase.

Cache-aware and Pre-fetching Policies. Since our model can be useful in a variety of contexts - from real-time visualization on a local host, to client-server transmission on a geographic network - and it is especially relevant for huge databases, then the amount of data transferred between different levels of the memory hierarchy is of utmost importance in assessing its performance. Network bandwidth can be critical for a web application, as well as bandwidth on the system bus for CPU-GPU communication. In all such contexts, suitable policies can be developed to optimize performance in terms of trade-off between speed and quality. Fast compression/decompression mechanisms [18] can be adopted to compress patches or groups of patches (subgrids), thus reducing bandwidth usage. Suitable cache-aware policies can be also developed to decide, depending on both bandwidth and amount of memory available on the "client" side, the amount of data to be transferred and cached, and how to discard data from local memory when memory becomes scarce. Finally, for applications such as dynamic view-dependent rendering, suitable pre-fetching techniques can be developed to foresee and transfer the data needed to render the next frames ahead of time.

References

1. Ammann, L., Génevaux, O., Dischler, J.-M.: Hybrid rendering of dynamic heightfields using ray-casting and mesh rasterization. In: Proceedings of Graphics Interface, GI 2010, Toronto, Ont., Canada, Canada, pp. 161–168. Canadian Information Processing Society (2010)
2. Bösch, J., Goswami, P., Pajarola, R.: Raster: simple and efficient terrain rendering on the gpu. In: Proceedings EUROGRAPHICS 2009 (Area Papers), Munich, Germany, pp. 35–42 (2009)
3. Carr, N.A., Hoberock, J., Crane, K., Hart, J.C.: Fast gpu ray tracing of dynamic meshes using geometry images. In: Gutwin, C., Mann, S. (eds.) Graphics Interface, pp. 203–209. Canadian Human-Computer Communications Society (2006)
4. Cignoni, P., Ganovelli, F., Gobbetti, E., Marton, F., Ponchio, F., Scopigno, R.: Bdam - batched dynamic adaptive meshes for high performance terrain visualization. Comput. Graph. Forum 22(3), 505–514 (2003)
5. Dick, C., Krüger, J., Westermann, R.: GPU ray-casting for scalable terrain rendering. In: Proceedings of Eurographics 2009 - Areas Papers, pp. 43–50 (2009)
6. Lindstrom, P., Cohen, J.D.: On-the-fly decompression and rendering of multiresolution terrain. In: Proceedings of the 2010 ACM SIGGRAPH Symposium on Interactive 3D Graphics and Games, I3D 2010, pp. 65–73. ACM, New York (2010)
7. Lindstrom, P., Koller, D., Ribarsky, W., Hodges, L.F., Faust, N., Turner, G.A.: Real-time, continuous level of detail rendering of height fields. In: SIGGRAPH 1996: Proceedings of the 23rd Annual Conference on Computer Graphics and Interactive Techniques, pp. 109–118. ACM, New York (1996)
8. Livny, Y., Sokolovsky, N., Grinshpoun, T., El-Sana, J.: A gpu persistent grid mapping for terrain rendering. Vis. Comput. 24(2), 139–153 (2008)
9. Losasso, F., Hoppe, H.: Geometry clipmaps: terrain rendering using nested regular grids. In: SIGGRAPH 2004: ACM SIGGRAPH 2004 Papers, pp. 769–776. ACM, New York (2004)
10. NVIDIA Corporation. NVIDIA CUDA C programming guide (2012) (Version 4.2)
11. Oh, K., Ki, H., Lee, C.-H.: Pyramidal displacement mapping: a gpu based artifacts-free ray tracing through an image pyramid. In: Slater, M., Kitamura, Y., Tal, A., Amditis, A., Chrysanthou, Y. (eds.) VRST, pp. 75–82. ACM (2006)
12. Pajarola, R., Gobbetti, E.: Survey of semi-regular multiresolution models for interactive terrain rendering. Vis. Comput. 23(8), 583–605 (2007)
13. Press, W.H., Teukolsky, S.A., Vetterling, W.T., Flannery, B.P.: Numerical Recipes, 3rd edn. The Art of Scientific Computing. Cambridge University Press (September 2007)

14. Samet, H.: Foundations of Multidimensional and Metric Data Structures. The Morgan Kaufmann Series in Computer Graphics and Geometric Modeling. Morgan Kaufmann Publishers Inc., San Francisco (2005)
15. Tevs, A., Ihrke, I., Seidel, H.-P.: Maximum mipmaps for fast, accurate, and scalable dynamic height field rendering. In: Haines, E., McGuire, M. (eds.) SI3D, pp. 183–190. ACM (2008)
16. Treib, M., Reichl, F., Auer, S., Westermann, R.: Interactive editing of gigasample terrain fields. Computer Graphics Forum (Proc. Eurographics) 31(2), 383–392 (2012)
17. USGS and The University of Washington. Puget sound terrain,
    http://www.cc.gatech.edu/projects/large_models/ps.html
18. van der Laan, W.J., Jalba, A.C., Roerdink, J.B.T.M.: Accelerating wavelet lifting on graphics hardware using cuda. IEEE Transactions on Parallel and Distributed Systems 22, 132–146 (2011)
19. Voorhies, D.: Triangle-cube intersection. Graphics Gems III, 236–239 (1992)
20. Weiss, K., De Floriani, L.: Simplex and diamond hierarchies: Models and applications. In: Hauser, H., Reinhard, E. (eds.) Eurographics 2010 - State of the Art Reports, Norrköping, Sweden. Eurographics Association (2010)
21. Wendland, H.: Piecewise polynomial, positive definite and compactly supported radial functions of minimal degree. Advances in Computational Mathematics 4(1), 389–396 (1995)

Visualization of Long Scenes from Dense Image Sequences Using Perspective Composition

Siyuan Fang and Neill Campbell

Department of Computer Science, University of Bristol, U.K.
fangs@cs.bris.ac.uk, Neill.Campbell@bristol.ac.uk

Abstract. This paper presents a system for generating multi-perspective panoramas for long scenes from dense image sequences. Panoramas are created by combining different perspectives, including both original and novel perspectives. The latter are rendered using our perspective synthesis algorithm, which employs geometrical information to eliminate the sampling error distortion caused by depth parallax of non-planar scenes. Our approach for creating multi-perspective panoramas is different from existing methods in that a perspective composition framework is presented to combine various perspectives to form a panorama without undesired visual artifacts, through suppressing both colour inconsistencies and structural misalignments among input perspectives. We show that this perspective composition can facilitate the generation of panoramas from user specified multi-perspective configurations.

Keywords: Image generation, Image based rendering, Visualization.

1 Introduction

A photograph can only capture a portion of long scenes, such as a street, since the field of view of a common camera is usually quite limited. With a single panorama combined from several different images, users are able to view scenes of interest simultaneously. More importantly, a panorama is an effective way of summarizing content of input images with much less redundant data.

Traditional panoramas are generated from images captured at a fixed viewpoint with pure rotational movement [1,2,3]. In this case, input images can be registered to a reference coordinate based on particular alignment models, of which the most general one is the homography. However, it is usually impossible to place the viewpoint far enough away to encompass the entire street, imagining that we wish to capture a long but narrow street. Obviously, to acquire more scenes, we have to change the viewpoint. Generating panoramas from images captured at different viewpoints is much more challenging, as in this case, the image registration cannot be parameterized by an uniform homography if scenes are not planar.

For non-planar scenes, registering and stitching images with different viewpoints may cause serious visual effects, such as ghost artifacts. To alleviate this problem, these images need to be properly combined, e.g., divide the overlapping area of multiple images into different segments, each of which is only rendered with a single image. The seam is optimized to go through areas that are at a low risk of producing unnatural visual

G. Csurka et al. (Eds.): VISIGRAPP 2012, CCIS 359, pp. 67–81, 2013.

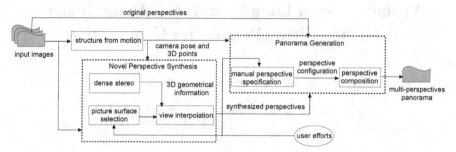

Fig. 1. The system framework

artifacts. However, with only original input images (or perspectives), such an optimized seam would not exist. In addition, being able to view a scene from any arbitrary possible perspective offers a great flexibility in allowing users to depict what they expect to convey in the resultant panorama. This gives rise to the requirement for synthesizing novel perspectives from input images.

Our novel perspective synthesis algorithm is based on the well-known strip mosaic [4,5], which offers an excellent solution to synthesize novel views from dense images. However, since each strip extracted from the input image is rendered from a regular pin-hole camera, the synthesized result usually exhibits a sampling error distortion, which is visually unacceptable. In our system, estimated 3D geometrical information is used to eliminate this kind of distortion.

The essence of generating multi-perspective panoramas is to properly combine different perspectives to make the result exhibit a natural appearance. In this paper, a perspective composition framework is presented to overcome visual effects brought by both colour (pixel value) discrepancies and structural misalignments. The framework consists of two steps: firstly, parts of various perspectives are selected such that visual discontinuities among those parts can be minimized, and then, remaining artifacts are further suppressed through a fusion process.

An overview of our system is presented in Fig 1. In our system, street scenes are captured by a video camera (with a fixed intrinsic camera parameter K) moving along the scene to capture it looking sideways. The camera pose of each input image (i.e., the translation vector T, the rotation matrix R and K) is recovered using our Structure from Motion (SfM) system, together with a sparse set of reconstructed 3D scenes points. From recovered camera poses, novel perspectives are synthesized based on 3D geometrical information estimated using our dense stereo algorithm. An interface for manually specifying the multi-perspective configuration is provided based on our perspective composition framework, which combines different perspectives (original or novel) to form the resultant panorama.

The rest of this paper is organized as follows. Section 2 presents background. Section 3 presents our algorithm for synthesizing novel perspectives. Section 4 describes our perspective composition framework. Results and discussions are presented in Section 5 and Section 6 concludes this paper.

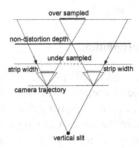

Fig. 2. The sampling error distortion is caused by the depth parallax

2   Background

The earliest attempt at combining images captured at different viewpoints is perhaps view interpolation, which warps pixels from input images to a reference coordinate using a pre-computed 3D scene geometry [6,7,8]. There are two main problems with these approaches: to establish an accurate correspondence for stereo is still a hard vision problem, and there will likely be holes in the resultant image due to sampling issues of the forward mapping and the occlusion problem. Another thread is based on optimal seam [2,10], which stitches input images with their own perspective and formulates the composition into a labeling problem, i.e., pixel values are chosen to be one of the input images. Results are inherently multi-perspective. However, these approaches only work well for roughly planar scene, as for scenes with large depth variations, it is often impossible to find an optimal partition that can create seamless mosaics.

The strip mosaic offers a better alternative. The basic idea is to cut a thin strip from a dense collection of images and put them together to form a panorama. In its early form, the push-broom model [11,4], the resultant image is parallel in one direction and perspective in the other, while the crossed-slits [5] model is perspective in one direction and is perspective from a different viewpoint in the other direction. Therefore, the aspect ratio distortion is inherent due to the different projections along the two directions.

In addition, because scenes within each strip are rendered from a regular pinhole perspective, given a certain strip width, there is a depth at which scenes show no distortion. For a further depth, scenes might be duplicately rendered, i.e., over-sampled, while for a closer depth, scenes cannot be fully covered, i.e., under-sampled. In the literature, this kind of artifact is named a sampling error distortion [11], see Fig 2.

Even for scenes with complex geometrical structures, strip mosaic can still produce visually acceptable results in spite of the fore-mentioned aspect ratio and sampling error distortions. Therefore, the strip mosaic provides a foundation upon which multi-perspective panoramas in a large scale can be constructed. An interactive approach is presented in [13], where several perspectives in the form of vertical slits are specified by users. Some other approaches attempt to automatically detect the multi-perspective configuration through minimizing metrics for measuring undesired effects, e.g., the colour discrepancy between consecutive strips [14] or the aspect ratio distortion [15,16].

3   Novel Perspective Synthesis

3.1   Single Direction View Interpolation

The novel perspective is rendered onto a 3D picture surface, which is assumed to be perpendicular to the ground plane of scenes. A working coordinate system (WCS) is fitted from camera poses of input sequence to ensure that the ground plane is spanned by the X and Z axes, so that the picture surface can be simplified as a line in the top-down view of scenes, and extruded along the up (Y) axis. Then input images are rectified according to WCS.

The picture surface is defined by a 3D plane π_f and the X-Z plane of WCS is denoted as π_c. If scenes are exactly located on the picture surface, a point (or pixel) of the resultant image $\mathbf{p}' = [x', y']^\top$ can be mapped to a point $\mathbf{p} = [x, y]^\top$ of the ith input image by a projective transformation, i.e., the homography:

$$\begin{bmatrix} x \\ y \\ 1 \end{bmatrix} = \mathbf{H}_i \begin{bmatrix} x' \\ y' \\ 1 \end{bmatrix} = \mathbf{K}[\mathbf{R}_i \mid \mathbf{t}_i]\mathbf{G} \begin{bmatrix} x' \\ y' \\ 1 \end{bmatrix} \tag{1}$$

where $\mathbf{G}$ is a 4×3 matrix that establishes the mapping between a 2D point of the resultant image and a 3D point $\mathbf{X}_p = [X_p, Y_p, Z_p]^\top$ on the picture surface, such that:

$$\begin{bmatrix} X_p \\ Y_p \\ Z_p \\ 1 \end{bmatrix} = \mathbf{G} \begin{bmatrix} x' \\ y' \\ 1 \end{bmatrix} = \begin{bmatrix} s_x \mathbf{V}_x & s_y \mathbf{V}_y & \mathbf{O} \\ 0 & 0 & 1 \end{bmatrix} \begin{bmatrix} x' \\ y' \\ 1 \end{bmatrix} \tag{2}$$

where $\mathbf{V}_x$ and $\mathbf{V}_y$ are vectors that parameterize X and Y axes of the plane coordinate of the picture surface and $\mathbf{O}$ is the origin of the plane coordinate. We choose $\mathbf{V}_x$ and $\mathbf{V}_y$ as projections of the X and Y axes of WCS onto the picture surface. s_x and s_y define the pixel size along the X and Y axes of the image coordinate. Given a point $\mathbf{p}$ on the picture surface, suppose that the corresponding distance deviating from the camera trajectory is represented by a function $d(\mathbf{p})$, then the pixel size at $\mathbf{p}$ is: $s_x = \frac{d(\mathbf{p})}{f} s_x'$. where f is the focal length, and s_x' is the pixel size of the input image. The pixel size along the Y (vertical) direction is: $s_y = \alpha s_x$, where α is the aspect ratio of the input image.

We assume that the (horizontal) projection center $\mathbf{C}_v$ of a novel perspective always lies on plane π_c and the vertical slit $\mathbf{L}$ is the line that passes through $\mathbf{C}_v$ and perpendicular to π_c, as shown in Fig 3. The mapping from a point $\mathbf{p} = [x, y]^\top$ in the ith image onto the picture surface is the intersection of 3 planes: the picture surface π_f, the plane π_v that contains $\mathbf{X}_d$ and the vertical slit $\mathbf{L}$ and the plane π_h that contains $\mathbf{X}_d$ and the X axis of the ith camera that is centered at $\mathbf{C}_i$, see Fig 3.

Once the intersection is recovered, it is mapped to the resultant image using $\mathbf{G}^+$, the *pseudo-inverse* of $\mathbf{G}$. This approach can be further simplified, since the Y component of $\mathbf{p}'$, i.e., y', can be directly computed using the homography $\mathbf{H}_i$. The value of the X component x' depends on the actual 3D point. Suppose that the picture surface π_f intersects π_v at a 3D line, and $\mathbf{X}_s$ and $\mathbf{X}_t$ are two points on that 3D line, then we have:

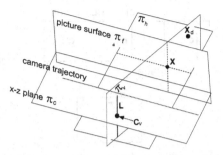

Fig. 3. Points warping based on the 3D geometry

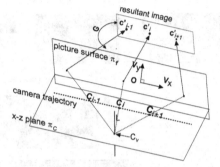

Fig. 4. Rendering from a novel perspective. The projection center of the novel perspective is projected onto the picture surface and then mapped to the final resultant image.

$$\begin{bmatrix} ((G^+)^{2\top} X_s)((G^+)^{3\top} X_t) - ((G^+)^{2\top} X_t)((G^+)^{3\top} X_s) \\ ((G^+)^{3\top} X_s)((G^+)^{1\top} X_t) - ((G^+)^{3\top} X_t)((G^+)^{1\top} X_s) \\ ((G^+)^{1\top} X_s)((G^+)^{2\top} X_t) - ((G^+)^{1\top} X_t)((G^+)^{2\top} X_s) \end{bmatrix} \begin{bmatrix} x' \\ y' \\ 1 \end{bmatrix} = 0 \qquad (3)$$

where $(G^+)^{k\top}$ denotes the kth row of the matrix G^+. With this equation, the value of x' can be solved from the known value of y'. Since with one direction the mapping adopts the original projective transformation, and the other is based on the real 3D geometry, this rendering strategy is named a "single direction view interpolation" as opposed to the full perspective interpolation.

The point mapping is followed by the determination of which input image is selected to render a point in the result. Such selection is inspired by the the strip mosaic. We project each camera center C_i onto a point in the resultant image c_i' along the line connecting C_i and the projection center of the novel perspective C_v, see Fig4. We define a vertical center line CL_i that passes c_i' on the resultant image. A vertical split line $BL_{i,i+1}$ is drawn between any consecutive camera center projections. The center line CL_i is then mapped to $\widehat{CL}_i$ in the corresponding input image I_i. We only examine pixels within a region around $\widehat{CL}_i$. For each row of I_i, we take the pixel on $\widehat{CL}_i$ as the starting point and search on both sides. Once the warped point onto the result is beyond the split line $BL_{i,i+1}$ or $BL_{i-1,i}$, we proceed to the next row, see Fig 5.

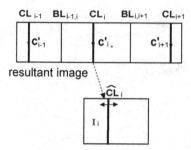

Fig. 5. Center lines and split lines on the resultant image. Pixel warping is carried out within a region around the center line mapping.

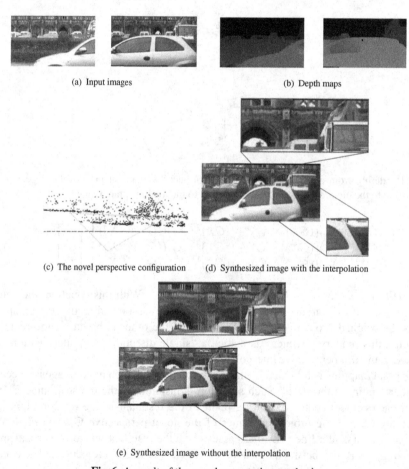

(a) Input images   (b) Depth maps

(c) The novel perspective configuration   (d) Synthesized image with the interpolation

(e) Synthesized image without the interpolation

Fig. 6. A result of the novel perspective synthesis

Fig 6(d) shows the result synthesized using our single direction view interpolation. As compared to that without the interpolation shown in Fig 6(e), the sampling error distortion is removed. However, the aspect ratio distortion still exists. For example, in Fig 6(d), the car in front of the middle low wall is apparently squashed.

3.2   Dense Stereo

To estimate the depth (or, 3D geometry) map for each point (pixel) in an image $\mathbf{I}_i$, a stereo process is performed to $\mathbf{I}_i$ and its neighboring image $\mathbf{I}_{i+1}$. The stereo is accomplished in two steps: firstly, a correspondence between $\mathbf{I}_i$ and $\mathbf{I}_{i+1}$ is detected, and then the depth map is computed from the correspondence together with camera poses of $\mathbf{I}_i$ and $\mathbf{I}_{i+1}$.

To construct the correspondence, we adopt the concept of the surface correspondence as suggested in [17]. A surface can be parameterized by the motion of its projections on $\mathbf{I}_i$ and $\mathbf{I}_{i+1}$, such that: $\mathbf{p} + S(\mathbf{p}) = \mathbf{p}'$. In this sense, the correspondence detection is converted to determining for each point $\mathbf{p}$ in $\mathbf{I}_i$ which surface it should belong to, and to calculating the motion parameter of that surface. Since the stereo pair is assumed to be rectified and the vertical movement is ignorable, the surface is represented by a 1D affine model:

$$S(\mathbf{p}) = \begin{bmatrix} a_1 * x + a_2 * y + b \\ 0 \end{bmatrix} \tag{4}$$

We adopt a similar framework to that proposed in [17]. The basic idea is to iteratively refine the estimation by alternating between two steps:

1. Given a labeled map of each point, we need to find the affine motion parameter for each connected segment. This is done by minimizing the cost function $\sum_{\mathbf{p} \in \Omega} (\mathbf{I}_i(\mathbf{p}) - \mathbf{I}_{i+1}(\mathbf{p} + S(\mathbf{p})))^2$, where Ω denotes the set of all points in a segment. This cost function is minimized using the the iterative method proposed in [18].

2. Given a set of surfaces characterized by their affine motion parameters, each pixel is labeled as belonging to one surface. The problem is solved by a Markov Random Field (MRF) optimization implemented using the Graph Cut algorithm [19]. The cost function of the MRF consists of a data term that computes the cost for a pixel $\mathbf{p}$ to be assigned with a surface $S(\mathbf{p})$, and a smooth term penalizing a pixel $\mathbf{p}$ and its neighboring point $\mathbf{q}$ for having different surface labels.

Fig 6(b) presents an example result of our dense stereo algorithm.

4   Perspective Composition

Our perspective composition consists of two steps. Firstly, for each point of the resultant panorama, its pixel value is selected from one input perspective, then, visible discontinuities along lines bordering adjacent segments rendered from different perspectives are suppressed.

4.1   Perspective Selection

Given n perspectives: $\{\mathbf{V}_i\}_0^{n-1}$, for each point $\mathbf{p}$ of the resultant panorama, the perspectives selection is represented by a labeling function: $L(\mathbf{p}) = i$. Labels of all points constitute a labeling configuration: $\mathbf{L}$, the cost of which is formulated as a Markov Random Field (MRF):

$$E(\mathbf{L}) = \sum_{\mathbf{p}} E_D(\mathbf{p}, L(\mathbf{p})) + \sum_{\mathbf{p}} \sum_{\mathbf{q} \in \mathcal{N}(\mathbf{p})} E_S(\mathbf{p}, \mathbf{q}, L(\mathbf{p}), L(\mathbf{q})) \tag{5}$$

E_S denotes the smooth term and E_D denotes the data term.

The smooth term E_S consists of three terms: a depth term, a colour term and a structure term, and the measuring function is a weighted sum of these three terms:

$$E_S(\mathbf{p}, \mathbf{q}, L(\mathbf{p}), L(\mathbf{q})) = E_{d\_S} + \mu_0 E_{c\_S} + \mu_1 E_{g\_S} \tag{6}$$

μ_0 and μ_1 are weights.

Depth Smooth Term. The depth smooth term encourages the seam to go through regions where 3D geometry coincides with the picture surface. We calculate for each pixel of a perspective the residual error with respect to the picture surface. Each point mapped from the input image onto the synthesized image of a perspective constitutes a point sample. Suppose that the point sample is extracted from the input image $\mathbf{I}_i$, and let us denote the depth under the camera coordinate of $\mathbf{I}_i$ as $d_{\mathbf{I}_i}(\mathbf{x})$. Then, we calculate the depth of the corresponding point projected onto the picture surface, denoted as $d_{\mathbf{I}_i}(\mathbf{x}')$. The residual error of the point sample is:

$$r_{\mathbf{I}_i}(\mathbf{x}') = \begin{cases} 1.0 - \frac{d_{\mathbf{I}_i}(\mathbf{x})}{d_{\mathbf{I}_i}(\mathbf{x}')} & d_{\mathbf{I}_i}(\mathbf{x}') \geq d_{\mathbf{I}_i}(\mathbf{x}) \\ 1.0 - \frac{d_{\mathbf{I}_i}(\mathbf{x}')}{d_{\mathbf{I}_i}(\mathbf{x})} & d_{\mathbf{I}_i}(\mathbf{x}') < d_{\mathbf{I}_i}(\mathbf{x}) \end{cases} \tag{7}$$

The residual error of a grid point $r_{\mathbf{V}_i}(\mathbf{p})$ of the ith perspective is computed by convolving these samples with the Gaussian filter. Given a pair of neighboring pixels $\mathbf{p}$ and $\mathbf{q}$ of the resultant panorama, with assigned labels as $L(\mathbf{p})$ and $L(\mathbf{q})$, the depth smooth term is:

$$E_{d\_S} = r_{\mathbf{V}_{L(\mathbf{p})}}(\mathbf{p}) + r_{\mathbf{V}_{L(\mathbf{q})}}(\mathbf{p}) + r_{\mathbf{V}_{L(\mathbf{p})}}(\mathbf{q}) + r_{\mathbf{V}_{L(\mathbf{q})}}(\mathbf{q}) \tag{8}$$

Colour Smooth Term. To place the seam in regions where pixel values from different perspectives are similar, the colour smooth term is defined as:

$$\begin{aligned} E_{c\_S} = \ & \frac{1}{N} \sum_{\mathbf{x} \in \mathbf{W}} | V_{L(\mathbf{p})}(\mathbf{p} + \mathbf{x}) - V_{L(\mathbf{q})}(\mathbf{p} + \mathbf{x}) | \\ & + \frac{1}{N} \sum_{\mathbf{x} \in \mathbf{W}} | V_{L(\mathbf{p})}(\mathbf{q} + \mathbf{x}) - V_{L(\mathbf{q})}(\mathbf{q} + \mathbf{x}) | \end{aligned} \tag{9}$$

where $\mathbf{W}$ is a window for the aggregation of difference, and N is the size of $\mathbf{W}$.

Structural Smooth Term. To suppress structural discontinuities, we define the structural smooth term as (assuming the gradient ∇. captures the most structural information of an image):

$$\begin{aligned} E_{g\_S} = \ & | \nabla \mathbf{V}_{L(\mathbf{p})}(\mathbf{p}) - \nabla \mathbf{V}_{L(\mathbf{q})}(\mathbf{p}) | \\ & + | \nabla \mathbf{V}_{L(\mathbf{p})}(\mathbf{q}) - \nabla \mathbf{V}_{L(\mathbf{q})}(\mathbf{q}) | \end{aligned} \tag{10}$$

The Data Term. A general form of the data term is written as:

$$E_D(\mathbf{p}, L(\mathbf{p})) = \begin{cases} U_{L(\mathbf{p})}(\mathbf{p}) & \mathbf{p} \in \mathbf{V}_{L(\mathbf{p})} \\ \infty & \mathbf{p} \notin \mathbf{V}_{L(\mathbf{p})} \end{cases} \tag{11}$$

$U_{L(\mathbf{p})}(\mathbf{p})$ measures the fitness of a pixel to be assigned with the label. We adopt a simple solution, i.e., use a uniform function such that: $U_{L(\mathbf{p})}(\mathbf{p}) \equiv 0$.

4.2 Perspective Fusion

To remove discontinuities along seams between two neighboring segments rendered from different perspectives, we adopt a local method, i.e., information of one segment along the boundary line is blended into the interior of the other one. Such information could simply be pixel values, or warping vectors compensating for structural misalignments.

The Fusion Paradigm. Segments of each input perspective are extracted from the result of the perspective selection. Let us assume that there are m such segments, and for each segment $k \in \{0, ..., m - 1\}$, the mapping function $L(k)$ denotes the index of the corresponding perspective i, $i \in \{0, ..., n - 1\}$. A segment Ω_k is enclosed by its boundary lines $\partial\Omega_k$. There are two kinds of boundary lines: 1) adjoining boundary lines that are adjacent to other segments, and 2) self-closure boundary lines that do not border with any other segments, see Fig 7. As for the former, information from other segments need to be blended into the interior part of Ω_k, whilst, for the latter, we only consider information from Ω_k itself.

We propose a monotonic fusion paradigm that only performs the boundary fusion in a single direction. Let us suppose that two neighboring segments Ω_j and Ω_k share a adjoining boundary line. Without losing generality, it is assumed that $L(j) < L(k)$. Information from Ω_j along the boundary line are blended into the interior part of Ω_k, while, Ω_j remains unchanged. Fig 7 illustrates this monotonic fusion.

A proper order of input perspectives is needed. We compute for each perspective the number of its neighboring perspectives $N(i)$, and then sort all input perspectives with an ascending order of $N(i)$. If two perspectives have the same value of $N(i)$, then the one with more pixel number is placed before the other.

Blending of Pixel Values. To achieve a smooth fusion, the pixel value blending is constrained by the gradient field of a segment Ω_k as suggested in [20]:

$$\min_{f'} \iint_{\mathbf{p} \in \Omega_k} |\nabla f'(\mathbf{p}) - \nabla f(\mathbf{p})|^2 \quad \mathbf{p} \in \partial\Omega_k : f'(\mathbf{p}) = f^\star(\mathbf{p}) \tag{12}$$

where $f(\cdot)$ is the original pixel value and $f'(\cdot)$ is the pixel value to be speculated in the blending process. $f^\star(\cdot)$ denotes the pixel value at the boundary line $\partial\Omega_k$.

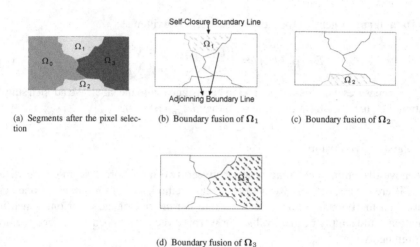

(a) Segments after the pixel selection

(b) Boundary fusion of Ω_1

(c) Boundary fusion of Ω_2

(d) Boundary fusion of Ω_3

Fig. 7. The boundary fusion in a monotonic order. The order of involved perspectives is: $L(0) < L(3) < L(1) = L(2)$.

Blending of Image Warping. Misalignments can be roughly grouped into two categories: a small structural misalignment, which is usually brought by breaking edges along the adjoining boundary line, and a large structural misalignment, which is mainly caused by significant geometrical misalignments. Fig 8(a) and 9(a) presents real examples of these two types of misalignments. We introduce two corresponding algorithms based on image warping. Our system enables these two optional algorithms to be selected by users for a given adjoining boundary line.

Structure Re-alignment. It is a common practice to compensate for small structural misalignments through locally re-aligning deviated edges, e.g., [21,22]. We match edges striding over the adjoining boundary line bordering Ω_j and Ω_k, by measuring their differences in edge directions and pixel values. For a pair of matched edges, we calculate the backward warping vector. Then we interpolate warping vectors for those non-edge points on the adjoining boundary line. For the self-closure boundary line, the warping vector is 0. Then, warping vectors are blended into the interior of Ω_k using the Poisson image editing [20]:

$$\min_{\mathbf{z}'} \iint_{\mathbf{p} \in \Omega_k} | \nabla z'(\mathbf{p}) |^2 \quad \mathbf{p} \in \partial\Omega_k : z'(\mathbf{p}) = z^\star(\mathbf{p}) \tag{13}$$

where $z'(\mathbf{p})$ denotes the warping vector to be speculated and $\mathbf{z}^\star(\mathbf{p})$ is warping vector from the boundary line.

Segment Shift. To fix the large structural misalignment, the image warping is based on a robust match, which is constrained by the geometrical information. Firstly a match region $\mathbf{R}$ is placed to enclose the adjoining boundary line between Ω_j and Ω_k in $\mathbf{V}_{L(k)}$ (the corresponding perspective of Ω_k), and for each point $\mathbf{p}$ in $\mathbf{R}$, its depth information is calculated as described in the novel perspective synthesis, and then it is used to guide the mapping of $\mathbf{p}$ onto the perspective $\mathbf{V}_{L(j)}$ as $\mathbf{p}'$. The similarity between $\mathbf{p}$ and $\mathbf{p}'$ is

(a) A small struc-   (b) After the structural misalignment   ture re-alignment

Fig. 8. A result of the structure re-alignment. In (a), edges are broken by the seam. After the structure re-alignment (b), edges are correctly aligned, and thus the structural discontinuity is eliminated.

measured, and if it is above certain threshold, then these two points are regarded as a correct match. A robust measuring function could be the Normalized Cross-Correlation (NCC), or SIFT feature matching [23], which is reliable but sometimes too sparse.

Two matched points provide a backward warping vector. For those without correct matches, their warping vectors are estimated using the convolution with a Gaussian filter, or if correct matches are sparse, a Radial Basis Function (RBF)-based interpolation with thin-plate spline kernel is adopted. Now, a warping vector is associated with each point on the adjoining boundary between Ω_j and Ω_k. These warping vectors are then blended into the interior of Ω_k using 13. This strategy often induces a large image deformation, which would cause parts of one segments shifted towards the other, and therefore we name it as "segment shift".

5   Results and Discussion

Experiments have been conducted on real urban scenes. We demonstrate in Fig 10 how the perspective composition can be used to create a multi-perspective panorama from a manually specified perspective configuration. The perspective configuration is shown in Fig 10(d), which is mixed with both novel and original perspectives. The original perspective is rendered through mapping the corresponding input image onto the picture surface using a projective transform as defined in 1. The novel perspective is synthesized using our single direction view interpolation. Fig 10(a) shows the result of the MRF optimization for the perspective selection, where adjoining boundary lines (seams) are highlighted. Fig 10(b) shows the map of residual error with respect to the picture surface, from which one can see that seams produced by the MRF optimization are roughly placed in areas with low residual errors. Fig 10(c) presents the final panorama after the boundary fusion. More results are shown in Fig 11.

We are not the first to generate multi-perspective panoramas through perspective composition. The approach presented in [10] takes original perspectives as input, and use the MRF optimization to select a perspective for rendering each pixel in the resultant panorama. This approach works quite well for mainly planar scenes. However, due to the lack of facility to synthesize novel perspectives that are wide enough to cover scenes not on the main plane (picture surface), a seam placed at the area corresponding

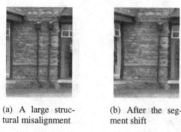

(a) A large struc-   (b) After the seg-
tural misalignment   ment shift

Fig. 9. A result of the segment shift. Due to the geometrical misalignment, a duplicate gutter is shown in (a), after the segment shift, the ghost gutter is eliminated.

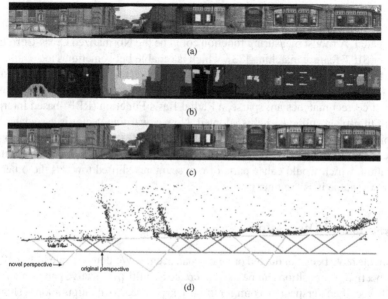

(a)

(b)

(c)

novel perspective →   original perspective

(d)

Fig. 10. A Panorama created from the perspective composition. In the multi-perspective config-uration (d), original perspectives are denoted as blue and novel ones are denoted as green. The result of MRF optimization is shown in (a) and the composed residual error map is shown in (b). The final panorama after boundary fusion is shown in (c).

to the off-plane scenes would induce serious visual artifacts. Fig 12 presents an example result of this approach, which is visually unacceptable [1].

There are several existing approaches that address the problem using synthesized novel perspectives. However, they assume that input perspectives are precisely regis-tered with each other, and therefore no further composition processing is required in their system. For example, the interactive approach described in [13] only allows a set of disjoint perspectives to be specified, and these disjoint perspectives are simply connected by a set of inverse perspectives in between them. Obviously, their approach

---

[1] Actually, they use a fish-eye camera to expand the filed of view (FOV) of input images. How-ever, the FOV of an image is still limited.

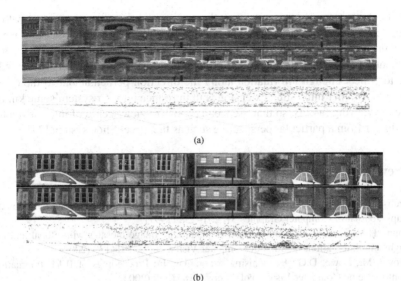

Fig. 11. Multi-perspective panoramas of urban scenes. For each result, the outcome of the MRF optimization (top) is blended using our boundary fusion algorithm (middle).

Fig. 12. A Panorama created from pure original perspectives [10]. Input image sequence is re-sampled to get a set of sparse original perspectives, which are combined using the MRF opti-mization. For scenes off picture surface, visual artifacts are noticeable.

restricts content that can be conveyed in the resultant panorama, e.g., the perspective configuration as presented in Fig 11(b) can never be achieved with their approach.

6 Conclusions

This paper presents a system for producing multi-perspective panoramas from dense video sequences. Our system uses estimated 3D geometrical information to eliminate the sampling error distortion in the synthesized novel perspective. Then a perspective composition framework is presented to combine different perspectives by suppress-ing their pixel value and structural discrepancy. Compared to the existing methods, the perspective composition not only removes noticeable artifacts, but also relieves some constraints imposed on the perspective configuration that a resultant panorama can be properly generated from.

The main problem of our approach is the aspect ratio distortion associated with the synthesized novel perspective. The cause of this problem lies in the fact that we are lack of information along the direction perpendicular to the direction of the camera movement. In the future, we shall look into the use of an array of cameras mounted on a pole to collect enough information along the direction perpendicular to the camera movement. Another interesting extension is to introduce into our system some kinds of interactive viewing facility, so that users can choose to view scenes of interest at a high resolution or from a particular perspective such as the Street Slide system [24].

References

1. Szeliski, R., Shum, H.Y.: Creating full view panoramic image mosaics and environment maps. Journal of Computer Graphics 31, 251–258 (1997)
2. Shum, H.Y., Szeliski, R.: Construction of panoramic image mosaics with global and local alignment. International Journal of Computer Vision 36(2), 101–130 (2000)
3. Brown, M., Lowe, D.G.: Recognising panoramas. In: Proceedings of IEEE International Conference on Computer Vision, vol. 2, pp. 1218–1225 (2003)
4. Peleg, S., Rousso, B., Rav-Acha, A., Zomet, A.: Mosaicing on adaptive manifold. IEEE Transactions on Pattern Analysis and Machine Intelligence 22(10), 1144–1154 (2000)
5. Zomet, A., Feldman, D., Peleg, S., Weinshall, D.: Mosaicing new views: the crossed-slits projection. IEEE Transactions on Pattern Analysis and Machine Intelligence 25(6), 741–754 (2003)
6. Szeliski, R., Kang, S.B.: Direct methods for visual scene reconstruction. In: Proceedings of IEEE Workshop on Representation of Visual Scenes, pp. 26–33 (1995)
7. Kumar, R., Anandan, P., Irani, M., Bergen, J., Hanna, K.: Representation of scenes from collections of images. In: Proceedings of IEEE Workshop on Representation of Visual Scenes, pp. 10–17 (1995)
8. Zheng, K.C., Kang, S.B.: Layered depth panoramas. In: Proceedings of the IEEE Conference on Computer Vision and Pattern Recognition, pp. 1–8 (2007)
9. Shum, H.Y., Szeliski, R.: Construction of panoramic image mosaics with global and local alignment. International Journal of Computer Vision 36(2), 101–130 (2000)
10. Agarwala, A., Agrawala, M., Cohen, M., Salesin, D., Szeliski, R.: Photographing long scenes with multi-viewpoint panoramas. ACM Transactions on Graphics 25(3), 853–861 (2006)
11. Zheng, J.Y.: Digital route panoramas. IEEE Multimedia 10(3), 57–67 (2003)
12. Peleg, S., Rousso, B., Rav-Acha, A., Zomet, A.: Mosaicing on adaptive manifold. IEEE Transactions on Pattern Analysis and Machine Intelligence 22(10), 1144–1154 (2000)
13. Roman, A., Garg, G., Levoy, M.: Interactive design of multi-perspective images for visualizing urban landscapes. In: Proceedings of IEEE Visualization, pp. 537–544 (2004)
14. Wexler, Y., Simakov, D.: Space-time scene mnifolds. In: Proceedings of the International Conference on Computer Vision, vol. 1, pp. 858–863 (2005)
15. Roman, A., Lensch, H.P.A.: Automatic multiperspective images. In: Proceedings of Eurographics Symposium on Rendering, pp. 161–171 (2006)
16. Acha, A.R., Eagel, G., Peleg, S.: Minimal Aspect Distortion (MAD) Mosaicing of long scenes. International Journal of Computer Vision 78(2-3), 187–206 (2008)
17. Birchfield, S., Tomasi, C.: Multiway cut for stereo and motion with slanted surfaces. In: Proceedings of the International Conference on Computer Vision, pp. 489–495 (1999)
18. Shi, J., Tomasi, C.: Good features to track. In: Proceedings of the IEEE Conference on Computer Vision and Pattern Recognition, pp. 593–600 (1994)

19. Kolmogorov, V., Zabih, R.: What energy functions can be minimized via graph cuts. IEEE Transactions on Pattern Analysis and Machine Intelligence 26(2), 147–159 (2004)

20. Pérez, P., Gangne, M., Blake, A.: Poisson image editing. In: Proceedings of SIGGRAPH, vol. 22, pp. 313–318 (2003)

21. Fang, H., Hart, J.C.: Textureshop: texture synthesis as a photograph editing tool. In: Proceedings of SIGGRAPH, vol. 23, pp. 354–359 (2004)

22. Jia, J., Tang, C.-K.: Image stitching using structure deformation. IEEE Transactions on Pattern Analysis and Machine Intelligence 30(4), 617–631 (2008)

23. Lowe, D.G.: Distinctive image features from scale-invariant keypoints. International Journal of Computer Vision 60(2), 91–110 (2004)

24. Kopf, J., Chen, B., Szeliski, R., Cohen, M.: Street-Slide: Browsing street level imagery. ACM Transactions on Graphics 29(4), 96:1–96:8 (2010)

Optimizations with CUDA: A Case Study on 3D Curve-Skeleton Extraction from Voxelized Models

Jesús Jiménez and Juan Ruiz de Miras

Department of Computer Science, University of Jaén,
Campus Las Lagunillas s/n, 23071 Jaén, Spain
{jjibanez,demiras}@ujaen.es

Abstract. In this paper, we show how we have coded and optimized a complex and not trivially parallelizable case study: a 3D curve-skeleton calculation algorithm. For this we use NVIDIA CUDA, which allows the programmer to easily code algorithms for executing in a parallel way on NVIDIA GPU devices. However, when working with algorithms that have high data-sharing or data-dependence requirements, like the curve-skeleton calculation, it is not always a trivial task to achieve acceptable acceleration rates. So we detail step by step a comprehensive collection of optimizations to be considered in this class of algorithms, and in general in any CUDA implementation. Two different GPU architectures have been used to test the implications of each optimization, the NVIDIA GT200 architecture and the Fermi GF100. As a result, although the first direct CUDA implementation of our algorithm ran even slower than its CPU version, overall speedups of 19x (GT200) and 68x (Fermi GF100) were finally achieved.

Keywords: Curve-skeleton, 3D Thinning, CUDA, GPGPU, Optimizations, Fermi.

1 Introduction

GPGPU (General-Purpose computing on Graphics Processing Units) has undergone significant growth in recent years due to the appearance of parallel programming models like NVIDA CUDA (Compute Unified Device Architecture) [1] or OpenCL (Open Computing Language) [2]. These programming models allow the programmer to use the GPU for resolving general problems without knowing graphics. Thanks to the large number of cores and processors present in current GPUs, high speedup rates could be achieved.

But not all problems are ideal for parallelizing and accelerating on a GPU. The problem must have an intrinsic data-parallel nature. Data parallelism appears when an algorithm can independently execute the same instruction or function over a large set of data. Data-parallel algorithms can achieve impressive speedup values if the *memory accesses / compute operations* ratio is low. If several memory accesses are required to apply few and/or light operations over the retrieved data, obtaining high speedups is complicated, although it could be easier with the automatic cache memory provided in the new generation of NVIDIA GPUs. These algorithms that need to consider a group of values in order to operate over a single position of the dataset are commonly known

G. Csurka et al. (Eds.): VISIGRAPP 2012, CCIS 359, pp. 82–96, 2013.

as data-sharing problems [3]. The case study of this paper, a 3D thinning algorithm, belongs to this class of algorithms and shares characteristics with many other algorithms in the areas of volume modelling or image analysis.

Some optimizations and strategies are explained in vendor guides [1,4], books [5,6] and research papers [3,7,8,9]. In most cases, the examples present in these publications are too simple, or are perfectly suited to the characteristics of the GPU. Furthermore, the evolution of the CUDA architecture has meant that certain previous efforts on optimizing algorithms are not completely essential with the new Fermi architecture [10]. None of those studies can assess the implications of the optimizations based on the CUDA architecture used. Recent and interesting works present studies in this respect, e.g. [11,12], but only loop optimization techniques, in the first paper, and simple matrix operations, in the second paper, are discussed.

For GPGPU, Fermi architecture has a number of improvements such as more cores, a higher number of simultaneous threads per multiprocessor, increased double-precision floating-point capability, new features for C++ programming and error-correcting code (ECC). But within the scope of data-sharing and memory-bound algorithms, the most important improvement of the Fermi architecture is the existence of a real cache hierarchy.

In the rest of the paper, we firstly describe our case study, a 3D thinning algorithm for curve-skeleton calculation. Later we expose our hardware configuration and the voxelized models that we used to check the performance of the algorithm. Next, we analyze one by one the main optimizations for two different CUDA architectures (GT200 and Fermi GF100), and show how they work in practice. Finally, we summarize our results and present our conclusions.

2   Case Study: A 3D Thinning Algorithm

A curve-skeleton is a simple and compact 1D representation of a 3D object that captures its topological essence in a simple and very compact way. Skeletons are widely used in multiple applications like animation, medical image registration, mesh repairing, virtual navigation or surface reconstruction [13].

Thinning is one of the techniques for calculating curve-skeletons from voxelized 3D models. Thinning algorithms are based on iteratively eliminating those boundary voxels of the object that are considered simple, e.g. those voxels that can be eliminated without changing the topology of the object. This process thins the object until no more simple voxels can be removed. The main problem that these thinning algorithms present is their very high execution time, like any other curve-skeleton generation technique. We therefore decided to modify and adapt a widely used 3D thinning algorithm presented by Palágyi and Kuba in [14] for executing on GPU in a parallel and presumably more efficient way. Thus, all previously exposed applications could benefit of that improvement.

The 3D thinning algorithm presented in [14] is a 12-directional algorithm formed by 12 sub-iterations, each of which has a different deletion condition. This deletion condition consists of comparing each border point (a voxel belonging to the boundary of the object) and its 3x3x3 neighborhood (26-neighborhood) with a set of 14 templates. If anyone matches, the voxel is deleted; if not, the voxel remains. Each voxel neighborhood is transformed by rotations and/or reflections, which depend on the study direction, thus changing the deletion condition.

In brief, the algorithm detects, for a direction d, which voxels are border points. Next, the 26-neighborhood of each border point is read, transformed (depending on direction d) and compared with the 14 templates. If at least one of them matches, the border point is marked as deletable (simple point). Finally, in the last step of the sub-iteration all simple points are definitely deleted. This process is repeated for each of the 12 directions until no voxel is deleted. The pseudo code of the 3D thinning algorithm is shown in the listing above, where $model$ represents the 3D voxelized object, $point$ is the ID of a voxel, d determines the direction to consider, $deleted$ counts the number of voxels deleted in each general iteration, nbh and $nbhT$ are buffers used to store a neighborhood and its transformation, and $match$ is a boolean flag that signals when a voxel is a simple point or not.

```
START;
do{ //Iteration
   deleted = 0;
   for d=1 to d=12 { //12 sub-iterations
      markBorderPoints(model, d);

      for each BORDER_POINT do{
         nbh =loadNeighborhood(model, point);
         nbhT =transformNeighborhood(nbh, d);
         match =matchesATemplate(nbhT);
         if(match) markSimplePoint(model, point);
      }

      for each SIMPLE_POINT do{
         deletePoint(model, point);
         deleted++;
      }
   }
}while(deleted>0);
END;
```

[Pseudo code of Palágyi and Kuba 3D thinning algorithm. General procedure]

Regarding the functions, $markBorderPoints()$ labels as "BORDER_POINT" for the direction d, all voxels which are border points, $markSimplePoint()$ labels the voxel point as "SIMPLE_POINT", and $deletePoint()$ deletes the voxel identified by point. This algorithm has an intrinsic parallel nature, because a set of processes are applied on multiple data (voxels of the 3D object) in the same way. But this is not fully parallelizable, since each sub-iteration (one for each direction) strictly depends on the result of the previous one and some CPU synchronization points will be needed to ensure a valid final result. In fact, we are dealing with a data-sharing algorithm, where processing a data-item (a voxel) needs to access other data-items (neighbors voxels). Therefore kernel functions will have to share data between them. This is a memory-bound algorithm with a high ratio of slow global memory reads to operations with

Table 1. GPU specifications (MP: Multiprocessor, SP: Scalar Processor)

	GTX 295	GTX 580
Architecture	GT200	GF100
Computing Capability	1.3	2.0
Number of MPs	30	16
Number of SPs	240	512
Thread Slots per MP	1,024	1,536
Warp Slots per MP	32	48
Block Slots per MP	8	8
Max. Block Size	512	1,024
Warp Size	32	32
Global Memory	895 MB	1,472 MB
Constant Memory	64 KB	64 KB
Shared Memory per MP	16 KB	48 KB / 16 KB
L1 Cache	0	16 KB / 48 KB
32-bit registers per MP	16K	32K

this read data, and it is not favourable in CUDA implementations. In addition, these operations are very simple (conditional sentences and boolean checks), so it is difficult to hide memory access latencies.

3 Hardware, 3D Models and Final Results

Two different GPUs, based on GT200 and GF100 CUDA architectures, have been used to test and measure the performance of our algorithm. The main specifications of these GPUs are exposed in Table 1. The GTX295 is installed on a PC with an Intel Core i7-920 @ 2.67GHz 64-bits and 12 GB of RAM memory (Machine A). The GTX580 is installed on a server with two Intel Xeon E5620 @ 2.40GHz 64-bits and 12 GB of RAM memory (Machine B). The GTX580 has two modes: (1) Set preference to L1 cache use (48 KB for L1 cache and 16 KB for shared memory), or (2) set preference to shared memory (16 KB for L1 cache and 48 KB for shared memory). We differentiate along this paper between these modes when testing our algorithm.

Regarding the models used to test the CUDA algorithm, we use a set of five 3D voxelized objects with different complexity, features and sizes. These models are: the *Happy Buddha* and *Bunny* models from the Stanford 3D Scanning Repository [15], *Female pelvis* and *Knot rings* obtained in [16], and *Nefertiti* from [17]. All values of speedup, time or other measures shown in this paper are the average value for these five 3D models.

As an example, Fig. 1 shows the *Happy Buddha* model and also the *Female Pelvis* model, and their curve-skeletons calculated at a high resolution of 512 x 512 x 512 voxels.

Table 2 summarizes the main data obtained when executing the 3D thinning algorithm. Time is represented in seconds. As could be seen, the improvement when executing on the GPU is impressive. By analyzing the data, when the algorithm runs on the CPU, running time directly depends on the number of iterations. However, when

Fig. 1. Stanford's Happy Buddha and Pelvis voxelized models, and their calculated 3D curve-skeletons

Table 2. Main data and final execution results for the test models at a resolution of 512 x 512 x 512. GTX580 in shared memory preference mode. MACHINE A: CPU Intel i7-920 + GT200 GPU. MACHINE B: CPU Intel Xeon + GF100 GPU.

Model	Initial Voxels	Final Voxels	Itertns.	MACHINE A			MACHINE B		
				CPU Time (s)	GTX295 Time (s)	GTX295 Speedup	CPU Time (s)	GTX580 Time (s)	GTX580 Speedup
Buddha	5,269,400	4,322	65	351.30	14.15	24.83x	376.34	5.19	72.51x
Bunny	20,669,804	7,088	125	676.09	37.24	18.15x	732.95	10.95	66.93x
Pelvis	4,942,014	9,884	102	552.66	28.59	19.33x	596.46	8.13	73.36x
Rings	19,494,912	12,309	59	332.58	24.43	13.61x	353.13	5.70	61.95x
Nefert.	11,205,574	858	53	288.32	12.83	22.47x	307.68	4.47	68.83x

executing on GPU, this fact is not true, e.g. *Knot Rings* model is more time consuming than *Happy Buddha* model, although it implies less iterations. Thus, we conclude that the GPU algorithm is more sensitive to the irregularities and the topology of the model.

In the next section we expose step by step the strategies and their practical implications that we have followed to achieve the optimal results showed in Table 2 with our CUDA implementation of the 3D thinning algorithm. It is important to remark that the single-thread CPU version of the thinning algorithm is the one provided by its authors.

4   Optimization Approaches

In this section we expose step by step the strategies and their practical implications that we have followed to achieve an optimal performance in our CUDA implementation of the 3D thinning algorithm. It is important to remark that as basic thinning CPU algorithm we use the one provided by its authors. In addition, we compile it on 64-bits mode to achieve the better execution time as possible.

4.1   Avoiding Memory Transfers

Input data must be initially transferred from CPU to GPU (global memory) through the PCI Express bus [5]. This bus has a low bandwidth when compared with the speed of the kernel execution, so one fundamental aspect in CUDA programming is to minimize these data transfers [9]. So once the data has been transferred to the device memory, it should not return to the CPU until all required operations and functions are applied. In our first naive CUDA implementation of the thinning algorithm, this fact was not taken into account, since some functions were launched on the GPU device and others on the CPU host, thus transferring several data between host and device. Therefore, the results of this first implementation are very poor, as could be seen in Fig. 4 ("Memory Transfers" speedup). The processing time was even worse than that obtained with the CPU version. This shows that direct implementations of not trivially parallelizable algorithms may initially disappoint the programmers expectations regarding GPU programming. This occurs regardless of the GPU used, which means that optimizations are necessary for this type of algorithms even when running on the latest CUDA architecture.

In our case, as previously mentioned, several intermediate functions, such as obtaining a transformed neighborhood, were initially launched on the CPU. Therefore we must move these CPU operations to the GPU, by transforming them into kernels. This way the memory transfer bottleneck is avoided, achieving a relative speedup of up to 1.43x on the GTX295. A speedup between 1.49x (L1 cache preference) and 1.58x (shared memory preference) is achieved for the GTX580 (see "All processes to GPU" speedup in Fig. 4).

4.2   Kernel Unification and Computational Complexity

As a result of assigning more operations to the GPU we can create several kernels, each one responsible for executing a simple function. Although data transfer to the CPU is not yet necessary, the kernels still need synchronization between them, and this class of synchronization needs the use of the slow global memory, by reading/writing from/to it. So this division of kernels does not seem to be a good idea.

In our case study, the first kernel marks whether voxels are border points or not, so that the second kernel can obtain and transform their neighborhoods. The third kernel detects which voxels are simple points, so the fourth kernel can delete them. The computational requirements of each kernel are very low (conditional sentences and a few basic arithmetic operations), therefore, the delays when reading from global memory cannot be completely hidden. It seems clear that this kernel division (a valid solution in a CPU scope) is not efficient and prevents a good general acceleration value. So we restructured the algorithm by unifying the first three kernels in only one, thus generating a new general kernel with an increased computational complexity, thus hiding the latency in accessing global memory. The kernel unification usually implies a higher register pressure. We take this fact into account later, when discussing the MP occupancy and resources in section 4.5.

The practical result for the GTX295 is a speedup increase of up to 5.52x over the previous CUDA version. The cumulative speedup so far is up to 7.89x over the original CPU algorithm. Higher speedup rates are achieved for the GTX580, due to the minimization of global memory read/write instructions and the automatic cache system. A speedup of 18.3x over the previous version is achieved, nearly 29x respect the CPU version (see "Kernel Unification" speedup in Fig. 4). For the first time we have overcome the performance of the original CPU algorithm for all our test models and model sizes.

4.3   Constant Memory

Constant memory is a 64 KB (see Table 1) cached read-only memory, both on GT200 and GF100 architectures, so it cannot be written from the kernels. Therefore, constant memory is ideal for storing data-items that remain unchanged along the whole algorithm execution and are accessed many times from the kernels [6]. Also, as a new improvement incorporated on the GF100 architecture, the static parameters of the kernel are automatically stored in constant memory. In our 3D thinning algorithm we store in constant memory the offset values indicating the position of the neighbours of each voxel. These values depend on the dimension of the model and do not change along the thread execution, so are ideal for constant memory. These values are accessed while checking if a voxel belongs to the 3D model boundary and when operating over a border point to obtain its neighbourhood. Thus, global memory bandwidth is freed. Our tests indicate that the algorithm is 11% to 18% faster, depending on the model size and the GPU used, when using constant memory (see "Constant Memory Usage" speedup in Fig. 4).

4.4   Shared Memory Usage

Avoiding memory transfers between devices and hiding the access memory latency time are important factors in improving CUDA algorithms, whatever GPU architecture, as outlined in sections 4.1 and 4.2. But focusing only on the GT200 architecture, the fundamental optimization strategy is, according to our experience, to use the CUDA memory hierarchy properly. This is mainly achieved by using shared memory instead of global memory where possible [1,5,9]. However, the use of shared memory on the newest GF100 GPUs may not be so important, as would be seen later.

Shared memory is a fast on-chip memory widely used to share data between threads within the same thread-block [8]. It can also be used as a manual cache for global memory data by storing values that are repeatedly used by thread-blocks. We will see that this last use is not so important when working on GF100-based GPUs, since the GF100 architecture provides a real cache hierarchy.

The access time to shared memory is at least 100x faster than to global memory, but it is a very limited resource (see Table 1). It could be dynamically allocated during the kernel launch, but not during the kernel execution. This fact avoids that each thread within a thread-block could allocate the exact amount of memory that it needs. Therefore, it is necessary to allocate memory to all the threads within a thread-block, although not all of these threads will use this memory. Several memory positions are wasted in this case.

Based on our experience we recommend the following steps for an optimal use of shared memory: A) identify the data that are reused (data-sharing case) or accessed repeatedly (cache-system case) by some threads, B) calculate how much shared memory is required, globally (data-sharing case) or by each individual thread (cache-system case), and C) determine the number of threads per block that maximizes the MP occupancy (more in section 4.5).

Focusing now on our case study, the neighborhood of each voxel is accessed repeatedly so it can be stored in shared memory to achieve a fast access to it. This way, each

Table 3. Block size and speedup relationship on the GTX295. Average values for the five test models.

Block Size	Thread Slots	Warp Slots	Warp Multiple	$Occupancy_T$	Divergent Branch	Throughput	Serialized Warps	Speedup
128	512	16	Yes	50.00%	**3.67%**	1.328 GB/s	**20,932**	13.82x
149	596	20	No	58.20%	3.75%	**2.198 GB/s**	23,106	**15.03x**
288	576	18	Yes	56.25%	3.89%	1.350 GB/s	25,074	14.15x
301	602	20	No	**58.79%**	3.77%	2.017 GB/s	27,758	14.56x
302	302	10	No	29.49%	3.79%	1.231 GB/s	30,644	10.24x

thread needs to allocate 1 byte per neighbour. This amount of allocated shared memory and the selected number of threads per thread-block determine the total amount of shared memory that each thread-block allocates.

We have tested our 3D thinning algorithm by first storing each 26- neighborhood in global memory and then storing it in shared memory. Testing on the GTX295 with our five test models, a relative speedup of more than 2x when using shared memory is achieved. On the contrary, for the GTX580, the relative speedup is minimal, achieving only a poor acceleration of around 10%, with shared memory preference mode. This indicates that the Fermi's automatic cache system works fine in our case. In other algorithms, e.g. those in which not many repeated and consecutive memory accesses are performed, a better speedup could be obtained by implementing a hand-managed cache instead of using a hardware-managed one. If the L1 cache preference mode is selected, using shared memory decreases the performance on a 25%, because less shared memory space is available. Despite this fact, the use of shared memory is still interesting because it releases global memory space, since the neighbourhood could be directly transformed in shared memory without modifying the original model, which permits us to apply new improvements later.

The overall improvement of the algorithm, up to 13.94x on GTX295 and 36.17x on GTX580, is shown in Fig. 4 (see "Shared Memory Usage" speedup)

4.5 MP Occupancy

Once the required amount of shared memory is defined, the number of threads per block that generates the better performance has to be set. The term MP occupancy refers to the degree of utilization of each device multiprocessor. It is limited by several factors. Occupancy is usually obtained as:

$$Occupancy_W = \frac{ResidentBlocks * \lceil BlockSize/WarpSize \rceil}{MaxMPWarps}$$

This estimation is the ratio of the number of active warps per multiprocessor to the maximum number of active warps. In this expression, empty threads generated to complete the warp when the block size is not a multiple of the warp size are considered as processing threads. We calculate MP occupancy based on the total resident threads as follows:

$$Occupancy_T = \frac{ResidentBlocks * BlockSize}{MaxMPThreads}$$

This expression offers a most reliable value of the real thread slot percentage used to process the data. We have considered both expressions in our analysis for the sake of a more detailed study. It is important to note that if the block size is a multiple of the warp size both expressions return the same value. With respect the parameters, $BlockSize$ represents the selected number of threads per thread-block. The $WarpSize$ parameter is the number of threads which forms a warp, $MaxMPThreads$ and $MaxMPWarps$ is the maximum number of threads and warps, respectively, which a MP can simultaneously manage, and $ResidentBlocks$ represents the number of blocks that simultaneously reside in an MP. We can obtain this last value as:

$$ResidentBlocks = min(\lfloor \frac{MaxMPThreads}{BlockSize} \rfloor, \lfloor \frac{MaxMPWarps}{\lceil BlockSize/WarpSize \rceil} \rfloor,$$
$$MaxMPBlocks)$$

$MaxMPBlocks$ represents the maximum number of thread-blocks that can simultaneously reside in each MP. All these static parameters are listed in Table 1. Obviously, if $MaxMPThreads/WarpSize$ is equal to $WarpSize$ (like for the GTX295), the second mathematical expression of $ResidentBlocks$ is not necessary.

But the block size is not the only factor that could affect the occupancy value. Each kernel uses some MP resources as registers or shared memory (see previous section), and these resources are limited [5,8]. Obviously, an MP occupancy of 1 (100%) is always desired, but sometimes it is preferable to lose occupancy if we want to take advantage of these other GPU resources.

Focusing now on registers, each MP has a limit of 16 K registers (on 1.x devices) or 32 K registers (on 2.x devices). Therefore, if we want to obtain a full occupancy then each thread can use up to 16 registers (16 K / 1024 = 16 registers). On the other hand, on the GTX580 each thread can use up to 21 registers (32 K / 1536 = 21.333 registers). Taking this into account, we calculate the number of simultaneous MP resident blocks in a more realistic way as follows:

$$ResidentBlocks = min(\lfloor \frac{MaxMPThreads}{BlockSize} \rfloor, \lfloor \frac{MaxMPWarps}{\lceil BlockSize/WarpSize \rceil} \rfloor,$$
$$\lfloor \frac{TotalSM}{RequiredSM} \rfloor, \lfloor \frac{MaxThreadReg}{RequiredReg * BlockSize} \rfloor, MaxMPBlocks)$$

Where $TotalSM$ represents the total amount of shared memory per MP; $RequiredSM$ is the amount of shared memory allocated in each thread-block; $MaxThreadReg$ is the number of MP registers; and $RequiredReg$ is the number of registers that each thread within a block needs.

In summary, there are three factors limiting the MP occupancy: (1) the size of each thread-block, (2) the required shared memory per block, and (3) the number of registers used per thread. It is therefore necessary to analyze carefully the configuration which maximizes the occupancy. To check the exact amount of shared memory and registers used by blocks and threads, we can use the NVIDIA Visual Profiler (NVP) tool [18], or we can set the '–ptxas-options=-v' option in the CUDA compiler. NVP also directly reports the MP occupancy value as the expression called $Occupancy_W$ in this paper.

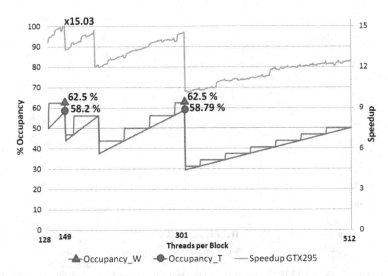

Fig. 2. Analysis of GTX295 MP Occupancy and the speedup achieved with different "threads per block" values. Average values for the five test models.

In our case study, when compiling for devices with a compute capability of 1.x, our threads never individually surpass 16 used registers (the highest value if we want to maximize occupancy on the GTX295), so this factor is obviated when calculating the number of resident bocks for this device. But when compiling the same kernel for 2.x devices, each thread needs 24 registers. This is because these devices use general-purpose registers for addresses, while 1.x devices have dedicated address registers for load and store instructions. Therefore, registers will be a limit factor when working on the GTX580 GPU.

If the block size increases, the required shared memory grows linearly because allocated shared memory depends directly on the number of threads launched. However, the MP occupancy varies irregularly when block size increases, as shown in Fig. 2 and Fig. 3. $Occupancy_W$ is always equal or greater than $Occupancy_T$ because $Occupancy_W$ gives equal weight to empty threads and real processing threads. However, $Occupancy_T$ only considers those threads that really work on the 3D model.

In brief, the amount of shared memory and the number of required registers determine the resident blocks, this number of blocks and the block size determine how many warps and threads are simultaneously executed in each MP, and the occupancy is then obtained.

Focusing on the algorithm running on the GTX295, the MP occupancy is maximized (62.5%) when a value of 301 threads per block is set. A block size of 149 obtains equal $Occupancy_W$ percentage, but 301 threads per block configuration also maximizes $Occupancy_T$ (58.79%). It seems clear that one extra thread in a block could be a very important factor. In our example, if we select 302 threads instead of 301, occupancy is reduced from 58.79% to 29.49%, which generates a reduction of the algorithm's performance. In the literature this is sometimes called a performance cliff [5], because a slight increase in resource usage can degenerate into a huge reduction in performance.

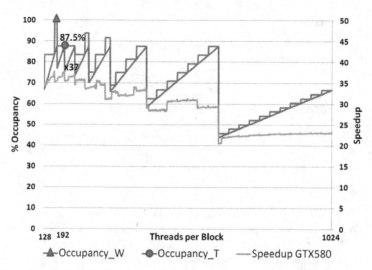

Fig. 3. Analysis of GTX580 MP Occupancy and the speedup achieved with different "threads per block" values. Average values for the five test models.

The highest occupancy is no guaranty for obtaining the best overall performance. Therefore, we perform an experimental test on the device for determining exactly the best number of threads per block for our algorithm. The analysis of the MP occupancy factor obtains a set of values that would lead to a good performance for our kernel execution. But if we want to maximize the speedup it is necessary to take into account other parameters. Table 3 shows, for different block sizes, the values obtained for the main parameters to be considered on the GTX295 GPU. In this table, Divergent Branch represents the percentage of points of divergence with respect to the total amount of branches (the lower the better). Overall Throughput is computed as (total bytes read + total bytes written) / (GPU time) and refers to the overall global memory access throughput in GB/s (the higher the better).

The value Serialized Warps counts the number of warps that are serialized because an address conflict occurs when accessing to either shared memory or constant memory (the lower the better). All these parameters are obtained with the NVP.

Table 3 also shows that the highest speedup is achieved with a configuration of 149 threads per block. Although that row does not have the highest occupancy value, it has a low number of Serialized Warps and also the highest memory throughput value. It is important to note that the achieved speedups are directly related to its corresponding memory throughput. This fact indicates that the algorithm is clearly memory bound, as previously mentioned. The best values of Divergent Branch and Serialized Warps appear with a size of 128 threads, but its low occupancy and throughput prevent its achieving a maximum speedup.

A very similar reasoning could be done by analyzing for the GTX580 with the shared memory preference mode. In Fig. 3 are represented the theoretical $Occupancy_T$ and $Occupancy_W$ trends.

According to our theoretical occupancy calculations, a block-size of 192 threads, which is a warp-size multiple, seems to be the better configuration, achieving an 87.5%

of $Occupancy_T$ and $Occupancy_W$. In fact, the best speedup is achieved with this last value. By selecting the L1 cache preference mode, we realize another equivalent analysis, concluding that for this case 631 threads per block is the ideal value.

Figure 2 and Fig. 3 also shows the evolution of the speedup when selecting different block sizes. These lines follow the same trend as the $Occupancy_T$ line, especially in Fig. 2, demonstrating that this is a good parameter to take into account when setting the thread-block size. The irregularities of the speedup line are due to the influence of the other parameters shown in Table 3.

Finally, "Block Size (Occupancy)" value in Fig. 4 represents the achieved speedup when we select: 149 threads per block instead of 128 for the GTX295, 192 threads per block instead of 149 for the GTX580 in shared memory preference mode, and 631 threads per block instead of 149 for the GTX 580 in L1 cache preference mode.

4.6 Device Memory. Buffers

At this moment of the programming process we have two kernels in our parallel CUDA algorithm: the first kernel determines which voxels are simple points and labels them, and the second one deletes all simple points, so we are performing some extra and inefficient writes to global memory. If the first kernel directly delete simple points, the final result would not be right because each kernel requires the original value of its neighbors. We can duplicate the structure which represents the 3D voxelized model taking advantage of the high amount of global memory present in GPU devices. Therefore, at this time we also beneficiates of the use of shared memory on both GPUs, since more global memory is released. In this way, a double-buffer technique is implemented and only one kernel must be launched.

This kernel directly deletes simple points by reading the neighborhood from the front-buffer and writing the result in the back-buffer. This ensures a valid final result and, according to our tests, improves the algorithm's performance. This improvement is greater if the voxelized 3D object has a high number of voxels. In the case of our 3D models, this optimization achieves an average improvement of 25% on the GTX295, and an acceleration of 52% and 83%, depending on the selected mode, on the GTX580 (see Double Buffer speedup in Fig. 4).

4.7 Other Strategies

There are other optimization strategies that could improve our parallel algorithm. One of them is to avoid that threads within the same warp follow different execution paths (divergence). Unfortunately, in our case study it is very difficult to ensure this because the processing of a voxel by a thread depends directly on whether the voxel is a border point or not, whether it is a simple point or not, or if the voxel belongs to the object or not. However, empty points and object points managed by a warp are consecutive except when in-out or out-in transition regarding the object boundary occurs.

This implies that the problem of divergence does not greatly affect our algorithm. In fact, as shown in Table 3, the percentage of divergent branches is quite low. However, it is interesting to try different combinations with our conditional sentences to get better speedup.

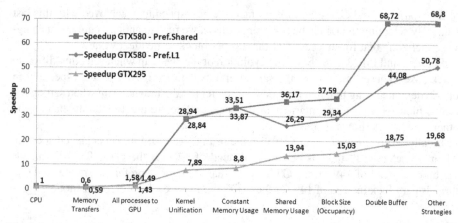

Fig. 4. Summary of the main optimization strategies applied and their achieved speedups. Average values for the five test models with size of 512 x 512 x 512.

It is also recommended to apply the technique of loop unrolling, thus avoiding some intermediate calculations which decrease the MP performance [8]. Shared memory is physically partitioned into some memory. To achieve a full performance of shared memory, each thread within a half-warp has to read data from a different bank, or all these threads have to read data from the same bank. If one of these two options is not satisfied then a partition camping problem occurs that decreases the performance [19].

By applying all these enhancements, our algorithm obtains a final speedup of up to 19.68x for the GTX295. For the GTX580, with the L1 cache preference mode, a final speedup of 50.78x is achieved. This GPU achieves a high speedup of 68.8x with the shared memory preference mode (see Other Strategies speedup in Fig. 4). It is important to note that both CPU and GPU applications are compiled in 64-bit mode.

5   Conclusions

We have detailed in a practical way the main CUDA optimization strategies that allow achieving high acceleration rates in a 3D thinning algorithm for obtaining the curve-skeleton of a 3D model. Two different GPU architectures have been used to test the implications of each optimization, the NVIDIA GT200 architecture and the new Fermi GF100. Unlike typical CUDA programming guides, we have faced to a real, complex and data-sharing problem that shares characteristics with many algorithms in the areas of volume modelling or image analysis.

We conclude that parallelizing a linear data-sharing algorithm by using CUDA and achieving high speedup values is not a trivial task. The first fundamental task when optimizing parallel algorithms is to redesign the algorithm to fit it to the GPU device by minimizing memory transfers between host and device, reducing synchronization points and maximizing parallel thread execution. Secondly, especially when working with GT200-based GPUs, the programmer must have a deep knowledge of the memory hierarchy of the GPU. This allows the programmer to take advantage of the fast shared memory and the cached constant memory. Also, the hardware model must be taken into account in order to maximize the processors occupancy, the influence of divergent paths to the thread execution, or which types of instructions have to be avoided.

It has been demonstrated that the use of shared memory as a manual cache may not be a fundamental task (it depends on the algorithm characteristics) with the new GF100 GPUs, due to the presence of a new memory hierarchy and its automatic cache system. Anyway, shared memory still is a faster mechanism necessary to share data between threads within a thread-block. The use of shared memory also allows the programmer to release global memory space, which can be used for the implementation of other optimizations. Obviously, if we decide to use shared memory in our algorithm with the GF100 architecture, we must select the shared memory preference mode to achieve the highest speedup rate. The rest of improvements exposed along this paper result in a speedup increase in both GT200 and GF100 based GPUs, so it is clear that the CUDA programmers have to apply them even if they only work with the latest Fermi GPUs.

We have shown the impressive speedup values that our GF100 GPU achieves with respect to the GT200. This is mainly due, in our case, to the high number of cores, a higher amount of simultaneous executing threads per MP, and the real cache L1 and L2 hierarchy present on the GT100 architecture.

A summary of the main optimization strategies detailed in this paper and their corresponding average speedup rate are presented in Fig. 4. These results show that very good speedups can be achieved in a data-sharing algorithm through the particularized application of optimizations and the reorganization of the original CPU algorithm.

Acknowledgements. This work has been partially supported by the University of Jaén, the Caja Rural de Jaén, the Andalusian Government and the European Union (via ERDF funds) through the research projects UJA2009/13/04 and PI10-TIC-5807.

References

1. NVIDIA: NVIDIA CUDA C Programming Guide, Version 4.2 (2012),
   http://developer.download.nvidia.com/compute/DevZone/docs/html/C/doc/CUDA_C_Programming_Guide.pdf
2. Khronos OpenCL Working Group: The OpenCL Specification, Version 1.2 (2012),
   http://www.khronos.org/opencl
3. Kong, J., Dimitrov, M., Yang, Y., Liyanage, J., Cao, L., Staples, J., Mantor, M., Zhou, H.: Accelerating MATLAB Image Processing Toolbox Functions on GPUs. In: Proc. of the Third Workshop on General-Purpose Computation on Graphics Processing Units (GPGPU-3), Pittsburgh, PA, USA (March 2010)
4. NVIDIA: NVIDIA CUDA Best Practices Guide v4.1 (2012),
   http://developer.download.nvidia.com/compute/DevZone/docs/html/C/doc/CUDA_C_Best_Practices_Guide.pdf
5. Kirk, D.B., Hwu, W.W.: Programming Massively Parallel Processors. Hands-on Approach. Morgan Kaufmann Publishers, Burlington (2010)
6. Sanders, J., Kandrot, E.: CUDA by Example. An Introduction to General-Purpose GPU Programming. Addison-Wesley (2010)
7. Huang, Q., Huang, Z., Werstein, P., Purvis, M.: GPU as a General Purpose Computing Resource. In: Proc. of the International Conference on Parallel and Distributed Computing. Applications and Technologies, pp. 151–158 (2008)

8. Ryoo, S., Rodrigues, C.I., Baghsorkhi, S.S., Stone, S.S., Kirk, D.B., Hwu, W.W.: Optimization Principles and Application Performance Evaluation of a Multithreaded GPU Using CUDA. In: Proc. of the 13th ACM SIGPLAN Symposium on Principles and Practice of Parallel Programming (2008)
9. Feinbure, F., Troger, P., Polze, A.: Joint Forces: From Multithreaded Programming to GPU Computing. IEEE Software 28(3), 51–57 (2011)
10. Wittenbrink, C.M., Kilgariff, E., Prabhu, A.: Fermi GF100 GPU Architecture. IEEE Micro 31, 50–59 (2011)
11. Reyes, R., de Sande, F.: Optimize or wait? Using llc fast-prototyping tool to evaluate CUDA optimizations. In: Proceedings of 19th International Euromicro Conference on Parallel, Distributed and Network-Based Processing, pp. 257–261 (2011)
12. Torres, Y., González-Escribano, A., Llanos, D.R.: Understanding the Impact of CUDA Tuning Techniques for Fermi. In: Proceedings of the 2011 International Conference on High Performance Computing and Simulation, HPCS, Number 5999886, pp. 631–639 (2011)
13. Cornea, N., Silver, D., Min, P.: Curve-skeleton Properties, Applications and Algorithms. IEEE Transactions on Visualization and Computer Graphics 13, 530–548 (2007)
14. Palágyi, K., Kuba, A.: A Parallel 3D 12-Subiteration Thinning Algorithm. Graphical Models and Image Processing 61, 199–221 (1999)
15. Stanford University: The Stanford 3D Scanning Repository (2012),
    http://graphics.stanford.edu/data/3Dscanrep
16. AIM: AIM@SHAPE REPOSITORY (2012), http://shapes.aimatshape.net
17. 3DVIA: 3DVIA REPOSITORY (2012), http://www.3dvia.com
18. NVIDIA: Compute Visual Profiler, User Guide (2011),
    http://developer.download.nvidia.com/compute/DevZone/docs/html/C/doc/Compute_Visual_Profiler_User_Guide.pdf
19. Price, D.K., Humphrey, J.R., Spagnoli, K.E., Paolini, A.L.: Analyzing the Impact of Data Movement on GPU Computations. In: Proc. of the SPIE - The International Society for Optical Engineering, vol. 7705 (2010)

Distance-Aware Bimanual Interaction for Large High-Resolution Displays

Anke Lehmann and Oliver Staadt

University of Rostock, Institute for Computer Science,
Albert-Einstein-Str. 22, 18051 Rostock, Germany
{anke.lehmann,oliver.staadt}@uni-rostock.de
http://vcg.informatik.uni-rostock.de

Abstract. Large high-resolution displays allow users to perceive the global context of information from a distance and to explore detailed information at close-up range. This enables the user to interact with displayed content at various distances. In this paper we introduce bimanual interaction techniques that enable users to manipulate virtual content with the suitable accuracy. The *separated-cursors* technique differentiates between the manipulation tasks while the *connected-cursors* technique allows performing the manipulation tasks simultaneously. We consider three relative mapping methods which map the physical hand motion to relative virtual object motion depending on the user–display distance (*interaction scaling*). Mapping is based on a continuous distance-related mapping factor or predefined mapping factors. We evaluated the separated-cursors technique with and without interaction scaling. The explorative study indicates that a distance-related continuous mapping factor performs better than predefined mapping factors. Furthermore, the participants often needed fewer object selections to sort objects with interaction scaling.

Keywords: 2D manipulation technique, large display, 3D interaction, distance-adapted.

1 Introduction

Large high-resolution displays (LHRD) combine a large physical display area with high pixel density. On the one hand LHRDs allow users to perceive the global context of complex information by simply stepping away. On the other hand the users are able to step closer to the display to see detailed information. In this context, interaction techniques for LHRDs should support mobility, accuracy and easy availability to carry out interaction tasks.

The interaction techniques described in this paper are developed in the context of our Tele-Presence System comprising a 24-panel LCD wall [1]. The setting allows us to display remote users at a natural scale, at a sufficient resolution, and to share interactive high-resolution content. For collaboration work, a shared virtual space with variable depth is located between the local and remote user.

For this environment we require intuitive user interaction that supports the large interaction volume in front of the LCD wall. The user should be able to carry out distant selection and manipulation as well as manipulation with high precision at close range.

G. Csurka et al. (Eds.): VISIGRAPP 2012, CCIS 359, pp. 97–111, 2013.

In general the user's distance in front of a large display is considered for selection and navigation tasks in previous work [2][3][4].

In our ongoing work we investigate how the user benefits from the user–display distance for simple 2D manipulation tasks. The main contribution of our work is the interaction scaling approach that allows the user to manipulate 2D objects with the appropriate accuracy in varying distance. Therefore, we explored different relative mapping functions which map the physical absolute hands motion to virtual relative objects motion supporting desired precision.

We developed two bimanual interaction techniques for 2D object manipulation: *separated-cursors* and *connected-cursors* method.

In explorative studies we evaluated the distance-adapted 2D manipulation techniques with different mapping functions. In a pre-study both interaction techniques are tested with a continuous mapping and a nonlinear mapping approach. Based on these results we re-adjusted the mapping approaches. In an explorative study, we evaluated the separated-cursors technique with revised continuous mapping and zone mapping approaches.

This paper extends our previous work [5].

2   Related Work

In large high-resolution display environments interaction techniques have to be customized that the user is able to interact with virtual content from various distances.

For instance, extended laser pointer techniques allow the user to interact with (physically) unreachable objects and small objects in large display environments [6][7][8][9]. Ahlborn et al. [7] have developed an effective detection algorithm of laser pointer interaction on large-scale display environments that works at various lighting conditions. Using a predictive searching reduces the amount of image processing to detect the laser pointer dot. Using infrared laser pointer techniques [10][11] the on-screen cursor is invisible, thus the problem of hand jitter and latency are hidden from the user. Those techniques use a visual representation of the invisible laser dot (e.g., hotspot, visual cursor). Vogel and Balakrishnan [4] investigated techniques for pointing and clicking using only the user's hand. For example, they developed a hybrid pointing technique that uses ray casting for coarse pointing interaction and relative pointing for more precise interaction.

Another challenge is the manipulation of virtual objects on large workspaces. In [12] dragging techniques use an acceleration method to overcome large distances. Grossmann et al. [13] provide a two-handed interaction technique for the creation of 3D models by drawing 2D profile curves on large displays. In [14] camera-equipped mobile phones are utilized by the users to interact with large displays. The virtual objects have been manipulated based on the motion gestures that are performed by the user with his mobile phone. The CGLXTouch project [15] supports multitouch device interaction by multiple users. A low-resolution screen image of the display wall is displayed on the multitouch device corresponding to the available pixel resolution of the device. Thus, users can indirectly manipulate data on the ultra-high-resolution display via multitouch gestures on their devices concurrently.

Previous work [2][3][4][16] has shown that the current distance of a user to a large display affects the usability and the user's performance. For example, when stepping closer to LHRDs it is helpful to refine the selection radius or to adjust the navigation speed. Kopper et al. [17] allow the user to switch between absolute and relative mapping for pointing interaction. Furthermore, the user can control a zoom window. It provides a magnified view of objects, where the user can precisely interact.

Multiscale interaction by Peck et al. [3] is a 3D interaction technique that uses the benefit of physical navigation in front of a large high-resolution display. Depending on the user's distance from the interaction object, he controls the scale of interaction in addition to the scale of perception. For example, when the user changes his physical position relative to the display, the multiscale cursor is changed, which rescales the data on the display interactively. The interactive public ambient display [18] utilizes the user distance to control public and personal information presentation. In [19] the user distance controls the virtual light-source position that affects the interactive user's shadow cast.

Our objective is to find a general approach for scalable interaction that adjusts the interaction precision to the user's position in front of a large high-resolution display.

3   Interaction Scaling

Interaction scaling means to adjust the technical precision of user interaction depending on the user's distance to the LHRD. Our objective is to find an adequate mapping of the user's movements to virtual movements. Interaction scaling allows the user to manipulate high-resolution content with the appropriate accuracy in varying distance.

We propose a customized mapping of the gesture to the virtual cursor movements taking into consideration the user's distance to the LHRD. The current distance is calculated using the average of the distance of both hands. For example, if the user stands farther away from the display he should be able to move an object across a large LCD wall with a small gesture. In contrast, if he steps closer to the display, the virtual object should be moved with high accuracy by using large physical movements.

In our initial experiments, we consider three relative mapping functions: continuous mapping, nonlinear mapping and zone mapping. The mapping functions are applied to the virtual cursors as visual representation of the user's hand. We use a nonisomorphic mapping technique meaning that users are able to manipulate objects quite differently than in real world. In contrast, the isomorphic method uses a strict one-to-one correspondence between hand movements in the physical and virtual world [20].

The *continuous mapping* function applies a linear factor to the physical movements. The mapping factor is equal to one at middle distance of the interaction space. The factor decreases linearly closer to the LHRD and grows linearly with increasing distance (see Figure 1, left). We use a simple linear equation to calculate the mapping factor (mf) depending on the current user–display distance (udd); m and b are designate constants:

$$mf = f(udd) = m \, udd + b. \tag{1}$$

For *nonlinear mapping* the interaction space in front of the display is divided into three regions (see Figure 1, middle). At distant and close-up range we use predefined mapping

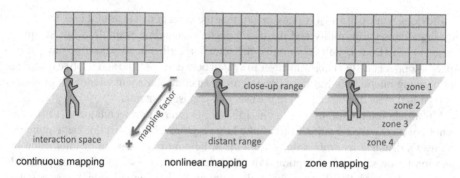

Fig. 1. Interaction scaling with different mapping functions: a) continuous mapping, b) nonlinear mapping and c) zone mapping

factors and in between the factor is linearly interpolated. This function uses the same linear equation (1), but the mapping factor grows faster with increasing distance than at continuous mapping.

For *zone mapping* we divide the interaction space into four zones with predefined mapping factors: close-up range, mid-range, distant, and farther region (see Figure 1, right). With zone mapping the mapping factor is increased in each region away from the display. There is no distance where the physical movements are equal to virtual movements as opposed to continuous or nonlinear mapping. In the first two regions (zone 1 and zone 2) the mapping factor is less than one. In these regions the user is able to manipulate objects precisely. In the other two regions (zone 3 and zone 4) the user handles object with coarse precision. Here, the mapping factor is greater than one.

Interaction scaling just manipulates the 2D position of the virtual cursor. The distance-related mapping factor is multiplied by the absolute hand position to determine the corresponding virtual cursor position. The parameters for the manipulation tasks (i.e., scaling, rotation, translation) are calculated by the virtual cursors behavior. Thus, the mapping factor influences the precision of the manipulation indirectly. For instance, similar to common two finger multitouch gestures, the scaling factor is calculated based on the distance change between both cursors. The rotation angle is computed from the angular rotation of the line between both cursors.

We developed two bimanual interaction techniques for 2D object manipulation that support the interaction scaling: *separated-cursors* and *connected-cursors*. We use tracked wireless input devices with multiple buttons to simplify the triggering of user interaction. Thus, the user is able to point at an object, push the button to start the interaction, and release the button to complete the interaction.

The *separated-cursors* technique differentiates the user's hands between dominant and nondominant hand. The dominant hand is used to select and move an object. The nondominant hand is used to scale and rotate the selected object (see Figure 2). The user switches the manipulation mode (i.e., select/move and scale/rotate) by a trigger. During scale/rotate mode the dominant hand's virtual cursor is fixed and the corresponding hand motion is ignored.

The *connected-cursors* technique uses an additional midpoint cursor that is located between both virtual cursors. This midpoint cursor is used to select an object. In order

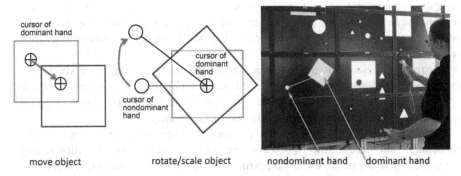

move object   rotate/scale object   nondominant hand   dominant hand

Fig. 2. Illustration of 2D object manipulation with separated-cursors technique, the crosshair cursor indicates the selected object

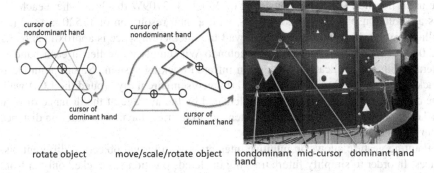

rotate object   move/scale/rotate object   nondominant mid-cursor dominant hand
                                                hand

Fig. 3. Illustration of 2D object manipulation with connected-cursors technique, the crosshair cursor indicates the selected object

to translate a selected object the virtual cursors have to move to the desired direction simultaneously. Increasing or decreasing the distance between the cursors resizes a virtual object. To rotate an object the user moves his hands in a fashion similar to turning a steering wheel. The object manipulation is illustrated in Figure 3. The connected-cursors method allows the user to select and manipulate a virtual object in a continuous manner without changing the interaction mode. Thus, the manipulation tasks are performed simultaneously.

4   Exploratory Study

We conducted an experiment to evaluate our interaction scaling techniques for large high-resolution displays. Our hypothesis is that interaction scaling improves the user performance compared to manipulation tasks that do not exploit the current user distance to the large display wall.

In a preliminary study we tested our bimanual interaction techniques (separated-cursors and connected-cursors) with two relative mapping functions (continuous mapping and nonlinear mapping), as described in Section 3. Based on these results we readjust the experiment and performed an explorative user study. Here, we investigated one interaction technique (separated-cursors) with two mapping functions of interaction scaling (continuous mapping and zone mapping).

The primary function of the explorative study is to discover parameters, which affect the application of interaction scaling for 2D manipulation tasks. Using these results we are able to develop a suitable interaction scaling depending on the LHRD setup and manipulation task in order to improve the user performance.

We implemented a 2D puzzle solver application to compare the user performance (e.g., task completion time, number of object selection) with and without interaction scaling. We use OpenGL for rendering and the Vrui toolkit for device and display handling[1].

4.1 Apparatus

We use a flat tiled LCD wall consisting of 24 DELL 2709W displays, where each tile has a resolution of 1920 x 1200 pixels, with a total resolution of 11520 x 4800 (55 million pixels). In front of the display wall the interaction space is approximately 3.7 x 2.0 x 3.5 meter. The user holds a Nintendo Wii remote controller in each hand to interact with the application. We use an infrared tracking system (Naturalpoint Opti-Track TrackingTools) with 12 cameras arranged semicircularly around the LCD wall. The current user–display distance is calculated by the average of the distance of both tracked input devices. The tracking system setup restricts the user interaction distance from 40 centimeters to 3 meters.

Pointing gesture allows an intuitive interaction with virtual objects at different distances. In order to simplify future tracking the hands position are tracked only in front of the LHRD and we do not consider the orientation of the hands or input devices. The hands' positions are projected orthogonally on the screen. Therefore, 3D position detection is quite possible by various optical tracking methods.

After a while a drift arises between absolute hand motion and relative cursor movements by using interaction scaling. Since the mapping factor is multiplied by the absolute hand position to determine the virtual relative cursor position. For this reason, the user can trigger a reset of the virtual cursors position corresponding to the hands position.

Since we use an LCD wall with bezels, the puzzle application is configured in such a way that no virtual content is occluded by the bezels. The virtual objects are limited by a minimum and maximum size (range size 1cm–50cm). The size limits were determined experimentally and the virtual objects are visible at distance. The virtual objects are generated with random size and position at application start without overlapping. The target objects will always be in the same place on the display and be of the same size.

4.2 Previous Study

In a pre-study we tested our 2D manipulation techniques with two distance-adapted mapping functions: continuous and nonlinear mapping.

---

[1] http://idav.ucdavis.edu/~okreylos/ResDev/Vrui/index.html

We developed a simple puzzle solver application where the user has to manipulate 2D objects with respect to position, size and orientation to fit into their corresponding 2D target (see Figure 2 and Figure 3). The user has to sort three 2D objects (i.e., square, circle, triangle) to solve the task. Therefore, the user selects an object onto his virtual cursor by pressing the device button on his dominant hand. At separated-cursors technique he can switch to scale/rotate mode by pressing the device button on his nondominant hand. We tested the interaction techniques with three different mapping functions – the described continuous and nonlinear mapping and for the purpose of comparison a static mapping function. The continuous mapping function uses a linear mapping factor that grows linearly from 0.3 to 3.0 with increasing distance in front of the display. The nonlinear mapping function utilizes a predefined mapping factor in close-up range (0.3) and distant range (3.0). Both regions are 50 centimeters deep. In between the mapping factor grows linearly from 0.3 to 3.0 with increasing distance. The static mapping function uses a mapping factor equal one at any distance, so the physical movements are mapped directly to virtual movements. In the preliminary study we measured the task completion time and the count of cursor resets. Our prediction is the user achieves a shorter task completion time with a distance-adapted mapping factor.

Six male subjects participated the preliminary study and their age ranges from 29 to 53 years. At the beginning the subject performs a five minutes tutorial to practice the interaction tasks with both interaction techniques. Afterwards the evaluation starts. The trial starts with the first object selection, and finishes with the last sorted object. Each subject tested both interaction techniques with three mapping functions and two repetitions (2x3x2 samples per subject).

The results of the separated-cursors technique are the mean task completion time was equal with continuous mapping (mean: 38 seconds, mean deviation: 7 seconds) and static mapping (mean: 37 seconds, mean deviation: 3 seconds), whereas the subjects achieved a larger mean task time (mean: 56 seconds, mean deviation: 24 seconds) at nonlinear mapping. In contrast, for connected-cursors technique the shortest mean task completion time was generated with static mapping (mean: 33 seconds, mean deviation: 2 seconds). The users needed a larger mean task time at continuous mapping scenario (mean: 45 seconds, mean deviation: 7 seconds) and nonlinear mapping scenario (mean: 45 seconds, mean deviation: 10 seconds). We observed no difference between the number of cursor reset and the interaction techniques. At both interaction techniques the nonlinear mapping required frequent cursor resets.

Besides measured quantitative results, the users were ask to answer some questions which interaction technique they preferred and which combination of technique and mapping scenario. All subjects were able to use both interaction techniques. Three subjects used the interaction scaling intentionally, but no subject was bothered by interaction scaling. Three subjects preferred the separated-cursors technique and the other three subjects favored the connected-cursors technique. Most of the subjects favored the continuous mapping approach over static mapping scenario.

In summary, the preliminary study showed the interaction scaling scenario with nonlinear mapping was not suitable There are three reasons for this drawback. The mapping factor grows too fast in the middle region that was difficult to handle for some subjects.

The user must not to use the entire interaction space by stepping forward or back to solve the task. Additionally, a kind of snapping function helps the user to sort the objects into targets. So the static mapping was utilizable to solve the task quite well.

Our conclusions of this preliminary test are the continuous mapping was suitable but the nonlinear mapping did not work well. Our prediction was not confirmed.

Consequently, we remodeled the nonlinear mapping approach and divided the interaction space into four zones with predefined mapping factors (zone mapping function). To divide the interaction space into five zones then the zones are to small. For continuous mapping function we only revised the limits of the mapping factor. Furthermore, we adjusted some application parameters. For example we use smaller objects and targets that are still visible from a distance. So the user has to use the entire interaction space to manipulate 2D objects. Besides, the tolerance value when an object fits to its target with respect to position, size and orientation was adjusted to 2 millimeters.

4.3   Experiment

In the next explorative study, we investigate one interaction technique (separated-cursors) with two mapping functions of interaction scaling. In this study, we would like to evaluate just one interaction technique to reduce the duration of an experiment for each participant. After initial tests, we expect that the separated-cursors technique provides promising results.

There are two interaction scaling scenarios: continuous mapping and zone mapping. Continuous mapping calculates a mapping factor that increases from 0.2 to 2.5 with increasing distance. The zone mapping scenario divides the interaction space into four even regions with a depth of 60 centimeters. The experimental mapping factors are 0.2 (close-up range), 0.7 (mid-range), 1.5 (distant region), and 2.5 (farther region). For instance, if the user moves his hand 10 centimeters in physical space at close-up range then the corresponding cursor is moved 2 centimeters in virtual space. Conversely, the virtual cursor is moved 25 centimeters while the physical hand movement is 10 centimeters at farther region.

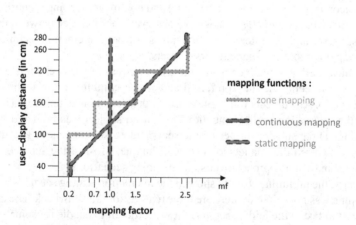

Fig. 4. Illustration of the distance-adapted mapping factor within the three scenarios

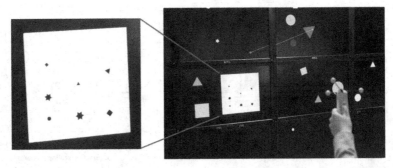

Fig. 5. Application with separated-cursors technique and the experiment's target box

For the purpose of comparison the scenario without interaction scaling uses a static mapping function. Here, the real hand movements are mapped directly to the virtual cursor motions by using a mapping factor of 1.0 at any distance. The used mapping functions are illustrated in Figure 4.

The implemented 2D puzzle solver application is used to compare the task completion time and the number of object selection with and without interaction scaling.

The experiment consists of two parts – a training phase and the test scenarios. At the beginning the subject performs a 10 minutes tutorial to practice the interaction tasks with and without interaction scaling. Afterwards the evaluation starts. The task is to sort eight objects (a couple of triangles, circles, squares, and stars) in the corresponding targets (see Figure 5). In the tutorial the subject sorts three various object types. The objects position, size and orientation are randomized.

The objects have to be manipulated to fit into the targets by dragging, scaling and rotating. Only when the user drops down the object onto the desired target by releasing the selection button, the application will test the fitting accuracy. The object tolerance is two millimeters regarding target size, position and orientation. The tolerance value was determined experimentally in order that users are able to sort objects without frustrating. Object orientation is described by the position of the vertices. If an object is sorted correctly, it will be locked to avoid undesired movements.

The trial starts with the first object selection, and finishes with the last sorted object. The experimental software measures the task completion time in seconds and the number of object selections. After the test, the subject fills in a subjective questionnaire.

We used a within-subject design. The independent variable was the interaction scaling with three levels (static mapping, continuous mapping, zone mapping). The presentation order was counter-balanced. Each participant performed three scenarios with two repetitions. The dependent variable was the task completion time and the number of object selections. The subject was informed whether interaction scaling is active or not.

The explorative study includes 15 participants but the test results of two persons were incomplete. Thus, we can only evaluate the results of 13 subjects. All 13 participants were volunteers that were college students (54%) or staff members (46%) from computer science department. The participants were 31% female and 69% male. The ages of the participants ranged from 20 years old to 39 years old with an average age of 27. The participants had less or no prior experience working with large display environments.

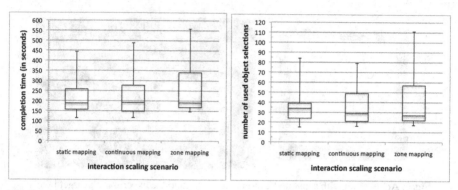

Fig. 6. Boxplots of completion times (left) and used object selections (right) within the scenarios in the first iteration

4.4 Results

We performed a one-way ANOVA to determine statistical significance in the explorative study. The parameter completion time shows no interesting results or no statistically significant differences between scenarios (mean task completion time: $F_{2,36} = 1.526, n.s.$). In general, the completion time is larger at the first run to solve the puzzle. About 10 participants (77%) improved their task completion time in the second run of the scenario. In the static mapping scenario the mean improvement was 47 seconds and in the scenarios with interaction scaling (i.e., continuous mapping and zone mapping) on average 20 seconds. We observed that the presentation order of the scenarios has an influence on the completion time. The puzzle generates a low training curve. The more the participant practiced the puzzle the faster he was able to solve the puzzle without interaction scaling.

There is a correlation between task completion time and number of used object selections. An increase in completion time is combined with a larger number of selections. Sometimes the user needed more time to sort in a specific object. For instance, the subject required 16 object selections to sort in one object (e.g., triangle) and then only 2 or 3 selections to sort another object (e.g., star or square) in the same scenario. We observed that the completion time is a less important parameter of user performance in our experiment.

The measured completion times in the first run are illustrated in Figure 6 (left). In general, the participants were faster on average without interaction scaling, i.e. static mapping scenario (mean: 209 seconds, mean deviation: 68 seconds) in comparison to the continuous mapping scenario (mean: 223 seconds, mean deviation: 85 seconds) and the zone mapping scenario (mean: 268 seconds, mean deviation: 116 seconds).

We identify interesting results in terms of used object selections. In particular, a difference is recognizable between using interaction scaling (i.e., continuous mapping, zone mapping) and without interaction scaling (i.e., static mapping) in the first iteration. The number of used object selections in each scenario is shown in Figure 6 (right). We captured 104 samples (8 objects x 13 subjects) within one run. Table 1 shows that more objects were sorted with two selections with interaction scaling by comparison without interaction scaling.

Table 1. Frequency of used object selections in each scenario in the first run

scenario	static mapping		continuous mapping		zone mapping	
selections	frequency of object selections (absolute and relative values)					
1	10	9.6%	11	10.6%	11	10.6%
2	27	26.0%	34	32.7%	31	29.85%
3	16	15.4%	17	16.3%	13	12.5%
4	15	14.4%	5	4.8%	9	8.6%
5	9	8.6%	7	6.7%	9	8.6%
> 5	27	26.0%	30	28.9%	31	29.85%

Table 2. Frequency of used object selections for each object type and scenario (static mapping (sm), continuous mapping (cm), zone mapping (zm)) in the first run

object type	squares			circles			triangles			stars		
selections	sm	cm	zm	sm	cm	zm	sm	cm	zm	sm	cm	zm
1	2	1	4	3	3	1	1	0	2	4	7	4
2	6	9	6	10	8	10	7	11	9	4	6	6
3	4	7	2	4	5	6	5	2	1	3	3	4
4	6	0	4	3	1	1	3	2	1	3	2	3
> 4	8	9	10	6	9	8	10	11	13	12	8	9

To select an object the user has to move the corresponding virtual cursor of his dominant hand onto the object and press the input device button. The user moves a selected object by moving his dominant hand. If the user presses the input device button of the nondominant hand then the scale/rotate mode is activated until the button is released. This mode allows the user to scale and rotate the selected object by moving his nondominant hand. The object is selected until the button of the dominant hand is released. However, a statistical significance between the scenarios is not present in the explorative study ($F_{2,36} = 0.124, n.s.$).

In addition, Table 2 indicates the difference between the object types. For instance, rotatable objects (e.g., square, triangle, star) were sorted with interaction scaling (continuous mapping and zone mapping) more frequently compared to the scenario with static mapping. We observed that most of subjects moved an object closer to the corresponding target at a distance and then they stepped closer to the display to adjust the object. Using this strategy, the subjects needed only two selections within interaction scaling scenarios. We observed that when participants used more than five object selections they were impatient or they did not go closer to the display.

The repetitions of the scenario with static mapping function more participants were also able to sort the objects with two selections. This suggests that object sorting without interaction scaling is a matter of practice. However, a lot of exercise is not required because the learning curve is low and finished after three solved puzzles. This observation is also reflected by the subjects' comments.

In the zone mapping scenario many users had difficulties solving the puzzle. The precision of the manipulation was very high in the close-up range; the participant took more physical movements to manipulate the objects. In addition, the mapping factor changed rapidly because of the small regions. In the continuous mapping scenario the fluent adjustment was less perceived by the users.

We used predefined mapping factors unequal one for zone mapping that are distinguish from the other mapping functions. However, the results showed a mapping factor of one is quite well for distant region in our setup that we should keep in mind.

Furthermore, we observed that the drift between hands and cursors unfavorably affects the participants. In the zone mapping scenario the difference between absolute hand position and relative cursor position is perceptible by the user, due to the rapid changes of the mapping factor. In the continuous mapping scenario the mapping factor changes continuously. Here, the drift is less pronounced and the users are able to compensate the effect. Users with virtual reality experience were able to compensate the drift and they specifically applied the cursor reset, whereas users without experience in virtual reality environments were dissatisfied with the drift effect.

Experimental tests with a few users indicated that the completion time improves considerably by exercise with interaction scaling. Primarily, users with a natural hand tremor could benefit from interaction scaling. This idea is supported by the participants' comments. For example, eight participants preferred the scenario with interaction scaling. Some users desired to interactively disable the automatic adjustment of the precision. For instance, then the user is able to resize quickly large objects to fit into a small target at close-up range.

5   Conclusions and Future Work

We presented distance-adapted 2D manipulation techniques that adjust the interaction precision to the user's position in front of a large high-resolution display. This interaction scaling allows the user to perform distant selection and manipulation in varying distance with the appropriate accuracy.

The introduced explorative study is supposed to prepare the user study, particularly by developing and attempting the suitable interaction scaling for 2D manipulation tasks. Therefore, we implemented a 2D puzzle solver application to evaluate the user performance (e.g., task completion time, number of used object selections). In a preliminary study we tested both bimanual interaction techniques (separated-cursors, connected-cursors) with two relative mapping functions (continuous mapping, nonlinear mapping) and a static mapping function. Based on these results we readjusted the mapping functions and some experimental application parameters. Afterwards, the separated-cursors technique was evaluated with two mapping functions of interaction scaling (continuous mapping, zone mapping) and without interaction scaling (static mapping).

The explorative study shows that the users accept interaction scaling. In particular, they preferred the higher precision close to the display and the reducing of their hand tremor. The results indicate that a distance-dependent continuous mapping factor is more utilizable than predefined mapping factors. For instance, the users were on average faster with continuous mapping compared to zone mapping. In addition, many participants completed the task faster without interaction scaling. One possible explanation is the short training curve of the puzzle application. The more the subjects practiced the puzzle the faster they were able to solve it.

An interesting result is that the participants needed less object selections to sort objects with interaction scaling compared to the scenario without interaction scaling. In particular, the subjects were more often able to sort objects at most two selections with interaction scaling scenarios. However, the number of used selections has shown that users required less object selections but generally they took more time to solve the puzzle with interaction scaling. Here, it needs to be checked, if more complex tasks or other tasks will improve the task completion time by using interaction scaling.

The explorative study indicates that the cursor drift strongly affects the user's performance. In particular, users without virtual reality experience were dissatisfied with the drift in the zone mapping scenario. The drift effect is less pronounced in the continuous mapping scenario than in the zone mapping scenario, because the mapping factor changes continuously and the user is able to compensate the difference between hands motion and cursors motion.

The reason we did not get statistical significant results, we suppose that the drift negatively affects the results. Thus, the drift has abolished the benefits of interaction scaling.

As future work we plan to involve intention recognition to obviate the drift between absolute hand motion and relative cursor motion. So the interaction precision is adjusted to the user's current position and his motion sequence. The drift problem occurs at both interaction techniques (separated-cursors, connected-cursors) and the available cursor reset is less intuitive. Thus, we will evaluate the connected-cursors technique with the reduced drift effect.

In our LHRD environment with a display wall width of four meters a maximum mapping factor of one is sufficiently good to reach objects from a distance. We expect using deeper zones; the differences between the mapping methods are clearly visible. So interaction scaling with zone mapping could improve the user's performance.

Since we use a Nintendo Wii remote controller as input device, we are able to utilize haptic feedback. For instance, the haptic feedback can be used to indicate a precision modification (e.g., change of current zone, switch between coarse and precise manipulation mode).

Additionally, we will readjust the tracking volume that the user is able to interact closer at the display. We will also test to calculate user–display distance based on the head position to adjust the precision factor as expected from the user, instead of using the average of the distance of both hands.

The next steps include utilizing the results of the explorative study (i.e., to minimize the drift, complex task, appropriate interaction zones, etc.). We will perform a user study to evaluate how the user benefits from the user–display distance for 2D manipulation tasks.

Acknowledgements. This work was supported by EFRE fond of the European Community and a grant of the German National Research Foundation (DFG), Research Training Group 1424 MuSAMA. We thank the anonymous reviewers for their valuable contribution. The research leading to these results has received funding from the People Programme (Marie Curie Actions) of the European Union's Seventh Framework Programme FP7/2007-2013/ under REA grant agreement no. 290227.

References

1. Willert, M., Ohl, S., Lehmann, A., Staadt, O.: The Extended Window Metaphor for Large High-Resolution Displays. In: JVRC 2010: Joint Virtual Reality Conference of EGVE - EuroVR - VEC, pp. 69–76. Eurographics Association, Stuttgart (2010)
2. Kopper, R., Bowman, D.A., Silva, M.G., McMahan, R.P.: A human motor behavior model for distal pointing tasks. International Journal of Human-Computer Studies 68(10), 603–615 (2010)
3. Peck, S.M., North, C., Bowman, D.: A Multiscale Interaction Technique for Large, High-Resolution Displays. In: Proceedings of the 2009 IEEE Symposium on 3D User Interfaces, 3DUI 2009, pp. 31–38. IEEE Computer Society, Washington, DC (2009)
4. Vogel, D., Balakrishnan, R.: Distant Freehand Pointing and Clicking on Very Large, High Resolution Displays. In: Proceedings of the 18th Annual ACM Symposium on User Interface Software and Technology, UIST 2005, pp. 33–42. ACM, New York (2005)
5. Lehmann, A., Staadt, O.: Distance-adapted 2D Manipulation Techniques for Large High-Resolution Display Environments. In: Proceedings of the International Conference on Computer Graphics Theory and Applications, pp. 387–394. SciTePress, Rome (February 2012)
6. Peck, C.H.: Useful Parameters for the Design of Laser Pointer Interaction Techniques. In: CHI 2001 Extended Abstracts on Human Factors in Computing Systems, CHI 2001, pp. 461–462. ACM, New York (2001)
7. Ahlborn, B.A., Thompson, D., Kreylos, O., Hamann, B., Staadt, O.G.: A practical system for laser pointer interaction on large displays. In: Proceedings of the ACM Symposium on Virtual Reality Software and Technology, pp. 106–109. ACM (2005)
8. Argelaguet, F., Andujar, C.: Efficient 3D Pointing Selection in Cluttered Virtual Environments. IEEE Computer Graphics and Applications 29(6), 34–43 (2009)
9. Fukazawa, R., Takashima, K., Shoemaker, G., Kitamura, Y., Itoh, Y., Kishino, F.: Comparison of Multimodal Interactions in Perspective-corrected Multi-display Environment. In: 2010 IEEE Symposium on 3D User Interfaces (3DUI), pp. 103–110 (2010)
10. Cheng, K., Pulo, K.: Direct Interaction with Large-Scale Display Systems using Infrared Laser Tracking Devices. In: Proceedings of the Asia-Pacific Symposium on Information Visualisation, APVis 2003, vol. 24, pp. 67–74. Australian Computer Society, Inc., Darlinghurst (2003)
11. König, W.A., Bieg, H.J., Schmidt, T., Reiterer, H.: Position-Independent Interaction for Large High-Resolution Displays. In: IHCI 2007: Proceedings of IADIS International Conference on Interfaces and Human Computer Interaction 2007, pp. 117–125. IADIS Press (July 2007)
12. Collomb, M., Hascoët, M., Baudisch, P., Lee, B.: Improving drag-and-drop on wall-size displays. In: Proceedings of Graphics Interface, GI 2005, School of Computer Science, University of Waterloo, Waterloo, Ontario, Canada, pp. 25–32. Canadian Human-Computer Communications Society (2005)
13. Grossman, T., Balakrishnan, R., Kurtenbach, G., Fitzmaurice, G., Khan, A., Buxton, B.: Interaction Techniques for 3D Modeling on Large Displays. In: ACM I3DG 1999 Symposium on Interactive 3D Graphics, pp. 17–23 (2001)
14. Jeon, S., Hwang, J., Kim, G.J., Billinghurst, M.: Interaction with large ubiquitous displays using camera-equipped mobile phones. Personal Ubiquitous Computing 14(2), 83–94 (2010)
15. Ponto, K., Doerr, K., Wypych, T., Kooker, J., Kuester, F.: CGLXTouch: A multi-user multi-touch approach for ultra-high-resolution collaborative workspaces. Future Generation Computer Systems 27(6), 649–656 (2011)

16. Jota, R., Pereira, J.A.M., Jorge, J.A.: A Comparative Study of Interaction Metaphors for Large-Scale Displays. In: Proceedings of the 27th International Conference Extended Abstracts on Human Factors in Computing Systems, CHI 2009, pp. 4135–4140. ACM, New York (2009)
17. Kopper, R., Silva, M.G., McMahan, R.P., Bowman, D.A.: Increasing the Precision of Distant Pointing for Large High-Resolution Displays. Technical report, Computer Science. Virginia Tech (2008)
18. Vogel, D., Balakrishnan, R.: Interactive public ambient displays: Transitioning from implicit to explicit, public to personal, interaction with multiple users. In: Proceedings of the 17th Annual ACM Symposium on User Interface Software and Technology, UIST 2004, pp. 137–146. ACM, New York (2004)
19. Shoemaker, G., Tsukitani, T., Kitamura, Y., Booth, K.S.: Body-Centric Interaction Techniques for Very Large Wall Displays. In: Proceedings of the 6th Nordic Conference on Human-Computer Interaction: Extending Boundaries, NordiCHI 2010, pp. 463–472. ACM, New York (2010)
20. Bowman, D.A., Kruijff, E., LaViola, J.J., Poupyrev, I.: 3D User Interfaces: Theory and Practice. Addison Wesley Longman Publishing Co., Inc., Redwood City (2004)

Visual Simulation of Magnetic Fluid Using a Procedural Approach for Spikes Shape

Tomokazu Ishikawa[1], Yonghao Yue[2], Kei Iwasaki[3], Yoshinori Dobashi[4], and Tomoyuki Nishita[2]

[1] Tokyo University of Technology, 1404-1, Katakura-cho, Hachiouji-shi, Tokyo, Japan
[2] The University of Tokyo, 5-1-5 Kashiwa-no-Ha, Kashiwa-shi Chiba, Japan
[3] Wakayama University, Sakaedani 930, Wakayama-shi, Wakayama, Japan
[4] Hokkaido University, Kita 14, Nishi 9, Kita-ku, Sapporo-shi, Hokkaido, Japan

Abstract. In this paper, we propose a model to simulate magnetic fluids. Magnetic fluids behave as both fluids and as magnetic bodies, and these characteristics allow them to generate 'spike-like' shapes along a magnetic field. However, the spike shapes could not be reproduced by using the simulation method in the field of magnetic fluids. The spikes are difficult to simulate using fully physical-based methods. Therefore, we propose a visual simulation method for magnetic fluids whose shapes change according to the magnetic field. The shapes of the magnetic fluids can be roughly simulated by incorporating the calculation of magnetic field into the SPH(smoothed particle hydrodynamics) method. We compute the spike shapes using a procedural approach, and map the shapes onto the fluid surface. Although our method is not strictly physical based, our method can generate visually plausible results within a reasonable computational cost and we demonstrate that our method can generate visually plausible results.

1 Introduction

In the field of computer graphics, fluid simulation is one of the most important research topics. Many methods have therefore been proposed to simulate realistic motion of fluids by introducing physical laws. Previous methods have attempted to simulate incompressible fluids, such as smoke, water and flames, as well as compressible fluids such as explosions and viscous fluids [1–4]. In this paper, we focus on visual simulation of magnetic fluids.

A magnetic fluid is a colloidal solution consisting of micro-particles of ferromagnetic bodies, a surfactant that covers the magnetic micro-particles, and a solvent that acts as the base (see Fig.1). Therefore, magnetic fluids behave as both fluids and as magnetic bodies and can be magnetized and attracted to a magnet. Magnetic fluids have been studied and developed by NASA. Since 1960 they have been used as the seals for movable parts in spacesuits, and for the positioning of objects under a gravity environment [5]. Thanks to the controllability of the shapes of the magnetic fluids by magnetic forces, magnetic fluids have been widely used for various products such as electrical and medical equipments. A more interesting application of the magnetic fluids have appeared for creating new works of art. When a magnet is located near a magnetic fluid, the magnetic fluid forms spiky shapes like horns along the direction of the magnetic

G. Csurka et al. (Eds.): VISIGRAPP 2012, CCIS 359, pp. 112–126, 2013.

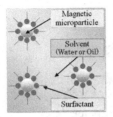

Fig. 1. Structure material of magnetic fluid

Fig. 2. Spiking phenomenon of magnetic fluid (photograph)

field generated by the magnet (see Fig. 2). This is known as the 'spiking phenomenon'. The art work using the magnetic fluids utilizes this phenomenon and generates interesting shapes by applying magnetic forces to the fluids.

Magnetic fluids have been studied extensively in the field of electromagnetic hydrodynamics. The phenomena covered by electromagnetic hydrodynamics can be further classified into plasma and magnetic fluids. A plasma is an electromagnetic fluid that generally has charge (i.e. an electric current flows) but does not have any defined interfaces (or free surfaces). The dynamics of aurora, prominence, and flares in the sun can be calculated by simulating a plasma. On the other hand, a magnetic fluid has usually interfaces but does not have any charges. We can find a few researches on the visual simulation of these phenomena in the field of computer graphics. However, to the best of our knowledge, no methods have been proposed for simulating the magnetic fluids in the field of computer graphics. Although we could use techniques developed in the field of magnetohydrodynamics, their computational cost is extremely high [6]. They typically require tens of hours to simulate a single spike only.

We therefore propose an efficient and visually plausible method for simulating the spiking phenomenon, aiming at the virtual reproduction of the art work. Our method combines a procedural approach and the SPH (smoothed particle hydrodynamics) method. The SPH method is used to compute overall surfaces of the fluid with a relatively small number of particles. Then, we generate the spike shapes procedurally onto the fluid surface. Although our method is not fully physically-based, it is easy to implement and we can reproduce spike shapes that are similar to those observed in the real magnetic fluids.

2 Related Work

Many methods have been proposed to simulate incompressible fluids such as smoke and flames [1, 2]. Goktekin et al. proposed a simulation method for viscoelastic fluids by incorporating an elastic term into the Navier Stokes equations [3].

Stam and Fuime introduced the SPH method into the CG field for representing flames and smoke [7]. Müller et al. proposed a SPH-based method based to simulate fluids with free surfaces [8]. Recently, many methods using the SPH method have been proposed, e.g., simulation of viscoelastic fluids [9], interaction of sand and water [10], and fast simulation of ice melting [11]. Our method also uses the SPH method and to simulate the magnetic fluids.

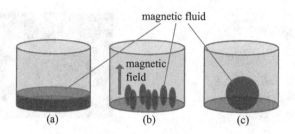

Fig. 3. Potentiality of shapes of magnetic fluid. (a), (b) and (c) show the state with minimum potential energy, minimum magnetic energy and minimum surface energy, respectively.

In computer graphics, no methods have been proposed for simulating electromagnetic hydrodynamics. Although a technique for simulating the magnetic field was proposed by Thomaszewski et al [12], only the magnetism of rigid bodies is calculated as an influence of magnetic fields. Baranoski proposed a visual simulation method for the aurora by means of simulating the interaction between electrons and the magnetic field using particles with an electrical charge [13, 14]. However, these methods do not take into account fluid dynamics.

In the field of physics, the characteristics of magnetic fluids have been studied since 1960. Rosenswig demonstrated spiking phenomena by using quantitative analysis [15]. Sudo et al. have studied the effects of instability, not only in the spiking phenomenon, but also on the surfaces of magnetic fluids [16]. Han et al. modeled the formation of a chain-shape between colloidal particles according to the magnetization of the particles[17]. Combined with a lattice Boltzmann method, they showed that the colloidal particles would form lines along the magnetic field. However, their method cannot represent the spike shapes. Yoshikawa et al. combined the MPS (Moving particle Semi-implicit) method with the FEM (Finite Element Method) and simulated magnetic fluids. Even when using 100,000 particles and a mesh with 250,000 tetrahedra, they were able to reproduce only a single spike [6]. Therefore, we believe that it is difficult to simulate the spike shapes using only fully physical-based methods. In this paper, we propose an efficient simulation method for the formation of spikes by animating the behavior of the fluid.

3   Spiking Phenomenon

Before explaining our simulation approach, we will describe the mechanism about the formation of the spike shape [15]. There are three important potential energies E_g, E_{mag} and E_s that relate to the formation mechanism.

E_g is the potential energy of gravity. If only the gravity is applied as an external force to the magnetic fluid, the fluid will form a horizontal surface at a constant height, as shown in Fig. 3 (a), since E_g is at the minimum level under this condition. E_{mag} is the magnetic potential energy. If only the magnetic force is applied as an external force, the fluid will form a certain number of spheroids that stand at the bottom of the vessel, as shown in Fig. 3 (b). E_{mag} is at a minimum level under these conditions. E_s is the

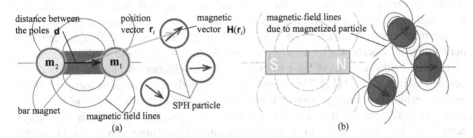

Fig. 4. Calculation of the magnetization and the magnetic force. (a) First, we calculate the magnetic field vector at each SPH particle induced by a magnetic dipole. (b) Next, we calculate the influence of other particles from the magnetized particles.

surface energy. If the surface tension alone is applied as the external force, the fluid will form into a spherical shape, as shown in Fig. 3 (c). E_s is at the minimum level under these conditions. The actual shape is the one that minimizes the summation of these three energies, resulting in spike-like shapes, as shown in Fig. 2.

Therefore, in order to simulate the spiking phenomena, the three forces need to be taken into account : the gravity, magnetic forces, and the surface tension. At the early stages of this research, we tried to simulate the spiking phenomenon by using the SPH method only. However, it turned out that we could not reproduce the spikes unless we used a significant number of particles, resulting in a very long computation time. Thus, we use the SPH method to simulate the overall behavior of the fluids and develop a new procedural method to generate the spike shapes. Details of our method is described in the following sections.

4 Our Simulation Method

As we described before, our method combines the SPH method and a procedural approach. In this section, we first describe the governing equations of the magnetic fluid that are solved by using the SPH method (Section 4.1). Next, we describe the computation of the magnetic force applied to each particle and a technique for generating the fluid surface by using the result of the SPH simulation (Section 4.2). Then, we describe the procedural method for computing the spike shape (Section 4.3).

4.1 Governing Equations

The behavior of incompressible fluids is described by the following equations.

$$\nabla \cdot \mathbf{u} = 0, \tag{1}$$
$$\frac{\partial \mathbf{u}}{\partial t} = -(\mathbf{u} \cdot \nabla)\mathbf{u} - \frac{1}{\rho}\nabla p + \nu \nabla^2 \mathbf{u} + \mathbf{F}. \tag{2}$$

Equation (1) is the continuity equation, and Navier-Stokes equation (Equation (2)) describes the conservation of momentum. $\mathbf{u}$ is the velocity vector, t is time, ρ is the fluid density, p is the pressure and ν is the kinematic viscosity coefficient. **F** is the external force that includes the gravity, the magnetic force, and the surface tension [11].

Our method solves the above equations by using the SPH method. That is, the magnetic fluids are represented by a set of particles and the motion of the fluids is simulated by calculating the motions of the particles. For this calculation, we use the method developed by Iwasaki et al [11]. This method is significantly accelerated by using the GPU and is capable of simulating water. We extend the method to the simulation of magnetic fluids. The difference of magnetic fluids from the non-magnetic fluids is that the magnetic force is induced when magnetic field exists. The computation of the magnetic force is described in the next subsection.

4.2   Calculation of Magnetization and Magnetic Force

Each particle represents a small magnetic fluid element, and its motion is calculated by taking into account the properties of both fluid and magnetic body. To calculate the magnetic force, our method assumes the paramagnetism, that is, each particle does not have any magnetic charges if there is no external magnetic field. However, if a magnetic field is applied, each particle becomes magnetized in the direction along the applied magnetic field.

In this paper, we assume that the magnetic field is induced by a bar magnet placed near the fluid. In order to handle a magnet with an arbitrary shape, we can use the method developed by Thomaszewski et al [12].

The magnetic field is calculated by approximating the bar magnet as a magnetic dipole. We assume that the north and south poles of the magnetic bar have an equal magnitude of magnetic charge but the signs are different (positive or negative). When computing the magnetic force working on each particle, it is not sufficient to calculate only the force induced directly by the magnetic bar. This is due to the paramagnetism. When each particle is placed in the magnetic field of the magnetic bar, the particle is magnetized and works as if it were a small spherical magnet. Therefore, our method first computes the magnetic field at equilibrium state, taking into account the magnetization of the particles. After that, the magnetic force for each particle is calculated. The details are described in the following.

The magnetic moment **m** due to a magnetic dipole is defined by the following equation:

$$\mathbf{m} = q_m \mathbf{d}, \tag{3}$$

where q_m is the magnitude of the magnetic charge and **d** is a vector connecting from the south to north poles. We call the magnetic vector induced by the magnetic bar as a background magnetic vector. Let us assume that the origin is at the midpoint between the north and the south poles. Then, the background magnetic vector $\mathbf{H}_{dipole}(\mathbf{r})$ at position **r** is expressed by the following equation.

$$\mathbf{H}_{dipole}(\mathbf{r}) = -\frac{1}{4\pi\mu}\nabla\frac{\mathbf{m}\cdot\mathbf{r}}{r^3}, \tag{4}$$

where μ is the permeability of the magnetic fluid and $r = |\mathbf{r}|$. Each particle is magnetized due to the background magnetic vector field and induces an additional magnetic vector field. Thus, in order to obtain the final magnetic vector $\mathbf{H}(\mathbf{r}_j)$ at particle j, the magnetic interactions between particles have to be computed by solving the following equation,

$$\mathbf{H}(\mathbf{r}_j) = \mathbf{H}_{dipole}(\mathbf{r}_j) - \frac{V}{4\pi\mu} \sum_{\substack{i=1 \\ i\neq j}}^{N} \nabla \frac{\chi\mathbf{H}(\mathbf{r}_i)\cdot\mathbf{r}_{ij}}{r_{ij}^3}, \tag{5}$$

where V is the volume of a particle and we assume that the volume of all particles are equal, $\mathbf{r}_i$ is the position of particle i, N is the total number of particles, χ is the magnetic susceptibility. $\mathbf{r}_{ij} = \mathbf{r}_j - \mathbf{r}_i$, and $r_{ij} = |\mathbf{r}_j - \mathbf{r}_i|$. The magnetic susceptibility changes due to the external magnetic field. It is known that the magnetization of the magnetic fluids is saturated when the magnitude of an external magnetic field is larger. We calculate the magnetization in all particles based on the actual relationship between the magnetization and an external magnetic field in [6]. The gradient part of the second term in Equation (5) is calculated by the following equation,

$$\nabla \frac{\chi\mathbf{H}(\mathbf{r}_i)\cdot\mathbf{r}_{ij}}{r_{ij}^3} = \nabla(\chi\mathbf{H}(\mathbf{r}_i))\cdot\frac{\mathbf{r}_{ij}}{r_{ij}^3} + \chi\mathbf{H}(\mathbf{r}_i)\cdot\nabla(\frac{\mathbf{r}_{ij}}{r_{ij}^3}). \tag{6}$$

We use the kernel function to calculate the partial differential of $\mathbf{H}$ $(\mathbf{r}_i)$, that is,

$$\nabla(\chi\mathbf{H}(\mathbf{r}_i)) = \sum_{\substack{j=1 \\ j\neq i}}^{N} \frac{m_j}{\rho_j}\chi\mathbf{H}(\mathbf{r}_j)\nabla w(r_{ij}), \tag{7}$$

where $w(r_{ij})$ is the kernel function. We use the following kernel function frequently refered in the SPH method [8],

$$w(r) = \begin{cases} \frac{315}{64\pi h^9}(h^2 - r^2)^3 & 0 \leq r \leq h \\ 0 & h < r, \end{cases} \tag{8}$$

where h is the effective radius of each particle. We calculate Equation (5) taking into account the influences from all the particles. We use the Gauss-Seidel method to solve Equation (5).

Next, the magnetic force $\mathbf{F}_{mag}(\mathbf{r}_i)$ is calculated by using the following equation [15],

$$\mathbf{F}_{mag}(\mathbf{r}_i) = -\nabla\phi_i(\mathbf{r}_i), \tag{9}$$

where,

$$\phi_i = \frac{\mu|\mathbf{H}(\mathbf{r}_i)|^2}{2}. \tag{10}$$

$\nabla\phi_i$ in Equation (9) is calculated by using the kernel function represented by Equation (8), that is,

$$\nabla\phi_i = \sum_{j} m_j \frac{\phi_j}{\rho_j}\nabla w(r_{ij}). \tag{11}$$

Fig. 5. Photograph of a real magnetic fluid surface

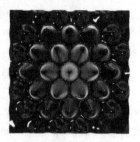

Fig. 6. The surface computed using Equation (13)

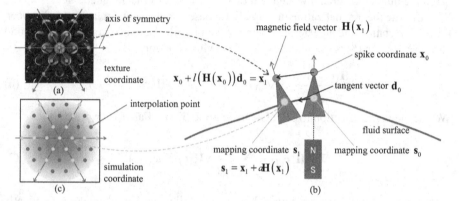

Fig. 7. (a) Spike texture coordinates are used as the height field. (b) To calculate the coordinates of the spike vertices, we trace along the fluid surface. (c) The coordinates other than an axis of symmetry are calculated by interpolation.

4.3   Computing Spike Shapes

The formation of the small spike shapes on the magnetic fluid surface can be explained by the balance among the forces of the surface tension, gravity and the stress due to magnetization [15]. As we described before, our method synthesizes the spike shapes by employing the procedural approach. The basic idea is as follows. We prepare a procedural height field representing the spike shapes generated on a flat surface. Next, during the simulation, the height field is mapped onto the curved surface calculated by using the SPH particles. When the fluid surface is flat and a magnetic field is perpendicular to the flat surface, the spike shapes can be represented as a height field $z(x, y)$ expressed by the following equation (see Appendix A for derivation).

$$z(x, y) = \sum C_0(\sin k_1 x + C_1 \cos k_1 x)(\sin k_2 y + C_2 \cos k_2 y), \quad (12)$$

where C_i ($i = 0, 1, 2$), k_1 and k_2 are parameters controlling the spike shapes. There is a constraint on k_1 and k_2: these need to be integers that satisfy $k_1^2 + k_2^2$ is the same for possible combinations of k_1^2 and k_2^2. Σ means the sum of the possible combinations. For the real magnetic fluids, a regular hexagonal pattern is often observed (see Fig. 5). Therefore, we choose the constants in Equation (12) so that such a pattern can be reproduced:

$$z(x, y) = C_0(\cos \frac{k}{2}(\sqrt{3}x + y) + \cos \frac{k}{2}(\sqrt{3}x - y) + \cos ky). \tag{13}$$

The above equation is used for the procedural height field representing the spike shapes on a flat surface. We set k to 50. Fig. 6 shows an example of the spike shapes synthesized by using Equation (13). Compared to Fig. 5, we can see that the synthesized shape is very similar to the real spike shapes. The size of the spike is controlled by adjusting C_0. We simply assume that C_0 is proportional to the magnitude of the magnetic field.

$$C_0 = \beta \mid \mathbf{H}(\mathbf{x}) \mid, \tag{14}$$

where, β is the proportional coefficient, $\mid \mathbf{H}(\mathbf{x}) \mid$ is the magnitude of the magnetic field at position $\mathbf{x}$.

In the real world, the following three structural features are observed: 1) positions of the spikes are symmetric as shown in Fig. 5, 2) distances between neighboring spikes become shorter when the magnetic force becomes stronger, and 3) the spikes are formed along the direction of the magnetic field lines. We develop a mapping method so that these three features are reproduced.

First, we set the intersection between the extended line connecting a magnetic dipole and the fluid surface to the origin of the texture coordinate defined by xy in Equation (13). This is because the magnetic field created from one magnet becomes symmetrical field with respect to a point centering on magnet. We trace six directions from the origin of the texture coordinates and calculate the mapping coordinates of the vertices of the spike because the height field reproduced by Equation (13) has three axes of symmetry (see Fig. 7 (a)). Let $\mathbf{x}_0$ be the position of the top of the spike just above the magnet. For each direction of six tangent vectors align to the three axes, the position of n-th spike $\mathbf{x}_n$ from the origin is calculated by the following equation,

$$\mathbf{x}_n = \mathbf{x}_{n-1} + l(\mathbf{H}(\mathbf{x}_0))\mathbf{d}_{n-1}, \tag{15}$$

where l is a function representing the distance between the tops of $n - 1$-th and n-th spikes and it is determined by $\mathbf{H}(\mathbf{x}_0)$. $\mathbf{d}_{n-1}$ is the tangent vector on the fluid surface at the mapping coordinate $\mathbf{s}_{n-1}$. Experimentally, we used $l = \frac{\alpha}{|\mathbf{H}(\mathbf{x}_0)|}$, where $\alpha = 0.15$.

To represent the characteristics that the spikes grow along the direction of the magnetic field lines, we calculate the magnetic field vector at $\mathbf{x}_1$, and we calculate the intersection between the fluid surface and the magnetic field vector. The intersection point is the mapping coordinate $\mathbf{s}_1$. By repeatedly applying this operation to a mapping area, we calculate the mapping coordinates.

The positions of the tops of the spikes between two adjacent symmetry axes (red points in Fig. 7 (c)) are calculated by interpolating the positions of two n-th spikes (yellow points in Fig. 7 (c)). The mapping area is determined by using the particles whose magnitudes of the magnetizations are greater than a threshold. The magnitude of magnetization is calculated by the balanced equation (Equation (B26)) for simple spike

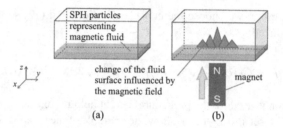

Fig. 8. The simulation space of our method. (a) The magnetic fluids, which are represented by a set of SPH particles, are stored in a cubic container. (b) The magnet is located underneath the container. Then the motions of the magnet fluids are simulated by moving the magnet.

shapes in equilibrium (see Appendix B). We use the minimum value of the magnetization M_c as the threshold. M_c is calculated by the following equation,

$$M_c^2 = \frac{2}{\mu}(1 + \frac{1}{\gamma})\sqrt{(\rho_1 - \rho_2)g\kappa}, \tag{16}$$

where ρ_1 and ρ_2 are the density of the magnetic fluid and air, respectively. κ is the magnitude of the surface tension.

5   Rendering

The surfaces of the magnetic fluids are extracted by using the method proposed by Yu et al. [18]. Since the magnetic fluids are colloid fluids, the transmitted light in the magnetic fluids is scattered. However, since the colors of the magnetic fluids are black or brown in general, the albedo of magnetic fluids is very small. Thus, the light scattering effects inside the magnetic fluids are negligible. Therefore, our method ignores the light scattering inside the magnetic fluids. We used POV-Ray to render the surfaces.

6   Results

For the simulation of our method, we used CUDA for the SPH method and the calculation of the magnetic force at each SPH particle. The number of particles used in the simulation shown in Figs. 9 is 40,960. The average computation time of the simulation for a single time-step is 6 milliseconds on a PC with an Intel(R) Core(TM)2 Duo 3.33GHz CPU, 3.25GB RAM and an NVIDIA GeForce GTX 480 GPU. The parameters used in the simulation are shown in Table 1. The average computation time of the surface construction for a frame is 2 minutes on the same PC. The initial fluid surface is shown in Fig. 8 (a). The fluid is contained in a box, which is not shown. Fig. 8 (b) shows how the shape of the fluid surface changes when a magnet approaches the bottom of the box. Fig. 9 shows an animation sequence of the magnetic fluid when we move the magnet in the vertical direction. As shown in Fig. 9, the spikes grow and increase when the magnet moves closer to the magnetic fluids. Fig. 10 shows an animation sequence of the magnetic fluid when we eliminate the magnet field. The surface becomes flat as

(a) t = 1.6 sec   (b) t = 3.2 sec   (c) t = 4.8 sec   (d) enlarged view of (c)

Fig. 9. Formation of spikes in the magnetic fluids. Spike shapes grow as the magnet approaches the bottom of the magnetic fluids.

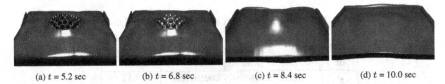

(a) t = 5.2 sec   (b) t = 6.8 sec   (c) t = 8.4 sec   (d) t = 10.0 sec

Fig. 10. Magnet fluids act as fluids when the magnetic field is reduced

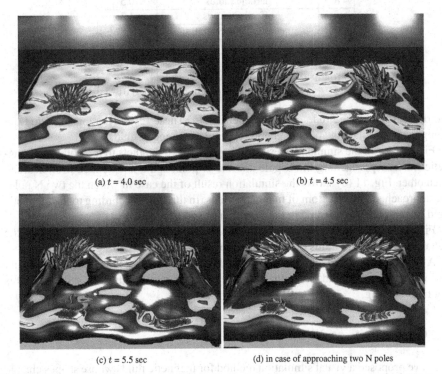

(a) t = 4.0 sec

(b) t = 4.5 sec

(c) t = 5.5 sec

(d) in case of approaching two N poles

Fig. 11. These figures show the simulation results to approach two magnets to the bottom of magnetic fluids. In cases of (a) to (c), approaching the S pole and the N pole, spike is extended to indicate to each other. (d) shows the simulation result of the case in which two N poles are approached to the bottom of magnetic fluids. In this case, according to the magnetic field lines, spike is extending in the direction of spike recede.

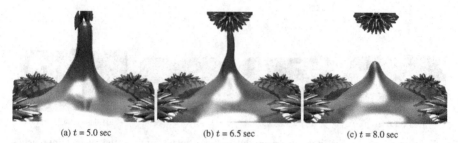

(a) $t = 5.0$ sec   (b) $t = 6.5$ sec   (c) $t = 8.0$ sec

Fig. 12. These figures show the simulation results to emulate a art work. We set one magnet on the ceiling, and four magnets on the bottom of the magnetic fluids.

Table 1. Parameter setting of magnetic fluid simulation

param.	meaning	value
dt	time step	0.00075
ν	kinematic viscosity coefficient	0.12
m	particle mass	0.016
R	particle radius	0.5
h	effective radius	1.3
g	gravitational acceleration	9.8
k	coefficient of surface tension	7.5
q_m	magnitude of the magnetic charge	5.0
μ	permeability of the magnetic fluid	$4\pi \times 10^{-7}$
χ	magnetic susceptibility	0.01

we decrease the magnitude of the magnetic field. These results demonstrate that our method can simulate the paramagnetic property of magnetic fluids.

Fig. 11 shows the simulation results to approach two magnets to the bottom of magnetic fluids. Approaching the S pole and the N pole, spike is extended to indicate to each other. Fig. 11 (d) shows the simulation result of the case in which the two N poles are approached to the bottom of magnetic fluids. In this case, according to the magnetic field lines, spike is extending in the direction of spike recede.

Fig. 12 shows the simulation results to emulate a art work. We can simulate the behavior of magnetic fluids that are pulled to a magnet on the ceiling.

A drawback of our method is that the spikes are not able to flow along the velocity and vorticity of the fluid, since the function used for representing the spike shapes is not time-varying.

7   Conclusions and Future Work

We have proposed a visual simulation method for magnetic fluids whose shapes change according to the magnetic field. We compute the spike shapes using a procedural approach, and map the shapes onto the fluid surface. Our method demonstrates that the magnitude of the magnet field influences the shapes of the magnet fluids and the magnet fluids act as fluids when the magnet field is eliminated. There are three limitations for our method. First, the conservation of the fluid volume is not considered when mapping the spike shapes onto the fluid surface. Second, our method cannot handle the fusion of more than one spike shapes, while we can observe such a fusion in real magnetic fluids. Third, our method does not simulate the flows of spikes along the velocity and vorticity of the magnetic fluid, since the function used for representing the spike shapes is not changed by the fluid behavior.

In future work, we would like to calculate the spike pattern other than regular hexagonal pattern dynamically using Equation (12) and represent the other spike shape arrangement. Moreover, to apply our method to works of art, we would like to control the magnetic field by using electric current flows.

References

1. Stam, J.: Stable fluids. In: Proceedings of SIGGRAPH 1999. Computer Graphics Proceedings. Annual Conference Series, pp. 121–128. ACM, ACM Press/ACM SIGGRAPH (1999)
2. Fedkiw, R., Stam, J., Jensen, H.W.: Visual simulation of smoke. In: Proceedings of SIGGRAPH 2001. Computer Graphics Proceedings. Annual Conference Series, pp. 15–22. ACM, ACM Press/ACM SIGGRAPH (2001)
3. Goktekin, T.G., Bargteil, A.W., O'Brien, J.F.: A method for animating viscoelastic fluids. In: Proceedings of SIGGRAPH 2004. Computer Graphics Proceedings. Annual Conference Series, pp. 463–468. ACM, ACM Press/ACM SIGGRAPH (2004)
4. Yngve, G.D., O'Brien, J.F., Hodgins, J.K.: Animating explosions. In: Proceedings of SIGGRAPH 2000. Computer Graphics Proceedings, Annual Conference Series, pp. 29–36. ACM, ACM Press/ACM SIGGRAPH (2000)
5. Kneller, E.: Ferromagnetisum. Springer (1962)
6. Yoshikawa, G., Hirata, K., Miyasaka, F., Okaue, Y.: Numerical analysis of transitional behavior of ferrofluid employing mps method and fem. IEEE Transactions on Magnetics 47(5), 1370–1373 (2011)
7. Stam, J., Fiume, E.: Depicting fire and other gaseous phenomena using diffusion processes. In: Proceedings of SIGGRAPH 1995. Computer Graphics Proceedings, Annual Conference Series, pp. 129–136. ACM, ACM Press/ACM SIGGRAPH (1995)
8. Müller, M., Charypar, D., Gross, M.: Particle-based fluid simulation for interactive applications. In: Proceedings of the 2003 ACM SIGGRAPH/Eurographics Symposium on Computer Animation, pp. 154–159. ACM (2003)
9. Clavet, S., Beaudoin, P., Poulin, P.: Particle-based viscoelastic fluid simulation. In: Proceedings of the 2005 ACM SIGGRAPH/Eurographics Symposium on Computer Animation, pp. 219–228. ACM (2005)
10. Rungjiratananon, W., Szego, Z., Kanamori, Y., Nishita, T.: Real-time animation of sand-water interaction. Computer Graphics Forum (Pacific Graphics 2008) 27(7), 1887–1893 (2008)
11. Iwasaki, K., Uchida, H., Dobashi, Y., Nishita, T.: Fast particle-based visual simulation of ice melting. Computer Graphics Forum (Pacific Graphics 2010) 29(7), 2215–2223 (2010)
12. Thomaszewski, B., Gumann, A., Pabst, S., Strasser, W.: Magnets in motion. In: Proceedings of SIGGRAPH Asia 2008. Computer Graphics Proceedings, Annual Conference Series, pp. 162:1–162:9. ACM, ACM Press/ACM SIGGRAPH Asia (2008)
13. Baranoski, G., Rokne, J., Shirley, P., Trondsen, T., Bastos, R.: Simulation the aurora. Visualization and Computer Animation 14(1), 43–59 (2003)
14. Baranoski, G., Wan, J., Rokne, J., Bell, I.: Simulating the dynamics of auroral phenomena. ACM Transactions on Graphics (TOG) 24(1), 37–59 (2005)

15. Rosensweig, R.: Magnetic fluids. Annual Review of Fluid Mechanics 19, 437–461 (1987)
16. Sudo, S., Hashimoto, H., Ikeda, A., Katagiri, K.: Some studies of magnetic liquid sloshing. Journal of Magnetism and Magnetic Materials 65(2), 219–222 (1987)
17. Han, K., Feng, Y.T., Owen, D.R.J.: Three-dimensional modelling and simulation of magnetorheological fluids. International Journal for Numerical Methods in Engineering 84(11), 1273–1302 (2010)
18. Yu, J., Turk, G.: Reconstructing surfaces of particle-based fluids using anisotropic kernels. In: Proceedings of the 2010 ACM SIGGRAPH/Eurographics Symposium on Computer Animation, pp. 217–225. ACM, Eurographics Association (2010)
19. Cowley, M.D., Rosensweig, R.E.: The interfacial stability of a ferromagnetic fluid. Journal of Fluid Mechanics 30(4), 671–688 (1967)

Appendix A

Surface Deformation of Magnetic Fluid

In this appendix, we consider the case where the liquid surface is initially horizontal (the surface is equal to the xy-plane as shown in Fig. 13(a)) [19]. We apply a vertical magnetic field (in z direction) and calculate how the liquid surface changes according to the magnetic field. We show that we can obtain Equation (12) for describing the surface displacement according to the magnetic field. The variables of the density and magnetic field are defined as shown in Fig 13(a). When the liquid surface is slightly deformed (Fig. 13(b)), the variation of the magnetic flux density inside the magnetic fluid, $\mathbf{b}_1 = \mathbf{B} - \mathbf{B}_0$, and the variation of the magnetic field, $\mathbf{h}_1 = \mathbf{H} - \mathbf{H}_{01}$ have the following relationship:

$$\mathbf{b}_1 = (\mu h_{1x}, \mu h_{1y}, \hat{\mu} h_{1z}), \tag{A17}$$

where the magnetic flux density and the magnetic field are parallel. μ is the permeability, $\hat{\mu}$ is the differential permeability, h_{1x}, h_{1y}, h_{1z} show the x, y and z components of $\mathbf{h}_1$, since the magnetic flux density and the magnetic field are parallel. By letting the magnetic potential inside the magnetic fluid be ϕ_1 the magnetic field $\mathbf{h}_1$ in case of no electric current can be expressed as:

$$\mathbf{h}_1 = \nabla \phi_1. \tag{A18}$$

If the electric current is flowing, the magnetic field due to electric currents must be considered and the potential term becomes complicate. By using the following equation,

$$\mathbf{H} = \nabla \cdot \mathbf{B}, \tag{A19}$$

the divergence of the variation of the magnetic flux density can be rewritten as:

$$\nabla \cdot \mathbf{b}_1 = \mu \left(\frac{\partial^2 \phi_1}{\partial x^2} + \frac{\partial^2 \phi_1}{\partial y^2} \right) + \hat{\mu} \frac{\partial^2 \phi_1}{\partial z^2}. \tag{A20}$$

On the other hand, the magnetic field potential ϕ_2 above the magnetic fluid satisfies the following equation:

$$\left(\frac{\partial^2 \phi_2}{\partial x^2} + \frac{\partial^2 \phi_2}{\partial y^2} + \frac{\partial^2 \phi_2}{\partial z^2} \right) = 0. \tag{A21}$$

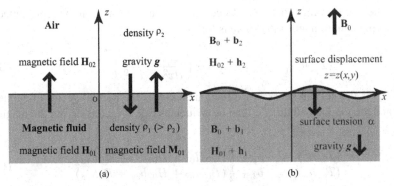

Fig. 13. (a) Horizontal interfacial boundary and vertical magnetic field. Each character equation of the fluid set as in the figure. (b) Deformation of the interfacial boundary by applied vertical magnetic field.

Moreover, $\phi_1 = 0$ ($z \to -\infty$) and $\phi_2 = 0$ ($z \to \infty$) can be used as boundary conditions because each magnetic field is not affected by the deformation of the interfacial boundary at $z \pm \infty$. Due to the condition that the tangential component of magnetic field **H** is equal on both sides of the liquid surface, and the surface normal component of magnetic flux density **B** has the same value on both sides of the interface, the following equation is satisfied on the deformed liquid surface.

$$\begin{cases} \phi_1 - \phi_2 = M_{01} z(x,y) \\ \hat{\mu}\frac{\partial \phi_1}{\partial z} - \mu_0 \frac{\partial \phi_2}{\partial z} = 0, \end{cases} \tag{A22}$$

where, $M_{01} = |\mathbf{M}_{01}|$, $z(x, y)$ is the height field of the deformed liquid surface. Then, the following equations satisfy Equation (A20), (A21) and (A22) and the boundary condition.

$$\phi_1 = \frac{M_{01}}{1+\gamma} z(x,y) \exp\left(k\sqrt{\frac{\hat{\mu}}{\mu}} z \right), \tag{A23}$$

$$\phi_2 = \frac{\gamma M_{01}}{1+\gamma} z(x,y) \exp\left(-kz\right), \tag{A24}$$

where, $\gamma = \sqrt{\frac{\hat{\mu}\mu}{\mu_0^2}}$ and $z(x, y)$ must satisfy the following equation:

$$\left(\frac{\partial^2}{\partial x^2} + \frac{\partial^2}{\partial y^2} + k^2 \right) z(x,y) = 0, \tag{A25}$$

The general solution of this equation is the one shown in Equation (12).

Equilibrium of Force Inside Spike Shape

In this appendix, we explain that the minimum value of the magnetization is represented as Equation (16) when the magnetic fluid forms a spike shape. Considering the balance between the surface tension and the difference in the stress on both sides of the liquid surface, the equilibrium equation of forces at the liquid surface can be represented by the following equation when the spike is formed.

$$(T_{zz}n_z)_1 - (T_{zz}n_z)_2 - \alpha \left(\frac{\partial^2}{\partial x^2} + \frac{\partial^2}{\partial y^2} \right) z = 0, \tag{B26}$$

where T_{zz} is the normal stress in z direction and n_z is the normal vector of z-axis. In the air and the magnetic fluid, T_{zz} can be written as follows, considering the magnetic pressure.

$$\begin{aligned} (T_{zz}n_z)_1 &= -p_1 + \tfrac{1}{2} (B_0 H_{01} + H_{01}b_{1z} + B_0 h_{1z}) \\ (T_{zz}n_z)_2 &= -p_2 + \tfrac{1}{2} (B_0 H_{02} + H_{02}b_{2z} + B_0 h_{2z}). \end{aligned} \tag{B27}$$

Substituting the following equation of pressure distribution in Equation (B26),

$$\begin{aligned} p_1 &= -\rho_1 g z + \tfrac{1}{2} (B_0 h_{1z} - H_{01}b_{1z}) \\ p_2 &= -\rho_2 g z + \tfrac{1}{2} (B_0 h_{2z} - H_{02}b_{2z}), \end{aligned} \tag{B28}$$

the following equation can be derived considering Equations (A22) and (A25),

$$\left\{ (\rho_1 - \rho_2)g - \frac{\gamma}{1+\gamma} k\mu_0 M_{01}^2 + \alpha k^2 \right\} z(x, y) = const. \tag{B29}$$

Because z is not zero when the spike is deformed, Equation (B29) holds only when the constant on the right side and the term in parentheses on the left side are zero. That is,

$$M_{01}^2 = \frac{1+\gamma}{\mu_0 \gamma} \left\{ (\rho_1 - \rho_2)\frac{g}{k} + \alpha k \right\}. \tag{B30}$$

If the magnetization of magnetic fluid is less than Equation (B30), the liquid surface does not change. When $k = \sqrt{\frac{(\rho_1 - \rho_2)g}{\alpha}}$, the right hand side of equation is minimum. The minimum value is shown in Equation (16).

Perspectives for Sketching Fluids Using Sketch-Based Techniques and Gradient Vector Flow for 3D LBM Initialization

Sicilia Judice, José Guilherme Mayworm, Pedro Azevedo, and Gilson Giraldi

National Laboratory for Scientific Computing, Petrópolis/RJ, Brazil
Faculty of Technical Education of the State of Rio de Janeiro, Petrópolis/RJ, Brazil
{sicilia,jmayworm,pedrovoa,gilson}@lncc.br
http://www.lncc.br

Abstract. This work is primarily concerned with sketch-based techniques to convert drawing input from the user into an initial fluid configuration. The application of sketching techniques is proposed in order to enable the user to freely draw the initial state of the fluid flow. This proposal has several issues which are discussed in this work. A combination of sketching techniques and Gradient Vector Flow (GVF) is explored to obtain a smooth initialization for the simulation of $2D/3D$ fluids using a Lattice Boltzmann Method (LBM). The LBM is based on the fundamental idea of constructing simplified kinetic models, which incorporates the essential physics of microscopic processes so that the macroscopic averaged properties satisfy macroscopic equations.

Keywords: Fluid simulation, Lattice-Boltzmann method, Gradient vector flow, Sketching modeling.

1 Introduction

Fluids are complex physical systems which macroscopical description involves concepts in continuous mechanics, kinetic theory and partial differential equations. In the last decades, techniques for fluid modeling and simulation have been widely studied for computer graphics applications. The motivation for such interest relies in the potential applications of these methods and in the complexity and beauty of the natural phenomena that are involved. In particular, techniques in the field of computational fluid dynamics (CFD) have been applied for fluid animation in applications such as virtual surgery simulators [14], visual effects [24], and games [13].

The traditional fluid animation methods in computer graphics rely on a top-down viewpoint that uses 2D/3D mesh-based approaches motivated by the methods of finite element (FE) and finite difference (FD) in conjunction with Navier-Stokes equations for fluids [8,17]. Alternatively, lattice methods comprised of the Lattice Gas Cellular Automata (LGCA) and Lattice Boltzmann (LBM) can be used. The basic idea behind these methods is that the macroscopic dynamics of a fluid are the result of the collective behavior of many microscopic particles. The LGCA follows this idea, but it simplifies the dynamics through simple and local rules for particle interaction and displacements.

G. Csurka et al. (Eds.): VISIGRAPP 2012, CCIS 359, pp. 127–141, 2013.

On the other hand, the LBM constructs a simplified kinetic model, a simplification of the Boltzmann equation, which incorporates the essential microscopic physics so that the macroscopic averaged properties obey the desired equations [4]. The LBM have provided significant successes in modeling fluid flows and associated transport phenomena. The methods simulate transport by tracing the evolution of a single particle distribution through synchronous updates on a discrete grid. Before starts the simulation, it is necessary to define the initial conditions, which can be an initial velocity field, pressure field or an initial distribution of particles.

In [11] we proposed an intuitive framework for $2D$ LBM fluid flow initialization. To implement this task, the LBM was combined with methods of sketch-based modeling [6], so the user can define an initial state for the fluid flow through free-hand drawing. The user draws sketch paths inside the fluid domain using the mouse. Each path defines a streamline and its corresponding tangent field is used to compute the fluid velocity over the path. In this way, this first velocity field is used as input to the Gradient Vector Flow (GVF) [25]. Finally, the field obtained by solving the GVF equations is a smooth version of the original one that tends to be extended very far from the user defined paths. Thus, the smoothed velocity field is used as an initial condition for the LBM method.

In this paper we discuss some issues and perspectives to extend this framework to a $3D$ environment. Firstly, we shall consider user interface issues. In the $\Re^2$, a drawing canvas is provided, which in the actual implementation is aligned with the computer screen, and the user draws sketch paths inside the fluid domain using the mouse. Such environment is not efficient for taking $3D$ drawings due to the ambiguities inherent to the process of accessing $3D$ positions through a $2D$ device. We can address this problem with a different hardware setup: mouse $3D$, virtual reality devices, among others. However, even such improvement might be not efficient if the user needs to draw too many streamlines to get the desired result. In this situations icons defined through singular points and the skeleton of a vector field would be worthwhile.

Then, following the idea presented in [11], the velocity field over the skeleton can be used as input to the $3D$ Gradient Vector Flow (GVF) [27]. Similarly to the $2D$ environment, the smoothed velocity field obtained by solving the GVF equations is used as an initial condition for the $3D$ LBM method.

This chapter is organized as follows. Firstly, we provide a brief review of related work in Section 2. We describe the methodology of the Lattice Boltzmann technique in section 3, the methodology of the Gradient Vector Flow in section 4 and the concepts behind sketch-based modeling in section 5. Then, we present the proposed technique in section 6. The results and advantages of the proposed framework are shown in section 7. Finally, section 8 gives the conclusions and future works.

2 Related Work

The Lattice Boltzmann Method (LBM) is based on the fundamental idea of constructing simplified kinetic models that incorporate the essential physics of microscopic processes so that the macroscopic averaged properties satisfy macroscopic equations. The LBM is especially useful for modeling complicated boundary conditions and multiphase interfaces [4]. Extensions of this method are described, including simulations of fluid turbulence, suspension flows, and reaction diffusion systems [22].

Lattice models have a number of advantages over more traditional numerical methods, particularly when fluid mixing and phase transitions occur [15]. Simulation is always performed on a regular grid, and can be efficiently implemented on a massively parallel computer. Solid boundaries and multiple fluids can be introduced in a straightforward manner and the simulation is done efficiently, regardless of the complexity of the boundary or interface [3]. In the case of Lattice-Gas Cellular Automata (LGCA), there are no numerical stability issues because its evolution follows integer arithmetic. For LBM, numerical accuracy and stability depend on the Mach number (max-speed/speed of sound). The computational cost of the LGCAs is lower than that for LBM-based methods. However, system parametrization (e.g., viscosity) is difficult to do in LGCA models, and the obtained dynamics is less realistic than for LBM.

To provide an intuitive modeling of the initial configuration of the fluid, sketching techniques can be applied. The first sketch-based modeling system was *Sketchpad* launched in 1963 by Ivan Sutherland [18]. An early approach was to use drawing input as symbolic instructions [28]. This method allows a designer access to the multitude of commands in a modeling interface, and was well suited to the limitations of early hardware. As technology has progressed, the evolution of these approach leads to a system that can interpret a user's drawing directly [21], a system that can use shading and tone to give a 2D drawing the appearance of 3D volume [23], and a system that can approach 3D modeling from the perspective of sculpture in which virtual tools are used to build up a model like clay, or cut it down with tools like a sculptor [2].

The sketch-based modeling systems SKETCH [28] and Teddy [10] are examples of how sketches or drawn gestures can provide a powerful interface for fast geometric modeling. However, the notion of sketching a motion is less well-defined than that of sketching an object. Walking motions can be created by drawing a desired path on the ground plane for the character to follow, for example. In [19], the authors present a system for sketching the motion of a character. Recently, the work of [16] proposed a sketch-based system for creating illustrative visualizations of 2D vector fields. The work proposed by [29] presents a sketching system that incorporates a background fluid simulation for illustrating dynamic fluid systems. It combines sketching, simulation, and control techniques in one user interface and can produce illustrations of complex fluid systems in real time. Users design the structure of the fluid system using basic sketch operations on a canvas and progressively edit it to show how flow patterns change. The system automatically detects and corrects the structural errors of flow simulation as the user sketches. A fluid simulation runs constantly in the background to enhance flow and material distribution in physically plausible ways.

The Gradient Vector Flow (GVF) method is based on a parabolic partial different equation (PDE) that may be derived from a variational problem [25]. The method was originally proposed for image processing applications: an initial value problem derived from image features is associated to that parabolic PDE [1]. The GVF has been applied together with active contours models (or snakes) for boundary extraction in medical images segmentation. Snakes are curves defined within an image domain that can move under the influence of internal forces within the curve itself and external forces derived from the image data. They are used in computer vision and image processing applications, particularly to locate object boundaries.

The key idea of GVF is to use a diffusion-reaction PDE to generate a new external force field that makes snake models less sensitive to initialization as well as improves the snakes ability to move into boundary concavities [25]. Also, there are results about the global optimality and numerical analysis of GVF in the context of Sobolev spaces [26]. In our work we take advantage of the GVF ability to generate a smooth version of the original field, that tends to be extended very far from the paths defined by the user, to get an initial velocity field constrained to the user sketch.

3   The Lattice Boltzmann Method

In recent years, Lattice Boltzmann Methods (LBM) have taken the attention of the scientific community, due to their ease of implementation, extensibility and computational efficiency. Specifically in computational fluid dynamic, LBM has been applied due to its ease implementation of boundary conditions and numerical stability in wide variety of flow conditions with various Reynolds numbers [5]. The LBM has evolved from the Lattice Gas Cellular Automata (LGCA), which, despite its advantages, has certain limitations related to their discrete nature: the rise of noise, which makes necessary the use of processes involving the calculation of average values and little flexibility to adjust the physical parameters and initial conditions [5].

The LBM was introduced by [12], where the authors showed the advantage of extending the boolean dynamics of cellular automata to work directly with real numbers representing probabilities of presence of particles. In the LBM, the domain of interest is discretized in a lattice and the fluid is considered as a collection of particles. These particles move in discrete time steps, with a velocity pointing along one of the directions of the lattice. Besides, particles collide with each other and physical quantities of interest associated with the lattice nodes are updated at each time step. The computation of each node depends on the properties of itself and the neighboring nodes at the previous time step [4,5]. The dynamic of this method is governed by the Lattice Boltzmann equation:

$$f_i(x + \Delta_x c_i, \ t + \Delta_t) \ - \ f_i(x, t) \ = \ \Omega_i(f) \,, \tag{1}$$

with $i = 1, ..., z$ and where f_i is the particle distribution function, x is the lattice node, c_i is one of the lattice directions, Δ_x is the lattice spacing, Δ_t is the time step, $\Omega_i(f)$ is the collision term, and z is the number of lattice directions.

In the work presented in [9], the authors proposed to linearize the collision term Ω_i around its local equilibrium solution:

$$\Omega_i(f) \ = \ -\frac{1}{\tau}\left(f_i(x, t) \ - \ f_i^{eq}(\rho, u) \right), \tag{2}$$

where τ is the relaxation time scale and f_i^{eq} is the equilibrium particles distribution that is dependent on the macroscopic density (ρ) and velocity (u). The parameter τ is related to diffusive phenomena in the problem, in this case with the viscosity of the fluid [4]. The general equation of the equilibrium function is given by [5]:

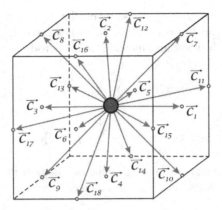

Fig. 1. The D3Q19 LB model, with 18 non-zero velocities

$$f_i^{eq} = \rho\omega_i \left[1 + \frac{(c_i \cdot u)}{c_s^2} + \frac{(c_i \cdot u)^2}{2c_s^4} - \frac{(u \cdot u)}{2c_s^2} \right], \tag{3}$$

where ω_i are weights and the c_s^2 is the lattice speed of sound, which is dependent on the lattice.

There are different LBM models for numerical solutions of various fluid flow scenarios, where each model has different lattice discretization. The LBM models are usually denoted as DxQy, where x and y corresponds to the number of dimensions and number of microscopic velocity directions (c_i) respectively. In this work we implement a 3D LBM model known as D3Q19. This model has 18 possibilities of non-zero velocities, as shown in Fig. 1, given by:

$$c_0 = (0,0,0),$$

$$c1 = (1,0,0)v, \quad c_2 = (0,1,0)v, \quad c_3 = (-1,0,0)v,$$

$$c_4 = (0,-1,0)v, \quad c_5 = (0,0,-1)v, \quad c_6 = (0,0,1)v,$$

$$c_7 = (1,1,0)v, \quad c_8 = (-1,1,0)v, \quad c_9 = (-1,-1,0)v,$$

$$c_{10} = (1,-1,0)v, \quad c_{11} = (1,0,-1)v, \quad c_{12} = (0,1,-1)v,$$

$$c_{13} = (-1,0,-1)v, c_{14} = (0,-1,-1)v, c_{15} = (1,0,1)v,$$

$$c_{16} = (0,1,1)v, \quad c_{17} = (-1,0,1)v, \quad c_{18} = (0,-1,1)v,$$

where v is the particle velocity related to each direction c_i. The lattice speed of sound and the weights for the lattice of the D3Q19 LBM model are given by:

$$c_s^2 = \frac{1}{3}, \quad \omega_0 = \frac{1}{3}, \quad \omega_{1-6} = \frac{1}{18}, \quad \omega_{7-18} = \frac{1}{36}, \tag{4}$$

where ω_0 is related to the rest particle. Replacing (4) in (3), gives us the equilibrium function for the D3Q19 LB model, where $i = 0, ..., 18$:

$$f_i^{eq} = \omega_i \left[\rho + 3\frac{(c_i \cdot u)}{v^2} + \frac{9}{2}\frac{(c_i \cdot u)^2}{v^4} - \frac{3}{2}\frac{(u \cdot u)}{v^2} \right]. \tag{5}$$

Our interest relies on the macroscopic scale, where the physical macroscopic quantities seem to show a continuous behavior. Then, the macroscopic density (ρ) and velocity (u) are calculated from the respective moments of the density distribution, as follows:

$$\rho(x, t) = \sum_{i=0}^{18} f_i(x, t) , \tag{6}$$

$$u(x, t) = \frac{1}{\rho(x, t)} \sum_{i=0}^{18} f_i(x, t) c_i . \tag{7}$$

The Lattice Boltzmann equation (1) contains the two steps of the simulation, namely: stream and collision. These two steps can be computed separately, through the following expressions:

$$f_i^*(x, \, t + \Delta_t) = f_i(x - \Delta_x c_i, t) , \tag{8}$$

and

$$f_i(x, t + \Delta_t) = (1 - \tau) f_i^*(x, \, t + \Delta_t) + \tau f_i^{eq}(\rho, u) . \tag{9}$$

The main steps of the simulation algorithm can be summarized as follows:

Algorithm I: D3Q19 LBM Model

1. **Initialization ($t = 0$):**
   (a) $\rho(x, 0) = 1.0$
   (b) $u(x, 0) = (0, 0, 0)$
   (c) $f_i(x, 0) = f_i^{eq}(\rho, u)$
2. **Main Loop ($t = 1$ to t_{max}):**
   (a) Stream Step (8)
   (b) Update macroscopic density (6) and velocity (7)
   (c) Collision Step (9)

Boundary conditions are fundamental features for fluid simulation. The standard boundary conditions for LBM simulations are no-slip walls [20]. It means that close to the boundary the fluid does not move at all. Hence, each cell next to a boundary should have the same amount of particles moving into the boundary as moving into the opposite direction. This will result in a zero velocity, and can be imagined as reflecting the particle distribution functions at the boundary. The reflection process is shown in Fig. 2. For the implementation, boundary and fluid cells need to be distinguished. Thus, in the streaming step, the previous algorithm must check the type of the cells: if the neighboring cell is a boundary, the opposite distribution function from the current cell would be taken, instead of applying the standard stream calculation (8).

4   The Gradient Vector Flow

The Gradient Vector Flow (GVF) fields were originally proposed in [25] as a new class of external forces for active contour models. They are dense vector fields derived from

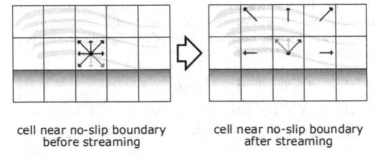

cell near no-slip boundary
before streaming

cell near no-slip boundary
after streaming

Fig. 2. No-slip obstacle cells directly reflect the incoming distribution functions. (*Source:* [20]).

images by minimizing an energy functional in a variational framework. These mini-mization are achieved by solving linear partial differential equations which diffuses the gradient vectors of a gray-level or binary edge map computed from the input image. In [27], the authors presented the $3D$ formulation for the GVF, which has the identical formulation as the $2D$, since it is written in a dimension-independent form.

The $3D$ Gradient Vector Flow (GVF) field is defined as the vector field $v(x, y, z) = (u(x, y, z), v(x, y, z), w(x, y, z))$ that minimizes the energy functional:

$$\varepsilon = \int \int \int \left(\mu |\nabla v|^2 + |\mathbf{F}|^2 |v - \mathbf{F}|^2 \right) dx dy dz , \qquad (10)$$

where $\mathbf{F} = (F_1(x, y, z), F_2(x, y, z), F_3(x, y, z))$ is a field defined over the domain of interest.

When $\mathbf{F}$ is small, the energy is dominated by partial derivatives of the vector field, yielding a smooth field. Otherwise, the second term dominates the integrand, and is minimized by setting $v = \mathbf{F}$. The parameter μ is a regularization parameter that should be set according to degree of smoothness required. The GVF can be found by solving the associated Euler-Lagrange equations given by:

$$\mu \nabla^2 u - (u - F_1)|\mathbf{F}|^2 = 0 , \qquad (11)$$

$$\mu \nabla^2 v - (v - F_2)|\mathbf{F}|^2 = 0 , \qquad (12)$$

$$\mu \nabla^2 w - (w - F_3)|\mathbf{F}|^2 = 0 , \qquad (13)$$

where ∇^2 is the Laplacian operator. Equations (11)-(13) can be solved by treating u, v and w as functions of time t and solving:

$$u_t(x, y, z, t) = \mu \nabla^2 u(x, y, z, t) - (u(x, y, z, t) - F_1(x, y, z))|\mathbf{F}|^2 , \qquad (14)$$

$$v_t(x, y, z, t) = \mu \nabla^2 v(x, y, z, t) - (v(x, y, z, t) - F_2(x, y, z))|\mathbf{F}|^2 , \qquad (15)$$

$$w_t(x, y, z, t) = \mu \nabla^2 w(x, y, z, t) - (w(x, y, z, t) - F_3(x, y, z))|\mathbf{F}|^2 , \qquad (16)$$

subject to some initial condition $v(x, y, z, 0) = v_0(x, y, z)$. The steady-state solution (as $t \to \infty$) of these parabolic equations is the desired solution of the Euler-Lagrange equations (11)-(13). These are reaction-diffusion equations and are known to arise in areas as heat conduction, reactor physics, and fluid flow. The field obtained by solving the above equation is a smooth and extended version of the original one. For convenience, the authors in [26] rewrite (14)-(16) as follows:

$$u_t(x, y, z, t) = \mu \nabla^2 u(x, y, z, t) - b(x, y, z)u(x, y, z, t) + c_1(x, y, z), \quad (17)$$

$$v_t(x, y, z, t) = \mu \nabla^2 v(x, y, z, t) - b(x, y, z)v(x, y, z, t) + c_2(x, y, z), \quad (18)$$

$$w_t(x, y, z, t) = \mu \nabla^2 w(x, y, z, t) - b(x, y, z)w(x, y, z, t) + c_3(x, y, z), \quad (19)$$

where:

$$b(x, y, z) = |\mathbf{F}|^2,$$
$$c_1(x, y, z) = b(x, y, z)F_1(x, y, z),$$
$$c_2(x, y, z) = b(x, y, z)F_2(x, y, z),$$
$$c_3(x, y, z) = b(x, y, z)F_3(x, y, z).$$

5 The Sketch-Based Modeling

The Sketch-Based Modeling (SBM) is a computational research area that focus on intuitive simplified modeling techniques. It is based on the sketch process made by traditional artist. Basically, the sketch-based modeling program has to provide a comfortable and intuitive environment where the artist can freely draw his object. Then, using the sketch as an input, the program must interpret the data and find an approximate representation [6].

The sketch process starts with the drawing done by the user through some input device (for example, mouse, tablet or touch screen). This drawing is then sampled and stored with some information such as position, velocity, pressure, among others. The type of information that can be stored depends on the device being used. For example, some devices provide pressure information, multiple touches or slope of the pen. Another device-dependent aspect is the sample frequency, which determines the sample distribution [7].

The goal of a sketch-based modeling program is to model the object intended by the user, not necessarily what was drawn on the input device. One issue with this type of system occurs when the user does not have much ability to design or handling the device. In this case, the tracing performed may be inaccurate. Another common issue is the noise from the device, which comes from an inaccurate drawing capture. Due to the presence of noise, it is common to perform a filtering of sampled data. Another feature is to perform a fitting of the data for a convenient curve [7].

The data are stored as a sequence of points, $T = \{p_1, ..., p_n\}$, where n is the number of samples and $p_i = (x_i, y_i, t_i)$ indicates the position (x_i, y_i) and instant t_i each point was sampled. If the data acquisition device captures more information, the point can be thought of as $(x_1, ..., x_k)$, where each element represents an attribute of the point. Besides the attributes captured, it is also possible to calculate a few others, such as velocity and acceleration. All this information can be useful to add features to the model.

The points are conveniently grouped together to build a two-dimensional model to which the system must infer some meaning. This model is called the *sketch*. The sketch can be used both for creating and editing of 3D graphic object being modeled, such as to control. In the latter case the application decides which task to perform, according to the interpretation of the sketch. This is known as sketch of gesture [19].

6 Proposed Method

This work proposes a combination of sketching techniques and Gradient Vector Flow to obtain a smooth initialization for the simulation of $3D$ fluids using a Lattice Boltzmann Method. For modeling a fluid through LBM we need to discretize the domain, set the initial and boundary conditions and then to apply the local rule of evolution. However, in the field of animation, it is common to generate scenes from advanced states of fluid dynamics generated through fluid simulation techniques. The initialization of the simulation is a fundamental step.

One of the goals of this work is primarily concerned with how to take drawing input from the user and convert it into an initial fluid configuration. We claim that such task can be implemented through an intuitive framework for fluid modeling using sketching techniques and GVF. In [11] we implemented a $2D$ environment where the sketching were made through simple lines draws using the mouse as input device. In this work, the main challenge remains in the task of convert drawing input from the user as an initial $3D$ fluid configuration.

As an example, much simpler then fluid dynamics, let us consider $2D$ electrostatic fields generated by punctual charges. In this case, we have two basic configurations: one for a positive charge and another one for a negative charge (Fig. 3).

The electrostatic field at point x given by one charge is:

$$ \mathbf{E} = \frac{kq_1}{x^2} e , \tag{20} $$

where k is a constant, q_1 is the charge and e is the unitary vector. Besides, given a distribution of charged particles we can compute the electrostatic field in a point through:

$$ \mathbf{E} = \sum \frac{kq_i}{x_i^2} e_i . \tag{21} $$

In the case of fluid dynamics the sketching of the initial configuration is much more complex because there are too many degrees of freedom to consider. However, in terms of high level features, the initialization of the LBM simulation can be performed through the initial velocity field and convenient boundary conditions that define the fluid behavior nearby the frontiers of the domain. In this work we propose to use an electrostatic field as a sketch icon to define the initial velocity field of the fluid.

Thus, given a $3D$ domain, a charge is located in some point within the volume, and the electrostatic field is calculated for all point x inside a neighborhood with radius r around the charge, through equation (20). If more then one charge is available, then the electrostatic field must be calculated through equation (21). In this way, the electrostatic

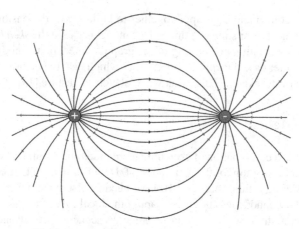

Fig. 3. Example of interaction of opposites charges

field gives the field **F** in expressions (11)-(13) and the initial condition v_0 of the GVF. Then, the iterative process of the GVF should compute many times as necessary until the initial field is smooth enough to act as an initial condition of the fluid simulation. Finally, the solution of GVF equations generates the initial velocity field that we need to set up the LBM simulation through the equilibrium function given by expression (5).

The computational system was developed in $C/C++$ language, using the object oriented paradigm. The visualization was implemented in OpenGL, a traditional library for computer graphics. The GLUT programming interface was used to implement the interactions between OpenGL and the window system of our application. The graphical user interface, composed by buttons, checkboxes, spinners, among others controls, is generated using the GLUI API, which is a GLUT-based $C++$ user interface library. The Fig. 4 shows the main window of the computational system.

7   Results

This section presents a $3D$ fluid flow example achieved by our framework, using a positive charge to represent an initial outflow within the fluid. For the results explained below the dimension of the grid is $128 \times 128 \times 128$. In this way, we start by defining a positive charge with $q = 5.0$, located exactly at the middle of the volume. So, the electrostatic field is calculated for all point x inside a neighborhood with radius $r = 32$. The Fig. 4 shows the visualization of the velocity vectors computed by the equation (20). Following all the procedure explained in section 6, we compute the GVF field through 100 iterations, and then use the solution of GVF equations to define the initial velocity field for the LBM simulation. Finally, we simulate the fluid until it reaches the equilibrium state. The Fig. 5 shows the visualization of the velocity vectors of the LBM in a step 100 of the fluid simulation.

The LBM simulation generates the density (scalar) and the velocity (vector) fields. The visualization of the density is performed through a color map for each cell of the lattice: we map the density range into a color scale and draw a single point. Therefore, the field is rendered as a color field in the display. The velocity field is visualized

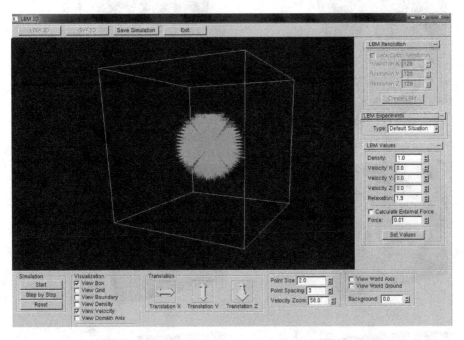

Fig. 4. The graphical user interface of the computational system

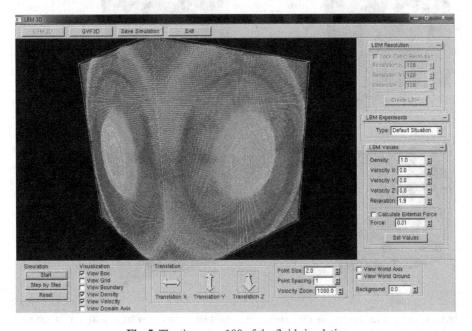

Fig. 5. The time step 100 of the fluid simulation

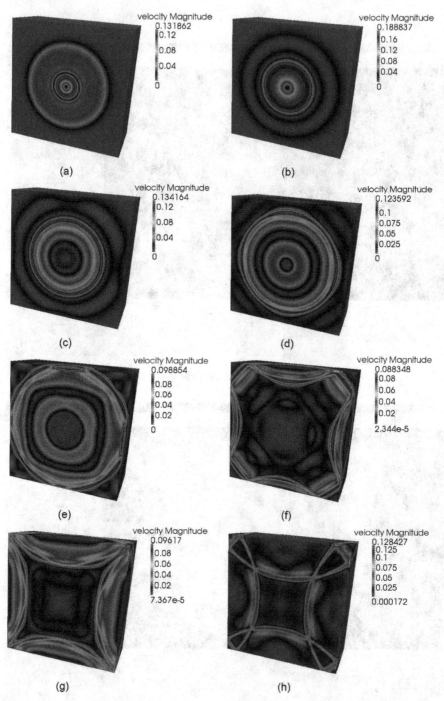

Fig. 6. Results for the respective time steps of the fluid simulation: (a) 20, (b) 40, (c) 60, (d) 80, (e) 100, (f) 120, (g) 140, (h) 160

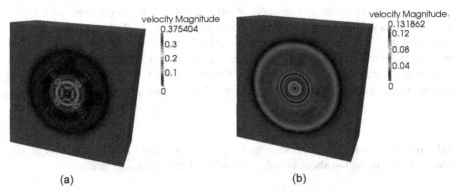

Fig. 7. Results for the the fluid simulation at time step 20 using: (a) 20 GVF iterations, (b) 100 GVF iterations

through oriented arrows for each cell, which size is scaled according to the velocity field intensity, as seen in Fig. 4 and Fig. 5. However, these visualizations are not comfortable in a $3D$ environment. Thus, to increase the visualization, we used the Paraview, as we can see in Fig. 6.

The Fig. 6 shows a sequence of the simulation proposed. We can see that the fluid behaves as expected, evolving toward the edges. To illustrate the advantage of the GVF methodology, the Fig. 7 (a) and (b) shows the same time step of the fluid simulation ($t = 20$) and both with the same configuration as explained in the beginning of the section. The difference between these images is that the first one used only 20 iterations of the GVF, while the second one used 100 iterations of the GVF. We observed that the Fig. 7 (b) reaches a smoother velocity field, with values nearly three times smaller than the Fig. 7 (a).

8 Conclusions and Future Works

In this work we presented a computational system that allows a $3D$ fluid flow initialization for computer graphics applications. We proposed a combination of sketching techniques with the $3D$ Gradient Vector Flow method to obtain a smooth initialization for the simulation. The fluid simulation is done using a three-dimensional Lattice Boltzmann Method (LBM). The results section illustrates an example of fluid flow simulated through our system. We observed that the combination proposed in section 6 worked well for the purposes of this work. Moreover, if we discard the GVF and use the initial field given by the electrostatic field tested in the results section as the initial condition of the LBM, the simulation destabilizes because of high velocity values. This fact confirms the advantage of using the GVF methodology for generating smooth initial conditions, without compromising the stability of the simulation model. However, it is necessary to conduct a study of the computational cost involved, since the GVF is also an iterative process.

The main contribution of this work is the implementation and combination of the three-dimensional methodologies involved. To validate this combination, a fixed scenario was implemented in the results section. However, to achieve completely our goals, the system must allow the user to generate different situations. In this way, a future direction for this work is to implement the $3D$ sketching process. With the sketching techniques the system enables the user to draw freely the initial state of the fluid flow using an intuitive interface. But, the user may sketch unstable configurations that changes too fast without adding extra machinery to the fluid flow model, which may be an undesirable behavior. Our system must check such problem and warn the user or automatically fix it.

Acknowledgements. The authors would like to thank Daniel Reis Golbert, for all the attention and discussion about visualization of $3D$ LBM fluid simulation.

References

1. Aubert, G., Kornprobst, P.: Mathematical Problems in Image Processing - Partial Differential Equations and the Calculus of Variations. Springer, New York (2002)
2. Bærentzen, J.A., Christensen, N.J.: Volume Sculpting using the Level-Set Method. In: Proceedings of the Shape Modeling International, p. 175. IEEE Computer Society (2002)
3. Buick, J.M., Easson, W.J., Greated, C.A.: Numerical Simulation of Internal Gravity Waves using a Lattice Gas Model. International Journal for Numerical Methods in Fluids 26, 657–676 (1998)
4. Chen, S., Doolen, G.D.: Lattice Boltzmann Method for Fluid Flows. Annual Review of Fluid Mechanics 30, 329–364 (1998)
5. Chopard, B., Luthi, P., Masselot, A.: Cellular Automata and Lattice Boltzmann techniques: an approach to model and simulate complex systems. Advances in Physics (1998)
6. Cook, M.T., Agah, A.: A Survey of Sketch-based 3D Modeling Techniques. Interact. Comput. 21, 201–211 (2009)
7. Cruz, L., Velho, L.: A sketch on sketch-based interfaces and modeling. In: Graphics, Patterns and Images Tutorials (SIBGRAPI-T), pp. 22–33 (2010)
8. Foster, N., Metaxas, D.: Modeling the Motion of a Hot, Turbulent Gas. In: ACM SIGGRAPH, pp. 181–188 (1997)
9. Higuera, F.J., Jimenez, J., Succi, S.: Boltzmann approach to Lattice Gas simulations. Europhys. Lett. 9 (1989)
10. Igarashi, T., Matsuoka, S., Tanaka, H.: Teddy - a Sketching Interface for 3D Freeform Design. In: ACM SIGGRAPH Courses, New York (2007)
11. Judice, S.F., Giraldi, G.A.: SKETCHING FLUID FLOWS - Combining Sketch-based Techniques and Gradient Vector Flow for Lattice-Boltzmann Initialization. In: International Conference on Computer Graphics Theory and Applications, GRAPP, pp. 328–337 (2012)
12. McNamara, G.R., Zanetti, G.: Use of the Boltzmann Equation to Simulate Lattice-Gas Automata. Phys. Rev. Lett. 61, 2332–2335 (1988)
13. Müller, M., Keiser, R., Nealen, A., Pauly, M., Gross, M., Alexa, M.: Point-based Animation of Elastic, Plastic and Melting Objects. In: ACM SIGGRAPH/Eurographics Symposium on Computer Animation, pp. 141–151 (2004)
14. Müller, M., Schirm, S., Teschner, M.: Interactive Blood Simulation for Virtual Surgery based on Smoothed Particle Hydrodynamics. Technol. Health Care 12, 25–31 (2004)
15. Rothman, D.H., Zaleski, S.: Lattice-Gas Models of Phase Separation - Interface, Phase Transition and Multiphase Flows. Rev. Mod. Phys. 66, 1417–1479 (1994)

16. Schroeder, D., Coffey, D., Keefe, D.: Drawing with the Flow - a Sketch-based Interface for Illustrative Visualization of 2D Vector Fields. In: Proceedings of the Seventh Sketch-Based Interfaces and Modeling Symposium, pp. 49–56. Eurographics Association, Aire-la-Ville (2010)

17. Stam, J.: Flows on Surfaces of Arbitrary Topology. In: ACM SIGGRAPH, pp. 724–731 (2003)

18. Sutherland, I.E.: Sketchpad - a Man-Machine Graphical Communication System. In: Proceedings of the SHARE Design Automation Workshop, pp. 6.329–6.346. ACM, New York (1964)

19. Thorne, M., Burke, D., van de Panne, M.: Motion Doodles - an Interface for Sketching Character Motion. ACM Trans. Graph. 23, 424–431 (2004)

20. Thürey, N.: A Lattice Boltzmann Method for Single-Phase Free Surface Flows in 3D. Master's Thesis, Dept. of Computer Science 10. University of Erlangen-Nuremberg (2003)

21. Varley, P.A.C., Martin, R.R., Suzuki, H.: Can Machines Interpret Line Drawings? In: EUROGRAPHICS Workshop on Sketch-Based Interfaces and Modeling (2004)

22. Wei, X., Member, S., Li, W., Mueller, K., Kaufman, A.E.: The Lattice Boltzmann Method for Simulating Gaseous Phenomena. IEEE Transactions on Visualization and Computer Graphics 10, 164–176 (2004)

23. Williams, L.: 3D Paint. ACM SIGGRAPH Comput. Graph. 24, 225–233 (1990)

24. Witting, P.: Computational Fluid Dynamics in a Traditional Animation Enviroment. In: ACM SIGGRAPH, pp. 129–136 (1999)

25. Xu, C., Prince, J.L.: Gradient Vector Flow: A new External Force for Snakes. In: Proceedings of the Conference on Computer Vision and Pattern Recognition, pp. 66–71 (1997)

26. Xu, C., Prince, J.L.: Snakes, Shapes, and Gradient Vector Flow. IEEE Transactions on Image Processing 7, 359–369 (1998)

27. Xu, C., Prince, J.L.: Gradient Vector Flow Deformable Models. In: Bankman, I. (ed.) Handbook of Medical Imaging. Academic Press (September 2000)

28. Zeleznik, R.C., Herndon, K.P., Hughes, J.F.: Sketch - an Interface for Sketching 3D Scenes. In: ACM SIGGRAPH Courses, New York (2006)

29. Zhu, B., Iwata, M., Haraguchi, R., Ashihara, T., Umetani, N., Igarashi, T., Nakazawa, K.: Sketchbased Dynamic Illustration of Fluid Systems. SIGGRAPH ASIA Technical Papers, Hong Kong (2011)

Part II

Information Visualization Theory and Applications

Space-Time Flow Visualization of Dynamics in 2D Lagrangian Coherent Structures

Filip Sadlo[1], Sven Bachthaler[1], Carsten Dachsbacher[2], and Daniel Weiskopf[1]

[1] University of Stuttgart, Germany
[2] Karlsruhe Institute of Technology, Germany
{sadlo,bachthaler,weiskopf}@visus.uni-stuttgart.de,
dachsbacher@kit.edu

Abstract. Stretching and compression in tangent directions of Lagrangian coherent structures (LCS) are of particular interest in the vicinity of hyperbolic trajectories and play a key role in turbulence and mixing. Since integration of hyperbolic trajectories is difficult, we propose to visualize them in 2D time-dependent vector fields by space-time intersection curves of LCS. LCS are present as ridge lines in the 2D finite-time Lyapunov exponent (FTLE) field and as ridge surfaces in its 3D space-time domain. We extract these ridge surfaces from the forward and reverse FTLE field and intersect them. Due to their advection property, LCS become stream surfaces in 3D space-time. This allows us to use line integral convolution on the LCS to visualize their intrinsic dynamics, in particular around hyperbolic trajectories. To reduce occlusion, we constrain the LCS to space-time bands around their intersection curves. We evaluate our approach using synthetic, simulated, and measured vector fields.

Keywords: Flow visualization, Lagrangian coherent structures, Hyperbolic trajectories.

1 Introduction

As science and engineering methods evolve, modeling of phenomena is shifting from stationary to time-dependent domains. 2D computational fluid dynamics (CFD) simulations are of major importance in several domains, such as the analysis of flow in films and on free-slip boundaries. To examine and understand such data, efficient tools for analysis and visualization are required. Feature extraction techniques, providing a condensed representation of the essential information, are often applied to the visualization of vector fields. A prominent concept revealing the overall structure is vector field topology [1]. Whereas vector field topology is directly applicable only to steady or quasi-stationary vector fields, Lagrangian coherent structures (LCS) [2] are popular for the analysis of time-dependent vector fields. LCS are a time-dependent counterpart to separatrices, which are streamlines started from separating regions of different behavior. LCS have been increasingly subject to research in the last decade and can be obtained as maximizing curves (ridges) in the finite-time Lyapunov exponent (FTLE), a scalar field measuring the separation of trajectories [2]. FTLE computation is, however, an expensive task because at least one trajectory needs to be computed per sample point.

G. Csurka et al. (Eds.): VISIGRAPP 2012, CCIS 359, pp. 145–159, 2013.
© Springer-Verlag Berlin Heidelberg 2013

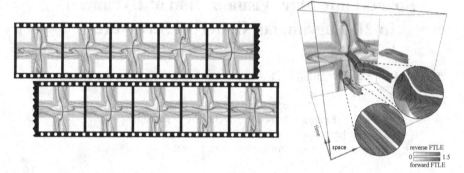

Fig. 1. Left: Traditional visualization of a time-dependent vector field by time series of the finite-time Lyapunov exponent is difficult to analyze and does not convey the dynamics inside its ridges (Lagrangian coherent structures). Right: Our space-time representation reveals the overall structure and makes the dynamics inside the Lagrangian coherent structures visible by line texture patterns. Close-ups: In contrast to the traditional 2D visualization, different dynamics along intersection curves (almost parallel flow on the left vs. strongly hyperbolic flow on the right) is apparent.

LCS behave as material lines under the action of time-dependent flow, i.e., they are advected and exhibit negligible cross-flow for sufficiently long advection time intervals, as reported by Haller [2], Lekien et al. [3], and Sadlo et al. [4]. This property gives rise, e.g., to the acceleration technique by Sadlo et al. [5] based on grid advection.

Our new method adopts the concept of hyperbolic trajectories and space-time streak manifolds, which we therefore discuss in the following. Previous work by Sadlo and Weiskopf for 2D fields [6] and Üffinger et al. for 3D fields [7] generalized vector field topology to time-dependent vector fields by replacing the role of streamlines by generalized streak lines [8]. This way, critical points turn into degenerate streak lines and separatrices into streak lines (space-time streak manifolds) converging toward these degenerate streak lines in forward or reverse time. It was found that these need to be distinguished degenerate streak lines identical to the previously discovered hyperbolic trajectories [9].

Hyperbolic trajectories can be seen as constituent structures in time-dependent 2D vector field topology. As mentioned, space-time streak manifolds—the time-dependent counterpart to separatrices—can be constructed alone from hyperbolic trajectories—no dense sampling is required in contrast to the FTLE approach. However, a major limitation with hyperbolic trajectories is the difficulty of their integration. Although the integration error tends to grow exponentially in linear vector fields, it is usually negligible due to comparably short advection times and low separation rates along common trajectories. Unfortunately, this is not the case in typical hyperbolic configurations due to large separation rates and the fact that both forward and reverse integration are subject to repulsion from one of the LCS (see Fig. 2). Hyperbolic trajectories coincide with the intersection of forward and reverse LCS; since ridges in forward FTLE represent repelling LCS whereas those in reverse FTLE are attracting, the trajectory is repelled from the former forward and from the latter in backward direction.

Our method has therefore a twofold objective: (1) avoiding the integration of hyperbolic trajectories by replacing them with intersections of LCS, and (2) revealing

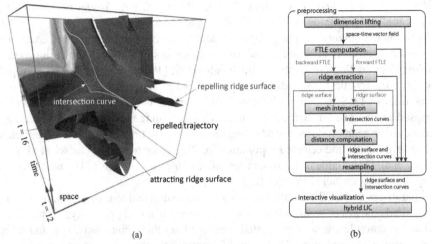

(a)   (b)

Fig. 2. (a) Space-time ridge surfaces in forward (red) and reverse (blue) finite-time Lyapunov exponent together with cross section at final time step (colored). The space-time intersection curve in the center (white) represents a hyperbolic trajectory. Traditional integration of the hyperbolic trajectory from the initial intersection is difficult due to exponential growth of error (yellow curve). (b) Overview of our technique, accompanied by the data that are passed between the stages of the pipeline.

tangential dynamics in LCS, accomplished by line integral convolution (LIC). By treating time as an additional dimension, we obtain a stationary visualization that conveys the overall structure in space-time. Several approaches for obtaining seeds for hyperbolic trajectories exist: by intersecting ridges in hyperbolicity time [9], ridges in FTLE [6], and constructing streak manifolds from them, or by building a time-dependent linear model from critical points [10]. This kind of visualization of hyperbolic trajectories is, however, restricted to LCS geometry, i.e., the dynamics in the vicinity of the hyperbolic trajectories is not conveyed. Furthermore, the hyperbolicity of the vector field is typically analyzed by requiring negative determinant of the velocity gradient. This approach fails in providing insight into the role and importance of hyperbolic trajectories. In contrast, our LIC-based visualization captures the configuration of the flow in the neighborhood of hyperbolic trajectories and also in general along LCS. One example is the discrimination of almost parallel flow configurations from strongly hyperbolic ones (Fig. 1, (right)). This provides increased insight in the overall dynamics, interplay, and importance of LCS. For example, this allows for a qualitative analysis of mixing phenomena. We refer the reader to fluid mechanics literature, e.g., [11] for the underlying concepts, e.g., for details on mixing and the Lagrangian skeleton of turbulence.

2   Related Work

Work that is closely related to our objectives was discussed in the previous section, here we give a short overview of work that is in weaker context.

Many applications of vector field topology in fluid mechanics have been presented by Perry et al. [12]. It was later introduced in visualization by Helman and Hesselink [1],

[13] again in the context of flow fields. For details, we refer the reader to the work by Globus et al. [14], Asimov [15], and Abraham and Shaw [16].

Vector field topology did also give rise to derived concepts and techniques. Examples are saddle connectors [17] and boundary switch curves [18], both augmenting vector field topology by line-type features. Bachthaler et al. [19] proposed a flux-based topology for 2D magnetic fields induced by point dipoles. Hlawatsch et al. [20] extended the concept of LCS to symmetric second-order tensor fields. Peikert and Sadlo [21] proposed a technique for extracting islands of stability in recirculating flow. Several approaches have been proposed for adopting the concepts to time-dependent vector fields, including the path line oriented topologies for 2D vector fields by Theisel et al. [22] and Shi et al. [23], Galilean-invariant alternatives for critical points [24], and basics for a Lagrangian vector field topology [25].

Separatrices and LCS are able to convey the structural and temporal organization of vector fields, however, at the same time, they suffer from this property; vector direction and magnitude are not represented, neither along these constructs, nor, and more importantly, in their vicinity. There are different approaches to overcome these drawbacks. Critical points are often visualized with glyphs representing the linearized flow. Another approach is to augment separatrices with arrows as presented by Weinkauf et al. [26]. However, the most common approach in 2D and 3D vector field topology is to combine the separatrices with line integral convolution (LIC), e.g., see Weiskopf and Ertl [27]. This vector field visualization with LIC can be either drawn between separatrices in the case of 2D vector fields, or on the separatrices themselves in the case of 3D vector fields. For time-dependent vector fields, this approach is not applicable because LIC visualizes transport along streamlines, i.e., instantaneous field lines, whereas LCS are usually obtained using true trajectories, i.e., from path lines. Therefore, other methods are required for visualizing the advection in the context of LCS, e.g., Shadden et al. [28] advect particles. We exploit the fact that 2D time-dependent vector fields can be turned into 3D stationary vector fields by dimension lifting. Since the resulting domain is steady, streamlines are then equal to path lines, which allows us to use LIC. Texture-based methods (like LIC) have the advantage of avoiding the seed point positioning problem by conveying the field structure in a dense fashion. Since there is no intrinsic, predefined surface parametrization available, image-space oriented methods like [29], [30], and [27] are predestined for our task (we build on the latter one). More background information on texture-based vector field visualization can be found in the survey by Laramee et al. [31].

3   Space-Time LCS Visualization

Our new visualization technique builds on the fact that time-dependent vector fields can be turned into stationary ones by treating time as additional dimension. This approach is common in the field of differential equations, where non-autonomous systems are made autonomous. Hence, 2D time-dependent vector fields $(u(x, y, t), v(x, y, t))^\top$ are converted into steady 3D vector fields $(u(x, y, t), v(x, y, t), 1)^\top$, which we denote as space-time vector fields. All following steps of our algorithm (see Fig. 2(b)) take place in this space-time domain. Since 2D path lines represent streamlines in space-time, we use 3D streamline integration over advection time T inside the space-time vector field to generate a flow map $\phi(x, y, t) \mapsto (x', y', t + T)^\top$. Then, for each time slice $\bar{t}$ of the space-time stack we compute the traditional 2D FTLE according to Haller [2] as $1/|T| \ln \sqrt{\lambda_{\max}[(\nabla_2 \phi(x, y, \bar{t}))^\top \nabla_2 \phi(x, y, \bar{t})]}$ with $\nabla_2 = (\partial/\partial x, \partial/\partial y, 0)^\top$ and major eigenvalue $\lambda_{\max}(\cdot)$. LCS are then extracted from the resulting stack of traditional 2D FTLE fields by ridge surface extraction, discussed in Section 3.1.

Due to the discussed material advection property of LCS, these surfaces represent stream surfaces in the space-time vector field, i.e., they are tangent to the space-time flow. This allows a direct application of LIC techniques, which we describe in Section 3.3. By this, LIC visualizes the dynamics of path lines along which the LCS are advected, and hence the dynamics within the LCS. As intersections of stream surfaces are streamlines, the space-time intersection of these LCS surfaces from forward and reverse FTLE represents a counterpart to hyperbolic trajectories. In Section 3.2, we address the investigation of these intersection curves in terms of hyperbolicity, again based on LCS. Restricting the LIC visualization to bands around the intersection curves comprises our second major contribution, detailed in Section 3.4.

3.1 Ridge Surface Extraction

We extract the ridge surfaces from the stack of 2D FTLE fields as height ridges [32] of codimension one from the 3D space-time FTLE field, according to Sadlo and Peikert [33]. We follow this approach to avoid the problems that would arise from stitching of the individual ridge curves from the 2D FTLE fields. Furthermore, ridges are typically non-manifold, which would cause further issues. Since Eberly's formulation [32] is local and relies on higher-order derivatives, it is subject to erroneous solutions. It is therefore common practice to apply filtering and we follow the filtering process described by Sadlo and Peikert [34]: since only sufficiently "sharp" FTLE ridges represent LCS, ridge regions where the modulus of the eigenvalue of the Hessian is too low are suppressed. Further, we require a minimum FTLE value, hence requiring a minimum separation strength of the LCS. Finally, to suppress small ridges, we filter the ridge surfaces by area. As described in [34], we also use a least-squares approach to prevent noise amplification during estimation of the gradient and Hessian. Figure 2 shows examples of ridges extracted from a stack of forward and reverse-time FTLE: repelling LCS (ridges in forward FTLE) colored red and attracting ones (ridges in reverse FTLE) blue. The space-time structure of the field is revealed including the intersection curves. However, this does not convey hyperbolicity aspects, e.g., it does not disambiguate intersection curves representing strong hyperbolic trajectories from weak hyperbolic ones. This motivates the visualization of hyperbolicity on LCS.

3.2 Visualizing Hyperbolicity

To help the user in the investigation of hyperbolic effects, and hyperbolic trajectories in particular, we map hyperbolicity to saturation, shown in Fig. 3(a). We have chosen the hyperbolicity definition by Haller [9], i.e., the sign of the determinant of the velocity gradient of the original 2D vector field at the respective space-time location. One can see how this technique not only reveals the presence of hyperbolicity but also allows for

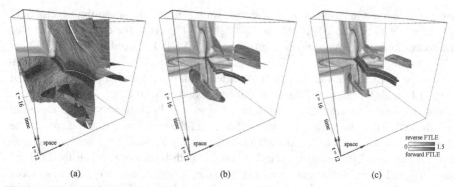

Fig. 3. Building blocks for space-time LCS visualization, shown with the example from Sec. 5.1. Advection time for forward and reverse FTLE is $T = 4s$. (a) Space-time LIC qualitatively visualizes LCS dynamics: hyperbolic behavior is apparent. In addition, hyperbolicity is encoded by color saturation. A minimum FTLE value of 0.5 is used. (b) Intersection bands by clipping with complementary FTLE reduce occlusion but still provide context, and convey structure of the reverse FTLE. The minimum complementary FTLE value is 0.41. (c) Intersection bands by clipping with distance to intersection curves further reduces occlusion and provides the topological skeleton.

the interpretation of the hyperbolic regions around the intersection curves. To examine hyperbolicity more precisely, we introduce a novel technique to visualize LCS dynamics in the next section.

3.3 Visualizing LCS Dynamics

The LCS in our space-time FTLE field are present as ridge surfaces and to fully capture the spatial variation of their dynamics they lend themselves to dense texture-based visualization such as LIC. Since LCS lack intrinsic surface parametrization and need to be analyzed in overview scales as well as in local detail, image-space oriented approaches are predestined to visualize the space-time structure. We use the hybrid physical/device-space LIC approach by Weiskopf and Ertl [27], which relies on particle tracing computed in the physical space of the object and in the device space of the image plane at the same time. The LIC pattern is based on the tangential part of the vectors attached to our surfaces. This dual-space approach combines the advantages of image-space methods with frame-to-frame coherence and avoids inflow issues at silhouette lines. For a detailed description of this visualization technique, we refer to the original paper.

In the context of our visualization of LCS dynamics, the goal is to visualize the space-time direction of the vector field. Hence, we normalize the space-time vectors during LIC computation to obtain LIC line patterns of uniform length for optimal perception. In contrast to traditional spatial LIC, we retain the visual encoding of velocity magnitude in the form of surface orientation in space-time. For example, small angles between surface normal and the time axis indicate high speed.

Figure 3(a) exemplifies the method again on the same data set. It is apparent how this technique conveys the time-dependent dynamics within LCS. Combining it with the saturation-based visualization of hyperbolicity (Section 3.2) supports the identification of hyperbolic intersection curves and still provides the LCS dynamics context. Since LCS are often convoluted, they typically exhibit many intersections that are, however, often occluded. We address this problem by the building block described next: the restriction of the technique to regions around space-time LCS intersection curves. At the same time, this approach explicitly addresses the analysis of the intersection curves.

3.4 LCS Intersection Bands

Even in the simple example shown so far, it is obvious that occlusion tends to be a problem in space-time visualization of LCS. To address this and to provide a method for analyzing intersection curves of LCS at the same time, we introduce two complementary approaches that have proven valuable in our experiments, both restricting the visualization to bands around the LCS intersection curves.

As discussed in Section 3.1, a common approach is to filter FTLE ridges by prescribing a minimum FTLE value. This way, the visualization is restricted to important LCS, i.e., those representing strong separation. This filter is applied to ridges in both forward and reverse FTLE fields. If we additionally prescribe a minimum value for the complementary FTLE, i.e., the reverse in case of forward FTLE ridges and the forward in case of reverse FTLE ridges, one typically restricts the visualization to bands around the intersection curves, shown in Fig. 3(b). This technique has the advantage that the profile of the complementary FTLE field is conveyed, allowing qualitative interpretation of the interplay of LCS. Furthermore, it often features additional bands that do not exhibit LCS intersections. They are generated if FTLE ridges are located in regions of high complementary FTLE. These additional bands are still of interest: the respective regions exhibit both high forward and reverse-time FTLE. Additionally, these bands may connect to other bands that feature intersection curves and hence convey the overall organization of the LCS. A drawback of this approach, however, is that the bands may get too narrow for appropriate LIC visualization or too wide to sufficiently reduce occlusion.

Therefore, we propose, as an alternative, to restrict the LCS to the neighborhood of their intersection curves. To avoid numerical issues, we first omit regions where the LCS intersect at small angle.

Furthermore, a minimum length of the intersection curves is required to obtain significant visualizations. The remaining intersection curves are then used for distance computation, leading to a distance field on the LCS that is then used for clipping. Figure 3(c) shows an example: the dynamics of the LCS is well depicted by LIC and at the same time occlusion is substantially reduced, allowing for the analysis of the intersection curves with respect to LCS dynamics and hyperbolicity. Since the resulting bands can still be too narrow due to perspective foreshortening, we also support depth-corrected width of the bands described in Section 4.2.

To sum up, these clipping approaches result in visualizations that can be seen as an extended topological skeleton of time-dependent flow. Note that we use equal thresholds for forward and reverse-time FTLE ridge filtering as well as for complementary FTLE band clipping, for ensuring consistent visualization. Finally, we would like to point out the similarity to saddle connectors [17], although our approach resides in space-time, whereas saddle connectors visualize 3D steady vector fields.

3.5 Combined Visualization

Our system allows the user to interactively switch on and off the clipping for intersection bands. When clipping is enabled, the remaining choice is between complementary FTLE and distance-based intersection bands. Depth-correction of intersection band width is always enabled. In summary, only three different modes (no clipping, complementary clipping, distance-based clipping) are required to cover the visualization needs.

4 Implementation

This section details the implementation of the different building blocks of our technique as well as modifications to existing approaches. The pipeline shown in Fig. 2(b) gives an overview of the steps and provides information about the data that are exchanged between different stages of the pipeline.

4.1 Preprocessing

Several steps in our technique are performed in a pre-processing phase, once per data set.

The original data set is given as a series of time steps of a 2D vector field. To create the stationary space-time 3D vector field, we apply dimension lifting, i.e., the time series of the 2D vector field are stacked and the time dimension is treated as additional third dimension. This space-time vector field is used to compute the 3D space-time FTLE field for forward and reverse time direction. Using this FTLE field, ridge surfaces are extracted. A detailed description of the ridge extraction method is given by Sadlo and Peikert [34].

The ridge surface meshes from forward and reverse–time FTLE are intersected to obtain the intersection curves. Once the geometry of all intersection curves is obtained, a distance field is computed that holds the distance of ridge surface vertices to the nearest intersection curve. Next, we compute vertex-based normals, which are used for shading in the interactive visualization. During this process, normals are reoriented if necessary; however, since ridge surfaces are not necessarily orientable, we may not succeed for all normals. Remaining inconsistencies for the normals are treated during interactive visualization using a shader. Finally, the space-time flow vectors are sampled at the vertex locations of the ridge surface mesh. This resampling is independent of the FTLE sampling grid, allowing for acceleration methods [35], [34], and [36]. Distance values, normals, resampled flow vectors, and additional scalars like FTLE values, hyperbolicity, and the minor eigenvalue of the Hessian (see Section 3.1) are attached to the ridge surface mesh that is then passed to the interactive visualization stage.

4.2 Interactive Visualization

The core of our interactive visualization is based on hybrid physical/device-space LIC [27] to create line-like texture on the ridge surfaces.

During rendering of the space-time ridge surfaces, we apply Phong illumination to enhance visibility and perception of the geometry. Since the ridge surfaces may be non-orientable, we have to ensure that local normal vectors are consistently oriented in order to avoid shading artifacts. Therefore, we make normal orientation consistent during fragment processing using the dot product between normal and view vector. This prevents inconsistent shading due to normal interpolation; however, ridge surfaces may still appear rippled. This happens because of FTLE aliasing effects at strong and sharp ridges, where very high FTLE gradients are present. To compensate for this, we correct the normals to be perpendicular to the space-time vector field and hence to its LCS during fragment processing.

We handle occlusion by attaching additional data (regular FTLE, complementary FTLE, distance to nearest intersection curve) obtained during the preprocessing stage (see Section 4.1) to each vertex of the ridge surface mesh and upload this data as additional texture coordinates to the GPU. Fragments that do not meet the filtering criteria are discarded. All thresholds used in this process are adjustable in real-time by the user. In addition to user controlled clipping, we adjust the width of our LCS intersection bands if they are clipped by the distance to the nearest intersection curve. We adjust the clipping threshold based on distance to the camera position. This results in intersection bands with constant image-space width, which reduces occlusion of intersection bands that are close to the camera. At the same time, intersection bands that are farther away are enlarged, which improves visibility of the LIC pattern.

5   Results

We apply the presented methods to different data sets. The first two data sets are synthetic, whereas the third is created by CFD simulation, and the fourth is obtained by remote sensing of ocean currents.

Our implementation was tested on a PC with an Intel Core Quad CPU (2.4 GHz), 4 GB of RAM and an NVIDIA GeForce 275 GPU with 896 MB of dedicated graphics memory. Each of the presented data sets is visualized at interactive rates. Since our implementation is based on the approach presented by Weiskopf and Ertl [27], it shows the same performance behavior—we refer to their paper for a detailed performance analysis.

A bounding box of the domain helps the user to navigate and orientate in space-time. This bounding box is color coded—the time dimension is indicated by a blue axis while the two spatial dimensions have a red and green axis, respectively. The last time step of the space-time region of interest is located at the back end of the bounding box which shows the FTLE field as a color–coded texture. In this texture, FTLE values are mapped to saturation, with full saturation mapping to the highest FTLE value. There, we use the same color-coding as for the space-time ridge surfaces.

5.1   Oscillating Gyre Saddle

The synthetic vector field that we use as an example in this section is due to Sadlo and Weiskopf [6]. It exhibits a non-linear saddle (Fig. 4(a)) that oscillates between the locations $(0.25, 0.25)$ and $(-0.25, -0.25)$ at a period of $\tau = 4$. Please refer to Fig. 1, Fig. 2, and Fig. 3 for resulting visualizations. To sum up, it exhibits a strongly hyperbolic intersection curve visualized in Fig. 1 (right) and several non-hyperbolic ones. This is

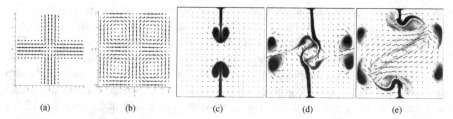

Fig. 4. (a) Gyre Saddle example at $t = 0$. (b) Quad Gyre example at $t = 0$. (c)–(e) Three time steps of the buoyant plume example, color indicates temperature (red maps to high temperature, blue to low temperature). (c) Two plumes build up and travel toward each other in vertical direction. (d) After collision, two new plumes are created that travel toward the walls. (e) After collision with the walls.

consistent with the Eulerian picture (Fig. 4(a)) showing distinguished saddle behavior at its center. As mentioned by Sadlo and Weiskopf [6], there are other ridges due to shear processes. These are of inferior importance for mixing and cannot give rise to hyperbolic trajectories, i.e., their LIC patterns do not show hyperbolic behavior. Note that we filter FTLE ridges to show the strongest and largest LCS. Supressing weaker ridges simplifies the resulting visualization which we use for depicting purposes.

5.2   Quad Gyre

The double gyre example was introduced by Shadden et al. [28] to examine FTLE and LCS, and to compare them to vector field topology. It consists of two vortical regions separated by a straight separatrix that connects two saddle-type critical points: one oscillating horizontally at the upper edge and the other synchronously oscillating horizontally along the lower edge. This is a prominent example where the vector field topology result substantially differs from LCS. This data set is temporally periodic. To avoid boundary issues, we use a larger range, resulting in four gyres. As proposed by Shadden et al., we use the configuration $\epsilon = 1/4$, $\omega = \pi/5$, and $A = 1/10$. Figure 4(b) shows a plot at $t = 0$ for these parameters.

Rendering the quad gyre without clipping (Fig. 5(a)) results in space-time ridges that heavily occlude each other. Please note that the $y = 0$ plane represents an LCS in both forward and reverse direction, which results in z-fighting. Nevertheless, the LIC line pattern is consistent in that region due to the image-based LIC technique. Reducing occlusion by clipping with the complementary FTLE (Fig. 5(b)) removes parts of the ridge surfaces, while preserving the context of the bands. Note, for example, that the red bands are connected at the upper edge of the domain and hence are part of the same LCS. If we clip the space-time ridge surfaces by distance to their intersection curves (Fig. 5(c)), occlusion is even more reduced, but less context is conveyed. However, this technique especially pays off in data sets with complex space-time dynamics, since the topological skeleton is well visible from most views. In all images, hyperbolicity is visualized by mapping it to the saturation of the ridge surface color. It can be seen that it readily guides attention to hyperbolic LIC patterns. As in the results by Sadlo and Weiskopf [6], we identify a hyperbolic trajectory at the center of the structure.

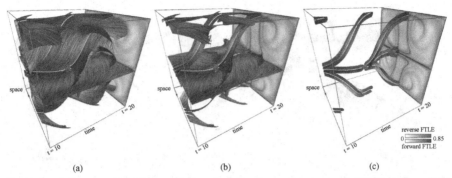

(a)   (b)   (c)

Fig. 5. Quad-Gyre example. The advection time for forward and reverse FTLE is $T = 7.5s$. (a) Full visualization of forward and reverse LCS. A lower FTLE threshold of 0.4 is used. (b) Visualization restricted to complementary FTLE bands. Minor artifacts appear due to aliasing effects of forward and reverse FTLE. The minimum complementary FTLE value is 0.19. (c) Restriction to distance-based LCS intersection bands reveals the topological space-time skeleton.

5.3 Buoyant Plumes

This data was obtained by a CFD simulation of buoyant 2D flow. A square container was modeled with a small heated region at its bottom wall and a small cooled region at its top wall. Figure 4(c)–4(e) illustrates the flow. Two plumes are developed, a hot one rising to the top and a cold one moving in reverse direction to the bottom. They then collide at the center and give rise to two new plumes traveling horizontally toward the side walls. As they approach the walls, they both split and produce plumes traveling in vertical direction. From that point on, the regular behavior is replaced by increasingly turbulent flow behavior.

Figure 6(a) shows the visualization of both forward- and reverse-time FTLE ridges. There is no clipping applied for this image but saturation already guides to the hyperbolic regions, however, many of them are occluded. In Fig. 6(b), the distance-based LCS intersection bands nicely visualize the hyperbolic mechanisms. One can see how the two plumes approach each other and merge, then divide and later give rise to turbulent flow. We finally identify several strong hyperbolic regions toward the end of the examined time interval. The multitude of hyperbolic regions approves the observation of strong buoyant mixing. The high intricacy and topological complexity of turbulent buoyant flow reflects in our visualization.

5.4 OSCAR

Ocean Surface Currents Analyses Real-time (OSCAR) [37] is a project to calculate ocean surface velocities from satellite data. The OSCAR product is a direct computation of global surface currents using satellite sea surface height, wind, and temperature. The OSCAR analyses have been used extensively in climate studies, such as for ocean heat storage and phytoplankton blooms.

We applied our technique to the gulf stream at the east coast of North America. We thereby focused on a strong hyperbolic LCS system involved in mixing (Fig. 7(a)). As expected, our technique revealed a complex Lagrangian skeleton of turbulence [11],

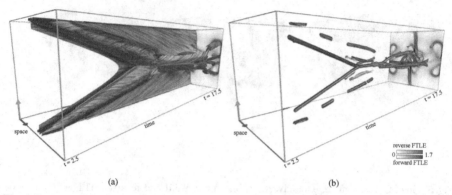

(a)   (b)

Fig. 6. Buoyant plumes example. The advection time for forward and reverse FTLE is $T = 1.5s$. (a) Full visualization of forward and reverse LCS. The dynamics of the two plumes is apparent in the first part of the examined time interval. A lower FTLE threshold of 0.87 is used. (b) LCS intersection bands clipped by distance, revealing the skeleton.

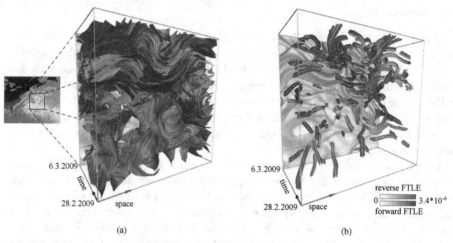

(a)   (b)

Fig. 7. OSCAR example. The advection time for forward and reverse FTLE is $T = 25$ days. The small map on the left hand side shows the atlantic ocean and the east coast of North America. It gives a frame of reference for our visualization results and exemplifies the prevalent mixing due to the gulf stream. Please note that this map does not show flow but rather water temperature mapped to colors and that it was generated outside of the investigated time interval. (a) Full visualization of forward and reverse LCS. A lower FTLE threshold of 9×10^{-7} is used. Flow around several intersection curves shows strong hyperbolic behavior. (b) LCS intersection bands clipped by distance.

shown in Fig. 7(a). Our LIC patterns allow a direct and qualitative inspection of the LCS with respect to hyperbolic mechanisms and mixing. Whereas many regions in the OSCAR data set exhibited inferior hyperbolic behavior, it is prominent in the selected region. Again, the LCS intersection bands dramatically reduce occlusion while still conveying topological structure and hyperbolic dynamics, see Fig. 7(b). Following the

LIC line patterns along the temporal axis directly conveys the action of the flow in terms of mixing, i.e., thinning and folding.

6 Conclusions

We have presented an approach for the visualization and analysis of the dynamics in LCS of time-dependent 2D vector fields. Compared to traditional approaches, we do not restrict the investigation of LCS to their geometric shape. We extend the visualization by allowing the user to analyze the intrinsic dynamics of LCS in terms of stretching and compression, in particular along hyperbolic trajectories. These dynamics are visualized by space-time LIC on space-time ridge surfaces of the 2D FTLE.

Occlusion problems due to convoluted and heavily intersecting LCS are reduced by clipping of the LCS, providing LCS intersection bands. Clipping can be based on the distance to the hyperbolic trajectories and on forward and reverse FTLE to suppress less important regions. A major numerical aspect of our method is the avoidance of the difficult direct integration of hyperbolic trajectories, we intersect FTLE ridge space-time surfaces instead. Still, the growth of the respective space-time streak manifolds is conveyed by the LIC.

Finally, we have demonstrated the applicability of our method with several synthetic and real-world data sets, also in the context of turbulent flow analysis, a topic of ongoing research. In future work, we plan to extend our technique to 3D time-dependent vector fields, i.e., investigate intersection curves of LCS and the surfaces they span over time.

Acknowledgements. The second and fourth author thank the German Research Foundation (DFG) for financial support within SFB 716 / D.5 at University of Stuttgart. The first author thanks DFG for financial support within the Cluster of Excellence in Simulation Technology, and SFB-TRR 75 at University of Stuttgart. This paper is an extended version of our previous work [38].

References

1. Helman, J., Hesselink, L.: Representation and display of vector field topology in fluid flow data sets. IEEE Computer 22, 27–36 (1989)
2. Haller, G.: Distinguished material surfaces and coherent structures in three-dimensional fluid flows. Physica D Nonlinear Phenomena 149, 248–277 (2001)
3. Lekien, F., Coulliette, C., Mariano, A.J., Ryan, E.H., Shay, L.K., Haller, G., Marsden, J.E.: Pollution release tied to invariant manifolds: A case study for the coast of Florida. Physica D Nonlinear Phenomena 210, 1–20 (2005)
4. Sadlo, F., Üffinger, M., Ertl, T., Weiskopf, D.: On the finite–time scope for computing Lagrangian coherent structures from Lyapunov exponents. In: Topological Methods in Data Analysis and Visualization II, pp. 269–281. Springer (2012)
5. Sadlo, F., Rigazzi, A., Peikert, R.: Time–dependent visualization of Lagrangian coherent structures by grid advection. In: Topological Methods in Data Analysis and Visualization, pp. 151–165. Springer (2011)
6. Sadlo, F., Weiskopf, D.: Time–dependent 2D vector field topology: An approach inspired by Lagrangian coherent structures. Comp. Graph. Forum 29, 88–100 (2010)

7. Üffinger, M., Sadlo, F., Ertl, T.: A Time-Dependent Vector Field Topology Based on Streak Surfaces. IEEE Transactions on Visualization and Computer Graphic 19, 379–392 (2013)
8. Wiebel, A., Tricoche, X., Schneider, D., Jaenicke, H., Scheuermann, G.: Generalized streak lines: Analysis and visualization of boundary induced vortices. IEEE Transactions on Visualization and Computer Graphics 13, 1735–1742 (2007)
9. Haller, G.: Finding finite-time invariant manifolds in two-dimensional velocity fields. Chaos 10, 99–108 (2000)
10. Ide, K., Small, D., Wiggins, S.: Distinguished hyperbolic trajectories in time-dependent fluid flows: Analytical and computational approach for velocity fields defined as data sets. Nonlinear Processes in Geophysics 9, 237–263 (2002)
11. Mathur, M., Haller, G., Peacock, T., Ruppert-Felsot, J.E., Swinney, H.L.: Uncovering the Lagrangian skeleton of turbulence. Physical Review Letters 98, 144502 (2007)
12. Perry, A.E., Chong, M.S.: A description of eddying motions and flow patterns using critical-point concepts. Annual Review of Fluid Mechanics 19, 125–155 (1987)
13. Helman, J., Hesselink, L.: Visualizing vector field topology in fluid flows. IEEE Computer Graphics and Applications 11, 36–46 (1991)
14. Globus, A., Levit, C., Lasinski, T.: A tool for visualizing the topology of three-dimensional vector fields. In: Proc. of IEEE Visualization, pp. 33–41 (1991)
15. Asimov, D.: Notes on the topology of vector fields and flows. Technical Report RNR-93-003, NASA Ames Research Center (1993)
16. Abraham, R.H., Shaw, C.D.: Dynamics, the Geometry of Behavior, 2nd edn. Addison-Wesley (1992)
17. Theisel, H., Weinkauf, T., Hege, H.C., Seidel, H.P.: Saddle connectors - An approach to visualizing the topological skeleton of complex 3D vector fields. In: Proc. IEEE Visualization, pp. 225–232 (2003)
18. Weinkauf, T., Theisel, H., Hege, H.C., Seidel, H.P.: Boundary switch connectors for topological visualization of complex 3D vector fields. In: Proc. Joint Eurographics - IEEE TCVG Symposium on Visualization (VisSym 2004), pp. 183–192 (2004)
19. Bachthaler, S., Sadlo, F., Weeber, R., Kantorovich, S., Holm, C., Weiskopf, D.: Magnetic Flux Topology of 2D Point Dipoles. Comp. Graph. Forum 31, 955–964 (2012)
20. Hlawatsch, M., Vollrath, J., Sadlo, F., Weiskopf, D.: Coherent structures of characteristic curves in symmetric second order tensor fields. IEEE Transactions on Visualization and Computer Graphics 17, 781–794 (2011)
21. Peikert, R., Sadlo, F.: Flow Topology Beyond Skeletons: Visualization of Features in Recirculating Flow. In: Hege, H.C., Polthier, K., Scheuermann, G. (eds.) Topology-Based Methods in Visualization II, pp. 145–160. Springer (2009)
22. Theisel, H., Weinkauf, T., Hege, H.C., Seidel, H.P.: Stream line and path line oriented topology for 2D time–dependent vector fields. In: Proc. IEEE Visualization, pp. 321–328 (2004)
23. Shi, K., Theisel, H., Weinkauf, T., Hauser, H., Hege, H.C., Seidel, H.P.: Path line oriented topology for periodic 2D time–dependent vector fields. In: Proc. Eurographics / IEEE VGTC Symposium on Visualization, pp. 139–146 (2006)
24. Kasten, J., Hotz, I., Noack, B., Hege, H.C.: On the extraction of long-living features in unsteady fluid flows. In: Topological Methods in Data Analysis and Visualization, Theory, Algorithms, and Applications, pp. 115–126. Springer (2010)
25. Fuchs, R., Kemmler, J., Schindler, B., Sadlo, F., Hauser, H., Peikert, R.: Toward a Lagrangian vector field topology. Comp. Graph. Forum 29, 1163–1172 (2010)
26. Weinkauf, T., Theisel, H., Hege, H.C., Seidel, H.P.: Topological construction and visualization of higher order 3D vector fields. Comp. Graph. Forum, 469–478 (2004)
27. Weiskopf, D., Ertl, T.: A hybrid physical/device-space approach for spatio-temporally coherent interactive texture advection on curved surfaces. In: Proc. Graphics Interface, pp. 263–270 (2004)

28. Shadden, S., Lekien, F., Marsden, J.: Definition and properties of Lagrangian coherent structures from finite-time Lyapunov exponents in two-dimensional aperiodic flows. Physica D Nonlinear Phenomena 212, 271–304 (2005)
29. Laramee, R.S., Jobard, B., Hauser, H.: Image space based visualization of unsteady flow on surfaces. In: Proc. IEEE Visualization, pp. 131–138 (2003)
30. van Wijk, J.J.: Image based flow visualization for curved surfaces. In: Proc. IEEE Visualization, pp. 123–130 (2003)
31. Laramee, R.S., Hauser, H., Doleisch, H., Vrolijk, B., Post, F.H., Weiskopf, D.: The state of the art in flow visualization: Dense and texture–based techniques. Comp. Graph. Forum 23, 203–221 (2004)
32. Eberly, D.: Ridges in Image and Data Analysis. Computational Imaging and Vision. Kluwer Academic Publishers (1996)
33. Sadlo, F., Peikert, R.: Visualizing Lagrangian coherent structures and comparison to vector field topology. In: Topology-Based Methods in Visualization II, pp. 15–30 (2009)
34. Sadlo, F., Peikert, R.: Efficient visualization of Lagrangian coherent structures by filtered AMR ridge extraction. IEEE Transactions on Visualization and Computer Graphics 13, 1456–1463 (2007)
35. Garth, C., Gerhardt, F., Tricoche, X., Hagen, H.: Efficient computation and visualization of coherent structures in fluid flow applications. IEEE Transactions on Visualization and Computer Graphics 13, 1464–1471 (2007)
36. Hlawatsch, M., Sadlo, F., Weiskopf, D.: Hierarchical line integration. IEEE Transactions on Visualization and Computer Graphics 17, 1148–1163 (2011)
37. Bonjean, F., Lagerloef, G.: Diagnostic model and analysis of the surface currents in the tropical pacific ocean. Journal of Physical Oceanography 32, 2938–2954 (2002)
38. Bachthaler, S., Sadlo, F., Dachsbacher, C., Weiskopf, D.: Space-Time Visualization of Dynamics in Lagrangian Coherent Structures of Time-Dependent 2D Vector Fields. In: Proc. International Conference on Information Visualization Theory and Applications, pp. 573–583 (2012)

GeoTemCo: Comparative Visualization
of Geospatial-Temporal Data with Clutter Removal
Based on Dynamic Delaunay Triangulations

Stefan Jänicke[1], Christian Heine[2], and Gerik Scheuermann[1]

[1] Image and Signal Processing Group, Institute for Computer Science,
University of Leipzig, Germany
[2] ETH Zürich, Switzerland
{stjaenicke,scheuermann}@informatik.uni-leipzig.de,
cheine@inf.ethz.ch

Abstract. The amount of online data annotated with geospatial and temporal metadata has grown rapidly in the recent years. Providers like Flickr and Twitter are popular, but hard to browse. Many systems exist that, in multiple linked views, show the data under geospatial, temporal, and topical aspects. We unify and extend these systems in a Web application to support comparison of multiple, potentially large result sets of textual queries with extended interaction capabilities. We present a novel fast algorithm using a dynamic Delaunay triangulation for merging glyphs in the map view into so-called circle groups to avoid visual clutter, which is critical for the comparative setting. We evaluate our design by qualitative comparison with existing systems.

Keywords: Visual data exploration, Geovisualization, Comparative visualization, Dynamic Delaunay triangulation.

1 Introduction

Although the amount and types of data available through public Web resources is seemingly endless, finding information is still largely performed by text queries. Popular search engines rank the typically huge amounts of query results based on relevance and popularity. When too many irrelevant items remain, the user is required to restate the query by adding or replacing search terms. Unfortunately, repeated refinement can lead to frustration. An alternative is to spatialize the data and allow the user to refine queries using mouse-based navigation.

While the data amount is increasing, data also become more structured. Websites such as Flickr and Twitter provide rich data sources annotated with geospatial and temporal metadata. This metadata can be used to provide a contextual overview of the data in many forms: topical, geospatial, and temporal, being some of the most popular. Users already familiar with searching in geographic environments like Google maps, can find results presented directly on a map rather than in a list, emphasizing the geospatial aspect. A tool providing more contextual overview and filter capabilities allows for synergetic effects.

G. Csurka et al. (Eds.): VISIGRAPP 2012, CCIS 359, pp. 160–175, 2013.

In this paper, we present a Web application that enables the synergetic exploration of multiple topical queries in a geospatial and temporal context. It employs a map view for the geospatial context, a time view for the temporal context, and provides on-demand tag clouds for topical refinements. All views provide linked brushing. This allows, for instance, to juxtapose and compare spatial distribution and temporal trends of multiple queries. Our design is based on a number of published systems that each allow only a subset of our requirements: comparing multiple datasets, refining temporal context, and scaling to a large number of items, both computationally and visually. We achieve the later by zoom-dependent aggregation of result locations into non-overlapping circles, thus avoiding visual clutter in the map view.

We extend our design, which we reported on in a previous version of this paper [1], to reflect the results of a usability study. In particular, we made circles transparent to mitigate potential occlusions of map labels, provide a new tag cloud design for detailed comparison of result sets, and present a novel aggregation algorithm that removes the run-time complexity in the start-up phase of our system from $O(n^2)$ to $O(n \log n)$.

2   Related Work

Our work can be placed in the domain of thematic cartography and geovisualization. Overviews of the field are given by, e.g. Dent [2] and Slocum *et al.* [3]. An overview of tools, principles, challenges, and the concept of the analysis of geotemporal data are given by Andrienko and Andrienko [4,5]. An important role plays the representation of data at multiple levels of detail to allow both gaining an overview and an interactive drilling down onto the details, as well as linking different views on the data, i.e. allowing interaction in one view to affect other views. This typically makes it easier to find causal relationships and unforeseen connections.

Because of limited space we can address only a few representative designs that exploit synergetic effects of linked views for geospatial-temporal data.

The Web application *VisGets* [6] employs four linked views: a location view, showing the result items as small glyphs on a map, a time view, showing histograms of results for year, month, and day resolution, a tag view, showing most-frequent words in a size proportional to their importance, and a results view, showing small textual or image thumbnails of results arranged as a table. VisGets offers query refinement in space (selecting a glyph), time (selecting a year, month, or day), and by topic (selecting a tag). Each refinement affects the presentation in all other views. VisGets also provides many mechanisms to interact with the results of a single query, but a comparison of different queries is not directly supported. Because no aggregation of closely positioned glyphs takes place, visual clutter often ensues. The time view supports only query refinement for months within the same year, or days within the same month. The provided time resolutions make it also inconvenient to work with datasets spanning centuries or just hours and minutes.

GeoVISTA CrimeViz [7] enables comparison and analysis of different crime incident types. The map view shows individual circles only when zoomed in. In overviews, the incidents of all types are aggregated into hexagonal bins, thereby disabling comparison. The display of the bins using transparency interacts with the map: in dense areas the map is occluded and the underlying map can bias the transparency perception. In the CrimeViz time view, the number of incidents per time period of different types are stacked. It can show the total trend well, but is insufficient for comparing the different incident types [8]. The supported linked interactions are asymmetric: a selection in the time view (year, month, week, no time ranges) filters items on the map but not vice versa. CrimeViz's data source offers 8 different incident types, of which only the 3 smallest (with a maximum total of 637 incidents per year) are used. The other 5 types, ranging from 2,600 to 9,300 incidents per year each, are omitted.

The problem with many results in a map view becomes apparent in the visualization of the Iraq conflict incidents by *The Guardian* [9]. It does not make use of the different casualty types present in the data source or time information, and suffers from "red-dot fever" [10]: glyphs overlap in the map to an extent where the spatial distribution can no longer be determined reliably. To support large datasets, our tool thus automatically aggregates result hits in the map to non-overlapping circles. It becomes indispensable when presenting glyphs of different visual properties, since overlaps could bias the perceived distributions.

The increasing data sizes to be shown in scatter plots, forced the development of binning strategies. Data-independent, top-down approaches like rectangular binning [11] and hexagonal binning [12] split the plane into rectangular or hexagonal bins. The number of items per bin can be reflected in different ways, e.g., a bin coloring with associated colors from a predefined color map. Furthermore, specific shapes (e.g., circles, hexagons) reflecting the bin count with size can be placed in the bin area. A special case for shapes are so called sunflower plots [13], which reflect the number of items in one bin of the scatter plot with a sunflower glyph, that has a specific number of petals for a specific number of points.

These top-down binning strategies are widely used in geoapplications [5]. However, Novotny [14] remarked that the result can be misleading since cluster centers might be split into distinct bins. He proposes K-means [15] as a bottom-up binning approach, but it requires an appropriate selection of the number of clusters. General clustering algorithms cannot make assumptions on the dimensionality of the data and can therefore be slow. In this paper, we propose to use a fast data-driven clustering employing a dynamic 2D Delaunay triangulation algorithm. Delaunay triangulations are typically used in geographic information systems to model terrain [3], but to the best of our knowledge, we are the first to employ it as a clustering algorithm for clutter removal of glyphs.

3   Design

Our system's design is inspired by Dörk *et al.* [6]. It also consists of a map view showing the position of query results, a time view showing the distribution of results in a time span, and a detail view showing textual contents or thumbnails of data items arranged in a table. Our system differs in that we allow comparison of multiple result sets from a classical keyword or term-based topical search, support time-span data, show tag clouds for selected data on demand in the map, provide more flexible selections in the time domain, and render glyphs in the map avoiding visual clutter. Internally, we support any simple statistical graph, with the time view being a special case, and a designer can add more views based on the data to show. Fig. 4(c) gives an example view composition.

We chose colors to mark the different result sets, because of their effective use to discriminate categorical data [16]. An alternative is to use small multiples similar to the system *LISTA-Viz* [17], but we found the use of small multiples makes comparison of scattered data with irregular spatial distribution difficult. Furthermore, colors can serve as the visual link between the different views. As the number of colors that can be easily distinguished by humans is limited to 12 [18], we restricted our method to four datasets, to ensure both a good distinction from the map, as well as allowing colors to mix in the time view. We presume map colors to be mostly dark, cold, or unsaturated, and select very light colors for deselected and very saturated colors for selected circles to ensure that the thematic overlay pops out in comparison to the base map. The four base colors used for datasets 1 through 4 are red, blue, green, and yellow – to accommodate color impaired users while preserving red for single type datasets.

Each view provides native navigation and selection that results in updates of the other views. The map and the time views provide simple zoom and pan. Because of the way we aggregate data in these views an animation between zoom levels or time resolution changes is not performed. We reflect selections by marking table entries and the corresponding fraction of map glyphs and time graphs with saturated versions of the datasets' base colors. When selections are performed by a mouse drag gesture, the impact of releasing the mouse at this point is immediately reflected in the other views. Selections can be modified by dragging shapes or clicking on table entries in the detail view.

3.1   Map View

The dominant view in our visualization in terms of screen space is the *map view*. It is a thematic map [3] comprising a base map and a thematic overlay. The base map can be a contemporary map or one of 23 different historical maps showing political borders from 2000 BC to 1994 AD provided by Thinkquest[1]. Overlaying data over historic maps can benefit applications in the humanities (see e.g. Tsipidis et al. [19] for archaeological data, or the HESTIA project [20], which investigates the differences between imagined geographic distances and real distances in ancient Mediterranean space). Because a dataset may span a time range for which multiple maps are available and there is no concept of "average political border" we show the map closest to the median time stamp occurring in the dataset as default and allow the user to switch maps.

For the overlay, we chose a proportional glyph map over isopleth and choropleph maps due to the scattered nature of our data. We can use neither dasymetric nor dot maps, as these require ancillary information and a cartographer to apply this information correctly. The spatial distribution could also be shown via heat map, but to preserve legibility of the base map and to show multiple datasets, color mixing would ensue, against which Ware [18] argues. Also, humans are more accurate judging areas than they are judging color tones, making areas a better candidate for quantitative values [8]. Using glyphs also allows to group glyphs and to make every data item individually accessible for interaction.

---

[1] http://library.thinkquest.org/C006628/

Fig. 1. Place name tag clouds with different levels of detail

We disallow the glyphs to overlap in order to avoid visual clutter. While drawing rules such as "always let the smaller overlap the larger" can reduce the risk of occluding small glyphs, this is only a solution if glyphs do not differ in their other visual attributes, like shape or color. Instead, we merge circles based on their size, distances, and the current scale in an iterative process.

The overlap removal algorithm, which can be directly attached for single input sets ($m = 1$), is described in the next section. In the case of multiple ($m = 2, 3, 4$) input sets, we compose multiple circles $c_1, \ldots, c_m$ into a more complex glyph – a *circle group* – whose bounding circle b will be used for the aggregation. We chose them over pie charts, because these improve comparisons of data at the same point at the expense of comparison of the global distribution.

The grouping process is illustrated in Fig. 2d-f. Initially we place the centers of m prototype circles on the vertices of a regular m-polygon. The prototype circles' radius is set equal to the largest circle to group. Then we move the m circles using their correct radius from their polygon vertex closest to the polygon center without leaving the prototype. Finally we construct the bounding circle by moving it from the polygon center towards the center of the largest circle until its boundary touches two circles. Although this wastes some space, it is quick to compute and allows the map to be seen through. To ensure the map legibility underneath large circles, we draw all circles semi-transparent.

Selections in the map view can be specified by clicking on items or by drawing circles, rectangles, polygons, or clicking on an administrative region (e.g. country), which then selects the items in the surrounding polygon. Each of the map's circles is associated with a details-on-demand tag cloud showing the most frequent place names in a font scaled proportional to their frequency. The cloud provides a preview of how a glyph arising from agglomeration would split if zoomed in. If the data offers different levels of detail for a place, we choose the label dependent on the current zoom level. We distinguish between country, region, city, and borough level. We replace missing levels by the next coarser or the next finer level. Fig. 1 gives example place name tag clouds. In the comparison setting we use lines to link tags between datasets, as can be seen in Fig. 5(b).

3.2 Time View

Using terminology of Harris [21], our time view is a segmented area graph with time for the x-axis. A segmented area graph is a line chart where the area under the line is filled.

$T_1, \ldots, T_n$ partition the interval $T = [t_{min}, t_{max}]$ of the given dataset into intervals of regular duration: either seconds, minutes, hours, days, weeks, months, quarters, years, or decades. It is chosen to maximize the number of intervals without exceeding 400. Short units typically arise from dynamic data sources and large units arise from data with historic context. The resolution unit changes automatically when the user zooms inside the time view.

Whereas the x-axis of the time view is directly defined by $T_1, \ldots, T_n$, the y-direction shows the number of data items that fall in each interval using binning. For data items with time stamps the counting is straight-forward, for data items with time spans we add a value proportional to the amount of overlap with each bin. Although this can lead to an over-representation of items with long time spans in the time view, we found this to be no problem. For the datasets we considered, either the effect was benign as the time spans had approximately the same duration or items with longer time spans were also more interesting.

In the comparative setting we perform the bin counting per group. In the final visualization the bins' sizes are shown as overlapping segmented area graphs rather than bar charts because the former is better suited to direct comparison of the groups' time distribution. We shade the area under each line using a semi-transparent version of that datasets color, ensuring that all curves are visible and also hinting at the area that would have been present in the bar chart. Through the use of blending, the limitation to four colors as well as the stacked area graphs' shape mitigates ambiguities. The user can switch to logarithmic scale if datasets to be compared have largely different totals.

The time view allows both the clicking on one bin and the selection of a time range using a mouse drag gesture. A toolbar is then shown, that offers to add a "gray zone" which blends between selected and unselected elements. A play button starts an animation mode causing the selected time window to loop.

3.3 Detail View

For inspection of single data items that match the current filtering we present small textual or image thumbnails presented as a table in the detail view. This view is the only one which does not include any aggregation, but results are presented on multiple pages if they exceed a certain fixed number.

The system also allows to export elements of a selection as a new dataset. This can be used for the temporal comparison of different geographical regions of one dataset or the geographical comparison of different time periods is possible.

4 Overlap Removal Algorithm

In the following let k denote the number of supported scales (i.e. magnifications). The scale doubles with each level l ($1 \leq l \leq k$). Furthermore, let N denote the number of points P, $p_i = (0.5 + lon_i/360°, 0.5 + lat_i/180°)$ in a normalized space. Each circle i represents n_i points. We define a minimum radius r_{min} dependent on the average font size of common Web mapping services' labels (e.g. Google Maps, Bing Maps) so that circles have salience no smaller than labels. The maximum radius was found empirically

---

Algorithm 1. OverlapRemoval(P)

$D \leftarrow$ empty Delaunay triangulation
for $i = 1$ to $|P|$ **do**
  if $p_i \in D$ **then**
    $p_j \leftarrow$ duplicate of p_i in D
    $n_j \leftarrow n_j + 1$
  else
    Insert(p_i,D)
    $n_i \leftarrow 1$
  end if
end for
for $l = k$ to 1 **do**
  $Q \leftarrow$ empty priority queue
  for all edges $\{p_i, p_j\}$ in D **do**
    $\psi \leftarrow (\epsilon + r_i + r_j)/(2^{7+l}\|p_i - p_j\|)$
    if $\psi > 1$ **then**
      Insert($\{p_i, p_j\}$,ψ,Q)
    end if
  end for
  while Q not empty **do**
    $\{p_i, p_j\} \leftarrow$ highest priority element of Q
    $n_{ij} \leftarrow n_i + n_j$
    $p_{ij} \leftarrow \frac{n_i}{n_{ij}}p_i + \frac{n_j}{n_{ij}}p_j$
    Delete(p_i,D)
    Delete(p_j,D)
    Insert(p_{ij},D)
    Update(Q)
  end while
end for

---

as $r_{max} = 4\log_2(N + 1)$. A circle's area A_i is a linear interpolation between the corresponding minimum and maximum circle areas A_{min} and A_{max} based on n_i:

$$A_i = A_{min} + \frac{n_i - 1}{N - 1}(A_{max} - A_{min}).$$

Because neighboring circles are most likely to overlap and we want to merge close circles before far circles, we use a dynamic Delaunay triangulation as supporting data structure, allowing us to quickly find and merge overlapping circles.

The algorithm is detailed in Algorithm 1 and illustrated in Fig. 2a-c. It initially creates a dynamic Delaunay triangulation of the given points in the normalized space merging duplicates. After initialization, all edges of the triangulation are inserted into a priority queue with a priority ψ depending on the amount of overlap. ψ relates the distances after transformation from normalized space to screen space and the radii of the circles in pixel. The factor containing l in the formula for ψ assumes that the map image for level 1 has dimensions 256×256. F or simplicity and speed we use the ratio of the minimum distance desired plus $\epsilon \geq 0$ and the real distance as priority. Circles overlap or are too close when $\psi > 1$. After constructing the priority queue, we repeatedly find

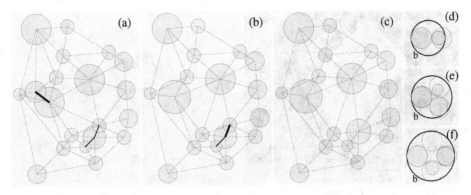

Fig. 2. Aggregation of single and multiple items. The next occlusion to be resolved is marked by line thickness.

the overlap of highest priority and remove it by merging the circles, which affects both the Delaunay triangulation and the priority queue, and finish when there are no more overlaps. Then we proceed with the next scale, which implicitly halves point distances but not radii in the formula for ψ.

In our implementation we use the algorithm proposed by Kao *et al.* [22]. It is a randomized incremental algorithm that constructs the initial triangulation in $O(N \log N)$ expected time, and can find a duplicate to a given point in $O(\log N)$. As the triangulation contains $O(N)$ edges, construction of the priority queue using a simple heap requires $O(N \log N)$ time. Each merging of circles requires 3 elementary operations on the triangulation, each with $O(\log N)$ expected time, and an expected constant number of updates to the priority queue, each with $O(\log N)$ time. As building the priority queue and merging circles takes place for each scale we can give the trivial upper bound of our algorithm as $O(kN \log N)$. This is a significant improvement over the agglomeration algorithm using clustering presented in the previous version of this paper [1].

5   Results

GeoTemCo is the main application which implements the design described in Section 3. *GeoTemCo* works completely within the client's browser, performing filtering, visualization, and interaction, and allows to load data locally or using a server that is an adapter for dynamic data source. Within the development phase for *GeoTemCo* we used among others the following three dynamic sources: Europeana[2], an online library of several million digitized objects of European's cultural heritage, eAQUA[3], a project studying topic migrations in the ancient Mediterranean based on words extracted from ancient Greek texts, and Flickr[4]: a database of millions of public user-provided photos. All items are annotated with creation place and date.

---

[2] http://www.europeana.eu/

[3] http://www.eaqua.net/

[4] http://www.flickr.com/

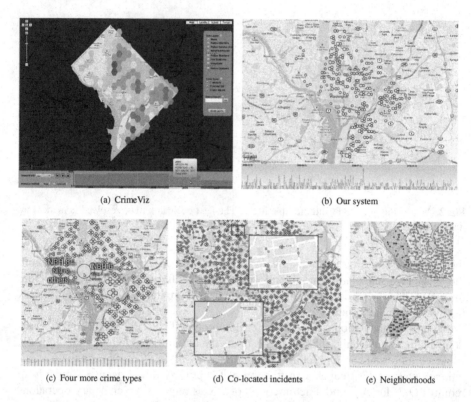

(a) CrimeViz

(b) Our system

(c) Four more crime types

(d) Co-located incidents

(e) Neighborhoods

Fig. 3. Crimes in Washington D.C. [Fig. 3(a) reproduced with permission from [7]]

GeoTemCo supports both KML and JSON exchange formats. Since the overall support for JavaScript as well as its browser performance has increased in the last years, we decided to implement *GeoTemCo* completely in JavaScript. We adapted two Open-Source JavaScript libraries for implementing our views: OpenLayers[5] is used to provide both the thematic layer and the base map from different Web mapping services, e.g., Google Maps, Open Street Map or historic maps, hosted on our own GeoServer[6] instance. Also, we extended the Simile Widgets Timeplot[7] for displaying statistical graphs to support our interaction.

5.1 Crime Incidents

We compared the *CrimeViz* application (Fig. 3(a)) to our visualization (Fig. 3(b)) for crime incidents in 2009. Both show the distribution of homicide, arson, and sex abuse incidents in the Washington D.C. metropolitan area. Our tool easily shows that there was

---

[5] http://openlayers.org/

[6] http://geoserver.org/

[7] http://www.simile-widgets.org/timeplot/

neither homicide (blue) nor arson (red) incidents in the north western neighborhoods, which is not directly visible in the CrimeViz map, because of the hexagonal binning, that furthermore causes a loss of map context in dense regions. When considering further crime types, we find patterns for thefts and robberies near populated places like metro stations or shopping centers. Unlike *CrimeViz*, we aggregate preserving incident types, hence we find more relations, e.g. by comparing the crime types stolen cars (red), burglaries (blue), thefts (green), and robberies (yellow) (Fig. 3(c)). We detect relatively few stolen car (20%) and burglary incidents (23%) in comparison to thefts (45%) and robberies (35%) in Washington D.C.'s downtown.

Crime analysts can use our visualization to detect connected crime incidents of different types. For instance, a daily exploration reveals, that stolen car incidents are often grouped with a theft, burglary or robbery incident, e.g., co-located incidents at 27th of June (Fig. 3(d)). The number of correlations increases further by choosing a two day time range. The original *CrimeViz* did not allow such fine-grained selection of time ranges. The analyst can furthermore compare different districts using the administrative region selection offered by the map view. Another application could be a decision making support for apartment search, based on regions of low burglary probability, or where it would be safe to rent a garage for a car. Fig. 3(e) indicates Neighborhood 13 (top) as substantially safer than Neighborhood 39 (bottom) with respect to stolen cars and burglaries.

5.2 Guardian Data

The *Iraq war logs* dataset as published by *The Guardian*, contains around 60,000 entries; one for each incident with at least one casualty during the Iraq conflict from 2004 to 2009. Each entry states place and time, as well as the number of casualties by type (civilian, enemy, Iraq forces, coalition forces).

The Guardian visualization [9] for the *Iraq war logs* is a map containing one circle for each incident. It produces a lot of clutter as the result of overlapping glyphs distorting perception of incident densities. In Fig. 4(a) three conflict centers can be guessed: Baghdad in the center, Al Mausi in the north, and Al Basrah in the south-east, but easily confirmed using the overlap removal algorithm (Fig. 4(b)) in our tool. Baghdad clearly stands out as the region with most incidents.

For comparison, we split all incidents based on the casualty type into four different datasets. Fig. 4(c) shows an increased number of incidents with civilian casualties (red) in 2006 and 2007. A second histogram using logarithmic scale shows the number of incidents by casualty total. We discover the incident with most casualties, which is known as the *2005 Baghdad bridge stampede*. In contrast to various newspaper reports of around 1,000 casualties, the data shows only 437 civilian and 7 Iraq forces casualties (green).

Furthermore, we prepared four datasets containing one item for each casualty to point out regions and time periods with lots of casualties. Fig. 4(d) (top) shows an increased number of casualties in 2007 compared to 2004, except for enemy casualties, in particular in Baghdad. The *Operation Imposing Law* (February 14th - November 24th 2007) reduced the overall number of victims, most notably in Baghdad. On March 14th 2007, the Iraq military stated, that there were only 265 civilian casualties in the first

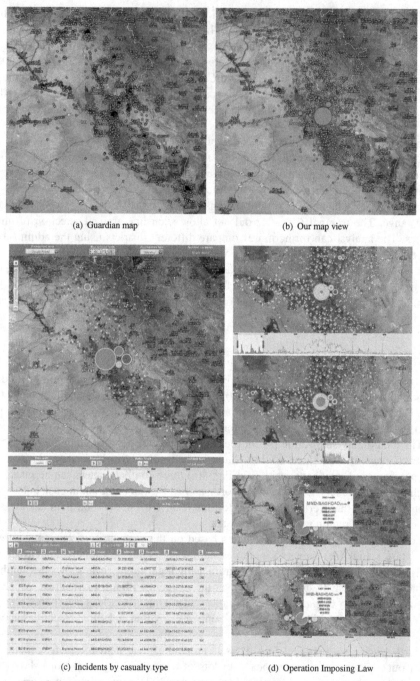

(a) Guardian map

(b) Our map view

(c) Incidents by casualty type

(d) Operation Imposing Law

Fig. 4. Iraq War Logs: Analysis [Fig. 4(a) reproduced with permission from [9]]

month of *Operation Imposing Law*, which is a low compared to the month before the operation (1440). By filtering using the proper time ranges and clicking the tag cloud for Baghdad, we find 2,540 and 997 civilian casualties, respectively, for these time periods in Fig. 4(d) (bottom).

5.3   Biodiversity Data

The European project *BioVeL*[8] combines several biodiversity databases with the goal to implement and provide flexible user interfaces for biologists for their research on biodiversity issues. In this context GeoTemCo is integrated into a complex workflow process as one of the major visual interfaces for researchers. Biologists select a list of specific species and initialize GeoTemCo with observation entries of different time periods used as different datasets. Exploration and filtering abilities help to detect geospatially migrating species over time. Furthermore, GeoTemCo is used to clean the underlying databases from wrong entries. The results of these user interactions are exploited for the onward workflow.

Fig. 5(a) gives an example for two observation cycles for marine organisms at the south-eastern coast of Sweden, the first from 1916 to 1938 and the second from 2006 to 2009. For each item, the species' identifier replaces the place name field, so that place name tag clouds show most frequently observed species for geographical areas (Fig. 5(b)). Hovering, a circle pack's boundary shows tag lists for both circles. Tags which occur in both lists are connected to each other. Hovering an unconnected tag in one list shows an additional link. If the tag also exists in the opposite list, it appears as a new entry (top). Otherwise, the information *"Not available"* is shown, which indicates migrated (middle) and non-native species (bottom).

5.4   Books from Google Ancient Places

Google Ancient Places (GAP) [23] is concerned with the analysis of books on history. *GapVis*[9] is a visualization from GAP where historic places mentioned in books are plotted onto a map. Page numbers are used as a second dimension, so that an analysis of geospatially migrating topics in books is possible. *GapVis* does not avoid visual clutter on the map and a comparative view for books is also lacking.

We use the same data and utilize our time view for the books' page dimension. Fig. 6 shows an example for two books about the Roman empire, written by Livy approximately 2000 years ago: *Roman History* and *The History of Rome, Vol. 5*. The political map of 1BC reflects proper historian circumstances. Instantly we see quite different geospatial references. Fig. 6(a) (bottom) clearly indicates that the second book thematizes the conflict between the ancient Rome and the Volscian territory starting at around page 100. In contrast, this period is not discussed in *Roman History*, rather we detect a thematic migration (Fig. 6(b)) from the ancient Italian (top) to the ancient Greek region (bottom).

---

[8] http://www.biovel.eu/.
[9] http://nrabinowitz.github.com/gapvis

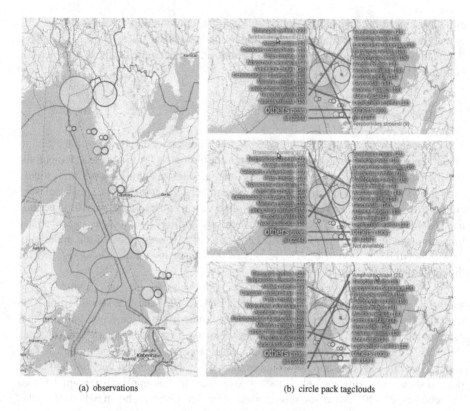

(a) observations

(b) circle pack tagclouds

Fig. 5. Observation cycles from 1916-1938 (red) and 2006-2009 (blue)

5.5   Timing Evaluation

We compared the performance of the Delaunay overlap removal algorithm (DOR) with the hierarchical agglomerative clustering method (HAC) as described in [1]. We used the *Iraq war logs* data as benchmark because of its high number of data items non-uniformly spread. We split the incidents randomly into sets of different size and performed several iterations in different browsers for each set. For the test with Ubuntu 12.04, we used a quadcore Intel(R) Core(TM) i5-2410M CPU @ 2.30GHz and 8GB memory. As Internet browsers, we chose Google Chrome 19 and Mozilla Firefox 13. The following table shows the median runtimes of 11 iterations for all datasets with both algorithms in both browsers.

	558	1,185	2,523	4,628	8,917	15,716	33,801	52,048
DOR (Chrome19)	0.08s	0.17s	0.42s	0.86s	1.69s	3.64s	6.85s	10.79s
DOR (FF13)	0.11s	0.26s	0.5s	1.03s	2.1s	3.98s	7.46s	12.45s
HAC (Chrome19)	0.16s	0.37s	1.56s	4.17s	14.41s	42.21s	193.38s	518.24s
HAC (FF13)	0.71s	0.16s	3.07s	7.58s	30.39s	110.35s	483.19s	1038.78s

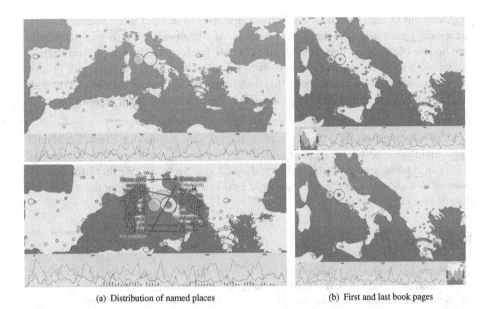

(a) Distribution of named places   (b) First and last book pages

Fig. 6. Livy books: *Roman History* (red) and *The History of Rome, Vol. 5* (blue)

6   Conclusions and Future Work

We presented a novel approach and Web application to show, compare, and explore multiple topical query results in a geographical and temporal context. We were able to utilize, combine, and improve approaches from several prior works. In contrast to CrimeViz [7], which also offers comparative visualization, we display items without aggregating them into the same representatives for coarser zoom levels. We aggregate map glyphs to avoid visual clutter, which is an issue in the Guardian visualization for the Iraq war logs [9]. Compared to the similar system VisGets [6], which only works for one set of results, we also made use of the linked views approach (map, time line, detail view) to extend the users exploration abilities. Furthermore, we enriched the filter capabilities in both geospatial (e.g., selecting all results inside a country) and temporal dimension (e.g., selecting dynamic time ranges).

Our case studies show that visually comparable datasets extend the exploration and analysis abilities of the user in an effective way. It helps to detect equalities and varieties between distinct data contents that unveil their relationships in space and time. Our method is limited to four datasets at a time mainly to ensure that the colors used for discrimination are properly distinguishable, the splitting of circles does not waste too much screen space, and the overlapping segmented area graphs do not occlude each other too much.

In the future we will direct our attention to the extension of our method to very large datasets by searching for client-server communication where most of the data remains on the server but a working set is transmitted to the client for quick interaction. We aim to extend our system to extract and show trajectories of distinct sets containing movement data, potentially leading to new insights. At some point we also want to support live update of dynamic data sources like Twitter feeds to see how topics proliferate. We would also like to extend our system to show the uncertainty in data with historic context, which is often annotated by hand and uses places' names instead of longitude and latitude. These names can be resolved, but often yield polygonal regions.

Acknowledgements. We thank Sebastian Bothe, Vera Hernandez-Ernst, Karl-Heinz Sylla, and Robert Kuwaliak from Fraunhofer IAIS for collaborating on the extension of GeoTemCo for several projects, and providing data for Section 5. We thank the contributors of Google Ancient Places, especially Leif Isaksen, for providing the underlying data of GapVis.

References

1. Jänicke, S., Heine, C., Stockmann, R., Scheuermann, G.: Comparative visualization of geospatial-temporal data. In: GRAPP/IVAPP, pp. 613–625 (2012)
2. Dent, B.D.: Cartography: Thematic Map Design, 5th edn. McGraw-Hill (1999)
3. Slocum, T.A., McMaster, R.B., Kessler, F.C., Howard, H.H.: Thematic Cartography and Geovisualization, 3rd international edn. Prentice Hall Series in Geographic Information Science. Prentice-Hall (2009)
4. Andrienko, G., Andrienko, N.: Visual Data Exploration: Tools, Principles, and Problems. Classics from IJGIS: Twenty Years of the International Journal of Geographical Information Science and Systems, 475–479 (2006)
5. Andrienko, N., Andrienko, G.: Exploratory Analysis of Spatial and Temporal Data: A Systematic Approach. Springer (2005)
6. Dörk, M., Carpendale, S., Collins, C., Williamson, C.: VisGets: Coordinated Visualizations for Web-based Information Exploration and Discovery. IEEE Transactions on Visualization and Computer Graphics 14, 1205–1212 (2008)
7. Roth, R.E., Ross, K.S., Finch, B.G., Luo, W., MacEachren, A.M.: A User-Centered Approach for Designing and Developing Spatiotemporal Crime Analysis Tools. In: Purves, R., Weibel, R. (eds.) Proceedings of GIScience (2010)
8. Cleveland, W.S., McGill, R.: Graphical Perception: Theory, Experimentation, and Application to the Development of Graphical Methods. Journal of the American Statistical Association 79, 531–554 (1984)
9. Rogers, S.: The Guardian - Wikileaks Iraq war logs: every death mapped (2010), http://www.guardian.co.uk/world/datablog/interactive/2010/oct/23/wikileaks-iraq-deaths-map (retrieved July 10, 2011)
10. Schuyler: Web map API roundup: Mapping hacks (2006), http://mappinghacks.com/2006/04/07/web-map-api-roundup/
11. Wilkinson, L.: The Grammar of Graphics (Statistics and Computing). Springer-Verlag New York, Inc., Secaucus (2005)
12. Carr, D.B., Littlefield, R.J., Nichloson, W.L.: Scatterplot matrix techniques for large n. In: Proceedings of the Seventeenth Symposium on the Interface of Computer Sciences and Statistics on Computer Science and Statistics, pp. 297–306. Elsevier North-Holland, Inc., New York (1986)
13. Cleveland, W.S., Mcgill, R.: The Many Faces of a Scatterplot. Journal of the American Statistical Association 79, 807–822 (1984)

14. Novotny, M.: Visually effective information visualization of large data. In: 8th Central European Seminar on Computer Graphics (CESCG 2004), pp. 41–48. CRC Press (2004)
15. Lloyd, S.P.: Least squares quantization in pcm. IEEE Transactions on Information Theory 28, 129–137 (1982)
16. Bertin, J.: Semiology of graphics. University of Wisconsin Press (1983)
17. Hardisty, F., Klippel, A.: Analysing Spatio-Temporal Autocorrelation with LISTA-Viz. Int. J. Geogr. Inf. Sci. 24, 1515–1526 (2010)
18. Ware, C.: Information Visualization: Perception for Design, 3rd edn. Morgan Kaufmann (2004)
19. Tsipidis, S., Koussoulakou, A., Kotsakis, K.: Geovisualization and Archaeology: supporting Excavation Site Research. In: Ruas, A. (ed.) Advances in Cartography and GIScience. Volume 2. Lecture Notes in Geoinformation and Cartography, vol. 6, pp. 85–107. Springer, Heidelberg (2011)
20. Barker, E., Bouzarovski, S., Pelling, C., Isaksen, L.: Mapping an ancient historian in a digital age: the Herodotus Encoded Space-Text-Image Archive (HESTIA). Leeds International Classical Studies 9 (2010)
21. Harris, R.L.: Information Graphics: A Comprehensive Illustrated Reference. Oxford University Press (1999)
22. Kao, T., Mount, D.M., Saalfeld, A.: Dynamic maintenance of delaunay triangulations. Technical report, University of Maryland at College Park, College Park, MD, USA (1991)
23. Barker, E., Isaksen, L., Byrne, K., Kansa, E.: GAP: a neogeo approach to classical resources. In: European Conference on Complex Systems 2010 (2011)

Scaffold Hunter: Facilitating Drug Discovery by Visual Analysis of Chemical Space

Karsten Klein[1,*], Nils Kriege[2,**], and Petra Mutzel[2]

[1] School of Information Technologies, The University of Sydney, Australia
[2] Department of Computer Science, Technische Universität Dortmund, Germany
kklein@it.usyd.edu.au,
{nils.kriege,petra.mutzel}@cs.tu-dortmund.de

Abstract. The search for a new drug to cure a particular disease involves to find a chemical compound that influences a corresponding biological process, e.g., by inhibiting or activating an involved biological target molecule. A potential drug candidate however does not only need to show a sufficient amount of biological activity, but also needs to adhere to additional rules that define the basic limits of druglikeness, including for example restrictions regarding solubility and molecular weight. The sheer size of the search space, i.e., the chemical space that contains the available compounds, the large number of potentially relevant data annotations per compound, the incomplete knowledge on those properties, and the complex relation between the molecular properties and the actual effects in a living organism, complicate the search and may turn the discovery process into a tedious challenge. We describe Scaffold Hunter, an interactive software tool for the exploration and analysis of chemical compound databases. Scaffold Hunter allows to explore the chemical space spanned by a compound database, fosters intuitive recognition of complex structural and bioactivity relationships, and helps to identify interesting compound classes with a desired bioactivity. Thus, the tool supports chemists during the complex and time-consuming drug discovery process to gain additional knowledge and to focus on regions of interest, facilitating the search for promising drug candidates.

Keywords: Scaffold tree, Chemical space, Chemical compound data, Integrative visualization, Interactive exploration.

1 Introduction

The search for a potential new drug is often compared to "searching a needle in a haystack". This refers to the fact that within the huge chemical space of synthesizable small organic compounds (approximately 10^{60} molecules), there is only a small fraction of potentially active compounds of interest for further investigation. Due to the cost and effort involved in synthesis and experimental evaluation of potential drugs, efficient

* Karsten Klein was partly supported by ARC grant H2814 A4421, Tom Sawyer Software, and NewtonGreen Software. Research was done while at TU Dortmund.
** Nils Kriege was supported by the German Research Foundation (DFG), priority programme "Algorithm Engineering" (SPP 1307).

G. Csurka et al. (Eds.): VISIGRAPP 2012, CCIS 359, pp. 176–192, 2013.
© Springer-Verlag Berlin Heidelberg 2013

identification of promising test compounds is of utmost importance. However, orientation within chemical space is difficult, as on the one hand there is only partial knowledge about molecule properties, and on the other hand a large number of potentially relevant annotations exist, as physical and chemical properties, target information, side effects, patent status, and many more. Some of these annotations also may be either predicted with a certain confidence or result from experiments, with uncertainty and sometimes even contradicting information. Nonetheless, there are some approaches to classify and cluster compounds for navigation. A number of properties might be good indicators for drug-like molecule characteristics, as, e.g., biological activity, and besides toxicity there are several physico-chemical properties that allow to discard molecules, as, e.g., stability and synthesizability.

The classical drug discovery pipeline, which aims at detecting small molecules that bind to biological target molecules involved in a disease process (e.g., proteins), does not only require a large amount of time, money, and other resources, but also suffers from a small and even decreasing success rate. Since the behavior and impact of a chemical compound often cannot be easily predicted or derived from simple molecular properties, the drug discovery pipeline involves high throughput screenings of large substance libraries with millions of compounds in the early stages to identify potentially active molecules. The results of a screening only give an incomplete picture on a restricted area of the possible solution space, and hence need to be analyzed to detect potential lead structures that can be used as the starting point of the further drug development.

As a result, the drug discovery process involves decisions based on expertise and intuition of the experienced chemist that cannot be replaced by automatic processes. Nonetheless this process can be greatly supported by computational analysis methods, an intuitive representation of the available data, and by navigation approaches that allow for organized exploration of chemical space. The chemist's workflow therefore can be supported by automatic identification of regions within the chemical space that may contain good candidates with high probability and by enriching the navigation with pointers to these region within a visual exploration and analysis process.

Even though the use of automated high throughput methods for screening and synthesis led to large compound libraries and a huge amount of corresponding data in pharmaceutical companies and academic institutions, this did not lead to a significant increase in the success rate. Sharing data among these actors might help to improve the understanding and therefore also the discovery process. Consequently, more and more data is made publicly available over a large number of online databases, and computational methods to analyze the data are used to an increasing extent. However, without adequate methods to integrate and explore the data, this wealth of possibly relevant information may even complicate the drug discovery process. In addition, information is spread across many resources, having different access interfaces, and even the unambiguous identification of compounds can be non-trivial. Integration of these data resources in a visual analysis tool with an intuitive navigation concept facilitates drug discovery processes to a large extent. Several initiatives try to improve the situation by fostering precompetitive collaboration [1] and open sharing of data and information [2]. Such efforts can be supported and complemented by open source analysis tools, and it can therefore be expected that the success of these initiatives will push both the development and the use of these tools.

Scaffold Hunter is a software tool for the exploration and analysis of chemical compound databases that supports the chemist in the search for drug candidates out of the structural space spanned by a possibly large pool of compounds. It allows navigation in this chemical space with the help of a hierarchical classification based on compound structure, and integrates a variety of views with complementary analysis methods. The views provide innovative graphical visualizations as well as established representations for data and analysis results. Combined with suitable interaction techniques, these components allow to assess the chemical data with respect to the various aspects of multidimensional data annotations in an integrated fashion. In addition, Scaffold Hunter allows to integrate data from multiple resources and formats over a flexible import plugin interface.

Scaffold Hunter was implemented as a prototype application in 2007, being the first tool that allows to navigate in the hierarchical chemical space defined by the scaffold tree [3]. The Scaffold Hunter prototype was successfully used in an experimental study that focused on the chemical aspects of using brachiation along scaffold tree branches, proving the effectiveness of the approach and the usefulness of our implementation [4]. Here, we focus on the visualization and analysis techniques used, including new views and a data integration concept, and on their interplay.

1.1 Related Work

Compared to other application areas, especially biology, the support of the analysis workflow in chemistry by integrated tools that combine both advanced interactive visualization as well as analysis methods is rather weak even though the need for such tools has been formulated quite often [1,5]. On the one hand tools based on a data pipelining concept like KNIME [6], which features several cheminformatics extensions, or the commercial product Accelrys Pipeline Pilot are applied. Although these approaches are more intuitive to use than cheminformatics software libraries, they nevertheless require a fair amount of expert knowledge in cheminformatics and lack integrated visual analysis concepts. On the other hand general purpose visualization tools like TIBCO Spotfire are used. Spotfire can be extended by a structure depiction plugin, but lacks sophisticated domain specific analysis methods. Concepts to classify molecules, e.g. based on clustering by common substructures, have first been proposed several years ago [7], but are often not supported in interactive visualization software. Recently there have been attempts to create software to remedy the situation: The server-based tool Molwind [8] has been developed by researchers at Merck-Serono and was inspired by Scaffold Hunter. While also based on the scaffold tree concept, Molwind uses NASA's World Wind engine to map scaffolds to geospatial layers. The application SARANEA [9] focuses on the visualization of structure-activity and structure-selectivity relationships by means of "network-like similarity graphs", but misses a structural classification scheme which is advisable for large data sets. Compared to these approaches, the web based tool iPHACE [10] introduces basic additional features for visual analysis, namely interaction heat maps, to focus on the drug-target interactions. Another recent approach to support the analysis of chemical data sets is Scaffold

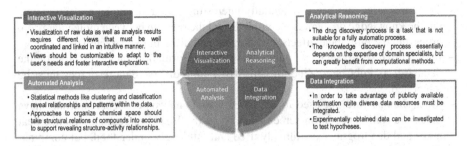

Fig. 1. Interactive visual analysis of the correlation between chemical structure and biological activity. The knowledge discovery process is a cyclic procedure: Analyzing known data may allow to generate new hypotheses which lead to further experiments. Results obtained here are again integrated into the tool for further investigation.

Explorer [11], which allows the user to define the scaffolds with respect to his task-specific needs, but is targeted more towards the analysis of small data sets.

Although these first approaches received a positive feedback from the pharmaceutical community, they are more or less in a prototypical stage with a small user base. The most likely explanation is that chemists first need to familiarize with such approaches, as there have not been established ways for the integrated visual analysis of chemical data so far.

1.2 Goals and Challenges

Our main goal in the development of Scaffold Hunter was to facilitate the interactive exploration of chemical space in an intuitive way also suitable for non-experts in cheminformatics. We wanted to develop a software tool that integrates drug discovery data and allows to browse through the structures and data in an interactive visual analysis approach.

Several goals guided the design and implementation of Scaffold Hunter:

- The user should be able to integrate data from public resources and from his own compound databases.
- Views that represent a space of chemical compounds in an intuitive fashion for chemists should be automatically created.
- Interaction with the views should be possible to adapt them to the needs of a specific task, and to allow an analysis of the underlying data.
- Guided navigation within the compound space should be possible, to focus on regions of interest and to drill down to promising drug candidates.

When these goals are satisfied, the tool enables a visual analysis workflow that supports the efficient identification of drug candidates based on the combined information available. See Figure 1 for a model of this workflow.

Several challenges make a straightforward realization of these goals difficult:

- The set of chemical compounds under investigation may contain several million compounds, raising both efficiency and visualization problems.

– There is a large number of potentially interesting data annotations per compound, but the knowledge on them is incomplete, and the relation between molecular properties and the biological effects are complex and difficult to characterize.
– In order to take advantage of publicly available information, including large online databases as PubChem, Zinc, or ChEMBL, quite diverse data resources must be integrated.
– Most chemists are not used to advanced visual analysis concepts and only have moderate confidence in on-screen analysis so far. Visual representations like heat maps and dendrograms are already used and intuitively understood, but combination in an integrated interactive environment is not yet widespread. New interaction and analysis concepts for the exploration of large chemical databases need to be developed that are suitable for chemists without expert knowledge in cheminformatics and statistics.

2   Scaffold Hunter

Scaffold Hunter addresses the above mentioned challenges by means of a flexible framework for the integration of data sources and several interconnected visual analysis components described in Sec. 2.1.

There are several workflows along the drug discovery process that are related, but require slightly different views on the data. Often, an overview on the database contents is needed, both for evaluation and for comparison. Applications include visualization of several data sets at the same time, for instance comparison of results from several assays, or data sets stemming from multiple databases to rate their overlap or coverage of chemical space. An internal and a commercial database could be compared to gauge to what extent purchasing would increase the coverage of promising regions of chemical space, or where patent issues might be relevant. It should be noted that the visualization of this space is not restricted to show what is contained in the database, but also indicates gaps in the structural coverage, which give hints on structurally simpler but still biologically active molecules for synthesis or purchase.

A further task is the search for biologically active molecules that may be promising for synthesis to check suitability as potential drugs. Here, spots of large potential biological activity have to be identified. Note that biological activity for the largest part of the chemical space is not known, as the molecules are not tested or not even synthesized, but can only be derived indirectly, e.g., from the values of similar molecules with known activity. In addition, there are also many other required or desired properties, as for example synthesizability or bio-availability, which need to be estimated, and are often approximated best by experienced chemists with the help of computational analysis methods. Hence, the dynamic generation of new hypotheses and the integration of additional experimental data during the discovery process requires a complex interplay between interactive visualization, analytical reasoning, computational analysis, and experimental evaluation and validation as illustrated in Figure 1. A recent work-flow based on the scaffold tree classification combines scaffolds that are not annotated with bioactivity with scaffolds of related small molecules with known bioactivity and targets [12]. The merging of the corresponding trees allows to prospectively assign bioactivity and to identify possible target candidates for non-annotated molecules.

Most of the use-cases include exploration of the chemical space, and therefore the core concept of Scaffold Hunter builds upon a corresponding navigation paradigm for orientation as described in Section 2.1. As many use-cases also rely on the import of data from heterogenous sources, Scaffold Hunter provides a flexible data integration concept, which is described in Sec. 2.3.

2.1 Visual Analysis Components

Since the search for drug candidates involves a complex knowledge discovery process there is no single best technique that reveals all relations and information that might be of interest to the chemists. Scaffold Hunter combines different approaches to categorize and organize the chemical space occupied by the molecules of a given compound set allowing the user to view the data from different perspectives. Two important aspects here are structural features and properties of compounds. Relating structural characteristics to properties like a specific biological activity is an important step in the drug discovery process. Therefore, Scaffold Hunter supports to analyze high-dimensional molecular properties by means of a molecular spreadsheet and a scatter plot module. Developing meaningful structural classification concepts is a highly challenging task and still subject of recent research. Two orthogonal concepts have emerged: Approaches based on unsupervised machine learning and *rule-based classification* techniques, which both have their specific advantages [7]. Therefore, Scaffold Hunter supports cluster analysis using structure-based similarity measures, a typical machine learning based technique, as well as a rule-based approach based on scaffold trees. Comprehensive linkage techniques foster the interactive study of different perspectives of a data set providing additional value compared to isolated individual views.

Scaffold Tree. In order to organize chemical space and to reduce the number of objects that have to be visualized, we use the *scaffold tree* approach [3]. This approach computes an abstraction of the molecule structures that allows to represent sets of molecules by single representatives, so-called *scaffolds*, for navigation. A scaffold is obtained from a molecule by pruning all terminal side chains. The scaffold tree algorithm generates a unique tree hierarchy of scaffolds: In a step-by-step process, each scaffold is reduced up to a single ring by cutting off parts that are considered less important for biological activity, see Figure 2. In each step a less characteristic ring is selected for removal by a set of deterministic rules, such that the residual structure, which becomes the parent scaffold, remains connected. By this means the decomposition process determines a hierarchy of scaffolds. As, depending on the task at hand, differing aspects may be crucial to define relevant relations between scaffolds, the user can customize the rules for scaffold tree generation. The resulting set of trees is combined at a virtual root to a single tree which can be visualized using graph layout techniques.

Each scaffold represents a set of molecules that are similar in the sense that they share a common molecular framework. Experimental results show that these molecules also share common biological properties, making the classification suitable for the identification of previously unknown bioactive molecules [3]. Furthermore the edges of the scaffold tree provide meaningful chemical relations along which such properties are preserved up to a certain extent and are therefore appropriate for navigation [13].

·**Fig. 2.** Creation of a branch in the scaffold tree

Compounds in a chemical database will not completely cover the chemical space spanned by the created scaffolds. Scaffolds that are not a representative of molecules, but solely created during the scaffold tree reduction step, are nonetheless inserted into the tree. These *virtual scaffolds* represent 'holes' in the database and may be of particular interest as a starting point for subsequent synthesis. They represent previously unexamined molecules that may for example exhibit higher potency.

Since the generation of a scaffold tree for a large data set is a time consuming task, Scaffold Hunter allows to compute and permanently store scaffold trees using the default rule set proposed in [3] or a customized rule set which can be compiled by means of a graphical editor.

Scaffold Tree View. Based on the scaffold classification concept, Scaffold Hunter's main view represents the scaffold tree. The implementation is based on the toolkit Piccolo [14] and supports to freely navigate in the scaffold tree view, as the user interface allows grab-and-drag operations and zooming. Zooming can be done either manually in direction of the mouse cursor, or automatically when the user switches between selected regions of interest. The system then moves the viewport in an animation to the new focus region, first zooming out automatically to allow the user to gain orientation. At the new focus region, the system zooms in again. For realization of the Overview-plus-Detail concept, we implemented a minimap. The minimap shows the whole scaffold tree and the position of the viewport and allows to keep orientation even at large zoom scales, see Figure 3(a). Both the main view and the minimap allow Pan-and-Zoom operations.

On startup, a user-defined number of levels is shown, and an expand-and-collapse mechanism allows the user to either remove unwanted subtrees from the view or to explore deeper into subtrees of interest. By default, the scaffold tree is laid out using a radial style and is always centered at the virtual root. We decided not to allow the selection of a new root for the following reason: As drug candidates need to meet certain requirements regarding their biological activity and bio-availability, it will rarely be necessary to explore trees over more than a few levels (typically < 8). The molecules on deeper levels will be too large and have too many rings to be relevant for further consideration. However, in the case that all molecules of the visualized subset share a common scaffold, the tree is centered on this scaffold and the virtual root is hidden, as shown in Figure 3(b). Such views allow to explore individual branches in detail.

In order to guide the chemist in his search for a new drug candidate, scaffolds can be annotated with property values derived from the associated molecules, e.g. the average biological activity, or values directly related to the structure of the scaffold, e.g. the number of aromatic rings. These properties can be represented by several graphical

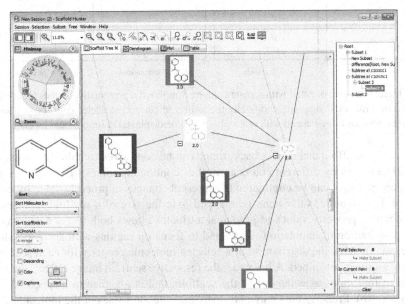

(a) Close-up view of a scaffold tree, where properties are represented by colored borders and text labels

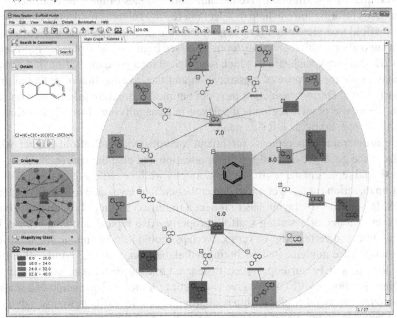

(b) Layout of a subtree rooted at a scaffold of interest with sorting and color shading. A sorting with respect to a scaffold property can be applied to define the clockwise order of a scaffold tree, a background color shading of segments reveals scaffolds with the same property value.

Fig. 3. Scaffold Tree View

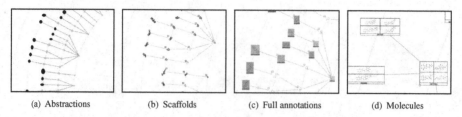

(a) Abstractions   (b) Scaffolds   (c) Full annotations   (d) Molecules

Fig. 4. Increasing level of detail with semantic zoom. Simplified representative shapes (a) are first replaced by structure images (b), and finally the full set of currently selected data annotations is shown (c). Molecules associated with scaffolds (d) can be displayed at lower zoom levels.

features: The scaffold and canvas background can be configured to indicate associated categorical values by different colors as well as continuous values by color intensity, see Figure 3. Edges can be configured to represent changes in property value by color gradient. Furthermore, values can be mapped onto the size of a scaffold representation. Mapping property values to graphical attributes allows both to get an overview on the distribution of annotation values and to focus on regions with specific values of interest. To show the distribution of a selected molecule property for each scaffold, property bins can be defined. A bar under the respective scaffold image reflects the proportion of molecules associated with the scaffold, that is assigned to a specified bin, see Figure 3(b). Property bins may optionally indicate the values of the molecule subset represented by a scaffold, or give the cumulative values of the subtree rooted at the scaffold. This information can help to select interesting subtrees for deeper exploration.

The scaffold tree view provides a semantic zoom that increases the level of graphical data annotations with increasing zoom level, see Figure 4. Scaffolds are represented using a 2D structure visualization, which is sufficient for a good estimation of the chemical behavior for the purpose of classification and the investigation of potential drugs in an early stage. During navigation in zoom out mode, structure information on scaffolds in the mouse pointer region is displayed in a magnifying glass window that can optionally be opened in the left side pane.

There are several requirements for layout methods within Scaffold Hunter which result from the goals we defined for the application and also the approach taken. The layouts should represent the scaffold tree hierarchy well, i.e., allow to easily follow the bottom-up direction for navigation, to detect the scaffold level, and to visually separate subtrees. In addition, the layout has to reflect a (circular) sorting of the subtrees based on the user's choice of a sorting scaffold property. Also typical aesthetic criteria like edge crossings and vertex-edge or vertex overlaps should be taken into account. Several layout methods are implemented, including radial, balloon, and tree layout. All of them easily allow to satisfy our edge order, distance, crossing restriction, and vertex size constraints, see Figures 3(b), 5. We give visual cues for the level affiliation of a scaffold by visualizing the radial circles as thin background lines. In addition, we use a dynamic distance between layers which is adapted according to the zoom level. This allows to achieve good separation of hierarchy levels and a clear depiction of the tree structure in lower zoom levels, whereas in close-up zooms scaffolds can still be represented together with at least one child level.

Cluster Analysis. In cheminformatics cluster analysis based on molecular similarity is widely applied since the 1980s and can now be considered a well-established technique [15] compared to the novel scaffold tree concept. However, computing an appropriate similarity coefficient of molecules is far from trivial and many similarity measures have been proposed [16]. Common techniques to compare the structure of chemical compounds include their representation by bit vectors, so-called *molecular fingerprints*, which encode the presence or absence of certain substructures, and allow the application of well known (dis)similarity measures like Euclidean distance or Tanimoto coefficient. The choice of an adequate similarity coefficient may depend on the specific task performed or the characteristics of the molecules which are subject to the analysis. To cope with the need for various molecular descriptors Scaffold Hunter supports their computation by plugins.

We implemented a flexible clustering framework including a generic interface which allows the user to select arbitrary numerical properties of molecules and to choose from a list of similarity coefficients. Furthermore specific properties and similarity measures for fingerprints and feature vectors are supported. Scaffold Hunter includes a hierarchical clustering algorithm and supports various methods to compute inter-cluster similarities, so-called *linkage strategies.*

Dendrogram View. The process of hierarchical clustering can be visualized by means of a *dendrogram*, a tree diagram representing the relation of clusters. The dendrogram is presented as another view and is supplemented by a modified spreadsheet which can be faded in on-demand below the dendrogram panel, see Figure 5. The spreadsheet is tightly-coupled with the dendrogram: The order of the molecules corresponds to the ordering of the leaves of the dendrogram and an additional column is added representing the cluster each molecule belongs to by its color. Scaffold Hunter fosters an interactive refinement of clusters by means of a horizontal bar which can be dragged to an arbitrary position within the dendrogram. Each subtree below the bar becomes a separate cluster. The spreadsheet dynamically adapts to the new partition defined by the position of the bar.

When clustering large data sets dendrograms tend to have a large horizontal expansion compared to the vertical expansion. To take this into account we implemented a zooming strategy that allows to scale both dimensions independently giving the user the possibility to focus on the area of interest. At higher zoom levels the leaves of the dendrogram are depicted by the structural formulas of the molecules they represent. The sidebar contains a zoom widget that displays the molecule belonging to the leaf at the horizontal position of the mouse pointer and is constantly updated when the mouse pointer moves within the dendrogram view. This allows the user to retain orientation at lower zoom levels.

Molecular Spreadsheet. A molecular spreadsheet depicts a set of compounds in table form, see Figure 5. Each row represents a molecule and each column a molecular property. Our implementation features an additional column showing the structural formula of each molecule. The rows of the table can be reordered according to the values of a specified column, which allows the user, for example, to sort the rows according to the biological activity of the molecules and to inspect the molecules successively, selecting

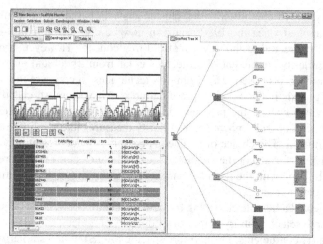

Fig. 5. Split view showing a dendrogram combined with a molecular spreadsheet (left) and a scaffold tree (right)

or marking molecules of interest. Deciding if a molecule is of interest for a specific task may, of course, depend on the expert knowledge of the user who also wants to take different properties of the molecules into account. Therefore the spreadsheet allows to freely reorder the columns and to make the leftmost columns sticky. Sticky columns always remain visible when scrolling in horizontal direction, but are still affected by vertical scrolling. The width and height of columns and rows, respectively, is adjustable. Just like the scaffold tree view the sidebar of the spreadsheet view features an overview map and a detail zoom, showing the cell under the mouse pointer in more detail. This is especially useful to inspect structural formulas that where scaled down to fit into a cell or to completely view long texts that were truncated to fit. The spreadsheet module is easily customizable and is reused as an enhancement of the dendrogram view to which it can be linked.

Scatter Plot. Scaffold Hunter includes a scatter plot view that allows for the analysis of multidimensional data. The user can freely map numerical properties to the axes of the plot and to various graphical attributes. At least two properties must be mapped to the x- and y-axis, respectively, but the user may optionally also map a property to the z-axis turning the 2D plot into a freely-rotatable 3D plot. In addition properties can be mapped to the dot size or be represented by the dot color, see Figure 8. This allows the user to visually explore the relationship of different properties, to identify correlations, trends or patters as well as clusters and outliers.

The sidebar contains several widgets showing additional information or provide tools to interactively manipulate the visualization of the data. When the user hovers the mouse cursor over a data point, the corresponding structural formula is shown in a detail widget. The visible data points can be filtered dynamically using range sliders and jitter can be introduced to detect overlapping points. Selected or marked molecules can be highlighted in the scatter plot and single data points as well as regions can be added to the selection.

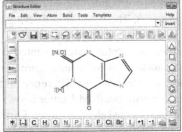

(a) Filter dialog to define constraints.   (b) Substructure search dialog.

Fig. 6. Filter dialog and integrated graphical structure editor for substructure search based on JChemPaint [17]

2.2 Coordination and Linkage of Views

When multiple views of the data are provided, intuitive linking is of utmost importance for acceptance by chemists. Brushing and switching of views, e.g., from classification representations like dendrograms to spreadsheets, are intuitive actions in the chemist's knowledge discovery process, and need to be supported in a way that allows to keep the orientation. Scaffold Hunter incorporates several techniques affecting all views in a similar manner.

Selection Concept. There is a global selection mechanism for molecules, i.e. if a molecule is selected in the spreadsheet view, for example, the same molecule is also selected in all other views (*Brushing and Linking*). All views support to select single or multiple molecules by dragging the mouse while holding the shift key. Since scaffolds represent a set of molecules, not all of which must be selected simultaneously, the coloring of scaffolds indicates if all, none or only a subset is selected. If a scaffold is selected, all associated molecules are added to the selection. At a lower zoom level it is also possible to select individual molecules, see Figure 4(d). Both, the scaffold tree view and dendrogram view, are based on a tree-like hierarchical classification. These views also allow to select sets of related molecules belonging to a specified subtree.

Subset Management and Filtering. In practice it is not sufficient to just manage a single set of selected scaffolds of interest. Therefore, Scaffold Hunter allows to create and manage arbitrary subsets of the initial data set. The user can create a new subset containing all the molecules that are currently selected to permanently store the selection for later use. Of course, it is possible to reset the selection to the molecules of a stored subset. However, the subset concept is much more powerful than suggested by this simple use-case. Subsets can be created by means of a flexible filter mechanism based on rules regarding scaffold and molecule properties deposited in the database, see Figure 6(a). Filter rules can be stored and reapplied to other molecule sets. A frequent task during the analysis of chemical compounds is the search for structurally similar compounds and to filter large compound databases by means of substructure search, i.e. to create a subset consisting only of molecules that contain a user-specified substructure. We have implemented a fast graph-based substructure search approach [18] and integrated a structure editor [17], which allows to create search patterns graphically, see Figure 6(b). The result of a filtering can be highlighted in the current view by setting the selection to the new subset.

All subsets created are presented at the right sidebar in a tree-like fashion that reflects the relation of subsets, see Figure 3(a). The user may perform the basic set operations union, intersection and difference on two or more sets leading to a new subset containing the result. Scaffold Hunter allows to create new views showing only the molecules contained in the selected subset. Furthermore the underlying subset of the current view can be changed to a different subset preserving the active mapping of properties to graphical attributes.

The subset concept is suitable for the typical drill-down approach in a chemical workflow, where the set of considered molecules is reduced step by step. The subset tree provides links back to upper levels of the drill-down process to get back from dead ends and fathomed areas of the chemical space under investigation. Restricting to subsets of medium-size helps the user to preserve orientation and at the same time allows for an efficient analysis and visualization. Although chemical databases may contain millions of compounds, the interface capabilities are designed and restricted to the visualization of dozens to only several thousand compounds. However, the visualization of all database entries as distinct entities simultaneously is hardly ever of interest for chemists.

Multiple Views and Connecting Elements. Scaffold Hunter allows to inspect sets of molecules with different views. Furthermore, it is possible to create several views of the same type based on different subsets. This is a prerequisite for the visual comparison of different subsets, but requires techniques to help the user to preserve orientation.

Scaffold Hunter supports labeling views to be able to identify their source and how they were created, e.g. by highlighting the underlying data set in the subset tree. Each view comes with a specific toolbar and sidebar (cf. Figure 3(a)) and the GUI is adjusted whenever another view becomes active. However, for several views the sidebar contains elements with a similar intended purpose, but implemented in a view specific manner. For example, all views offer a detail widget, that works as a magnifying glass in the scaffold tree view, as a zoom to the leaf node of the dendrogram, shows a complete cell of a spreadsheet or details of a dot in the scatter plot, respectively. A tooltip containing a user-defined list of properties of a molecule or scaffold as well as comments is consistently presented across views, see Figure 7. It is possible to annotate specific molecules or scaffolds of interest and persistently store comments, which can then also be viewed by other users, if desired, to support joint work on a project. In addition visual features like setting flags to support orientation when moving back and forth through several views are supported. Especially when working with large molecule sets, it can be hard to relocate selected molecules in a different view. Therefore all views support to focus the current selection, e.g. by automated panning and zooming such that all selected molecules are contained in the viewport.

Scaffold Hunter arranges multiple views by means of a tabbed document interface, which most users are familiar with and which allows to quickly switch between different views. To fully exploit the additional benefit of different visual analysis components it is important to consider multiple views at the same time. Therefore, the tab pane can be

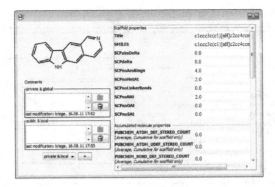

Fig. 7. Hovering over a scaffold or molecule image with the mouse pointer opens a tooltip window that shows the corresponding structure view and user-selectable property information. Private or public comments can be entered and stored persistently.

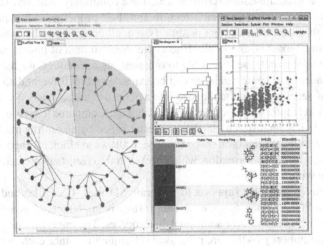

Fig. 8. Several views showing data and statistical analysis results complementary to the scaffold tree navigation

split horizontally or vertically and views can be moved from one tab pane to the other, see Figure 5. Furthermore it is possible to open additional main windows (cf. Figure 8) to support work on multiple monitors.

Since the creation of subsets and the customization of views is an important step in the knowledge discovery process that should be preserved, the current subset tree as well as the state of each view is stored as a session and can be resumed later.

2.3 Data Integration

Chemical data on compounds is collected in different databases that are accessible over web or programmatical interfaces. The information stored as well as the interfaces to retrieve them are highly heterogeneous. However, there are various standardized

Fig. 9. Importing an SD file allows the specification of a mapping from the properties contained in the SD file to the internal properties

file formats like structure data (SD) files which are commonly used and store sets of molecules with information on their structure and their properties. Most public databases support to export their content or subsets, e.g. all compounds that where investigated in the same bioassay, as SD file. Due to the sheer amount of information and the need to prepare the data to be accessible to our analysis techniques, we rely on a data warehouse concept, i.e. compound data can be extracted from different data sources, is transformed, if necessary, and then loaded into a central database once in a preprocessing step. Scaffold Hunter only operates on this database. Compared to a virtual database, where a unified view on different databases is established by an on-line transformation of queries and results, the data warehouse approach allows to efficiently access data and to precompute additional information, which is essential to facilitate interactive analysis and navigation within the data.

Scaffold Hunter currently supports to integrate SD files, CSV files and databases via customized SQL queries. Since each data format is implemented as a plugin, it is easily possible to add support for additional data sources. The import framework allows to define several import jobs that are processed subsequently. Since each imported data source may have a different set of properties, defining an import job includes specifying a mapping to internal properties and a merging strategy to cope with possible conflicts, cf. Figure 9. It is also possible to specify a transformation function that can, e.g., be used to adjust the order of magnitude of the imported property values to the scale expected for the internal property.

After an initial data set has been stored, it is still possible to add additional properties for each molecule. This allows to integrate new experimental data at a later stage in the knowledge discovery process, cf. Figure 1. In addition, it is possible to calculate further properties that can be derived from the structure of each molecule.

3   Conclusions and Outlook

We presented Scaffold Hunter, a tool for the analysis of chemical space. There is already an active user community that provides valuable feedback, and the main concept of bioactivity guided navigation of chemical space seems to be promising, which is also backed by recent results [13].

Nonetheless the software could be extended by features to address a broader community, with a smooth integration into additional chemical workflows. Support for additional views and further analysis capabilities could help to boost the use of Scaffold Hunter. The development and integration of additional functionality is encouraged by a modular software architecture designed to be easily extendable and by providing the software as open source.

A promising direction to enhance the currently supported classification concepts based on tree-like hierarchies is to support network-like structures. Recently an extension of the scaffold tree approach was proposed taking all possible parent scaffolds into account [19]. This creates so-called scaffold networks, which were shown to reveal additional scaffolds having a desired biological property. Furthermore networks can be used to represent structural similarities, e.g. derived from maximum common substructures, and might prove to be more flexible when ring-free molecules are considered or functional side-chains should be taken into account. However, visualizing networks instead of tree-like hierarchies without compromising the orientation is challenging. New navigation concepts have to be developed and graph layout techniques must be customized to the specific characteristics of such networks. We plan to make use of the Open Graph Drawing Framework [20] for that purpose.

Due to the dynamic nature and the growing extent of publicly available chemical data it might be helpful to also allow direct access to public resources from within the GUI, e.g., by providing direct links to PubChem web pages for database compounds.

Scaffold Hunter is implemented in Java and freely available under the terms of the GNU GPL v3 at `http://scaffoldhunter.sourceforge.net/`.

Acknowledgements. We would like to thank the participants of student project group PG552, the group of Prof. Waldmann, in particular Claude Ostermann and Björn Over, as well as Stefan Mundt, Stefan Wetzel, and Steffen Renner for their valuable suggestions and their contributions to the project.

References

1. IMI: Innovative Medicines Initiative 2nd Call, Knowledge Management – Open Pharmacological Space (2009)
2. OpenWetWare (2012), `http://www.openwetware.org`
3. Schuffenhauer, A., Ertl, P., Roggo, S., Wetzel, S., Koch, M.A., Waldmann, H.: The Scaffold Tree - Visualization of the Scaffold Universe by Hierarchical Scaffold Classification. J. Chem. Inf. Model. 47, 47–58 (2007)
4. Wetzel, S., Klein, K., Renner, S., Rauh, D., Oprea, T.I., Mutzel, P., Waldmann, H.: Interactive exploration of chemical space with Scaffold Hunter. Nat. Chem. Biol. 5, 581–583 (2009)
5. Irwin, J.J.: Staring off into chemical space. Nat. Chem. Biol. 5, 536–537 (2009)
6. Berthold, M.R., Cebron, N., Dill, F., Gabriel, T.R., Kötter, T., Meinl, T., Ohl, P., Sieb, C., Thiel, K., Wiswedel, B.: KNIME: The Konstanz Information Miner. In: Studies in Classification, Data Analysis, and Knowledge Organization, GfKL 2007 (2007)

7. Schuffenhauer, A., Varin, T.: Rule-Based Classification of Chemical Structures by Scaffold. Molecular Informatics 30, 646–664 (2011)
8. Herhaus, C., Karch, O., Bremm, S., Rippmann, F.: MolWind - mapping molecule spaces to geospatial worlds. Chemistry Central Journal 3, 32 (2009)
9. Lounkine, E., Wawer, M., Wassermann, A.M., Bajorath, J.: SARANEA: A freely available program to mine structure-activity and structure-selectivity relationship information in compound data sets. J. Chem. Inf. Model. 50, 68–78 (2010)
10. Garcia-Serna, R., Ursu, O., Oprea, T.I., Mestres, J.: iPHACE: integrative navigation in pharmacological space. Bioinformatics 26(7), 985–986 (2010)
11. Agrafiotis, D.K., Wiener, J.J.M.: Scaffold Explorer: An Interactive Tool for Organizing and Mining Structure-Activity Data Spanning Multiple Chemotypes. Journal of Medicinal Chemistry 53, 5002–5011 (2010)
12. Wetzel, S., Wilk, W., Chammaa, S., Sperl, B., Roth, A.G., Yektaoglu, A., Renner, S., Berg, T., Arenz, C., Giannis, A., Oprea, T.I., Rauh, D., Kaiser, M., Waldmann, H.: A Scaffold-Tree-Merging Strategy for Prospective Bioactivity Annotation of γ-Pyrones. Angew. Chem. Int. Ed. 49, 3666–3670 (2010)
13. Bon, R., Waldmann, H.: Bioactivity-Guided Navigation of Chemical Space. Acc. Chem. Res. 43, 1103–1114 (2010)
14. Bederson, B.B., Grosjean, J., Meyer, J.: Toolkit design for interactive structured graphics. IEEE Trans. Softw. Eng. 30(8), 535–546 (2004)
15. Downs, G.M., Barnard, J.M.: Clustering Methods and Their Uses in Computational Chemistry, pp. 1–40. John Wiley & Sons, Inc. (2003)
16. Maggiora, G.M., Shanmugasundaram, V.: Molecular similarity measures. Methods in Molecular Biology 672, 39–100 (2011)
17. JChemPaint chemical 2D structure editor (2012), http://jchempaint.github.com
18. Klein, K., Kriege, N., Mutzel, P.: CT-Index: Fingerprint-based Graph Indexing Combining Cycles and Trees. In: IEEE 27th International Conference on Data Engineering (ICDE), pp. 1115–1126 (2011)
19. Varin, T., Schuffenhauer, A., Ertl, P., Renner, S.: Mining for Bioactive Scaffolds with Scaffold Networks: Improved Compound Set Enrichment from Primary Screening Data. J. Chem. Inf. Model. 51, 1528–1538 (2011)
20. The Open Graph Drawing Framework (2012), http://www.ogdf.net

Structural Decomposition Trees:
Semantic and Practical Implications

Daniel Engel[1], Hans Hagen[1], Bernd Hamann[2], and René Rosenbaum[3]

[1] Department of Computer Science, University of Kaiserslautern, Germany
[2] Institute for Data Analysis and Visualization (IDAV), Department of Computer Science,
University of California, Davis, U.S.A.
[3] Institute for Computer Science, University of Rostock, Germany
{d_engel,hagen}@cs.uni-kl.de,hamann@cs.ucdavis.edu,
rrosen@informatik.uni-rostock.de

Abstract. The visualization of high-dimensional data is a challenging research topic. Existing approaches can usually be assigned to either relation or value visualizations. Merging approaches from both classes into a single integrated strategy, Structural Decomposition Trees (SDTs) represent a completely novel visualization approach for high-dimensional data. Although this method is new and promising, statements on how to use and apply the technique in the context of real-world applications are still missing. This paper discusses how SDTs can be interpreted and interacted with to gain insights about the data more effectively. First, it is discussed what properties about the data can be obtained by an interpretation of the initial projection. These statements are also valid for other projections based on principal components analysis, addressing a frequent problem when applying this technique. Further, a detailed and task-oriented interaction guideline shows how provided interaction methods can be utilized effectively for data exploration. The results obtained by an application of these guidelines in air quality research indicate that much insight can be gained even for large and complex data sets. This justifies and further motivates the usefulness and wide applicability of SDTs as a novel visualization approach for high-dimensional data.

Keywords: High-dimensional data visualization, Projections, Interaction.

1 Introduction

The visualization of high-dimensional data is a common but still unsolved problem. Structural decomposition trees (SDTs) [1] represent a novel approach to this challenge. SDTs combine value and relation visualizations into one approach and thus provide a variety of benefits not available in related visualization technology. Research concerning SDTs, however, is constrained to the introduction and description of fundamental aspects of this novel displaying approach only. Although, research concerned with main utilization strategies have recently been published [2], the eligibility of SDTs when extensively applied in complex real-world visual data analysis has not been discussed in literature so far.

This paper provides guidance and an example for the successful application of SDTs in data visualization. After reviewing related work in the area of high-dimensional data

G. Csurka et al. (Eds.): VISIGRAPP 2012, CCIS 359, pp. 193–208, 2013.
© Springer-Verlag Berlin Heidelberg 2013

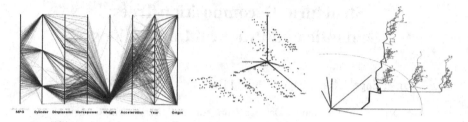

Fig. 1. The two classes of visualizations for high-dimensional data (value (left) and relation (center) visualizations) are brought together by SDTs (right). All visualizations represent the well-known "cars" data set. The SDT highlights the five distinct clusters by its branch structure also conveying the respective differences in the data values.

visualization (Section 2), the first part of this paper (Section 3) is particularly concerned with the interpretation of an SDT. Thereby, we focus on alignment and length of the different dimensional anchors and provide practical implications supporting the users in their understanding of high-dimensional data projections. Classifying and discussing means for interaction provided by SDTs from a functional point of view, the second part (Section 4) is concerned with appropriate data exploration. For each listed interaction, distinct aims and guidelines for its appropriate application are stated. The third part (Section 5), discusses results we obtained from an application of SDTs in the visual analysis of air quality data. It shows that by taking advantage of the introduced methods much insight can be gained even for complex and large data sets. We conclude (Section 6) that SDTs are a valid means for visualizing and gaining insight into high-dimensional data, but must be understood and applied in the right way in order to avoid misinterpretation and wrong conclusions. Here, we provide the necessary information to accomplish this objective successfully.

2   Related Work

2.1   Visualization of High-Dimensional Data

As a result of most data acquisition tasks today, high-dimensional data are of strong interest to the visualization community. Many different approaches and techniques have been proposed. According to [1], they can be categorized into *value* or *relation visualizations*. By focusing on the conveyance of data coordinate values for every data point, **value visualizations** allow for a detailed analysis of the data. The parallel coordinates plot (see Figure 1, left) is a typical representative of this category. Due to their focus on value representation for each data point, a common problem with all associated techniques is that they are often not scalable with regard to the amount and dimensionality of the data. As a result this usually leads to clutter and long processing times as the number of dimensions and amount of data points increase. In order to overcome these issues, cluster-based approaches [3–5], appropriate means for interaction [6, 7], and better utilization of the available screen space [8] have been proposed. Clutter reduction is also achieved by dimension ordering arranging the dimensions within the visual representation based on correlations within the data. After the initial formal problem statement [9], this technique has been expanded in [10] and [11]. Although these methods are great improvements to reduce clutter, the displayed information is often too detailed and a meaningful representation can generally not be obtained for large data sets.

Instead of aiming at communicating data values, **relation visualizations** are designed to convey data relationships. They are mostly point mappings, projecting the m-dimensional (m-D) data into the low-dimensional presentation space. As relations within the data may be too complex to be completely conveyed in presentation space, projections are usually ambiguous. A well-known point projection approach is principal components analysis (PCA) conveying distance relations in m-D space by projecting into a plane that is aligned to capture the greatest variance data space without distorting the data (see Figure 1, center). Multi-dimensional scaling (MDS) commonly uses general similarity measures to represent the data, but leads to distortion and a visualization that may be difficult to interpret. Interpretation of the representation is a general issue with point projections as long as no means to comprehend the parameters used for the projection are available. One such option are dimensional anchor (DA) visualizations [12] projecting and displaying the basis vectors along the data points (see Figure 1, center). These DAs are also an appropriate means to adjust the projection interactively [13]. Relation visualizations usually lead to a meaningful overview of the data. Their effectiveness, however, strongly depends on the quality of the initial projection and the means provided to interpret and interact with it. Current research mainly focuses on improved representation of specific data structures, e.g., scientific point cloud data [14], a better incorporation of domain-appropriate analysis techniques, e.g., brushing and filtering [15], or computational speed gains [16].

Due to the rather diverse properties of value and relation visualizations, they each have distinct application domains. Thus, they are often used simultaneously in exploratory multi-view systems [17]. Few publications tackle the problem of combining both classes into a single approach. Most of them have been proposed for value visualizations, such as the technology described in [10, 18, 19], [20], or [21]. SDTs represent a completely different approach that promises to bridge the existing gap between both classes.

2.2   Structural Decomposition Trees

SDTs are founded on a sophisticated data projection, but provide additional means to represent the dimension contributions for each data point (see Figure 1, right). This is achieved by introducing a tree structure showing the projection path for each displayed data point and thus its individual dimension values. The projection paths also allow for an unambiguous identification and interpretation of data points that reside at different locations in *m*-D space, but have been projected in close proximity in the projection space. A main problem in showing the different projection paths is the introduced clutter. SDTs overcome this issue by introducing a multi-stage processing pipeline. Hierarchical clustering is used to identify, aggregate, and bundle common line segments. The resulting tree has minimal overall branch length, reducing the redundancies considerably. Appropriate representation of the individual dimension contributions is accomplished by a well-designed drawing order. The tree itself is represented by colored lines, whereby the number of elements within this subtree is encoded by branch

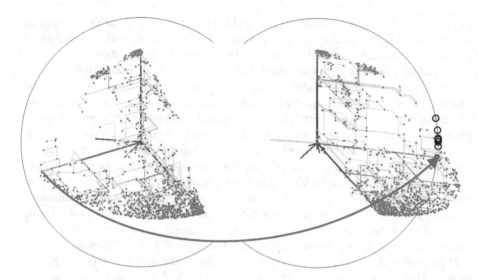

Fig. 2. The main interactions provided by SDTs: *Repositioning of DAs* (green arrow) allows for an intuitive adjustment of the projection. *Dimension highlighting* (yellow DA) conveys the individual contributions of a dimension in the data (yellow tree segments). *Path highlighting* (purple tree branch) is intended to emphasize interesting tree branches and substructures.

thickness (see Figure 1, right). The initial SDT projection maximizes the space between tree paths and allows for a better interpretation of the visualization [1].

Different means for interaction, either on individual or groups of data points or the whole representation, make possible for further exploration of the data (see Figure 2). The projection can be significantly changed by a re-arrangement of the end points of the DAs. These dimension vectors can be independently modified in their lengths and angles relative to each other. Thereby, so-called variance points are placed along the unit circle in order to indicate angles that lead to other promising projections. Different means to emphasize and filter dimensions and line segments are provided to facilitate investigation and interpretation of the structural decomposition of the data. Published research concerned with SDTs mainly focuses on its technical foundations. Although, semantic aspects of an SDT representation were discussed in [2], the authors were mainly concerned with the application of SDTs in visual cluster analysis. General statements to practical implications, guidelines, and a concrete use case were not provided.

3 Interpretation of the Initial Layout

Projections are a powerful means to convey relations in high-dimensional data. Due to the characteristics of dimension reduction, however, they are often difficult to interpret. In previous work it was shown that SDTs are specifically suited to depict data coordinates in a way that aims at intuitive interpretation. Experimental studies of PCA-based projections showed that the projection conveys properties of the data by the length and relation of the DAs to each other. This, however, has never been explicitly quantified.

In this section, we investigate in full detail how the initial arrangement of DAs in SDTs relates to the corresponding variables in the data and how the user can interpret this arrangement to infer knowledge about the data. Due to the use of a PCA-related projection method for SDTs, the given statements apply to all PCA-based projections. We shortly recall *dimensional anchors and their arrangement*, after which we are *linking the properties of DAs to those of the data*. We first outline why DAs are used to reflect a PCA projection and how their initial arrangement is defined. This is expressed by latent features in the data, i.e., the eigenvectors and eigenvalues of the data's covariance matrix indicating the information content within the different data dimensions. In order to understand which data properties are visually encoded in a projection, we investigate how the projection is defined by these features and what information is thereby depicted. This is expressed by a derivation of the *spectral decomposition of the covariance matrix*. After these steps, we show that the specific DA arrangement allows one to derive *conclusions* and data properties that are of keen interest to the user but not depicted by the common plotting of principal components. Finally, statements to *implications* of these properties aim for a better understanding of an arbitrary PCA-based projection avoiding its misinterpretation.

DAs and Their Arrangement. Since SDTs can be computed and visualized both in 2D or 3D space, the following considerations are made for an arbitrary display dimensionality p. We assume that n m-dimensional data points are stored row-wise in X so that $X \in \mathbb{R}^{(n \times m)}$. The projection of X to $\widetilde{X} \in \mathbb{R}^{(n \times p)}$ is defined by the linear mapping of m-D data points X_i to p-D display points $\widetilde{X}_i$, for $1 \leq i \leq n$, by the linear combination of DAs $a_j \in \mathbb{R}^p$ with the corresponding coordinate $X_{i,j}$, for $1 \leq j \leq m$:

$$\widetilde{X}_i = \sum_{1 \leq j \leq m} a_j X_{i,j}. \tag{1}$$

This technique, the mapping in star coordinates [13], can be understood as a generalization of drawing 3D objects on paper to arbitrary dimensions. In the original work, however, the DAs are initially arranged in a uniform distribution along a unit circle. In general, this leads to a non-orthogonal projection. This can be misleading because the distance in display space does not reflect distance in $\mathbb{R}^m$. To avoid this, a projection is designed to minimize this mapping error. This error is commonly expressed as the sum of squared pairwise distance differences arising from the mapping from m to p dimensions, $\sum_{1 \leq i,j \leq n} (D(X_i, X_j) - d_2(\widetilde{X}_i, \widetilde{X}_j))^2$, where d_2 is the Euclidean distance metric and D is an appropriate distance metric of the application domain. This error can be minimized, for example, by PCA in the case $D = d_2$. Instead of expressing the data by the original unit vectors, PCA computes new orthogonal directions (principal components) in which the data has maximal variance and re-expresses all data points in coordinates of these principal components. The projection is defined by the p principal components that capture the highest variance in the data. Although distance relations between data points are captured well in this projection, the interpretation of principal components is not intuitive. In almost all applications, the link to the original data is essential for analysis. Therefore, the depiction of the original data coordinates and relations between the original data dimensions is an important aspect for a projection.

Linking Properties of DAs to Those of the Data. In previous work [1], both approaches have been combined and the initial arrangement of DAs has been defined to reflect a (weighted) PCA projection into p-dimensional display coordinates. We utilize DAs to make possible a better interpretation and more intuitive understanding of the underlying projection without losing any of the underlying projection's benefit. In this research, we investigate the properties of this DA projection in more detail and deduct which properties of the DAs link to which properties in the data. The following considerations are based on the data's covariance matrix. Without loss of generality, we assume X to be centered and, since the used weighting scheme in previous work changes the covariance matrix (to be weighted) a priori, we can neglect the weighting in the following. We also neglect the global scaling by n^{-1} that does not influence relations in the data.

The PCA projection $\widetilde{X}$ of X is defined as $\widetilde{X} = X\,\widehat{\Gamma}$, with $\widehat{\Gamma} = (\gamma^{(1)}, ..., \gamma^{(p)}) \in \mathbb{R}^{(m \times p)}$ being the matrix storing column-wise the eigenvectors of the corresponding p largest eigenvalues of the covariance matrix S of X. Equation (1) implies that the linear mapping of DAs $A = (a_1, ..., a_m)^T \in \mathbb{R}^{(m \times p)}$ is defined as $\widetilde{X}_i = X\,A$. In order to initially arrange the DAs such that their mapping is equivalent to that of the PCA, we define each DA as a row vector of $\widehat{\Gamma}$:

$$a_i = \left(\gamma_i^{(1)}, ..., \gamma_i^{(p)} \right)^T . \tag{2}$$

This step is equivalent to the projection of the original unit vectors $\mathbf{1}_i \in \mathbb{R}^m$ to $\mathbb{R}^p$ subject to the same rotation, i.e., $a_i^T = \mathbf{1}_i^T \widehat{\Gamma}$. It is important to note that PCA projects X by reducing its dimensionality to p in an optimal variance-preserving way. Thus, the information that is actually displayed by this projection is that of the inherently defined best rank-p approximation $\widehat{X}$ of X.

Spectral Decomposition of the Covariance Matrix. The process of dimensionality reduction by maximizing variance becomes clear when considering the spectral decomposition of S. That is the decomposition of the combined variances of all elements in X into successive contributions of decreasing variance: $S = \lambda_1 \gamma^{(1)} \gamma^{(1)^T} + ... + \lambda_r \gamma^{(r)} \gamma^{(r)^T}$, with λ_k being the k highest eigenvalue of S and $\gamma^{(k)}$ the corresponding eigenvector for $1 \leq k \leq r = rank(X)$.

Each contribution $S^{(k)} = \lambda_k \gamma^{(k)} \gamma^{(k)^T}$ thereby increases the rank of the matrix summation by one. λ_k holds the variance of the contribution, whereas $\gamma^{(k)} \gamma^{(k)^T}$ defines the mixing of this variance, i.e., how this contributes to S. Consequently, the covariance matrix of the PCA's p-dimensional best rank-p approximation $\widehat{X}$ of X equals the sum over the first p contributions, where usually $p \ll rank(X)$. The covariance between dimensions i and j of the projected data $\widehat{X}$ is

$$\widehat{S}_{i,j} = \sum_{1 \leq k \leq p} \lambda_k \gamma_i^{(k)} \gamma_j^{(k)} . \tag{3}$$

Similarly, $\widehat{X}$ can be defined by $\widehat{X} = X\,\widehat{\Gamma}\widehat{\Gamma}^T$. For the dimensions (columns) in $\widehat{X}$ the following equation holds: $\widehat{X}_{\bullet,i} = \sum_{1 \leq j \leq m} X_{\bullet,j} (\widehat{\Gamma}\widehat{\Gamma}^T)_{i,j}$, $\widehat{X}_{\bullet,i}$ is constructed from X by the linear combination of all $X_{\bullet,j}$ with coefficients $(\widehat{\Gamma}\widehat{\Gamma}^T)_{i,j} = \sum_{1 \leq p \leq p} \gamma_i^{(k)} \gamma_j^{(k)}$. Consequently, these coefficients define the orthogonal projection of the data and account for the similarities between columns in $\widehat{X}$, i.e., for $rank(\widehat{X})$.

Conclusions. With the above considerations in mind, we show in the following that the length of each DA and the angles between them reflect specific properties of the projection and of the projected data $\widehat{X}$. The mixing matrix $\widehat{\Gamma}\widehat{\Gamma}^T$ holds normalized contributions to $\widehat{S}$ and relates to the DA's arrangement in the sense that $(\widehat{\Gamma}\widehat{\Gamma}^T)_{i,j} = \sum_{1 \leq k \leq p} S_{i,j}^{(k)}/\lambda_k = \widetilde{S}_{i,j}$, whereas $\widetilde{S}_{i,j} = \cos \angle(a_i, a_j) \, \|a_i\|_2 \, \|a_j\|_2$. We can draw the following conclusions:

1. The length of DAs equals the standard deviation of the respective dimension in $\widehat{X}$, normalized for each contribution $\widehat{S}^{(k)}$ by its variance λ_k.

$$\|a_i\|_2 \overset{(2)}{=} \sqrt{\sum_{1 \leq k \leq p} (\gamma_i^{(k)})^2}$$

$$\overset{(3)}{=} \sqrt{\widetilde{S}_{i,i}} = \tilde{s}_i$$

2. The cosine of the angle between two DAs equals the correlation of the respective dimensions in $\widehat{X}$, where both covariance and standard deviation are normalized for each contribution $\widehat{S}^{(k)}$ by its variance λ_k.

$$\cos \angle(a_i, a_j) = \frac{a_i^T a_j}{\|a_i\|_2 \|a_j\|_2}$$

$$\overset{(2)}{=} \frac{\sum_{1 \leq k \leq p} \gamma_j^{(k)} \gamma_i^{(k)}}{\tilde{s}_i \, \tilde{s}_j}$$

$$\overset{(3)}{=} \frac{\widetilde{S}_{i,j}^{(k)}}{\tilde{s}_i \, \tilde{s}_j} = \tilde{r}_{i,j}$$

Implications. It is important to emphasize that $\widehat{X}$ does not represent the whole data X but only its best rank-p approximation. That is, $\widehat{X}$ is the approximation of X that can be optimally depicted in p dimensions with regard to its variance. Therefore, $\widehat{X}$ is the orthogonally projected data on the subspace $\mathbb{R}^p$ which is spanned in a way that the projection reflects the dominant trends in X. However, $\mathbb{R}^p$ can only cover the most important information in the data. While other subspaces that are left out globally account for less variance in the data, relations therein may still be of importance for the user. Unfortunately, this information cannot be captured in a single projection and, consequently, parts of the relations between the original data dimensions in $\mathbb{R}^m$ are lost. The user has to be aware of this issue because it may lead to possible misinterpretations stemming from the visual assessment of the DAs' properties.

Because principal components are mutually orthogonal, it is possible that the depicted standard deviation of certain dimensions is lower in the initial projection than in other projections. This depends on the overall information content of this dimension in the subspaces collapsed by dimensionality reduction. Thus, the knowledge derived from the DAs can only be a subset of the hidden information and usually represents a high-level view only. To avoid misinterpretation, they must be further evaluated. The quality of the projection, with regard to one dimension, is reflected by the amount of its lost variance due to dimension reduction. To indicate this information, an SDT display provides *variance points* for each dimension. Each variance point consists of two circles. While the outer circle's radius represents s_i, the dimension's standard variation, the inner circle represents $\widehat{s_i}$, the part of the dimension's standard variation that is reflected by the projection. Assessing the ratio between both circles, $(\widehat{s_i}/s_i)^2$, thereby allows one to infer the quality of the projection with regard to a data dimension. Thereby, variance points provide guidance for interactive exploration.

Commonly, the user is aware of the fact that projections have an inherent information loss. Projections that map different points in $\mathbb{R}^m$ to the same location in $\mathbb{R}^p$ make this fact clear. Ambiguity is often a severe problem and stems from the principal illustration of "collapsed" subspaces. Points that only differ in the subspaces that are disregarded by dimensionality reduction are consequently projected onto the same location. By visualizing the projection path of each data point, SDTs prevent possible misinterpretations by assuring the user that data points are only equal when they share the same path. This display, however, introduces further graphical primitives into the data representation, leading to occlusion problems and visual clutter. How to solve these issues by proper interactive exploration is discussed in the following sections.

4   Means for Interaction: Purpose and Guidelines

Interactions within SDTs can be mainly classified as interactions with the *data* or the *dimensional anchors* as well as *changes of the view*. In this section, we describe the available interaction methods from a general, functional standpoint, state their individual aims, and complete with novel guidelines on how to interact with SDTs. This will provide users with quick insight and reference to the available methods. Using these guidelines, SDTs convey an intuitive visual mapping that can be remembered and from which the user can quickly learn

- how the data is assembled, spread, where clusters are, or which pattern they follow,
- how parts of the data are connected, differ, or how they relate to each other, and
- what properties they have, e.g., intra-cluster variances, shape, or alignment.

4.1   Interactions with the Data

This class of interactions allows the user to highlight or filter parts of the data. Associated techniques are usually strongly task and application depend.

Interaction: **Dimension highlighting**
Aim: Emphasizing dimension contributions of the data
Guidelines: This interaction (see Figure 2) allows the user to emphasize all line segments corresponding to the coordinates of a dimension and thus helps to investigate the structural decomposition of the data. The selection of too many dimensions decreases its usefulness. Only DAs of current importance to the user should be selected.

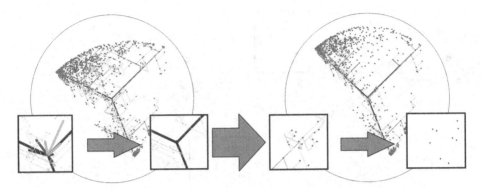

Fig. 3. Interactive complexity and clutter reduction taking advantage of the capabilities of SDTs: dimension filtering (left) reduces the number of branch segments in the tree, node collapsing (right) the number of displayed subtrees. Additional means for zoom and pan interaction allow the users to drill-down into the presentation and data to obtain momentary detail (bottom).

Interaction: **Path highlighting**
Aim: Emphasizing data points and subtrees
Guidelines: Path highlighting (see Figure 2) emphasizes interesting pathes and branches within the SDT. During selection the user should focus on paths that lead through cluttered regions as they might no be easily followed and take unexpected ways.

Interaction: **Node collapse**
Aim: Data filtering
Guidelines: This interaction causes subtrees and data points to disappear from the SDT representation. A single subtree is then represented by a characteristic point only (see Figure 3, right). After collapsing, the main value contributions of all associated data points are still visible and can be used and interpreted, e.g., for comparison with other subtrees. Most appropriate regions to apply node collapse are cluttered areas or uninteresting subtrees. The user, however, should always bear in mind that data filtering was applied.

4.2 Interactions with the Dimensional Anchors

The layout of an SDT visualization consists of the different DAs. As their alignment strongly influences the projection of the data, allowing for their interactive modification is a powerful means for a variety of purposes. As there is no restriction on their placement, interactions can change the (1) *angle* or (2) *length* of an DA, or (3) *both*. Each kind of modification can be used to achieve a distinct aim.

Interaction: **Move of a DA to a corresponding variance point**
Aim: Exploration of hidden subspaces
Guidelines: Subspaces hidden by dimension reduction can contain further information important for the analyst. They are made available by a successive exploration of individual dimensions via their respective variance points. This leads to different but still

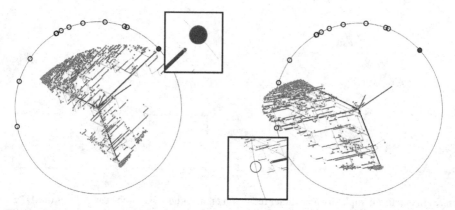

Fig. 4. Variance points help to find other promising projections of the data. Large variance points (left) indicate projections most suited to convey the variance in the data. Opposite variance points (right), even when not accounting for much variance, often lead to strongly different projections helping to identify unexpected data properties.

orthogonal projections of the data. To explore most important information first, it is meaningful to use large variance points indicating a strong inherent information content. We also propose to use variance points placed at opposite positions on the unit circle. Although position has no meaning regarding the amount of information content, this leads to strong changes in the projection and may reveal unexpected and important insight (see Figure 4). Switching between close points does not significantly change the projection and can usually be skipped even for large variance points.

Interaction: **Move of the SDT stem to another position**
Aim: Solving occlusion issues
Guidelines: Sometimes only the orientation of the tree or of large branches is to be changed, e.g., to overcome visibility and occlusion issues. To support this, we propose to find and relocate a dimension with strong contribution to the stem of the SDT, e.g., a dimension with low variance. This leaves the initial crone structure of the SDT widely unaltered for further analysis.

Interaction: **Orthogonal placement of two DAs**
Aim: Discovery or verification of correlation between two dimensions
Guidelines: The orthogonal placement of two DAs emphasizes potential correlation between two dimensions and thus enables the viewer for its visual discovery or verification. Correlations can be identified by following the development of the point contributions from the origin along the direction of the respective dimension vectors. As an example, increasing contributions for both dimensions indicate a linear correlation for the associated dimensions (see Figure 5, left). Visual emphasis of the involved dimension contributions by dimension highlighting helps revealing such characteristic patterns. Due to the fact that SDTs are projected into a two-dimensional presentation space, correlations between more than two dimensions must be explored successively.

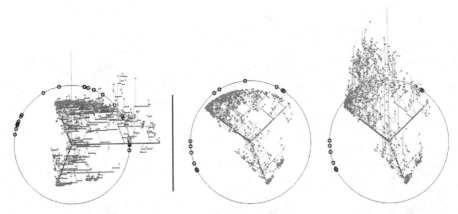

Fig. 5. The orthogonal placement of two DAs (red and yellow color) in the presentation can simplify the evaluation of correlations between the associated dimensions (left). In order to overcome potential point cluttering within the initial projection (center), a DA (green color) can be interactively stretched (right).

Interaction: **Enlarging or shrinking a DA**

Aim: Exploration of data distribution, discovery of data clusters, conveyance of value contributions

Guidelines: As the length of a DA proportionally influences the position of the projected data, the associated points can be stretched or compressed easily (see Figure 5, center/right). This allows for an investigation of the data distribution of the associated dimension. Thereby, it is useful to enlarge and shrink the DA multiple times and in different directions to discover the representation where the distribution is conveyed best. Dimensions causing a visual separation of data points usually contribute to clustering. Enlarging the length of a DA enhances separation and thus can help identifying such clusters. All points of a potential cluster show a similar behavior during length changes. Path highlighting can be used for further verification. In case of a valid m-D cluster, all associated points must share the same projection path.

Length modification is also particularly useful to visually emphasizing value contributions in the tree. Strong contributions can easily be identified by their strong response to length changes.

Interaction: **Move of a DA to the origin of the projection**

Aim: Dimension filtering

Guidelines: To reduce clutter, it is meaningful to filter out less interesting dimensions by placing their anchors at the origin of the projection (see Figure 3, left). Appropriate candidates are dimensions that are correlated or show similar characteristics. They can be substituted by a single *super*-DA, whereby its angle is determined by the average and the length by the sum of all associated DAs. This changes the point projections only slightly, but removes many SDT branches from the representation. We further propose to remove dimensions having (1) very small variance points or (2) many, very small branches of similar length at high tree levels indicating little structure in the data.

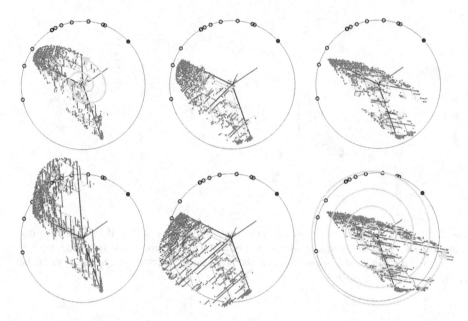

Fig. 6. Moving a DA in circles activates the motion parallax effect of the human visual system letting the tree and the data points appear more "plastic". By providing many different coordinated projections, characteristics of the data can be identified or verified. Best results are obtained by using a DA corresponding to a dimension with high variance.

Interaction: **Continuous circular movement of a DA**

Aims: Discovery of m-D data clusters, exploration of data distribution

Guidelines: The movement of a DA enables the motion parallax effect of the human visual system to create a pseudo three-dimensional impression of the two-dimensional SDT representation (see Figure 6). This lets the points and the tree appear more "plastic" and results in more insight about the structure and potential clusters in the data. During the interaction, point clusters can be identified by their constant grouping. Circular movement leading to similar projections at each turn helps the human visual system to memorize the gained insight. Continuously changing diameter stretches or compresses potential clusters allowing for improved identification or verification. Not every dimension is equally suited to achieve this. We propose to select a dimension that strongly contributes to higher tree branches, e.g., one that has a high variance in data values. As such a dimension strongly affects the top of the SDT leaving its stem nearly unchanged, it can increase motion parallax. Appropriate dimensions can easily be found by dimension highlighting emphasizing all line segments corresponding to the coordinates of a dimension and thus conveying their distribution.

4.3   Interactions to Change the View

Interaction: **Zoom&Pan of the current viewing region**

Aim: Providing overview or detail

Guidelines: Changing view point and direction is a common means in interactive data exploration. Following the information visualization mantra [22] visual data analysis should successively repeat the stages: (1) providing an overview to the data, (2) filtering data that are of minor interest, and (3) drilling-down to uncover interesting details. Overview and detail within this process can be obtained by panning and zooming into the representation (see Figure 3).

5   Results and Use Case

In the following, the guidelines and implications described in this paper are applied in the form of a case study on a real-world data set from the application of air quality research. Data has been provided by the Air Quality Research Center of UC Davis and obtained by single particle mass spectrometry [23]. We discuss the application of SDTs to wood stove source sampling data from Pittsburgh, Pennsylvania. The focus for this investigation lies in quantifying the relationship between isotopes ambient during biomass combustion. Biomass combustion emits copious amounts of gases and particles into the atmosphere and plays a key role in almost all present day environmental concerns including the health effects of air pollution, acid rain, visibility reduction, and stratospheric ozone depletion. The raw 256-dimensional data has undergone application-specific data transformations as well as dimension reduction to the dimensions most important for the investigation purposes of our collaborators: m/z 24 (C_2^+), 27 ($C_2H_3^+$), 36 (C_3^+), 39 ($^{39}K^+$ / $C_3H_3^+$), and 41 ($^{41}K^+$ / $C_3H_5^+$). The data are highly unstructured. Due to this characteristic, the SDT consists of a small stem and many small branches. The achieved representation of individual coordinate values, however, still allows for an accurate data investigation as shown by the following findings.

Figure 7 a), shows the initial projection for 1000 particles randomly selected from the sampling campaign. This first view clearly reveals two main clusters corresponding to m/z 39 and to a mixture of m/z 24, 27, 36, and 41, respectively. The *Dimensional Anchor arrangement* suggests a positive correlation between m/z 24 and 36 by their DAs' co-location, as well as low variance in m/z 41 by the DAs low length. Verification of both indicators based on *dimension highlighting* and *variance points* reveals that the variance in m/z 39 is only partially reflected in the projection. This can be seen in Figure 7 b), where a secondary placement of the DA is suggested at the bottom of the circle. Highlighting and *circular movement* of the DA, however, reveals that the overall variance is considerably lower than in other dimensions.

Further investigation of the large cluster on the ride side of the view reveals that two stems branching of in dimensions 27 ($C_2H_3^+$) and 39 ($^{39}K^+$ / $C_3H_3^+$) are the primary contributors to this cluster. Detailed investigation by *zooming and panning* reveals that these points indeed show mixtures of all dimensions, mainly residing in mid-value ranges and of similar intra-cluster variance. This is shown in Figure 7 c), where a parallel coordinates plot of these dimensions is included for reference. By using *dimension and branch filtering*, further insight is gained in the relationship between dimensions 24, 27 and 39. In Figure 7 d), DA 36 is moved at the center of the projection due to its correlation with these dimensions. In the figure, the selection of dimensions 24 and 39 reveals that low value contributions of $^{39}K^+$ / $C_3H_3^+$ are present in the majority of

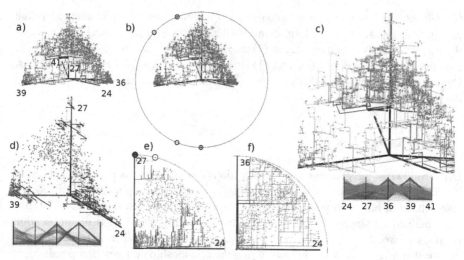

Fig. 7. SDT of 1000 mass spectra obtained from a source sampling campaign in Pittsburgh, Pennsylvania: (**a**) Initial projection of the dimensions relevant to analysis indicates correlation between 24 and 36, as well as low variance in 41. (**b**) Verification of 41's variance points conveys the information loss for this dimension due to dimension reduction. (**c**) Navigation and selection options allows to quickly identify the cluster residing in mid-value ranges of the dimensions. (**d**) Options for filtering allow to further adjust the view to current needs. (**e**) The display of the data's structure avoids misconceptions while (**f**) adjusting the projection for verification of assumptions.

the cluster located along the DA of 24 (C_2^+), while in the clusters of 27 ($C_2H_3^+$) and 39 ($^{39}K^+$ / $C_3H_3^+$), these mixtures are filtered out. Successive investigation of the relationship between 24 (C_2^+) and 27 ($C_2H_3^+$) is conducted by the *orthogonal placement of DAs*, as shown in Figure 7 e).

Next to its highly interactive capabilities, the SDT's strength lies in displaying the underlying structure of the data, thus, enhancing the projection by conveying proximities in high-dimensional space, as well as in projective space. While the point projection, as shown in Figure 7 e), does not display any relationship between the two dimensions, the SDT shows two main branches. After investigation, it is revealed that the upper and lower branch structures originate from samples showing values in 39 ($C_3H_3^+$) and 36 (C_3^+), respectively. The co-occurrence of $C_2H_3^+$ and $C_3H_3^+$, as well as C_2^+ and C_3^+ is in perfect agreement of the wood stove source sampling study [23], where correlations between C_x^+ and $C_xH_y^+$ isotopes have been verified based on manual data analysis. Figure 7 f) shows this correlation for C_2^+ and C_3^+.

6   Conclusions

SDTs are a valid means to visualize and explore high-dimensional data. However, several questions important for a broad adoption still remain to be answered. Our paper addresses several of these questions. We were particularly interested in practical implications and insight that can be gained from an interpretation of the initial projection of the data. We showed that the length and relation of DAs allow one to draw meaningful conclusions about the information content of a single and correlations between multiple dimensions of the data. We also provided a functional view and novel guidelines for effective interaction with SDTs. To illustrate their meaningful appliance, we performed a case study on highly complex real-world data. The results demonstrate that SDTs can be successfully used in a variety of real-world application domains to cope with the challenging problem of high-dimensional data analysis, visualization, and interactive exploration.

Acknowledgements. The authors gratefully acknowledge the support of the German Research Foundation (Deutsche Forschungsgemeinschaft, DFG) for funding this research (grants #RO3755/1-1, #RO3755/2-1, and #1131).

References

1. Engel, D., Rosenbaum, R., Hamann, B., Hagen, H.: Structural decomposition trees. Computer Graphics Forum 30, 921–930 (2011)
2. Rosenbaum, R., Engel, D., Mouradian, J., Hagen, H., Hamann, B.: Interpretation, interaction, and scalability for structural decomposition trees. In: Proceedings of International Conference on Information Visualization Theory and Applications, Rome, Italy (2012)
3. Johansson, J., Ljung, P., Jern, M., Cooper, M.: Revealing structure within clustered parallel coordinates displays. In: Proceedings of the Proceedings of the 2005 IEEE Symposium on Information Visualization, pp. 125–132. IEEE Computer Society, Washington, DC (2005)
4. Zhou, H., Yuan, X., Qu, H., Cui, W., Chen, B.: Visual Clustering in Parallel Coordinates. Computer Graphics Forum 27, 1047–1054 (2008)
5. Artero, A.O., de Oliveira, M.C.F., Levkowitz, H.: Uncovering clusters in crowded parallel coordinates visualizations. In: Proceedings of the IEEE Symposium on Information Visualization, pp. 81–88. IEEE Computer Society, Washington, DC (2004)
6. Elmqvist, N., Dragicevic, P., Fekete, J.D.: Rolling the dice: Multidimensional visual exploration using scatterplot matrix navigation. IEEE Transactions on Visualization and Computer Graphics 14, 1141–1148 (2008)
7. Hauser, H., Ledermann, F., Doleisch, H.: Angular brushing of extended parallel coordinates. In: INFOVIS 2002: Proceedings of the IEEE Symposium on Information Visualization (InfoVis 2002), pp. 127–130. IEEE Computer Society, Washington, DC (2002)
8. McDonnell, K.T., Mueller, K.: Illustrative parallel coordinates. Computer Graphics Forum 27, 1031–1038 (2008)
9. Ankerst, M., Berchtold, S., Keim, D.A.: Similarity clustering of dimensions for an enhanced visualization of multidimensional data. In: INFOVIS 1998: Proceedings of the 1998 IEEE Symposium on Information Visualization, pp. 52–60. IEEE Computer Society, Washington, DC (1998)
10. Yang, J., Peng, W., Ward, M.O., Rundensteiner, E.A.: Interactive hierarchical dimension ordering, spacing and filtering for exploration of high dimensional datasets. In: Proceedings of the Ninth Annual IEEE Conference on Information Visualization, pp. 105–112. IEEE Computer Society, Washington, DC (2003)
11. Peng, W., Ward, M.O., Rundensteiner, E.A.: Clutter reduction in Multi-Dimensional data visualization using dimension reordering. In: Proceedings of the IEEE Symposium on Information Visualization, pp. 89–96. IEEE Computer Society, Washington, DC (2004)

12. Hoffman, P., Grinstein, G., Pinkney, D.: Dimensional anchors: a graphic primitive for multidimensional multivariate information visualizations. In: NPIVM 1999: Proceedings of the 1999 Workshop on New Paradigms in Information Visualization and Manipulation, pp. 9–16. ACM, New York (1999)

13. Kandogan, E.: Visualizing multi-dimensional clusters, trends, and outliers using star coordinates. In: Proceedings of the ACM International Conference on Knowledge Discovery and Data Mining, pp. 107–116. ACM, New York (2001)

14. Oesterling, P., Heine, C., Jänicke, H., Scheuermann, G.: Visual analysis of high dimensional point clouds using topological landscapes. In: 2010 IEEE Pacific Visualization Symposium (PacificVis), pp. 113–120 (2010)

15. Jänicke, H., Böttinger, M., Scheuermann, G.: Brushing of attribute clouds for the visualization of multivariate data. IEEE Transactions on Visualization and Computer Graphics 14, 1459–1466 (2008)

16. Ingram, S., Munzner, T., Olano, M.: Glimmer: Multilevel mds on the gpu. IEEE Transactions on Visualization and Computer Graphics 15, 249–261 (2009)

17. Paulovich, F.V., Oliveira, M.C.F., Minghim, R.: The projection explorer: A flexible tool for projection-based multidimensional visualization. In: Proceedings of the XX Brazilian Symposium on Computer Graphics and Image Processing, pp. 27–36. IEEE Computer Society, Washington, DC (2007)

18. Yang, J., Ward, M.O., Rundensteiner, E.A., Huang, S.: Visual hierarchical dimension reduction for exploration of high dimensional datasets. In: Proceedings of the Symposium on Data visualisation, VISSYM 2003, pp. 19–28. Eurographics Association, Aire-la-Ville (2003)

19. Yang, J., Patro, A., Huang, S., Mehta, N., Ward, M.O., Rundensteiner, E.A.: Value and relation display for interactive exploration of high dimensional datasets. In: Proceedings of the IEEE Symposium on Information Visualization, pp. 73–80. IEEE Computer Society, Washington, DC (2004)

20. Johansson, S., Johansson, J.: Interactive dimensionality reduction through user-defined combinations of quality metrics. IEEE Transactions on Visualization and Computer Graphics 15, 993–1000 (2009)

21. Yuan, X., Guo, P., Xiao, H., Zhou, H., Qu, H.: Scattering points in parallel coordinates. IEEE Transactions on Visualization and Computer Graphics 15, 1001–1008 (2009)

22. Shneiderman, B.: The eyes have it: A task by data type taxonomy for information visualizations. In: Proceedings of the IEEE Symposium on Visual Languages, pp. 336–343 (1996)

23. Bein, K., Zhao, Y., Wexler, A.: Conditional sampling for source-oriented toxicological studies using a single particle mass spectrometer. Environmental Science and Technology 43, 9445–9452 (2009)

Part III
Computer Vision Theory and Applications

Photometric Linearization by Robust PCA
for Shadow and Specular Removal

Takahiro Mori[1], Ryohei Taketa[2], Shinsaku Hiura[2], and Kosuke Sato[1]

[1] Graduate School of Engineering Sciences, Osaka University
1-3 Machikaneyama, Toyonaka, Osaka 560-8531, Japan
[2] Graduate School of Information Sciences, Hiroshima City University
3-4-1 Ozukahigashi, Asaminamiku, Hiroshima 731-3194, Japan
hiura@hiroshima-cu.ac.jp

Abstract. In this paper, we present an efficient method to remove shadow and specular components from multiple images taken under various lighting conditions. We call the task photometric linearization because Lambert's law of diffuse component follows linear subspace model. The conventional method[1] based on a random sampling framework make it possible to achieve the task, however, it contains two problems. The first is that the method requires manual selection of three images from input images, and the selection seriously affects to the quality of linearization result. The other is that an enormous number of trials takes a long time to find the correct answer. We therefore propose a novel algorithm using the PCA (principal component analysis) method with outlier exclusion. We used knowledge of photometric phenomena for the outlier detection and the experiments show that the method provides fast and precise linearization results. Additionally, as an application of the proposed method, we also present a method of lossless compression of HDR images taken under various lighting conditions.

Keywords: Photometric linearization, Reflection components, Shadow removal, Lossless compression.

1 Introduction

Most photometric analysis methods assume that the input images follow the Lambert's law. It is therefore important to generate images with only diffuse reflections from the input images with other photometric components, such as specular reflections and shadows.

Several methods have already been proposed for separation of photometric components. The dichromatic reflection model[2] is often used[3–5] for the separation. If the colors of the objects are quite different from the color of the light source, the model is very effective. However, if the two colors are similar, the separation becomes unstable. This method is of course not applicable for monochromatic images.

The polarization is also useful for the separation process. Wolff and Boult[6] proposed a method to separate specular reflections by analyzing the reflected polarization, while Nayar et al.[7] used combined color and polarization clues to separate the specular reflections. These methods, however, have a common restriction in that they cannot

G. Csurka et al. (Eds.): VISIGRAPP 2012, CCIS 359, pp. 211–224, 2013.

handle shadows. The geometry of the scene is useful for the analysis of specular reflections and shadows. Ikeuchi and Sato[8] proposed a method to classify photometric components based on the range and brightness of the images. A shadowed area can be distinguished using the shape of the object, but it is not easy to measure the shape of the scene even in the occluded areas.

However, there are some methods that use the characteristics of diffuse reflection, which lies in a linear subspace. Shashua[9] showed that an image illuminated from any lighting direction can be expressed by a linear combination of three basis images taken from different lighting directions, and assuming a Lambertian surface and a parallel ray. This means that an image can be perfectly expressed in a 3D subspace. Belhumeur and Kriegman[10] showed that an image can be expressed using the illumination cone model, even if the image includes attached shadows. In the illumination cone, the images are expressed by using a linear combination of extreme rays. Georghiades et al.[11] extended the illumination cone model so that cast shadows can also be expressed using shape reconstruction. Although any photometric components can ideally be expressed using the illumination cone, large numbers of images corresponding to the extreme rays are necessary.

Based on Shashua's framework, Mukaigawa et al.[1, 12] proposed a method to convert real images into linear images with diffuse components using only the random sample consensus algorithm. The method can also classify each pixel into diffuse, specular, attached shadow and cast shadow areas. However, because their method starts from three manually selected input images, the result depends heavily on the image selection. Their algorithm also takes a very long time to find an adequate combination of diffuse pixels from an enormous set of random samples. Therefore, in this paper, we propose a novel algorithm using the PCA (principal component analysis) method with outlier exclusion. This method automatically generates basis images, and the deterministic algorithm guarantees much a shorter execution time. The outliers are distinguished by using the knowledge of photometric phenomena, and the results show that out algorithm provides better results than those using RANSAC-based outlier exclusion.

2   Classifying Reflection Using Photometric Linearization

From the viewpoint of illumination and reflection phenomena, each pixel on the input image is classified into several areas, as shown in Fig.1. According to the dichromatic reflection model[2] shown in Fig.2, reflection consists of diffuse and specular reflections. While the observed intensity caused by diffuse reflection is independent of the viewing direction, specular reflection is only observed from a narrow range close to the mirror direction of the incident light. Shadows are also classified into attached shadows and cast shadows[9]. If the angle between the surface normal and the light direction is larger than a right angle, the intensity of the surface is zero and is called attached shadow. If there is an object between the light source and the surface, the incoming light is occluded by the object. This is called cast shadow.

In the following, we discuss the reflection phenomena using a linear model of diffuse reflection.

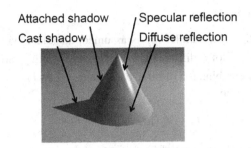

Attached shadow / Specular reflection
Cast shadow / Diffuse reflection

Fig. 1. Common photometric phenomena observed in a scene

Reflection = Diffuse + Specular

Fig. 2. Dichromatic reflection model

2.1 Classification of Reflections

The Lambertian model is a most basic reflection model of a matte surface, such as plaster. The intensity of the surface is represented as

$$i = \mathbf{n} \cdot \mathbf{s} \tag{1}$$

where $\mathbf{n}$ denotes the surface property vector, which is a product of a unit normal vector and the diffuse reflectance. Similarly, $\mathbf{s}$ represents the lighting property vector, which is a product of a unit vector towards the lighting direction and the brightness of the light.

In Eq.(1), if the angle between $\mathbf{n}$ and $\mathbf{s}$ is greater than 90°, the intensity i becomes negative, but, of course, there cannot be a negative power of light. In this case, the area on the object is observed as being attached shadow, and the intensity becomes zero instead of the negative value. To deal with the attached shadows as well as the diffuse reflections, the following equation is commonly used[10].

$$i = max\,(\mathbf{n} \cdot \mathbf{s}, 0) \tag{2}$$

In contrast, as shown in Fig. 1, the angle between $\mathbf{n}$ and $\mathbf{s}$ is smaller than 90° in the area of a cast shadow. If there is no inter-reflection, the intensities of both shadowed areas are zero, and we can distinguish between two shadow phenomena by using the sign of $\mathbf{n} \cdot \mathbf{s}$ if we know the surface normal and the lighting direction.

As shown in Fig. 2, the intensity of the specular reflection is an additional component to the diffuse reflection. Therefore, the intensity at the specular reflection is always greater than the value calculated with the Lambertian model. To summarize, we can distinguish the illumination and reflection components using the following criterion.

$$\begin{cases} \text{Diffuse reflection}: & i = \mathbf{n} \cdot \mathbf{s} \\ \text{Specular reflection}: & i > \mathbf{n} \cdot \mathbf{s} \\ \text{Attached shadow}: & i = 0 \cap \mathbf{n} \cdot \mathbf{s} \leq 0 \\ \text{Cast shadow}: & i = 0 \cap \mathbf{n} \cdot \mathbf{s} > 0 \end{cases} \tag{3}$$

2.2 Photometric Linearization

Shashua[9] showed that if a parallel ray is assumed, an image with N pixels $I_k = \left(i_{(k,1)}\ i_{(k,2)}\ \cdots\ i_{(k,N)}\right)^T$ of a diffuse object under any lighting direction can be expressed using a linear combination of three basis images, $(\hat{I}_1, \hat{I}_2,\ and\ \hat{I}_3)$ taken using different lighting directions;

$$I_k = c_k^1 \hat{I}_1 + c_k^2 \hat{I}_2 + c_k^3 \hat{I}_3 \tag{4}$$

Here, let $C_k = \left(c_k^1\ c_k^2\ c_k^3\right)^T$ be a set of coefficients of the image I_k.

However, real images do not always satisfy Eq.(4), because specular reflections and shadows are commonly observed. Therefore, in this paper, we discuss the conversion of real images into linear images which include diffuse reflection components only. This conversion process is called photometric linearization and the converted images are called linearized images. Because linearized images should satisfy Eq.(4), all M input images could be expressed by using linear combination of the three basis images[9] as

$$\left(I_1^L\ I_2^L\ \cdots\ I_M^L\right) = \left(\hat{I}_1\ \hat{I}_2\ \hat{I}_3\right)\left(C_1\ C_1\ \cdots\ C_M\right) \tag{5}$$

where $i_{(k,p)}^L = i_{(k,p)}$ at the pixel of diffuse reflection. In other words, $i_{(k,p)}^L = \mathbf{n}_p \cdot \mathbf{s}_k$ is satisfied in linearized images, and we can lead relationships such that a set of basis images $\mathbf{B} = \left(\hat{I}_1\ \hat{I}_2\ \hat{I}_3\right)$ and a set of coefficients $\mathbf{C} = \left(C_1\ C_1\ \cdots\ C_M\right)$ can be represented as $\mathbf{B} = \left(\mathbf{n}_1\ \mathbf{n}_2\ \cdots\ \mathbf{n}_N\right)^T \cdot \Sigma$ and $\mathbf{C} = \Sigma^{-1} \cdot \left(\mathbf{s}_1\ \mathbf{s}_2\ \cdots\ \mathbf{s}_M\right)$ respectively, using the common 3×3 matrix Σ.

2.3 Classification Using Linearized Images

As described above, each pixel of the input images can be classified into areas of diffuse reflection, specular reflection, attached shadow and cast shadow using the surface normal $\mathbf{n}$ and the lighting direction $\mathbf{s}$. Fortunately, we only use the product of these vectors $\mathbf{n} \cdot \mathbf{s}$, and we can also classify them by comparing the pixel values of the input and linearized images, $i_{(k,p)}$ and $i_{(k,p)}^L$ respectively. The classification does not need any additional information, such as 3D shapes, lighting directions, or color information.

In reality, captured images are affected by various types of noise. For example, imaging devices produce a dark current even if the intensity of the scene is zero. Also, the pixel intensity values are not perfectly linear in actual sensors, and so we often model these noises sources with additive and multiplicative noise models.

As shown in Figure 3, we classify each pixel with the following criteria.

$$\begin{cases} \text{Specular Reflection: } i_{(k,p)} > i_{(k,p)}^L * T_1 \cap i_{(k,p)} > i_{(k,p)}^L + T_2 \\ \text{Attached Shadow: } \quad i_{(k,p)} < T_s \cap i_{(k,p)}^L \le 0 \\ \text{Cast Shadow: } \qquad i_{(k,p)} < T_s \cap i_{(k,p)}^L > 0 \\ \text{Diffuse Reflection: } \quad otherwise \end{cases} \tag{6}$$

The thresholds T_1 and T_2 shown in Fig.3 are used to check the equality of $i_{(k,p)}$ and $i_{(k,p)}^L$ with certain multiplicative and additive noises. The threshold T_S is used to distinguish shadows. These thresholds can be determined through experiments with real

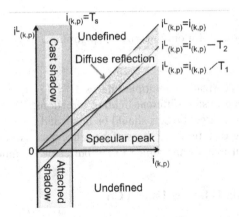

Fig. 3. Criterion for photometric classification

Fig. 4. Specular lobe arise around specular peak

images. In the linearization algorithm described below, we gradually decrease these thresholds to exclude the outliers properly.

2.4 Handling Specular Lobe

As mentioned in section2.1, the intensity observed at specular reflection points is greater than that at the points with diffuse reflection only. However, in reality, the difference is not always sufficiently large, and the thresholds T_1 and T_2 against noise will improperly include specular reflections to the inliers. More specifically, this phenomenon is commonly observed at specular lobes. As shown in Fig.4, specular lobes surround the specular peaks, so we use spatial information to exclude such areas. While the linearization method using PCA described in the next section does not use the information about the neighboring relationships between pixels, we can exclude the erroneous area by increasing the area of the specular peaks by using the dilation operation. It is therefore important not only to exclude outliers during linearization, but also to use classification of optical phenomena to expand the specular reflection area only.

3 Photometric Linearization Using PCA

In this section, we present our linearization algorithm derived from principal component analysis (PCA). More specifically, we combine an outlier exclusion process based on the classification of photometric phenomena with repetitive PCA.

3.1   Algorithm

The following is the process for our linearization algorithm.

(A) Initialize

For the photometric linearization, multiple images $\mathbf{I} = \begin{pmatrix} I_1 & I_2 & \cdots & I_M \end{pmatrix}$, $M > 3$ as shown in Fig.5 are taken using different lighting directions. While taking these images, the camera and the target objects should be fixed, and the information about the 3D shape, the lighting direction and the surface reflectance is not necessary. As an initialization, the input images are copied to the buffer of the inlier images, $\mathbf{I}^{IN} = \begin{pmatrix} I_1^{IN} & I_2^{IN} & \cdots & I_M^{IN} \end{pmatrix}$.

(B) Calculate Three Basis Images Using PCA

In the conventional method[1], three manually selected images are converted into linearized images using the RANSAC algorithm[13]. However, as discussed earlier, this method has a problem in that the quality of the result depends heavily on the image selection. In contrast, we use all images to calculate the linearized image using PCA. More specifically, we calculate the 1st, 2nd, and 3rd principal components $\mathbf{B} = \begin{pmatrix} \hat{I}_1 & \hat{I}_2 & \hat{I}_3 \end{pmatrix}$ of the matrix $\mathbf{I}^{IN}$ by analyzing the eigenvectors of the covariance matrix $\mathbf{I}^{IN}\mathbf{I}^{IN^T}$ without subtracting the mean of the input images. Because the principal components are orthogonal to each other, we can obtain linearly independent basis images as shown in Fig.6, where negative values are shown in red.

(C) Generate Linearized Images

The coefficients of the linear combination $\mathbf{C}$ are determined by minimizing the root mean square errors between the input and linearized images as

$$\mathbf{C} = \mathbf{B}^T \mathbf{I}^{IN} \tag{7}$$

because $\mathbf{B}$ is the orthonormal basis and $\mathbf{B}^T\mathbf{B} = I$. The linearized images are then calculated by using the basis images and coefficients,

$$\mathbf{I}^L = \mathbf{B} \cdot \mathbf{C} \tag{8}$$

(D) Classification of Photometric Components

As described in section 2.3, each pixel of each input image is classified into four photometric components, diffuse, specular peak, attached shadow and cast shadow, by comparing the pixel values of the input image $i_{(k,p)}$ and the linearized image $i^L_{(k,p)}$ based on the photometric classification criterion Eq.(6), as shown in Fig.3.

(E) Extension to Specular Lobe Area

As shown in Fig.4, specular lobes arise around specular peaks. Therefore, pixels around the specular peak area are classified as outliers by the specular lobe. Fig.7 shows an example of classification for a scene with a sphere.

Fig. 5. Input images

Fig. 6. Three basis images (red color represents negative value)

Red: Specular peak
Yellow: Specular lobe
Green: Attached shadow
Blue: Cast shadow

Fig. 7. Classification of photometric components

(F) Pixel Value Replacement

Pixels affected by nonlinear illumination and reflection phenomena should be excluded as outliers for the next iteration of the PCA calculation,

$$\begin{cases} i^{IN}_{(k,p)} = i_{(k,p)} \text{ pixel of diffuse reflection} \\ i^{IN}_{(k,p)} = i^{L}_{(k,p)} \text{ pixel of specular reflection, specular lobe,} \\ \qquad\qquad\qquad \text{attached and cast shadows} \end{cases} \tag{9}$$

(G) Tighten Thresholds and Iterate

The algorithm starts from very loose thresholds to exclude the explicit outliers only. If such evident outliers are removed, the result of the next calculation becomes closer to the correct answer. Therefore, at this stage, thresholds T_1 and T_2 are slightly tightened towards the values determined for the sensor's noise level, as shown in Fig.8. Then, the process sequence from (B) to (G) is repeated until the thresholds reach the predetermined minimum values.

3.2 Example

Here, we show an example of each step of the linearization process for the input image shown in Fig.5. In Fig.9, ① shows one of the input images. Because the initial image

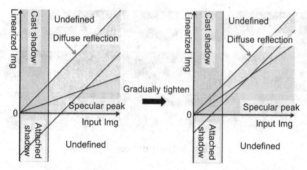

Fig. 8. Tightening thresholds during iteration

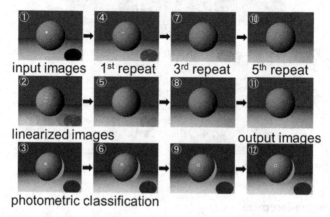

Fig. 9. Example of the process of linearization by replacing outliers

contains nonlinear components, the linearized images calculated by step (C) contain artifacts, as shown in ②. By using the classification result shown in ③, the pixel values at the outlier pixels of image ① are replaced by a linearized image ② in step (F), and the next input image ④ is generated. Here, the pixel intensities in the specular and cast shadow areas are relaxed, so the next linearized result ⑤ is better than the result calculated using the raw input images. The processes are repeated with tighter thresholds, and finally we obtain a clear linearized image ⑪ and correct classification results ⑫.

4 Experiments

In this section, we show several experimental results. Computationally generated images are used for the quantitative evaluation because we can also render the images without specular reflection and shadows as the ground truth. Results using real images show the robustness and feasibility of our method for the actual task.

4.1 Evaluation Using Synthetic Images

First, we evaluated our proposed method by comparing the conventional method[1] with our method using synthetic images. The input images were generated by POV-Ray

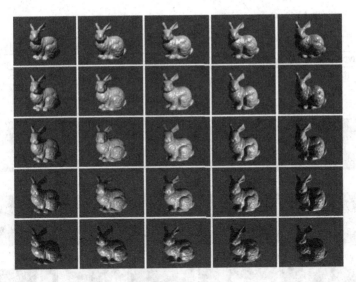

Fig. 10. Input images

ray-tracing rendering software. The object shape is that of the Stanford Bunny, as shown in Fig.10. Twenty-five images were generated, using a different lighting direction for each image. In most images, cast shadows are observed on the object itself.

Fig.11(a) shows three manually selected images to be converted as basis images using the conventional method. As described above, the conventional method requires manual selection, which heavily affects the result. The selection shown in the figure is one of the adequate selections. Fig.11(b) shows the ground truths without specular reflection and shadows, corresponding to the three selected images. While we obtain linearized images for all input images in the final result, we will show these three images in the paper for comparison purposes.

The result of linearization by the conventional method are shown in Fig.11(c), with a corresponding error map (Fig.11(d)). Because the algorithm based on random sampling, the result shows heavy noise and failed estimation caused by the probabilistic fluctuation and unstableness.

Unlike the conventional method, our algorithm does not require manual selection. Fig.11(e) shows the results of the linearization of the three input images corresponding to the manually selected images for the conventional method. The colored error map shown in Fig.11(f) shows fewer errors when compared to that of the conventional method. Fig.11(g) shows the three basis images $\mathbf{B} = \begin{pmatrix} \hat{I}_1 & \hat{I}_2 & \hat{I}_3 \end{pmatrix}$ where the red color indicates negative values. The classification results from our method shown in Fig.11(h) also show that our method correctly works.

A quantitative evaluation is shown in Table 1. Not only much lesser error but also more than 300 times faster calculation are achieved by our method, compared to the previous method. This is because the conventional method uses the RANSAC[13] algorithm to remove the non-Lambertian components and runs an enormous number of iterative calculations. If the number of iterations is limited, the result is degraded.

Table 1. Quantitative evaluation of the linearization result

	Mean error	Variance of error	Maximum error	Calculation time[s]
Conventional	9.634	410.740	255	5.132×10^3
Proposed	3.716	28.107	151	1.488×10^1

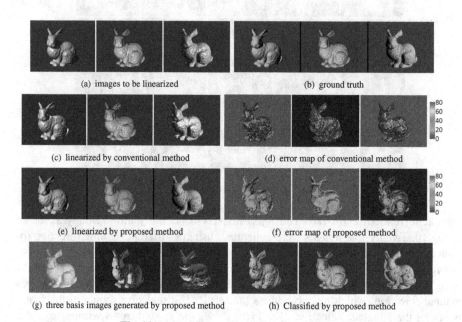

(a) images to be linearized   (b) ground truth

(c) linearized by conventional method   (d) error map of conventional method

(e) linearized by proposed method   (f) error map of proposed method

(g) three basis images generated by proposed method   (h) Classified by proposed method

Fig. 11. Linearization of complex shaped object

Fig. 12. Input images

4.2 Evaluation Using Real Images

In this section we use real images taken with a camera. The scene contains a pot, as shown in Fig.12. Twenty-four images were captured, using a different lighting direction for each one.

Fig.13(a) shows the three input images selected for linearization by the conventional method. Fig.13(b) shows the linearization result generated by the conventional method,

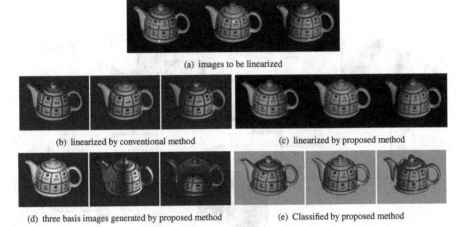

(a) images to be linearized

(b) linearized by conventional method   (c) linearized by proposed method

(d) three basis images generated by proposed method   (e) Classified by proposed method

Fig. 13. Linearization of real images

Table 2. Comparison of the calculation time

	Calculation time[s]
Conventional	8.028×10^3
Proposed	1.675×10^1

while Fig.13(c) shows the linearization result generated by the proposed method. Both results are similar, however, we can see some noisy fluctuations on the results from the conventional method. In contrast, the proposed method provides smooth images without specular reflections. Figure 13(e) shows that our algorithm properly classifies the phenomena observed on the object. The proposed method also has an advantage of being much faster than the conventional method as shown in Table2.

5   Lossless Compression of HDR Images under Various Lighting Conditions

As an application of proposed photometric linearization method, we present a method of lossless compression for HDR images taken under various lighting conditions. For digital archiving of fine arts or ancient relics, high quality images of the object should be recorded without any loss of information. In this case, HDR images are commonly used, however, there are very few achievements of lossless compression of HDR images. Therefore, we incorporate our method into efficient image compression method.

In general, most part of object appearance is covered by diffuse reflection, and specular reflection is observed in limited area. Therefore, as shown in Fig. 14, non-diffuse components of images contain many zero or very small values. Since the performance of lossless compression directly reflects the entropy of the pixel values, the compression rate is much improved by using the residuals of linear approximation.

In this experiments, we captured 32 HDR images under different lighting conditions using Apogee Alta 16000 cooled CCD camera. In Fig.15, 15 of 32 input images

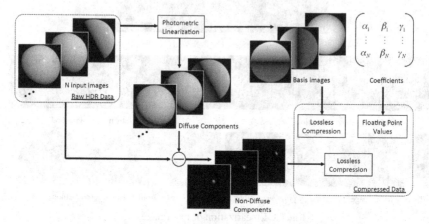

Fig. 14. Lossless compression of HDR images using photometric linearization

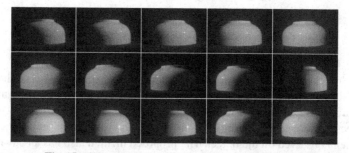

Fig. 15. HDR Images for the experiment of compression

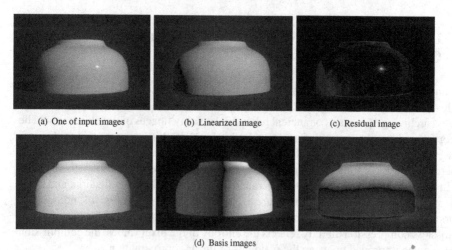

(a) One of input images   (b) Linearized image   (c) Residual image

(d) Basis images

Fig. 16. Result of photometric linearization for HDR pictures

Table 3. Comparison of compression rate

Method	Overall file size [kbyte]	Compression rate[%]
Huffman coding	48,448	78
Proposed	41,783	68

are shown. Result of photometric linearization for HDR images are shown in Fig.16. Although our method has an overhead to record basis images, the compression ratio is improved as shown in Table 3.

6   Conclusions

We focused on the approach of the conventional photometric linearization method[1], which selects three basis images from real images, including not only diffuse reflections but also specular reflections and shadows. The conversion accuracy thus becomes unstable and is seriously influenced by the selection of the three basis images, and it also takes a long time to remove the non-Lambertian components, e.g. the specular reflections and shadows.

We therefore proposed a novel pixel value replacement algorithm using photometric classification, which enables us to uniquely generate three ideal basis images, including only diffuse reflections from real images, and enables us to generate accurate ideal images stably and quickly. We then confirmed the effectiveness of the proposed method experimentally.

Acknowledgements.   The authors are grateful to Prof. Mukaigawa and Mr. Ishii for providing their source codes and real images presented in their paper (Mukaigawa et al,, 2007) for our comparisons shown in Section 4. This work was partially supported by Grant-in-Aid for Scientific Research (B:21300067) and Grant-in-Aid for Scientific Research on Innovative Areas (22135003).

References

1. Mukaigawa, Y., Ishii, Y., Shakunaga, T.: Analysis of photometric factors based on photometric linearization. JOSA A 24, 3326–3334 (2007)
2. Shafer, S.: Using color to separate reflection components from a color image. Color Research and Applications 10, 210–218 (1985)
3. Klinker, G., Shafer, S., Kanade, T.: The measurement of highlights in color images. International Journal of Computer Vision 2, 7–32 (1988)
4. Sato, Y., Ikeuchi, K.: Temporal-color space analysis of reflection. JOSA A 11, 2990–3002 (1994)
5. Sato, Y., Wheeler, M., Ikeuchi, K.: Object shape and reflectance modeling from observation. In: Proceedings of the 24th Annual Conference on Computer Graphics and Interactive Techniques, pp. 379–387. ACM Press/Addison-Wesley Publishing Co. (1997)
6. Wolff, L., Boult, T.: Constraining object features using a polarisation reflectance model. IEEE Trans. Patt. Anal. Mach. Intell. 13, 635–657 (1991)

7. Nayar, S., Fang, X., Boult, T.: Removal of specularities using color and polarization. In: Proceedings of the IEEE Computer Society Conference on Computer Vision and Pattern Recognition, CVPR 1993, pp. 583–590. IEEE (1993)

8. Ikeuchi, K., Sato, K.: Determining reflectance properties of an object using range and brightness images. IEEE Transactions on Pattern Analysis and Machine Intelligence, 1139–1153 (1991)

9. Shashua, A.: Geometry and photometry in 3D visual recognition. PhD thesis, Citeseer (1992)

10. Belhumeur, P., Kriegman, D.: What is the set of images of an object under all possible lighting conditions? In: CVPR, p. 270. IEEE Computer Society (1996)

11. Georghiades, A., Belhumeur, P., Kriegman, D.: From few to many: Illumination cone models for face recognition under variable lighting and pose. IEEE Transactions on Pattern Analysis and Machine Intelligence 23, 643–660 (2001)

12. Mukaigawa, Y., Miyaki, H., Mihashi, S., Shakunaga, T.: Photometric image-based rendering for image generation in arbitrary illumination. In: Proceedings of the Eighth IEEE International Conference on Computer Vision, ICCV 2001, vol. 2, pp. 652–659. IEEE (2001)

13. Fischler, M., Bolles, R.: Random sample consensus: a paradigm for model fitting with applications to image analysis and automated cartography. Communications of the ACM 24, 381–395 (1981)

A Robust People Tracking Algorithm Using Contextual Reasoning for Recovering Detection Errors

Rosario Di Lascio[1,*], Pasquale Foggia[2], Alessia Saggese[2], and Mario Vento[2]

[1] A.I.Tech s.r.l., A Spin-off Company of the University of Salerno, Italy
[2] Dipartimento di Ingegneria Elettronica e Ingegneria Informatica, University of Salerno, Italy
dilascio@aitech-solutions.eu,
{pfoggia,asaggese,mvento}@unisa.it
www.aitech-solutions.eu

Abstract. In this paper we propose an efficient and robust real-time tracking algorithm, able to deal with the common errors occurring in the object detection systems, like total or partial occlusions. Most of the common tracking algorithms make their tracking decisions by comparing the evidence at the current frame with the objects known at the previous one; the main novelty of our method lies in the fact that it takes into account also the history of each object. To exploit this idea, the algorithm adopts an object model based on a set of scenarios, implemented by a Finite State Automaton (FSA), in order to differently deal with objects depending on their recent history. An experimental evaluation of the algorithm has been performed using the PETS2010 database, comparing the obtained performance with the results of the PETS2010 contest participants.

1 Introduction

Object tracking algorithms are devoted to the task of reconstructing the object trajectories given the evidence collected from a video sequence. Although this task is apparently simple, several problems may hamper its performance: problems with the detection of the objects in each frame (objects missing or partially detected, spurious objects, objects split in parts), occlusions (a person is totally or partially covered by an element of the scene, or by another person), noise due to light changes or camera motion. Thus, many algorithms have been proposed in the literature for facing these problems, but none of them is both sufficiently reliable to operate in the complexity of a real world scenario, and sufficiently fast to work in real time.

The algorithms present in the literature can be roughly divided into two categories. In the first one, tracking is performed after an object detection phase: objects are detected in each frame using either some form of change detection (e.g. differences from a background model) or an a priori model of the objects. Algorithms in this category are usually faster, but they have to consider also the errors of the detection phase, such as spurious and missing objects, objects split into pieces, multiple objects merged into a single detected *blob*). As an example, [1] and [2] use a greedy algorithm that matches

---

* This research has been partially supported by A.I.Tech s.r.l., a spin-off company of the University of Salerno (www.aitech-solutions.eu).

G. Csurka et al. (Eds.): VISIGRAPP 2012, CCIS 359, pp. 225–241, 2013.
© Springer-Verlag Berlin Heidelberg 2013

each object to its nearest neighbor, with constraints based on proximity. The first method assumes that the number of objects is constant, so it does not deal with object entries, exits and occlusions; the latter method adds the ability to deal with entering or exiting objects and to recognize that an occlusion has occurred (without restoring the object identities after the occlusion).

The W^4 system [3] uses the overlap of the areas as a criterion to find a correspondence between the objects at the current and at the previous frame. When this criterion selects multiple objects, the algorithm considers split or merge hypotheses to deal with detection errors or with occlusions. After an occlusion, an appearance model of the objects is used to reassign the original object identities. Also, when an object is seen for the first time, the algorithm waits for a fixed number of frames before assigning it an object identifier, in order to filter out spurious objects due to detection errors. The use of overlap works well with high frame rates and objects that are not very fast, but might fail in other conditions.

The method by Pellegrini et al. [4] tries to predict the trajectories on the scene using a set of behavior models learned using a training video sequence. The method is very effective for repetitive behaviors, but may have some problems for behaviors that do not occur frequently. The method by Ess et al. [5] uses stereo vision, coupled with a motion dynamic model and an object appearance model to perform the tracking. The method is not applicable where a stereo camera is not available; furthermore its computational cost is significant, requiring 0.3 seconds per frame only for the tracking part. Dai et al. [6] have proposed a method able to track pedestrians by using shape and appearance information extracted from infra-red imagery. The method may have some problems when objects quickly change their appearance or during occlusions.

Several recent methods [7], [8], [9], [10], use the information from different cameras with overlapping fields of view in order to perform the occlusion resolution. The data provided by each camera are usually combined using a probabilistic framework to solve the ambiguities. This kind of technique is limited to the cases where multiple cameras are available; furthermore, most of the methods adopting this approach require a full calibration of each camera, which could make the deployment of the system more complicated.

In the second category, detection and tracking are performed at once, usually on the basis of an object model that is dynamically updated during the tracking. These methods are computationally more expensive, and often have problems with the initial definition of the object models, that in some cases has to be provided by hand. In [11], Comaniciu et al. propose the use of Mean Shift, a fast, iterative algorithm for finding the centroid of a probability distribution, for determining the most probable position of the tracking target. It requires a manual selection of the objects being tracked in the initial frame, and deals only with partial occlusions. Tao et al. [12] have proposed a method based on a layered representation of the scene, that is created and updated using a probabilistic framework. Their method is able to deal with occlusions, but is extremely computational expensive. The method by [13] tracks people in a crowded environment. However it uses an a priori model of a person, that is not extendable to other kind of objects. Several recent methods ([14], [15], [16], [17], [18]) have investigated the use of Particle Filters, that are a tool based on the approximate representation of a probability distribution using a finite set of samples, for solving the tracking problem in a Bayesian formulation. Particle Filters look very promising, since they make tractable a very general and flexible framework. However, the computational cost is still too high for real-time applications, especially with multiple occluding targets.

In this paper we propose a real-time tracking algorithm belonging to the first category; it assumes that an object detection based on background subtraction generates its input data. Most of the algorithms in the same category make their tracking decisions by comparing the evidence at the current frame with the objects known at the previous one. Our algorithm, instead, uses objects' past history to obtain useful hints on how they should be tracked: for instance, for objects stable in the scene, information such as their appearance should be considered more reliable. To exploit this idea, our algorithm adopts an object model based on a set of scenarios, in order to differently deal with objects depending on their recent history; the scenarios are implemented by Finite State Automata, each describing the different states of an object and the conditions triggering the transition to a different state. The state is used both to influence which processing steps are performed on each object, and to choose the most appropriate value for some of the parameters involved in the processing. As a result, the algorithm is robust with respect to the errors generated by the object detection (spurious or missing objects, split objects) and is able to work with partial and total occlusions.

2 Rationale and Overview of the Algorithm

Before starting the description of the algorithm, we need to introduce some terminology and notations.

A *blob* is a connected set of foreground pixels produced by a detection algorithm, which usually finds the foreground pixels by comparing the frame with a background model; then the foreground pixels are filtered to remove noise and other artifacts (e.g. shadows); finally, the foreground pixels are partitioned into connected components, which are the blobs. The tracking algorithm receives in input the set of blobs detected at each frame. We assume that the detection phase uses a dynamic background model dealing with lighting changes; noise reduction, shadow and small blob removal are further carried out. See details in [19].

An *object* is any real-world entity the system is interested in tracking. Each object has an *object model*, containing such information as the object class (e.g. a person or a vehicle), state (see subsection 4.1), size, position, trajectory and appearance (see subsection 4.4). A *group object* corresponds to multiple real-world entities tracked together; if a group is formed during the tracking (i.e. it does not enter the scene as a group), its object model mantains a reference to the models of the individual objects of the group.

The task of the tracking algorithm is to associate each blob to the right object, in such a way as to preserve the identity of real-world objects across the video sequence; in the process the algorithm must also create new object models or update the existing ones as necessary.

In real cases, the detection phase produces some common errors: spurious or missing blobs, objects split into several parts, etc. In addition the algorithm must also handle partial or total occlusions, ensuring that object identities are not lost across the occlusion.

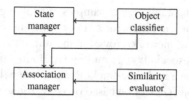

Fig. 1. An overview of the tracking system

A key idea behind the proposed algorithm is to base the decisions regarding an object not only on its current conditions, but also on its past history; in this way spurious observations can be easily ignored, and the decisions can be based on stable properties of the object. To this aim, the object history is encoded using a *state*, belonging to a finite set of possible values. The transitions between states are explicitly described through a Finite State Automaton, and are triggered by such events as the permanence of the object in the scene, its disappearance, the outcome of the object classification and the participation to an occlusion.

Figure 1 shows the modules composing the tracking system (detailed in the following sections) and their interdependencies:

- the *state manager*, which mantains and updates an instance of the FSA for each object;
- the *association manager*, which establishes a correspondence between objects and blobs, solving split-merge events and performing occlusion reasoning;
- the *object classifier*, which assigns objects to a set of predefined classes; the object class is used both during the update of the FSA state and during the association between objects and blobs to solve split/merge cases;
- the *similarity evaluator*, which computes a similarity measure between objects and blobs, considering position, size and appearance; this similarity is used during the association between objects and blobs.

3   Common Problems Encountered by Tracking Algorithms

In this section we examine some typical problems of people detection, in order to see how they can be solved at the tracking level by incorporating information about the history of the objects.

One of the most frequently encountered issues is related to the objects entering the scene, which have a very unpredictable appearance during the first frames of their life. Figure 2 shows a typical example, in which the person is split by the detection phase into two different blobs (i.e. legs and arms). The problem here is that after a few frames the parts appear to merge forming a new group of objects; since the occlusion resolution requires that object identities are preserved within a group, the tracking algorithm would continue to keep track of two separate objects (labeled 1 and 2 in the figure). To solve this problem, the tracking algorithm has to use different rules for dealing with merging objects when they are just entering or when they are stably within the scene.

Another typical issue, either caused by an error in the detection phase or by a total occlusion of an object, is the occurrence of missing blobs. Figure 3 shows an example:

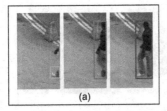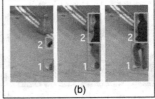

(a)   (b)

Fig. 2. Problems with entering objects. (a) The detection output across three adjacent frames. (b) The tracking performed without considering the object history.

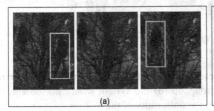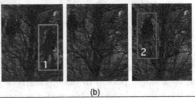

(a)   (b)

Fig. 3. Problems with totally occluded objects. (a) The detection output across three adjacent frames. (b) The tracking performed without considering the object history.

the person passing behind the tree is not detected in the second frame of the sequence. Thus the algorithm, at the third frame frame, would assign a newly created id to the blob, if it does not keep some memory about objects that have disappeared. On the other hand, the algorithm should not preserve information about objects that are truly leaving the scene, to avoid the risk of reassigning the same id to a different object entering from the same side.

Other issues are related to objects occluding each other, forming a group. In Figure 4.a it is shown a problem with the stability of group classification: in the first frame, the two persons in the group are perfectly aligned, and so a classifier would not be able to recognize that the object is a group. On the other hand, in the following frames the object is easier to recognize as such. Thus, in order to obtain a reliable classification the tracking algorithm has to wait that the classifier output becomes stable, before using it to take decisions.

Another problem related to groups is the loss of the identities of the costituent objects. An example is shown in Figure 4.b, where objects 1 and 2 first join a group and then are separated again. When the objects become separated, the tracking algorithm would incorrectly assign them new identities, if the original ones where not preserved and associated with the group. Notice that in this case it would not have been possible to simply keep tracking separately the two objects using some kind of motion prediction until the end of the occlusion, because as a group the objects have performed a drastic change of trajectory (a 180° turn).

The analysis conducted in this Section about the typical problems in a real-world setting shows that in a lot of situations a tracking system cannot be able to correctly follow the objects without knowing additional information about their history. In the next section, we will see how the proposed FSA is able to provide this information.

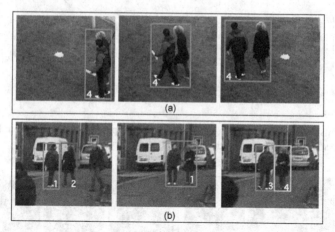

Fig. 4. Occlusion related problems. In (a) the appearance of a group of people change from being identical to a single person to being clearly a group. In (b) the system would not be able to correctly track the individual objects if it only uses the uniformity of the motion.

4 System Architecture

In this section we will describe in more details the four subsystems composing the proposed tracking algorithm.

4.1 Object State Management

The state manager has the task of maintaining and updating the FSA state of each object; the FSA state embodies the relevant information about the past history of the object, which can be used by the other parts of the tracking system. What pieces of information are actually relevant is a decision depending somewhat on the specific application. Although we present only a single formulation of the FSA, it should be considered that the methodology is more general, and easily extendable to other cases, since the knowledge about the states and the transitions between them is declaratively specified in the automaton definition, and not hidden within procedural code.

In order to deal with the issues discussed in Section 3, we propose a state manager based on the Finite State Automaton depicted in Figure 5, formally defined as: $\mathcal{A} = \langle S, \Sigma, \delta, s_0, F \rangle$, where $S = \{s_0, \ldots, s_m\}$ is the set of the states; $\Sigma = \{a_0, \ldots, a_m\}$ is the set of the transition conditions, i.e. the conditions that may determine a state change; $\delta : S \times \Sigma \to S$ is the state-transition function; $s_0 \in S$ is the initial state and $F \subset S$ is is the set of final states.

The proposed Finite State Automaton states and transitions are shown in Table 1. In particular, the set of states S is shown in Table 1.a; we choose s_0 as initial state, since each object enters the scene by appearing either at the edge or at a known entry region (e.g. a doorway). Furthermore we choose s_5 as final state, since each object necessarily has to leave the scene. The set Σ of transition conditions is shown in Table 1.b.

It is worth noting that each state has been introduced in order to correctly solve one of the issues described earlier, as we will detail below. So it is possible to extend the

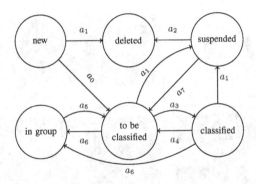

Fig. 5. The state diagram of the object state manager

Table 1. The Finite State Automaton. (a) The set S of the states. (b) The set Σ of the transition conditions.

(a)		(b)	
Id	**Description**	**Id**	**Description**
s_0	new object	a_0	obj enters completely within the scene
s_1	to be classified object	a_1	obj disappears from the scene
s_2	classified object	a_2	obj does not reappear in the scene for a time T_d
s_3	suspended object	a_3	obj classification changes
s_4	in group object	a_4	obj classification remains the same for two frames
s_5	deleted object	a_5	obj leaves the group
		a_6	obj occludes with one or more objects
		a_7	obj reappears inside the scene

FSA with the addition of other states and transitions, in order to deal with some other problem that should rise in a specific application context.

The meaning of the states and the conditions triggering the transitions are detailed below:

– *new* (s_0): the object has been just created and is located at the borders of the frame; if it enters completely, and so does not touch the frame borders (a_0), it becomes *to be classified*; otherwise, if it leaves the scene (a_1), it immediately becomes *deleted*; The introduction of the *new* state solves the problem related to the instability of entering objects, since it makes the system aware of such scenario and then capable to react in the best possible way, as shown in Figure 6.a. Moreover, this state allows the algorithm to quickly discard spurious objects due to detection artifacts, since they usually do not persist long enough to become *to be classified*.
– *to be classified* (s_1): the object is completely within the scene, but its class is not yet considered reliable; if the classifier assigns the same class for at least two frames (a_3), it becomes *classified*; if the association manager detects that the object has joined a group (a_6), it becomes *in group*; if the object disappears (a_1), it becomes *suspended*;
– *classified* (s_2): the object is stable and reliably classified; if the classifier assigns a different class (a_4), it becomes *to be classified*; if the association manager detects

Fig. 6. Output of the tracking algorithm based on the proposed FSA, when applied to the problems discussed in Section 3. (a) The entering object is correctly recognized as a single object, and not a group. (b) The object identity is preserved when the person passes behind the tree. (c) A group initially classified as a single person is correctly handled when classification becomes stable. (d) The group object maintains the constituent object identities.

that the object has joined a group (a_6), it becomes *in group*; if the object disappears (a_1), it becomes *suspended*;

- *in group* (s_4): the object is part of a group, and is no more tracked individually; its object model is preserved to be used when the object will leave the group; if the association manager detects that the object has left the group (a_5), it becomes *to be classified*;
- *suspended* (s_3): the object is not visible, either because it is completely occluded by a background element, or because it has left the scene; if the object gets visible again (a_7), it becomes *to be classified*; if the object remains suspended for more than a time threshold T_d (a_2), it becomes *deleted*; currently we use $T_d = 1$ sec; this state avoids that an object is forgotten too soon when it momentarily disappears;
- *deleted* (s_5): the object is not being tracked anymore; its object model can be discarded.

Figure 7 shows in a very simple example how the object state management works.

4.2   Object Classification

The tracking system needs an object classifier to determine if a blob corresponds to a group, an individual object, or an object part. Currently we have applied our system to people tracking, so we have only two classes of individual objects: person and baggage.

For these classes, the width and the height are a sufficiently discriminant feature vector; if the algorithm should be applied to a problem with more classes, other features could be added, for example based on the shape of the blob. In order to obtain the actual width and height of the object, removing the scaling introduced by the perspective, we perform an Inverse Perspective Mapping (IPM) based on camera calibration data, that reconstructs the 3D position of the object from its 2D position in the image plane [20].

The classifier we have implemented is a simple Nearest Neighbor classifier, that has a reference set of a few objects for each class (including groups of people). The

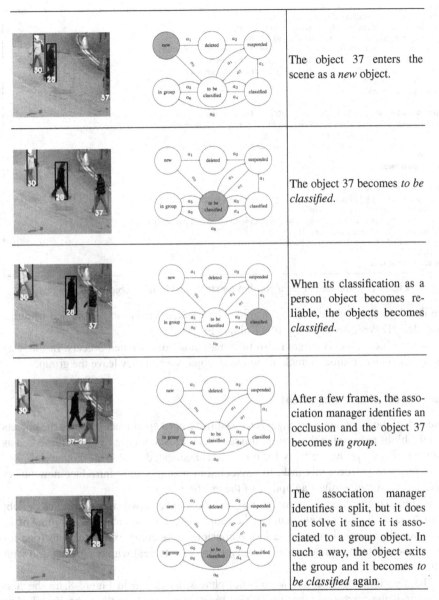

Fig. 7. Each object is associated to a Finite State Automaton that aims to manage the history of an object. We focus attention on the object identified by number 37 since it is entering the scene.

Euclidean distance is used to compare the feature vector of a reference object with the blob to be classified.

For individual objects, the object model keeps information about appearance and shape: we consider the area and the perimeter of an object, its color histograms and its actual width and height. Moreover the model keeps information about the observed and

```
procedure TrackingAlgorithm (obj_models, blobs)
  AssociationStableObjs (obj_models, blobs)
  pending_blobs := SearchPendingBlobs(blobs)
  AssociationInstableObjs (obj_models, pending_blobs)
  unassociated_blobs := SearchPendingBlobs(pending_blobs)
  CreateObjFromPendingBoxes(obj_models,unassociated_blobs)
  UpdateObjectsState(obj_models)
end procedure

procedure AssociationInstableObjs (obj_models, blobs)
  sim_mat := ObjInstableSimilarityMatrix(obj_models, blobs)
  for all obj in obj_models:
    (best_boxes, best_objs) := BestAssociation(sim_mat)
  end
end procedure

procedure AssociationStableObjs (obj_models, blobs)
  sim_mat := ObjStableSimilarityMatrix(obj_models, blobs)
  for all obj in obj_models:
    (best_boxes, best_objs) := BestAssociation(sim_mat)
    SolveMerge(best_boxes, best_objs)
    SolveSplit(best_boxes, best_objs)
  end
end procedure
```

Fig. 8. The structure of the algorithm for stable and instable objects associations

predicted position of the object centroid. The predicted position is obtained using an extended 2D Position-Velocity (PV) Kalman Filter.

Group object models contain also information about occluded objects. In this way the system can continue to track the *in group* objects when they leave the group.

4.3 Association Management

The task of the association manager is to establish a correspondence between the objects and the blobs detected at the current frame. This correspondence can be represented as a matrix $T = \{t_{ij}\}$, where t_{ij} is 1 if object o_i is associated to blob b_j, 0 otherwise.

In order to perform this task, the association manager may introduce new object models, and it may request an update of the existing ones.

In simple cases, there is a one-to-one correspondence between an object and a blob; in such cases, at most one element has the value 1 in each row and in each column of T. However, the association manager has to consider more complex associations (one-to-many, many-to-one, and even many-to-many) in order to deal with occlusions and with split blobs.

The algorithm operates in two distinct phases, as shown in Figure 8: in the first one it finds the correspondence for stable objects (i.e. objects in the *to be classified* or *classified* state); in the second phase it tries to assign the remaining blobs to objects in the *new* state, possibly creating such objects if necessary.

The algorithm for the association of stable objects is shown in Figure 8. It is a greedy algorithm, based on the use of a similarity matrix. Rows and columns of the similarity matrix are respectively used to represent the objects and the blobs. In this way each element s_{ij} of the matrix represents a similarity measure between the blob b_j and the object o_i. The construction of the similarity matrix and of the similarity index is described in detail in subsection 4.4.

The algorithm starts by choosing the maximum element of the matrix, s_{kl}; if its value is above a given threshold τ, the algorithm records the corresponding association:

$$t_{k,l} = 1 \text{ if } s_{kl} > \tau \tag{1}$$

Then the algorithm checks if the blob b_l of this association has other objects that are close to it and are not similar enough to different blobs, as an evidence that an occlusion is starting, or that a detached object part (or a baggage) is becoming attached to the object; this condition can be formulated as:

$$\exists o_m \neq o_k : s_{ml} > \tau \wedge s_{ml} = \max_j s_{mj} \tag{2}$$

The association manager uses the current state and the output of the classifier to discriminate between the two kinds of event, and in the first case it creates a group object and links it with the individual objects forming the occlusion.

At this point the algorithm verifies if the object of the selected association o_k has other blobs that are close to it and are not similar enough to different objects; this may be caused by either the end of an occlusion, or by a split blob; more formally:

$$\exists b_n \neq b_l : s_{kn} > \tau \wedge s_{kn} = \max_i s_{in} \tag{3}$$

Again, the association manager uses the current state and the classifier outputs to recognize the correct event; in the case of an ending occlusion, the algorithm uses the individual object models linked to the group object to reassign the correct identity to the objects leaving the group, changing their state from *in group* to *to be classified*.

Finally, the algorithm removes from the similarity matrix all the rows and columns corresponding to objects and blobs it has used, and repeats the choice of the maximum element in the matrix. If no element is above the threshold τ, all the remaining unassigned objects are put in the *suspended* state and the first phase terminates.

The second phase is shown in Figure 8. It follows a similar scheme, except that it considers only the objects in the *new* state, and does not perform the checks for merges, splits, starting and ending occlusions. Moreover, the similarity matrix is built using less features than in the first phase since we have experimentally verified that only the position information (see section 4.4) is sufficiently reliable for such objects. At the end of this phase, any remaining unassigned blobs are used to create new object models, initialized to the *new* state.

4.4 Similarity Evaluation

The similarity matrix is used to match one or more blobs with one or more objects. In order to measure the similarity between an object o_i and a blob b_j, the tracking system uses an index based on three kinds of information, i.e. the position, the shape and the appearance:

$$s_{ij} = \sqrt{\frac{\alpha_p \cdot (s_{ij}^p)^2 + \alpha_s \cdot (s_{ij}^s)^2 + \alpha_a \cdot (s_{ij}^a)^2}{\alpha_p + \alpha_s + \alpha_a}} \tag{4}$$

where s_{ij}^p is the position similarity index, that is the distance between the estimated centroid of an object o_i and the centroid of a blob b_j; s_{ij}^s is the shape similarity index between an object o_i and a blob b_j; s_{ij}^a is the appearance similarity index between an object o_i and a blob b_j, based on color histograms; α_p, α_s and α_a are the weights of position, shape and appearance similarity index respectively.

All α values have been chosen by experimentation over a training set. Namely, in the first phase, selected values for objects in the *to be classified* and *classified* state are $\alpha_p = \alpha_s = \alpha_a = 1$ while for objects in the *in group* state selected values are $\alpha_s = \alpha_a = 1$; $\alpha_p = 0$ since in this context shape and appearance similarity perform better than position one. Finally, in the second phase that evaluates *new* objects, we choose to consider the only reliable feature, that is the position. Thus selected α values are $\alpha_s = \alpha_a = 0$; $\alpha_p = 1$.

For the position, the coordinates predicted by a Kalman filter are compared with the center of the blob, using Euclidean distance, obtaining for each object o_i and each blob b_j the distance d_{ij}. The position similarity index is then computed as:

$$s_{ij}^p = 1 - d_{ij}/d_{\max} \tag{5}$$

where $d_{\max}$ is a normalization factor depending on the maximum velocity of objects representing the maximum displacement of an object between two frames.

For characterizing the shape similarity, the system uses the real height and the area of the blob and of the object model; in particular if we denote as Δh_{ij} the relative height difference between o_i and b_j, and as ΔA_{ij} the relative area difference, the considered shape similarity index is:

$$s_{ij}^s = 1 - \sqrt{((\Delta A_{ij})^2 + (\Delta h_{ij})^2)/2} \tag{6}$$

Finally, as a representation of the appearance we have used the color histograms computed separately for the upper half and for the lower half of the object or blob (*Image Partitioning*). We have experimented with several criteria for comparing the histograms, and we have found that the most effective value is the χ^2 distance:

$$q_{ij} = \frac{1}{M} \sum_k \frac{\left(h_i^o(k) - h_j^b(k)\right)^2}{h_i^o(k) + h_j^b(k)} \tag{7}$$

where index k iterates over the bins of the histogram, h_i^o is the histogram of object o_i, h_j^b is the histogram of blob b_j, and M is the number of bins. The appearance similarity index is:

$$s_{ij}^a = 1 - \sqrt{\left((1 - q_{ij}^{up})^2 + (1 - q_{ij}^{low})^2\right)/2}. \tag{8}$$

where q_{ij}^{up} is the value of q_{ij} computed using only the upper half of the object/blob, and q_{ij}^{low} is the value computed using only the lower half.

5   Experimental Validation

In order to assess the performance of the method with respect to the state of the art, we have used the publicly available PETS 2010 database [21], currently adopted by

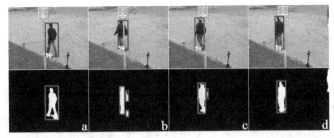

Fig. 9. The output of the method on a PETS2010 sequence containing a split, caused by the presence of a pole in the scene. The first row shows the result of the method, while the second one the list of the detected blobs. Note that the object is correctly tracked, notwithstanding the split in frames (b) and (c).

Fig. 10. The output of the proposed method on a PETS2010 sequence containing an occlusion. Note how the object 9 is correctly tracked inside the different groups although it quickly changes its direction in the frame (c).

many research papers. It is made of seven videos captured in a real-world environment, containing several occlusions between a person and an object, two persons or among several persons.

We have computed in each view the maximum velocity of the objects, from which we have derived the optimal values of the d_{max} parameter of equation 5, that are $d_{max} = 100$ for views 1, 3 and 4 and $d_{max} = 150$ for view 5, 6, 7 and 8.

Figures 9 and 10 show two excerpts, respectively containing a split pattern and a complex occlusion pattern among three persons, correctly handled by our algorithm. A quantitative evaluation has been carried out using the performance indexing proposed in the PETS 2010 contest [22]. In particular, we have used the following indices: the *Average Tracking Accuracy* (ATA), the *Multiple Object Tracking Accuracy* (MOTA) and the *Multiple Object Tracking Precision* (MOTP). In the following we introduce some notations useful to formally define them.

Let $G_i^{(t)}$ and $D_i^{(t)}$ be the i-th ground truth object and the detected one in frame t; $N_G^{(t)}$ and $N_D^{(t)}$ denote the number of ground truth objects and detected ones in frame t, respectively, while N_G and N_D denote the number of ground truth objects and unique detected ones in the given sequences. N_{frames} is the number of frames in the sequences.

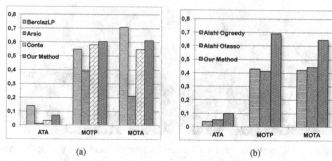

(a)   (b)

Fig. 11. Performance of the method compared with the PETS 2010 contest participants on all the views (a) and on a set of selected views (1, 5, 6 and 8) (b)

Finally, N_{mapped} refers to the mapped system output objects over an entire reference track, taking into account splits and merges and and $N_{mapped}^{(t)}$ refers to the number of mapped objects in the t-th frame.

ATA is a spatiotemporal measure that penalizes fragmentations in spatiotemporal dimensions while accounting for the number of objects detected and tracked, missed objects, and false positives. ATA is defined in terms of Sequence Track Detection Accuracy STDA:

$$ATA = \frac{STDA}{[(N_G + N_D)/2]}, \quad \text{where} \ \ STDA = \sum_{i=1}^{N_{mapped}} \frac{\sum_{t=1}^{N_{frames}} \frac{|G_i^{(t)} \cap D_i^{(t)}|}{|G_i^{(t)} \cup D_i^{(t)}|}}{N_{G_i \cup D_i \neq 0}}. \quad (9)$$

MOTA is an accuracy score computing the number of missed detects, false positives and switches in the system output for a given ground truth track. It is defined as:

$$MOTA = 1 - \frac{\sum_{t=1}^{N_{frames}} \left(c_m \cdot m_t + c_f \cdot fp_t + c_s \cdot is_t \right)}{\sum_{t=1}^{N_{frames}} N_G^{(t)}}, \quad (10)$$

where m_t is the number of misses, fp_t is the number of false positives, and is_t is the number of ID mismatches in frame t considering the mapping in frame $(t-1)$; c values are weights chosen as follow: $c_m = c_f = 1; c_s = log_{10}$.

Finally, MOTP is a precision score calculating the spatiotemporal overlap between the reference tracks and the system output tracks:

$$MOTP = \frac{\sum_{i=1}^{N_{mapped}} \sum_{t=1}^{N_{frames}^{(t)}} \frac{|G_i^{(t)} \cap D_i^{(t)}|}{|G_i^{(t)} \cup D_i^{(t)}|}}{\sum_{t=1}^{N_{frames}} N_{mapped}^{(t)}}. \quad (11)$$

Before analysing the performance of the method, let us point out some properties of the considered views. The first view presents interactions among two or three objects; the only difficulty is due to the presence of the pole and of the sign hanged on it, which causes a lot of splits. Note that the proposed method proves to be particularly robust with respect to the split situations on this view.

Table 2. The real number of occurrences of the objects in the scenes and the number of id switches

View	Objs	Objs Occurrences	Correctly Identified Objs	Id Switch
1	22	4840	4592 (95%)	92 (3%)
3	21	6377	4925 (77%)	294 (5%)
4	22	6076	4440 (73%)	158 (3%)
5	28	2722	2344 (86%)	76 (3%)
6	32	3141	2621 (84%)	156 (5%)
7	29	4578	3225 (70%)	147 (3%)
8	26	4310	3406 (79%)	107 (2%)

Views 3 and 4 are the most complex; in particular, view 3 is characterized by the presence of a large tree (about one-third of the scene), occluding a lot of individual or group objects. The situation is further complicated by the complexity of interactions among the objects, which involves in the average 2–5 objects for view 3 and 2–6 for view 4. Another problem in view 4 is the presence of a white-orange ribbon, continuously moving because of the wind. Such situation causes a lot of problems also in the detection phase. The problem of the moving ribbon is also present in views 5, 6, 7 and 8, even if it is less visible. We can note that the performance obtained in views 6 and 7 is generally lower than that obtained on other sequences; this is related to more complex interactions between the tracked objects, having a very high number of occlusions associated to objects that are entering the scene (unstable objects).

It is worth noting that the method, during an occlusion, does not attempt to find the exact position of an object inside a group; it continues to track the group as a whole, using the Kalman filter for obtaining a prevision of the position of each object inside the group itself; this choice obviously causes a degradation of the performance if it is measured using indices defined assuming that objects are always tracked individually.

Figures 11.a and 11.b show the performance of the method, compared with the participants on the PETS 2010 competition. It is worth noting that the results presented to the PETS 2010 by other competitors in some cases only refer to a subset of the views (Views 1, 5, 6 and 8). For such reason, in order to have a proper comparison with these methods, we present the experimental results computed both over all the views and over the same subset of views as these methods. In particular, the results in Figures 11.a refer to all the views of the database, while Figure 11.b only refers to views 1, 5, 6 and 8. We can note that in the first comparison our method outperforms the others on the precision index (MOTP), while in the second one it clearly outperforms all the other participants of the context on these views on all the indices. Table 2 presents for each view a detail of the performance of our algorithm.

As for the computational cost, the system runs at 16 milliseconds per frame on 4CIF images, using an Intel Xeon processor at 3.0GHz.

6   Conclusions

In this paper we have presented a real-time tracking algorithm able to overcome many of the problems of the object detection phase, as well as total or partial occlusions. It has been experimentally validated on a public database, showing a significant performance improvement over the participants to an international competition.

References

1. Seth, I., Jain, R.: Finding trajectories of feature points in a monocular image sequence. IEEE Trans. on Pattern Analysis and Machine Intelligence 9, 56–73 (1987)
2. Intille, S.S., Davis, J.W., Bobick, A.F.: Real-time closed-world tracking. In: IEEE Conf. on Computer Vision and Pattern Recognition, pp. 697–703 (1997)
3. Haritaoglu, I., Harwood, D., David, L.S.: W4: Real-time surveillance of people and their activities. IEEE Trans. on Pattern Analysis and Machine Intelligence 22, 809–830 (2000)
4. Pellegrini, S., Ess, A., Schindler, K., van Gool, L.: You'll never walk alone: Modeling social behavior for multi-target tracking. In: 2009 IEEE 12th International Conference on Computer Vision, pp. 261–268 (2009)
5. Ess, A., Leibe, B., Schindler, K., van Gool, L.: Robust multiperson tracking from a mobile platform. IEEE Transactions on Pattern Analysis and Machine Intelligence 31, 1831–1846 (2009)
6. Dai, C., Zheng, Y., Li, X.: Pedestrian detection and tracking in infrared imagery using shape and appearance. Computer Vision and Image Understanding 106, 288–299 (2007)
7. Tong, X., Yang, T., Xi, R., Shao, D., Zhang, X.: A novel multi-planar homography constraint algorithm for robust multi-people location with severe occlusion. In: Fifth International Conference on Image and Graphics, ICIG 2009, pp. 349–354 (2009)
8. Khan, S., Shah, M.: Tracking multiple occluding people by localizing on multiple scene planes. IEEE Transactions on Pattern Analysis and Machine Intelligence 31, 505–519 (2009)
9. Berclaz, J., Fleuret, F., Turetken, E., Fua, P.: Multiple object tracking using k-shortest paths optimization. IEEE Transactions on Pattern Analysis and Machine Intelligence 33, 1806–1819 (2011)
10. Delamarre, Q., Faugeras, O.: 3d articulated models and multiview tracking with physical forces. Computer Vision and Image Understanding 81, 328–357 (2001)
11. Comaniciu, D., Ramesh, V., Meer, P.: Real-time tracking of non-rigid objects using mean shift. In: Proc. of the IEEE Conf. on Computer Vision and Pattern Recognition, vol. 2, pp. 142–149 (2000)
12. Tao, H., Sawhney, H., Kumar, R.: Object tracking with bayesian estimation of dynamic layer representations. IEEE Trans. on Pattern Analysis and Machine Intelligence 24, 75–89 (2002)
13. Wu, B., Nevatia, R.: Detection of multiple, partially occluded humans in a single image by bayesian combination of edgelet part detectors. In: Tenth IEEE Int. Conf. on Computer Vision., vol. 1, pp. 90–97 (2005)
14. Hu, W., Zhou, X., Hu, M., Maybank, S.: Occlusion reasoning for tracking multiple people. IEEE Transactions on Circuits and Systems for Video Technology 19, 114–121 (2009)
15. Saboune, J., Laganiere, R.: People detection and tracking using the explorative particle filtering. In: 2009 IEEE 12th International Conference on Computer Vision Workshops (ICCV Workshops), pp. 1298–1305 (2009)
16. Yin, S., Na, J.H., Choi, J.Y., Oh, S.: Hierarchical kalman-particle filter with adaptation to motion changes for object tracking. Computer Vision and Image Understanding 115, 885–900 (2011)
17. Medeiros, H., Holguin, G., Shin, P.J., Park, J.: A parallel histogram-based particle filter for object tracking on simd-based smart cameras. Computer Vision and Image Understanding 114, 1264–1272 (2010)

18. Breitenstein, M., Reichlin, F., Leibe, B., Koller-Meier, E., Van Gool, L.: Online multiperson tracking-by-detection from a single, uncalibrated camera. IEEE Transactions on Pattern Analysis and Machine Intelligence 33, 1820–1833 (2011)
19. Conte, D., Foggia, P., Percannella, G., Tufano, F., Vento, M.: An experimental evaluation of foreground detection algorithms in real scenes. EURASIP Journal on Advances in Signal Processing 11 (2010)
20. Muad, A., Hussain, A., Samad, S., Mustaffa, M., Majlis, B.: Implementation of inverse perspective mapping algorithm for the development of an automatic lane tracking system. In: 2004 IEEE Region 10 Conference, TENCON 2004, vol. A, 1, pp. 207–210 (2004)
21. 13th IEEE Int. Workshop on Performance Evaluation of Tracking, Surveillance: The PETS 2010 benchmark data (2010), http://www.cvg.rdg.ac.uk/PETS2010/
22. Ellis, A., Ferryman, J.: PETS2010 and PETS2009 evaluation of results using individual ground truthed single views. In: IEEE Int. Conf. on Advanced Video and Signal Based Surveillance, pp. 135–142 (2010)

Artifact-Free Decompression and Zooming of JPEG Compressed Images with Total Generalized Variation*

Kristian Bredies and Martin Holler

Institute of Mathematics and Scientific Computing,
University of Graz, Heinrichstr. 36, A-8010 Graz, Austria

Abstract. We propose a new model for the improved reconstruction and zooming of JPEG (Joint Photographic Experts Group) images. In the reconstruction process, given a JPEG compressed image, our method first determines the set of possible source images and then specifically chooses one of these source images satisfying additional regularity properties. This is realized by employing the recently introduced *Total Generalized Variation (TGV)* as regularization term and solving a constrained minimization problem. Data fidelity is modeled by the composition of a color-subsampling and a discrete cosine transformation operator. Furthermore, extending the notion of data set by allowing unconstrained intervals, the method facilitates optional magnification of the original image. In order to obtain an optimal solution numerically, we propose a primal-dual algorithm. We have developed a parallel implementation of this algorithm for the CPU and the GPU, using OpenMP and Nvidia's Cuda, respectively. Finally, experiments have been performed, confirming a good visual reconstruction quality as well as the suitability for real-time application.

Keywords: Artifact-free JPEG decompression, Total generalized variation, Image reconstruction, Image zooming.

1 Introduction

This paper presents a novel method for artifact-free reconstruction and zooming of given JPEG compressed images. Being a lossy compression, a given JPEG compressed object does not provide exact information about the original source image, but can be used to define a convex set of possible source images. Our method reconstructs an image in accordance with this given data and minimal total generalized variation (TGV) of second order. This recently introduced functional [1] is well-suited for images as it is aware of both edges and smooth regions. In particular, its minimization discourages blocking and ringing artifacts which are typical for JPEG compressed images. It not only yields a significantly better approximation of the original image compared to standard decompression, but also outperforms, in terms of visual quality, existing similar variational approaches using different image models such as, for instance, the total variation. Moreover, the proposed method can easily be extended to simultaneous decompression and zooming, yielding an effective approach that is conceptually new and superior to standard zooming methods applied on decompressed images.

---

* Support by the Austrian Science Fund *FWF* under grant SFB F032 ("Mathematical Optimization and Applications in Biomedical Sciences") is gratefully acknowledged.

G. Csurka et al. (Eds.): VISIGRAPP 2012, CCIS 359, pp. 242–258, 2013.
© Springer-Verlag Berlin Heidelberg 2013

The proposed model can be phrased as an infinite dimensional minimization problem which reads as

$$\min_{u \in L^2(\Omega)} \mathrm{TGV}^2_\alpha(u) + \mathcal{I}_{U_D}(u) \tag{1}$$

where TGV^2_α is the total generalized variation functional of second order and $\mathcal{I}_{U_D}$ a convex indicator function corresponding to the given image data set U_D.

The reason for using the second order TGV functional is that for the moment it provides a good balance between achieved image quality and computational complexity. This is true especially since the improvement in the step from order one to order two, where order one corresponds to TV regularization, is visually most noticable (see [1]). Generalizations to higher orders, however, seem to be possible and might lead to further improvements.

Among the continuous formulation, we also present a discretized model and an efficient solution strategy for the resulting finite-dimensional minimization problem. Moreover, we address and discuss computation times of CPU and GPU based parallel implementations.

Due to the high popularity of the JPEG standard, the development of improved reconstruction methods for JPEG compressed images is still an active research topic. In the following, we briefly address some of those methods. For a further review of current techniques we refer to [2–4]. A classical approach is to apply filters, which only seems effective if space varying filters together with a pre-classification of image blocks is used. Another approach is to use algorithms based on projections onto convex sets (POCs), see for example [5–7], where one defines several convex sets according to data fidelity and regularization models. Typical difficulties of such methods are the concrete implementation of the projections and its slow convergence.

Our approach, among others, can be classified as a constrained optimization method, where the constraints are defined using the available compressed JPEG data. One advantage of this method is that, in contrast to most filter based methods, we do not modify the image, but choose a different reconstruction in strict accordance to the set of possible source images. Since data fidelity is numerically realized by a projection in each iteration, we can ensure that at any iteration, the reconstructed image is at least as plausible as the standard JPEG reconstruction. Furthermore, the proposed method can easily be extended to a combined decompression and zooming method. Tackling these two problems simultaneously has the advantage that more freedom in data fidelity for the zooming process can be allowed, where, in contrast to that, a zooming process separate from decompression will always be forced close to an artifact-corrupted image. This gives a reconstruction method for obtaining higher resolution images which is superior to standard zooming methods such as cubic interpolation applied on standard as well as improved reconstructions of JPEG compressed images.

Let us stress that the idea of pure reconstruction of JPEG images by minimizing a regularization functional under constraints given by the compressed data is not new. In [8–10] this was done using the well known total variation (TV) as regularization functional. In contrast to quadratic regularization terms, this functional is known to smooth the image while still preserving jump discontinuities such as sharp edges. But still, total variation regularized images typically suffer from the so called *staircasing effect* [11–13], which limits the application of this method for realistic images.

The total generalized variation functional (TGV), introduced in [1], does not suffer from this defect. As the name suggests, it can be seen as a generalization of the total variation functional: The functional may be defined for arbitrary order $k \in \mathbb{N}$, where in the case $k = 1$, it coincides with the total variation functional up to a constant. We will use the total generalized variation functional of order 2 as regularization term. As we will see, the application of this functional has the same advantages as the total variation functional in terms of edge preserving, with the staircasing effect being absent. Nevertheless, evaluation of the TGV functional of second order yields a minimization problem itself and non-differentiability of both the TGV functional as well as the convex indicator function used for data fidelity make the numerical solution of our constrained optimization problem demanding.

The outline of the paper is as follows: In Section 2 we briefly explain the JPEG compression standard and introduce the TGV functional, in Section 3 we define the continuous and the discrete model, shortly introduce an extension to image zooming and present a numerical solution strategy, in Section 4 we present experiments including computation times of CPU and GPU based implementations and in Section 5 we give a conclusion.

2   Theoretical Background

2.1   The JPEG Standard

At first we give a short overview of the JPEG standard which is partly following the presentation in [8]. For a more detailed explanation we refer to [14]. The process of JPEG compression is lossy, which means that most of the compression is obtained by loss of data. As a consequence, the original image cannot be restored completely from the compressed object.

Let us for the moment only consider JPEG compression for grayscale images. Figure 1 illustrates the main steps of this process. At first, the image undergoes a blockwise discrete cosine transformation resulting in an equivalent representation of the images as the linear combination of different frequencies. This makes it easier to identify data with less importance to visual image quality such as high frequency variations. Next the image is quantized by pointwise division of each 8×8 block by a uniform quantization matrix. The quantized values are then rounded to integer, which is where the loss of data takes place, and after that these integer values are further compressed by lossless compression. The resulting data, together with the quantization matrix, is then stored in the JPEG object.

The standard JPEG decompression, as shown in Figure 2, simply reverses this process without taking into account incompleteness of the data, i.e., that the compressed object delivers not a uniquely determined image, but a convex set of possible source images. Instead it just assumes the rounded integer value to be the true quantized DCT coefficient which leads to the well known JPEG artifacts as can be seen, for example, in Figure 3.

In the case of color images, typically a subsampling of color components is performed as part of JPEG compression. For that, color images are processed in the $YCbCr$

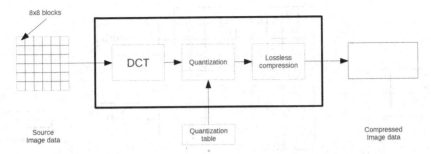

Fig. 1. Schematic overview of the JPEG compression procedure, taken from [8]

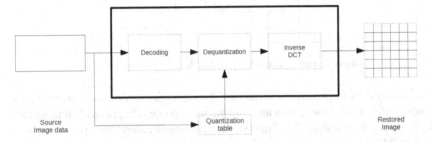

Fig. 2. Schematic overview of the standard JPEG decompression procedure, taken from [8]

Fig. 3. JPEG image with typical blocking and ringing artifacts

color space, i.e., the images are given as $u = (y, cb, cr)$, where y is the luminance component and cb, cr are chroma components. Subsampling is then applied to the chroma components cb and cr, which reflects the fact that the human eye is less sensitive to

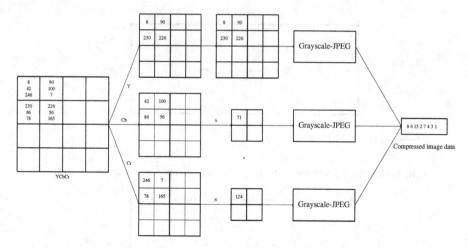

Fig. 4. Chroma subsampling during JPEG compression

color variations than to brightness variations. The resulting three image components, which now differ in resolution, then undergo the same process as grayscale images (see Figure 4). Again, the standard JPEG decompression simply reverts this process, now by applying an additional chroma-upsampling as last step.

An integral part of the model we propose is taking the set of all possible source images associated with a given JPEG object as a constraint. This set can be mathematically described as follows. With the integer coefficient data $(d_{i,j}^c)$, where the range of i, j depends on the resolution of the color component $c \in \{0, 1, 2\}$, and the quantization matrix $(Q_{i,j}^c)_{0 \leq i,j < 8}$, both provided by the compressed JPEG object, the set of numbers which yield $d_{i,j}^c$ in the quantization and rounding step is given by the interval

$$J_{i,j}^c = \left[Q_{i,j}^c(d_{i,j}^c - \frac{1}{2}), Q_{i,j}^c(d_{i,j}^c + \frac{1}{2}) \right]. \tag{2}$$

Note that for this notation we extend the quantization matrices up to the image dimensions simply by repeating the 8×8 coefficients. Having this, the coefficient data set D can be defined as

$$D = \left\{ (z_{i,j}^c) \mid z_{i,j}^c \in J_{i,j}^c \text{ for all } c, i, j \right\} \tag{3}$$

and the set of possible source images of the compression process as

$$U_D = \left\{ u = (u_{i,j}^c) \mid ASu \in D \right\} \tag{4}$$

where A is a color-component-wise blockwise DCT operator and S is a subsampling operator (see Subsection 3.2 for the definition of A and S).

2.2 The TGV Functional

Another building block of the model is the total generalized variation functional (TGV) as proposed in [1], in particular of second order. We give here a short definition and sum up some important results, for details and proofs however, we refer to [1, 15]. The pre-dual formulation of second-order TGV is given by

$$
\text{TGV}_\alpha^2(u) = \sup \left\{ \int_\Omega u \operatorname{div}^2 v \, dx \, \Big| \, v \in C_c^2(\Omega, \mathcal{S}^{2\times2}), \right.
$$

$$
\left. \|v\|_\infty \le \alpha_0, \|\operatorname{div} v\|_\infty \le \alpha_1 \right\}, \quad (5)
$$

where $\alpha = (\alpha_0, \alpha_1) \in \mathbb{R}^2$, $u \in L^1(\Omega)$ and $\mathcal{S}^{2\times2}$ is the space of symmetric 2 by 2 matrices. Given a function $u \in L^1(\Omega)$, the second-order TGV functional takes into account, as the test functions have the form $\operatorname{div}^2 v$, the generalized derivative of u up to order 2. Its kernel is the set of polynomials with degree less than 2. Evaluation of TGV_α^2 can be also interpreted as an optimal balancing of the first and second generalized derivative of u among themselves. This becomes obvious, considering an equivalent representation of TGV_α^2:

$$
\text{TGV}_\alpha^2(u) = \inf_{v \in \text{BD}(\Omega, \mathbb{R}^d)} \alpha_1 \|\nabla u - v\|_1 + \alpha_0 \|\mathcal{E}(v)\|_1. \quad (6)
$$

Here, $\mathcal{E}(v)$ denotes the symmetrized derivative of the vector field v and $\text{BD}(\Omega)$ the space of vector fields of bounded deformation. As one can also see in (6), the ratio between the parameters α_1 and α_0 weights the balancing between the first and second derivative of u and will later also influence possible solutions of TGV_α^2 regularized optimization problems. The TGV functional possesses several properties which support its usage as regularization term, such as convexity and lower semi-continuity with respect to L^1 convergence. It also satisfies a Poincaré-Wirtinger type inequality which can be used to obtain coercivity of the objective functional.

3 The Method

This section is devoted to present the TGV-based JPEG reconstruction method. Let us at first state the associated minimization problem in an infinite dimensional setting. Note that we abuse notation by using the same symbols for the continuous setting as for the discrete one.

3.1 The Continuous Setting

For convenience we only consider grayscale images for the continuous setting. Hence, our images are represented by real valued functions $u \in L^2(\Omega)$ with Ω a bounded Lipschitz domain, typically a rectangle. Using the definition of the TGV functional given in (5) we can formulate the infinite dimensional minimization problem as follows:

$$
\min_{u \in L^2(\Omega)} \text{TGV}_\alpha^2(u) + \mathcal{I}_{U_D}(u) \quad (7)
$$

where

$$
\mathcal{I}_{U_D}(u) = \begin{cases} 0 & \text{if } u \in U_D, \\ \infty & \text{else.} \end{cases}
$$

The data set U_D can be defined as

$$U_D = \{u \in L^2(\Omega) \mid Au \in D\}$$

where A is a basis transformation operator related to a general orthonormal basis $(a_n)_{n \geq 0}$ of $L^2(\Omega)$. The coefficient data set $D \subset \ell^2$ reflects interval restrictions on the coefficients:

$$D = \{z \in \ell^2 \mid z_i \in J_i \, \forall i \in \mathbb{N}_0\}$$

where $J_i \subset \mathbb{R}$ is a non-empty, closed (not necessarily bounded) interval for any $i \in \mathbb{N}_0$. Note that this model allows arbitrary orthonormal bases $(a_n)_{n \geq 0}$ of $L^2(\Omega)$ and constraints on infinitely many coefficients. However, for JPEG decompression, one usually chooses an infinite block-cosine orthonormal basis, and lets only the J_i associated with the first 8×8 blockwise coefficients be bounded and $J_i = \mathbb{R}$ for the remaining i, see [8] for details.

Under assumptions which are satisfied in the application of this model to JPEG decompression, we can show existence of a solution to (7). More generally, as necessary for the extension of this model to a reconstruction method combined with zooming, if we assume that U_D has non-empty interior and that $J_{n_0}, J_{n_1}, J_{n_2}$ are bounded for certain n_0, n_1, n_2, existence of a solution can be guaranteed.

3.2   The Discrete Model

Based on the equivalent formulation of the TGV functional in (6) and the data set U_D as in (4) we will now formulate our discrete model.

For $k, l \in \mathbb{N}$, we set the space of discrete color images $U = \mathbb{R}^{8k \times 8l \times 3}$ and further $V = U^2$ and $W = U^3$. The dimension $8k \times 8l \times 3$ results from the three color components and reflects the fact that any JPEG image is processed with its horizontal and vertical number of pixels being multiples of 8.

Now for $u \in U$, a discrete vector-input version of the TGV_α^2 functional can be defined as

$$\text{TGV}_\alpha^2(u) = \inf_{v \in V} \alpha_1 \|\nabla(u) - v\|_V + \alpha_0 \|\mathcal{E}(v)\|_W, \tag{8}$$

where $\nabla : U \to V$ denotes a discrete, color-component-wise gradient operator using forward differences and $\mathcal{E} : V \to W$ denotes a discrete, color-component-wise symmetric gradient operator using backward differences, i.e., $\mathcal{E}(v) = \frac{1}{2}(J(v) + J(v)^T)$ with $J(v)$ a discrete color-component-wise Jacobian of v. Note that in $\mathcal{E}(v)$, the off-diagonal entries need to be stored only once, thus $\mathcal{E}(v) \in U^3$. For $v = (v_{i,j})_{0 \leq i,j < 8k}$ with $v_{i,j} \in \mathbb{R}^{3 \times 2}$ the norm on V is defined as

$$\|v\|_V := \sum_{i,j} |v_{i,j}|$$

with $|\cdot|$ the Frobenius norm on $\mathbb{R}^{3 \times 2}$. The norm $\|\cdot\|_W$ is defined similarly.

In order to avoid extensive indexing, we will now give just a local, component-wise definition of the operators S and A, necessary to describe the data set U_D. The subsampling operator S depends on the foregoing chroma subsampling process, but typically is defined on disjoint 2×2 blocks of each chroma component, denoted by $(z_{i,j})_{0 \leq i \leq 1}$, as

$$Sz = \frac{1}{4} \sum_{m,n=0}^{1} z_{m,n}, \tag{9}$$

reducing the resolution of the chroma components by the factor 4. Since the resolution of the brightness component is not reduced, S is the identity for this component. The discrete cosine transformation operator is defined, for each color component, on each disjoint 8×8 block $(z_{i,j})_{0 \leq i,j \leq 7}$, as

$$(Az)_{p,q} \quad = \quad C_p C_q \sum_{n,m=0}^{7} z_{n,m} \cos\left(\frac{\pi(2n+1)p}{16}\right) \cos\left(\frac{\pi(2m+1)q}{16}\right),$$

for $0 \leq p, q \leq 7$ and

$$C_s = \begin{cases} \frac{1}{\sqrt{8}} & \text{if } s = 0, \\ \frac{1}{2} & \text{if } 1 \leq s \leq 7. \end{cases}$$

With the operators S and A, the set U_D can now be defined as already done before in (4) by

$$U_D = \{u \in U \mid ASu \in D\},$$

where the coefficient data set D is obtained from the compressed JPEG object as in (3).

With these prerequisites, the finite dimensional optimization problem for artifact-free JPEG decompression reads as

$$\min_{u \in U} \mathrm{TGV}_\alpha^2(u) + \mathcal{I}_{U_D}(u), \tag{10}$$

where again

$$\mathcal{I}_{U_D}(u) = \begin{cases} 0 & \text{if } u \in U_D, \\ \infty & \text{else.} \end{cases}$$

Using the boundedness of the data intervals $J_{i,j}^c$ defined in (2) it can be shown that there exists a solution to (10) and that this problem is equivalent to

$$\min_{(u,v) \in U \times V} F(K(u,v)) + \mathcal{I}_{U_d}(u), \tag{11}$$

where $K : U \times V \to V \times W$,

$$K = \begin{bmatrix} \nabla & -1 \\ 0 & \mathcal{E} \end{bmatrix}$$

and $F : V \times W \to \mathbb{R}$,

$$F(v,w) = \alpha_1 \|v\|_V + \alpha_0 \|w\|_W.$$

This formulation will now be the basis for the numerical approach.

3.3   Extension for Image Zooming

The purpose of this subsection is to show how our model for artifact-free reconstruction of JPEG images can easily be extended for zooming. For that, remember that in the reconstruction process, the set of possible source data was defined as

$$U_D = \{u \in U \mid ASu \in D\}.$$

If U is given by $U = \mathbb{R}^{8k \times 8k \times 3} \cong \mathbb{R}^{192k}$, the restriction $ASu \in D$ can be described component-wise by bounded intervals $J_n \subset \mathbb{R}$, $0 \leq n < 192k$, as

$$(ASu)_i \in J_i \quad \text{for all } 0 \leq i < 192k.$$

Here, the operator A is a component-wise discrete block-wise cosine transformation operator, applying a cosine transformation on k^2 blocks of size 8×8 for each image component.

Assume now that we have a higher resolution image given, say $\tilde{u} \in \tilde{U} = \mathbb{R}^m$, $192k < m \in \mathbb{N}$. If we again split each component into k^2 blocks, but of size $l > 8$, and define $\tilde{A} : \tilde{U} \to \ell^2$ to be a blockwise DCT operator for this larger blocks, the first 8×8 coefficients of each block of $\tilde{A}\tilde{u}$ can be expected to coincide, up to a uniform factor, with the coefficients of each 8×8 block of Au, where u is a sub-sampled version of $\tilde{u}$. The remaining coefficients of $\tilde{A}\tilde{u}$ then reflect the high-resolution information.

Thus, if we now want to reconstruct a high resolution image $\tilde{u} \in \tilde{U}$ from a low-resolution data set D, we can define an index set $N \subset \mathbb{N}$ corresponding to the coefficients where the data intervals J_n are known, and simply set $J_i = \mathbb{R}$ for $0 \leq i < m, i \notin N$. Then, by defining the data set

$$\tilde{D} = \{z \in \ell^2 \mid z_i \in \tilde{J}_i\},$$

where $\tilde{J}_i$ is given by the JPEG data for $i \in N$ and $\tilde{J}_i = \mathbb{R}$ else, we can reconstruct higher resolution images fitting to the low resolution data. Note that with the same technique, we can also upsample the color components. Thus, the set of possible high resolution source images of a given JPEG file can simply be given as

$$U_D = \{u \in \tilde{U} \mid \tilde{A}u \in \tilde{D}\},$$

where now for the color components even more intervals $\tilde{J}_i$ describing $\tilde{D}$ may be unconstrained than for the brightness component, reflecting color upsampling. As already mentioned in Subsection 3.1, existence of a solution can still be guaranteed in the case that some intervals J_n are unbounded, since in the combined decompression-zooming approach at least three suitable intervals are bounded.

Including this extension, without further modification of the model, we can now decide prior to the reconstruction process whether we only want to reconstruct the original-sized image or even increase its resolution. As one can notice in the following, this generalization works basically with the same algorithmic implementation as the pure reconstruction method and in Section 4 we will confirm its effectivity compared to other zooming methods.

3.4   A Primal-Dual Algorithm

We numerically solve our minimization problem using a primal-dual algorithm presented in [16], for which convergence can be ensured. This algorithm is well-suited for this problem because, as we will see, all necessary steps during one iteration reduce to simple arithmetic operations and the evaluation of a forward and inverse block-cosine transformation, for which highly optimized code already exists. This makes the algorithm fast and also easy to implement on the GPU.

As first step we note that (11) is equivalent to the following saddle-point problem:

$$\min_{x \in X} \max_{y \in Y} \left((y, Kx)_{Y,Y} - F^*(y) + \mathcal{I}_{U_D}(x) \right) \tag{12}$$

where $X = U \times V$, $Y = V \times W$, $(\cdot, \cdot)$ is the scalar product on Y and F^* is the convex conjugate of F. The primal-dual strategy for finding saddle points presented in [16] amounts to performing the abstract iteration shown in Algorithm 1. Note that ∂F^* and $\partial \mathcal{I}_{U_D}$ refers to the subdifferential of F^* and $\mathcal{I}_{U_D}$, respectively, and the operator K^* denotes the adjoint of K and is given by

$$K^* = \begin{bmatrix} -\operatorname{div} & 0 \\ -1 & -\operatorname{div}_2 \end{bmatrix}$$

with $\operatorname{div} = -\nabla^*$ and $\operatorname{div}_2 = -\mathcal{E}^*$ denoting discrete divergence operators.

Algorithm 1. Abstract primal-dual algorithm

- Initialization: Choose $\tau, \sigma > 0$ such that $\|K\|^2 \tau \sigma < 1$, $(x^0, y^0) \in X \times Y$ and set $\bar{x}^0 = x^0$
- Iterations ($n \geq 0$): Update $x^n, y^n, \bar{x}^n$ as follows:

$$\begin{cases} y^{n+1} = & (I + \sigma \, \partial F^*)^{-1}(y^n + \sigma K \bar{x}^n) \\ x^{n+1} = & (I + \tau \, \partial \mathcal{I}_{U_D})^{-1}(x^n - \tau K^* y^{n+1}) \\ \bar{x}^{n+1} = & 2x^{n+1} - x^n \end{cases}$$

Using standard arguments from convex analysis, it can be shown that the resolvent-type operators $(I + \sigma \, \partial F^*)^{-1}$ and $(I + \tau \, \partial \mathcal{I}_{U_D})^{-1}$ take the following form:

$$(I + \sigma \partial F^*)^{-1}(v, w) = \left(\operatorname{proj}_{\alpha_1}(v), \operatorname{proj}_{\alpha_0}(w) \right)$$

where

$$\operatorname{proj}_{\alpha_1}(v) = \frac{v}{\max(1, \frac{\|v\|_\infty}{\alpha_1})},$$

$$\operatorname{proj}_{\alpha_0}(w) = \frac{w}{\max(1, \frac{\|w\|_\infty}{\alpha_0})}$$

and

$$(I + \tau \partial \mathcal{I}_{U_D})^{-1}(u, v) = \left(u + S^{-1}(\operatorname{proj}_{U_A}(Su) - Su), v \right)$$

where

$$\operatorname{proj}_{U_A}(u) = A^* z$$

with

$$z_{i,j}^c = \begin{cases} u_{i,j}^c & \text{if } (Au)_{i,j}^c \in J_{i,j}^c = [l_{i,j}^c, r_{i,j}^c] \text{ or } J_{i,j}^c = \mathbb{R} \\ r_{i,j}^c & \text{if } (Au)_{i,j}^c > r_{i,j}^c \\ l_{i,j}^c & \text{if } (Au)_{i,j}^c < l_{i,j}^c, \end{cases}$$

$A^* = A^{-1}$ the adjoint of A and S^{-1} denoting the upsampling operator associated with S, given locally by replication of $z \in \mathbb{R}$, i.e.,

$$S^{-1}z = \begin{pmatrix} z \cdots z \\ \vdots \quad \vdots \\ z \cdots z \end{pmatrix}.$$

Having this, we can now give the concrete implementation of the primal-dual algorithm for JPEG decompression in Algorithm 2. Note that the step-size restriction $\sigma\tau \leq \frac{1}{12}$ results from the estimate $\|K\|^2 < 12$. As one can see, all steps of Algorithm 2 can be evaluated by simple, mostly pixel-wise operations making each iteration step fast.

Algorithm 2. Scheme of implementation

1: **function** TGV-JPEG(J_{comp})
2:     $(d, Q) \leftarrow$ Decoding of JPEG-Object J_{comp}
3:     $d \leftarrow d \cdot Q$
4:     $u \leftarrow S^{-1}(A^*(d))$
5:     $v \leftarrow 0, \overline{u} \leftarrow u, \overline{v} \leftarrow 0, p \leftarrow 0, q \leftarrow 0$
6:     choose $\sigma, \tau > 0$ such that $\sigma\tau \leq 1/12$
7:     **repeat**
8:         $p \leftarrow \text{proj}_{\alpha_1}(p + \sigma(\nabla\overline{u} - \overline{v}))$
9:         $q \leftarrow \text{proj}_{\alpha_0}(q + \sigma(\mathcal{E}(\overline{v}))$
10:       $u_+ \leftarrow u + \tau(\text{div}\, p)$
11:       $v_+ \leftarrow v + \tau(p + \text{div}_2\, q)$
12:       $u_+ \leftarrow u_+ + S^{-1}(\text{proj}_{U_A}(Su_+) - Su_+)$
13:       $\overline{u} \leftarrow (2u_+ - u), \overline{v} \leftarrow (2v_+ - v)$
14:       $u \leftarrow u_+, v \leftarrow v_+$
15:     **until** Stopping criterion fulfilled
16:     **return** u_+
17: **end function**

---

4   Numerical Experiments

We implemented and tested the proposed TGV-based JPEG decompression method. First of all, we have compared the standard JPEG decompression with our method for three images possessing different characteristics. The outcome can be seen in Figure 5, where also the image dimensions and the memory requirement of the JPEG compressed image is given in *bits per pixel (bpp)*. As one can see, our method performs well in reducing the typical JPEG artifacts and still preserves sharp edges.

Table 1. Computation times in seconds to perform 1000 iterations for different devices and image sizes. CPU: AMD Phenom 9950. GPUs: Nvidia Quadro FX 3700 (compute capability 1.1), Nvidia GTX 280 (compute capability 1.3), Nvidia GTX 580 (compute capability 2.0). Note that on the Quadro FX 3700 and GTX 280, not enough memory was available to perform the algorithm for the 3200×2400 pixel image.

Device	512×512	1600×1200	3200×2400
CPU Single-core	53.22	672.51	1613.44
CPU Quad-core	28.32	263.70	812.18
GPU Quadro FX 3700	4.92	35.52	-
GPU Nvidia GTX 280	2.2	10.22	-
GPU Nvidia GTX 580	1.2	6.6	25.70

Figure 6 then allows to compare our results with the reconstruction using TV instead of TGV as regularization functional as proposed in [8]. As one can see, in particular in the surface plots, the TV-based method also maintains sharp edges. However, it leads to a staircasing effect in regions that should be smooth. In contrast to that, the TGV-based method yields a more natural and visually more appealing reconstruction in such regions.

Figure 7 serves as an example of an image containing texture. It can be seen that our method preserves fine details and does not lead to additional smoothing of textured regions.

Finally, Figure 8 shows effectivity of the extension of our approach to image reconstruction combined with zooming. As one can see, the TGV-based high resolution reconstruction outperforms not only cubic interpolation of the standard reconstruction, but also cubic interpolation of a low-resolution image obtained with the TGV-based reconstruction technique. This indicates that not only the combination of TGV-based reconstruction with DCT-based zooming yields improved results, but also DCT based zooming of an uncompressed image itself is an effective zooming method, as has also been confirmed in [17].

We also developed a parallel implementation of the reconstruction method for multi-core CPUs and GPUs, using OpenMP [18] and Nvidia's Cuda [19], respectively. For the GPU implementation we partly used kernel functions adapted to the compute capability of the device. The blockwise DCT was performed on the CPU and the GPU using FFTW [20] and a block-DCT kernel provided by the Cuda SDK, respectively. Computation times of those implementations for multiple image sizes are given in Table 1. As one can see, especially the GPU implementation yields a high acceleration and makes the method suitable for real-time applications. The given computation times correspond to the computation of 1000 iterations, which is in most cases more than enough for a reconstruction visually almost indistinguishable from one obtained as optimal solution satisfying a suitable stopping criterion. Since the decrease of the TGV-value of the image is typically very high especially during the first iterations of the algorithm, and since a fit-to-data can be ensured for any iteration step image, one could use the image obtained after only a few number of iterations as intermediate reconstruction and then iteratively update the solution.

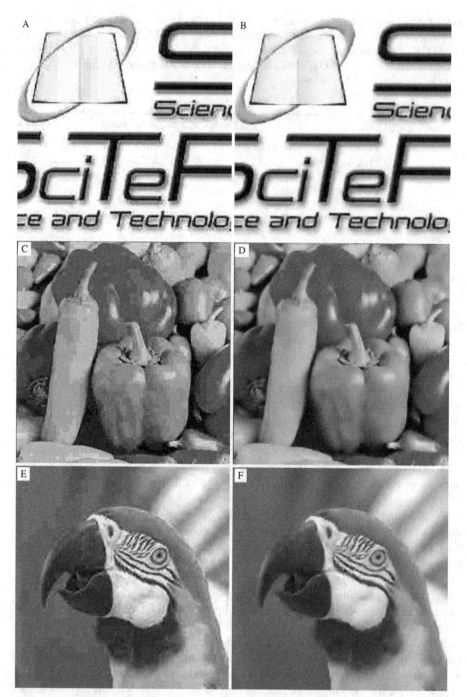

Fig. 5. On the left: Standard decompression, on the right: TGV-based reconstruction after 1000 iterations. A-B: SciTePress image at 0.5 bpp (256 × 256 pixels). C-D: Peppers image at 0.15 bpp (512 × 512 pixels). E-F: Parrot image at 0.3 bpp (256 × 256 pixels).

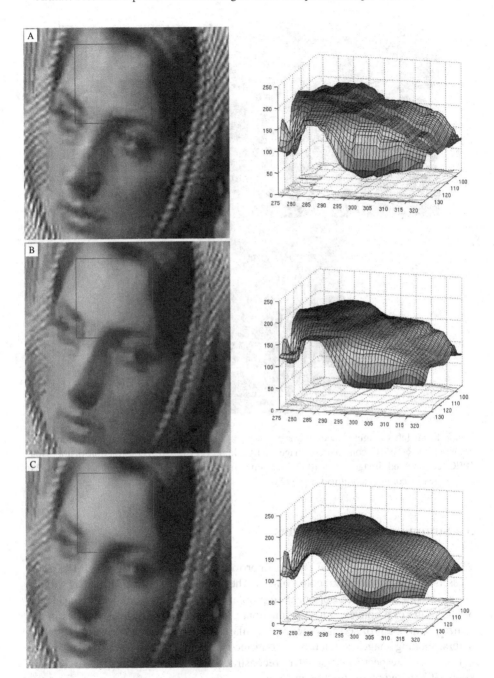

Fig. 6. Close-up of Barbara image at 0.4 bpp at 1000 iterations. The marked region on the left is plotted as surface on the right. A: Standard decompression. B: TV-based reconstruction. C: TGV-based reconstruction.

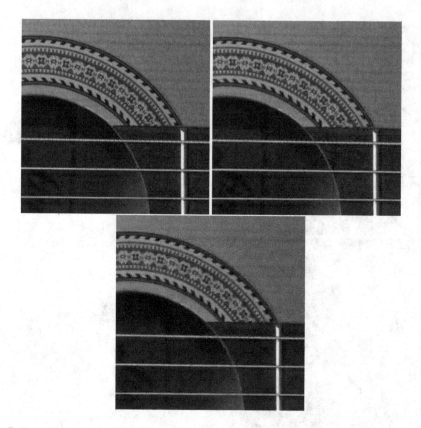

Fig. 7. From left to right: Uncompressed image at 24 bpp (256 × 256 pixels), standard decompression of JPEG compressed image at 1.06 bpp, TGV-based reconstruction of the same JPEG compressed image after 1000 iterations. Image by [21], licensed under CC-BY-2.0 (http://creativecommons.org/licenses/by/2.0/).

5   Summary and Conclusions

We proposed a novel method for the improved reconstruction of given JPEG compressed images, in particular, color images. The reconstruction is performed by solving a non-smooth constrained optimization problem where exact data fidelity is achieved by the usage of a convex indicator functional. The main novelty, however, lies in the utilization of TGV of second order as a regularization term which intrinsically prefers natural-looking images, as it has been confirmed in Section 4. This was shown to be true not only with respect to the standard reconstruction, but also with respect to already-known TV-based reconstruction methods.

The extension of the method to a combined reconstruction and zooming process allows to reconstruct even high resolution images from a compressed, low resolution data file and indicates the potential of our general framework also for different applications in image processing. Moreover, a parallel implementation for multi-core CPUs

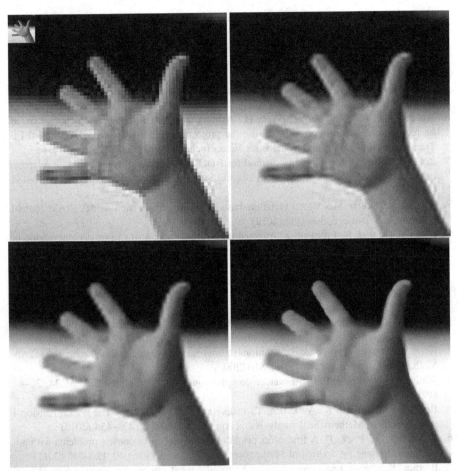

Fig. 8. Top left: Original, compressed image (64×64 pixels) together 8 times magnification by pixel repetition (512×512). Top Right: 8 times magnification by cubic interpolation. Bottom left: 8 times magnification of TGV-decompression using cubic interpolation. Bottom right: 8 times magnification using TGV-decompression plus zooming. Image by [22], licensed under CC-BY-2.0 (http://creativecommons.org/licenses/by/2.0/).

and GPUs showed that the reconstruction process can be realized sufficiently fast in order to make the method also applicable in practice.

Motivated by these promising results, the focus of further research will be the development of a theory for a more general model using the TGV functional of arbitrary order.

References

1. Bredies, K., Kunisch, K., Pock, T.: Total generalized variation. SIAM Journal on Imaging Sciences 3, 492–526 (2010)
2. Nosratinia, A.: Enhancement of JPEG-compressed images by re-application of JPEG. The Journal of VLSI Signal Processing 27, 69–79 (2001)

3. Singh, S., Kumar, V., Verma, H.K.: Reduction of blocking artifacts in JPEG compressed images. Digital Signal Processing 17, 225–243 (2007)
4. Shen, M.Y., Kuo, C.C.J.: Review of postprocessing techniques for compression artifact removal. Journal of Visual Communication and Image Representation 9, 2–14 (1998)
5. Kartalov, T., Ivanovski, Z.A., Panovski, L., Karam, L.J.: An adaptive POCS algorithm for compression artifacts removal. In: 9th International Symposium on Signal Processing and Its Applications, pp. 1–4 (2007)
6. Weerasinghe, C., Liew, A.W.C., Yan, H.: Artifact reduction in compressed images based on region homogeneity constraints using the projection onto convex sets algorithm. IEEE Transactions on Circuits and Systems for Video Technology 12, 891–897 (2002)
7. Zou, J.J., Yan, H.: A deblocking method for BDCT compressed images based on adaptive projections. IEEE Transactions on Circuits and Systems for Video Technology 15, 430–435 (2005)
8. Bredies, K., Holler, M.: A total variation–based JPEG decompression model. SIAM Journal on Imaging Sciences 5, 366–393 (2012)
9. Alter, F., Durand, S., Froment, J.: Adapted total variation for artifact free decompression of JPEG images. Journal of Mathematical Imaging and Vision 23, 199–211 (2005)
10. Zhong, S.: Image coding with optimal reconstruction. In: International Conference on Image Processing, vol. 1, pp. 161–164 (1997)
11. Nikolova, M.: Local strong homogeneity of a regularized estimator. SIAM J. Appl. Math. 61, 633–658 (2000)
12. Caselles, V., Chambolle, A., Novaga, M.: The discontinuity set of solutions of the TV denoising problem and some extensions. Multiscale Model. Simul. 6, 879–894 (2007)
13. Ring, W.: Structural properties of solutions to total variaton regularization problems. M2AN Math. Model. Numer. Anal. 34, 799–810 (2000)
14. Wallace, G.K.: The JPEG still picture compression standard. Commun. ACM 34, 30–44 (1991)
15. Bredies, K., Kunisch, K., Valkonen, T.: Properties of $L^1 - TGV^2$: The one-dimensional case. Journal of Mathematical Analysis and Applications 398(1), 438–454 (2013)
16. Chambolle, A., Pock, T.: A first-order primal-dual algorithm for convex problems with applications to imaging. Journal of Mathematical Imaging and Vision 40, 120–145 (2011)
17. Bredies, K.: Recovering piecewise smooth multichannel images by minimization of convex functionals with total generalized variation penalty. SFB Report 2012-006, Institute of Mathematics and Scientific Computing, University of Graz (2012)
18. OpenMP Architecture Review Board: Openmp application program interface, version 3.1 (2011), http://www.openmp.org
19. NVIDIA: NVIDIA CUDA programming guide 2.0. NVIDIA Cooperation (2008)
20. Frigo, M., Johnson, S.G.: The design and implementation of FFTW3. Proceedings of the IEEE 93, 216–231 (2005); Special issue on Program Generation, Optimization, and Platform Adaptation
21. Dawgbyte77 (2005), http://www.flickr.com/photos/dawgbyte77/3052164481/
22. Kubina, J. (2008), http://flickr.com/photos/kubina/42275122

Efficient Rapid Prototyping of Particle Filter Based Object Tracking on Homogenous System

Hanen Chenini[1,2], Jean Pierre Dérutin[1,2], and Thierry Chateau[1,2]

[1] Clermont Université, Université Blaise Pascal, Institut Pascal,
BP 10448, F-63000 Clermont-Ferrand
[2] CNRS, UMR 6602, IP, F-63171 Aubiére

Abstract. This paper presents a multi-processor approach for rapid prototyping of computer vision application and illustrates its advantages using a generic implementation of a real-time object tracking application. We propose to use such a particle filter with color-based image features. As our application should estimate the probability distribution of an object position, the target model is compared with the current hypotheses of the particle filter using an approximation of the Kullback-Leibler coefficient from the K-Nearest Neighbor framework. Based on new methodology on rapid design and prototyping, we present the parallelization of the proposed algorithm on Homogeneous Network of Communicating Processors architecture. The aim of the proposed design methodology was to raise the abstraction level of the specifications, by developing the appropriate models and tools supporting the design from the specification down to the embedded implementation. The proposed method has been evaluated for face detection and tracking application in several video sequences.

1 Introduction

In most of computer vision application, prior knowledge about the phenomenon being modeled is available. This knowledge allows us to formulate Bayesian models. Within this setting, Monte-Carlo simulation methods (particle filtering) can be used in order to implement the Bayesian framwork. PFs are Bayesian in nature and their goal is to find an approximation to the Posterior Density Functions (PDF) of the states of interest (e.g. position of a moving object in tracking) based on observations corrupted by additive gaussian white noise which are inputs to the filter. This is done using the principle of Importance Sampling (IS) whereby, multiple copies (particles) of the variable of interest are drawn from a known density (Importance Function (IF)), each one associated with a weight that signifies the quality of that specific particle based on the received observations. An estimation of the variable of interest is obtained by the weighted sum of all the particles. In this context, particle filters provide a robust tracking framework as they are neither limited to linear systems nor require the noise to be Gaussian. It can keep its options open and consider multiple state hypotheses simultaneously. Here, we propose to track objects based on their color information using the particle filter. The proposed algorithm considered in our approach, uses a Gaussian approximation to the full-posterior as the importance function. Also, we propose to compute the Kullback-Leibler distance using the K-Nearest Neighbor (KNN) framework to evaluate likelihood

G. Csurka et al. (Eds.): VISIGRAPP 2012, CCIS 359, pp. 259–273, 2013.
© Springer-Verlag Berlin Heidelberg 2013

that further increases the complexity of the algorithm. Depending on the state-space model proposed, the complexity is related to the prediction of M sampled particles and weight evaluation stage. Translating an algorithm for real-time implementation requires making specific choices so that the design meets the constraints. Some of the main constraints are speed of execution, power dissipation, accuracy of the results, cost and time involved in the implementation. Dedicated hardware implementation may be useful for high speed processing but it does not offer the flexibility and programmability required for system evolution. Applications with stringent resource-consumption and runtime constraints are increasingly resorting to MP-SoC (Multi- Processors System on Chip) architectures. Generally, the MP-SoC architecture has become a solution for designing embedded systems dedicated to applications that require intensive computations. As more processing elements are integrated in a single chip, the mapping of software tasks to hardware resources is important since it affects the degree of parallelism among multiple processors and the utilization of hardware resources.

With regard to the latter, our design flow for the fast prototyping of image processing algorithm on a MP-SoC architecture is based upon meeting algorithm processing power requirements and communication needs with refinement of a generic parallel architecture model. This parallel architecture contains multiple homogenous processors, memory blocks, DMA (Direct memory access) and several I/O resources in the same chip. In addition, it can be beneficial to take advantage of the parallelism, low cost, and low power consumption offered by FPGAs. The design and implementation of a real-time object tracking algorithm on a FPGA focuses on minimizing resource utilization to allow functionality of the application that uses the tracking information to be added. Here, we propose a real-time, embedded vision solution for object tracking, implemented on an FPGA-based Homogeneous Network of Communicating Processors (HNCP) architecture [10]. The remained structure of this paper is arranged as follows. Section 2 describes the theory behind the PFs and the survey of existing related efforts. In Section 3, we briefly describe and present the face tracking algorithm with particle filter framwork, including face model, dynamic model and observation model. Section 4 is mainly concerned with outlining our proposed design flow for implementing the developed image processing application. Evaluation of resource utilization and latency of the parallel implementation on FPGA platform to speed up the tracking process is presented in section 5. Section 6 concludes the paper.

2   State of the Art

Sequential Monte Carlo (SMC) methods [1] are a set of simulation based methods which provide a convenient and attractive approach to computing a posterior probability distribution. PFs are used to perform filtering for dynamic state-space problem that can be described as a sequential representation. State-space model depends on physics of this problem. In most practical scenarios, these models are non-linear and the densities involved are non-Gaussian. In computer vision, particle filtering has been proven very successful for non-linear and non-Gaussian estimation problems. Their complexity is related to the number of particles N, the nonlinear functions in the model and weight evaluation stage. Hence for meeting speed requirements of real time applications, it is necessary to have high throughput designs with ability to process a larger number of particles in a given time. In the hardware implementation of PFs algorithms, the choices available are to either use a digital signal processor (DSP), a field-programmable gate array (FPGA) or an application specific IC (ASIC). Recently, many approaches on the hardware implementation of particle filters have drawn attention [5], resulting in an FPGA prototype for a particle filter algorithm but without any parallelization. As part of that effort, the authors have developed an architecture for a digital hardware implementation of particle filters along with efficient resampling algorithms. Their initial attempt was evaluated on TI TMS320C54x DSP for bearings-only tracker algorithm. By using a Xilinx Virtex II Pro FPGA, they achieved a maximum sampling frequency of 50 kHz for a similar application. This later led to an application specific integrated circuit (ASIC) implementation for realizing certain stages in the particle filter algorithm.

Regarding parallel implementation of the particle filter, many works have shown that the particle filter is immediately parallelizable since there are no data dependencies among particles. The resampling, which is inherently sequential, has been modified in order to allow for parallel implementation. Therefore, most of the works on parallel particle filters focus on designing a resampling step suitable for parallel implementation. Efficient methods to address this in hardware can be found in [6], [9]. Furthermore, in a recent paper [7], the authors present an implementation on an SIMD parallel processor of an object tracker based on a color-based particle filter. They proposed different parallel resampling methods and proposed architectures for effective implementation of these methods. Other interesting implementation strategy was done using General Purpose Graphical Processing Units (GP-GPUs) [8]. The authors explored the implementation of multi-cue based face tracking algorithm on dedicated processors and demonstrated the efficiency of two parallel computing techniques.

3   Face Tracking with Particle Filter

In our approach, we develop a real time moving object tracking algorithm through a sequence of video that relies on particle filter. Tracking objects in video involves the modeling of non-linear and non-gaussian systems. The particle filter can be employed by using a probabilistic framework which formulates tracking problems as a Hidden Markov Model (HMM). The state of the tracked object at time t is donated s_t, which represents unobserved state (hidden position) of the object, and its history is $S = \{s_1...s_t\}$. Similarly, the temporal data sequence (images) features at time t is z_t with history is $Z = \{z_1...z_t\}$. From a Bayesian perspective, the tracking problem is to recursively compute the posterior state-density of the state s_t at time t, taking different values, given the data $z_{0:t}$ up to time t.

Generally, the particle filter consists of four main steps: 1) Sampling step, Generation of new particles around the estimated state of the previous frame, in which M particles s_t^m for $m = \{1...M\}$ are generated from old sample set s_{t-1}^m using an importance function

$$\hat{s}_t^m \approx \pi(s_t \backslash s_{0:t-1}^m, z_t) \tag{1}$$

2) Weight measurement, assigns importance weights ω_t^m for each newly generated samples based on the received observation. This step is the most computationally intensive

and generally involves the computation of transcendental trigonometric and exponential functions.

$$\hat{\omega}_t^m \propto \omega_{t-1}^m \frac{P(z_t \backslash s_t^m) P(s_t \backslash s_{t-1}^m)}{\pi(s_t^m \backslash s_{0:t-1}^m, z_{1:t-1})} \tag{2}$$

3) State estimation obtains the final state vector of face by newly generated samples and its weights 4) Resampling step where the input is an array of the weights of the particles and the output is an array of indices of which particles are going to propagate forward. The first three steps form the particle filter Sequential Importance Sampling (SIS) filter. The filter that performs all the four operations is the Sample Importance Resampling Filter (SIRF). To start object tracking, the proposed application is based on skin color detection which is performed on the input image. A SIRF is applied then for tracking the position s_t of the region of interest (in this paper we are interested in tracking the human face). In the following, the steps contained in this proposed tracking approach will be described in further detail.

3.1 Skin Detection Using Color

In the following, we present a conceptually simple approach for face detection. Skin color [2] is a distinguishing feature of human faces. In a controlled environment, the skin detection can be efficient to locate faces in images. The skin detection technique is summarized in figure 1. This method used the thresholding(a) of RGB color space for skin detection, segmentation technique (b) and region labeling (c) in order to separate the face region (d). The rectangular region of the face (e) is used as the reference face model through a sequence of video.

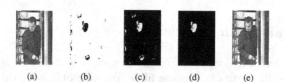

(a)   (b)   (c)   (d)   (e)

Fig. 1. Face detection using skin color

3.2 Color Based Tracking Approach

We have developed a color based particle filter. We have modeled the states, as it location and color in each frame of the video. For implementation of particle filter, we pick M rectangular regions $\{s_t^0 ... s_t^M\}$ within the object to be tracked. Each rectangle s_t^m is represented by the mean (x, y, h, s, v) position and color of the pixels within region s_t^m (other color spaces can be considered similarly). Since we use the SIRF, the importance density becomes only dependent on z_t) and s_{t-1}) which is given by:

$$\pi(s_{0:t} \backslash z_{0:t}) = p(s_t \backslash s_{t-1}^m, z_t) \tag{3}$$

Consequently, the recurrence relations (1) and (2) are simplified and formed the basis for the optimal Bayesian solution:

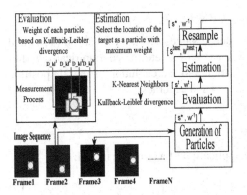

Fig. 2. Particle filter scheme

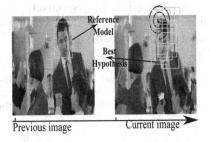

Fig. 3. Particle generation within the search window

- For the mth sample

$$s_t^m \approx p(s_t \backslash s_{t-1}^m) \qquad (4)$$

- For the mth sample, the weight assignment equation is :

$$\omega_t^m = \omega_{t-1}^m p(z_t \backslash s_t^m) \qquad (5)$$

Figure 2 outlines an iteration of the particle filter algorithm. The performance of the filter has been tested on a rolling ball sequence. The actual frame (example we take here frame 2) of the sequence is loaded and M samples are taken using (x,y) coordinates of upper-left corner stored in each particle. Particle weights computation is based on the distinctive features that can be followed from frame to frame around the region of interest instead of performing an exhaustive search over the whole image. In order to improve weights computation, we have chosen to get an estimation of the Kullback-Leibler divergence from the Kth Nearest Neighbor (KNN). The particle with the maximum weight s_t^{max} is selected as best candidate for the state of the system in the iteration. In order to track moving objects efficiently, we perform a resampling stage (see Figure 2) evaluating previous particle weights and concentrating particles around the most probable states, discarding those with lower weights. For subsequent frames, the tracking algorithm confines its search space to an area centered on the location found in the previous frame(see Figure 3). A detailed description of the tracking algorithm is presented in the following sections.

3.3 Face Model

The Object model for tracking in image processing is based on properties of the object (i.e. the object motion, shape, color or appearance from the model between consecutive video frames). To define the problem of tracking, we consider that the state sequence s_t of a target given by: $s_t = \{X_t, Y_t, W, H\}$ where s_t is a rectangle which represents the Region-of-Interest (ROI), (X_t, Y_t) is the position of upper-left corner of the rectangle and W, H are the width and the height of the rectangle respectively. In our methods, the face model is defined by:

$$P_t = \alpha_x P_x + \alpha_y P_y + \alpha_h P_h + \alpha_s P_s + \alpha_v P_v \tag{6}$$

where $\alpha_x, \alpha_y, \alpha_h, \alpha_s$ and α_v are the confidence values of the 2D position (x, y) and color space (H, S, V) respectively. The values can be determined empirically by human. The combination of the color information and the evolution of the 2D position achieve excellent performance in term of speed and accuracy.

3.4   Evolution and Observation Model

The sample set is propagated through the application of a dynamic model:

$$s_t = s_{t-1} + \Omega_{t-1} \tag{7}$$

where Ω_{t-1} indicates the Gaussian noises. To weigh the sample set, we will estimate the state vector s_t at discrete times with the help of system observations which are realizations of the stochastic process z_t governed by the measurement equation. The observations are available at discrete times according to:

$$p(z_t \backslash s_t) \approx \exp(-\mu D_{kl}) \tag{8}$$

where D_{kl} is the Kullback-Leibler divergence between the reference and the target frames. The aim of the likelihood distribution $p(z_t \backslash s_t)$ is to determine in successive frames the region which best matches, in terms of a similarity measure. This similarity between the template and the current image can be measured by the distance between them. As we will see later, this distance is expressed from the samples using the Kth Nearest Neighbour framework (KNN). Then, the samples are located around the maximum of the Kullback-Leibler coefficient which represents the best match to the target model.

3.5   Kullback-Leibler Divergence Approximation Using the Kth Nearest Neighbour Algorithm

As we want to favor samples whose color distributions are similar to the target model, the Kullback-Leibler divergence is used for the weighting[3]:

$$D_{kl}(R, T) = \int_R f_T(s) \frac{\log(f_T(s))}{\log(f_R(s))} \, ds \tag{9}$$

Distance (10) can be decomposed as follows:

$$D_{kl}(R, T) = \int_R f_T(s) \log(f_T(s)) \, ds - \int_R f_T(s) \log(f_R(s)) \, ds = -H(T) + H_X(T, R) \tag{10}$$

where H is the differential entropy and H_X is the cross entropy, also called relative entropy or likelihood. Initially, ROI is defined in a reference frame and the purpose is to determine the ROI in subsequent target frames in video sequences. The proposed algorithm tracks a ROI by determining the similarity measures between the reference and the target model using the Kullback Leibler Divergence. In this paper, we propose to

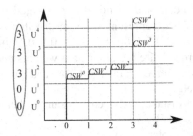

Fig. 4. Systematic resampling with non-normalized weights (M=5)

compute the Kullback-Leibler distance between two high-dimensional PDFs using the KNN framework. Since the Kullback- Leibler is a distance, the KNN-based expression of the Kullback-Leibler distance proposed for ROI tracking is the difference between a cross entropy and differential entropy [4]. The KNN estimate of this distance is given by:

$$D_{kl}(T,R) = H_{KNN}^{X}(T,R) - H_{KNN}(T) = \log(\frac{|R|}{|T-1|}) + \frac{d}{|T|}\sum_{s \in T}\log(\frac{\rho_k(R,s)}{\rho_k(T,s)}) \quad (11)$$

where $\rho_k(R,s)$, $\rho_k(T,s)$ are the distance to the Kth nearest neighbor of s in R and T respectively excluding the sample located at s if any.

3.6   Systematic Resampling in SIR

The particles are resampled to generate an unweighted particle set according to their importance weights to avoid degeneracy. Standard algorithms used for resampling such as residual resampling (RR), branching corrections, systematic resampling (SR)[4]. The proposed algorithm in this paper uses the systematic resampling algorithm. The Resampled particles are drawn proportional to this distribution to replace the original set. The SR concept for a PF that used 5 particles is shown in figure 3. First the cumulative sum of weights (CSW) of sampled particles is computed. Then, as shown on the y axis of the graph, a function u(m) called the resampling function is systematically updated and compared with the CSW of the particles. The corresponding particles are replicated to form the resampled set which for this case is $\{x(0), x(0), x(3), x(3), x(3)\}$. This method eliminates particles with low weight and keeps more particles in more probable regions.

3.7   The Proposed Particle Filter Algorithm

We can now specify the algorithm in detail as fellows. The face tracking algorithm is separated into two main stages: automatic initialization and particle filter tracking. The principle of the proposed algorithm is described in detail bellow.

1. Initialization(automatic)(Reference face template updating).
2. Particle filter tracking:
   Using cumulative measurement up to time t, $Z = (z_1...z_t)$, our aim is to estimate $[s_t^m, \omega_t^m]_{m=0}^{M} = Function([s_{t-1}^m, \omega_{t-1}^m]_{m=0}^{M}, z_t))$.

- Simulate M independent and identically distributed random samples (Randomly chosen particles to represent posterior distribution by generating a random number $\delta_x \in \;]-0.5, 0.5[$, $\delta_y \in \;]-0.5, 0.5[$ uniformly distributed). $[s_t^m, \omega_t^m]_{m=0}^M$ (where ω_t^m are the associated weights and M is the number of particles). Given the observed data z_t at t, for each particle $m = 0 ... M$ do:
- Calculate face model.
- Calculate Euclidean distance between the sample feature vector P_t and the reference feature vector P_r.
- Calculate Kullback-Leibler distance.
- Weight measurement: For the mth, we obtain its weights ω_t^m by a Kullback-Leibler similarity function as shown in Equation (10). So we obtain the final weight for the mth as:
$$\omega_t^m \approx \exp(-\mu D_{kl})$$
3. Estimating state parameters at time step: calculate mean position of each target using a weighted average of the particles.
4. Resampling step $[s_t^m, \omega_t^m]_{m=0}^M$ to obtain new set of particles $[s_t^m, \hat{\omega}_t^m]_{m=0}^M$ (using the above-mentioned resampling algorithm).

4   The Proposed Multi-processors System on Chip Design Methodology

Due to the increasing complexity of MP-SoC architectures, software and hardware designers as well as system architects are facing completely new challenges. Optimization of interconnects among processors and memories becomes important as multiple processors and memories can be integrated on a MP-SoC since it may target multiple objectives: application performance, power consumption/energy, temperature, small chip area, etc. Consequently, high performance embedded design must aim to obtain an ideal balance between hardware constraints and performance constraints. As well, developing processors network systems tailored to a particular application domain is critical and design-time consuming in order to achieve high performance customized solutions. The effectiveness of such approaches largely depends on the availability of an ad hoc design methodology. To meet the performance and cost constraints, architectures are often heterogeneous with multiple differentiated processors, complex memory hierarchy and hardware accelerators. However, for programming these architectures efficiently, hardware description languages (HDL), such as Verilog or VHDL, have to be used. Many application developers are not familiar with these HDL languages, because they traditionally develop their applications using high-level and software related design languages such as C, C++ or Matlab. Consequently, the programmers have to focus on low-level system issues and they have to manage low level communication problems such as deadlocks. This not only distracts the programmer from the application software, but also requires a technical background rarely found among application domain experts. The need for appropriate high-level programming abstractions, capable of simplifying the programming chore without sacrificing efficiency, is forcing a move to more powerful dedicated hardware architecture and minimizing the modeling effort.

To achieve the challenge of an improved programmability, a high level design methodology for FPGA-based multiprocessor architectures is introduced. Therefore, our research interests are based mainly on fast prototyping tools which enable the parallelization of real-time signal and image algorithms in a homogeneous communicating processor network. The ultimate aim is to propose new optimized design methodology under performance constraints. Based on Multi-Processors concept, our approach proposes an original design flow for the fast prototyping of image processing on a MP-SoC architecture. The proposed MP-SoC methodology is based on two essential concepts. First, it consists in the derivation of a generic architecture based on a HNCP (Homogeneous Network of Communicating Processors). The second feature, parallelization of the sequential code on the different soft-core performed using specific communication functions based on Parallel Skeleton concept, such as SCM (Split Compute and Merge) for data or static task parallelism, FARM for dynamic data sharing (or dynamic task sharing) and PIPE for task-parallel parallelism. In fact, PIPE represents staged computation where parallelism can be achieved by computing different stages simultaneously and each stage may be a nested skeleton pattern.

4.1   The HNCP (Homogeneous Network of Communicating Processors)

Since architectures for real-time image processing need to manage a large amount of data and work within real-time requirements, the use of parallelism is a fundamental part of most of these systems. In our approach, we have only concentrated to MIMD-DM (Multiple Instruction Multiple Data with Distributed Memory) architectures which permit the design of several types of parallelism (data, task and flow parallelism). Communication between nodes is realized thanks to the well-known message passing communication model. We chose this architecture because of its ability to execute a large range of parallel scheme efficiently (data and task parallelism, pipeline). The interconnection network is a static network with regular hypercube topology. This kind of topology is characterized by a dimension D which is related to the number of processors (nodes) N by the formula $N = 2^D$ (diameter D is maximum distance between two processors).

In order to enable communication between processors, we have also provided the choice of several communication link types, ranging from a simple FIFO point to point communication, to more complex solutions such as DMA point to point links or a Network on Chip (NoC) based on a packet router. This architecture is homogeneous. As seen from the figure 4, each node comprises the same identical components (soft processor, with local memory for application software and data storage, and a communication device).

4.2   Architecture Generation and HNCP Configuration via CubeGen Tool

In order to reduce the time and effort needed to design a network of communicating processors, we have developed a tool called CubeGen (see figure 5). It enables to automate the configuration file creation dedicated to the Embedded Development Kit (EDK) of Xilinx Company. This .mhs file contains the description of the system with the connection between the different IPs. The designer has to specify, via a graphical interface, the different parameters chosen for the network: network dimension, number of stages, MicroBlaze parametrization, memory size allocated to each processor, type of communication link and use or not of the special IP for I/O (VHDL block designed to control the

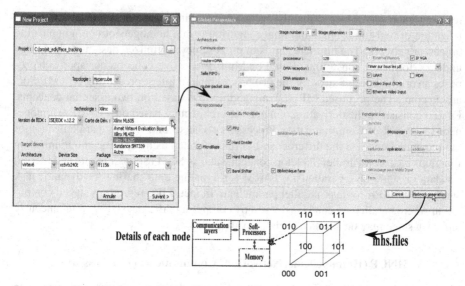

Fig. 5. GUI of the CubeGen tool

I/O directly from the video flow). CubeGen automates the high level description of the HNCP in few seconds. The designer launches the synthesis of the system with specific target to check if this configuration of the HNCP can be implemented. This methodology matches perfectly with the concept of fast prototyping on SoPC. The designer obtains quickly an architecture tailored for the target application. Moreover, CubeGen provides a well-suited library (regarding architecture configuration choice) of specific lightweight communication functions that facilitate conversion from sequential algorithm to a parallel C code.

4.3   Proposed Design Flow

Fig. 6 shows the proposed design flow starting from a high-level description for both: the FPGA-based multiprocessor systems and the sequential algorithm. In fact, this applications are programmed using imperative languages such as C, C++. Thanks to a CubeGen tool, an Homogeneous Network of Communicating Processors (HNCP) is automatically generated using a set of available IPs. CubeGen also generates specific lightweight communication functions that are tuned to the network configuration (number of processors, communication links, parallelization scheme...). With these communication functions, designer can easily convert sequential algorithm into a parallel C code. Thus the whole system is instantiated on SoPC Xilinx platform. If HW architecture does not meet area constraints, a first loop enables to re-configure the HNCP thanks to CubeGen. Furthermore, our approach offers the possibility to simulate the whole system before synthesizing the code. Using ModelSim, the application is executed on the architecture and the execution behavior is captured. All the relevant characteristics for performance estimation can then be easily extracted: application throughput, maximum latency, utilization rate of resources, etc. According to the estimated performance, the

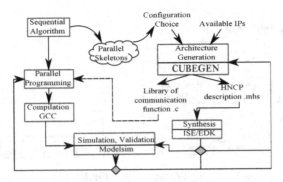

Fig. 6. The proposed design flow

designer can change the architecture configuration and/or modify the parallel application to converge to a suitable solution. Finally, the complete architecture is implemented using high-level design tools such as the Embedded Development KIT (EDK) from Xilinx to generate the bitstream that configures the FPGA and even upload it.

5   Parallel Particle Filter Algorithm on HNCP

In our implementation of face tracking algorithm, several independent parallel data (particles) are generated. In practice, we generate M number of particles in the region of high interest (i.e. around the tracked object) for each iteration. As shown in figure 3, this search window is variable from one frame to another . A straight-forward method to apply the farm skeleton with this specific application is to associate a work element for each generated particle since all the particles are independents. Therefore, we will focus to implement our tracking algorithm using dynamic data with the enhanced Farm skeleton provided by our skeleton library. Our skeleton library offers a pre-implemented function dedicated to farm implementation for initialisation (init-farm), synchronization (synchro) and work distribution (farm). The designer can use directly these functions to shorten parallel programming.In the data-farming case, work-item represents a sub data set (the particles in this case). Typically, the farmer starts by sending a work-item to each worker. Then it waits for a result from a worker and immediately sends another work-item to it. This repeats until no work-items are left and the workers are no longer processing data. On the other side, each worker simply waits for a work-item, processes it and returns the result to the farmer until it receives a stop condition from the farmer. Each worker calculates the weights measurements for one sample, including three measurements from face model, Kullback-Leibler distance and weight importance.

One can see in figure 7 the parallel tracking algorithm scheme using Farm skeleton. The proposed algorithm is executed in N processors. Since M particles are generated and because the processing time is regular, each worker eventually process M/N sample. Finally, the sample weights from all processors are collected and the sample parameter with maximum weight is selected to be the final estimation for the target face. Resampling requires knowledge of sum of all particle weights. Hence it cannot begin before the weights of all the particles have been calculated. Figure 8 shows the whole

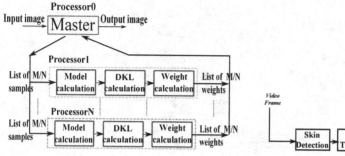

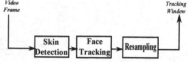

Fig. 7. Parallel face tracking using FARM

Fig. 8. FPGA Face Detection and Tracking implementation

application steps of the face detection and tracking methods (including the skin detection step) of the FPGA implementation. The skin detection is delivered sequentially by the master processor. The advantage of the hardware implementation of this type of detector is that it entails very small amounts of memory (mainly the 128 bytes for the BRAM) and it gives sensible results with a much lower computational cost.

6 Experimental Results

This section is mainly dedicated to provide a few results concerning resource costs and the performance of the proposed architectures instantiated using CubeGen tool. We made several experiments on sequential and multi-core parallel implementation. Given a video sequence centered around the human figure, each tracking task has been initialized by manually marking the target object in the first frame. We assume in our approach the image to be recorded with stationary camera. The performance (speed) depends on the size of the search region which we have defined by enlarging the target region by one third in each direction (the model representations of all the particles are generated inside this region).

6.1 Sequential Implementation

The time of latency in the developed algorithm depends on the number of particles. For implementation of particle filter, M samples randomly generated consisting of rectangular regions are taken from the input image (Figure 9). So each particle m carries information of $\{x_t^m, y_t^m\}$ subwindow coordinates $m = 0...M$ and a weight between the target color window in the current frame and the reference color window. The color window with the maximum weight s_t^{max} is chosen as best candidate for the face. As first step, for each image, the results produced by a C implementation of the face tracking running on a standard 3 GHz PC with 3 GB RAM, is below $35ms$. The number of search window (particles) is set to 100 in order to be better concentrated around the true state. The size of the search window (face) $H_{Particle}$x$W_{Particle}$ varies among different video sequence. For the sequential implementation on FPGA platform, we use a 32-bit RISC soft core processor, MicroBlaze, which is developed as soft IP by Xilinx Company, running at 200 MHz with 128k data and instruction memory (BRAM).

(a)   (b)   (c)   (d)   (e)

Fig. 9. A color-based target model and the different hypotheses (Blue rectangle) that are calculated with the particle filter. The yellow rectangle represents the expected object location.

The proposed hardware architecture has been implemented on a Xilinx ML605 FPGA development board. In a video sequence, this implementation has an output latency of approximately $160ms$ with 20 particles. The resampling step is a bottleneck in the SIRF execution as it cannot be parallelizable with other operations. Regarding the computation times, it should be mentioned that the proposed tracking algorithm requires more than 94% of the total execution time without the resampling. Consequently, one can often expect and frequently achieve an improvement in performance by using far more particle. Thus, the benefit of the parallel implementation becomes much important to propose a faster and more efficient real-time particle filters.

6.2   Parallel Implementation

To first get a sense of the presented architecture implementations in terms of FPGA resource usage and clock frequency, we present a number of experiments in which we show the FPGA synthesis results and the execution times of the proposed algorithm. Table 1 shows FPGA resource usage and synthesis results for different size of HNCP architecture configurations targeting a Xilinx Virtex-6 XC6VLX240T FPGA. For each node of the hypercube, there is one processor (MicroBlaze) with 128Kb of local memory. This tables shows that the router-DMA communication device takes a significant part of the resources needed by the whole network of processors. This proportion increases progressively from nearly 66% for a 4 nodes network to more than 75% for a 32 nodes network [10]. As expected, increasing the number of core leads to higher speed up and negatively impacts the area occupied. We would like to make a comparison in terms of number of particles and the speedup. In order to investigate the performance with different sizes of network, we set the particle number to 65 particle and the computing core from 1 to 16 (dimension of HNCP D=1...4 i.e. 2^D node). The performance figure is shown in figure 10. The computing result is from one person (one face) in the investigate frame. In each experiment, we vary the number of particles evaluations that can be processed in real-time with different sizes of HNCP. Example speedup graph for an image resolution of 256x192 is shown in figure 11. Some differences in processing time between experimental findings and theoretical assumptions are due mainly to communication effects. The ideal graph represents a parallel implementation in which all processors operate 100% efficiency, communication overheads could be ignored between processors and assumes static task execution times. In reality, efficiency will be less than 100% due the communication cost and the residual sequential overheads are taken into account by applying Amdahl's law. For this parallel implementation and from up to 16 processors, communication cost (which is a sequential part) becomes

Table 1. FPGA Resource utilization of target device(Xilinx xc6v2x240tff 1156-1)

Dimension	Slice Registers	Slice LUTs	Block RAM/FIFO
1	12057(4%)	15720(10%)	104(25%)
2	27626(9%)	27312(18%)	288(68%)
3	56458(18%)	52909(35%)	381(91%)
4	114547(38%)	102489(68%)	405(97%)

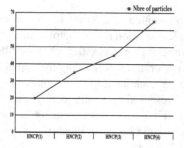

Fig. 10. FPGA particle number

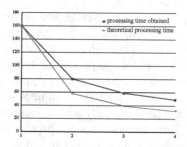

Fig. 11. FPGA processing time results

significant. In practice, the speedup of a program using multiple processors in parallel computing is limited by the time needed for the sequential fraction of the program. However, the remaining sequential algorithm part in the parallel algorithm (sample generation and resampling steps) represents a minor part of the processing time in the sequential implementation. Hence, the performance of the proposed algorithms is rarely close to the theoretical speedup. From figure 11, we can observe that effectively the number of particles M increases with the size of HNCP architecture. There is significant gain in increasing the level of parallelism when M/N becomes small. The time of resampling (including the time needed to select the location of target as a particle with maximum weight) use less than 7% of the execution time so does not significantly affect the total time of execution. Consequently, it is possible to implement the major bottleneck of the algorithm (the computation of the color model and, the particle weights) in a parallel manner suitable for our HNCP architecture, but also that the non-parallelizable steps can be implemented efficiently. The experimental results demonstrate that the parallel Farm scheme can achieve a good speedup compared to the corresponding sequential algorithms. In real practice, we can achieve a speed of at least 17 frames per second. The percentage of correct face tracking is over 95%, depended on the number of particles M. As a conclusion, the presented architecture achieves the best performance and its throughput scales very well as the number of cores increases.

7   Conclusions

The proposed design methodology addresses the challenging problem of efficient design of embedded systems for complex and demanding high performance applications. Our overall hardware implementation method is based upon meeting algorithm processing power requirements and communication needs. The hardware architecture, which is the physical support for execution, is generated with a graphic environment called CubeGen. This tool is the key to enhance the flexibility and the performance during design space exploration. Furthermore, our strategy uses specific communication functions based on a parallel skeleton library which enables users to develop parallel programs as if they were sequential ones by composing suitable skeletons. To evaluate the entire design flow of the current approach, this article shows with a practical case (tracking object) a real time embedded vision application and presents both software and hardware implementation with performance results on a Xilinx SoPC target. The prototyping results show that the proposed architecture speeds up significantly the execution time and has shown a good performance with real images. This allows us to propose a particle filter framwork for fast face tracking to achieve real time performance using our HNCP architecture.

References

1. Diaconis, P.: Sequential monte carlo methods in practice. Journal of the American Statistical Association 98, 496–497 (2003)
2. Vezhnevets, V., Sazonov, V., Andreeva, A.: A survey on pixel-based skin color detection techniques. In: Proc. GRAPHICON 2003, pp. 85–92 (2003)
3. Boltz, S., Debreuve, É., Barlaud, M.: High dimensional statistical measure for region-of-interest tracking. IEEE Transactions on Image Processing 18, 1266–1283 (2009)
4. Bolić, M.: Architectures for efficient implementation of particle filters. PhD thesis, Stony Brook University, New York (2004)
5. Athalye, A., Bolić, M., Hong, S., Djurić, P.M.: Generic hardware architectures for sampling and resampling in particle filters, EURASIP J. Applied Signal Processing 17, 2888–2902 (2005)
6. Bolić, M., Athalye, A., Djuric, P., Hong, S.: Algorithmic modification of particle filter for hardware implementation. In: Proceedings of the European Signal Processing Conference (EUSIPROC), Vienna, Austria (2004)
7. Medeiros, H., Park, J., Kak, A.: A parallel implementation of the color-based particle filter for object tracking. In: IEEE Computer Society Conference on Computer Vision and Pattern Recognition Workshops, Anchorage, AK, pp. 1–8 (2008)
8. Liu, K., Zhang, T., Wang, L.: A new parallel video understanding and retrieval system. In: ICME 2010, pp. 679–684 (2010)
9. Sutharsan, S., Sinha, A., Kirubarajan, T., Farooq, M.: An optimization based parallel particle filter for multitarget tracking. In: Proceedings of the Spie, vol. 5913, pp. 87–98 (2005)
10. Damez, L., Siéler, L., Dérutin, J.P., Landrault, A.: Embedding of a real time image stabilization algorithm on a parameterizable SoPC architecture a chip multiprocessor approach. Journal of Real-Time Image Processing (February 2010)

Veridical Perception of 3D Objects in a Dynamic Stereoscopic Augmented Reality System

Manuela Chessa, Matteo Garibotti, Andrea Canessa, Agostino Gibaldi,
Silvio P. Sabatini, and Fabio Solari

Department of Informatics, Bioengineering, Robotics, and Systems Engineering,
University of Genoa, Italy
manuela.chessa@unige.it
http://www.pspc.unige.it

Abstract. Augmented reality environments, where humans can interact with both virtual and real objects, are a powerful tool to achieve a natural human-computer interaction. The recent diffusion of off-the-shelf stereoscopic visualization displays and motion capture devices has paved the way for the development of effective augmented reality systems at affordable costs. However, with the conventional approaches an user freely moving in front of a 3D display could experience a misperception of the 3D position and of the shape of virtual objects. Such distortions can have serious consequences in scientific and medical fields, where a veridical perception is required, and they can cause visual fatigue in consumer and entertainment applications. In this paper, we develop an augmented reality system, based on a novel stereoscopic rendering technique, capable to correctly render 3D virtual objects to an user that changes his/her position in the real world and acts in the virtual scenario. The proposed rendering technique has been tested in a static and in a dynamic augmented reality scenario by several observers. The obtained results confirm the improvement of the developed solution with respect to the standard systems.

Keywords: Stereoscopic display, Virtual reality, 3D Visualization, Eye tracking, Dynamic stereoscopic rendering, 3D Position judgment, Human-computer interaction.

1 Introduction

In the last decade, there has been a rapidly growing interest in technologies for presenting stereo 3D imagery both for professional applications, e.g. scientific visualization, medicine and rehabilitation system [1–3], and for entertainment applications, e.g. 3D cinema and videogames [4].

With the diffusion of 3D stereo visualization techniques, researchers have investigated the benefits and the problem associated with them. Several studies devised some specific geometrical parameters of the stereo acquisition setup (both actual and virtual) in order to induce the perception of depth in a human observer [5]. In this way, we can create stereo pairs that are displayed on stereoscopic devices for human observers

G. Csurka et al. (Eds.): VISIGRAPP 2012, CCIS 359, pp. 274–285, 2013.

which do not introduce vertical disparity, and thus causing no discomfort to the users [6]. Yet, other factors, related to spatial imperfections of the stereo image pair, that yield visual discomfort have been addressed. In [7] the authors experimentally determined the level of discomfort experienced by a human observer viewing imperfect binocular image pairs, with a wide range of possible imperfections and distortions. Moreover, in the literature there are several works that describe the difficulty of perceptually rendering a large interval of 3D space without a visual stress, since the eyes of the observer have to maintain accommodation on the display screen (i.e., at a fixed distance), thus lacking the natural relationship between accommodation and vergence eye movements, and the distance of the objects [8]. The vergence-accommodation conflict is out of the scope of this paper, however for a recent review see [9].

Besides the previously cited causes of discomfort, another well-documented problem is that the 3D position of objects, thus their 3D shape, and the scene layout are often misperceived by a viewer freely positioned in front of stereoscopic displays [10]. Only few works in the literature address the problem of examining depth judgment in augmented or virtual reality environments in the peripersonal space (i.e. distances less than 1.5 m). Among them, [11] investigated depth estimation via a reaching task, but in their experiment the subjects could not freely move in front of the display. Moreover, only correcting methods useful in specific situation, e.g. see [12, 13], or complex and expensive systems [14] are proposed in the literature. Nevertheless, to the knowledge of the authors, there are no works that aim to quantitatively analyze the 3D shape distortions, their consequences on the perception of the scene layout, and to propose an effective and general solution for an observer that freely moves in front of a 3D monitor.

In entertainment applications such distortions can cause visual fatigue and stress. Moreover, in medical and surgery applications, or in cognitive rehabilitation systems and in applications for the study of the visuo-motor coordination, they can have serious implications. This is especially true in augmented reality (AR) applications, where the user perceives real and virtual stimuli at the same time, thus it is necessary that the rendering of the 3D information does not introduce undesired distortions.

In this paper, we propose a rendering technique, the True Dynamic 3D (TD3D), and an AR system capable to minimize the 3D shape misperception problem that arises when the viewer changes his/her position with respect to the screen, thus yielding a natural interaction with the virtual environment. The performances of the developed system are quantitatively assessed and compared to the results obtained by using a conventional system, through experimental sessions with the aim of measuring the user's perception of the 3D positions of virtual objects and the effectiveness of his/her interaction in the AR environment.

The paper is organized as follow: in Section 2 we describe the geometry of the standard stereoscopic 3D rendering technique, the misperception associated with the movements of the observer, and the developed TD3D solution; Section 3 describes the AR system we have developed; Section 4 presents two experimental studies designed to validate the proposed approach; the conclusions are discussed in Section 5.

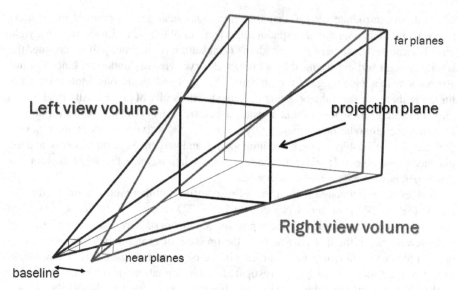

far planes

Left view volume

projection plane

Right view volume

near planes

baseline

Fig. 1. The two skewed frustums for the off-axis technique

2   The Geometry of the Stereoscopic 3D Rendering Technique

2.1   The Standard Approach

To create the stereo 3D stimuli for the conventional approach, we have adopted the stereo rendering, based on the method known as "parallel axis asymmetric frustum perspective projection", or off-axis technique [5, 15], the technique usually used to generate a perception of depth for a human observer. In the off-axis technique, the stereo images are obtained by projecting the objects in the scene onto the display plane for each camera; such projection plane has the same position and orientation for both camera projections (see Fig. 1).

We have also taken into account the geometrical parameters necessary to correctly create stereo pairs displayed on stereoscopic devices for human observer [5]. In particular:

- the image planes have to be parallel;
- the optical points should be offset relative to the center of the image;
- the distance between the two optical centers have to be equal to the interpupillary distance;
- the field of view of the cameras must be equal to the angle subtended by the display screen;
- the ratio between the focal length of the cameras and the viewing distance of the screen should be equal to the ratio between the width of the screen and of the image plane.

Moreover, as in [7], one should take into account the problem of spatial imperfection that could cause visual discomfort to the user, such as:

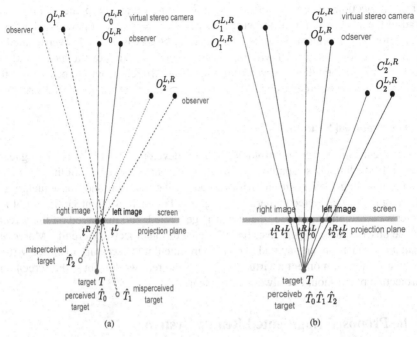

Fig. 2. A sketch of geometry of the stereoscopic augmented reality environment when using the standard stereo rendering technique (a), and when using the proposed TD3D approach (b). (a) In the virtual environment a target is positioned in T, and a stereo camera is placed in $C_0^{L,R}$, thus generating the left and right projections t^L and t^R on the projection plane. A real observer in the same position $O_0^{L,R}$ of the virtual camera will perceive the target correctly, whereas he/she will misperceive the position ($\hat{T}_1$ and $\hat{T}_2$) of the target when looking at the screen from different positions ($O_1^{L,R}$ and $O_2^{L,R}$). (b) In the proposed technique, the virtual camera is moved accordingly to the different positions of the observer's eyes. This yields different projections of the target ($t_0^L, t_0^R; t_1^L, t_1^R; t_2^L, t_2^R$) on the projection plane, thus allowing a coherent perception of the target for the observer.

- crosstalk, that is a transparent overlay of the left image over the right image and vice versa;
- blur, that is different resolutions of the stereo image pair.

2.2 Misperception with the Standard Approach

The previously mentioned rules are commonly considered when designing stereoscopic virtual reality systems. Nevertheless, when looking at a virtual scene, in order to obtain a veridical perception of the 3D scene layout, the observer must be positioned in the same position of the virtual stereo camera. If the observer is in the correct position, then the retinal images originated by viewing the 3D stereo display, and the ones originated by looking at the real scene are identical [10]. If this constraint is not satisfied, a misperception of the object's position and depth occurs (see Fig. 2a).

In Figure 2a, a virtual stereo camera positioned in C_0 (for the sake of simplicity, denoting both the positions of the left (C_0^L) and right (C_0^R) cameras) determines the left and right projections t^L and t^R of the target T on the projection plane. An observer located in the same position of the virtual camera ($O_0 = C_0$) will perceive the target in a position $\hat{T}_0$ coincident with the true position. Otherwise, an observer located in a different position ($O_i \neq C_0$) will experience a misperception of the location of the target ($\hat{T}_i \neq T$). When the observer is in a location different from the position of the virtual camera, he misperceives both the position of the object and its spatial structure.

2.3   The Proposed Solution

To overcome the misperception problem, we have developed the TD3D rendering technique. Such a technique is capable of compensating for the movement of the observer's eyes by computing their positions with respect to the monitor, and consequently repositioning the virtual stereo camera (see Fig. 2b). For each different viewpoint of the observer a corresponding stereo image pair is generated, and displayed on the screen. Thus, the observer always perceives the 3D shape of the objects coherently. Moreover, to maintain a consistent augmented reality environment it is necessary to have a virtual world that is at each moment a virtual replica of the real world. Thus, the screen and the projection plane should be always coincident.

3   The Proposed Augmented Reality System

3.1   Software and Hardware Components

Considering the availability of commercial products with high performances and affordable costs, we decided to use off-the-shelf devices to design and develop our AR system. Specifically, we use the Xbox Kinect, a motion sensing input device developed by Microsoft for the Xbox 360 video game console. Based on an RGB camera and on an infrared (IR) depth sensor, this RGB-D device is capable of providing a full-body 3D motion capture. The depth sensor consists of an IR projector combined with a monochrome camera.

All the software modules are developed in C++, using Microsoft Visual Studio 10. To render the stereoscopic virtual scene in quad buffer mode we use the Coin3D graphic toolkit[1], a high level 3D graphic toolkit for developing cross-platform real time 3D visualization. To access the data provided by Microsoft XBox Kinect, we use the open source driver, released by PrimeSense[2], the company that developed the 3D technology of the Kinect. The localization and the tracking of the head and the hand rely on the framework OpenNI[3], a set of open source Application Programming Interfaces (APIs). These APIs provide support for access to natural interaction devices, allowing the body motion tracking, hand gestures and voice recognition.

The processing of the images acquired by Kinect RGB camera is performed through the OpenCV 2.4[4] library.

---

[1] www.coin3D.org
[2] www.primesense.com
[3] www.openni.org
[4] opencv.willowgarage.com

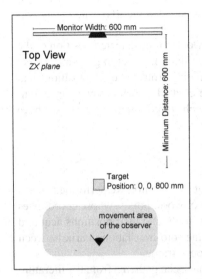
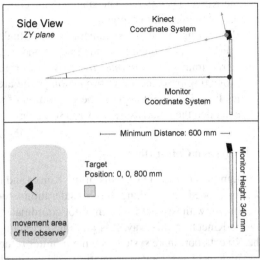

Fig. 3. The developed setup for the augmented reality system. The reported measures refer to the specific setup considered for the experimental results. The position of the target is the same of the one of the experiment shown in Figure 4.

Both the development and the testing phases have been conducted on a PC equipped with an Intel Core i7 processor, 12 GB of RAM, a Nvidia Quadro 2000 video card enabled to 3D Vision Pro with 1 GB of RAM, and a Acer HN274H 3D monitor 27-inch.

3.2   System Description

Figure 3 shows the setup scheme of our system. The XBox Kinect is located on the top of the monitor, centered on the X axis, and slightly rotated around the same axis. This configuration was chosen because it allows the Kinect to have good visibility on the user, without having the Kinect interposed between the user and the monitor.

The proposed system, during the startup phase, is responsible to recognize and track the position of the skeleton of the user. After the startup phase, each time new data is available from the Kinect, the system performs a series of steps to re-compute the representation of the 3D virtual world, and to achieve the interaction with the user. These steps can be summarized as follows:

- Detection of the positions of the user's eyes and index finger, through colored markers, in the image plane of the Kinect RGB camera. This can be achieved first by obtaining the positions of the head and of the hand from the skeleton, produced by OpenNI libraries, and then performing a segmentation and a tracking of the colored markers in the sub-images, centered in the detected positions of the head and of the hand. This image processing step is based on the color information, and is performed by using OpenCV libraries.
- Computation of the position of the eyes and of the finger in real world coordinates by combining their positions in the image plane and the corresponding depths (from

the Kinect D camera). The spatial displacement between the RGB and D cameras has been taken into account.

- Positioning of the stereo camera of the virtual world in the detected position of the user's eyes, obtained from the images and depth map. In order to generate correct stereo images, two *asymmetric frustums* originating from the eyes' positions and projecting onto the same *projection plane* are created. Since the existing graphics libraries do not support the generation of such stereoscopic frustums, we have extended the behavior of the Coin3D camera class.

3.3 System Calibration

To align the coordinate systems of the Kinect and of the monitor, we performed a calibration procedure by taking into consideration a set of world points, whose coordinates are known with respect to the monitor coordinate system, and their positions acquired by the Kinect. In this way, it is possible to obtain the roto-translation matrix between the Kinect coordinate system and the monitor reference frame.

The Kinect accuracy in estimating world points has been gathered from the literature [16]. In order to evaluate the precision of the algorithm, described in Section 3.2, in the estimation of the 3D position of the observer's eyes and of his/her finger, we performed a test session, by placing the colored marker at different distances, ranging from 500 mm to 1600 mm, from the Kinect sensor. For each position we acquired and processed several samples, Table 1 shows the uncertainty range on the localization of the 3D points.

Table 1. The uncertainty range (i.e. the standard deviations of the measures, expressed in mm) of the position estimation of the user's eyes and finger through our procedure that combines color based segmentation and depth map from the Kinect

	std min [mm]	std max [mm]
X	0.22	1.16
Y	0.24	1.44
Z	0.11	1.73

4 Experiments and Results

To quantitatively assess the proposed TD3D rendering technique and the augmented reality system, and to verify if it effectively allows a veridical perception of the 3D shape and a better interaction with the user, we have performed two types of experiments. In the first one, the observer was asked to reach a virtual target (i.e. the nearest right bottom vertex of a frontal cube whose width is 25 mm), in the second one, the task was to track the right bottom vertex of a cube along an elliptical path. In both cases, the scene has been observed by different positions, and we have acquired the position of the observer's eyes and of the finger during the execution of the tasks. The experiments have been performed both by using a standard rendering technique and the proposed

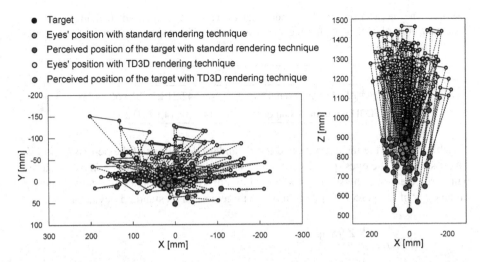

Fig. 4. Perceived positions of the target point, and the related eyes' positions for the reaching task. The perceived positions of the target with our tracking system enabled (green circles) are less scattered than the ones using a conventional system (red circles).

TD3D rendering technique that actively modifies the rendered images with respect to the position of the observer's eyes. The virtual scenes have been designed in order to minimize the effects of the depth cues other than the stereoscopic cue, such as shadows and perspective. It is worth noting that since we use a real finger to estimate the perceived depth of a virtual object, we obtain a veridical judgment of the depth. If the task is performed by using a virtual finger (a virtual replica of the finger), we obtain a relative estimation of the depth, only.

For the first experiment 12 subjects were chosen, with ages ranging from 22 to 44. The second experiment has been performed by 6 subjects, with ages ranging from 28 to 44. All participants (males and females) had normal or corrected-to-normal vision. Each subject performed the two tasks looking at the scene from different positions both with the standard and the TD3D rendering techniques.

4.1 First Experiment: 3D Position Estimation of a Static Object

Figure 4 shows the results of the first experiment.

With the TD3D rendering technique, the positions of the observer's eyes (represented by yellow circles) are spread in a smaller range than the positions acquired with the standard rendering technique (represented by cyan circles). This happens since, as a consequence of the active modification of the point of view, the target could not be visible from lateral views. This behaviour is consistent with real world situations, in which objects that are seen through a window disappear when the observer moves laterally. Nevertheless, the perceived target points with the TD3D technique and our system (green circles) are less scattered than the perceived positions of the target point with the standard rendering technique (red circles).

Table 2. The mean error and the standard deviation values (expressed in mm) of the perceived position of the target for the first experiment. The actual position of the target is $(12.5, -12.5, 812.5)$.

	X	Y	Z
standard rendering technique	49±42	31±18	81±66
TD3D rendering technique	14±10	14±7	18±14

Table 2 shows the mean errors and their standard deviations of the perceived points. The tracking of the eyes' position of the observer and the re-computation of the stereo pairs projected onto the screen, performed by our system, yield a consistent reduction in the error of the perceived position of the target and in its standard deviation.

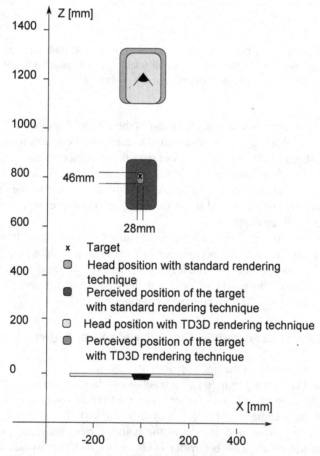

Fig. 5. Graphic representation of the results of the first experiment. The boxes are centered in the mean values of the eyes' positions and of the perceived positions of the target. The size of the boxes is represented by the standard deviation values. The smaller size of the green box represents a veridical perception (i.e. without misperception) of the position of the target.

TD3D rendering technique

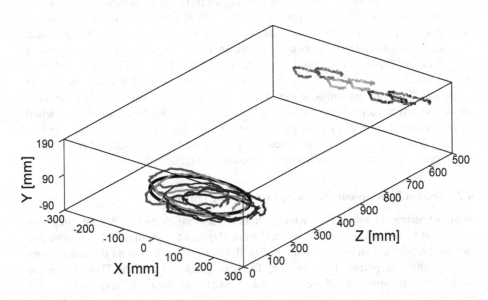

standard rendering technique

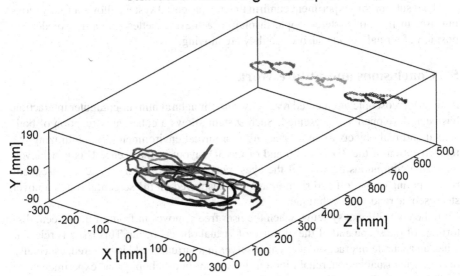

Fig. 6. Tracking of an object moving along an elliptical path, with the developed TD3D technique (top) and with the standard rendering technique (bottom). The average positions of the observers' eyes for 3 different points of observation are plotted (curves marked with circles).

A graphic representation of the scattering areas of the perceived points with respect to the movements of the observer in the two situations is shown in Figure 5. It is worth noting that the area where the target is perceived, when our tracking system is enabled, is very small, thus indicating a veridical perception of the virtual object. In particular, with the standard rendering technique, the mean and the standard deviation values of the perceived 3D points, expressed in mm, are $(18 \pm 65, -16 \pm 22, 775 \pm 102)$, whereas we obtain $(21 \pm 14, -2 \pm 7, 799 \pm 23)$ with the developed system and the TD3D technique. Since the positions of the observers are uniformly distributed in the work space, the perceived positions of the target are uniformly distributed around the actual target position (see Fig. 2), thus yielding mean values comparable between the two systems. The misperception is represented by the spread of the perceived positions of the target, that it can be quantified by the standard deviation values.

4.2 Second Experiment: Tracking of a Moving Object

In this experiment a cube whose width is 20 mm is moving along an elliptical path, from -150 mm to 150 mm in the X axis, and from 100 mm to 300 mm in the Z axis. The obtained results are shown in Figure 6. The different colors represent the acquisitions from the different points of observation. The tracks acquired with the TD3D technique are closer to the true path of the object (black line), than the tracks acquired by using the standard rendering technique. We also computed the mean errors and the standard deviations with respect to the true path of the object, obtaining a value of 50 ± 10 mm for the developed TD3D technique and of 90 ± 43 mm for the standard rendering technique.

The results of this experiment confirm that the proposed system allows a freely moving user in front of a stereoscopic display to achieve a better perception of the 3D position of virtual objects, also when they are moving.

5 Conclusions and Future Work

A novel stereoscopic augmented reality system for natural human-computer interaction has been developed and presented. Such system allows a coherent perception of both virtual and real objects to an user acting in a virtual environment, by minimizing the misperception of the 3D position and of the 3D layout of the scene. This is achieved through a continuous tracking of the eyes' position of the observer and a consequent re-computing of the left and right image pair displayed on the screen, through a novel stereoscopic rendering technique.

In the conventional systems, when the user freely moves in front of the screen, distortions of the shape and of the distance of virtual objects occur. This issue is relevant when an accurate interaction of a real observer in a virtual world is required, especially in scientific visualization, rehabilitation systems, or in psychophysical experiments.

The proposed system relies on off-the-shelf technologies (i.e., Microsoft XBox Kinect for the tracking, and a 3D monitor with shutter glasses for the rendering) and it allows a natural interaction between the user and the virtual environment, without adding significant delay in the rendering process.

The performances of the developed augmented reality system has been assessed by a quantitative analysis in reaching and tracking tasks. The results have been compared with the ones obtained by using a conventional system that does not track the position of the eyes. The results confirmed a better perception of the 3D position of the objects obtained with the proposed system.

Acknowledgements. This work has been partially supported by "Progetto di Ricerca di Ateneo 2010", and by the Italian National Project "PRIN 2008".

References

1. Subramanian, S., Knaut, L., Beaudoin, C., McFadyen, B., Feldman, A., Levin, M.: Virtual reality environments for post-stroke arm rehabilitation. Journal of NeuroEngineering and Rehabilitation 4, 20–24 (2007)
2. Ferre, P., Aracil, R., Sanchez-Uran, M.: Stereoscopic human interfaces. IEEE Robotics & Automation Magazine 15, 50–57 (2008)
3. Knaut, L.A., Subramanian, S.K., McFadyen, B.J., Bourbonnais, D., Levin, M.F.: Kinematics of pointing movements made in a virtual versus a physical 3-dimensional environment in healthy and stroke subjects. Archives of Physical Medicine and Rehabilitation 90, 793–802 (2009)
4. Kratky, A.: Re-viewing 3D – Implications of the Latest Developments in Stereoscopic Display Technology for a New Iteration of 3D Interfaces in Consumer Devices. In: Cipolla Ficarra, F.V., de Castro Lozano, C., Pérez Jiménez, M., Nicol, E., Kratky, A., Cipolla-Ficarra, M. (eds.) ADNTIIC 2010. LNCS, vol. 6616, pp. 112–120. Springer, Heidelberg (2011)
5. Grinberg, V., Podnar, G., Siegel, M.: Geometry of binocular imaging. In: Proc. of the IS&T/SPIE Symp. on Electronic Imaging, Stereoscopic Displays and Applications, vol. 2177, pp. 56–65 (1994)
6. Southard, D.: Transformations for stereoscopic visual simulation. Computers & Graphics 16, 401–410 (1992)
7. Kooi, F., Toet, A.: Visual comfort of binocular and 3D displays. Displays 25, 99–108 (2004)
8. Wann, J.P., Rushton, S., Mon-Williams, M.: Natural problems for stereoscopic depth perception in virtual environments. Vision Research 35, 2731–2736 (1995)
9. Shibata, T., Kim, J., Hoffman, D.M., Banks, M.S.: The zone of comfort: Predicting visual discomfort with stereo displays. Journal of Vision 11, 1–29 (2011)
10. Held, R.T., Banks, M.S.: Misperceptions in stereoscopic displays: a vision science perspective. In: Proceedings of the 5th Symposium on Applied Perception in Graphics and Visualization, APGV 2008, pp. 23–32 (2008)
11. Singh, G., Swan, I.J.E., Jones, J.A., Ellis, S.R.: Depth judgment measures and occluding surfaces in near-field augmented reality. In: APGV 2010, pp. 149–156. ACM (2010)
12. Lin, L., Wu, P., Huang, J., Li, J.: Precise depth perception in projective stereoscopic display. In: The 9th International Conference for Young Computer Scientists, ICYCS 2008, pp. 831–836 (2008)
13. Vesely, M., Clemens, N., Gray, A.: Stereoscopic images based on changes in user viewpoint. US 2011/0122130 Al (2011)
14. Cruz-Neira, C., Sandin, D., DeFanti, T.: Surround-screen projection-based virtual reality: the design and implementation of the cave. In: Proceedings of the 20th Annual Conference on Computer Graphics and Interactive Techniques, pp. 135–142 (1993)
15. Bourke, P., Morse, P.: Stereoscopy: Theory and practice. In: Workshop at 13th International Conference on Virtual Systems and Multimedia (2007)
16. Khoshelham, K.: Accuracy analysis of Kinect depth data. GeoInformation Science 38 (2010)

Orientation-Based Segmentation of Textured Images Using Graph-Cuts

Maria Sagrebin-Mitzel and Til Aach*

Institute of Imaging and Computer Vision, RWTH Aachen University, 52056 Aachen, Germany
http://www.lfb.rwth-aachen.de/

Abstract. In this work we present a hierarchical segmentation algorithm for textured images, where the textures are composed of different number of additively superimposed oriented patterns. The number of superimposed patterns is inferred by evaluating orientation tensor based quantities which can be efficiently computed from tensor invariants such as determinant, minors and trace. Since direct thresholding of these quantities leads to non-robust segmentation results, we propose a graph cut based segmentation approach. Our level dependent energy functions consist of a data term evaluating orientation tensor based quantities, and a smoothness term which assesses smoothness of the segmentation results. We present the robustness of the approach using both synthetic and real image data.

Keywords: Orientation-based segmentation, Textured images, Superimposed oriented patterns, Orientation tensor, Energy minimization, Graph cut.

1 Introduction

Various problems in the analysis of digital images require the analysis of textured image contents, such as segmentation or classification [17,27,28,23,22,21]. Basically texture classification and segmentation deal with the discrimination of regions which contain textures which are distinct according to some criterion, while each region corresponds to a homogeneous texture.

We consider here textures, which are composed of different numbers of additively superimposed oriented patterns. Such textures occur, for instance, in X-ray images of car tires, which contain different numbers of metal gratings superimposing each other (Fig. 1). Our goal is to segment these images into regions according to the number of superimposed patterns. The analysis of orientations is often based on orientation tensors computed from image gradients, such as in [6,18,29] for single oriented patterns, and in [2,24] for multiple orientations. The number of oriented patterns superimposed across a local image patch can then be determined by the rank of these tensors, specifically by testing orientation tensors for rank deficiency. In particular, the assumption that a local image patch exhibits a given number of oriented patterns holds if the corresponding orientation tensor is rank-deficient by one. The tests can thus be performed based on criteria computed from the eigenvalues of the orientations tensors, or from other invariants

---

* The authors gratefully acknowledge funding of this work by the Deutsche Forschungsgemeinschaft (DFG, AA5/3-1).

G. Csurka et al. (Eds.): VISIGRAPP 2012, CCIS 359, pp. 286–300, 2013.
© Springer-Verlag Berlin Heidelberg 2013

such as determinants, minors and trace. One approach, taken in [2,24] is to sequentially test for one, two and more orientations by hierarchical thresholding of these criteria. Such purely data-driven thresholding, however, is prone to generate isolated decision errors, in particular in more noisy image data. To achieve robust segmentation results, we follow here the approach of deriving energy functions consisting of a data term evaluating tensor rank, and a smoothness term which assesses the smoothness of the image regions. Similarly as above for the thresholding approach, the data term depends on the number of orientations tested for. We therefore develop here a hierarchical algorithm to minimize the energy using graph cuts [8].

In the following, we first review the tensor-based analysis of single and multiple orientations. We then illustrate the hierarchical structure of our general approach. This is followed by a derivation of the data energy terms. On each level of the hierarchy, the corresponding data term is complemented by a smoothness term, specifically the Potts model, to assess region smoothness. The total energy is then approximately minimized by a graph cut algorithm. We evaluate the algorithm qualitatively and quantitatively using both synthetically generated and real image data.

2   Analysis of Single and Multiple Orientations

Since orientation estimation plays an important role in wide areas like texture analysis, adaptive filtering and image enhancement, a number of different approaches have been proposed. These include among others quadrature filter based methods [19,14,1], the structure tensor [13,29,6,18,7] and its extensions to orientation tensors for multi-oriented patterns [2,24], the energy tensor [10] or the boundary tensor [20]. Yet another alternative, particularly for orientation-adaptive filtering and feature detection by matched filtering, are single-steerable [12,16] and multi-steerable filters [25].

In the following, we summarize the orientation-tensor based approach to orientation analysis, and a hierarchical, purely data-driven procedure for estimating the number of superimposed oriented patterns.

2.1   Single Orientation

The bivariate gray-level image $f(\mathbf{x})$ is said to be oriented in a local region Ω if and only if

$$f(\mathbf{x}) = f(\mathbf{x} + k\mathbf{v}) \ \forall k \in \Re \ and \ \forall \mathbf{x}, \mathbf{x} + k\mathbf{v} \in \Omega \tag{1}$$

where the case of $f(\mathbf{x})$ being constant over Ω is excluded. The unit vector $\mathbf{v} = (\cos\theta, \sin\theta)^T = \mathbf{v}(\theta)$ describes the orientation of $f(\mathbf{x})$ in terms of the angle θ.

Eq. 1 states that a given image is locally constant with respect to $\mathbf{v}$ if its directional derivative $\frac{\partial f}{\partial \mathbf{v}} = \langle \nabla f, \mathbf{v} \rangle$, i.e., the scalar product between the image gradient ∇f and $\mathbf{v}$, is zero for all gradients computed in the neighborhood Ω.

Because of noise in real image data and to allow for slight model violations, one seeks to find the solution of the following equation

$$\theta = \arg \min_{-\pi/2 < \phi \leq \pi/2} \int_{\Omega} \left(v^T(\theta) \nabla f(x)\right)^2 d\Omega \tag{2}$$

which leads to the so-called *structure tensor* approach for orientation estimation found in the pioneering work of [6], [29], [18] and others.

Using the image gradient $\nabla f = (f_x, f_y)^T$, we define the structure tensor $\mathbf{T}^{(1)}$: $\mathfrak{R}^N \to \mathfrak{R}^{N \times N}$ (where $N = 2$ for bivariate images) as a local integration over the outer product of the gradient

$$\mathbf{T}^{(1)} = \int_\Omega (\nabla f)(\nabla f)^T d\Omega = \int_\Omega \begin{bmatrix} f_x^2 & f_x f_y \\ f_x f_y & f_y^2 \end{bmatrix} d\Omega \qquad (3)$$

If the image signal is perfectly oriented according to (1) over Ω, the structure tensor $\mathbf{T}^{(1)}$ has one zero eigenvalue and $rank(\mathbf{T}^{(1)}) = 1$. In the presence of more than one orientation, both eigenvalues have a high value and $rank(\mathbf{T}^{(1)}) = 2$. Only in the case of $f(\mathbf{x})$ being perfectly constant over Ω, both eigenvalues vanish and $rank(\mathbf{T}^{(1)}) = 0$.

2.2 Higher-Order Orientations

As shown in [2] and [24] the detection of higher-order oriented structure can be treated in a similar manner. Let the image $f(\mathbf{x})$ be composed from several single oriented signals $f_i(\mathbf{x})$, $i \in [1, 2, ..., M]$ within a local region Ω:

$$f(\mathbf{x}) = \sum_{i=1}^M \alpha_i f_i(\mathbf{x}) \ \forall \mathbf{x} \in \Omega \qquad (4)$$

where the α_i denote weighting constants.

For $M = 2$, the composite image $f(\mathbf{x})$ then satisfies:

$$\frac{\partial^2 f(\mathbf{x})}{\partial \mathbf{u} \partial \mathbf{v}} = 0 \ \forall \mathbf{x} \in \Omega \qquad (5)$$

where the unit vectors $\mathbf{u} = (\cos\theta, \sin\theta)^T = (u_x, u_y)$ and $\mathbf{v} = (\cos\gamma, \sin\gamma)^T = (v_x, v_y)$ denote the orientations of $f_1(x)$ and $f_2(x)$, respectively. In the same way, (5) holds if the oriented patterns occur in mutually exclusive subregions Ω_1 and Ω_2 of Ω at a region boundary according to

$$f(\mathbf{x}) = f_i(\mathbf{x}) \ \forall \mathbf{x} \in \Omega_i \qquad (6)$$

where $\bigcup_i \Omega_i = \Omega$ and $\bigcap_i \Omega_i = \emptyset$.

Constraint (5) can be rewritten as the inner product $\mathbf{a}^T \mathbf{g}^{(2)}(\mathbf{x}) = 0 \ \forall \mathbf{x} \in \Omega$, where $\mathbf{a}$ is a three-dimensional vector encoding the orientations given by

$$\begin{aligned} \mathbf{a}^T &= (u_x v_x, u_x v_y + u_y v_x, u_y v_y) \\ &= (\cos\theta \cos\gamma, \sin(\theta + \gamma), \sin\theta \sin\gamma) \end{aligned} \qquad (7)$$

and where $\mathbf{g}^{(2)}$ can be viewed as a higher-order gradient given by

$$\mathbf{g}^{(2)} = (f_{xx}, f_{xy}, f_{yy})^T \qquad (8)$$

The components of $\mathbf{a}$ represent the mixed orientation parameters, which, if needed, can be decomposed into the sought orientation angles θ and γ as shown in [24].

Constraint (5) can now be rewritten to

$$Q\left(\mathbf{a}\right) = \int_{\Omega} \left(\mathbf{a}^T \mathbf{g}^{(2)}\right)^2 d\Omega = 0, \quad \mathbf{a}^T \mathbf{a} > 0. \tag{9}$$

Minimizing this expression subject to the constraint $\mathbf{a}^T \mathbf{a} > 0$ leads again to an eigensystem analysis, this time of the orientation tensor $\mathbf{T}^{(2)}$ defined as follows:

$$\begin{aligned} \mathbf{T}^{(2)} &= \int_{\Omega} \left(\mathbf{g}^{(2)}\right) \left(\mathbf{g}^{(2)}\right)^T d\Omega \\ &= \int_{\Omega} \begin{bmatrix} f_{xx}^2 & f_{xx}f_{xy} & f_{xx}f_{yy} \\ f_{xx}f_{xy} & f_{xy}^2 & f_{xy}f_{yy} \\ f_{xx}f_{yy} & f_{xy}f_{yy} & f_{yy}^2 \end{bmatrix} d\Omega \end{aligned} \tag{10}$$

Confidence in the double orientation hypothesis is high if one eigenvalue is small and the other two are large. Moreover, if the image $f(\mathbf{x})$ exhibits two ideal orientations in Ω, one eigenvalue is zero and $rank(\mathbf{T}^{(2)}) = 2$.

In the case of three orientations, $M = 3$ and $\mathbf{g}^{(3)}$ has the form

$$\mathbf{g}^{(3)} = \left(f_{xxx}, f_{xxy}, f_{xyy}, f_{yyy}\right)^T \tag{11}$$

which leads to the 4×4 orientation tensor $\mathbf{T}^{(3)}$ defined as

$$\mathbf{T}^{(3)} = \int_{\Omega} \left(\mathbf{g}^{(3)}\right) \left(\mathbf{g}^{(3)}\right)^T d\Omega \tag{12}$$

Again the presence of three different orientations in the image region Ω can be tested for by an eigensystem analysis of the above orientation tensor.

2.3   Hierarchical Orientation Estimation

Following the above discussion, the estimation of a number of superimposed oriented patterns in a single image patch can be achieved by testing the rank of the orientation tensors, which was based above on an eigensystem analysis. For $M \geq 2$, calculating eigenvectors and eigenvalues of a tensor may require iterative numerical methods. To avoid this step, [24] derived a hierarchical algorithm where rank testing employs tensor invariants such as determinant and trace.

The hierarchical testing of the algorithm was achieved by comparing the ratios

$$s_M = \frac{\sqrt[M+1]{\lambda_1^{(M)} \cdots \lambda_{M+1}^{(M)}}}{\sqrt[M]{\frac{1}{M+1} \sum_{i=1}^{M+1} \lambda_1^{(M)} \cdots \lambda_{i-1}^M \lambda_{i+1}^{(M)} \cdots \lambda_{M+1}^M}} \tag{13}$$

against predefined thresholds ϵ_M. $\lambda_i^{(M)}$ denotes the i-th eigenvalue of the orientation tensor $\mathbf{T}^{(M)}$. Note that both numerator and denominator can be computed without an eigensystem analysis from quantities such as trace, determinant and minors of the corresponding tensor $\mathbf{T}^{(M)}$. Both the numerator and denominator of s_M can be interpreted as mean eigenvalues, with the numerator being the geometric mean of all eigenvalues.

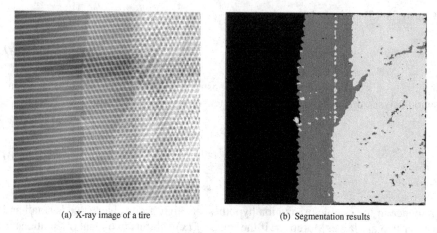

(a) X-ray image of a tire　　　　　　　　　(b) Segmentation results

Fig. 1. Segmentation results based on the segmentation procedure, proposed by [24]

The upper bound for s_M is one, which is reached when all eigenvalues are equal. The lower bound is zero, which is obtained when at least one eigenvalue vanishes.

The procedure for the hierarchical decision making is as follows: Starting with $M = 1$, compute the orientation tensor $\mathbf{T}^{(M)}$ and the value of s_M. If s_M is smaller than the predefined threshold ϵ_M, mark the region as M-oriented. Otherwise increment M by one and go to the next decision level by computing $\mathbf{T}^{(M+1)}$ and the corresponding value s_{M+1}.

Applying this procedure with $M_{max} = 3$ results in a segmentation of the image into areas with one, two or three orientations, plus a region with more than three orientations. Fig. 1 (a) shows a part of a X-ray image of a tire, revealing its internal metal grating structure. Fig. 1 (b) shows the corresponding region map obtained for $\epsilon_1 = 0.5$, $\epsilon_2 = 0.6$ and $\epsilon_3 = 0.7$, where the area in dark gray represents single orientations, the area in medium gray double orientations and the area in light gray three orientations.

While the overall estimated region structure corresponds well to the original image, the segmented regions itself are corrupted by small isolated decision errors. On these image parts, a different number of superimposed oriented patterns have been assigned than in the surrounding area.

This behavior is predominantly caused by the fact that each decision considers only local information from the data inside the small image patch Ω. This purely data-driven approach thus ignores region assignments of neighboring image patches. In other words, when making a decision at a specified image patch, no context from decisions for neighboring patches is taken into account (cf. [3,15,9,4]).

However, in most applications the assumption of real object being represented through coherent and continuous regions in an image is valid. To incorporate this knowledge into the segmentation procedure, we develop in the following an algorithm which additionally to the data term also uses a regularization term. This additional regularization term imposes further constraints concerning the sought segmentation. It favors segmentation results with coherent larger regions with smooth boundaries rather than small, ragged regions.

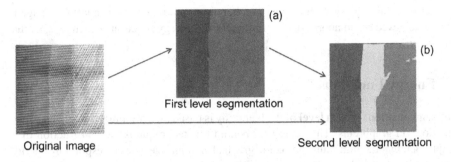

Fig. 2. Overview of the approach

The newly developed segmentation algorithm consists of a hierarchy of energy functions, each containing a data and a smoothness term. The definitions of the data terms are based on the ratios defined in (13). The smoothness term is the same in each function.

The hierarchical structure of the proposed approach is described in the next section.

3   Approach Overview

The hierarchical principle of the proposed approach is motivated by the structure of the orientation estimation algorithm discussed in the previous section. On the first level of the hierarchy the image is segmented into two regions corresponding to single and higher order oriented image parts. Further segmentation steps for the second and higher levels of the hierarchy consider only image regions which did not pass the test for a single orientation. Fig. 2 illustrates this procedure exemplarily.

Figs. 2 (a) and (b) show the results of the first and second level segmentation, respectively. In the first step the image is segmented into two regions, where the darker area corresponds to the image region with a single orientation and the brighter area to the image region containing a structure with more than one orientation pattern.

On the second level of the hierarchy, only the image part exhibiting more than one orientation is considered. This region is again divided into two regions, one containing double orientations and the other one containing more than two orientations. The image part with a single oriented structure is disregarded from this step onwards. Following this procedure the segmentation step on the third level of the hierarchy would divide the previously determined higher order oriented image part again into two regions corresponding to image areas with three orientations and those with more than three superimposed patterns.

On every level of the hierarchy, the segmentation is based on a minimization of a level dependent energy function. The data term of these functions incorporates the ratio s_M defined in (13), where M corresponds to the level of the hierarchy. The regularization term is the same in all functions and imposes smoothness constraints on the segmentation results.

To not disturb the neighborhood relationships between adjacent regions, all energy functions of the developed approach are defined over P, which is the set of all image pixels. When testing for a specified number of orientations at the corresponding level of the hierarchy, all regions with a lower number of orientations should be left unchanged. This is achieved by an appropriate definition of the energy function at each level of the hierarchy.

4 Energy Functions

The segmentation on each level of the hierarchy is based on a minimization of an energy function via graph cuts. The basic idea behind this technique is the construction of a graph such that the minimum cut on the graph also minimizes the corresponding energy function [8]. Here, the optimal segmentation of the underlying image is computed by using the *expansion* algorithm, developed by [8]. The energy functions they consider in their work have the form

$$E(l) = E_{data}(l) + E_{smooth}(l) \tag{14}$$

where l denotes the labeling of the observed data. For image segmentation, l is a function which assigns to each pixel $p \in P$ the corresponding label $l_p \in L$. The form of $E_{data}(l)$ is given by

$$E_{data}(l) = \sum_{p \in P} D_p(l_p) \tag{15}$$

where D_p measures how well label l_p fits the pixel p. $E_{smooth}(l)$ is the smoothness term of the energy function and measures the extent to which the labeling function l is not piecewise smooth. $E_{smooth}(l)$ has the form

$$E_{smooth}(l) = \sum_{\{p,q\} \in N} V_{p,q}(l_p, l_q) \tag{16}$$

where N is the set of adjacent pairs of pixels and $V_{p,q}(l_p, l_q)$ denotes the penalty for pixels p and q having different labels.

The *expansion* algorithm seeks to find an optimal labeling l^* such that the energy function given in (14) is minimized. It starts with an initial labeling and *moves* in every step toward the labeling with a lower energy until it reaches its minimum. In this context a new labeling l^{new} is said to lie within a single α-*expansion move* of l if only a finite set of pixels have changed their labels to α, where $\alpha \in L$. For more details on this approach, see [8].

The main task is now the definition of appropriate functions $E_h(l)$, $h \in [1, \cdots, h_{max}]$ where h denotes the segmentation level.

As already stated above, all energy functions in our approach have the same smoothness term $E_{smooth}(l)$. Here we have used the Potts model [26] as a discontinuity preserving function:

$$V(\alpha, \beta) = K \cdot T(\alpha \neq \beta) \tag{17}$$

where $T(\cdot)$ is 1 if its argument is true and otherwise 0. This model encourages partitions consisting of larger, smoothly shaped regions.

The definition of the corresponding data terms $E_{data}(l)$ is given in the next sections.

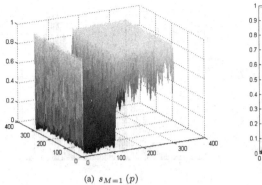

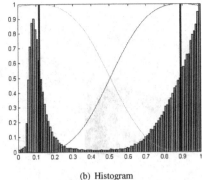

(a) $s_{M=1}(p)$

(b) Histogram

Fig. 3. Spatial distribution of the ratios $s_{M=1}(p)$, $p \in P$ and the corresponding histogram with cluster centers and membership functions

4.1   First-Order Data Term

As stated above, the data term $E_{data}(l)$ of an energy function measures how well the given labeling l fits the underlying image data. To obtain such an initial labeling, from which the necessary parameters can be estimated as well as to derive an appropriate data term, we applied the fuzzy c-means algorithm [5] to the ratios $s_{M=1}(p)$, $p \in P$ defined in (13), where p denotes the center of the image region Ω.

Fig. 3 shows the spatial distribution and the corresponding histogram of the $s_{M=1}(p)$ values computed from the original image shown in Fig. 1 (a).

Evidently, large values of $s_{M=1}(p)$ indicate a multiple oriented structure in an image, whereas small values correspond to image areas with a single orientation. The histogram in Fig. 3(b) reflects this situation by two clearly separable clusters.

Since in this context the order of the labeling set is $|L| = 2$, we apply the fuzzy c-means algorithm to separate the values into two clusters, which correspond to the labels l^{single} and l^{multi}, respectively. The results of this clustering procedure are also shown in Fig. 3(b). The two black bars correspond to the positions of the computed centers, while the curves depict the membership functions μ^{single} and μ^{multi} of the respective cluster:

$$\mu^{single}(s_{M=1}(p)) : P \rightarrow [0, 1]$$
$$\mu^{multi}(s_{M=1}(p)) : P \rightarrow [0, 1] \tag{18}$$

The results of a membership function are numerical values in $[0, 1]$ that correspond to the degrees to which the pixel $p \in P$ belongs to one or the other cluster. A large value complies with a high degree of affiliation to the corresponding cluster.

We can now define the data term $E_{data}(l)$ of the first energy function to

$$E_{data}(l) = \sum_{p \in P} (1 - \mu^{l_p}(s_{M=1}(p))) \tag{19}$$

where

$$D_p(l_p) = (1 - \mu^{l_p}(s_{M=1}(p))) \tag{20}$$

measures how well the label l_p fits the pixel p. Since we seek to minimize the overall energy function, a good fit is represented by a small value.

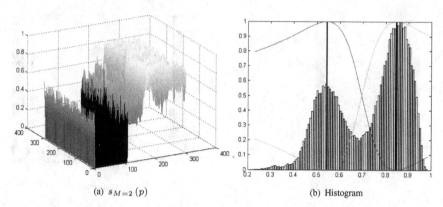

(a) $s_{M=2}(p)$ (b) Histogram

Fig. 4. Spatial distribution of the values $s_{M=2}(p)$ and the corresponding histogram with cluster centers and membership functions

4.2   Second-Order Data Term

The data term $E_{data}(l)$ of the second level energy function is obtained similarly, with the fuzzy c-means algorithm now being applied to the values $s_{M=2}(p)$, $p \in P$, where again p denotes the center of the image region Ω. Fig. 4 shows the spatial distribution and the corresponding histogram of the $s_{M=2}(p)$ values computed from the original image shown in Fig. 1 (a). As one can see, the $s_{M=2}(p)$ values have been computed only for pixels which have been marked as belonging to the image area of multiple orientations, $p \in \Omega^{multi} \subset P$. Pixels of the single oriented image part, $p \in \Omega^{single} \subset P$, have been disregarded in this step. The corresponding histogram shows that in contrast to the $s_{M=1}$ histogram, the two main clusters are here much closer to each other, having their centers around 0.53 and 0.85, respectively.

Application of the fuzzy c-means to these values results in two clusters and two membership functions μ^{double} and μ^{multi}, which in this case correspond to the labels l^{double} and l^{multi}, respectively.

To take into acount the neighborhood relationships between the two regions Ω^{multi} and Ω^{single}, the energy function $E_{h=2}(l)$ is defined over the entire pixel set P. To leave Ω^{single} unchanged during this and the following segmentation steps, this region is considered as being labeled by a fixed label l^{img}, where the corresponding membership function is defined as:

$$\mu^{img}(p) = \left\{ \begin{array}{l} 1,\ p \in \Omega^{single} \\ 0,\ p \in \Omega^{multi} \end{array} \right\} \tag{21}$$

Additionally, the two membership functions μ^{double} and μ^{multi} are modified according to

$$\mu^{double\_mod}(p) = \left\{ \begin{array}{ll} 0 & ,p \in \Omega^{single} \\ \mu^{double}(s_{M=2}(p)) & ,p \in \Omega^{multi} \end{array} \right\}$$

$$\mu^{multi\_mod}(p) = \left\{ \begin{array}{ll} 0 & ,p \in \Omega^{single} \\ \mu^{multi}(s_{M=2}(p)) & ,p \in \Omega^{multi} \end{array} \right\} \tag{22}$$

With these membership functions, the data term $E_{data}(l)$ of the second level energy function can be defined similarly to that of the first level energy function. Adding the third fixed label with the above defined membership function (21) ensures that the *expansion* algorithm does not relabel the single oriented region and treats the neighborhood relationships of the two regions Ω^{single} and Ω^{multi} in the same manner as inside these regions.

4.3 Higher-Order Data Terms

The data term of the higher-order energy function $E_h(l)$, $h \in [3, \cdots, h_{max}]$ is defined in analogy to that of the second order data term. After computing the membership functions of the two labels l^h and l^{multi}, the support of the fixed label l^{img} is extended to cover all regions with an already detected number of orientations, with membership function

$$\mu^{img}(p) = \left\{ \begin{array}{l} 1, \ p \in \Omega^{h-1} \\ 0, \ p \in \Omega^{multi} \end{array} \right\}$$

where in the case of $h = 3$ the image region Ω^{h-1} is a union of the two image regions Ω^{single} and Ω^{double}. Here, Ω^{double} denotes the image region which was labeled as being double oriented in the previous hierarchy level.

The two membership functions μ^h and μ^{multi} are also modified in analogy to (22):

$$\mu^{h\_mod}(p) = \left\{ \begin{array}{ll} 0 & , p \in \Omega^{h-1} \\ \mu^h \left(s_{M=h}(p) \right) & , p \in \Omega^{multi} \end{array} \right\}$$

$$\mu^{multi\_mod}(p) = \left\{ \begin{array}{ll} 0 & , p \in \Omega^{h-1} \\ \mu^{multi} \left(s_{M=h}(p) \right) & , p \in \Omega^{multi} \end{array} \right\}$$

As one can see the ratios s_M are also computed depending on the hierarchy level.

5 Experiments and Results

To test the performance and robustness of the described algorithm quantitatively and qualitatively, we applied it to both synthetic and real image data to detect up to three orientations. The regularization parameter K in (17) was set to $K = 1$ in all cases. Fig. 5 b) shows the segmentation result for the synthetically generated image shown in Fig. 5 a).

This synthetic image contains several parts, each with a different number of superimposed oriented patterns. The structure consists of two additive orientations in each of the two larger rectangles, whereas in the two smaller rectangles the number of superimposed oriented patterns is three. The background of the image is single-oriented.

Evidently, the algorithm segments the image well into three different types of regions. The black area represents the single-oriented image part. The area in dark gray represents image regions where two different orientations have been detected, and the area in medium gray corresponds to image regions containing structures with three different orientations. At the boundary between the double-oriented regions and the single-oriented background, the algorithm detects three occludingly superimposed orientations, also represented by medium gray.

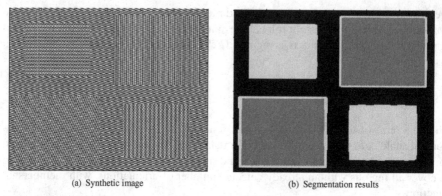

(a) Synthetic image   (b) Segmentation results

Fig. 5. Segmentation result for the synthetic image with several multi-oriented regions. No noise was added to the image.

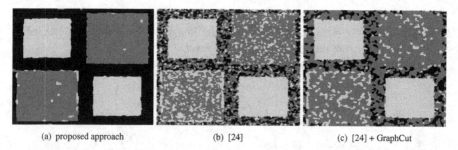

(a) proposed approach   (b) [24]   (c) [24] + GraphCut

Fig. 6. Segmentation results for the synthetic image with added noise ($SNR = 3dB$)

This segmentation result was obtained on the image to which no noise was added. Decreasing the signal-to-noise ratio (SNR) leads first to segmentation results where the mentioned border region around the double-oriented image parts starts to vanish. The uniformity of the regions is disturbed only when the SNR is as low as $SNR = 3dB$. Fig. 6 shows the segmentation results obtained by three different approaches including the one presented in this work.

Evidently, the described approach produces more stable results than the segmentation procedure based solely on the comparison of the ratios in (13) with the predefined thresholds, as a comparison between Figs. 6 (a) and (b) shows. In Fig. 6 (b), only image parts with three different orientations were segmented properly. The rest of the image contains many misclassified regions. The subsequent application of the *expansion* algorithm to these data, shown in Fig. 6 (c), could not reach the performance of our approach. The initial labeling for the *expansion* algorithm was in this case obtained by the hierarchical thresholding algorithm developed in [24].

Additionally, Fig. 7 shows the development of the F-score values [11] computed from the segmentation results while decreasing the SNR value of the original image shown in Fig. 5 (a). The F-score is a measure of the segmentation accuracy. It is computed from precision p and recall r via $F = 2 \cdot (pr)/(p+r)$. Each one of the three plots in Fig. 7 shows three different F-curves corresponding to the segmentation accuracy of the single-, double- and triple-oriented image parts, respectively.

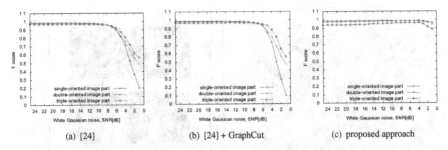

Fig. 7. F-score computed from the segmentation results while decreasing the SNR value of the original image

Obviously, SNR-values lower than 8 dB result in a very poor segmentation when using the thresholding procedure in [24]. Subsequent application of a graph cut optimization technique could not improve these results substantially. However, the F-score values shown in the third plot testify that the segmentation results obtained with the algorithm developed in this paper are significantly better. Another interesting point is the behavior of the different F-curves relative to each other. In the first two plots the F-curves corresponding to the single oriented image parts decline faster than the other two curves of the same plot. However, in the third plot the F-curve corresponding to the triple oriented image part declines faster, meaning that the segmentation accuracy of the corresponding image regions is getting worse. The following two facts are responsible for this behavior. Adding Gaussian noise to the image tends to lead to higher values of the ratio defined in (13). Thresholding these values by the same threshold leads therefore to a segmentation with more image regions which have been assigned a double-oriented structure. Since we used in our approach an adaptive fuzzy c-means algorithm for the initial cluster labeling, no declining of the red F-curve can be observed in the third plot. Still, experiments have shown that the distance between the two clusters varies strongly depending on which hierarchy level the segmentation is performed. On the first level the distance is relatively large, meaning that the centers lie in $[0, 0.5]$ and $[0.5, 1]$ interval, respectively. On the second level, both cluster centers were in $[0.5, 1]$ interval, which is the main reason for the poor segmentation of the higher-order oriented image structures.

We tested our algorithm also on texture images. In Fig. 8, the original image is composed of three different textures. Both the background texture and the texture on the lower part of the image were taken from the Brodatz database. The resulting segmentation is shown in Fig. 8 (b). It consists of two classes corresponding to single- and multi-oriented image regions, respectively.

More results are provided in Fig. 9, where the proposed segmentation approach could robustly separate single- and multi-oriented regions.

The conducted experiments also revealed the fact, that the presented segmentation approach yields plausible segmentation results only if the sizes of differently textured regions in the image are almost equal. In this case the histograms of the level dependent eigenvalue ratios show two clearly separable clusters (s. Fig. 3, 4 (b)). The fuzzy c-means algorithm detects the two clusters robustly and the computed membership functions can be used in the definition of the corresponding energy function. However in the

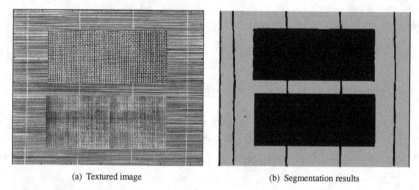

(a) Textured image   (b) Segmentation results

Fig. 8. Segmentation results of the textured image with several multi-oriented regions

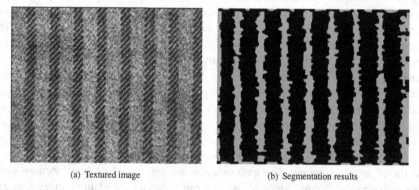

(a) Textured image   (b) Segmentation results

Fig. 9. Segmentation results of the textured image taken from the Brodatz database

case of differently sized regions, where one region greatly dominates the another one, the cluster corresponding to the smaller region cannot be distinguished from interfering noise and the algorithm fails to detect this region robustly. Additional histogram analysis and appropriate modification of the underlying data distribution has to be performed in order to increase the saliency of the second cluster.

6   Conclusions

We have developed a hierarchical segmentation algorithm, which separates an image into different regions based on the number of superimposed oriented patterns within each region. The algorithm combines the tensor-based analysis of multiple oriented patterns in [2,24] with a Potts region model [26] and energy minimization via graph cuts [8]. On every level of the hierarchy, the segmentation is thus achieved through a minimization of the corresponding energy function. The data term of the energy function evaluates the hypothesis that a given image part exhibits a particular number of superimposed orientations, and employs criteria testing the rank of the corresponding orientation tensor. The data term is complemented by a smoothness term derived from the Potts model, which serves as a regularization term. The smoothness energy acts as a discontinuity preserving term, encouraging labellings where adjacent pixels exhibit identical labels except across region boundaries. The energy functions were minimized via graph cuts. The algorithm was evaluated quantitatively and qualitatively on both synthetic and real image data. The quantitative evaluation verified the robustness of the algorithm against image noise in signal-to-noise ratios as low as $3dB$. Similarly, a strong performance of the algorithm was observed in real image data, such as textures and texture mosaics from the Brodatz database. In particular, the occurrence of isolated segmentation errors could be significantly reduced in comparison to the non-regularized thresholding approaches in [24].

We concentrated here on the segmentation of single- and multi-oriented textures according to the number of oriented patterns present in a region. We therefore did intentionally not consider the orientations themselves, which are encoded in the eigenvectors (particularly in the eigenvector corresponding to the lowest eigenvalue of an orientation tensor) rather than the eigenvalues. Future work is directed at including explicit orientation information into the framework, thus allowing to divide a region with a given number of orientations further according to the orientation estimates.

Acknowledgements. The authors gratefully acknowledge funding of this work by the Deutsche Forschungsgemeinschaft (DFG, AA5/3-1).

References

1. Aach, T., Kaup, A., Mester, R.: On texture analysis: Local energy transforms versus quadrature filters. Signal Process 45, 173–181 (1995)
2. Aach, T., Mota, C., Stuke, I., Mühlich, M., Barth, E.: Analysis of superimposed oriented patterns. IEEE Transactions on Image Processing 15(12), 3690–3700 (2006)
3. Besag, J.: Spatial interaction and the statistical analysis of lattice systems. Journal Royal Statistical Society B 36(2), 192–236 (1974)
4. Besag, J.: On the statistical analysis of dirty pictures. Journal Royal Statistical Society B 48(3), 259–302 (1986)
5. Bezdek, J.C.: Pattern Recognition with Fuzzy Objective Function Algorithms (Modern Perspectives in Energy). Springer (1981)
6. Bigün, J., Granlund, G.H.: Optimal orientation detection of linear symmetry. In: ICCV 1987, pp. 433–438 (1987)
7. Bigün, J., Granlund, G.H., Wiklund, J.: Multidimensional orientation estimation with applications to texture analysis and optical flow. IEEE Transactions on Pattern Analysis and Machine Intelligence 13(8), 775–790 (1991)
8. Boykov, Y., Veksler, O., Zabih, R.: Fast approximate energy minimization via graph cuts. IEEE Transactions on Pattern Analysis and Machine Intelligence 23(11), 1222–1239 (2001)
9. Derin, H., Cole, W.S.: Segmentation of textured images using Gibbs random fields. Computer Vision, Graphics, and Image Processing 35, 72–98 (1986)
10. Felsberg, M., Granlund, G.H.: POI Detection Using Channel Clustering and the 2D Energy Tensor. In: Rasmussen, C.E., Bülthoff, H.H., Schölkopf, B., Giese, M.A. (eds.) DAGM 2004. LNCS, vol. 3175, pp. 103–110. Springer, Heidelberg (2004)
11. Frakes, W.: Information Retrieval Data Structure & Algorithms. Prentice-Hall, Inc. (1992)
12. Freeman, W., Adelson, E.: The design and use of steerable filters. IEEE Trans. PAMI 13(9), 891–906 (1991)

13. Förstner, W.: A feature based corresponding algorithm for image matching. Intl. Arch. of Photogrammetry and Remote Sensing 26, 150–166 (1986)
14. Granlund, G.H., Knutsson, H.: Signal Processing for Computer Vision. Kluwer, Dordrecht (1995)
15. Haralick, R.M.: Decision making in context. IEEE Transactions on Pattern Analysis and Machine Intelligence 5(4), 417–429 (1983)
16. Jacob, M., Unser, M.: Design of steerable filters for feature detection using Canny-like criteria. IEEE Transactions on Pattern Analysis and Machine Intelligence 26(8), 1007–1019 (2004)
17. Jain, A.K., Farrokhnia, F.: Unsupervised texture segmentation using Gabor filters. Pattern Recognition 24(12), 1167–1186 (1991)
18. Kass, M., Witkin, A.: Analyzing oriented patterns. Comput. Vis., Graph., Image Process. 37, 362–385 (1987)
19. Knutsson, H., Granlund, G.H.: Texture analysis using two-dimensional quadrature filters. In: IEEE Workshop on Computer Architecture for Pattern Analysis and Image Data-Base Management, Pasadena, CA (1983)
20. Köthe, U.: Integrated edge and junction detection with the boundary tensor. In: ICCV, vol. 1, pp. 424–431 (2003)
21. Lategahn, H., Groß, S., Stehle, T., Aach, T.: Texture classification by modeling joint distributions of local patterns with gaussian mixtures. IEEE Transactions on Image Processing 19(6), 1548–1557 (2010)
22. Lazebnik, S., Schmid, C., Ponce, J.: A sparse texture representation using local affine regions. IEEE Transactions on Pattern Analysis and Machine Intelligence 27, 1265–1278 (2005)
23. Liu, X., Wang, D.: Texture classification using spectral histograms. IEEE Transactions on Image Processing 12(6), 661–670 (2003)
24. Mühlich, M., Aach, T.: Analysis of multiple orientations. IEEE Transactions on Image Processing 18(7), 1424–1437 (2009)
25. Mühlich, M., Friedrich, D., Aach, T.: Design and implementation of multi-steerable matched filters. IEEE Transactions on Pattern Analysis and Machine Intelligence 34(2), 279–291 (2012)
26. Potts, R.: Some generalized order-disorder transformation. Proc. Cambridge Philosophical Soc. 48, 106–109 (1952)
27. Randen, T., Husoy, J.H.: Filtering for texture classification: A comparative study. IEEE Transactions on Pattern Analysis and Machine Intelligence 21(4), 291–309 (1999)
28. Randen, T., Husoy, J.H.: Texture segmentation using filters with optimized energy separation. IEEE Transactions on Image Processing 8(4), 571–582 (1999)
29. Di Zenzo, S.: A note on the gradient of a multi-image. Comput. Vis., Graph., Image Process. 33, 116–125 (1986)

High Resolution Surveillance Video Compression Using JPEG2000 Compression of Random Variables

Octavian Biris and Joseph L. Mundy

Laboratory for Engineering Man-Machine Systems, Brown University, Providence, RI, U.S.A.

Abstract. This paper proposes a scheme for efficient compression of wide-area aerial video collectors (WAVC) data, based on background modeling and foreground detection using a Gaussian mixture at each pixel. The method implements the novel approach of treating the pixel intensities and wavelet coefficients as random variables. A modified JPEG 2000 algorithm based on the algebra of random variables is then used to perform the compression on the model. This approach leads to a very compact model which is selectively decompressed only in foreground regions. The resulting compression ratio is on the order of 16:1 with minimal loss of detail for moving objects.

Keywords: JPEG2000, Compression, Background modeling, Surveillance video.

1 Introduction

Recent development of wide-area aerial video collectors (WAVC) that acquire 1.5 Gpixel images at ten frames per second [7] imposes novel challenges for compression and transmission of the video data. Acquisition and manipulation of wide area aerial surveillance video is a challenging task due to limited on-board storage and bandwidth available for transferring video to the ground. A collection mission of two hours produces 350 TeraBytes of data and a bandwidth of 50 Giga Bytes/sec to record a three-channel video at 10 frames per second. These high bandwidth processing and storage requirements warrant the need for an efficient compression scheme.

The current approach to managing WAVC data is to encode the video with JPEG2000 on a frame-by-frame basis using multiple Analog Devices ADV212 chips, operating on sections of the video frame in parallel. However, with lossless compression this approach results in only a 3:1 compression ratio and cannot achieve the required frame rate. Applying higher compression ratios is not feasible since the loss of fidelity for small moving objects significantly reduces the performance of automated algorithms, such as video tracking.

The overall objective of this paper is to describe an approach to the compression of high resolution surveillance video using a background model that tolerates frequent variations in intensity and also apparent intensity change due to frame mis-registration. Since total pixel area of moving objects in a scene is relatively small, an approach based on selectively encoding moving objects in each frame and only transmitting a full frame occasionally is likely to produce a high compression factor. The success of this strategy depends on the ability to accurately detect foreground. It is proposed to

G. Csurka et al. (Eds.): VISIGRAPP 2012, CCIS 359, pp. 301–312, 2013.

use a background model based on a mixture of Gaussians (GMM), where the model is compressed using JPEG2000. This approach leads to an efficient foreground detection algorithm and a model that is relatively inexpensive to compute and store.

Alternative strategies such as Motion JPEG and MPEG-4 Part 10/AVC (also known as H264) video compression standards are not practical in this application. Both methods require the memory storage of past frames, especially in the case of H-264 which uses up to 16 bi-predictive frames in motion estimation as well as multiple motion vectors for each block which point to different reference frames. These reference frames would have to be stored in high-speed memory, which is very limited and largely occupied with the formation of video frames, e.g. Bayer color restoration.

Several methods of surveillance video compression based on background-foreground segmentation exist [1] [9] but none suggest a practical solution for the case of ultra-high resolution aerial video. Moreover, pixel-based background models which are less computationally demanding than block-based models require very large memory. For example, the robust pixel-based background modeling scheme proposed by C. Stauffer and W. Grimson [10] uses a mixture of weighted normal distributions at each pixel. Consequently, for a 3-channel video a model with three mixture components at every pixel requires 21 floating point numbers per pixel, or a storage of over 130 GBytes per frame.

W.R. Schwartz and H. Pedrini [9], extend the motion estimation approach of Babu on foreground objects by projecting intra-frame blocks on an eigenspace computed using PCA over a set of consecutive frames, thus exploiting the spatial redundancy of adjacent blocks. The cost of estimating the PCA basis as well as the requirement of observing foreground-free frames during the estimation process renders this approach unsuitable.

2   Surveillance Video Compression

In the approach to be described, foreground pixels are detected using a Gaussian mixture model (GMM), which provides rapid adaptation to changing imaging conditions as well as a probabilistic framework. Since a GMM is stored at each pixel, the storage requirement would be prohibitive without some strategy for model compression. In the following, a technique for significant model data reduction without loss in detection accuracy is described. The description starts with a review of the GMM background model.

2.1   Background Modeling

The extensive literature on background modeling methods can be assigned to two major categories. The first one exploits temporal redundancy between frames by applying a statistical model on each pixel. Model parameters are estimated either on-line recursively or off-line using maximum likelihood. Although the normal distribution seems sound and inexpensive at first, it cannot cope with wide variations of intensity values such as reflective surfaces, leaf motion, weather conditions or outdoor illumination changes. A natural improvement is to use a mixture of weighted normal distributions(GMMs), a widely used appearance model for background and foreground modeling. However, the amount of storage required to maintain a GMM at each pixel is impractically large for the WAVC application. In order for the GMM representation to be effective, the storage requirement must be reduced by at least an order of magnitude. This paper presents an innovative approach to the compression of such models in order to detect moving objects in very large video frames. Before presenting the new compression method, a survey of the GMM background modeling approach is provided as background. Without compression, such models would require an impractically large amount of storage.

Friedman and Russell successfully implemented a GMM background model over a traffic video sequence, each parameter being estimated using the general Expectation-Maximization algorithm [2]. However, the most popular pixel-based modeling scheme is that implemented by Stauffer and Grimson [10], which uses a fast on-line K-means approximation of the mixture parameters. Several variations of this method were developed improving parameter convergence rate and overall robustness [6][15].

The second category of background models analyzes features from neighboring blocks thus exploiting spatial redundancy within frames. Although Heikkilä, and Pietikäinen [3] implemented an operator that successfully depicts background statistics through a binary pattern, the relatively high computational cost prevent its use in this application. W.R. Schwartz and H. Pedrini [9], propose a method in which intra-frame blocks are projected on an eigenspace computed using PCA over a set of consecutive frames, thus exploiting the spatial redundancy of adjacent blocks. The cost of estimating the PCA basis as well as the requirement of observing foreground-free frames during the estimation process renders this approach unsuitable. The same reason makes other block-based methods that capture histogram,edge, intensity [4][5] and other feature informations unsuitable for high resolution surveillance video.

In the proposed approach, the background model is based on a fast-converging extension of the Stauffer and Grimson approximation presented by Dar-Shyang Lee [6] to model background. The extension of Lee is explained by starting with a summary of the basic Stauffer and Grimson algorithm. The value of each pixel is described by a mixture of normal distributions. Thus, the probability of observing a particular color tuple $\mathbf{X}$ at time t is given by

$$\mathbf{Pr}(\mathbf{X}_t) = \sum_{i=0}^{K-1} \omega_{i,t} \cdot \mathcal{N}\left(\mathbf{X}_t, \boldsymbol{\mu}_{i,t}, \Sigma_{i,t}\right) \tag{1}$$

K is the number of distributions in the mixture (typically 3 to 5) and $\omega_{i,t}$ represents the weight of distribution i at time t. Each distribution in the mixture (also referred to as mixture component) is normal with *Pdf*:

$$\mathcal{N}\left(\mathbf{X}_t, \mu, \Sigma\right) = \frac{1}{(2\pi)^{\frac{n}{2}}|\Sigma|^{\frac{1}{2}}} \exp\left(-\frac{1}{2}\left(\mathbf{X}_t - \mu_t\right)^T \Sigma^{-1}\left(\mathbf{X}_t - \mu_t\right)\right) \tag{2}$$

The proposed method checks to see if a new incoming pixel color tuple $\mathbf{X}_{t+1}$ is within a factor f (typically 2.5) standard deviations from a normal distribution in the mixture. If no match is found the least weighted component is discarded in favor of a new one with mean $\mathbf{X}_{t+1}$ and a high variance. The weights change according to:

$$\omega_{i,t+1} = (1 - \alpha)\omega_{i,t} + \alpha \cdot M_{i,t} \tag{3}$$

The value of $M_{i,t}$ is 1 for the distribution with the closest match (if more than one distribution matches, the one with the highest match ratio (i.e. $\omega_i/|\Sigma_i|$) is chosen and 0 for the rest of the distributions. The learning rate α represents how fast should the new weight change when a match is found. Each component i in the mixture will be updated as follows:

$$\mu_{t+1,i} = (1 - \rho_{t,i})\mu_{t,i} + \rho_{t,i}\mathbf{X}_t \tag{4}$$

$$\Sigma_{t+1} = (1 - \rho_{t,i})\Sigma_{t,i} + \rho_{t,i}(\mathbf{X}_t - \mu_t)^T(\mathbf{X}_t - \mu_t) \tag{5}$$

Essentially, ρ is the probability of observing the tuple X_t given the mixture component i scaled by the learning rate.

$$\rho_{i,t} = \alpha\mathbf{Pr}(\mathbf{X}_t|i, \theta_{i,t}) = \alpha\mathcal{N}(\mathbf{X}_t, \mu_{i,t}, \Sigma_{i,t}) \tag{6}$$

The parameter α causes many inaccuracies in various applications since a small value leads to slow convergence and a large value will make the model sensitive to rapid intensity variations. This problem is addressed by Lee's implementation in which each mixture component i has its own adaptive learning rate which is a function of a global parameter α and a match count $c_{i,t}$ (i.e. the number of times component i was a match up until the current time t). Let $q_{i,t}$ be 1 if component i is the closest match at time t and 0 otherwise. The weight is updated as follows:

$$\omega_{i,t+1} = (1 - \alpha)\omega_{i,t} + \alpha q_{i,t} \tag{7}$$

The key difference from the Stauffer and Grimson algorithm is the following update equation,

$$\rho_{i,t} = q_{i,t}\alpha\left(\frac{1 - \alpha}{c_{i,t}} + \alpha\right) \tag{8}$$

Since each component maintains a history of observations, the convergence rate of the true background distribution can be achieved much faster while maintaining robustness in the early stages of learning. The background model for video frames of dimension $w \times h$ at time t can be regarded as an image of random variables

$$\mathbb{I} = \left\{\mathcal{P}df\left(\mathbf{X}_t^{ij}\right) | i < w, j < h, \mathbf{X}_t^{i,j} \sim \mathcal{M}(\omega_t^r, \mu_t^r, \Sigma_t^r)\right\} \tag{9}$$

The sample space for each pixel, X_t^{ij} is the set of all possible color tuples (e.g. all 8-bit RGB value combinations) and the probability function is the mixture of normal distributions $\mathcal{M}(\omega_t^r, \mu_t^r, \Sigma_t^r)$. Storing $\mathbb{I}$ losslessly requires a large memory space is not a practical solution. A highly compressed representation of $\mathbb{I}$ will make implementations tractable but with the risk of inaccurate classification of foreground objects. As will be seen, JPEG2000 provides an effective compression scheme, since regions that are detected to contain foreground based on a highly compressed model can be refined locally without decompressing the entire model, and thus obtain the accuracy of the original background model.

2.2 The JPEG2000 Standard

JPEG2000 applies a transform (DWT) to the image and then truncates the bit resolution of the wavelet coefficients. The coefficients are then encoded using image neighborhood context analysis followed by entropy coding. In the case of large single frames, JPEG2000 has better compression quality, compared to other coding schemes such as JPEG or H264. The standard also supports the concept of levels, where quality can be flexibly balanced with compression ratio. Additionally the hierarchical nature of the DWT intrinsically provides an image pyramid, which is useful for visualizing large images.

A discrete wavelet transform (DWT) decomposes a signal into low and high frequency coefficients. A single level of the 2-d transform divides the image in four high and low frequency subbands along each direction (e.g. the HL subband emphasizes the high frequencies in the horizontal direction and low frequencies in the vertical direction). The subband that contains low frequencies in both horizontal and vertical directions (LL) represents a low-pass filtered and downsampled representation of the original image. A recursive application of the transform on the LL band yields a pyramid with multiple levels of decomposition of the original image. The subband size in each level is one fourth the size of corresponding one from the level before.

The effective tiered decomposition of the original image in JPEG2000 permits its decompression at various intermediate resolutions before reaching the original image resolution. Once the wavelet domain is computed via the lifting scheme with the Daubechies 9/7 or 5/3 wavelet filters, the coefficients are quantized and entropy coded. To further achieve scalability, JPEG2000 introduces the concept of coding passes when sending wavelet coefficients' bits to the entropy encoder. Instead of using a raster-scan order to code the nth bit of each sample, the coding passes prioritize the coding of bits that will reduce distortion the most from the overall image. In the case of lossy encoding, instead of truncating the same number of bits for every sample in a region, JPEG2000 truncates a certain number of coding passes, effectively performing a "selective" bit truncation per sample. Furthermore, JEPG2000 has a highly hierarchic partitioning policy which permits random access and decoding of spatial regions in the codestream.

2.3 Compression of Background Models Using JPEG 2000

In order to compress the background model, which is an array of GMM distributions, it is necessary to derive the associated GMM distribution for the DWT coefficients at each subband at each level of the wavelet decomposition. Since the wavelet transform involves basic arithmetic operations such as addition and scalar multiplication, the required transform of the GMM will be evaluated according to the presented novel technique based on the algebra of random variables.

Algebra of Random Variables. To obtain the distribution of the sum of two independent random variables knowing each of their distribution, one must convolve one pdf with the other. Mathematically,

$$P_{X+Y}(z) = P_X(x) \otimes P_Y(y) \tag{10}$$

The operator $\otimes$ stands for convolution. Similarly, one can determine the distribution of an invertible function g of a random variable as such [12]:

$$P_{g(X)}(y) = P_X(g^{-1}(y)) \cdot \frac{dg^{-1}(y)}{dy} \tag{11}$$

for our purposes let g be a linear function of the form $Y = g(X) = s \cdot X$. Thus (11) becomes

$$P_Y = \frac{1}{s} P_{Y/s} \tag{12}$$

Extending these to normally distributed random variables we have for the sum operator [13]:

$$\mathcal{N}(X, \mu_X, \Sigma_X) \otimes \mathcal{N}(Y, \mu_Y, \Sigma_Y) = \tag{13}$$
$$= \mathcal{N}(X + Y, \mu_X + \mu_Y, \Sigma_X + \Sigma_Y) \tag{14}$$

Similarly for scaling:

$$\frac{1}{s} \mathcal{N}\left(\frac{Y}{s}, \mu, \Sigma\right) = \mathcal{N}(Y, s \cdot \mu, s^2 \cdot \Sigma) \tag{15}$$

The order of summation and integration can transposed thus obtaining,

$$\mathcal{M}(\theta^r) \otimes \mathcal{M}(\theta^q) = \int_z \sum_{i=0}^{m} \omega_i^r P_{X_i}(z) \sum_{j=0}^{n} \omega_j^q P_{Y_j}(x - z) dz \tag{16}$$

$$= \sum_{j=0}^{n} \sum_{i=0}^{m} \omega_i^r \omega_j^q \int_z P_{X_i}(z) P_{Y_j}(x - z) dz \tag{17}$$

$$= \sum_{j=0}^{n} \sum_{i=0}^{m} \omega_i^r \omega_j^q \mathcal{N}(X_i, \theta_i^r) \otimes \mathcal{N}(X_j, \theta_j^q) \tag{18}$$

Note that the convolution of two mixtures of size m and n generally yields $m \cdot n$ modes. The scalar multiplication of mixtures simply scales each mode thus:

$$s \cdot \mathcal{M}(\omega^r, \mu^r, \Sigma^r) = \mathcal{M}(\omega^r, s\mu^r, s^2 \Sigma^r) \tag{19}$$

The Wavelet Transform of Random Variables. Based on these operations over random variables, the distribution for each wavelet coefficient can be obtained. One issue is that convolution of distributions produces a number of components equal to the product of the number of components in each distribution. It is necessary to prune back the extra components. One approach is to delete the lowest weight components and then renormalizing the weights of the remaining components. Alternatively Z. Zhang et al.[14] propose an elegant way of merging modes in a mixture. Essentially, two mixture modes with weights ω_i and ω_j will yield a new mode with weight $\omega_k = \omega_i + \omega_j$ after the merger. The underlying property of the newly obtained mode is:

$$\omega_k \mathbf{Pr}(\mathbf{X}|k) = \omega_i \mathbf{Pr}(\mathbf{X}|i) + \omega_j \mathbf{Pr}(\mathbf{X}|j) \tag{20}$$

Taking the expectation operator on each side will give out the mean μ_k of the new distribution. The covariance is similarly obtained by solving $\Sigma_k = \mathbf{E}[\mathbf{X}\mathbf{X}^T|k] - \mu_k\mu_k^T$ Finally we end up with the following merger relationships:

$$\omega_k\mu_k = \omega_i\mu_i + \omega_j\mu_j \tag{21}$$

$$\omega_k\left(\Sigma_k + \mu_k\mu_k^T\right) = \omega_i\left(\Sigma_i + \mu_i\mu_i^T\right) + \omega_j\left(\Sigma_j + \mu_j\mu_j^T\right) \tag{22}$$

After each addition operation, the extra modes are merged until the desired mixture size obtained, e.g. three or five components. Using the lifting scheme the approximate distribution of wavelet coefficients is obtained. For each frame $\mathbf{F}$ in the video, the probability map $\mathbb{P}$ is obtained by evaluating at every pixel (i,j) $\mathbf{Pr}(\mathbf{X}_t^{i,j} = F^{ij})$, i.e. $\mathbb{P} = \mathbf{Pr}(\mathbb{I} = \mathbf{F})$. Thresholding and binarizing $\mathbb{P}$, a mask is obtained to select the foreground pixels which will be encoded using standard JPEG2000. According to A. Perera et al.[8] H.264 is reputed to have better performance in encoding foreground blocks. However, as mentioned earlier, its memory costs preclude its application in wide area aerial video collection.

It is desirable to work with a JPEG2000 compressed representation of $\mathbb{I}$ when obtaining $\mathbb{P}$. A sound implementation is to store in high speed memory the lowest resolution LL band (typically LL5) and and use its random variables to evaluate the probability map. Let the lowest LL band in the wavelet transform decomposition of $\mathbb{I}$ be $\mathbb{L}$. Because the size of $\mathbb{L}$ is $2^5 = 32$ times smaller than $\mathbb{I}$, each distribution in $\mathbb{L}$ will be used to measure the probability of the pixels in a 32x32 patch in the video frame $\mathbf{F}$. A less accurate probability map will result than the one obtained using the full model $\mathbb{I}$. However, by taking advantage of/harnessing the scalability features of JPEG 2000, the accuracy of this probability map can be increased according to the method described below. Low probability pixels are assumed to be due to the result of actual foreground or possibly due to the inaccuracy of the distribution in $\mathbb{L}$. Distributions from $\mathbb{L}$ are refined by local decompression from the codestream in order to distinguish true foreground from model inaccuracy. Pixels that are found to have low probability in a frame will have their corresponding distribution from $\mathbb{I}$ determined via local JPEG2000 decompression. The probability for those pixels is then re-evaluated with the decompressed distributions which are close to the distributions of the in original model $\mathbb{I}$, as shown in Figure 1. The model will not be exactly recovered due to the fact that JPEG2000 irreversible compression is employed on $\mathbb{I}$.

It is safe to assume that foreground pixels exist in coherent regions. Therefore it is efficient that a pixel needing local decompression causes the neighboring distributions to also be decompressed due to the pyramid structure of the DWT. Thus, the overhead involved with performing the inverse DWT and bitplane de-coding is minimized.

3   Experiments

In the first experiments, data that has been obtained from a high-definition video camera is used to evaluate the proposed scheme. In a final experiment, the compression performance is evaluated on ARGUS wide-area aerial video data taken from one of the focal

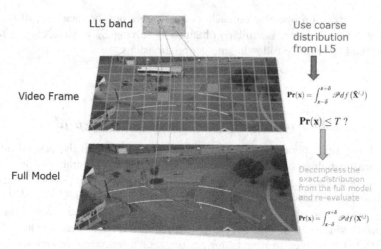

Fig. 1. Probability map evaluation using LL5

planes. [11] As mentioned above, if the probability of a certain pixel measured with $\mathbb{L}$ falls below a certain value, the pixel's corresponding distribution from the compressed $\mathbb{I}$ is extracted from the codestream. Several experiments have been run with different decision thresholds, namely $\{0.01 , 0.1 , 0.3 , 0.5 , 0.7 , 0.9 , 0.99\}$. Background models were encoded at various bitrates also starting at 0.05 and ending at 32 bps(bits per sample). A 1280 x 720 background model having a maximum of three components per mixture and each component having an independent covariance matrix takes up 5.5 KB of storage when JPEG2000 compressed at 0.05 bps. A higher rate like 32 bps will increase the storage cost per frame to 3184 KB. On the other hand, higher bitrate models require a smaller number of local decompressions when evaluating foreground probability. It can be noted that even the higher rate produces a model that is approximately 100 times smaller than the original GMM and comparable in storage to a single uncompressed color video frame. The JPEG 2000 library used was D Taubman's "Kakadu" 2.2 library [11].

Figure 3 shows the pixels which require local decompression when evaluating the probability map on one of the frames with two differently encoded background models. Figure 2 (a) shows that the number of lookups drops dramatically as bitrate increases from a fractional value to an integer one. Moreover, the receiver operator characteristic (ROC) curves in figure 2 (b) depict that the True Positive Rate (TPR) vs. False Positive Rate (FPR) pairs approach the top left corner rapidly as a function of the bitrate of the model used to measure foreground probability. From both figures, it is clear that models encoded at bitrates ranging from 5bps and above exhibit very similar characteristics both in the ability to correctly identify background and the in number of local decompressions required during probability evaluation.

3.1 Results

After each probability map is evaluated with the method described above, a binary mask is derived from it via probability thresholding and is applied on the corresponding

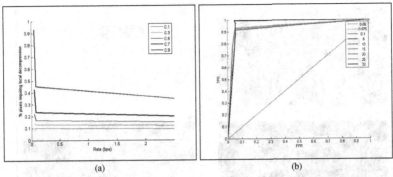

Fig. 2. (a) Percent of pixels requiring local refinement vs. bit rate and (b) ROC characteristic curves for various bitrates

(a)   (b)

Fig. 3. Number of local refinements required with a decision threshold of 0.7 and a model compressed at a rate of (a) 0.05 bps and (b) 32 bps

Table 1. Compression Ratios for two Video Sequences

Video id	Model II	Video (Lossless)	Video (lossy @ 0.05 bps)
Still 720p Camera	96	4	31
ARGUS City Scene	96	16	87

frame. The resulting foreground objects are encoded using JPEG2000. Once every 50 frames the mean image $M_{t,k}$ of the highest weighted component of the background model is encoded, where

$$M_{t,k} = \{\mu_{tk}^{ij} | i < w, \, j < h, \, k = \arg\max_r (\omega_t^r),$$

$$X_t^{i,j} \sim \mathcal{M}(\omega_t^r, \mu_t^r, \Sigma_t^r)\}$$

Figure 4 shows a video frame and associated probability map, foreground set and its reconstruction post compression. A 600 frame 720p video , having each foreground object losslessly compressed according to the described method, will reduce its overall storage reduced by a factor of 4. Each foreground frame has an average of 0.02 bps. The lossy encoding of foreground objects is possible, at the expense of reconstruction artifacts. These are due to the fact that JPEG2000 smooths with each DWT level abrupt

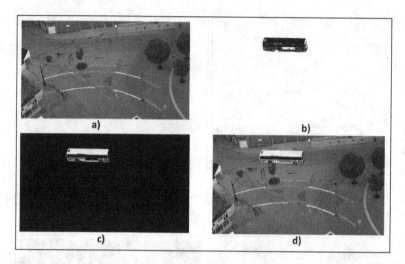

Fig. 4. (a) Mean image $M_{k,50}$ (b) probability map evaluated with model encoded at 5 bps (c) Segmented Foreground (d) Reconstructed Frame $d = a + c$

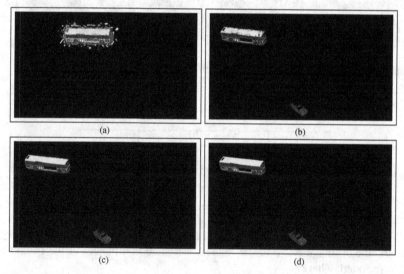

Fig. 5. Encoded foreground (a) lossy 0.01 bps (no mask), (b) lossy at 0.01 bps , (c) lossy at 0.05 bps and (d) lossless

transitions from RGB values at foreground edges to the 0-value background label. This behavior has been reported by Perera *et al.* [8]. One solution is to losslessly encode a binary mask corresponding to the foreground and apply it on the decoded foreground to eliminate the smoothing artifacts. The results of this masking technique are shown in Figure 5. A second aerial video sequence, acquired from one of the ARGUS focal planes, has frame size 2740x2029 and the pixel resolution of moving objects is 25 times lower than for the stationary camera.

As a consequence, a high compression ratio is achieved since the relative area of moving objects is much smaller. Scaling the results to the full 1.5 GByte ARGUS sequence, the encoding of moving objects requires only 90 MBytes. The results for video and background model compression are summarized in Table 1. In each case, moving objects are encoded with no compression. It should be noted that in the ARGUS sequence additional bits were spent on encoding pixel intensities near discontinuities (edges) that are labeled as foreground due to frame misalignment.

4 Conclusions

It has been demonstrated that efficient foreground detection and frame encoding can be achieved by exploiting the intrinsic mechanisms of the JPEG2000 coding scheme. By encoding the probability distributions it is possible to reduce the storage cost of GMM per pixel to the same order as a single video frame. The resulting accuracy in foreground detection, even for video that is registered to a single ground plane, enables a significant advance in compression ratio without sacrificing the quality needed for computer vision algorithms such as tracking.

Future work will focus on a GPU implementation of the proposed algorithm. Pixelwise and frame-wise parallelism is inherent will be exploited in the implementation. Another consideration is to develop algorithms for the lossy encoding of foreground objects to further improve the compression ratio. As noted by Perera *et al.* [8], such compression is not a trivial task since JPEG2000 smooths with each DWT level abrupt transitions from RGB values at foreground edges to the 0-value background label . Moreover, such encoding will inevitably require closer integration with the computer vision algorithms, such as encoding only the information that is actually used in tracking.

References

1. Venkatesh Babu, R., Makur, A.: Object-based Surveillance Video Compression using Foreground Motion Compensation. In: 2006 9th International Conference on Control, Automation, Robotics and Vision, pp. 1–6 (2006)
2. Friedman, N., Russell, S.: Image segmentation in video sequences: A probabilistic approach 1 Introduction. In: UAI, pp. 175–181 (1997)
3. Heikkilä, M., Pietikäinen, M.: A texture-based method for modeling the background and detecting moving objects. IEEE Transactions on Pattern Analysis and Machine Intelligence 28(4), 657–662 (2006)
4. Jabri, S., Duric, Z., Wechsler, H., Rosenfeld, A.: Detection and location of people in video images using adaptive fusion of color and edge information. In: ICPR 2000, pp. 4627–4631 (2000)
5. Javed, O., Shafique, K., Shah, M.: A hierarchical approach to robust background subtraction using color and gradient information. In: Proceedings Workshop on Motion and Video Computing, pp. 22–27 (2002)
6. Lee, D.-S.: Effective gaussian mixture learning for video background subtraction. IEEE Transactions on Pattern Analysis and Machine Intelligence 27(5), 827–832 (2005)
7. Leininger, J., Edwards, B.: Autonomous real-time ground ubiquitous surveillance-imaging system (argus-is). In: Defense Transformation and Net-Centric Systems 2008, vol. 6981 (2008)

8. Perera, A.G.A., Collins, R., Hoogs, A.: Evaluation of compression schemes for wide area video. In: 37th IEEE Applied Imagery Pattern Recognition Workshop, AIPR 2008, pp. 1–6 (2008)

9. Schwartz, W.R., Pedrini, H., Davis, L.S.: Video Compression and Retrieval of Moving Object Location Applied to Surveillance. In: Kamel, M., Campilho, A. (eds.) ICIAR 2009. LNCS, vol. 5627, pp. 906–916. Springer, Heidelberg (2009)

10. Stauffer, C., Grimson, W.E.L.: Adaptive background mixture models for real-time tracking. In: Proceedings of the IEEE Computer Society Conference on Computer Vision and Pattern Recognition (Cat. No PR00149), pp. 246–252 (1999)

11. Taubman, D.S., Marcellin, M.W.: JPEG 2000: Image Compression Fundamentals, Standards and Practice, Third Printing 2004. Kluwer Academic Publishers (2004) ISBN: 9780792375197

12. Scheaffer, W., Wackerly, R., Mendenhall, D.: Mathematical statistics with applications. Duxbury, Thomson Learning (2002) ISBN: 0534377416 9780534377410

13. E.W. Weisstein: Normal sum distribution. MathWorld–A Wolfram Web Resource, http://mathworld.wolfram.com/NormalSumDistribution.html

14. Zhang, Z.: EM algorithms for Gaussian mixtures with split-and-merge operation. Pattern Recognition 36(9), 1973–1983 (2003)

15. Zivkovic, Z.: Improved adaptive Gaussian mixture model for background subtraction. In: Proceedings of the 17th International Conference on Pattern Recognition, ICPR 2004, vol. 2, pp. 28–31 (2004)

Automatic Human Age Estimation Using Overlapped Age Groups

Merve Kilinc[1,2] and Yusuf Sinan Akgul[2]

[1] National Research Institute of Electronics and Cryptology (UEKAE)
TUBITAK - BILGEM, 41470, Kocaeli, Turkey
[2] GIT Vision Lab., Department of Computer Engineering,
Gebze Institute of Technology, 41400, Kocaeli, Turkey
merve.kilinc@tubitak.gov.tr, akgul@bilmuh.gyte.edu.tr
http://vision.gyte.edu.tr/

Abstract. Facial aging effects can be perceived in two main forms; the first one is the growth related transformations and the second one is the textural variations. Therefore, in order to generate an efficient age classifier, both shape and texture information should be used together. In this work, we present an age estimation system that uses the fusion of geometric features (ratios of distance values between facial landmark points) and textural features (filter responses of the face image pixel values). First the probabilities of a face image belonging to each overlapping age groups are calculated by a group of classifiers. Then an interpolation based technique is used to produce the final estimated age. Many different textural features and geometric features were compared in this study. The results of the experiments show that the fusion with the geometric features increases the performance of the textural features and the highest age estimation rates are obtained using the fusion of Local Gabor Binary Patterns and Geometric features with overlapping age groups.

Keywords: Age estimation, Age classification, Geometric features, LBP, Gabor, LGBP, Cross ratio, FGNET, MORPH.

1 Introduction

Human age estimation is one of the most challenging problems in computer vision and pattern recognition. Estimating human age from his or her face is a hard problem not only for the existing computer vision systems but also for humans in some circumstances.

Aging is not a general progress, different individuals age in different ways. Aging pattern of each person is determined by many internal and external factors such as genetics, health, lifestyle, and even weather conditions [9] [10]. In order to achieve successful results in applications like age estimation or age classification, the data set that will be used to train the algorithm must contain all these factors. Therefore, the collection of training data is another difficulty of research on age progression and estimation. It is really hard to collect face images of the same person at different ages and it is highly important to assign each instance to the right age class. In order to have a

G. Csurka et al. (Eds.): VISIGRAPP 2012, CCIS 359, pp. 313–325, 2013.

general and qualified aging pattern that overcomes the negative influences of individual differences, a complete and accurately labeled face aging database is needed.

In spite of these present difficulties, age estimation can be used in a wide range of smart human-machine applications, e.g. limiting access to age-appropriate Internet or television contents or creating a general characteristics of a typical customer in a required age range to be used to develop a marketing strategy. Besides, facial aging is a subproblem in face recognition, because simulating the appearance of a person across years may help recognizing his or her face [17] [18].

Some earlier work has been reported on different aspects of age progression and estimation. Kwon and Lobo [14] proposed an age classification method that focuses on both the shape and the wrinkles of human face to classify input images into only one of the three age groups: babies, young adults and senior adults. Lanitis [15] presented comparative results of different classifiers; shortest distance classifier, neural network based classifier and a quadratic function classifier. The face images are represented by the AAM method and the best results were obtained when classifiers based on quadratic function and neural network based classifiers are used. Guo and Fu [11] presented a locally adjusted regressor which uses age manifold learning to map pixel intensity of the original face images into a low dimensional subspace for the learning and the prediction of the aging patterns. Yang [21] used Real AdaBoost algorithm to train a classifier by composing a sequence of Local Binary Pattern (LBP) features as a representation of face texture. Age is classified into only three periods: child, adult and old people. Gao [9] used Gabor features as face representation and the Linear Discriminant Analysis (LDA) to construct the age classifier that classifies human faces as baby, child, adult, or elder people. Images in the training set are labeled without the age information.

There exists some other work concerning face recognition with aging variations on human faces. For example, Burt and Perrett [3] described a method for the simulation of aging effects on male faces only by using facial composites which blend shape and color information. Ramanathan and Chellappa [17] proposed a craniofacial growth model that characterizes growth related shape variations observed in human faces. They used age-based facial measurements and proportion indices.

Age estimation can be considered either a classification or a regression problem [8]. We can see that for different experiment cases, the classification based age estimation can be much better or much worse than the regression based techniques. Therefore a hybrid approach which combines the classification and regression methods is the most effective solution for the age estimation problem.

Although the aging pattern is dissimilar for each person, individuals belonging to the same age group share some facial shape and texture similarities. This paper presents an extension of our previous work with a set of experiments [13]. Our original systems uses overlapping age groups (Figure 1 and Figure 2) and a classifier that measures the probability of a given image belonging to each group. Since our task is to estimate the human age, we use the interpolated probabilities to reach the final estimated age.

We formed our age groups non-uniformly to take advantage of facial feature developments of different age phases. During the formative years, facial aging effects are more pronounced, therefore we partition the formative years to smaller ranges. For the older age groups, the ranges get larger because the changes are smaller compared to

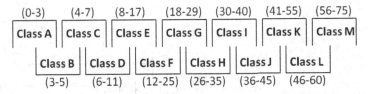

Fig. 1. The overlapping age groups for FG-NET Database [6]

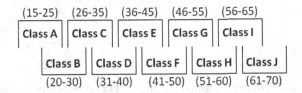

Fig. 2. The overlapping age groups for MORPH Database

the formative age groups. The age groups are chosen to overlap so that it is possible to employ an interpolation based technique to estimate the final age.

For the feature extraction process, first we calculate various ratios of the Euclidean distances between facial points to be used as geometric features. Some of these distances are calculated in a way that they are not affected by head poses and perspective distortion effects of cameras. Second, to extract textural features, we use face representation techniques such as LBP, Gabor, Local Gabor Binary Pattern (LGBP) which are commonly used by the face recognition community. Then we combine geometric and textural features and use AdaBoost algorithm to construct the final classifier. While textural features play an important role to distinguish age classes between middle age and older people, geometric features become more important to classify younger subjects.

The rest of this paper is organized as follows: Section 2 describes the proposed age estimation method. Section 3 introduces the geometric features which are used for the description of the growth related shape variations for the classification. In Section 4, textural feature extraction methods are presented. Section 5 shows comparative experimental results in age estimation for two databases (FG-NET and MORPH) and Section 6 provides some concluding remarks.

2   The Fusion of Geometric and Textural Features

Facial aging effects can be perceived in two main forms; the first one is the growth related transformations in facial shape during formative years. The other is, the textural variations such as wrinkles, creases, and other related skin artifacts that occur during adulthood. Therefore, while some earlier work deal with only facial texture to construct an age classifier [9], some use shape and texture information separately to distinguish one age class from the others [14] [21].

We tested 8 different classifiers that use different facial feature vectors. Some of these classifiers use textural features, some of them use geometric features and others

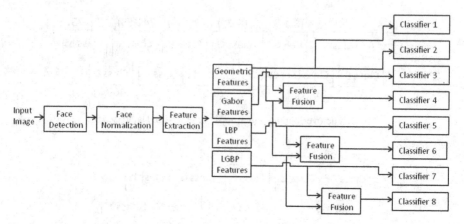

Fig. 3. The overall diagram of the proposed age classification system

use fusion of textural and geometric features. The overall feature sets of each classifier is shown in Figure 3.

Before the feature extraction phase of the training, samples in the training data set are assigned group labels. Most of the samples are assigned two group labels because our age groups overlap (Figure 1 and Figure 2). For the training, first, face boundaries are automatically detected, and face image patches are cropped from images in the training dataset. Prior to feature extraction, all images undergo geometric and illumination normalization. After the preprocessing phase, several feature extraction methods are applied to the normalized face images: 1) Ratios of the distances between facial landmarks are extracted to be used as geometric features. 2) The LBP operator is applied to every pixel of the face image and then resulting values are used as the feature vectors. 3) After convolving the face image with a range of Gabor filters, the magnitude responses are used to represent the Gabor features. 4) The LGBP representations of the face images are used as LGBP features. In addition to these extracted features, we combine each textural feature with geometric features at the feature level to enhance the representation power of the face image.

After the feature extraction phase, the AdaBoost learning algorithm [7] is used to model the age classifiers. AdaBoost algorithm combines the weak classifiers to construct a strong classifier. In every iteration, it reweighs each instance according to the output of the classifier. Finally we obtain 8 distinct classifiers; Classifier 1 uses Geometric features without cross ratio features, Classifier 2 uses Geometric features, Classifier 3 uses Gabor features, Classifier 4 uses the fusion of Geometric and Gabor features, Classifier 5 uses LBP features, Classifier 6 uses the fusion of Geometric and LBP features, Classifier 7 uses LGBP features and Classifier 8 uses the fusion of Geometric and LGBP features.

For testing, an input face image goes through the same face detection, normalization and feature extraction phases. Then, the probabilities of each age group assignment is obtained from the age group classifier. The probabilities of the highest scoring group and its two neighbors are used to calculate an interpolated age value using a weighted average of the three group centers. Age calculation function is defined as:

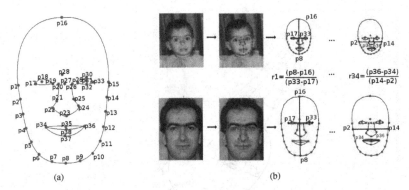

(a)   (b)

Fig. 4. (a) 38 facial landmarks which are read from point files that are provided for face images in FG-NET Aging Database (b) Geometric Features Extraction Process

$$age = X_{med} + ((Y_{med} - X_{med})/2)P_y + ((Z_{med} - X_{med})/2)P_z \qquad (1)$$

where X_{med}, Y_{med} and Z_{med} are the median age values of the age classes with the highest probabilities respectively. In the equation P_y and P_z are the second and the third highest probability values of the age classes. We found that overlapping age groups performs better with our implementation method than the non-overlapping age groups.

3 Geometric Features

Aging causes significant variations in the anatomy of human face especially during the transition period from childhood to adulthood. Changes in the shape of the face across ages can play a critical role in age estimation. In order to describe the human face geometrically, ratios of distance values between facial landmark points according to face anthropometry can be used [14]. Face anthropometry is the science of measuring size and proportions on human faces [17]. Anthropometric data have been widely used in generating geometric models of human face [4], in characterizing growth related shape variations [17] for the face recognition applications and in constructing face models for computer graphics.

In our age estimation as illustrated in Figure 4(a), we obtain 38 facial landmarks from 68 points which are read from point files that are provided for every face image in Face and Gesture Recognition Research Network (FG-NET) [6] Aging Database. In order to further test the method on the MORPH database [16], same facial landmarks are extracted automatically for each face image in the database. Then, to model the geometric shapes of human faces at different ages, we extract 34 facial proportions, ratios of distances between above mentioned facial landmarks as shown in Figure 4(b). Some of the facial proportions which are used as geometric features of the classifier are; $r_1 : (\frac{p8-p16}{p33-p17})$, $r_2 : (\frac{p8-p38}{p11-p5})$, ..., $r_{34} : (\frac{p36-p34}{p8-p27})$.

Although the geometric features of a face image are insensitive to the changes in illumination, they might be affected by head pose variations and camera distortions. In order to addres this problem, the two of the geometric features that we use in age

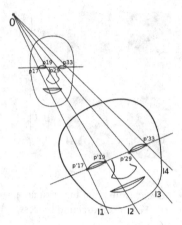

Fig. 5. Cross ratio for the eye corner points

classification are based on cross ratio of the face image. If p_1, p_2, p_3 and p_4 are four distinct points on the same line, then the cross ratio is computed as:

$$(p_1, p_2; p_3, p_4) = \frac{(p_1 - p_3)(p_2 - p_4)}{(p_2 - p_3)(p_1 - p_4)} \tag{2}$$

The cross ratio is invariant to the projective transformations. As illustrated in Figure 5, l_1, l_2, l_3 and l_4 are four coplanar lines passing through the same point O. The cross ratio of these lines is defined as the cross ratio of the intersections of these lines with any other line that does not pass through O. Therefore, the cross ratios $(p_{17}, p_{19}; p_{29}, p_{33})$ and $(p_{17}', p_{19}'; p_{29}', p_{33}')$ are equal.

In our work, we model these lines as the lines passing through the central projection of the camera and the facial points. For the first cross ratio, we use the eye corner points; $(p17, p19; p29, p33)$ (Figure 5). For the second cross ratio, we use the head point, center point of eye brows, mouth mid point and chin point; $(p16, p28; p38, p8)$. These two geometric features make our classification system robust against the perspective distortions, because the cross ratio between four colinear points stays constant under perspective transformations.

4   Textural Features

Facial aging effects, especially in older age groups, are mostly perceived in the form of textural variations such as wrinkles, creases, and changes in skin tone. Textural changes in human face provide fundamental information for the estimation of human age. Thus, the effectiveness of the textural face representation method is highly important for age estimation. In face recognition applications, the LBP operator and Gabor filters are among the most popular techniques for face representation [1] [5] [2] [19]. We use LBP, Gabor and LGBP features as textural features in age estimation as explained below.

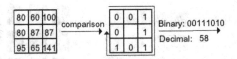

Fig. 6. The original LBP operator

4.1 LBP Features

Local Binary Pattern is a non-parametric kernel which summarizes the local spatial structure of an image [1]. The original LBP operator labels the pixel of the image by comparing it with the surrounding pixels in its 3×3-neighbourhood as illustrated in Figure 6.

The decimal form of the resulting 8-bit word (LBP code) can be expressed as follows [1]:

$$LBP(x_c, y_c) = \sum_{n=0}^{7} s(i_n - i_c)2^n \qquad (3)$$

where i_c corresponds to the gray value of the center pixel (x_c, y_c), i_n to the gray value of the 8 surrounding pixels, and function $s(x)$ is defined as:

$$s(x) = \begin{cases} 1 \ if x \geq 0 \\ 0 \ if x < 0 \end{cases} \qquad (4)$$

Local binary pattern based face recognition has been proposed as a robust face recognition algorithm [1] [5]. Therefore, we use the LBP values of the pixels rather than the raw intensities as the feature vector for the classifier.

4.2 Gabor Features

Gabor filters are one of the most effective texture representation techniques for analyzing an image into a detailed local description. Gabor features are commonly used in face representation for the face recognition applications due to their robustness to image variations [2] [19].

The Gabor representation of a face image is generated by convolving it with the Gabor filters [2]. Applying a Gabor filter $\Psi_{f,\Theta}(x, y)$ to the pixel at the (x, y) pixel position in the image can be defined as:

$$g_{f,\Theta}(x, y) = f(x, y) * \Psi_{f,\Theta}(x, y) \qquad (5)$$

where $f(x, y)$ corresponds to the intensity value of the pixel, f and Θ are used for controlling the scale and the orientation of the Gabor filters, respectively, and $*$ is referred as the convolution operator.

When convolving a face image with a range of Gabor filters at different orientations and scales, we can get a set of filter responses that characterize the local texture of the face image. In our method, we use 12 Gabor filters with the following parameters: $f \in \{1, 1.5, 2\}$ and $\Theta \in \{\frac{\pi}{8}, \frac{2\pi}{8}, \frac{4\pi}{8}, \frac{6\pi}{8}\}$. After convolving the face image with the Gabor filters, we obtain 12 Gabor magnitude images with 3 distinct scales and 4 distinct orientations as shown in Figure 7.

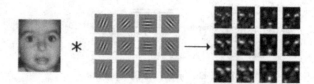

Fig. 7. Convolution of the face image with the Gabor filters

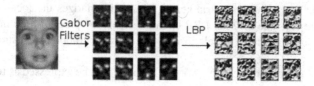

Fig. 8. LGBP face representation process

4.3   LGBP Features

Local Gabor Binary Pattern which is the combination of Gabor filters and the LBP operator, is used to enhance the information in the Gabor magnitude image. LGBP representation combines the local intensity distribution with the spatial information [22]. In order to generate the LGBP representation of a face image; the face image is convolved with multi-scale and multi-orientation Gabor filters first. Then, the LBP operator is applied to each pixel of the Gabor magnitude images as illustrated in Figure 8.

In order to obtain the LGBP representation of face images, the LBP operator is applied to each pixel of each 12 Gabor magnitude images. Then, we use the pixel values of 12 LGBP representations as LGBP features of the face image.

5   Experimental Results

We performed age classification experiments on the FG-NET Aging Database [6] and MORPH Database [16] which are the most popular databases in the face age estimation research community. The FG-NET Aging database contains 1002 high-resolution color or grayscale face images from 82 subjects ranging from age 0 to 69. Images in the database display facial appearance changes in pose, illumination, expression, etc. Also there are only few images of persons older than 40 in the database. Table 1 shows the age range distribution of the images that are used in the FG-NET experiment. The MORPH Database contains more than 55000 images of more than 13000 individuals ranging from age 16 to 77. The average number of images per individuals is 4. For MORPH experiment, we use 20 randomly selected samples for each age value which range from age 16 to 65.

In FG-NET experiment, for each sample in dataset, the age class values are labeled according to the exact age information. We used the age class scheme which is illustrated in Figure 1. Then for each classifier, Leave-One-Person-Out (LOPO) evaluation scheme is used. In each fold, all samples of a single person are used as the testing set

Table 1. The age range distribution of the images in the FG-NET Database

Age Classes	Number of Samples
(0-3)	141
(3-5)	120
(4-7)	156
(6-11)	201
(8-17)	321
(12-25)	361
(18-29)	210
(26-35)	100
(30-40)	88
(36-45)	55
(41-55)	49
(46-60)	27
(56-75)	9

Table 2. MAE of age estimation on FG-NET Database

Age Estimation Method	MAE
Classifier1 (Geometric-no cross ratio)	7.86
Classifier2 (Geometric)	6.68
Classifier3 (Gabor)	10.24
Classifier4 (Geometric+Gabor)	9.35
Classifier5 (LBP)	8.94
Classifier6 (Geometric+LBP)	8.18
Classifier7 (LGBP)	9.55
Classifier8 (Geometric+LGBP)	5.05

and the remaining samples are used as the training set. For comparison purposes, we used the Mean Absolute Error (MAE) [15] which is the most commonly used metric for age estimation. Table 2 shows the MAE of age estimation for different kinds of features which are used as face image feature vectors for the age classifiers.

It can be observed in Table 2 that, using all textural features in combination with the geometric features, contributes positively to the performance of age estimation. The combination of LGBP and Geometric features achieves 5.05 MAE on the FG-NET Aging Database. Note also that, cross ratio is a very important feature, because it improves the overall geometric estimation results.

As previously mentioned, the images in the FG-NET Database, are not equally distributed over age ranges. For a detailed analysis of the age estimation method, we calculated the MAE for each decade seperately. The comparative results of the MAEs per decade (MAE/D) for different kinds of features are shown in Table 3.

As we previously mentioned, overlapping age groups performs better with our interpolation method than the non-overlapping age groups. In order to verify this, we also tested our method with non-overlapping age class scheme. The age is partitioned into seven different classes such that ClassA (0-3), ClassB (4-7), ClassC (8-17), ClassD (18-29), ClassE (30-40), ClassF (41-55), ClassG (56-70), ClassH (70+). The samples are

Table 3. MAE/D of age estimation on FG-NET Database

Age Ranges	Feature Set							
	Geometric	LBP	Gabor	LGBP	Geo+LBP	Geo+Gabor	Geo+LGBP	Geo+LGBP (no overlap)
(0-10)	4.35	6.8	8.62	8.24	5.46	6.17	3.34	5.16
(11-20)	4.72	5.32	7.53	7.4	6.13	7.95	3.28	6.1
(21-30)	8.87	9.71	9.31	6.13	11.87	13.37	7.17	7.67
(31-40)	13.18	18.48	20.21	19.45	12.71	13.46	10.25	16.75
(41-50)	16.08	25.38	22.76	22.51	18.91	20.97	13.4	16.3
(51-60)	24.83	38.7	30.45	27.82	28.58	26.13	14.57	30.99
(61-70)	31.85	37.6	36.9	45.23	38.52	34.9	24.81	34.1

Table 4. MAE of age estimation on MORPH Database

Age Estimation Method	MAE
Classifier2 (Geometric)	15.15
Classifier3 (Gabor)	9.73
Classifier4 (Geometric+Gabor)	8.11
Classifier5 (LBP)	12.33
Classifier6 (Geometric+LBP)	10.93
Classifier7 (LGBP)	8.58
Classifier8 (Geometric+LGBP)	6.28

assigned one group label. Our best MAE for non-overlapping age groups was obtained using the fusion of LGBP and Geometric features as expected. The experimental results are shown in the last column of Table 3. The comparative results reveal that overlapping age groups performs remarkably better than the non-overlapping age groups.

The age class scheme which is used in FG-NET experiment is not adequate for MORPH experiment, because the face image dataset that is used in MORPH experiment does not contain samples for age values which range from 0 to 15. Therefore in MORPH experiment, for age class labeling process, we used another age class scheme which is illustrated in Figure 2. Then for each classifier, Leave-One-Out evaluation scheme is used. In each fold, one sample is used as the testing set and the remaining samples are used as the training set. Table 4 shows the MAE of age estimation on MORPH Database. As can be observed from Table 4, the combination of LGBP and Geometric features achieves 6.28 MAE on MORPH Database.

For a detailed analysis of the age estimation method, we calculated the MAE for each decade seperately for the MORPH Database. The comparative results of the MAEs per decade (MAE/D) for different kinds of features are shown in Table 5.

We can say that, the effectiveness of the fusion of LGBP and Geometric features result from many aspects. These include the LBP descriptor that captures small texture details, multi-scale and multi-orientation Gabor features that encode facial texture over a range of coarser scales. Finally, geometric proportions that are used for the characterization of the variations in facial shape contribute positively to the age estimation.

Table 5. MAE/D of age estimation on MORPH Database

Age Ranges	Feature Set						
	Geometric	LBP	Gabor	LGBP	Geo+LBP	Geo+Gabor	Geo+LGBP
(10-20)	21.37	16.66	13.96	9.29	13.8	11.62	9.13
(21-30)	14.65	13.76	9.19	8.33	11.69	8.04	6.5
(31-40)	11.42	8.2	9.27	7.36	8.02	7.57	5.34
(41-50)	12.49	12.03	10.7	7.97	11.11	8.38	7.06
(51-60)	16.26	12.31	7.15	9.62	10.77	6.44	5.23
(61-70)	20.5	14.13	10.78	10.03	12.32	8.57	5.43

Facial aging causes the most noticable variations in one's appearance during the formative years. As a result, the estimated age of a young person is more accurate than the older persons. As can be observed from Table 3, the MAE of age estimation at young ages is lower than the MAE of age estimation at old ages. Besides, in FG-NET experiment, there are only few old person images are used which are not enough for creating a general age estimation model. In MORPH experiment, we used same number of images for each age value and we get similar MAE values for each decade.

In this paper, we also tested the age estimation system according to the ethnicity of the subjects. For this purpose, we generated 4 different subsets of the MORPH database: Subset1(250 Black people images), Subset2(250 White people images), Subset3(250 Black people images), Subset4(250 White people images) and Subset5(Subset1+ Subset2). In these experiments Subset1, Subset2 and Subset5 were used as training sets, Subset3 and Subset4 were used as testing sets. All the face images in the subsets belong to different individuals and each subset contains equal number of samples for each gender. The experiments for different test scenarios are performed just for the fusion of LGBP and Geometric features, which was found to be the best combination by our previous experiments. Analyzing the results illustrated in Table 6, it can be observed that when the test images and the training imagesare of different races, MAE of the age estimation increases. Also when we compared the results with the Table 4, MAE of age estimation increases from 6.28 to 7.15 for black people and 7.95 for white people. In Table 4, number of training samples that were used for the experiments are 999, on the other hand it is 500 in Table 6. Therefore, this could be the reason that the MAE in Table 4 is lower than MAE in Table 6.

We also compared our results with the state of the art methods that follow the same popular Leave-One-Person-Out (LOPO) test strategy. As shown in Table 7, our method performs comparably with the state of the art approaches on age estimation.

Table 6. MAE of Different Test Scenarios on MORPH Database According to race information

Test Scenarios(Train/Test)	MAE
Subset5/Subset3 (Black+White/Black)	7.15
Subset5/Subset4 (Black+White/White)	7.95
Subset1/Subset3 (Black/Black)	6.19
Subset1/Subset4 (Black/White)	11.42
Subset2/Subset3 (White/Black)	8.96
Subset2/Subset4 (White/White)	6.62

Table 7. MAE of Different Methods on FG-NET Database

Method	MAE
Geng et al.[10]	6.77
Geng et al.[10]	8.06
Guo et al.[11]	5.07
Yan et al.[20]	4.95
Guo et al.[12]	4.77
Our Method	5.05

6 Conclusions

We presented an age estimation method that combines the geometric and textural features of human face. We propose to use overlapping age groups and a classifier to assign probabilities of a face image belonging to each group. The interpolation of the classifier probabilities produces the final estimated age. This method has the advantage of using robust classifiers in the process of numerical age estimation.

Our age group classifiers employ textural features, geometric features, and fusion of these features. Comparative experiments for different features show that for each textural feature, the fusion with the geometric features provides significant improvements. In this paper, we used the combination of geometric features and one textural feature set (LBP, Gabor, LGBP). The fusion of more than two feature sets might achieve better results. Employment of the cross ratio technique in geometric features improved the classification rates considerably. When we use the combination of LGBP and Geometric features in the AdaBoost algorithm, we obtain 5.05 and 6.28 MAE of age estimation for FG-NET and MORPH Databases, respectively. We formed different age class schemes for different datasets by using a heuristic approach. Our future work will concentrate on generating age class scheme automatically according to the characteristics of the dataset that is used in the age estimation experiments. As mentioned before, age estimation is a challenging problem even for human. Therefore we will compare performance our system with the human ability in age estimation as a future work.

Acknowledgements. The authors would like to thank Dr. K. Ricanek of UNCW for providing the MORPH Face Aging Database [16] and they would also like to thank the FG-NET consortium for providing the FG-NET Aging Database [6].

References

1. Ahonen, T., Hadid, A., Pietikäinen, M.: Face Recognition with Local Binary Patterns. In: Pajdla, T., Matas, J(G.) (eds.) ECCV 2004. LNCS, vol. 3021, pp. 469–481. Springer, Heidelberg (2004)
2. Bhuiyan, A., Liu, C.H.: On face recognition using gabor filters. World Academy of Science, Engineering and Technology (2007)
3. Burt, D.M., Perrett, D.I.: Perception of age in adult caucasian male faces: Computer graphic manipulation of shape and colour information. Proceedings of the Royal Society of London. Series B: Biological Sciences 259(1355), 137–143 (1995)

4. DeCarlo, D., Metaxas, D., Stone, M.: An anthropometric face model using variational techniques. In: Proceedings of the 25th Annual Conference on Computer Graphics and Interactive Techniques, SIGGRAPH 1998, pp. 67–74. ACM, New York (1998)
5. Ekenel, H., Fischer, M., Tekeli, E., Stiefelhagen, R., Ercil, A.: Local binary pattern domain local appearance face recognition. In: IEEE 16th Conference on Signal Processing, Communication and Applications, SIU 2008, pp. 1–4 (2008)
6. FGNET: The FG-NET Aging Database (2010), http://www.fgnet.rsunit.com/
7. Freund, Y., Schapire, R.E.: Experiments with a New Boosting Algorithm. In: Proceedings of the Thirteenth International Conference on Machine Learning, pp. 148–156 (1996)
8. Fu, Y., Guo, G., Huang, T.: Age synthesis and estimation via faces: A survey. IEEE Transactions on Pattern Analysis and Machine Intelligence 32(11), 1955–1976 (2010)
9. Gao, F., Ai, H.: Face Age Classification on Consumer Images with Gabor Feature and Fuzzy LDA Method. In: Tistarelli, M., Nixon, M.S. (eds.) ICB 2009. LNCS, vol. 5558, pp. 132–141. Springer, Heidelberg (2009)
10. Geng, X., Hua Zhou, Z., Smith-Miles, K.: Automatic age estimation based on facial aging patterns. IEEE Transactions on Pattern Analysis and Machine Intelligence 29, 2234–2240 (2007)
11. Guo, G., Fu, Y., Dyer, C., Huang, T.: Image-based human age estimation by manifold learning and locally adjusted robust regression. IEEE Transactions on Image Processing 17(7), 1178–1188 (2008)
12. Guo, G., Mu, G., Fu, Y., Huang, T.: Human age estimation using bio-inspired features. In: IEEE Conference on Computer Vision and Pattern Recognition, CVPR 2009, pp. 112–119 (2009)
13. Kilinc, M., Akgul, Y.S.: Human age estimation via geometric and textural features. In: Proc. International Conference on Computer Vision Theory and Applications (VISAPP), vol. 1, pp. 531–538 (2012)
14. Kwon, Y.H., Lobo, N.D.V.: Age classification from facial images. In: Proc. IEEE Conf. Computer Vision and Pattern Recognition, pp. 762–767 (1999)
15. Lanitis, A., Draganova, C., Christodoulou, C.: Comparing different classifiers for automatic age estimation. IEEE Trans. Systems, Man, Cybernetics Part B 34(1), 621–628 (2004)
16. Ricanek Jr., K., Tesafaye, T.: MORPH: A longitudinal image database of normal adult age-progression. In: Proceedings of the 7th International Conference on Automatic Face and Gesture Recognition, FGR 2006, Washington, DC, USA, pp. 341–345 (2006)
17. Ramanathan, N., Chellappa, R.: Modeling age progression in young faces. In: IEEE Computer Society Conference on Computer Vision and Pattern Recognition, vol. 1, pp. 387–394 (2006)
18. Ramanathan, N., Chellappa, R.: Modeling shape and textural variations in aging faces. In: 8th IEEE International Conference on Automatic Face Gesture Recognition, FG 2008, pp. 1–8 (2008)
19. Shan, S., Gao, W., Chang, Y., Cao, B., Yang, P.: Review the Strength of Gabor Features for Face Recognition from the Angle of Its Robustness to Mis-Alignment. In: International Conference on Pattern Recognition, vol. 1, pp. 338–341 (2004)
20. Yan, S., Zhou, X., Liu, M., Hasegawa-Johnson, M., Huang, T.: Regression from patch-kernel. In: IEEE Conference on Computer Vision and Pattern Recognition, CVPR 2008, pp. 1–8 (2008)
21. Yang, Z., Ai, H.: Demographic Classification with Local Binary Patterns. In: Lee, S.-W., Li, S.Z. (eds.) ICB 2007. LNCS, vol. 4642, pp. 464–473. Springer, Heidelberg (2007)
22. Zhang, W., Shan, S., Gao, W., Chen, X., Zhang, H.: Local gabor binary pattern histogram sequence (lgbphs): a novel non-statistical model for face representation and recognition. In: Tenth IEEE International Conference on Computer Vision, ICCV 2005, vol. 1, pp. 786–791 (2005)

Single Camera Railways Track Profile Inspection Using an Slice Sampling-Based Particle Filter

Marcos Nieto[1], Andoni Cortés[1], Javier Barandiaran[1],
Oihana Otaegui[1], and Iñigo Etxabe[2]

[1] Vicomtech-ik4, Paseo Mikeletegi 57, E20009, San Sebastian, Spain
[2] Datik, San Sebastian, Spain
{mnieto,acortes,jbarandiaran,ootaegui}@vicomtech.org,
ietxabe@datik.es

Abstract. An automatic method for rail inspection is introduced in this paper. The method detects rail flaws using computer vision algorithms. Unlike other methods designed for the same goal, we propose a method that automatically fits a 3D rail model to the observations. The proposed strategy is based on the novel combination of a simple but effective laser-camera calibration procedure with the application of an MCMC (Markov Chain Monte Carlo) framework. The proposed particle filter uses the efficient overrelation slice sampling method, which allows us to exploit the temporal coherence of observations and to obtain more accurate estimates than with other sampling techniques. The results show that the system is able to robustly obtain measurements of the wear of the rail. The two other contributions of the paper are the successfull introuction of the slice sampling technique into MCMC particle filters and the proposed online and flexible method for camera-laser calibration.

Keywords: Computer vision, Particle filter, Slice sampling, Laser, Calibration, Rail inspection.

1 Introduction

Defect detection systems for rail infrastructure are utterly needed to reduce train accident and associated costs while increase transport safety. The early detection of wear and deformation of tracks optimises maintenance scheduling and reduces costs of periodic human inspections. For that purpose it is required the introduction of new technological developments that make these systems more efficient, easier to install and cheaper for rail operators. Specifically, some magnitudes are of vital importance, such as the wear of the rails, and the widening of the track, which may cause catastrophic derailment of vehicles [1].

Traditionally, this problem has been faced using human inspection, or tactile mechanical devices which analyse the profile of the tracks while installed in dedicated rail vehicles running at low speed. Current technological trends try to avoid using contact-based devices to avoid their practical problems. Some works are based on the use of ultrasonic guided waves [2], which allow the detection of surface-breaking cracks and

G. Csurka et al. (Eds.): VISIGRAPP 2012, CCIS 359, pp. 326–339, 2013.

sizing of transverse; and vision-based systems, that determine the presence and magnitude of visible flaws [3]. Due to the rail geometry, lasers are typically used to project a line on the rail to ease the detection of its profile.

Regarding vision systems applied in this field, massive amounts of data are typically acquired and stored for a supervised posterior analysis stage to actually identify and locate defects. A major lack in this type of applications is the automatic fit of the model of the rail to the detections so that the potential wear of the rail could be automatically analyzed to see if it falls within the tolerances. The challenge of a vision-system in this field is to fit a planar 3D model of a rail to a set of 2D observations of laser projections in the abscence of reliable visual features that generate metric patterns (a pair of points with known distance, or a known angle between imaged lines). Some authors [3] [4] have omitted this problem and work at image level, which includes the inherent projective distortion into their measurements. Popular computer vision tools fail in this task, such as POSIT [5] since it does not work for planar structures, or optimisation methods, such as gradient-descent of Levenberg-Marquardt algorithm [6], which are extremely sensitive to local minima.

In this paper we propose an automatic method for rail auscultation using a vision-based system that fits a 3D model of the rail to the observations using a MCMC (Markov Chain Monte Carlo) particle filter. The method performs estimates of the probability density function of the model through time by applying the overrelaxation slice sampling technique, which provides accurate and robust fits while reducing the number of required evaluations of the posterior function compared to other schemes such as importance sampling or Metropolis-Hastings.

This paper is organized as follows: section 2 illustrates the architecture of the method; in section 3 the image processing techniques used for laser detection are explained; section 4 shows in detail the proposed particle filter strategy to fit the 3D model to the observations and section 5 depicts the procedure to project the 2D image elements into 3D to retrieve the actual metric error measurements. Tests and discussion are presented in section 6.

2 System Description

The system has been devised to measure two important magnitudes: the wear of the rails, and the widening of the track. For that purpose, one camera and a laser are installed for each rail, which are set-up as depicted in figure 1. As shown, the only requirement is that the laser line is orthogonally projected to the rail, i.e. the laser plane coincides with $Y = 0$. The camera monitorises the projected line with a certain angle to acquire images as those shown in figure 2. This angle can be any that guarantees that the laser line is observed in its projection on both the head and web of the rail.

It is noteworthy that the system does not require an exact positioning or simmetry of the cameras with respect to the rails, since the vision-based algorithm automatically determines the relative position and rotation $\{R, \mathbf{t}\}$ of the cameras with respect to their corresponding rail.

Figure 3 shows a block diagram of the system. The first stage comprises the proposed method for laser line detection, which feeds the 3D modeling stage that projects

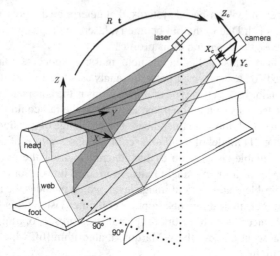

Fig. 1. Set-up of the elements of the system. The laser is installed orthogonal to the rail, while the camera shows some rotation and translation $\{R, \mathbf{t}\}$.

(a)   (b)   (c)

Fig. 2. Examples of images captured by the acquisition system: (a) typical static image; (b) image captured during regular service, with sun reflections; and (c) severe rail head wear

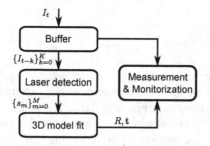

Fig. 3. Block diagram of the proposed method

a specific rail model (for instance we use the UIC-54 flat-bottom rail model) and finds the best translation and rotation parameters that makes the model fit to the observations. The last step is the reprojection of the detected points given the estimate of the model parameters to quantitatively determine the wear of the rail and the existing widening.

3 Laser Detection

This section describes the proposed procedure to extract the information relative to the rail profile from the images acquired by the system. In this harsh scenario two main problems arise. On the one hand, achieving a good isolation between the projection of the laser line and other illuminated elements (e.g. background elements reflecting the direct sun radiation). On the other hand, obtaining time coherent information despite the relative movement that the rails will show during regular services. The movement is caused by vibrations, curvature (the width of the track changes accordingly to the curve radius), or the relative position of the cameras with respect to the wheels (the more distance to the wheel, the more movement of the rail with respect to the bogie).

The laser line can be described by its visual characterizes. First, since we do use an infrared filter, the laser line is imaged as a bright stripe compared to the rest of the image, which remains dark (save for the reflective surfaces). Second, the laser line width can be considered fixed independently of the position in the image, since the relative distance between the different points in the rail is too low and causes no significant perspective effect.

According to these two considerations, the proposed method carries out the following actions (which are depicted with images in figure 4). First, we apply the Canny edge detector, which identifies the edges of the image, and we keep the gradient values (G_x, G_y) it internally computes using the Sobel operator [7]. From each identified edge pixel, we search in the gradient direction the closest edge pixel and store the obtained distance as a measure of the width of the stripe (see figure 5 8a)). Since we do have edges that do not belong to the laser stripe, a histogram analysis is carried out to select the most repeated distance value w_t. An example histogram is shown in figure 5 (b), where the ground truth value is shown with a dashed line. As shown, the detected maximum of the histogram is very close to the ground truth. This value is averaged in time to adapt the system measurements to the observations, so that we obtain $\hat{w}_{t,K} = \frac{1}{K} \sum_{k=1}^{K} \hat{w}_{t-k}$.

Since we do have an instantaneous estimate of $\hat{w}_{t,K}$ at each time instant (except for the very first frame), we can as well characterise the intensity level of the laser line by analyzing the intensity level of the middle pixels between pairs of edge points whose distance is close to $\hat{w}_{t,K}$. With this analysis we obtain the mean μ_I and standard deviation σ_I of the intensity values $I(x, y)$ of the pixels likely belonging to the laser stripe.

From the information extracted at pixel-level, it is possible to search for the laser stripes at a higher level. The search is carried out locating pairs of edge points that likely belong to the laser. A pair p_i is defined as a couple of points which define the left and right limit of the projected laser line and whose distance is close to $\hat{w}_{t,K}$. To reduce the algorith complexity, we define pairs at row level, i.e.

$$p_i = \{(x_l, x_r, y) \setminus |x_r - x_l - \hat{w}_{t-K}| < \epsilon\} \tag{1}$$

where x_l and x_r are the x-coordinates of the points of the pair, y is their common vertical coordinate; and ϵ is an error limit that can be safely set as a percentage of the width value, e.g. $\epsilon = 0.05\hat{w}_{t-K}$.

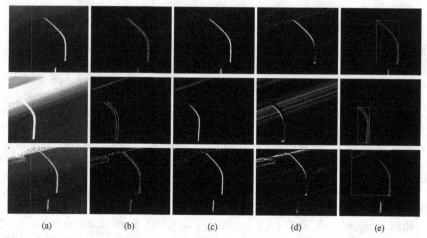

(a)   (b)   (c)   (d)   (e)

Fig. 4. Examples of the proposed laser detection methodology for different cases (shown in rows): (a) original image; (b) Canny edges; (c) G_x, magnitude of gradient x-component; (d) G_y, magnitude of gradient y-component; and (e) connected component analysis.

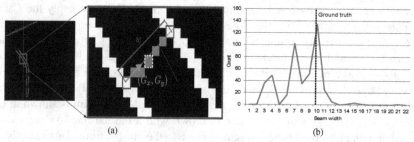

(a)   (b)

Fig. 5. Laser detection: (a) estimation of the width of the laser beam. The middle point between the start and end points is used to compute the mean intensity level of the laser line; (b) Histogram of width values for the example images of figure 4 middle row.

The intensity level information is used to classify pairs in connected groups so that the different parts of the laser projection (the corresponding to the head and the web of the rail) can be identified. This classification will allow having a better model fit. For that purpose a thresholded image is created from I using as threshold $\mu_{t,K} - 2\sigma_{t,K}$. For each pair we can define a label that identifies the connected component it belongs to, $c_i = m$.

Finally we obtain stripes as sets of pairs which belong to the same connected component of the intensity binarized image: $s_m = \{p_i \setminus c_i = m\}$. From here on we will denote a pair p_i as $p_{m,i}$ where m identifies the cluster or stripe s_m it belongs to.

To reduce the impact of outliers those sets of pairs whose cardinality is lower than 3 are removed, i.e. there must be at least 3 connected pairs to define a stripe. Two main stripes are finally identified amongst the stripes. As shown in figure 4 (e) the lower vertical stripe corresponds to the rail web, and the largest one defines the head of the rail. The lower point of the head stripe will be denoted as anchor point, and used as a reference point to fit the 3D model.

4   3D Model Fit

To actually be capable of determining the existing wear of the rail, it is necessary to fit the rail model to the observations extracted from the images. The observation of image I_t is defined as $\mathbf{z}_t = \{s_m\}_{m=1}^M$, i.e. a set of M stripes.

The model fit must be such that describes the relative movement between the rail and the camera, so that we obtain a common coordinate system for the model and the observation and measure the potential defects.

From the projective geometry point of view, there is an unsolved ambiguity in the projection of a 3D planar model to a 2D observation with unkown scale: a single 2D observation can be the projection of the model at different positions and distances.

Therefore, the problem consists on finding the relative traslation and rotation between each camera with its corresponding rail. This way, for each camera we can define the state vector to be estimated at each time instant t as $\mathbf{x}_t = (x, y, z, \theta, \dot{x}, \dot{y}, \dot{z}, \dot{\theta})^\top$, where (x, y, z) are the translation components of each coordinate axis and θ is the rotation in the y-axis (the rotation of the other angles can be considered negligible). The last four elements correspond to the first derivative of each of the four former parameters. We will assume that the intrinsic parameters of the camera are computed at the set-up and installation stage so that the projection matrix is already computed and available.

In this work we propose to apply Bayesian inference concepts that allow us to propagate the probability density function of the state vector conditioned to the knowledge of all observations up to time t, $p(\mathbf{x}_t | \mathbf{z}_{1:t})$. Within this framework we will be able to overcome the mentioned ambiguity and achieve accurate estimates of the target coordinate systems so that the rail defects can be measured.

4.1   MCMC Particle Filter

MCMC methods have been successfully applied to different nature tracking problems [8,9]. They can be used as a tool to obtain maximum a posteriori (MAP) estimates provided likelihood and prior models. Basically, MCMC methods define a Markov chain, $\{\mathbf{x}_t^{(s)}\}_{s=1}^{N_s}$, over the space of states, $\mathbf{x}$, such that the stationary distribution of the chain is equal to the target posterior distribution $p(\mathbf{x}_t | \mathbf{z}_{1:t})$. A MAP, or point-estimate, of the posterior distribution can be then selected as any statistic of the sample set (e.g. sample mean or robust mean), or as the sample, $\mathbf{x}_t^{(s)}$, with highest $p(\mathbf{x}_t^{(s)} | \mathbf{z}_{1:t})$, which will provide the MAP solution to the estimation problem. Compared to other typical sampling strategies, like sequential-sampling particle filters [10], MCMC directly sample from the posterior distribution instead of the prior density, which might be not a good approximation to the optimal importance density, and thus avoid convergence problems.

If we hypothesize that the posterior can be expressed as a set of samples

$$p(\mathbf{x}_{t-1} | Z^{t-1}) \approx \frac{1}{N_s} \sum_{s=1}^{N_s} \delta(\mathbf{x}_{t-1} - \mathbf{x}_{t-1}^{(s)}) \tag{2}$$

then

$$p(\mathbf{x}_t | Z^{t-1}) \approx \frac{1}{N_s} \sum_{s=1}^{N_s} p(\mathbf{x}_t | \mathbf{x}_{t-1}^{(s)}) \tag{3}$$

We can directly sample from the posterior distribution since we have its approximate analytic expression [8]:

$$p(\mathbf{x}_t|Z^t) \propto p(\mathbf{z}_t|\mathbf{x}_t) \sum_{s=1}^{N_s} p(\mathbf{x}_t|\mathbf{x}_{t-1}^{(s)}) \tag{4}$$

For this purpose we need a sampling strategy, such as the Metropolis-Hastings (MH) algorithm, which dramatically improves the performance of traditional particle filters based on importance sampling.

Nevertheless, there are other sampling strategies that can be applied in this context and that improve the performance of MH, reduce the dependency on parameters and increase the accuracy of the estimation using the same number of evaluations of the target posterior. Next subsection introduces the slice sampling algorihtm, that was designed to remove the problem of random walk detected in MH [12,14].

4.2 Markov Chain Generation

Particle filters infer a point-estimate as an statistic (typically, the mean) of a set of samples. Consequently, the posterior distribution has to be evaluated at least once per sample. For high-dimensional problems as ours, MCMC-based methods typically require the use of thousands of samples to reach a stationary distribution. This drawback is compounded for importance sampling methods, since the number of required samples increases exponentially with the problem dimension.

In this work we propose to use the overrelaxated slice sampling strategy [12], which avoids random walks in the generation of the Markov Chains and thus allows obtaining better descriptions of the posterior distribution.

Slice Sampling. This technique generates a chain of samples, $\{\mathbf{x}_k\}_{k=1}^N$ from a arbitrary target pdf, $p(\mathbf{z})$ [14]. The only requirement to apply this algorithm is that the value $p(\mathbf{x})$ can be evaluated for any given value of $\mathbf{x}$. As described by [13], the slice sampling improves the results, in terms of efficiency, of typical sampling approaches based on the Metropolis-Hastings (MH) algorithm [11]. MH has an important drawback that makes it inefficient for the proposed application as it is sensible to the step size, given by the proposal distribution. If it is chosen too small, the process behave as a random walk, which makes the algorithm converge very slowly and, on the contrary, if it is too large, the rejection rate may be very high, hence not achieving accurate results. The advantage of the slice sampler is due to its ability to automatically adapt its step size according to the characteristics of the probability density function.

For a better understanding of the slice sampler, let us consider first the univariate case. Slice sampling works by augmenting x with an auxiliary random variable u and then sample from the joint (x, u) space. Given the previous sample x_{k-1}, u is uniformly drawn in the range $[0, p(x_{k-1})]$. Fixed u, the sample x_{k-1} is obtained from the "slice" through the distribution defined by $\{x : p(x) > u\}$. This criterion is illustrated in figure 6 (a). Nevertheless, it is difficult to find the limits of the slice and thus to draw a sample from it. For that reason an approximation is done by means of creating a

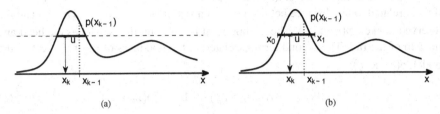

(a)   (b)

Fig. 6. Univariate slice sampling: (a) the uniform u value determines the slice through $p(x)$; and (b) the practical implementation uses fixed length steps to determine the range in which x is uniformly sampled

quantized local slice, delimited by x_0 and x_1 as shown in figure 6 (b). To obtain these limits, the value $p(x)$ is evaluated at left and right of x_{k-1} using fixed length steps (the quantification step) until $p(x) < u$. The next sample, x_k, is obtained by uniformly sampling on this range (iteratively until $p(x_k) > u$).

For multidimensional problems, the one-dimensional strategy can be applied repeatedly on every single dimension to obtain the samples.

Overrelaxated Slice Sampling. The overrelaxation method consists on the automatic generation of a new sample given the defined slice without the need of using a uniform random sample between the slice limits. When the slice is defined, the next sample value x_{t-1} is defined as the symmetric point between the middle of the slice limits and the start point x_{k-1}.

This simple step reduces the rejection rate of samples in many situations, since the probability of the symetric point x_{t-1} to have a function value lower than u is very reduced (it only will occur if the previous point was actually in the limit of the slice).

4.3   Likelihood Function

The likelihood function determines the evaluation of each sample of the chain $\mathbf{x}_t^{(s)}$ with respect to the observation at each time instant. Formally, this function determines the probability of observing $\mathbf{z}_t$ given a certain state vector hypothesis $\mathbf{x}_t^{(s)}$.

In our case, the observations correspond to the detected laser stripes, while each sample $\mathbf{x}_t^{(s)}$ determines a hypothesized position and rotation of the 3D model. With the camera calibration information we can project this model to the image and define a cost function that determines how good the projected models fit to the detected stripes.

The model can be defined as $\{c_i = (X_i, 0, Z_i)\}_{i=1}^N$ in $Y = 0$, a set of coplanar control points. In homogeneous coordinates we have $\{\mathbf{X}_i = (X_i, 0, Z_i, 1)^\top\}_{i=1}^N$. For each sample proposed by the particle fitler, we do have a traslation and rotation of the model which is applied to each control point:

$$\mathbf{X}_i^{(s)} = R^{(s)}\mathbf{X}_i + \mathbf{C}^{(s)} \tag{5}$$

The result is projected into the image plane using the camera projection matrix: $\mathbf{x}_i^{(s)} = P\mathbf{X}_i^{(s)}$.

The likelihood function can be defined as the weighted sum of two functions. One of them related to the distance between the anchor point of the projected model and the observed strokes, $p(\mathbf{z}_t, \mathbf{x}_{t,a}^{(s)})$. The anchor point is the point that separates the head and the web of the rail. The second term is related to the goodness of fit of the rest of the model, $p(\mathbf{z}_t, \mathbf{x}_{t,b}^{(s)})$:

$$p(\mathbf{z}_t | \mathbf{x}_t^{(s)}) = \alpha p(\mathbf{z}_t, \mathbf{x}_{t,a}^{(s)}) + (1 - \alpha) p(\mathbf{z}_t | \mathbf{x}_{t,b}^{(s)}) \qquad (6)$$

The first term, related to the anchor point is defined as a normal distribution on the distance between the observed and reference point:

$$p(\mathbf{z}_t | \mathbf{x}_{t,a}^{(s)}) = \frac{1}{\sqrt{2\pi}\sigma_a} \exp\left(-\frac{1}{2} \frac{d^2(\mathbf{x}_{t,a}^{(s)}, \mathbf{z}_{t,a})}{\sigma_a^2} \right) \qquad (7)$$

where $\mathbf{z}_{t,a}$ is the 2D position of the anchor point and σ_a is the standard deviation that characterizes the expected observation noise of the anchor point.

For the second term we first loop over the projected model points and search for the closest left and right points of a pair p_i. In case there is no pair closer than a defined threshold, no points are associated with that model point. When the points are found, the counters N_l and N_r are increased, and the distance between the model point and the left and right points are accumulated as d_l and d_r.

The second term can be then described as:

$$p(\mathbf{z}_t | \mathbf{x}_{t,b}^{(s)}) = \frac{1}{\sqrt{2\pi}\sigma} \sum_{i=\{l,r\}} \frac{N_i}{2N_{model}} \exp\left(-\frac{d_i^2}{\sigma^2} \right) \qquad (8)$$

where N_{model} is the number of model points. Since this function uses both left and right fitting, it gives high likelihood values for models that project between the left and right edges of the laser beam, which enhances the accuracy of the fit compared to using only one of the edges.

For a better visualization, we have computed the likelihood value of all the possible values of the model state vector spanning its x and y-coordinates for an example image. The result can be seen in figure 7 where the likelihood map is depicted as an intensity image, where the brighter pixels correspond to (x, y) positions with higher likelihood value, and darker ones with lower value. As shown, the likelihood function is a peaked and descending function that can be easily sampled with the proposed slice sampling procedure. In figure 7 (b) we can see as well the obtained samples, which actually fall in the regions of the space with higher likelihood values. In figure 8 an example model fit is depicted. The color code of the axes of the coordinate frame helps to understand the likelihood map of figure 7.

5 Rail Wear and Widening

When the model fit has been obtained, we know the new coordinate system $\{X', Y', Z'\}$ that best fit to the observations, and that can be different from the initial coordinate system $\{X, Y, Z\}$ according to the potential relative movements of the rail with respect

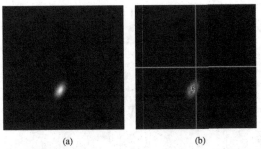

(a)   (b)

Fig. 7. Visualization of the likelihood map of the (x, y) dimension: (a) likelihood map; (b) likelihood map and the set of samples obtained with the slice sampling strategy

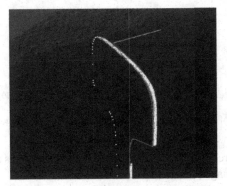

Fig. 8. An example hypothesis drawn by the sampler

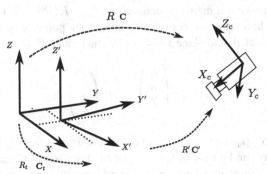

Fig. 9. Relationship between the initial coordinate system $\{X, Y, Z\}$, the camera coordinate system, $\{X_c, Y_c, Z_c\}$ and the coordinate system defined after the application of the correction provided by the particle filter $\{X', Y', Z'\}$

to the camera (typically when the train is in a curve). Figure 9 illustrates the different coordinate systems involved.

To analyze the observed profile and compare it with the reference profile it is necessary to transform back the observations from the 3D plane defined by $Y' = 0$. We can do that by obtaining the new extrinsic parameters of the camera coordinate system, $\{R', C'\}$, recompute the projection matrix P' that links 3D points in $\{X', Y', Z'\}$ to

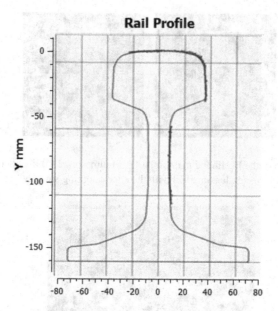

Fig. 10. Comparison of the reference UIC-54 model and the backprojected laser points

points in the image and reduce it to a 3×3 homography that defines the correspondence between points in the image plane and points in the $Y' = 0$.

The new extrinsic parameters can be computed using the initial extrinsic parameters and the values given by the filter as $\mathbf{C}' = R_t^{-1}(\mathbf{C} - \mathbf{C}_t)$ and $R' = RR_t$.

The corrected projection matrix is defined as $P' = K[R'| - R'\mathbf{C}']$, a matrix that links 3D points in homogeneous coordinates into image points as $\mathbf{x} = P'\mathbf{X}'$. Given that the laser is projected onto plane $Y' = 0$, we can reduce P' to a 3×3 homography H' as:

$$\mathbf{x} = P' \begin{pmatrix} X \\ 0 \\ Z \\ 1 \end{pmatrix} = H' \begin{pmatrix} X \\ Z \\ 1 \end{pmatrix} \tag{9}$$

where $H' = (\mathbf{p}_1, \mathbf{p}_3, \mathbf{p}_4)$ and $\mathbf{p}_i$ is the i-th column of P'.

The homography can be used to backproject the laser points detected in the image into a rectified view of plane $Y' = 0$ where metric measurements of the rail wear can be generated as shown in figure 10.

Finally, the widening of the track can be as well computed as the X component of the relative traslation between the coordinate system $\{X', Y', Z'\}$ of the left camera and the right camera.

6   Tests and Discussion

We have evaluated the performance of the proposed strategy applying different sampling methods but using for them all the proposed likelihood function: sequential

Table 1. Eficiency comparison between slice sampling (SS) and overrelaxated slice-sampling (OSS)

Step = 1 (mm)	SS		OSS			
Num. Samp.	Num. Evals.	Error(mm)	Num. Evals.	Error(mm)	$\Delta Evals(\%)$	$\Delta Error(\%)$
10	287	3.364	266	3.213	7.32	4.49
15	430	2.732	419	2.572	2.56	5.86
25	695	1.198	650	1.363	6.47	-13.77
50	1345	1.345	1221	1.635	9.22	-21.56
100	2977	1.057	2869	1.101	3.63	4.16
Step = 2 (mm)	SS		OSS			
Num. Samp.	Num. Evals.	Error(mm)	Num. Evals.	Error(mm)	$\Delta Evals(\%)$	$\Delta Error(\%)$
10	249	3.454	283	3.553	-13.65	-2.87
15	354	2.235	313	2.322	11.58	-3.89
25	632	1.332	561	1.554	11.23	-16.67
50	1229	1.112	1095	1.223	10.90	-9.98
100	2477	0.988	2171	1.212	12.35	-22.67
Step = 4 (mm)	SS		OSS			
Num. Samp.	Num. Evals.	Error(mm)	Num. Evals.	Error(mm)	$\Delta Evals(\%)$	$\Delta Error(\%)$
10	195	5.391	166	5.489	14.87	-1.82
15	395	3.325	312	2.665	21.01	19.85
25	602	2.156	481	1.559	20.10	27.69
50	1124	1.285	901	1.082	19.84	15.80
100	2229	0.998	1844	1.001	17.27	-0.30

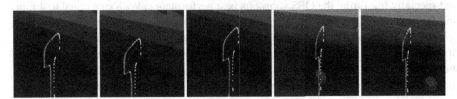

Fig. 11. Example fitting of the UIC-54 model to a test rail section

importance resampling (SIR) [10], Metropolis-Hastings (MH) [13], Slice Sampling [14] and Overrelaxed Slice Sampling (OSS) [12].

Due to the dimensionality of the problem (6 DoF), the SIR particle filter requires too many samples to keep a low error fit. It has been shown that the number of samples SIR requires to that end grows exponentially with the dimensionality of the problem. In our case we have observed that SIR does not provide stable results using the proposed likelihood function for a reasonable number of particles (up to 10^4).

We have implemented three MCMC sampling methods that create Markov Chain, which are known to be the solution to the dimensionality problem of SIR: MH, SS and OSS. The MH, as explained in [13][14], suffers from the problem of the selection of the proposal function. If a gaussian function is used, the problem is to find the adequate standard deviation for that proposal. We have observed that we have a trade-off problem: on the one hand we need small deviations (less than 0.5 mm) to appropriately model the posterior function, while MH requires high values to move quickly in the state space and avoid the random-walk problem. This trade-off is not solved satisfactorily by the MH for the proposed problem.

On the contrary, slice sampling is capable of finding this trade-off, since its sampling methodology relies on finding slices which guarantees a good adaptation to the posterior function shape. This capability allows obtaining very accurate results, specially when using small values for the steps that defines the slice. The only problem of using small steps is that the definition of the slice requires often a significant number of evaluations of the posterior, which in turn reduces the performance of the system. This drawback can be partially solved using the overrelaxated slice sampling, which reduces the number of evaluations to be carried out.

We have carried out a test to compare the performance of the system using the SS and the OSS methods. The test is run to fit the UIC-54 model on a sequence with movement, to evaluate how good the sampling alternatives fit when the posterior function is changing from one frame to the next one. The comparison is based on the computation of the fit error. The results are shown in table 1. As can be observed, we have run the tests for different step values (1, 2 and 4 mm), and for different number of effective samples to be drawn by the sampling methods. The tables shows the number of evaluations required by the methods to obtain such number of effective samples, and the fit error, which is computed as the average distance of the detected laser points reprojected into plane $Y' = 0$. The last two columns show the relative difference between these parameters for the SS and the OSS.

As we can see, for small steps both methods perform similarly, requiring the OSS between 2 and 9% less evaluations. Nevertheless, for larger steps, such as for 2 mm and specially for 4 mm, the OSS shows its best performance. With step equal to 4 mm, and 100 samples, OSS evaluates the posterior 1844 times, while SS needs 2229, both of them obtaining almost the same error fit. These results show that the OSS is capable of more efficiently representing a probability density function using the slice method, which allows faster computation without sacrifying accuracy, which remains close to 1 mm average fit error (some examples of the model fitting are shown in Fig. 5).

6.1 Future Work

This paper summarizes the achievements reached during the development of a system for the automatic inspection of rail wear and widening. At the time of submitting this paper the project is in a development stage, so that the results have been obtaining with a preliminar prototype system. In the further stages of the project, several improvements are planned and a more detailed evaluation analysis which will integrate localisation data to the detection of rail defects.

7   Conclusions

In this paper we have introduced a new methodology for the early detection of rail wear and track widening based on projective geometry concepts and a probabilistic inference framework. Our approach presents a scenario where its usage in regular services is possible, with low cost acquisition and processing equipment, which is a competitive advantage over other manual or contact methodologies. For that purpose, we propose the use of powerful probabilistic inference tools that allow us to obtain 3D information of the magnitudes to be measured from uncomplete and ambiguous information. In this proposal we use the overrelaxated slice sampling technique, which implies a step forward in MCMC methods due to its reliability, versatility and greater computational efficiency compared to other methods of the literature that build Markov Chains.

Acknowledgements. This work has been partially supported by the Basque Government under the INTEK2011 strategic project TRACKINSPECTOR.

References

1. Cannon, D.F., Edel, K.-O., Grassie, S.L., Sawley, K.: Rail defects: an overview. Fatigue & Fracture of Engineering Materials & Structures 26(10), 865–886 (2003)
2. Lanza di Scalea, F., Rizzo, P., Coccia, S., Bartoli, I., Fateh, M., Viola, E., Pascale, G.: Non-contact ultrasonic inspection of rails and signal processing for automatic defect detection and classification. Insight - Non-Destructive Testing and Condition Monitoring 47(6), 346–352 (2005)
3. Alippi, C., Casagrande, E., Scotti, F., Piuri, V.: Composite Real-Time Image Processing for Railways Track Profile Measurement. IEEE Transactions on Instrumentation and Measurement 49(3), 559–564 (2000)
4. Alippi, C., Casagrande, E., Fumagalli, M., Scotti, F., Piuri, V., Valsecchi, L.: An Embedded System Methodology for Real-Time Analysis of Railways Track Profile. In: IEEE Technology Conference on Instrumentation and Measurement, pp. 747–751 (2002)
5. DeMenthon, D., Davis, L.S.: Model-Based Object Pose in 25 Lines of Code. International Journal of Computer Vision (15), 123–141 (1995)
6. Nocedal, J., Wright, S.J.: Numerical Optimization. Springer (2006)
7. Gonzalez, R.C., Woods, R.E.: Digital Image Processing. Prentice Hall (2002)
8. Khan, Z., Balch, T., Dellaert, F.: MCMC-Based Particle Filtering for Tracking a Variable NUmber of Interacting Targets. IEEE Transactions on Pattern Analysis and Machine Intelligence 27(11), 1805–1819 (2005)
9. Bardet, F., Chateau, T.: MCMC Particle Filter for Real-Time Visual Tracking of Vehicles. In: IEEE International Conference on Intelligent Transportation Systems, pp. 539–544 (2008)
10. Arulampalam, M.S., Maskell, S., Gordon, N., Clapp, T.: A Tutorial on Particle Filters for Online Nonlinear/Non-Gaussian Bayesian Tracking. IEEE Transactions on Signal Processing 50(2), 174–188 (2002)
11. Gilks, W., Richardson, S., Spiegelhalter, D.: Markov Chain Monte Carlo Methods in Practice. Chapman and Hall/CRC (1996)
12. Neal, R.M.: Suppressing Random Walks in Markov Chain Monte Carlo Using Ordered Overrelaxation. In: Learning in Graphical Models, pp. 205–228 (1998)
13. Bishop, C.M.: Pattern Recognition and Machine Learning (Information Science and Statistics). Springer (2006)
14. Neal, R.M.: Slice sampling. Annals of Statistics 31, 705–767 (2003)

Foreground Segmentation from Occlusions
Using Structure and Motion Recovery

Kai Cordes, Björn Scheuermann, Bodo Rosenhahn, and Jörn Ostermann

Institut für Informationsverarbeitung (TNT), Leibniz Universität Hannover,
Appelstr. 9, 30167 Hannover, Germany
{cordes,scheuermann,rosenhahn,ostermann}@tnt.uni-hannover.de
http://www.tnt.uni-hannover.de

Abstract. The segmentation of foreground objects in camera images is a fundamental step in many computer vision applications. For visual effect creation, the foreground segmentation is required for the integration of virtual objects between scene elements. On the other hand, camera and scene estimation is needed to integrate the objects perspectively correct into the video.

In this paper, discontinued feature tracks are used to detect occlusions. If these features reappear after their occlusion, they are connected to the correct previously discontinued trajectory during sequential camera and scene estimation. The combination of optical flow for features in consecutive frames and SIFT matching for the wide baseline feature connection provides accurate and stable feature tracking. The knowledge of occluded parts of a connected feature track is used to feed an efficient segmentation algorithm which crops the foreground image regions automatically. The presented graph cut based segmentation uses a graph contraction technique to minimize the computational expense.

The presented application in the integration of virtual objects into video. For this application, the accurate estimation of camera and scene is crucial. The segmentation is used for the automatic occlusion of the integrated objects with foreground scene content. Demonstrations show very realistic results.

1 Introduction

Camera motion estimation and simultaneous reconstruction of rigid scene geometry from video is a key technique in many computer vision applications [1–3] A popular application in movie production is the integration of virtual objects. For the perspectively correct view of these objects in each camera, a highly accurate estimation of the camera path is crucial [4]. State of the art techniques use a pinhole camera model and image features for the camera motion estimation. The camera motion estimation workflow consists of feature detection, correspondence analysis, outlier elimination, and bundle adjustment as demonstrated in [1], for example. For the occlusion of the virtual objects with foreground scene content, a segmentation is required which is usually done manually [4].

Most scene reconstruction techniques rely on feature correspondences in consecutive frames. Thus, temporarily occluded scene content causes broken trajectories. A reappearing feature induces a new 3D object point which adopts a different and

G. Csurka et al. (Eds.): VISIGRAPP 2012, CCIS 359, pp. 340–353, 2013.

Fig. 1. *Playground* sequence (1280 × 720 pixels), top row: example frames 11, 33, 44, 76 with temporarily occluded scene content resulting from static and moving foreground objects. Feature trajectories discontinue and their features reappear after being occluded; center row: for integrating virtual objects, it is essential to handle foreground occlusions in the composition of virtual and real scenes; bottom row: correct occlusion of the virtual objects.

therefore erroneous position. Recent approaches solve this problem by incorporating non-consecutive feature correspondences [5–8]. The additional correspondences and their trajectories are used to stabilize the bundle adjustment and improve the reconstruction results. The reconstructed object points of these feature trajectories are not seen in several camera views. In many cases, they are not seen because of occlusion with foreground objects. This information has not been used for further scene understanding so far.

We regard the occlusion and reappearance of scene parts as valuable scene information. It can be used to detect occlusions in video and result in a meaningful foreground segmentation of the images. The foreground segmentation can be used for the automatic occlusion of integrated virtual objects.

A typical input example is shown in Fig. 1, top row. In this sequence, the background scene is temporarily occluded by a part of the swing rack and the swinging child. For the application of integrating virtual objects into the video, the foreground objects have to occlude the correct augmented image parts throughout the sequence. This is essential to provide realistic results. Otherwise the composed sequence does not look satisfactory as shown in the center row of Fig. 1. The desired result is shown in the bottom row.

In literature, some approaches have been proposed for occlusion handling in video. A comparable objective is followed in [9]. Occlusion edges are detected [10] and used for the video segmentation of foreground objects. However, no 3D information of the scene is incorporated and only edges of one foreground object are extracted which is not advantageous for the following image based segmentation. In [11], the complete hull of occluded objects is reconstructed. For this approach, video streams from multiple, calibrated cameras are required in a shape from silhouette based 3D reconstruction. In [12], differently moving objects in the video are clustered by analyzing point trajectories for a long time. In this approach, a dense representation of the images is needed [13]. In [14], a sparse image representation is used. The background trajectories span a subspace, in which foreground trajectories are classified as outliers. The idea is to distinguish between camera induced motion and object induced motion. These two classes are used to build background and foreground appearance models for the following image segmentation. However, many foreground trajectories are required to provide a reliable segmentation result. The approach presented in [15] computes depth maps which are combined with a structure from motion technique to obtain stable results.

Our approach is designed for the integration of virtual objects, and can make use of the extracted 3D information of the reconstructed scene. It is not restricted to certain foreground object classes and allows for arbitrary camera movements. A very important step is the feature tracking. For the demanded accuracy, long and accurate trajectories are desired. In contrast to [12, 16], our approach relies on a sparse representation of the images using reliable image feature correspondences as required for the structure and motion estimation. We propose a combination of wide-baseline feature matching for feature correspondences in non-consecutive frames and optical flow based tracking for frame to frame correspondences. The resulting trajectories are incorporated in an extended bundle adjustment optimization for the camera estimation. The additional constraints lead to an improved scene reconstruction [7, 8].

We identify foreground objects in the camera images as regions which occlude already reconstructed scene content. Resulting from the structure and motion recovery approach, reconstructed scene content is represented by 3D object points. In contrast to [9], this approach provides occlusion points inside the foreground objects, which is very desirable for the following segmentation procedure. The image segmentation is obtained by efficiently minimizing an energy function consisting of labeling and neighborhood costs using a contracted graph [17, 18]. The algorithm is initialized with the automatically extracted information about foreground and background regions. The presented approach eases the integration of virtual objects into video significantly.

In the following Sect. 2, the structure and motion recovery approach is explained. Sect. 3 shows the automatic detection of foreground regions using correspondences in non-consecutive frames and their object points. In Sect. 4, the application of integrating virtual objects into video is demonstrated. Sect. 5 shows experimental results on natural image data. In Sect. 6, the paper is concluded.

2   Structure and Motion Recovery

The objective of structure and motion recovery is the simultaneous estimation of the camera parameters and 3D object points of the observed scene [1]. The camera parameters of one camera are represented by the projection matrix A_k for each image I_k, $k \in [1 : K]$ for a sequence of K images. For the estimation, corresponding feature points are required. In case of video with small displacements between two frames, feature tracking methods like KLT [19] tend to produce less outliers and provide increased localization accuracy compared to feature matching methods [20].

Methods as presented in [6–8] additionally make use of feature correspondences in non-consecutive frames as shown in Fig. 2 and therefore increase the reconstruction reliability. Establishing non-consecutive feature correspondences is especially important if scene content disappears and reappears, e.g. if foreground objects temporarily occlude

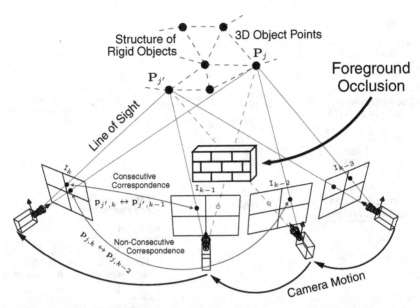

Fig. 2. Common structure and motion estimation techniques use corresponding feature points in consecutive images only, for example $\mathbf{p}_{j',k} \leftrightarrow \mathbf{p}_{j',k-1}$. Due to foreground occlusion, trajectories discontinue and the corresponding scene content reappears in a later image. These trajectories are connected using a wide-baseline correspondence analysis, for example $\mathbf{p}_{j,k} \leftrightarrow \mathbf{p}_{j,k-2}$. A real world example is shown in Fig. 1.

the observed scene. It follows, that non-consecutive correspondences induce occlusion information which is explicitly used in our approach for automatic foreground segmentation as explained in Sect. 3. The developed feature tracking scheme is presented in Sect. 2.1, and the bundle adjustment scheme is shown in Sect. 2.2.

2.1   Feature Detection and Tracking

The presented feature tracking scheme is designed for even large foreground occlusions while the camera is moving freely. Hence, a wide baseline analysis is required for establishing correspondences in non-consecutive frames. For a reliable feature matching, the SIFT descriptor [21] is used for this task. Consequently, the feature selection uses the scale space for the detection of interest points. For a complete scene representation, the features in an image should be spatially well-distributed. For the results shown in this paper, the SIFT detector is used for newly appearing features and provides sufficiently distributed points. For sequences with very low texture content, a combination of different scale invariant feature detectors should be considered [21–23]. For the tracking from frame to frame, the KLT tracker provides higher accuracy and less outliers than feature matching techniques.

The tracking workflow is shown in Fig. 3. Newly detected SIFT features are tracked using KLT. The KLT tracked features are validated with RANSAC and the epipolar constraint. Inliers are used for the bundle adjustment leading to the estimation of the

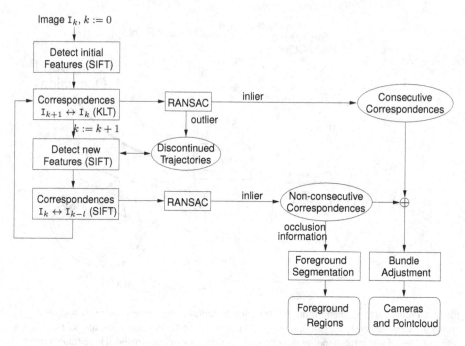

Fig. 3. Workflow overview: features are tracked in consecutive frames by KLT while nonconsecutive correspondences are established using the SIFT descriptor. Features of the current frame I_k are matched to features of previously discontinued trajectories in the images I_{k-l}, $l = 2, \ldots, L, L \leq k$. For validation, RANSAC and the epipolar constraint between I_k and I_{k-l} is used. The bundle adjustment is based on consecutive and non-consecutive correspondences. The occlusion information is extracted from the non-consecutive correspondences and their trajectories. It is used to initialize the foreground segmentation algorithm which is described in detail in Fig. 5.

current camera A_k as well as to an update of the point cloud. Outliers and lost tracks with an already reconstructed valid 3D object point are stored for a later match with the possibly reappearing feature. To represent newly appearing and reappearing scene structures, SIFT features are detected. They are at first compared to the stored discontinued trajectories. Validation with RANSAC and the epipolar constraint between A_k and A_{k-l}, $l > 1$ result in non-consecutive correspondences of the current frame I_k. They are used to stabilize the bundle adjustment as well as to extract occlusion information. The occlusion information leads to the automatic foreground segmentation as explained in Sect. 3.

The combination of SIFT detection for newly appearing features, SIFT matching for non-consecutive frames, and KLT tracking for frame to frame tracking provides optimal performance for the presented occlusion handling and accurate scene reconstruction.

2.2   Bundle Adjustment

The main idea of bundle adjustment [24] in structure and motion recovery approaches is that a reprojected 3D object point $\mathbf{P}_j$ should be located at the measured feature point $\mathbf{p}_{j,k}$ for each image $\mathtt{I}_k$, in which $\mathbf{P}_j$ is visible. The 3D-2D correspondence of object and feature point is related by

$$\mathbf{p}_{j,k} \sim \mathtt{A}_k \mathbf{P}_j \tag{1}$$

where $\sim$ indicates that this is an equality up to scale. The bundle adjustment equation to be minimized is

$$\epsilon = \sum_{j=1}^{J} \sum_{k=1}^{K} d(\mathbf{p}_{j,k}, \mathtt{A}_k \mathbf{P}_j)^2 \tag{2}$$

The covariance of the positional error which is derived from the gradient images is incorporated in the estimation [25] using the Mahalanobis distance for $d(\dots)$. The minimization of (2) results in the final camera parameters and object points.

3   Automatic Foreground Segmentation

The non-consecutive feature tracking connects discontinued trajectories to newly appearing features as shown in Fig. 2. If the trajectory is discontinued because of an occlusion with foreground objects, the image coordinates of occluded scene content can be derived by reprojecting the corresponding reconstructed 3D object point onto the image planes. These image locations are used to feed an interactive algorithm [17, 18], which is designed to segment an image into foreground and background regions with the help of initially known representative foreground and background image parts, called user strokes.

In [17, 18], the segmentation is initialized with manually drawn user strokes. In our work, the *strokes* are restricted to small discs and created automatically using the extracted occlusion information as explained in Sect. 3.1.

3.1   Occlusion Information

Let us assume, that foreground objects temporarily occlude the background scene. Thus, non-consecutive correspondences are established between the last occurrence of the tracked and the reappearing feature after being occluded. By reprojecting their 3D object points onto the image planes, occluded locations of these points can be measured. A successfully established non-consecutive correspondence $\mathbf{p}_{j,k} \leftrightarrow \mathbf{p}_{j,k-l-1}$ in the current frame $\mathtt{I}_k$ is a part of a feature trajectory $\mathbf{t}_j^*$ as follows:

$$\mathbf{t}_j^* = (\mathbf{p}_{j,k}^{visible}, \mathbf{p}_{j,k-1}^{occluded}, \dots, \mathbf{p}_{j,k-l}^{occluded}, \mathbf{p}_{j,k-l-1}^{visible}, \dots)$$

The object point $\mathbf{P}_j^*$ of $\mathbf{t}_j^*$ is occluded in l frames. It is visible in the current image $\mathtt{I}_k$ and in some previous images $\mathtt{I}_{j,k-l-1}, \dots$. It is occluded in the images $\mathtt{I}_{k-1}, \dots, \mathtt{I}_{k-l}$. It may has been occluded several times before. The coordinates of each of the occluded image locations $\mathbf{p}_{j,k-1}^{occluded}, \dots, \mathbf{p}_{j,k-l}^{occluded}$ can be estimated with relation (1) after selecting

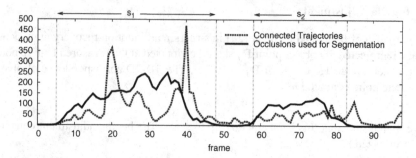

Fig. 4. *Playground* sequence (see Fig. 1): The number of connected trajectories in each frame (dotted blue line) and the number of occlusions used for the segmentation for each frame (black line). The intervals s_1, s_2 depict the parts with foreground occlusions in the sequence. If a connected trajectory results from occlusion, several reprojections of the corresponding 3D object point are usable for the segmentation.

a scale factor for the reconstruction. These coordinates are used to extract occlusion information which provides the initialization for the automatic foreground segmentation.

If the object point $\mathbf{P}_j^*$ is invisible in the current image I_k because of occlusion, its reprojection $A_k \mathbf{P}_j^*$ belongs to the foreground. However, experiments have shown, that many non-consecutive feature tracks are established without occluded scene content. To verify the occlusion property, a similarity constraint between each *invisible* point of $\mathbf{t}_j^*$ and the current feature point $\mathbf{p}_{j,k}^{visible} = A_k \mathbf{P}_j^*$ is evaluated. If the similarity constraint is fulfilled, the object point is not occluded in the camera view. Otherwise, the reprojection is an occluded image position. As similarity measure, the color histogram in a $d \times d$ window around each reprojection $A_{k-1} \mathbf{P}_j^*, A_{k-2} \mathbf{P}_j^*, \ldots$ is computed. For the measurement, the Bhattacharyya histogram distance metric is chosen. This metric provides best results for comparing histograms [20]. Based on the size of the region used for a SIFT descriptor [21], the size d is chosen to $d = 15 \ pel$. This step is important because the correspondence may be established a few frames after the feature reappears. Furthermore, non-consecutive feature correspondences may arise if a track is temporarily lost due to ambiguities in the image signal (repeated texture patterns, noise) or if scene content leaves and re-enters the field of view.

In Fig. 4, the number of occlusions used for the segmentation for each frame is shown (black line) for the *Playground* sequence from Fig. 1. The frame interval in which the child and the swing rack occlude the scene for the first time is denoted with s_1. The second occlusion interval is denoted with s_2. Within these intervals, many trajectories are connected (dotted blue line). The numbers of occlusions used for the segmentation in each frame are plotted with the black line. One connected trajectory may provide several useful occlusions in the previous frames. On the other hand, no useful occlusion is induced if the trajectories discontinue without occluding scene content, e. g. frames 48-57 and 83-98, respectively.

The visualization of the occlusion information is shown in Fig. 6, center row and Fig. 7, second row, respectively. The occluded image locations are visualized as white discs, the visible locations of the non-consecutive correspondences are black. The diameter of

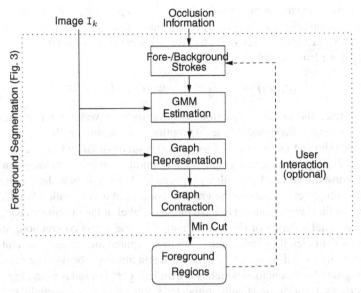

Fig. 5. Foreground Segmentation in detail (refer to Fig. 3): The occlusion information of the current frame k automatically generates strokes associated to foreground or background. Their Gaussian Mixture Model (GMM) is obtained by extracting the corresponding color information of image I_k. Before computing the Minimum Cut, the graph is contracted to minimize the computation time. The resulting foreground regions may be guided by the user by adding additional strokes manually.

a disc is set to d, $d = 15$ *pel* as described before. These images provide the initialization for the segmentation procedure as explained in Sect. 3.2.

3.2 Foreground Segmentation

The occlusion information (Fig. 6, center row) is used to initialize an efficient image segmentation algorithm [17, 18]. This algorithm provides the segmentation as the minimum of the discrete energy function $E : \mathcal{L}^n \to \mathbb{R}$:

$$E(x) = \sum_{i \in \mathcal{V}} \varphi_i(x_i) + \sum_{(i,j) \in \mathcal{E}} \varphi_{i,j}(x_i, x_j), \tag{3}$$

where $\mathcal{V}$ corresponds to the set of all image pixels and $\mathcal{E}$ is the set of all edges between neighboring pixels. For the problem of foreground segmentation the label set $\mathcal{L}$ consists of a foreground (fg) and a background (bg) label. The unary term φ_i is given as the negative log likelihood using a Gaussian mixture model (GMM) model [26], defined by

$$\varphi_i(x_i) = -\log Pr(I_i \mid x_i = S), \tag{4}$$

where S is either fg or bg and I_i describes the feature vector of pixel i. The GMM's for foreground and background are estimated by image regions that are assigned to either fore- or background. Usually this information is given by the user marking foreground and background with strokes or bounding boxes. In this paper the GMM's are estimated using the occlusion information that is derived automatically as described in Sect. 3.1. Hence, no user interaction is needed. The pairwise term $\varphi_{i,j}$ of (3) takes the form of a contrast sensitive Ising model and is defined as

$$\varphi_{i,j}(x_i, x_j) = \gamma \cdot [x_i \neq x_j] \cdot \exp(-\beta \|I_i - I_j\|^2) . \tag{5}$$

where [.] denotes the indicator function. The parameter γ weights the impact of the pairwise term and β corresponds to the distribution of noise among all neighboring pixels. It has been shown that the energy function (3) is submodular and can be represented as a graph [17]. Represented as a graph, the minimum cut minimizes the given energy function. We use the efficient algorithm proposed in [18] to compute the minimum cut. Based on the graph representation the graph is contracted to a so called *SlimGraph* by merging nodes that are guaranteed to have the same label in the minimum energy state. Hence, the optimal solution of (3) is not changed by the graph contraction. Since the graph becomes smaller, the segmentation can be computed much more efficiently. Figure 5 reviews the workflow of the foreground segmentation process. The result is the desired foreground segmentation which is shown in Fig. 6, bottom row and Fig. 7, third row, respectively. If the automatically initialized segmentation fails partially or lacks in accuracy, the user is able to guide the segmentation by providing additional information about foreground or background, i.e. by placing additional strokes. This additional information is then used to refine the GMM's describing the regions and the segmentation is updated.

4   Application: Occlusion of Integrated Virtual Objects

An often used technique in movie production is the integration of virtual objects into a video. This technique allows the editor for including scene content that has not been there during image acquisition. The required data for this step are accurate camera parameters and a coarse reconstruction of the scene. This is the objective of structure and motion recovery approaches. If the integrated virtual object has to be occluded by real scene content, a segmentation is required, which is usually done manually [4].

Our approach provides automatically segmented foreground regions. These regions have two properties: (1) their scene content temporarily occludes the background scene (see Sect. 3.1). (2) they are visually homogeneous (see Sect. 3.2). The resulting segmentation as shown in Fig. 7, third row, is used in a compositing step for the occlusion of the augmented objects. The white regions are copied from the input, the black regions are copied from the augmented sequence (Fig. 1, center row).

5   Experimental Results

The presented approach of foreground segmentation is tested using footage of a freely moving camera. Here, two example sequences are demonstrated.

The first sequence (270 frames) is recorded from a driving bus. Several foreground objects such as trees, bushes, signs, and a bus station occlude the background scene

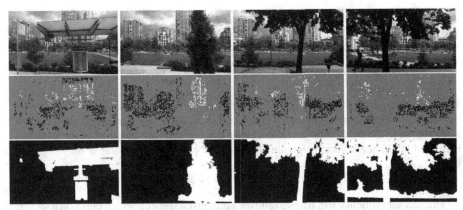

Fig. 6. Foreground segmentation results of the *Bus* sequence (1280 × 720 pixels), top row: input sequence; center row: occluded (white) and not occluded (black) object points; bottom row: automatic segmentation of foreground objects using the occlusion information as initialization

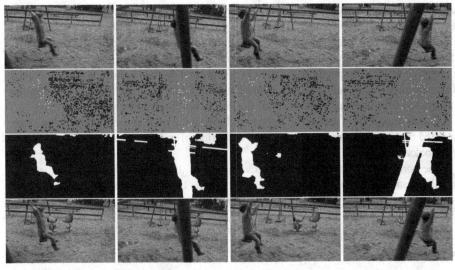

Fig. 7. Result examples of *Playground* sequence from Fig. 1: Top row: occluded (white) and not occluded (black) object points. center row: segmentation of foreground objects as described in Sect. 3.1 which is needed for the composition of real and virtual scenes; bottom row: final result of the integration of the virtual objects into the video sequence using the composition of the input sequence from Fig. 1, top row and the augmented sequence from Fig. 1, bottom row.

temporarily as shown in Fig. 6, top row. The center row of Fig. 6 shows the extracted occlusion information. The white discs depict foreground locations, the black ones are classified as background locations as described in Sect. 3.1. These images provide the initialization for the segmentation algorithm (Sect. 3.2). As shown in the bottom row, arbitrary and complex foreground object are segmented successfully, for example the structure of leaves of the trees.

(a)   (b)

Fig. 8. Errors resulting from a misleading segmentation. (a): although there is no occlusion information in the fence, the segmentation classifies it to the foreground because of its appearance being similar to the swing rack; (b): although the point is correctly classified as foreground, it is isolated by the segmentation algorithm because of the strong motion blur of the foreground object.

The second sequence (98 frames) shows a playground scene with a child on a swing. The foreground objects are the swinging child and some parts of the swing rack as shown in Fig. 7, top row. The occlusion information in the second row results from evaluating the non-consecutive correspondences. Again, the white discs belong to the foreground and the black discs belong to the background. These images initialize the segmentation algorithm, which leads to the foreground segmentation result shown in the third row. In the bottom row, the application of integrating virtual objects into the video sequence is demonstrated. This sequence is the composition of the rendered sequence from Fig. 1, center row, and the input sequence. The composition is done using the foreground segmentation result. The pixels segmented as foreground regions (white pixels) are copied from the input sequence (Fig. 1, top row) while the black labeled background regions are copied from the augmented sequence (Fig. 1, bottom row).

The swinging child as well as the parts of the swing rack in the foreground are segmented reliably. The integration and the occlusion of the virtual objects is convincing and looks realistic.[1]

The computational expense for the evaluation of the occlusion information is marginal. It consists of reprojections of the object points $\mathbf{P}_j^*$, histogram calculations of their surrounding windows, and the image segmentation which is done in less than a second per image.

5.1 Limitations

Although the foreground is segmented reliably, some background regions are classified as foreground as well because of their visual similarity. Fig. 8 shows two examples in detail. On the left, a small part of the fence which belongs to the background occlude the augmented objects because of a misleading segmentation. Here, the fence is visually very similar to the part of the swing rack which is a foreground region. On the right, the segmentation algorithm assigns a small part of the child to the background, although it has attached a correctly classified foreground disc. This is due to the strong motion blur. In these cases, the segmentation algorithm leads to suboptimal solutions. Even in the erroneous frames, the presented approach provides a meaningful initial solution

---

[1] The video can be downloaded at:

http://www.tnt.uni-hannover.de/staff/cordes/

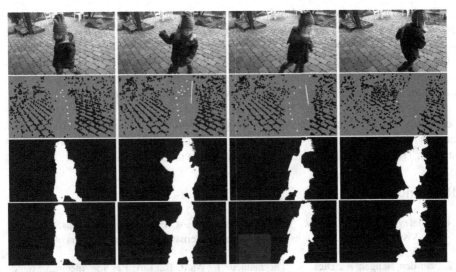

Fig. 9. The *Throw* sequence (1280 × 720 pixels): Top row: Input sequence. second row; segmentation of foreground objects and two additional strokes. third row: result without the manually added strokes, bottom row: result with the additional strokes.

within a few seconds which can easily be refined by adding a few user strokes and restarting the segmentation procedure. Note, that the results presented in this Sec. 5 are fully automatic.

5.2 User Interaction

The presented approach can easily be guided by the user if the segmentation results are not satisfactory. The additional link in the workflow is the dashed line in Fig. 5. The images with the resulting occlusion information are used as a starting point and some strokes are manually added to the images. These strokes may be foreground or background and should cover the critical regions in the images. An example is shown in Fig. 9. In this sequence, some regions that belong to the foreground are classified as background for two reasons: (1) no occlusion information available for the colors values in the critical regions, e.g. face and hair, (2) the boundary between foreground and background is smooth due to motion blur. The final result achieved by adding one more stroke in two images is shown in Fig. 9, third row.

6   Conclusions

The paper presents an approach for video segmentation. It incorporates 3D scene information of sequential structure and motion recovery. Occlusions are extracted from discontinued feature trajectories and their 3D object points. The presented feature tracking combines the highly accurate and reliable KLT tracker for correspondences in consecutive frames with wide-baseline SIFT correspondences for non-consecutive frames.

The localization of occluded and not occluded scene content is gained from the re-projection of 3D object points onto the camera planes. This data is successfully used as initialization of an efficient segmentation algorithm which results in visually homogeneous foreground regions. The results are demonstrated using the application of the integration of virtual objects into the scene. The foreground segmentation enables the automatic occlusion of the integrated objects with foreground scene content.

The effectiveness of the approach is demonstrated using challenging image sequences. Virtual object are accurately integrated and their occlusion with foreground objects is convincing. It is shown that the user can easily guide the algorithm by placing strokes. This additional information is used to refine the segmentation result.

References

1. Pollefeys, M., Gool, L.V.V., Vergauwen, M., Verbiest, F., Cornelis, K., Tops, J., Koch, R.: Visual modeling with a hand-held camera. International Journal of Computer Vision (IJCV) 59(3), 207–232 (2004)
2. van den Hengel, A., Dick, A., Thormählen, T., Ward, B., Torr, P.H.S.: Videotrace: rapid interactive scene modelling from video. In: SIGGRAPH, vol. 86, ACM, New York (2007)
3. Hasler, N., Rosenhahn, B., Thormählen, T., Wand, M., Seidel, H.P.: Markerless motion capture with unsynchronized moving cameras. In: IEEE Conference on Computer Vision and Pattern Recognition, CVPR (2009)
4. Hillman, P., Lewis, J., Sylwan, S., Winquist, E.: Issues in adapting research algorithms to stereoscopic visual effects. In: IEEE International Conference on Image Processing (ICIP), pp. 17–20 (2010)
5. Cornelis, K., Verbiest, F., Van Gool, L.: Drift detection and removal for sequential structure from motion algorithms. IEEE Transactions on Pattern Analysis and Machine Intelligence (PAMI) 26(10), 1249–1259 (2004)
6. Engels, C., Fraundorfer, F., Nistér, D.: Integration of tracked and recognized features for locally and globally robust structure from motion. In: VISAPP (Workshop on Robot Perception), pp. 13–22 (2008)
7. Zhang, G., Dong, Z., Jia, J., Wong, T.-T., Bao, H.: Efficient Non-consecutive Feature Tracking for Structure-from-Motion. In: Daniilidis, K., Maragos, P., Paragios, N. (eds.) ECCV 2010, Part V. LNCS, vol. 6315, pp. 422–435. Springer, Heidelberg (2010)
8. Cordes, K., Müller, O., Rosenhahn, B., Ostermann, J.: Feature Trajectory Retrieval with Application to Accurate Structure and Motion Recovery. In: Bebis, G. (ed.) ISVC 2011, Part I. LNCS, vol. 6938, pp. 156–167. Springer, Heidelberg (2011)
9. Apostoloff, N.E., Fitzgibbon, A.W.: Automatic video segmentation using spatiotemporal t-junctions. In: British Machine Vision Conference, BMVC (2006)
10. Apostoloff, N.E., Fitzgibbon, A.W.: Learning spatiotemporal t-junctions for occlusion detection. In: IEEE Conference on Computer Vision and Pattern Recognition (CVPR), vol. 2, pp. 553–559 (2005)
11. Guan, L., Franco, J.S., Pollefeys, M.: 3d occlusion inference from silhouette cues. In: IEEE Conference on Computer Vision and Pattern Recognition (CVPR), pp. 1–8 (2007)
12. Brox, T., Malik, J.: Object Segmentation by Long Term Analysis of Point Trajectories. In: Daniilidis, K., Maragos, P., Paragios, N. (eds.) ECCV 2010, Part V. LNCS, vol. 6315, pp. 282–295. Springer, Heidelberg (2010)
13. Brox, T., Malik, J.: Large displacement optical flow: Descriptor matching in variational motion estimation. IEEE Transactions on Pattern Analysis and Machine Intelligence (PAMI) 33(3), 500–513 (2011)

14. Sheikh, Y., Javed, O., Kanade, T.: Background subtraction for freely moving cameras. In: IEEE International Conference on Computer Vision and Pattern Recognition (ICCV), pp. 1219–1225 (2009)

15. Zhang, G., Jia, J., Hua, W., Bao, H.: Robust bilayer segmentation and motion/depth estimation with a handheld camera. IEEE Transactions on Pattern Analysis and Machine Intelligence (PAMI) 33(3), 603–617 (2011)

16. Liu, C., Yuen, J., Torralba, A.: Sift flow: Dense correspondence across scenes and its applications. IEEE Transactions on Pattern Analysis and Machine Intelligence (PAMI) 33(5), 978–994 (2011)

17. Boykov, Y., Jolly, M.P.: Interactive graph cuts for optimal boundary & region segmentation of objects in n-d images. In: IEEE International Conference on Computer Vision (ICCV), vol. 1, pp. 105–112 (2001)

18. Scheuermann, B., Rosenhahn, B.: SlimCuts: GraphCuts for High Resolution Images Using Graph Reduction. In: Boykov, Y., Kahl, F., Lempitsky, V., Schmidt, F.R. (eds.) EMMCVPR 2011. LNCS, vol. 6819, pp. 219–232. Springer, Heidelberg (2011)

19. Lucas, B., Kanade, T.: An iterative image registration technique with an application to stereo vision. In: International Joint Conference on Artificial Intelligence (IJCAI), pp. 674–679 (1981)

20. Thormählen, T., Hasler, N., Wand, M., Seidel, H.P.: Registration of sub-sequence and multi-camera reconstructions for camera motion estimation. Journal of Virtual Reality and Broadcasting 7(2) (2010)

21. Lowe, D.G.: Distinctive image features from scale-invariant keypoints. International Journal of Computer Vision (IJCV) 60(2), 91–110 (2004)

22. Matas, J., Chum, O., Urban, M., Pajdla, T.: Robust wide baseline stereo from maximally stable extremal regions. In: British Machine Vision Conference (BMVC), vol. 1, pp. 384–393 (2002)

23. Dickscheid, T., Schindler, F., Förstner, W.: Coding images with local features. International Journal of Computer Vision (IJCV) 94(2), 1–21 (2010)

24. Triggs, B., McLauchlan, P.F., Hartley, R.I., Fitzgibbon, A.W.: Bundle Adjustment – A Modern Synthesis. In: Triggs, B., Zisserman, A., Szeliski, R. (eds.) ICCV-WS 1999. LNCS, vol. 1883, pp. 298–372. Springer, Heidelberg (2000)

25. Hartley, R.I., Zisserman, A.: Multiple View Geometry, 2nd edn. Cambridge University Press (2003)

26. Rother, C., Kolmogorov, V., Blake, A.: Grabcut: interactive foreground extraction using iterated graph cuts. ACM SIGGRAPH Papers 23(3), 309–314 (2004)

A Model for the Restoration of Semi-transparent Defects Based on Lie Groups and Human Visual System

Vittoria Bruni[1], Elisa Rossi[2], and Domenico Vitulano[2]

[1] Dept. SBAI University of Rome La Sapienza, Via A. Scarpa 16, 00161 Rome, Italy
[2] Ist. per le Applicazioni del Calcolo, C.N.R., Via dei Taurini 19, 00185 Rome, Italy
bruni@dmmm.uniroma1.it, {e.rossi,d.vitulano}@iac.cnr.it

Abstract. This paper presents a new model for the restoration of semi-transparent blotches on archived sepia-toned images. Its main feature is the combination of Human Visual System mechanism and Lie groups transformations properties. The former allows to define restoration as a gradual reduction of the visual perception of the defect. The latter allows to easily select the transformation that better performs this reduction exploiting Lie groups properties. Extensive experimental results on original photographs of the Alinari Archive affected by semi-transparent blotches show the potential of the proposed approach.

Keywords: Image restoration, Lie group transformations, Semi-transparent blotches.

1 Introduction

Digital image restoration is an increasing and popular area of research. In the last years a lot of research effort has been devoted to propose novel and adaptive digital restoration methods, able to deal with image defects like noise, line-scratches, tear, moire, blotches, shake and flicker [12]. The model proposed in this paper focuses on the class of semi-transparent degradation, whose main peculiarity is that part of the original information still survives in the degraded area [4]. In particular, blotch restoration has been investigated.

The main goal is the definition of a general framework that is as much as possible independent of a priori assumption on the degradation under exam, in order to easily generalize the restoration process to different kind of defects. The only assumptions are: i) the knowledge of the detection mask, that is a map defined on image pixels whose value is 1 if the pixel is damaged and 0 if not; the semi-transparency of degradation. In fact, in order to preserve the artistic and historical value of artworks, it is necessary to remove the damage preserving the original image content and without creating new artifacts. To this aim, the Human Visual System (HVS) mechanism has been involved in the restoration process [21]. In fact, image defects are detected by human eyes 'at first glance' even in complicated cases as they are perceived as an anomaly in any natural image. Therefore, it is expected that the reduction of the visual contrast of the degraded region (visual anomaly) reduces the visual contribution of the degraded area. Hence, degraded pixels having the same visual contrast are classified by means of the Successive Mean Quantization Transform (SMQT) [16] and for points in the same

G. Csurka et al. (Eds.): VISIGRAPP 2012, CCIS 359, pp. 354–368, 2013.

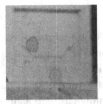

Fig. 1. Examples of semi-transparent blotches in real photographs

class the restoration transform is selected inside a suitable set of transformations. The latter is chosen as the Lie group of projective transformations since its useful algebraic and geometrical properties. Moreover, infinitesimal operations in Lie algebras and their integration in global transform in Lie groups are able to model some HVS phenomena, as deeply investigated in [11] and [6].

The proposed approach is two-fold innovative: *i)* the combination of HVS and Lie groups allows the proposed model to have not a precise target to converge — as it usually happens in Lie groups based approaches (see, for instance, [7,18,14,15]). The exact final solution is not known in advance and the model is only required to force the visual contrast of the final solution to be in a suitable range of values according to 'typical' contrast of the surrounding clean image — blotch has to be invisible; *ii)* the rich set of Lie groups transformations overcomes the search of the solution of the restoration problem through simple translation and shrinking operations, that are commonly used by existing competitors.

The reminder of the paper is the following. Next section contains the motivations of the work and a short state of the art of image restoration methods. Section 3 briefly introduces Lie group transformations. Section 4 presents the proposed restoration model. Finally, Section 5 contains results and concluding remarks.

2 Blotch Restoration: Problem Setting

Blotches are usually caused by dirt or moisture on archived material that partially or completely obscures some image regions. They appear as irregularly shaped regions with a darker average intensity and a slight variation in color, as shown in Fig. 1. Hence, the lack of distinctive features, like shape and color, makes their detection and restoration not trivial tasks. Blotches must be restored using clean information from the immediate vicinity of the blotch, although this is not essential. However, part of the original information still survives even after the degradation process. This is due to its physical formation that can be modeled by the spreading and penetration of water droplets into material. During the spreading process, the radius of the wet region grows to an equilibrium point. From this point on, the liquid is absorbed depending on the porosity of the considered medium. In ideal conditions, the central pores absorb more than the external pores, since they come in contact with the liquid earlier. This can be seen in many blotches, where the effects of the blotch are more evident towards its centre. For complete spreading and absorption processes, one can expect a smooth transition to the unaffected area; on the contrary a spurious edge is evident. Hence, the degraded image J at the point $\mathbf{x} = (x, y)^T$ can be modeled as

$$J(\mathbf{x}) = \mathcal{T}(I(\mathbf{x})),$$

where $\mathcal{T}$ is a proper composition of transformations and I is the original image. The goal of the restoration process should be to find the inverse of $\mathcal{T}$ in order to reconstruct the original image I. Unfortunately, the evolution of a drop involves different parameters, such as drop geometry and the regularity of paper surface, that are unknown in real applications. Hence, $\mathcal{T}$ unknown as well as its inverse $\mathcal{T}^{-1}$. Inpainting methods or texture synthesis approaches [1,2,5,8,13] are not appropriate for the restoration of partially missing data regions, since they completely discard the original information that is still contained in those regions. On the contrary, existing approaches that exploit the semi-transparency property, like [4,19,9,3], make implicit or explicit assumptions on the physical model that causes the degradation so that their restoration consists of 'ad hoc' operations. For example, in [19] semi-transparency is modeled as a linear dependence between the intensity values of the degraded and original region, assuming similar statistic features inside and outside the degraded one. A non linear model closer to the visual appearance of degradation is used in [9]: it uses *flattening* to emphasize blotches darkness and *enhancement* to exploit the local image statistics. Affine pointwise transformations are employed in [4] and [3]. While the former involves a minimization algorithm that emphasizes the propagation of information from the outside-in, the latter relies on a precise model of both physical and visual characteristics of the specific degradation kind.

To address the restoration problem in a less constrained manner, the proposed model employs the Lie group of projective transformations as a redundant set of transformations where automatically select the best $\mathcal{T}^{-1}$. The selected transformations are not global but they are adapted to the local properties of the damaged area, according to a contrast-based classification. External information is involved just in the definition of the admissible range values for degraded pixels and for comparing global measures like the inner contrast between the damaged area and its surrounding regions, making the model quite independent of external features.

3   A Short Review about Lie Algebra

Definition. A finite *Lie group* G is a set of elements equipped with a group multiplication $* : G \times G \to G$, that is:

- $\forall g_1, g_2, g_3 \in G\ (g_1 * g_2) * g_3 = g_1 * (g_2 * g_3)$
- $\exists\, e \in G$, identity element, such that $\forall\, g \in G\ e * g = g * e = g$
- $\forall\, g \in G\quad \exists\, g^{-1} \in G : g * g^{-1} = g^{-1} * g = e$

and a differentiable manifold of finite dimension, i.e. a space locally diffeomorphic to R^n, if n is the dimension of G. Moreover the group operation $*$ and the inverse map $(G \to G, g \mapsto g^{-1})$ are C^∞ with respect to the differentiable structure of the manifold.

So a Lie group G has algebraic properties coming from the group structure and geometric properties coming from the differentiable structure and they are deeply related. Finally, every finite Lie group can always be viewed as a matrix group.

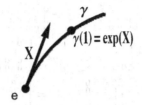

Fig. 2. Definition of the exponential map

Definition. A *Lie algebra* $\mathfrak{g}$ is a vector space endowed with a bilinear operation, $[\,,\,]$: $\mathfrak{g} \times \mathfrak{g} \to \mathfrak{g}$, $(X, Y) \mapsto [X, Y]$, called Lie bracket, antisymmetric and satisfying Jacobi identity, that is

- $\forall X, Y \in \mathfrak{g}$, $[X, Y] = -[Y, X]$
- $\forall X, Y, Z \in \mathfrak{g}$ $[X, [Y, Z]] + [Z, [X, Y]] + [Y, [Z, X]] = 0$.

If G is a Lie group, its tangent space at identity, $\mathfrak{g}$, which is a vector space, has a Lie algebra structure. Hence, $\mathfrak{g}$ is a vector space of the same dimension of G, endowed with a Lie bracket. If G is a matrix group, the Lie bracket is the matrix commutator, i.e. $[X, Y] = XY - YX$. Since G is a differentiable manifold, there exists a correspondence between its tangent space at identity (the Lie algebra $\mathfrak{g}$) and G itself, that is the exponential map exp : $\mathfrak{g} \to G$. Let $X \in \mathfrak{g}$ be a tangent vector at e in G; locally there exists the integral curve of X, that is a smooth curve starting from the identity with tangent vector X, i.e. $\gamma : [0, T_0] \to G$ such that $\gamma(0) = e$ and $\dot{\gamma}(0) = X$; we define $\exp(X)$ as the point on G reached by the curve γ at time 1, that is $\exp(X) = \gamma(1)$, see Fig. 2. The exponential map is a local diffeomorphism around the origin of $\mathfrak{g}$ and it gives a natural way to move from $\mathfrak{g}$ (vector space) to G (manifold). For matrix groups, it corresponds to matrix exponential: $\exp(X) = \sum_{n=0}^{\infty} \frac{X^n}{n!}$. For a complete treatment of Lie groups and Lie algebras see, for instance, [20] and [10].

3.1 Lie Group Transformations

Most of the matrix Lie groups can be used to describe transformations in the plane or in the space. For instance, rotations in the plane are represented by the group $SO_2 R = \left\{ \left(\begin{smallmatrix} \cos\theta & \sin\theta \\ -\sin\theta & \cos\theta \end{smallmatrix} \right), \theta \in R \right\}$. The dimension of the group can be thought as the number of free parameters needed to describe the transformations. In case of plane rotations we just need one parameter, the angle θ, so the dimension of $SO_2 R$ is 1. We can think about its Lie algebra elements, which are tangent vectors at the identity, as the infinitesimal transformations (rotation of an 'infinitesimal angle') of the points. In this paper we are interested in using projective transformations in the space and they can be described as a matrix group, P_3, acting on space points expressed in homogeneous coordinates, with the convention that the fourth value in the coordinates is always scaled back to 1. Projective transformations are characterized by 15 parameters, that is the dimension of P_3, described by the following basis of its Lie algebra representing translations, rotations, scaling, shear and projections:

$$t_1 = \begin{bmatrix} 0&0&0&1 \\ 0&0&0&0 \\ 0&0&0&0 \\ 0&0&0&0 \end{bmatrix} \quad t_2 = \begin{bmatrix} 0&0&0&0 \\ 0&0&0&1 \\ 0&0&0&0 \\ 0&0&0&0 \end{bmatrix} \quad t_3 = \begin{bmatrix} 0&0&0&0 \\ 0&0&0&0 \\ 0&0&0&1 \\ 0&0&0&0 \end{bmatrix} \quad translations$$

$$t_4 = \begin{bmatrix} 0&0&0&0 \\ 0&0&1&0 \\ 0&-1&0&0 \\ 0&0&0&0 \end{bmatrix} \quad t_5 = \begin{bmatrix} 0&0&-1&0 \\ 0&0&0&0 \\ 1&0&0&0 \\ 0&0&0&0 \end{bmatrix} \quad t_6 = \begin{bmatrix} 0&1&0&0 \\ -1&0&0&0 \\ 0&0&0&0 \\ 0&0&0&0 \end{bmatrix} \quad rotations$$

$$t_7 = \begin{bmatrix} 1&0&0&0 \\ 0&0&0&0 \\ 0&0&0&0 \\ 0&0&0&0 \end{bmatrix} \quad t_8 = \begin{bmatrix} 0&0&0&0 \\ 0&1&0&0 \\ 0&0&0&0 \\ 0&0&0&0 \end{bmatrix} \quad t_9 = \begin{bmatrix} 0&0&0&0 \\ 0&0&0&0 \\ 0&0&1&0 \\ 0&0&0&0 \end{bmatrix} \quad scaling$$

$$t_{10} = \begin{bmatrix} 0&1&0&0 \\ 0&0&0&0 \\ 0&0&0&0 \\ 0&0&0&0 \end{bmatrix} \quad t_{11} = \begin{bmatrix} 0&0&0&0 \\ 0&0&0&0 \\ 1&0&0&0 \\ 0&0&0&0 \end{bmatrix} \quad t_{12} = \begin{bmatrix} 0&0&0&0 \\ 0&0&1&0 \\ 0&0&0&0 \\ 0&0&0&0 \end{bmatrix} \quad shear$$

$$t_{13} = \begin{bmatrix} 0&0&0&0 \\ 0&0&0&0 \\ 0&0&0&0 \\ 1&0&0&0 \end{bmatrix} \quad t_{14} = \begin{bmatrix} 0&0&0&0 \\ 0&0&0&0 \\ 0&0&0&0 \\ 0&1&0&0 \end{bmatrix} \quad t_{15} = \begin{bmatrix} 0&0&0&0 \\ 0&0&0&0 \\ 0&0&0&0 \\ 0&0&1&0 \end{bmatrix} \quad projections$$

Hence, every real linear combination of $t_1, ..., t_{15}$ is an infinitesimal projective transformation in the space that corresponds to a transformation of the group P_3 thanks to the exponential map.

The infinitesimal transformation of a generic point $p = \begin{bmatrix} x \\ y \\ z \end{bmatrix}$ is $\tilde{L}_j = t_j \begin{bmatrix} x \\ y \\ z \\ 1 \end{bmatrix}$ $j = 1, ..., 15$ whose affine coordinates L_j respectively are:

$$L_1 = \begin{bmatrix} 1 \\ 0 \\ 0 \end{bmatrix} \quad L_2 = \begin{bmatrix} 0 \\ 1 \\ 0 \end{bmatrix} \quad L_3 = \begin{bmatrix} 0 \\ 0 \\ 1 \end{bmatrix} \quad L_4 = \begin{bmatrix} 0 \\ z \\ -y \end{bmatrix} \quad L_5 = \begin{bmatrix} -z \\ 0 \\ x \end{bmatrix} \quad L_6 = \begin{bmatrix} y \\ -x \\ 0 \end{bmatrix}$$

$$L_7 = \begin{bmatrix} x \\ 0 \\ 0 \end{bmatrix} \quad L_8 = \begin{bmatrix} 0 \\ y \\ 0 \end{bmatrix} \quad L_9 = \begin{bmatrix} 0 \\ 0 \\ z \end{bmatrix} \quad L_{10} = \begin{bmatrix} y \\ 0 \\ 0 \end{bmatrix} \quad L_{11} = \begin{bmatrix} 0 \\ 0 \\ x \end{bmatrix} \quad L_{12} = \begin{bmatrix} 0 \\ z \\ 0 \end{bmatrix}$$

$$L_{13} = \begin{bmatrix} x^2 \\ xy \\ xz \end{bmatrix} \quad L_{14} = \begin{bmatrix} xy \\ y^2 \\ yz \end{bmatrix} \quad L_{15} = \begin{bmatrix} xz \\ yz \\ z^2 \end{bmatrix}.$$

3.2   Surfaces Distance Minimization by Projective Transformation

The relation between Lie algebras and Lie groups allows us to define an iterative procedure able to map a given surface S_1 in $\mathbb{R}^3$ to another one, S_2. $\forall p \in S_1$, let n_p be the unit normal at S_1 in the point p and d_p the distance between p and S_2 along n_p, as in Fig. 3. Hence, $\sum_{p \in S_1} d_p$ is the distance between S_1 and S_2. Let L_j^p, for $j = 1, ..., 15$, be the infinitesimal projective transformation L_j applied to the point p. The goal is to estimate 15 real parameters, $\alpha_1, ..., \alpha_{15}$, such that the infinitesimal projective transformation $\sum_{j=1}^{15} \alpha_j L_j^p$, projected onto the normal direction n_p, minimizes the distance between S_1 and S_2, i.e.

$$(\alpha_1, ..., \alpha_{15}) = \arg\min_{\alpha_j} \sum_{p \in S_1} \left(d_p - \sum_{j=1}^{15} \alpha_j \left(L_j^p \cdot n_p \right) \right)^2.$$

It is easy to check that $\alpha = (\alpha_1 \dots \alpha_{15})^T$ is such that

$$\alpha = A^{-1}b,$$

where the elements of the matrix A and the column vector b respectively are

$$A_{jk} = \sum_{p \in S_1} \left(L_j^p \cdot n_p \right) \left(L_k^p \cdot n_p \right)$$

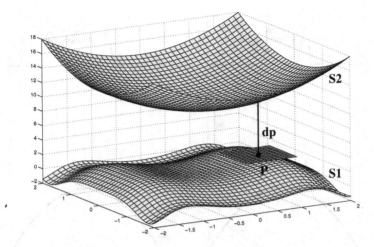

Fig. 3. Distance d_p between a point p in S_1 and S_2 along the normal direction

and

$$b_k = \sum_{p \in S_1} d_p \left(L_k^p \cdot n_p \right).$$

$t = \sum_{j=1}^{15} \alpha_j t_j$ is the infinitesimal transformation living in the Lie algebra $\mathfrak{g}$ (vector space) that minimizes the distance between S_1 and S_2 along the normal direction. The exponential map transforms t into a projective transformation T of the group, i.e. $T = \exp(t) = \sum_{n=0}^{\infty} \frac{t^n}{n!}$. Finally, S_1 is updated applying T to its points: $S_1^{(1)} = T(S_1)$. The minimization process can be then iterated using the couples of surfaces $(S_1^{(1)}, S_2)$, and so on.

For the numerical computation of $\exp(t)$ applied to a generic point $\mathbf{x}$, a 4th order Runge Kutta algorithm can be used — see [7] for details. It is equivalent to cut the 4th order series expansion of the matrix exponential and apply it to the point $\mathbf{x}$, that is $T(\mathbf{x}) \approx \left(Id + t + (\frac{1}{2})t^2 + (\frac{1}{6})t^3 + (\frac{1}{24})t^4 \right) (\mathbf{x})$, but it directly manages affine coordinates.

4   The Proposed Model

The degraded image can be modeled as a surface in $\mathbb{R}^3$, in a obvious way: pixels locations are x and y coordinates, while the intensity value is the z coordinate. If the real clean image is known, we could apply the minimization algorithm described in the previous section, in order to select the projective transformation that minimizes the distance between the degraded surface and the clean one. It is clear that the minimization algorithm is independent of the choice of the Lie group. We can replace the Lie group of projective transformations with some other Lie group, without change the algorithm structure. However, projective transformations seem to be able to recover details more

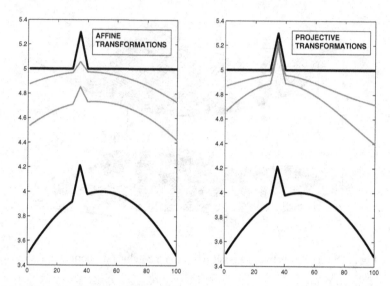

Fig. 4. Synthetic original information (*top solid dark line*) and its degraded version (*bottom solid dark line*). Two iterations (*solid line*) of the recovery process that peaks transformations in two different groups: affine group (*left*) and projective group (*right*).

precisely than, for instance, affine transformations. In Fig. 4, the minimization algorithm has been applied to two curves in $\mathbb{R}^2$, instead of two surfaces in $\mathbb{R}^3$ for a better visualization, using both Lie groups of affine and projective transformations. If the affine group is used, the solution becomes closer to the right one: the hat (i.e., the original image detail) is straight but it has a lower energy than the original one. If the whole projective group is considered, the restoration algorithm converges toward the right solution: the hat is straight and its intensity does not decrease. Moreover, as Fig. 4 shows, the iterative procedure has the good property to preserve the structure of the curve. This is very useful for restoration process since semi-transparency of the blotch means that some part of original information is preserved under the damage: the minimization algorithm is able to preserve the main structure of the surface, that is the original image survived to the degradation process.

Coming back to restoration, the problem is that the real clean image is unknown in real applications. That is why some basic rules of HVS are used for defining suitable ranges of intensity values for the damaged area to be not visible with respect to its neighborhood: a target surface to be reached is defined based on visibility properties. HVS is also involved in the model in order to overcome the structural rigidity of the minimization algorithm. In fact, despite the wide flexibility of Lie transformations, the minimization process is global. In other words, at each step the parameters $\{\alpha_j\}_{j=1,\ldots,15}$ are the same for each point. Hence, if on the one hand global transformations preserve the original information contained in the degraded region, on the other hand they forget that pixels may have been subjected to a different amount of degradation. In order to find a tradeoff between preservation of original information and model flexibility, it is

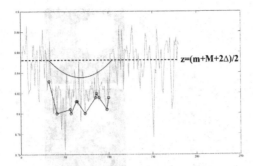

Fig. 5. Plane section of a blotch (*light gray*), the surface of the $i - th$ group (*piecewise curve*) and the corresponding paraboloid (*dark and solid line*)

necessary to classify damaged pixels accounting for their visual importance and restore them accordingly.

4.1 Processing of the Damaged Area

The restoration process has two goals: points classification in order to process in the same way those equally perceived by human eye, and definition of the target surfaces to use in the minimization procedure (points having the same visual contrast have to converge to the same target surface). Both require HVS perception mechanism to be embedded in the model.

Let I be the analyzed image, B its damaged area and let E be a sufficiently small neighborhood of B such that we can assume that E and B share the same information. In order to classify the points in B according to their contrast properties, the SMQT algorithm [16] is used. It groups pixels having comparable visual contrast. More precisely, SMQT builds a binary tree using the following rule: given a set of data D and a real parameter L (number of levels), split D into two subsets, $D_0 = \{x \in D | D(x) \leq \overline{D}\}$ and $D_1 = \{x \in D | D(x) > \overline{D}\}$, where $\overline{D}$ is the mean value of D. D_0 and D_1 are the first level of the SMQT. The same procedure is recursively applied to D_0 and D_1 and so on until the Lth level, that is composed of 2^L subsets. We set $L = 3$ in order to obtain a $\log_2$ quantization of the damaged pixels (i.e. $2^3 = \log_2(256)$ groups, where $[0, 255]$ is the gray scale range). Each group in B corresponds to a surface (defined by interpolation).

Let M and m be respectively the maximum and the minimum value for E (except for outliers). $[m, M]$ is the range of admissible values for the final solution. In fact, a natural scene component is required to not exceed the range of values of the surrounding information in terms of visibility bounds. $[m, M]$ is proportional to the global contrast of the whole image I, i.e. $\frac{M-m}{\mu_I}$ where μ_I is the mean value of I. Since we are dealing with a local degradation, we can think that any transformation of the degraded region does not influence too much μ_I, so that it can be considered constant. That is why from now on we will just deal with ranges instead of contrasts. The target surface of the i-th group is defined as a paraboloid cut by the plane $z = \frac{m+M}{2} + \Delta$, where Δ accounts for the global visibility of the degraded area B with respect to the external one E, and

Fig. 6. Complicated cases: Area selected by the detection mask (*Right*) contains pixels darker than the damaged pixel. (*Left*) original image

whose vertex is proportional to the mean value of the group, according to the interval values. Each surface converges to the corresponding paraboloid, as shown in Fig. 5. The iterative minimization process stops when the target surface has been reached in agreement with visibility bounds. More precisely, let S be the initial surface, $S^{(n)}$ the solution at the n-th iteration and P the target paraboloid; $S^{(n)}$ is the final solution if

$$\frac{\sum_{x \in S} |S^{(n)}(x) - P(x)|}{\sum_{x \in S} P(x)} \leq k \,, \tag{1}$$

where k is the least detection threshold given by Weber's law, see [21]. The first member of previous equation corresponds to Weber's contrast evaluated at the points of the analysed surfaces.

In order to avoid annoying artifacts, especially in complicated cases as the ones in Fig. 6, and to better preserve the original image content, a preprocessing step is required, as described in the following section.

4.2 Preprocessing of the Damaged Area

HVS mechanism and SMQT algorithm are again exploited to split the degraded region B into three regions: the darkest, D_1, the brightest, D_3 and the central one, D_2, where most of information lives. Each region will be restored separately.

SMQT is applied to the whole degraded surface B, with $L = 3$, so 8 groups of pixels are defined: $B_1, \ldots, B_8$, ordered from the darkest to the brightest pixels. We compute the inner contrast $C_j = \frac{\sigma_j}{\mu_j}$ of each B_j, with σ_j the standard deviation and μ_j the mean of B_j. Let $\eta = \{C_1, \cdots, C_8\}$ be the discrete contrast curve of B, as in Fig. 7. Darker pixels in B, say D_1, are those sets B_j whose inner contrast is greater than k (where k is the least detection threshold given by the Weber's law). On the contrary, brighter pixels in B, say D_3, are those B_j whose inner contrast curve has positive first derivative. Let D_2 be the union of the remaining groups. Summing up, SMQT quantization of the degraded region B combined with its contrast properties allows to split the whole range of values of damaged pixels into three intervals: $[b_0, b_1]$, $]b_1, b_2[$ and $[b_2, b_3]$, corresponding to regions D_1, D_2 and D_3, respectively.

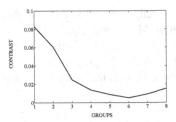

Fig. 7. Contrast curve η of B

Hence, HVS manages the restoration process of each of them. In particular, it determines whether restoration is really necessary or not. In fact, even though the damaged area B appears darker than the neighborhood E, it is important to check if the intersection between E and B values contains points that are darker than the blotch, as in Fig. 6. To this aim, it is necessary to check if the darker region of E, corresponding to those pixels whose value is in the interval $[b_0, b_1]$, masks D_1. Setting the just noticeable threshold $\epsilon = .33$ [17], if their contrast ratio is included in $[1 - \epsilon, 1 + \epsilon]$, then the same information lives outside the blotch, and D_1 must be left unchanged; otherwise D_1 must be transformed and mapped into the range $[m, M - \delta]$, where δ is such that $[M - \delta, M]$ and is proportional to $[b_2, b_3]$. It is worth stressing that we choose to move D_1 values in $[m, M - \delta]$ and not in $[m, M]$ in order to preserve eventual original information. The restoration algorithm, as described in the previous section, is applied to D_1, instead of the whole B, and the target surfaces are paraboloids cut by the plane $z = \frac{m+M-\delta}{2}$.

With regard to D_3, i.e. the brightest region of B, we check if it is masked by the region in E corresponding to the values in the interval $[b_2, b_3]$. D_3 mostly corresponds to the transition area from E to B, according to the physical properties of the damaged area. Hence, the ratio between the inner contrasts is included in $[1 - \epsilon, 1 + \epsilon]$ and with high probability we don't need to transform it.

Finally, D_2 contains most of degradation and it must be mapped into the interval $[m, M]$. However, because of some rigidity of the model, it will be better to shift the interval, i.e. $[m + \delta, M + \delta]$. δ measures the darkness of the damaged area and it is well represented by the difference between the mean values of B and E. So the restoration algorithm in Section 4.1 is applied to D_2 and paraboloids are cut by plane $z = \frac{m+M+2\delta}{2}$.

4.3 Masking Refinement

The iterative restoration algorithm tends to preserve the original information at the expense of some rigidity (solutions tend to be dark). As a result, we need to stress the range values relative to D_2 in order to have sufficiently bright solutions and a sufficiently large range values to avoid oversmoothed solutions. This requires a final masking operation. Specifically, let S_2 be the output of the minimization algorithm applied to D_2. Let V be the set of pixels in S_2 whose value is greater than $M - \epsilon$, that is $V = \{p \in S_2 \mid v(p) > M - \epsilon\}$, where $v(p)$ is the value of the pixel p in S_2 and V^C its complementary set in S_2. The ratio between V and V^C is the inner contrast of S_2. If this ratio is included in $[1 - \epsilon, 1 + \epsilon]$, we don't need masking; otherwise, we have to replace the values of some pixels in V with their original ones. The main idea is to replace those pixels that originally were sufficiently bright and that became too bright in the minimization algorithm. More precisely, let $H = \{p \in V \mid v_{orig}(p) > \tau\}$ and $V_{orig} = \{v_{orig}(p) \mid p \in V\}$ where $v_{orig}(p)$ is the original value of the pixel p in D_2 and τ is a suitable constant related to the properties of V_{orig}, then $S_2(H) = V_{orig}(H)$. Note that $\tau = \bar{V}_{orig} + \epsilon$, where $\bar{V}_{orig}$ is the mean value of V_{orig}.

4.4 Algorithm

Let set $I =$ initial image, $B =$ degraded area and $E =$ neighborhood of B.

Step 1. Split B into the groups D_1, D_3 and D_2 using SMQT;
Step 2. Estimate the range of the solution $[m, M]$ from the surrounding information;
Step 3. Check if D_1 has to be processed; if so, go to step 4, otherwise go to step 7;
Step 4. Apply SMQT to D_1;
Step 5. Compute paraboloids including the solution whose vertices are set according to the mean amplitudes of the groups computed in step 4 and the output of step 2;
Step 6. For each group in step 4, apply the iterative procedure in Section 3.2 where the target surfaces are the ones computed in step 5, until eq. (1) is satisfied;
Step 7. Apply steps 4-5-6 to D_2;
Step 8. Perform masking refinement.

Figs. 8-9-10 show the results of some steps of the algorithm. In Fig. 8 D_1 must be processed: the initial contrast ratio between D_1 and its corresponding external area is 2.5. On the contrary, the one between D_3 and its corresponding external region is 0.8; hence it is not necessary to process it. For the blotch in Fig. 9, both D_1 and D_3 don't need to be processed — contrast ratios respectively are 1.1 and 0.9. Also in Fig. 10 both D_1 and D_3 don't need to be processed — contrast ratios respectively are 1.1 and 0.9; moreover, in this case also masking refinement is not necessary.

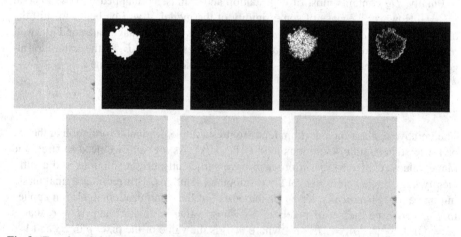

Fig. 8. (*Top: from left to right*) Degraded image, its detection mask, D_1, D_2 and D_3 masks. (*Bottom*) Restored images after: processing D_1 (*left*), processing also D_2 (*middle*) and final masking (*right*)

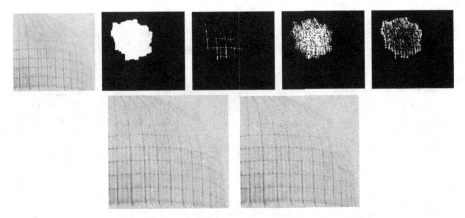

Fig. 9. (*Top - from left to right*) Original degraded image, its detection mask, D_1, D_2 and D_3 masks. (*Bottom*) Restored image after processing D_2 (*left*) and final masking (*right*)

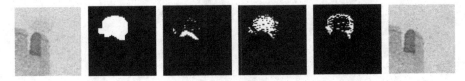

Fig. 10. (*From left to right*): Original degraded image, its detection mask, D_1, D_2 and D_3 masks and final solution

5 Experimental Results and Concluding Remarks

The proposed approach has been tested on selected images from the photographic Alinari Archive in Florence, affected by semi-transparent defects. It is worth stressing the importance of testing the method on real damages. In fact, since the real physical process is unknown, artificial defects are not representative of real applications on archived material. Some results are shown in Fig. 11. In all tests, the size of the neighbouring area of the degraded region is about three times the one of the degraded area. As it can be observed, the visual appearance of the recovered images is very good: no artifacts appear, the texture of the background is well recovered as well as eventual details of the original image (see, for example, the edges of the dome). The use of a selective algorithm avoids annoying halo effects at the border of the defect along with over-smoothing in the inner part of the restored region. As a result, the restored region is not still perceived as an anomaly on the image. The convergence process is different for each group of points so that it could happen that some groups converge after one or two iterations while others require longer convergence time. In that way the over-smoothing is avoided and the preservation of the inner information is guaranteed via the visibility based stopping criterion in eq. (1). Moreover, the preprocessing of the damaged area and masking procedures allow the detection mask to be not precise (it can be larger than the degraded region) and to manage complicated cases where the degraded area

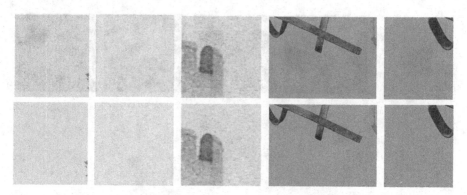

Fig. 11. Original (*Top*) and restored (*Bottom*) images

Fig. 12. *(Top to bottom - left to right)*: Original image, restored image with the present method and restored using methods in [9], [19] and [3]

intersects a darker region of the image, as in Figs. 9 and 10, so that restoration does not create artifacts in correspondence to not degraded pixels. This is a great advantage, since the detection mask heavily influences restoration results of available restoration frameworks. It is also worth highlighting that even though the proposed algorithm involves iterative procedures, it uses simple and fast operations and 4/5 iterations on average to converge. The time of each iteration depends on both the dimension of the image and the degraded area. For instance, in the case of blotch in Fig. 8, each iteration takes 45 seconds on average.

For the sake of completeness, the restoration results have been compared with some others restoration methods [3,4,9,19]. Since the clean image is not available in real applications, comparison is based on the perceived visual quality: some results are shown in Figs. 12 and 13.

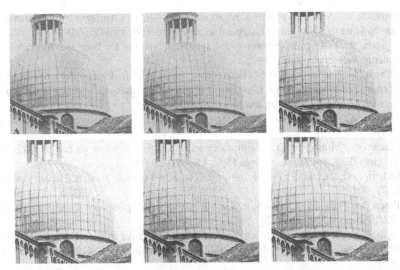

Fig. 13. Blotch on a textured image. *(Top to bottom - left to right)*: degraded, restored image with the present method and restored using methods in [9], [19], [4] and [3].

Future research will be oriented to refine the proposed model to make it more flexible and adaptive to different amount of degradation while faithfully preserving original image information and to generalize it in order to include in a common framework a wider class of degradations kinds.

Acknowledgements. Authors would like to thank Alinari Archive for kindly providing images.

References

1. Bertalmio, M., Sapiro, G., Caselles, V., Bellester, B.: Image inpainting. In: Proc. of SIGGRAPH 2000, pp. 417–424 (2000)
2. Bertalmio, M., Vese, L., Sapiro, G., Osher, S.: Simultaneous structure and texture image inpainting. IEEE Trans. on Image Proc. 12(8), 882–889 (2003)
3. Bruni, V., Crawford, A., Kokaram, A., Vitulano, D.: Semi-transparent blotches removal from sepia images exploiting visibility laws. Sig. Image and Video Proc. (2011)
4. Crawford, A.J., Bruni, V., Kokaram, A., Vitulano, D.: Multiscale semitransparent blotch removal on archived photographs using bayesian matting techniques and visibility laws. In: Proc. ICIP 2007, St. Antonio, Florida (2007)
5. Criminisi, A., Perez, P., Toyama, K.: Region filling and object removal by exemplar-based image inpainting. IEEE Trans. on Image Proc. 13(9), 1200–1212 (2004)
6. Dodwell, P.C.: The Lie transformation group model of visual perception. Perception and Psychophysics 34(1), 1–16 (1983)
7. Drummond, T., Cipolla, R.: Application of Lie algebras to visual servoing. Int. J. of Computer Vision 37(1), 21–41 (2000)
8. Efros, A., Freeman, W.: Image quilting for texture synthesis and transfer. In: Proc. of SIGGRAPH, pp. 341–346 (2001)

9. Greenblatt, A., Agaian, S., Panetta, K.: Restoration of images damaged by semi-transparent water blotches using localized image enhancement. In: Proc. of SPIE (2008)
10. Helgason, S.: Differential geometry and symmetric spaces. In: Pure and Appl., vol. XII, Academic Press, New York (1962)
11. Hoffman, W.: The Lie algebra of visual perception. J. of Math. Psycho. 3(1), 65–98 (1966)
12. Kokaram, A.: Motion Picture Restoration. Digital Algorithms for Artifact Suppression in Degraded Motion Picture Film and Video. Springer (1998)
13. Kokaram, A.: Parametric texture synthesis for filling holes in pictures. In: Proc. of ICIP (2002)
14. Mansouri, A., Mukherjee, D.: Constraining active contour evolution via Lie groups of transformation. IEEE Trans. Image Proc. 13(6), 853–863 (2004)
15. Mukherjee, D., Acton, S.: Affine and projective active contour models. Pattern Rec. 40(3) (2007)
16. Nilsson, M., Dahl, M., Claesson, I.: The successive mean quantization transform. In: Proc. of ICASSP, pp. 429–432 (2005)
17. Pappas, T.N., Safranek, R.J., Chen, J.: Perceptual criteria for image quality evaluation. In: Bovik, A. (ed.) Handbook of Image and Video Processing, pp. 939–959. Academic Press (2005)
18. Porikli, F., Tuzel, O., Meer, P.: Covariance tracking using model update based on Lie algebra. In: Proc. of the IEEE Conf. on Comp. Vis. and Patt. Rec., CVPR (2006)
19. Stanco, F., Tenze, L., Ramponi, G.: Virtual restoration of vintage photographic prints affected by foxing and water blotches. J. of Electronic Imaging 14(4) (2005)
20. Varadarajan, V.: Lie groups, Lie algebras and their representations. Prentice-Hall Series in Modern Analysis. Prentice-Hall (1974)
21. Winkler, S.: Digital Video Quality. Vision Models and Metrics. Wiley (2005)

3D Structure Estimation from a Single View Using Generic Fitted Primitives (GFP)

Tiberiu T. Cocias, Sorin M. Grigorescu, and Florin Moldoveanu

Department of Automation, Transilvania University of Braşov, Braşov, Romania
{tiberiu.cocias,s.grigorescu,moldof}@unitbv.ro

Abstract. This paper presents a method for surface estimation applied on single viewed objects. Its goal is to deliver reliable 3D scene information to service robotics application for appropriate grasp and manipulation actions. The core of the approach is to deform a predefined generic primitive such that it captures the local geometrical information which describes the imaged object model. The primitive modeling process is performed on 3D *Regions of Interest* (ROI) obtained by classifying the objects present in the scene. In order to speed up the process, the primitive points are divided into two categories: *control* and *regular points*. The control points are used to sculpt the initial primitive model based on the principle of active contours, or snakes, whereas the regular points are used to smooth the final representation of the object. In the end, a compact volume can be obtained by generating a 3D mesh based on the newly modified primitive point cloud. The obtained *Point Distribution Model*s (PDM) are used for the purpose of precise object manipulation in service robotics applications.

Keywords: Robot vision, 3D object reconstruction, Object structure estimation, Primitive modeling, Service robotics.

1 Introduction

Nowadays most service robotics applications use depth perception for the purpose of environment understanding. In order to precisely locate, grasp and manipulate an object, a robot has to estimate as good as possible the pose and the structure of that object of interest. For this reason different visual acquisition devices, such as stereo cameras, range finder or structured light sensors, are used [14].

For online manipulation, together with the pose of the object, it is needed to determine the 3D particularities of the viewed structure in order to estimate its shape [5].

There are several types of methods that focus on the 3D reconstruction of objects using multiple perspectives. Such methods try to reconstruct the convex hull of the object [11], or to recover its photo-hull [9]. Other algorithms explore the minimization of the object's surface integral with a certain cost function over the surface shape [10].

On the other hand, the reconstruction can be addressed also from a single view. This technique is usually efficient when applied to regular surface objects. An early approach for this challenge was investigated for piecewise planar reconstructions of paintings and photographs [6]. Subsequent improvements of the technique [3], [13]

G. Csurka et al. (Eds.): VISIGRAPP 2012, CCIS 359, pp. 369–382, 2013.
© Springer-Verlag Berlin Heidelberg 2013

increased the geometric precision especially for scenes with multiple vanishing planes.

In terms of reconstruction resolution and accuracy, range images (e.g. from laser scanners) provide one of the best surface estimations data. However, it has speed deficiency, sensor dimension and power consumption [8]. The main challenge encountered during 3D reconstruction is the automatic computation of the 3D transformations that align the range data. Thus, the registration of different perspective point clouds into one common coordinate system represents one of the most researched topics in the computer vision community [8], [12].

The rest of the paper is organized as follows. In Section 2 a brief description of the image processing chain is provided. The main contribution of the paper, that is the 3D shape modeling approach, is given in Section 3. Finally, before conclusions, performance evaluation results are presented in Section 4.

2   Machine Vision Apparatus

The block diagram of the proposed scene perception system can be seen in figure 1.

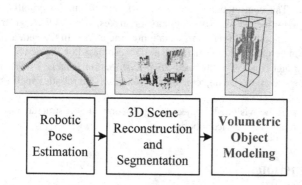

Fig. 1. Block diagram of the proposed scene perception system

The reference coordinates of the obtained visual information is related to the online determined *position and orientation* (pose) of a robot which perceive the environment through a stereo camera configuration [4] or using and RGBD sensor [17]. Since the robot can operate both in indoor and outdoor environments, the use of stereo-vision, for outdoor scenes, and MS Kinect® [17] for indoor scenarios, is well justified. Once a certain pose is determined, the imaged scene can be reconstructed and segmented for the purpose of environment understanding. The main objective here is to get the depth, or disparity, map which describes the 3D structure of an imaged scene. This information is further used by the final *object structure estimation* algorithm, which is actually the main focus of this paper. One of the main algorithms used in the proposed vision system is the object classification method which delivers to the volumetric modeling method the object class and the 2D object ROI. The classification procedure is based on color and depth information. A detailed description of the approach can be found in [4].

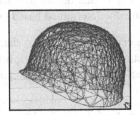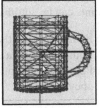

Fig. 2. Examples of meshed GFPs; (from left to right) chair, duck, helmet and mug

3   Modeled Based Object Structure Estimation

The object structure estimation system is based on the active contour principle used to manipulate a set of pre-defined *Point Distribution Models* (PDM) by stretching them over a point cloud describing an object in a given 3D *Region of Interest* (ROI). In the considered process, three main challenges arise: the sparse nature of the disparity maps, for the case of stereo-vision configuration, the calculation of the 3D ROI and the nonlinear object modeling.

3.1   The Generic Fitted Primitive (GFP)

In the presented work, a Generic Fitted Primitive (GFP) is defined as a PDM model which serves as a backbone element for constructing a particular object, or shape. The generic PDM primitive is represented by a data structure that has as background component a shape vector X which contains 3D feature points describing the model of an object class. In order to keep the initial structure compact, a second vector Y is used to store the indexes of the un-deformed primitive triangulation such that after the modeling process the moving points can be easily followed. Such example models are shown in figure 2. Additionally, the structure contains a scale factor s, a rotation matrix R and a translation matrix t that relates the PDM to a canonical reference coordinate system.

Since in the considered source of visual information, that is disparity images or depth maps, only one perspective of the imaged object is available, the PDM model is actually used to augment the missing information. In this case, we consider objects that have a symmetrical shape. Nevertheless, the proposed approach can be applied on irregular shaped entities. Depending on the complexity and regularity of the surface object, the primitive model can be defined either by a low or a high number of 3D feature points. For example, the mug shown in figure 2 is described by 412 feature points. Since the PDM describing such an object represents an almost regular surface, not all these points are important for the object modeling process. In this sense, primitive points can be divided into two main categories. The first category is represented by *regular points*, or points with low discriminative power which usually form constant geometrical surfaces. The second category assembles the so-called *control points*, namely those points that define the shape of an object. Furthermore, control points can be automatically determined based on three main characteristics [2]:

1. Points marking the center of a region, or sharp corners of a boundary;
2. Points marking a curvature extreme or the highest point of an object;
3. Points situated at an equal distance around a boundary between two control points obeying rule 1.

In the same time, control points can be determined manually under the guidance of a human [16]. This last method captures the features of an object more efficiently but suffers from subjectivity on features definition since the process is controlled by a human person. Depending on the modeled object, in our approach we used both the automatic and the manual techniques to determine control points. Using the introduced points, the computation time is increased since the number of points describing the shape of an object is usually much lower than the total number of points from the GFP. The 3D positions of the GFP points are actually directly dependent on the positions of the control points, as it will later be shown in this section. For example, from a total of 1002 points describing the helmet primitive from figure 2, only 473 of them (marked with red dots) are considered to be control points. On the other hand, for a complex object, this number can be equal to the initial PDM features number, meaning that all points from the primitive are considered to be control points since all of them are needed to capture a specific feature. Taking into account a lower number of control points will considerably increase the computational speed of the modeling process.

3.2   Disparity Map Enhancement

The presented modeling principle accepts as input information a dense point cloud of the object which structure will be estimated. In this sense, the MS Kinect® [17] sensor has no problem in providing such dense information, whereas the stereo camera configuration outputs a sparse disparity maps. Namely, it contains "holes" or discontinuities in areas where no stereo feature matching exists [1]. Such discontinuities are present in low textured regions or constant color areas from the environment.

To overcome this issue we propose an enhancement method which deals with disparity maps discontinuities. Basically, the idea is to scan each point from a disparity image and determine if there is a gap between the considered point and a neighboring point situated at a certain distance, as shown in figure 3(a). Since we apply the principle on disparity maps, which are defined on the 2D domain, there are only 5 main neighboring directions from a total of 8 in which we search for discontinuities. The untreated 3 directions refer to the back of the centered point and it is assumed that are no discontinuities in that direction since the position is already searched.

The disparity map is actually a grey scale image with pixel intensities inverse-proportional to the distance between the considered 3D world point and the camera's position. Having in mind that the disparity image is represented using 8 bits, we sample it using 256 layers, each corresponding to certain intensity in the disparity domain. The enhancement process searches for discontinuities only in one layer at a time,

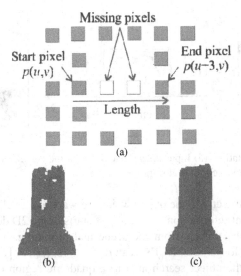

Fig. 3. Disparity enhancement algorithm. (a) Missing pixels searching principle. (b)Original disparity map. (c) Enhanced disparity image.

since there is no information about the connectivity of the intensities. In this sense, the layers are stored using a 256 bins histogram. For each pixel in each layer the number of the same intensity along a direction is calculated. In order not to merge two different objects, the search area is reduced to a finite value, dynamically calculated. The search process starts from the lowest neighboring distance value, which has a two pixels length, and ends when a discontinuity is found or the maximum length is reached. The discontinuity is determined by comparing the length of the direction with the number of the same intensity pixels found along this direction. If the number of pixels found is below the length of the considered direction, the missing positions are filled with pixels with the same intensity as the ones already found.

There is a slight chance that two closely positioned objects are merged by the algorithm. In order to overcome this challenge, a variance driven image of the disparity map has been used [15]. From the variance image only object contours are extracted. In this way it can be determined if the points which take part in the fill process belong to one single region or to a neighboring region. The result of the presented method will be a compact and dense representation of the disparity image, as shown in figure 3(c). On the other hand, it is needed to connect the layers which are very close (in terms of disparity) in the 3D model. This can be achieved by diffusing the gradient separating two neighboring intensities. In order to preserve the 3D features of the object, the diffusing process will occur only for regions with translation of intensity no grater then 5 intensities layers. In this way, the obtained layers are smoothly connected.

3.3   3D ROI Definition

Because of the complexity of the scene, it is difficult to apply the modeling process directly on the entire scene. To overcome this issue, we propose the definition of a

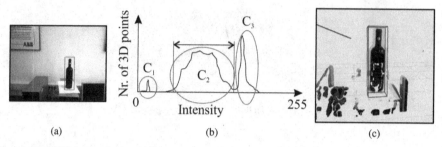

(a)   (b)   (c)

Fig. 4. 3D ROI computation. (a) Input image together with the calculated 2D ROI. (b) Histogram cluster segmentation. (c) 3D ROI re-projection.

local frame attached directly to the object which we want to model, rejecting from the scene all the redundant information. This process starts in the 2D domain by segmenting and classifying the objects from the scene and providing, besides the class to which the object belongs, 2D ROI's feature vectors $[p_l, p_R]$, $i = 1,2,3,4$. This description restricts the object search area to a quadratic region of interest. For the stereo-vision configuration the 3D ROI is determined by computing the disparity between the left and right ROI points. In this way only a planar representation (slice) in the 3D space is obtained. The volumetric property is evaluated starting with the assumption that the pixels inside the 2D ROI describe only the object. The depth is determined statistically by finding the highest density of 3D points which lie inside the planar ROI along the Z 3D Cartesian axis. A 3D representation of the ROI can be seen in figure 4. However, there is a possibility that the highest density of 3D points belongs to a noise entity outside the object border but still inside the ROI.

To overcome this problem, a histogram of the disparity image is calculated. Instead of searching only the top density value of the intensities in histogram, we check also the highest aperture of the histogram for the considered top density. Basically we determine the highest distribution of connected points by summing all the densities from the slices of the aperture belonging to a top value of the histogram as:

$$d = \sum_{i+a}^{i+b} \max(h(i)),$$ (1)

where d represent the highest cluster of 3D points, $h(i)$ is the number of pixels for a certain bin i and a, b are the closest and farthest non zero $h(i)$ relatively to the considered intensity i, respectively. The margin of the aperture is actually defining the first and last planes of the 3D ROI volume along the Z axis, respectively.

For the case of the MS Kinect sensor, the ROI formulation is trivial. The final bounding box can be easily extracted by a simple selection, from the depth map, of the points laying inside the segmented 2D ROI.

3.4   PDM Shape Alignment

The 3D alignment process deals with the calculation of the rotation and translation of the primitive shape with respect to the point cloud distribution inside the 3D ROI. Because each PDM, that is primitive and point cloud, is defined in its own coordinates system, a similarity transformation is used to align the two models. Since the ROI's PDM is related to the same coordinate system as the 3D virtual environment, we have chosen to bring the primitive's PDM into a reference 3D environment coordinate system. The reference coordinate system is given by the on-line determined pose of the stereo camera [4]. In this sense, the primitive is considered to be a translational shape, while the 3D ROI is marked as a static cube. The similarity transformation is described by:

$$X_{new} = sR(X_{old} - t), \qquad (2)$$

where, X_{old} and X_{new} represent the 3D coordinate of a point before and after the similarity transformation, s is a scale factor, while R and t are the matrices defining the rotation and translation of a point, respectively. These coefficients represent the Degrees of Freedom (DoF) of a certain shape.

The scale factor is determined based on the 3D point cloud information inside the ROI. Since a disparity enhancement is considered before the 3D re-projection process, it can be presumed that inside the ROI exist one or more large densities of points which describe the object of interest. For each model or point cloud is determined the radius of a centered sphere which embeds the respective point cloud. By computing a ration between these radiuses, a scale factor can be determined.

The translation of the moving shape is easily determined by adding the center of gravity of the points inside the 3D ROI from the center of gravity of the primitive PDM, as follows:

$$t = \frac{1}{n_p}\sum_{i=1}^{n_p} a_i + \frac{1}{n_p}\sum_{j=1}^{n_p} b_j, \qquad (3)$$

where, n_p represent the number of points of the model and a and b are the two densities of points, that is of the object's shape (primitive model) and of the fixed point cloud inside the 3D ROI. The rotation between the two models is not so trivial to obtain. Because one of the models represents only a perspective of the second one, the rotation can be determined by matching these two entities. This operation starts by computing the shape descriptors for each model based on the FPFH descriptor [18]. Next, a Sample Consensus Initial Alignment (SAC-IA) algorithm [18] is used to determine the best transformation between the two entities. This transformation contains also the rotation of the primitive relative to the reference point cloud, which is the scene object.

By using the proposed alignment method, a rough object volumetric estimation is obtained based on the fitting primitive principle. An example result of the similarity transformation can be seen in figure 5, where, the red silhouette represents the PDM primitive shape whereas the blue model represent the object from the scene.

3.5   PDM Primitive Modeling

The points which drive the modeling process are the control points described in a previous subsection. The behavior of the other points in the PDM model is automatically derived from the movement of the control points. The modeling process is achieved by dragging after each control point the neighbors from the surrounding

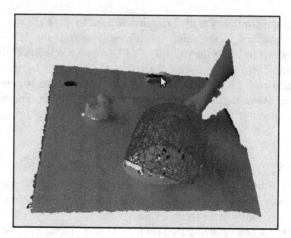

Fig. 5. Primitive PDM shape alignment example

area. Each of the neighbor point is moved based on a physical relation describing the property of the considered object. This relation can be either linear, as in equation 4, or non-linear for more complex surfaces. For simplicity if explanations, we have considered in this work a linear relation between control and the rest of the PDM points:

$$x_{new} = x_{old}\left(1 + \frac{d_{curr}}{d_{max}}\right),\qquad(4)$$

where, x_{new} and x_{old} represent the new and old 3D coordinates of the considered neighboring points, respectively, d_{max} is the distance between the control point and the farthest neighbor within the affected area and d_{curr} represent the distance between the control point and the translated neighbor. The results of such a linear modeling are shown in figure 6, where control points are marked with red, their neighbors are labeled with blue the rest of the PDM points are green. The surrounding dragged area has the shape of a cube centered on the control point 3D coordinate and has its area defined as double the distance between the initial and the new position of the control point, as depicted in figure 6.

The proposed approach for estimating an object's volume starts with a generic object PDM model, namely a primitive, and ends by capturing by each primitive control point the local features of the modeled object of interest. As explained, this is achieved by minimizing the distance between the control point and the PDM in a respective neighborhood. The minimization procedure is based on the *active contours* principle, better known as *snakes* [7]. This approach represents a deformable contour model of the considered object.

In an image, an active contour is a curve parameterized by the minimization of and energy functional:

$$\varepsilon(c) = \varepsilon_{int}(c) + \varepsilon_{ext}(c) = \int_0^1 \big[E_{int}\big(c(s)\big) + E_{ext}\big(c(s)\big)\big]ds,\qquad(5)$$

where, E_{int} and E_{ext} are the internal and external energies, respectively and $c(s) = [x(s), y(s), z(s)]$ represents the curve describing the object's surface, while $s \in [0,1]$. By defining an initial contour within an image, it will move under the influence of

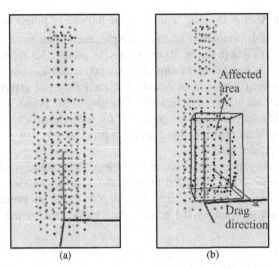

(a)   (b)

Fig. 6. A linear dependency between a control point and its neighbors. (a) Initial PDM shape model.(b) Point deformation along a considered direction.

internal forces computed based on the derivatives from the active contour an also under the influence of the external forces captured from the image.

In the presented 3D object modeling approach, the image domain is equivalent to the 3D representation of the scene. For this reason the same energy minimization principle has been used to model the shape of an object. Instead of using an initial active contour, as in the original method, we propose the use of a 3D generic primitive PDM model. The movement of the contour surface is thus described by the direction of the lowest functional energy, that specific region actually corresponding to a probable contour in the image [19]. In the considered 3D case being the highest density of points from the 3D scene.

The idea of using forces to move the primitive points is that the primitive PDM must be attracted and fitted on the border of the object. The internal forces, which refer exclusively to the primitive PDM, are responsible for supervising the shape smoothness and continuity. As described in the equation 6, the continuity property is controlled by the first derivate while smoothens is define by the second derivate of the surface.

$$E_{int} = E_{cont} + E_{curv} = \tfrac{1}{2}(\alpha(s)|v'(s)|^2 + \beta(s)|v''(s)|^2), \qquad (6)$$

where, E_{cont} is the energy responsible for the continuity of the surface and E_{curv} deals with the bending property of the hull of the object. α and β are two parameters which influence the E_{cont} and E_{curv} forces, while $v(s) = [x(s), y(s), z(s)]$ represent the coordinates of a point from the shape vector X. In the discreet domain the two energies can be rewritten as:

$$E_{cont} = (x_i - x_{i-1})^2 + (y_i - y_{i-1})^2 + (z_i - z_{i-1})^2, \qquad (7)$$

$$E_{curv} = (x_{i-1} - 2x_i + x_{i+1})^2 + (x_{i-1} - 2x_i + x_{i+1})^2 + (x_{i-1} - 2x_i + x_{i+1})^2, \quad (8)$$

where, $x_i, y_i, z_i \in \mathbf{X}$, $i = 0, ... n_p$ and n_p is the number of points in the shape PDM vector. In the original formulation of the principle, each point from the shape can be moved in one of the eight possible 2D directions. In current 3D approach, because of the third dimension, a number of 24 directions are taken into account.

The correct moving direction is mainly influenced by the external energy E_{Ext} which evaluates for each direction the highest density of 3D points. Because this density can be spatially very close, a weight factor for the external energy is introduced. Thus, if these candidate positions have an appropriate number of points, the weight factor will be considered zero.

Since we have only one perspective of the object, there are large object areas with no 3D point cloud description needed to drive the contour energies. The un-imaged back side of an object represents such an example. In the proposed approach, the missing information is filled by the generic data introduced by the PDM primitive model.

4   Experimental Results

The main objective of the presented approach is robust 3D object structure estimation for appropriate object grasping and manipulation in service robotics. In order to prove the reliability of the concept, different types of objects were estimated, starting from more simple models (e.g. mug and bottle) and ending with high irregular geometrical shapes (duck, chair or helmet). Since the robot can operate in any environment, the experiments were conducted both outdoor, using a Point Grey Bumblebee® stereo camera system [20], and indoor using a MS Kinect® RGBD sensor [17]. The sensing devices were mounted on a Pioneer P3 – DX robotic platform [21] equipped with a 7 DOF Cyton 2 robotic arm [22]. The grasp plan action was performed using *GraspIt!* library [23].

The *Ground Truth* (GT) data against which the proposed method has been tested is composed of a number of manual measurements conducted on the objects: width, height, thickness, translation and rotation. The translation and rotation was measure with respect to a fixed reference coordinate system represented by an ARToolKit® [24] marker.

4.1   Mug Modeling

The mug primitive structure is defined by 412 points out of which only 258 are defining the actual structure of the shape (control points). Three different mugs were placed on a flat surface, in and indoor scenario. The scene was perceived using the MS Kinect sensor. The structure estimation method was applied independently on each segmented mug. The time consumed for the entire estimation process, including segmentation, classification, initial raw alignment and modeling process of all considered shapes, was 11.76 seconds on an Intel Pentium I5 2.30 GHz platform. The result obtained is depicted in figure 7.

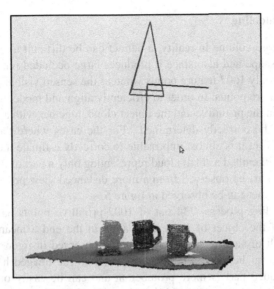

Fig. 7. Segmented modeled mugs

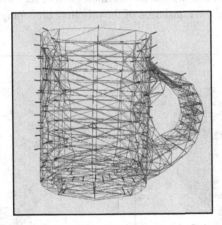

Fig. 8. Mug GFP meshes before (green) and after (red) the fitting process. The blue lines represent the directions of the features normals.

The first two mugs (red and blue) were accurately positioned, with a pose error below 3%, while the green mug positioning produced an increased error because of the occluded part of the handle. Lacking distance information, the handle was positioned randomly in the unseen part of the model, producing in the end a 3D volume with a low confidence for grasping. Regarding the first two models, more than 65% of primitive points were repositioned during the structure estimation process, leaving the rest of 35% points to generally estimate the occluded parts of the mugs. Based on the new 3D definition of the model, the grasp action had a successfully grasp rate of over 95%. In figure 8, the difference between the initial 3D structure of the primitive (presented as a green mesh) and the modeled one (red mesh) can be intuitively observed.

4.2   Helmet Modeling

Representing a large volume in reality, a helmet can be difficult to estimate because of the elongated shape and also since it produces large occluded regions. The primitive is defined by only 1002 feature points whereas the sensed visible part is described through 15378 feature points. In order to efficiently align and model the primitive, the scale ratio between the primitive and the object cloud, together with a raw transformation matrix, must be correctly determined. For the cases where the object is seen directly from the front it is almost impossible to correctly estimate the scale since the centered sphere will embed a small cloud representing only a part of the object. In this sense, the object must be observed from a more distanced view point. An initial raw alignment for a helmet can be observed in figure 5.

After the modeling process, 734 out of 1002 primitive points have captured the local geometry of the object of interest, creating in the end a meaningful compact volume. The result of such reshape action can be observed in figure 9. Because the primitive helmet (war helmet) is rather different from the imaged helmet (climbing helmet), the occluded part is more protuberant and can be easily observed. During tests, the presented modeling method has proved its efficiency and robustness as long as the observed object does not have more than 60% of its surface occluded. Above this value, the scale and the translation of the primitive are ambiguous.

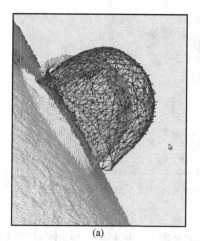 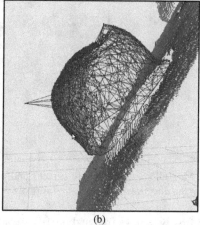

(a)   (b)

Fig. 9. Object structure estimation. (a) Initial primitive alignment between the primitive (red mesh) and object point cloud (blue point cloud). (b) Final modeled primitive.

The statistical measures of achieved errors in all the experiments are given in Table 1.

Table 1. Performance evaluation results for the proposed GFP estimation approach

Object	Alignement						Modeling			
	Rotation (%)			Translation (%)			Primitive Points		Volumetric error (%)	Ocluded region (%)
	ϕ	θ	φ	x	y	z	Total	Modeled		
Mug	4.1	1.2	2.4	0.1	0.74	1.7	412	258	2.78	47
Helmet	2.5	0.7	2.4	0.25	0.14	1.2	1002	734	3.12	28
Duck	5.1	3.2	4.2	1.3	2.1	3.1	2329	1452	5.72	45
Chair	0.7	1.3	1.5	2.01	0.1	0.8	842	548	1.35	19
Bottle	0.1	0.4	0.3	0.5	0.6	1.15	382	305	2.71	36

5   Conclusions

In this paper, an object volumetric modeling algorithm for objects of interest encountered in real world service robotics environments has been proposed. The goal of the approach is to determine as precisely as possible the 3D particular surface structure of different objects. The calculated 3D model can be further used for the purpose of visually guided object grasping. As future work the authors consider the time computation enhancement of the proposed procedure through parallel computational devices (e.g. Graphic Processors), as well as the application of the method to other computer vision areas, such as 3D medical imaging.

Acknowledgements. This Paper Is Supported by the Sectoral Operational Program Human Resources Development (SOP HRD), Financed from the European Social Fund and by the Romanian Government under the Projects POSDRU/107/1.5/S/76945 and POSDRU/89/1.5/S/59323.

References

1. Brown, M., Burschka, D., Hager, G.: Advances in Computational Stereo. IEEE Transaction on Pattern Recognition and Machine Intelligence 25(8), 993–1008 (2003)
2. Cootes, T., Taylor, C., Cooper, D., Graham, J.: Active Shape Models-Their Training and Application. Comp. Vision and Image Understanding 61(1), 38–59 (1995)
3. Criminisi, A., Reid, I., Zisserman, A.: Single View Metrology. International Journal on Computer Vision 40(2), 123–148 (2000)
4. Grigorescu, S., Cocias, T., Macesanu, G., Puiu, D., Moldoveanu, F.: Robust Camera Pose and Scene Structure Analysis for Service Robotics. Robotics and Autonomous Systems 59(11), 899–909 (2011)
5. Hartley, R., Zisserman, A.: Multiple View Geometryin Computer Vision. Cambridge University Press, Great Britain (2004)
6. Horry, Y., Anjyo, K., Arai, K.: Tour into the Picture: Using a Spidery Mesh Interface to Make Animation from a Single Image. In: Proc. ACM SIGGRAPH, New York, pp. 225–232 (1997)

7. Kass, M., Witkin, A., Terzopoulos, D.: Snakes: Active Contour Models. International Journal of Computer Vision 1(4), 321–331 (1998)
8. Kim, T., Seo, Y., Lee, S., Yang, Z., Chang, M.: Simultaneous Registration of Multiple Views with Markers. Computer-Aided Design 41(4), 231–239 (2009)
9. Kutulakos, K., Seitz, S.: A Theory of Shape by Space Carving. International Journal of Computer Vision 38(3), 199–218 (2000)
10. Lhuillier, M., Quan, L.: A Quasi-Dense Approach to Surface Reconstruction from Uncalibrated Images. IEEE TPAMI 27(3), 418–433 (2005)
11. Matsuyama, T., Wu, X., Takai, T., Wada, T.: Real-Time Dynamic 3-D Object Shape Reconstruction and High-Fidelity Texture Mapping for 3-D Video. IEEE Transactions on Circuits and Systems for Video Technology 14(3), 357–369 (2004)
12. Stamos, I., Liu, L., Chao, C., Wolberg, G., Yu, G., Zokai, S.: Integrating Automated Range Registration with Multi-view Geometry for the Photorealistic Modeling of Large-Scale Scenes. International Journal of Computer Vision 78(2/3), 237–260 (2008)
13. Sturm, P., Maybank, S.: A Method for Interactive 3D Reconstruction of Piecewise Planar Objects from Single Images. In: BMVC, United Kingdom (1999)
14. Trucco, E., Verri, A.: Introductory Techniques for 3-D Computer Vision. Prentice Hall PTR (1998)
15. Turiac, M., Ivanovici, M., Radulescu, T.: Variance-driven Active Contours. In: International Conference on Image Processing, Computer Vision, and Pattern Recognition, Las Vegas, Nevada, USA (2010)
16. Zheng, Y., Barbu, A., Georgescu, B., Scheuering, M., Comaniciu, D.: Four-Chamber Heart Modeling and Automatic Segmentation for 3D Cardiac CT Volumes Using Marginal Space Learning and Steerable Features. IEEE Transaction on Medical Imaging 27(11), 1668–1681 (2008)
17. Microsoft motion sensing devices, http://en.wikipedia.org/wiki/Kinect
18. Rusu, R.B., Blodow, N., Beetz, M.: Fast Point Feature Histograms (FPFH) for 3D Regis-tration. In: International Conference on Robotics and Automation, Kobe, Japan, pp. 3212–3217 (2009)
19. Nixon, M.S., Aguado, A.S.: Feature extraction and image Processing. Academic Press (2002)
20. Point Grey Research's,
   http://www.ptgrey.com/products/bumblebee2/bumblebee2_stereo_camera.asp
21. Autonomous mobile robots, software and accessories,
   http://www.mobilerobots.com
22. Autonomous mobile robots, manipulators,
   http://www.mobilerobots.com/accessories/manipulators.aspx
23. Miller, A., Allen, P.K.: Graspit!: A Versatile Simulator for Robotic Grasping. IEEE Robotics and Automation Magazine 11(4), 110–122 (2004)
24. Augmented Reality (AR) research department,
   http://www.hitl.washington.edu/artoolkit/

Facial Landmarks Detector Learned by the Structured Output SVM

Michal Uřičář, Vojtěch Franc, and Václav Hlaváč

Center for Machine Perception, Department of Cybernetics,
Faculty of Electrical Engineering, Czech Technical University in Prague,
Technická 2, 166 27 Prague 6, Czech Republic
{uricamic,xfrancv,hlavac}@cmp.felk.cvut.cz

Abstract. We propose a principled approach to supervised learning of facial landmarks detector based on the Deformable Part Models (DPM). We treat the task of landmarks detection as an instance of the structured output classification. To learn the parameters of the detector we use the Structured Output Support Vector Machines algorithm. The objective function of the learning algorithm is directly related to the performance of the detector and controlled by the user-defined loss function, in contrast to the previous works. Our proposed detector is real-time on a standard computer, simple to implement and easily modifiable for detection of various set of landmarks. We evaluate the performance of our detector on a challenging "Labeled Faces in the Wild" (LFW) database. The empirical results show that our detector consistently outperforms two public domain implementations based on the Active Appearance Models and the DPM. We are releasing open-source code implementing our proposed detector along with the manual annotation of seven facial landmarks for nearly all images in the LFW database.

Keywords: Facial Landmarks Detection, Deformable Part Models, Structured Output Classification, Structured Output SVM.

1 Introduction

The detection of facial landmarks like canthi nose and mouth corners (see Fig. 1) is an essential part of face recognition systems. The accuracy of the detection significantly influences its final performance [1–3]. The problem of the precise and robust detection of facial landmarks has received a lot of attention in the past decade. We briefly review only the approaches relevant to the method proposed in this paper.

Among the most popular are detectors based on the Active Appearance Models (AAM) [4] which use a joint statistical model of appearance and shape. Detectors build on AAM provide a dense set of facial features, allowing to extract whole contours of facial parts like eyes, etc. However high resolution images are required for both training and testing stage and the detection leads to solving a non-convex optimization problem susceptible to local optima unless a good initial guess of the landmark positions is available.

A straightforward approach to landmark detection is based on using independently trained detectors for each facial landmark. For instance the AdaBoost based detectors

G. Csurka et al. (Eds.): VISIGRAPP 2012, CCIS 359, pp. 383–398, 2013.

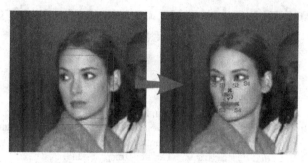

Fig. 1. Functionality of the facial landmark detector

and its modifications have been frequently used [5]. If applied independently, the individual detectors often fail to provide a robust estimate of the landmark positions. The weakness of the local evidence can be compensated by using a prior on the geometrical configuration of landmarks. The detection is typically carried out in two consecutive steps. In the first step, the individual detectors are used to find a set of candidate positions for each landmark separately. In the second step, the best landmark configuration with the highest support from the geometrical prior is selected. The landmark detectors based on this approach were proposed for example in [6–9].

The Deformable Part Models (DPM) [10–13] go one step further by fusing the local appearance model and the geometrical constraints into a single model. The DPM is given by a set of parts along with a set of connections between certain pairs of parts arranged in a deformable configuration. A natural way how to describe the DPM is an undirected graph with vertices corresponding to the parts and edges representing the connections between the pairs of connected parts. The DPM detector estimates all landmark positions simultaneously by optimizing a single scoring function composed of a local appearance model and a deformation cost. The complexity of finding the best landmark configuration depends on the structure of underlying graph. Acyclic graph allows efficient estimation by a variant of the Dynamic Programming.

An instance of finely tuned facial landmark detector based on the DPM has been proposed in [14]. The very same detector was also used in several successful face recognition systems described in [15] and [16]. In this case, the local appearance model is learned by a multiple-instance variant of the AdaBoost algorithm with Haar-like features used as the weak classifiers. The deformation cost is expressed as a mixture of Gaussian trees whose parameters are learned from examples. This landmark detector is publicly available and we use it for comparison with our detector.[1] Importantly, learning of the local appearance model and the deformation cost is done in two independent steps which simplifies learning, but may not be optimal in terms of detectors accuracy.

We propose to learn the parameters of the DPM discriminatevly in one step by directly optimizing accuracy of the resulting detector. The main contributions of this paper are as follows:

---

[1] There also exists a successful commercial solution OKAO Vision Facial Feature Extraction API (http://www.omron.com) which is used for example in Picasa™ or Apple iPhoto™ software.

1. We treat the landmark detection with the DPM as an instance of the structured output classification problem whose detection accuracy is measured by a loss function natural for this application. We propose to use the Structured Output SVM (SO-SVM) [17] for supervised learning of the parameters of the landmark detector from examples. The learning objective of the SO-SVMs is directly related to the accuracy of the detector. In contrast, all existing approaches we are aware of optimize surrogate objective functions whose relation to the detector accuracy is not always clear.
2. We empirically evaluate accuracy of the proposed landmark detector learned by the SO-SVMs on a challenging "Labeled Faces in the Wild" (LFW) database [18].
3. We provide an empirical comparison of two popular optimization algorithms — the Bundle Method for Regularized Risk Minimization (BMRM) [19] and the Stochastic Gradient Descend (SGD) [20] — which are suitable for solving the convex optimization problem emerging in the SO-SVM learning.
4. We provide an open source library which implements the proposed detector and the algorithm for supervised learning of its parameters. In adidtion we provide a manual annotation of the facial landmarks for all images from the LFW database.

The paper is organized as follows. Section 2 defines the structured output classifier for facial landmark detection based on the DPM. Section 3 describes the SO-SVM algorithm for learning the parameters of the classifier from examples. Experimental results are presented in Sect. 4. Section 5 shortly describes the open source implementation of our detector and the provided manual annotation of the LFW database. Section 6 concludes the paper.

2   Structured Output Classifier for Facial Landmark Detection

We treat the landmark detection as an instance of the structured output classification problem. We assume that the input of our classifier is a still image of fixed size containing a single face. In our experiments we construct the input image by cropping a window around a bounding box found by a face detector (enlarged by a fixed margin ensuring that the whole face is contained) and normalizing its size. The classifier output are estimated locations of a set of facial landmarks. A formal definition is given next.

Let $\mathcal{J} = \mathcal{X}^{H \times W}$ be a set of input images with $H \times W$ pixels, where $\mathcal{X}$ denotes a set of pixel values which in our experiments, dealing with 8bit gray-scale images, is $\mathcal{X} = \{0, \ldots, 255\}$. We describe the configuration of M landmarks by a graph $G = (V, E)$, where $V = \{0, \ldots, M-1\}$ is a set of landmarks and $E \subset V^2$ is a set of edges defining the neighboring landmarks. Each landmark is assigned a position $s_i \in \mathcal{S}_i \subset \{1, \ldots, H\} \times \{1, \ldots, W\}$, where $\mathcal{S}_i$ denotes a set of all admissible positions of the i-th landmark within the image $I \in \mathcal{J}$. The quality of a landmark configuration $\mathbf{s} = (\mathbf{s}_0, \ldots, \mathbf{s}_{M-1}) \in \mathcal{S} = \mathcal{S}_0 \times \cdots \times \mathcal{S}_{M-1}$ given an input image $I \in \mathcal{J}$ is measured by a scoring function $f \colon \mathcal{J} \times \mathcal{S} \to \mathbb{R}$ defined as

$$f(I, \mathbf{s}) = \sum_{i \in V} q_i(I, \mathbf{s}_i) + \sum_{(i,j) \in E} g_{ij}(\mathbf{s}_i, \mathbf{s}_j) \ . \tag{1}$$

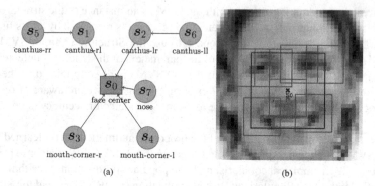

(a)   (b)

Fig. 2. Definition of (a) the underlying graph $G = (V, E)$ for the landmark configuration and (b) the components of the proposed detector

The first term in (1) corresponds to a local appearance model evaluating the match between landmarks on positions $\mathbf{s}$ and the input image I. The second term in (1) is the deformation cost evaluating the relative positions of the neighboring landmarks i and j.

We assume that the costs $q_i: \mathcal{J} \times \mathcal{S}_i \to \mathbb{R}, i = 0, \ldots, M - 1$ and $g_{ij}: \mathcal{S}_i \times \mathcal{S}_j \to \mathbb{R}, (i, j) \in E$ are linearly parametrized functions

$$q_i(I, \mathbf{s}_i) = \langle \mathbf{w}_i^q, \Psi_i^q(I, \mathbf{s}_i) \rangle \tag{2}$$

$$g_{ij}(\mathbf{s}_i, \mathbf{s}_j) = \langle \mathbf{w}_{ij}^g, \Psi_{ij}^g(\mathbf{s}_i, \mathbf{s}_j) \rangle , \tag{3}$$

where $\Psi_i^q: \mathcal{J} \times \mathcal{S}_i \to \mathbb{R}^{n_{iq}}, \Psi_{ij}^g: \mathcal{S}_i \times \mathcal{S}_j \to \mathbb{R}^{n_{ig}}, i = 0, \ldots, M - 1$ are predefined maps and $\mathbf{w}_i^q \in \mathbb{R}^{n_{iq}}, \mathbf{w}_{ij}^g \in \mathbb{R}^{n_{ig}}, i = 0, \ldots, M - 1$ are parameter vectors which will be learned from examples. Let us introduce a joint map $\Psi: \mathcal{J} \times \mathcal{S} \to \mathbb{R}^n$ and a joint parameter vector $\mathbf{w} \in \mathbb{R}^n$ defined as a column-wise concatenation of the individual maps Ψ_i^q, Ψ_{ij}^g and the individual parameter vectors $\mathbf{w}_i^q, \mathbf{w}_{ij}^g$ respectively. With these definitions we see that the scoring function (1) simplifies to $f(I, \mathbf{s}) = \langle \mathbf{w}, \Psi(I, \mathbf{s}) \rangle$.

Given an input image I, the structured output classifier returns the configurations $\hat{\mathbf{s}}$ computed by maximizing the scoring function $f(I, \mathbf{s})$, i.e.

$$\hat{\mathbf{s}} \in \arg\max_{\mathbf{s} \in \mathcal{S}} f(I, \mathbf{s}) . \tag{4}$$

We assume that the graph $G = (V, E)$ is acyclic (see Fig. 2(a)), which allows efficient solving of the maximization problem (4) by dynamic programming.

A complete specification of the structured classifier (4) requires to define:

– The maps $\Psi_i^q(I, \mathbf{s}_i), i = 0, \ldots, M - 1$ where $\Psi_i^q(I, \mathbf{s}_i)$ defines a local feature descriptor of i-th landmark computed on a rectangular window centered at $\mathbf{s}_i$. We call the rectangular window a component (see Fig. 2(b)). The size of the component and its feature descriptor are crucial design options which have to be made carefully. In Sect. 2.1 we describe a list of feature descriptors we have considered.

– The fixed maps $\Psi_{ij}^g(\mathbf{s}_i, \mathbf{s}_j), (i, j) \in E$ defining the parametrization of the deformation cost. Section 2.2 describes the parametrization which we have considered.

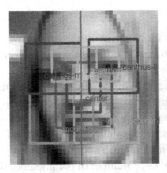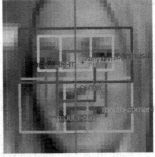

Fig. 3. Left: optimal search spaces for each component. Right: the same search spaces made symmetrical along the vertical magenta line.

- The set $\mathcal{S} = (\mathcal{S}_0 \times \cdots \times \mathcal{S}_{M-1})$ defining the search space of the landmark positions. These sets can be interpreted as hard constraints on the admissible configurations of the landmarks, i.e. the landmark positions outside these sets corresponds to $-\infty$ value of the deformation cost $g_{ij}(\mathbf{s}_i, \mathbf{s}_j)$.
  We tune the size of these search spaces experimentally — we keep track of the axis aligned bounding box (AABB) for each component throughout the whole database excluding the images whose components does not fit in the image. We set the size of components in order to keep at least 95% images of the original database. Consequently, the AABB of each component is made vertically symmetric along the center y-axis in order to remove bias to certain positions. Figure 3 visualizes the found search spaces.
- The joint parameter vector $\mathbf{w} \in \mathbb{R}^n$ learned from the training examples by the SO-SVM algorithm described in Sect. 3.

Finally we would like to stress that the particular number of landmarks and their neighborhood structure can be arbitrary as long as the inference problem (1) can be solved efficiently. In this paper we experiment with the 8-landmarks variant of the graph $G = (V, E)$ shown in Fig. 2(a).

2.1 Appearance Model

We have experimented with several feature descriptors Ψ_i^q for the local appearance model $q_i(I, \mathbf{s}_i)$. In particular, we considered i) normalized intensity values, ii) derivatives of image intensity values, iii) histograms of Local Binary Patterns (LBP) [21] and iv) the LBP pyramid feature descriptor [22]. We obtained the best results with the LBP pyramid feature descriptor which is used in the experiments. The LBP pyramid descriptor is constructed by concatenating binary encoded LBP features computed in each pixel (up to boundary pixels) and in several scales. In particular, we use the LBP pyramid computed in 4 scales starting from the original image and consequently downscaling the image 3 times by $1/2$. The resulting feature vector is high dimensional but very sparse.

2.2 Deformation Cost

We have experimented with two parametrizations of the deformation cost $g_{ij}(s_i, s_j)$: i) a table representation and ii) a quadratic function of a displacement vector between landmark positions.

The table representation is the most generic form of the deformation cost useful when no prior knowledge is available. Table elements specify cost for each combination of s_i and s_j separately. $\Psi_{ij}^g(s_i, s_j)$ is a sparse vector with all elements zero but the element corresponding to the combinations (s_i, s_j) which is one. Such a representation of the deformation cost is very flexible and easy to implement. Though the table representation is very flexible its main disadvantage is a very large number of parameters to be learned. In turn, a large number of training examples is required to avoid over-fitting. In fact, each combination (s_i, s_j) should be present in training examples at least once to make the corresponding cost non-zero.

As the second option, we considered the deformation cost $g_{ij}(s_i, s_j)$ to be a quadratic function of a displacement vector $s_j - s_i$. Following [12], we define the deformation cost as

$$\left. \begin{aligned} \Psi_{ij}^g(s_i, s_j) &= (dx, dy, dx^2, dy^2) \\ (dx, dy) &= (x_j, y_j) - (x_i, y_i) \end{aligned} \right\} \tag{5}$$

This representation accounts for the distance and the direction of the j-th landmark with respect to i-th landmark. This representation is determined only by four parameters which substantially reduces the risk of over-fitting.

We found experimentally the quadratic deformation cost to give slightly better results compared to the table representation, therefore experiments described further use only this parametrization of deformation cost.

3 Learning the Parameters of the Structured Output Classifier

We learn the joint parameter vector w by the SO-SVM algorithm [17]. The requirements on the classifier are specified by a user defined loss-function $\ell \colon \mathcal{S} \times \mathcal{S} \to \mathbb{R}$. The value $\ell(s, s^*)$ penalizes the classifier estimate s provided the actual configuration of the landmarks is s^*. The SO-SVM requires loss function to be non-negative and zero iff the estimate is absolutely correct, i.e. $\ell(s, s^*) \geq 0$, $\forall s, s^* \in \mathcal{S}$, and $\ell(s, s^*) = 0$ iff $s = s^*$. In particular, we use the mean normalized deviation between the estimated and the ground truth positions as the loss function, i.e.

$$\ell(s, s^*) = \kappa(s^*) \frac{1}{M} \sum_{j=0}^{M-1} \|s_j - s_j^*\| . \tag{6}$$

The normalization factor $\kappa(s^*) = \|\frac{1}{2}(s_{eyeR} + s_{eyeL}) - s_{mouth}\|^{-1}$ is reciprocal to the face size which we define as the length of the line connecting the midpoint between the eye centers s_{eyeR} and s_{eyeL} with the mouth center s_{mouth}. The normalization factor is introduced in order to make the loss function scale invariant which is necessary because responses of the face detector used to construct the input images do not allow accurate estimation of the scale. Figure 4 illustrates the meaning of the loss function (6). Finally, we point out that any other loss function meeting the constraints defined above can be readily used, e.g. one can use maximal normalized deviation.

Given a set of training examples $\{(I^1, \mathbf{s}^1), \ldots, (I^m, \mathbf{s}^m)\} \in (\mathcal{J} \times \mathcal{S})^m$ composed of pairs of the images and their manual annotations, the joint parameter vector $\mathbf{w}$ of the classifier (4) is obtained by solving the following convex minimization problem

$$\mathbf{w}^* = \arg \min_{\mathbf{w} \in \mathbb{R}^n} \left[\frac{\lambda}{2} \|\mathbf{w}\|^2 + R(\mathbf{w}) \right] , \text{ where} \tag{7}$$

$$R(\mathbf{w}) = \frac{1}{m} \sum_{i=1}^{m} \max_{\mathbf{s} \in \mathcal{S}} \left(\ell(\mathbf{s}^i, \mathbf{s}) + \langle \mathbf{w}, \Psi(I^i, \mathbf{s}) \rangle \right) - \frac{1}{m} \sum_{i=1}^{m} \langle \mathbf{w}, \Psi(I^i, \mathbf{s}^i) \rangle . \tag{8}$$

The number $\lambda \in \mathbb{R}^+$ is a regularization constant whose optimal value is tuned on a validation set. $R(\mathbf{w})$ is a convex piece-wise linear upper bound on the empirical risk $\frac{1}{m} \sum_{i=1}^{m} \ell(\mathbf{s}^i, \arg \max_{\mathbf{s} \in \mathcal{S}} f(I^i, \mathbf{s}))$. That is, the learning algorithm directly minimizes the performance of the detector assessed on the training set and at the same time it controls the risk of over-fitting via the norm of the parameter vector.

Though the problem (7) is convex its solving is hard. The hardness of the problem can be seen when it is expressed as an equivalent quadratic program with $m|\mathcal{S}|$ linear constrains (recall that $|\mathcal{S}|$ is the number of all landmark configurations). This fact rules out off-the-shelf optimization algorithms.

Thanks to its importance a considerable effort has been put to a development of efficient optimization algorithms for solving the task (7). There has been an ongoing discussion in the machine learning community trying to decide whether approximative online solvers like the SGD are better than the accurate slower solvers like the BMRM. No definitive consensus has been achieved so far. We contribute to this discussion by providing an empirical evaluation of both approaches on the practical large-scale problem required to learn the landmark detector. The empirical results are provided in Sect. 4.5. For the sake of self-consistency, we briefly describe the considered solvers, i.e. the BMRM and the SGD algorithm, in the following two sections.

3.1 Bundle Methods for Regularized Risk Minimization

The BMRM is a generic method for minimization of regularized convex functions [19], i.e. BMRM solves the following convex problem

$$\mathbf{w}^* = \arg \min_{\mathbf{w} \in \mathbb{R}^n} F(\mathbf{w}) := \frac{\lambda}{2} \|\mathbf{w}\|^2 + R(\mathbf{w}) , \tag{9}$$

where $R : \mathbb{R}^n \to \mathbb{R}$ is an arbitrary convex function. The risk term $R(\mathbf{w})$ is usually the complex part of the objective function which makes the optimization task hard. The core idea is to replace the original problem (9) by its reduced problem

$$\mathbf{w}_t = \arg \min_{\mathbf{w} \in \mathbb{R}^n} F_t(\mathbf{w}) := \frac{\lambda}{2} \|\mathbf{w}\|^2 + R_t(\mathbf{w}) . \tag{10}$$

The objective function $F_t(\mathbf{w})$ of the reduced problem (10) is obtained after replacing the risk $R(\mathbf{w})$ in the original objective $F(\mathbf{w})$ by its cutting plane model

$$R_t(\mathbf{w}) = \max_{i=0,1,\ldots,t-1} \left[R(\mathbf{w}_i + \langle R'(\mathbf{w}_i), \mathbf{w} - \mathbf{w}_i \rangle \right] , \tag{11}$$

where $R'(\mathbf{w}_i) \in \partial_{\mathbf{w}_i} R(\mathbf{w}_i)$ denotes an arbitrary sub-gradient of R evaluated at the point $\mathbf{w}_i \in \mathbb{R}^n$.

Starting from an initial guess $\mathbf{w}_0 = \mathbf{0}$, the BMRM algorithm computes a new iterate $\mathbf{w}_t$ by solving the reduced problem (10). In each iteration t, the cutting plane model (11) is updated by a new cutting plane computed at the intermediate solution $\mathbf{w}_t$ leading to a progressively tighter approximation of $F(\mathbf{w})$. The BMRM algorithm halts if the gap between $F(\mathbf{w}_t)$ (an upper bound on $F(\mathbf{w}^*)$) and $F_t(\mathbf{w}_t)$ (a lower bound on $F(\mathbf{w}^*)$) falls below a desired ε, meaning that $F(\mathbf{w}_t) \leq F(\mathbf{w}^*) + \varepsilon$. The BMRM algorithm stops after at most $\mathcal{O}(1/\epsilon)$ iterations for arbitrary $\varepsilon > 0$ [19].

The reduced problem (10) can be expressed as an equivalent convex quadratic program with t variables. Because t is usually small (up to a few hundreds), off-the-shelf QP solvers can be used.

Before applied to a particular problem, the BMRM algorithm requires a procedure which for a given $\mathbf{w}$ returns the value of the risk $R(\mathbf{w})$ and its sub-gradient $R'(\mathbf{w})$. In our case the risk $R(\mathbf{w})$ is defined by (8) and its sub-gradient can be computed by the Danskin's theorem as

$$R'(\mathbf{w}) = \frac{1}{m} \sum_{i=1}^{m} \left(\Psi(I^i, \hat{\mathbf{s}}^i) - \Psi(I^i, \mathbf{s}^i) \right) \tag{12}$$

$$\hat{\mathbf{s}}^i = \arg\max_{\mathbf{s} \in \mathcal{S}} \left[\ell(\mathbf{s}^i, \mathbf{s}) + \langle \mathbf{w}, \Psi(I^i, \mathbf{s}) \rangle \right] . \tag{13}$$

Note that the evaluation of $R(\mathbf{w})$ and $R'(\mathbf{w})$ is dominated by the computation of the scalar products $\langle \mathbf{w}, \Psi(I^i, \mathbf{s}) \rangle$, $i = 1, \ldots, m$, $\mathbf{s} \in \mathcal{S}$, which, fortunately, can be efficiently parallelized.

3.2 Stochastic Gradient Descent

Another popular method solving (7) is the Stochastic Gradient Descent (SGD) algorithm. We use the modification proposed in [20] which uses two neat tricks. Starting from an initial guess $\mathbf{w}_0$, the SGD algorithm iteratively changes $\mathbf{w}$ by applying the following rule:

$$\mathbf{w}_{t+1} = \mathbf{w}_t - \frac{\lambda^{-1}}{t_0 + t} g_t, \quad g_t = \lambda \mathbf{w}_t + \mathbf{h}_t . \tag{14}$$

t_0 is a constant and t is the number of the iteration. The SGD implementation proposed in [20] tunes the optimal value of t_0 on a small portion of training examples subsampled from training set. The sub-gradient is computed in almost the same manner as in (12), but only for one training image at a time, i.e. $\mathbf{h}_t = \Psi(I^t, \hat{\mathbf{s}}^t) - \Psi(I^t, \mathbf{s}^t)$.

In addition, [20] propose to exploit the sparsity of the data in the update step. Equation (14) can be expressed as

$$\mathbf{w}_{t+1} = \mathbf{w}_t - \alpha_t \mathbf{w}_t - \beta_t \mathbf{h}_t, \text{ where} \tag{15}$$

$$\alpha = \frac{1}{t_0 + t}, \quad \beta = \frac{\lambda^{-1}}{t_0 + t} . \tag{16}$$

Note that if $\mathbf{h}_t$ is sparse then subtracting $\beta_t \mathbf{h}_t$ involves only the nonzero coefficients of $\mathbf{h}_t$, but subtracting $\alpha_t \mathbf{w}_t$ involves all coefficients of $\mathbf{w}_t$. In turn, it is beneficial to reformulate (15) as

$$\mathbf{w}_{t+1} = (1 - \alpha_t)\mathbf{w}_t - \beta_t \mathbf{h}_t \ . \tag{17}$$

By using this trick, the complexity $\mathcal{O}(d)$ corresponding to the naïve implementation of the update rule (14) reduces to the complexity $\mathcal{O}(d_{\mathrm{non-zero}})$ corresponding to the reformulated rule (17), where d is the dimension of the parameter vector and $d_{\mathrm{non-zero}}$ is the number of the non-zero elements in $\mathbf{h}_t$. Typically, like in our case, $d_{\mathrm{non-zero}}$ is much smaller than d.

A considerable advantage of the SGD algorithm is its simplicity. A disadvantage is a lack of any certificate of optimality and thus also of the theoretically grounded stopping condition.

4 Experiments

In this section, we present experimental evaluation of the proposed facial landmark detector and its comparison against three different approaches. We considered the detector estimating positions of the eight landmarks: the canthi of the left and right eye, the corners of the mouth, the tip of the nose and the center of the face. The corresponding graph (V, E) is shown in Fig. 2(a).

In Sect. 4.1, we describe the face database and the testing protocol used in the experiments. The competing methods are summarized in Sect. 4.2. The results of the comparison in terms of detection accuracy and basic timing statistics are presented in Sect. 4.4. Finally, in Sect. 4.5 we compare two algorithms for solving the large-scale optimization problems emerging in the SO-SVM learning, namely, the BMRM and the SGD algorithm.

4.1 Database and Testing Protocol

We use the LFW database [18] for evaluation as well as for training of our detector. This database consists of $13,233$ images each of size 250×250 pixels. The LFW database contains a great ethnicity variance and the images have challenging background clutter. We augmented the original LFW database by adding manual annotation of the eight considered landmarks.

We randomly split the LFW database into training, testing and validation sets. Table 1 describes this partitioning. The experimental evaluation of all competing detectors was made on the same testing set. The training and the validation parts were used for learning of the proposed detector and the base line SVM detector. The other competing detectors had their own training databases.

In order to evaluate the detectors, we use two accuracy measures: i) the mean normalized deviation $\ell(\mathbf{s}, \mathbf{s}')$ defined by equation (6) and ii) the maximal normalized deviation

$$\ell^{\max}(\mathbf{s}, \hat{\mathbf{s}}) = \kappa(\mathbf{s}) \max_{j=0,\ldots,M-1} \|\mathbf{s}_j - \hat{\mathbf{s}}_j\| \ , \tag{18}$$

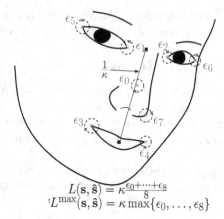

$$L(\mathbf{s}, \hat{\mathbf{s}}) = \kappa \frac{\epsilon_0 + \cdots + \epsilon_8}{8}$$
$$L^{\max}(\mathbf{s}, \hat{\mathbf{s}}) = \kappa \max\{\epsilon_0, \ldots, \epsilon_8\}$$

Fig. 4. The illustration of two accuracy statistics used to benchmark the detectors. The green and the red crosses denote the manually annotated landmarks and the detected landmarks, respectively. The deviations $\epsilon_0, \ldots, \epsilon_7$ correspond to radii of the dashed circles.

Table 1. The partitioning of the LFW database into training, validation and testing set

Data set	Training	Validation	Testing
Percentage	60%	20%	20%
# of examples	6,919	2,307	2,316

where $\mathbf{s} = (\mathbf{s}_0, \ldots, \mathbf{s}_{M-1})$ are the manually annotated landmark positions and $\hat{\mathbf{s}} = (\hat{\mathbf{s}}_0, \ldots, \hat{\mathbf{s}}_{M-1})$ are the landmark positions estimated by the tested detector. Figure 4 illustrates both accuracy measures.

4.2   Competing Methods

In this section, we outline all detectors that were used in the experimental evaluation.

Proposed Detector. The proposed detector estimates the landmark positions according to (4). As the feature descriptor $\Psi_i^q(I, \mathbf{s}_i)$ defining the local appearance model $q_i(I, \mathbf{s}_i)$, we use the LBP pyramid described in Sect. 2.1. As the parametrization $\Psi_{ij}^g(\mathbf{s}_i, \mathbf{s}_j)$ of the deformation cost $g_{ij}(\mathbf{s}_i, \mathbf{s}_j)$, we use the quadratic function described in Sect. 2.2. The parameter vector $\mathbf{w}$ of the classifier (4) is trained from the training part of the LFW database using the BMRM algorithm (c.f. Sect. 3.1). The regularization constant λ appearing in the learning problem (7) was selected from the set $\{10, 1, 0.1, 0.01, 0.001\}$ to minimize the average mean normalized deviation R_{VAL} computed on the validation part of the LFW database.

Independently Trained SVM Detector. This detector is formed by standard two-class linear SVM classifiers trained independently for each landmark. For training, we use the SVM solver implemented in LIBOCAS [22]. For each individual landmark we created a different training set containing examples of the positive and negative class. The positive class is formed by images cropped around the ground truth positions of the respective component. The negative class contains images cropped outside the ground truth regions. Specifically, the negative class images satisfy the following condition

$$\left| P_-^x - P_{\text{GT}}^x \right| > \frac{1}{2} \text{width}_{\text{GT}}, \ \left| P_-^y - P_{\text{GT}}^y \right| > \frac{1}{2} \text{height}_{\text{GT}} \ , \tag{19}$$

where P_-^x and P_{GT}^x is the x-coordinate of the negative and the ground truth component respectively. $\text{height}_{\text{GT}}$ and width_{GT} denote the width and the height of the component.

We use the LBP-pyramid descriptor (see Sect. 2.1) as the features. The parameters of the linear SVM classifier are learned from the training part of the LFW database. The SVM regularization constant C was selected from the set $\{10, 1, 0.1, 0.01, 0.001\}$ to minimize the classification error computed on the validation part of the LFW database.

Having the binary SVM classifiers trained for all components, the landmark position is estimated by selecting the place with the maximal response of the classifier scoring function, evaluated in the search regions defined for each component differently. The search regions as well as the sizes of the components are exactly the same as we use for the proposed SO-SVM detector.

Note that the independently trained SVM detector is a simple instance of the DPM where the deformation cost $g_{ij}(\mathbf{s}_i, \mathbf{s}_j)$ is zero for all positions inside the search region and $-\infty$ outside. We compare this baseline detector with the proposed SO-SVM detector to show that one can improve the accuracy by learning the deformation cost from data.

Active Appearance Models. We use a slightly modified version of a publicly available implementation of the AAM [23]. As the initial guess of the face position required by the AAM, we use the center of the bounding box obtained from a face detector. The initial scale is also computed from this bounding box. The AAM estimates a dense set of feature points which are distributed around important face contours like the contour of mouth, eyes, nose, chin and eyebrows. The AAM requires a different training database which contains high resolution images along with annotation of all contour points.

For training the AAM model we use a publicly available IIM Face database [24]. The IIM database consists of 240 annotated images (6 images per person). Each image is 640×480 pixel in size and comes with 58 manually annotated points which are distributed along the main face contours. Note that the creation of training examples for the AAM put much higher demands on the annotator who has to click a large number of uniformly distributed points. In contrast, our method requires annotation of only a small number of well defined points. Specifically, the whole IIM database requires to annotate 13920 points, carefully distributed along each contour, while the LFW database requires to annotate 48433 points, which are well defined and easy to annotate.

To compare the AAM based detector with our detector, we have to transform the output of the AAM, i.e. the points on contours around important face parts, to the landmark positions returned by our detector. We simply select the relevant points on the corresponding contours.

4.3   Detector of Everingham et al.

The last competing detector is the DPM based detector of [25]. This detector was trained on a collection of consumer images which, however, are not available. This detector returns canthi of both eyes (4 landmarks), corners of the mouth (2 landmarks) and 3 landmarks on the nose. To compare this detector, we consider only the relevant landmarks for our detector. Note that unlike the proposed SO-SVM detector, this detector learns the local appearance model and the deformation cost of the DPM independently.

4.4   Results

In this section, we describe results of the experimental evaluation of the detection accuracy of all competing detectors. We have measured the mean and the maximal normalized deviation computed on the test part of the LFW database.

Table 2 shows the average mean normalized deviation R_{TST} and the the average maximal normalized deviation $R_{\text{TST}}^{\max}$ for each individual detector. The results show that the proposed detector consistently outperforms all other competing methods irrespective to the accuracy measure. Surprisingly, the independently trained SVM detector is comparable with the DPM based detector of [25]. The far worst results were obtained for the AAM based detector which can be attributed to a relatively low resolution input images.

In Fig. 5 we show the cumulative histograms of the mean and maximal normalized deviation. Table 3 shows the percentage of examples from the test part of the LFW database with the mean/maximal normalized deviation less or equal to 10% (this corresponds to the line at 10% of x-axis taken from Fig. 5. It is seen that the proposed detector estimates around 97% of images with the mean normalized deviation less than 10%. This results is far better than was achieved for all other competing methods. In

Table 2. Average mean normalized deviation and the average maximal normalized deviation computed on the test part of the LFW database

	R_{TST}	$R_{\text{TST}}^{\max}$
AAM	17.6042	31.2715
Independent SVMs	7.1970	18.3601
Everingham et al.	7.9975	15.9451
proposed detector	**5.4606**	**12.4080**

Table 3. The percentage of images from the test part of the LFW database where the mean/maximal normalized deviation of the estimated landmark positions was less or equal to 10%

	Mean	Maximal
AAM	8.98%	0.62%
Everingham et al.	85.28%	22.93%
binary SVM	85.66%	34.50%
proposed detector	**96.59%**	**53.23%**

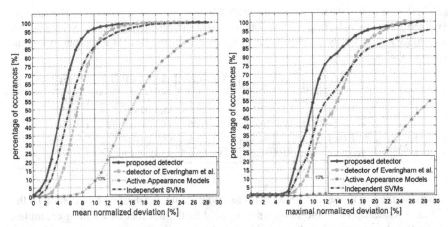

Fig. 5. Cumulative histograms for the mean and the maximal normalized deviation shown for all competing detectors

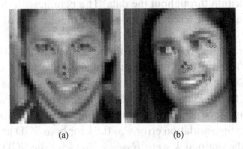

(a)   (b)

Fig. 6. Sample images where the estimated landmark positions have the mean normalized deviation equal to 10%. The green and red points denote the manually annotated and estimated landmarks, respectively.

Fig. 6, we show examples of images with the mean normalized deviation equal to 10% for better understanding of these statistics.

We have also measured the average time required by the proposed detector to process a single image. The measurements were done on a notebook with Intel Core 2 Duo T9300 2.50 GHz. The average detection time was 7 ms per face.

4.5 Comparison of BMRM and SGD

In this section, we compare performance of the BMRM and the SGD algorithm on the problem emerging when learning the proposed detector.

The task of the solvers is to minimize the problem stated in (7). Besides the value of the objective function $F(\mathbf{w})$ of the task (7) we also measured the validation risk $R_{\text{VAL}}(\mathbf{w})$ being another important criterion characterizing convergence of the learning algorithm.

Table 4. Comparison of the BMRM and the SGD. We show the value of primal objective function $F(\mathbf{w})$ and validation risk R_{VAL} for the 50th iteration (assuming termination of SGD after this iteration) as well as for the number of iterations needed by the BMRM algorithm to find the ϵ-precise solution.

	λ	$\lambda = 1$		$\lambda = 0.1$		$\lambda = 0.01$		$\lambda = 0.001$	
	# of iterations	50	106	50	201	50	462	50	1200
BMRM	$F(\mathbf{w})$	77.48	62.19	45.13	29.68	35.33	14.62	34.35	7.459
	$R_{\text{VAL}}(\mathbf{w})$	23.24	10.48	9.054	6.067	9.054	5.475	9.054	5.876
SGD	$F(\mathbf{w})$	50.88	50.44	20.62	20.52	13.72	10.80	12.86	6.309
	$R_{\text{VAL}}(\mathbf{w})$	9.719	9.627	6.156	6.142	5.577	5.496	5.544	5.818

To make the iterations of both algorithms comparable, we define one iteration of the SGD as a sequence of single update steps equal to the number of training examples. This makes the computational time of both solvers approximately proportional to the number of iterations. The optimal value of parameter t_0 for SGD was selected to minimize the objective function $F(\mathbf{w})$ computed on 10% of the training examples after one pass of the SGD algorithm throughout the data. The parameter t_0 have to be tuned for each value of λ separately. We fixed the total number of iterations of the SGD algorithm to 50.

We run both solver on the problem (7) with the parameters $\lambda \in \{0.001, 0.01, 0.1, 1\}$ recording both $F(\mathbf{w})$ and $R_{\text{VAL}}(\mathbf{w})$. Results of the experiment are summarized in Table 4.

It can be seen that the SGD converges quickly at the beginning and it stalls as it approaches the minimum of the objective F. Similarly for the validation risk. The optimal value of λ minimizing the validation error was 0.01 for both SGD and BMRM. The test errors computed for the optimal λ were $R_{\text{TST}} = 5.44$ for the SGD and $R_{\text{TST}} = 5.54$ for the BMRM, i.e., the difference is not negligible. The results for the SGD could be improved by using more than 50 iterations, however, in that case both algorithms would require the comparable time. Moreover, without the reference solution provided by the BMRM one would not know how to set the optimal number of iterations for the SGD. We conclude that for the tested problem the BMRM produced more accurate solution, but the SGD algorithm was significantly faster. This suggests that the SGD is useful in the cases when using the precise but slower BMRM algorithm is prohibited. In the opposite case the BMRM algorithm returning a solution with the guaranteed optimality certificate is preferable.

5   Open-Source Library and LFW Annotation

We provide an open-source library implementing the proposed DPM detector including the BMRM algorithm for supervised learning of its parameters. The detector is implemented in C and we also provide the MEX interface to MATLAB. The library comes with several toy example applications, e.g. running the detector on still images or a video stream and displaying the landmarks. The library is licensed under the GNU/GPL version 3 and was tested on GNU/Linux and Windows platform.

In addition, we provide a manual annotation of the LFW database for noncommercial use. The following set of landmarks is annotated for each face: canthi for both eyes, the tip of the nose and the corners of mouth, i.e. 7 annotated landmarks in total for each image. Both the library and the annotation can be downloaded from: http://cmp.felk.cvut.cz/~uricamic/flandmark

6 Conclusions

In this paper, we have formulated the detection of facial landmarks as an instance of the structured output classification problem. Our structured output classifier is based on the DPM and its parameters can be learned from examples by the SO-SVM algorithm. In contrast to the previous works, the learning objective is directly related to the accuracy of the resulting detector. Experiments on the LFW database show that the proposed detector consistently outperforms a baseline independently trained SVM detector and two public domain detectors based on the AAM and DPM.

Acknowledgements. The first two authors were supported by EC projects FP7-ICT-247525 HUMAVIPS and PERG04-GA-2008-239455 SEMISOL. The third author was supported by the Grant Agency of the Czech Republic under Project P103/10/0783. All authors were supported by The Grant Agency of the CTU Prague project SGS12/187/OHK3/3T/13. Any opinions expressed in this paper do not necessarily reflect the views of the European Community. The Community is not liable for any use that may be made of the information contained herein.

References

1. Beumer, G., Veldhuis, R.: On the accuracy of EERs in face recognition and the importance of reliable registration. In: 5th IEEE Benelux Signal Processing Symposium (SPS 2005), pp. 85–88. IEEE Benelux Signal Processing (2005)
2. Cristinacce, D., Cootes, T., Scott, I.: A multi-stage approach to facial feature detection. In: 15th British Machine Vision Conference (BMVC 2004), pp. 277–286 (2004)
3. Riopka, T., Boult, T.: The eyes have it. In: Proceedings of ACM SIGMM Multimedia Biometrics Methods and Applications Workshop, pp. 9–16 (2003)
4. Cootes, T.F., Edwards, G.J., Taylor, C.J.: Active appearance models. IEEE Trans. Pattern Analysis and Machine Intelligence 23, 681–685 (2001)
5. Viola, P., Jones, M.: Robust real-time face detection. International Journal of Computer Vision 57, 137–154 (2004)
6. Beumer, G., Tao, Q., Bazen, A., Veldhuis, R.: A landmark paper in face recognition. In: 7th International Conference on Automatic Face and Gesture Recognition (FGR 2006). IEEE Computer Society Press (2006)
7. Cristinacce, D., Cootes, T.: Facial feature detection using AdaBoost with shape constraints. In: 14th Proceedings British Machine Vision Conference (BMVC 2003), pp. 231–240 (2003)
8. Erukhimov, V., Lee, K.: A bottom-up framework for robust facial feature detection. In: 8th IEEE International Conference on Automatic Face and Gesture Recognition (FG 2008), pp. 1–6 (2008)

9. Wu, J., Trivedi, M.: Robust facial landmark detection for intelligent vehicle system. In: IEEE International Workshop on Analysis and Modeling of Faces and Gestures (2005)

10. Crandall, D., Felzenszwalb, P., Huttenlocher, D.: Spatial priors for part-based recognition using statistical models. In: CVPR, pp. 10–17 (2005)

11. Felzenszwalb, P.F., Huttenlocher, D.P.: Pictorial structures for object recognition. Internatinal Journal of Computer Vision 61, 55–79 (2005)

12. Felzenszwalb, P.F., Girshick, R.B., McAllester, D., Ramanan, D.: Object detection with discriminatively trained part based models. IEEE Transactions on Pattern Analysis and Machine Intelligence 99 (2009)

13. Fischler, M.A., Elschlager, R.A.: The representation and matching of pictorial structures. IEEE Transactions on Computers C-22, 67–92 (1973)

14. Everingham, M., Sivic, J., Zisserman, A.: "Hello! My name is.. Buffy" – automatic naming of characters in TV video. In: Proceedings of the British Machine Vision Conference (2006)

15. Everingham, M., Sivic, J., Zisserman, A.: Taking the bite out of automatic naming of characters in TV video. Image and Vision Computing 27 (2009)

16. Sivic, J., Everingham, M., Zisserman, A.: "Who are you?" – learning person specific classifiers from video. In: Proceedings of the IEEE Conference on Computer Vision and Pattern Recognition (2009)

17. Tsochantaridis, I., Joachims, T., Hofmann, T., Altun, Y., Singer, Y.: Large margin methods for structured and interdependent output variables. Journal of Machine Learning Research 6, 1453–1484 (2005)

18. Huang, G.B., Ramesh, M., Berg, T., Learned-Miller, E.: Labeled faces in the wild: A database for studying face recognition in unconstrained environments. Technical Report 07-49, University of Massachusetts, Amherst (2007)

19. Teo, C.H., Vishwanthan, S., Smola, A.J., Le, Q.V.: Bundle methods for regularized risk minimization. J. Mach. Learn. Res. 11, 311–365 (2010)

20. Bordes, A., Bottou, L., Gallinari, P.: SGD-QN: Careful quasi-newton stochastic gradient descent. Journal of Machine Learning Research 10, 1737–1754 (2009)

21. Heikkilä, M., Pietikäinen, M., Schmid, C.: Description of interest regions with local binary patterns. Pattern Recognition 42, 425–436 (2009)

22. Franc, V., Sonnenburg, S.: LIBOCAS — library implementing OCAS solver for training linear svm classifiers from large-scale data (2010),
http://cmp.felk.cvut.cz/~xfrancv/ocas/html/index.html

23. Kroon, D.J.: Active shape model (ASM) and active appearance model (AAM). MATLAB Central (2010),
http://www.mathworks.com/matlabcentral/fileexchange/
26706-active-shape-model-asm-and-active-appearance-model-aam

24. Nordstrøm, M.M., Larsen, M., Sierakowski, J., Stegmann, M.B.: The IMM face database - an annotated dataset of 240 face images. Technical report, Informatics and Mathematical Modelling, Technical University of Denmark, DTU (2004)

25. Everingham, M., Sivic, J., Zisserman, A.: Willow project, automatic naming of characters in tv video. MATLAB implementation (2008),
http://www.robots.ox.ac.uk/~vgg/research/nface/index.html

Efficient Estimation of Human Upper Body Pose
in Static Depth Images

Brian Holt and Richard Bowden

Centre for Vision, Speech and Signal Processing, University of Surrey, Guildford, U.K.
B.Holt@surrey.ac.uk
http://info.ee.surrey.ac.uk/Personal/B.Holt/

Abstract. Automatic estimation of human pose has long been a goal of computer vision, to which a solution would have a wide range of applications. In this paper we formulate the pose estimation task within a regression and Hough voting framework to predict 2D joint locations from depth data captured by a consumer depth camera. In our approach the offset from each pixel to the location of each joint is predicted directly using random regression forests. The predictions are accumulated in Hough images which are treated as likelihood distributions where maxima correspond to joint location hypotheses. Our approach is evaluated on a publicly available dataset with good results.

1 Introduction

Human pose estimation is a challenging problem to which a fast, robust solution would have wide ranging impact in gaming, human computer interaction, video analysis, action and gesture recognition, and many other fields. The problem remains a difficult one primarily because of the human body is a highly deformable object. Additionally, there is large variability in body shape among the population, image capture conditions, clothing, camera viewpoint, occlusion of body parts (including self-occlusion) and background is often complex.

In this paper we cast the pose estimation task as a continuous non-linear regression problem. We show how this problem can be effectively addressed by Random Regression Forests (RRFs). Our approach is different to a part-based approach since there are no part detectors at any scale. Instead, the approach is more direct, with features computed efficiently on each pixel used to vote for joint locations. The votes are accumulated in Hough accumulator images and the most likely hypothesis is found by non-maximal suppression.

The availability of depth information from real-time depth cameras has simplified the task of pose estimation [1–4] over traditional image capture devices by supporting high accuracy background subtraction, working in low-illumination environments, being invariant to colour and texture, providing depth gradients to resolve ambiguities in silhouettes, and providing a calibrated estimate of the scale of the object. However, even with these advantages, there remains much to done to achieve a pose estimation system that is fast and robust.

One of the major challenges is the amount of data required in training to generate high accuracy joint estimates. The recent work of Shotton et al. [3] uses a training set

G. Csurka et al. (Eds.): VISIGRAPP 2012, CCIS 359, pp. 399–410, 2013.
© Springer-Verlag Berlin Heidelberg 2013

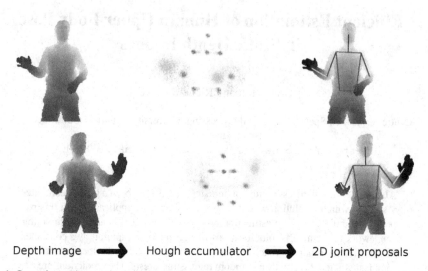

Depth image ➡ Hough accumulator ➡ 2D joint proposals

Fig. 1. Overview. Given a single input depth image, evaluate a bank of RRFs for every pixel. The output from each regressor is accumulated in a Hough-like accumulator image. Non-maximal suppression is applied to find the peaks of the accumulator images.

of one million computer generated depth images of people of various shapes and sizes in a variety of poses. A distributed decision tree algorithm is deployed on a proprietary distributed training architecture using 1000 cores to train their decision trees. This vast computing power makes the problem tractable, but is not suitable for researchers without access to these sorts of facilities. We therefore propose an approach that is in many ways similar to Shotton et al's approach, but requires significantly less data and processing power.

Our approach applies advances made using RRFs reported recently in a wide range of computer vision problems. This technique has been demonstrated by Gall and Lempitsky [5] to offer superior object detection results, and has been used successfully in applications as diverse as the estimation of head pose [6], anatomy detection and localisation [7], estimating age based on facial features [8] and improving time-of-flight depth map scans [9]. To the best of our knowledge Random Regression Forests have not been applied to pose estimation.

Our contributions are the following. First, we show how RRFs can be combined within a Hough-like voting framework for static pose estimation, and secondly we evaluate the approach against state-of-the-art performance on publicly available datasets. The chapter is organised as follows: Section 2 discusses related work, Section 3 develops the theory and discusses the approach, Section 4 details the experimental setup and results and Section 5 concludes.

2   Related Work

A survey of the advances in pose estimation can be found in [10]. Broadly speaking, static pose estimation can be divided into global and local (part-based) pose estimation. Global approaches to discriminative pose estimation include direct regression using

Relevance Vector Machines [11], using a parameter sensitive variant of Locality Sensitive Hashing to efficiently lookup and interpolate between similar poses [12], using Gaussian Processes for generic structured prediction of the global body pose [13] and a manifold based approach using Random Forests trained by clustering similar poses hierarchically [14].

Many of the state of the art approaches to pose estimation use part-based models [15–17] . The first part of the problem is usually formulated as an object detection task, where the object is typically an anatomically defined body part [18, 19] or Poselets (parts that are "tightly clustered in configuration space and appearance space") [4, 20, 21]. The subsequent task of assembly of parts into an optimal configuration is often achieved through a Pictorial Structures approach [18, 19, 22], but also using Bayesian Inference with belief propagation [23], loopy belief propagation for cyclical models [15, 24, 25] or a direct inference on a fully connected model [16].

Work most similar to ours includes

– Gall and Lempitsky [5] apply random forests tightly coupled with a Hough voting framework to detect objects of a specific class. The detections of each class cast probabilistic votes for the centroid of the object. The maxima of the Hough accumulator images correspond to most likely object detection hypotheses. Our approach also uses Random Forests, but we use them for regression and not object detection.
– Shotton et al. [3] apply an object categorisation approach to the pose estimation task. A Random Forest classifier is trained to classify each depth pixel belonging to a segmented body as being one of 32 possible categories, where each category is chosen for optimal joint localisation. Our approach will use the same features as [3] since they can be computed very efficiently, but our approach skips the intermediate representation entirely by directly regressing and then voting for joint proposals.
– The work of [4] serves as a natural baseline for our approach, since their publicly available dataset is designed for the evaluation of static pose estimation approaches on depth data. They apply an intermediate step in which Poselets are first detected, whereas we eliminate this step with better results.

3   Proposed Approach

The objective of our work is to estimate the configuration of a person in the 2D image plane parametrised by B body parts by making use of a small training set. We define the set of body parts $\mathbb{B} = \{\mathbf{b}_i\}_{i=1}^{B}$ where $\mathbf{b}_i \in \Re^2$ corresponding to the row and column of $\mathbf{b}_i$ in the image plane. The labels corresponding to $\mathbb{B}$ comprise $\mathbb{Q} = \{$head, neck, shoulder$_L$, shoulder$_R$, hip$_L$, hip$_R$, elbow$_L$, elbow$_R$, hand$_L$, hand$_R\}$ where $|\mathbb{Q}| = B$.

The novelty in our approach is twofold. Firstly, our approach is able to learn the relationship between the context around a point x in a training image and the offset to a body part $\mathbf{b}_i$. Given a new point x' in a test image, we can use the learned context to predict the offset from x' to $\mathbf{b}'_i$. Secondly, since the image features that we use are weak and the human body is highly deformable, our second contribution is to use Hough accumulators as body part likelihood distributions where the most likely hypothesis $\hat{\mathbf{b}}_i$ is found using non-maximal suppression.

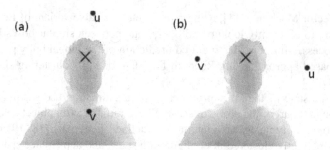

Fig. 2. Image features. The most discriminative feature ϕ is that which yields the greatest decrease in mean squared error, and is therefore by definition the feature at the root node of the tree. In (a) the pixel x is shown with these offsets $\phi = (u, v)$ that contribute most to $head_y$ (the row) and in (b) the offsets ϕ that contribute most to $head_x$ (the column).

3.1 Image Features

We apply the randomised comparison descriptor of [3, 26, 27] to depth images. While this is an inherently weak feature, it is both easy to visualise how the feature relates to the image, and when combined with many other features within a non-linear regression framework like Random Regression Forests it yields high accuracy predictions. Given a current pixel location x and random offsets $\phi = (u, v)$ $|u| < w, |v| < w$ at a maximum window size w, define the feature

$$f_\phi(I, x) = I(x + \frac{u}{I(x)}) - I(x + \frac{v}{I(x)}) \tag{1}$$

where $I(x)$ is the depth value (the range from the camera to the object) at pixel x in image I and $\phi = (x_1, x_2)$ are the offset vectors relative to x. As explained in [3], we scale the offset vectors by a factor $\frac{1}{I(x)}$ to ensure that the generated features are invariant to depth. Similarly, we also define $I(x')$ to be a large positive value when x' is either background or out of image bounds.

The most discriminative features found to predict the head are overlaid on test images in Figure 2. These features make sense intuitively, because in Figure 2(a) the predictions of the row location of the head depend on features that compute the presence or absence of support in the vertical direction and similarly for Figure 2(b) in the horizontal direction.

3.2 Random Regression Forests

A decision tree [28] is a non-parametric learner that can be trained to predict categorical or continuous output labels.

Given a supervised training set consisting of p F-dimensional vector and label pairs (S_i, l) where $S_i \in R^F$, $i = 1, ..., p$ and $l \in R^1$, a decision tree recursively partitions the data such that impurity in the node is minimised, or equivalently the information gain is maximised through the partition.

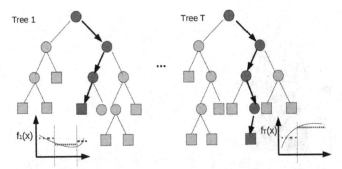

Fig. 3. Random Regression Forest. A forest is an ensemble learner consisting of a number of trees, where each tree contributes linearly to the result. During training, each tree is constructed by recursively partitioning the input space until stopping criteria are reached. The input subregion at each leaf node (shown with rectangles) is then approximated with a constant value that minimises the squared error distance to all labels within that subregion. In this toy example, the single dimension function $f(x)$ is approximated by constant values (shown in different colours) over various regions of the input space.

Let the data at node m be represented by Q. For each candidate split $\theta = (j, \tau_m)$ consisting of a feature j and threshold τ_m, partition the data into $Q_{left}(\theta)$ and $Q_{right}(\theta)$ subsets

$$Q_{left}(\theta) = (x, l)|x_j \leq \tau_m \qquad (2)$$

$$Q_{right}(\theta) = Q \setminus Q_{left}(\theta) \qquad (3)$$

The impurity over the data Q at node m is computed using an impurity function $H()$, the choice of which depends on the task being solved (classification or regression). The impurity $G(Q, \theta)$ is computed as

$$G(Q, \theta) = \frac{n_{left}}{N_m} H(Q_{left}(\theta)) + \frac{n_{right}}{N_m} H(Q_{right}(\theta)) \qquad (4)$$

Select for each node m the splitting parameters θ that minimise

$$\theta^* = \arg\min_{\theta} G(Q, \theta) \qquad (5)$$

Given a continuous target y, for node m, representing a region R_m with N_m observations, a common criterion $H()$ to minimise is the Mean Squared Error (MSE) criterion. Initially calculate the mean c_m over a region

$$c_m = \frac{1}{N_m} \sum_{i \in N_m} y_i \qquad (6)$$

The MSE is the sum of squared differences from the mean

$$H(Q) = \frac{1}{N_m} \sum_{i \in N_m} (y_i - c_m)^2 \qquad (7)$$

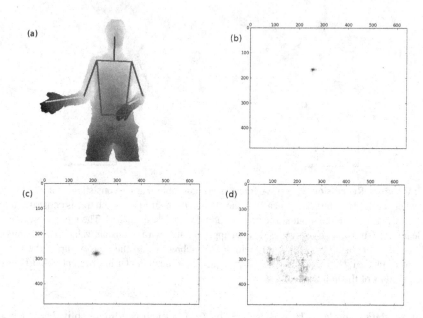

Fig. 4. Hough accumulator images. The Hough image is a probabilistic parameterisation that accumulates votes cast by the RRFs. The maxima in the parameterised space correspond to the most likely hypotheses in the original space. In this example the Hough accumulator shows the concentration of votes cast for the (b) left shoulder, (c) left elbow and (d) left hand.

Recurse for subsets $Q_{left}(\theta^*)$ and $Q_{right}(\theta^*)$ until the maximum allowable depth is reached, $N_m < min\_samples$ or $N_m = 1$.

Given that trees have a strong tendency to overfit to the training data, they are often used within an ensemble of T trees. The individual tree predictions are averaged

$$\hat{y} = \frac{1}{T} \sum_{t=0}^{T} \hat{y}_t \qquad (8)$$

to form a final prediction with demonstrably lower generalisation errors [29].

3.3 Hough Voting

Hough voting is technique that has proved very successful for identifying the most likely hypotheses in a parameter space. It is a distributed approach to optimisation, by summing individual responses to an input in an parameter space. The maxima are found to correspond to the most likely hypotheses.

Our approach uses the two dimensional image plane as both the input and the parameter space. For each body part $q_j \in \mathbb{Q}$ we define a Hough accumulator $\{\mathbb{H}_q\}, \forall q \in \mathbb{Q}$, where the dimensions of the accumulator correspond to the dimensions of the input image I: $\mathbb{H} \in \Re^{I_w} \times \Re^{I_h}, \mathbb{H} = 0$ for all pixels.

An example of the Hough voting step in our system can be seen in Figure 4 where the final configuration is shown alongside the accumulator images for the left shoulder, elbow and hand. Note that the left shoulder predictions are tightly clustered around the groundtruth location, whereas the left elbow is less certain and the left hand even more so. Nevertheless, the weight of votes in each case are in the correct area, leading to successful predictions shown in Figure 4(a).

3.4   Training

Before we can train our system, it is necessary to extract features and labels from the training data. Firstly, we generate a dictionary of F random offsets $\phi_j = (u_j, v_j)_{j=1}^F$. Then, we construct our training data and labels. For each image in the training set, a random subset of P example pixels is chosen to ensure that the distribution over the various body parts is approximately uniform. For each pixel x_p in this random subset, the feature vector S is computed as

$$S = f_{\phi_j}(I, x)_{j=1}^F \tag{9}$$

and the offset $o_i \in \Re^2$ from every x to every body part q_i is

$$o_i = x - \mathbf{b}_i \tag{10}$$

The training set is then the set of all training vectors and corresponding offsets. With the training dataset constructed, we train $2B$ RRFs $R_i^1 i \in 1..B$, to estimate the offset to the row of body part $\mathbf{b}_i$ and $2B$ RRFs $R_i^2 i \in 1..B$, to estimate the offset to the column of body part $\mathbf{b}_i$.

3.5   Test

Since the output of a RRF is a single valued continuous variable, we let $f(R_i^{1,2}, I, x)$ be a function that evaluates the RRF $R_i^{1,2}$ on image I at pixel x.

We apply the following algorithm to populate the Hough parameter space $\mathbb{H}_q \forall q \in \mathbb{Q}$.

Algorithm 1. Compute probability distribution $\mathbb{H}_q$

Input: Image I,

  for each pixel x **do**
    for each label $q_i \in \mathbb{Q}$ **do**
      $o_i^1 \Leftarrow R_i^1(x)$
      $o_i^2 \Leftarrow R_i^2(x)$
      increment $\mathbb{H}_{q_i}(x + o_i^1, x + o_i^2)$
    end for
  end for

The key idea is that for each pixel in a test image, each RRF will be evaluated to estimate the the location of the body part by adding the prediction (which is the offset) to the current pixel.

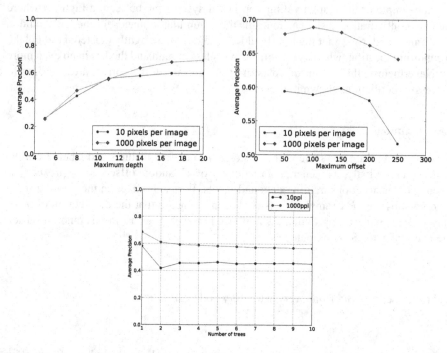

Fig. 5. Parameter tuning. Experiments on accuracy when (a) the depth of the trees are varied, (b) the maximum offset is varied and (c) the number of trees in the forest is varied.

4   Experimental Results

In this section we evaluate our proposed method and describe the experimental setup and experiments performed. We compare our results to the state-of-the-art [4] on a publicly available dataset, and evaluate our results both quantitatively and qualitatively.

For each body part $q_i \in Q$, a Hough accumulator likelihood distribution is computed using Algorithm 1. Unless otherwise specified, we construct our training set from 1000 random pixels x per training image I, where each sample has $F = 2000$ features $f_\phi(I, x)$. This results in a training set of 5.2GB.

4.1   Dataset

A number of datasets exist for the evaluation of pose estimation techniques on appearance images, for example Buffy [30] and Image Parse [31], but until recently there were no publicly available datasets for depth image pose estimation. *CDC4CV Poselets* [4] appears to be the first publicly available Kinect dataset, consisting of 345 training and 347 test images at 640x480 pixels, where the focus is on capturing the upper body of the subject. The dataset comes with annotations of all the upper body part locations.

Table 1. Percentage of Correctly Matched Parts. Where two numbers are present in a cell, they refer to left/right respectively.

	Head	Shoulders	Side		Waist	Upper arm		Forearm		Total
[4]	**0.99**	0.78	**0.93**	0.73	0.65	0.69	0.66	0.22	0.33	0.67
Our method	0.97	**0.81**	0.82	**0.83**	**0.71**	**0.74**	**0.72**	**0.28**	**0.37**	**0.69**

4.2   Evaluation

We report our results using the evaluation metric proposed by [30]: "A body part is considered as correctly matched if its segment endpoints lie within $r = 50\%$ of the length of the ground-truth segment from their annotated location." The percentage of times that the endpoints match is then defined as the Percentage of Correctly Matched Parts (PCP). A low value for r requires to a very high level of accuracy in the estimation of both endpoints for the match to be correct, and this requirement is relaxed progressively as the ratio r increases to its highest value of $r = 50\%$. In Figure 6 we show the effect of varying r in the PCP calculation, and we report our results at $r = 50\%$ in Table 1 as done by [30] and [4]. From Table 1 it can be seen that our approach represents an improvement on average of 5% for the forearm, upper arm and waist over [4], even though our approach makes no use of kinematic constraints to improve predictions.

In Figure 5(a) we show the effect of varying the maximum depth of the trees. Note how the Random Regression Forest trained on the training set with less data (10 pixels per image) tends to overfit to the data on deeper trees. Figure 5(b) shows the effect of varying the maximum window size w for the offsets ϕ. Confirming our intuition, a small window has too little context to make an accurate prediction, whereas a very large window has too much context which reduces performance. The optimal window size is shown to be 100 pixels. Figure 5(c) show the effect of varying the number of trees in the forest. The accuracy decreases sharply for the first few trees and then more or less plateaus. The intuition behind this result is is that a single tree can account for extremes in the data, whereas a forest using a euclidean measure is well suited to predicting data that is distributed normally, will sometimes struggle to estimate data that is not and will consistently underestimate extremal values.

Example predictions including accurate estimates and failure modes are shown in Figure 7.

4.3   Computation Times

Our implementation in python runs at ~ 15 seconds per frame on a single core modern desktop CPU. The memory consumption is directly proportional to the number of trees per forest and the maximum depth to which each tree has been trained. At 10 trees per forest and a maximum depth of 20 nodes, the classifier bank uses approximately 4 gigabytes of memory. The code is not optimised, meaning that further speed-ups could be achieved by parallelising the prediction process since the estimates of each pixel are independent of each other, by reimplementing the algorithm in C/C++, or by making use of an off the shelf graphics card to run the algorithm in parallel in the GPU cores.

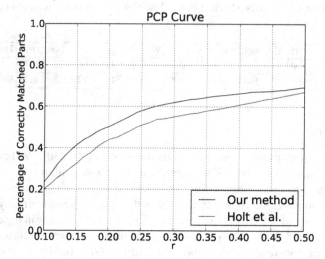

Fig. 6. PCP error curve against [4]. Our method clearly beats theirs for all values of r, even though we do not impose kinematic constraints.

Fig. 7. *Top three rows:* Example predictions using the proposed method. *Bottom row:* Failure modes.

5   Conclusions and Future Work

We have shown how Random Regression Forests can be combined with a Hough voting framework to achieve robust body part localisation with minimal training data. We use data captured with consumer depth cameras and efficiently compute depth comparison features that support our goal of non-linear regression. We show how Random Regression Forests are trained, and then subsequently used on test image with Hough voting to accurately predict joint locations. We demonstrate our approach and compare to the state-of-the-art on a publicly available dataset. Even though our system is implemented in an unoptimised high level language, it runs in seconds per frame on a single core. As future work we plan to apply these results with the temporal constraints of a tracking framework for increased accuracy and temporal coherency. Finally, we would like to apply these results to other areas of cognitive vision such as HCI and gesture recognition.

Acknowledgements. This work was supported by the EC project FP7-ICT-23113 Dicta-Sign and the EPSRC project EP/I011811/1. Thanks to Eng-Jon Ong and Helen Cooper for their insights and stimulating discussions.

References

1. Zhu, Y., Fujimura, K.: A bayesian framework for human body pose tracking from depth image sequences. Sensors 10, 5280–5293 (2010)
2. Ganapathi, V., Plagemann, C., Koller, D., Thrun, S.: Real time motion capture using a single time-of-flight camera. In: [36], pp. 755–762
3. Shotton, J., Fitzgibbon, A., Cook, M., Sharp, T., Finocchio, M., Moore, R., Kipman, A., Blake, A.: Real-time human pose recognition in parts from a single depth image. In: [34]
4. Holt, B., Ong, E.J., Cooper, H., Bowden, R.: Putting the pieces together: Connected poselets for human pose estimation. In: Proceedings of the IEEE Workshop on Consumer Depth Cameras for Computer Vision, Barcelona, Spain (2011)
5. Gall, J., Lempitsky, V.: Class-specific hough forests for object detection. In: [32], pp. 1022–1029
6. Fanelli, G., Gall, J., Van Gool, L.: Real time head pose estimation with random regression forests. In: [34], pp. 617–624
7. Criminisi, A., Shotton, J., Robertson, D., Konukoglu, E.: Regression Forests for Efficient Anatomy Detection and Localization in CT Studies. In: Menze, B., Langs, G., Tu, Z., Criminisi, A. (eds.) MICCAI 2010. LNCS, vol. 6533, pp. 106–117. Springer, Heidelberg (2011)
8. Montillo, A., Ling, H.: Age regression from faces using random forests. In: Proceedings of the, Cairo, Egypt, pp. 2465–2468 (2009)
9. Reynolds, M., Doboš, J., Peel, L., Weyrich, T., Brostow, G.: Capturing time-of-flight data with confidence. In: [34]
10. Moeslund, T., Hilton, A., Krüger, V.: A survey of advances in vision-based human motion capture and analysis. Computer Vision and Image Understanding 104, 90–126 (2006)
11. Agarwal, A., Triggs, B.: Recovering 3D human pose from monocular images. IEEE Transactions on Pattern Analysis and Machine Intelligence 28, 44–58 (2006)
12. Shakhnarovich, G., Viola, P., Darrell, T.: Fast pose estimation with parameter-sensitive hashing. In: Proceedings of the IEEE International Conference on Computer Vision, Nice, France, p. 750 (2003)
13. Bo, L., Sminchisescu, C.: Twin gaussian processes for structured prediction. International Journal of Computer Vision 87, 28–52 (2010)
14. Rogez, G., Rihan, J., Ramalingam, S., Orrite, C., Torr, P.H.S.: Randomized trees for human pose detection. In: [35], pp. 1–8
15. Sigal, L., Black, M.: Measure locally, reason globally: Occlusion-sensitive articulated pose estimation. In: Proceedings of the IEEE Computer Society Conference on Computer Vision and Pattern Recognition, New York, NY, USA, pp. 2041–2048 (2006)

16. Tran, D., Forsyth, D.: Improved human parsing with a full relational model. In: [33], pp. 227–240
17. Sapp, B., Jordan, C., Taskar, B.: Adaptive pose priors for pictorial structures. In: [36], pp. 422–429
18. Felzenszwalb, P., Huttenlocher, D.: Pictorial structures for object recognition. International Journal of Computer Vision 61, 55–79 (2005)
19. Andriluka, M., Roth, S., Schiele, B.: Pictorial structures revisited: People detection and articulated pose estimation. In: [32], pp. 1014–1021
20. Bourdev, L., Maji, S., Brox, T., Malik, J.: Detecting people using mutually consistent poselet activations. In: [33], pp. 168–181
21. Wang, Y., Tran, D., Liao, Z.: Learning hierarchical poselets for human parsing. In: [34]
22. Eichner, M., Ferrari, V., Zurich, S.: Better appearance models for pictorial structures. In: Proceedings of the BMVA British Machine Vision Conference, London, UK, vol. 2, p. 6 (2009)
23. Singh, V.K., Nevatia, R., Huang, C.: Efficient inference with multiple heterogeneous part detectors for human pose estimation. In: [33], pp. 314–327
24. Wang, Y., Mori, G.: Multiple Tree Models for Occlusion and Spatial Constraints in Human Pose Estimation. In: Forsyth, D., Torr, P., Zisserman, A. (eds.) ECCV 2008, Part III. LNCS, vol. 5304, pp. 710–724. Springer, Heidelberg (2008)
25. Tian, T.P., Sclaroff, S.: Fast globally optimal 2d human detection with loopy graph models. In: [36], pp. 81–88
26. Amit, Y., Geman, D.: Shape quantization and recognition with randomized trees. Neural computation 9, 1545–1588 (1997)
27. Lepetit, V., Fua, P.: Keypoint recognition using randomized trees. IEEE Transactions on Pattern Analysis and Machine Intelligence 28, 1465–1479 (2006)
28. Breiman, L., Friedman, J., Olshen, R., Stone, C.: Classification and regression trees. Chapman and Hall (1984)
29. Breiman, L.: Random forests. Machine Learning 45, 5–32 (2001)
30. Ferrari, V., Marin-Jimenez, M., Zisserman, A.: Progressive search space reduction for human pose estimation. In: [35], pp. 1–8
31. Ramanan, D.: Learning to parse images of articulated bodies. In: Proceedings of the NIPS, Vancouver, B.C., Canada, vol. 19, p. 1129. Citeseer (2006)
32. IEEE Computer Society Conference on Computer Vision and Pattern Recognition. In: Proceedings of the IEEE Computer Society Conference on Computer Vision and Pattern Recognition, Miami, FL, USA (2009)
33. European Conference on Computer Vision. Proceedings of the European Conference on Computer Vision, Heraklion, Crete (2010)
34. IEEE Computer Society Conference on Computer Vision and Pattern Recognition. Proceedings of the IEEE Computer Society Conference on Computer Vision and Pattern Recognition, Colorado Springs, USA (2011)
35. IEEE Computer Society Conference on Computer Vision and Pattern Recognition. Proceedings of the IEEE Computer Society Conference on Computer Vision and Pattern Recognition, Anchorage, AK, USA (2008)
36. IEEE Computer Society Conference on Computer Vision and Pattern Recognition. Proceedings of the IEEE Computer Society Conference on Computer Vision and Pattern Recognition, San Francisco, USA (2010)

Plant Root System Analysis from MRI Images

Hannes Schulz[1], Johannes A. Postma[2], Dagmar van Dusschoten[2],
Hanno Scharr[2], and Sven Behnke[1]

[1] Computer Science VI: Autonomous Intelligent Systems, University Bonn,
Friedrich-Ebert-Allee 144, 53113 Bonn, Germany
[2] IBG-2: Plant Sciences, Forschungszentrum Jülich, 52425 Jülich, Germany
{schulz,behnke}@ais.uni-bonn.de,
{j.postma,d.van.dusschoten,h.scharr}@fz-juelich.de

Abstract. We present a novel method for deriving a structural model of a plant root system from 3D Magnetic Resonance Imaging (MRI) data of soil grown plants and use it for plant root system analysis. The structural model allows calculation of physiologically relevant parameters. Roughly speaking, MRI images show local water content of the investigated sample. The small, local amounts of water in roots require a relatively high resolution, which results in low SNR images. However, the spatial resolution of the MRI images remains coarse relative to the diameter of typical fine roots, causing many gaps in the visible root system. To reconstruct the root structure, we propose a three step approach: 1) detect tubular structures, 2) connect all pixels to the base of the root using Dijkstras algorithm, and 3) prune the tree using two signal strength related thresholds. Dijkstras algorithm determines the shortest path of each voxel to the base of the plant root, weighing the Euclidean distance measure by a multi-scale vesselness measure. As a result, paths running within good root candidates are preferred over paths in bare soil. We test this method using both virtually generated MRI images of Maize and real MRI images of Barley roots. In experiments on synthetic data, we show limitations of our algorithm with regard to resolution and noise levels. In addition we show how to use our reconstruction for root phenotyping on real MRI data of barley roots and snow pea in soil. Extending our conference publication [1], we show how to use the structural model to remove unwanted structures, like underground weeds.

Keywords: Root modeling, Plant phenotyping, Roots in soil, Maize, Barley.

1 Introduction

In this paper, we present a method for deriving a structural model of plant roots from MRI measurements of roots in soil (cmp. Fig. 1). From this model, we then derive local root mass and diameter together with suitable statistics.

Plant roots are 'the hidden half' of plants [2] because non-invasive root imaging in natural soils is hampered by a wide range of constrictions. For a full, non-destructive 3D assessment of root structure, topology and growth, only two main techniques are currently available, Computer Tomography, using X-Rays or neutron [3–5] and Nuclear Magnetic Resonance Imaging (MRI) [6–8]. Both X-ray CT and MRI are volumetric 3D

G. Csurka et al. (Eds.): VISIGRAPP 2012, CCIS 359, pp. 411–425, 2013.
© Springer-Verlag Berlin Heidelberg 2013

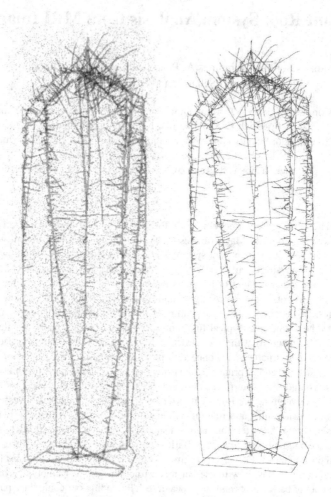

Fig. 1. A simulated maize root MRI image at SNR 150 (left) and its true and fitted structure model overlayed, with missing/additional pieces marked in strong red/blue (right)

imaging techniques, where CT is based on absorption and MRI is an emission-based technique.

For MRI, most signal stems from water in the roots and to a lesser extend from soil water. Even though MRI contrast can be adapted such that discrimination between root water and soil water is maximized (see Sec. 3), signal-to-noise ratio (SNR) remains relatively low. In addition, contrast can be enhanced by manipulating the soil mixture such that mainly signal from the roots is detected.

With the same equipment, MRI measurements can be done at different spatial resolutions, where lower resolution results in a significant reduction in measurement time. This is relevant for root phenotyping studies, where larger quantities of plants need to be measured repeatedly over a longer period. Thus, one of our main concerns is in how far a diminishing resolution and low SNR reduces the accuracy of a root reconstruction algorithm. For plant root studies, this algorithm should produce from the MRI measurements estimates for local and overall root mass, root length, and diameter. Here, we examine the capability of a novel root reconstruction algorithm to obtain these estimates at different image resolutions and noise levels.

As root diameters may be of subvoxel size, voxel-wise segmentation would be brittle. We therefore reconstruct a structural, i.e. zero-diameter model of the root system and subsequently derive parameters like local root mass and diameter, without finding step edges in the data. To construct the root structure, we first find tubular structures on multiple scales. We then determine the plant shoot position and connect every root candidate element to it by a shortest path algorithm. Finally, we prune the graph using two intuitive thresholds, and adjust node positions with subvoxel accuracy by a mean-shift procedure. For root mass and diameter estimation, we use the scale value σ giving maximum response of the [9] tubularness measure $\mathcal{V}(\sigma)$ (see Eq. 1). Root mass can then be derived by locally summing image intensities within a cylinder of the found diameter around the root center.

After reviewing related work, we start by giving a short overview of the MRI method applied (Sec. 3), followed by a description of the novel root reconstruction algorithm (Sec. 4) and how to use the reconstructed root to derive root statistics (Sec. 5). Experiments in Sec. 6 demonstrate the performance of our approach.

2 Related Work

Data similar to ours has been analyzed extensively in the biomedical literature, e.g. using the multi-scale "vesselness" measure of [9]. Of many suggested approaches for finding and detecting vessels, [10] is most similar to ours. Our approach is less heuristic, however, and uses knowledge of global connectedness. While the primary focus of most approaches is visualization, we aim at fully automated extraction of root statistics, such as length and water distribution, to model roots and biological processes of roots.

So far, only few image processing tools are available for plant root system analysis [11–13]. For these tools, however, roots need to be well visible, e.g. by invasively digging them out, washing, and scanning them or by cultivating plants in transparent agar [14]. Analysis is restricted to 2D data. Large root gaps, artifacts due to low SNR, or reconstruction in 3D have not yet been addressed.

Classical, non-invasive image-based root system analysis tools in biological studies are e.g. 2D rhizotrons [4]. 3D MRI has already been used in root-soil-systems for the analysis of e.g. waterflow [15]. Semi-automated reconstruction of roots by 3D CT based on a multivariate grey-scale analysis has recently been shown to work [16]. However, to the best of the authors knowledge, fully automatic root system reconstruction in 3D data is new.

3 Imaging Roots in Soil by MRI

MRI is an imaging technique well-known from medical imaging and general background information is available in textbooks, see e.g. [17]. The MRI signal is proportional to the proton density per unit volume, modulated by an NMR relaxation phenomenon called T_2 relaxation. It causes an exponential signal decrease after excitation that can be partially refocused into an echo. Plant root analysis in soil was so far hampered by a relatively poor contrast between roots and surrounding soil water. However, soil water contribution to the echo signal can be reduced to less than 1%, increasing contrast significantly. This is achieved by mixing small soil particles (a loamy sand) and larger ones and keeping the water saturation of the soil at moderate levels. Thus, the soil water T_2 (relaxation time) is only a few milliseconds whereas the root water T_2 is several tens of milliseconds. Using an echo time of 9 ms, the signal amplitude of soil water is damped severely, whereas the root water signal intensity is only mildly affected. Additionally, as magnetic particles disturb MRI signals heavily, such particles should be removed from the soil beforehand to assure a high-fidelity 3D image reconstruction.

The MRI experiments were carried out on a vertical 4.7 Tesla spectrometer equipped with 300 mT/m gradients and a 100 mm r.f. coil (Varian, USA). 3D images were generated using a so-called single echo multi slice (SEMS) sequence, with a field of view of 100 mm and a slice thickness of 1 mm. A barley plant was grown in a 420 mm long 90 mm diameter PVC tube with a perforated bottom to prevent water clogging. Measurements where performed about 6 weeks after germination. Because the tube is longer than the homogeneous r.f. field, it was measured in five stages. The resulting image stacks were stitched together without any further corrections. The final $192 \times 192 \times 410$ volumetric image has a lateral spatial resolution of 0.5 mm and a vertical resolution of 1 mm. Additionally a 3 week old snow pea plant inside a container of 300 mm length was studied, in the same manner as the barley plant. After excavation the snow pea roots were scanned and analysed using WinRhizo (Regent Instruments, Canada).

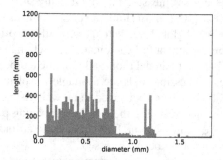

Fig. 2. Root diameter distribution of the root shown in Figure 1

3.1 Synthetic MRI Images

Synthetic MRI images were generated using *SimRoot*, a functional-structural model capable of simulating the architecture of plant roots [18, 19]. Virtual root models of 15 day old maize plants[1] were converted into scalar valued images in which the pixel value corresponds to the root mass within the 0.5 mm cubed pixels. Five images were generated from five runs, which only varied due to variation in the model's random

---

[1] Barley plants are not yet available in SimRoot. 15 day old maize roots come closest to the barley root data.

number generators. We added variable amounts of Gaussian noise to the images at SNRs of 10, 50, 100, 150, 200, and 500. Note that even images with high SNR cannot simply be thresholded, since roots thinner than a voxel would not be detected anymore. The resolution of the images with SNR of 150, i.e. an achievable SNR in real MRI data, were scaled down in the two horizontal dimension to voxel dimensions of 0.5, 0.67, 1, and 1.3 mm to see how the resolution of the MRI image might affect the results. Figure 1, left, shows one of the simulated maize root images, and Figure 2 its root diameter distribution. Please note, that as for real roots not all diameters are populated in the histogram.

4   Reconstruction of Root Structure

We build a structural root model from volumetric MRI measurements in four main steps. First, we find tubular structures on multiple scales. Secondly, we determine the shoot position (the horizontal position of the plant at ground level). Thirdly, we use a shortest path algorithm to determine connectivity. Finally, we prune the graph using two intuitive thresholds.

Finding Tubular Structures. We follow the approach proposed by [9], which is widely used in practice. MRI images typically do not contain isotropic voxels. The axes are therefore first scaled up using cubic spline interpolation. The result $L(\mathbf{x})$ (Fig. 3(b)) is then convolved with a three-dimensional isotropic derivative of a Gaussian filter $G(\mathbf{x}, \sigma)$. The standard deviation σ determines the scale of the tubes we are interested in:

$$\frac{\partial}{\partial x} L(\mathbf{x}, \sigma) = \sigma^\gamma L(\mathbf{x}) * \frac{\partial}{\partial x} G(\mathbf{x}, \sigma).$$

In the factor σ^γ, introduced by [20] for fair comparison of scales, γ is set to 0.78 (for a tubular root model as in [21]). Differentiating again yields the Hessian matrix $H_o(\sigma)$ for each point $\mathbf{x}_o$ of the image. The local second-order structure captures contrast between inside and outside of tubes at scale σ as well as the tube direction. Let $\lambda_1, \lambda_2, \lambda_3$ ($|\lambda_1| \leq |\lambda_2| \leq |\lambda_3|$) be the eigenvalues of $H_o(\sigma)$. For tubular structures in L holds: $|\lambda_1| \approx 0$, $|\lambda_1| \ll |\lambda_2|$, and $|\lambda_2| \approx |\lambda_3|$. The signs and magnitudes of all three eigenvalues are combined in the medialness measure $\mathcal{V}_o(\sigma)$ proposed in [9] (Fig. 3(c)), determining how similar the local structure at $\mathbf{x}_o$ is to a tube at scale σ:

$$\mathcal{V}_o(\sigma) = \begin{cases} 0 & \text{if } \lambda_2 > 0 \text{ or } \lambda_3 > 0 \\ \underbrace{\left(1 - \exp \frac{-\lambda_2^2}{2\alpha^2 \lambda_3^2}\right)}_{\mathcal{R}_A} \underbrace{\exp \frac{-\lambda_1^2}{2\beta^2 |\lambda_2 \lambda_3|}}_{\mathcal{R}_B} \underbrace{\left(1 - \exp \frac{-\sum_i \lambda_i^2}{2c^2}\right)}_{S} \end{cases}.$$

Here, $\mathcal{R}_A$ distinguishes between plate-like and line-like structures, $\mathcal{R}_B$ is a measure of how similar the local structure is to a blob, and S is larger in regions with more contrast. The relative weight of these terms is controlled by the parameters α and β, which we both fix at 0.5. Finally, we combine the responses of multiple scales by selecting the maximum response

$$\mathcal{V}_o = \max_{\sigma \in \{\sigma_0, \ldots, \sigma_S\}} \mathcal{V}_o(\sigma). \tag{1}$$

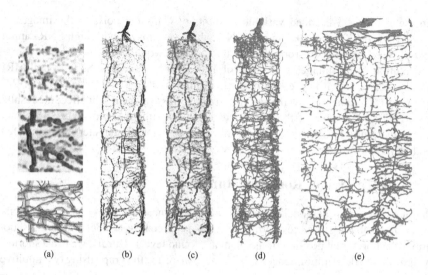

(a)   (b)   (c)   (d)   (e)

Fig. 3. Root model reconstruction. (**a**) Raw data, tubeness-measure [9], structural model. Volume rendering of (**b**) raw data and (**c**) tubeness-measure. (**d**) 3D rendering of model, edges weighted by estimated diameter. (**e**) Cylindrical projection of model.

where $\sigma_i = (\sigma_S/\sigma_0)^{i/S} \cdot \sigma_0$. For our experiments, we select $\sigma_0 = 0.04\,\text{mm}$, $\sigma_S = 1.25\,\text{mm}$, and $S = 20$.

Finding the Shoot Position. In our model, we utilize the fact that plant roots have a tree graph structure. The root node of this tree is a point at the base of the plant shoot, which has, due to its high water content and large diameter, a high intensity in the image. To determine the position of the base of the plant shoot $\mathbf{x}_r$, we find the maximum in the ground plane slice p convolved with a Gaussian $G(\mathbf{x}, \sigma)$ with large σ,

$$\mathbf{x}_r = \arg\max_{\mathbf{x}} \left\{ L(\mathbf{x}, \sigma) \mid x_3 = p \right\}.$$

Determining Connectivity. So far, we have a local measure of vesselness $\mathcal{V}$ at each voxel and an initial root position $\mathbf{x}_r$. What is lacking, is whether two neighboring voxels are part of the same root segment and how root segments are connected. In contrast to some medical applications, we can use the knowledge of global tree connectedness. For this purpose, we first define a graph on the voxel grid, where the vertices are the voxel centers and edges are inserted between all voxels in a 26-neighborhood. We further define an edge cost w for an edge between $\mathbf{x}_s$ and $\mathbf{x}_t$ as

$$w(\mathbf{x}_s, \mathbf{x}_t) = \exp\left(-\omega(\mathcal{V}_s + \mathcal{V}_t)\right)$$

with $\omega \gg 0$. For each voxel $\mathbf{x}_o$, we search for the minimum-cost path to $\mathbf{x}_r$. This can efficiently be done using the Dijkstra algorithm [22], which yields a predecessor for each node in the voxel graph, determining the connectivity.

Model Construction. Every voxel $\mathbf{x}_o$ is now connected to $\mathbf{x}_r$, but we already know that not all voxels are part of the root structure. The voxel graph needs to be pruned to represent only the roots. For this purpose, it is sufficient to select leaf node candidates that exceed the two thresholds explained below. The nodes and edges on the path from leaf node $\mathbf{x}_l$ to $\mathbf{x}_r$ in the voxel graph are then added to the root graph.

In a first step we cut away all voxels from the graph with $L(\mathbf{x}) < L_{\min}$, meaning that a leaf node candidate needs to contain a minimum amount of water.

In a second step, we find leaf nodes of the tree, i.e. root tips. To do so, we search for high values in a median-based 'upstream/downstream ratio' D for voxel $\mathbf{x}_o$

$$D_o = \mathrm{median}_{\mathbf{u} \in N_m^+(\mathbf{x}_o)}(L(\mathbf{u})) / \mathrm{median}_{\mathbf{d} \in N_m^-(\mathbf{x}_o)}(L(\mathbf{d})),$$

where neighborhood $N_m^-(\mathbf{x}_o)$ denotes the m predecessor voxels of $\mathbf{x}_0$ with highest $\mathcal{V}$ when following the graph for m steps away from $\mathbf{x}_r$ (i.e. into the soil), and $N_m^+(\mathbf{x}_o)$ are the m successor voxels with highest $\mathcal{V}$ when following the graph for m steps towards $\mathbf{x}_r$ (i.e. into the root). Thus, D_o is approx. 1 for voxels surrounded by soil and voxels lying in a root since there, the only variations of $L(\mathbf{x})$ are due to noise. D_o is largest and in the range of SNR for voxels indicating a root tip as we encounter 'signal' on the one side of the voxel and 'noise' on the other. Thus root tips are voxels where $D_o > D_{\min}$, where $D_{\min}$ is a tuning parameter.

The tree constructed in this manner cannot distinguish between parts of the root and bits of underground weed which are not connected to the main root. This is not desirable. In a final pruning step, we remove all branches for which the optimal path crosses more than five consecutive millimeters of water-free soil, where water-free means below a two standard deviations from the estimated noise level.

In roots with large diameter, there are still multiple paths from the outer rim to the root center. In a final step, we remove segments which contain a leaf and are shorter than the maximum root radius from the root graph. This step is iterated as long as segments can be removed from the graph.

5   Estimation of Root Parameters

In most biological contexts local and global parameters describing the phenotype of a root are needed, e.g. to derive species-specific models of roots. In this section, we show how to derive such parameters supported by our model.

Root Lengths. To determine the root lengths, high-precision positioning of vertices is essential. So far, vertices are positioned at voxel centers. We now apply a mean-shift procedure to move the nodes to the center of the root with subvoxel precision. At each node n at position $\mathbf{x}_n$, we estimate the inertia tensor in a radius of 3 mm and determine its eigenvalues $\lambda_1 \leq \lambda_2, \leq \lambda_3$ as well as corresponding eigenvectors $\mathbf{v}_1, \mathbf{v}_2, \mathbf{v}_3$. If $\lambda_3 > 1.5\lambda_2$, we assume $\mathbf{v}_3$ to correspond to the local root direction. We then move the node to the mean of a neighborhood in the voxel grid weighted by the vesselness measure $\mathcal{V}$ (Eq. 1). To do so, we choose a 4-neighborhood of $\mathbf{x}_n$ in the plane spanned by $\mathbf{v}_1$ and $\mathbf{v}_2$, and evaluate $\mathcal{V}$ by linear interpolation. Nodes where no main principal axis can be determined ($\lambda_3 < 1.5\lambda_2$) are moved to the mean of their immediate neighbors in the root graph. We iterate these steps until convergence. The resulting structural model is shown in Fig. 3(a). Finally, we can determine the total root lengths by summing over all edge lengths.

Root Radius. For estimation of the local root radius $r(\mathbf{x})$, we use the argument leading to the maximum response $\mathcal{V}_o$ in Eq. 1

$$r_o = \arg \max_{\sigma \in \{\sigma_0, \ldots, \sigma_S\}} \mathcal{V}_o(\sigma) \tag{2}$$

at location $\mathbf{x}_o$. The radius assigned to a node is calculated by averaging r in each segment. A root segment is a list of all vertices connected to each other by exactly two connections, meaning they are either ended by a junction or a root tip.

Root Mass. Root mass is derived by sampling along segments in 0.2 mm steps. We mark for each sampling location $\mathbf{x}_o$ all voxels within the local radius r_o. The mass of a root segment is the sum of values L of all marked voxels.

For constant water density ρ in the roots the mass of a root slice of length l can be calculated from its radius and vice versa as

$$m_o = \rho \pi r_o^2 l \tag{3}$$

Thus especially for subvoxel roots mass estimate may be used as a radius measure.

6   Experiments

6.1   Synthetic Maize Roots

Of the five synthetic root systems, one root system is set aside to tune the two thresholding parameters from Sec. 4 so that they maximize the $F_{0.5}$ measure [23]

$$F_{0.5} = \frac{1.25 P \cdot R}{0.25 P + R}. \tag{4}$$

with precision P and recall R. Precision P is the fraction of true positives in all found positives (true and false positives), while recall is the fraction of true positives in all elements that should have been found (true positives and false negatives). The precision P has double the weight of recall R in the $F_{0.5}$ measure in order to reduce the chance of false positives. As a result the chance of false negatives increases, however this error is relatively small compared to the current detection error of fine roots by the MRI.

To determine true/false positives and false negatives for precision and recall, we sample synthetic and reconstructed roots in 0.2 mm steps and determine the closest edge of the respective other model. A 'match' occurs when this distance is smaller than one voxel size.

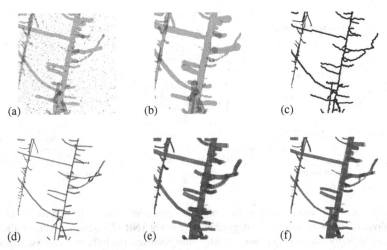

Fig. 4. Example of a reconstructed root (detail): false positives, false negatives, and diameter estimates. (a) Raw data at SNR 150, (b) tubular structures enhanced using Eqn. (1), (c) extracted structure model before subvoxel positioning, (d) true and fitted structure model overlayed, with missing/additional pieces marked in strong red/blue, (e) diameter estimates, (f) mass estimates.

6.2   Sensitivity to Resolution and Noise

For quantitative analysis of our reconstruction algorithm, we use synthetic data of maize roots (see Sec. 3). Fig. 4 shows a typical detail view of such data at SNR 150. At this SNR Frangi's tubularness measure (Eq. (1), Fig. 4b) gives a reasonable indication of where the root is. Figs. 4c, d show the found positions before and after subvoxel positioning. In Fig. 4d we see that most parts of the root system are correctly detected, however, at junctions and crossings the algorithm sometimes prefers shortcuts over the true root path. For root length the effect has not much influence, however branching angles are slightly biased towards 90°. In addition, as short (< 3 mm) root elements are suppressed for the sake of robustness with respect to noise and uncorrect skeletonization of thick roots, true short root elements are non-surprisingly missing.

Diameter and mass of the roots are shown in Fig. 4e, f, where in Fig. 4e diameter is estimated from the Frangi scales (Eq. 2), and in Fig. 4f diameter is calculated from the estimated mass (by inverting Eq. 3). We observe that radius from mass, i.e. from the measured image intensities, is much more reliable than the geometry-based estimate—especially for smaller roots. However, this is only possible under the assumption of constant water density in the root, being perfectly true for our synthetic data. While for healthy roots this is also well fulfilled, the radius of drying roots will unavoidably be systematically underestimated by this method.

In the next sections we investigate the statistical properties of the found root systems with respect to root length, volume, and diameter.

Root Length. Data acquisition time for MRI scales with image resolution. Therefore, image resolution should be selected as low as possible with respect to the measurement

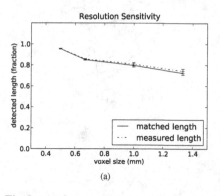
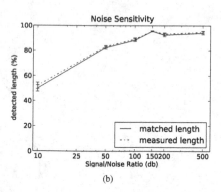

(a)   (b)

Fig. 5. (a) Influence of image resolution: fraction of detected overall root length versus voxel size, for five individual data sets showing 15 day old maize roots at SNR 150. Matched length indicates true positives only, measured length also includes false positives. (b) Influence of noise: fraction of detected overall root length versus signal to noise ratio, for five individual data sets showing 15 day old maize roots at 0.5 mm voxel size. Matched length indicates true positives only, measured length also includes false positives.

task at hand. In order to test sensitivity of our root reconstruction algorithm with respect to image resolution, we calculated root length from the synthetic MRI data (see Sec. 3) with $SNR = 150$ and varying image resolution and compared to the known ground truth. Fig. 5(a) shows how detected root length decreases with larger voxel sizes. For the highest resolution provided (0.5 mm), 95.5% of the true overall root length is detected with standard deviation 0.3%, which is well acceptable for most plant physiological studies. Increasing voxel size quickly decreases found root length to 80% at 1 mm voxel size and to ≈72% at 1.33 mm voxel size. For larger voxels, false positives have a measurable influence of about 2%. For highest resolutions, false positives have no significant influence. We conclude, that voxel size should not be greater than 0.5 mm.

As with other imaging modes, SNR of MRI data increases with acquisition time. Thus, to keep acquisition time short, image noise should be selected as high as possible with respect to the measurement task at hand. We calculated root length from the synthetic MRI data (see Sec. 3) with 0.5 mm voxel size and varying noise levels and compared to the known ground truth (see Fig. 5(b)). For the lowest SNR (10), only 50% of the roots are detected. Detection rate quickly increases with increasing SNR and levels off to 95% at an SNR of about 150. At the given resolution, an SNR of 150–200 seems to give the best balance between detection accuracy and measuring time.

Root Mass and Diameter. Root biologists commonly divide the root system into diameter classes. The derived root diameter distribution and the corresponding volume and mass distributions give insight in the soil exploration strategy of the plant. In Fig. 6, we show scatter plots (i.e. 2D histograms) for true versus measured diameter and volume for SNR 500, 150, and 50. The drawn slope 1 line indicates perfect matches. In the high SNR case (Fig.6a) diameters between approx. 1 and 1.6 voxels (0.5 mm to 0.8 mm) are reliably measured. Diameters between 0.5 and 1 voxel are slightly overestimated and

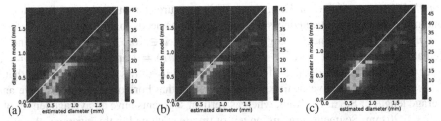

Fig. 6. Histograms of true versus measured diameter at resolution 0.5 mm and (**a**) SNR 500, (**b**) SNR 150, and (**b**) SNR 50. Diameter was measured using Eq. 2. For matching, each root was sampled in 0.2 mm steps and counted as "matched" if a corresponding line segment in the other root was closer than one voxel size.

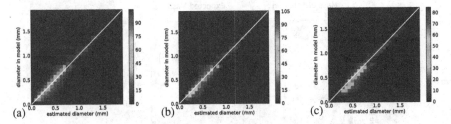

Fig. 7. Same as Fig. 6, however with diameter estimated from local mass (cmp. end of Sec. 5)

smaller diameters are strongly biased towards 1 voxel (0.5 mm) diameter. For diameters larger than 1.6 voxels much less root elements are available (cmp. Fig. 2), thus the shown scatter plots are less populated there. We observe however, that diameters are slightly overestimated there. Comparing Figs. 6a and 6b shows that for roots thicker than 1 voxel diameter estimates do not significantly change when increasing noise from SNR 500 to SNR 150. Subvoxel diameters are more strongly biased towards 1 voxel, meaning that such roots are still found reliably but their diameter cannot be estimated accurately. For SNR 50 overestimation becomes even stronger and is also well visible for diameters up to approx. 0.75 mm. Root mass estimates and diameters derived from them are much more robust (see Fig. 7). For SNR 500 and 150 almost no difference is visible, while for SNR 50 results are slightly worse, but still much better than the ones derived via the Frangi scale σ, even at SNR 500.

6.3   Real MRI Measurements

Barley. We calculate statistical properties of barley roots in order to demonstrate the usefulness of our algorithm on real MRI images of roots. Obviously, there are a wealth of possibilities of how statistics on the modeled root system may be built. In the following, we give two examples where

1. the plausibility of the results can easily be checked visually,
2. results cannot be achieved from the MRI images directly, and
3. structural information on the roots is needed.

Length Distribution between Furcations. This measure cannot be derived from local root information, as connectedness between furcations needs to be ensured. We define a *segment* as list of connected edges $\{e_i(n_i, n_{i+1})\}$, $i \in \{0, \dots, N\}$ where all intermediate nodes n_k, $k \in 1, \dots, N - 1$ have indegree(n_k) = 1 and outdegree(n_k) = 1. A segment is horizontal/vertical if the vector $n_N - n_0$ draws an angle smaller than $45°$ with the horizontal/vertical axis. Here, we find that horizontal segments have an average length of 8.8 ± 7.77 mm, whereas vertical segments have an average length of 5.10 ± 5.20 mm. Segments containing a root tip are excluded in this average. We conclude, that vertical roots have greater branching frequency than the horizontal (higher order) roots.

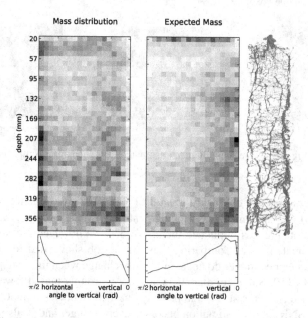

Fig. 8. Mass distribution in root, w. r. t. depth and root angle. Darker regions represent more mass. Left: Unnormalized mass, shows that horizontal roots are prevalent and bind most of the water. Middle: Mass normalized by number of roots, shows that vertical roots tend to have more mass than horizontal ones. Directly beneath the soil surface, roots tend to have more mass regardless of direction. Bottom plots depict the marginal mass distribution of angle. Right: Model visualization weighted by estimated mass (cmp. Fig. 3).

Distribution of Mass. The MRI voxel grid allows to calculate the total mass of a plant. Using the model constructed above, this mass distribution can now be analyzed in new ways, which may be useful when building statistical models of root growth. In Fig. 8, we show the distribution of mass under the model (as derived in Sec. 5) as a function of the depth and the root angle. We distinguish between expected mass of a root at a certain depth/angle and the total mass at this point. The data clearly shows that horizontal roots bind most water (left), while vertical roots are less abundant, but are expected to be heavier (middle). These results agree with current biological understanding of the

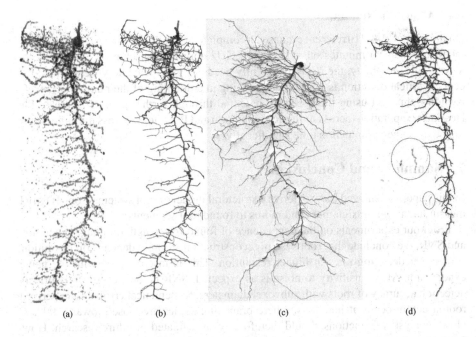

(a)   (b)   (c)   (d)

Fig. 9. Root system of a 3 week old snow pea grown in a 90×300 mm cylinder. (a) Projection image of 3D MRI data. (b) Mass-weighted visualization of reconstructed model. (c) A scan of the excavated root system. (d) Overlay of a MRI scan and a reconstructed model of a younger snow pea root system of 2 weeks. The underground weeds are clearly visible in the MRI scan (red circles), but do not show up in the model (blue).

root architecture of barley plants, which is characterized by a small number of thick, vertically growing nodal roots and a large number of fine horizontally growing lateral roots, branching off the nodal roots.

Snow Pea. In a final experiment a snow pea plant was studied using the above protocols. After excavation of the root system the roots were scanned in a traditional way to determine the root length. Both the MRI image and the scan (Fig. 9) show small nodules attached to the roots of the snow pea that are formed in a symbiotic relationship between the plant and nitrogen-fixing bacteria. Winrhizo (Fig. 9(c)) yields an overall root length of 608 cm, of which 491 cm are composed by roots with a diameter exceeding 200 μm. According to our analysis of the MRI scans we have a root length of 495 cm which clearly shows that we observe roots with a diameter that is considerable smaller than the image resolution. Roots with a diameter of less than 200 μm, however, are not detected. Due to the less complicated nature of this particular root system it is much easier to perform a visual comparison of the graph and the raw MRI data, which also shows that most of the gaps in the MRI data are properly bridged by our software.

6.4 Algorithm Runtime

On the $192 \times 192 \times 410$ reference dataset, a complete, partially parallelized run currently takes less than 20 minutes on a $12 \times 2.67\,$GHz core Intel machine. For the sake of algorithmic simplicity, the dataset currently needs to provide cubic voxels. Thus, the coarse vertical direction is upsampled resulting in a doubling of the number of voxels. Avoiding this and using the speed up potential through further parallelization of the Hessian computation (across multiple computers) and later steps (across multiple cores) may reduce the computation time significantly.

7 Summary and Conclusions

In this paper, we showed how to derive a structural model of root systems from 3D MRI measurements and assign mass and radius to found root segments.

From our experiments on the dependence of found root length on image resolution and SNR, we conclude that root system reconstruction strongly depends on resolution, with better detection rates at higher resolution. This is in coherence with the naïve expectation. Also sensitivity to noise is as expected. SNR below 100 severely effects detection accuracy of roots with subvoxel diameters. Systematical errors of the derived root structure occur at junctions, where branching angles are biased towards 90°. A closer analysis of junctions should therefore be investigated in future research. However other measures are already well applicable. Especially mass estimation (and radius estimation when water density in roots is constant) turned out to be robust against SNR reduction, while geometry-based diameter estimates from Frangi scales become less and less reliable. For healthy roots, radius from mass is an excellent alternative to geometry-based measures, but in drying roots water density is nonconstant and more sophisticated radius measurements should be investigated.

For real data of barley roots we showed, how the derived structural and local quantities can readily be used for plant root phenotyping.

References

1. Schulz, H., Postma, J.A., van Dusschoten, D., Scharr, H., Behnke, S.: 3D Reconstruction of Plant Roots from MRI Images. In: Proceedings of the International Conference on Computer Vision Theory and Applications (VISAPP), Rome, Italy (2012)
2. Waisel, Y., Eshel, A., Kafkafi, U. (eds.): Plant Roots: The Hidden Half. Marcel Dekker, Inc. (2002)
3. Nakanishi, T., Okuni, Y., Furukawa, J., Tanoi, K., Yokota, H., Ikeue, N., Matsubayashi, M., Uchida, H., Tsiji, A.: Water movement in a plant sample by neutron beam analysis as well as positron emission tracer imaging system. Journal of Radioanalytical and Nuclear Chemistry 255, 149–153 (2003)
4. Pierret, A., Doussan, C., Garrigues, E., Kirby, J.M.: Observing plant roots in their environment: current imaging options and specific contribution of two-dimensional approaches. Agronomy for Sustainable Development 23, 471–479 (2003)
5. Ferreira, S., Senning, M., Sonnewald, S., Keßling, P.M., Goldstein, R., Sonnewald, U.: Comparative transcriptome analysis coupled to x-ray ct reveals sucrose supply and growth velocity as major determinants of potato tuber starch biosynthesis. BMC Genomics. Online Journal 11 (2010)

6. Brown, J.M., Kramer, P.J., Cofer, G.P., Johnson, G.A.: Use of nuclear-magnetic resonance microscopy for noninvasive observations of root-soil water relations. Theoretical and Applied Climatology, 229–236 (1990)

7. Southon, T.E., Jones, R.A.: NMR imaging of roots – methods for reducing the soil signal and for obtaining a 3-dimensional description of the roots. Physiologia Plantarum, 322–328 (1992)

8. Jahnke, S., Menzel, M.I., van Dusschoten, D., Roeb, G.W., Bühler, J., Minwuyelet, S., Blümler, P., Temperton, V.M., Hombach, T., Streun, M., Beer, S., Khodaverdi, M., Ziemons, K., Coenen, H.H., Schurr, U.: Combined MRI-PET dissects dynamic changes in plant structures and functions. Plant Journal, 634–644 (2009)

9. Frangi, A.F., Niessen, W.J., Vincken, K.L., Viergever, M.A.: Multiscale Vessel Enhancement Filtering. In: Wells, W.M., Colchester, A.C.F., Delp, S.L. (eds.) MICCAI 1998. LNCS, vol. 1496, pp. 130–137. Springer, Heidelberg (1998)

10. Lo, P., van Ginneken, B., de Bruijne, M.: Vessel tree extraction using locally optimal paths. In: Biomedical Imaging: From Nano to Macro, pp. 680–683 (2010)

11. Dowdy, R., Smucker, A., Dolan, M., Ferguson, J.: Automated image analyses for separating plant roots from soil debris elutrated from soil cores. Plant and Soil 200, 91–94 (1998)

12. Mühlich, M., Truhn, D., Nagel, K., Walter, A., Scharr, H., Aach, T.: Measuring Plant Root Growth. In: Rigoll, G. (ed.) DAGM 2008. LNCS, vol. 5096, pp. 497–506. Springer, Heidelberg (2008)

13. Armengaud, P., Zambaux, K., Hills, A., Sulpice, R., Pattison, R.J., Blatt, M.R., Amtmann, A.: Ez-rhizo: integrated software for the fast and accurate measurement of root system architecture. Plant Journal 57, 945–956 (2009)

14. Nagel, K.A., Schurr, U., Walter, A.: Dynamics of root growth stimulation in nicotiana tabacum in increasing light intensity. Plant Cell and Environment 29, 1936–1945 (2006)

15. Haber-Pohlmeier, S., van Dusschoten, D., Stapf, S.: Waterflow visualized by tracer transport in root-soil-systems using MRI. In: Geophysical Research Abstracts, vol. 11 (2009)

16. Tracy, S., Roberts, J., Black, C., McNeill, A., Davidson, R., Mooney, S.: The X-factor: visualizing undisturbed root architecture in soils using X-ray computed tomography. Journal of Experimental Botany 61, 311–313 (2010)

17. Haacke, E., Brown, R., Thompson, M., Venkatesan, R.: Magnetic Resonance Imaging, Physical Principles and Sequence Design. John Wiley & Sons (1999)

18. Postma, J.A., Lynch, J.P.: Root cortical aerenchyma enhances the acquisition and utilization of nitrogen, phosphorus, and potassium in zea mays l. Plant Physiology 156, 1190–1201 (2011)

19. Postma, J.A., Lynch, J.P.: Theoretical evidence for the functional benefit of root cortical aerenchyma in soils with low phosphorus availability. Annals of Botany 107, 829–841 (2011)

20. Lindeberg, T.: Edge detection and ridge detection with automatic scale selection. In: CVPR, pp. 465–470 (1996)

21. Krissian, K., Malandain, G., Ayache, N., Vaillant, R., Trousset, Y.: Model based multiscale detection of 3d vessels. In: Proceedings of the Workshop on Biomedical Image Analysis, pp. 202–210. IEEE (1998)

22. Dijkstra, E.: A note on two problems in connexion with graphs. Numerische Mathematik 1, 269–271 (1959)

23. van Rijsbergen, C.: Information Retrieval, 2nd edn. Butterworth, London (1979)

Region Growing: When Simplicity Meets Theory – Region Growing Revisited in Feature Space and Variational Framework

Chantal Revol-Muller[1], Thomas Grenier[1], Jean-Loïc Rose[1], Alexandra Pacureanu[1,2], Françoise Peyrin[1,2], and Christophe Odet[1]

[1] CREATIS, CNRS UMR 5220, Inserm U1044, Univ. de Lyon 1, INSA-Lyon,
7 Av. Jean Capelle 69621, Lyon, France
[2] ESRF, BP 220, 38043 Grenoble Cedex, France
{muller,grenier,rose,odet}@creatis.insa-lyon.fr,
{joitapac,peyrin}@esrf.fr

Abstract. Region growing is one of the most intuitive techniques for image segmentation. Starting from one or more seeds, it seeks to extract meaningful objects by iteratively aggregating surrounding pixels. Starting from this simple description, we propose to show how region growing technique can be elevated to the same rank as more recent and sophisticated methods. Two formalisms are presented to describe the process. The first one derived from non-parametric estimation relies upon feature space and kernel functions. The second one is issued from a variational framework, describing the region evolution as a process which minimizes an energy functional. It thus proves the convergence of the process and takes advantage of the huge amount of work already done on energy functionals. In the last part, we illustrate the interest of both formalisms in the context of life imaging. Three segmentation applications are considered using various modalities such as whole body PET imaging, small animal µCT imaging and experimental Synchrotron Radiation µCT imaging. We will thus demonstrate that region growing has reached this last decade a maturation that offers many perspectives of applications to the method.

Keywords: Region growing, Feature space, Scale parameters, Variational approach, Shape prior energy, Vesselness.

1 Introduction

Life imaging by means of many modalities (X-ray Computed Tomography, Magnetic Resonance Imaging (MRI), Ultrasounds, Positron Emission Tomography (PET), etc.) allows a three-dimensional exploration of the anatomical structures with an increasing precision and provides the doctors or biologists with a huge amount of data to analyze. In order to leverage these high-tech imaging systems, it is of the utmost importance to have efficient software to automatically extract the objects of interest. This process called "image segmentation" is fundamental, since it determines the quality of the ulterior study, in terms of accuracy of measurements and quantitative analysis carried out on the explored anatomical structures. Image segmentation is a strenuous problem,

G. Csurka et al. (Eds.): VISIGRAPP 2012, CCIS 359, pp. 426–444, 2013.

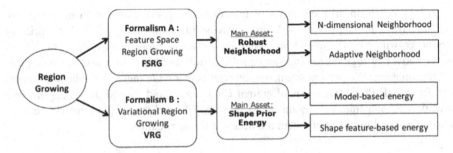

Fig. 1. Two formalisms of region growing process

strenuous problem, especially in life imaging, due to complexity of the anatomical objects, weak spatial resolution, special nature of the physical processes involved in the formation of the images as well as presence of noise and specific artifacts according to the imaging modalities and the imaged structures (artifacts of movement, physical artifacts of interface, inhomogeneity of the background....).

Since the first definition of segmentation given by Zucker in "Region Growing: Childhood and Adolescence" [1], many techniques have been proposed in literature to solve the problem : region growing [2-6], snakes and active contours [7-10] , level sets [11,12], graph cuts [13,14], etc. Among region-based approaches, region growing is often used in semi-interactive segmentation software. This technique is appreciated by the users for its simple, flexible and intuitive use. Generally, it consists in extracting a region of interest by aggregating all the neighboring pixels considered as homogeneous, starting from an initial set of seeds created manually [15] or automatically [16,17]. The criterion of homogeneity is evaluated from the grey levels of the region (statistical moments, parameters of texture, Bayesian approaches). However, the main disadvantage of region growing is to be badly affected by unwanted spread or leak outside the sought object since the process cannot distinguish connected structures with similar intensities or statistic properties. In order to solve problems due to objects connectivity, the integration of geometrical constraints during the growth is essential. Whereas some techniques are well suitable to take into account shape prior [18-21], region growing in its original description is not supported by a mathematical framework that could help it to do so, and thus sparse solutions are mainly ad-hoc [22,23].

In this paper, we propose to underpin region growing by means of two formalisms (see Fig. 1). The first formalism is feature space oriented. It allows to process whatever kind of data (e.g. grey levels, physical parameters, spatial coordinates). Its major advantage is to define a robust neighborhood i.e a set of points belonging to the targeted population without considering outliers. Furthermore, this approach allows to describe adaptive approach since the neighborhood can be locally adjusted to the variation of the underlying probability density of data. We will demonstrate the interest of this approach by describing a multidimensional and an adaptive region growing. The second formalism describes region growing in a variational framework. The region growing is viewed as an iterative and convergent process driven by an energy minimization. This formalism is especially useful to take into account whatever kind of energy based on different types of information e.g. contour, region or shape. We will illustrate this approach by detailing two solutions for integrating shape prior in region growing via: i) a model-based energy and ii) a feature shape energy. In Section 4, we show that region growing can be successfully used in the context of experimental life imaging. We present segmentation results in a wide range of applications starting from NaF PET images, small animal CT-imaging and also SRμCT imaging. We will thus demonstrate that by means of these two formalisms, region growing can be easily designed to positively meet the needs of the applications.

2   Formalism A: Feature Space Region Growing (FSRG)

In this formalism, region growing aims to segment points that belong to a multidimensional space called feature space. We call this approach FSRG. The number of features used to describe a point determines the dimension of this space. This approach is especially useful in the context of medical imaging, where data to process comes from multimodality imaging techniques such as PET-CT devices or from maps of physical parameters such as ρ, T1, T2 in MRI or echogenicity, elasticity, diffusors density in ultrasound imaging. In FSRG, region growing seeks to group similar points together by using techniques stemmed from non-parametric density estimation based on kernel function. After some definition reminders, we set up the principle of FSRG.

2.1   Definitions

Region. A region R (resp. $\bar{R}$) is the set of the segmented (resp. non-segmented) points of a d-dimensional space $\mathbb{R}^d$. As region growing is an iterative process, the content of a region at an iteration t is noted $R^{[t]}$. The initial region $R^{[0]}$ is usually called the set of seeds.

FSRG formalism derives from the framework of non-parametric density estimation based on kernel function (for further details, see [24]) which consists in reconstructing the underlying density $\hat{f}$ of multidimensional data $\left(\mathbf{x}_i \in \mathbb{R}^d, i = 1..n \right)$ by means of $K_{\mathbf{H}}$ a multivariate kernel function normalized by $\mathbf{H}$ a matrix of scaled parameters as reminds in (1):

$$\hat{f}(\mathbf{x}; \mathbf{H}) = \frac{1}{n} \sum_{i=1}^{n} K_{\mathbf{H}}(\mathbf{x} - \mathbf{x}_i) \tag{1}$$

Kernel. In FSRG, K also denotes a kernel function but with weaker constraints than in (1) (especially, no normalization requirement):

$$K(\mathbf{x}) : \begin{cases} \mathbb{R}^d \to [0,1] \\ K(\vec{0}) = Max(K(\mathbf{x})) \\ K(\vec{\infty}) \to 0 \end{cases} \tag{2}$$

For convenience, a profile k can be associated to K a radially symmetric kernel :

$$K(\mathbf{x}) = k(\mathbf{x}^T \mathbf{x}) \tag{3}$$

In particularly, the special profile k_{rect} will be used :

$$k_{rect}(u) = \begin{cases} 1 & if \ \ |u| \le 1 \\ 0 & otherwise \end{cases} \quad u \in \mathbb{R}^+ \tag{4}$$

In our case, u corresponds to a squared distance between two points in the feature space such as:

$$d_M^2(\mathbf{x}, \mathbf{y}, \mathbf{H}) = (\mathbf{x} - \mathbf{y})^T \mathbf{H}^{-1}(\mathbf{x} - \mathbf{y}) \tag{5}$$

also called the Mahalanobis distance, where $\mathbf{H}$ the matrix of scaled parameters, is symmetric and positive-definite. If $\mathbf{H}$ is chosen diagonal, the computed distance is called the normalized Euclidian distance.

The points $\mathbf{x} \in \mathbb{R}^d$ can be separated in c sub-vectors $\mathbf{x}_j$ associated to their c features $(j \in [1, c])$. The matrix $\mathbf{H}$ can similarly be decomposed in c submatrices $\mathbf{H}_j$:

$$\mathbf{H} = \begin{bmatrix} \mathbf{H}_1 & & 0 \\ & \ddots & \\ 0 & & \mathbf{H}_c \end{bmatrix} \tag{6}$$

Then, a multivariate kernel built from a product of spherical kernels can be expressed as a product of one-dimensional kernels K_j :

$$K_\mathbf{H}(\mathbf{x}) = \prod_{j=1}^{c} K_j \left(\left(\mathbf{x}_j^T (\mathbf{H}_j)^{-1} \mathbf{x}_j \right)^{1/2} \right)$$
$$K_\mathbf{H}(\mathbf{x}) = \prod_{j=1}^{c} k_j \left(\left(\mathbf{x}_j^T (\mathbf{H}_j)^{-1} \mathbf{x}_j \right) \right) \tag{7}$$

By convention, s (resp. r) index will represent spatial (resp. range) feature.

Robust Neighborhood. We call $N(\mathbf{y})$ the robust neighborhood of a point $\mathbf{y}$, the set of points that contains all those, which satisfy a special condition and lets apart the outliers.

$$N(\mathbf{y}) = \left\{ \mathbf{x} \in X \mid k_{rect}(d^2(\mathbf{x}, \mathbf{y}, \mathbf{H})) = 1 \right\} \tag{8}$$

where X is a subset of $\mathbb{R}^d$ such as: $X \subset \mathbb{R}^d$.

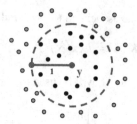

Fig. 2. Robust neighborhood N(y) represented by the set of black points

This writing is powerful since it allows to deal with data represented in a feature space through a distance associated to each feature. Moreover, similarly to non-parametric estimation, the scale parameters can be adapted to each point of the space by means of a local matrix $\mathbf{H}_{|y}$. For instance, in case of spatial and range features, the adaptive robust neighborhood $N(\mathbf{y})$ can be written as a product of profiles with adaptive scale parameters:

$$N(\mathbf{y}) = \left\{ \mathbf{x} \in X \,\middle|\, k_{rect}\left(d^2\left(\mathbf{x}_s, \mathbf{y}_s, \mathbf{H}_{s|y}\right)\right).k_{rect}\left(d^2\left(\mathbf{x}_r, \mathbf{y}_r, \mathbf{H}_{r|y}\right)\right) = 1 \right\} \qquad (9)$$

2.2   Principle of FSRG

Iterative Process. Region growing is an iterative process that aims to agglomerate new points to an existing region while a special condition is checked. The set of new points at each iteration will be denoted $B^{[t]}$ since this set is spatially included in a narrow band around the current region $R^{[t]}$. Starting from an initial region $R^{[0]}$, the evolution process can be described by (10) :

$$R^{[t+1]} = R^{[t]} \cup B^{[t]} \qquad (10)$$

This step is repeated until convergence, i.e. the current region does not evolve anymore: $R^{[t+1]} = R^{[t]}$.

Narrow Band. $B^{[t]}$. The set $B^{[t]}$ is tightly related to the notion of robust neighborhood previously defined in section 2.1. It can be defined as the set of points $\{\mathbf{y}\}$, which do not belong to $R^{[t]}$, but whose robust neighborhood $N(\mathbf{y})$ contains at least a point of $R^{[t]}$.

$$B^{[t]} = \left\{ \mathbf{y} \in \overline{R}^{[t]} \,\middle|\, N(\mathbf{y}) \cap R^{[t]} \neq \varnothing \right\} \qquad (11)$$

It can be noted that the selection of the new points and the behavior of the region growing rely entirely upon the robust neighborhood $N(\mathbf{y})$.

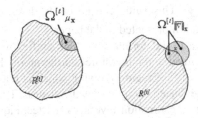

Fig. 3. Local information used in Road RG

In the next section, we take advantage of the open formalism of FSRG to describe two kinds of region growing: i) a multidimensional region growing and ii) a locally adaptive region growing.

2.3   Two Illustrations of FSRG

In the following, the definition of the narrow band $B^{[t]}$ (11) and the principle of evolution (10) stay identical; the methods differ only by their specific robust neighborhood.

Multidimensional Region Growing (MRG). The description of a multidimensional region growing as mentioned in [25] is straightforward with FSRG. The multivariate kernel used in the robust neighborhood can process both spatial and range features of the set X.

$$N(\mathbf{y}) = \left\{ \mathbf{x} \in X \mid k_{rect}\left(d^2\left(\mathbf{x}_s, \mathbf{y}_s, \mathbf{H}_s\right)\right) \cdot k_{rect}\left(d^2\left(\mathbf{x}_r, \mathbf{y}_r, \mathbf{H}_r\right)\right) = 1 \right\} \qquad (12)$$

$N(\mathbf{y})$ contains the points spatially close to $\mathbf{y}$ and with a range feature similar to $\mathbf{y}_r$. The maximum extents are controlled by the matrices $\mathbf{H}_s$ and $\mathbf{H}_r$.

Adaptive Region Growing (ARG). In [6], the authors present a Robust Adaptive Region Growing (Road RG) which can be rewritten within FSRG framework. This method integrates local information about the average grey levels of near points belonging to $R^{[t]}$ and the average norm of the gradient in some vicinity of the tested point (see **Fig. 3**).
Thus, the robust neighborhood can take the following form:

$$N(\mathbf{y}) = \left\{ \mathbf{x} \in X \mid k_{rect}\left(d^2\left(\mathbf{x}_s, \mathbf{y}_s, \mathbf{H}_s\right)\right) \cdot k_{rect}\left(d^2\left(\mathbf{x}_r, \mathbf{y}_r, \mathbf{H}_{r|\mathbf{y}}\right)\right) = 1 \right\} \qquad (13)$$

The scale parameters in matrix $\mathbf{H}_s$ are constant for the spatial features but those of the matrix $\mathbf{H}_{r|\mathbf{y}}$ for the range features are adapted to each point $\mathbf{y}$. In the context of RoAd RG, the range feature is one-dimensional, so $\mathbf{H}_{r|\mathbf{y}}$ is simply a scalar value updated for each point $\mathbf{y}$. This value can be easily determined from the adaptive range of the tolerate variation presented in the paper.

To sum up, FSRG is a useful formalism which unifies many region growing approaches previously presented in the literature. Furthermore, the description in feature space widens the possibilities of region growing which is not restricted anymore to a segmentation method dedicated to grey level images. The robust neighborhood grounded on kernel density estimation leverages the technique and offers many advantages such as the ability to describe adaptive approach by means of scale parameters. In the next section, we present a second formalism for region growing which profits from the powerful variational framework.

3   Formalism B: Variational Region Growing (VRG)

Variational Region Growing formalism (VRG) describes the region growing as an optimization process that aims to minimize some functional called energy, by analogy with many physics phenomena. It relies upon the hypothesis that for an energy judiciously chosen, the segmented region corresponds to pixels that minimizes the energy. This approach is widely used in many segmentation techniques e.g. Bayesian segmentation, active contours, level sets, graph-cuts, but so far, not fully capitalized by region growing [2,26,27,6,23]. It was only in 2009 that VRG was firstly described in literature by [28,29].

3.1   Definitions

Region Representation. The evolving region is represented by a characteristic function $\Phi_{\mathbf{x}}$ defined as:

$$\Phi_{\mathbf{x}} = \Phi(\mathbf{x}) = \begin{cases} 1, & if \ \mathbf{x} \in \Omega_{in} \\ 0, & if \ \mathbf{x} \in \Omega_{out} \end{cases} \tag{14}$$

where $\mathbf{x} \in \mathbb{R}^d$ is an element of the image domain Ω, Ω_{in} the subset representing the segmented region in Ω and $\Omega_{out} = \Omega \setminus \Omega_{in}$ the absolute complement of Ω_{in} representing the background.

The initial region $(t = 0)$ is described by the characteristic function Φ^0:

$$\Phi^0 = \left\{ \mathbf{x} \in \Omega \,|\, \Phi(\mathbf{x}, t = 0) = 1 \right\} \tag{15}$$

ε-Neighborhood. The ε-neighborhood of a point $\mathbf{u}$ of the metric space Ω is the set of all points close to $\mathbf{u}$ in accordance with Euclidian distance:

$$N_\varepsilon(\mathbf{u}) = \left\{ v \in \Omega \,|\, \|v - u\| \le \varepsilon \right\} \tag{16}$$

The outer (resp. inner) boundary δ_ε^+ (resp. δ_ε^-) of Ω_{in} is defined as follows:

$$\partial_\varepsilon^+ = \left\{ v \in \Omega_{out} \mid \exists u \in \Omega_{in}, \; v \in N_\varepsilon(u) \right\}$$
$$\partial_\varepsilon^- = \left\{ v \in \Omega_{in} \mid \exists u \in \Omega_{out}, \; v \in N_\varepsilon(u) \right\} \tag{17}$$

The union of inner and outer boundaries can also be noted $\delta_\varepsilon^\pm$.

3.2   Principle of VRG

VRG aims to achieve the desired image partition by switching the discrete function Φ_x, in order to minimize an energy functional which models the structure to detect. Of course, this energy functional must be correctly designed in such a way that its minimum corresponds to the solution of the segmentation i.e. the sought object.

Segmentation by Variational Approach. In a variational approach, the segmentation is expressed as an optimization process:

$$\Phi^* = \arg \min_\Phi J(\Phi) \tag{18}$$

where Φ^* is the optimal partition of image obtained by minimizing the energy $J(\Phi)$.

In order to iteratively find the solution, an artificial time-variable t is introduced, thus allowing to relate $\Delta_t \Phi$ the time-dependent variation of Φ with $\Delta J(\tilde{\Phi})$ the estimated variation of the energy for $\tilde{\Phi}$ a small alteration of Φ as follows:

$$\Delta_t \Phi + F(\Phi, \Delta J(\tilde{\Phi})) = 0 \tag{19}$$

where F is a functional controlling the region evolution.

Equation of Evolution. In VRG, the evolution of the region is a discrete process in both spatial and time domains because elements of Ω are sampled on a grid and iterations depend on a discrete-time variable n.

In this case, the aim of F is to induce the switch of Φ values, each time that yields a reduction of the energy i.e. $\Delta J(\tilde{\Phi}) < 0$. Thus, F can be expressed as a function of $\Delta J(\tilde{\Phi})$ and $c(\Phi)$ the switch state command expressed in (22), as follows:

$$F(\Phi, \Delta J(\tilde{\Phi})) = -c(\Phi) \cdot H(-\Delta J(\tilde{\Phi})) \tag{20}$$

where H stands for the one-dimensional Heaviside function:

$$H(z) = \begin{cases} 0 & \text{if } z < 0 \\ 1 & \text{if } z \geq 0 \end{cases} \tag{21}$$

The command $c(\Phi)$ leads to the switch of Φ_x at a point $\mathbf{x}$ by means of the next operation:

$$c(\Phi_x) = 1 - 2\Phi_x \tag{22}$$

From (19) and (20) the evolution of the region can be written as:

$$\Delta_t \Phi - c(\Phi) \cdot H(-\Delta J(\tilde{\Phi})) = 0 \tag{23}$$

The equation (23) is solved iteratively by numerical methods starting from Φ^0. We note Φ^n the region function at iteration n. The values of the function Φ at the iteration $n+1$ are evaluated at each point as follows:

$$\Phi_x^{n+1} = \Phi_x^n + c(\Phi_x^n) \cdot H(-\Delta J(\tilde{\Phi}_x^n)) \tag{24}$$

Depending on the sign of $\Delta J(\tilde{\Phi}_x^n)$, the value of Φ_x^{n+1} is switched or remains unchanged. The evolution stops when Φ^n does not encounter any modification at the assessed points.

Vicinity to Assess. In VRG, at each iteration, only a limited set of voxels are evaluated for possible aggregation. These voxels are selected by defining a vicinity which surrounds the boundary of the segmented region. The width of this vicinity depends on the size of the ε-neighborhood (16) used to defined the outer and inner boundaries (17). The aim of this vicinity is similar to the narrow band used in level sets. Most of the time, only the outer boundary is considered for the evolution of the region. However, if the inner boundary is included in the vicinity, that means that points belonging previously to the evolving region can be tested at the next iteration and possibly ejected. The vicinity is taken into account in the equation of evolution (24) by replacing $c(\Phi_x^n)$ by $c_\varepsilon(\Phi_x^n)$:

$$c_\varepsilon(\Phi_x^n) = \begin{cases} c(\Phi_x^n) & \text{if } \mathbf{x} \in \delta_\varepsilon^\pm \\ 0 & \text{otherwise} \end{cases} \tag{25}$$

Energy Variation. Since the evolution of the region depends on the energy variation $\Delta J(\tilde{\Phi}_x^n)$, it is of interest to find out a common expression of this variation for a wide class of energies. Among the plethora of energies proposed in the literature, we restrict the study on region-based energies. In [30], the author presents a general expression of a region-based energy obtained from a "region-independent" descriptor k_x as:

$$J(\Omega_{in}) = \int_{\Omega_{in}} k_x d\mathbf{x} \tag{26}$$

In our discrete case, the expression of the energy becomes:

$$J(\Phi^n) = \sum_{x \in \Omega} k_x \Phi_x^n \qquad (27)$$

Given the energy $J(\Phi^n)$ at the iteration n, we evaluate the energy $J(\tilde{\Phi}^n)$ that would result from the state switch of a candidate voxel v.
The assessed state switch of v is defined by:

$$\tilde{\Phi}_v^n = 1 - \Phi_v^n \qquad (28)$$

Thus:
$$\tilde{\Phi}_x^n = \Phi_x^n \qquad \text{for all } x \neq v \qquad (29)$$

From the relations (27), (28), (29) the evaluated energy can be then written as:

$$J(\tilde{\Phi}^n) = k_v \cdot \tilde{\Phi}_v^n + \sum_{x \neq v, x \in \Omega} k_x \cdot \Phi_x^n \qquad (30)$$

$$J(\tilde{\Phi}^n) = k_v \cdot (1 - \Phi_v^n) - k_v \cdot \Phi_v^n + \underbrace{k_v \cdot \Phi_v^n + \sum_{x \neq v} k_x \cdot \Phi_x^n}_{J(\Phi^n)} \qquad (31)$$

Therefore, the energy variation $\Delta J(\tilde{\Phi}_v^n)$, associated to a single voxel v have the following formulation:

$$\Delta J(\tilde{\Phi}_v^n) = (1 - 2\Phi_v^n) \cdot k_v \qquad (32)$$

This expression for the evolution of the energy functional is valid for any region-independent descriptor k_v.

Example of Region-Based Energy. In [31], the authors propose a region-based energy based on the average grey level calculated inside and outside the segmented region:

$$J_I(\Phi_x) = \lambda_{\text{int}} \sum_x |f(x) - \mu_{in}|^2 \Phi_x + \lambda_{\text{ext}} \sum_x |f(x) - \mu_{out}|^2 (1 - \Phi_x) \qquad (33)$$

where μ_{in} (resp. μ_{out}) is the average intensity in Ω_{in} (resp. Ω_{out}) and $f(x)$ the intensity value of the pixel x.

According to (32), the variation of this energy expresses as following:

$$\Delta J_I(\tilde{\Phi}_v^n) = (1 - 2\Phi_v^n)\left[|f(v) - \mu_{in}|^2 - |f(v) - \mu_{out}|^2\right] \qquad (34)$$

To sum up the section 3.2, VRG formalism describes region growing as an iterative process that converges towards a minimum of energy. VRG is a powerful formalism since it allows to deal with whatever kind of energies. The next section presents two solutions to constrain region growing by shape prior from: i) a model-based energy and ii) a feature shape energy.

3.3   Integration of Shape Prior

Model-Based Energy. The definition of a model-based energy is conceivable when a reference shape is available. This approach was successfully implemented by [32,20]. It consists in describing the shape by descriptors such as Legendre or Chebyschev moments. Then, a shape distance based on these descriptors must be carefully defined in order to compare the shape of the evolving region with the one of the reference object. The shape energy governing the region growing is tightly related to this distance. In the following, we briefly remind the approach proposed by [32] that relies on a shape energy based on Chebyschev moments.

Chebyschev Moments. The Chebyschev moments of order $p+q$ of a binary image of size $N \times N$ defined by a characteristic function Φ_x are expressed using the scaled orthogonal Chebyschev polynomials $t_{p,N}(.)$, as follows:

$$T_{pq} = C_{pq} \cdot \sum_{x \in \Omega} t_{p,N}(x_1) t_{q,N}(x_2) \Phi_x \qquad p, q = 0,1,2,..,\eta-1 \quad \eta \leq N \qquad (35)$$

where the p-th order Chebyschev polynomial is given by:

$$t_{p,N}(x_1) = \frac{p!}{N^p} \sum_{k=0}^{p} (-1)^{p-k} \binom{N-1-k}{p-k} \binom{p+k}{p} \binom{x_1}{k} \qquad (36)$$

These moments are made invariant by using an affine transformation T^{aff} [33] such as $\mathbf{u} = T^{\text{aff}} \mathbf{x}$, thus allowing shape alignment during the segmentation:

$$V_{pq} = C_{pq} \cdot \sum_{x \in \Omega} t_{p,N}(u_1) t_{q,N}(u_2) \Phi_x \qquad \text{with } \mathbf{u} = [u_1, u_2] \qquad (37)$$

Shape prior energy. The shape prior energy is based on the weighted Frobenius distance. It measures the difference between the set of moments describing the inside of the evolving region Φ^n and the set of moments of the reference object.

$$J_{prior}(\Phi^n) = \sum_{p,q}^{p,q < \eta} H_{pq}(\sigma)^2 \cdot \left(T_{pq}(\Phi^n) - T_{pq}^{ref} \right)^2 \qquad (38)$$

where H_{pq} is a weighting positive function used to adapt the criterion to the Chebyschev moment hierarchy:

$$H_{pq}(\sigma) = \frac{1}{\sqrt{2\pi\sigma^2}} \exp^{-\frac{(p+q)^2}{2\sigma^2}} \qquad (39)$$

Variation of the Shape Prior Energy. The principle used to determine the variation of energy $\Delta J\left(\tilde{\Phi}_v^n\right)$ is the same as 3.2. The variation at the voxel **v** is given by the following equation:

$$\Delta J_{prior}\left(\tilde{\Phi}_v^n\right)=\left(1-2\Phi_v^n\right)\cdot\sum_{p,q}^{p,q<\eta}H_{pq}\left(\sigma\right)\cdot\left(2T_{pq}^n R_v+\left(1-2\Phi_v^n\right)R_v^2-2T_{pq}^{ref}R_v\right) \qquad (40)$$

where $R_v=C_{pq}t_{p,N}\left(u_1\right)t_{q,N}\left(u_2\right)$.

Depending on the sign of $\Delta J\left(\tilde{\Phi}_v^n\right)$ value, the region function Φ^n will evolve by aggregating or rejecting a point belonging to the vicinity of Φ^n.

Total Energy. In order to define a process of segmentation that depends on both grey levels of the image and shape prior given by the reference model, a mixed energy $J_T\left(\Phi_x\right)$ must be introduced in VRG:

$$J_T\left(\Phi_x\right)=J_I\left(\Phi_x\right)+\alpha.J_{prior}\left(\Phi_x\right) \qquad (41)$$

with $J_I\left(\Phi_x\right)$ the energy of Chan and Vese presented in (33) and $J_{prior}\left(\Phi_x\right)$ the shape prior-energy defined in (38). The hyper-parameter α balances the influence of shape prior and image data.

The variation of the total energy at the voxel **v** will take into account the variation of each energy:

$$\Delta J_T\left(\tilde{\Phi}_v^n\right)=\Delta J_I\left(\tilde{\Phi}_v^n\right)+\alpha.\Delta J_{prior}\left(\tilde{\Phi}_v^n\right) \qquad (42)$$

In the next section, another kind of shape prior energy is proposed. This energy derives from special shape features of the sought structure.

Energy Based on Shape Features. The energy based on a shape feature is defined by a functional, which takes into account some information on the geometry of the structure to detect. For instance, the structure of the object can be mainly tubular. Such an energy is presented in [34], the authors propose to introduce vesselness information in the energy functional in order to improve the spread of the region growing into tubular structures. The vesselness information is obtained by a special filtering based on Hessian matrix [35,36], which yields a probability map of the tubular-like structures in the image. The filter can be tuned to enhance tubular features of a particular size. The energy functional $J_{FS}\left(\Phi_x\right)$ combines $f\left(\mathbf{x}\right)$ the intensity information in the original image and $v\left(\mathbf{x}\right)$ the vesselness information obtained from Sato or Frangi filtered image. Each term of the energy is weighted by the likelihood that the current element belongs to a tubular structure, which is given by the value of $v\left(\mathbf{x}\right)$.

$$J_{FS}\left(\Phi_x\right)=J_f\left(\Phi_x\right)+J_v\left(\Phi_x\right) \qquad (43)$$

Where:

$$J_v(\Phi_x) = \sum_x v(x)|v(x) - \mu_{v_{in}}|^2 \Phi_x + \sum_x v(x)|v(x) - \mu_{v_{out}}|^2 (1 - \Phi_x) \qquad (44)$$

$$J_f(\Phi_x) = \sum_x (1 - v(x))|f(x) - \mu_{f_{in}}|^2 \Phi_x + \sum_x (1 - v(x))|f(x) - \mu_{f_{out}}|^2 (1 - \Phi_x) \qquad (45)$$

with $v(\mathbf{x})$ the vesselness similarity measure at the voxel $\mathbf{x}$ and $\mu_{v_{in}}, \mu_{v_{out}}$ (respectively $\mu_{f_{in}}, \mu_{f_{out}}$) the average grey levels of the domains Ω_{in} and Ω_{out} in the filtered image $v(\mathbf{x})$ (respectively in the original image $f(\mathbf{x})$).

The variation of the energy functional at the voxel $\mathbf{v}$ expresses as follows:

$$\Delta J_{FS}(\tilde{\Phi}_v^n) = (1 - 2\Phi_v^n)(k_v(J_v) + k_v(J_f)) \qquad (46)$$

Where:

$$k_v(J_v) = v(\mathbf{v})\left(|v(\mathbf{v}) - \mu_{v_{in}}|^2 - |v(\mathbf{v}) - \mu_{v_{out}}|^2\right) \qquad (47)$$

$$k_v(J_f) = (1 - v(\mathbf{v}))\left(|f(\mathbf{v}) - \mu_{f_{in}}|^2 - |f(\mathbf{v}) - \mu_{f_{out}}|^2\right) \qquad (48)$$

$v(\mathbf{v}) \in [0,1]$ can be seen as a measure of the probability of the voxel $\mathbf{v}$ to be part of a tube-like structure. During the segmentation evolution, when a tested voxel belongs to a tubular structure $v(\mathbf{v})$ is close to 1, therefore, the term $k_v(J_v)$ in the equation (46) is preponderant. If the considered voxel is part of the background or of non-tubular structure, $v(\mathbf{v})$ is close to 0 and the term $k_v(J_f)$ becomes preponderant, hence the intensity in the original image is taken into account. As we will see in the section 4.3, this energy permits to detect both lacunae and canaliculi and, by propagation on the line enhancement provided by Sato's filter, it makes possible to reconnect parts of the same canaliculus.

4   Applications to Medical and Biomedical Imaging

In this section, we illustrate the use of region growing in the context of life imaging. Three region growing methods derived from FSRG and VRG formalisms were applied to segment images from various modalities such as whole body PET images, small animal μCT images and SRμCT images of lacuno-canicular network.

4.1   FSRG ARG: Whole Body PET Images of Bone Activity

[18F]Fluoride Ion PET Images. Fig. 4a displays an example of a whole body [18F]fluoride ion PET study, obtained with a standard protocol of [18F]fluoride ion PET acquisition described in [37]. The dimensions of the volume are 128x128x349

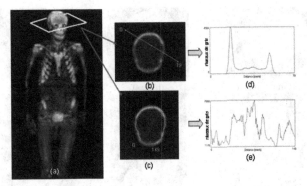

Fig. 4. (a) Whole body [18F]fluoride ion PET image; (b), (c) the same slices in the skull; (d), (e) two profiles of intensity

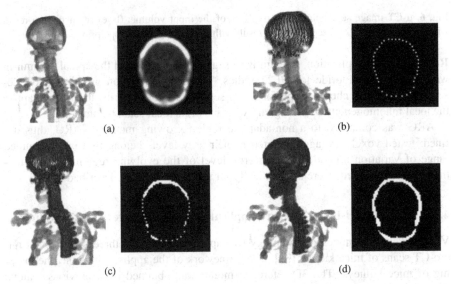

Fig. 5. Segmentation of [18F]fluoride ion PET image: a) original data, b) initial seeds, c) NARG results, d) ARG results. For each subfigure, 3D representation is given on the left and a slice located in the skull is given on the right.

pixels and the grey levels are coded in short format (16 bits). The intensity values are proportional to the tracer uptake. Through the plots of two profiles, Fig. 4d and Fig. 4e highlight the high variations of the intensity and the strong inhomogeneity of the tracer uptake due to bone metabolism. The white line and curve used for the profiles were drawn on the same slice located in the skull (Fig. 4b and Fig. 4c).

Fig. 5c and Fig. 5d display the results of the segmentation with NARG and ARG. For both methods, tuning parameters were experimentally adjusted. In the skull, ARG leads to a better segmentation than NARG, since the evolving region has successfully spread over the whole structure despite the high variations of the intensities. That demonstrates the improvements provided by the use of the adaptive parameters.

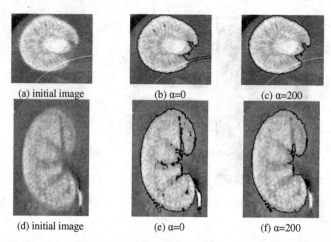

(a) initial image   (b) α=0   (c) α=200

(d) initial image   (e) α=0   (f) α=200

Fig. 6. μ-CT image segmentation: (a,d) slices of the input volume; (b, e) segmentation result without shape prior; (c, f) segmentation result with the model-based shape prior

Results. In this application, the aim is to segment the skull and the spinal column in whole body [18F]fluoride ion PET studies. The adaptive region growing ARG described in 2.3 was chosen to perform this segmentation due to its ability to adapt to the local inhomogeneity of the signal by means of its local scale parameter.

ARG was compared to a non-adaptive region growing method NARG, thus defined: tested voxels are agglomerated if their grey levels belong to a predetermined range of variation around the mean grey level of the evolving region. In both methods, the initial seeds were automatically set up by a procedure described in [37].

4.2   VRG-Model-Based Energy: Application to μCT Images of Mice Kidney

VRG driven by a model-based energy was applied to segment three dimensional micro-CT scans of mice kidney [32]. The framework of the application is the phenotyping of mice kidneys. The 3D reference model was obtained by a previous manual segmentation of a reference volume. The method was tested on a random input volume. Slices of x-plane and y-plane are shown in Fig. 6a and Fig. 6d.

We compare the results of VRG with and without shape prior i.e using $J_T(\Phi_x)$ or only $J_I(\Phi_x)$. Fig. 6b, Fig. 6e and Fig. 7a show the resulting segmentation without shape prior $(\alpha=0)$. The segmentation fails to segment the kidney due to strong inhomogeneities in the image. Moreover, the final contour spreads through the leaking points induced by an artifact. Fig. 6c, Fig. 6f and Fig. 7b illustrate VRG results with shape prior constraint. The parameter σ stepping in $J_{prior}(\Phi_x)$ was set to 1.5. This value was not chosen too low in order to take into account enough information about the reference model. The hyper-parameter α was fixed to 200 and achieves a good compromise between $J_{prior}(\Phi_x)$ and $J_I(\Phi_x)$ since the kidney surface has been recovered more accurately and without any leakage.

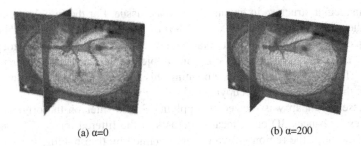

(a) α=0   (b) α=200

Fig. 7. Segmentation results: a) without shape prior; b) with model-based shape prior

4.3   VRG-Feature Shape Energy: Application to SRμCT Images of Canaliculi Network

VRG driven by a feature shape energy was applied to segment experimental data obtained with very high resolution SR-μCT at ESRF, representing 3D images of the

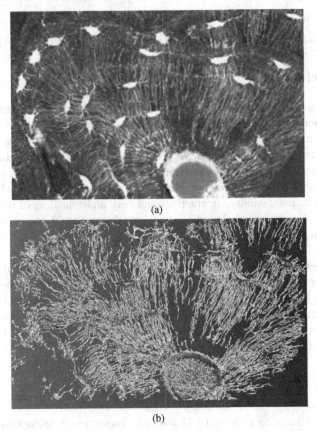

Fig. 8. Volume of interest showing the lacuno-canalicular system in a human femur bone sample (image width ~ 224 μm): a) Maximum Intensity Projection of the original (inverted) volume; b) Isosurface of the segmentation obtained with VRG and the feature shape energy $J_{FS}(\Phi_x)$.

lacuno-canalicular structure in human femur bone tissue. For the sample presented in Fig. 8a, the acquisition resolution was 0.28μm, the energy was set at 20.5keV and 2000 projections were taken with a counting time of 0.8 seconds. The osteocyte cell network is essentially composed of ellipsoidal objects interconnected through tubular structures. The main difficulty in segmenting this formation arises from the slender canaliculi, the linear features occupying only a few voxels in diameter.

The vesselness map was created by applying Sato's filter on the original image. This process enhances 3D curvilinear structures in the filtered image. The seeds for the initialization of the region growing were obtained by thresholding the vesselness map. The parameters used for the vesselness filter were determined from a previous study based on a phantom. Fig. 8 displays the results obtained for a 800x500x100 sub-volume extracted from a $(2048)^3$ volume. Fig. 8a shows a Maximum Intensity Projection of the original sub-volume. In Fig. 8b, VRG has efficiently yielded the first segmentation results of the lacuno-canalicular system in 3D from SR-μCT. Moreover, a quantitative study carried on synthetic data mimicking lacunae interconnected by canaliculi showed that VRG driven by the shape feature energy $J_{FS}(\Phi_x)$ over performs VRG only driven by $J_I(\Phi_x)$, since it can detect correct tubular structures at a rate 20% higher and lead to better connection of the caniculi network [34].

5   Conclusions

We have presented two visions of region growing. The first one can easily deal with multidimensional data in the feature space and specify locally adaptive segmentation. The second one leverages the powerful mathematical tools of variational framework. One major advantage is to bring convergence properties through the minimization of the energy functional. Various approaches derived from both formalisms have been successfully applied to life imaging, yielding quite satisfying results while enabling simple initializations, intuitive interactions and easy understanding of tuning parameters by users. To our knowledge, these two formalisms should encompass the entire spectrum of region growing approaches.

Acknowledgements. The authors thank the Animage department of the CERMEP (Lyon, France) for supplying [18F]fluoride ion PET images and micro-CT scans of mice kidney, Pr. M Lafage-Proust (Inserm U890, St Etienne, France) for providing the bones samples and the ESRF ID19 group for help during data acquisition. This work was conducted in the framework of the LabEX PRIMES "Physics Radiobiology Medical Imaging and Simulation".

References

1. Zucker, S.W.: Region growing: Childhood and adolescence. Computer Graphics and Image Processing 5(3), 382–399 (1976)
2. Adams, R., Bischof, L.: Seeded region growing. IEEE Transactions on Pattern Analysis and Machine Intelligence 16(6), 641–647 (1994)

3. Mehnert, A., Jackway, P.: Improved seeded region growing algorithm. Pattern Recognition Letters 18(10), 1065–1071 (1997)
4. Revol, C., Jourlin, M.: New minimum variance region growing algorithm for image segmentation. Pattern Recognition Letters 18(3), 249–258 (1997)
5. Chuang, C.H., Lie, W.N.: Region growing based on extended gradient vector flow field model for multiple objects segmentation. In: IEEE International Conference on Image Processing, Thessaloniki, pp. 74–77. Institute of Electrical and Electronics Engineers Computer Society (2001)
6. Grenier, T., Revol-Muller, C., Costes, N., Janier, M., Gimenez, G.: 3D robust adaptive region growing for segmenting [18F] fluoride ion PET images. In: IEEE Nuclear Science Symposium Conference Record, San Diego, CA, United States, pp. 2644–2648. Institute of Electrical and Electronics Engineers Inc., Piscataway (2007)
7. Kass, M., Witkin, A., Terzopoulos, D.: Snakes: active contour models. In: Proceedings - First International Conference on Computer Vision, London, Engl., pp. 259–268. IEEE, New York (1987)
8. Xu, C., Prince, J.L.: Generalized gradient vector flow external forces for active contours. Signal Processing 71(2), 131–139 (1998)
9. Paragios, N., Deriche, R.: Geodesic active regions: A new framework to deal with frame partition problems in computer vision. Journal of Visual Communication and Image Representation 13(1-2), 249–268 (2002)
10. Freedman, D., Zhang, T.: Active contours for tracking distributions. IEEE Transactions on Image Processing 13(4), 518–526 (2004)
11. Malladi, R., Sethian, J.A., Vemuri, B.C.: Shape modeling with front propagation: a level set approach. IEEE Transactions on Pattern Analysis and Machine Intelligence 17(2), 158–175 (1995)
12. Paragios, N., Deriche, R.: Geodesic active regions and level set methods for motion estimation and tracking. Computer Vision and Image Understanding 97(3), 259–282 (2005)
13. Boykov, Y.Y., Jolly, M.P.: Interactive graph cuts for optimal boundary and region segmentation of objects in N-D images. In: Proceedings of the 8th IEEE International Conference on Computer Vision, vol. I, pp. 105–112 (2001)
14. Rother, C., Kolmogorov, V., Blake, A.: "GrabCut" - Interactive foreground extraction using iterated graph cuts. Acm Transactions on Graphics 23(3), 309–314 (2004)
15. Olabarriaga, S.D., Smeulders, A.W.M.: Interaction in the segmentation of medical images: A survey. Medical Image Analysis 5(2), 127–142 (2001)
16. Fan, J., Yau, D.K.Y., Elmagarmid, A.K., Aref, W.G.: Automatic image segmentation by integrating color-edge extraction and seeded region growing. IEEE Transactions on Image Processing 10(10), 1454–1466 (2001)
17. Lin, Z., Jin, J., Talbot, H.: Unseeded region growing for 3D image segmentation. International Conference Proceeding Series (2000)
18. Chan, T., Zhu, W.: Level set based shape prior segmentation. In: Proceedings - 2005 IEEE Computer Society Conference on Computer Vision and Pattern Recognition, CVPR 2005, San Diego, CA, United States, pp. 1164–1170. Institute of Electrical and Electronics Engineers Computer Society, Piscataway (2005)
19. Cremers, D., Sochen, N., Schnörr, C.: Towards Recognition-Based Variational Segmentation Using Shape Priors and Dynamic Labeling. In: Griffin, L.D., Lillholm, M. (eds.) Scale-Space 2003. LNCS, vol. 2695, pp. 388–400. Springer, Heidelberg (2003)
20. Foulonneau, A., Charbonnier, P., Heitz, F.: Affine-invariant geometric shape priors for region-based active contours. IEEE Transactions on Pattern Analysis and Machine Intelligence 28(8), 1352–1357 (2006)

21. Gastaud, M., Barlaud, M., Aubert, G.: Combining shape prior and statistical features for active contour segmentation. IEEE Transactions on Circuits and Systems for Video Technology 14(5), 726–734 (2004)

22. Dehmeshki, J., Ye, X., Costello, J.: Shape based region growing using derivatives of 3D medical images: Application to semi-automated detection of pulmonary nodules. In: IEEE International Conference on Image Processing, Barcelona, Spain, pp. 1085–1088. Institute of Electrical and Electronics Engineers Computer Society (2003)

23. Rose, J.L., Revol-Muller, C., Almajdub, M., Chereul, E., Odet, C.: Shape Prior Integrated in an Automated 3D Region Growing method. In: IEEE International Conference on Image Processing, ICIP 2007, San Antonio, USA, pp. 53–56 (2007)

24. Silverman, B.W.: Density Estimation for Statistiques and Data Analysis. Monographs on Statistics and Applied Probability, vol. 26. Chapman and Hall, London (1986)

25. Comaniciu, D., Meer, P.: Mean shift: A robust approach toward feature space analysis. IEEE Transactions on Pattern Analysis and Machine Intelligence 24(5), 603–619 (2002)

26. Zhu, S.C., Yuille, A.: Region competition: unifying snakes, region growing, and Bayes/MDL for multiband image segmentation. IEEE Transactions on Pattern Analysis and Machine Intelligence 18(9), 884–900 (1996)

27. Revol-Muller, C., Peyrin, F., Carrillon, Y., Odet, C.: Automated 3D region growing algorithm based on an assessment function. Pattern Recognition Letters 23(1-3), 137–150 (2002)

28. Rose, J.L., Revol-Muller, C., Reichert, C., Odet, C.: Variational region growing. In: VISAPP 2009 International Conference on Computer Vision Theory and Applications, Lisboa, Portugal, pp. 166–171 (February 2009)

29. Rose, J.L., Grenier, T., Revol-Muller, C., Odet, C.: Unifying variational approach and region growing segmentation. In: 18th European Signal Processing Conference (EUSIPCO 2010), Aalborg, Denmark, pp. 1781–1785 (August 2010)

30. Jehan-Besson, S., Barland, M., Aubert, G.: DREAM2S: Deformable regions driven by an Eulerian accurate minimization method for image and video segmentation. International Journal of Computer Vision 53(1), 45–70 (2003)

31. Chan, T.F., Vese, L.A.: Active contours without edges. IEEE Transactions on Image Processing 10(2), 266–277 (2001)

32. Rose, J.L., Revol-Muller, C., Charpigny, D., Odet, C.: Shape prior criterion based on Tchebichef moments in variational region growing. In: IEEE International Conference on Image Processing, ICIP 2009, Cairo, Egypt, pp. 1077–1080 (November 2009)

33. Pei, S.-C., Lin, C.-N.: Image normalization for pattern recognition. Image and Vision Computing 13(10), 711–723 (1995)

34. Pacureanu, A., Revol-Muller, C., Rose, J.L., Sanchez-Ruiz, M., Peyrin, F.: A Vesselness-guided Variational Segmentation of Cellular Networks from 3D Micro-CT. In: IEEE International Symposium on Biomedical Imaging: From Nano to Macro, Rotterdam, Netherlands, pp. 912–915 (June 2010)

35. Sato, Y., Nakajima, S., Shiraga, N., Atsumi, H., Yoshida, S., Koller, T., Gerig, G., Kikinis, R.: Three-Dimensional Multi-Scale Line Filter for Segmentation and Visualization of Curvilinear Structures in Medical Images. Medical Image Analysis 2(2), 143–168 (1998)

36. Frangi, A.F., Niessen, W.J., Vincken, K.L., Viergever, M.A.: Multiscale Vessel Enhancement Filtering. In: Wells, W.M., Colchester, A.C.F., Delp, S.L. (eds.) MICCAI 1998. LNCS, vol. 1496, pp. 130–137. Springer, Heidelberg (1998)

37. Grenier, T., Revol-Muller, C., Costes, N., Janier, M., Gimenez, G.: Automated seeds location for whole body NaF PET segmentation. IEEE Trans. Nuc. Sci. 52(5), 1401–1405 (2005)

Author Index